Donegal

HISTORY & SOCIETY

Interdisciplinary Essays on the
History of an Irish County

 GEOGRAPHY PUBLICATIONS

The editors and publisher are very grateful to Donegal County Council for its generous subvention to this publication.

Published in Ireland by
Geography Publications,
Templeogue, Dublin 6W

ISBN 0 906602 45 9

Cover design by Christy Nolan
Typesetting by Phototype-Set Ltd., Dublin
Printed by ColourBooks Ltd.

Contents

List of Figures

List of Plates

Editor's Foreword and Acknowledgements

Donegal: History & Society follows *Tipperary* (1985), *Wexford* (1987), *Kilkenny* (1990), *Dublin* (1992), *Waterford* (1992), *Cork* (1993) and *Wicklow* (1994) in the Irish County History and Society series. It is the first volume to deal with a northern county and therefore brings a fresh spatial perspective to the study of the regional dimension in history.

In the companion volume, *Cork: History & Society*, T.C. Barnard questioned the validity of using the county as a point of entry into late seventeenth century Ireland. His perceptive comment may be applied with even greater emphasis to earlier periods when Ireland was partitioned into a complex network of gaelic lordships. Donegal is, like Cork, a big county, 'an unwieldy and contrived construct'. It is deeply fissured on its northern shores by the Atlantic; great mountain ranges limit communication and force the fringes of east, west and north outward. Historically Donegal has looked to Scotland and Spain rather than to Dublin or London. More than any Irish county Donegal's story has to take account of beyond.

Donegal's ancient fractured surfaces are overlain with the rich humus of geography and history. Its large Gaeltacht, the most populous in Ireland, and its considerable non-Catholic population afford insights to the greater Ireland, north and south. This county is however a place of proud belonging and is a valid and convenient measure of area to harvest history. Donegal has an ample store of scholarship in both the Irish and English languages which is constantly being replenished. Local groups, such as the County Donegal Historical Society, through their publications ensure the vitality of the past. *Donegal: History & Society* brings together a *meitheal* of scholars to gather its history. It is not an easy task. There are many fragments, great silences and some voices which are too loud. This book is dedicated to the living and the dead who have made Donegal.

In producing *Donegal: History & Society* we have drawn on the resources and generosity of many people. Chief among them have been the contributors who responded so positively when we issued our initial invitations to join us in this endeavour. We are grateful to the County Donegal Historical Society, and in particular to Kathleen Emerson and Seamus Gildea, for organising a seminar in Ballybofey in October 1994 at which some of the chapters in this volume were given a public airing. Donegal County Council has been very supportive and gave a generous financial subvention towards the cost of production.

We wish to express our gratitude to the elected members of the County Council and the County Manager, Michael McLoone. The late Tom O'Reilly, former County Secretary, assisted the project in every way possible and for that we wish to record our thanks. We owe a very special debt to the staff of Donegal County Library, especially Mary Monaghan and Mary McCole.

We are deeply grateful to the staff of the many archives, libraries and museums who have facilitated research for this book especially to Fergus Gillespie of the Genealogical Office, Gerry Lyne, Kevin Brown and Eugene Hogan of the National Library of Ireland and Ken Hannigan of the National Archives of Ireland. David Dickson kindly supplied a print of the painting, 'Rathmullan Street with Inishowen hills in distance' by Elizabeth Otway, which is depicted on the front cover and Fergus Gillespie provided the print of the 'arms of Rory O'Donnell' for the back cover from the archives of the Genealogical Office. We are grateful to the Ulster Museum, Belfast, the Public Record Office of Northern Ireland, the National Library of Ireland and the many individuals who kindly provided photographs for this volume.

All of the production work for this book was done in Ireland and we wish to thank our typesetters, Phototype-Set, Glasnevin, especially Michael Lynam and Noel Murphy and our printer, ColourBooks, who were both unsparing in their efforts to ensure that this volume matched the high quality of its predecessors. Christy Nolan of Phototype-Set designed the cover. Deasún FitzGerald indexed the volume and provided editorial assistance. Stephen Hannon and Ciarán Lynch of the Geography Department, University College Dublin were unsparing in their efforts to ensure the high quality of cartography throughout the book.

Réamhrá

'Tá mé ro-óg do sheanchuimhní,' a dúirt fear scoth-aosta de chuid na gCroisbhealaí liom nuair a bhí mé á cheistiú faoi chuimhní a óige agus chúlaigh sé siar isteach i sean-nós an tsearbhadais. De réir cosúlachta, bhí sé cruaidh i gcónaí fána chuid seanchais. B'fhéidir gur cineál de 'anal retentiveness' ba chúis lena chuid ainnise. Agus mé ag inse an scéil dona chomharsa beal dorais, arsa sise liom, amach díreach, gan fiacail a chur ann, 'Órú a thaiscigh, cha scarfadh an t-ógánach sin lena chac, chan amháin a chuimhní.'

Seanchuimhní! Mar chine, tá said linn i dtólamh. Ó leanbh go liath, tá said ár gcomóradh. Seanchuimhní sinseartha. Tá said fite fuaite i bhfíodóireacht ár n-aigne, i ngréasán ár sícé. Thig linn iad a sheachaint ach cha dtig linn iad a scrios. Amanta, cuireann said daoine áirithe glan as a meabhair, go speisialta nuair a thosaíonn siad ag éileamh a gceart; nuair a thosaíonn said ag iarraidh teanga a thabhair don tost a thacht iad. Nach as an bhrú sin sa Sícé spreagadh na filíochta go minic. Tig na seanchuimhní seo anuas chugainn ó ghlúin go glúin agus ó *gene* go *gene*. Agus le casadh a chur i seanfhocal, 'níl a fhios ag duine ar bith cá háit a bhfuil na *genes* ag teannadh ar an duine eile.'

Is fada an bealach ó inné go dtí amárach agus níl compánach níos fearr leis an bhóthar sin a ghiorrú ná Gobán Saor na Cuimhne. Taitníonn an leabhar seo liom mar gur ceiliúradh é ar an chuimhne, cuimhne na gConallach orthu féin mar chine. Sa tsaothar seo, tá saol agus saoithiúlacht s'againn féin a thabhairt chun an tsolais agus chun na cuimhne. Chuala mé máthair ag rá lena mac óg, *teenybopper trendyáilte*, de chuid na Bealtaine, nuair nach raibh sé ábalta cuimhniú cá háit ar fhág sé eochracha an tí; 'O thúsaigh tú ag cur an *ghrease* sin i do chuid gruaige, tá achan rud ag sleamhnú as do chuimhne.' Coinnímis greim ar ár gcuimhne mar sé atá ann ná an snaidhm bheag a chuireann muid ar snáithe na staire agus é ag sleamhnú uainn trí pholl snáthaide na síoraíochta. Cúis bhróid dúinn uilig go bhfuil pobail bheaga ar fud an Chontae ag fógairt a bhféiniúlachta féin; ag fógairt don tsaol mhór go bhfuil meas acu ar a dtréithe agus ar a ndúchas; go bhfuil said bródúil as a n-achmainní cultúrtha féin. Tá seo á chur i gcrích acu le foilseacháin agus le féilte. Seo an rud a nglaonn an file Liam Ó Muirthile, 'náisiúntacht na mbailte fearainn' air. Is cuimhneach liomsa agus mé ag teacht i méadaíocht go mbíodh beagmheas ag na húdaráis ar an tsaíocht áitiúil seo. Go romhinic, dhéantaí neamart ann agus neamhiontas dó. Mura mbeadh ann ach mioneachtraí beaga barrúla na mbailte fearainn; *trivia* tíriúla na treibhe; is fiú an seanchas seo a chruinniú agus a chaomhnú. Tá saoithiúlacht ár sinsear le sonrú sna scéalta seo fosta.

Tá sé tábhachtach i ré seo an Idirnáisiúnachais go ndéanfadh gach paróiste, gach pobal beag a mbratach féin a ardú ar chrann a bhféiniúlachta; go ndédanfadh siad suaitheantas a sainiúlachta a chaitheamh os comhair an tsaoil. Agus tá pobail bheaga sa Chontae seo á dhéanamh sin le dearfacht agus le dóchas. Cé acu i nGleann Cholmcille, i nDún Lúiche, i gCarn Domhnaigh, tá na pobail bheaga seo sásta stiúir a ghlacadh ar a gcinniúint féin; sásta cor agus casadh úr a chur ina ndán féin. Dá mhéad a mhothaíonn pobal ar bith go bhfuil rud inteacht suntasach, rud inteacht pearsanta dá gcuid féin le bronnadh acu ar an chine daonna i gcoitinne, is amhlaidh is mó a bheas meas acu orthu féin agus, dá réir sin, tá súil agam, meas acu ar dhaoine eile chomh maith. Sé an mana atá ag na pobail seo, i ngan fhios daofa féin, déarfainn, ná 'bogfaidh mise agus bogfaidh tusa agus bogfaith muid le chéile.'

Thar na blianta, tá Údarás na Gaeltachta an-fheidmiúil san fheachtas féin-slánaithe seo. Tá cuidiú agus cinnireacht agus comhairle á chur ar fáil acu d'eagraíochtaí áitiúla ar fud na Gaeltachta; polasaí a chuir brí agus borradh i ngníomhaíocht na bpobal seo. Agus níl ansin ach dream amháin de *Delphic Oracles* an Dúchais, anseo i nDún na nGall. Dar ndóigh, má tá muid ag iarraidh ár mbrionglóidí a fhíorú, caithfimid fanacht múscailte. Caithfimid fanacht foscailte. I ré seo an bheaguchtaigh, chan daoine díograiseacha amháin atá uainn ach daoine dúisithe.

Ná bímis ródhoicheallach roimh athruithe – cuid thábhachtach den tsaol is ea an bhreith – an bás – athnuachan agus athrú. Is fearr coiscéim amháin chun tosaigh ná choiscéim chun deiridh. Tá gach ní, beo agus neamhbheo, ag síorathrú. Tá ár gCultúr Gaelach mar an gcéanna – ag sní de shíor i dtreo na síoraíochta. Tabhar cluas éisteachta ar feadh bomaite do Hermann Hesse:

> All life is a becoming, not a being. It's motion not static. Consequently, what you call culture is not something finished once and for all that we inherit and preserve or throw away and destroy. Only so much of our culture remains alive and effective as each generation is able to gain possession of and breathe life into.

Na bíodh imní ar bith ort, dá bhrí sin, más i *microwave* a dhéanann tú do chuid brúitíní, más thart ar *radiators* a bhíonn tú ag scéalaíocht; más ar *ghettoblaster* a éisteann tú leis an sean-nós. Tá tú ag cur saoithiúlacht do shinsear in oiriúint do riachtanais do shaoilse. Na

Dúchasóirí is mó a thógann mo chroí-se – ná iad siúd atá leath – réamhstairiúil agus leath *post-modern* ina ndóigh agus ina ndearcadh. Inniu, d'fhéadfadh said a bheith ag buachailleacht *dinosaurs* le Fionn Mac Cumhaill agus, amárach, thiocfá orthu ag imirt *strip-poker* le Méabh Chonnacht.

Seo mo chuid *Role Models*; daoine atá dílís dá ndúiche agus dá ndúchas ach, ag an am chéanna, daoine nach bhfuil teannta taobh istigh de sheanmhúnlaí agus de sheanstruchtúir. Tá siad ina ndúiseacht – anseo, anois – san aimsir láithreach.

Agus os ag trácht ar an dúchas atá mé, nach iontach an téagar agus an teacht aniar atá sa teanga. In ainneoin gach iarracht le í a dhíothú, tá sí go fóill ar a cosa agus ag ciceáil. Agus is ardú meanman agus cúis dóchais do phobal na Gaeilge ar fud na tíre an seasamh dearfach atá glactha ag Uachtarán na hÉireann, Máire Mhic Roibín, i leith na teanga. Mheabhraigh sí dúinn, san aitheasc a thug sí nuair a hinsealbhaíodh í mar uachtarán, nach raibh an teanga ar a toil aici ach gheall sí go ndéanfadh sí an easpa sin a leasú. Rud a rinne. Agus í ag teacht ar an teanga i nDáil Éireann, dúirt sí féin:

> Tá sé ráite ag go leor daoine ó shoin liom gur thug an dea-shampla sin misneach dóibh mé a leanúint. Agus mhéadaigh sin mo mhisneach féin. Táimid ag dul ar aghaidh le chéile, ag cabhrú le chéile agus ag tabhairt cuireadh do dhaoine eile muid a leanúint ar an aistear cultúrtha seo is dual d'Éireannaigh.

Agus creideann sí go láidir go dtuilleann an teanga an cúram agus an chosaint chéanna atá á thabhairt don timpeallacht. 'Tá an ghluaiseacht faoi shlánú na timpeallachta,' a dúirt sí, 'tar éis greim a fháil ar shamhlaíocht na hóige. Anois, is gá dúinn a áiteamh ar ár muintir óg gur cuid den timpeallacht í an teanga freisin; gur rud beo í atá faoi strus agus faillí déanta ina leith'.

Thar aon ní, ba mhaith liom go mbeadh ár gcóras oideachais i nGaeilge saor ó luachanna seargtha agus ó nósanna calctha. Ba mhaith liom go mbeadh ár gcuid múinteoirí Gaeilge ag fáiltiú roimh fheiniméan na beatha. Ba mhaith liom go ndéanfadh said foscailteacht aigne a chothú is a chleachtadh. Chan tairbhe ar bith don teanga má mbhíonn ár gcuid múinteoirí ina bpríosúnaigh taobh istigh de bhallaí Berlin na seanaimsearthachta. Ba mhaith liom go ndéanfadh siad spiorad na fiontraíochta agus spiorad na fiosrachta a spreagadh ina gcuid scoláirí. Ba chóir go mbeadh na cáilíochtaí seo ar thús Cadhnaíochta gus muid ag caint ar chur chun cinn na Gaeilge. Agus chan fhuil láthair níos fearr leis na tréithe seo a fhorbairt agus a fhairsingiú ná sa scoil. Tá géarghá le foscailteacht agus le fiosracht agus le fiontraíocht i ngach ngé de shaol na Gaeilge. Go rómhinic, bíonn ár gcuid díograiseoirí teanga scoite amach ón saol sa dún dainséarach sin ar a dtugtar an Aimsir Chaite – áit nach bhfuil fás ná forbairt i ndán daofa – áit nach bhfuil i ndán daofa féin agus a gcuid aislingí ach an bás. Tá go leor daoine amuigh ansiúd a bhfuil an Ghaeilge ina codladh i gcúl a gcinn. Caithfear cuidiú leis na daoine sin a gcuid Gaeilge a mhúscailt as an tromshuan ina bhfuil sí. Go leor de na daoine seo, ní bhíonn muinín acu an méid den teanga atá acu a úsáid. Síleann siad go bhfaighimid locht ar a gcuid cainte, go mbéimid ag magadh faoina gcuid *gibberish* Gaeilge. Caithfimid fáiltiú roimh achan fhocal Gaeilge a chluinimid – achan abairt, is cuma cé chomh briste, bliotach agus atá sí. Sa dóigh sin, béimid ag tabhairt misnigh do na daoine seo an teanga a úsáid. Tá go leor daoine ar fud an Chontae a bhfuil a gcuid Gaeilge ceilte sa *chloset* acu. Caithfimid cuidiú leo 'a theacht amach' léithe go poiblí. Agus ní dhéanfar sin ach amháin le cineáltas agus le *counselling*. Caithfimid a chur ina luí ar dhaoine atá ag foghlaim Gaeilge gan eagla a bheith orthu roimh mheancóg a dhéanamh go poiblí, gan náire ar bith a bheith orthu má shleamhnaíonn said ar shiolla éigin; gan taom croí a bheith acu má bhaineann an tuiseal ginideach tuisle astu. Nílimid anseo le cigireacht teanga a dhéanamh ar dhuine ar bith. Mar a dúirt Máirtín Ó Cadhain, 'Ná cuireadh canúinteoirí ná cantalóirí ná ollúin ollscoile ná cainteoirí dúchais de bhur mbuille sibh. Ní le cantalóirí ná le hollúin ná leis an nGaeltacht féin an Ghaeilge. Is leis an gcine í. Mar theanga cine, agus ní mar theanga ollún ná cúpla ceantar iargúlta atá beatha i ndán di. Pér bith cén sort teanga a bheas á labhairt – Gaeilge ghlan nó neamhghlan – ach í a bheith sách forleathan – is teanga bheo í'.

Tá an t-ádh dearg orainn go bhfuil dornán de dhaoine gnaíúla, gealgháireacha ag cur na Gaeilge chun cinn sa Chontae: Liam Ó Cuinneagáin, cuir i gcás – Gúrú Ghleann Cholm Cille; stiúrthóir agus spreagthóir Oideas Gael, agus Liam Lillis Ó Laoire, curadh ceoil Chloich Cheann Fhaola; scríbhneoir agus scoláire. Seo díograiseoirí dúchasacha. Seo dúchasóirí atá dúisithe. Tá foscailteacht aigne agus fairsingeacht samhlaíochta ag baint leo beirt. Cinnte, tá grabhrógaí beaga dár gcultúr, a déarfadh siad beirt, caillte idir 'An Greim Gasta agus *An Golden Grill*' ach os a choinne sin, má tá a bolg thiar ar a tóin leis an fhéar gortach, thig leis an tSeanbhean Bhocht a theacht chuici féin, i gcónaí le bocstaí *microwaveáilte* agus le brúitíní *smasháilte*. Caithfimid ár dtodhchaí a fhí as ár ndúchas chomh fada agus is féidir a leithéidí a dhéanamh ag deireadh an fhichiú haois. Cha dtig linn ligean do shnáithe ár scéil a ghabháil in aimhréidhe idir Túirne Mháire agus *Fruit of the Loom*. Tuigeann siad beirt go gcaithfear leanúnachas a chothú. B'fhéidir go bhfuil Balor Béimeann na cianta sa chré ach tá *Cyclops* an tseomra suí deabheo. Tá iarracht an-mhór á déanamh i láthair na huaire le é a Ghaelú i gceart sa dóigh nach mbeidh sé de nós aige súil nimhe an drochmheasa a chaitheamh ar ár nDúchas. Is é an dúshlán, a déarfadh Liam agus Lillis, atá amach romhainn, mar thír agus mar threabh, ná a bheith ábalta dual den rud a shnaidhmeadh go néanta i ngréasán sóisialta ár saoil. De bhrí sin, cha chuirfeadh sé iontas ar bith orm dá bhfeicinn an bheirt acu ag *joyrideáil* i gceann de chuid carbaid Chú Chulainn. Lena chois sin, cuireann siad faoi gheasa mé lena gcuid gramadaí. Seo cainteoirí a bhfuil a gcuid consan caol níos caoile ná Twiggy; múinteoirí a bhfuil stiúir agus smacht acu ar a gcuid h-annaí; daoine dáimhiúla atá i dtiúin lena gcuid tuiseal. Agus cén fáth nach mbéadh? Níl siolla Gaeilge ina gceann nach ndéantar a shruthlú achan mhaidin i dTobar An Dúchais. Cé bith fá dhaoine eile, níl rian ar bith de *Phlaque* ar Ghaeilge na beirte seo.

Agus tá Oideas Gael, an t-eagras a bhunaigh Liam Ó Cuinneagáin i nGleann Cholm Cille, le cúrsaí teanga agus cultúir a chur ar fáil do dhaoine fásta, ag bláthú in aghaidh na bliana agus ag síolrú, de réir cosúlachta. Tá An Chrannóg, a mhacasamhail d'áras agus d'ionad againn anois i nGaoth Dobhair. Agus is maith ann iad. Cineál de Acadaimh i gcúrsaí Gaeilge atá sna hionaid seo. Tá polasaí teanga á chur chun cinn acu ar bhonn proifisiúnta.

Thar rud ar bith eile, turas atá sa leabhar seo turas cultúrtha timpeall na contae. Déantar muid a thionlacan go sibhialta agus go scolártha go dtí suíomh staire agus seandálaíochta, go dtí láithreacha léinn agus litríochta. Tugtar le fios dúinn go bhfuil muid mar dhream daoine, áitiúil agus idirnáisiúnta; go bhfuil muid seanaimseartha agus nua-aoiseach; go bhfuil muid seanteach ceanntuí-ach agus *bungalow modcon-ach*. Agus is aoibhinn liom turais mar seo – *mystery tours* sa tsaol agus sa tsamhlaíocht. Cuimhním ar mo sheanchara – Maggie Neddie Dhonncaidh, mo chomarsa béal dorais i Mín 'A Leá; bean nár fhág an baile ach an t-aon uair amháin ina saol, aistear fada eipiciúil a rinne sí go hiarthar Chontae an Chláir agus aríst chun a bhaile ar an lá céanna i mí Mheán An tSamhraidh sa bhliain 1963. Bhí Biddy, deirfiúir daoithe, pósta ar fhear de chuid an Chláir, agus iad ag cur fúthu thall i Londain Shasana. Is cosúil gur shocraigh siad saoire na bliana sin a chaitheamh le bunadh s'aigsean in Iarthar an Chláir agus tugadh cuireadh do Mhaggie a ghabháil síos chucu ar cuairt. Rud a rinne ach de ruaig reatha. Fuair sí Charlie John Óig, tiománaí cairr de chuid na háite agus fear a bhí gar go maith i ngaol díthe féin le í a thiomáint síos agus ar ais aríst aníos ar an lá céanna. Agus ina dhiaidh sin, cha raibh as a béal ach 'An lá a chuaigh mise go Contae an Chláir'. Agus bhéarfadh sí cuntas iomlán duit ar gach cor agus casadh den aistear sin; gach eachtra, mion, mór agus measartha a tharla díthe ar a turas.

Bhí gach gné den turas clóbhuailte ar a cuimhne … an méid a chonaic sí; an méid a chuala sí agus an méid a mhothaigh sí. Agus mise agus mo chairde, na blianta ina dhiaidh sin ag insint díthe fá eachtraí a tharla dúinn agus muid ag taisteal ar an mhór-Roinn nó i Meiriceá, thiocfadh aoibh áthais ar a haghaidh shoineanta, agus déarfadh sí, 'Bhuel, nach bhfuil sin iontach – tá sé go díreach cosúil leis an rud a tharla domhsa an lá a chuaigh mé go Contae an Chláir'. B'shin í ar shiúl faoi lánseoil ar aistear an aobhnis. Agus de réir mar a chuaigh sí anonn i mblianta, d'éirigh an *Odyssey* lae seo níos draíochtúla agus níos eipiciúla. Chruthaigh Maggie Neddie Dhonncaidh miotas dúinne i Mín 'A Leá; miotas a lonraíonn mar a bheadh réaltóg os cionn leadránacht laethúil ár saoil; miotas a thugann ardú meanman dúinn nuair a bhíonn an saol sa mhullach orainn. Níl le déanamh againn ach cuimhneamh 'ar an lá a chuaigh mise go Contae an Chláir" agus tá a fhios againn go bhfuil bealach éalaithe as an bhuaireamh. Faraor géar, tá Maggie Neddie Dhonncaidh ag iompar na bhfód i Reilig Ghort A' Choirce ach tá mise siúrailte go bhfuil a spiorád óigeanta ag siobhiúl sa tsíoraíocht.

Agus tú ag déanamh do thurais fríd an tsaothar seo, mholfainn duit do chuid adharca a bheith amuigh agat, adharca na teagmhála agus adharca na tuigbheála; *Sensors* na samhlaíochta. Macasamhail Mhaggie, bí i do *See - r*. Bí ag lorg brí. Cha nochtann an fhírinne í féin ach daofa siúd a théann ar a tóir, agus chan fheiceann tú í mura bhfuil do shúile foscailte. Chan súil cinn amháin atá i gceist ach súile na haigne chomh maith.

Fadó, fadó, bhí laoch ann – fear óg ábalta arb é mian gach mná é. Bhíodh sé amuigh ag fiach achan lán san fhoraois agus san fhiántas.

Tráthnóna amháin, le buíú gréine, tháinig tart air go tobann agus chrom sé síos le deoch a ól i lochán sléibhe a bhí ina shlí, agus é sínte síos ar a bholg ag ól an uisce seo a thug fluichadh agus fuaradh dó i dteas an tráthnóna, chonaic sé an scáile is áille dár leag sé a shúil ariamh air ag lonrú thíos faoi san uisce. Scáile éin a bhí ann. D'fhéach sé ar feadh tamaill fhada ar an scáile seo ag soilsiú san uisce. Má bhí an scáile chomh hálainn seo, an bhféadfaí amharc ar an éan é féin – iontas na n-iontas – gan titim i bhfanntais le haoibhneas? De bhrí sin, d'árdaigh sé a cheann go ciúin agus go cúramach go bhfeicfeadh sé an t-éan a bhí ag foluain os a chionn sa spéir. Ní raibh faic le feiceáil. Bhí an t-éan imithe i bhfaiteadh na súl is ní raibh le feiceáil ach aoibh ghriandóite na spéire ag spléachadh anuas air. Bhí sé iontach buartha gur imigh an aisling seo as radharc. Rinne sé amach láithreach go rachadh sé ar thóir an éin iontaigh seo agus go ndéanfadh sé é a aimsiú, in ainneoin na n-ainneoin. Le scéal fada a dhéanamh gairid, rinne sé sin. Chaith sé an chuid eile dá shaol ag tóraíocht an éin – thíos agus thuas; i gcéin agus i gcóngar. Is iomaí teorainn a thrasnaigh sé; is iomaí críoch a chonaic sé. Fuair sé leid anseo faoin éan; nod ansiúd. Casadh daoine air a chonaic an t-éan; daoine a chuala faoi dhaoine a chonaic é; daoine a shíl go bhfaca siad é. Sa deireadh, agus é ag titim ar a bhata ... tháinig sé ar cheantar álainn i measc na gcnoc agus dúradh leis go raibh an t-éan éachtach seo, a raibh sé ar a lorg leis na blianta, ag neadú ar bharr an tsléibhe ab airde san áit. Suas leis comh maith agus a bhí ar a chumas, ag streachailt ar a lámha agus ar a chosa; ag tarraingt ar an bharr, ar bhuaic na mistéire. Bhí sé ag éirí tuirseach traochta. Bhí a anáil i mbarr a ghoib. Sa deireadh, agus é beagnach ag barr, thit sé as a sheasamh. Bhí sé sna smeacharnaí deireanacha. Ag an bhomaite sin, is na súile ag druid air, chuala sé cleitearnach éin os a chionn ... cineál de shioscadh caoin, ceolmhar agus thit cleite anuas as na spéarthaí ar a bhrollach – an cleite ab áille dár leag sé a shúil ariamh air. Tháinig aoibh na hóige aríst ina aghaidh agus é ag fáil bháis is an cleite ag spréacharnaigh ar a bhrollach ...

Tá súil agam go ndéanfar rudaí a bhí doiléir a shoiléiriú duit ar d'aistear léitheoireachta fríd an leabhar seo ... Guím go dtitfidh cleite nó dhó i do threo ...

Cathal Ó Searcaigh

List of Abbreviations

A.F.M.
: *Annála ríoghachta Éireann; Annals of the kingdom of Ireland by the Four Masters from the earliest period to the year 1616*, ed. and trans. John O'Donovan (7 vols, Dublin, 1851; reprint, New York, 1966).

A.L.C.
: *The Annals of Loch Cé: a chronicle of Irish affairs, 1014-1690*, ed. W. M. Hennessy (2 vols, London, 1871; reflex facsimile, Irish Manuscripts Commission, Dublin, 1939).

A.U.
: *Annála Uladh, Annals of Ulster; otherwise Annála Senait, Annals of Senat: a chronicle of Irish affairs, 431-1131, 1155-1541*, ed. W. M. Hennessy and B. MacCarthy (4 vols, Dublin, 1887-1901).

A.U.2
: The Annals of Ulster (to A.D. 1131), part I, ed. Seán Mac Airt and Gearóid Mac Niocaill (Dublin, 1983).

Anal. Hib.
: *Analecta Hibernica, including the reports of the Irish Manuscripts Commission* (Dublin, 1930-).

Ann. Clon.
: *The Annals of Clonmacnoise, being annals of Ireland from the earliest period to A.D. 1408, translated into English, A.D. 1627, by Conell Mageoghagan*, ed. Denis Murphy (Royal Society of Antiquaries of Ireland, Dublin, 1896).

Ann. Inisf.
: *The Annals of Inisfallen (MS Rawlinson B 503)*, ed. and trans. Seán Mac Airt (Dublin Institute for Advanced Studies, 1951).

Ann. Tig.
: 'The annals of Tigernach', ed. Whitley Stokes, in *Rev. Celt.*, xvi-xvii (1895-7).

Archiv. Hib.
: *Archivium Hibernicum: or Irish historical records* (Catholic Record Society of Ireland, Maynooth, 1912-).

Arch. Jn.
: *Archaeological Journal* (London, 1844-).

B.M.
: British Museum.

B.M. cat. Ir. MSS
: *Catalogue of Irish manuscripts in the British Museum*, vol. i, by S. H. O'Grady; vol. ii, by R. Flower (London, 1926).

B.N.B., index 1950-54 [etc.]	*The British national bibliography, cumulated index 1950-54*, ed. A. J. Wells [etc.] (London, 1955-).
Belfast Natur. Hist. Soc. Proc.	*Proceedings and Reports of the Belfast Natural History and Philosophical Society* (Belfast, 1873-).
Bigger cat.	*Catalogue of books and bound MSS of the Irish hsitorical, archaeological and antiquarian library of the late Francis Joseph Bigger, presented to the Belfast Public Library* (Belfast, 1930).
Bk. Arm.	*Liber Ardmachanus; The Book of Armagh*, ed. John Gwynn (Royal Irish Academy, Dublin, 1913).
Bk. Fen.	*The Book of Fenagh*, ed. W. M. Hennessy and D. H. Kelly (Dublin, 1875; reflex facsimile, Irish Manuscripts Commission, Dublin, 1939).
B.L.	British Library.
Breifne	*Breifne: journal of Cumann Seanchais Bhreifne* (*Breifne Historical Society*) (Cavan, 1958-).
Brit. Acad. Proc.	*Proceedings of the British Academy* (London, 1903-).
Cal.	*Calendar; Cal.* is here used as the first word in the short titles of calendared series issued by the English and Irish Public Record Offices.
Cal. Carew MSS, 1517-74 [etc.]	*Calendar of the Carew manuscripts preserved in the archiepiscopal library at Lambeth, 1515-74* [etc.] (6 vols, London, 1867-73).
Cal. doc. Ire., 1171-1251 [etc.]	*Calendar of documents relating to Ireland, 1171-1251* [etc.] (5 vols, London, 1875-86).
Cal. justic. rolls Ire., 1295-1303 [etc.]	*Calendar of the justiciary rolls, or proceedings in the court of the justiciar of Ireland . . . [1295-1303]* [etc.], ed. J. Mills (2 vols, Dublin, 1905, 1914).
Cal. papal letters, 1198-1304 [etc.]	*Calendar of entries in the papal registers relating to Great Britain and Ireland: papal letters, 1198-1304* [etc.] (London, 1893-).
Cal. pat. rolls, 1232-47 [etc.]	*Calendar of the patent rolls, 1232-47* [etc.], (London, 1906-).
Cal. pat. rolls Ire., Hen. VIII-Eliz.	*Calendar of patent and close rolls of chancery in Ireland, Henry VIII to 18th Elizabeth*, ed. James Morrin (Dublin, 1861).

Cal. pat. rolls Ire., Eliz.	*Calendar of patent and close rolls of chancery in Ireland, Elizabeth, 19 year to end of reign,* ed. James Morrin (Dublin, 1862).
Cal. pat. rolls Ire., Jas I	*Irish patent rolls of James I: facsimile of the Irish record commissioners' calendar prepared prior to 1830,* with foreword by M. C. Griffith (Irish Manuscripts Commission, Dublin, 1966).
Cal. S.P. dom., 1574-80 [etc.]	*Calendar of state papers, domestic series, 1547-80* [etc.], (London, 1856-).
Cal. S.P. Ire., 1509-73 [etc.]	*Calendar of the state papers relating to Ireland, 1509-73* [etc.] (24 vols, London 1860-1911).
Cal. S.P. Scot., 1547-63 [etc.]	*Calendar of state papers relating to Scotland and Mary queen of Scots, 1547-63* [etc.] (Edinburgh, 1898-).
Camb. Hist. Jn.	*Cambridge Historical Journal* (Cambridge, 1923-57, 13 vols).
C.B.E.	*Cnuasach Bhéaloideas Éireann,* Roinn Bhéaloideas Éireann, Coláiste na hOllscoile, Baile Átha Cliath.
Celtic Rev.	*The Celtic Review* (Edinburgh, 1904-16, 10 vols).
Celtica	*Celtica* (Dublin, 1950-).
Census Ire., 1659	*A census of Ireland* circa *1659, with supplementary material from the poll money ordinances (1660-1661),* ed. S. Pender (Irish Manuscripts Commission, Dublin, 1939).
Census Ire., 1841	*Report of the commissioners appointed to take the census of Ireland for the year 1841* [504], H.C. 1843, xxiv.
Census Ire., 1851, I, I [etc.]	*The census of Ireland for the year 1851: part I, showing the area, population and number of houses by townlands and electoral divisions,* vol. i, province of Leinster, H.C. 1852-3, xci [etc.].
Chron. Scot.	*Chronicum Scotorum: a chronicle of Irish affairs . . . to 1135, and supplement . . . 1141-1150,* ed. W. M. Hennessy (London, 1866).
Civil Survey	*The Civil Survey, A.D. 1654-56,* ed. R. C. Simington (Irish Manuscripts Commission, 10 vols, Dublin, 1931-61), vol. iii, Counties of Donegal, Londonderry and Tyrone (Dublin, 1937).

Clogher Rec.	*Clogher Record* ([Monaghan]), 1953-).
Colgan, *Acta SS Hib.*	John Colgan, *Acta sanctorum veteris et maioris Scotiae, seu Hiberniae sanctorum insulae . . .* (2 vols, Louvain, 1645; reflex facsimile, with foreword by Brendan Jennings, Irish Manuscripts Commission, Dublin, 1948).
Collect. Hib.	*Collectanea Hibernica: sources for Irish history* (Dublin, 1958-).
Commons' jn.	*Journals of the house of commons* [of England, Great Britain, or United Kingdom].
Commons' jn. Ire.	*Journals of the house of commons of the kingdom of Ireland . . .* (1613-1791, 28 vols, Dublin, 1753-91; reprinted and continued, 1613-1800, 19 vols, Dublin, 1796-1800).
Comp. bk Conn.	*The compossicion booke of Conought*, ed. A. M. Freeman (Irish Manuscripts Commission, Dublin, 1936).
Cork Hist. Soc. Jn.	*Journal of the Cork Historical and Archaeological Society* (Cork, 1892-).
D.N.B.	*Dictionary of national biography*, ed. Sir Leslie Stephen and Sir Sidney Lee (66 vols, London, 1885-1901; reprinted with corrections, 22 vols, London, 1908-9).
Devon comm. rep.	*Report from her majesty's commissioners of inquiry into the state of the law and practice in respect to the occupation of land in Ireland* [earl of Devon, chairman], H.C. 1845 (605), xix, 1-56.
Docwra, *Narration*	Sir Henry Docwra, 'A narration of the services done by the army ymployed to Lough-Foyle . . .' in *Miscellany of the Celtic Society*, ed. John O'Donovan (Dublin, 1849).
Donegal Annual	*Journal of the County Donegal Historical Society; iris Cumann Seanchais Dún na nGall* (vol. i, Londonderry, 1947-50); continued as *The Donegal Annual, incorporating the journal of the County Donegal Historical Society* (Londonderry, [1951]-).
Dublin Hist. Rec.	*Dublin Historical Record* (Dublin, 1938-).
E.H.R.	*English Historical Review* (London, 1886-).
Econ. Hist.	*Economic History; or supplement of the Economic Journal* (London, 1926-).

Econ. Hist. Rev.	*Economic History Review* (London, 1927-).
Éire-Ireland	*Éire-Ireland: a journal of Irish studies* (Irish American Cultural Institute, St Paul, Minn., 1965-).
Études Celt.	*Études Celtiques* (Paris, 1936-).
Fiants Ire., Hen. VIII [etc.]	'Calendar to fiants of the reign of Henry VIII . . .' [etc.] in *P.R.I. rep. D.K. 7-22* (Dublin, 1875-90).
Galway Arch. Soc. Jn.	*Journal of the Galway Archaeological and Historical Society* (Galway, 1900-).
Gen. synod Ulster rec.	*Records of the general synod of Ulster, 1691-1820* (3 vols, Belfast, 1890-98).
H.C.	House of commons sessional paper.
H.M.C.	Historical Manuscripts Commission.
Hansard I, i [etc.]	*Cobbett's parliamentary debates, 1803-12* (vols i-xxii, London, 1804-12); continued as *The parliamentary debates from the year 1803 to the present time,* 1812-20 (vols xxiii-xli, London, 1812-20; from vol. xxvii, 1813-14, the title includes: *published under the superintendence of T. C. Hansard*).
Hist. Jn.	*The Historical Journal* (Cambridge, 1958).
I.E.R.	*Irish Ecclesiastical Record* (Dublin, 1864-).
I.H.S.	*Irish Historical Studies: the joint journal of the Irish Historical Society and the Ulster Society for Irish Historical Studies* (Dublin, 1938-).
I.M.C.	Irish Manuscripts Commission, Dublin.
Inq. cancell. Hib. repert.	*Inquisitionum in officio rotulorum cancellariae Hiberniae . . . repertorium* (2 vols, Dublin, 1826-9).
I.F.C.	Irish Folklore Commission.
Ir. Geneal.	*The Irish Genealogist: official organ of the Irish Generalogical Research Society* (London, 1937-).
Ir. Geography	*Irish Geography* (*bulletin of the Geographical Society of Ireland*) (vols i-iv, Dublin, 1944-63); continued as *The Geographical Society of Ireland, Irish Geography* (vol. v- , Dublin, 1964-).
Ir. texts	*Irish texts,* ed. J. Fraser, P. Grosjean, and J. G. O'Keefe (fasc. 1-5, London, 1931-4).
Jn. Brit. Studies	*Journal of British Studies* (Hartford, Conn., 1961-).

L. & P. Hen. VIII, *1509-13* [etc.]	*Letters and papers, foreign and domestic,* *Henry VIII* (21 vols, London, 1862-1932).
Lr Cl. Aodha Buidhe	*Leabhar Cloinne Aodha Buidhe*, ed. Tadhg Ó Donnchadha (Irish Manuscripts Commission, Dublin, 1931).
Misc. Ir. Annals	*Miscellaneous Irish annals* (A.D. 1114-1437), ed. Séamus Ó hInnse (Dublin Institute for Advanced Studies, 1947).
N.A.I.	National Archives Ireland
N.A.I. 620	Rebellion papers
N.A.I. C.B.S.	Chief Secretary's Office, Crime Branch Special files
N.A.I. D/JUS.	Department of Justice
N.A.I. D./L.G.	Department of Local Government
N.A.I. D./T.	Department of the Taoiseach
N.A.I. O.P.	Official papers [1st series]
N.A.I. O.R.	Chief Secretary's Office, Outrage Reports
N.A.I. Q.R.O.	Quit Rent Office
N.A.I. RLF. COM.	Relief Commission
N.A.I. SOC.	State of the Country Papers [1st and 2nd series – consecutive numbering, 2nd series begins at 3000]
N.H.I.	A New History of Ireland, under the auspices of the Royal Irish Academy, ed. T. W. Moody, T. D. Williams, J. C. Beckett, F. X. Martin (Dublin, 1968-).
N.L.I.	National Library of Ireland
N.M.I.	National Museum of Ireland
O.S. name-books, *Donegal*	[*Books containing information relative to the* *place-names of the county of Donegal collected* *during the progress of the ordnance survey in* *1834* [etc.], ed. Rev. Michael O'Flanagan, from the originals in the Ordnance Survey, Phoenix Park (typescript, 76 vols, Bray)].
P.R.O.	Public Record Office of England.
P.R.O.I.	Public Record Office of Ireland.
P.R.O.N.I.	Public Record Office of Northern Ireland.
Pat. rolls Ire., Jas I, ed. Erck	*A repertory of the inrolments of the patent rolls* *of chancery in Ireland commencing with the* *reign of James I,* ed. J. C. Erck (2 pts, Dublin, 1846-52).
Prehist. Soc. Proc.	*Proceedings of the Prehistoric Society* (Cambridge, 1935-).

R. Hist. Soc. Trans.	*Transactions of the Royal Historical Society* (London, 1872-).
R.I.A.	Royal Irish Academy.
R.I.A. cat. Ir. MSS	T. F. O'Rahilly and others, *Catalogue of Irish manuscripts in the Royal Irish Academy* (Dublin, 1926-).
R.I.A. Proc.	*Proceedings of the Royal Irish Academy* (Dublin, 1836-).
R.S.A.I. Jn.	*Journal of the Royal Society of Antiquaries of Ireland* (Dublin, 1892-).
Rec. comm. Ire. rep., 1811-15 [etc.]	*Reports of the commissioners appointed by his majesty to execute the measures recommended in an address of the house of commons respecting the public records of Ireland; with supplement and appendixes* (3 vols, [London, 1815-25]; i, rep. 1-5, 1811-15; ii, rep. 6-10, 1816-20; iii, rep. 11-15, 1821-5).
Red Bk Kildare	*The Red Book of the earls of Kildare*, ed. G. Mac Niocaill (Irish Manuscripts Commission, Dublin, 1964).
Reg. privy council Scot., 1545-69 [etc.]	*Register of the privy council of Scotland, 1549-69* [etc.] (Edinburgh, 1877-).
Rot. pat. Hib.	*Rotulorum patentium et clausorum cancellariae Hiberniae calendarium* (Dublin, 1828).
S.P. Hen. VIII	*State papers, Henry VIII* (11 vols, London, 1830-52).
S.R.O.	Scottish Record Office.
Studia Hib.	*Studia Hibernica* (Dublin, 1961-).
T.C.D.	Trinity College, Dublin.
U.J.A.	*Ulster Journal of Archaeology* (Belfast, 3 series: 1853-62, 9 vols; 1895-1911, 17 vols; 1938-).
Ulster Folklife	*Ulster Folklife* (Belfast, 1955-).
Z.C.P.	*Zeitschrift für celtische Philologie* (Halle, 1896-1943, 23 vols; Tübingen, 1953-).

Contributors and Editors

*Cathal Ó Searcaigh
File, Mín a'leá, Gort a' Choirce

Brian Lacy
Museum Services, Derry City Council

*Michael Herity
University College Dublin

Helen Lanigan-Wood
Fermanagh County Museum

Eithne Verling
Formerly Donegal County Museum now Galway Theatre Project

Raghnall Ó Floinn
National Museum of Ireland

*Dónal Mac Giolla Easpaig
Ordnance Survey, Dublin

*Katherine Simms
Trinity College Dublin

*Darren Mac Eiteagáin
University College Dublin

Robert J. Hunter
Magee College, University of Ulster, Derry

*John J. Silke
Diocesan Archivist, Diocese of Raphoe

Kevin McKenny
Institute of Irish Studies, Belfast

Graeme Kirkham
Swindon, Wiltshire

William Crawford
The Federation for Ulster Local Studies, Belfast

*David Dickson
Trinity College Dublin

*James Anderson
The Open University, Milton Keynes

Jonathan Bell
Ulster Folk and Transport Museum, Belfast

James S. Donnelly, Jnr.
University of Madison, Wisconsin

*Martina O'Donnell
University College Dublin

*Brendán Mac Suibhne
Carnegie-Mellon Institute, Pittsburgh

*Jim MacLaughlin
University College Cork

Anne O'Dowd
National Museum of Ireland

Pat Bolger
Former County Development Officer, Donegal

*John Tunney
Heritage consultant, Dublin

Nollaig Mac Congháil
University College Galway

*Damhnait Nic Suibhne
University College Cork

*Lillis Ó Laoire
University of Limerick

*Fergus Gillespie/Fergus Mac Giolla Easpaig
Genealogical Office, Dublin

Liam Ronayne
County Library, Donegal

*Máiread Dunlevy
Hunt Museum, Limerick

William Nolan
University College Dublin

*either native of the county or have family connections with Donegal.

Chapter 1

PREHISTORIC AND EARLY HISTORIC SETTLEMENT IN DONEGAL

BRIAN LACY

Donegal is a very large and geographically varied county extending over almost 500,000 hectares. In its present form and area the county dates back only to the mid seventeenth century, which raises the question as to what extent it can be a meaningful unit for the analysis of settlement in remote times. The county is, however, made up of a number of ancient territories which appear to have had distinct geographical and political identities in earlier historic and (almost certainly for some of them) in prehistoric periods.[1] It is worth noting in this context that the enclave of territory on the west bank of the river Foyle immediately surrounding the city of Derry, which was delimited at the time of the Plantations in Ulster, was in previous times very much part of the patrimony of Donegal. The archaeology of this area must also be kept in mind when assessing the early settlement patterns of Donegal.

The amount and standard of archaeological research in Donegal have been mixed and discontinuous.[2] The county has been well served in terms of professional and amateur site surveying,[3] although detailed field walking has only been carried out to a limited extent. Several important Donegal artifacts and collections have been recorded and preserved,[4] but the exact findspot of many of these is not known. In addition, few modern excavations have been carried out in the county, so we are dependent largely on the evidence recovered from other parts of the country to flesh out the local detail.

The various field surveys probably provide a reasonably accurate picture of the overall distribution of ancient monuments and sites in the county. Some caution, however, must be observed. The surveys have revealed that, approximately one third of all ancient monuments shown on Ordnance Survey maps of the county since the 1830s have been destroyed, with destruction rates in some important areas, such as east Donegal, being as high as 50 per cent.[5] The loss in east Donegal is highly significant, since, being some of the best agricultural land in the region, we would assume that the area was inhabited, since Neolithic times at least, by some of the wealthier local communities. These are likely to have had the most elaborate settlements and monuments, the remains of many of which must have been removed or severely disfigured.

There is archaeological evidence of human settlement in Donegal throughout all periods of Irish prehistory from the later Mesolithic period onwards (i.e. post 5500 BC). However, it is also clear that some parts of the county were not occupied at all and others were not settled simultaneously or continuously. The complex geological structure of the county[6] has resulted in a number of geographical areas which were not conducive to human settlement at various periods in the past. Even today only about a third of the land of the county is suitable for agriculture. In addition, some geographical features in the county, such as the lowlying wetlands and the mountains, acted as substantial barriers to communication until modern times.

The centre of Donegal is dominated by the dramatic, granitic mountain ranges of Derryveagh and Glendowan situated, respectively, to the west and east of the great Gweebarra rock fault which splits Donegal from Gweebarra Bay to Sheep Haven. This central mountainous region, and the equally isolated area of the Bluestack mountains to the south of it, is virtually unenclosed and uninhabited today. The absence of surviving archaeological sites and monuments from these areas seems to demonstrate that, despite their great natural beauty, they were not seen as inviting habitats for human settlement at any time in the past.[7]

To the west of these mountains lie the Gaeltacht parishes of The Rosses, Gweedore and Cloghaneely. Although this region has been intensively settled in modern times (a congested district in the terminology of the nineteenth century), distribution maps of archaeological sites dating to earlier periods emphasise the relative scarcity of settlement. Significantly, the same absence of settlement can be discerned for the triangle of poor land around the pilgrimage destination of Lough Derg in the south-east of the county.[8]

The Mesolithic period

As might be expected in this northern county, there is some limited evidence to be found in Donegal of the oldest identified phases of human occupation in Ireland during the Mesolithic period. The earliest unambiguous Irish site associated with these hunter/gatherer people is at Mount Sandel near Coleraine in the adjoining county Derry. The stone implements found at that site, which dates to about 7000 BC, show local characteristics which are quite different to similar contemporary objects from Britain. This would seem to imply that there could be an earlier initial phase of indigenous Mesolithic culture in Ireland which has yet to be recognised.[9]

The distribution of known sites in Donegal where Mesolithic material has been found reflects more, however, the activity of modern archaeological collectors and investigators rather than the movements of our early ancestors. Systematic searches for this type of evidence would almost certainly extend the range of these sites and material. Although it has been suggested by Woodman, the leading authority on the subject, that the shores of the loughs and estuaries of north Donegal would have been very suitable areas for settlement during the Mesolithic period, no such habitation sites have yet been found in the county. A number of Mesolithic flint objects from Donegal have been documented, particularly finds of individual Bann Flakes from the latter part of the period, but a collection of narrow blades found at the base of the peat at Raws Bog near Castlefinn 'could be Early Mesolithic' in date,[10] i.e. pre 5500 BC.

The location of this find close to the River Finn, which in turn links into the system of the River Foyle and Lough Foyle, is quite consistent with the riverine and estuarine habitats apparently favoured by Mesolithic settlers. The recent find of several Bann Flakes on the western river shoreline just north of Derry seems to confirm the viewpoint that the Foyle and its tributaries served as a water highway into the interior of the country during the Mesolithic period.[11] The find of a possible early Mesolithic axe in the late nineteenth century at Dunfanaghy strengthens the likelihood that early as well as later Mesolithic settlers were established in the region. Unfortunately this axe has not been identified in any museum collection in recent times, so its authenticity cannot be verified by modern scholars.[12]

Despite palynological analysis of samples from Aranmore Island suggesting the possibility of very early prehistoric human settlement there,[13] only one definite Mesolithic site has been found in Donegal. At Urrismenagh, on the shore of Dunaff Bay at the north-west corner of the Inishowen peninsula, what has been interpreted as a temporary site of Mesolithic activity was identified and partially excavated in the 1960s.[14]

Dunaff Bay lies near the mouth of Lough Swilly where it opens out to the Atlantic Ocean. There are numerous traces of post-glacial raised beaches around the bay. During the course of geological investigations researchers noted 'an almost complete section of the lowest ancient beach exposed in a disused gravel pit'.[15] Flint objects were found in the upper levels of the section and the site was subsequently re-investigated by archaeologists.

A number of stratified flints were systematically collected from the section, as well as loose finds from the surface of the gravel pit and from three small hillocks to the east and south of the site. The stratified material came from the shingle layers of the ancient beach and from the overlying soil. No significant differences were noted between the finds from the individual layers or between stratified and unstratified material.

The flints, which for the most part consisted of waste material, were subsequently re-examined by Woodman.[16] They were mainly derived from 'uniplane single-platformed cores'. Four rough scrapers or spokeshaves were discovered in the collection. Most of the flints were unabraded and unrolled and thus their deposition was deemed to have been contemporary with the formation of the beach. The raw material from which these objects were produced consisted of light grey, well-rounded, flint beach pebbles, from 2 inches to 8 inches in diameter. It is most likely that instead of being transported by natural agencies such as glaciation, these pebbles were brought to the site by Mesolithic people from the adjacent chalk/flint areas in counties Antrim and Derry. Recently, on the basis of these Dunaff finds, it has been suggested that 'already by the Late Mesolithic we may presume some form of coastal trade in flint'.[17]

The age of this fossil beach at Dunaff Bay is uncertain. It could be an ancient, high storm beach but, according to Addyman and Vernon,[18] it was most likely formed by the post-glacial maximum marine trans-gression (when the sea rose to its highest level *vis-à-vis* the land) contemporary with the Atlantic pollen zone and the end of the Mesolithic period (i.e. *c.* 3500 BC). Pollen analysis carried out on a sample from a nearby bog[19] showed heavy afforestation during the milder conditions in the area during the Atlantic period, with a mixture of birch, pine, oak, alder and hazel, and traces of elm and willow.

The site has been interpreted as the location of a small flint industry, perhaps the part-time activity of a group of offshore Mesolithic fisher-men, whose boats had the technical capacity to return home with cargoes of flint as well as fish. Alternatively the site could represent similar activity by a Mesolithic group drawn to that location for the annual salmon run up Lough Swilly in May or June, or for seal-hunting or some other form of food-gathering appropriate to the area. Unfortunately no evidence of dwelling huts or cooking places was found during the investigations of the site.

Neolithic period

If evidence of Mesolithic settlement is scarce in Donegal this is not the case for the succeeding period. Donegal is exceptionally rich in megalithic tombs of the Neolithic and Early Bronze Age (fig. 1.1). In both number and quality these are among the best of their kind in

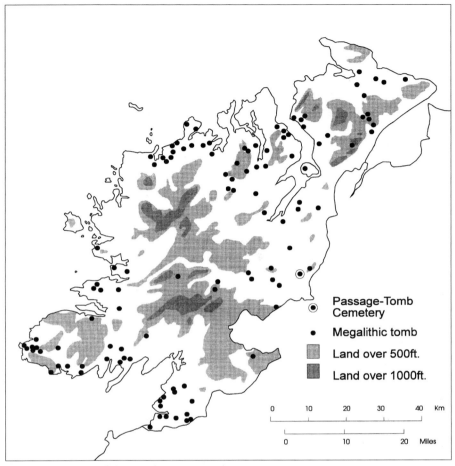

Fig. 1.1   Megalithic tombs in Donegal.

Ireland. Approximately 10 per cent of all known megalithic tombs from the whole of Ireland can be found in county Donegal, indicating the relative importance of this area and the wealth and sophistication of its communities, throughout the Neolithic and into the Early Bronze Age.

We cannot be certain of the origins of the Neolithic way of life in Ireland, the beginnings of which are discernible from about 4500 BC. This new culture, the economic foundation of which was based on farming rather than hunting and gathering, included the construction of elaborate funerary monuments and the making of pottery for both domestic and ritual purposes. Traditional assumptions that Neolithic culture must have been introduced to Ireland by groups of immigrants from Britain and/or France are increasingly being challenged. While firm evidence is certainly not available yet, it is no longer possible to

5

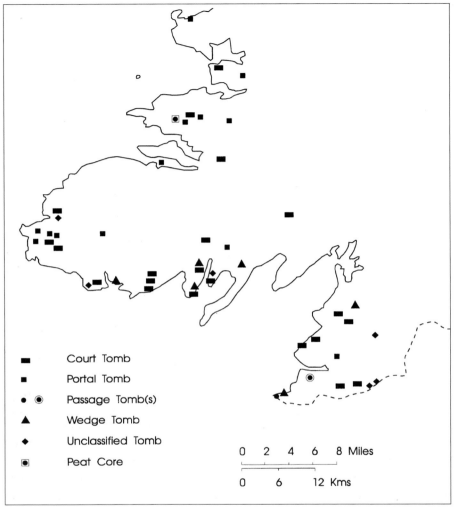

Court Tomb

Portal Tomb

Passage Tomb(s)

Wedge Tomb

Unclassified Tomb

Peat Core

0   2   4   6   8 Miles

0   6   12 Kms

Fig. 1.2   Megalithic tombs in south-west Donegal (after Keeling).

dismiss totally the case for an indigenous evolution to an agricultural economy here by the aboriginal Mesolithic people, based on ideas, and certainly on animals, imported from abroad.[20]

Megalithic tombs of the Neolithic period are widespread throughout county Donegal. However, they are absent from the barren areas already alluded to above; in the high Slieve Tooey and Slieve League areas to the north and south of Glencolumbkille, and surprisingly in the curve of good land around Donegal Bay from south of Donegal town westward along the coast to the unusually shaped peninsula of St John's Point (fig. 1.2). This is an area of glacial drift, drumlins and rich

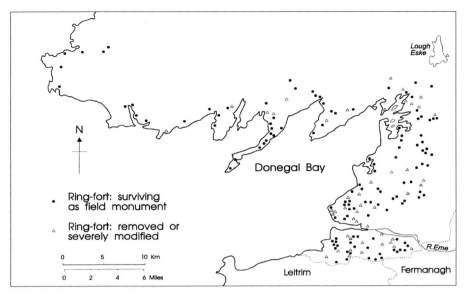

Fig. 1.3   Ring-forts located in south Donegal (after Barrett).

carboniferous limestone land resulting in good pasture which was exploited successfully in later times[21] (fig.1.3). It is likely that this lowland remained thickly forested during the earlier part of the prehistoric period. The absence of megalithic tombs, for whatever reason, suggests that the region was shunned by the pioneering agriculturalists of the Neolithic and Early Bronze Age. However, the possibility that these areas were settled by Neolithic communities which did not erect tombs cannot be discounted; such an explanation has been provided for a 'megalith-free' zone in county Kilkenny.[22]

A few miles west of Killybegs, paradoxically almost at the junction point where the good limestone land gives way to the hard quartzite of mountainous Slieve League peninsula, a small, steep, rocky valley slopes down from about 400 feet, opening out onto Donegal Bay at Shalwy Strand below. Close together in the valley can be found the remains of three court-tombs which were excavated in the 1960s and 1970s by Laurence Flanagan. Only traces of the highest (Bavan tomb) had survived but excavation revealed almost the entire ground plan, and produced a number of leaf-shaped arrowheads, stone beads, a hollow scraper and sherds of Western Neolithic pottery.[23]

The two other tombs, named Croaghbeg and Shalwy respectively, are much better preserved and can be found lower down the valley. Both are very impressive structures and consist of long cairns with full courts and main burial galleries divided into two chambers. The Croaghbeg tomb in addition has a single subsidiary chamber which opens directly onto the court beside the entrance. In both cases massive lintels span the entrance jambs to the burial galleries. Excavation of the tombs produced a range of flint implements including knives and scrapers.[24] Finds from the Shalwy tomb also included portions of a shale bracelet and sherds of pottery. The concentration of these three tombs, two at least of which are major monuments by any standards, seems to suggest the location of a fairly wealthy, self-confident community living in this immediate area during the Neolithic period.

Megalithic tombs of various types can be found in several of the other valleys opening out onto the sea from this otherwise high, mountainous peninsula, most notably at Malinmore and Glencolumbkille where some of the most extraordinary tombs in Ireland are located. The coastal distribution hints at cultural connections with the other dense concentrations of such tombs around much of Donegal Bay, in the northern parts of counties Mayo and Sligo. The similarity of material culture identified at all these sites, as in other parts of the country, suggests that contact and communication of various kinds were maintained over great distances as well as more locally.

There is an apparent paradox nowadays in the location of some of these tombs, arising from the impoverishment of the land in which they are now situated and the ostentation of the original megalithic design and construction. This, however, can be reconciled when we appreciate that they were built by successful agriculturalists at a time of drier and warmer weather conditions, and in a far better endowed landscape than exists today.[25] The countryside was yet to acquire, at least to any significant extent, the blanket of peat which is such a major feature in the area now.

The well-preserved and unique Cloghanmore tomb, one of two court-tombs in Malinmore, is almost 40 metres long with a 3-metre long passage leading from its east end into an oval court 14 metres x 11 metres. At the west end of the court there are two parallel galleries, each roughly 5 metres long and divided into two burial chambers. Opening off the court at each side of the entrance passage is a single subsidiary chamber and beside the entrance to each of these a decorated stone forms part of the wall of the court on which 'curvilinear ornament thought to be similar to that of passage-tombs' is carved.[26] These stones have the only examples of such decoration known from any of the Irish court-tombs.

A few miles away at Farranmacbride on the northern side of the Glencolumbkille valley is an enormous court-tomb set in a cairn 57 metres in length. The tomb is partially destroyed but its oval-shaped central court, at 20.5 metres along its main axis, is the largest feature of its kind from the entire series of such monuments in Ireland. Two galleries, each 5 metres in length and each divided into two chambers, are situated opposite each other at each end of the court. Three subsidiary chambers survive around the court and it is likely that there was also a fourth which has since been destroyed.[27]

Among several other megalithic structures in these valleys, the Malinmore portal-tomb (or tombs) is unique in Ireland. The monument consists of a group of six related portal-tomb chambers. A large portal tomb stands at each end of the group in an east-west line 90 metres long. Between these, but 5 metres north of the axis line, are set four smaller chambers. The orientation of each of the end tombs and one of the smaller is towards the east. Another of the smaller chambers faces north but because of disturbance it is not possible to determine the orientation of the remaining two. The site has not been excavated, but 'it has been suggested that all six chambers were originally incorporated in the one long cairn.'[28] It has also been calculated that one of the roofstones of the western end tomb (unfortunately fallen from its original position) weighs about 40 tons.[29]

In all, over 40 court-tombs (fig. 1.4) and over 20 portal-tombs (fig. 1.5) can be found scattered throughout county Donegal.[30] Among the more impressive of these is the well-preserved Ballymunterhiggin central court-tomb located a few miles south of Ballyshannon.[31] Attention is often drawn also to one of the two portal-tombs at Kilclooney More because of its 4.2 metres long, strikingly-shaped roofstone. Another interesting aspect of this latter monument is that it consists of two tombs about 9 metres apart, incorporated in a 25-metre long cairn. The larger of these, in which sherds of Neolithic pottery have been found, is at the north end of the cairn, but the smaller chamber is also unusual because of 'the presence of a lintel above the portals'.[32]

The sheer scale and elaboration of such monuments in Donegal, particularly those in the south, inevitably force us to the conclusion that a highly sophisticated society was established here by the third millenium BC.

Passage-tombs in Donegal are confined to two areas, presumably indicating some kind of localisation of the particular communities which erected them. At Finner and nearby Magheracar close to Bundoran there are the remains of two tombs. However, records from the last century suggest the existence of at least another two in the townland of Finner, whose precise location cannot now be determined.[33] The partially eroded, so-called Giant's Grave, standing on the edge of a sea-cliff at Magheracar was excavated,[34] to reveal an

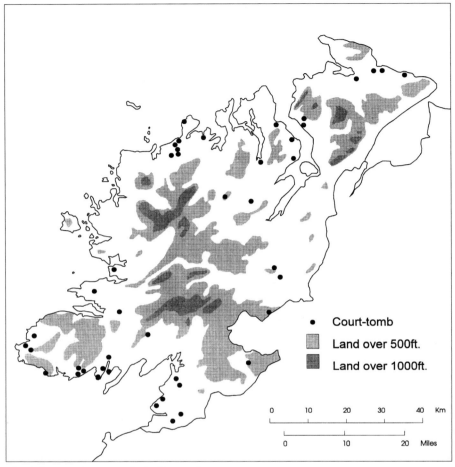

Fig. 1.4   Court-tombs in Donegal.

undifferentiated passage-tomb. Finds from the tomb included flint scrapers, prehistoric pottery sherds, a miniature stone axe, fragments of a stone bead and a piece of bone with concentric semi-circular scores as well as other fragments of bone scattered throughout the monument. A layer of 'sticky earth' and small stones which 'contained flecks of charcoal and occasional fire-reddened stones, reflecting pre-cairn activity' was found also. Waste flakes of flint and other types of stone were found in this layer as was a leaf-shaped flint arrowhead.

Careful fieldwork along with the examination of nineteenth century records brought to light a previously unknown passage-tomb cemetery in the vicinity of Kilmonaster near Raphoe on the good lands of east Donegal.[35] At 700 feet on the summit of Croaghan Hill, inside what is almost certainly a hill-fort of the Iron Age or Late Bronze Age, there is a

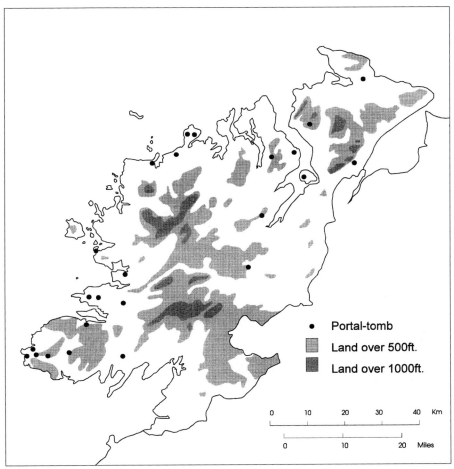

Fig. 1.5   Portal-tombs in Donegal.

mound 3 metres in height and 21 metres in diameter. This seems to be the dominant monument related to a much-damaged Neolithic passage-tomb cemetery consisting of the Croaghan Hill mound and a further twelve tombs scattered across the countryside below the hill.

Many of the tombs in this group are either partially or totally destroyed, as are many other monuments of all periods in this part of Donegal. The excellent farmland in the area has produced a more intensive form of agriculture here in modern times which unfortunately has resulted in a high degree of destruction of archaeological sites and monuments.

Nevertheless a study of the accumulation of stray finds of flint and stone objects from the same general district of east Donegal seems to strengthen the conclusion that the area was intensively settled by a strong and comparatively wealthy farming community during the Neolithic period.[36] The good quality of the flint from which many of these objects were made seems to indicate that plentiful supplies, other than the stray nodules found in the natural drift sources, were available for exploitation. Large quantities of flint are not known in Donegal and, as was suggested earlier in connection with the Mesolithic industrial site at Dunaff Bay, it is likely that supplies were obtained from the neighbouring flint-rich areas in counties Antrim and Derry. This availability of good flint was also observed at the excavations of the Bavan and Shalwy court-tombs in the south-west of the county. The examination of a separate collection of similar artifacts from Straleel, also in south-west Donegal, led to the observation that 'the quantity of implements once again indicates that flint was not by any means in such short supply in the west as has sometimes been suggested. The means by which this flint arrived in the west is, of course, quite another problem.'[37]

On the other hand, the variety of material, from which the polished stone axes in the east Donegal collection were made, suggested that no specific stone was quarried, and 'that any more or less suitable rock-type that came to hand was utilised for the manufacture of the axes'.[38] Other researchers had noted the use of a greenstone from near Creeslough in north-west Donegal for the manufacture of polished axes.[39]

The extent to which the siting of megalithic tombs indicated a preference by the original builders for particular types of location was tested in a recent study in south-west Donegal.[40] In the absence of known house and habitation sites of the period from the area, the likelihood that the tombs were located close to the settlements of the people who built and used them was also examined in the same study. The environments of fifty tombs were examined (fig. 1.2). These consisted of twenty-one court-tombs; thirteen portal-tombs; seven wedge-tombs; three passage-tombs and six unclassified tombs.

It was found that forty-four of the tombs lay below 500 ft with the greatest number (eighteen) lying between 100-200 ft. Although some contrasts in siting patterns between the various types of monuments were noted, the majority of the tombs were situated on ridges or in valleys with a definite preference 'for the warmer southerly facing slopes.' More than 65 per cent were located in areas of Brown Earth, Brown Podzolic and Grey-Brown Podzolic soils, types considered among the best for agricultural purposes today. With the exception of three examples, all the tombs were situated within 200 metres of a fresh-water source. The researchers concluded that the distribution of the tombs suggested a correspondence with the general locations of contemporary settlements. This conclusion may be particularly significant in relation to the discussion about the 'megalith-free' area from St John's Point to south of Donegal town discussed above.

A pollen analysis was carried out as part of the same study. This revealed that the pre-Neolithic period landscape in this area of south-west Donegal had been dominated by mixed deciduous woodland which included oak, birch, hazel, alder and pine, a similar mix to that found in the Atlantic period landscape at the Dunaff Bay Mesolithic site discussed above. This tree-covered landscape gradually gave way to a more open countryside, most probably the result of deliberate forest clearance by the Neolithic community. Grasses, plantain, buttercup, bramble and heather were present, but the virtual absence of elm pollen suggested that the final stage of the elm decline occurred here around 3800 BC. Analysis of pollen taken from soils buried beneath three of the tombs, i.e. from the ground surface on which the tombs had been originally built, indicated a very high presence of grasses, plantain, mugwort, dandelion, thistle and legumes. There was a very low presence of arboreal pollen, indicating that the tombs had been built in open clearances adjacent to areas of pasture.

Cereal-type pollen at two of the tombs suggested that 'cereal production was taking place in the very close vicinity'. More direct evidence of prehistoric agriculture in Donegal can be found in the pre-bog field systems which have been recorded at various sites in the county[41] and which are discussed elsewhere in this volume.

The Bronze Age

Evidence for Bronze Age settlement is well attested in Donegal, both in terms of field monuments[42] and finds of contemporary artifacts.[43] At least twenty-five wedge-tombs are known from the county (fig. 1.6). Their distribution tends to parallel that of the spread of other megalithic structures but with a slight emphasis towards the northern end of the county, a pattern which appears to be repeated, with other Bronze Age sites. Indeed there is a marked tendency for Bronze Age sites to be located in the northern districts of the county. One group of five tombs in Glentogher, Inishowen corresponds with the pattern, noted elsewhere in the country, of wedge-tombs frequently coinciding with mineral deposits.

Approximately seventy-five cists have come to light in Donegal (fig. 1.7). Although not all of them have produced datable evidence, it is most probable that the bulk can be assigned to the Bronze Age. Among these is the typical cist grave discovered in 1987 at Lisnamulligan near Castlefinn. This consisted of a trapezoidal space, 0.95 metres x 0.65 metres, defined by standing slabs which were

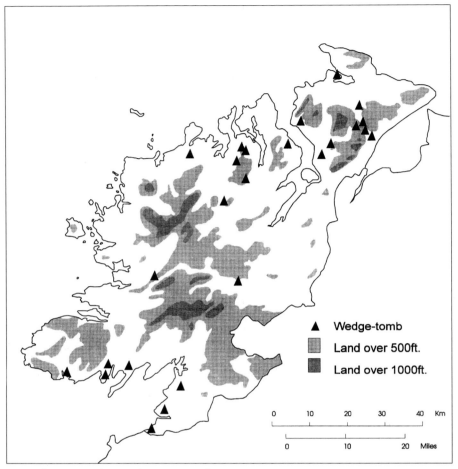

Fig. 1.6   Wedge-tombs in Donegal.

inserted into an oval pit dug in the subsoil. The floor of the cist was made up of flat stones. Two slabs were placed 'corbel-fashion', one at each end of the cist and on these the top capstone was placed. Inside was 'a single crouched inhumation with the head facing east'. A bowl food vessel was placed in the north-east corner beside the head.[44]

The distribution map of cists in Donegal also shows a concentration towards the northern end of the county, a pattern which is strengthened when we add in the known sites on the west bank of the River Foyle but on the Derry side of the border. As already noted, not all of these cists can be dated, or indeed accurately located, but the map does seem to confirm the trend already referred to in the context of other Bronze Age sites.

Among the monuments included in this category are several

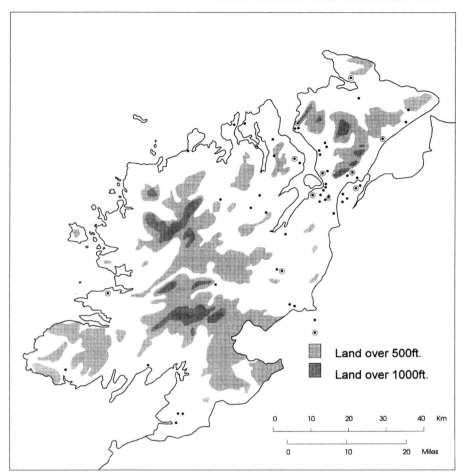

Fig. 1.7   Cists in Donegal.

cemeteries containing multiple numbers of cists and burials, as at Carrontlieve, Drumhaggart and Drung.[45] A cairn 2 metres high and 12 metres in diameter at Killycolman near Rathmullan may have contained as many as twenty-five cists,[46] an indication, surely, of a thriving Bronze Age community in that vicinity. At Drung, near the northern end of Inishowen, the skeletal remains of an adult male, an adult female and an infant were found respectively in three separate cists. A bronze awl, a piece of rock crystal and a pygmy cup were found also at the site.[47] At Lough Fad, a few miles north of Ardara, a cist divided into two compartments was found in a low oval mound roughly 6 metres x 5 metres and 1 metre high.[48] Each compartment contained an individual disarticulated burial, which seems to suggest that the skeletons of the corpses in question were defleshed elsewhere before their final interment. Other skeletal material was found in the mound also, but this may derive from the re-use of the site (up to the middle of the last century) as a Cillín or burial ground for unbaptized children.

The date of the Lough Fad cists is not certain but spectacular evidence of Early Bronze Age activity comes from nearby Naran in the form of two gold lunulae. A similar gold lunula is known from Gartan, further north in the county. Gold objects dating to the Later Bronze Age have been found in other north Donegal sites. At Largatreany a hoard of six gold ribbon torcs was found[49] while the finding of a hoard of fourteen similar objects was reported from Inishowen late in the last century.[50] Taken together, these objects clearly imply a society in which wealth and status were enjoyed and displayed.

Coastal habitation sites (also known as sandhill-sites or midden-sites) seem to be particularly common in county Donegal.[51] They probably range in date from the Mesolithic period to medieval and early modern times, reflecting the universal economic practice of sea-food harvesting by coastal dwellers. As they are often located in areas of shifting sand and dunes, individual sites tend to appear and disappear, time and time again. They have produced a wide range of debris and artifacts. At Magheragallan bones of ox, sheep, pig, horse, and red deer were found as well as shellfish and sherds of an Early Bronze Age bowl food vessel.[52] On the other hand, a site excavated at Carrickfin which produced a bone or horn, harp peg, a bronze pin and a rimsherd of handmade pottery, as well as large quantities of bones and shells, can probably be dated to the thirteenth or fourteenth century.[53] A similar date seems likely for the destroyed site at Tonebane at the northern end of the Fanad Peninsula.[54]

There are over twenty unclassified megalithic structures and more than forty cairns and mounds of various types scattered throughout county Donegal. Approximately 300 existing or former standing stones and stone alignments are known, with a distribution mainly concentrated in the northern and eastern parts of the county[55] (fig. 1.8). Without excavation it is very difficult to assign particular dates to most of these. Some of the standing stones, such as those at Ardmore in Inishowen and Barnes Lower, can probably be assigned to the Bronze Age because of the range of decorative motifs carved on them. This probably applies to the numerous examples of rock art found at various sites in the northern half of the county.[56]

Fulachta Fiadha or ancient cooking places, which may belong to the Bronze Age, are extremely common in other parts of Ireland.[57] However, only three examples are known from Donegal.[58] It is not clear if this low number is related more to the absence of detailed field-work than to the non-existence of these sites elsewhere in the county. The

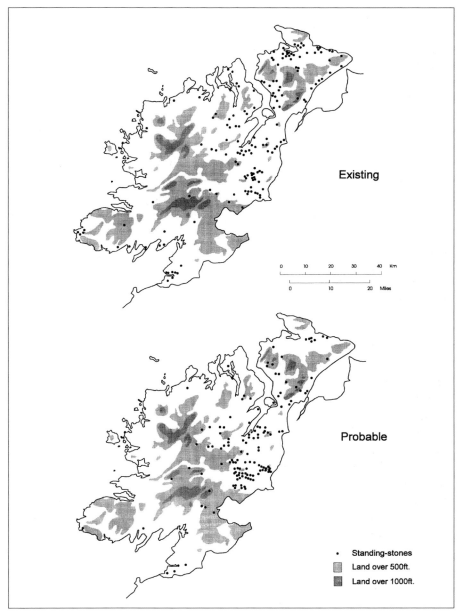

Fig. 1.8   Standing-stones (existing and probable) in Donegal.

three known examples are located in the north-west of the county close to the distribution of known rock art, again emphasising the concentration of Bronze Age sites in north Donegal.

17

Donegal is situated on the margins of one of the two concentrations of Bronze Age stone circles found in Ireland. One group is concentrated in the Cork/Kerry region while another occurs in central and south-western Ulster. Stone circles are not common in Donegal but two relatively large examples can be found in the county: at Glackadrumman in Inishowen (the Bocan circle) and at what is called the Beltany stone circle near Raphoe.[59] The latter is one of the largest monuments of its kind in Ireland but it has been greatly interfered with so that its exact nature cannot be stated with absolute certainty without excavation. It now consists of a large, disturbed platform, 0.5 metres in height, delimited by a circle of sixty-four remaining stones. Originally, the circle may have been formed by as many as eighty of these orthostats. Several of the surviving stones are decorated with cupmarks.[60]

A little outside the circle on the south-east side there is an outlying stone 2 metres in height. A line bisecting the circle and extended through this outlier is aligned with the sunrise of the mid-winter solstice, in a manner similar to that at the great Neolithic passage-tomb at Newgrange, county Meath. It has been claimed that alignments with other astronomical events can be detected at Beltany also,[61] particularly with the sunrise on May day (Lá Bealtaine) which may explain the popular name of the site. Sixty metres to the south-west of the circle is another partially destroyed circular area, 35 metres in diameter, formed by field boundaries.[62] Older editions of the Ordnance Survey maps refer to this area as a graveyard. Its precise connection, if any, with the better-known stone circle is not clear.

The Iron Age

The unusual carved stone head from Beltany, wearing a torc or similar neck-ornament, and which can be assigned to the Iron Age,[63] is associated with the stone circle. Six other carved stone heads from this area of east Donegal probably date to the Iron Age[64] as does the beautiful bronze sword hilt, in a stylised human shape, from Ballyshannon Bay which was probably imported about the first century BC.[65]

The transition from the Late Bronze Age to the Early Iron Age can be detected in Europe north of the Alps from the last decades of the eighth century BC with the emergence and spread of the so-called Hallstatt Culture across the continent. There is very little trace of the Hallstatt Culture in Ireland, with no evidence of any 'invasion' or migration of population groups into the country around that time. Although this is often referred to as a 'Dark Age' in Irish archaeology, the available information for the period suggests the gradual acquisition by the indigenous people of the knowledge of iron-working instead of a wholesale change of population and culture.[66]

As is the case in other parts of the country, without excavation there is great difficulty in assigning specific monuments or even types of monuments to the Iron Age. Sites found in Donegal clearly range in date over many of the archaeological 'periods' including the Iron Age. Individual sites and types of sites were re-used by different cultures for both similar and different purposes, and monuments which appear superficially the same to us today may have had very different functions and meanings for the various groups of people who constructed them. However, with that caution, and on the basis of present knowledge we can tentatively assign certain sites in the county to the end of the first millenium BC or the first few centuries of the present era.

Three definite hillforts which can be assigned almost certainly to the Late Bronze Age or Iron Age, have been identified in Donegal: the earthworks at The Grianán of Aileach on the summit of Greenan Mountain (800 feet) overlooking Lough Swilly and Lough Foyle; the enclosure surrounding the passage-tomb on the summit of Croaghan Hill (700 feet); and McGonigles Fort at Glasbolie in the extreme south of the county (c. 150 feet). About one third of all Irish hillforts have within them older mounds or cairns with probable funerary functions.[67] All three sites in Donegal fall within this category if we include the destroyed 'tumulus' recorded at The Grianán of Aileach early in the last century.[68]

There is another group of eleven large hill-top or hill-slope enclosures in Donegal[69] which do not fit neatly into the category of hillfort but which share many similarities and which may overlap in date. They appear to have had a defensive or even a military purpose. This seems very evident at the large circular site of Cashelnavean, overlooking (and probably originally defending) the northern end of the Barnesmore Gap which anciently served (and still serves) as one of the most important routeways from Connacht into north Donegal. A similar defensive function for the enclosure on a ridge overlooking the Glentogher valley in Inishowen seems almost certain. This commands the junction of several routes among which is the main road leading north across Inishowen to the important monastic site at Carndonagh. Several of the monuments such as those at Balleeghan Upper, Ballymagan, Ballynarry and Lisfannon, are located on cliff edges and inland promontories and again may share some similarities in date and function with the five inland promontory forts known in the county.[70] This is possibly the case also with the thirty or so promontory forts scattered along Donegal's convoluted coastline and on a number of offshore islands.[71]

The Early Medieval period

Many of the sites potentially assigned to the Iron Age may well have continued in use into the Early Medieval (Christian) period. This is almost certainly the case at The Grianán of Aileach where the centre of the hillfort is occupied by the impressive, restored cashel. This monument is usually identified with The Grianán of Aileach of early Irish literature, the principal fortification of the powerful northern Uí Néill dynasty. Some commentators have contended that a nearby site at Elagh (Aileach), county Derry is the one referred to in the ancient documentation. Such a claim seems unlikely as Elagh contains the remains of a later medieval castle built by the O'Doherty family and there are no monuments of the Early Medieval period there. The extensive range of monuments, including the site of a prehistoric 'tumulus', the hillfort, the cashel and a holy well, combined with its commanding position, suggests that popular tradition is correct in identifying the better-known and exceptionally important archae-ological site as the royal fort of ancient times.[72]

The cashel at The Grianán is only one of approximately 200 such structures which are to be found throughout Donegal. Another similar monument, the oval (36.6 metres x 25.8 metres) O'Boyles' Fort, which encloses the entire area of a small island in Doon Lough, has also been reconstructed. Many of the other cashels are in a poor state of preservation, although several have at least some sections of their original stone walling intact. Cashels are distributed widely through the county. The cashel at Rinnaraw in north-western Donegal has been excavated.[73] Grass-covered mounds in the north-west sector of the enclosure turned out to be 'the foundations of a dry-built structure, probably some form of house site'. An area of paving consisting of 'well laid slabs or flagstones' on which lay 'a number of large structural stones' was found in the southern sector of the site. Pieces of iron slag, furnace bottoms and part of a small lignite bracelet were also found as were 'traces of firing and charcoal'.

Approximately 250 earthen ringforts have been identified in county Donegal. Their distribution coincides broadly with that of the stone-built cashels (fig. 1.9). They vary in size, shape and defining features and while some, such as that at Dunwiley near Stranorlar, are clearly defensive in nature, others were probably no more than minimally protective. A number of these sites, such as that at Dooballagh, had associated souterrains, as did a number of cashels and contemporary church sites.[74] In addition, over seventy 'isolated' souterrains have been found in the county; these were probably associated with types of settlement which have left no obvious trace of an enclosure.[75] Their distribution broadly parallels that of the cashels and ringforts (fig. 1.9)

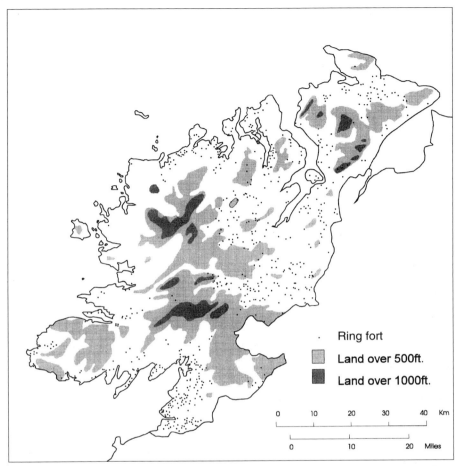

Fig. 1.9   Known ring forts (including those of stone and those known only from cropmarks) in Donegal (Mytum).

and this pattern is replicated in the location of the 250 enclosures, now destroyed, but for which various forms of evidence have been preserved.[76]

Some twenty lake habitation sites of various types have also been identified in Donegal. No doubt some of these belong to different archaeological periods: sites such as the partially excavated Moylederg Island in Lough Eske, for example, is assumed to have been occupied through successive archaeological periods.[77] This is a natural island which was artificially extended. Finds from the site ranged in date from the Neolithic to early modern times but the bulk of the occupation material was dated to the Medieval period.

Some lake habitation sites in Donegal seem to be true crannog in

21

that they were totally artificial constructions. Although the name crannog derives from the use of brushwood and timber in their building, it seems that all of the Donegal crannogs so far identified were constructed by laying down cairns of stone on the lake bed.[78] Although the number of sites is restricted, their distribution in Donegal parallels those of the other sites such as ringforts and cashels with which they are usually associated.

There is, therefore, ample evidence of human settlement in Donegal from the Mesolithic period through to Early Medieval times. Much of this evidence has still to be analysed and teased out for what it can tell us about where and how people lived in the past. Indications have been given as to how this research might proceed in future.[79] It is clear that Donegal will remain a fertile area for archaeological research for a long time to come.

References

1. B. Lacy *et al, Archaeological survey of Donegal* (Lifford, 1983), pp 1-2.
2. L. N. W. Flanagan, 'Accumulations of neolithic flint and stonework from near Raphoe, county Donegal' in *U.J.A.,* vol. 31 (1968), p. 9.
3. Lacy, *Archaeological survey;* pp 10-12. B. Lacy, 'Archaeological survey of Donegal', in *Donegal Annual,* 1979, pp 445-6.
4. S. P. Ó Ríordáin, 'Recent acquisitions from county Donegal in the National Museum' in *R.I.A. Proc.,* vol. 42, C (1935), pp 145-91.
5. B. Lacy, 'The archaeological survey of county Donegal' in T. Reeves-Smith and F. Hamond, *Landscape archaeology in Ireland* (Oxford, 1983), pp 16-21.
6. W. S. Pitcher and A. R. Berger, *The geology of Donegal: a study of granite emplacement and unroofing* (New York, 1972); J. B. Whittow, *Geology and scenery in Ireland* (Middlesex, 1974), pp 57-62.
7. Lacy, *Archaeological survey,* p. 3.
8. Ibid., p. 5.
9. P. C. Woodman, *Excavations at Mount Sandel 1973-77* (Belfast, 1985), p. 171.
10. Ibid., *The Mesolithic in Ireland* (Oxford, 1978), p. 286.
11. Brian Lacy, *Siege city – the story of Derry and Londonderry* (Belfast, 1990), pp 6-7.
12. Woodman, *Mesolithic,* p. 286.
13. B. Lacy, 'Inishowen', Irish Association for Quaternary Studies, Field Guide no. 7 (1984), p. 22.
14. P. V. Addyman and P. D. Vernon, 'A beach pebble industry from Dunaff Bay, Inishowen, Co. Donegal' in *U.J.A.,* vol. 29 (1966), pp 6-15.
15. N. Stephens and F. M. Synge, 'Late Pleistocene shorelines and drift limits in North Donegal' in *R.I.A. Proc.,* 64, sect. B (1965).
16. Woodman, *Mesolithic,* p. 283.
17. J. P. Mallory and T. E. McNeill, *The archaeology of Ulster* (Belfast, 1991), p. 49.
18. Addyman and Vernon, 'Beach pebble', p. 13.
19. J. Pilcher, 'Report on samples from Dunaff' in Addyman and Vernon, 'Beach pebble', pp 14-5.
20. M. Gibbons, 'The archaeology of early settlement in county Kilkenny' in

W. Nolan and K. Whelan (eds), *Kilkenny: history and society* (1990), pp 2-3.

21. G. F. Barrett, 'A field survey and morphological study of ring-forts in southern county Donegal' in *U.J.A.,* 43 (1980), pp 39-51.

22. Gibbons, 'Early settlement', p. 3.

23. L. N. W. Flanagan and D. E. Flanagan, 'The excavation of a court cairn at Bavan, county Donegal' in *U.J.A.,* 29 (1966), pp 16-38.

24. Lacy, *Archaeological survey,* pp 20, 29.

25. M. Ó hOireachtaigh, *Gleann Cholm Cille: 5000 bliain greanta i gcloch* (Gleanncholmcille, 1990), p. 5.

26. S. Ó Nualláin in Lacy, *Archaeological survey,* p. 26.

27. Ibid., p. 22.

28. Ibid., pp 32-3.

29. Ó hOireachtaigh, *Gleann Cholm Cille,* p. 16.

30. Lacy, *Archaeological survey.*

31. S. Ó Nualláin in Lacy, *Archaeological survey,* p. 16.

32. Ibid., p. 32.

33. M. Herity, *Irish passage graves* (Dublin, 1974), pp 215-6.

34. Eamon Cody, 'Giant's Grave, Magheracar' in *Excavations: summary accounts of archaeological excavations in Ireland,* vols for 1986 and 1987.

35. S. Ó Nualláin, 'A ruined megalithic cemetery in county Donegal' in *R.S.A.I. Jn.,* 98 (1968), pp1-29.

36. Flanagan, 'Neolithic flint', pp 9-15.

37. L. N. W. Flanagan, 'Flint implements from Straleel, county Donegal' in *U.J.A.,* 29 (1966), pp 91-4.

38. Flanagan, 'Neolithic flint', p. 15.

39. E. M. Jope, 'Porcellanite axes from factories in north-east Ireland: Tievebulliagh and Rathlin' in *U.J. A.,* 15 (1952), pp 31-55.

40. D. Keeling, K. Molloy and R. Bradshaw, 'Megalithic tombs in south-west Donegal' in *Archaeology Ireland,* 3, no. 4 (1989), pp 152-4.

41. Lacy, *Archaeological survey,* pp 50-4.

42. Ibid.

43. Ó Ríordáin, 'Recent acquisitions'.

44. R. Ó Floinn, 'Lisnamulligan' in *Excavations: summary accounts of archaeological excavations in Ireland* (1989).

45. Lacy, *Archaeological survey,* pp 65-6.

46. Ó Ríordáin, 'Recent acquisitions', pp 173-4.

47. E. Rynne, 'Bronze Age burials at Drung, county Donegal' in *R.S.A.I. Jn.,* 93 (1963), pp 169-79.

48. J. Raftery, 'A Bronze Age burial mound at Loughfad, county Donegal' in *U.J.A.,* 5 (1942), pp 122-6.

49. G. Eogan, 'The Later Bronze Age in Ireland in the light of recent research'. *Prehist. Soc. Proc.,* 30 (1964), pp 268-351.

50. Day, *R.S.A.I. Jn.,* 16 (1883), pp 182-5.

51. Lacy, *Archaeological survey,* pp 55-8.

52. E. E. Evans, 'A sandhill site in Magheragallan, county Donegal' in *U.J.A.,* 4 (1941), pp 71-5.

53. B. Raftery, 'Carrickfin – coastal midden' in *Excavations: summary accounts of archaeological excavations in Ireland* (1985).

54. B. Lacy, 'Tonebane Glebe' in *The Journal of Irish Archaeology,* v (1989/90), p. 72.

55. Lacy, *Archaeological survey,* pp 74-97.

56. Ibid., pp 98-101; M. and E. Van Hoek, 'A new group of cup and ring marked

rocks in Inishowen, county Donegal' in *R.S.A.I. Jn.*, 114 (1984), pp 144-9; M. Van Hoek, 'The prehistoric rock art of county Donegal (parts I and II)' in *U.J.A.*, 50 and 51 (1987 and 1988), pp 23-46, 21-47; R. Crumlish, 'An example of rock art from Inishowen, county Donegal' in *R.S.A.I. Jn.*, 121 (1991), p. 171.

57. Gibbons, 'Early settlement', pp 13-5.

58. Lacy, *Archaeological survey*, pp 102-3.

59. Ibid., pp 69-74.

60. Van Hoek, 'Rock art', pp 25-6.

61. T. Boyle-Somerville, 'Instances of orientation in prehistoric monuments of the British Isles' in *Archaeologia*, 73 (1922-23), pp 193-224.

62. Lacy, *Archaeological survey*, p. 73.

63. B. Raftery, *La Tene in Ireland – problems of origin and chronology* (Marburg, 1984), pp 309-10.

64. E. Rynne, 'Celtic stone idols in Ireland' in C. Thomas (ed.), *The Iron Age in the Irish Sea province* (London, 1972), pp 86-8.

65. Mallory and McNeill, *Ulster*, p. 156.

66. B. Raftery, 'The Early Iron Age' in M. Ryan (ed.), *The illustrated archaeology of Ireland* (Dublin, 1991), p. 107.

67. B. Raftery, 'Irish hillforts' in Thomas, *Iron Age*, pp 37-58.

68. Col. Colby, *Ordnance Survey of Ireland – county of Londonderry, i* (Dublin, 1837), illustration after page 216.

69. Lacy, *Archaeological survey*, pp 116-8.

70. Ibid., pp 218-9.

71. Ibid., pp 219-30.

72. B. Lacy, 'The Grianán of Aileach' in *Donegal Annual* (1984), pp 5-24.

73. T. Fanning, 'Rinnaraw – Cashel and house site' in *Excavations: summary accounts of archaeological excavations in Ireland*, vols. for 1987, 1988, 1989, 1990.

74. Lacy, *Archaeological survey*, p. 231.

75. Ibid., pp 231-9.

76. Ibid., pp 197-217.

77. O. Davies, 'Excavations on Moylederg Island, Lough Eske, county Donegal' in *U.J.A.*, 9 (1946), pp 91-9.

78. Lacy, *Archaeological survey*, pp 104-6.

79. Keeling *et al*, 'Megalithic tombs'; L. N. W. Flanagan, 'Peat, forest and field systems in S.W. Donegal: a preliminary survey' in *Irish Archaeological Research Forum*, iv, Pt. 1 (1977), pp 31-5.

Chapter 2

EARLY CHRISTIAN DECORATED SLABS IN DONEGAL: *AN TURAS* AND THE TOMB OF THE FOUNDER SAINT

MICHAEL HERITY

The early Christian cross-ornamented slabs and pillars found in such great numbers throughout Ireland, particularly in the counties along the western seaboard, have been the subject of many studies from the point of view of their art and their affiliations outside Ireland.[1] Recent work by the writer has attempted to take this study further[2] by emphasising the function of the slabs in systems of ritual, examining them as monuments of the pilgrimage ritual known as *an turas* at sites like Inishmurray, Gleanncholmcille and Tory Island, and also in their role as marking and celebrating the tomb of the founder saint, which is of focal importance at so many ancient sites. This paper documents the slabs and monuments of *Turas Chonaill* (fig. 2.1), between Inishkeel and Gleanncholmcille, and examines the art and context of a number of imposing slabs and pillars, many of them ornamented on both broad faces, in west and north Donegal.

Turas Chonaill, St Connell's pilgrimage, and the Loughros early Christian slabs

A concentration of small cross-slabs, together with a number of simple crosses inscribed on rock-faces and a cross-decorated stone slab with rudimentary arms in the townlands of Drumirrin, Kilcashel, Cloghboy, Newtownburke and Crannogeboy, document an early Christian presence on the Loughros peninsula, west of Ardara. Though the stone slab in Kilcashel, called St Connell's cross and the small cross-inscribed block near the water's edge in the same townland (fig. 2.3 (2, 3)), might be associated with a possible early ecclesiastical foundation now repre-sented by the graveyard on the roadside below St Connell's Cross on the east (fig. 2.2a), the only other possible early foundation on the peninsula, marked Loughros Church on the Ordnance Survey six-inch map, at the east edge of Shanaghan Lough, is too far from the concentration around Newtownburke to account plausibly for their presence in that area (fig. 2.2f). If a third early Christian foundation ever

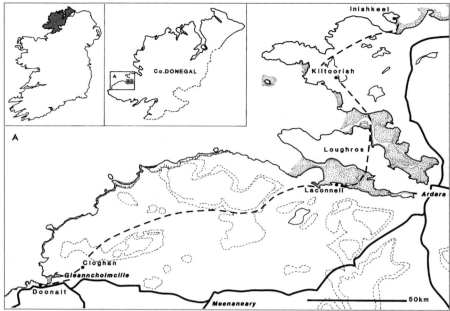

Fig. 2.1   Reconstructed route of *Turas Chonaill* between Inishkeel and Gleanncholmcille.

existed there, it appears now to be lost without trace in the archaeology of Loughros. Its existence is not even hinted at in local lore or in placenames, unlike references to an ancient church and its priest suggested by Sruhaunnaheglish *(Sruthán na h-Eaglaise)* which flows into the sand south of Loughros between Laconnell and Barkillew townlands from the east slopes of Croaghataggart *(Cruach an t-sagairt)*.

Strong local tradition in the area points to Laconnell, a cross-marked boulder on the south side of the sands of the estuary near Sand Island, as marking the line of an heroic *turas* or pilgrimage undertaken by Conall Caol, founder of Inishkeel in the sixth century and a contemporary of Colmcille. It has given its name to the townland, just like the early Christian foundation of Kiltoorish *(Cill turais)* on the Dawros Peninsula, north of Loughros. Tradition describes this arduous *turas* of Conall's as crossing the sandy expanses from Inishkeel to the mainland, of crossing Ballinreavy strand at the inner end of Loughros More Bay, where *Oitir Chonaill* (Conall's sandbank) is situated, and finally the sands between Loughros and Laconnell. Séamus Mac Giolla Cearra of Straboy has recalled for me how the old people described Conall's legendary pilgrimage: *Dhein sé na trí feirsde le trághadh amháin* (he forded the three tidal sands at one low tide).

After reaching land at Laconnell the pilgrim wishing to emulate Conall

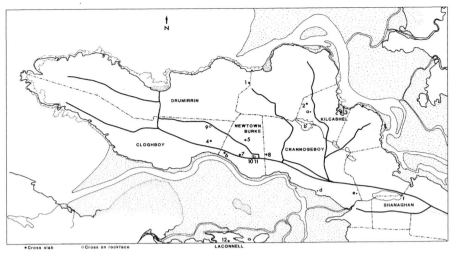

Fig. 2.2   Map of the Loughros peninsula showing positions of cross-slabs, numbered 1 to 11, and other monuments.

made across the hills towards the Glen. Here a group of cross-slabs and a well near the early foundation of Cill Chaoimhín *(Cill an Spáinnigh)* in Drum and Clogher townlands were recognised locally as belonging to *Turas Chonaill* by informants of Dr Seán Ó h-Eochaidh more than fifty years ago,[3] notably Seán Gillespie of Kinnakillew, and probably also Peigí Mhór Ní Ghadhra of Cloghan. Séamus Mac Giolla Cearra has helped reconstruct the probable route from Laconnell to Drum (fig. 2.1).

Leaving the coast about the village of Maghera, the pilgrims followed the line of the Owenwee river up Granny, climbing south of west out of the valley towards Craiganiller in Meenacurrin townland. The best route follows a westerly direction over an area known locally as Curraghmore *(An Currach Mór)*, and crosses the source of the Glen river at a height of about one thousand feet into the south end of Straboy townland, from where the pilgrim could see south of west into the Glen. It continues into Lougheraherk, passing north of the lake of that name, north again of Kiltyfanned Lough, apparently associated with St Fanad of Kilaned *(Cill Fhanaid)* in the Glen, beyond which an old track runs from the south end of Meenasillagh townland over the north-west shoulder of Croaghacullion before descending into Drum. Here the first pilgrims would have found themselves on the north side of the little stream which runs noisily westward immediately beside the tiny early foundation of St Cavan.

Description of the group of cross-slabs on and near the Loughros peninsula best begins with the most northerly slab, that in Drumirrin townland.

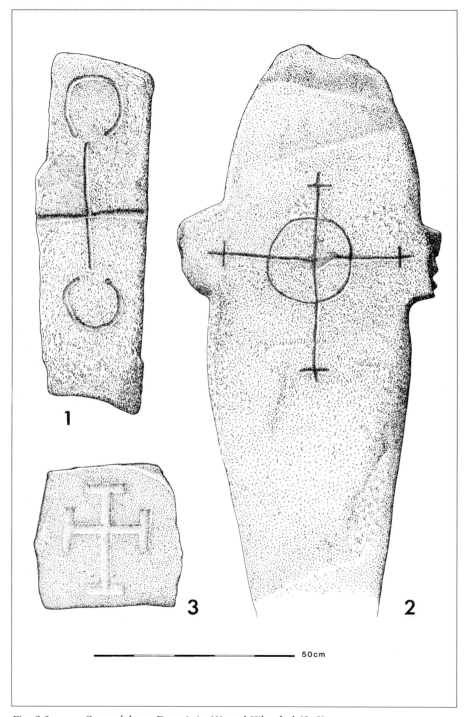

Fig. 2.3   Cross-slabs at Drumirrin (1) and Kilcashel (2, 3).

1. Drumirrin, Cross-slab (fig. 2.3 (1))
This slab is at present lying loose, 17m north of the townland boundary
with Liskeeraghan where it turns west. It is a regular rectilinear slab,
88cm high, 27cm in greatest width, 8cm thick, with a cross incised on
one broad face towards the upper end.

   This is a simple incised cross, 33.5cm high, 27cm across the arms,
which run to the edges of the slab, with penannular features, each 15-
16cm in diameter, inscribed above and below the shaft. At the crossing
of shaft and transom are traces of a small circular drilled hole. The
overall height of the carved ornament including the penannular
features is 66.3cm.

2. St Connell's Cross, Kilcashel (fig. 2.3 (2))
Large slab, 1.61m high, 31.5cm wide near the butt and 11cm in
maximum thickness, with rudimentary arms creating a cross-shaped
outline, the span across the arms 64.5cm. The slab faces north and
south (185°) and has an incised Latin cross, 54cm high, 49.5cm across
the arms, centrally placed at the level of the rudimentary arms of the
slab on the south face. Towards the ends of the arms and shaft of the
cross short incised lines cut the limbs; an incised circle 22.5/24cm in
diameter encloses the crossing. Around the foot of the slab, particularly
on the south side, is a rough setting of stones, possibly the remains of a
leacht. This and the fact that it looks south suggests that here is the
cross-slab of a *turas*, placed so as to face pilgrims approaching from
the south.

3. Kilcashel, Cross-slab (fig. 2.3 (3))
Small block of stone, the decorated face almost square, 37cm in height,
37cm in greatest width and 31.5cm in thickness across the upper
surface. A Latin cross, 28.5cm high, 21cm across the arms, with T-bar
terminals on all four limbs, is deeply incised in broad grooves on the
south-east face.

   The slab lies at the south foot of a steep rise, at the top of which is a
small thick-walled *caiseal* (fig. 2.2c), at the edge of the small sheltered
basin of Garrybeg in which there are suitable landing-places. About
one hundred metres west by north of the basin the land rises in a
series of apparently uncultivated terraces lying on either side of a small
stream. This cross-inscribed stone appears to mark a landing-place
south of the sand-bank known as *Oitir Chonaill*.

4. Newtownburke or Cloghboy, Cross-slab (fig. 2.4 (4))
Now in a private house in Cloghboy, possibly found in Newtownburke
nearby, this is a very irregular slab, maximum dimensions 68 by 31.5cm

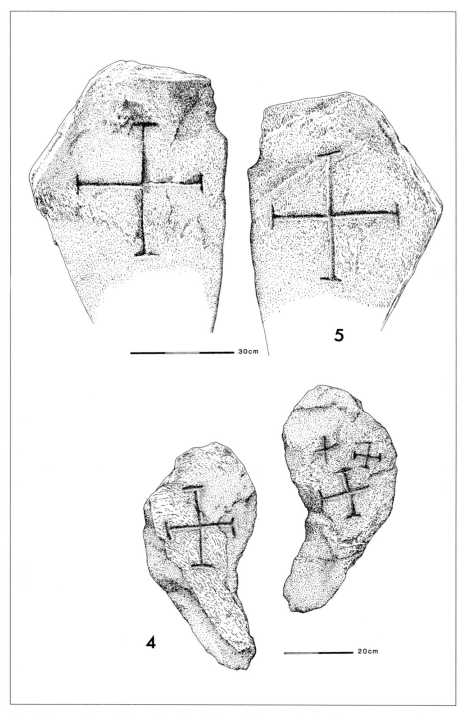

Fig. 2.4   Cross-slabs at Cloghboy (4) and Newtownburke (5).

and about 6cm thick, with three crosses on one broad convex face, a single cross on the other broad flat face.

Face A (left) has a single incised cross, 24.3cm high and 20.4cm across the arms, with T-bar terminals. Face B has three incised crosses: the largest, towards the mid-point of the slab, is 15cm high and has three T-bar terminals, the fourth terminal being flaked off. Above this are two smaller incised crosses: left: a simple equal-armed cross 7.4 by 7.4cm wide; right: a small cross with four T-bar terminals, 8.4 by 8.25cm wide.

5. Newtownburke, Cross-slab (fig. 2.4 (5))

An irregular slab, 64cm high above the ground, 56.5cm in maximum width, 6-8cm in thickness, is fixed in a field fence north of the road to Drumirrin village on the slope on the south side of Drumirrin Hill, immediately north of Slab 7. The slab is decorated towards the upper end of both broad east and west faces.

Face A (left) is a cross with T-bar terminals, 40.5cm high, 36.8cm wide across the arms. Face B (right) is a more regularly incised cross, 38.5cm high, 37.4cm wide across the arms, also with T-bar terminals.

6. Newtownburke, Cross-slab (fig. 2.5 (6))

This slab stands on a tiny cairn of field-stones south of the road, apparently found nearby and erected there in this century. The slab, 75.5cm high, 26cm wide across the arms of the incised cross and 11-13cm thick, is decorated on both broad faces near the upper, broader end of the slab. Both inscribed crosses are Latin in form.

The cross on Face A (left) is 32cm high and 22.5cm across the arms with three 'fishtail' terminals and a T-bar at the lower end of the shaft. The cross on Face B (right) is 29.1cm high, 20.3cm wide across the arms and has four T-bar terminals.

7. Newtownburke, Cross-slab (fig. 2.6 (7))

This slab is lying loose against a field fence north of the roadway. It is a regular slab, 1.04m high, 28cm wide at the butt, 34cm wide immediately below a slightly gabled apex and 16cm thick. Two crosses, their stems longer than the arms, are incised on the main broad faces of the slab a little above centre.

Cross A (left) is the less well-marked of the two, 35.5cm high, 29.7cm across the arms, the arms cutting the shaft below its centre-point, with three T-bar terminals and a 'fishtail' on the lower limb. Cross B (right), is a more deeply cut, balanced cross, 41.4cm high and 24.9cm across the arms, with T-bar terminals on the transom and 'fishtails' on the upper and lower ends of the shaft.

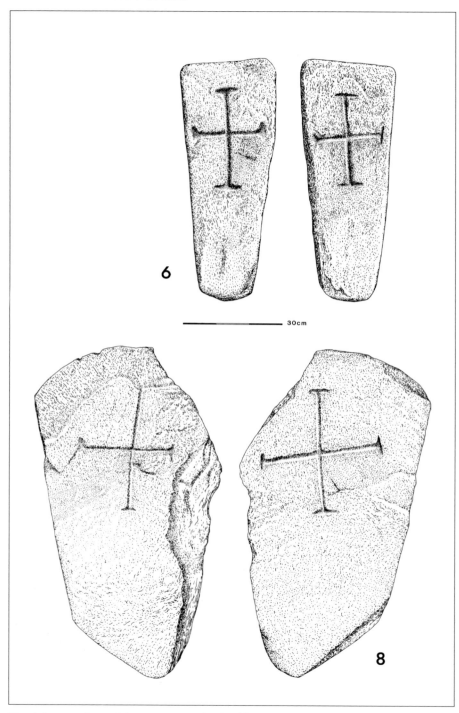

Fig. 2.5   Cross-slabs at Newtownburke (6) and Crannogeboy (8).

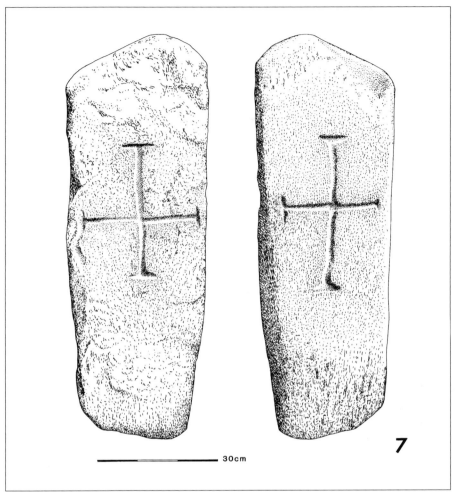

30cm

7

Fig. 2.6   Cross-slabs at Newtownburke (7).

8. Crannogeboy, Cross-slab (fig. 2.7 (6))
Large slab of irregular shape, 1.03m high, with incised crosses on both
flat faces near the upper end of the slab. It lies loose against a field
fence behind a farmhouse close to the west boundary of Crannogeboy
townland, which takes its name from a crannog or lake-dwelling
marked on the map (fig. 2.2b); three saddle-querns and some polished
stone axeheads from the crannog suggesting a pre-Christian date are
now in the National Museum of Ireland.

Both incised crosses are very similar in form: the shaft tends to be
equally divided by the transom, and there are T-bar terminals at the
ends of the limbs. On Face A the cross, which is the better-preserved of

the two, is 39.3cm high and 36.9cm across the arms; the surface of Face B is badly flaked and the cross, 37.5cm high by 28.3cm across the arms, is less clearly marked.

9. Cloghboy, rock-inscribed Cross (fig. 2.7)

On the north-west vertical face of a rock outcrop, 15m south of the road leading to Drumirrin from the south side of the Loughros peninsula, 500m west of Slab 5 in Newtownburke is a thinly incised Latin cross, 36.9cm high and 18.9cm across the arms, with T-bar terminals at the ends of shaft and transom.

10, 11. Newtownburke, rock-inscribed Crosses (fig. 2.7 (10, 11))

Two crosses incised on the south face of a rock outcrop north of the road west to Cloghboy and 80m west of number 8.

Cross 11 is a Latin cross, 24.9cm high and 16cm across the arms, weathered and faintly marked; there are T-bar terminals at the ends of arms and shaft, that on the lower end of the shaft now very faint. Cross 10, below Cross 11 and about 5m to the west, is a well-marked Latin cross, 25.5cm high and 18.6cm across the arms, with terminals resembling fishtails.

12. Laconnell, *Leac Chonaill* (fig. 2.7)

A large earthfast boulder, maximum dimensions 1.29m, is the eponymous *Leac Chonaill*. On it is engraved an irregular cross with T-bar terminals, 26.5cm by 25.8cm.

What can we know of the date at which the crosses described above were carved, most on slabs, one on a boulder, some on the living rock? Is it possible that they date back to the time of Conall Caol in the sixth century? And does *Turas Chonaill* date to this time also?

The crosses represented are almost entirely of the type with T-bar terminals, normally made with narrow grooves or, on the small regular block above the shore at Kilcashel, with broader, bolder grooving. The engraved cross with fishtail terminals on the rock-face at Newtownburke (fig. 2.7 (10)) belongs to a type much more common at early Christian foundations along the west coast as far south as Kerry and also among the early cross-slabs at Iona in Scotland. This type with T-bar terminals is not so common, but is known in the area at Toome, near Inishkeel,[4] on a tall pillar marking the station of a *turas* on a height in Drum townland above the early foundation of Teampall Chaoimhín, associated with the south-west terminus of *Turas Chonaill* in the Glen.[5] It is also found on Rathlin O'Birne island, in the hermitage founded by Assicus (Tassach), favourite disciple of St Patrick, who was

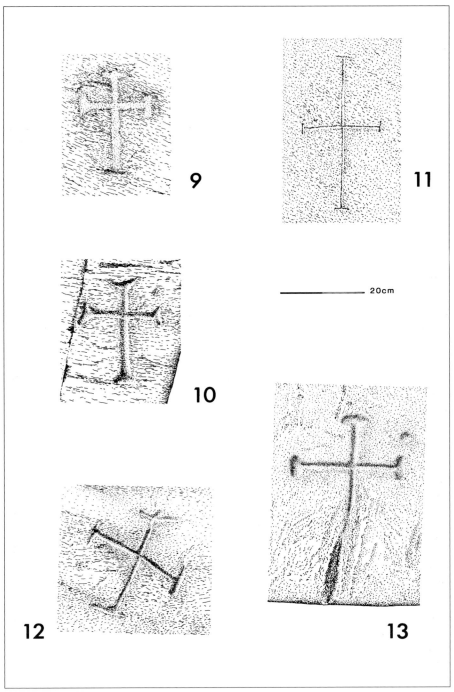

Fig. 2.7   Crosses incised on rock face at Cloghboy (9) and Newtownburke
(10, 11), on boulders at Laconnell (12) and Beefan (13).

a hermit there for seven years about the year 500. Here the type occurs in the form of an encircled equal-armed cross with T-bar terminals on the west side of the principal decorated slab beside the holy well and on a slab, one of a pair set up at the east side of the slab-shrine within the tiny oratory in the inner enclosure.[6]

Further afield, the type with bolder grooving like Kilcashel is known on a *leacht* beside the Bronze Age *gallán* engraved with a Christian cross-in-circle and associated locally with St Patrick in Lankill townland, east of Croagh Patrick in Mayo.[7] W. F. Wakeman drew an example of the type in the last century, probably at Mainistir Chiaráin on Aran,[8] and the type is also known as far south as Teampall na Cluanach in Lateevemore townland on the Dingle peninsula.[9] Iona, founded by Colmcille in 563, also has two examples of the T-barred cross on a slab, No. 17, 1.65m long, now lying about 7m south of St Martin's Cross.[10] Four others in mid-Argyll have recently been published, at Achadh na Cille, at the head of Lough Sween, and Barnakill, now at Poltalloch in the Crinan area. Two, now at Duntaynish House and Inverneill House and possibly originally from Eilean Mór at the mouth of Lough Sween, belong also to this group.[11]

The Loughros/Laconnell/Drum group appear to stand between the early sixth century, when the Rathlin O'Birne slab might reasonably be dated, and the beginning of the seventh century, where the Iona slabs can be placed. They could thus be reasonably assigned to Conall Caol, contemporary of Colmcille. There would be no chronological difficulty in holding that the Newtownburke group originally belonged to a group of stations set around an early foundation in that area before being incorporated in *Turas Chonaill*; such a hypothetical foundation can be as early as the time of Assicus on Rathlin O'Birne, about the year 500.

Four of the slabs have crosses engraved on both faces, nos 5, 6 and 7 in Newtownburke townland and 4, now in Cloghboy a little to the east. In the same area are the rock-engraved crosses (fig. 2.7 (9, 10, 11)) *Turas* slabs decorated on both faces are unusual but are found at Stations 2 and 12 of *Turas Cholmcille* at Gleanncholmcille. Could it be that these Newtownburke and Cloghboy slabs marked stations which were to be visited twice by pilgrims, both going south to the Glen and returning north to Inishkeel, so that a decorated face presented itself to pilgrims going north or south?

The slab at Kilcashel has what appears to be a wreathed cross with T-bar terminals and a single incised circle at the crossing of arms and shaft, the cross inscribed on the south face occupying part of the additional space created by the carving of extensions resembling arms on the sides of the slab at this point. It is 1.61m tall. A close parallel is to be found on the Dingle peninsula on a cross with more clearly carved arms with rounded ends, a tall head and a total height of over 1.72m. At the crossing is a Latin cross with T-bar terminals, a double wreath at the centre, the ends of the arms of the incised cross reaching into the space created by the arms.[12] This cross stands within the sub-rectangular enclosure of a burial ground, An Cheallúnach in Reenconnell (*Rinn Chonaill*) townland, north of Dingle. The close resemblance in form and ornamentation of these two rare monuments in Donegal and Kerry, 400 kilometres apart by sea, suggests that they belong to a common tradition represented only at Dingle and Loughros. But is the association of the sites at which they stand with a Conall only coincidence? And is the Conall of Reenconnell Conall Caol?

An Turas is normally performed at a holy well or at an ecclesiastical foundation, the circuit followed by the pilgrim being restricted to a small number of stations in a relatively small area. Rathlin O'Birne, where a small number of stations are found in and immediately outside the two earliest enclosures at the foundation, conforms to this model, the holy well being here, as at many other sites, covered with a well-house.[13] Foundations where the pilgrim visited a number of stations relatively close to the focal foundation are those of Caher Island and Tory Island.[14] The two sites where the pilgrim covers the greatest circuit are those of Inismurray and Gleanncholmcille; it has been argued that at this latter site the present *Turas Cholmcille* is a composite based on an early, restricted set of stations arranged around a hermitage with the tomb-shrine of Colmcille, Station 5, and a holy well, Station 7, not far removed in style and date from Tassach's stations on Rathlin O'Birne. To this, it appears, a set of stations was added around the year 700 at the eastern and more accessible end of the valley, now numbered 9 to 15 and 1 and 2, which are in most cases marked by cross-pillars ornamented in a style akin to jewelled metalwork and manuscripts of the period immediately before and around 700. This *Turas Cholmcille* and the stations known as *An Turas Mór* on the island of Inismurray[15] follow a circuit requiring about four hours to traverse and covering five kilometres of ground. Both appear to be developments of the seventh century.[16]

The evidence for the linear *Turas Chonaill* is all of simple cross-engraved slabs, boulders or the living rock with incised crosses which suggest that they were carved in Conall's time in the sixth century. Even if it were argued that the Newtownburke group belongs to a separate early foundation later incorporated into *Turas Chonaill,* the crosses carved on *Leac Chonaill* which marked the successful crossing of *na trí feirsde* going south-west, and on the slabs above the landing place at Kilcashel and Drumirrin, are sufficiently close to the general range to date the establishment of this linear *Turas Chonaill* to the sixth century. The Lankill slab in Mayo suggests a similar date in the life of another linear *turas* followed from Ballintubber on the east to Croagh Patrick along a routeway known as *Tóchar Phádraig.*

Above Station 7 of *Turas Cholmcille* in Beefan, a boulder with incised cross stands immediately north of the roadway as it runs west. The cross has weathered T-bar terminals at the ends of the arms and of the upper shaft and is 27cm across the arms. Its form and position would appear to associate it with the western stations of *Turas Cholmcille* below (fig. 2.7 (13)).

Developments in An Turas towards the year 700

The pilgrim arriving at the end of the sixth century from Inishkeel at Drum at the east end of the Glen would in all likelihood have found a *dísert,* a truly deserted place ideal for hermits. At that early time, during and immediately after the lifetime of Colmcille and Conall Caol, the round of *Turas Cholmcille* was probably followed entirely beyond the great salt-marsh at the west end of the valley under Beefan, extending between the stations now designated numbers 3 to 8. The cross-slabs at the stations of this *turas* are exclusively primitive, ascetic in style and in keeping with a date in the sixth century.[17] These were centred on the focal *Teampall Cholmcille* and its slab-lined *Leaba Cholmcille* in their tiny circular enclosure (Station 5), and the holy well and great stone cairn of Station 7; at the present Stations 3 and 5 the pilgrim followed a ritual using prayer-stones.[18]

The series of tall cross-pillars marking many of the stations now located at the east end of the valley between Stations 9 and 15 and including Station 2 had yet to be erected, probably by a powerful abbot who celebrated the enlargement of the compass of *Turas Cholmcille* close to the year 700 by commissioning the series of tall cross-pillars with highly accomplished ornament in contemporary style in that area which reached close to the end of *Turas Chonaill* in the townland of Drumroe.[19] When erected, these proclaimed Gleann-cholmcille as a centre of art in touch with the great centres in the east of the country, like Durrow, and like the centres where the Derrynavlan paten, the Tara Brooch, the Moylough Belt-shrine and other important works were already being made or were fore-shadowed. This enlargement extended *Turas Cholmcille* into a *Turas Mór* like that followed at Inismurray Island close to the feast of Molaise, the founder, on 12 August. On 9 June, Colmcille's Day, every year since, this *Turas Mór* has been followed in the Glen by thousands of pilgrims.

The Inishkeel/Lough Swilly slab tradition, 600-700

At Conall Caol's Inishkeel at the north end of *Turas Chonaill,* a number of slabs bear a developed art different in idiom and style from the unique pillar art of Gleanncholmcille. East of St Mary's church, two sculptured stones stand 2.25m apart.

The first is a large upright cross-slab, 1.20m tall, with rounded outline at the top, carved on two faces. The upper, west face of the slab is filled by a Latin cross with expanded terminals having a convex curve at the ends of the shaft and concave curves on both sides of each of the limbs. Inside the cross is a loose interlace design which ends in pairs of pointed loops in the arms and pairs of pointed loops on either side of a ring-knot at the foot and head. This cross stands above a depiction of a horse-drawn chariot with a driver sitting on the draught-pole. In the two upper quadrants of the cross there are two birds opposed, possibly swans, and above them faint traces of two stylised human figures apparently in long robes.

On the east face of the slab is a larger cross, slightly more angular in design, with a greatly enlarged foot. It is filled with a more expertly executed interlace composed from three plaited stands which expand into the enlarged foot as circular knots drawn out to the corner. Below the arms are two stylised cloaked figures. Under the foot of the cross a pair of clerics stand bowed low on either side of an altar, possibly representing Paul and Anthony (fig. 2.8).

The second and more easterly sculpted stone now stands to about the same height, but appears to be broken off at the top and may originally have had projecting arms at the top, suggesting a cross shape.[20] Its east face is decorated with a broad-band interlace;[21] its west, facing the figure-ornamented slab described above, has a band 8cm wide and 2cm deep cut back all around its edge. Did these two stones once form part of a composite monument?

This accomplished west slab at Inishkeel introduces us to a homogeneous series of similar slabs in the west and north of the county, which are among the finest carved Christian slabs in Ireland and are rivalled only by broadly similar elaborate gabled stones in Scotland, like one of the ornamented slabs standing in the churchyard at Nigg in Rosshire.[22] The first of these is in the churchyard at Fahan Mura, on the east shores of Lough Swilly.

Fahan Mura

This great tall slab, shaped on all four sides and carved to a gable shape on top, stands 2.19m tall and 90cm wide and is 3.20m from the south-east corner of the present church. A pair of carved tenons project 7cm from the sides at a height of 1.10m above ground; it seems this, like the slabs at Inishkeel, may also have formed part of a composite monument.[23]

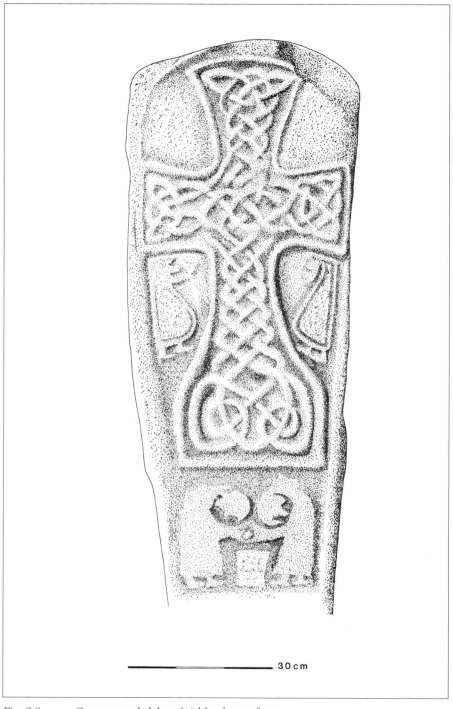

30cm

Fig. 2.8   Cross-carved slab at Inishkeel, east face.

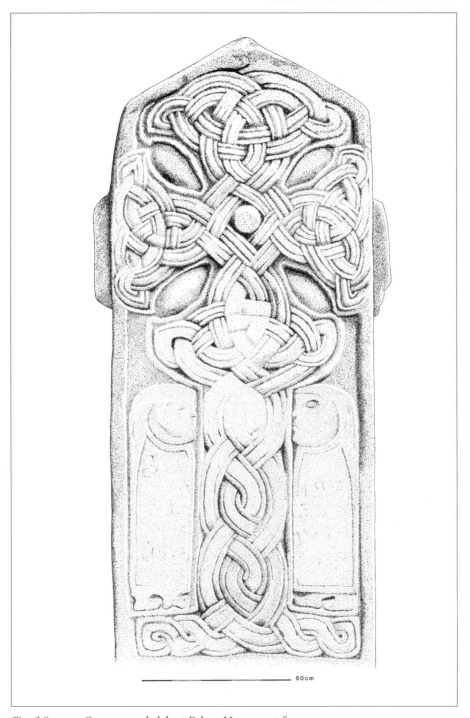

50cm

Fig. 2.9   Cross-carved slab at Fahan Mura, west face.

On the west face (fig. 2.9) an equal-armed cross covered with carved interlace stands on a vertical pillar drawn out at the foot to make a horizontal plinth or base; pillar and base are also carved with a continuation of the upper interlaced design. The interlace is of a woven broad band with a narrow border on either side, lower and flatter on pillar and base, tighter and narrower on the head. At the centre of the cross is a circular boss, around which the bands sweep, appearing to lift and adapt to the curves of the cross by narrowing and forming a tighter interlace, more convex in section, particularly on the arms, thus appearing in great relief. In the spaces between the limbs of the cross the stone is dressed into convex pointed ovals.

On either side of the pillar two figures stand above the plinth at the base. They are dressed in ankle-length robes, their feet apparently shod. The heads are shown in profile with short nose and square jutting chin, the eye of the figure on the right clearly marked as an oval in relief. Both have long hair falling down their backs to below the shoulder; the figure on the left appears to be bearded above the line of the chin. On each figure, within a border going all the way round the robes, is an inscription in six horizontal lines.

The opposite, east face of the slab shows the same border around the edge, inside which is a similar equal-armed cross standing on a stem widening towards a trapezoid foot and filled with a less elaborate interlace, also of bordered bands. Four triple-circle discs fill the spaces between the arms and the head and foot of the cross; at the centre is a smaller, possibly double-circle disc. A pair of birds, with curved beaks engaged, are carved in a triangular pediment above the cross. Françoise Henry has indicated the proximity of Fahan to the important Columban monastery of Derry and the strong impulses from as far away as the Coptic world which lie behind the complexity of the iconographical programme of this and other monuments in Inishowen, and the preponderance of motifs such as marigolds and interlace found on them.[24] On the narrow north face of the slab Macalister read a doxology in Greek,[25] the unusual form of which is to be found in the mid-seventh century Antiphonary of Bangor; this form is quoted in Canons 13 and 15 of the fourth Council of Toledo held in 633.[26]

Drumhallagh

A sculptured slab at Drumhallagh, worked on all four faces and with carved cross-designs on the two broader faces, is 1.33m tall and stands near a field fence on a raised stony platform on a height above the west shore of Lough Swilly. Local tradition attests the former existence of a church here. The east face of the slab is divided by the limbs of a Latin cross with expanded ends, the sides of the slab curving out and back as if to contain the transom. The cross is filled with a loose interlace design, created with a double band, with pointed knots in the ends of the arms and shaft. The interlace is more tightly knitted at the centre of the head and is apparently confused in the right arm. The moulding which makes the outline of the cross turns outwards at the foot to create an open field, possibly suggesting a plinth.

In the lower quadrants of the slab, standing one on either side of the cross, is a pair of ecclesiastics with croziers. Each has a flat hairstyle or cap on the head and is clothed in an ankle-length cloak drawn up into a high collar or hood behind the head. Each cloak is bordered all round and ornamented with a pair of opposed C-curves inside the border at the lower end. The figure on the left holds a short crooked crozier at chest-height; the one on the right holds a tau crozier. Both appear to be shod. A pair of squatting figures are apposed, thumb in mouth, in the upper quadrants. Their outer garments sit up behind the head with the same high collar, and each is decorated with a triangular key design on the body with a curved extension drawn over the hip and thigh.

Contrasting with this, on the west face of the slab, is a Latin cross with curved expanded ends to the limbs and with a carved boss at the centre of the crossing. The limbs of the cross are filled with bosses so that it resembles a *crux gemmata*. In each of the four angles is a carved circular boss in low relief. This cross stands on a base which is slightly trapezoid. This face too is bordered.

Carndonagh

The marigold slab at Carndonagh stands near the edge of a terrace on the south-east side of the present church on the site. It is 1.68m tall, parallel-sided, is elegantly carved on all four sides, and is 42.9cm wide at the top. On the west face a pair of figures stand on either side of a flabellum, the head of which is a seven-petalled marigold in a circle (fig. 2.10). At the centre of the marigold is a double circle in relief; there is a small boss in each of the webbed spaces between the petals. The handle is shown with a stepped design, ending in a pair of great loops at the bottom. These loops straddle a peltoid extension of a circle below, which stands on a horizontal foot with a stepped design like that of the handle of the flabellum. Threaded through the circumference of the circle is a regular four-looped interlace resembling a marigold.

The figure on each side is shown in knee-length robes and, as at Fahan, with hair dressed back over the ears to fall over the nape of the neck. That on the right holds in the hand nearest the viewer, raised in front of his chest, a crooked crozier. The figure on the left holds in a

Fig. 2.10   Cross-carved slab at Carndonagh, west face and north side.

similar position what may be a tau crozier with a vertical slot carved above the pointed foot.

The east face of the pillar shows an unusual Crucifixion. The figure of Christ is placed on an equal-armed cross from whose foot develops a twisted interlace stem which ends in a tripartite knot. The Christ, dressed in a long robe, has a greatly enlarged head which protrudes through the upper surface of the slab. Standing below the cross on either side are two figures, each dressed in knee-length robes which are ornamented with an equal-armed cross on the body. Beneath this composition the lower part of the pillar is filled by an equal-armed cross, ornamented with a twisted interlace, which stands on a plinth filled with a step-pattern. There are traces of two equal-armed crosses in the upper angles of this cross.

The close resemblance in style and composition of the Inishkeel, Drumhallagh and Fahan slabs suggests the existence of a tradition of carving in these areas of west and north Donegal which appears to have been developing during the course of the seventh century, concerned with the veneration of the cross. A somewhat earlier date, closer to 600, can be argued for the very accomplished Carndonagh slab, with its flabellum, its marigold, and its clerics, apparently bishop and abbot with crooked and T-shaped croziers respectively. This Carndonagh slab shares with the great Fahan Mura slab its siting a little to the south-east of the present church; the Inishkeel slab stands due east of St Mary's church. This similarity in siting raises the question of the function of these monuments, displayed as they are in very public positions apparently close to the contemporary principal church.

Examination of a pair of roughly contemporary slabs of the same large slab tradition on the islands of Duvillaun More and Inishkea North in an area of strong Columban influence off the Mullet peninsula in north-west Mayo may help in elucidating this question of their function. These were respectively 1.85m and 1.52m in height and each has a great Crucifixion scene rudely carved on its west face. The Duvillaun slab stands at the west end of a grave with rectangular outline immediately south of the small rectangular oratory, both at the east end of an ovoid enclosure; the Inishkea slab stands within one of a pair of conjoined houses with rectilinear interior and curved exterior investigated by Françoise Henry in 1938 on the Bailey Mór, a large sandhill.[27] Local tradition interpreted the Duvillaun grave as the tomb of the [founder] saint, whose name is forgotten;[28] it is possible that the Inishkea slab marked a similar tomb.

Could it be that the roughly contemporary Donegal slabs described above, sited as they are in the open, close to the east end of their respective churches at three sites, and near the focus of the enclosure at Drumhallagh, were erected to mark in the same idiom the tombs of the respective founders?

The tomb of the saint

The evidence for the form and ornamentation of the tomb-shrine of the saint has recently been briefly reviewed by the writer and a rough sequence proposed.[29] An early stage is indicated by graves marked by cross-inscribed stones on which ogham inscriptions in proto-Irish have been engraved, like the one at Teampall Mhanacháin (Teampall Geal), Ballymorereagh, on the Dingle peninsula.[30] The linguistic evidence suggests that these might belong for the most part to the period before 600 and the cross-marked slab at Inchagoill on Lough Corrib has an inscription following a similar formula.[31] Such graves are also marked by upright and recumbent cross-slabs, like *Leaba Phádraig* on Caher Island. Slabs at Tigh Mhóire, near Vicarstown on the Dingle peninsula,[32] in the burial enclosure north of the large oratory on Sceilg Mhichíl, and at Termons, Dromkeare and Loher near Waterville, all in Kerry,[33] appear also to mark the founders' graves in their respective enclosures; indeed the slabs at Tigh Mhóire may have resembled the pair at Inishkeel in that they were apparently upright slabs at the head and foot of a grave.

A different fashion seems to be indicated by the appearance of ornamented box-shrines, of A-roofed form like the Kerry/Clare/Galway group represented by the shrines at Killabuonia and Kilreelig, or of ornamented box-shrine form, like the one described by George Petrie in 1820 at Ardoileán, off the Galway coast,[34] that documented by the existence of four corner-posts at Kilnaruane, Bantry[35] or the reconstruction of four of the slabs found at Carrowntemple in Sligo.[36]

This ornamented group appears to be parallel in date to the ornamented series of cross-pillars which have the different function of marking the stations of the pilgrimage round or *turas* in Gleanncholmcille, and also to the Inishkea and Duvillaun Crucifixions, occurring at the end of the seventh century. In what appears to be a later development, the *leaba* (literally, bed) of the saint is often incorporated in a small stone building, often with antae, designated as the house (*teach, tigh*) of the founder saint, like *Teach Molaise* at Inismurray, *Teach Chiaráin* at Clonmacnois and St Columba's Shrine at Iona. The focal position of these monuments underlines the importance of the founder saint's relics and his/her shrine in the devotional life of the monastery. It is no surprise that the small building of *Teach Molaise* marks the beginning and end of *An Turas Mór* at Inismurray.

It is now possible to envisage a theoretical framework and a notional sequence into which the Donegal slabs will fit: just as we assign many of the Loughros and Gleanncholmcille slabs to a framework based on *an Turas* and its development and enlargement between about 500 and 700, so we assign the slabs of the Lough Swilly/Inishkeel group to developments in marking the tomb of the founder saint set in roughly the same two centuries. Two other slabs, at Killaghtee and Kilrean in the south of the country, may be interpreted also as marking the tomb of the founder at their respective sites and can also be placed in the seventh century.

The cross-inscribed slab at Killaghtee, 1.75m in height, stands south-west of the remains of the late medieval church. It has a sophisticated outline, cut to a rounded shape at the apex. Within this upper area on the west face of the slab is a Maltese cross, slightly concave, the arms having 'a hardly perceptible curve',[37] encircled by a raised moulding; at its centre are two concentric incised circles with a hollow in the centre. Below and to the right of the cross-design, a loosely worked triquetra knot is cut. Although identified by Françoise Henry as a possible Chi-rho, the evidence does not appear to support this identification. The east face of the slab is plain.

In the graveyard at Kilrean, near Glenties, 5m north-east of the north-east corner of the present church, a cross-slab decorated on both faces stands 1.57m in height. On the west face of the slab is an elaborate ringed Latin cross which covers most of the dressed surface, its arms breaking through the line of the long sides of the stone. The cross outline is created by a broad band in false relief; at the centre of the head two concentric incised circles represent a boss. The segments of the ring appear in a plane behind that of the body of the cross; within the segments the stone is cut away to create the impression of hollowed angles. At the apex of the upper shaft is an angular four-lobed interlace knot; the same design is carved on the lower shaft a similar distance below the central boss. These knots closely resemble that of the lower element of the design on the west face of the tall pillar at Station 15 of *Turas Cholmcille* at Gleanncholmcille, where the motif is presented in a circular frame, and suggest that pillar and cross-design are contemporary. A square enamelled stud from a brooch at Freswick Links, Caithness, bears a similar motif.[38]

At the level of the protruding arms on the east face, which is largely undressed, is carved a much weathered cruciform design consisting of four oval pointed petals, each with a lentoid hollowed centre, enclosed within a broad band which interlaces at the crossing. This design is paralleled in Scotland on a cross-slab at Cill Eileagáin, Mulreesh, on the island of Islay,[39] and echoed also in the design of the west face of the cross-pillar on Station 2 of *Turas Cholmcille*.[40]

The word *Martartech* is sometimes applied to the house in which the relics of a martyr are laid, as in Martry *(martartech)* in Meath and

Castlemartyr (*martre,* DIL, s.v. martrae) in Cork.[41] Many placenames listed by Hogan[42] consist of the word *tech* preceding the name of a saint as *t. Aeda guairi* in Connacht, *t. Airindáin* (Tyfarnham) in Westmeath, *t. Caoin* (Tagheen) in Mayo, *t. Damnata* (Tedavnet) in Monaghan, *t. Eoin* (St John's Point) in Down, *t. Fainche* (Tyance) in Derry, *t. Mo-chua* (Timahoe) in Laois, *t. Molaga* (Timoleague) in Cork, *t. Munnu* (Taghmon) in Wexford, *t. Scuithín* (Tiscoffin) in Kilkenny. Flanagan has noted that within the total count of her documented instances the formation pattern is almost invariably *tech* qualified by a personal name, as in the examples quoted here.[43] Three names of this family *(t. Baithín)* commemorate saints named Baithín at Taghboyne in Westmeath, Tibohine near Frenchpark in Roscommon and Taughboyne in Donegal. At this Donegal site, *Baithín Mór,* successor of Colmcille as abbot of Iona, previously abbot of Magh-lunge in Tiree, is commemorated.[44] The name suggests that a building to house the founder's relics like *Teach Molaise* on Inismurray and *Teach Chiaráin* at Clonmacnois was built at a mature stage in the monastery's history, probably replacing an earlier form of tomb-shrine at the site. With *Leaba Cholmcille* at Beefan, and possibly also with many of the accomplished cross-slabs described above, it suggests that the custom of marking the resting-place or shrine of the founder saint was widespread if not universal in Donegal, as elsewhere in Ireland and Scotland, in the early centuries of christianity and that the shrine marking the spot assumed one of the standard forms.

References
1.   H. C. Crawford, *Irish carved ornament* (Dublin, 1926); F. Henry, 'Early christian slabs and pillar stones in the west of Ireland' in *R.S.A.I., Jn.,* lxxvii (1937), pp 265-279.
2.   M. Herity, 'The antiquity of *an turas* (the pilgrimage round)' in A. Lehner and W. Berschin (ed.), *Lateinische Kultur im VIII Jahrhundert* (St Ottilien, 1989), pp 95-143; ibid., *Gleanncholmcille, guide to 5,000 years of history in stone;* ibid., 'Carpet pages and Chi-rhos, some depictions in Irish early Christian manuscripts and stone carvings' in *Celtica* xxi (1990), pp 208-22; ibid., 'The forms of the tomb-shrine of the founder saint in Ireland' in M. D. Spearman and J. Higgitt (ed.), *The age of migrating ideas* (Edinburgh, 1993), pp 188-95; ibid., *'Les premiers ermitages et monastéres en Irlande, 400-700'* in *Cahiers de Civilisation Médiévale* xxxvi (1993), pp 219-61.
3.   L. Price, 'Glencolumbkille, county Donegal, and its early christian cross slabs' in *R.S.A.I. Jn.,* lxxi (1941), pp 78-80.
4.   B. Lacy, *Archaeological survey of county Donegal* (Lifford, 1983), p. 296, fig. 147 c.
5.   Herity, *Gleanncholmcille,* pp 37-8.
6.   Ibid., pp 41-3.
7.   F. Henry, 'Megalithic and early christian remains at Lankill, county Mayo' in *R.S.A.I. Jn.,* lxxxii (1952), pp 68-71.

8. W. F. Wakeman, 'On the earlier forms of inscribed christian crosses found in Ireland' in *R.S.A.I. Jn.*, xxi (1890-1), pp 350-8.
9. J. Cuppage, *Archaeological survey of the Dingle peninsula* (Ballyferriter, 1986), pp 329, 332 and fig. 199 c.
10. *The royal commission on the ancient and historical monuments of Scotland, Argyll, iv, Iona* (Edinburgh, 1982), pp 181-2 (hereafter *R.C.A.H.M.S.*).
11. Ibid., vii, pp 45-6, 50, 66, 83.
12. Cuppage, *Dingle peninsula*, p. 345, fig. 207.
13. P. Walsh, 'The monastic settlement on Rathlin O'Birne Island, county Donegal' in *R.S.A.I. Jn.*, cxiii (1983), p. 59; Herity, 'The antiquity of *an turas*', pp 106-7, 120.
14. Herity, 'The antiquity of *an turas*', pp 107-11, 118-9.
15. P. Heraughty, *Inishmurray, ancient monastic island* (Dublin, 1982), p. 29; Herity, 'The antiquity of *an turas*', p. 96.
16. Herity, 'The antiquity of *an turas*', pp 212-22.
17. Ibid., p. 121.
18. Ibid., p. 120.
19. Herity, *Gleanncholmcille*, p. 31.
20. F. Henry, *Irish art in the early christian period to 800 A.D.* (London, 1965), p. 130.
21. Lacy, *Archaeological survey*, pl. 47.
22. J. R. Allen and J. Anderson, *The early christian monuments of Scotland* (Edinburgh, 1903), fig. 72.
23. M. Herity, 'The forms of the tomb-shrine', p. 191, fig. 23.3a.
24. Henry, *Irish art*, pp 125-8.
25. R. A. S. Macalister, 'The inscription on the slab at Fahan Mura, county Donegal' in *R.S.A.I. Jn.*, lix (1929), pp 89-98.
26. Henry, *Irish art*, pp 125-8.
27. F. Henry, 'Remains of the early christian period on Inishkea North, county Mayo' in *R.S.A.I. Jn.*, lxxx (1945), pp 127-55.
28. F. Henry, 'Early christian slabs and pillar stones in the west of Ireland' in *R.S.A.I. Jn.*, lxvii (1937), p. 272.
29. Herity, 'The forms of the tomb-shrine'.
30. Cuppage, *Dingle peninsula*, pp 268-70.
31. Herity, 'The antiquity of *an turas*', fig. 17a; Herity, 'The forms of the tomb-shrine', p. 188, fig. 23.2b.
32. Cuppage, *Dingle peninsula*, pp 345-6, pl. 46.
33. F. Henry, 'Early monasteries, beehive huts and dry-stone houses in the neighbourhood of Caherciveen and Waterville' in *R.I.A. Proc.*, lviii (1957), C, pp 126, 134, 136, 144.
34. M. Herity, 'The ornamented tomb of the saint at Ardoileán, county Galway' in M. Ryan (ed.), *Ireland and insular art, A.D. 500-1200* (Dublin, 1987), pp 141-3; Herity, *Gleanncholmcille*, pp 97-8.
35. Herity, 'The forms of the tomb-shrine', pp 191-3, fig. 23.5a.
36. M. A. Timoney and P. F. Wallace, 'Carrowntemple, county Sligo, and its inscribed slabs' in E. Rynne (ed.), *Figures from the past* (Dublin, 1987), pp 43-61; Herity, 'The forms of the tomb-shrine', p. 191, fig. 23.4 e-h.
37. Henry, *Irish art*, p. 120.
38. C. Bourke and J. Close-Brookes, 'Fine insular enamelled ornaments' in *P.S.A.S.*, (1989), pp 229-30.
39. *R.C.A.H.M.S.*, v, p. 166.
40. Herity, 'The antiquity of *an turas*', p. 106.

41. E. Hogan, *Onomasticon Gaedelicum* (Dublin, 1910), pp 536-7.
42. Ibid., pp 622-7.
43. D. Flanagan, 'The Christian impact on early Ireland: the place-names evidence' in P. Ní Chatháin and M. Richter (eds), *Ireland and Europe, the early church* (Stuttgart, 1982), p. 37.
44. W. Reeves, *The life of St. Columba* (Dublin, 1957), p. 43.

Chapter 3

STONE SCULPTURE IN DONEGAL

HELEN LANIGAN WOOD AND EITHNE VERLING

Celtic idols

The oldest stone sculptures in Donegal belong to the Iron Age, to pagan Celtic times, when images of gods and goddesses were created in wood and stone. The majority of these stone carvings have been found in the northern half of the country, where they are often concentrated in particular geographical areas.[1]

One of these concentrations is in east Donegal, in the vicinity of Raphoe, an area of good agricultural land which has been occupied successively since the Late Stone Age. Three stone idols are known from this area, one of them published here for the first time. There is also an unfinished bust which may belong to the same period.

Three other stone busts from this locality, formerly displayed outside a house in Woodlands, were previously thought to be pre-Christian.[2] However, we now think they were carved much later, in the Post-Medieval period.

The best known sculpture from the Raphoe area and one generally accepted as pre-Christian is the head from Beltany, now in the National Museum (Plate 3.1). It belonged at one time to the Wilson family (of Drumaneny House near Beltany Stone Circle) who sold it about 1948 at an auction.[3] It is not known where it came from originally although it is reputed to have been found in the vicinity of Beltany Stone Circle.[4]

The Beltany head is a well executed piece carved with great assurance. Its most compelling features are large staring eyes and a prominent mouth. These create the same kind of strong visual impact evoked by the janiform idol on Boa Island in Fermanagh, one of the masterpieces of the Celtic world. The Beltany head is carved on an unusually thin piece of stone. Around its neck are traces of decoration which could possibly represent a torc, a gold collar worn by Celtic heroes and deities.[5]

The second stone head from east Donegal, formerly at Creaghadoos, is now in a private collection[6] (Plate 3.2). Made from a beautifully rounded boulder, its features are carefully cut into the stone, incised to such a shallow depth that they almost blend into the smooth surface of the stone. A number of other Celtic idols such as the three-faced head

51

Plate 3.1   Stone Head, Beltany (N.M.I.).

from Corleck in county Cavan and the three-faced head from Glejbjerg in Jutland, Denmark, also appear to have been carved from natural rounded boulders. Another carved stone from Creagadoos is now in Donegal County Museum. It is a roughly shaped bust, possibly a stone rejected by the carver before it was finished.[7]

The third stone head from the Raphoe area was found in the 1940s during a field clearance operation between the village of Convoy and

Plate 3.2   Stone Head, Creaghadoos (Donegal County Museum).

Plate 3.3   Stone Head, Convoy/Ballybofey (Donegal County Museum).

the town of Ballybofey (Plate 3.3). All its features – wide oval eyes, thick oval lips, large grotesque ears and wedge-shaped nose – are carved in relief above an exceptionally flat face. This is a powerful carving, almost certainly pre-Christian.

The non-naturalistic traditions of Celtic sculpture, so well illustrated in these heads from the Raphoe area, continued into the Early Christian/Early Medieval period and are exhibited not only in stone carvings but also in metalwork and illuminated manuscripts. The Early Christian figurative art can be securely dated by its context and often the facial features on stone and metal figures of this period bear striking resemblances to those on the earlier head idols – for example the figures on the Athlone Crucifixion plaque,[8] the figure on the Irish-made hanging-bowl mount from a Viking grave at Myklebostad in Norway,[9] the gilded face on the bell shrine mount from the Killua Castle collection,[10] the figures depicted on the Donegal book shrine, the Misach,[11] the statues from White Island in Fermanagh[12] and one of the carved figures on the south pillar at Carndonagh (Plate 3.4).

None of the pre-Christian head carvings in Ireland comes from securely dated contexts. The pre-Christian dating of the janiform figure on Boa Island has recently been questioned with comparisons being made between its design of two figures set back to back and Early Christian filigree patterns of kneeling men with backs turned to each other on the paten from Derrynaflan.[13] Indeed other Early Christian comparisons could be found for the Boa Island figure, for example the two crossed-legged figures on the Irish ninth-century wooden bucket from a Norwegian grave at Oseberg[14] and the figure with outsized head and crossed arms on one of the Early Christian pillars from Carndonagh (Plate 3.5).

These links between pagan and Christian are generally interpreted as echoes from the past and in some cases may have been a deliberate attempt to impose a Christian meaning on a pagan image. However, if the Iron Age dating of these heads and figure carvings remains unproven, ascribing them to later periods is equally tentative. In the case of the Boa Island carving, the presence of a phallus on one of the figures makes a Christian interpretation difficult and unlikely.

The group of head carvings from the Raphoe area points to the strength of religious practice in that locality in pre-Christian times. Later, Raphoe became an important Christian centre. Perhaps, as in Armagh city, the Christian monastery of Raphoe was built on the site of a Celtic sanctuary. Indeed, in the medieval papal chancery documents there is a strange reference to laymen in the Raphoe diocese being censored in 1265 AD for worshipping idols.[15] This makes one wonder if pagan beliefs were still alive here in the thirteenth century.

The Early Christian period

While few traces of pagan religion survive in Donegal, over 130 early church sites are known, testifying to the strength of Christianity in the county at this time. Many simple cross-inscribed slabs can be found on these sites but carvings of real sculptural quality are rare.

However, at Carndonagh, on the Inishowen peninsula, carvings of remarkable quality have survived on the site of an early Patrician church located in the area around the present eighteenth-century Church of Ireland church. There is a High Cross standing between two decorated pillars, a cross slab known as 'the Marigold Stone' and a decorated lintel from an Early Christian church.

The High Cross

The High Cross, known as St Patrick's or Donagh Cross,[16] has a simple and pleasing shape with short arms curving gently from the shaft (Plate 3.6). Its decoration is unusual, combining bands of interlaced ribbon with simplified figures in low relief, shown frontally and in profile.

The most prominent scene on the cross is a Crucifixion accompanied by two figures representing either Stephaton and Longinus, sponge and lance bearers, or the two thieves crucified with Christ. Below it are three figures wearing cowls and long robes. These may represent the holy women who visited Christ's tomb after the Resurrection.[17] The two pillars are carved in the same style as the cross and apart from spiral ornament on the north pillar are covered exclusively with figures and other representational images.

The harpist on the north pillar, representing King David, is the only figure that can be identified with any certainty (Plate 3.5). The figure of the warrior on the same pillar may also be David although it could alternatively represent Goliath (Plate 3.6). The remaining side of the north pillar contains a baffling image of a large fish with a small bird, perhaps an eagle, perched on its head.

On the south pillar is a figure holding a bell and a book or satchel (Plate 3.4). Below this is a crozier, shepherd's crook or walking staff lying on its side. This figure is usually identified by the episcopal emblem as a saintly bishop or abbot. However, it has been suggested that the crozier is a walking staff and that the figure represents a pilgrim or a pilgrim saint.[18]

The figure on the south side of this pillar continues to be enigmatic (Plate 3.8). Controversy surrounds the interpretation of the two 'horns' rising from the forehead. If they are intended to represent horns, then the figure may take on either the pre-Christian symbolism of a horned god[19] or possibly the Christian symbolism of a devil.

Plate 3.4   South Pillar, Carndonagh, west face (Peter Harbison).

Plate 3.5   North Pillar, Carndonagh, east face (Office of Public Works).

Plate 3.6   St Patrick's High Cross, Carndonagh, east face (Peter Harbison).

Plate 3.7   North Pillar, Carndonagh, west face (Peter Harbison).

Plate 3.8   South Pillar, Carndonagh, south face (Peter Harbison).

It seems more plausible to accept the 'horns' as locks of hair, in which case one could identify the objects on the lower part of the stone as three loaves and a poorly carved fish, and interpret the image as The Miracle of the Loaves and Fishes.[20] On the north side of this pillar is a carving interpreted as Jonah and the Whale.[21] It consists of a large human head shown in profile above a fish-like body. Only a face has been carved on the remaining side of this pillar.[22]

The 'Marigold' stone

The 'Marigold' stone takes its name from the well preserved design which dominates the west face of this cross slab. The design, framed by a circle, can be viewed as a floral motif with seven petals – in which case it is closer to the six-petalled asphodel than to a marigold with its multiplicity of petals. Alternatively, if one sees the shapes between the petals as predominant, the design becomes a star-shaped motif with seven rays. Emanating from this circular shape is a long stem or handle. This design may represent a 'flabellum' – a fan used during Mass in warm climates to keep flies away from the altar. There are two figures on either side of this 'flabellum'. Both appear to be carrying a staff or crozier and may represent two pilgrims or possibly St Paul and St Anthony.[23]

On the opposite side of this slab is an unusual depiction of the Crucifixion (Plate 3.9). Christ's head protrudes above the top line of the slab and placed low down below his feet are two figures possibly representing the thieves crucified with Christ.

Carved lintels

The carved lintel at Carndonagh is one of three similar church lintels in the county.[24] They would have surmounted the main west doorways of pre-Romanesque churches built during the period between the tenth and the early twelfth centuries. The two other lintels are at Clonca and Raphoe.[25]

The decoration on the Carndonagh lintel is very weathered. In the centre is a ringed cross. On the right is some clumsily carved interlacing and on the left are at least four figures. Two of these appear to be holding on to a crozier or a post set between them. On the extreme left is another figure clasping a staff or crozier.

The lintel at Clonca has been re-used over the west doorway of a seventeenth-century church, now in ruins. The stone is so badly weathered that although one can detect a number of figures, it is impossible to identify which scenes are portrayed.

The lintel at Raphoe Cathedral is now in two fragments and part of the centre is missing. The left piece, now in the vestibule of the

Plate 3.9   'Marigold' Stone Cross Slab, Carndonagh, east face (Peter Harbison).

cathedral, depicts the Arrest of Christ and St Peter cutting off the ear of Malchus, servant of the High Priest. The missing central piece almost certainly represented the Crucifixion. Part of this – Christ's head and left arm – can be traced on the badly weathered right side of the lintel which is now built into the outer north wall of the church. Above Christ's extended arm is a small angel, and below it are faint traces of the sponge or lance-bearer. To the right are two bearded men holding something, perhaps a crozier, between them. The other figures further to the right are too badly damaged to be identified.

The early ecclesiastical site of Clonca on the Inishowen peninsula contains several interesting stone sculptures in addition to the lintel already described. There are the remains of two High Crosses, one of which is a solid-ringed cross-head without figurative decoration. The other High Cross, called St Buadan's Cross, is a remarkably tall slender cross, almost four metres high.

St Buadan's Cross, Clonca

Apart from three figurative panels, this cross is entirely covered in abstract ornament – well carved interlacing, fret patterns and one unusual panel of spirals with animal head terminals (Plate 3.10). One of the figurative panels can be clearly identified as the Miracle of the Loaves and Fishes.[26] This wonderful composition shows Jesus in profile with a caricaturish face, sitting on a high backed chair and holding up the five loaves on a circular platter. Below this the two fishes have been carefully placed to fill the remaining space within the panel.

On one of the arms of the cross is carved a small figure with hands stretched upwards in an attitude of prayer. A similar figure is inscribed on one of the cross slabs from the Early Christian site at Conwal, near Letterkenny.[27]

The third figurative panel contains two figures sitting side by side (Plate 3.10). Their arms may be crossed and interlinked or they may be holding two crossed staffs. It has been suggested that these represent St Paul and St Anthony in the desert and that the two animals above them, with almost human faces, are the lions that dug St Paul's grave.[28] To complete the symmetrical design of this panel, the carver has filled the free spaces beside the lions' heads with the spiral heads of two croziers.

St Mura's Cross slab, Fahan

One of the outstanding Early Christian monuments in Donegal is the cross slab at Fahan on the eastern shores of Lough Swilly (Plate 3.11). Known as St Mura's Cross, it is believed to mark the grave of St Mura, first abbot of Fahan. St Mura was a disciple of St Colmcille who founded the monastery of Fahan in the sixth century.

Plate 3.10   St Buadan's High Cross, Clonca, west face (Anthony Weir).

Plate 3.11   St Mura's Cross Slab, Fahan, east face (Office of Public Works).

The cross slab has a pointed top and is unusual in having short arms protruding from each side. It is decorated on both sides with splendidly carved crosses of intricate bands of interlacing. On the west side two figures, now quite weathered, stand facing each other on either side of the cross shaft. At one time their garments were thought to bear inscriptions but no trace of any inscription can now be seen. On the north side, however, there is an inscription, in Greek, which is translated as: 'Glory and Honour to the Father, the Son and the Holy Ghost'.

Across the Swilly, at Drumhallagh on the western shores of the lough, stands another interesting cross slab decorated on both sides with Latin crosses.[29] The sides of the slab bulge outwards at the ends of the cross arms, echoing the protrusions on St Mura's Cross.

The cross on the west side of the slab is decorated with pellets – a design perhaps inspired by metal crosses studded with jewels.[30] On the opposite face an angel is carved above the arms of the cross, each angel shown with a hand raised in front of its face. Below the arms of the cross two long-robed figures with croziers stand facing each other, like the two figures on St Mura's Cross.

Two figures without croziers are carved in a similar position under the cross arms on one of the cross slabs at Inishkeel Island off the north coast.[31] A second cross slab at Inishkeel has a Crucifixion scene with what appear to be two angels above the cross arm and the lance and sponge bearers below.[32] The slab is broken and only the legs of the lance-bearer survive.

At Carrowmore east of Carndonagh the west face of the High Cross contains a badly weathered incised carving interpreted as Christ in Majesty accompanied by two angels.[33] A similar design occurs on a Scottish cross, at Camuston in Forfarshire.[34]

There is still some uncertainty about the date of many of these carvings. Because of similarities in form and/or decoration, the High Cross, pillars and cross slab at Carndonagh are probably roughly contemporary with the cross slabs from Drumhallagh, Inishkeel and Fahan.

This group of Donegal carvings has long been recognised as highly distinctive and very different from High Crosses and cross slabs in other parts of the country. The broad ribbon interlacing on the Donegal carvings has been compared with the interlacing in the seventh-century Book of Durrow and these monuments have been dated to the late seventh or early eighth-century.[35]

It has also been suggested that the Donegal cross and cross slabs mark a transitional stage in the evolution of High Crosses – from simple cross slabs to slabs with protruding arms (as at Fahan) to free-standing ringed crosses.[36] However, Harbison has argued that these Donegal carvings are more likely to be ninth century in date, and hence roughly contemporary with some of the other Irish High Crosses. We would agree with his view that these monuments are best regarded as 'a highly distinctive and individualistic regional group of carvings'.[37] Their special characteristics include figure carvings of exceptionally large scale, bold ribbon interlacing of high quality and cross slabs and crosses of unusual shape.

They are the work of highly creative sculptors who probably drew inspiration from many sources including illuminated manuscripts, metalwork and stone carving. Their outstanding achievements were the High Cross and 'Marigold' stone at Carndonagh and St Mura's Cross slab at Fahan. Sculptors living and working in a geographically isolated region, remote from the larger monastic centres and the artistic fashions of the day, gave coherence and individuality to Donegal carvings.

St Buadan's Cross at Clonca is different from the other carvings. The small scale of the figures in the three figurative panels is exceptional in Donegal and is closer to that on High Crosses in other parts of the country. The tall slender shape of the cross is also distinctive. Yet this carving, like those at Carndonagh and Fahan, also portrays the work of a highly individualistic carver with an equally assured sense of design.

Medieval sculptural traditions

The early part of the Medieval period – the thirteenth and fourteenth centuries – was a time when there was little produced by Donegal stonecarvers. This decline was in marked contrast with the vitality and originality of sculpture in the preceding period.

Two heads now in Rossnowlagh Museum are said to have come from the Cistercian Abbey of Assaroe,[38] a daughter house of Boyle Abbey and founded in 1178. One of these (Plate 3.12) made of badly weathered sandstone, is carved in the Romanesque style, and although it could be contemporary with the first building activity on the site, it is more likely to belong to the early thirteenth century, to a time when the strict Cistercian rules forbidding sculpture in their churches were being widely infringed. In parts of the west of Ireland the Romanesque style was current in the thirteenth century[39] and in places like Devenish in Fermanagh its influence was still apparent in the fifteenth century.[40]

The second stone from Assaroe, also badly weathered, is a mask-like head carved in relief on a rectangular slab of fine-grained light-coloured stone (Plate 3.13). The hair is carved in a most unusual way to suggest a beard, side-locks and a leafy crown. So little of Assaroe Abbey has survived that it is only possible to hazard a guess as to its architectural context. Although it lacks the usual characteristics of a voussoir – a narrower and curved bottom – it could have been inserted as a keystone in a relieving arch. Keystones with similar flat bases are found at Killydonnell and Balleeghan friaries.[41] A close dating is equally difficult to establish, but a thirteenth century date would not be unlikely.[42]

There is a round headed window built into Tullyaughnish seventeenth century parish church in Ramelton which is probably another Late Romanesque carving of the early thirteenth century.[43] Decorated with bosses and a foliage pattern of fleur de lys set between two animals, a lion and possibly a winged dragon, the window fragment came from a former church at Aughnish Isle in Lough Swilly.

Another stone head, now on loan to Donegal County Museum, came from the town of Raphoe (Plate 3.14). It was found during the first half of the nineteenth century buried in a field next to the Cathedral graveyard. It may represent a woman. Its face is well moulded with high cheekbones, a strong rounded chin and a naturalistic lip channel above well-shaped lips. The nose has been broken off. However, the most dominant features are the protruding eyebrows and blank thick-lidded eyes. These appear strange and other-worldly alongside the naturalistic treatment of the rest of the face and the hair line.

There are no close parallels for this head and while the non-naturalistic eyes and brows would be at home in a pre-Christian context, the rest of the carving is closer to the Medieval style. Given its discovery close to Raphoe Cathedral, it is probably best considered as Medieval in date, possibly thirteenth or fourteenth century.

Late Medieval resurgence

In the fifteenth and sixteenth centuries Donegal experienced a major expansion of monasticism. Franciscan friaries of the Third Order Regular were established at Killydonnell, Balleeghan, Magherabeg and Ballysaggart; a foundation of the stricter Franciscan Observantine Order was built in Donegal and a Carmelite Friary at Rathmullan. Stone carvers were again assured of patronage and examples of their decorative work have survived in all but one of these friaries. The stonecarvers usually decorated church doors and windows and occasionally they embellished a tomb for a member of the founder's family.

The founders were drawn from the ruling O'Donnell sept and from the MacSweenys. The latter were descendants of an Argyle chieftain Suibhne O'Neill and became distinguished gallowglasses or mercenaries for the O'Donnells.[44]

Decorative heads in churches

The position most favoured for decorative heads and foliage was on the terminals of hood mouldings; good examples can be seen on the large traceried east windows of Killydonnell and Balleeghan friaries, both O'Donnell foundations of the later fifteenth century.[45] At Killydonnell there are more headstops on the south chancel window and at Balleeghan another head is used in the relieving arch overhead. At Raphoe Cathedral in addition to the typical head stops on the hood moulding of the south chancel window (Plate 3.15), two other stone heads are set above slit windows in the tower.[46]

Plate 3.12   Stone Head, Assaroe (Donnelly Photographers).

Plate 3.13   Stone Head, Assaroe
             (Donegal County Museum).

Plate 3.14   Stone Head, Raphoe
             (Donegal County
             Museum).

The Carmelite Friary of Rathmullan, founded by Owen Roe MacSweeny in 1516, has typical head stops on the hood moulding of its south chancel window (Plate 3.16). Originally it also had an unusual large carving of a mitred figure set above the hood moulding of the east window. This badly weathered carving is now inside the Catholic church at Rathmullan.[47] Another carved head with stylised foliage below it, now on the gatepost of Clondevaddock Church of Ireland church at Rosnakill, may also have been a head stop on a late Medieval church.[48]

One other carved head from a graveyard at Doorin Point in Drimcoe townland may also be Medieval. It is now missing but a photograph of it survives showing a grimacing gargoyle-like face with mouth wide open and with deep scores cut on the forehead to suggest wrinkles. The head was inserted in a wall above a stone bearing the inscription 'Patrick Millar 1789'. A somewhat similar head, now very weathered, is set high up on the east wall of Derrybrusk Late Medieval church in Fermanagh where it seemed to have had only a decorative function.[49]

Animal carvings

A number of interesting Late Medieval animal carvings are associated with Donegal churches. All are carved on dressed stones but none of these stones is in its original position.

Two of them came from the Franciscan Tertiary Friary at Magherabeg which was founded in the fifteenth century by O'Donnell. One, now missing, was incomplete when it was drawn by the Ordnance Survey team between 1845-48.[50] Their sketch shows the body of what appears to be a lion, with its genitalia being attacked by a dog. The second stone still to be seen at St Ernan's Hotel at Muckross is a strange carving of a monstrous beast with two bodies and a single head.[51] The bodies are shown in profile while the face with its wide staring eyes and gloomy expression is portrayed frontally.

Two remarkably similar animals, this time with separate heads, were carved many centuries earlier on Clonca High Cross (Plate 3.10), and again there is a strange combination of front-facing heads with bodies shown in profile.A second monster, very like the one from St Ernan's, can be seen outside the Church of Ireland parish church at Ramelton, alongside a carving of a heraldic lion. Both are dressed bevelled stones. Where these two stones came from or how they might have been used is not known. They were formerly in Tullyaughnish seventeenth-century parish church which stands in ruins adjacent to the present Church of Ireland church.[52]

In the 1920s or 1930s another stone with animal carvings was found in the vicinity of Tullyaughnish church and is now in a private

Plate 3.15   Hood moulding, south chancel window, Raphoe Cathedral (Helen Lanigan Wood).

Plate 3.16   Stone Head, south chancel window, Rathmullan Carmelite Friary (Helen Lanigan Wood).

Plate 3.17   Terminal of Hood Moulding, Tullyaughnish, Ramelton (Donegal County Museum).

collection. It is an incomplete terminal of a hood moulding, made of limestone, with the point of the terminal ending in a leaf spray (Plate 3.17). Above the leaves is a lion regardant, its head turned to face a boar standing on its back. The boar is probably playing the bagpipes, the latter shown as a rounded bladder-like object with two long stems.

A pig playing bagpipes is carved on an early sixteenth century misericord seat in Beverley Minster, on seat number 18, one of the seats reserved for canons vicars.[53] On the same seat are carved a pig playing a harp, a saddled pig and young pigs dancing. There is also a boar on one of the Medieval oak misericord seats in Limerick Cathedral.[54] The boar was a symbol of gluttony but it was also an English royal badge used by Richard III and his Yorkist followers. Between the lion and the stem of the hood moulding is a strange quadruped, probably an antelope with a collar around its neck. Below the collar a limb is stretched towards something at the top centre of the stone which is now broken off. A collared antelope was an English royal badge used by King Henry VI and occurs on one of the misericord seats in Limerick Cathedral.

Two other interesting animal carvings come from Raphoe Cathedral. One is a sheep's head on a corbel now lying outside the Cathedral porch. The other is a terminal stone from a hood moulding showing a dragon biting the point of the terminal; above it a stag with a dog on top attacking its antlers.[55] This stone was stolen from the Cathedral in 1980.

Four Late Medieval grave-slabs

Four grave-slabs of Late Medieval date are known from Donegal. Like their counterparts in the West Highlands of Scotland they were probably laid flat over graves dug into the ground.[56] It is now generally accepted that these are the work of Irish carvers who, although probably familiar with Scottish carvings, developed their own repertoire of motifs including animals, humans, interlace and foliate patterns.[57]

In Clonca church the grave-slab in memory of Magnus Mac Orristin with its distinctive Medieval sword is closest in style to the Scottish carvings but even here details such as the foliate ornament and the two winged beasts on top of the central cross appear to be Irish in inspiration.

Two of the other Donegal grave-slabs commemorate members of different MacSweeny septs, both with strong Scottish connections. The one from Fan an Charta, Franciscan Tertiary Friary at Ballysaggart (Plate 3.18) and now at Killybegs Roman Catholic Church is, although uninscribed, traditionally in memory of a MacSweeny Banagh of Rahan Near Castle close to St John's Point.

This is divided into nine panels, the largest containing an impressive carving of a soldier armed with sword and battle axe, wearing a helmet with an unusual fan-shaped plume, and obviously intended to represent a MacSweeny gallowglass. In the same panel are two or three small animals, now very weathered but clearer in a rubbing of the stone published in 1872 (Plate 3.18). In the next panel below this is a pair of opposed beasts, possibly representing lions. Below this is a small interlaced design which closely resembles the main cross head on the MacSweeny slab from Doe Castle with its arms ending in spear points. In the bottom panel are two figures apparently fighting each other and the five remaining panels contain interlace and foliate ornament.

The grave-slab from Castledoe graveyard, now displayed at Doe Castle (Plate 3.19), has an indecipherable inscription but has long been accepted as the tomb slab of a MacSweeny na dTuath of Doe Castle. In 1903 the antiquarian Bigger deciphered the name of the sculptor as Madoniuf Oravaity and suggested a date of 1544.[58] The two MacSweeny grave-slabs are quite different in style although interlace, foliate and animal motifs are common to both.

Animals feature more prominently on the MacSweeny slab from Doe Castle. It is possible to identify an eagle with two fish in its claws, a bull or calf, a boar and possibly a fox and a lion. The fourth grave-slab was found recently in Clonmany graveyard.[59] It is covered in foliage patterns and is uninscribed.

Plate 3.18   Grave Slab, Fan an Charta Friary, Ballysaggart, now at Killybegs (Rubbing
by Patterson, published in 1872).

Plate 3.19   Grave Slab, Castledoe Graveyard, now at Doe Castle (R. Welch, courtesy
of Ulster Museum).

To a large extent the significance of these Medieval carvings eludes
us today. The headstops may be purely decorative although those from
the friaries seem to represent friars. Sometimes as in the case of the
mitred figure from Rathmullan Carmelite Friary the rank can be
identified while the figure remains nameless.

75

The same is true of the animal carvings and most interpretations must remain tentative. Real animals as well as mythical beasts are found. It seems to be the world of the Medieval bestiaries, of moral tales and Christian allegories, based on biblical and classical sources. In this world the lion, the stag and the eagle become symbols of Christ and the fishes caught by the eagle personify souls drawn to God. The fox and the griffin become symbols of the devil; the dragon symbolises evil, the boar gluttony.[60]

However, some of the animals may have heraldic symbolism. For example, the boar on the Castle Doe grave-slab could be an allusion to the three boars on the MacSweeny coat of arms. The boar also appears to have been used on the Tullyaughnish hood moulding terminal as an emblem of Richard III and the Yorkist cause. The royal emblem of the collared antelope on the same stone apparently refers to King Henry VI. The occurrence together of the two royal badges could perhaps refer to the War of the Roses, begun in the reign of Henry VI, which ended in that of Richard III. Some, however, hold the view that certain depictions such as hunting scenes are purely representational and without any underlying symbolism.[61]

Exhibitionist figure

Only one exhibitionist figure is known from Donegal and regrettably it is now missing. It was recorded and drawn by the Ordnance Survey team in 1846-7 when it was in the side of the coach house at Lougheask Castle.[62] The drawing shows an acrobatic figure with legs raised to ear level and a hand placed in the genital area. Thomas Fagan, writing in the Ordnance Survey Memoirs for Donegal, observed that the figure was female and that it had been taken from the castle on Lough Eske Island, a stronghold occupied by the O'Donnells in the sixteenth and the early years of the seventeenth centuries.

The interpretation of exhibitionist figures is still a much debated topic. In Ireland female exhibitionists – the so-called Sheela-na-gigs – are found not only on churches as in France, Spain and Britain but are also carved on the walls of Late Medieval castles. Sometimes they are set above doors or windows, sometimes on quoins, often almost out of sight on the upper wall levels. The Irish examples found on churches – Romanesque and Medieval churches – are generally regarded as having had a moral function, to warn the faithful against the sin of lust and against the seductive powers of women.

It has been suggested that the sheela-na-gigs on castles may have had the additional purpose of warding off evil and it is possible that the Donegal exhibitionist was carved with the idea of bringing protection to the O'Donnells within their castle. The exhibitionist from

Loch Eske Castle is not included in the two principal publications on this subject.[63]

Post-Medieval: new styles and folk art

The seventeenth century brought new planter settlers to Donegal, one of whom was Richard Hansard from Lincolnshire, a Cambridge graduate and professional soldier who founded the town of Lifford under the terms of the Plantation of James I.

When Sir Richard died in 1619, a fine Renaissance monument was erected in Clonleigh Church of Ireland parish church in memory of himself and his wife, Dame Alice, who died two days before him. Husband and wife are shown as in life, Richard wearing armour, both clad in contemporary Jacobean costume and kneeling opposite each other at a prie-dieu or praying desk. Between them is an inscribed tablet recording Hansard's military exploits in Ireland which helped to bring about the new order and an end to the old Gaelic world.

The new style of monument reflects the vigour and optimism of the young colony and the inscription is of some historic significance in that it records that Hansard's executors carried out his instructions to build a church, school and school-house for the new town of Lifford. None of these buildings survives today.[64]

Compared with the near-contemporary Chichester monument in Carrickfergus or the O'Connor Don monument in Sligo Abbey, the Hansard monument is modest in scale. The two Lifford figures are stiffly carved and slightly squat, less naturalistic than those on the Chichester and O'Connor Don tombs. Very few seventeenth-century tombs have survived in Ireland and the Hansard tomb is the only one of its kind in Donegal.[65]

It has been suggested that the designs for some of these seventeenth-century tombs were supplied by the College of Arms and that the work was carried out by local stonecarvers.[66] This may have been the case for the Hansard monument and the sculptor may have been Irish rather than one of the new planter settlers. However, whether for Irish, Scottish or English stonecarvers, the seventeenth century in Ireland was a period of decline with few commissions for monumental or decorative carving. The craft began to revive in the eighteenth century when the general populace began to erect family gravestones.

Folk art

Between the seventeenth and nineteenth centuries a number of Donegal sculptors with varying skills turned their hands to carving stone heads and busts. Three of these busts, now in the National Museum, formerly decorated a gate-post and garden wall of a house in

Woodlands, near Raphoe.[67] According to tradition they were carved by a member of a local family called Gordon, who had lived in the house during the nineteenth century.

One of the busts from Woodlands is particularly interesting. It has three faces and has been described by two writers as a pre-Christian idol of the Early Iron Age[68] (Plate 3.20). However, the bust, no longer obscured by plaster and whitewash, was quite clearly designed originally as a well balanced single bust with a flattish face. Subsequently another face was carved in a very different style in high relief on the back of the bust and finally a third face, again in high relief, was carved between the two, resulting in a three-faced sculpture of great imbalance, clumsiness and ugliness. The original single bust almost certainly had a second ear similar to the one remaining. This would have been removed when the side face was carved.

The Woodlands bust was not conceived as a three-faced bust and it can no longer be accepted as a Celtic triple god or goddess. Even as a single bust it may be no older than the nineteenth century although the possibility remains that the original bust may have been a pre-Christian idol and may have been reworked and added to by Gordon in the nineteenth century.

There is little reason for doubting the local tradition that the two other busts from Woodlands were carved by a member of the Gordon family. One of the busts known locally as 'The Sailor' has a caricaturish appearance, with a flat beret on its head and with lips pursed as though whistling. The other is distinctively ape-like with a protruding jaw, deep-set eyes and a low forehead. While simple carvings like these are notoriously difficult to date, the absence of any early characteristics combined with the tradition that they were carved locally in the recent past suggests that these two busts are more likely to belong to the nineteenth century than to the Iron Age.

Another group of stone heads, four in all, is built into the wall of an outbuilding attached to Drumnacroil Cottage near Ballintra.[69] These have rugged faces carved in a primitive manner, almost certainly by the same hand. They may have been carved for the local parish priest, Father Daniel Kelly, who built or extended Drumnacroil Cottage and lived there until his death in 1860.

It has been suggested that these heads came from a Medieval church at nearby Truman West which Fagan described in the Ordnance Survey Memoirs of 1847 as having been 'recently demolished'.[70] According to Fagan this church had 'doors and windows of the gothic order, cased with cut stone, and preserving some human heads and other devices'.[71] However, the Drumnacroil heads are quite different in style from the heads decorating Medieval churches and are very unlikely to have come

Plate 3.20   Stone three-faced bust. Woodlands, face on back (N.M.I.).

Plate 3.21   Padraic Mac Mághnusa Grave-stone, Old Killymard Graveyard, near Mountcharles, carved by Brian Monaghan and son (Catherine Gallagher).

from this church or to be any earlier than the Post-Medieval period.

Stonecarving in the twentieth century
Donegal's long tradition of stonecarving continued into the twentieth

century with fine examples of monumental sculpture (Plate 3.21) and some good decorative work in churches. Much skilled work can be seen in St Eunan's cathedral in Letterkenny which was completed in 1901. Of exceptional quality is the carving by a German sculptor of the 'Columban Arch' between the nave and transepts, which commemorates the lives of Saints Columba, Eunan and Patrick.

In this survey of Donegal stonecarving, the work of certain artists stands out: the pre-Christian head from Beltany, St Mura's cross slab at Fahan and the Early Christian carvings in Carndonagh. The words of the Kilkenny artist Tony O'Malley, expressing his appreciation of the Medieval carvings at Jerpoint Abbey, could as aptly be applied to these monuments: 'Carvings like these are full of energy still but it is the energy of the mind that made them – the stones are still alive.'[72]

Acknowledgments

We are much indebted to those who provided us with photographs and gave us permission to reproduce them: Dr Peter Harbison, Catherine Gallagher, Anthony Weir, Arthur Spears, Lucius Emerson, Donnelly Photographers, The National Museum of Ireland, The Ulster Museum, The Office of Public Works and Donegal County Museum.

References

1. E. Rynne, 'Celtic stone idols in Ireland' in *The iron age in the Irish sea province: C.B.A. Research Report,* 9 (1972), pp 79-98.
2. E. Rynne, 'The three stone heads at Woodlands near Raphoe, Co. Donegal' in *R.S.A.I. Jn.* (1964), pp 105-9.
3. Pers. Comm. from Mrs A. Northridge, former owner of the head.
4. Rynne, 'Celtic stone idols in Ireland', p. 88.
5. Idem.
6. O. Davies, 'Carved stones from near St Johnston in Co. Donegal' in *R.S.A.I. Jn.* (1947), pp 157-8.
7. Ibid., pl. XLI.
8. F. Henry, *Irish art in the early Christian period to A.D. 800* (London, 1965), pl. 46.
9. S. Youngs (ed.), *The work of angels* (London, 1989), p. 61.
10. Ibid., pl.137.
11. H. P. Swan, *'Twixt Foyle and Swilly* (Dublin, 1949), pp 188-9.
12. H. Hickey, *Images of stone* (1985), pp 35-42.
13. M. Ryan, 'A suggested origin for the figure representations on the Derrynaflan paten' in E. Rynne (ed.), *Figures from the past* (Dublin, 1987).
14. M. Mac Namidhe, 'The "buddha bucket" from the Oseberg final' in *Irish Arts Review* (1989-90), pp 77-82.
15. A. Gwynn and R. N. Hadcock, *Medieval religious houses in Ireland* (Dublin, 1988), p. 95.
16. Swan, *Foyle and Swilly,* p.11.
17. P. Harbison, 'A Group of early Christian carved stone monuments in county Donegal' in J. Higgitt (ed.), *Early medieval sculpture in Britain and Ireland,* B.A.R., British Series 152 (1986), pp 50.

18. P. Harbison, *Pilgrimage in Ireland* (London, 1991), p. 217.
19. Henry, *Irish art,* p. 130.
20. Harbison, 'Carved stone monuments', p. 57.
21. Henry, *Irish art,* p. 130.
22. Harbison, 'Carved stone monuments', p. 78.
23. Ibid., p. 54.
24. B. Lacy, *Archaeological survey of county Donegal* (Donegal, 1983), p. 249.
25. Ibid., pp 254-5, 284-5.
26. Harbison, 'Carved stone monuments', p. 83.
27. H. Roe, 'The orans in Irish christian art' in *R.S.A.I. Jn.* (1970), pp 213-4.
28. Harbison, 'Carved stone monuments', p. 62.
29. Ibid., p. 63.
30. Idem.
31. Ibid., p. 64, pl.4.14a.
32. Ibid., p. 65, pl.4.13c.
33. Ibid., p. 61, pl.4.10c.
34. Ibid., p. 61.
35. F. Henry, *La sculpture Irlandaise pendant les douze premiers siècles de l'ère Chrétienne* (Paris, 1932), pp 16, 96, 164.
36. Henry, *Irish Art,* pp 117-58.
37. Harbison, 'Carved stone monuments', p. 67.
38. A. Spears and L. Emerson 'The deity by the well' in *Donegal Annual* (1990), pp 86-107. Spears and Emerson argue unconvincingly that this head belongs to the early Iron Age.
39. R. Stalley, *The Cistercian monasteries of Ireland* (Yale, 1987), pp 184-9.
40. Hickey, *Images of stone,* pp 63-4.
41. Lacy, *Archaeological survey,* p. 328, pl. 64.
42. Our thanks to Professor Roger Stalley for helpful discussion about this carving.
43. Lacy, *Archaeological survey,* pp 242, 342, pl.VI, 3.
44. E. MacLysaght, *Irish families* (Dublin, 1978), pp 271-2.
45. Lacy, *Archaeological survey,* pp 328-9, 336-8.
46. Ibid., pp 284,286.
47. Ibid., pp 343-6.
48. Ibid., p. 288.
49. Hickey, *Images of stone,* pp 81-82.
50. Lacy, *Archaeological survey,* pp 342, 349.
51. Ibid., p. 342. The illustration on pl. II (4) is of the stone at Ramelton Church of Ireland church, not, as captioned, the one at St Ernan.
52. Ibid., p. 343. Pl VI (4) and II (4). See note 51.
53. T. Tanfield, *Beverley minster misericord seats* (booklet).
54. J. Hunt, 'The Limerick cathedral misericords' in *Ireland of the welcomes,* 20 (1971).
55. Lacy, *Archaeological survey,* pp 284-6.
56. K. A. Steer and J. W. M. Bannerman, *Late monumental sculpture in the West Highlands,* The Royal commission the ancient and historical monuments of Scotland (1977).
57. Ibid., p. 43.
58. F. J. Bigger, 'The MacSwyne grave slab' in *U.J.A.* (1903), pp 139-40.
59. Publication forthcoming.
60. J. Romilly Allen, E*arly christian symbolism in Great Britain and Ireland* (London, 1887), pp 342-8.

61. Steer and Bannerman, *Monumental sculpture,* p. 186.
62. Lacy, *Archaeological survey,* pp 349, 361.
63. J. Andersen, *The witch on the wall* (London, 1977). A.Weir and J. Jerman, *Images of lust* (London, 1986).
64. Lacy, *Archaeological survey,* p. 340.
65. H. Potterton, *Irish church monuments 1570-1880,* Ulster Arch. Heritage Soc. (1975), pp 17, 19.
66. Ibid., p. 8.
67. Rynne, 'Stone heads at Woodlands', pp 105-9.
68. Idem and A. Ross, *Pagan celtic Britain* (London, 1967); pp 75, 114-15.
69. A. Spears and L. Emerson, 'Carved stone heads from Drumnacroil, Ballintra' in *Donegal Annual* (1991), pp 50-61.
70. Ibid., pp 58-60.
71. Lacy, *Archaeological survey,* p. 298.
72. T. O'Malley, 'Inscape – life and landscape in Callan and county Kilkenny' in W. Nolan, and K. Whelan (ed.), *Kilkenny: history and society* (Dublin, 1990), p. 631.

Plate 3.22   'Marigold Stone' cross slab, Carndonagh, west face (Peter Harbison).

Chapter 4

SANDHILLS, SILVER AND SHRINES – FINE METALWORK OF THE MEDIEVAL PERIOD FROM DONEGAL

RAGHNALL Ó FLOINN

Introduction

Many factors have contributed towards shaping the personality of Donegal and some of these will be evident in the study which follows: an examination of the fine metalwork from the county dating from the period between the close of the Iron Age and the Reformation. While relatively rich in field monuments of all periods,[1] there is a dearth of archaeological objects from the county. The relatively small proportion of good arable land and correspondingly large area of rough pasture and upland bog has resulted in only a small number of stray finds being discovered and reported to museums, with the notable exception of those found in sandhills sites. The scarcity of archaeological excavations of any period in the county has also been a contributory factor. Yet the interest of antiquarians goes back to the late eighteenth century when people such as General Charles Vallancey and Daniel Grose reported the discovery of archaeological finds from the county. In the nineteenth century, apart from locally-based collectors like Wybrands Olphert of Ballyconnell House and Major Nesbitt of Wood Hill, Ardara, John Harvey of Malin Hall, Lord George Hill of Gweedore and George Young of Culdaff House,[2] finds from the county were already to be found in the cabinets of collectors outside the county, especially those based in and around Belfast. Some of these can now be traced in museum collections in Ireland and Britain but others, such as the 'Small hollow silver Case found in a tumulus, Co. Donegall; figures of Adam and Eve on one side' exhibited in Belfast in 1852 by James Carruthers of Belfast cannot now be traced.[3] The strong tradition of local collectors continued into the present century, the collections of Henry Morris of Springville, Derry and Harry Swan of Buncrana being particularly rich in Donegal finds, both now in the National Museum of Ireland.

For the study of the metalwork of the medieval period, three aspects stand out which will be dealt with in turn. In rough chronological order these are: the large number of stray finds from coastal sandhills sites ranging in date from the fourth to the fifteenth centuries, a number of Viking age (ninth to tenth century) silver hoards and a fine collection of ecclesiastical objects of tenth- to sixteenth-century date. Although chronologically distinct, these three strands of evidence cannot offer a coherent picture of fine metalwork over the course of the medieval period. Rather than provide a catalogue or description of the metal-work, this paper concentrates on its physical and historical context and, in particular, on the implications of stray finds for the study of settlement history and the importance of ecclesiastical metalwork for the study of lay and ecclesiastical patronage and power politics in the middle ages.

Sandhills sites

Sandhills settlement sites are particularly common on the coast of counties Kerry, Galway, Donegal, Derry, Antrim and Down. Few have been scientifically excavated but because of their instability, habitation levels, usually visible as layers of charcoal and shells, are constantly being exposed. Archaeological objects of all periods are weathered out of these layers and it is these stray finds that first attracted the attention of antiquarians from the early nineteenth century.[4] In Donegal these sandhills sites stretch from Bundoran in the south to Malin Head in the north[5] and have produced finds of all periods from as early as the Later Mesolithic to modern times.[6]

The earliest record of the discovery of finds from Donegal sandhills is a watercolour by George du Noyer in the National Museum of Ireland dated September 1838 (Pl. 4.1). It is entitled 'From the Museum of Major Nesbitt of Ardara, found at Magheramore'. Although a sandhills context is not explicitly stated, the townland of Magheramore near Ardara contains an extensive area of sand-dunes in which habitation material has been found.[7] The collection contains objects of various periods ranging from the dagger of the Early Bronze Age (Pl. 4.1, 3) to the rowel of a medieval spur (Pl. 4.1, 9) and is typical of the range of types from other Donegal sites. Two of the items illustrated, an ibex headed and an omega pin (Pl. 4.1, 1 and 4) have made their way into the collections of the National Museum of Ireland.[8] Other early collectors of sandhills finds included Mr. Wybrants Olphert of Ballyconnell House, county Donegal who amassed a large collection of artefacts from around Ballyness Bay (Pls 4.2, 4.3), some of which are now in the Ulster Museum[9] and Lord George Hill who collected finds from the Magheraclogher, Gweedore area much of which he presented to the Royal Irish Academy.[10] In the published accounts of these finds, the writers note that objects of different periods were found mixed together and that they were sometimes associated with structural

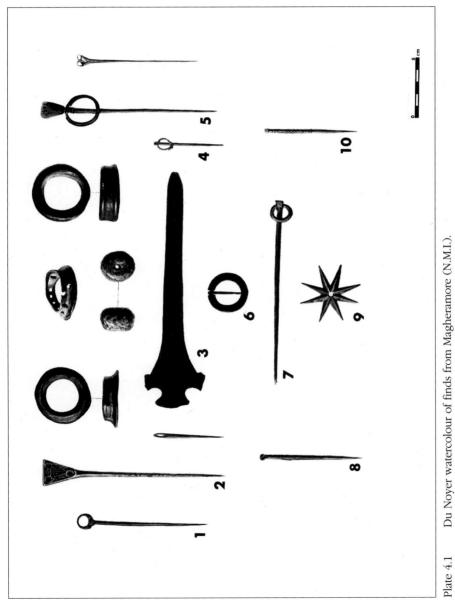

Plate 4.1   Du Noyer watercolour of finds from Magheramore (N.M.I.).

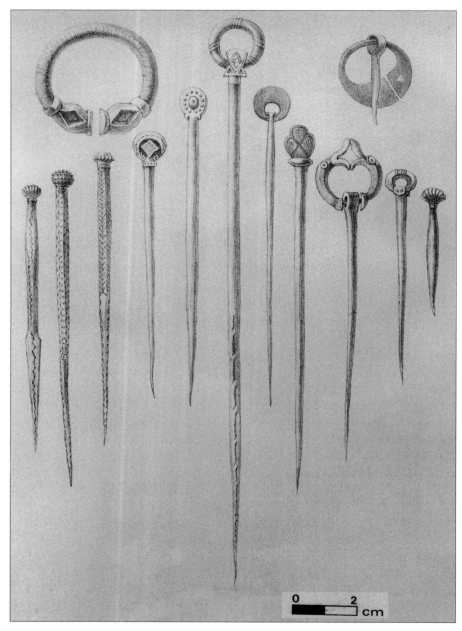

Plate 4.2   Finds from Ballynass sandhills (1:3).

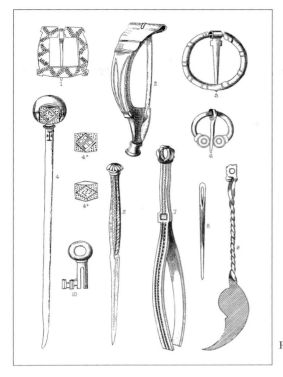

Plate 4.3   Finds from Ballynass sandhills (1:0.5).

features such as hearths and stone settings resembling houses. Without excavation it is not possible to say whether the finds were directly associated with the visible structures or whether the latter represent permanent settlements or temporary coastal encampments. The quality and quantity of finds from some sites – for example, over fifty pins from Ballyness Bay alone – makes it likely, however, that some represent permanent settlements on the fertile light shell sand *machair* which is easily tilled. This has also been recognised in the Hebrides where similar coastal *machair* attracted settlement from prehistoric times.[11]

An examination of the stray finds from sandhills in Donegal in museum collections and in published accounts shows that objects of medieval date occur in all areas where middens have been recognised with the exception of the extreme south of the county around Killybegs and Bundoran (fig. 4.1). The latter area has produced a small number of prehistoric finds but none of medieval date.[12] This absence may simply reflect the pattern of collecting in the county as most collectors seem to have concentrated on the more productive sites in the north and west which were recognised as early as the mid-nineteenth century. It is also possible that the sandhills around Donegal Bay, being

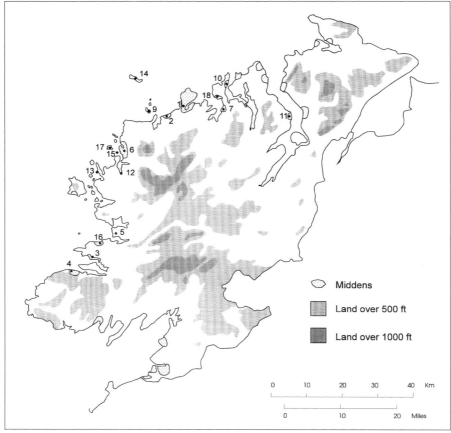

Fig. 4.1   Distribution of sandhills sites yielding metalwork of the early medieval period. Shaded areas represent distribution of midden sites after Lacy, *Archaeological Survey*, fig. 24. Numbers refer to Table 4.1.

more sheltered, are less susceptible to erosion and are therefore likely to yield less material. Table 4.1 plots the object types of early medieval date found at each site, arranged roughly in chronological order by object type. The sites are grouped somewhat arbitrarily as the find locations are often imprecise. Material from 'Gweedore', for example, includes finds from Magheraclogher and Bunbeg. Finds from Dunfanaghy come from at least three separate locations and the precise findplace of the early finds of Iron Age and sub-Roman date from there are not recorded. Although circular hut sites measuring 5m and 8m in diameter are recorded at Dunfanaghy it is not known exactly where these were located or if any of the surviving finds were associated with them. The finds from Maghera came from a mound known as 'Ardnaglough' in which the stones of two 'huts' were visible while some of the finds from Ballyness, Rosapenna and Magheraclogher also appear to have been found in the vicinity of stone structures.

Table 4.1
List of sandhills sites which have produced metalwork of medieval date (Numbers refer to fig. 4.1)

	Iron Age/ Roman brooch	Ibex pin	Hand pin	Toilet impl.	Omega pin	Pen. brooch	Ringed pin	Stick pin	Late Med. misc.
1. Dunfanaghy[13]	X	X			X	X	X	X	X
2. Ballyness[14]	X			X		X	X	X	X
3. Magheramore[15]		X			X	X	X	X	X
4. Maghera[16]			X		X	X	X	X	
5. Dooey[17]			X	X	X	X	X	X	
6. Gweedore/Bunbeg[18]			X	X	X		X		
7. Glenree[19]			X						
8. 'Castleport'[20]						X			
9. Inishbofin[21]						X		X	
10. Tranarossan[22]						X		X	
11. Kinnegar[23]							X		
12. The Rosses[24]							X	X	
13. Cruit Is.[25]								X	
14. Tory[26]								X	
15. Braade[27]								X	
16. Naran/Middletown[28]								X	
17. Inishfree Is.[29]								X	
18. Rosapenna[30]								X	X

The first thing to note is that, with the exception of the material from the Dooey excavations, all the finds are of bronze or brass and consist for the most part of various types of pins and brooches, indicating a bias on the part of collectors in favour of easily recognisable object types. One would expect to find brooches, pins and knives of iron and pins and combs of bone in such a collection but these are not represented. In fact very few non-metal objects have been collected from these sites. Pottery of late medieval date has been found at a number of sites.[31] Furthermore, again with the exception of the Dooey excavations, no site has produced stray finds of clay crucibles, moulds or other metalworking debris. Table 4.1 nevertheless shows that the most productive sites, such as Dunfanaghy, Ballyness and Magheramore, have produced not only the widest range of types but also the earliest dateable finds. Conversely, where sites (such as Tory, Braade, Naran and Rosapenna) have produced only single finds or finds in small quantities, these tend to be late in date and usually belong to only one chronological phase. This suggests that the absence of earlier finds at these latter sites is a result of their being less intensively searched. The pattern revealed by these 'stray' finds, therefore, is one of a fairly continuous settlement of the coastlands of the county at various stages during the first millenium AD and into the early second millenium.

The clearest evidence for this is provided by the excavations at Dooey, Lettermacaward, carried out in 1959.[32] The site was excavated as a result of the large number of stray finds which had come in to the National Museum of Ireland over the previous twenty years.[33] The excavators identified four phases of occupation – the first three interpreted as habitation and the last as a cemetery. They felt that the occupation at Dooey which 'probably did not last for more than a century or two at the most and that, furthermore, it was of fairly continuous duration' could be dated to the 'early centuries AD'.[34] It would now seem that the earliest levels date to the fifth or sixth century and the latest to the eleventh or twelfth century.[35] Evidence for the production of fine metalwork on the site from all three occupation levels survived in the form of clay moulds for brooches and other objects, a lead model of the head of a brooch pin for impressing into a clay mould, clay crucibles, metal slag and an antler motif-piece (Pl. 4.4). The latter came from Phase I on the site and is probably the earliest dated Irish example.[36] The lead model is of interest as it bears the same design as that for the head of a bronze brooch-pin from Raphoe, some forty kilometres to the east of Dooey, formerly in the collection of the late Harry P. Swan (fig. 4.2).[37] The presence of luxury items such as finger rings and toilet implements indicates a community of high status and the excavators felt that these items along with some bone pins suggested contacts with post-Roman Scotland.[38] The importance of the Dooey excavations which have produced stratified contexts for object types occurring as stray finds elsewhere cannot be overemphasised and it is unfortunate that these excavations still remain unpublished. They are unique in that they provide evidence of successive phases of metalworking activity on the same site.

It must be remembered, however, that only the higher status sites such as Dooey – which were always in the minority – are likely to produce fine metalwork objects and that the vast majority of settlements would have been at subsistence level, yielding few diagnostically dateable finds. A more typical site has been revealed through recent excavations of a coastal settlement at Rinnaraw, near Portsalon, including a substantial house with attached byre surrounded by an enclosure. Finds were few and included quern-stones and spindle

Plate 4.4   Motif-piece from Dooey.

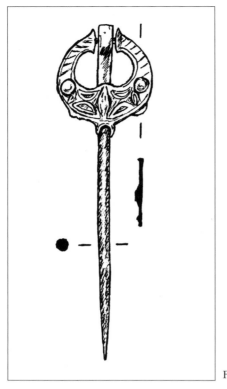

Fig. 4.2   Brooch-pin from Raphoe (1:1).

whorls, a few undiagnostic iron objects and some coarse pottery, none of them easily dateable. A series of radiocarbon dates obtained from charcoal samples gave the clearest evidence that the site dated to the early medieval period.[39] Rescue excavation of another sandhills site at Tonbane Glebe yielded no structural evidence but a date in the later middle ages was suggested by the presence of a quern fragment and some sherds of pottery known as Everted Rim Ware.[40]

Some of the individual finds deserve comment. The Iron Age/sub-Roman period is scarcely represented in county Donegal and only four objects of definite Iron Age date are known.[41] One of these, a brooch of Navan type dating to the century on either side of the birth of Christ, comes from the sandhills at Dunfanaghy.[42] Further early activity on the north coast is indicated by the presence of two Roman brooches from Dunfanaghy[43] and Ballyness (Pl. 4.3, 2) both dating to the first or second century AD. Two Roman coins of third century date come from a midden at Dunfanaghy near where the brooch was found.[44] To these early finds may be added a glass bead from the sandhills at Rosapenna, perhaps dating to the early centuries AD.[45] A hooked toilet implement from Ballyness (Pl. 4.3, 9) is a rare piece derived from Roman prototypes which have been interpreted as toothpicks and it may date as early as the fourth or fifth century. Other early finds include ibex-headed pins from Dunfanaghy[46] and Magheramore (Pl. 4.1, 1) which are otherwise rare in Ireland – the only other provenanced Irish find being that from the sandhills at Ballyeagh, Ballybunnion, county Kerry.[47] These pins are probably of Scottish origin and have been dated to the fourth century AD by Stevenson.[48] Warner interpreted the presence of such exotic material in sandhills on the north coast as objects deposited by refugees.[49] However, the contacts with Scotland and northern Britain implied by the ibex-headed pins continue in later centuries. Witness for example an early penannular brooch from Maghera, omega pins found at five sandhills sites and a Pictish style pin of a brooch from Tranarossan. Combined with the historically documented contacts between the north-west of Ireland and Scotland in the early medieval period, the evidence suggests that there is no need to invoke refugees to explain this material but rather that its presence is a product of exchange and trade between two areas separated by a seaway used since prehistoric times.

A considerably greater amount of material survives for the sixth and seventh centuries, consisting of various types of brooches and pins. Omega pins are known from five sandhills sites in the county, including several of bronze and iron from the Dooey excavations. As with the ibex-headed pins this type is otherwise rarely found in Ireland, emphasising again the wealth of the Donegal sites. Omega pins are, however, likely to be of Irish manufacture although their form may have been inspired by Roman brooches of the early centuries AD[50] and the earliest dateable examples are from Dooey perhaps of fifth- or sixth-century date.[51] The only other Irish omega pins from excavation contexts are an unstratified find from Lagore crannog[52] and an iron example from Cahercommaun.[53] The latter is of interest as the pin is short in relation to the size of the ring – a feature of some of the Dooey iron omega pins. An elaborate silver omega pin from the Aran Islands has been dated to the seventh/eighth century,[54] a plain bronze example from Bunbeg has been assigned the same date while a third, with a head of blue glass from Ervey, county Meath has been dated to the eighth or ninth centuries.[55] These silver and bronze pins all have long shanks and relatively small heads. If the typological development of omega pins mirrors that of zoomorphic penannular brooches, where the early examples have a large ring in proportion to the length of the pin and the later examples have progressively longer pins and smaller heads, then the earliest omega pins are the iron examples from Dooey and Cahercommaun and the later examples are of bronze and silver. The dates suggested above for some of the latter, however, may be too late and the majority of Irish examples are probably of fifth/seventh century date. Also predominantly of sixth/seventh century date are the four hand pins[56] and two of the three zoomorphic penannular brooches from sandhills sites.[57] The third, from Maghera, is an early type and may date to the fifth or sixth century.[58]

Elaborate silver brooches of eighth or ninth century date are absent from the county although a catalogue of reproductions by the Dublin jewellers Edmond Johnson, Ltd., of *c.*1900 contains a drawing of a penannular brooch called 'The Innishowen Brooch' (fig. 4.3).[59] The drawing shows many features in common with the Cavan Brooch but differs from it in that the 'Innishowen Brooch' is penannular, the terminals are lobed and the arrangement of the panels at the centre of the hoop is repeated at either end. Said to have been in a private collection at the time, this object is otherwise unknown. Without further details it must be concluded that the 'Innishowen Brooch' is, in fact, a nineteenth-century creation, being a variant design of the well-known Cavan Brooch.[60] A small gilt silver brooch of ninth-century date from an unknown locality in the county is in the British Museum.[61]

The decorated triangular pinhead of a penannular brooch found at Magheramore (Pl. 4.1, 2) belongs to a small group of Irish brooches of gilt or tinned bronze of eighth century date which represent simplified versions of brooches of the 'Tara' type. They are widely distributed throughout Britain and Ireland and also occur in Viking graves in Norway.[62] A pinhead which is almost identical to that from Maghermore is known from a ninth-century woman's grave at Mindresunde, Norway.[63] In most cases these brooches lack either the pin or the hoop or are otherwise incomplete. It is tempting to view this fact and the dispersed distribution of the group as the result of Viking activity and this indeed may be the case. One of these brooches, from a Viking grave at Pierowall in Orkney, was fitted with a Pictish-style looped pin

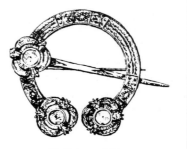

THE INNISHOWEN BROOCH –
This Brooch is believed to be twelfth century work, and is now in a private collection.

Silver, quite solid 16/-

Silver gift 18/-

Solid Silver, with stones, from 22/-

Half Actual Size

Fig. 4.3   Drawing of 'Innishowen Brooch' replica (scale refers to replica).

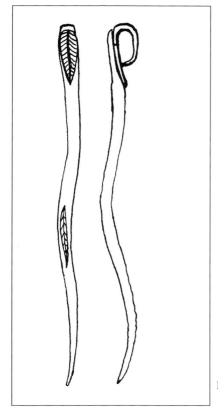

Fig. 4.4   Pin of penannular brooch from Tranarossan (1:1).

to cater for local tastes. From Tranarossan on the Rosguill peninsula there is a similar looped pin for a brooch (fig. 4.4) which is likely to be a Scottish import or at least influenced by Pictish-style brooches.

Ringed and stick pins are by far the most common artefacts from the Donegal sandhills and all types seem to be represented. There are a few early ringed pins such as the spiral-ringed, baluster-headed example from Magheramore (Pl. 4.1, 5) of probable seventh- or eighth-century date[64] but most of the ringed pins are of the polyhedral-headed and kidney-ringed type dating to the tenth, eleventh and twelfth centuries (Pls 4.1, 7, 4.2 and 4.3, 4). It is interesting to note that a large proportion of ringed pins from Scotland also come from sandhills sites and that many of them are associated with Viking graves.[65] Although it remains a possibility that some of the ringed pins from sandhills sites in Donegal may have been associated with burials there is as yet no certain recorded instance of a Viking burial from the county.[66]

It is hard to quantify the numbers of stick pins from sandhills sites but an indication of how common they are is given by the fact that

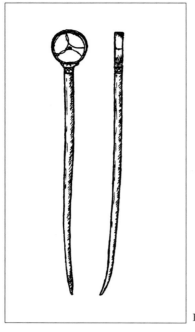

Fig. 4.5   Disc-headed pin, Tory Island (1:2).

they are present on all but four sites. In addition to those listed above, the collection of the late Henry Morris of Springtown, Derry, now in the National Museum of Ireland contains some thirty-three stick pins from coastal sites in the county, at least twelve of which are of early medieval date.[67] Most of the stick pins can be only generally dated to the eleventh, twelfth and early thirteenth centuries. Pins of the later types with decorated shanks predominate. Earlier types dating to the eleventh and twelfth centuries include the non-functional kidney ringed pin from Ballyness (Pl. 4.2) and disc-headed pins from the same site and from Tory Island (fig. 4.5).

Finds of later medieval date are not very common. Medieval ring brooches dating to the thirteenth to fifteenth centuries are known from Magheramore (Pl. 4.1, 6), Ballyness (Pl. 4.3, 1 and 3) and Maghera and medieval finger rings from Dunfanaghy and Bunbeg. It is possible that later medieval types are under-represented as collectors were less interested in them.

Stray finds not from sandhills

Only a few finds of early medieval date are recorded from the county which are not from sandhills sites. Among these are two bog finds – the pin of a zoomorphic penannular brooch from Crovehy near Dungloe[68] and a brooch-pin with amber insets from Grousehall, near

Plate 4.5   Brooch-pin from Grousehall (2:3, N.M.I.).

Pettigo (Pl. 4.5).[69] The ring of a silver annular brooch of ninth-century date in the British Museum comes from an unknown locality in the county.[70] More recently, a bronze ringed pin of late tenth- or eleventh-century date was found at Ballintemple close to Tullaghobegly church.[71]

With the exception of the additions to early medieval shrines, metalwork of the later medieval period is poorly represented. An iron axehead inlaid with silver arranged in step and zig-zag patterns from the Swan collection is said to have been found in the county in 1910 (Pl. 4.6). The shape of the blade is similar to axes on Scottish tombs dated to the fifteenth century but the inlaid decoration suggests that it might date as early as the twelfth century.[72] There is also a pair of rowel spurs of the sixteenth century which were found at Donegal Castle[73] and a set of three brewing pans of similar date from a bog at Coolcholly, near Assaroe.[74]

Viking Age silver

Four hoards of silver ornaments of c.850-950, one coin hoard of c.970 and one single find of a silver ingot (from the sandhills at Tramore Strand, townland of Murroe, near Dunfanaghy) are known from the

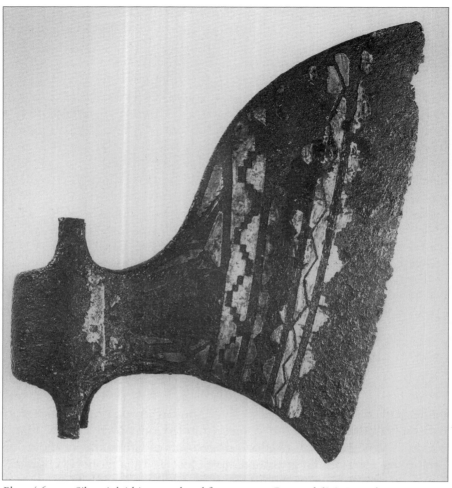

Plate 4.6   Silver inlaid iron axehead from county Donegal (2:3, N.M.I.).

county. These have been recorded in detail elsewhere.[75] It has often been assumed that finds of silver are indicators of Viking settlement in Ireland but in more recent times it has become apparent that much of this silver ended up in Irish hands. Examination of the find circumstances of the Donegal finds confirms this and shows that they were buried with care, sometimes in, or in the vicinity of, settlement sites. The hoard of four arm rings from Roosky was found in the walls of a cashel[76] while the group of five silver arm rings from Carrowmore were found in or beside a large stone enclosure.[77] The seven pieces of silver 'squared and perfectly plain' found in 1848 while demolishing the fort of Liss Cor may have constituted an ingot hoard. The 'fort of Liss Cor' is in fact a double-walled cashel, located on a rock outcrop close to the sea shore.[78] The hoard of ingots and arm rings from near Raphoe were said to have been found 'at the base of a dry stone ditch'; the ditch may perhaps have been associated with a cashel or other enclosure. The Carrowmore arm rings and those from a hoard from north-west Inishowen were found linked together, a feature of silver hoards found elsewhere in the Viking world. The former were secreted under a large stone which had markings on its upper surface and the Carrowen hoard of Anglo-Saxon coins was found 'covered by a small flat stone, beside or partly under a very large isolated rock'.[79] It is likely, therefore, that the hoards were deposited not by Norse settlers but by their Irish owners who had acquired them from the Vikings either by trade or as booty. One of the Roosky arm rings certainly passed through Viking hands before being buried as it has the letter 'R' carved in runes on the inside – perhaps the initial of its owner?[80]

A particular feature of the distribution of Viking Age silver in north-west Ireland is the concentration of finds in Inishowen (fig. 4.6). In fact, Viking age silver hoards of any kind are otherwise rare in the north-west, there being none from Sligo, Leitrim or Fermanagh and only one each from counties Tyrone and Derry.[81] Graham-Campbell sought a historical context for the deposition of the hoards in the annalistic references to Viking activity on the north-west coast in the later ninth and early tenth centuries, concluding that the four Inishowen hoards of arm rings were most likely deposited during the 920s and 930s by their Irish owners.[82] Further evidence of this is contained in a eulogy in praise of Eichnechán mac Dálaig, king of Cenél Conaill, who died in 906 which begins *Ard na scéla, a mheic na ccuach*. This has been ascribed to the poet Flann mac Lonáin whose death is recorded in 918[83] but Ó Corráin would date the poem much later, perhaps in the eleventh or twelfth century.[84] Nevertheless, the poem does provide useful information on Viking activity along the north coast and on the relationship between the Vikings and the local inhabitants, albeit through a piece of Ua Domnaill propaganda.[85] The historical background to the events recorded in the poem may be reconstructed from the annalistic references in the Annals of Ulster and the Annals of the Four Masters under the years 921 and 919 respectively. They record the presence of a Viking fleet of twenty ships under the command of the son of Uathmharan, son of Barid which landed at the place at the centre of the activities described in the poem – Cenn Maghair – in the year 921. They were defeated by Fergal mac Domnaill who 'killed the crew of one of their ships and wrecked the ship and took its booty'. In the same year another fleet of thirty-two ships under the Viking Acolb, whose base was at a site called Cenn Ríg, was abandoned. In the poem it is Eichnechán who is the

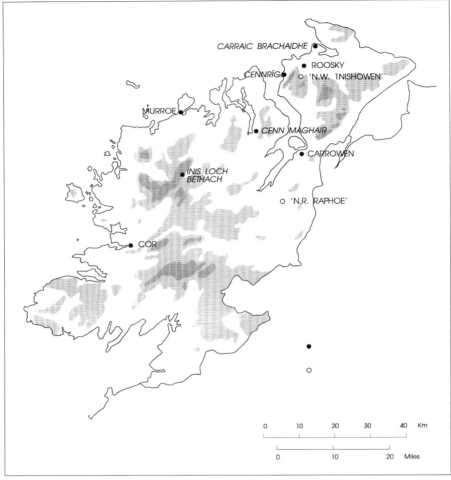

Fig. 4.6   Distribution of Viking age silver objects and hoards and *(in italics)*
placenames mentioned in poem in praise of Eichnechán mac Dálaigh.

victorious hero. It relates how he was forced to marry his three
daughters to the Viking chiefs Cathais, Tuirgeis and Galltor in order that
his territory be spared from giving them tribute. It describes the escape
of the daughter married to Cathais (the 'Acolb' of the annals?),
apparently the leader of the Vikings, to Carraic Brachaidhe along with
the treasure of the Norsemen, consisting of a thousand ounces of red
gold, including gold armlets. The Vikings attack Eichnechán at his base
at Cenn Maghair where they are defeated and their wealth divided
among the Cenél Conaill, 'ten ounces to every strong *túath*, five ounces
to every great church', the poet himself receiving five gold armlets and
five drinking horns as well as 'a hundred ounces of gold and pure

white silver'. The text suggests that the Vikings' 'gold' (which should be seen as a metaphor for treasure of all kinds, including silver) was accumulated outside Cenél Conaill territory. The setting of the poem in the Fanad and Inishowen peninsulas provides a context for the silver hoards which occur in the same area and indicates one way in which such bullion could be acquired by the Irish and divided among local kings and churches. The poem also documents a number of important secular settlement sites – both native and Viking – in the area which may well have been occupied in the early tenth century when the events recounted in the poem took place (fig. 4.6). These include the stronghold of the Uí Maíl Fábhaill at Carraic Brachaidhe, a rocky outcrop at Carrickabraghy in Inishowen, now occupied by the ruins of a medieval castle[86] and two strongholds of the Cenél Conaill: Cenn Maghair, now Kinnaweer at the head of Mulroy Bay in Fanad and Inis Loch Bethach, a crannóg in Lough Veagh also occupied into the late medieval period.[87] The site at Kinnaweer appears to have been occupied since at least the early eighth century as it is referred to in the Annals of the Four Masters in the year 702. It is possible that Cenn Ríg may be equated with the site of Dunree Fort on the western side of the Inishowen peninsula with a commanding view of the approaches to Lough Swilly.[88] Smyth has identified Cenn Ríg with an island off the coast of Inishowen[89] but this is based on a confusion of two placenames by the editor of the Annals of Ulster.[90]

While there is no archaeological evidence that the Viking settlement in the Fanad and Inishowen peninsulas was permanent, the annalistic evidence and the eulogy to Eichnechán mac Dálach with its references to marriage alliances and payments of tribute to the Vikings does suggest that Viking bases were occupied on something more than a temporary basis around Lough Foyle in the late ninth and early tenth century.[91] A foothold in Lough Foyle was sufficiently secure for a fleet to raid as far as Armagh in 898. Despite this, the Norse settlement in Donegal was not sufficiently strong to influence placenames and only one – Sheep Haven, for the bay between Horn Head and the Rosguill peninsula – seems to be derived from Old Norse.

Ecclesiastical metalwork, relics and shrines

By far the most important items of fine metalwork to have survived from the county are objects used in the service of the church. Many of these were in the possession of their hereditary keepers who were often the descendants of the stewards – *airchennaigh* or erenaghs – of church lands. These erenagh families continued as farmers in occupation of these lands after the church reforms of the twelfth

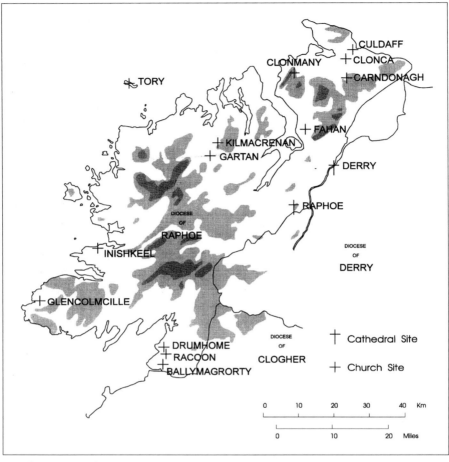

Fig. 4.7   Ecclesiastical sites mentioned in the text.

century which they held from the bishop subject to the payment of rents.[92]

Politically, county Donegal in the later first millennium AD was divided between the Cenél Conaill and the Cenél Eógain and this was reflected in the later middle ages by the boundaries of the medieval dioceses of Raphoe and Derry, respectively (fig. 4.7).[93] Originally the diocese of Raphoe included the Inishowen peninsula, the homeland of the Cenél Eógain but it was transferred to the diocese of Derry in the mid-thirteenth century. The complex relationship between Raphoe and Derry during the twelfth and thirteenth centuries coupled with the lack of sources for the early history of Raphoe make it difficult to locate where a number of the most important shrines were kept during the medieval period.[94] Derry and Raphoe were among the least anglicised of dioceses in the later middle ages and the pattern and continuity of land ownership, especially of the church lands of the *airchennaigh* or erenagh families was established as early as the eleventh or twelfth centuries. For example, the family of Ua Daighri (anglicised O'Deery) is recorded in the Annals of Ulster from the twelfth century as one of the *airchennaigh* of Derry.[95] The family of Ua Doireid (anglicised O'Dowry) were *airchennaigh* of Domnach Mór Magh Ithe (Donaghmore) from the eleventh to at least the thirteenth centuries,[96] and are recorded as vicars or rectors in the fifteenth.[97] An Inquisition of 1602 at Derry found 'the two herenachs of St Columbkill's lands to be O'Dery and O'Dowry'.[98] The 1609 Inquisition is a unique document of these erenagh lands in the Ulster dioceses and often the names of the families are recorded.[99] Forty-two out of the forty-seven parishes in the diocese of Derry were divided between the parson (rector), vicar and erenagh.[100] It is clear from the papal records that the office of rector and vicar in a parish changed hands regularly and was often the subject of dispute, usually between members of local families. For example, in 1418 the rectories of Clonmany and Clonca were in dispute between Solomon Ó Brolchain and David Omurgisan and Clonmany was in addition claimed by Luke Ó Molmochair.[101] Vicars and rectors were ecclesiastical benefices supported by tithes.

Like their counterparts elsewhere in Ireland, most of the surviving ecclesiastical objects are first recorded by nineteenth century anti-quarians although for Donegal these are fortunately augmented by a number of earlier texts, most notably Manus O'Donnell's *Betha Colaim Chille* and John Colgan's *Acta Sanctorum* and *Triadis Thaumaturgae*, dating to the sixteenth and seventeenth centuries, respectively. In a number of cases, outlined below, the family who were the hereditary keepers are known. Where the keeper's name is not recorded, it can sometimes be suggested from the contemporary written records.

The ecclesiastical metalwork can be divided into two groups. The first consists of objects which were functional such as bells, croziers or books but which at some point were considered relics by virtue of an association with a saint and were often enshrined – such as the *Cathach*, associated with St Colmcille, patron saint of the O'Donnells or the Bearnán Conaill, an iron bell with a later protective cover or shrine associated with St Conall of Inishkeel. The second consists of artefacts such as bells and eucharistic vessels of Donegal provenance but which have no traditional association with a saint or church or are not known to have been used as relics. For convenience, however, the objects are discussed by type.

The account which follows concentrates on the significance of these relics as social and historical documents rather than on their art historical importance. As might be expected, a large proportion of the surviving metalwork is associated with churches belonging to the Columban federation or those which in the later medieval period were subsumed into Colmcille's cult.

Bells

The most numerous ecclesiastical objects to have survived are hand-bells of iron and bronze of early medieval date. The typology of these bells has been examined by Bourke[102] and his classification is followed here. Bells of Class 1 are made from single forged sheets of iron, coated with bronze, and are regarded as the earliest type of hand-bell dating to between the seventh and the ninth centuries. There are two certain examples of Donegal provenance. The first was found in a bog 'near the ruins of an old Chapel'.[103] Its findplace is not recorded but as it was acquired from a Mr Tredennick of Camlin, near Ballyshannon it may have been found somewhere in that area.

The most important iron bell of this type is associated with St Conall of Inishkeel (Pls 4.7, 4.8). Known as the 'Bearnán Conaill' it is now preserved in the British Museum.[104] It was provided with a cap of tinned(?) bronze which was riveted directly on to the bell. This bears an incised cross in the spandrels of which are panels of ribbon and animal interlace and a design derived from the so-called 'vertebral' ring-chain pattern common on insular Viking sculpture in the Irish Sea area and this enables us to date this mount to the tenth century. The iron bell must have been of some antiquity by this time as its handle had been lost. In the later medieval period, perhaps the fifteenth century, a hollow box of bronze covered with decorated silver plates was made to enclose the bell. The back-plate was engraved with figures of the Apostles (fig. 4.8). The framing silver bands on the front and around the top bear inscriptions in Gothic script. These appear to be in Latin, those around the top identifying the figures of the Evangelists, the Virgin and Child and the Archangel Michael. The lengthy inscription around the front is now illegible. John O'Donovan stated that 'the names of Mahon O'Meehan and – O'Breslan' were still legible in the middle of the last century[105] but these names, if they were ever visible, can no longer be read. Subsequently, two silver strips carrying an inscription were added to the short sides near the base. The script of this later inscription differs from that of the front and appears to be in Irish. Again, it is difficult to make any sense of it. The large rock crystal was probably added at this time.

When first recorded in modern times, the bell and its shrine were in the possession of a senior member of the O'Breslins.[106] During the pattern or *turas* at Inishkeel the bell was held forth by its keeper to be

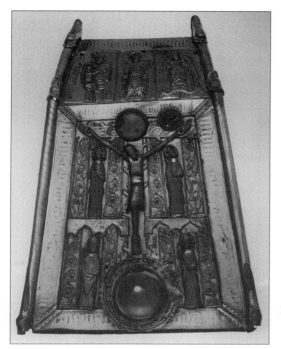

Plate 4.7   Bearnán   Conaill
shrine   –   front
(British Museum).

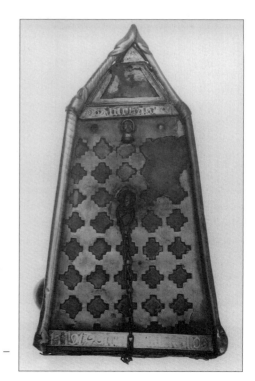

Plate 4.8   Bearnán Conaill shrine –
side (British Museum).

Plate 4.9   Bronze bell from Gartan (N.M.I.).

kissed by pilgrims. According to another source, however, the original keepers were the Gearan family from whom it passed to the O'Breslins at a later date.[107] While the O'Breslins were rectors of Inishkeel in the fifteenth century,[108] the Inquisition of 1609 mentions three erenaghs of Inishkeel: O'Breslin, O'Keran (Gearan) and O'Moyney (Mooney).[109] It may well be that the keepership alternated between members of these families. After the suppression of the *turas* by the local clergy, Conal O'Breslin of Glengesh parted with it *c*.1833 to Major Nesbitt of Wood Hill, Ardara for three cows and an annuity. It was stolen *c*.1845 and re-appeared in Birmingham in 1858 and was finally acquired by the British Museum.

Two large quadrangular cast bronze bells of Class 2 are known from the county. Bells of this type are usually dated to the period 700-900.[110] The most important, in view of its historical associations with St Colmcille, is a bell from Gartan sold by its (unfortunately unnamed) hereditary keeper in 1847 for £3 to buy a passage to America (Pl. 4.9). It passed into the hands of the Rev G.H. Reade of Iniskeen and is now in the National Museum.[111] O'Nahan (Nawn) was the coarb and erenagh of Gartan in the early seventeenth century and the bell may have been in the possession of a member of the same family. Of O'Nahan it was said in the 1609 Inquisition that he 'carrieth Collumkillie's read [red?] stone' although there is no reference to a bell.[112] There is no further reference to this 'red stone' or description of what it was – it may have been a luck stone or even part of a portable altar of red marble.[113] The second bell is preserved in the Parochial House at Culdaff. It is known as 'St Buadan's Bell'.[114] It was preserved by the O'Duffy or Dooghie family until the late nineteenth century when it passed by marriage into the hands of an O'Dogherty. The O'Duffys were probably the hereditary keepers of the bell as the erenagh of Culdaff in 1609 was an O'Doghie.[115] In modern times it is recorded that on completion of the pattern or *turas* to St. Buadan's Well at Culdaff, water was lifted with the bell and taken away.[116]

The small bronze bell of St Mura of Fahan with its decorated mounts, now in the Wallace Collection in London, is well known (Pls 4.10-4.12).[117] Water drunk from the bell was said to have curative powers. The earliest detail recorded about the bell is that it was purchased by a collector called Reynolds for the Dungannon collector, John McLelland, from its unnamed keeper, 'a poor fisherman' in Inishowen for £6 in 1850.[118] Elsewhere it is said that it was purchased at Lisfannan, Fahan.[119] A letter in the Wallace Collection's file states that the bell was acquired from an O'Morresson in whose family it had been for generations.[120] If this is the case then it would be the second relic in the hands of this family, the other being the shrine known as the Misach. Colgan makes

Plate 4.10   Bell of St Mura – front
(Wallace Collection,
London).

Plate 4.11   Bell of St Mura – oblique
view of side and back
(Wallace Collection,
London).

Plate 4.12   Bell of St Mura – detail of
eleventh-century work on
front (Wallace Collection,
London).

no reference to the bell in mentioning the relics of Fahan preserved in the area in the seventeenth century. Bonner states that the erenagh family of Fahan in the later middle ages was Mac Céile.[121] Three erenagh families are mentioned as holding land at Fahan in the 1609 Inquisition – Mounterheiles *(Muintir Uí Éilithe)* or Healys, and two septs of O'Donnells.[122]

The bell consists of a small quadrangular bell of cast bronze to which decorated mounts have been applied. The earliest of these, now covered by later mounts, consist of the curved cap and a series of cast panels with interlaced foliate ornament added to the front (Pl. 4.11). The style of these mounts has been compared to the Cathach and Misach shrines and they are therefore dated to the late eleventh century.[123] The silver mounts added to the cap and to the lower half of the front may perhaps be of fourteenth or fifteenth century date. At this stage also two loops were added, presumably to enable the bell to be carried on a chain suspended from the neck. The rock crystal setting and the stamped silver foils of the upper half of the front are later additions of perhaps the sixteenth century.

The original handle of the bell is obscured by the later cap (Pl. 4.12) and Bourke included the Bell of St Mura among his Class 2 bells. An examination of X-ray photographs taken recently for the Wallace Collection, however, reveals that the bell originally had a handle with two finger holes. This feature, combined with its small size, suggests that it belongs to bells of Bourke's Class 3 – a group of small cast bronze bells with handles incorporating two or three finger-holes which Bourke would regard as transitional between the bronze bells of Class 2 and the round-mouthed bells of twelfth century and later date.[124]

Fahan was the principal monastery of the Cenél Eógain – Mura's own genealogy links him with the Cenél Eógain.[125] Its principal ecclesiastical family in the eleventh and twelfth century was the Uí Cellaig who provided three abbots – Cucairce, Mael Martain and Robartach.[126] They may be the Uí Cellaig listed in the genealogies as descended from the Cenél Eógain king Aed Allán.[127] The eleventh-century decoration of the shrine is so close to the Cathach and Misach shrines that it is possible that it was, like the other two objects, done at Kells. If so it is significant that objects associated with both Cenél Conaill and Cenél Eógain monasteries were being enshrined by crafts-men working in the same style if not actually in the same workshop in the later eleventh century and that this style was associated primarily with monasteries affiliated to the Columban federation.

Another small bell similar to that of St Mura, provided with three finger-holes in the handle, and known variously as the 'Bell of

Drumholm', the 'Ballymagroarty Bell' or the 'Bell of St Ernan of Drumholm', now in Rossnowlagh Museum, was found in Racoon graveyard around the year 1840.[128] The association with St Ernan appears to be a modern invention based on its find place and should caution against accepting such attributions uncritically.

Finally, there is one other bell which may be of this type. Doherty gives the history of a bell formerly in the possession of the McColgans which was found in the early eighteenth century at a place called Ceannaclug in the parish of Carndonagh 'where it had been hidden away'.[129] He identifies it with the reference in the 1609 Inquisition to 'the keeper of the saint's bell' at Carndonagh and calls it 'The Donagh Bell'. The bell was acquired by the Royal Irish Academy in 1847, the published account stating that it was 'found in the townland of Carnaclug'.[130] No townland of that name is recorded by the Ordnance Survey but the placename 'Keenaglog' occurs in the townland of Churchland Quarters on the east bank of the Donagh River, 1.5km north-east of Carndonagh. As the bell acquired by the Academy in 1847 was never registered, there is no independent description of it. Bourke argues that the bell illustrated by Doherty as the Keenaglog bell is, in fact, a bell in the Petrie collection found near Devenish.[131] This may be the case but there are two other, unlocalised bells of this type in the National Museum's collections and the Keenaglog bell may well be one of them.[132] The association of the bell with the 1609 reference to a bell at Carndonagh must remain problematical.[133] Whatever the problems of identifying the Keenaglog bell, it is clear that provenanced bells of Class 3 are concentrated in the north-west and may well represent a distinctive regional type.

There are a number of other bells which cannot now be located or identified. Doherty referred to a bronze bell of St Finian of Moville, but nothing more is known of it.[134] He also mentioned two other Donegal bells – the 'Long Island bell' and the 'Donegal bell' – in a lecture to the Royal Irish Academy.[135] The oral tradition of a bell at Glencolmcille, known locally as the 'Dubh Duaibhseach' (the black, gloomy bell)' and associated with Colmcille, is recorded in the Ordnance Survey Letters. It was not known in the area for centuries but its iron tongue had latterly been found by a farmer 'who, not knowing what it was, got nails made of it in a forge'![136] It may well be that this is the iron bell with a similar-sounding name associated with Colmcille preserved by the Mc Guirks at Termon Maguirk, county Tyrone. This was a foundation attributed to Colmcille and his bell there was known as 'Dia Díoltais', i.e. 'God of Vengeance'. It is possible that the latter, which is now in the National Museums of Scotland, was transferred during the later middle ages from Glencolmcille to Termon Maguirk.[137] Yet another bell associated with Colmcille is mentioned by the antiquarian George Petrie, in a letter to the Earl of Dunraven in 1843. Writing of Donegal antiquities he stated, 'They had a bell of St Columb's in Tory Island, but a tinker stole it away some thirty or forty years ago.'[138]

Crozier and chain of St Mura

One of the relics captured at the Battle of Down in 1178 was a crozier called *Bachall Mhura*.[139] John Colgan, a native of Inishowen writing in 1645, described as still extant 'the Crozier or Pastoral staff of this holy Prelate (which is commonly called Bachull Mura, i.e. Baculus Murani) which is covered over and adorned with gems and laid in a case which is guilt with gold. By this several miracles were wrought, and by it as the revenger of falsehood and the true indicator of virtue, the pious people and the nobles in particular, those descended from the family of O'Neills, when they would have all ambiguity removed from their assertions or terminate any dissention by the solemnity of an Oath, were accustomed to swear'.[140] Colgan mentions the former existence in the neighbourhood of other relics of St Mura. John O'Donovan, writing in 1835 in the Ordnance Survey Letters (p. 36) could get no account of the crozier and concluded that it was either destroyed in the disturbances of 1688 or had been carried to the Continent.

There is no further reference to the crozier until the mid-nineteenth century when two different croziers are attributed to St Mura. In neither case is the Bell of St Mura connected with the crozier and it would appear that bell and crozier were in separate hands by this time. A crozier and chain attributed to St Mura are preserved in the Petrie Collection in the National Museum of Ireland. According to the MS catalogue of the Petrie collection, the two objects were presented to Petrie by a Mr Woods of Sligo.[141] From a list of croziers in Petrie's collection published elsewhere, we know that Petrie acquired it before February 1851.[142] Doherty, citing Wakeman as his source, states that a portion of the crozier of St Mura, comprising the head or crook and about 18 inches of the staff, was preserved in the vicinity of Sligo 'whither in all likelihood it was carried about the time of the flight of the earls in 1607'.[143] The crozier (Pl. 4.13) now consists of three pieces – the crook with an integral knop to which is attached portion of the shaft with a plain knop, a detached plain knop and portion of the shaft with two decorated knops. No early detailed description of the crozier is known but annotations (undated but perhaps of the 1890s) by William Wakeman to the manuscript Petrie catalogue in the National Museum of Ireland describe its length, including the crook, as 2 feet 11½ inches. This measurement accords with the present length of the

crozier although an old photograph of the crozier in the Museum's archives of perhaps the 1880s or 1890s shows that the upper plain knop was in a different position to where it is today. It is not certain if all the pieces belong to the one crozier. The crozier as it is assembled at present has five knops which would be unusual for an early Irish crozier. On the basis of its decoration it can be dated to the eleventh or early twelfth century.[144] The chain (Pl. 4.14) consists of a length of linked, riveted brass rings from a suit of chain armour, measures 2.40m in length and is unlikely to be much earlier than the fifteenth century.[145]

John McLelland, writing in 1853 of the Bell of St Mura, says that the saint's crozier 'is believed to be the one now in the collection of Mr John Bell, Dungannon' and this statement is repeated verbatim by Ellacombe.[146] This crozier head is now in the National Museums of Scotland, Edinburgh.[147] Later nineteenth century writers were unsure as to which of the two was the crozier mentioned by Colgan and more recently Bourke has questioned whether either have any connection with Fahan.[148]

The Bell collection crozier head can be easily dismissed. McLelland is the only source for attributing it to St Mura. The crozier is only localised to Ireland in the National Museums of Scotland register and is not mentioned in Bell's manuscript notebook.[149] Bell himself makes no reference to it in a letter to J.H. Todd in November 1851 about the Bell of St Mura and appears to accept that the crozier in the Petrie collection is the Bachall Mura, making no mention of

Plate 4.13   Crozier of St Mura (N.M.I.).

114

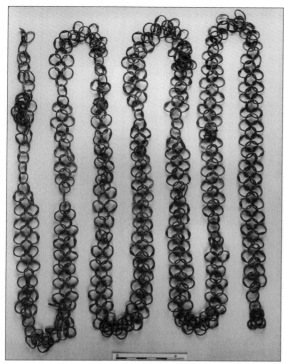

Plate 4.14   Petrie's Chain of St Mura (N.M.I.).

the crozier head in his possession.[150]   In September of the following year, Bell's crozier head was exhibited in Belfast as 'Portion of a brass Crozier, Saint's Staff, or Bachall'   while McLelland exhibited The Bell of Saint Muran'.[151] Bell would surely have alluded to its connection with St Mura if this were the case. Against this, and in favour of accepting the Petrie crozier, we have Petrie's own record in his letter of February 1851 and Todd's and Bell's implicit acceptance of this. O'Donovan, in a note on Fahan in the Annals of the Four Masters in 1856 refers to the Bachall Mura 'preserved in Mr Petrie's Cabinet, together with a bronze chain, said to have belonged to the same saint'.[152] With the single exception of McLelland, then, all other scholars in the mid nineteenth century would appear to have accepted the Petrie crozier as that of St Mura. As for their acquisition in Sligo, the objects could have been brought there by an Inishowen family during the transplantations from Donegal and other parts of the north of Ireland to Connacht in the seventeenth and eighteenth centuries. Petrie, in turn, had many connections with the Sligo area, having stayed at Rathcarrick House in 1835 and 1837 while working on the Ordnance Survey and had interviewed the keeper of the Soiscél Molaisse who was a tenant farmer in the county.[153]

There is one piece of evidence, however, which casts doubt on the Petrie objects' association with Fahan. This is contained in the miscellaneous notes to the *Martyrology of Donegal,* a work completed in 1630. Writing of St Lommán of Portloman, a church site on the shores of Lough Owel, county Westmeath, it is said, 'His staff is extant, as also his chain, by which women labouring in childbirth, when girt with it, are healed.'[154] It is difficult to believe in the existence in Ireland in the

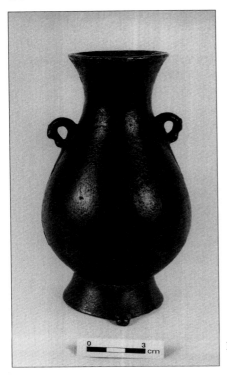

0   3 cm

Plate 4.15   Bronze eucharistic vase from Fahan (N.M.I.).

early seventeenth century of two croziers and chains associated with two different saints. Stylistically it must also be admitted that the ornament of the crozier of St Mura is closer to other work of north Munster and midland provenance and differs very much from the other objects associated with Donegal, including the Bell of St Mura.[155] The question may be resolved by the discovery of further documentation in Petrie's surviving papers concerning the acquisition from Mr Woods. In the meantime, all one can say is that the Fahan provenance is doubtful and that it may well be that Petrie's crozier and chain are in fact to be associated with St Lommán of Portloman and have no connection with Donegal.

Eucharistic vessel from Fahan

A bronze vase was found in the late eighteenth century near the church at Fahan (Pl. 4.15).[156] Acquired by the National Museum in 1920 from Prof R.A.S. Macalister of University College, Dublin,[157] it consists of a single-piece casting of bronze in the form of a tall bulbous vase, 15.8cm high. It is provided with a pair of loop handles which terminate in animal heads and originally rested on three feet formed of animals' heads, only one of which now survives. Two projecting spurs on the

116

rim indicate that the vessel was provided with a lid. Originally thought to be of oriental workmanship, the style of the animal heads is comparable to that found on Irish metalwork of the late eleventh and early twelfth centuries. The feet of the vessel with their projecting cat-like ears are very close in style to those on the sides of the Cross of Cong and on the front of the Shrine of St Patrick's Tooth. It is difficult to be certain of its function but in shape it is similar to the small globular, two-handled ampulla found in the ruins of an old church in Island Magee, county Antrim, which bears an inscription of the type found on ecclesiastical objects.[158] This was probably used as a container for holy oil or chrism and the Fahan vessel probably had a similar function.

The Cathach

The traditions associated with the Cathach and its shrine were first described by Manus O'Donnell in his *Life of St Colmcille* written in 1532. It was 'Colmcille's chief relic in the land of Cinel Conaill Gulban. It is encased in gilded silver, and it is not lawful to open it. And if it be taken thrice right-hand wise round the host of Cinel Conaill, when about to engage in battle, they always return safe in triumph. It is on the bosom of a comharba or a cleric who is as far as possible free from mortal sin that it should be borne around the host.'[159] It was regarded as the very book which Colmcille copied and which led to the battle of Cúl Dréimne and Colmcille's exile to Iona and was the chief relic of Colmcille's kinsmen, the O'Donnells.

The relic consists of part of a psalter considered to be of late sixth or early seventh century date and which therefore could be contemporary with the saint.[160] It is contained in a cover or shrine in the form of a hinged box of wood covered with metal plates added at various dates (Pls 4.16-4.17). The earliest of these consist of the cast silver plates on the narrow sides and a plaque bearing an openwork pattern of crosses on the back. This work is dated by an inscription on the latter to between 1062 and 1098.[161] The front is covered with a gilt silver mount with repoussé and engraved ornament of fourteenth century date.[162] Other mounts and settings were added subsequently.

The history of the shrine in the later middle ages is well-documented. It was captured along with hostages of the O'Donnells and its *maor* or steward, Mac Robhartaigh, slain at the battle of Belach Buidhe (Ballyboy near Boyle) in 1497 by Mac Dermott, only to be returned in 1499. It was present at the battle of Fersat Mór fought between O'Neill and O'Donnell in 1567 when its custodian, another Mac Robhartaigh, was slain.[163] Colgan wrote that the Cathach was kept in his time at Ballymagrorty in the parish of Drumhome, county Donegal.[164] It was reportedly brought to France by one Daniel O'Donnell after the Treaty

Plate 4.16   The Shrine of the Cathach – front (N.M.I.).

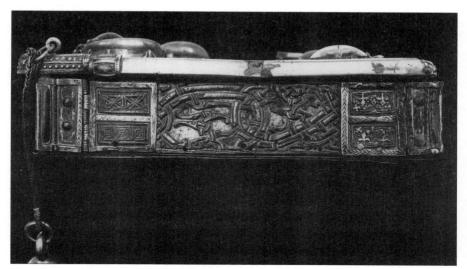

Plate 4.17   The Shrine of the Cathach – side (N.M.I.).

of Limerick and a silver case was made for it there in 1723. Brought back to Ireland sometime after 1802 by Sir Capel Molyneux, it came into the hands of Sir Neal O'Donel of Newport House, county Mayo and was eventually transferred to the Royal Irish Academy in 1842.[165]

An interesting sidelight on the presence of the Cathach in county Mayo is a local tradition that there was a relic preserved at Ballycroy in the late eighteenth century which was called *Cochall Choluim Chille,* i.e. the cowl of Colmcille.[166] This is described as being in the possession of two old men of the name Clery and Freel, 'a box with some gems inserted into its cover, which resembled glass eyes, and that whenever any one perjured himself these eyes were wont to turn round to roll like human eyes, and make signs of melancholy disapprobation of the conduct of the profane perjurer, that these two men left Ballycroy and took the Cochall (Cecullus) with them, and that no one heard of it nor of anything like it until some years ago Lady O'Donnell got a relic somewhere called the Cathach of Columbkille, but that there is no certainty of its being the same, with the Cochall taken away by the two old men about 60 years before'. Elsewhere, it is recorded that 'a colony of the Kinel-Connell were established here [i.e. at Erris] about two centuries since, and it was among them the Caah of St Columbkille was found'.[167] If this tradition is reliable (and its authority was questioned by Petrie),[168] the relic in question must have been the Cathach and O'Donovan's informant mistakenly gave it the name of the *Cochall Colmcille* – a relic which is otherwise unknown. This tradition of the presence of the shrine in Ballycroy in the late eighteenth century appears at variance with the accepted version of events which places it in France until 1802 but the mention of an O'Friel, whose family were erenaghs of Kilmacrenan, and an O'Clery, who held lands at Drumhome, county Donegal, where the shrine was known to have been in the later middle ages, suggests that it may have been the Cathach. The shrine would therefore appear to have been brought back to Ireland before 1802 and that by this time it had passed out of the hands of the Mac Robhartaigh family, its hereditary keepers throughout the middle ages.

There is considerable disagreement also as to where the Cathach might have been kept in the early middle ages. Because of its con-nection with the O'Donnells, whose inauguration site was at Kilmacrenan, Petrie suggested that at an early date the psalter may have come into the possession of the O'Friels, the erenagh family of Kilmacrenan who, among other duties, inaugurated the chief of the O'Donnells.[169] Reeves suggested that it was kept by the family of Mac Robhartaigh of Tory Island from the fifteenth to the seventeenth centuries.[170] There is, however, no independent evidence for the presence of the manuscript or shrine at either of these locations. In Henry's view, the Cathach and possibly the Misach also remained in the hands of the O'Donnells throughout the middle ages and 'were probably deposited, when the clan and its army did not need them, in monasteries of Inishowen, such as Fahan and perhaps Clonmany, close to Aileach, their chief fortress'.[171] This suggestion is untenable as Inishowen and Aileach were in Cenél Eógain, not Cenél Conaill, territory. Herbert was more circumspect, suggesting that the former abbot of Kells, Domnall mac Robartaigh, mentioned on the shrine's inscription, returned north with the Cathach 'and remained afterwards in a northern Columban monastery'.[172] Some writers have stated that it was kept in a crypt at Ballymagrorty, in the parish of Drumhome,[173] while others have suggested that it was originally kept at Derry by the Mac Robhartaigh family at Ballymagrorty, near Derry, and that it later transferred to the church of the same name in the south of county Donegal.[174]

The inscription on the Shrine of the Cathach asks for prayers for Cathbarr Ua Domnaill who commissioned it, for Sitric Mac Meic Aedha who made it and for Domnall mac Robartaigh 'successor of Kells'.[175] From this Henry and others deduced that the shrine was made at Kells between the years c.1062 and 1098, effectively the presumed period of Domnall mac Robartaigh's abbacy of Kells.[176] It has been shown that mac Robartaigh was replaced as abbot by 1094 so that the date of the shrine can be narrowed slightly to between 1062 and 1094.[177] A more precise dating is hindered by the uncertainty of what exactly is meant at this period by the terms *comarba Cenansa, comarba Colmcille* and *comarba Colmcille ⁊ Adamnáin* and it is difficult therefore to ascertain the exact abbatial succession at the key Columban monasteries of Iona, Kells, Derry and Raphoe.[178]

We have no information on the mac Robartaigh genealogies although they are generally accepted as being of the Cenél Conaill.[179] There is one small piece of evidence, however, which suggests that they were probably descended from the Cenél Lugdach, the Cenél Conaill branch from which Cathbharr Ua Domnaill who commissioned the shrine is descended. The Cathach was kept in the later middle ages at Ballymagrorty in the parish of Drumhome[180] and there is a Ballymagrorty townland in Templemore parish on the outskirts of Derry.[181] Both have sites associated with Colmcille[182] and it is surely no coincidence that in the early tenth century, Cináed mac Domnaill, who is recorded as joint abbot of Derry and Drumhome, is of a collateral branch of the Cenél Lugdach.[183] It seems possible, therefore, that the mac Robartaigh traced their ancestry to the Cenél Lugdach through Cináed, a churchman associated with Derry in the early tenth century.

The Cenél Lugdach through the mac Robartaigh family of clerics may therefore have been involved in the ecclesiastical politics of Derry in the tenth century and by the succeeding century were firmly established in Kells. Herbert suggests that Domnall mac Robartaigh may have been the son of Robartach, an abbot of Kells who died in 1057, who in turn may have been the son of another abbot, Ferdomnach, who died in 1007/8.[184] Máel Maire Ua Robartaigh was another Kells monastic official in the early twelfth century[185] and it has also been suggested that Muiredach mac Robartaigh – alias Marianus Scottus, founder of Ratisbon – was of this family.[186]

Cathbarr Ua Domnaill was head of the Cenél Conaill sept of the Cenél Lugdach (also known as Clann or Síl Dálach)[187] from whom the O'Donnell kings of Tír Conaill in the later middle ages were descended. The eponymous ancestor of the Cenél Lugdach was, according to the genealogies, related to Colmcille and several abbots of Iona from the sixth to the eighth centuries.[188] The Cenél Lugdach provided an abbot of Iona in the ninth century, briefly gaining the kingship of Cenél Conaill in the late ninth and early tenth centuries. During this time the sept provided at least two abbots of Derry, one being the son of the king, Eichnechán mac Dálaig, the other being Cináed mac Domnaill, who was also abbot of Drumhome, where the Cathach was kept in the later middle ages.[189] Otherwise they appear only rarely in the annals, not rising to prominence again until the eleventh century, the few early references usually recording internecine strife.[190] Cathbarr's death as king of Cenél Lugdach is recorded in 1106 but his claim was not unchallenged. Mac meic Gilla Coluim Ua Domnaill, slain by his own kinsmen in 1100, was accorded the title of king of Cenél Lugdach.[191] There is not enough information to say whether the Cenél Lugdach were allied to either of the two Cenél nAeda septs who monopolised the kingship of Cenél Conaill in the eleventh and twelfth centuries – the Ua Cannannáin and Ua Máel Doraid. It has been suggested that they were allied to the Ua Cannannáin claimants in the late eleventh century although there is no documentary evidence to support this.[192] If this were indeed the case then it is of interest that Domnall mac Robartaigh's immediate predecessor as abbot of Kells was Gilla Críst Ua Máel Doraid. The Ua Máel Doraid seem to have had an interest also in Iona. Gilla Críst was styled '*comarba* Colmcille in Ireland and Scotland' on his death in 1062 and the son of the abbot Ua Máel Doraid – possibly Gilla Críst's son – killed the abbot of Iona, Mac Meic Báethéne, in 1070.[193] It would be interesting to know what Mac Meic Báethéne's family affiliations were and it is possible that the Ua Cannannáin/Ua Máel Doraid struggle for the kingship of Cenél Conaill also spilled over into the appointment of the abbots of the important monasteries under their influence such as Kells, Iona and Derry. In this context, the enshrinement of the Cathach may have been part of the Ua Domnaill/mac Robartaigh claim to the office of *comarba* Colmcille.

Alternatively, the relic may have been enshrined at this time as part of the Cenél Conaill response to the growing threat posed by Domnall mac Lochlainn, king of the neighbouring Cenél Eógain since 1083, who had ambitions to the high kingship. In 1093 he blinded the Cenél Conaill king Aed Ua Cannannáin and inflicted a crushing defeat on the Cenél Conaill at Fersat Mór five years later. By 1113 he had intruded his own son into the Cenél Conaill kingship[194] and was also responsible for bringing the monastery of Derry under Cenél Eógain control.[195] The enshrinement of an important relic associated with its founding saint may have been part of the Cenél Conaill's attempts to retain control over Derry.

It is tempting to identify the Cathach as one of the relics of Colmcille brought south from Tír Chonaill to Kells by Aonghus Ua Domhnalláin in the year 1090 and the date would fit well with that suggested by those named on the inscription.[196] The relics are listed as a bell called *Clog na Rígh*, a flabellum[197] and 'the two gospel books', along with one hundred and forty ingots of silver for their enshrinement. Of these the bell and the flabellum are known from other sources as being associated with Colmcille (see below). Henry suggested that the bell alias *Clog na Rígh* is probably to be identified as the Bell of St Mura since the decoration of the latter is so similar to that of the Cathach and the Misach; but there is no evidence that the Fahan bell was ever known by that name.[198] Given the fact that the Shrine of the Cathach was made at Kells in the later eleventh century and that Ua Domhnalláin was a member of the Kells community, it seems reasonable to suggest that it was one of the gospel books referred to in the annalistic entry.

This brings us back to the question of where the Cathach was kept in the early middle ages. To reconstruct where it might have been we need to work back from the later medieval sources. There seems no doubt that the shrine was kept at Ballymagrorty near Drumhome in the later middle ages and one must assume that its keepers were descended from the Domnall mac Robartaigh of the late eleventh century inscription. While the principal church of the Cenél Conaill from the early eleventh century was Raphoe – which became the diocesan see sometime after the synod of Rath Breasail in 1111 – there is not a single piece of evidence that the Cathach was ever preserved there or that the Mac Robhartaigh family were associated with it. Given the likely Cenél Lugdach origin of the family and their association with

Derry in the tenth century, it seems reasonable to infer that the family's original lands were at Ballymagrorty near Derry as their kinsmen the Uí Domnaill did not become kings of Cenél Conaill until the time of Eignechán c.1200 and hence could not have extended their influence into the south of the county until then. The Mac Robhartaigh family was probably given lands at Ballymagrorty in south Donegal in the thirteenth century by their patrons when the centre of O'Donnell power moved from Kilmacrenan to Assaroe as part of their policy of planting 'the former Ua Cannannáin and Ua Máel Doraid lands among themselves, their supporters (chiefly in the professional families), and the church'.[199] The granting of lands at Drumhome to the Mac Robhartaigh family would be particularly appropriate as it had been formerly in the hands of the abbots of Derry in the tenth century and by the twelfth had become the chief church of the Ua Domnaill's Cenél nAeda rivals (Ua Máel Doraid and Ua Cannannáin) for the overkingship and had been the burial place of one of these, Flaithbertach Ua Máel Doraid in 1197, only three years before Eignechán became the first of the Ó Domnaill kings of Tír Chonaill.[200]

We cannot be sure when the Cathach was transferred to Drumhome but it could have been as early as the mid-thirteenth century. The earliest dated documentary reference to the Cathach's association with Colmcille is contained in the *Book of Fenagh* in a text which is probably no earlier than the mid-thirteenth century.[201] In a poem in which Colmcille, after a battle, comes to Caillin and prophesies the coming of a great abbot to Fenagh, it is claimed that he bequeaths to St Caillin of Fenagh, county Leitrim, a number of items including the Cathach 'which he wrote himself' and a copy of the Gospels called the *Cethir lebor*.[202] The poem mentions Drumhome, and prophesies that the abbot would come in the time of Domnall Mór Ó Domnaill (+1241) and Conchobar Ó Ruairc (+1257), suggesting a composition date for the poem in the mid-thirteenth century. There is no doubt that it is the Cathach of the O'Donnells that is being referred to here and it is possible that the episode was invented to explain the (no doubt temporary) presence of the shrine at Fenagh, perhaps captured by the O'Rourkes, the patrons of Fenagh, from the O'Donnells. A possible occasion for this was when the Cenél Conaill surrendered hostages to a combined force of Anglo-Normans and their Connacht allies at Drumhome in 1242.[203] This is far from certain, however, and the picture is complicated by the fact that the text also refers to a cross of hazel belonging to Caillin himself which is also called *cathach*.[204]

There is an important reference to the Cathach in a text called *Aided Muirchertaigh Meic Erca* – the death of Muirchertach mac Erca – a complex text dated by Byrne to the fourteenth century[205] although others have suggested that its core may date as early as the eleventh century.[206] Here, the Cathach is one of three battle standards given by St Cairnech, patron saint of Dulane, county Meath, to the Cenél Conaill and Cenél Eógain, along with the Bell of the Will (St Patrick's Bell) and Cairnech's Misach.[207] The date and historical context of this text is critical to the history of both the Cathach and the Misach but until a critical edition of the text is made it is difficult to assess its significance. The inclusion of an Armagh relic – the Bell of St Patrick – as a battle standard of the Cenél Conaill and Eógain may point to an earlier date for the text as the latter was enshrined by Domnall Ua Lochlainn during the abbacy of Domnall Mac Amalgada between 1091 and 1105, making it almost contemporary with the enshrinement of the Cathach.[208] Whatever its date, the important point here is that the text makes no association between the Cathach and Colmcille.

It follows from the above that the name 'Cathach' attached to the manuscript cannot – with the possible exception of *Aided Muirchertaigh meic Erca* – be found in documents earlier than the thirteenth century, nor is there any earlier text associating it with Colmcille. It is not mentioned in any of the earlier lives of Colmcille, including an Irish *Life* composed in Derry *c*.1150, which rules out its presence there in the twelfth century (or at least the presence of a relic *known* as the Cathach). It is surprising also that an object of such importance is ignored in all texts, annalistic and hagiographical, anterior to the mid thirteenth century. If the tradition associating the manuscript with Colmcille and the battle of Cúl Dréimne was an early one, why is it not mentioned by Adamnán? In fact, in the annalistic accounts of Cúl Dréimne only the late Annals of the Four Masters refer to the manuscript as part of the cause of the battle. The name Cathach and the traditions ascribing its composition to Colmcille and its association with the battle of Cúl Dréimne could therefore be late inventions.

The term *cathach* was not used exclusively for the manuscript of the O'Donnells and was applied to a number of other relics during the middle ages. The *cathach* of Cailinn already mentioned took the form of a hazel cross and a *cathach* of St Iarlaith was kept at Tuam in the twelfth century.[209] Compounds of the word *cath* were applied to other objects: a crozier of Colmcille preserved in Scotland was known as the *cathbuaid* ('battle triumph')[210] and another *cathbuaid* associated with St Brigid appears to have been a trumpet.[211] The crozier of Findchú of Brigown, county Cork, was known as the *Cennchathach* and, like the Cathach of Colmcille, was carried thrice round his host before battle.[212] Still others were battle standards – *meirge catha* – such as the crozier of St Grellan, the battle standard of the Uí Mhaine. The name *cathach* is therefore a motif associated with a number of warrior-saints and may not have been the original name of the psalter which now bears the name.

Is it possible that the relic was known by some other name before the thirteenth century? If we are correct in assuming that the keepers of the shrine held lands at Ballymagrorty on the outskirts of Derry before transferring to Drumhome, was it perhaps there that the shrine was kept in the early middle ages? If so, can it be identified in the sources? In an Irish *Life of Colmcille,* composed at Derry *c.*1150, there is a passage which relates how the saint brought back from Tours 'the Gospel which had been on Martin's breast in the grave for a hundred years'.[213] This prized manuscript was known as *Soscéla Martain* ('Gospels of St Martin') and was one of the great treasures of the monastery of Derry. In an annalistic entry relating to the death in 1166 of the king of Ireland, Muirchertach Ua Lochlainn, as a result of the dishonouring of the abbot of Armagh and the *Bachall Íosa* and the abbot of Derry and the *Soscéla Martain* it would appear that the two relics were of parallel, if not equal, importance.[214] The cult of St Martin seems to have been particularly strong in Derry as there are references to a cemetery and a well dedicated to the saint there.[215] The last we hear of the *Soscéla Martain* is in 1182 when it was carried off by the foreigners after the battle of Drumbo, county Antrim, between the Cenél Eógain and the Normans.[216] Herbert assumed that, as nothing more is heard of it, its loss may be presumed from that year.[217] Could it be, however, that the sacred manuscript known as *Soscéla Martain* is, in fact, the Cathach and that it reappears in the following century as the *Cathach* and that its name and use as a battle talisman associated with their patron saint suited the needs of Clann Domnaill more than its earlier association with the more distant Martin of Tours? The invention of an evocative association with the much earlier battle of Cúl Dréimne, a site in county Sligo within the theatre of war of the expanding ambitious Clann Domhnaill would also be appropriate. The gospels of Martin were, to judge from the Irish *Life*, of considerable antiquity by the twelfth century and a late sixth/early seventh century psalter in Insular script could have been taken equally as having been written by Colmcille in the thirteenth century. The fact that the manuscript is a psalter and not a gospel book should pose no difficulty as the manuscript said to have been copied by Colmcille was a gospel book. It is also significant that the *Soscéla Martain* are last heard of effectively being used as a battle standard or *cathach*.

One can only speculate as to the person responsible for inventing the Cathach's associations with Colmcille's expulsion and its use as a battle standard in the thirteenth century. We have seen that the earliest reference occurs in the *Book of Fenagh* which may have been written

125

during the reign of Domnall Óg Ó Domnaill. The same Domnall, on his accession in 1258, broke with time-honoured tradition in that he was inaugurated not at Kilmacrenan but in the church at Raphoe.[218] Such a bold gesture may well have been accompanied by other changes including, perhaps, the invention of the traditions associated with the Cathach.

All this is merely speculation, however, and it must be admitted that there are potential difficulties in equating the Cathach with the Gospels of Martin. If the reference to the former in *Aided Muirchertaigh Meic Erca* is as early as the eleventh century then clearly there was a relic known as the Cathach associated with the Cenél Conaill and Cenél Eógain at that date. However, it is still possible that the relic could have been known by both names – the *Soscéla Martain* always associated with the Cenél Eógain (Derry in the early twelfth century was under the control of the Cenél Eógain and the Gospels were in Cenél Eógain hands when last mentioned at the battle of Drumbo in 1182) while the term Cathach was the one which was ultimately to become associated with the relic. The substitution of Colmcille for Martin as the saint with which the relic was associated should not be surprising – the shrine known as the Misach was transferred from St Cairnech to Colmcille in popular tradition by the early seventeenth century and only serves to demonstrate the dominance of the cult of Colmcille in this part of Ireland.

The Misach
The shrine known as the Misach, associated with St Cairnech, is a rectangular wooden box to which metal mounts of varying dates have been added (Pls 4.18, 4.19).[219] It was opened and repaired by Sir William Betham in the early nineteenth century who recorded that the box consisted of a hollowed block of yew open at one side in the manner of a slip case for a book. He also stated that considerable damage had been done to some of the metal plates. It is now sealed and it is difficult to be certain which parts are original and which nineteenth century copies. The contents of the shrine were already lost in the last century but it is generally accepted that the shape of the shrine, which resembles other book shrines, suggests that it contained a manuscript. It is also generally agreed that the word *misach* derives from the word *mí* ('month') and perhaps means a calendar and it has therefore been suggested that the shrine may have contained a calendar of saints' lives.[220]

The workmanship is principally of two periods. The cast copper-alloy plates on the sides compare very closely in style with the shrine of the Cathach and is therefore probably of the late eleventh century.

Plate 4.18 The shrine of the Misach – front (N.M.I.).

One of the plates on the long side appears to be a copy of the other, no doubt one of the repairs carried out for Betham. The openwork plate on the back may also be of this date but copying the original which was perhaps discarded. The front is covered with stamped silver foils containing a number of repeated designs. Stylistically difficult to date, they appear to be earlier than the inscription of 1534. It is possible, however, that the dies from which they were struck were in

Plate 4.19 The shrine of the Misach – side (N.M.I.).

circulation for a long time and that they were added, along with the silver filigree rock crystal settings and the crucifix figure, in the early sixteenth century.

The later history of the shrine is well documented. The inscription on the shrine itself is in Irish and translates 'Brian son of Brian Ó Muirgheasa covered me AD 1534'.[221] In the Inquisition of 1609 the erenagh of Clonmany, Donogh O'Morreeson, was described as 'keeper of the missagh or ornaments left by Columkill'.[222] Several writers have noted that the name of the relic is mis-translated as 'ornaments' and that the relic was associated with Colmcille rather than Cairnech. This, however, is not surprising, as the cult of Cairnech seems never to have been particularly widespread in Donegal and it is likely that the shrine was absorbed into the stronger cult of Colmcille at an early date. The shrine was obtained in the vicinity of Fahan by Dr Thomas Barnard, dean of Derry, before 1760. It subsequently passed through Lord Dunraven to St Columba's College, Rathfarnham and is currently on loan to the National Museum of Ireland.[223]

The inscription on the shrine and the Inquisition entry link the object with the Ó Muirgheasa family and with Clonmany by at least the late sixteenth century. The earliest reference to an Ó Muirgheasa erenagh is the obit in 1516 of *an toircinneach Ó Muirgheasa .i. Niall décc.*[224] Presumably Niall was erenagh of Clonmany and was a kinsman of the Brian mac Briain of the inscription and of Donogh O'Morreeson mentioned in the Inquisition, although this cannot be proven conclusively.

The Ó Muirgheasa family of ecclesiastics can be traced back to the late fourteenth century. The earliest is one David O'Moryson of the chapter of Derry in 1397[225] and members of the family are listed as rectors of Clonmany in 1417, 1426 and 1455.[226] They were also associated throughout the fifteenth century with the other Inishowen churches of Clonca, Fahan, Culdaff and Donaghmore.[227] Only a few are mentioned as vicars and rectors of churches outside Inishowen.[228] Many maintained a connection with Derry, there being six canons of the Ó Muirgheasa family listed between 1397 and 1538 and of these, three were rectors of parishes elsewhere.[229] The family was thus intimately connected with the church in Derry and with Inishowen and in particular the parishes of Clonmany and Clonca.

Little is known of the family before the fourteenth century and their earlier genealogical affiliation has eluded modern scholars. The *Laud* genealogies, under the Cenél Eógain sept of Cenél Tigernaigh, record the name Tnúdach *a quo Hui Muirgusa ⁊ Hui Chonnicáin.*[230] According to the genealogies, the eponymous Tigernach was one of four (or five) sons of Erc, the most famous being Muirchertach mac Erca. His other brothers are listed as Moen, ancestor of the Cenél Moen (Ua

Gairmledaigh) and Feradach, from whom the Cenél Feradaigh (Mac Cathmhail) were descended.[231] These three septs are said in the *Book of Fenagh* to hold land 'between Eogain and Conaill' – that is the border land between the Cenél Eógain and Cenél Conaill.[232] The descendants of Moen held lands in *Magh nIthe* – roughly the barony of Raphoe while those of Feradach occupied the barony of Clogher in county Fermanagh. The Cenél Tigernaigh lands are less easily located but they included an area called *Fernmagh*.[233] Hogan was uncertain as to the location of their lands, placing *Fernmagh* in the diocese of Derry or Raphoe and the Cenél Tigernaigh in Tír Eoghain or Inis Eogain.[234] The Uí Muirgheasa could therefore have originally held lands anywhere from the area of the lower Foyle to Inishowen but we cannot be sure of this as there are no early historical references to Clonmany. If, however, the association between the Misach and Clonmany is late, this might explain the transfer of the Misach from Cairnech to Colmcille, founder of Clonmany, in the Inquisition of 1609. There seems to be no other historical connection between Clonmany, or indeed Inishowen, and Cairnech.[235]

Unlike the Cathach, the Misach is recorded in the twelfth century annals, although the reference appears to have eluded all modern writers. In Mac Cárthaigh's Book under the year 1166 (recte 1165) Muirchertach mac Lochlainn violates the hospitality of Eochaidh mac Duinnsléibhe, king of Ulaidh, at his Easter house at *Camus Comhghaill* (Camus Macosquin, county Derry). The latter is carried off to Muirchertach's crannog at *Inis Aonaigh* (Lough Enagh, county Derry) where he is blinded. In a revenge killing Muirchertach is slain. The two kings were under the protection of the relics of the north of Ireland including the Crozier and Bell of Patrick, the Gospels of Martin, the Misach of Cairnech and the three shrines in Teampall na Scrín and in the presence of the king of Airghialla, the Cenél Conaill and Cenél Eógain and their clerics.[236] The Misach was obviously by this time regarded as an important relic of the northern church and was associated with Cairnech. It was sufficiently important to be mentioned by name ranking in importance with the relics of St Patrick and the Gospel of St Martin. The Misach is next referred to as one of the battle standards of the Cenél Conaill and Cenél Eógain given by Cairnech along with the Cathach and St Patrick's Bell in *Aided Muirchertach Meic Erca*, a text which we have seen is dated variously to the eleventh and the fourteenth centuries. If the text is as early as the eleventh century, then it would be the earliest reference to the shrine.

Cairnech's principal church in Donegal was at *Cluain Lighean* (Clonleigh), near Lifford and a second church at *Domhnach Mór Magh Ithe* (Donaghmore) some 10km to the south-east is also associated with him.[237] Both are in the disputed border area between Cenél Conaill and Cenél Eógain territory. The chiefs of Druim Lighean from at least the twelfth century were the Uí Donnghaile.[238] Unfortunately, the Uí Muirgheasa are connected with neither Clonleigh or Donaghmore, the erenaghs in the later medieval period being the Uí Cearbhalláin and Uí Doireidh respectively.

Cairnech's Donegal connections are explained in two late texts associating him with his maternal aunt, Erc, wife of Muiredach mac Eoghain (also the ancestor of the Uí Mhuirgheasa).[239] The first of these is in the Book of Mac Firbis (MacFirbhisigh) in which Cairnech is placed at Ros Ailigh (near Aileach) and blesses a church for Erc at an unidentified place called Cell Erca.[240] The second, in the Book of Fenagh, relates how Erc granted him lands at Druim Lighean, identified with Drumleen townland in Clonleigh parish.[241]

There is another more famous Cairnech, said to have been a Cornish Briton, who founded Dulane, county Meath. The Dulane Cairnech is mentioned in the prologue to the Senchas Már (where he is said to have been a companion of Patrick)[242] and in the Félire Oengusso,[243] suggesting that his is the earlier cult. The traditions surrounding both saints have not yet been the subject of critical study but they have several points in common. Both are non-Irish in origin, both are associated with Erc and both have successors called Casán and Masán. The Misach's inclusion in Aided Muirchertach Meic Erca, a tale set firmly in Meath but containing references to the Cenél Eógain and Conaill is the final proof that the Dulane saint and that associated with the Misach in Donegal can be regarded as one and the same person.

How, then, did his cult get transferred to Donegal? The answer may lie with a family who were once associated with Dulane but who, at an early stage, moved into Kells (a distance of only 3km to the south). The clerical family of the Uí Uchtáin were, along with the Uí Dúnáin, from an early date attached to Dulane. Maelfinnén mac Uchtáin was bishop of Kells and successor of Ultán (i.e. abbot of Ardbraccan) and Cairnech (i.e. abbot of Dulane) at his death in 969.[244] The family provided two abbots and two fir léiginn of Kells in the early eleventh century and their presence in Kells was probably due to the desire of the Clann Cholmáin kings to counter the influence of Armagh.[245] That the family was involved in the promotion of the cult of relics is clear from an episode in 1034 in which Maicnia Ua Uchtáin, fer légind of Kells, was drowned coming from Scotland along with the Cuilebad or flabellum of Colmcille and three shrines of St Patrick.[246] It is probable, therefore, that the cult of Cairnech was attached to that of Colmcille at Kells and that one of his relics was brought north sometime in the eleventh or twelfth centuries – a time when Kells was gradually being replaced by Derry as the head of the Columban *paruchia*. The Cuilebad itself, by the end of the century, had been transferred to the north as it was recorded as one of the relics of Colmcille in Tír Chonaill brought south for enshrinement in 1090.[247] Was the Misach perhaps one of the two gospel books mentioned in the same episode and therefore also transferred north by the end of the eleventh century?

The Misach was in the north by the mid-twelfth century and was of sufficient importance to deserve special mention in 1166 on a par with the principal relics of Armagh and Derry – St Patrick's Crozier and Bell and The Three Shrines and the Gospels of Martin. Is it not likely that by this time it was in the possession of *comarba Colmcille* and therefore kept at Derry, at least in the twelfth century? This is supported by the fact that when they first emerge in the documentary sources, the Uí Muirgheasa are connected with Derry. The evidence does not allow us to say whether the shrine was ever kept at either of Cairnech's two Donegal churches of Clonleigh or Donaghmore[248] before its next recorded presence at Clonmany in the early seventeenth century.

Cuilebad Cholmcille

We have noted above references to an object known as Cuilebad *Cholmcille*. It is first mentioned in 1034 when it was reputedly lost at sea along with relics of St Patrick while being brought from Scotland (probably from Iona) by Maicnia Ua Uchtáin, *fer légind* of Kells. It appears to have been recovered for in 1090 it is listed as one of the relics of Colmcille brought south from Tír Conaill. This object was, in fact, a liturgical fan or flabellum.[249] Confirmation that this relic was kept at Kells comes from a voyage tale known as *Immram Snedgusa ocus Maic Riagla*. Two main versions of the text exist – a verse text of ninth or tenth century date and a prose version of the eleventh century.[250] The prose version of the tale relates how Donnchadh mac Domnaill, king of Cenél Conaill, seeks advice from the *comarba* of Colmcille in Iona. Two clerics, Snedghus and Mac Riaghla, are sent to Ireland. On their return to Iona they are carried to an island in which there was an immense tree with a flock of white birds. A great bird with a golden head and silver wings gives them a leaf as large as the hide of an ox and he orders them to take it away and lay it on Colmcille's altar. The prose version ends, 'And it is St. Colmcille's *Cuilefaidh* at this day in Cennanas'.[251] The references to the Cenél Conaill and to Kells occur only in the later prose version and it is likely that the episode was invented to explain the presence at Kells of the Columban relic and that its composition dates either to the 1034 or the 1090 episodes related in the annals. Although the object no longer survives, there are a number of cross-slabs and pillars which bear handled discs inscribed with crosses of arcs or marigold patterns which are interpreted as representing flabella, including the so-called 'Marigold Stone' at Carndonagh.[252]

Treasury at Derry

We have seen that the relic known as *Soscéla Martain* was preserved at Derry in the twelfth century and it is argued that this may have been the manuscript which was subsequently known as the Cathach. It is possible that the Misach may have also been kept at Derry.

Gifts of secular objects and altar plate were regularly made to the church by local kings and these are of interest as they allow us to identify the patrons of individual churches. For Derry we get a unique glimpse of such donors of secular ceremonial or drinking horns in an annalistic entry for 1196. This records the robbery from the altar of the Tempall Mór at Derry by Mac Giolla Eidigh of Cianachta of the four best horns in Ireland which were known as *Mac Riabhach*, *Mac Solais*, the horn of Ua Maéldoraid and the *Cam Coruinn*, that is, the horn of Uí Dochartaigh. He broke them and took off their precious mounts. The articles were recovered on the third day after being stolen and the thief was hanged at Cros na Ríg in Derry.[253] Of the horn known as *Mac Riabhach* an earlier entry explains how it was acquired.[254] The king of Magh Ithe and Cenél nEnna, Niall Ua Gairmledaigh, was killed by Donnchadh Ua Cairelláin in the centre of Derry. In recompense Ua Cairelláin offered to the community of Derry the monastic service (*mainchene*) of himself and his sons and grandsons, a grant of land near Donaghmore and *Mac Riabhach*, described as the best goblet in Ireland. Of the four horns therefore we can identify the donors of three of them: Uí Cairelláin of Clann Diarmata, a Cenél Eógain sept; Uí Maél Doraid, who were intermittently kings of Cenél Conaill until 1197 and Uí Dochartaigh, a Cenél Conaill sept belonging to the Cenél Lugdach from Inishowen who were briefly kings of Cenél Conaill in the late twelfth and early thirteenth century before being replaced by the Uí Domnaill. Derry was therefore in receipt of gifts from both Cenél Conaill and Eógain sub-kings of the region. The rich treasury of Derry enjoyed only a brief period of peace, however, as the monastery was completely plundered in 1214 by the combined forces of Tomás mac Uchtrach, earl of Athol, and Ruaidhri mac Raghnaill who made off with 'the treasures of the community of Daire and of the North of Ireland' from the Tempall Mór.[255]

Reliquary crosses

There were two great wooden crosses, probably both adorned with gilt mounts and gems, venerated in the county in the middle ages. The first of these is the Great Cross of Colmcille which was preserved in Manus

O'Donnell's time on Tory Island as the chief treasure of that saint on the island and called then the *crux magna*.[256] It was reputedly a gift to the saint from Pope Gregory and had been brought to Tory from Iona. It was also known as the 'Great Gem of Colmcille' which suggests that it was a jewelled cross. It appears to have been of some size to judge from its name and also by the fact that in 1542 it was 'broken' by Brian Mac Conmhidhe who died as a result 'through the miracles of God and St Colmcille, and the curse of Ó Robhartaigh'.[257] The latter was presumably its keeper. It is not clear if this is the same as 'holy Collamkille's cross, a god of great veneration with Sorleyboy and all Ulster' mentioned in a letter from the lord-deputy, Sir John Perrot to the secretary, Lord Burghley in 1584 as part of the booty taken at Somhairle Buidhe mac Domhnaill's stronghold at Dunluce Castle, county Antrim.[258] This took the form of a pectoral cross to judge from Perrot's suggestion to Burghley that 'you may, if you please, bestow him [i.e. the cross] upon my good Lady Wallsingham or my Lady Sydney *to wear as a jewel* of weight and bigness, and not of price and goodness, upon some solemn feast or triumph day at the court'. Perhaps the Dunluce cross consisted of an enshrined fragment of the larger cross from Tory.

The second cross was kept in Raphoe Cathedral in the later middle ages and was known as the 'Holy Cross'. In 1397 it cured the eyesight of Aodh mac Mathghamhna, probably a king of Oriel, and in 1411 rained blood miraculously from its wounds.[259] We learn more about this cross from a petition made in 1600 by the clergy of Raphoe to Pope Clement VIII requesting a relic of the True Cross because the most sacred image of the cross (*sanctissima crucis imagine*), venerated at Raphoe Cathedral for centuries and which attracted pilgrims from all over Ireland, was burnt by English looters along with its books and countless ornaments.[260] These references suggest that it was made of wood with a figure of the crucified Christ. According to the petition it had been used for special devotion on the Feast of the Exaltation of the Cross (14 September) indicating that it contained a relic of the True Cross.

Conclusion

Despite the lack of excavated sites of the early medieval period, a surprisingly large *corpus* of material has survived from the county. The sandhills finds are among the richest from any Irish county. They are important pointers to coastal settlement sites of the early medieval period which are not associated with either ringforts or church sites and which do not appear to be recorded in the written sources. A more intense analysis of these finds, their precise locations and the exact

Fig. 4.8   Engraved figures of the Apostles, Bearnán Conaill shrine (1:1).

nature of associated structures backed up by field survey and excavation would give us a clearer picture of these coastal settlements. It is
clear, however, from the quality of material casually recovered from
some sites, that a number represent substantial, permanent high status
settlements.

The modest number of silver Viking Age hoards must be set against
the relative paucity of such material from the north-west of Ireland and
the find contexts indicate that some silver made its way into native
hands. There is also some indication that the Viking presence, at least

in Inishowen, may have been more permanent than previously thought.

The county is particularly rich in ecclesiastical metalwork. This is mainly due to the continuity of possession of relics among their hereditary keepers and contrasts with the relatively few objects of this type from the more anglicised areas of the country where the effects of the Reformation and the plantations were greater. The remarkable group of objects associated either directly or indirectly with the cult of Colmcille – the Cathach and Misach shrines and the Bell of St Mura – is unique in that stylistically they are so close and their place of manufacture (Kells) can be proposed on the basis of the historical sources. Apart from the objects listed, a bell crest from the lower reaches of the river Bann is stylistically of this group, further emphasising its northern distribution.[261] Another product of this group has recently been found at the site of an Augustinian priory at Inchaffray in Perthshire, Scotland. This consists of the crest of a bell or bell-shrine similar to that from the river Bann. Inchaffray is known to have had a community of Culdees prior to the adoption of the Augustinian rule and it is perhaps through Iona that the object came to Scotland.[262]

It is not possible to deal here with the later medieval work which is found on the Cathach and Misach shrines, the Shrine of the Bearnán Conaill and the Bell of St Mura. Several different phases of late medieval decoration are evident on these pieces. The quality of the silver casting on the Bearnán Conaill shrine and on the Bell of St Mura, the engraved work on the back of the Bearnán Conaill shrine (fig. 4.8) and the repoussé silver panel on the front of the shrine of the Cathach suggests the presence of skilled metalworkers in the county in the fourteenth, fifteenth and sixteenth centuries. It is unfortunate that the inscriptions on the front and side of the Bearnán Conaill shrine are now so worn as one or both almost certainly recorded the name of the craftsman. As no craftsman's name occurs on the shrine of the Misach we cannot be sure if the work was done locally. It seems likely that locally based goldsmiths were involved and this is emphasised by the survival of other major pieces of late medieval goldsmiths' work from the region such as the Cross of Clogher and the ceremonial drinking vessel of the Maguires known as the Dunvegan Cup, both from county Fermanagh, the Domnach Airgid shrine from county Monaghan and the Shrine of St Cailinn from county Leitrim.[263] That some of the main families of the region employed their own goldsmiths is evident from the description in 1479 of Matha Ua Maelruanaidh as 'the master-wright of the Maguire ... and a man of great hospitality and an eminent goldsmith'.[264] It is hard to suggest precise dates for this later work but it appears that the best work is of the fourteenth and fifteenth centuries with a noticeable decline in the sixteenth.

Acknowledgements

I wish to record my thanks to Dr Edel Bhreathnach for bringing a number of important texts to my attention and for much helpful discussion on the secular and ecclesistical politics of Donegal in the eleventh and twelfth centuries. I am grateful to the Trustees of the British Museum for permission to publish plates 4.7-4.8 and to the Trustees of the Wallace Collection for permission to reproduce plates 4.10-4.12.

References

1. B. Lacy, *Archaeological survey of county Donegal* (Lifford, 1983).
2. Harvey, Hill and Young exhibited antiquities at a meeting of the British Association for the Advancement of Science in Belfast in 1852; see *Descriptive catalogue of the collection of antiquities* (Belfast, 1852), pp 35, 40. For the Olphert and Nesbitt collections, see below.
3. Ibid., p. 18, no. 43.
4. For the most recent discussion of early medieval sandhill sites in Ireland see N. Edwards, *The archaeology of early medieval Ireland* (London, 1990), pp 46-7.
5. Lacy, *Archaeological survey*, pp 55-8.
6. The sites producing Mesolithic finds are listed in P.C. Woodman, *The Mesolithic in Ireland: hunter-gatherers in an insular environment*, *B.A.R.*, British Series 58 (Oxford, 1978), pp 285-6.
7. Lacy, *Archaeological survey*, p. 58, no. 229.
8. These are registered as 1959:214 and 1959:216 respectively. They were acquired from Mr Henry Naylor, an antique dealer, of Lower Liffey St, Dublin, as part of a larger collection of antiquities. Although provenanced by Naylor and published as from county Wexford (*R.S.A.I. Jn.*, 91 (1961), fig. 23b, c and p. 98) their shape and dimensions match exactly those of the du Noyer watercolour. Naylor was dealing in antiquities from at least 1920 and the collection acquired in 1959 contained material from other nineteenth-century collectors from the north of Ireland. A county Wexford provenance for these two objects would be unusual in view of the absence of material of similar date from that county. With the exception of the *Bearnán Conaill* from Inishkeel, now in the British Museum, the remainder of the Nesbitt collection, which disappeared in mysterious circumstances c.1845, remains to be identified in modern collections.
9. *U.J.A.*, 4 (1856), p. 240 and 6 (1858), pp 351-3. W.J. Knowles, 'Second report on the remains from the sandhills of the north coast of Ireland' in *R.I.A. Proc.*, 17 (1889-91), pp 614-6 and pl. xxiv. See L.N.W. Flanagan, R.B. Warner and P.C. Woodman, 'Department of antiquities – The Ulster Museum, Belfast archaeological acquisitions of Irish origin for the year 1966' in *U.J.A.*, 31 (1968), pp 44-51. This group of 134 objects, mainly pins and brooches, was formerly in the collection of the Cork collector, Robert Day, and contains some of the Ballyness finds from the Olphert collection.
10. *R.I.A. Proc.*, 7 (1857-61), pp 41, 159.
11. See, for example, I. Crawford and R. Switsur, 'Sandscaping and C14: the Udal, N. Uist' in *Antiquity*, 60 (1977), pp 124-36. For a distribution of *machair* soils in Scotland see B.E. Crawford, *Scandinavian Scotland* (Leicester, 1987), p. 28 and fig. 10.
12. D. Keeling, 'Neolithic and Early Bronze Age artefacts from south-west Donegal' in *Donegal Annual*, pp 55-74.
13. Lacy, *Archaeological survey*, No. 216. The Iron Age and Roman finds published in *U.J.A.*, 13 (1950), pp 54-6 and pl. 6 and *U.J.A.*, 24-25 (1961-62), p. 34 and pl. 11, d,

now in the Ulster Museum, are said to be from sandhills 'near Dunfanaghy'. The finds mentioned in *R.I.A. Proc.*, 22 (1900-2), p. 349, forming part of the group N.M.I. Reg. No. 1934:10399-10405, appear to come from sandhills in Muntermellan townland. One ringed pin and several stick pins of medieval and later date from Pollaguill townland, formerly in the Swan Collection, are in the National Museum (Reg. No. E92:270 and E92:231-243 respectively). Five others in the same collection are labelled as from Dunfanaghy (E92:222-3, 228, 250 and 252). Material in private hands from Tramore Strand, Murroe townland recorded in the National Museum include bronze stick- and ringed pins, a Viking-Age silver ingot and a silver stirrup finger ring of twelfth-or thirteenth- century date.

14. Lacy, *Archaeological survey*, No. 205; *U.J.A.*, 6 (1858), pp 351-3; *R.I.A. Proc.*, 17 (1889-91), pp 614-6 and pl. xxiv.

15. Lacy, *Archaeological survey*, No. 229; Du Noyer watercolour of 1838, see pl. I above.

16. Lacy, *Archaeological survey*, No. 227; *R.S.A.I. Jn.*, 63 (1933), p. 98 and pl. viii; *R.S.A.I. Jn.*, 91 (1961), pp 90-2 and fig. 23a.

17. A.B. Ó Ríordáin and E. Rynne, 'A settlement in the sandhills at Dooey, Co. Donegal' in *R.S.A.I. Jn.*, 91 (1961), pp 58-64; *R.S.A.I. Jn.*, 96 (1966), p. 17 and fig. 5.

18. Lacy, *Archaeological survey*, No. 207; *R.I.A. Proc.*, 7 (1857-61), pp 41, 159. These were recovered from Magheraclogher townland and are now in the National Museum of Ireland and include a hand pin (W.142), toilet implement (W.96), ringed pin (W.324) and stick pins (W.381-2). Finds from Bunbeg consist of an omega pin and a finger ring (1879:21, 22).

19. Lacy, *Archaeological survey*, No. 220. Hand pin: Reg. No. 1959:699.

20. *R.I.A. Proc.*, 22 (1900-2), pp 387-8. The brooch was found 'while pulling bent in sandhills near Castleport, county Donegal.' I have not been able to locate the placename Castleport. The brooch is now in the Ulster Museum.

21. Penannular brooch, N.M.I. Reg. No. 1931:16; see S.P. Ó Ríordáin, 'Recent acquisitions from county Donegal in the National Museum' in *R.I.A. Proc.*, 42C (1934-5), pp 182-3 and C. Newman, 'Fowler's type F3 early medieval penannular brooches' in *Medieval Archaeol.*, 33 (1989), fig. 2.2; stick pin – N.M.I. Reg. No. 1941:528.

22. Lacy, *Archaeological survey*, Nos 214, 215. In Dundooan Lower townland: *R.S.A.I. Jn.*, 32 (1902), p. 227 – stick pin. There is also the pin of a penannular brooch from the same site (N.M.I. Reg. No. 1941:1879).

23. Lacy, *Archaeological survey*, Nos. 225, 310. Ulster Museum Rec. Spec. 1990.38.

24. Not precisely located, these finds could have come from either the Gweedore or Braade/Carrickfin sandhills. *R.I.A. Proc.*, 42 (1934-5), p. 183, fig. 13, 77. Now N.M.I. Reg. No. 1930:556-7.

25. Three stick pins, two with thistle-shaped heads are in the Donegal County Museum (E. Verling pers comm).

26. A disc-headed stick pin, N.M.I. Reg. No. 1956:432.

27. Lacy, *Archaeological survey*, Nos 206, 209. From Braade townland, *R.S.A.I. Jn.*, 100 (1970), p. 156 and fig. 6a, b: *R.S.A.I. Jn.*, 102 (1972), pp 16-7 and fig. 5.

28. Lacy, *Archaeological survey*, No. 210; *R.S.A.I. Jn.*, 63 (1933), p. 252.

29. Ms. catalogue of antiquities in the collection of H. Morris, N.M.I., p. 50. This may be N.M.I. Reg. No. 1941:536.

30. Lacy, *Archaeological survey*, No. 230. Located in Rosapenna and Magheramagorgan townlands; *R.I.A. Proc.*, 19 (1893-6), p. 651; *R.S.A.I. Jn.*, 32 (1902), p. 227 – stick pin and medieval annular brooch.

31. From Moylederg Island, Lough Eske, *U.J.A.*, 9 (1946), p. 94, fig. 3; Bloody Foreland, *U.J.A.*, 13 (1950), p. 87, fig. 4, 3 and Ardpattan, *R.S.A.I. Jn.*, 72 (1942), p. 105, fig. 4.

32. For a preliminary account of the excavations see Ó Ríordáin and Rynne, 'Dooey,' pp 58-64. For a recent interpretation of the chronology of the site see U. O'Meadhra, *Early christian, viking and romanesque art: motif-pieces from Ireland. 2. A discussion*. Theses and papers in north-European archaeology 17 (Stockholm, 1987), pp 36-8.

33. P.J. McGill, 'Notes on shore dwellers and sandhill settlements (Dooey, Lettermacaward, Co. Donegal)' in *Donegal Annual*, 1 (1946), pp 27-31.

34. Ó Ríordáin and Rynne, 'Dooey,' pp 61, 64.

35. The later date is suggested by the presence of a number of ringed- and stick pins from the excavations (Unpublished, National Museum of Ireland).

36. Ó Floinn in S. Youngs (ed.), *The work of angels' Masterpieces of celtic metalwork, 6th-9th centuries* A.D. (London, 1989), pp 174-5, No. 152.

37. N.M.I. Reg. No. E92:259. The lead model was not found in the excavations but was a surface find from the site found in 1963 – see R. Ó Floinn in Youngs (ed.), *The work of angels*, p. 193, No. 185.

38. Ó Ríordáin and Rynne, 'Dooey,' p. 64.

39. For Rinnaraw, see T. Fanning, 'Rinnaraw,' in I. Bennett (ed.), *Excavations 1990* (Dublin, 1991), pp 21-2.

40. B. Lacy, 'Tonbane Glebe' in C. Manning and D. Hurl (ed.), 'Excavations bulletin 1980-84; summary accounts of archaeological excavations in Ireland' in *Jn. Irish Archaeol.*, v (1989/90), p. 74.

41. B. Raftery, *A catalogue of Irish Iron Age antiquities* (Marburg, 1983), Nos 2, 199, 244 and 391.

42. Raftery, *Iron Age antiquities*, No. 391.

43. T.B. Graham and E.M. Jope, 'A bronze brooch and ibex-headed pin from the sandhills at Dunfanaghy, Co. Donegal' in *U.J.A.*, 13 (1950), pp 54-6.

44. D. Bateson, 'Roman material from Ireland: a re-consideration' in *R.I.A. Proc.*, 73C (1973), p. 43.

45. *R.S.A.I. Jn.*, 32 (1902), p. 228.

46. Graham and Jope, 'Bronze brooch,' pl. 6.

47. J. Raftery, 'New early Iron Age finds from Kerry' in *Cork Hist. Arch. Soc. Jn.*, 45 (1940), pl. iv, p. 2 and p. 56. For the ibex-headed pin said to be from county Wexford see note 8 above.

48. R.B.K. Stevenson, 'Pins and the chronology of brochs' in *Proc. Prehist. Soc.*, 21 (1955), p. 291. This latter date is also accepted by R. Warner, 'Early Roman imports in Ireland' in *R.I.A. Proc.*, 76C (1976), p. 289. E. Fowler, 'Celtic metalwork of the fifth and sixth centuries AD: a re-appraisal' in *Archaeol. Jn.*, 120 (1963), pp 123-5 would assign ibex-headed pins to the Sub-Roman period.

49. Warner, 'Early Roman imports,' p. 280.

50. E. Fowler, 'The origins and development of the penannular brooch in Europe' in *Proc. Prehist. Soc.*, 26 (1960), pp 166-7.

51. The type has not yet been fully studied. For a preliminary list and discussion see Fowler, 'Celtic metalwork,' pp 145-6. Omega pins belong to Fowler's Type B3.

52. H. O'Neill Hencken, 'Lagore Crannóg' in *R.I.A. Proc.*, 53C (1950), p. 75 and fig. 17.

53. Ibid., *Cahercommaun, a stone fort in Co. Clare (R.S.A.I. Jn.*, special volume, 1938), p. 37 and fig. 22.

54. M. Ryan and M. Cahill, *Gold aus Irland* (Munich, 1981), No. 49.

55. N. Brady in *Kilian Mönch aus Irland- Aller Franken Patron* Exhibition catalogue (Würzburg, 1989), pp 174-5.

56. All in the National Museum of Ireland: Maghera – 1909: 34; Gweedore W.192; Dooey – 1955: 16 and Glenree – 1959:699.

57. 'Castleport': *R.I.A. Proc.,* 22 (1900-2), pp 387-8 and Inishbofin: *R.I.A. Proc.,* 42 (1934-5), pp 182-3.

58. *R.S.A.I. Jn.,* 63 (1933), p. 98 and pl. viii.

59. *Epitome of reproductions of ancient Celtic ornaments by Edmond Johnson Ltd., 94 Grafton St., Dublin,* p. 21.

60. A drawing of the Cavan Brooch, listed as such, appears on p. 13 of the same catalogue.

61. J. Graham-Campbell, 'Two groups of ninth-century Irish brooches' in *R.S.A.I. Jn.,* 102 (1972), pp 117-121, 124.

62. Youngs (ed.), *The work of angels,* pp 199-200, Nos 194-5.

63. E. Wamers, *Insularer metallschmuck in wikingerzeitlichen Gräbern Nordeuropas* (Neumünster, 1985), Taf. 34.4.

64. There are two others of this type from Gweedore (N.M.I. Reg. No. W.324) and Dunfanaghy (1934:10401). On the date of this type see T. Fanning, 'Some aspects of the bronze ringed pin in Scotland' in A. O'Connor and D.V. Clarke (ed.), *From the stone age to the forty-five* (Edinburgh, 1983), p. 325. Fanning states that the type could date as early as the fifth or sixth century.

65. Ibid., pp 334-42.

66. There is no evidence that the ringed pin from Kinnegar Strand was associated with human remains *pace* Warner in B. Lacy, *Archaeological survey,* pp 8, 66 and repeated in J. Graham-Campbell, 'A Viking-age silver hoard from near Raphoe' in G. MacNiocaill and P.F. Wallace (ed.), *Keimelia- studies in medieval archaeology and history in memory of Tom Delaney* (Galway, 1988), p. 109 and Edwards, *Archaeology of early medieval Ireland,* p. 191.

67. N.M.I. Reg. No. 1941: 534-566.

68. N.M.I. Reg. No. 1978: 248.

69. R. Ó Floinn in Youngs (ed.), *The work of angels,* p. 105, No. 91.

70. J. Graham-Campbell, 'Ninth-century Irish brooches,' pp 124-5 and pl. 19a,b.

71. T. Fanning and R. Crumlish, 'A bronze ringed pin from Ballintemple, Tullaghobegley, Co. Donegal' in *Donegal Annual,* 44 (1992), pp 83-7.

72. A. Mahr, 'The gallóglach axe' in *Galway Arch. Hist. Soc. Jn.,* 18 (1938-9), p. 66 and fig. 2, N.M.I. Reg. No. 1937:3633; D. H. Caldwell, 'Some notes on Scottish axes and long bladed weapons' in D. H. Caldwell (ed.), *Scottish weapons and fortifications 1100-1800* (Edinburgh, 1981), pp 262-276.

73. N.M.I. Reg. No. 1877:27, 28. Formerly in the collection of Mr W. Bloomfield of Castle Caldwell, county Fermanagh.

74. R. Stalley (ed.), *Daniel Grose (c.1766-1838) – the antiquities of Ireland* (Dublin, 1991), p. 168, and pl. 72, 1-3. One of these, from the Bloomfield Collection, is now in the National Museum (Reg. No. 1877:23).

75. J. A. Graham-Campbell, 'The Viking-age silver hoards of Ireland' in B. Almqvist and D. Greene (ed.), *Proceedings of the seventh Viking congress* (Dublin, 1976), pp 39-74; J.A. Graham-Campbell, 'Silver hoard from near Raphoe,' pp 102-11.

76. J. Raftery, 'A hoard of Viking silver bracelets from Co. Donegal' in *R.S.A.I. Jn.,* 99 (1969), pp 133-6.

77. Lacy, *Archaeological survey,* No. 709.

78. Lacy, *Archaeological survey,* No. 789, fig. 68. *Numismatic Chronicle,* n.s. iv (1864), 156.

79. *Numismatic Chronicle,* N.S., iv (1864), 156.

80. Raftery, 'Hoard of Viking silver bracelets,' fig. 1, No. 1966:23. The rune was not noted by Raftery but it can clearly be seen in the drawing of the arm ring.

81. The most recent map of Viking age silver hoards in Ireland is in Edwards, *Archaeology of Early Medieval Ireland*, fig. 88.

82. Graham-Campbell, 'Silver hoard from near Raphoe,' pp 109-10.

83. M. E. Dobbs, 'A poem ascribed to Flann Mac Lonáin' in *Ériu,* 17 (1955), pp 16-34. See also M. E. Dobbs, 'The site Carrickabraghy' in *U.J.A.,* 10 (1947), pp 63-5. I am grateful to Dr Edel Bhreathnach for bringing this text to my attention and for discussing it with me.

84. D. Ó Corráin, 'Nationality and kingship in pre-Norman Ireland' in T.W. Moody (ed.), *Historical Studies,* xi (Belfast, 1978), p. 32.

85. Eichnechán Mac Dálaig was one of only two Cenél Lugdach kings of Cenél Conaill before the Ua Domnaill rise to power at the beginning of the thirteenth century, the other being his father, Dálach Mac Muirchertach, who died in 870 (*A.U.*). Cenél Lugdach thereafter disappear from the annals until the mid-eleventh century.

86. Carrickabraghy townland; see Lacy, *Archaeological survey,* No. 1910.

87. Both places remained as Ó Domhnaill settlements in the later middle ages – for Cenn Maghair see *A.L.C.,* 1461 and 1522 and for Loch Bethach see *A.U.,* 1005 and *A.F.M.,* 1258. According to the Ordnance Survey Letters, p. 103, Ceann Maghair 'is the local name of a considerable tract of country in the north-east of the parish of Kilmacrenan adjoining Mulroy Lough'.

88. The fort may occupy the site of an earlier promontory fort although it is not listed in Lacy, *Archaeological survey.* The latter, p. 56, reports the discovery of 'brass pins' in the sandhills at Dunree but these cannot be traced.

89. A.P. Smyth, *Scandinavian York and Dublin* (New Jersey, 1979), ii, p. 19.

90. Hennessy *A.U.,* i, p. 187, n.11 equates Cenn Ríg with an island called Cuilen Rigi in entries for 732 and 802 and suggests that both are to be identified with Inch Island, off Inishowen in Lough Swilly. There is no reason, however, to suggest that Cenn Ríg and Cuilen Rigi are, in fact, the same place.

91. *Pace* Graham-Campbell, 'Silver hoard from near Raphoe,' p. 109.

92. D. Ó Corráin, *Ireland before the Normans* (Dublin, 1972), p. 94.

93. See J.A. Watt, 'Gaelic polity and cultural identity,' pp 336-40 and K. Nicholls, 'Gaelic society and economy in the high middle ages,' pp 433-5 in A. Cosgrove (ed.), *A new history of Ireland, ii, medieval Ireland 1169-1534* (Oxford, 1987).

94. On the relationship between the two dioceses see A. Gwynn, 'Raphoe and Derry in the twelfth & thirteenth centuries' in *Donegal Annual,* 4 (1959), pp 84-100.

95. *A.U.,* 1180; 1219; 1220; 1233. *A.U.,* 1062 records the death of Maelruanaid Ua Daighri, *prím anmchara tuaisceirt Eirenn,* who may also have been associated with Derry.

96. *A.U.,* 1064, 1206.

97. *Cal. pap. letters,* vii (1417-1431), p. 105, 1420 Geoffry Odoredi; pp 228-9, 1422 Odo Odoreid.

98. W. Reeves, *Acts of Archbishop Colton* (Dublin, 1850), p. 60, note v.

99. Donegal is best summarised in P. Ó Gallachair, 'Coarbs and erenaghs of county Donegal' in *Donegal Annual,* 4 (1960), pp 272-281.

100. Reeves, *Archbishop Colton,* p. 118.

101. *Cal. pap. letters,* vii (1417-1431), p. 96.

102. C. Bourke, 'Early Irish hand-bells' in *R.S.A.I. Jn.,* 110 (1980), pp 52-66 and C. Bourke, *Early Irish bells and bell-shrines* (M.A. thesis, U.C.D., 1980).

103. N.M.I. Reg. No. 1909:78. Illustrated in H.T. Ellacombe, *The church bells of Devon* (Exeter, 1872), p. 369, fig. 16.

104. Its history is outlined by H.S. Crawford, 'Notes on the Irish bell-shrines in the British Museum and the Wallace Collection' in *R.S.A.I. Jn.,* 52 (1922), pp 5-9.

105. *Annals of the kingdom of Ireland,* vi (Dublin, 1856), pp 2372-3, note w. O'Donovan refers to Petrie's (unpublished) lecture on bells which was to have been published in the *Transactions of the Royal Irish Academy.* Lithographs of the shrine were produced, however, showing that the condition of the inscription was much the same as it is today.

106. Ordnance Survey Letters, Donegal, pp 202-3, 206-7.

107. E. Ó Muirgheasa, 'The holy wells of Donegal' in *Béaloideas,* vi (1936), p. 151.

108. Murianus Ó Breslen, rector in 1428, see M. A. Costello, *De annatibus Hiberniae,* i, Ulster (Maynooth and Dublin, 1912), p. 261; Ó Breslen, rector in 1443 see E. Maguire, *A history of the diocese of Raphoe* (Dublin, 1920), i, p. 476.

109. Ó Gallachair, 'Coarbs and erenaghs,' p. 279.

110. Bourke, 'Early Irish hand-bells', p. 59.

111. N.M.I. Reg. No. 1883:122. Ellacombe, *Church bells of Devon,* pp 341-2 and fig. 14.

112. Ó Gallachair, 'Coarbs and erenaghs,' pp 277-8.

113. Two other healing stones are known from the county. The healing stone of St Conall was kept at a site called 'The Relig' near Bruckless; see W. G. Wood Martin, *Traces of the elder faiths of Ireland* (2 vols London, 1902), ii, p. 69 and fig. 18. The Holy Stone of Malin was in the custody of the O'Gormans and also had a curing effect; see B. Bonner, *Our Inis Eoghain heritage* (Dublin, 1972), pp 75-8, 248.

114. H. Morris, 'Some Ulster ecclesiastical bells' in *R.S.A.I. Jn.,* 61 (1931), p. 64 and pl. IIb.

115. Reeves, *Archbishop Colton,* p. 65. Arhalt and Nemias Odufaghy were vicars of Culdaff in the early fifteenth century: *Cal. pap. letters.,* vii, 1417-31, pp 395-6.

116. Little is known of this saint but his feast day is 22 July which suggest that he is associated with Mobiu (Mobhí) of Inis Cuscraigh (Inch, county Down), see Ó Muirgheasa, 'Holy wells of Donegal,' pp 159-60. This is hardly plausible. The Ó Cléirigh Saints' genealogies mention a *Baodain Cluana Dobhair* alias *Mobaoi* associated with Killeigh, county Offaly whose feast day is 13 December; see P. Walsh, *Genealogiae regum et sanctorum Hiberniae* (Maynooth and Dublin, 1918) p. 105. B. Bonner, 'Sidelights on the parishes of Culdaff and Clonca' in *Donegal Annual,* 9 (1970), pp 224-6 and Bonner, *Inish Eoghain heritage,* pp 83-4, 87-9 cites local tradition that the saint accompanied Colmcille to Scotland suggesting that he may be identified with Baíthéne, the saint's first cousin and successor as abbot of Iona.

117. *R.I.A. Proc.,* 5 (1850), p. 260; J. McLelland, 'The bell of St Mura' in *U.J.A.,*1 (1853), pp 274-5; Crawford, 'Notes on Irish bell shrines', pp 4-5.

118. W. J. Doherty, *Inishowen and Tirconnell* (Dublin, 1895) 2nd ed., p. 337, n. 1, quoting a letter of McLelland as his source. Other accounts appear to suggest that Reynolds was the fisherman from whom the bell was bought but this appears to be incorrect.

119. A. Spence, 'The antiquities of Fahan in Inish-Eogain' in *U.J.A.,* 17 (1911), p. 23; H. P. Swan, 'Historical associations of Fahan' in *Donegal Annual,* 5 (1962), p. 145.

120. Dated 21 May 1902 from a J. Knox of Dublin.

121. B. Bonner, 'Mac Colgan: airchinneach of Domhnach Mór Mhaigh Ithe' in *Donegal Annual,* 39 (1987), p. 25.

122. Ó Gallachair, 'Coarbs and erenaghs,' p. 274. Bonner, 'Mac Colgan: airchinneach' p. 25 renders the name Healy as *Mac Céile.*

123. F. Henry, *Irish Art in the romanesque period 1020-1170* (London,1970), pp 93-4; R. Ó Floinn, 'Schools of metalworking in eleventh- and twelfth-century Ireland' in M. Ryan (ed.), *Ireland and insular art A.D 500-1200* (Dublin, 1987), pp 180-1.

124. Bourke, 'Early Irish hand-bells,' pp 54-5.

125. P. Ó Riain, *Corpus genealogiarum sanctorum Hiberniae* (Dublin, 1985), p. 620: *Mura Othna Móre m. Feradaigh m. Ronain m. Eogain Merchruim m. Muredaig m. Eogain m. Neill Noigiallaig.*

126. *A.U.*, 1074, 1098 and 1136. Caínchomhrach Ua Cel... of the Cenél Eógain described as 'celibate, priest and favourite disciple of Máel Isu Ua Brolcháin' may have been of this family (*A.I.*,1091).

127. M. A. O'Brien, *Corpus genealogiarum Hiberniae* (Dublin, 1976), p. 135 (140a46).

128. Ellacombe, *Church bells of Devon*, p. 346 and fig. 22. Doherty, *Inishowen and Tirconnell*, pp 329-330 calls it the 'Bell of St Ernan of Drumholm' and H. Morris, 'Some Ulster ecclesiastical bells,' pp 63-4 and pl. d, calls it 'The Ballymagroarty bell.'

129. Doherty, *Inishowen and Tirconnell*, pp 337-8. H. S. Crawford, 'The crosses and slabs of Inishowen' in *R.S.A.I. Jn.*, 45 (1915), pp 196-7 refers to the find place as 'Keenaglug'. Both state that the McColgans kept the bell at Priestown. This is Priest Town, a small settlement 1km north-east of Carndonagh.

130. Presented on 13 December, 1847 by J. Connellan Deane, *R.I.A. Proc.*, 4 (1847-50), p. 24 where it is stated that the bell was acquired from an O'Donnell.

131. Bourke, *Bells and bell-shrines*, p. 223.

132. N.M.I. Reg. Nos. W. 12 and W. 20. Doherty's measurements, however, do not correspond exactly to either of these, nor does it correspond to the Devenish bell (Reg. No. P.1009) illustrated in M. Rogers, *Prospect of Erne* (Enniskillen, 1967), p. 55.

133. There is a church bell of fifteenth- or sixteenth-century date called the 'Sancta Maria bell' in the Protestant church at Donaghmore which has a Gothic inscription identifying its maker as 'Ricardus Pottar de Vrucin' which is likely to be of continental manufacture – see W. J. Doherty, 'Some ancient crosses and other antiquities of Inishowen, county Donegal' in *R.I.A. Proc.*, 18 (1891-3), pp 103-4. This could be the bell referred to in the 1609 Inquisition and also in Bishop Montgomery's Survey of 1607-9 of Derry, Raphoe and Clogher which, in describing Carndonagh, states 'In that place is a good bell', see *Anal. Hib.*, 12 (1943), p. 97.

134. Doherty, 'Some ancient crosses,' p. 115.

135. Quoted in Milligan, 'Ancient ecclesiastical bells in Ulster,' p. 49. This lecture was never published.

136. Ordnance Survey Letters, Donegal, pp 208, 212-6. It may be significant that the wife of Muirchertach mac Erca – the reputed sixth-century king of Tara who appears in a number of late texts linked with Colmcille – was called Duaibhseach.

137. D. Wilson, *Prehistoric annals of Scotland* (2nd ed., 2 vols, London and Cambridge, 1863), ii, pp 462-4. However, an alternative tradition states that this bell was found among the ruins of an unnamed church by one of the McGuirks; see S. Lewis, *A topographical dictionary of Ireland* 2 vols (London, 1837), ii, p. 620.

138. W. Stokes, *The Life and labours in art and archaeology of George Petrie, LL.D, M.R.I.A.* (London, 1868), p. 206.

139. *M.I.A.*, 1178.

140. *Acta sanctorum veteris et maioris Scotiae seu Hiberniae* (Louvain, 1645 reprinted Dublin, 1948), p. 587. Translated in Ordnance Survey Letters, Donegal, p. 35.

141. Petrie Collection MS Catalogue. The relevant entries, ii, pp 2-3, dictated by Petrie's daughter read: P.1015 *'Crozier of Saint Muruss of Fahan, Co. Donegal –*

patron saint of the O'Neills – Celtic ornamental design interlacing. At the time Colgan wrote the life of this saint, his shrine and books were in existence as well as his crozier, chain and bell. The shrine and books have been destroyed – the bell was bought for the British Museum for fifty pounds, and the chain in the museum of my father, to whom they were presented by Mr Woods of Sligo.' P.1015 *'Chain of Saint Murus'*. There are some inaccuracies in this account: the crozier, chain and bell of St Mura are not mentioned by Colgan and the bell was acquired by the Wallace Collection, not by the British Museum. Of Mr Woods nothing further is known but a William Abbott Woods, Hide Merchant, Leather Seller, Seedsman and Tanner of 7 Castle St., Sligo is the only Woods mentioned in the contemporary commercial directories and may have been Petrie's source – see *I. Slater's national commercial directory of Ireland* (Manchester and London, 1846), pp 139-40.

142. Stokes, *Life of George Petrie*, pp 303-4.
143. W. J. Doherty, 'The abbey of Fahan' in *R.I.A. Proc.*, 15 (1879-88), pp 98-9.
144. Henry, *Irish art*, p. 114; Ó Floinn, 'Schools of metalworking,' p. 185.
145. Chain mail consisting exclusively of riveted brass rings did not become common until *c.*1400; see D. Tweddle, *The anglian helmet from 16-22 Coppergate* (York, 1992), p. 1080.
146. McLelland, 'Bell of St Mura,' p. 274; Ellacombe, *Church bells of Devon*, p. 363.
147. R. H. Brash, 'The sculptured crosses of Ireland, what we learn from them' in *R.S.A.I. Jn.*, 12 (1872-3), p. 106.
148. C. Bourke, 'Irish croziers of the eighth and ninth centuries' in M. Ryan (ed.), *Ireland and insular art A.D. 500-1200* (Dublin, 1987), p. 168.
149. Ibid., p. 168.
150. *R.I.A. Proc.*, 5 (1850-3), pp 206-7.
151. *Descriptive catalogue of the collection of antiquities and other objects, illustrative of Irish history, exhibited in the museum, Belfast* (Belfast, 1852), p. 5, no. 37 and p. 39, no. 20 respectively.
152. J. O'Donovan, *Annals of the Kingdom of Ireland*, iv, pp 876-7, note d.
153. Stokes, *Life of George Petrie*, p. 240; R. Ó Floinn, 'The Soiscél Molaisse' in *Clogher Record*, 13, no. 2 (1989), p. 51.
154. J.H. Todd and W. Reeves (ed.), *Martyrology of Donegal* (Dublin 1864), xli-ii.
155. Ó Floinn, 'Schools of metalworking,' p. 185 where the closest objects are a crozier head perhaps from county Kilkenny and St Senan's Bell Shrine from Scattery Island, county Clare.
156. C. Vallancey, *Collectanea de rebus hibernicis* (Dublin, 1786), iv, pp 68-71 and pl. xiii. It is also illustrated in G. Petrie, 'Historic sketch of the past and present state of the fine arts in Ireland' in *Dublin Penny Jn.*, i, No. 11 (1832), pp 83-4. I am grateful to my colleague, Mr Paul Mullarkey, for bringing this to my attention.
157. Reg. No. 1920: 19.
158. *Dublin Penny Journal*, i, No. 52 (1833), pp 412-3. Petrie, *Christian inscriptions*, ii, pp 119-20 and fig. 102. For the inscription see M. Ní Bhrolcháin, 'Maol Íosa Ó Brolcháin: his work and family' in *Donegal Annual*, 38 (1986), p. 9.
159. H.J. Lawlor, 'The Cathach of St Columba' in *R.I.A. Proc.*, 33 (1916), pp 241, 443.
160. A full bibliography on the manuscript is contained in J. G. Alexander, *Insular manuscripts – 6th to the 9th century* (London, 1978), pp 28-9.
161. For the significance of the inscription see below.
162. The best description of the shrine is contained in Lawlor 'The Cathach,' pp 390-6. The work on the front of the Cathach is comparable to that on other dated fourteenth-century metalwork such as the Shrine of the Stowe Missal, the

Domnach Airgid and the Shrine of St Patrick's Tooth; see Mahr and Raftery, *Christian art in ancient Ireland*, 2 vols (Dublin, 1932 and 1941), pls. 65, 115 and 119-20 respectively.

163. *A.F.M.*, 1497, 1499, 1567.
164. J. Colgan, *Triadis thaumaturgae seu divorum Patriccii, Columbae, et Brigidae ... acta* (Louvain, 1647), p. 495.
165. Lawlor, 'The Cathach,' pp 243-5.
166. Ordnance Survey Letters, county Mayo, i, pp 333-5.
167. Ibid., pp 156-7.
168. Ibid., pp 216-7.
169. G. Petrie, *Christian inscriptions in the Irish language*, M. Stokes (ed.) (2 vols, Dublin, 1878), ii, p. 91.
170. W. Reeves, *The life of St Columba* (Dublin and Edinburgh, 1857), p. 320. Also J. F. Kenney, *The sources of the early history of Ireland: ecclesiastical* (New York, 1929), p. 629, n. 8. Manus O'Donnell makes no mention of it when he refers to the Great Cross of St Colmcille as being the chief relic of the saint on Tory (see below). The Tory Island surname in any case is Ó Robhartaigh (O'Rorty) and not Mac Robhartaigh.
171. Henry, *Irish art*, p. 90.
172. M. Herbert, *Iona, Kells and Derry* (Oxford, 1988), p. 93.
173. Dr Maguire, *History of the diocese of Raphoe* (2 vols, Dublin, 1920), i, 412-3, ii, pp 349-50; R.S. Ó Cochláin, 'The Cathach, Battle Book of the O'Donnells' in *The Irish Sword*, 8 (1968), p. 161. There is some confusion over where exactly this crypt was. Maguire and Ó Cochláin say this is at Ballymagrorty Church (Ballymagrorty Scotch townland); see Lacy, *Archaeological survey*, No. 1518. This is the site of *Rath Cunga*, an early ecclesiastical Patrician foundation, later brought under Columban control (A. Gwynn and R. N. Hadcock, *Medieval religious houses, Ireland* (London, 1970), pp 374, 400. Davies erroneously locates this crypt in the townland of Ballymagrorty Irish; see Lacy, *Archaeological survey*, No. 1598.
174. Ó Cochláin, 'The Cathach,' pp 161-2.
175. The inscription reads: *Oroit do [Chat]bharr Ua Domhnaill lasin dernad in cumtachsa ⁊ do Sittruic Mac Meic Aeda dorigne 7 do Dom[nall] mac [Rob]artaig do comarba Cenansa lasin dernad.*
176. Henry, *Irish art*, pp 89-90. His obit in *A.U.* states that he was *comarba Coluimcille fri ré*, that is 'successor of Colmcille for a long time.'
177. G. Mac Niocaill, *Notitiae as Leabhar Cheanannais* (Galway, 1962), pp 13-4. Mac Niocaill suggests that Domnall mac Robartaig retired to Derry as abbot and that the title *comarba Coluim Cille* in his obit was an honorary one given to abbots of the main monasteries of the Columban *familia.* It is therefore still possible that the shrine was made at any time up to his death in 1198. See also Herbert, *Iona, Kells and Derry*, p. 93.
178. Gwynn and Hadcock, *Medievial religious houses,* p. 94, for example, state that the abbots of Raphoe were given the title *comarba Coluim Cille & Adomnain* but only in the case of Maelduin (+817 *A.U.*) is Raphoe specifically mentioned. All the others were, in fact, abbots of Kells. Whether they were abbots of Raphoe at the same time is open to question. See Herbert, *Iona, Kells and Derry*, p. 80 on this question.
179. Reeves, *St Columba*, pp 400-1.
180. There are three townlands, Ballymagrorty, Ballymagrorty Irish and Ballymagrorty Scotch in the parish (O.S. 6" Sheet 103).
181. County Derry O.S. 6" Sheets 13, 20.

182. Gwynn and Hadcock, *Medieval religious houses*, p. 374.

183. *A.U.*, 921; Herbert, *Iona, Kells and Derry*, pp 73-4. For his genealogy see O'Brien, *Corpus*, p. 164 (144f 18).

184. Herbert, *Iona, Kells and Derry*, pp 91-3.

185. Ibid., p. 99.

186. Kenney, *Sources*, pp 616-7. The annals mention an abbot of Durrow, Diarmait Ua Robartaigh, who died in 1190 *(A.U.)* and another Ua Robartaigh, airchinneach of Connor, who died in 1081 (*A.U.*) but it is unclear what connection, if any, they had with the mac Robartaigh family of Kells.

187. From Dálach mac Muirchertaigh, chief of Cenél Conaill who was slain by his own sept in 870 (*A.U.*). Cathbarr's own genealogy is preserved; see M.A. O'Brien, *Corpus*, p. 164 (144 f 1).

188. See table in Byrne, *Irish kings and high kings*, p. 258.

189. Herbert, *Iona, Kells and Derry*, p. 74.

190. *A.U.*, 1011; 1038; 1100; 1106.

191. *A.U.*, 1106; 1100; *A.I.*, 1100.

192. T. Cannon, 'A history of the O'Cannons of Tir Chonaill', *Donegal Annual*, 12, 2 (1978), p. 291.

193. *A.U.*, 1062; 1070.

194. *A.U.*, 1093; 1098; 1113.

195. B. Lacy, 'The development of Derry, 600-1600' in Mac Niocaill and Wallace (ed.), *Keimelia*, pp 383-4; Herbert, *Iona, Kells and Derry*, pp 110-3.

196. *Ann. Tig.*, 1090: *M. Coluim Cille i. Clog na Rígh ocus an Chuilebaigh, ocus in da sosscéla do tabairt a Tir Chonaill, ocus seht fichit uinge d'airged, ocus Aenghus Ua Domnallán isse dos-fuc atuaidh.* Ua Domhnalláin's genealogy has not been preserved but he was a member of the community of Kells and died in 1109 (*A.U.*).

197. The word *cuilebad* means a flabellum, not a tunic, as in Henry, *Irish art*, p. 90, see *R.I.A. dictionary of the Irish language: C*, p. 587.

198. *Irish art*, pp 93-4. Henry curiously makes no reference to the gospel books as being listed in the *A. Tig.* entry.

199. T. Ó Canann, 'Trí saorthuatha Mhuintire Chanannáin: a forgotten medieval placename' in *Donegal Annual*, 38 (1986), p. 39. The mac Robhartaigh were never to become *airchennaigh* of Drumhome; the 1609 Inquisition states that the erenagh family was the O'Dorrianun. A Domhnall Ua Robhartaigh who was prior of the nearby Cistercian monastery of Assaroe was rector of Drumhome in 1425: Costello, *De annatibus*, pp 259-60.

200. *A.U.* 1197; Ó Canann, 'Trí saorthuatha Mhuinntire Chanannáin,' p. 38.

201. *Bk. Fen.* The original text, according to the editors (p. vi) 'must have been compiled ... about or previous to AD 1300.' T. Ó Cannan, 'Trí saorthuatha mhuinntire Channanáin,' p. 34 reckons that it was compiled during the reign of Domnall Óg Ó Domnaill (1258-81).

202. *Bk. Fen.*, pp 166, 168.

203. *A.L.C.*, 1242.

204. *Bk. Fen.*, p. 194. Of the *Cethir lebor* nothing more is known unless it is the shrine known as the 'Shrine of St Caillin' now preserved in the Diocesan Museum in Longford; see D. Murphy, 'The shrine of St Caillin of Fenagh' in *R.S.A.I. Jn.*, 22 (1892), pp 151-3. The monastery of Fenagh was in possession of another northern relic – a bell called *Clog na Rí* which tradition states originally belonged to the Cenél Eógain and which was given to Caillin by St Patrick; see *Bk. Fen.* pp 140, 232-8. This bell is now preserved at Foxfield, near Mohill, county Leitrim;

see J. Hynes, 'St Caillin' in *R.S.A.I. Jn.*, 61 (1931), pp 39-54. This bell is referred to as being present at Fenagh in *A.F.M.*, 1244, that is, roughly contemporary with the poem describing Colmcille's gift of the Cathach and other objects.

205. L. Nic Dhonnchada (ed.) *Aided Muirchertaig Meic Erca* (Dublin, 1964); F. J. Byrne, 'Historical note on Cnogba (Knowth)' in *R.I.A Proc.*, 66C (1967-8), p. 394, n. 46. I am grateful to Dr Edel Bhreathnach for helpful discussion of this and other texts relating to the Cathach.

206. K. McCone, *Pagan past and Christian present* (Maynooth, 1990), p. 147.

207. Nic Dhonnchada (ed.), *Aided Muirchertaig Meic Erca*. The relevant section, par.12, reads: *Ro bennaig Cairnech iat ⁊ ro fhágaib fágbála dóib .i. do c[h]landaib Conaill ⁊ Eógain ... ⁊ co rabat trí mergi acu .i. in Chatach ⁊ in Clog .i. in udachta Pádraig, in Mísach C[h]airnig ...* See also Henry, *Irish art*, p. 90.

208. Henry, *Irish art*, pp 94-7.

209. *Chron. Scot.*, 1130.

210. Reeves, *St Columba*, pp 332-4. The origin of the name of Colmcille's *cathbuaid* is explained in an undated entry in the Osraige Chronicle – see J. N. Radner (ed.), *Fragmentary annals of Ireland* (Dublin, 1978), p. 170.

211. *Z.C.P.*, 19 (1937), p. 120. I am grateful to Dr Edel Bhreathnach for this reference.

212. K. Hughes, *Early Christian Ireland: introduction to the sources* (Cambridge, 1972), p. 243.

213. Herbert, *Iona, Kells and Derry*, p. 23 (translated p. 257).

214. *A.U.*, 1166. See also Herbert, *Iona, Kells and Derry*, pp 190-1. The episode is treated in more expansive form in *Misc. Ir. Annals* under the year 1165 (recte 1166); see below.

215. B. Lacy, 'The development of Derry, 1600,' pp 387, 395. Lacy has made the ingenious suggestion that the cult of Martin may have arisen from a similarity between the Irish word for Tours – *Toirinis* – and Tory Island; see B. Lacy, *Siege city: The story of Derry and Londonderry* (Belfast, 1990), p. 43.

216. *A.U.*, 1182.

217. Herbert, *Iona, Kells and Derry*, p. 193.

218. K. Simms, *From kings to warlords* (Woodenbridge, 1987), pp 28-9.

219. E. C. R. Armstrong and H. J. Lawlor, 'The reliquary known as the Misach' in *R.S.A.I. Jn.*, 52 (1922), pp 105-12.

220. E. O'Curry, *Lectures on the manuscript materials of ancient Irish history* (Dublin, 1861), p. 336; Petrie, *Christian inscriptions*, p. 102; *R.I.A. dictionary of the Irish language:* M, p. 148. However, the accepted derivation of the word is by no means certain, as it appears to be otherwise unknown. It is possible that the word *Misach* could perhaps be derived from the Latin *mensa* / Irish *mias*, suggesting that the object may originally have been a portable altar, and later adapted as a book shrine. Enshrined portable altars were known elsewhere in Ireland, see for example references to the altar of Ciarán of Clonmacnoise and the marble altar of St Patrick, the latter preserved at Christchurch Cathedral, Dublin in R. Ó Floinn 'Innovation and conservatism in Irish metalwork of the Romanesque period' in C. Karkov and M. Ryan (eds), *Studies in insular art and archaeology* (American Early Medieval Studies: Oxford, Ohio), forthcoming.

221. Petrie, *Christian inscriptions*, ii, pp 102-3. It reads: *Brian mac Briain i Muirgiussa do cumdaig me AD MCCCCCXXXIIII.*

222. Reeves, *Archbishop Colton*, p. 45.

223. Armstrong and Lawlor, 'The Misach,' pp 109-12. See also Stokes, *Life of George Petrie*, pp 291-3.

224. *A.F.M.*, 1516.

225. Reeves, *Archbishop Colton*, p. 45.
226. David Omurgisan, rector of Clonmany and Clonca 1417: *Cal. Pap. Letters*, vii, p. 96; Solomon Omuirgisan, 1426: Costello, *De Annatibus*, p. 189; Rouelinus O'Muirgessan, 1455: *Cal. Pap. Letters*, xi, p. 284.
227. Clonca: 1417, David Omurgisan, *Cal. Pap. Letters*, vii, p. 96; 1447, Henry O'Murigesa, *Cal. Pap. Letters*, x, 287; 1470, Comedinus Omurgyssan, Costello, *De Annatibus*, p. 199. Fahan: 1412, Metrach Omuirgissan, *Cal. Pap. letters*, vi, p. 255. Culduff: 1429, Henry Omuirgissan, *Cal. Pap. Letters*, vii, p. 124.
228. Henricus Ó Morrisson, rector of Donaghmore, 1438-40; Magonius O'Murrgsa, vicar of Termonamongan, county Tyrone, 1466; William O'Moryssa, rector of Longfield (*Leamcoill*), county Tyrone, 1508 – J. B. Leslie, *Derry clergy and parishes* (Enniskillen, 1937), pp 198, 222, 247.
229. Leslie, *Derry clergy and parishes*, pp 68-72. Henry was also vicar of Culdaff and rector of Clonca.
230. K. Meyer, 'The Laud genealogies and tribal histories' in *Z.C.P.*, 8 (1912), p. 297. The Rawl. B502 genealogy for Cenél Tigernaigh is more complete and lists the eponymous ancestor, Muirgius, as a descendant of Tigernach – see O'Brien, *Corpus*, p. 180 (146 d 41).
231. O'Brien, *Corpus*, p. 134 (140 a 7-9).
232. *Bk. Fen.*, pp 332-3.
233. J. Carney (ed.), *Topographical poems* (Dublin, 1943), p. 8 (lines 207-8).
234. E. Hogan, *Onomasticon Goidelicum* (Dublin and London, 1910) pp 223, 411.
235. B. Bonner, *Where Aileach guards* (Dublin, 1974), p. 91, citing local tradition, says that there is an early church site called Boharny (*Both Chairnigh*) in Clonmany parish. This is not marked on the Ordnance Survey maps.
236. *Misc. Ir. Annals*, 1165.2: *Muircheartach mac Neil h. Lochlainn, ri Oilidh, do gabhail Eochadha mic Con Uladh Mic Duinn [Sh]leibe, ri Uladh, a cairdis Crist fein, a Camus Cumguill na tigh casga iar mbeith doibh fa aenmeis oidid gonuigi sin, ⁊ a breith lais gu hInis Aenaigh ⁊ a dalladh ann sin tar slanaigacht cumarba Padraic ⁊ na Bacla Isa ⁊ Cluig an Udhachta ⁊ Sosgela Marta[in] ⁊ Misaighi Cairnigh ⁊ na Tri Sgrin a Teampoll na Sgrin go minnaibh tuaisgirt Ereann umpu...*
237. E. Ó Doibhlin, 'O'Neills "own country" and its families' in *Senchas Ardmhacha*, 6, 1 (1971), pp 14-5. Colgan, *Acta Sanctorum*, pp 782-4 (quoted by Gwynn and Hadcock, *Medieval religious houses*, pp 33, 377) states that the church of Donaghmore, 10km south-east of Clonleigh, was also dedicated to Cairnech. Both churches however, have other foundation traditions. The patron saint of Clonleigh is said to be Lughaid, one of Colmcille's missionaries, while Donaghmore is said to be a Patrician foundation – see Leslie, *Derry clergy and parishes*, pp 159, 200.
238. J. H. Todd, *The Irish version of the Historia Britonum of Nennius* (Dublin, 1848), p. cix; *A.F.M.*, vi, pp 2426-30.
239. Cairnech's genealogy in the Book of Lecan gives his father as Sarán and his mother as Bébona, daughter of Loarn and sister of Erc. See Ó Riain, *Corpus*, p. 90.
240. E. Ó Doibhlin, 'O'Neills "own country" and its families,' pp 14-5.
241. *Bk. Fen.*, p. 338; Todd, *Historia Britonum*, pp ci-cx.
242. J. Carney, *Studies in Irish literature and history* (Dublin, 1955), pp 407-12.
243. W. Stokes, *Félire Oengusso* (London, 1905), p. 124: *Cairnig. i. a Tuilen. Cairnech do Bretnaib Corrn dó*, p. 132: *Cairnech o Thuilen hi fail Cenansa nar rig*. For further information on this saint see Nic Dhonnchadha, *Aided Muirchertaig Meic Erca*, pp xv-xvi and 71 and Kenney, *Sources*, pp 351-2.

244. *A.U.*, 969. The editors of *A.U.* mistakenly take the phrase *comarba Cairnigh* to refer to the abbot of Clonleigh, county Donegal. It is clear from a previous entry in *A.U.*, 945 recording the death of Maeltuile mac Dúnáin *comarba Tighernaigh ocus Cairnigh* that the term relates to the abbots of Dulane – see D. Ó Corráin, 'Mael Muire Ua Dúnáin (1040-117), Reformer' in P. de Brún, S. Ó Coileáin and P. Ó Riain (ed.), *Folia Gadelica* (Cork, 1983), pp 51-2.

245. Herbert, *Iona, Kells and Derry*, pp 85-9.

246. *A.U.*, 1034: *Maicnia Ua Uchtáin fer leiginn Cenannsa, do bathad ic tiachtain a hAlbain, 7 culebad Coluim Cille 7 tri minna do minnaib Patraicc 7 tricha fer impu.*

247. *Ann. Tig.*, 1090.

248. Donaghmore possessed other important relics in the twelfth century: the 'relics of Donaghmore' were present along with those of Ardstraw and St Ernan of Urney as witnesses to the peace made between Ua Cairellain and Ua Gairmledaigh in 1179 (*A.U.*).

249. See T. Olden, 'On the Culebath' in *R.I.A. Proc.*, 16 (1879-88), pp 355-8; O'Curry, *Lectures on the manuscript materials*, pp 332-5, where references to other Irish *cuilebaid* are to be found.

250. Kenney, *Sources*, pp 447-8.

251. A. G. Van Hamel (ed.), *Immrama* (Dublin, 1941), pp 78-85.

252. Lacy, *Archaeological survey*, No. 1532, pl. 25. See also Ibid., figs. 140, 158, and pls. 42 and 62 for other possible representations of flabella. For sculptural representations elsewhere, see F. Henry, *Irish art in the early christian period (to A.D. 800)* (London, 1965), pp 118, 120, 130 and fig. 14.

253. *A.L.C.*, 1196.

254. *A.L.C.*, 1177.

255. *A.U.*, 1214.

256. A. O'Kelleher and G. Schoepperle, *Betha Colaim Chille* (Urbana, 1918); Reeves, *St Columba*, pp 318-9; Maguire, *Diocese of Raphoe*, ii, pp 291-4.

257. *A.F.M.*, 1542.

258. C. McNeill, 'The Perrot Papers' in *Anal. Hib.*, 12 (1943), p. 12. See also *R.S.A.I. Jn.*, 17 (1885-6), p. 140.

259. *A.F.M.*, 1397; *A.F.M.*, *A.U.*, 1411.

260. *Archiv. Hib.*, ii (1913), pp 294-5. See also a translation in Maguire, *Diocese of Raphoe*, i, pp 11-17. I am grateful to Dr Edel Bhreathnach for this reference.

261. W. Reeves, 'On an ancient inscribed shrine-arch' in *R.S.A.I. Jn.*, 10 (1868-9), pp 353-6.

262. I. B. Cowen, 'Early Ecclesiastical Foundations' in P. McNeill and R. Nicholson (eds.) *An Historical Atlas of Scotland c.400-c.1600* (St Andrews, 1975), pp 17-9 and map 15.

263. For the Cross of Clogher, the Domnach Airgid and the Shrine of St Caillin, see Raftery, *Christian art*, ii. pl. 110, pls. 115-8 and pl. 126 respectively.

264. *A.U.*, 1479: *Matha hUa Mailruanaigh d'eg in bliadhain si, idon, ollam cerda Meg Uidhir ... 7 fer tighi aidhedh...*

Chapter 5

PLACENAMES AND EARLY SETTLEMENT IN COUNTY DONEGAL

DÓNALL MAC GIOLLA EASPAIG

County Donegal was one of the last of the counties of Ireland to be established by the English administration in the sixteenth century. The order of the first of September 1585, under which the county was created, declares:

> The meets and boundes, lymytts and precincts of the countye of Donnyngall, as foloweth:-
> Firste, it conteynath the whole countrye of O'Donell and all that surname.
> Item, it conteynath O'Doghertye's countrye, meeringe upon Lye-fferr-ffynne, and Farmanaghe, towards the southe.
> Item, it extendeth eastwarde and northwarde, uppon the mayne sea.
> Item, it also extendeth and joyneth uppon the countye of Slygo towards the weste.
> Finallye, the towne of Donnyngall is the only place for her majestie's gaole and sheere towne, for her highnes' cessions and jaile deliverye, within the said countye of Donnyngall.[1]

The 'countrye of O'Donell' above refers to the historic territory of Tír Chonaill, which comprised all of the present county of Donegal excluding the Inishowen peninsula. This area is more usually referred to in sixteenth century English sources as Tireconnell, or one of the other variant anglicisations of Tír Chonaill. 'O'Doghertye's country' was co-extensive with the whole peninsula of Inishowen, including the portion of the city and county of Derry which lies on the west bank of the River Foyle. These two territories are connected physically by the narrow neck of land which separates Lough Foyle and Lough Swilly. Despite this geographical link, however, the two regions have followed separate political paths for most of their history, with Inishowen looking southwards and eastwards to Tyrone and Derry rather than westwards towards Tír Chonaill. This historical fact is reflected in the current ecclesiastical divisions under which Inishowen forms part of the diocese of Derry while the rest of the county is in the diocese of Raphoe.

Whatever about their long-standing mutual animosity, the names of these two territories, Inishowen and Tír Chonaill, are actually related from both the historical and onomastic standpoint. From the early historical period, the present county of Donegal was dominated by two branches of the Uí Néill dynasty, *Cinéal Eoghain*, 'the kindred of Eoghan', and *Cinéal Conaill*, 'the kindred of Conall'. According to the genealogies Eoghan and Conall were sons of Niall Naoighiallach 'Niall of the nine hostages', the eponymous ancestor of the Uí Néill, who was reputedly king of Tara in the fourth century. Evidence suggests, however, that the Uí Néill originated in Connacht, probably at Rathcroaghan in Roscommon, from where various branches of the dynasty expanded eastwards into the midlands and northwards into Sligo and Donegal.[2] Conall is usually referred to as *Conall Gulban* 'Conall of Gulban' his epithet being the same word as that found in the placename *Binn Ghulban*, now Benbulbin in Sligo, a fact which would support a western provenance for the dynasty.

By the sixth century, the northern Uí Néill had gained political domination over the whole of the present county and were already expanding southward. The two principal branches, Cinéal Eoghain and Cinéal Conaill, are first mentioned in the *Annals of Ulster* under the year 563 when they are recorded as taking part in the great battle of Móin Daire Lothair: *Bellum Mona Daire Lothair for Cruithniu re nUib Neill in Tuaisceirt. Baetan m. Cinn co ndib Cruithnibh nod-fich fri Cruithniu, Genus Eugain 7 Conaill mercede conducti inna Lee 7 Airde Eolargg.* (The battle of Móin Daire Lothair was won over the Cruithin by the Ui Néill of the North. Baetán son of Cenn with two branches of the Cruithin fight it against the Cruithin. Cenél nEógain and Cenél Conaill were hired, being given the Lee and Ard Eolarg as recompense.) The placename *Móin Doire Lothair* is no longer extant, but from the context it apparently lay in the present county Derry. *Ard Eolarg*, one of the places which the Uí Néill were given for their participation in the battle, is now Magilligan, which lies on the Derry side of the entrance to Lough Foyle.

Cinéal Eoghain and *Inis Eoghain*

The Cinéal Eoghain established their headquarters at Aileach in Inishowen and initially their territory did not extend beyond the bounds of that peninsula. As mentioned above, however, they were already expanding southward and eastward into the present counties of Derry and Tyrone from the mid-sixth century. The Cinéal Eoghain were arguably the most powerful political dynasty in Ireland in early medieval times; eighteen of the high-kings of Tara beween the sixth and the twelfth centuries belonged to that dynasty.[3] In the later period, their descendants, notably the O'Neills, dominated the politics of Ulster until the Plantation of Ulster. Although originally the name of a ruling family, Cinéal Eoghain also referred to the territory ruled by that family, especially in the later medieval period. The name is found with territorial reference in the anglicised form *Keneleon* in an Anglo-Norman document under the year 1235.[4] From the tenth century, the wider territory of the Cinéal Eoghain became known as *Tír Eoghain*, 'the land of Eoghan', from which county Tyrone derives its name. The name of the original territory of the sept, *Inis Eoghain*, 'the island of Eoghan', Inishowen is first recorded in the eighth century in a curious entry in the annals: *Tri frosa do ferthain i Crich Muiredaigh i nInis Eugain .i. fross do argut ghil 7 fros do cruithniucht 7 fros do mhil.* (Three showers fell in Críoch Muireadhaigh in Inishowen, i.e. a shower of pure silver, a shower of wheat, and a shower of honey).[5] The peninsula is also sometimes referred to in the sources as *Tír Eoghain na hInse*, 'Tír Eoghain of the island'.[6]

Cinéal Conaill and *Tír Chonaill*

The territory of the Cinéal Conaill comprised west and south Donegal in the early historical period. The medieval bounds of the territory are described in an interesting document preserved in the *Book of Fenagh* as follows: *Teora fuind crichi Conaill;/ O Fertuis co Dobar ndil,/ Odta Dobar co hEidnig./ Ota Eidnig ni slicht cam,/ co roich fodes co Cromchall;/ O Bernas gan taisi threb,/ Co Ros itir da inber* (The three districts of Conall's territory, from Feartas to constant Dobhar, and from Dobhar to Eidhneach. From Eidhneach, not a crooked track, till it reaches southwards to Cromchall; From Bearnas,without weakness of tribes, to Ros idir dá inbhear).[7] Almost all of the placenames cited in the above entry are still extant or their location may be identified from other sources. The name *Feartas* lives on as Farsetmore, *Fearsaid Mhór* in Irish, the name of a townland in the parish of Leck, about two miles from Letterkenny. The word *feartas*, or in its modern form, *fearsaid*, occurs frequently in placenames including *Béal Feirste*, Belfast. The word is explained as 'a tidal (sandbank) ford', and the name *Feartas* originally referred to an important crossing point on the Swilly estuary. *Dobhar* is now the name of a townland in Gweedore, *Gaoth Dobhair*, in the civil parish of Tullaghobegly. As its meaning, 'water', implies, however, Dobhar was originally the name of a river, that known officially as the Gweedore River, or locally as *Abhainn Chroithlí*, Crolly River, which separates Gweedore from the Rosses district to the south.[8] *Eidhneach* is the name of another river, the Eany Water, which flows into Donegal Bay at Inver. The name *Cromchall* is now obsolete, but was apparently near Assaroe on the Erne at Ballyshannon which, according to other sources, marked the southern limit of Conall's lands: *Gabais Conall cona droing/siar co hEss Ruaid mic Baduirn* (Conall with his band possessed westwards to Eas Ruaidh son of Badharn).[9] *Bearnas,* Barnesmore, is the name of the important mountain gap on the main east-west route through the south-centre of the county which marked the south-eastern limit of Tír Chonaill. Significantly, Saint Patrick's biographer, Tírechán, who wrote in the last quarter of the seventh century, refers to Barnesmore as *Bernas filiorum Conill* 'the gap of the sons of Conall'.[10] *Ros idir dá inbhear,* which can be translated as 'the headland between two inlets', appears to be a description rather than a true placename. It is undoubtedly to be identified with the Ros Goill peninsula, which lies between the inlets of Mulroy Bay and Sheephaven Bay. This identification is supported by documentary evidence elsewhere in the *Book of Fenagh* which gives the bounds of Conall's lands as: *O Eas Ruaid co Rus Irguill* (From Eas Ruaid to Ros Iorghoill).[11]

Tír Chonaill, 'the land of Conall', the name by which the territory of the Cinéal Conaill became known is not recorded until the early tenth century: *Longus aile i Ciunn Maghair a n-airer Thire Conaill, .i. mc. Huathmaran m. Bairith, cum .xx. nauibus* (Another naval force [of Vikings] was at Ceann Maghair on the coast of Tír Chonaill, i.e. under the son of Uathmarán son of Barid, with twenty ships).[12] It is impossible to say when the placename *Tír Chonaill* was formed but comparative evidence suggests that it cannot have been much earlier than its first attestation, and was most certainly a good deal later than Conall Gulban's time.

Historically, Tír Chonaill was divided into four cantreds, or *triúcha céad,* and it is these ancient divisions which form the basis of the modern baronies. The extent of the individual cantreds is described in both native and non-native sources from the thirteenth century. In a text dating from the year 1289 in the Anglo-Norman, *Red Book of the Earls of Kildare* it is stated: *In Tirconyll sunt iiii cantreda terre ... ii cantreda de Tirconyll que iacent prope mare a Roscule usque ad Thethnegall .... ii cantreda de Tirconyll que iacent a Locherne usque Kynalmogn et versus Dery...* (In Tír Chonaill there are four cantreds of land ... two cantreds which lie near the sea from Roscule as far as Thethnegall ... two cantreds of Tír Chonaill which lie between Lough Erne and Cinéal Moghain and in the direction of Derry).[13] The first two cantreds mentioned were co-extensive with the western coastal half of Tír Chonaill, that is the modern baronies of Kilmacrenan, Boylagh and Banagh. *Roscule* is the Ros Goill peninsula, which, as has already been noted, was the northern limit of Tír Chonaill. The other two cantreds were co-extensive with the modern baronies of Raphoe North, Raphoe South and Tirhugh, north of the River Erne. *Kinelmogn*, which derives from Irish *Cinéal Moain*, was the name of a small sept, whose territory originally lay along the Foyle between Derry and Lifford.

Cinéal Éanna and Tír Éanna

Cinéal Éanna 'the kindred of Éanna' were descended from a brother of Conall and Eoghan, Éanna son of Niall Naoighiallach. This branch of the Uí Néill was absorbed into the Cinéal Conaill at an early period[14] certainly by the time the name of their territory, *Tír Éanna*, 'the land of Éanna' is first recorded in the early eleventh century: *Flaithbertach Ua Neill do techt i Tír Conaill coro ort Tir nEnna 7 Tír Lughdach* (Flaithbheartach Ó Néill came into Tír Chonaill and destroyed Tír Éanna and Tír Lughdhach).[15] In a poem dated to the thirteenth century in the *Book of Fenagh*, which gives the extent of the various cantreds of Tír Chonaill, the bounds of Tír Éanna are given as: *Tricha Enna siar arsin,/ co Bernus Mór co Sruthair/ Tarbach Tír Enna na nGread,/ soir co Fernach na feinnidh* (the cantred of Éanna spreads westwards from there [i.e. the Swilly] to Bearnas Mór [Barnesmore] to Sruthair, profitable Tír Éanna of the studs extends eastwards to Fearnach of the warrior bands).[16] *Sruthair* is now the name of a townland, Sruell, in the parish of Killymard, but the name suggests that it may have originally referred to a river, perhaps one of the tributaries of the Eany Water. *Fearnach* may refer to the townland of Farnagh in the parish of Aughnish, which lies on the western shore of Lough Swilly, but, from the context, the name is more likely to have referred to some place on the southern side of the lough on the northern border of Raphoe North barony. The name, Tír Éanna, did not survive into modern times, but from the above description, it was roughly co-extensive with the modern baronies of Raphoe North and Raphoe South.[17] This agriculturally rich geographical area is now popularly known as The Lagan, or, in Irish, *An Lagán*, which signifies 'the lowlying country'.

Cinéal Luighdheach and Tír Luighdheach

Tír Lughdhach or *Tír Luighdheach* 'the land of Lughaidh', the last placename mentioned in the annalistic entry of 1019 quoted above, was the territory of the *Cinéal Lughdhach,* or *Cinéal Luighdheach,* 'the kindred of Lughaidh'.[18] The cantred of Tír Luighdheach extended from the Gweedore River in the west to the River Swilly in the east: *On Dobar disgir cedna/Tricha Luigdhech mic Sedna/cus in abainn is glan li/Danup comainm Suilidi* (From the same impetuous Dobhar, the cantred of Lughaidh son of Seadna, [extends] to the river of clear aspect, the name of which is Súiligh).[19] The two rivers referred to, the

153

Swilly and the Gweedore River, mark the boundaries of the modern barony of Kilmacrenan, but it is unclear whether Tír Luighdheach was originally co-extensive with the whole of that barony, particularly whether it included the Fanad Peninsula. The name Tír Luighdheach is not recorded in the annals after the thirteenth century. After that time, most of the territory is referred to simply as *Na Tuatha, Na Trí Tuatha,* or *Tuatha Toraighe: Sidhraidh H. Baighill .i. taoiseach na Trí Túath fer beodha deigh einigh, do mharbhadh dia braithribh fein a bhfioll* (Siodhraidh Ó Baoighill, chieftain of the three Tuaths, a vigourous hospitable man, was killed by his own brothers).[20] *Na Tuatha* is simply the plural of *tuath,* a word which signifies the territory ruled by a local chieftain or petty king. The name is recorded in anglicised form in seventeenth century documentation as *Toa.* It survives today in the form Doe, the name of a district near Creeslough. Doe derives from the genitive form, *na dTuath,* which is found, for example, in the placename *Caisleán na dTuath,* 'the castle of Na Tuatha', which occurs in English as Doe Castle or Castle Doe.

Cinéal Luighdheach claimed descent from Lughaidh mac Séadna of the Cinéal Conaill: *Setna mac Fergusa Fáil / O fuil sil Sedna saer nair/ Cenel Lugdach thair sa bos/ Sluag Fanad co fir follus* (Seadna son of Fergus of Fál, from whom are the noble Síol Séadna, Cinéal Lughdhach are in the East and here, and the host of Fanad manifestly).[21] According to the genealogies Lughaidh was a great-grandson of Conall Gulban: *[Lugaid] m. Sétnai m. mic Fergusa m. Conaill Gulban m. Néill Noígiallaig.*[22] Séadna, Lughaidh's father,was a brother of Feidhilmidh, father of Colmcille: *Colum m. Feidlimid m. Fergusa m. Conaill Gulban.*[23] As is well known, Colmcille is traditionally associated with a number of places within Tír Luighdheach, notably Kilmacrenan, Templedouglas, and Gartan, his supposed birthplace.

The names *Cinéal Luighdheach* and *Tír Luighdheach* would appear, on the surface at least, to follow the same pattern as the other cantred-names met with so far. Whether it is possible to take Lughaidh's genealogy at face value is another matter. The north-western part of the barony of Kilmacrenan, particularly the Cloghaneely district, is also closely associated in folklore with the mythological Lughaidh Lámhfhada and his father Balar, whom he supposedly killed and beheaded at Dunlewey, *Dún Lúiche,* 'the fort of Lughaidh'.[24] The name *Lughaidh* replaced the name *Lugh* in later medieval times; in origin it is actually a derivative of Lugh. As is well known, Lugh Lámhfhada is the name of one of the most important figures in pre-Christian Irish mythology. He is identical with the pan-Celtic pagan deity *Lugus,* whose name occurs in a number of Celtic placenames, notably *Lugudunon,* which is the origin of several placenames on the continent, including Leyden in Belgium and Lyon in France.[25] *Lugudunon* signifies 'the fort of Lugus' and is, therefore, to be equated in meaning with the name *Dún Lúiche*. Apart from the evidence of local folklore, onomastic evidence exists to connect Lugh with the western part of Cinéal Luighdheach. In the *Papal Taxation* of 1302-6, the name of the parish of Tullaghabegly, in which Cloghaneely and Dunlewey are located, is given as *Talgalug*. This form could reflect an original Irish form *Tulcha Logha,* 'the mound of Lugh'.

A significant number of early Irish population-groups derived their names from certain pre-christian mythological figures. The *Conmhaicne* group, whose name signifies 'the descendants of Conmhac' were called after the mythological figure Conmhac, otherwise known as Lughaidh mac Con, who is very likely to be identified as Lugh Lámhfhada. The name survives in the placename Conamara, which is from an original *Conmhaicne Mara*, 'Conmhaicne of the sea'. The baronies of Leyny in county Sligo and Lune in county Meath derive their names from *Luighne*, a tribal name which signifies 'the descendants of Lugh'. Given the evidence for the strong mythological background of Tír Luighdheach, it is very probable that Lugh Lámhfhada was also the eponymous ancestor of Cinéal Luighdheach. The name and genealogy of the original population group would have been refashioned by the medieval genealogists in order to show direct descent from Conall Gulban.

Cinéal Baghaine and Tír Baghaine

Tír Baghaine, the name of the second of the coastal cantreds mentioned in the Anglo-Norman document of 1289, was the territory of the Cinéal Baghaine, a sub-division of the Cinéal Conaill, who claimed descent from Éanna Baghaine, one of the seven sons of Conall Gulban: *Énna Bóghuine ... ótát Cenél mBógáne (Éanna Boghaine* from whom are the *Cinéal Bóghaine*).[26] Cinéal Boghaine are first mentioned in the annals in the late eighth century: *Bellum re nDonnchad m. Aedho Muindeirg for Cenel mBoghaine* (A battle by Donnchad son of Aodh Muindearg against Cinéal Baghaine).[27] According to the *Book of Fenagh* poem already quoted, Tír Baghaine extended from the Gweedore River in the north-west of the county to the Eany Water in the south: *Triucha Baguine mblechta/Eolchai de luchd na questa;/ O Ednich co Dobar ndil/ Silius asna garbsleibtib* (The cantred of Baghaine of the milk, as inquiring people know, [extends] from Eidhnigh to constant Dobhar which flows from the rough mountains).[28] *Eidhnigh*, or the Eany Water, rises in the Blue Stack Mountains and flows south-westwards into the sea at Inver. The *Book of Fenagh* suggests here that Tír Baghaine did not originally include all of the modern barony of Banagh. The present south-eastern limit of that barony, as well as that given in seventeenth century official sources is the River Eske, which flows into the sea at Donegal and not the River Eany. This latter boundary is more likely to represent the historical reality. The *Red Book of the Earls of Kildare* gives the southern limit of the coastal cantreds of Tír Chonaill as a place called *Thethnegall*, which, as will be shown below, can be identified with Donegal. As it is most unlikely that a native poet and historian would confuse the names of two such well-known rivers as the Eske and Eany, the *Book of Fenagh* text may reflect a medieval territorial claim, rather than the contemporary political reality.

In the poem *Triallom timcheall na Fódla*, which was written by Seán Mór Ó Dubhagáin about the year 1400, Tír Baghaine is described as part of *tír Ó mBaoighill*, 'the land of the Ó Baoighill or O'Boyle'.[29] The O'Boyles were driven out of most of the southern part of Tír Baghaine in the thirteenth and fourteenth centuries by a branch of the Clann tSuibhne, the Mac Sweeneys, whose chief is variously described in the annals as *Mac Suibhne Thíre Baghaine* (Mac Suibhne of Tír Baghaine),[30] or more frequently as *Mac Suibhne Baghaineach*. The word *baghaineach* is an adjectival derivative of *Baghaine* which could also be used as a noun to refer to an inhabitant of Tír Baghaine. The plural form, *Baghainigh*, had replaced Tír Baghaine as a territorial name by the sixteenth century.[31] It is from the genitive plural of *Baghainigh* that the anglicised barony-name Banagh is derived.

The word *baghaine* or *bóghuine* is of infrequent occurrence in Irish. It is otherwise only found in the placename *Beann Bóghuine*, the name of an unidentified mountain. In the *Dindsenchas* of *Beann Bóghuine*, which seeks to show how the place received its name *Beann Bóghuine*, the second element is explained as being from a compound of *bó* 'cow' and *guine* 'slaying'. The hill is said to have received its name 'the peak of the cow-slaughter' from an incident in which one of the cows belonging to the female mythological figure, Flidais, was killed there.[32] As with most of the fabulous speculation that is to be found in the *Dindsenchas*, this explanation can be safely dismissed as a piece of fanciful folk-etymology. It is of interest however that Conall Gulban and his son Éanna Boghaine both have epithets which occur as second elements in mountain-names, *Beann Ghulban* in the case of the former and *Beann Bhaghaine* in the case of the latter.

Tír Ainmhireach

Following the seizure of their territories in the southern part of Tír Baghaine by the Mac Sweeneys, the O'Boyles were largely confined to the northern part of the cantred from the fourteenth century on, in what is now the barony of Boylagh. This area was known as *Tír*

Ainmhireach 'the land of Ainmhire': *Aindeles O Baighill taisech Tiri hAinmireach* (Aindeles Ó Baoighill chieftain of Tír Ainmhireach).[33] Ainmhire, from whom the territory takes its name, was, according to the genealogies, a son of Séadna and therefore a brother Lughaidh, the supposed ancestor of Cinéal Luighdheach. It is of note that O'Boyle's territory originally included Cloghaneely in the west of Tír Luighdheach according to Ó Dubhagáin: *Cloch Cinn Fhaoladh na ngeileach/ is Tír áloinn ainmireach/..... is Tír mborbdha mBághuine* ([The land of O'Boyle includes] Cloghaneely of the bright steeds and beautiful Tír Ainmhireach and fierce Tír Baghaine).[34]

As in the case of the names Tír Luighdheach and Tír Baghaine, the name Tír Ainmhireach did not survive beyond the medieval period but was replaced by the name *Baoigheallaigh* by the sixteenth century: *Conchobhar ócc O Baoicchill tanaise Baoigheallach do mharbhadh la cloind Uí Bhuighill* (Conchobhar Óg Ó Baoighill the tanist of the Baoigheallaigh was killed by the Ó Baoighill clan).[35] *Baoigheallaigh* is the plural of *Baoigheallach* which may be explained as 'a descendent of Baoigheall' from whom the Ó Baoighill are named. *Baoigheallaigh* would have originally referred to the collective members of the Ó Baoighill clan, but later it was applied to the territory over which they ruled. The anglicised barony-name, Boylagh, derives from the genitive plural, as in the case of Banagh. The modern Irish form of the barony name is *Baollaigh*.

Tír Aodha

The most southerly territory of Tír Chonaill was known as *Tír Aodha,* which became anglicised as the barony-name Tirhugh. Its bounds are given in the *Book of Fenagh*, where it is referred to as *Triocha Easa Ruaidh* 'the cantred of Assaroe': *Tricha Esa Ruaid re baigh,/ Maigrich iasgaich inberaich,/o Chall cháin na crobung cas/ Co hEdnich torainn dtrenglais* (The cantred of Assaroe the famous, abounding in salmon, fish, and inlets, [extends] from Callchain of the twisted clusters to the green loud-sounding Eidhnigh).[36] Assaroe on the river Erne marked the southern limit of Tír Chonaill and *Callcháin*, like the name *Cromchall* in other sources, was probably located on that river. According to the seventeenth century English sources the barony of Tirhugh lay between the River Drowes on the Leitrim border and the River Eske.[37] However, it is clear from all the earlier sources already cited that *Tír Aodha* did not originally extend south of the Erne. The later sources are historically correct, however, in setting the Eske as the northern limit of the barony, contrary to that given in the *Book of Fenagh* above. The limits of Tirhugh are confirmed in the *Annals of the Four Masters* in an entry for the year 1419: *Mórsluaicceadh la Brian Ua Concobhair*

*7 la híochtar Connacht uile co ngallaibh iomdhaibh leo tria forcongra
7 toghairm Uí Néill gor ro mhillset Tír Aodha uile otha Áth na nGall co
hÁth Seanaigh eitir fhér, arbhar, 7 foirccneamh 7 ro loisccseat
Murbhach longphort Uí Dhomhnaill an ccéin baoí Ó Domhnaill cona
shloghaibh i tTír Eoghain* (A great army was led by Brian Ó
Conchobhair and all of Lower Connacht with many of the English at
the request and solicitation of Ó Néill; and they spoiled all of Tirhugh
from Áth na nGall to Áth Seanaigh including its grass, corn, and
buildings, and burned Murbhach, Ó Domhnaill's fortress while Ó
Domhnaill was with his forces in Tír Eoghain). *Áth Seanaigh,* which is
the basis of the name *Béal Átha Seanaigh,* Ballyshannon in English,
was originally the name of a ford on the River Erne, which marked the
southern extent of Tirhugh. The name *Áth na nGall* is now obsolete
but it also referred to a ford, the one marking the northern limit of the
territory. The names *Áth na nGall* and *Thethnegall,* the name given in
the *Red Book of the Earl of Kildare* as marking the southern extent of
the two maritime cantreds of Tír Chonaill, obviously refer to the same
place. Both names contain the same second element as that found in
Dún na nGall. It is reasonable to assume, therefore, that *Áth na nGall*
referred to a ford on the River Eske somewhere near the original
settlement of *Dún na nGall,* probably near the ruins of Donegal Castle.

Tír Aodha differs from the names of the other ancient territories of
Tír Chonaill in several respects. Firstly, it is the only original cantred-
name to have survived the medieval period and to have become the
name of a barony. More importantly, it is the only one of the early
territories not to have been named after any of the various descendants
of Niall Naoighiallach. According to tradition, the personage from
whom *Tír Aodha,* 'the land of Aodh', is named was one *Aodh Ruadh
mac Badhuirn,* a mythological figure from whom also derived the
placename *Eas Ruaidh,* 'the cataract of (Aodh) Rua' now Assaroe on
the Erne outside Ballyshannon. The *Dindsenchas* relates how the
waterfall was named: *Eas Ruaid, canas rohainnmniged? Ni ansa. Aed
Ruad mac Baduirnd ri Erind robaided and oc faircsin a delba oc snam
an esa, a quo Eas Ruaid nominatur. Is e a sid, Sith Aeda, ar ur an easa.*
(Eas Ruaidh,[the waterfall of Ruadh], how was it so called? Not difficult.
It was Aodh Ruadh, son of Badhurn, king of Ireland, that was drowned
there while gazing at his image while swimming the waterfall. From
him Eas Ruaidh is named. His fairymound, Síodh Aodha [Aodh's
fairymound] is on the waterfall's bank.[38]

Dún na nGall/Donegal

The creation of the county in 1585 united for the first time the historic
territories of Tír Chonaill and Inishowen under the common name of

Donegal. It also gave the placename Donegal a broader reference than it had had previously, as, until then, the name referred exclusively to the town at the foot of the River Eske and it did not have any territorial application.[39] The designation county Donegal was adopted immediately by the English administration for official and legal purposes. The name Inishowen continued in official use as a barony-name and, of course, as a geographical name. On the other hand, Tír Chonaill, in all its various anglicised forms, had all but disappeared from official documents by the early seventeenth century. The name, seemingly, was not used even to designate the unofficial geographical area by the newly arrived English-speakers in the area.

The native Irish-speaking inhabitants of the county were much slower to adopt the new name, however. For them, the name *Dún na nGall* still referred exclusively to the town of Donegal while the name Tír Chonaill was adopted as the name of the county. Even today, Irish speakers are more inclined to refer to the county as Tír Chonaill in preference to *Contae Dhún na nGall*. It is only through the influence of outside forces, such as central government agencies and, more importantly, the Gaelic Athletic Association that the designation *Contae Dhún na nGall* has been slowly adopted by native Irish speakers in the county over the past few decades.

The choice of Donegal as the name for the new county was not surprising in the context of political realities of the late sixteenth century. Donegal was the principal seat of one the most powerful native Irish chieftains at that time, *Ó Domhnaill*, or O'Donnell, to whom 'all the principal gentlemen of Tireconell ...[gave] obedience... as their chief lord'.[40] Donegal was also one of the few places in the new county that resembled a town at the period – its only rival was Ballyshannon, as the other possible contenders for the description, Raphoe, Castlefinn and Lifford lay in ruins.[41] The English had already noted the potential of developing Donegal town twenty years before the creation of the county, as testified by Sydney's description of the town in 1566:

> This castle [Donegal] is one of the greatest that ever I saw in Ireland in any Irishman's hands, and would appear in good keeping one of the fairest, situated in a good soil, and so nigh a portable water as a boat of ten tons may come within twenty yards of the castle; the town with all ruined, which heretofore had been great and inhabited with men of traffic, specially with Englishmen; and so the name signifies, for Donegal is to say the English town.[42]

The anglicised name-form, *Donnyngall,* found in the order of 1585 reflects as faithfully as could reasonably be expected the original Irish form *Dún na nGall*. The name *Dún na nGall* is well attested in native Irish sources from the late fifteenth century and the importance of the place in the sixteenth century can be gauged from the many references to it in the annals of the period. The town of Donegal was, however, less than a century old when Sydney visited it in 1566. The earliest reference to the placename does not occur until 1474, when the Monastery or Abbey of Donegal, *Mainistir Dúin na nGall,* was founded by Aodh Ruadh Ó Domhnaill and his wife Nuala.[43] It was Aodh Ruadh who first built a castle at Donegal, probably about the same time as the monastery.[44] The earliest reference to O'Donnell having his residence there does not occur until 1495: *O Domhnaill do theacht cum a bhaile fein idon co Dun na nGall* (O'Donnell came to his own house, that is, Dun na nGall).[45] Until then, O'Donell's principal residence had been at *Murbhach,* or Murvagh, now a townland lying about four miles to the south-west of Donegal.[46]

There is no historical or archaeological evidence to say whether there had been any settlement at Donegal before Aodh Ruadh Ó Domhnaill built the castle and monastery. It would be surprising had there not been, when one considers the strategic location of the site, situated at the head of a navigable channel on Donegal Bay at the foot of river Eske, and at the crossroads of the main routes linking most of Tír Chonaill with Connacht and Fermanagh. Indeed these considerations must have influenced O'Donnell in his decision to move his seat of power to Donegal in the first place.

The placename *Dún na nGall* would also indicate that there had been some type of fortified structure on the site at an earlier period. The word *dún,* 'a fort', is one of the most important settlement terms in Irish placenames as, indeed, are its cognates in the early Celtic placenames in Britain and continental Europe. In Irish placenames, the term generally refers to an enclosed settlement or ringfort and in the earlier historical period it appears to designate the principal residence of a chieftain. The term would not have been used to refer to a late medieval castle and most certainly not to the one founded in the fifteenth century.

Placenames containing the element *dún* are found throughout Ireland and we find a number of important early examples in county Donegal. The name *Dún Lúiche*, 'the fort of Lughaidh', which has already been discussed, probably contains the name of the eponymous ancestor of the Cinéal Luighdheach, whether that was Lughaidh mac Séadna of the Cinéal Conaill or the mythological Lughaidh Lámhfhada. *Dún Cionnaola,* Dunkineely, signifies 'the fort of Cionnaola'. *Cionnaola* is the modern reflex of the Old Irish personal name *Ceann Faoladh*, several instances of which are to be found in the early genealogies of Cinéal Conaill. The same name is found in the placename *Cloich Chionnaola,* Cloghaneely, which is attested as *Cloch Chinn Fhaoladh* in Ó Dubhagáin's poem of c.1400 cited earlier. The presence of personal names such as Lughaidh and Ceann Faoladh suggest that a placename is of a comparatively early date. *Dún Fionnachaidh,* Dunfanaghy, can be explained as 'the fort of Fionnachadh'. *Fionnachadh,* 'the white or fair field', is attested frequently as a placename in its own right, for example, Finaghy near Belfast. However, a most interesting explanation of Dunfanaghy has been postulated recently by Alan Mac an Bhaird. He argues that the second element of this placename is actually a tribal name, Fionnchaidhe, which was recorded by the geographer Ptolemy in the first century of the Christian era.[47]

The name *Dún na nGall* is not as early as those mentioned above. The presence of the definite article, *na,* in the name makes it unlikely that it can predate the ninth century as it was only from then that the definite article becomes common in placenames.[48] The final element of the placename *Dún na nGall* is the genitive plural of the word *gall* 'foreigner' and *Dún na nGall* is usually explained as 'the fort of the foreigners', although at least one other interpretation is possible.[49] The word *gall,* plural *gaill,* signified various outsiders at different periods in history.[50] By the sixteenth century it would have denoted an Englishman as suggested by Sydney's explanation of the placename Donegal as 'the English Town'.[51] However, as has already been shown, two other placenames containing the term *gaill* are associated with Donegal at an earlier period, certainly before the English had gained a foothold in the county. The first is *Áth na nGall,* 'the ford of the foreigners', which is recorded in the entry in the *Annals of the Four Masters* under the year 1419; the other is *Thethnegall* which is found in the Anglo-Norman document of 1289 referred to previously. The form *Thethnegall* could be explained as a scribal error of the name *Áth na nGall,* but it is more likely to represent Irish *Teach na nGall,* 'the house of the foreigners'. As *teach* 'house' and *dún* 'fort' are both settlement terms, it is quite probable that the placenames *Thethnegall* and *Dún na nGall* referred to the same place. Given the early attestation of these placenames, *Dún/Áth/Teach na nGall,* it is reasonable to infer that the 'foreigners' referred to in them were either Anglo-Normans or Vikings. Historical evidence shows that the Anglo-Normans held lands in Tír Chonaill as early as 1235 and it is quite possible that they had established a number of permanent settlements within the terrritory during the thirteenth century.[52] Placenames require time to become established, however. For that reason, it is most improbable that the second element of the placename *Thethnegall,*

Teach na nGall, would refer to the Anglo-Normans, given its attestation in an Anglo-Norman source a mere fifty years after their arrival in the county. The evidence would therefore suggest that the foreigners referred to in the placename actually belong to an earlier period, that is, between the ninth and the thirteenth centuries. That being so, the *gaill* referred to were in all probability Vikings. There is some historical evidence to show that the Vikings were active in Donegal Bay in the early ninth century.[53] It is not unlikely that these Vikings would have established a number of semi-permanent trading settlements on the adjoining coast. Donegal offered a site that would have been attractive to Viking traders in the ninth and tenth centuries for the same reasons as it was attractive to the English in the seventeenth. The only evidence for the existence of a Viking settlement at Donegal, however, is in the actual placename *Dún na nGall,* 'the fort of the foreigners'.[54]

Early Christian settlement names

The introduction of Christianity into Donegal was probably contemporaneous with the northward expansion of Uí Néill during the late fifth and early sixth centuries. According to his seventh century biographer, Tírechán, Saint Patrick established a number of churches within the confines of the present county. It is certain that a number of early churches such as that at Carndonagh belonged to the Patrician mission but these were more likely to have been established by Patrick's followers in the generations following the saint's death. Whatever about the precise time of its introduction, there can be little doubt that Christianity was well established throughout the county by the time of Colmcille's death in the late sixth century. Many of the early ecclesiastical foundations in Donegal undoubtedly date from the pre-seventh century period. A large number of the names of these establishments are still extant, particularly in the parish-names of the county.

Names of early church sites generally contain a generic term that has specific reference to ecclesiastical settlement.[55] The earliest stratum of Irish ecclesiastical placenames does not contain such terms, however; the church simply assumed the name of the place in which it was situated. It is significant that the majority of names of early church sites in Donegal belong to this latter category; less than a quarter of the parish-names of the county contain elements specific to ecclesiastical settlement. The structure of these placenames, particularly the absence of the definite article, would indicate that they belong to the earliest period of Irish placenames and that most of them predate the establishment of the churches to which they refer. Certain patterns are discernible in the generic elements found in these names.

The word *cluain* is one of the most common elements in early Irish placenames. The term is generally explained as a 'meadow', 'pasture' or 'clearing' and it is often associated with human settlement. *Cluain* is not a particularly common element in the placenames of Donegal. It is significant, therefore, that five of the parish-names of the county contain this element. The parish of Clonleigh comes from Irish *Cluain Laogh,* 'the meadow of (the) calves', a name that has no ecclesiastical connotation whatsoever. Likewise the name of the parish of Clonca, which is from Irish *Cluain Catha.* The second element of this name is the genitive of the word *cath,* which is normally explained as 'battle'. In many of the placenames in which the element is found, however, *cath* would appear to have a different meaning.[56] *Cluain Catha* was dedicated to Breacán, an associate of Colmcille: *Brecan, Cluana Catha i nInis Eoghain, espucc Arda Brecain, acus ab Maighi Bili, do shliocht Eoghain, mic Néill* (Brecan of Cluain Catha in Inis Eoghain, bishop of Ard Breacáin and abbot of Maigh Bhile [Movilla] of the race of Eoghan son of Niall).[57]

The name *Cluain Dabhaodóg,* 'the meadow of Dabhaodóg', the original name of Clondavaddog Parish in Fanad does have ecclesiastical associations. It is named from a saint whose feast, according to the martyrologies, was celebrated on 22 July: *Dabhaotócc, Cluana da Bhaotócc a bhFanaid a dTír Conaill* (Dabhaodóg of Cluain Dabhaodóg in Fanad in Tír Chonaill).[58] Nothing else is known of this saint, but the name Dabhaodóg is one of the many hypocoristic or pet forms of the Old Irish personal name Baoth.

The patron saint of Culdaff in Inishowen was Baodán. The name Baodán is also a pet form of Baoth and, significantly, the saint was commemorated locally on 22 July, evidence that suggests that he and Dabhaodóg of Clondavaddog are identical. Although Culdaff does not contain the saint's name, it can be shown that the placename actually has associations with Baodán. The original Irish form of Culdaff is *Cúil Dabhcha* which signifies 'the corner of the vat or large vessel'. In the middle of the Culdaff River near the site of the early church is a large stone. This stone was formerly known as Baodán's Boat, and tradition holds that Baodán sailed from Scotland to Ireland in this 'boat'.[59] Undoubtedly, it is to Baodán's Boat, which Énrí Ó Muirgheasa has aptly described as 'a trough-shaped stone', that the second element *dabhach* of the placename *Cúil Dabhcha* refers.[60] This local tradition of Baodán's voyaging reflects closely that recorded by Adhamhnán in the seventh century:

At another time, a man Baitan (i.e. Baodán), by family a descendant of Nia-Taloirc, asked to be blessed by the saint on going to seek with the others a desert place in the sea. Bidding him farewell, the saint pronounced the following prophecy concerning him:

'This man, who goes to seek a desert place, but will be buried in that place in which a woman will drive sheep across his grave'. The same Baitan, after long circuitous voyaging through windy seas, having found no desert place, returned to his country; and for many years he continued there as the head of a small church, which in Irish is called Lathreg-inden. After some seasons in Derry (*in roboreto Calcagi*) he died and was buried there. And about the same time, it happened that because of an attack by enemies the neighbouring lay-people, with their women and children, took refuge in the church of that place. And so it came about that one day a woman was observed driving her sheep through the burial-place of that man, who had recently been buried there.[61]

Adjacent to the parishes of Clonca and Culdaff is the parish of Clonmany, *Cluain Maine,* 'the meadow of Maine'. Like the placename Clondavaddog, Clonmany also contains an early personal name and the evidence suggests that the individual to whom it refers also had ecclesiastical associations. There are several persons of the name Maine mentioned in the early sources, the most illustrious of whom was Maine Caol, father of Conall of *Inis Caoil,* or Inishkeel. Placename evidence intimates that it is this particular Maine who is referred to in the name Clonmany. Of particular interest is the fact that there is a townland called Crosconnell, *Cros Chonaill,* which signifies 'the cross of Conall' in the parish of Clonmany. It is also of note that almost directly across Lough Swilly in the parish of Killygarvan there is a townland called Clondallan, *Cluain Dalláin,* 'the meadow of Dallán'. This placename may celebrate Dallán Forgaill the illustrious author of *Amhra Cholm Cille,* the seventh century eulogy of Colmcille, who was Conall's teacher and associate at *Inis Caoil.* Dallán's principal church, which was in county Down, and was also known as *Cluain Dalláin.*[62]

Dallán Forgaill is apparently also commemorated at *Tulaigh Dhalláin,* 'the mound or hill of Dallán', now the townland of Tullygallan in the parish of Drumhome.[63] The word *tulach* signifies 'a low hill' or 'mound' and appears to have had significance as an assembly-place or place of inauguration in early Irish society. There are a number of placenames with *tulach* in the county which refer to ecclesiastical sites. Tullaghobegly, *Tulacha Beigile* in Irish, appears originally to have referred to an enclosed mound containing a church and graveyard in the parish of that name.[64] The first element is a reflex of the word *tulcha,* which can be explained as either an old dative or genitive form of *tulach*, or as a derivative of that word.[65] The second element is the name of a local saint who is apparently commemorated as *Bigill, Tulcha* 'Bigill of Tulach' in the *Martyrology of Donegal* under 1 November. As shown earlier, the first reference to this site suggests that the original name was *Tulcha Logha*, 'the mound of the Lugh', the pagan deity who had associations with several places within the parish, including *Dún Lúiche*. This would suggest that Tullaghobegly was initially a pre-christian religious site.

The parish-name of Tullyfern derives from Irish *Tulach Fheargna*, 'the mound or hill of Feargna'. *Feargna* is a common old Irish personal name and it is not possible to say from whom this placename is named. There was a place or territory called *Tír Fheargna*, 'the land of Feargna', in the neighbourhood of Kilmacrenan which may have originally referred to what is now the civil parish of Tullyfern.[66] There are several saints named Feargna mentioned in ecclesiastical sources, one of whom was successor of Colmcille as abbott of Iona: *Fergna Britt mac Failbe, epscop acus abb Ia Cholaim Cille é fós. Do Chenel gConnill Gulban mic Neill do AD 622* (Feargna Briott, son of Failbhe, Bishop; and he was also abbot of Iona. He was of the race of Conall Gulban, son of Niall AD 622).[67]

According to tradition, Colmcille was baptised at *Tulach Dhúghlaise*, now Templedouglas, an early church site in the townland of the same name. It takes its name from the river originally called *Dúghlaise*, 'the black stream', now the Glashagh River which flows past the old church. The substitution of the element *Temple-* for *Tully-* as first element is late and is due to English influence.

Colmcille's birthplace was at *Gartán*, Gartan. The name is a derivative of the word *gart*, a variant of *gort*, 'a field'. The name does not have any ecclesiastical connotations. Despite the number of churches associated with Colmcille within county Donegal, the only major ecclesiastical site which is actually named after him is *Gleann Cholm Cille*, Glencolumbkille. Literary references to Glencolumbkille are comparatively late despite the obvious antiquity of the site, with its impressive early Christian monuments including those associated with its famous *turas*. The evidence suggests that the dedication to Colmcille in this placename is late. The name is recorded simply as *Glend* in the *Papal Taxation* of 1302 and it is not until Maghnas Ó Domhnaill's *Betha Colaim Chille* of 1532 that the full name is first recorded: *ag abuind tSenglenda a crich Ceneoil Conill ris a raiter Glend Colaim Cilli aniug* (at the river of *Seanghleann*, 'old glen', which is called *Gleann Cholm Cille* today).[68]

Next to Colmcille, Conall was probably the most widely venerated saint in Donegal, particularly in the south-west of the county where his cult was widespread until comparatively recently.[69] He is particularly associated with *Inis Caoil*, Inishkeel, an island in the parish of the same name situated in the bay off Narin. In the earliest sources he is referred to simply as *Conall Insi Caíl*, 'Conall of Inis Caoil'.[70] In popular tradition, Conall is occasionally referred to as *Conall Caol*, which means 'Conall the slender'.[71] On the surface there would appear to be a connection between Conall's popular epithet, *caol* 'slender', and the placename; *Inis Caoil* contains the genitive singular of the adjective *caol* 'slender' used as a noun and the placename could be explained as 'the island of the slender one', that is, Conall. However, the form *Conall Caol* is not met with in pre-seventeenth sources and it is undoubtedly a product of folk etymology. The placename may be explained more plausibly without any reference to Conall. The word *caol* is found as a noun meaning a 'strait' or 'narrow', and it is with this sense it is often found in placenames elsewhere, for example, *An Caol*, the original name of Narrow Water near Newry and of Keel in Achill. *Inis Caoil* would therefore signify 'the island of the strait', the strait in question being the narrow passage between the island and the mainland which is fordable at low water.

Secular habitation sites as ecclesiastical sites

Archaeological evidence indicates that many early medieval churches were built within enclosures or ringforts.[72] Some of these enclosures belonged to the pre-christian period and were adopted as church-sites by the new religion. Others were undoubtedly built specifically for the church. Whatever their origin, a generic term denoting a ringfort, usually *ráth,* is often found in the names of early ecclesiastical sites of this type.

The word *ráth* is almost identical in meaning to the word *dún* and has almost as widespread a distribution as a placename element. Most of the placenames in which the term *ráth* is found refer to early secular habitation sites, usually ringforts. Many of the earliest of these names evidently indicate the dwelling places of petty kings or chieftains. Several of the Donegal placenames having *ráth* as first element may fall into this category. *Ráth Maoláin*, Rathmullen, contains the common early personal name, Maolán, and it may be translated as 'the fort of Maolán'. The name of the neighbouring town of Ramelton, *Ráth Mealtain*, contains a rare old personal name, Mealtan. Neither of these placenames, nor the sites to which they refer, have any apparent early ecclesiastical significance. On the other hand, a number of Donegal *ráth*-names do in fact refer to early church sites.

Two of the churches which were recorded in the seventh century by St Patrick's biographer, Tírechán, contain the element *ráth*. One of these was reputedly established by Patrick: *intrauit in campum Sereth trans amnem iter Es Ruaid et mare et fundauit aeclessiam hirRaith Argi* (he entered Magh Sereth across the river between Assaroe and the sea and founded a church in Ráith Argi).[73] The name *Raith Argi* is now obsolete but from the context it apparently referred to a place in either the parish of Kilbarron or Drumhome, possibly the townland of Rath in the latter. The name may signify 'the fort or enclosure of the milking-place'.

The other site mentioned by Tírechán is *Raith Chungai,* 'the fort or enclosure of the yoke or ridge'. It was here that Assicus, Patrick's coppersmith, was buried.[74] This name still survives in the form Racoo, the name of a burial-ground in the townland of Ballymagrorty in Drumhome parish.[75] While Tírechán asserts that *Ráith Chonga* was originally a Patrician foundation, he significantly mentions that the church was claimed by the Columban community of Ardstraw.[76]

The most important Columban foundation within the bounds of the present county was *Ráth Bhoth,* or Raphoe, which gave its name to the diocese. This site is particularly associated with Adhamhnán, or Eunan, the patron saint of the diocese, who was abbott of Iona and whose death is recorded in the *Annals of Ulster* under the year 704. Adhamhnán, or Adomnan in Old Irish, was a kinsman of Colmcille and author of the seventh century Latin biography of the saint. The second element of the placename *Ráth Bhoth* is the genitive plural of the word *both,* which is usually translated as a 'a hut or booth' but which may also refer to an ecclesiastical cell or oratory.[77] It occurs in the names of several early ecclesiastical sites in other parts of the country, for example, *Teampall Seanbhoth,* Templeshanbo, in Wexford and *Cill Seanbhotha,* Kilshanvy parish in Galway. The placename *Ráth Bhoth,* therefore, probably signifies 'the fort or enclosure of the huts or cells'. The comparative onomastic evidence would suggest that Raphoe was a purpose-built ecclesiastical enclosure containing a number of earthen cells or oratories.

Raymunterdoney is another early ecclesiastical establishment which gave its name to a parish. The second part of the name, *-munterdoney,* is not found until the seventeenth century and is apparently a late accretion.[78] The parish and the townland in which the church is situated is known locally in Irish as *Ráith.* Likewise, the parish is recorded simply as *Rath* in the *Papal Taxation* of 1302. The patron of the parish is Fionán, whose feast is the 25 November according to the *Martyrology of Donegal: Fionan, mac Piopain o Thempall Ratha i cCenel Conaill* (Fionan son of Piopan from Teampall Ratha [i.e. the church of Ráith] in Cinéal Conaill). He was also known as *Fionán Rátha,* 'Fionán of *Ráith'.* As with the majority of saints associated with

Tír Chonaill, the genealogists make him a descendent of Conall Gulban: *Fionan m. Piopain m. Amhalghadha m. Duaich m. Fearghosa m. Ninneadha m. Feargosa m. Conaill Gulban.*[79] Despite this assertion, Fionán of Raymunterdoney is undoubtedly the same saint Fionán whose cult is found in other parts of the country, particularly in Kerry and in the Midlands.[80] It is worth noting that Fionán's principal church in Kerry was located on Church Island in Waterville Lake. The original name of this lake was *Loch Luighdheach*, 'the lake of Lughaid'. Evidence shows that the personage referred to in this placename is Lughaidh Lámhfhada, that is the pagan god Lugh. Lugh's associations with the Cloghaneely district, of which the parish of Ray forms a part, have already been established. The possibility exists that the pagan cult of Lugh was replaced by the christian cult of Fionán in both north-west Donegal and south-west Kerry.

Fionán's name is commemorated in the parish in *Eas Fionáin,* 'the waterfall of Fionán', the name of a little waterfall on the shore about a mile from his church, where an annual *turas* was held until recently. Maghnas Ó Domhnaill tells how the saint came to be associated with this place:

> Once when Colmcille was saying his office and prayers beside the sea at Port Toraighe in the north of the territory of Cinéal Conaill a great thirst overcame a young cleric who was a fosterling of his, that is Fionán Rátha (Fionán of Ráith). There was no water near them at that time. When Colmcille noticed that Fionán was near death with thirst, he struck three blows with his crozier on a rock which was near him and three streams of water leapt out of it so that Fionán satisfied his thirst with that water. And those streams still come out of that rock today as they did on the first day and that water performs great miracles every day since; and God's name and Colmcille's are magnified thereby. And Colmcille granted an honour to Fionán that that place should be named after him so that its name today is Eas Fionáin (the waterfall of Fionán).[81]

Early churches were commonly established near pre-christian religious sites and the names of a number of these churches provide evidence of this. The church of *Droim Thuama,* from which the parish-name Drumhome derives, is one of Donegal's earliest recorded ecclesiastical sites. It is the only definite Donegal church mentioned by Adhamhnán, who refers to it as *Dorso Tómme,* which represents a semi-translation of the name into Latin. The second part of the name is the genitive singular of *tuaim,* which is found frequently as a placename element, signifying 'a (pagan) burial place or tumulus'. *Droim Thuama* therefore signifies 'the ridge of the burial mound or tumulus' and it is significant that Adhamhnán refers to the site as the burial place of one of Colmcille's disciples: *Ernene, gente mocu Fhir-roide, qui inter aliorum sancti Columbae monacorum reliquias, et ipse sanctus monacus, in dorso Tómme sepultus cum sanctis resurrectionem exspectat* (Ernene of the family of Mocu Fir-roide, himself a holy monk, lies buried among the remains of other monks of Saint Columba, and awaits the resurrection with the saints in Droim Thuama).[82]

The early church of Fahan was, in all probability, also built on the site of a pre-christian cemetery. The Irish form of the name is *Fathain*, which is a development of original Old Irish form *Othain*, the dative form of *Othan*. The word *othan* is of unknown etymology but it appears to refer to a grave of burial-place.[83] The church is said to have been founded in the seventh century by Mura. The site is often referred to as *Fathain Mhura*, 'Fathain of Mura', in the later medieval period in commemoration of its founder and this has led to the misinterpretation of the name as 'the burial-place of Mura'. The evidence suggests that the name of the site predates Mura, and that the form Fathain Mhura is but another example of the later practice of attaching the name of the patron to the name of the foundation with which he was associated.[84]

Generic ecclesiastical settlement terms

A small number of elements are found in the names of early church sites which refer specifically to ecclesiastical settlement. The most important of the elements attested in the ecclesiastical placenames of the earlier period of church development are *domhnach, cill, díseart*, and *teach*. Each of these terms can be loosely translated as 'church' when it occurs as an early placename element.[85]

Domhnach

The word *domhnach* is a borrowing of Latin *dominicum*, a word which had a specialised meaning of 'church-building' in pre-fifth century continental Latin. The Irish word *domhnach* is only found in the sense of 'church' in placenames and is not attested with this meaning in the general vocabulary of Irish, a fact that suggests that the word had become obsolete before the first written records. In toponomy, the term is associated with church-sites belonging to the earliest phase of Christianity, particularly those belonging to the Patrician period. It has been suggested that *domhnach* was the equivalent of a regional parish church, one founded to serve a settled community. In placenames the term *domhnach* is often qualified by the name of the district in which the church to which it refers is situated.

Saint Patrick founded a number of churches in Donegal according to the earliest Patrician sources. The names of four of these church-sites originally contained the element *domnach*. Tírechán's states in his seventh century *Collectanea* that Patrick crossed the River Drowes into what is now Donegal and founded a church in a place called *Magh nEine*. *Et perrexit ad campum Aine et posuit aeclessiam ibi* (And he proceeded to Magh nEine and founded a church there).[86] In the early tenth century Irish Life of St. Patrick, *Bethu Phátraic,* this church is referred to as *Domnach Mór Maigi Eni,* 'the great *domnach* or church of Magh nEine'.[87] *Magh nEine* was the old name of the plain between the Drowes and the Erne, which was not historically part of Tír Chonaill. The name of the church no longer survives but it is recorded as Donoghmore in the early seventeenth century.[88]

In his tendency to translate the placenames of his text into Latin, Tírechán refers to *domnach* as *aeclesia* or *aeclesia magna* and the two other Donegal churches mentioned by him are thus described: *Et perrexit for Bernas filiorum Conill in campo Itho et fundavit ibi aeclessiam magnam* (he proceeded over the gap of the sons of Conaill (Bearnas Mór) to Magh nIotha and founded there a great church).[89] This 'great church' is *Domhnach Mór Maighe Iotha,* now, Donaghmore, the name of a parish in the barony of Raphoe South. The name *Magh nIotha* is no longer in use, but it was apparently co-extensive with the Lower Finn Valley. Tírechán translates the church mentioned in *Bethu Phátraic* as *Domhnach Mór Maighe Tóchair* in similar fashion: *exiit ad campum Tochair et fecit aeclessiam ibi* (he went to Magh Tóchair and built a church there).[90] This name lives on in the parish-name Donagh, *Domhnach,* and in the name Carndonagh, *Carn Domhnach*, the site of the original church. *Magh Tóchair,* 'the plain of the causeway', was the name of the plain surrounding the church. The name no longer survives but the second element, *tóchar* 'causeway', is found in the name Glentogher, *Gleann Tóchair* 'the valley of the causeway', the name of the glen running eastwards from Carndonagh. Colton records the name of the parish as *Townaghglyntachyr* in his *Visitation of the Diocese of Derry* of 1392. This form, which reflects *Domhnach Glinne Tóchair,* suggests that the name *Magh Tóchair* had become obsolete by the late medieval period.

Bethu Phátraic refers to another *domhnach*-church, one which is not mentioned by Tírechán: *Is ed doluid Pátraic ó Domnach Mór Maigi Tochair isin mBretaig. Is and faránic na tri Dechnán, maicc sethar do Pátraic, hi crích Ailella maicc Eogain, ro ordnestar Óengus macc Ailella isin baili sin ⁊ fiú and fó domnach. Domnach Bile a ainm* (Then Patrick came from Domnach Mór Maighe Tóchair into Bréadach. There he found the three Deachnáns, sons of Patrick's sister, in the territory of Ailill son of Eoghan and he ordained Aonghas son of Ailill in that place, and he slept there on a Sunday: Domhnach Bile is its name).[91] *Bréadach* was the name of a well-known territory which was seemingly co-extensive with the original civil parish of Moville. The name survives in the form Bredagh River, which flows into the sea at Moville. *Domhnach Bile* is unquestionably a reference to the church of *Maigh Bhile*, which was situated in the townland of Cooley in the parish of Moville Upper. The name *Maigh Bhile*, from which derives Moville, signifies 'the plain of the sacred tree'.[92] The word *bile*, 'a sacred tree', is usually only found in names of pre-christian religious sites.[93] It is probable, therefore, that *Maigh Bhile* was originally the name of a pagan religious site, similar to a number of those sites discussed earlier.

Díseart

Díseart is a borrowing of Latin *desertum*, which is explained as 'an isolated place', or 'a desert'. The Irish word is generally translated as 'a hermitage', but not all *díseart*-churches were necessarily located in isolated places. The element *díseart* usually denotes a church associated with the Céile Dé reform movement of the eighth to ninth century, but several placenames containing the element may predate that period. It has been suggested that the *díseart* was attached, or in close proximity, to the monastic church, 'where the more devout monks ... might lead the life of recluses and at the same time share in the religious work of the church'.[94]

County Donegal has only two placenames containing the element *díseart*. The first of these is the townland of Disert in the parish of Inver. This placename is found unqualified in all sources, which makes it almost impossible to say to whom the church was dedicated. The site of the church is now marked by a disused graveyard, in which are a number of penitential cairns. There is a holy well dedicated to Colmcille nearby.[95]

The parish of Desertegny in Inishowen is from Irish *Díseart Éignigh*. The second part of the placename is undoubtedly a personal name, Éigneach, but it is not possible to identify the person referred to. Only one individual of the name is found in ecclesiastical sources, *Eicnech mac Con Cathrach* (Éigneach son of Cú Chathrach), but nothing more of this individual is known.[96] The name Éigneachán, a derivvative of Éigneach, was a popular name among the O'Dohertys and other Donegal families.

Teach

The word *teach*, 'a house', is the only widely attested native Irish element to designate a church or monastic site in placenames. The term is found in placenames of all periods but, generally speaking, it is only in the earliest names that it has ecclesiastical reference, with the meaning '(monastic) church'. The element *teach* is only attested in one ecclesiastical placename in Donegal.

Taughboyne in Cinéal Éanna takes its name from Irish *Teach Baoithín*, which signifies 'the house of Baoithín'. According to all the sources, Baoithín was the immediate successor of Colmcille as abbott of Iona: *Baoithín, abb Ia Cholaim Chille indiaidh Coluim Chille fén, acus Tech Baoithin i cCenel Conaill a prímh cheall, ár ba do chenel Conaill Gulban do ...... Ro fhaidh Baoithín a ainm iarsna ceithre bliadhnaibh remhráite do chum nimhe i ccomhainm an laoi do deachaidh Colum Cille do chum nimhe Ao. Di. 600* (Baoithín, abbot of Iona after Colmcille himself; and Teach Baoithín, [Taughboyne], in Cinéal Conaill was his chief church, for he was of the race of Conall Gulban. ... Baoithín resigned his soul to heaven after the four years aforesaid, on the same day of the month that Colmcille went to Heaven, AD 600).[97]

Cill

The element *cill* was the most productive term in ecclesiastical place-names in the pre-twelfth century Christian period. The word, which is a borrowing of Latin *cella*, has a range of meanings in Irish, 'church, monastic settlement or foundation, churchyard, graveyard'. In place-names, the term almost always refers to a monastic settlement particularly in pre-twelfth century names.[98] Donegal has a comparatively small number of placenames with the element *cill*; only six parish-names contain this element and, significantly, not one of these is located in Inishowen.

The most illustrious of the *cill*-names in the county is undoubtedly Kilmacrenan, through its association with Colmcille. It was here that Colmcille was fostered, according to Maghnas Ó Domhnaill in his sixteenth-century Life of the saint, *Betha Coluim Chille*. Further evidence for the saint's association with the church is attested elsewhere. The annals mention *Teach Choluim Cille,* 'the house of Colmcille', in connection with the site: *Teach Choluim Cille i cCill mic Nénain do ghabháil dUa Tairchert for Aodh mac Cathbairr Uí Domhnaill₇ a losccadh fair* (Teach Choluim Cille, 'the house of Colmcille' at Kilmacrenan was taken by Ó Taircheirt from Aodh son of Cathbharr Ó Domhnaill and it was burned over him).[99] Maghnas Ó Domhnaill remarks that Kilmacrenan was originally called *Doire Eithne,* 'the oak-wood of Eithne'. As is well known, Eithne was Colmcille's mother. She is still commemorated in *Tobar Eithne,* 'Eithne's well', the name of a holy well in the townland of Barnes Lower about four miles from Kilmacrenan. According to Ordnance Survey documents, a pilgrimage known as *Turas an Bhearnais* or *Turas Cholm Cille* was held annually at this well on 9 June, Colmcille's feast day.[100]

The name Kilmacrenan comes from Irish *Cill Mhic Réanáin,* which in turn is a late medieval development of the original form, *Cill Mhac nÉanáin,* through the process of dissimilation. *Cill Mhac nEanáin* signifies 'the church of the sons of Éanán'. Tradition is silent as to the identity of Éanán, but, according to Adhamhnán, one of Colmcille's sisters was the mother of his sons: *Consobrini sancti Columbe. Mincholeth mater filiorum Enain quorum unus Colmaan dicebatur* (Saint Columba's kindred. Mincholeth mother of the sons of Éanán one of whom was called Colmán).[101] Colmán was one of the most common Irish saint-names and it would be almost impossible to identify any one of them as Colmcille's nephew. *Cill Cholmáin,* 'the church of Colmán', now Killycolman in the parish of Killygarvan, commemorates one individual named Colmán. The martyrologies provide some clues to the identity of this particular saint, however. The *Martyrology of Tallaght* commemorates a saint named *Colmán Imramha,* 'Colmán of the Voyage', on 8 July. According to the later commentaries, this saint belonged to Fahan in Inishowen, which lies almost directly across Lough Swilly from Killygarvan: *Colman Iomramha, ó Faithin Bicc i nInis Eoghain.*[102] The feast day of Garbhán, the patron of the parish of Killygarvan, fell on 9 July. The circumstantial evidence suggests, therefore, that it is Colmán Iomramha who is commemorated in the placename of Killycolman.

Killygarvan is originally *Cill Gharbháin,* 'the church of Garbhán.' There are eight saints of the name Garbhán listed in the martyrologies. One of them is commemorated in the *Martyrology of Tallaght* on 9 July: *Garbán sac. Cinn tSaile* (Garbhán a priest of Ceann Sáile). The later commentaries identify the placename *Ceann Sáile* as Kinsealy in county Dublin: *ó Chinn tSaile leith aniár do Shurd, no i niarthur Erenn* (from Ceann Saile to the west of Sord, or in the western part of Ireland).[103] Placename evidence, however, suggests that this entry refers to Garbhán, the patron of Killygarvan. No trace of the original church of *Cill Gharbháin* now remains but it apparently lay in the modern townland of Glebe which was originally part of the townland of Killygarvan Upper.[104] There was a holy well known as *Tobar Garbháin* near the churchyard which those leaving home would visit as a cure for loneliness.[105] The townland adjoining the townland of Glebe is called Kintale, which derives from Irish *Cionn tSáile.* On balance, therefore, it is more probable that *Ceann Sáile* cited in the entry above refers to the townland of Kintale in Killygarvan Parish than to Kinsealy in county Dublin.

There is a saint named Conall commemorated in the townland of

Kilconnell, *Cill Chonaill*, 'the church of Conall', near Kilmacrenan. This name may commemorate Conall of Inis Caoil or perhaps another saint of the same name. Adhamhnán mentions a saint Conall in association with Colmcille: *Conallus episcopus Cule-rathin* (Conall bishop of Coleraine),[106] and it is possibly he who is commemorated here.

There is another bishop of Coleraine called Cairbre commemorated in the martyrologies on 15 November. This is surely the same Bishop Cairbre mentioned on 1 November, whom the *Martyrology of Donegal* associates with *Cill Chairbre*, Kilcarbery, a church in the townland of Ardgillew in the parish of Kilbarran:[107] *Cairpre, epscop. Ata Cill Chairpre a dTír Aodha, a ngar dEsruaidh agus do Sith Áodha Easa Ruaidh* (Cairbre, Bishop. There is a Cill Cairbre in Tirhugh near Assaroe and the Fairymound of Aodh of Assaroe).

The name of the parish of Kilbarron is from Irish *Cill Bharrainn*, 'the church of Barrann'. Barrann's feast day was celebrated on 21 May according to the martyrologies: *Bairrfhionn epscop7 ab ó Druim Cuilinn7 ó Chill Bhairrfhinn fri hEss-ruaidh atuaidh. Do chenel Conaill Gulban meic Néill dó* (Bairrfhionn bishop and abbot of Druim Cuilinn and of Cill Bhairrfhinn to the north of Assaroe. He was of the kindred of Conall Gulban).[108] The genealogies assert that Barrann was a great grandson of Conall Gulban but, as is the case with most of the saints' genealogies, this is undoubtedly a fiction.[109] Barrann is a regular reflex of earlier *Bairrfhind*, which is a compound of *barr* 'top or head' and *find* 'fair'. The name would therefore mean 'the fair headed one'. In his major study of Saint Finbar, Pádraig Ó Riain has shown that the name *Barrann* is interchangeable with *Fionnbharr*, a name composed of the same elements and with the same meaning. Ó Riain argues convincingly that both Fionnbharr, Finbar of Cork, and Barrann are one and the same saint, whose cult originated in north-east Ulster and which spread to many parts of Ireland under various names.[110]

Maghnas Ó Domhnaill relates the circumstances under which Barrann came to be associated with the parish of Kilbarron:

> Colmcille went towards Assaroe and he stopped at the mouth of little river called the Fuinnseannach (now Abbey River) that flows into the sea to the north of it. And he spoke to a certain holy man who was with him, who was a kinsman of his, Barrann son of Muireadhach son of Eochu son of Conall Gulban and he asked him where his crozier was. Barrann answered, 'I threw it at the demons as they went into the sea when we were drawing them out of Seanghleann (Glencolumbkille) and I have not found it since.' 'It is my will if it is God's will', said Colmcille, ' that your crozier should come here to you.' With that they saw the crozier

rising up towards them out of a rock before them. And a stream of water gushed out after it and there is a fresh-water well in that place to this day. Colmcille said that as an honour to Barrann the well should be named after him. So that its name is Ballán Barrainne from that day to this.[111]

Ballán Barrainne signifies 'the bullaun of Barrann', a bullaun being a naturally carved well in a rock. The name *Ballán Barrainne* no longer survives but the well is still in the place described, that is, on the shore of the townland of Abbeyland near Ballyshannon. It is marked on the Ordnance Survey six-inch map as Tobernaboghilla, that is, *Tobar na Bachaille*, which signifies 'the well of the crozier'. Thomas Fagan of the Ordnance Survey, writing in the middle of the last century, describes the well as 'a holy well of great antiquity and of much celebrity as a place of religious station, and still well attended about midsummer by the natives as well as those of remote districts. It is at full tide inundated by the adjoining sea'.[112]

Several explanations are possible as to why the stations at *Tobar na Bachaille* were held at midsummer and not on Barrann's feast-day of 21 May. It is clear that the association of Barrann with this well had been forgotten by the time of the Ordnance Survey. In that context the transfer of the celebrations to coincide with those held on St. John's Eve would have been easy. A more plausible explanation for the change of date may be suggested, however. Twenty-third June is the feast-day of Mochaoi of Nendrum in county Down: *Mochaoi, abb Naon dromma i nUltoibh. Caolán a chéd ainm* (Mochaoi Abbot of Nendrum in Ulster. Caolán was his first name).[113] It was at Nendrum that the cult of Barrann originated, according to Ó Riain. It is worth noting that Mochaoi, under his alternative name, Caolán, was also the patron of *Eachnais*, Aughnish on Lough Swilly. Caolán and Fionnbharr of Cork, under his hypocoristic form Bairre, both share a feast-day on 25 September.[114] It is very probable, therefore, that Barrann of Kilbarron was also commemorated on Mochaoi's principal feast day of 23 June, which would explain the celebrations at *Tobar na Bachaille*, otherwise *Ballán Barrainne* on that date.

Placename evidence indicates that Barrrann was venerated at two other sites in Donegal. Kilwarry in the parish of Tullyfern reflects an original Irish form *Cill Bhaire*, 'the church of Bairre'. However, the seventeenth century forms, *Killwarrin*,[115] and *Kilbarran*,[116] would indicate that *Cill Bharrainn* was the original form. Kilwarry is situated on the shore of a small lake called Lough Columbkille in which there is a natural feature known as Columbkille's Chair. There is no tradition to indicate whether there was any ritual attached to this lake but it would be surprising had there not been. The name of the lake illustrates once more how Barrann's cult had become intertwined with that of Colmcille in Donegal.

The other placename in which Barrann is commemorated is Killyverry in the parish of Raymoghy in the barony of Raphoe. Once again seventeenth century documentary forms such as *Killvarrin*,[117] *Kilbarry* and *Kilvarry*[118] show that *Cill Bhairre* and *Cill Bharrainn* could alternate. Killyverry lies in the heart of the Lagan, an area that was heavily planted by Scottish settlers in the seventeenth century, a fact that made it unlikely for any traditions about the saint to survive. It is significant, however, that Killyverry lies near Raphoe, which was one of the most important Columban foundations in the county, being particularly associated with Adhamhnán. Adhamhnán's feast-day falls on 23 September. It is worth noting that there is a Barrfhinn commemorated in the martyrologies on 22 September and that the feast of Finbar of Cork falls on 25 September.[119]

Despite his east Ulster origins, Barrann's pedigree was stitched into those of the Cinéal Conaill, like most of the other saints associated with Donegal. The parish of Kilcar, on the other hand, is dedicated to a saint for whom the medieval genealogists did not find a place in the local scheme of things. *Cill Charthaigh*, 'the church of Carthach', is named after Carthach, who was a son of the king of Cashel in Munster. He was a bishop and a pupil of Ciarán of *Saighir*, now Seirkeeran in county Offaly. His feast-day is 5 March, the same day as that of his mentor Ciarán: *Carthach, epscop, dalta Ciarain Saighre. Ba dia bhailtibh Druim Fertain, acus a cCairpre Ua Ciardha ata Druim Fertain, acus is leis Inis Uachtair for Loch Sileann, acus Cill Carthaigh i Tír Boghaine i cCenel Conaill. Mac dAonghus, mac Nadfraoich ri Mumhan eisium* (Carthach, Bishop, alumnus of Ciaran of Saighir. One of his places was Druim Fertain and Druim-fertain is in Cairbre Ua Ciardha; and to him belongs Inis Uachtair in Loch Sileann and Cill Charthaigh in Tír Boghaine in Cinéal Conaill. He was son of Aenghus, son of Nadfraech king of Munster).[120] It is of interest that both saints, Ciarán as well as Carthach, were venerated in the parish of Kilcar until recently. Stations were performed at *Tobar Charthaigh*, 'Carthach's well', on the eve of the saint's feast day, 4 March. These were followed by stations held at *Tobar Chiaráin*, 'Ciarán's well', in the townland of Bawan on 5 March.[121] There apparently was a church dedicated to Ciarán near his well. It is of interest that the parish of Kilcar was alternatively known as *Cill Chiaráin* until the seventeenth century, a fact that would indicate that Ciaran's cult had been as strong in the locality as that of his pupil.

Not all of the ecclesiastical sites of the county have patrons as easily identifiable as those discussed previously. The name of the parish of

Kilteevoge in the Finn Valley is a case in point. The modern Irish form of the name is *Cill Taobhóg* which signifies 'the church of Taobhóg'. Local tradition asserts that Taobhóg was a woman, the daughter of one Ó Duibheannaigh, a local chieftain.[122] This explanation is undoubtedly a late invention influenced by the termination *-óg*, which normally signifies a female in modern Irish. There is no saint named Taobhóg listed in the martyrologies. Attempts to identify him with Dabheóg of Lough Derg are not tenable.[123]

The name Taobhóg may be best explained as a late dialectal reflex of an original *Taodhóg*. This name occurs in two entries in the martyrologies. One entry is found under 13 July: *T'Aedoc .i. ó Thigh t'Áodócc* (Taodhóg of Teach Taodhóg).[124] Nothing more is known of this saint and his church, *Teach Taodhóg*, 'the house of Taodhóg', has not been identified. The other entry offers more clues to the identification of the saint. It occurs on 31 January: *da-Thaedoc .i. Da-Tháodhócc mac Colgan ó Achadh Dumha* (da-Thaedoc *i.e.* Da-Tháodhóg son of Colgu of Achadh Dumha).[125] The earlier *Martyrology of Tallaght* gives the name of this saint as *Taeda mac Colgan* (Taodh son of Colgu).[126] The names *Taodh* and *Taodhóg* are both hypocoristic forms of the name *Aodh*; *Taodh* comes from *Do-Aodh* 'your Aodh', while *Taodhóg* reflects *Do-Aodh-óg,* 'your little Aodh'. It is of interest that 31 January is also the feast of Maodhóg of Ferns: *Forba in mís do Mhaedócc* (the completion of the month to Maodhóg).[127] *Maodhóg* is also a hypocoristic form of *Aodh*, in this case from *Mo-Aodh-óg,* 'my little Aodh'. In the two earliest martyrologies, which were both compiled about the year 800, Maodhóg is referred to as simply Aodh: *Eda episcopi Ferna,* 'Aodh bishop of Ferns'[128] and *Aed fortrén Ferna,* 'strong Aodh of Ferns'.[129] The evidence suggests that Maodhóg and Taodhóg are one and the same saint, particularly the fact that both names are hypocoristic forms of Aodh, and the fact that they share the same feast day on 31 January.

Maodhóg was an associate of Náile, whose name is commemorated in the placename *Cill Náile,* now Kinawley in Fermanagh and in the name *Inbhear Náile,* now the parish of Inver in south Donegal.[130] It is possible that the cult of Maodhóg, under his alternative name Taodhóg, was introduced into Donegal along with that of Náile. It is of some significance that there is a saint named Aodh commemorated in the name of the parish adjoining Inver, Killaghtee, *Cill Leachta Aodha,* which signifies 'the church of Aodh's tomb'. Tradition is of no help in identifying the particular Aodh referred to in this placename. One possibility is that he is to be identified as Aodh mac Bric the patron of Sliabh Liag near Glencolumbkille. The alternative explanation is that the placename Killaghtee actually commemorates Aodh alias Maodhóg of Ferns.

Further evidence exists to connect Maodhóg with west Donegal. The sources attest that Maodhóg was a cousin of Dallán Forgaill. Significantly, Dallán's feast day is on 29 January, two days before that of Maodhóg.[131] Dallán was an associate of Conall and he is reputed to be buried on the island of Inishkeel. The parish of Inishkeel lies immediately to the west of Kilteevoge parish. Given the evidence for his association with this part of Donegal, it is reasonable to infer that it is Maodhóg, under his alternative hypocoristic name Taodhóg, who is commemorated in the placename *Cill Taodhóg*, 'the church of Taodhóg', now *Cill Taobhóg* or in English, Kilteevoge.

Acknowledgement

This paper is based on my work in the Placenames Branch, Ordnance Survey and I wish to thank the Director of the Ordnance Survey for permission to publish it.

References

1. *Inquisitionum in officio rotulorum ca cellariae asservatarum repertorium*, 2 vols. (Dublin, 1826-9), ii: *Ultonia*, p. xvii (hereafter *Inq. Ult.*).
2. Byrne, *Irish Kings*, p. 83.
3. Ibid., pp 283-4.
4. *Red Bk. Kildare*, 26.
5. *A.U.*, 764.
6. *Luid Patraic hi Tír nEugain na Insi.i. hi crích Fergussa* (Patrick went to Tír Eoghain of island, i.e. to the terrritory of Fergus) *Bethu Phátraic*, p. 94.
7. *Bk. Fen.*, p. 315.
8. For a discussion of the name Dobhar and its relationship to the name Gaoth Dobhair see Dónall Mac Giolla Easpaig, 'Logainmneacha Ghaoth Dobhair' in *Scáthlán* 3 (1986), pp 66-71.
9. *Bk. Fen.*, 402.
10. *Tírechán*, #47. It is worth noting that the association of Barnesmore with the Uí Néill persists in the names of two hills on the north-western and south-western sides of Barnesmore Gap, Croaghconnellagh, *Cruach Chonallach*, 'the mountain of the people of Cinéal Conaill', and Croaghonagh, *Cruach Eoghanach*, 'the mountain of the people of Cinéal Eoghain'.
11. *Bk. Fen.*, p. 400. See also the reference to Roscule in *Red Bk. Kildare* below.
12. *A.U.*, 921.
13. *Red Bk. Kildare*, pp 113-5.
14. Byrne, *Irish Kings*, p. 85.
15. *A.U.*, 1019.
16. *Bk. Fen.*, p. 396. In another poem in the same source, it is suggested that Derry lay in Cinéal Éanna territory: *Gabas Enna nDoiri dil,/ Dun Calgaich mic Aithemuin* (Éanna settled in faithful Derry, the fort of Calgach son of Aithemhan) *Bk. Fen.*, 396.
17. The division of the barony of Raphoe into North and South did not occur until the nineteenth century.
18. Both the forms *Luighdheach* and *Lughdhach* are recorded as the genitive of *Lughaidh*.

19. *Bk. Fen.*, p. 396.

20. *A.L.C.*, 1259.

21. *Bk. Fen.*, p. 336.

22. *Corp. Gen. Hib.*, 164.

23. *C.G.H.S.*, 4ff. His father is described merely as *Fedilmithum filium Fergusa*, 'Fedilmith son of Fergus', in *Adomnan* #4a.

24. See O.S. Letters, Donegal, pp 57-63. *Lúiche* is a late dialectal genitive form of *Lughaidh*.

25. A. Holder, *Alt-celtischer Sprachschatz*, ii, pp 308-45.

26. *Corp. Gen. Hib.*, p. 163.

27. *A.U.*, 784.

28. *Bk. Fen.*, p. 396 The area described is almost co-extensive with the modern baronies of Boylagh and Banagh. It is of interest that these two baronies are considered as one in official seventeenth-century sources, see, for example, the description of 'Ye Barrony of Boylogh and Banogh' in *Civil Survey*, iii, p. 72.

29. *Top Poems*, ii, 455-462. There is a townland of Ballyboyle, *Baile Uí Bhaoill*, 'the town of O'Boyle' in the parish of Killymard, about two miles south-west of Donegal town and six miles east of Inver. This placename is recorded in *A.F.M.* under the year 1440: *Caislén Baile Ui Baoighill do ghabhail la Mac Domnaill ui Domhnoill iar bfaghbhail bhaoghail fair 7 édala mora do fagbhail ann dairgeatt 7 dedach 7 deideadh 7 an caislen cedna do ghabail doiridhisi la hua nDomhmoill 7 a thabhairt dua Baoighill 7 clann domhnaill ui Domhnaill do ghabháil ann 7 a mbeith illaimh ag ua nDomhnaill ina mighníomhaibh* (The castle of Ballyboyle was taken by the son of Domhnall who was the son of O'Donnell, when he found it unguarded; and he found therein great spoils in money, apparel, and armour. The same castle was again taken by O'Donnell and given back to O'Boyle; and the sons of Domhnall O'Donnell were taken prisoners therein and detained in captivity by O'Donnell for their evil deeds). This evidence supports the suggestion that the territory between the rivers Eske and Eany was part of Tír Baghaine in the medieval period.

30. *A.U.*, 1496.

31. *A.F.M.*, 1590.

32. *Rennes Dindsenchas* #142. The prose tales in the Rennes Dindsenchas, ed. by Whitley Stokes in *Revue Celtique* xv, xvi (1894-5).

33. *A.U.*, 1343.

34. *Top Poems*, i, 455.

35. *A.F.M.*, 1588.

36. *Bk. Fen.*, p. 396.

37. *Civil Survey*, iii, p. 55; see also 'Survey of Ulster 1608 in *Anal. Hib.*, no. 3 (1931), pp 183-4.

38. *Rennes Dindshenchas* # 81.

39. The civil parish of Donegal was not created until after the mid-seventeenth century.

40. 'Contemporary account of Sydney's expedition to Ulster, 1566' in *R.S.A.I. Jn.*, xi (1870-1), p. 21.

41. Ibid., pp 19-20.

42. Ibid., p. 22.

43. *A.F.M.*, 1474.

44. Ibid., 1505.

45. *A.U.*, 1495.

46. *Murbach do loscadh leis, idon, longport hUi Domhnaill* (Murvagh that is,

Ó Domhnaill's stronghold was burned by him [that is, O'Connor]) *A.U.*, 1419.

47. Alan Mac an Bhaird, 'Ptolemy Revisited' in *Ainm* 5 (1991-93), p. 5. *Fionnchaidh* and *Fionnchaidhe* would have identical pronunciation in Donegal Irish.

48. Deirdre Flanagan 'Place-names in early Irish documentation: structure and composition' in *Nomina* 4 (1980), pp 41-4.

49. *Gall* can also signify 'a standing stone'. See DIL and compare Modern Irish *gallán*.

50. For a discussion of the term *gaill* in the early annals, see Diarmuid Ó Murchadha, 'Nationality names in the Irish annals' in *Nomina* 16 (199), pp 64-6.

51. 'Sydney's expedition', p. 22.

52. *Red Bk. Kildare*, no. 21.

53. *The Annals of Ulster* record that the Vikings burned the monastery of Inishmurry in Donegal Bay in the year 807: *Gentiles combuserunt Insolam Muiredaigh 7 invadunt Ross Comain.*

54. *Dún na nGall* is found as the name of several places throughout the country, one of which is mentioned in the annals: *Sluaigheadh oile la Muircheartach. co Connachtaibh, ocus ro loiscseat Dún Mór, Dún Ciarraighe, Dún na nGall, ocus ro mhillseat mór don tír archeana* (Another army was led by Muircheartach into Connacht, and they burned Dunmore, Dún Ciarraighe, and Dún na nGall, and destroyed a great part of the country generally). *A.F.M.*, 1159. *Dún na nGall* can be identified with a fort in the townland of Ballynacarragh, *Baile na Cathrach*, 'the town of the fort', in the barony of Kilmaine, county Mayo. It is referred to in the year 1625 as '1/2 qr of Caherendoonangall in Ballynecarragh' in *The Strafford Inquisition of Co. Mayo*, p. 56. This place is located many miles from the coast, where one would not expect to find Viking influence.

55. See Deirdre Flanagan, 'The Christian impact on early Ireland: placenames evidence' in P. Ní Chatháin and M. Richter (eds), *Irland und Europa/Ireland and Europe* (Stuttgart, 1984).

56. Many of the placenames containing this element refer to remote mountainous areas, unlikely situations for battles, for example, *Leitir Catha* in the Rosses in Donegal and *Beitheach Chatha* and *Glinn Chatha* in the Conamara area of county Galway.

57. *Mart. Don.*, 16 July.

58. *Mart. Don.*, 22 July.

59. Énrí Ó Muirgheasa, 'The holy wells of Donegal' in *Béaloideas*, 7 (1936), pp 143-162.

60. Several examples of 'saints' boats' have been recorded around the coast. The best known is probably that called Bád Cholm Cille, a boat-shaped boulder lying on the beach at Maíros near Rossaveal, county Galway, in which Colmcille is reputed to have sailed from Aran.

61. *Adomnan*, ##25b-26a.

62. G. Toner and M. B. Ó Mainnín, *Placenames of Northern Ireland, volume i: county Down I* (1992) pp 49-56.

63. See *Mart. Don.*, p. 30, n.1: *Ata Tulaigh Dalláin fos i tir Conaill*, 'There is a Tulaigh Dhalláin still in Tír Chonaill'.

64. For a description of the site see Lacy, *Archaeological survey*, p. 242.

65. See *D.I.L.*, *tulach*.

66. *Acus dorindedh flegh mór iarsin le macuib Ferghossa san inadh re n-abartar Both Brain, a tir Fergna aniugh, a termon Cille mic Nenain* (And a great feast was made by the sons of Fergus in the place that is called Both Brain in Tír Fheargna, 'the land of Feargna', today in the church-lands [tearmann] of

Kilmacrenan) A. O'Kelleher and G. Schoepperle (eds), *Betha Colaim Chille: Life of Columcille compiled by Manus O Donnell in 1532* (Chicago, 1918) (hereafter B.C.C.) #93.

67. *Mart.Don.*, 2 March.
68. *B.C.C.* #42.
69. For a comprehensive account of Conall's cult in Donegal see Lochlann McGill, *In Conall's footsteps* (1992).
70. *Mart. Tall.*, 22 May. The form *Conaill* is the genitive case.
71. See, for example, Niall Ó Dónaill, *Na Glúnta Rosannacha* (1952), p. 21: *Conall Mac Caolmháine b'ainm ó cheart dó, ach tugadh Caol, nó Conall Caol, mar leasainm air.*
72. Leo Swan, 'Enclosed ecclesiastical sites and their relevance to settlement patterns of the first millennium AD' in T. Reeves-Smyth and Fred Hamond (eds), *Landscape archaeology in Ireland* (1983), pp 269-280.
73. *Tírechán*, #47.
74. Ibid., #22.
75. See Lacy, *Archaeological survey*, p. 200. The development of *-onga* to *-oo* is well attested as in, for example, the name Inishcoo near Aranmore which derives from *Inis Conga.*
76. *Tírechán*, # 22. Drumhome was a Columban foundation.
77. See *D.I.L.*, *both.*
78. cf. *Rathmuinterdoinne* in '*Survey of Ulster, 1608*', p. 178.
79. *Gen.Reg. et SS*, p. 41. P. Walsh (ed.), *Genealogiae regum et sanctorum Hiberniae* (Dublin, 1918).
80. Both *Fionán* and *Fíonán* are attested as forms of the name and there is a good deal of confusion between them in early sources.
81. *B.C.C.*, #114.
82. *Adomnan*, #132a.
83. see *D.I.L.*, *othan.*
84. For full documentation and discussion of the name *Fathain* see *Dinnseanchas*, iii (1968-9), pp 52-5.
85. For a discussion of these elements see Flanagan, 'The Christian impact on early Ireland: placenames evidence'.
86. *Tírechán*, #46.
87. *Bethu Phátraic*, p. 89.
88. '*Survey of Ulster, 1608*, p. 183. For the identification of *Magh nEine* see Rev P. Ó Gallchobhair, 'Where is Magh Ceidne and Magh Ene?' in *Donegal Annual*, iii (1954-5), pp 70-3, and Diarmuid Ó Murchadha, 'Mag Cetne and Mag Ene' in *Éigse*, xxvi (1993), pp 33-46.
89. *Tírechán*, #47.
90. *Tírechán*, #47.
91. *Bethu Phátraic*, p. 95.
92. *Bun an Phobail*, the official Irish name of Moville town is not recorded until the early nineteenth century. The name is shown as Bunnaphobble on the first edition of sheet 22 Ordnance Survey six-inch map. It originally referred to a small village at the foot of the Bredagh River. John O'Donovan, writing in the Ordnance Survey Letters in 1835, mentions the village as follows: 'A neat village has sprung up of late years at the mouth of this little river, called by the natives Bunaphobble, but by the inhabitants of Derry and by strangers, Moville. Moville, has, however, become the general name of it these three or four years, and I think that we should adopt that name, as the village lies so very close to the old

church called Maghbile or Movilla.' Montgomery adopted the parish name as the name of the new town which he established in the mid-nineteenth century. Native Irish-speakers in the locality continued to refer to the place as Bun an Phobail, which signifies 'the bottom of the parish'.

93. For a discussion of *bile* in placenames, see D. Mac Giolla Easpaig, 'Lough Neagh and Tynagh revisited' in *Ainm* i (1986), pp 35-6.
94. Kenney, *Sources*, p. 468.
95. Lacy, *Archaeological survey*, p. 261.
96. *Mart. Tall.*, 24 April.
97. *Mart. Don.*, 9 June.
98. *Cill* usually designates a graveyard in late minor placenames.
99. *A.F.M.*, 1129.
100. Ordnance Survey, Hill drawing antiquity namebook, Donegal, no. 5.
101. *Adomnan*, p. 548.
102. *Mart. Don.*, 8 July.
103. *Mart. Gorm.*, 9 July, n. 3.
104. The 'antient Church called Killgarvan' is mentioned in *Civil Survey*, iii, p. 103,.
105. Ó Muirgheasa, *'Holy wells of Donegal'*, p. 144.
106. *Adomnan*, 51a.
107. Kilcarbery was apparently the name of the townland until the end of the seventeenth century: 'The Quarter of Cillcarbare' is mentioned in *Civil Survey*, iii, p. 57.
108. *Mart.Gorm.*, 21 May.
109. *C.G.H.S.*, 27.
110. Pádraig Ó Riain, 'St. Finnbarr: a study in a cult' in *Cork Hist. Soc. Jn.*, 82 (1977), pp 63-82.
111. *B.C.C.*, #133.
112. Ordnance Survey, Hill drawing antiquity namebook, Donegal, no. 107. Ó Muirgheasa, *'Holy wells of Donegal'*, p. 144, refers to this well as St Patrick's holy well and states that stations were still made there from 10 June to 20 September.
113. *Mart. Don.*, 23 June.
114. Ibid., 25 Sept.
115. *Inq. Ult.*, 1609.
116. *Civil Survey*, iii, p. 101.
117. *'Survey of Ulster, 1608'*, p. 187.
118. *Inq. Ult.*, 9 C I.
119. *Mart. Don.*, 22, 23, and 25 Sept.
120. Ibid., 6 March.
121. Ó Muirgheasa, *'Holy wells of Donegal'*, p. 147.
122. James O'Kane, 'Placenames of Inniskeel and Kilteevoge', p. 134 in *Zeitschrift fur Celtische Philologie*, Band 31(1970).
123. *Diocese of Raphoe*, pp 56-8.
124. *Mart. Gorm.*, July 13.
125. Ibid., 31 Jan.
126. *Mart. Tall.*, 31 Jan. The form *Taeda* represents the genitive case of *Taed.*
127. *Mart. Gorm.*, 31 Jan.
128. *Mart. Tall.*, 31 Jan.
129. *Mart. Oeng.* (1905), 31 Jan.
130. *Beatha Naile*, ##16-17.
131. *Mart. Don.*, 29 Jan.

Chapter 6

LATE MEDIEVAL DONEGAL

KATHARINE SIMMS

It was during the later medieval period, from the fourteenth to the end of the sixteenth centuries, that the modern county of Donegal gradually took shape as the traditional boundaries of Tír Chonaill were extended. As defined by twelfth- or thirteenth-century poems from the 'Old Book of Fenagh', the original territory allotted to the prehistoric Conall, son of Niall of the Nine Hostages, consisted of three districts or cantreds, the cantred of the O'Donnells' ancestor Lughaidh son of Séadna stretching from Farsetmore on the river Swilly to Gweedore, the cantred of Conall's son Boghuine from Gweedore to Inver, and the cantred of Assaroe extending from Inver east to the Barnesmore Gap and south to a certain hazelwood in the neighbourhood of the Erne estuary. Two further cantreds are described by the poems as closely associated with this heartland of the Cineál Conaill, namely the cantred of Conall's brother Cairbre, stretching westwards from the hazelwood by the Erne to near Ballysadare in county Sligo, and the cantred of his brother Éanna, east of the Barnesmore Gap and south of Inishowen.[1] Inishowen itself had been allotted to Conall's other brother Eoghan, whose descendants conquered Tír Eoghain (counties Derry and Tyrone) and became powerful and dangerous rivals to the Cineál Conaill.

What we have in the foregoing, of course, is simply a statement of tradition, though undoubtedly tailored to reflect the political realities of the poet's own period. For instance, whatever the earlier position, in the days of the high-king Brian Bóraimhe (d. 1014) the southern limits of the power of Maolruanaidh Ó Maoldoraidh, then king of Tír Chonaill, stretched down to the modern Ballysadare and Ballymote,[2] and in the late eleventh-century *Book of Rights* the territory of Cairbre Droma Cliabh (barony of Carbury Drumcliff, county Sligo) is described as subject to the king of Aileach. For most of the eleventh and twelfth centuries this title 'King of Aileach' which implied overlordship of all the northern Uí Néill, both Cineál Conaill and Cineál Eoghain, was attached to the MacLochlainn dynasty of Inishowen, where Grianán Ailigh itself was situated. However, the Munster *Annals of Inisfallen* call the powerful Maolruanaidh Ó Maoldoraidh 'king of the North (of

Ireland)' in 1026, and another high point was reached when his descendant Flaithbheartach Ó Maoldoraidh (d. 1197) was described as 'King of Cineál Conaill, Cineál Eoghain and of the territories as far as Ballysadare and Loch Gill (county Sligo)'.[3]

This control was built on fragile foundations, however. The Ó Maoldoraidh kings of Tír Chonaill had long alternated in power with a related and rival dynasty, the Uí Chanannáin,[4] and when Flaithbheartach Ó Maoldoraidh died apparently without any direct heir in 1197, other noble families put forward claimants to the kingship, and a brief period of confusion intervened before the first O'Donnell king of Tír Chonaill, Éigneachán (c. 1200-1208), ascended the throne.

The battles that raged at this time were not all dynastic in origin. In the late twelfth century Ulster was in the process of being invaded and partially conquered by Sir John de Courcy, while Richard Mór de Burgh and his Anglo-Norman allies conquered Connacht after prolonged fighting in 1236. Domhnall Mór O'Donnell, the second of his family to rule Tír Chonaill, was married to a daughter of the late king of Connacht, and it is significant that when his brother-in-law, King Felim O'Conor, fled to take refuge with O'Donnell in 1235, the English army pursued him no further than Ballysadare, which still marked the southern limits of the king of Tír Chonaill's power. On his death in 1241 Domhnall Mór was described as 'King of Tír Chonaill, Fir Mhanach, Cairbre, and Oirghialla from the plain northwards (i.e. the county Monaghan area)'.[5]

However, in the course of the Anglo-Norman conquest of Connacht, Maurice FitzGerald, second Baron Offaly and for a number of years the justiciar of Ireland, was rewarded for his services to the Anglo-Irish magnates by a grant (c. 1235-6) of lands in southern Sligo from Richard Mór de Burgh, lord of Connacht, while he received a further grant of the cantred of Cairbre from Hugh de Lacy, earl of Ulster, together with a speculative grant of the as yet unconquered kingdom of Tír Chonaill, which may have given him the pretext for his further claim to the kingdom of Fir Mhanach.[6] FitzGerald's vigorous attempts to enforce his claims led to repeated invasions of Tír Chonaill, the imposition of his own candidates as kings there, the successful exaction of hostages and tribute, even at one stage the colonisation of land in the modern barony of Tirhugh, though whether this episode gave rise to the place-name Dún na nGall, 'the Fort of the Foreigners', on the site of Donegal town itself has never been conclusively proven. The O'Donnells and their galloglass troops not only resisted these incursions with considerable success but counter-attacked by invading the Sligo lordship. Subsequently the threat to their independence diminished when in 1286 the second lord of Sligo, Maurice the Bald, died, leaving only heiresses, whose territorial claims were coveted by the second Richard de Burgh, the 'Red' Earl of Ulster and Lord of Connacht (d. 1326). In documents relating to the ensuing division of the inheritance we find a new definition of the boundaries of Tír Chonaill. It was now described as composed of four cantreds, two on the sea-coast from 'Roscule' to 'Thethnegall' (Rosguill to Donegal?) and two inland, stretching from Loch Erne to Cineál Moáin (around Lifford) and thence up to Derry.[7] Evidently by this time the formerly separate cantred of Tír Éanna was considered an integral part of Tír Chonaill, a development Tomás Ó Canann has traced back to the early eleventh century.[8]

Even so, these four cantreds as described in 1289 represent an underestimate. Although the river Erne may have marked the southern boundary of Tír Chonaill when it was first granted to Maurice FitzGerald, the Register of Clogher records a complaint in 1278 by the Fermanagh chief O'Flanagan of Tuath Rátha (barony Clanawley, county Fermanagh) that the sea-coast between the Erne and the river Drowes, known as Magh Éine, although once a part of his own sub-kingdom, had been overrun and occupied by King Gofraidh O'Donnell (1247-58) in the course of his war against the FitzGerald Lord of Sligo.[9] This controversy lived on to become the theme of a fifteenth-century poem by the little-known bard Giolla Íosa Ó Sléibhin: 'Cá sealbh is fearr ar Eas Ruaidh?' – which asks who had the best right to the Falls of Assaroe and the Erne estuary. Inevitably the poet decides the historical right belongs to his patron, Aodh Maguire (d. 1428), Tánaiste of Fir Mhanach, but he admits that in his own time the area was a hotly disputed battleground between Connacht and Tír Chonaill.[10] By the end of the sixteenth century English administrators were still in doubt as to where the interprovincial boundary should come. In 1585 the *Compossicion Booke of Conought* described Magh Éine as a part of county Sligo, but in the hands of O'Donnell,[11] while the cartographer Mercator made confusion worse by labelling the Erne estuary as 'Trowis flu' (River Drowes) in his Atlas of 1585. Although Bundrowse and its river are correctly identified by Baptista Boazio in his 1599 Map of Ireland, Mercator's error was repeated in 1610 by the Englishman John Speed.[12] On 26 November 1603 a commission set up by King James I to determine the 'Boundes of Tirconnell' which interrogated the historian Lughaidh Ó Cléirigh among other jurors, limited itself to defining the borders of Termonmagrath, the churchlands attached to St Patrick's Purgatory, held to belong to the king.[13] At that time the boundaries of the embryonic county were so closely identified with the lordship of Rughraidhe O'Donnell that the English government favoured a minimalist interpretation of the evidence. After the plantation, attitudes naturally changed, and in the Civil Survey of 1654 the plain between the Drowes and the Erne, the property of Thomas Lord ffolliott, is firmly described as part of the barony of Tirhugh and the county of Donegal.[14]

Another potential area for expansionist ambitions was the peninsula of Inishowen, once the seat of the powerful MacLochlainn kings of Aileach. Its political importance had been reduced when kingship of the Cinéal Eoghain passed in the course of the late twelfth and early thirteenth centuries to the O'Neills, who were based around Tullahogue and Dungannon, and Flaithbheartach Ó Maoldoraidh and his immediate successors, including the early O'Donnells, took advantage of this weakness to encroach on the peninsula repeatedly.[15] However, by 1300 the territory was claimed not by O'Neill or O'Donnell, but by William de Burgh, a kinsman of Richard de Burgh, the 'Red Earl' of Ulster. The earl took Inishowen back into his own hands that year, and subsequently built the great castle of Northburgh on the shores of the Foyle to guard his planned settlement at the port of Derry which he intended to build on churchlands he had recently extorted from the bishops of Derry and Raphoe.[16] It was not until after this man's grandson, William 'the Brown Earl', was murdered by his own vassals in 1333 as part of a general uprising which included the Gaelic chiefs, that the castle of Northburgh was gradually abandoned and O'Donnell's vassal chief, O'Dogherty of Ardmire, extended his lordship into the peninsula in the course of the fourteenth century.[17]

To the south lay Cinéal Moáin, the ancient Cinéal Eoghain sub-kingdom occupying the fertile lowlands between the modern Castlefinn and Newtownstewart. This had been debatable ground from the thirteenth century onwards, but following a series of agreements drawn up from the mid-fifteenth to early sixteenth centuries between O'Neill and O'Donnell, it was eventually to be divided in two by the Mourne-Foyle river, only the western boundaries of the diocese of Derry remaining to show the original territorial claims of O'Neill's forebears.[18]

Another diocesan boundary, that of Clogher, reminds us that as late as 1603 the extensive church-lands of the bishop of Clogher's tenant, Magrath of Termon Magrath, or Saint Patrick's Purgatory, were described as neutral territory lying between the borders of the O'Donnell, Maguire and O'Neill lordships. They were not listed among the churchlands of Donegal in 1609, but it is interesting that John Speed's map of Ulster locates St Patrick's Purgatory in the 'Countye of Tyr Connele' in 1610, and the area, described as the 'parish of Carne', was officially included in county Donegal by the Civil Survey of 1654.[19]

Over the same period in which the county boundaries gradually assumed their present shape, society in Tír Chonaill was to acquire that heavy emphasis on militarism which was to be such a characteristic aspect of its organisation during the Nine Years' War. Little enough is known about the military arrangements of the area in the early middle ages. An apparently late twelfth- or thirteenth-century poem from the 'Old Book of Fenagh' on the equal status of the kingdoms of Tír Chonaill and Tír Eoghain, describes the army of Tír Chonaill as composed of sub-kings, chieftains and 'brughadha' or non-noble landowners, who received wages when they went on hosting outside their own territory at the summons of the over-king.[20] Another poem in the twelfth-century *Book of Leinster* describes the King of Aileach as advancing into battle flanked by the fighting-men of the various territories subject to his rule, but adds that the king's own person was guarded by foreign mercenaries, most probably recruited even at this early date from the Hiberno-Norse inhabitants of the Hebrides.[21] While this was addressed to a Cinéal Eoghain patron, it is quite possible that a powerful twelfth-century king of Tír Chonaill such as Flaithbheartach Ó Maoldoraidh (d. 1197) could also have employed a small permanent force, a household cavalry troop or bodyguard of foreign mercenaries. However, it is not until the thirteenth century that we have records of alliances formed by the new O'Donnell dynasty with the Scots of the Isles, to invade Inishowen in 1212, to resist the FitzGerald lord of Sligo in 1247, and to participate in the fratricidal succession conflict between Aodh and Toirdhealbhach O'Donnell 1290-1303.[22]

In the course of this latter war, the annals specifically state that large numbers of *gallóglaigh,* that is, 'foreign warriors' or 'galloglass' belonging to the MacDonnells of the Isles supported the cause of Toirdhealbhach, whose mother was a MacDonnell, while his half-brother Aodh O'Donnell was similarly linked to the MacSweenys of Knapdale in Argyle.[23] 'The Ramifications of Clann Sweeny', an early sixteenth-century traditional history, tells us that in those early days 'no lord had a claim on them [the MacSweenys] for a rising-out or hosting *(slógadh)*, but they might serve whomsoever they wished',[24] and there is some evidence that mercenary commanders from this family were employed by O'Neill of Tír Eoghain and the O'Rourkes and O'Reillys of Breifne in the late thirteenth and early fourteenth centuries,[25] as part of a general influx of troops from the Highlands and Islands of Scotland into Connacht and Ulster at this time. Later, however, Scotland's War of Independence (1286-1314) had the double effect of first training the Highland nobility to take part in international warfare and then disinheriting those who had fought in opposition to the victorious Robert Bruce. Galloglass commanders who might earlier have crossed the sea in search of temporary freelance employment now sought a permanent new home in Ireland, and sufficient grants of land to maintain their noble status.

None were to be more successful in this quest than the MacSweeny family, who acquired military commands or constableships in Tír Chonaill, Connacht and Kerry, endowed with land-grants, and billeting-rights among the local population for the troops under their command. In this they compared with the MacDonnell galloglasses of North Connacht and Tír Eoghain, or the MacCabes of Fir Mhanach and Oirghialla.[26] In Tír Chonaill, however, where a fierce war of succession raged among the O'Donnell family from 1333 to 1380, and claimants to the kingship from opposing sides wooed the MacSweenys with land-grants and privileges,[27] the galloglass family ended up occupying three major sub-chieftaincies within the O'Donnell lordship, that of Fanad, the Trí Tuatha and Tír Boghaine, having suppressed or displaced the native dynasts. In the sixteenth century all three MacSweeny chieftains are found taking part in the political councils of Tír Chonaill as fully as any of the other local rulers such as O'Boyle, O'Dogherty or the junior members of the O'Donnell family themselves[28] and the head of the senior branch, MacSweeny Fanad, was inaugurated by O'Donnell at his own ceremonial site of Kilmacrenan, just as O'Cahan, the most power-ful sub-chief of Tír Eoghain, was inaugurated by the Great O'Neill.[29]

Right to the end of the medieval period, however, the MacSweeny chieftains of Tír Chonaill remained professional military commanders. A statement of tributes paid during the reign of Aodh Ruadh II O'Donnell (1592-1602) shows MacSweeny of Fanad as owing not merely a food-rent of cattle, and a cash payment for the support of billeted mercenaries or *buannaidhe* ('bonaghts'), like his neighbour O'Boyle, but also the service of 120 armoured galloglass. A like number was demanded of MacSweeny na Doe *('na dTuath')* and a further 60 from MacSweeny Banagh ('of Tír Bhoghaine'), making 300 heavy-armoured footsoldiers in all. In the same text O'Dogherty of Inishowen is held liable for what seems an unusually large cavalry contingent of 60 horsemen along with 120 ordinary foot-soldiers, whenever O'Donnell should summon him for a hosting, or 'rising-out' to war.[30] It is possible that the O'Dogherty chiefs had a traditional role as cavalry commanders, since in 1342 Domhnall O'Dogherty, the first of his line to rule Inishowen, is lamented in the *Annals of Ulster* with the words 'there was scarcely in Ireland a chief that had more people and a larger horse-host and a better spirit and valour, hospitality and bestowal than he'. In 1600 Sir Henry Docwra estimated that 'O Dogherty of his natural born people is able to make about 300 foot and 40 horse (handsome and soldier-like men) besides his bonnaughts which are sometimes one, sometimes two hundred more.'[31]

It has already been noted that each of O'Donnell's sub-chiefs was expected to make a cash contribution towards the maintenance of their overlord's hired mercenaries. These 'bonaghts' were normally full-time soldiers of Irish origin,[32] but in addition the O'Donnells led the field in the short-term importation of Scots regiments in large numbers to be used for particular campaigns, the troops sometimes known as 'redshanks', whose employment did so much to shape the politics of northern Ireland in the second half of the sixteenth century.[33] As early as 1428, Sir James White, constable of Carrickfergus Castle, in an appeal for help to the Dublin government, stated he had information 'that O'Donnell has sent to have a great multitude of Scots along with his own force to come in a short while against the aforesaid castle'.[34] The involvement of Scots in Ulster politics had been greatly increased since about the year 1400 by the marriage of Marjory Bisset, the heiress to the Glens of Antrim, with Eoin Mór MacDonnell, younger brother of the Lord of the Isles, and the consequent colonisation of the Glens by Scots from the Western Isles, but the O'Donnells did not limit their contacts to Scots already settled on the Irish mainland. For instance, in 1523 the young Maghnus O'Donnell went over to visit Scotland, and the following year the annals state that he and his father were assisted by the forces of a number of nobles from Scotland in their war against O'Neill and the earl of Kildare. Soon after came a series of marriage alliances between the O'Donnells and the Scottish chieftains, each sealing a contract for military assistance, culminating in the marriage of Iníon Dubh, daughter of James MacDonnell of the Isles, with Aodh Dubh the son of Maghnus, and the subsequent birth and battling career of their son, Aodh Ruadh or Red Hugh O'Donnell.[35]

Such comparatively large armies were no light burden on the inhabitants of an agriculturally unproductive area such as Tír Chonaill and in a poem addressed to Niall Garbh II O'Donnell, probably late in his reign c.1429-34, his taxation (*cáin*) is repeatedly referred to as *trom,* 'heavy, oppressive',[36] while the same theme crops up in a poem addressed to his brother and successor, Neachtain O'Donnell (reigned 1439-52): 'Let there be no scarcity of troops for the fight; O prince of Murbhach, think not too heavy thy burden of (paying) hired troops to meet the foreigners; make all preparations before the need arises.'[37]

The poets of course assured O'Donnell's vassals that this was money well spent, because their lord's military might ensured law and order within the kingdom, and security from outside invasion and conquest. Allusions were made in this mid-fifteenth-century period to an alleged prophecy of St Columba that he would never turn his back on his kinsfolk; it was claimed that the saint had pledged the English would never conquer the Cinéal Conaill.[38] This is a triumphalist version of the Columban prophecies, contrasting with the more usual messianic promises current in the thirteenth and sixteenth centuries that the

English tyranny would one day be rolled back by a king sometimes identified as a member of the Cinéal Conaill, or as bearing the name Aodh, who would reign victorious with the blessing of the saints.[39] A triumphal mood came naturally to the fifteenth-century O'Donnells whose political influence extended beyond the Donegal area across the territories of Fermanagh, Leitrim and Sligo, and who led their armies on occasion to attack the towns of Louth and Dundalk in the Pale.[40] It would seem, however, that Tír Chonaill owed its invincibility as much to its physical geography as to its heavily militarised society, or to the blessing of the saints. Even at the height of Cinéal Conaill's prosperity, the O'Neills of Tír Eoghain were always in a position to raid the accessible lowlands in the barony of Tirhugh to the south,[41] and the Lagan area bordering the Mourne-Foyle river to the east,[42] whereas the sea-coast west of the Bluestacks and the Derryveagh mountains remained largely undisturbed.[43]

The vulnerable lowlands were also the richest part of the O'Donnell lordship and this fact is reflected in two statements made in Irish about the tributes collected in the reign of Aodh Ruadh II, or 'Red Hugh' (d. 1602), and attributed respectively to Domhnall O'Gallagher, aged 81 in 1626, and Tadhg son of Theobald MacLinshy, O'Donnell's *maor*, or bailiff, who was said to have survived as an old man in 1620.[44] Although these statements are extant today only in eighteenth-century paper copies, with partial nineteenth-century translations, their contents are consistent with what little is otherwise known of O'Donnell's rights of lordship[45] and there seems no reason to suspect them of being deliberate forgeries. They imply that territories in the lordship of Tír Chonaill fell into three main categories. In the first place there was land directly under the control of whoever held the title of king or lord of the Cinéal Conaill, which was exempt from ordinary taxation and has been plausibly deduced by Tomás Ó Canann to have lain in the barony of Tirhugh.[46] This deduction fits in well with the events of 1343, when at the height of the succession struggle then raging the new king Aonghus O'Donnell granted out the whole of Tirhugh, both grazing and arable lands, to the nomadic O'Conor sept of Clann Muircheartaigh, in return for their military support against his deposed rival, Niall Garbh I, at one stroke reinforcing his army and depriving his rival of income from that area.[47] Later, we find lands in this district being used to endow the chief's poets and historians.[48]

Secondly, there were the sub-chieftaincies strung out along the barren west and north. In 1592 Archbishop Miler Magrath, who originally hailed from Termon Magrath before he took office in the Anglican church, reported to Queen Elizabeth: 'In O'Donnell's country and under him are divers men of great scope of land and good forces, specially five viz. O'Dogherty, O'Boyle and the three M'Sweenies, and every one of these five have their castles and lands by the sea side, and each of them will be glad to be free from O'Donnell's exaction.'[49] Some years later the correspondence of Captain Docwra, the commander of the English garrison in Derry, gives us a few details of O'Donnell claims over O'Dogherty of Inishowen. In March 1601 Docwra prevented the newly-appointed Feidhlim Óg O'Dogherty from paying O'Donnell 1,200 cows levied from his subjects as the price of his nomination to the sub-chieftainship.[50] In April Niall Garbh III O'Donnell, the English government's candidate for headship of his family, 'began with his own little broken English and the help of Captain Willis to interpret for him to demand the possession of Ennisowen to be delivered into his hands', claiming arbitrary rights to billeting, purveyance of goods and labour services from the inhabitants. 'The country is mine,' saith he, 'and so is all Tyrconnell, and I will use and govern it to my own pleasure.'[51] However, the proprietary rights of the overlord apparently ran concurrently with those of his sub-chief. In September of the same year, when Docwra attempted to seize the property of those inhabitants of Inishowen who had fled the country as a result of the war, and to use it for the benefit of the English garrison, he was prevented by the local population, who insisted 'all the country, goods and people whatsoever was O'Dogharty's, and whatsoever fell confiscate belonged of right unto him.' The frustrated Docwra protested, 'Undoubtedly if this tyrannical lordship of the Irish be not taken away, and the tenant allowed a propriety in his own goods (for thereon they ground their demand of all forfeitures and confiscations) according to the laws and customs of England, this people will never, while the world stands, be brought either unto civility or obedience.'[52]

Docwra's expressions of horror were to be echoed by James I's attorney-general in Ireland, Sir John Davies. He remarked of the Maguire lordship of Fermanagh in 1607:

> Touching the inferior gentlemen and inhabitants, it was not certainly known to the state here whether they were only tenants-at-will to the chief lords, whereof the uncertain cutting [taxation at will] which the lords used upon them might be an argument, or whether they were freeholders yielding of right to their chief lord certain rights and services, as many of them do allege, affirming that the Irish cutting was an usurpation and a wrong.

Davies was shown a document since lost, giving a traditional statement of Maguire's rights of lordship comparable to the accounts of O'Donnell's rights mentioned above, which compelled him to admit that Maguire's rights were subject to customary limitations in peacetime, though he added, 'Marry in time of war he made himself owner of all, cutting what he listed, and imposing as many bonaghts or hired soldiers upon them as he had occasion to use.' The problem was that in the late sixteenth and early seventeenth centuries war conditions had become the rule rather than the exception, a state of affairs not unconnected with the presence of the English administrators themselves. Later on in 1610, with the Plantation of Ulster in full swing, Davies cast subtle distinctions aside, stating emphatically in relation to East Breifne, or county Cavan,

> He that was O'Reilly, or captain of the country, had power to cut upon all the inhabitants, high or low, as pleased him; which argues they held their lands of the chief lord in villeinage ... Thus, then, it appears that, as well by the Irish custom as the law of England, His Majesty may, at his pleasure, seize these lands and dispose thereof.[53]

A number of interesting points arise from these outsiders' criticisms of the relationship between the overlords of Ulster and their vassals. Unlike the native authors, their strictures did not concern the actual amount of the lords' exactions, but rather their arbitrary powers of taxation, unlimited by the machinery of representation and consent, so that the nobility and gentry of Gaelic Ireland had as little constitutional protection against their rulers as the peasant classes in England. This was to import into the Irish situation the ongoing debate between the Stuart kings and the English House of Commons, eventually to erupt in civil war. The earlier letter of Archbishop Miler Magrath hints that chieftains and nobles of the middle rank in Ulster might have been interested in acquiring added rights and security of status under an extension of English Common Law uncomplicated by confiscations and plantation, but this choice was never really made available to them. The immediate consequence of suppressing Rughraidhe O'Donnell's Gaelic rights of lordship after the Treaty of Mellifont in favour of the title earl of Tirconnell was, as Sir Francis Shaen wrote in 1607, 'the Earl imposed a rent fourfold more than any O'Donnell had'.[54] Even if this remark is exaggerated, it implies the traditional exactions of Red Hugh and his predecessors cannot have reached the limits of their subjects' endurance. Indeed, the tract on the 'Ramifications of Clann Sweeny' shows successful resistance to taxation as the origin of one of the fixed contributions named in the O'Donnell rentals:

> When Ruaidhri [MacSuibhne Fanad] had been a long time in that chieftainship, Neachtain Ó Domhnaill [kg. 1439-52] came on a visit

to his house, and all the country thought his maintenance a great oppression. Ó Domhnaill had never until then a particular claim on them, and it was at that time they decided on a king's *martaigheacht* [contribution of beeves] for Ó Domhnaill. And this is the *martaigheacht,* namely, six beeves; and, as a fine, twenty cows instead of any beef deficient, and the beeve itself to be delivered in the end; and there is no determining by the lord as to the particular beeve, but the person himself may deliver whatever beeve he wishes to send; and that martaigheacht to be sent to Léim Í Thirchirt [Ó Tirchirt's Leap] on the borders of Fanad and the termon [of Kilmacrenan]; and Ó Domhnaill's steward himself to come for them to that place; and one half of the hides of the *martaigheacht* to be given to the steward of MacSuibhne; and it should not be allowed that they should remove these beeves out of the *cill* [Kilmacrenan], but they should be killed therein; and Ó Domhnaill himself to come to the *cill* to kill them; and if he should remain on the further side of the river of the *cill,* he should not get any beeve of them; and even this much he should not have except three times in the year, however frequently he should come to the *cill,* namely, in summer, and in harvest, and in winter.[55]

Clearly the multitude of conditions attaching to this agreement were designed to prevent the overlord using a traditional right to the provision of food for himself and his followers when he visited in person[56] as a mere excuse for a cattle tax, to be levied regularly whether he visited or not; and indeed it is as a simple cattle tax of 18 beeves yearly that the 'king's *martaigheacht*' figures later in the memoranda of Domhnall O'Gallagher and Theobald MacLinshy, the steward of Red Hugh. The precision of detail recorded in the 'Ramifications of Clann Sweeny' suggests that one or more brehon lawyers had a hand in drawing up the text of the original compromise. In the case of a vassal as powerful as MacSweeny Fanad, it is evident that the O'Donnell was not in a position to make unlimited exactions, and that 'all the country' under the rule of this sub-chief benefited from his strong position, just as the inhabitants of Inishowen had sheltered behind the absolute authority of O'Dogherty to protect themselves from the claims of Captain Docwra and the English garrison in Derry, true to the spirit of the saying then current, 'Spend me and defend me'.[57]

Besides all these sub-chieftaincies, and the apparently tax-free royal mensal lands in the barony of Tirhugh, a third category of lands mentioned in the O'Donnell rentals was the area directly subject to his tribute, in the form of annual cash payments assessed by land area, e.g.

36 groats per 'quarter' in the Lagan, 45 groats a 'quarter' in Tír Éanna, and so forth.[58] The named districts or tuatha vary slightly in the two lists, but roughly speaking comprise the whole of what became the barony of Raphoe, and most of the central and more fertile parts of the barony of Kilmacrenan. Politically speaking, this represents on the one hand the original homeland of the O'Donnell family, whose inauguration site was at Kilmacrenan, and whose ancestors figured in the annals as local kings of Cinéal Lugdach or Cinéal Luighdheach in the Kilmacrenan area long before they rose to become kings of all Tír Chonaill,[59] and on the other hand Magh Íotha and west Cinéal Moáin, the new lands conquered by the O'Donnells from the O'Neills in the course of the middle ages.[60]

The lands directly controlled by the chief of the O'Donnells thus fell into two very distinct segments – the royal lands south of the Barnesmore Gap in Tirhugh, and the family lands and new acquisitions to the north-east. This geographical separation threatened from time to time to become the basis of a permanent split inside the O'Donnell family, particularly in the fifteenth century. In 1423 Niall Garbh II, the new king of Tír Chonaill, fortified his royal estates by building the castle of Ballyshannon, while his brother Neachtain, who acted as his deputy, later succeeded him on the throne and almost certainly bore the official title of tánaiste of Tír Chonaill, was to build his own castle on the river Finn. When a succession struggle broke out between Niall Garbh's sons and their uncle Neachtain, the annals show Neachtain's sons raiding Tirhugh, while Niall Garbh's sons made war throughout the Finn Valley.[61] After the latter eventually killed King Neachtain himself in 1452, the powerful Henry O'Neill intervened, divided the land in half between the cousins and kept Castlefinn and Cinéal Moáin for himself. Naturally this solution satisfied neither party, and a bloody feud continued to eliminate most of the claimants on either side until in 1497 Éigneachán son of Neachtain O'Donnell, nominal tánaiste of Tír Chonaill, was slain by a son of Aodh Ruadh I (reigned 1461-1505, a son of Niall Garbh II O'Donnell). Aodh Ruadh I was the king who first built Donegal Castle and founded the Franciscan Abbey there, whereas annalistic references to Éigneachán clearly associate him with the Castlefinn and Lifford area.[62]

Similarly in the sixteenth century Lifford Castle, built in 1527 by Maghnus O'Donnell when he was still merely heir apparent to the kingship, tended with its surrounding area to become a base for alternative claims to authority, first under Maghnus himself in the last years of his father's reign, then in 1543-4 under Aodh son of Maghnus O'Donnell in opposition to his father the chief, and his elder brother Calbhach.[63] Later Lifford and Castlefinn were to be allotted to Conn, son of the Calbhach, tánaiste and disappointed claimant to kingship during the reign of Aodh son of Maghnus.[64] Although the newly-inaugurated Aodh Ruadh II, or Red Hugh, made Lifford one of his own chief residences in 1593, in 1600 in the course of the Nine Years' War Niall Garbh III, son of Conn son of the Calbhach, was to occupy and fortify it as a centre from which he made war on Red Hugh in alliance with the English forces, claiming the kingship of Tír Chonaill for himself.[65]

However, none of these incidents succeeded in permanently splitting the O'Donnell dynasty into separate lordships, as had happened to the MacCarthys, to the O'Conors of Connacht, and to a certain extent to the O'Neills of Tír Eoghain, most notably in the case of the Clandeboy branch. The widely scattered O'Donnell family lands were constantly being brought back under the control of a single chief, at the expense of prolonged and savage feuds which ruthlessly eliminated rival claimants.[66] This centralisation of authority under a long line of iron-fisted rulers was one reason for the surprisingly strong influence exercised by the barren and peripheral lordship of Tír Chonaill over neighbouring territories. Another was its large army comprising a high proportion of professional soldiers, kept not only in order to maintain central authority, but perhaps also necessary because the most fertile lands in the lordship were those most open to outside attack.

The military success of the O'Donnells brought with it a measure of wealth in the later middle ages. In addition to the tributes they collected from vassal territories, they could lay claim to the cocket of the port of Sligo,[67] and in 1560 we are told O'Donnell was known abroad as 'the king of the fish' because he controlled the greatest share in the Irish fish trade, buying wine in exchange from foreign merchants.[68] The notice in the annals of the sudden death of the wealthy Sligo merchant, Domhnall Ó Croidhean, while attending mass at Donegal Abbey in 1506[69] may be a hint that a market was already growing up beside the castle and abbey there. At the end of the sixteenth century Fearghal Óg Mac an Bhaird praised the Franciscan friars of Donegal for making extensive purchases of wine to serve to their guests.[70]

A part of the chieftains' surplus wealth was expended in patronage of the arts. It has already been noted that various learned families received grants of land within the taxfree royal district of Tirhugh. It is a singular fact that the learned septs of later medieval Donegal – Uí Sgingín, Uí Chléirigh, Mac an Bhaird, Ó Duinnshléibhe and so on were almost without exception brought into the area from other parts of Ireland.[71] The absence of native lay schools here in the twelfth and thirteenth centuries may be connected with the absence of references in the annals to sages, scribes or monastic teachers in any pre-Norman monasteries within the later diocese of Raphoe, though Derry appears to have maintained a monastic school of the old style into the 1220s and a coarb of Fahan in Inishowen was described as a learned sage at his death in 1098.[72] More intriguingly a noble from west Tír Chonaill, Tadhg son of Ceallach O'Boyle, was praised at his death in 1223 as the most munificent in the north of Ireland, dispensing valuables and wealth to men of every art.[73] It is not clear where such men of art would have come from, though since one source of our existing annals was being compiled in Derry about this time,[74] the remark may reflect the fact that some of Tadhg's wealth went to reward the local MacConmidhe poets from Cinéal Moáin.

Later in the thirteenth century an anonymous poet addressing a Roscommon lady, Cailleach Dé Ní Mhannacháin, may imply that his school of poets came from Assaroe,[75] and this may be an early reference to the Ó hUiginn school just south of the river Erne. The first Mac an Baird poet known to have composed for the O'Donnells was Eoghan, author of an elegy for the prince Domhnall O'Donnell, a son of Toirdhealbhach of the Wine, who was killed in 1420.[76] This poet's son, Gofraidh mac Eoghain Mhic an Bhaird, who died of the plague in 1478, was the first of whom the annals used the formal title 'the Mac an Bhaird of Tír Chonaill'.[77] Similarly Tadhg Cam Ó Cléirigh, who died in 1492 was the first of his family to be styled 'historian of the Cinéal Conaill' or 'ollamh of O'Donnell in poetry and history',[78] both these innovations occurring during the long reign of Aodh Ruadh I O'Donnell (1461-1505), the founder of Donegal Abbey.

A feature of bardic learning in the sixteenth century which was to be very marked in Tír Chonaill was an ever closer alliance with the Counter-Reformation wing of the church. The chief Maghnus O'Donnell, poet and compiler of the great *Life of Columba,* claimed that his views had been moulded by the friars of Donegal Abbey.[79] On 8 March 1527 the annals say *an Giolla Riabhach* Ó Cléirigh, O'Donnell's *ollamh* of history, died in the habit of St Francis, while in 1542 his nephew, Cormac Ó Cléirigh, a friar minor of Donegal, was described at his death as the most accomplished scholar of his time. In 1597 another member of the family was a Cistercian monk at Assaroe.[80] As the traditional sources of patronage were drying up at the end of the sixteenth and the beginning of the seventeenth century, some of the most distinguished bardic scholars of the day were recruited into the service of the Franciscan College at Louvain under the direction of Flaithrí Ó Maolchonaire, once confessor to Aodh Ruadh II, or 'Red Hugh' O'Donnell, and later Catholic archbishop of Tuam. The Louvain college, with its printing press and team of poets, authors and translators,[81] proved an essential source of theological instruction for the much neglected Irish-speaking church, but it was also the nursery of a new nationalist ideology, which was to find its political expression during the wars of the Confederation of Kilkenny (1641-50).[82] This group of scholars provided the intellectual context for the Four Masters' famous compilation of *Annals of the Kingdom of Ireland* under the direction of Friar Mícheál Ó Cléirigh in 1636. The same combination of Franciscan scholarship and nationalism surfaced during the 'Contention of the Bards', a war of words that erupted in 1616 between Tadhg mac Dáire Mhic Bhruaideadha, *ollamh* of history and poetry to the prosperous, Protestant O'Brien, earl of Thomond, and a number of poets hired by Aodh Óg O'Donnell, the great-uncle of Red Hugh, to defend the claims of his exiled O'Donnell kinsmen to be true heirs to a theoretical high-kingship of Ireland. Since King James I sat so firmly on the thrones of Scotland, England and Ireland at the time, the contending bards were derided even by Archbishop Flaithrí Ó Maolchonaire as 'hounds wrangling over an empty dish'[83] but Ó Maolchonaire's own abortive plans for the young Aodh O'Donnell to invade Ireland in 1630, and the rumours during the Confederate Wars that Owen Roe O'Neill would be made king[84] demonstrate that the views of Friar Roibéard mac Artúr and the other poets of the Contention were forwardlooking rather than backwardlooking. In making this brief excursus I have been trespassing beyond the middle ages, but only to establish the existence of a significant intellectual movement in seventeenth-century Ireland and Louvain which had its roots in the fusion of bardic and Franciscan scholarship under the patronage of the O'Donnell family in early sixteenth-century Donegal. Throughout the sixteenth century, it is an undeniable fact that Tír Chonaill played an unusually prominent part in Irish history as a whole, whether this is to be ascribed to its disproportionate military strength, its intellectual leadership or indeed the temporary prosperity brought to this area and other regions along the west coast by the expansion of the herring fisheries from the second half of the fifteenth century, a prosperity Timothy O'Neill[85] would see reflected in the large stone buildings, friaries and castles, which were erected at this period in the west of Ireland generally, and certainly in county Donegal.[86]

References

1. *Bk. Fen.*, pp v-vi, 314-315, 396-7. See the illuminating discussion by T. Ó Canann, 'Trí saorthuatha mhuinntire Chanannáin: a forgotten medieval place-name' in *Donegal Annual*, no. 38 (1986), pp 22-3.
2. *A.U.*, 1011, 1012. Annals are cited by the AD year of the entry, unless otherwise stated.
3. *Ann. Inisf.*, 1026; *Misc. Ir. Annals.*, 1197.

4. T. G. Cannon, 'History of the O'Cannons of Tír Chonaill' in *Donegal Annual*, xii (1978), pp 276-315.

5. *A.U., A.L.C.*, 1241.

6. *Red Bk. Kildare*, nos 21-2, 24, 31.

7. Ibid., no. 129; see G. H. Orpen, 'The Normans in Tirowen and Tirconnell' in *R.S.A.I. Jn.*, xlv (1915), pp 275-88.

8. Ó Canann, 'Trí saorthuatha,' p. 41 note 24.

9. K. W. Nicholls, 'The register of Clogher' in *Clogher Rec.*, vii (1971/2), p. 392. See P. Ó Gallchobhair, 'Where is Magh Céidne and Magh Ene?' in *Donegal Annual*, iii, (1954-5), pp 70-3.

10. *Ca sealbh as ferr ar Es Ruaidh*, Book of O'Conor Don, fo. 241b.

11. *Comp. Bk. Conn.*, pp 120, 126.

12. G. Mercator, *Atlas sive cosmographicae meditationes* (Duisburg, 1585), 'Hibernia': Tabulae 1 & 11; Boazio's 1599 Map of Ireland is printed on the end-papers of the Royal Irish Academy's *Atlas of Ireland* (Dublin, 1979); Speed's 1610 Map of Ulster is reproduced in T. Mathews, *The O'Neills of Ulster* (3 vols., Dublin, 1907), iii, facing page 192.

13. *Pat. rolls. Ire., Jas 1*, pp 47-8. See also *Inq. cancell. Hib. repert.*, ii, p. xvii.

14. *Civil Survey*, iii, pp 55-6. See letter of Sir Francis Shaen in 1607, *S.P. Ire., 1606-8*, p. 340. Ecclesiastically the area was part of the Fermanagh parish of Inishmacsaint.

15. *A.F.M.*, 1186, 1197, 1208, 1247; *A.L.C.*, 1208, 1209, 1211, 1212.

16. 'The muniments of Edmund Mortimer, Earl of March' B.L., Add. MS no. 6041, section on Ultonia nos xxxv, xxxvi, xliv, xlix; Theiner, *Vetera mon.*, p. 237; *Cal. pat. rolls 1307-13*, pp 292-3. See Otway-Ruthven, *Med. Ire.*, p. 214; T. McNeill, *Anglo-Norman Ulster* (Edinburgh, 1980), pp 31-2.

17. G. H. Orpen, 'The Earldom of Ulster' in *R.S.A.I. Jn.*, xliii (1913), p. 46; *A.U.*, 1342, 1413.

18. *A.U.*, 1442, 1452, 1456, 1480; *Ann. Conn.*, 1512.7, 1514.13; *S.P. Hen. VIII: Ire., 1538-46*, pp 478-9. B. Lacy, *Archaeological survey of county Donegal* (Lifford, 1983), p. 8, Fig. 4.

19. See notes 12 and 13 above and P. Ó Gallchobhair, 'The parish of Carn' in *Clogher Rec.*, viii (1975), pp 310-12.

20. *Bk. Fen.*, pp 358-9. See K. Simms, *From kings to warlords* (Woodbridge, 1987), p. 102.

21. T. O'Donoghue (ed.), 'Cert cech ríg co réil' in O. Bergin and C. Marstrander (ed.), *Miscellany presented to Kuno Meyer* (Halle, 1912), p. 268. See Simms, *From kings to warlords*, p. 118.

22. *A.U., A.L.C.*, 1212, 1247, 1290, 1291, 1295, 1303; *A.F.M.*, 1295.

23. P. Walsh (ed.), *The life of Aodh Ruadh O Domhnaill* (2 vols, Dublin, 1948, 1957), ii, p. 158; see D. Meek, 'The MacSween poem in "The Book of the dean of Lismore"', in *Notes and Queries of the Society of West Highland and Island Research*, no. xxv (1984), pp 3-12.

24. P. Walsh (ed.), *Leabhar Chlainne Suibhne* (Dublin, 1920), p. 45.

25. *Ann. Conn.*, 1305, 1346; *Lr Cl. Aodha Buidhe*, p. 31. See Simms, *From kings to warlords*, p. 122.

26. G. A. Hayes-McCoy, *Scots mercenary forces in Ireland 1565-1603* (Dublin, 1937), pp 26-37; *B.M., cat. Ir. MSS*, i, 386.

27. Walsh (ed.), *Leabhar Chlainne Suibhne*, pp 30-33, 38-45, 50-51; *Ann. Conn*, 1343:13, 1351:7, 1366:8, 1388:3, 1399:5; *A.F.M.*, 1351, 1359, 1380, 1398, 1400.

28. E.g. *Cal. Carew MSS*, 1515-74, p. 308; Walsh (ed.), *Life of Aodh Ruadh*, i, pp 38-41; W. Betham, *Irish antiquarian researches* (Dublin, 1827), i, p. 197.

29. Walsh (ed.), *Leabhar Chlainne Suibhne*, pp 50-1, *B.M.*, *cat. Ir. MSS*, i, p. 386; *Cal. S.P. Ire.*, *1606-8*, pp 155-6.

30. Cambridge Add., MS 2766 (20) (7); see P. de Brún and M. Herbert, *Catalogue of Irish manuscripts in Cambridge libraries* (Cambridge, 1986), pp 4-5. There is an imperfect English translation of this text in R.I.A., MS 14/B/7, pp 423-5.

31. *Cal. S.P. Ire.*, *1600-1*, p. 95.

32. E.g. 'The order and manner how O Neale doth cesse his Bownies', 2 Feb. 1602 (*Cal. Carew MSS 1601-3*, p. 212) names Tadhg O'Rourke and Diarmait O'Conor as two of the bonaghts in question. See Hayes-McCoy, *Scots mercenary forces*, pp 72-6.

33. Hayes-McCoy, *Scots mercenary forces*, p. 13.

34. *Rot. pat. Hib.*, p. 246, no. 21.

35. W. D. Lamont, 'The Islay charter of 1408' in *R.I.A. Proc.*, lx (1960) C, p. 170; *A.F.M.*, 1523, 1524, 1544, 1588; R. Bagwell, *Ireland under the Tudors* (London, 1885-90, 1963), ii, pp 21, 77.

36. J. Fraser and J. G. O'Keefe (ed.), 'Poems on the O'Donnells' in *Ir. texts*, ii, pp 46, 49, verses 5, 28, 33. See K. Simms, 'Niall Garbh II O'Donnell' in *Donegal Annual*, xii (1977), pp 17-18.

37. L. McKenna (ed.), *Aithdioghluim dána* (2 vols, Dublin 1939, 1940), ii, p. 57.

38. Fraser and O'Keefe, 'Poems on the O'Donnells,' pp 80, 87-8.

39. N. J. A. Williams (ed.), *The poems of Giolla Brighde Mac Con Midhe* (London, 1980), poems v & vi; *Ann. Conn.*, 1537, *A.F.M.*, 1602. See B. Ó Buachalla, 'Aodh Eanghach and the Irish king-hero' in D. Ó Corráin, L. Breatnach, K. McCone (eds.), *Sages, saints and storytellers: Celtic studies in honour of Professor James Carney* (Maynooth, 1989), pp 202-3, 206-7, 220.

40. *A.F.M.*, 1423, 1434, 1439, 1470, 1475, 1483, 1493, 1505. See Simms, 'Niall Garbh II,' passim.

41. *A.U.*, *A.F.M.*, 1436, 1477; *Ann. Conn.*, 1464:26.

42. *A.U.*, *A.F.M.*, 1432, 1442, 1471.

43. A possible instance of O'Neill's army reaching the Rosses in 1435 (*A.U.*, *A.F.M.*) would appear to arise from a similar placename in the Cinéal Moáin area of east Donegal, but see N. Ó Dónaill, *Na glúnta Rosannacha* (Bale Átha Cliath, 1952), pp 77-81.

44. See above, note 30.

45. *Cal. S.P. Ire.*, *1606-8*, pp 342-3; Walsh (ed.), *Leabhar Chlainne Suibhne*, pp 44-5, 58-9. See Ó Canann, 'Trí saorthuatha mhuinntire Chanannáin,' pp 24, 41, n. 28.

46. Ó Canann, 'Trí saorthuatha mhuinntire Chanannáin,' passim.

47. *Ann. Conn.*, 1343:13. See K. Simms, 'Nomadry in medieval Ireland: the origins of the creaght or *caoraigheacht*' in *Peritia*, v (1986), p. 382.

48. Ó Canann, 'Trí saorthuatha mhuinntire Chanannáin,' p. 39.

49. *Cal. S.P. Ire.*, *1588-92*, p. 500.

50. *Cal. S.P. Ire.*, *1600-1*, p. 213.

51. Ibid., p. 289.

52. *Cal. S.P. Ire.*, *1601-3*, p. 94.

53. Morley (ed.), *Ire. under Eliz. & Jas 1*, pp 348, 368-70, 386-7.

54. *Cal. S.P. Ire.*, *1606-8*, p. 339.

55. Walsh (ed.), *Leabhar Chlainne Suibhne*, p. 59.

56. K. Simms, 'Guesting and feasting in Gaelic Ireland' in *R.S.A.I. Jn.*, cviii (1978), pp 74, 79-82.

57. Edmund Spenser, *A view of the state of Ireland ... in 1596*, ed. W.L. Renwick (Oxford, 1970), p. 35. See Simms, *From kings to warlords*, p. 112.

58. See above, note 30. A 'quarter' was a very approximate unit of land measurement. For this part of Donegal the *Civil Survey* lists quarters varying from under eighty acres to over two hundred, but most fall between 120 and 180 acres.

59. *A.U.*, 1010, 1100, 1106, 1129. See above, note 1.

60. See above, note 18.

61. *A.F.M.*, 1423, 1431, 1434, 1464, 1477. See K. Simms, 'Niall Garbh II' (above note 36), p. 17, and *From kings to warlords*, pp 56, 59.

62. *A.U.*, *A.F.M.*, 1452, 1454, 1456, 1461, 1477, 1480, 1497, 1505. See L. McKenna, 'Some Irish bardic poems' in *Studies*, xxxix (1950), pp 437-45.

63. *Ann. Conn.*, 1527: 12, 13; 1531: 8; 1536: 14; 1537: 8, 10; 1543: 8, 11; 1544: 3. See J. G. Simms, 'Manus O'Donnell' in *Donegal Annual*, v (1962), pp 115-21.

64. E. Knott (ed.), *The bardic poems of Tadhg Dall O hUiginn* (2 vols, Dublin, 1922, 1926), poems i & v, and notes.

65. *A.F.M.*, 1593, 1600; Walsh (ed.), *Beatha Aodha Ruaidh*, i, pp 58-9, 262-81; Bagwell, *Tudors*, iii, pp 375-7, 427.

66. My attention was drawn to this aspect of the O'Donnell lordship by one of my students, Mr Noel Ward, who made a special study of the medieval history of Tír Chonaill as part of his B.A. Mod. degree at Trinity College Dublin, 1992.

67. M. Carney, 'Agreement between Ó Domhnaill and Tadhg Ó Conchubhair concerning Sligo Castle (23 June 1539)' in *I.H.S.*, iii (1942-3), pp 288 and 290, n. 5.

68. *Cal. Carew MSS 1515-74*, p. 308; T. O'Neill, *Merchants and mariners in medieval Ireland* (Dublin, 1987), pp 33-6, 46-7.

69. *Ann. Conn.*, 1506: 4.

70. McKenna (ed.), *Dioghluim dána*, no. 81, verses 15, 16.

71. Walsh, *Irish men of learning* (Dublin, 1960), pp 151-9; Idem, *The O'Clery family of Tír Conaill* (Dublin, 1938). On the Ó Duinnshleibhe family of physicians see O'Donovan in *A.F.M.*, iv, p. 742, note f, and K. Simms, 'Brehons in later medieval Ireland' in D. Hogan and W. N. Osborough (ed.), *Brehons, serjeants and attorneys* (Dublin, 1990), p. 60, n. 49.

72. *A.F.M.*, 1162, *A.U.*, 1098, 1185, 1189, 1207, 1220. There was also an earlier reference to learning at Both Chonais or Bodoney in Inishowen at *A.U.*, 852.

73. *A.F.M.*, *A.L.C.*, 1222, *A.U.*, 1223.

74. See G. MacNiocaill, *The medieval Irish annals* (Dublin, 1975), p. 29.

75. McKenna, *Aithdioghluim dána*, i, p. 4, ii, p. 3. For the MacConmidhe family see Williams, *The poems of Giolla Brighde Mac Con Midhe*, p. 2.

76. McKenna, 'Bardic poems,' pp 187-93; see Simms, 'Niall Garbh II' (above note 36), p. 12.

77. *Ann. Conn.*, 1478: 9.

78. *Ann. Conn.*, *A.F.M.*, 1492.

79. B. Bradshaw, *The dissolution of the religious orders in Ireland under Henry VIII* (London, New York, 1974), pp 13-14; idem, 'Manus the Magnificent' in A. Cosgrove and D. McCartney (ed.), *Studies in Irish history* (Dublin, 1979), pp 18-20.

80. *Ann. Conn.*, *A.L.C.*, *A.U.*, *A.F.M.*, 1527; *A.L.C.*, *A.F.M.*, 1542; *A.F.M.*, 1597.

81. Walsh, *Irish men of learning*, pp 246-51.

82. P. J. Corish (ed.), *The origins of Catholic nationalism* (*A history of Irish Catholicism*), (Dublin and Sydney, 1968), iii, pt. viii, pp 26-9.

83. L. McKenna (ed.), *Iomarbhágh na bhfileadh; the contention of the bards* (2 vols, London, 1918); B. Ó Cuív, 'The Irish language in the early modern period' in T. W. Moody, F. X. Martin and F. J. Byrne (ed.), the *New history of Ireland*, iii, (Oxford, 1976), p. 539.

84. B. Jennings, 'The career of Hugh son of Rory O'Donnell, earl of Tirconnell in the Low Countries 1607-1642, in *Studies* xxx (1941), pp 231-2; Bagwell, *Stuarts*, ii, p. 168.
85. O'Neill, *Merchants and mariners*, p. 36; see above, note 68.
86. Lacy, *Archaeological survey*, pp 326-84.

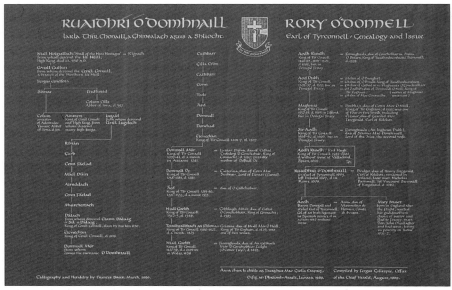

Plate 6.1   Pedigree of Ruaidhrí Ó Domhnaill, earl of Tyrconnell, *obit* 1608, by Fergus Gillespie. (From Collections of Genealogical Office).

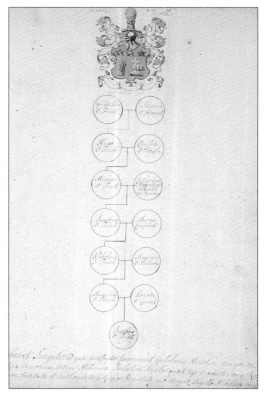

Plate 6.2   Copy of first page of certificate of arms and pedigree of Jacobus O'Friell, descendant of Gildusius Ó Firghil of Kilmacrenan, Genealogical Office Ms. 162 (Genealogical Office).

Chapter 7

THE RENAISSANCE AND THE LATE MEDIEVAL LORDSHIP OF TÍR CHONAILL; 1461-1555

DARREN MAC EITEAGÁIN

The late medieval lordship of Tír Chonaill reached the height of its power during the years 1461-1555. The lords of Tír Chonaill became the dominant force in Gaelic Ireland for almost a century and the lordship itself was in close contact with many centres of the Renaissance in Europe. For the purposes of this article I intend to build on the work of the historian Brendan Bradshaw, by focusing on three lords or princes of Tír Chonaill, Aodh Ruadh, Aodh Dubh and Maghnus Ó Domhnaill, who between them ruled the lordship of Tír Chonaill from 1461-1555 in an almost unbroken line of direct succession.[1] These princes of Tír Chonaill, father, son and grandson are three of the most remarkable men ever to have been produced in county Donegal. Able and gifted, they have been described as the great soldier-statesmen of their respective generations in Gaelic Ireland (fig. 7.1). Their grasp of military strategy and political intrigue fashioned a major expansion of Tír Chonaill influence, and a historian of late medieval Ireland has stated that: 'the family in the fifteenth and sixteenth centuries consistently showed a hardness and a sense of political purpose absent from most Irish rulers.'[2] It is important to remember that the historian in this period is dealing with what could be termed 'Greater Tír Chonaill' when the lands of the Cinél Conaill incorporated the peninsula of Inis Eoghain and the tract of land between Letterkenny and Lifford (Cinél Moen). This means that the marches of the lordship of Tír Chonaill at this time were almost coterminous with the modern county boundary, if Derry city and its lands to the west of the Foyle were incorporated and a small triangular tract of land around Lough Derg in the south of the county was excluded (fig. 7.2).

The rise to power of the lords of Tír Chonaill after 1461 was quite unusual. Following a long war with the Ó Neill lords of Tír Eoghain, Cinél Moen and Inis Eoghain were finally wrested from the Ó Neill sphere of influence and became integral parts of Tír Chonaill. Furthermore, with the development of a long-term strategic alliance

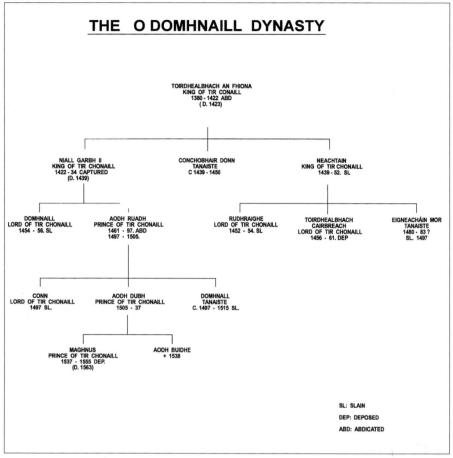

Fig. 7.1   The Ó Domhnaill dynasty.

between the lords of Tír Chonaill and the Ó Neill lords of Clann Aodha Buidhe, much of west Tír Eoghain, Oireacht Uí Cathain and the Ruta, in north-east Antrim was for long periods under Ó Domhnaill overlordship. There was also a parallel expansion of Tír Chonaill power in north Connacht and Fermanagh, where the Ó Domhnaill armies were spearheaded by dynastic propaganda and political intrigue. The area known as Iochtair Connacht was under the immediate overlordship of Tír Chonaill; the important port and castle of Sligo being in Ó Domhnaill hands so often that it became almost an appendage of Tír Chonaill itself. At the height of their power the lords of Tír Chonaill also subjugated Breifne Ó Ruairc, Moylurg and much of the modern counties of Mayo and Roscommon, making them immediate overlords of nine north-western counties.

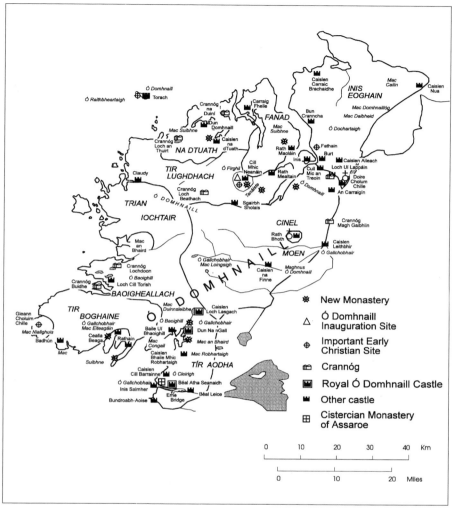

Fig. 7.2   Tír Chonaill, c.1530.

Ó Domhnaill power was built on the great loyalty shown to them by the inhabitants of Tír Chonaill. The three Mac Suibhne gallowglass families, Mac Suibhne Fanad, Mac Suibhne na dTuath and Mac Suibhne of Tír Boghaine, were the solid pillars on which the lords of Tír Chonaill built their military strength. The ruling Ó Domhnaill dynasty also relied heavily on families such as Ó Baoighill, Ó Gallchobhair and Ó Dochartaigh, with the O'Gallaghers in particular rising to prominence in Tír Chonaill. Because the lords of Tír Chonaill had an unusually large body of household or Lucht Tighe families, they were able to garrison many castles with military dependants who could be dismissed at will.

As a result, a defensive chain of castles guarding the borders of Tír Chonaill from Derry to Bun Droabhaoise on the southern frontier of the lordship was constructed. This line of fortifications included the major castles of Lifford, Castlefinn, Belleek and Ballyshannon, as well as smaller crannogs and tower houses. In addition, the power and cohesion of the Ó Domhnaill dynasty brooked no hint of rebellion from any internal faction thereby preventing any fragmentation during the late medieval period. Ruthless executions and mutilations of rivals, often including the brothers or even sons of the ruling lord, allowed the O'Donnells to preserve law and order and prevent dynastic civil wars which tore apart families such as the O'Connors of Connacht or the Ó Neills. Eigneachán Ó Domhnaill, who was made Tánaiste of Tír Chonaill in 1480 almost succeeded in splitting the dynasty and establishing a splinter lordship. However, he was assassinated in 1497 along with his entire retinue. The massacre of Eigneachán and his followers in 1497 poses the question as to the extent of Renaissance influences on Tír Chonaill.[3] Close examination of the trading, diplomatic and religious links of Tír Chonaill in late medieval times shows how these European networks influenced military, political and cultural innovations.

County Donegal was certainly not a depressed economic region in late medieval times. Its natural resources were then utilised by a relatively small population concentrated in the fertile lowlands. Late medieval Tír Chonaill was famous for its vast herds of cattle and flocks of sheep, as well as large unenclosed areas sown with oats. The uplands and the rugged western coastlands were then largely uninhabited, providing its lowland inhabitants with booley pastures, turf banks, large woodlands and extensive reserves of all types of wild game. Rivers and sheltered inlets were also a very valuable natural resource, giving salmon, eel, oyster and seal fisheries.[4] Many sheltered bays attracted large numbers of foreign merchants and fishermen exploiting an immensely valuable salmon and herring fishery, which developed during the course of the early sixteenth century into one of the biggest of its kind in Europe.

Tir Chonaill had long and well-established trading links with ports such as Bristol in the south of England, St Malo and Morlaix in Brittany and Ayr, Wigtown and Glasgow in Scotland. It had an equally well-established trade with home ports such as Galway and Drogheda. Imports into Tír Chonaill were primarily wine, luxury clothes and modern weapons and armour while the main exports were fish and hides. Trade with Bristol is well documented and it is known that the Bristol merchants traded fine quality cloths and other luxury goods for herrings and hides. Salmon, however, was the premier export from Tír Chonaill to Bristol and a detailed record of the trading procedure has been recorded in the English state papers. The Bristol merchants visited Tír Chonaill on an annual basis, staying two months at the Ó Domhnaill port of Assaroe, trading their goods and buying salmon. Records indicate that the Bristol merchants spoke Irish and were well known, on a personal basis, to the lord of Tír Chonaill. The merchants had free access to O'Donnell's court and carried correspondence directly to the king of England. It is also possible that the Bristolmen maintained resident agents or factors in Tír Chonaill, and one of the Bristol merchants, John Fagan, became secretary to both Aodh Dubh and Maghnus Ó Domhnaill.[5]

Trade with Bristol was not the only important element in the commercial network. Bretons and French supplied the O'Donnells with wine, salt, iron, gunpowder and firearms, trading them for fish, tallow and hides. Agreements were conducted at a very formal level, with documents being signed aboard ship to ensure compliance. Breton agents resided in Tír Chonaill, and the O'Donnells had men of their own on the continent.[6] The exploitation of the herring fishery was a lucrative trade in which the Spanish were important players, as hundreds of their fishing boats were known to frequent the west coast. Not only did the Spanish pay tribute of between a tenth and a sixth of their catch for protection while they fished, but they also paid for onshore facilities to cure their catch. Enterprises connected with the herring fishery were concentrated in the north-west, with Ó Domhnaill ports such as Aranmore and Claudy doing an extensive trade.[7] Information for the other ports is scant. All that is known about commerce with Scotland is that firearms and wine were involved and that both Glasgow and Wigtown were very protective of their trade.[8] The Lynchs of Galway plied the wine trade while the merchants of Drogheda came to Tír Chonaill to fish. Danish ships put in to Tír Chonaill occasionally (fig. 7.3).[9]

On the continent the lord of Tír Chonaill was famed for his wealth, one contemporary describing him as the: 'best lord of fish in Ireland, and he exchangeth fish always with foreign merchants for wine, by which [he] is called in other countries, the king of [the] fish.'[10] At the peak of their influence the lords of Tír Chonaill exerted varying degrees of control over the coastline from Erris head in Mayo to Dunluce Castle in Antrim.[11] They took particular care to control the Moy estuary, the cockets of Sligo and the valuable fishery of the river Bann. In fact Ó Domhnaill revenue was so great that it began to attract pirates, from Iar Chonnacht, Umhall, and the Hebrides, who raided the ports and sea lanes of Tír Chonaill from time to time.[12] Appreciation of O'Donnell wealth is evident in the verses of a bardic poem in which the poet urges them not to forsake ancient prizes such as Tara:

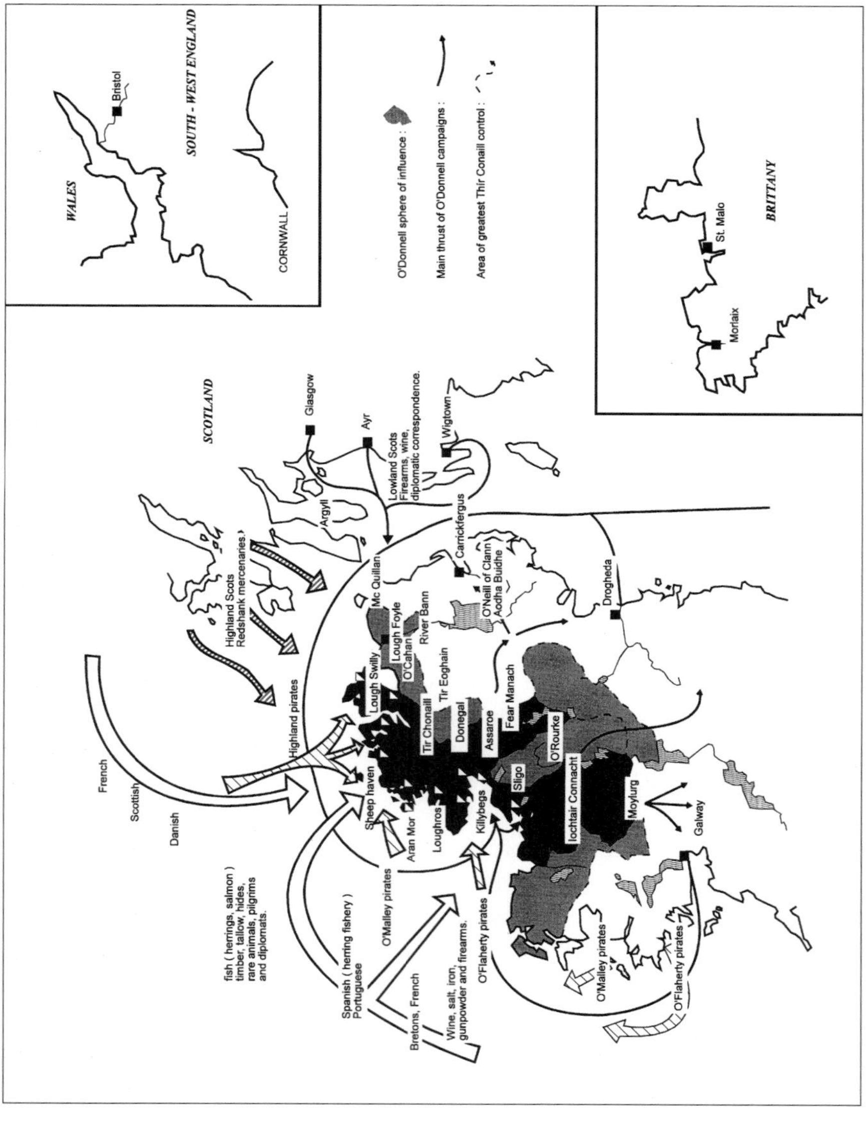

Fig. 7.3   The European contexts.

Forsake not for Donegal,
or the bay of Eas Da Eagann,
or ancient Loch Foyle, of the sparkling wines,
the royal rampart of Tara in the east.

Alas, if anyone found that for the cocket of Sligo Bay,
or for bright Croghan of the fair equipment
thou wouldst abandon
ancient Tara of Tuathal Teachtmhar.[13]

However, the lords of Tír Chonaill had long realised that there was no profit in taking Tara and that the north-western seaboard was where the customs dues and tributes were to be found.

The pilgrim trade between the north-west of Ireland and the continent was another important form of contact between Renaissance Europe and Tír Chonaill. St Patrick's Purgatory in Tearmann Dabheog was one of the most exotic pilgrimage sites in western Europe. Many important visitors came to the site, not least 'Pers Yonge, Master of the Magdalen of London', who brought a letter from Aodh Dubh Ó Domhnaill to Henry VIII in 1515, and the French knight who came via Scotland in 1516.[14] This particular individual was so hospitably entertained by Ó Domhnaill that he returned with artillery and royal soldiers from the king of Scotland, which enabled Aodh Dubh to capture Sligo and three other castles in Tír Oilella. Pilgrims from the north-west in turn visited Santiago de Compostela in Spain, the holy site associated with St James. Many of these pilgrims were undoubtedly from Tír Chonaill, as Aodh Dubh in 1507 told James IV of Scotland that he had intended to visit Galicia himself, but that his advisors had urged him not to:

> ... *nam licet nos vester sumus inferior et nobis minor imminet cura, cum Sanctum Jacobum Zebedaei in instanti anno visitare desidera [vi]mus per juris peritos et terrerum nostrarum conscientiae viros, et praecipue per fratres Minores de Observantia impediti fuimus ....*[15]

Once there, Tír Chonaill pilgrims must have been very impressed with the great Renaissance inspired Royal Hospice for Pilgrims built by King Ferdinand and Queen Isabella.[16]

It is evident therefore that Tír Chonaill did not depend on the Pale or southern England for its links with Renaissance-Europe. Of much more importance was contact with lowland Scotland, Brittany and Rome which brought the region into direct contact with centres of humanist thought. Two intertwining strands were of crucial importance in this; developments within the late medieval church and the subsequent enhancement of diplomatic skills at the court of Ó Domhnaill itself.

The wealth of the church in Tír Chonaill has long been seriously underestimated. Medieval sources such as the annates of Raphoe and Derry and the papal records, give a poverty-stricken picture of clerical life because cash revenues – and these were indeed paltry – only are taken into account. Other sources, however, indicate that clerical revenues from fisheries, eel weirs, food rents and tithes were enormous. For example, the yearly revenue of the bishop of Raphoe was 4 marks, £34, 5s, 379 meathers of butter and 350 meathers of meal.[17] Revenue accruing to parish clergy and various comharba (coarb) and airchinneach (erenagh) families was also substantial, ensuring that clerical salaries in the dioceses of Raphoe and Derry were quite lucrative, leading to intense competition for benefices which resulted in contact between local clergy and the heart of Renaissance Europe. This contact stemmed from the practice of 'Rome running' which was always strong in Gaelic Ireland. Competition between such clerical families as Ó Firgil, Ó Gallchobhair, Mac Congail, Mac Giolla Bhrighe and Ó Muirgheasain, who were allied to the ruling dynasty of Tír Chonaill, and declining families, such as Mac Maongail, and the Mac Meanmans (a discarded branch of the Ó Domhnaill dynasty), was so intense, that it led to an increasing diplomatic sophistication in church circles. Letters accusing rivals of corruption and papal replies passed to and fro between Tír Chonaill and Rome, usually via merchants from Scotland, Brittany and Bristol, with some clergy even making personal visits to Rome. For example, in 1463, one Uilliam Mac Giolla Brighe informed the pope that a certain: 'Donald Macmeriman Ydomnayll, dean of Raphoe, has ... sacrilegiously and of his own temerity broken the paten of a silver chalice for divine worship, melted it down and used the silver for the evil uses of his concubine, for her ornaments.'[18] Foreign contact not only improved the intellectual calibre of cleric, but fostered the adoption of diplomatic skills and the use of good Latin and seals. Clerics who were allied to the lord of Tír Chonaill were usually victorious, having the advantages of powerful patronage, better education and financial security.[19]

There were also strong links between the late medieval church in Tír Chonaill and many famous European educational centres. Clerics from here attended Glasgow university and Meanma Mac Carmaic, bishop of Raphoe from 1483-1514, was educated at Oxford. Other clerics such as Cú Chonnacht Ó Siaghail, the Augustinian abbot of Easdara in Sligo, was described in 1541 as: 'a right sober yong man; well lernyd, and hathe bene brought up in France'.[20] Bradshaw regards such educational ventures as part of O'Donnell policy to advance 'their own diplomatic, administrative and commercial needs'.[21]

Developments such as these ensured that the ruling dynasty had a well educated and very sophisticated clerical civil service at its disposal. The Observantine friars of the monastery of Donegal cultivated a very close relationship with the lords of Tír Chonaill, becoming both their spiritual and political advisors. In a letter to James IV dated 13 March, 1507, Aodh Dubh Ó Domhnaill expressly stated that the Observantines counselled him strongly not to go on pilgrimage to Santiago, while towards the end of his life they tried to heal the rift between himself and his son Maghnus Ó Domhnaill, by getting him to put away his concubine. Maghnus Ó Domhnaill's biography of St Columcille, the *Betha Colaim Chille,* was partly compiled by the Observantines, while Maghnus Ó Domhnaill, in 1537, specifically state: 'the freres consaillede me'.[22] In 1539, the agreement between Maghnus Ó Domhnaill and O'Connor Sligo, concerning Sligo Castle, was actually signed in the monastery of Donegal and witnessed by the guardian of the friary and the entire monastic community.[23]

This led to a flourishing of diplomatic contact between the lords of Tír Chonaill and various Irish leaders as well as with the courts of many European kings, as can be seen from the English and Scottish state papers. All three lords of Tír Chonaill had links with Irish magnates such as Ó Neill of Tír Eoghain, the earls of Desmond and the earls of Kildare, Irish families such as Ó Conchobhair Failghe and the many Hebridean mercenary dynasties who took service with them. However, by far the most important Ó Domhnaill diplomatic contacts were with the court of the king of Scotland.[24] Aodh Ruadh Ó Domhnaill built on traditional contacts with the Stuart kings of Scotland to establish strong links with King James IV, visiting the Scottish court at Edinburgh in 1495.[25] Aodh Dubh made the trip in 1513, staying for three months. Good evidence survives to indicate the sophisticated nature of Ó Domhnaill diplomatic links with the Scottish court. Aodh Dubh's preparations for his visit began as early as 1507 when his ambassador, Aeneas Mc Donayll, accompanied by two servants, delivered letters to James IV, returning with James's replies a month later. In 1508 Ó Domhnaill presented James with a gift of some prized Irish hawks, while in March 1513 the same ambassador, accompanied by a priest, was again sent to the Scottish court. Aodh Dubh arrived in July accompanied by a force of bodyguards and a retinue which included his harper. Ó Domhnaill was showered with gifts and liberally entertained, first by the earl of Argyll and then at Edinburgh, by the Scottish king. The *Annals of Ulster* record this event, stating:

O Domhnaill, namely Aodh, son of Aodh Ruadh, went, [with a] small force, to Scotland, at invitation by letters of the king of Scotland, when he received great honour and donatives from the king. And, on his being a quarter with the king and having changed the king of Scotland's intent as to going to Ireland, Ó Domhnaill comes safe to his house, after encountering great peril on sea.

Maghnus Ó Domhnaill built on these links although he never visited the Scottish court, despite trips to the Scottish highlands and islands.[26] Through these contacts they sought to monopolise access to Scottish 'Redshank' mercenaries, as well as acquiring military aid such as artillery and other equipment. Clerical appointments for Ó Domhnaill patronised clergy were also facilitated by support from the Scots faction at Rome. In return the Scottish king acquired a very powerful ally in the north of Ireland who could be of immense help in staging an Irish diversion to any Scottish invasion of the north of England.

Aodh Dubh and Maghnus Ó Domhnaill attempted to establish direct diplomatic links with the papacy and the king of England. Aodh Dubh personally visited both Pope Julius II and King Henry VIII in 1510-11. He continued to have direct correspondence with Henry VIII, cultivating English officials sent to govern Ireland, from time to time. Maghnus Ó Domhnaill continued this diplomatic policy with great aplomb, scoring great success in the 1530s by exploiting James V of Scotland's rapacious attitude to the papacy. In the 1540s and 1550s, Maghnus began to have some contact with King Francis I and King Henry II of France, respectively.[27] All of this diplomacy was of a very sophisticated nature, as the use of charters and the many surviving letters, indentures and agreements in the Scottish and English state papers show. The Latin style of writing used by the lords of Tír Chonaill was of a very high standard, being described by one Scottish historian as: 'a kingly style',[28] and some letters even retain Maghnus Ó Domhnaill's personal seal, a wolf with the red hand of Ulster, surrounded by the letters M+O.D.[29]

Aodh Ruadh, Aodh Dubh and Maghnus Ó Domhnaill were able military strategists, winning many battles by careful preparation and clever tactics. Aodh Dubh and Maghnus Ó Domhnaill were also noted for their intelligent use of fleets of ships, with which they roamed the Erne, often sailing deep into the heart of county Cavan.[30] It was the foreign contacts built through trade and diplomacy that opened the territory to many innovations in late medieval warfare. The first mention of firearms in any of the Irish annals occurs in 1487 when an Ó Domhnaill musketeer in Aodh Ruadh's army shot dead an Ó Ruairc during an incursion into Breifne.[31] Later both Aodh Dubh and Maghnus Ó Domhnaill were pioneer exponents of the use of artillery. In 1513, Aodh Dubh Ó Domhnaill was in negotiation with James IV of Scotland for a large quantity of munitions, including artillery in Ireland. The inventory of this shipment, although it never reached Tír Chonaill, is quite impressive. A record, fortunately preserved in the accounts of the lord high treasurer of Scotland, states that it included one canon drawn by twenty-six horses, one large culverin drawn by eight horses, two carts with eight barrels of powder, two carts with gunstands, one cart with pikes, skulls, mattocks and a trellis for the canon, as well as two Scottish wrights to operate the canon, a French wright to supervise the setting up of the artillery and eight Scottish sappers to undermine castles, all of whom were paid one month's wages, the projected duration of the expedition.[32] A canon did arrive from Scotland in 1516 and in 1536. Aodh Dubh had 'a great gun', which he used to overawe his enemies during an invasion of north Connacht. In 1537-8, Maghnus Ó Domhnaill was in contact with the king of Scotland looking for artillery and sending ambassadors back and forth across the north channel in an effort to speed things up.[33] Later in 1543-4 he turned to the lord deputy in Dublin, who sent artillery and one hundred soldiers to help Ó Domhnaill recapture Lifford Castle, which was in the hands of dissident O'Gallaghers.[34] This suggests that of all the Gaelic Irish lords, the O'Donnells were the most accustomed to the use of firearms and artillery. It is difficult to reconcile this evidence, that the O'Donnells were using firearms and artillery in the early years of the sixteenth century, with the claims of Lughaidh Ó Clerigh, the author of *Beatha Aodha Ruaidh Uí Dhomhnaill,* who asserted that they knew nothing of guns or 'strange arms'[35] at the beginning of the Nine Year's war.

External links had many other important consequences for the society of the lordship. A religious revival pioneered by the Franciscan Observantines swept the Atlantic seaboard in the late medieval period. A very strict, pious and humble order, they were brought into Tír Chonaill in 1474 by Aodh Ruadh and his wife Fionnghuala Ní Briain, who built a beautiful monastery for the friars at their capital, Donegal. The Observantine friars had a significant impact on society here. Their preaching is known to have deeply influenced the nobility, such as Tuathail Balbh Ó Gallchobhair, chieftain of the O'Gallaghers who died in 1541. Described as a pious and christian man, the *Annals of the Four Masters* state that he was greatly influenced while very young by the friars of Donegal, and that as a result he always tried to take his enemies prisoner while in battle.[36] Both Aodh Ruadh and Fionnghuala were very religious people, the lord of Tír Chonaill being a great church reformer, protecting the clergy during his reign and getting at least one bishop of Raphoe rehabilitated. His queen spent twenty-two years in the habit of St Francis following her husband's death, before she too was buried alongside him in the monastery of Donegal.[37] The friars also seem to have had a great influence on Máire Ní Máille, wife of Mac Suibhne Fanad, who died in 1522. In return she built a great hall for the Observantines at Donegal. Indeed Máire, and her husband, Ruaidhri Mac Suibhne, lord of Fanad from 1472-1518, appear to have been deeply religious, bringing the Carmelites to Rathmullan. Máire amassed a great deal of religious literature which included a tract on the finding of the true cross, a life of St Margaret, the Gospel of Nicodemus and a version of the Vision of St Paul. One record states that 'she went to mass once a day and fasted three days a week on bread and water as well as observing the Lentan, winter and Golden Friday fasts.'[38] The influence of the Observantines extended into other parts of Ulster and as a result the Observantine friary at Donegal became a prestigious resting place for many of the nobility of northern Ireland. The lords of Tír Chonaill, their immediate families, sub-chieftains such as the O'Boyles, bishops, neighbouring chieftains and the Cistercian abbot of Assaroe, were all buried in the monastery.[39]

The Observantines may have been responsible for many subtle developments in Tír Chonaill society at this time. An entertaining humorous text known as the 'Ceithearnach Caoilriabhach' in which a supernatural vagabond kerne visits the court of Aodh Dubh Ó Domhnaill at Ballyshannon, has hitherto been recognised as a surprisingly accurate story. Recent research, however, suggests that the text may in fact be a clever Observantine polemic against the vices of drunkenness and card playing, where the kerne, the knave in contemporary decks of cards, is in fact the devil in disguise come to wreak havoc amongst O'Donnell's household and soldiers. If the text dates from the 1530s, then the fact that Aodh Dubh's gallowglass and cavalry soldiers are cheekily massacred by the devil may have been used to bolster the morale of Maghnus Ó Domhnaill's men, as he and the Observantine Franciscans were in opposition to Aodh Dubh at this time.[40] Observantine friars were also used to promote the power and authority of the lordship in more overt ways. Testimony from a Galway merchant trading in Donegal in 1539 recounts how this was done. Maghnus Ó Domhnaill, about to raid the Pale in support of the Geraldine Confederacy, enlisted the spiritual support of the friars who preached that:

> every man ought, for the salvacion of his sowle, fight and make warr ayenste Our Soverayne Lord the Kinges Majestie, and his

trewe subjectes; and if any of theym, which soo shall fight ayenste His said Majestie, or his subjectes, dy in the quarrell, his sowle, that so shalbe dedd, shall goo to Heven, as the sowle of Saynt Peter, Pawle, and others, which soffered death and marterdom for Godes sake.[41]

In 1497, the guardian of the monastery of Donegal assisted the lord of Tír Chonaill, then in dispute with enemies in Fermanagh and the MacGraths of Tearmann Dabheog, by officiating over the closing and destruction of St Patrick's Purgatory on Lough Derg. The O'Donnells reciprocated handsomely. Aodh Ruadh supplied an important chapter of the Observantine friars, held in Donegal in 1488, while Aodh Dubh maintained an even larger chapter in 1530.[42]

Other outside influences blew through Tír Chonaill society like a much needed breath of fresh air. The lordship experienced massive building activity, so that by 1555 there were at least forty castles in the territory, as well as nine monasteries of recent construction (Donegal, Magherabeg, Ballysaggart, Killybegs, Balleeghan, Cill Ó dTomhrair, Killmacrenan, Rathmullan and Ballymacsweeney), not counting the late medieval re-edification of many parish churches such as St Columcille's chapel at Gartan and St Mary's church on Inishkeel.[43] For this to happen, Tír Chonaill must have been conditioned by 'the social propensity towards the acceptance of new fashions'.[44] Many of these structures were very large and imposing by Irish standards. Indeed, the Franciscan Observantine monastery of Donegal, the Third Order Regular houses at Machaire Beg and Cill Ó dTomhrair, and the regal Ó Domhnaill castles at Donegal and Lifford must have been impressive Renaissance-inspired buildings.

Trade led to the development of ports and towns such as Assaroe, Killybegs, Aranmore and Claudy and settlements on the shores of Lough Swilly and Lough Foyle. It is clear that Donegal, Lifford, Killybegs, Raphoe, Derry and the Ó Dochartaigh capital at Aileach were becoming true urban sites, with many buildings and significant populations, just as Sligo, yet another port in the Tír Chonaill sphere of influence, was a small town in late medieval times. The market at Donegal was frequented by merchants, but especially the O'Creans of Sligo and the Lynchs of Galway. Quite an amount of evidence survives for Donegal. The *Annals of the Four Masters* indicate that not only was there a large castle here, but a smaller one as well and two monasteries. The same source refers to another house belonging to the Franciscans known as *Mur na mBrathair*, which may have been a hospital. These annals also record a lime-kiln hill and hint at a substantial population – an entry for 1575 stating that a riot of the local inhabitants occurred. Other sources give additional information. The *Leabhar Chlainne Suibhne* refers to a great hall built for the Franciscans, while the *Short Annals of Tír Chonaill* record the existence of a 'faithe' or fairgreen, which may explain the presence of so many merchants in the town.[45] There is no doubt that the O'Donnells self consciously regarded Donegal as their capital. The *Annals of Connacht* record in 1537, that the capture of the castle: 'threw the country into confusion'.[46] The lords addressed most of their diplomatic correspondence from the castle and entertained dignitaries there. However, the best evidence that the centre was a real town occurs in a letter written by King James IV of Scotland in 1507, when he refers to Donegal as 'oppido Drumnangall'.[47] This is an interesting Latin term, being a learned classical reference to the great urban sites of the Celts of ancient Gaul. Donegal exhibited many of the characteristics of an urban central place. It possessed a defensive function, a complex religious organisation, a diversified economic base, as well as a socially differentiated population.

The Ó Domhnaill lords of Tír Chonaill had by late medieval times acquired great wealth and military and political power. With great wealth came acquired taste and sophistication. This is as true of Aodh Ruadh, Aodh Dubh and Maghnus Ó Domhnaill, as it was of contemporary kings of Scotland or Renaissance princes in Italy. Increased sophistication is evident in a certain individualistic flair associated with each prince of Tír Chonaill. One of the first things Aodh Ruadh Ó Domhnaill did on subjugating the O'Connors of Sligo in 1470, was to take back the historic books, the *Leabhar Gearr* and *Lebor na hUidre*, as well as a set of chairs belonging to a famous ancestor which had been looted over a century before.[48] Aodh Ruadh's introduction of the Observantines and the architectural elegance of Donegal castle and monastery are also monuments to his good taste. Aodh Dubh shared his father's interest in collecting ancient Irish manuscripts, accepting the *Book of Ballymote* from Mac Donnchadha in 1522 in lieu of 140 milch cows.[49] Indeed, there are few better examples of Renaissance influence on Tír Chonaill than his penchant for foreign travel, evident in his epic pilgrimage to Rome in 1510-11 where he arrived just as the Sistine chapel was nearing completion. Aodh Dubh had an audience with Pope Julius II and spent thirty-two weeks at the English court where he received a knighthood from Henry VIII.

A number of direct innovations made in Tír Chonaill may stem from contact with Renaissance Europe. In 1512, the year after Aodh Dubh returned, the annals refer to him hiring 1,500 axemen in Fermanagh and north Connacht. Although the O'Donnells had previously hired Hebridean mercenaries, the immense scale, suggestive date and unusual source of origin of these mercenaries hint that Aodh Dubh may have been directly influenced by the *condottieri* system, which he must have observed while in Italy.[50] It has been pointed out that there are two Tudor roses in the frontispiece portrait of Maghnus Ó Domhnaill's *Betha Colaim Chille* which depicts St Columcille in the robes of a late medieval bishop. The inspiration for the roses may have come from one of the lavish decorations Seán Ó Faolain so graphically depicts in his account of the knighting of Aodh Dubh at Westminster. Indeed, it is not too fanciful to picture Henry VIII presenting the new knight with a gold rose decoration, which Aodh Dubh kept as a family heirloom to eventually inspire the painter of this portrait thirty years later.[51]

The library of ancient Irish manuscripts in Donegal provides a parallel to the collection of classical Greek and Roman texts assembled by humanist rulers on the continent. It is almost certain that the O'Donnells had a substantial library, the only difference with the collections of continental rulers, such as Lorenzo de Medici or Francis I of France, being that they were harking back to an Irish golden age. Although aware of the interest in ancient Greece and Rome, it was Brian Boru, Cathal Crobhdhearg or other more ancient Irish kings who captured their imagination. Patronage was extended to the learned classes in Tír Chonaill, with families such as Ó Cleirigh and Mac an Bhaird enjoying a very privileged position. This lavish patronage may be Renaissance inspired. Simms writes that:

> ... the surplus wealth which the Gaelic Irish chieftains directed entirely towards feasting and poetry corresponded to funds laid out by the ruling classes of other European countries partly on entertainment, but also on magnificent processions, statues, pictures, jewellery and imposing architecture.[52]

The backward look to a past Irish golden age is evident in hints from contemporary works such as the *Beatha Colaim Chille* and the *Annals of Ulster,* the *Annals of Connacht* and the *Annals of Loch Ce.* In particular the O'Donnells appear to have modelled themselves on Brian Boru, finding parallells between their own careers and what they saw as Brian Boru's protection of the church and the weak in society, as well as his epic war with the foreigner. These aspirations were probably taken from that great Ó Briain propaganda work of the twelfth century, the *Cocad Gaedel re Gallaib.* Maghnus Ó Domhnaill in 1532 states that he had read it, and the fact that Aodh Ruadh married a Ní Briain, who was Aodh Dubh's mother, suggests that the O'Donnells did not need to look far for inspiration in this regard. The parallels for Aodh Dubh in this context are the strongest. The *Annals of Ulster* lauded Aodh Dubh, stating that: '... there came not from Brian Boruma downwards a king of better sway and rule than he.'[53] In the same vein the *Annals of Connacht* state that he was a 'veritable worthy kinsman of Brian Boruma mac Ceinneididh both in lineage and in actions', his actions including 'the exalting of Orders and churchmen', 'destroying rebels and lawless men' and 'attacking and conquering his foes'.[54] The *Annals of Ulster* refer to Aodh Ruadh in almost identical terms, stating that '... there came not from Brian Borumha ... down a king, or lord, that was of better sway and rule and was of more power than that king.' In true Renaissance style the same source also likens Aodh Ruadh to an 'Augustus of the whole north-west of Europe'.[55] These examples, Renaissance inspired, harken back to a long lost golden age before 'the folk across the sea came to smite Erin'.[56]

For sophisticated taste and progressive innovation, however, there are few better late medieval examples than that of Maghnus Ó Domhnaill. Bradshaw compares him favourably to the exemplary type of Renaissance prince documented by such contemporary authors as Machiavelli, Erasmus or Baldesare Castiglione. Indeed if Maghnus Ó Domhnaill had only been a man of letters, he would still have been one of the greatest Irish men of his generation. Eight of his poems have survived and they indicate a real and graceful talent as well as a biting wit. His poem beginning *'Cridhe so da ghoid uainne'* (Heart full of thoughts), has been described as having 'a rare gem-like quality', as have his other poems such as *'Dar liom, is galar e an gradh'* and *'Goirt anocht dereadh mo sgeal-'*. On the other hand, his satires of the friars of Donegal, while demonstrating the same genuine talent, are very humorous.[57] Ó Domhnaill's epic work, his *Betha Colaim Chille* (Life of St Columcille), which was written at Lifford in 1532, is a similarly talented and immensely important text.[58] Although Maghnus may not have actually written all the manuscript, he certainly commisioned and edited it, and probably had a great deal of control over all aspects of its compilation. As he wrote himself:

> And be it known to the readers of this life that it was Maghnus Ó Domhnaill mac Aodha mac Aodha Ruaidh mac Niall Garbh mac Toirrdhealbhach an Fhiona, that bade put into Gaelic the part of this Life that was in Latin, and bade make easy the part thereof that was hard Gaelic, to the end it might be clear and easy of understanding to all.[59]

This work laid the basis for the development of modern Irish, and as such provides a parallel to the poetry of Lorenzo de Medici which played a crucial role in the transformation of the Tuscan dialect into the literary language of Italy. It is also worth bearing in mind that other near contemporary rulers such as Philip the Good of Burgundy took a personal hand in the preparation of such works as the *Histoires de Troye*.[60] Although much of the content of the Life is medieval in character, in many other ways it is a true product of the Renaissance. Ó Domhnaill names thirty-five sources used in the compilation of the biography, demonstrating the comprehensive process of this procedure. The text states:

> And he collected and assembled the part thereof that was scattered throughout the ancient books of Erin, and he set it forth with his own lips. And passing great labor had he therewith. And much time did he give thereto, conning how he might put each part thereof in its own fitting place as it is writ here below.[61]

This statement illustrates the Renaissance research techniques used, giving a good indication of a new thoroughness and sense of direction evident in much of the Gaelic Irish scholarship of Tír Chonaill and indeed Fermanagh during the late medieval period. The slightly isolated paragraphs of the *Betha Colaim Chille* have been patterned on printed books, one expert going so far as to state that:

> The writing, obviously the work of the best scribe available, is a beautiful formal hand, very even and rhythmic. The text is laid out in paragraphs, which is unusual but may have been influenced by page layout in printed books in O'Donnell's library.[62]

In this the *Betha Colaim Chille* has many similarities to the *Annals of Ulster*, which Ruaidhri Ó Luinin meticulously compiled, using new Renaissance research techniques, the 'printlike clarity' of his hand being described as 'the ultimate evolution of the practicle miniscule'.[63] The decoration of the beautiful illustration of St Columcille in the *Betha Colaim Chille*, may also have been influenced by a Tudor decoration kept by Aodh Dubh Ó Domhnaill as an heirloom. Colmcille's portrait has other unusual decorative features such as acanthus leaves and fleur-de-lys terminations, which may be imitations of Franco-Flemish miniatures or even stained glass windows.[64]

The *Betha Colaim Chille* is a very important source as it not only contains much information on its erstwhile subject, St Columcille, but also many valuable hints about ordinary life in late medieval Tír Chonaill. A great deal of contemporary folklore found its way into the biography, while many glimpses of early sixteenth-century Gaelic Irish life are inadvertently given by the compiler. For example in paragraph 92, Ó Domhnaill records that iron was used in ploughs in Tír Chonaill, while in paragraphs 188-9, Ó Domhnaill or one of his assistants forgets that the conquest of Inishowen by the Cinél Conaill was only a recent historical phenomenon, stating that the Cinél Conaill bid farewell to Columcille on one side of Lough Foyle, while the Cinél Eoghan did so on the other. In fact one of the most intriguing statements occurs in paragraph 132 of the Life where Ó Domhnaill states that the people of Tír Chonaill believed that lobsters were in fact the demons of Glencolumbcille, cast into the sea by St Columcille, and turned into fish that were: 'blind of an eye and red'. Ó Domhnaill proceeds: 'fishers oft take them today, and they do naught to them when they perceive them, save to cast them again into the sea.'[65]

There are a number of significant parallels between the careers of Maghnus Ó Domhnaill and his father Aodh Dubh. Maghnus, because he was such a pivotal figure, was credited with innovations such as the first taxation of comharba and airchinneach families probably influenced by the example of King James V of Scotland. Similarly, Maghnus's castle of Lifford completed in 1527 must have been a very important Renaissance-inspired building. Although no trace of the structure survives today, one bardic poet has left a description of its 'delightful, lofty buildings, its tables, its coverlets, its cupboards; its wondrous, handsome, firm walls, its smooth marble arches ... the fortress of smooth-lawned Lifford'.[66] Here the inhabitants indulged in the very civilised pursuits of chess and reading, and indeed this should come as no surprise as Maghnus is described in his obit as 'a learned man, skilled in many arts, gifted with a profound intellect, and the knowledge of every science'.[67] However, an equally impressive description of the court of Aodh Dubh at Ballyshannon gives an indication of its well ordered nature and refined habits. Seating arrangements were very structured, with the most privileged closest to the lord. Guests were well supplied with 'new of all meats and with old of all liquors' by O'Donnell's many stewards, commanded by a major-domo. Music was provided by four harpists and there was a gatekeeper and a bodyguard of twenty horsemen, and forty gallowglasses.[68] Both Ó Domhnaill princes had a taste for sartorial splendour. In 1541, Lord Deputy St Leger was astounded to see Maghnus being rowed across a lake towards him, resplendent in: 'a cote of crymoisin velvet with aggllette of gold, 20 or 30 payer, over that a greate doble cloke of right crymoisin saten, garded with blacke velvet a bonette, with a fether, sette full of agglettes of gold'.[69] Less well-known, but in a similar vein, is the gift of an equally splendid suit of clothes to Aodh Dubh Ó Domhnaill, upon the visit of the latter to Edinburgh in 1513. Both the name of the tailor, one 'Turnebule, hemsman' and the cost, £15 16s 8d, are also recorded. Aodh Dubh's outfit consisted of a gown of twenty-eight ells of satin lined with taffeta, a coat made up of three ells of furred russet, scarlet trousers lined with half an ell of velvet, three and a half ells of fustian and a doublet of cream satin.[70]

Let us now turn to the political philosophy of the O'Donnells and the extent of their knowledge and involvement in Renaissance high diplomacy. Far from being isolated in the north-west of Ireland, the O'Donnells were heavily involved in many national and mainstream European alliances. As early as 1464 Aodh Ruadh visited Thomas FitzGerald, the eighth earl of Desmond.[71] From 1493-7, Aodh Ruadh was heavily involved in a Yorkist plot to put Perkin Warbeck on the throne of England. At this time the English were describing him as 'notoriously disloyal', which is really no surprise as not only was Aodh Ruadh building an Ulster Yorkist Confederacy and hiring Hebridean mercenaries, but he was in alliance with the tenth earl of Desmond, Seán Burke of Clanricard and James IV of Scotland. Ó Domhnaill even visited the court of the king of Scotland in 1495 to arrange for the reception of Warbeck, Aodh Ruadh sheltering the pretender, before spiriting him to Scotland.[72] In 1513, Aodh Dubh Ó Domhnaill intended to mount an Irish diversion to facilitate James IV's invasion of the north of England which was to end disastrously for the Scots at the battle of Flodden. Again the lord of Tír Chonaill visited the Scottish court and the annals state that Aodh Dubh personally persuaded James IV not to invade Ireland. Eventually the two leaders arranged that the Scottish king would give Aodh Dubh a large supply of munitions, to be shipped from Glasgow, with which Ó Domhnaill would launch a major military expedition, probably against Sligo or the Pale.[73] Maghnus also had contact with James V of Scotland, the papacy and the kings of France. His involvement in the Geraldine Confederacy has overtones of an ideological counter-reformation nature, while his alliance with Conn Bacach Ó Neill, his marriage to Eleanor FitzGerald and the sheltering of Gearóid, the only surviving Geraldine heir, broke bold new ground in diplomatic and military initiatives.

Naturally enough, the over-riding political philosophy of the lords of Tír Chonaill was to maintain their supremacy within Tír Chonaill and the O'Donnell sphere of influence in north Connacht and west Ulster. It is not surprising therefore, that they resurrected the ancient title of 'rí Leithe Cuinn,' (king of the northern half of Ireland), to glorify and give historical justification to their achievements.[74] The prime Ó Domhnaill objective was to keep the O'Neills of Tír Eoghain divided, weak and surrounded, so as to allow them to extend their influence into Fermanagh and north Connacht at will. In Fermanagh and Connacht, the O'Donnells were generally successful with only Mac Diarmada of Moylurg, from his base in the Curlew mountains, proving to be a long-term thorn in their side. However, the rivalry between Tír Chonaill and Tír Eoghain led to constant warfare, which has been described as 'the most important single fact in the history of Ulster in this period'.[75]

The lords of Tír Chonaill conducted a long-term strategy of allying with any potential enemy of Tír Eoghain, thus allowing them to outflank their great rivals. An alliance with the O'Neills of Clann Aodha Buidhe was very successful, as was an arrangement first agreed between Aodh Ruadh Ó Domhnaill and Gearóid Mor, the eighth earl of Kildare, which lasted from the late 1490s to about 1512. Ó Domhnaill and FitzGerald recognised each other's sphere of influence, Tír Conaill being paramount in north Connacht, west Ulster and north-east of the Bann, while Kildare dominated the rest of the island. Aodh Ruadh agreed to stop raiding the Pale and drop links with King James IV of Scotland. In return Kildare and Ó Domhnaill set about keeping Ó Neill in check by raiding Tír Eoghain simultaneously from the west and south, while FitzGerald, also, assisted Ó Domhnaill against Mac Diarmada of Moylurg. Kildare, Aodh Ruadh and Aodh Dubh Ó Domhnaill were then enabled to combine against their mutual enemies in Clanricard and Thomond in 1504 and 1510.[76]

The arrangement appears to have broken down in the time of Aodh Dubh Ó Domhnaill and Gearóid Óg, the ninth earl of Kildare. Aodh Dubh established direct contact with Henry VIII in 1511-12 which angered the FitzGeralds who wanted to control all contact between powerful Gaelic Irish potentates and the king. In any case, the earl of Kildare switched his support to the O'Neills of Tír Eoghain, a shift in emphasis which became much stronger when Conn Bacach, whose mother was a Geraldine, and he himself, a close kinsman of Gearóid Óg, became lord of Tír Eoghain in 1519. As a result there was large-scale warfare between Tír Chonaill and Tír Eoghain, almost continuously from 1513. This war reached its climax in a number of spectacular engagements in 1522-4, when Aodh Dubh and Maghnus Ó Domhnaill, because of access to vast numbers of Scottish Highland mercenaries, not only crushed Ó Neill, in a major battle just inside Tír Eoghain, but utterly humiliated a vast alliance of Connacht and north Munster enemies who had tried to attack Tír Chonaill from the south.[77] Gearóid Óg in turn was humbled when he tried to invade Tír Chonaill the following year to avenge O'Neill's defeat.

Aodh Dubh Ó Domhnaill was not reconciled with Gearóid Óg until 1531 and maintained his sphere of influence in the north of Ireland despite him. Instead Aodh Dubh pursued an alternative policy of maintaining good relations with English administrators, sent over periodically to govern Ireland when Gearóid Óg was in disfavour. This policy can be summed up by Aodh Dubh's own statement recorded in

1520: 'If ever the Kyng send the Erl of Kildare hether in auctoritie agayne, let the King make him an assurance, by indenture of this land, to him and to his heires for ever.'[78] An indenture was duly agreed at Drogheda in 1531. Maghnus Ó Domhnaill successfully reverted to this policy after the disaster of the battle of Bellahoe in 1539. In this the O'Donnells were pragmatic rather than pro-English or even anglophile. Sentiments expressed in the *Betha Colaim Chille*, bardic poetry and contemporary annals record that all three lords of Tír Chonaill, Aodh Ruadh, Aodh Dubh and Maghnus, harboured ambitions of driving the foreigner from Ireland, just as Brian Boru had supposedly done in a golden past. As the *Annals of Connacht* so eloquently put it in relation to Aodh Dubh Ó Domhnaill in 1537:

> ... there is no doubt that if the Gaels had not been growing feeble and fickle he would have made a bid for the sovereignty of Ireland, and it is probable he would have succeeded; but since he saw that the Gaels were becoming men of bad faith, trusting no man, unruly and froward, he made an alliance with the King of England, so that he was not oppressed by the might of the Galls but held sway in Leth Chuind without cavil, after the manner of the men of Ireland.[79]

All three lords of Tír Chonaill concluded that, to maintain their position of power, it was best to come to an arrangement with whoever had control of the administration in Dublin. By 1523 the O'Donnells believed they had the measure of Gearóid Óg; no invading English army ever set foot in Tír Chonaill, or even challenged the lord of Tír Chonaill in his wider sphere of influence and the fact that Maghnus Ó Domhnaill wanted to be made earl of Sligo in the 1540s, demonstrates that he was laying claim to a much wider area of authority than just the modern county of Donegal.[80]

In summary therefore the lords of Tír Chonaill were innovative, sophisticated and receptive to outside influences, while at the same time having a political and cultural self-confidence which enabled them to become the dominant force in Gaelic Ireland for three generations. In the contemporary Gaelic world the only adequate parallel was the rise of the Mac Ailin earls of Argyll in Scotland. Because the Ó Domhnaill polity collapsed so suddenly and left such little trace, it has led to its impact being somewhat forgotten, just as powerful political entities, such as the lordship of the Isles, Brittany or Burgundy, have also been overlooked because they have not bequeathed modern nation states. In relation to the question of Renaissance influence on Tír Chonaill, many trends are clear. I believe that what is true of Maghnus must be equally true of his father and grandfather, Aodh Dubh and

Aodh Ruadh. It is evident that the Irish culture of Tír Chonaill flourished in late medieval times and was influenced in many ways by direct and constant contact with centres of Renaissance activity. Contact with the Scottish court was undoubtedly the most important link, the impact of the Renaissance on this kingdom being for too long underestimated. The loss of Renaissance-inspired buildings such as most of the Observantine monastery at Donegal and Maghnus Ó Domhnaill's castle at Lifford has deprived us of important testimony in stone. In this Tír Chonaill provides a graphic parallel with Hungary where the great Matthias Corvinus (r. 1458-90) reconstructed the chateau at Buda in Renaissance style. This impressive building was subsequently buried beneath later accretions and its rediscovery in 1949 forced scholars to reassess the Renaissance in an area once thought to be outside its sphere of influence.[81]

References

1. Aodh Ruadh ruled Tír Chonaill from 1461 to 1497, when he abdicated, and again from 1497 to his death in 1505. Aodh Dubh reigned from 1505-37. Maghnus was in power from 1537 until his deposition in 1555.

2. K. Nicholls, *Gaelic and gaelicised Ireland in the middle ages* (Dublin, 1972), p. 136.

3. See N. Machiavelli, *The Prince* (Penguin Classics, 1981), pp 37-8, 59-60.

4. *Ann. Conn.*, 1343, no. 13, p. 295; *A.L.C.*, 1588, pp 488-9; Sir Conyers Clifford to the Lord Deputy and council, 1597 (*Cal. S. P. Ire.*, *1598-99*, pp 375-6); Preface – Captain Mostyn (*Cal. S. P. Ire.*, *1598-99*, pp xv-xvi); *Inquisitionum in officio rotulorum cancellariae Hiberniae asservatarum, repertorium*, ii, app. v, Donagall; 'The O'Kane Papers' in *Anal. Hib.*, no. 12 (January, 1943), pp 96-7, 101, 103.

5. *L. & P., Hen. VIII*, x, no. 1013; ibid., xv, nos 321 and 994; *S. P., Hen. VIII, iii, continued*, p. 98; ibid., no. cccix; W. Childs and T. O'Neill, 'Overseas trade' in *N.H.I.*, ii, pp 492, 505-6, 522; E. M. Carus-Wilson, *The overseas trade of Bristol* (London, 1967), pp 34, 45-6, 57, 86, 110; D. Harris Sacks, *Trade, society and politics in Bristol, 1500-1640* (USA, 1985), pp 256, 347, 355, 362.

6. *S. P. 3, Hen. VIII, iii*, continued, no. cccvi, p. 211; ibid., ccclxxxv, p. 446; ibid., no. cccxliv, p. 320; Captain Charles Plessington to the earl of Nottingham etc., 3 Sept, 1601 (*Cal. S. P. Ire.*, *1601-10*, p. 54).

7. The herring fishery was so profitable that in 1543 Henry VIII was offered a share of the revenue. Trade with Tír Chonaill must have been mutually beneficial as the merchants showed a great deal of loyalty to the lords of Tír Chonaill. On many occasions merchants from Bristol and Brittany refused to become involved in English adventures designed to bring the O'Donnells to heel. In fact, only the Galway merchants appear ill-disposed to the lords of Tír Chonaill and this may have stemmed from Ó Domhnaill military activity in Connacht. K. Simms, *Gaelic lordships in Ulster in the later middle ages* (unpublished Phd. thesis, T.C.D., 1976), i, p. 161; *S. P. 3, Hen. VIII, iii, continued*, no. cccxcvii, p. 481; ibid, no. cccxxii, p. 142; Sir Richard Bingham to the Lord Deputy (*Cal. S. P. Ire.*, *1588-92*, p. 545); ibid., 1592-96, p. 259.

8. Robert Bowes to Lord Burghley (*Cal. S. P. Scot., 1509-1603*, ii, p. 591); Mary Queen of Scots to Queen Elizabeth (ibid., i, p. 198).

9. *S. P. 3, Hen VIII, iii*, continued, no. cclxxii, p. 140; Sir Richard Bingham to the Lord Deputy (*Cal. S. P. Ire., 1592-96*, p. 259); The Lord Chancellor Loftus etc. to the Privy Council (ibid., 1596-97, p. 125).

10. Notes on Ulster (*Cal. Carew MSS, 1515-74*, no. 229, p. 181).

11. *S. P., Hen. VIII, iii*, continued, no. ccclxxxv, p. 447.

12. The lords of Tír Chonaill appear to have had a fleet of twelve or thirteen wooden ships, which were much more substantial than currachs, to protect their territorial waters. Although there is no record of any naval engagement with pirates, many robber gangs were surprised on islands or as they came ashore. *A.U.*, 1513; *A.F.M.*, 1542; ibid., 1543; ibid., 1551; ibid., 1200; *Cal. S. P. Ire., 1509-73*, no. 48, p. 210.

13. E. Knott (ed.), *The bardic poems of Tadhg Dall Ó hUigínn* (London, 1922), i, pp 8, 50-51, ii, pp 5-6, 50-1.

14. *L. & P., Hen. VIII*, ii, no. 224, 21, p. 6; *A.U.*, iii, 1516, pp 520-21.

15. *Letters and papers of the reigns of Richard II and Henry VII*, ed. J. Gairdner, i (London, 1863), p. 240, xxxvi. James IV to O'Donnel, [Mss. Royal 13 b.ii. no. 42. ADV. 172.] *The Letters of James the Fourth, 1505-1513*, calendared by R. Kerr Hannay, ed. R. L. Mackie, assisted by A. Spilman (Edinburgh, 1953), pp 63, 89. O'Donnel, Prince of Ulster, to James IV, Drunangall [Donegal], March 13, 1506-7, N.L. 53; g. 237.

16. *Letters of James IV*, no. 89, pp 63-4; G. R. Potter, 'The Arts in western Europe' in *The new Cambridge modern history*, i, *the Renaissance* (Cambridge, 1957), p. 167.

17. *Inquisitionum in officio*, app. v.

18. *Cal. papal letters*, xii, 1458-71. Lateran Regesta, dlxxxv. 5. Pius II, 18 Kal, July (June 14), St. Peter's Rome (f.10d) 1463, p. 178.

19. Ibid., *1458-1471*, f. 10 d., p. 178; ibid., *1484-92*, f. 21 r, p. 70; *L. & P., Hen. VIII*, xiii, ii, no. 1164; *Letters of James V*, f. 88, p. 321; ibid, f. 109, p. 348.

20. *The O'Kane papers*, pp 101-4; *De Annatis Hiberniae*, i, p. 288. Ó Siaghail was chaplain to Maghnus Ó Domhnaill and may be the 'Domnum Connatium Ofraghill, Abbatem Dirrensem', mentioned as being one of the ambassadors of Aodh Dubh Ó Domhnaill in 1531. *S. P. 3, Hen. VIII, iii*, continued, no. cccxliv, p. 320; *S. P. Hen. VIII*, no. lviii, p. 151, Submission of O'Donnell; M. Carney, 'Agreement between Ó Domhnaill and Tadhg Ó Conchobhair concerning Sligo Castle (23 June, 1539)' in *I.H.S.*, iii (1942-3), (hereafter cited as *Agreement*) p. 296.

21. B. Bradshaw, 'Manus the magnificent' in A. Cosgrove and D. McCartney (eds), *Studies in Irish history* (Dublin, 1978), p. 21.

22. *S. P. 2, Hen. VIII*, no. clxxviii, O'Donnell's letter, p. 472.

23. *Agreement*, pp 288-91.

24. There was a very important historical axis between the north of Ireland and the south of Scotland. It was of prime importance when the great Columban centre of Iona was the umbilical cord between the northern Uí Neill and the Anglo-Saxon kingdom of Northumbria during the seventh and eighth centuries. The link became very strong again in the late medieval period as the lords of Tír Chonaill and the kings of Scotland built up a powerful alliance in the north of these islands.

25. *A.U.*, 1513; ibid., 1523; P. F. Tylter, *History of Scotland*, iv, p. 322, note +; *Accounts of the lord high treasurer of Scotland*, i, p. 242 (hereafter cited as

Accounts).

26. *Letters of James IV*, nos 89, 104, 105, 106, pp 63-4, 70-1; *Accounts*, iii, p. 383; ibid., iv, pp. 135, 406, 415 -6.

27. *Letters of James V*, pp 275, 321, 348, 435; *L. & P., Hen. VIII*, xix, ii, no. 324, p. 169.

28. *Accounts*, iii, plxxvii.

29. *S. P. 2, Hen. VIII*, iii, p. 472; ibid., 3, iii, no. cccix, p. 217.

30. *A.U.*, 1508; ibid., 1514; *S. P. 3, Hen. VIII*, iii, continued, no. cccxliii, p. 313.

31. *A.F.M.*, 1487.

32. *Accounts*, iv, p. 527.

33. *A.L.C.*, 1536; *Letters of James V*, f. 101, p. 339.

34. *L. & P., Hen. VIII*, xix, i, no. 240, p. 128.

35. *B.A.R.*, i, 17, p. 35.

36. *A.F.M.*, 1541.

37. *A.F.M.*, 1470, note x; *A.U.*, 1487; *A.F.M.*, 1528.

38. *L.C.S.*, i, Craobhsgaoileadh Chlainne Suibhne, 50, p. 67.

39. *A.F.M.*, 1591; ibid., 1519.

40. I am very grateful to Dr Daithí Ó hÓgáin of the Department of Irish Folklore, U.C.D. for assistance with this tract. Dr Ó hÓgáin has also told me that inhabitants of the Hebrides knew that Knockainey was twelve miles from Limerick city because the story of the 'Ceithearnach Caoilriabhach' was very popular in the Gaelic-speaking Highlands. S. H. O'Grady, 'Cetharnach Uí Dhomnaill' in *Silva Gadelica*, i (London, 1892), pp xii-xiii, 276-89, 311-24; D. Ó hÓgáin, 'An Ceithearnach Caoilriabhach' in *Myth, legend and romance, an encylopaedia of the Irish folk tradition* (London, 1990), pp 81-3; J. F. Campbell, 'The slim swarthy champion' in *Popular tales of the west Highlands*, i (Edinburgh, 1860), pp 289-319.

41. Not surprisingly, the merchant goes on to state that when he stood up in church to protest: 'I was caste oute of church ..... for an heretike; and I was gretly affraide.' *S. P. 3, Hen. VIII*, iii, continued, no. cclxxii, p. 141.

42. *A.U.*, 1488; *A.F.M.*, 1530; *A.U.*, 1497; M. Haren, 'The close of the medieval pilgrimage: the papal suppression and its aftermath' in M. Haren and Y. de Pontfarcy (ed.), *The medieval pilgrimage to St Patrick's purgatory; Lough Derg and the European tradition* (Eniskillen, 1988).

43. 'Early ecclesiastical sites', 'Ecclesiastical architecture' and 'Castles and Defensive buildings' in B. Lacy (ed.), *Archaeological survey of county Donegal* (Lifford, 1983), pp 252, 272, 328, 331, 337, 341, 345, 362-3.

44. C. Ó Danachair, 'Irish tower houses and their regional distribution' in *Béaloideas* (Dublin, 1979), p. 160.

45. *A.F.M.*, 1564; ibid., 1512, note y; ibid., 1495; ibid., 1575; *C.C.S.*, 51, p. 67; 'Short annals of Tír Chonaill' in *B.A.R.*, ii, 40, p. 93.

46. *Ann. Conn.*, 1537.

47. *L. & P., Rich. II and Hen. VII*, i, no. xxxvi, p. 240.

48. *A.F.M.*, 1470; *R.I.A. Cat. Ir. MSS, fasc. 27*, pp 3369-70.

49. *Book of Ballymote*, memorandum on f. 333 a.

50. *A.U.*, 1510-11; *L. & P.*, i, ii, no. 26, p. 1556; *A.U.*, 1512; J. Burckhardt, *The civilisation of the Renaissance in Italy* (Zalsburg), pp 11, 63-5.

51. I am greatly indebted to my supervisor Professor F. J. Byrne of the Department of Medieval Irish History at U.C.D. for bringing this to my attention.

52. K. Simms, 'Guesting and feasting in Gaelic Ireland' in *R.S.A.I., Jn., 108* (1978), p. 93.

53. *A.U.*, 1537.

54. *Ann. Conn.*, 1537.
55. *A.U.*, 1505.
56. *Beatha Colaim Chille*, 8, p. 5.
57. T. Ó Rathaille, *Dánta Grádha*, nos 49-53, pp 70-4; C. MagCraith, *Dán na mBráthar Mionúr* (Dublin, 1967), nos 114-6, pp 375-6.
58. It has been stated that St Columcille was 'the unassailable pride of the O'Donnell family, the tutelary figure which justified the unique importance they attributed to themselves'. Certainly the cult of Columcille was extremely strong in late medieval Tír Chonaill. The population of Tír Chonaill had great respect for their illustrious kinsman and ancient ecclesiastical families associated with the saint, such as Ó Firghil and Ó Muirgheasain, enjoyed a very prestigious place in Tír Chonaill society. The *Cathach*, an ancient manuscript associated with Columcille, which was kept in a beautiful silver-plated box shrine, was also carried into battle by the late medieval lords of Tír Chonaill, as a kind of battle standard to ensure victory.
59. *B.C.C.*, 9, p. 7.
60. E. B. Fryde, 'Lorenzo de Medici' in A. G. Dickens (ed.), *The courts of Europe, politics, patronage and royalty, 1400-1800* (London, 1977), p. 92; H. C. Darby, chapter 2, in G. R. Potter (ed.), *The new Cambridge modern history*, ii, p. 58.
61. *B.C.C.*, 9, p. 7.
62. T. O'Neill, *The Irish hand* (Portlaoise, 1984), pp 84-5.
63. Ibid., p. 84.
64. F. Henry and G. Marsh-Micheli, 'Manuscripts and illuminations, 1169-1603' in *N.H.I.*, pp 807-9; K. Simms, 'The Norman invasion and the Gaelic recovery' in R. F. Foster (ed.), *The Oxford illustrated history of Ireland* (Oxford, 1991), p. 101.
65. *B.C.C.*, 92, p. 87; 188-9, p. 193; 132, p. 131.
66. Knott, *Bardic poems*, i, pp 36-7, ii, pp 24-5.
67. *A.F.M.*, 1563.
68. *Cetharnach Uí Dhomnaill*, pp 276-9, 311-4.
69. The same Englishman was surprised to note that O'Donnell's advisors were also well dressed, stating that Maghnus was accompanied by: 'fyve or sex parsonnes right honestely apparayled'. *S. P. 3, Hen. VIII, iii*, continued, no. cccxliv, p. 320.
70. *Accounts*, iv, pp 434-5.
71. *A.F.M.*, 1464.
72. *Accounts*, i, pp 242, 303, 339; *History of Scotland*, iv, p. 323; A. Conway, *Henry VII's relations with Scotland and Ireland, 1485-98* (Cambridge, 1932), pp 61, 78-80, 86.
73. Unfortunately for Ó Domhnaill, the supplies never arrived in Ireland. It appears that they were to be transported by some French ships expected in Glasgow with wine. Although Aodh Dubh captured Dunluce, apparently in an effort to speed up Scottish assistance, he did not get Scottish artillery until 1516.
74. P. Walsh, 'Craebhscaoileadh Cloinne Dalaigh' in *Anal. Hib., no. 8* (March, 1938), pp 380-1.
75. D. B. Quinn, '"Irish Ireland" and "English Ireland"' in *N.H.I.*, p. 621.
76. *A.U.*, 1504; ibid., 1510.
77. *A.U.*, 1522; *A.F.M.*, 1523; ibid., 1524.
78. *L. & P.*, iii, no. 924. p. 339.
79. *Ann. Conn.*, 1537.
80. *S. P. 3, Hen. VIII, iii, 3, continued*, no. cccxliii, p. 317. In the end Tír Chonaill's collapse came about due to factors within the Gaelic world. Maghnus Ó Domhnaill fell ill and was deposed by his son who was supported by a force

of Mac Ailin mercenaries with artillery. After almost a century of dynastic unity the O'Donnells became increasingly split, allowing Seán Ó Neill to tear the heart out of the Tír Chonaill lordship. With the collapse of O'Donnell power, the Mac Donnells filled the vacuum east of the Bann, the English doing the same in Connacht. However, the foundations laid by the Lords of Tír Chonaill from 1461-1555, were strong enough to ensure an Ó Domhnaill resurgence during the Nine Years' war, even though there had been an intervening period of thirty-five years of strife and turmoil within the lordship of Tír Chonaill itself.

81.   Dickens (ed.), *The courts of Europe*, pp 30-1.

Chapter 8

THE END OF O'DONNELL POWER

R. J. HUNTER

When Rory O'Donnell, created earl of Tyrconnell in September 1603, received a patent from the crown of 'all the territories or countries in the precinct of Tyrconnell' the following February, it could appear that he had been handsomely endowed in the pacification which ended the Nine Years' War.[1] To a substantial extent this was, of course, true. The O'Donnells had been, with the O'Neills, leading confederates in a major rebellion (and one which had drawn the Spaniards into Ireland as well) which, though defeated, was being terminated, not with confiscation and plantation but with restoration and the creation of an earldom. The explanation is not far to find. The crown was seeking a way to end the Irish dimension of the broader, protracted and expensive Anglo-Spanish war; it was not inflexibly committed to large-scale plantation as the only solution to its Irish problems.[2]

An examination of the patent reveals, however, that it represented, in a variety of ways, a very substantial curb on O'Donnell power. In the first place, the long-established O'Donnell pretensions to overlordship in areas beyond the main land mass of Donegal (west and south of Lough Swilly) were being overturned. The patent contained a specific 'injunction' that the earl and his successors 'should renounce and relinquish all claim or right which they had or might pretend to have over O'Doghertie's and O'Connor Sligoe's countries'. In fact, these claims to political overlordship over a grander region, based on the historic powers of earlier O'Donnell kings but analogous in royal eyes to an exercise of the overmighty practice of bastard feudalism, had extended even further, both southwards and eastwards, than the restriction in the patent would suggest. In 1607 Rory himself asserted that he had been deprived, southwards into Connacht, of long-accustomed tributes not only from Sligo but from Tirawley (in Mayo) and Moylurg (in Roscommon), and also from Dartry (in Monaghan) and Fermanagh, both in south Ulster.[3] The claim to overlordship in North Connacht had, indeed, been the breaking point in the crown's negotiations with Manus O'Donnell at the time of surrender and regrant in the early 1540s and the principle was established then that the crown would not normally concede to one lord a permanent

229

overlordship over others beyond the bounds of his own territory.[4] While the establishment of that principle meant that Manus O'Donnell received no patent, the attempt to make it effective in practice proved a slow and protracted one. However, with the establishment of the presidency and council of Connacht and more particularly the composition there in 1585, O'Donnell influence in north Connacht was being curtailed. Similarly, the crown's policy towards the *uir-ri* lordships in south Ulster and especially its success in bringing about the 'settlement' of Monaghan in 1591 had major implications for the exercise of any overlordship there by either of the two bigger lords to the north: O'Neill or O'Donnell. These progressive changes being brought about by the crown had contributed to the outbreak of the Nine Years' War, and in the course of it, Rory's brother, Red Hugh, had re-asserted O'Donnell overlordship in north Connacht.[5]

The claim to overlordship, eastward, in O'Doherty's country of Inishowen had been but part of the longstanding dispute of the O'Donnells with the O'Neills as to which of them, Ceneál Conaill or Ceneál nEogain, should control both it and a long stretch of territories on either side of the river Foyle.[6] In the sixteenth century each had sought to maintain their authority on either side of that river by lines of small castles or tower houses. Thus, for example, the O'Donnell strongholds at Carrigans and Mongavlin matched the O'Neill Dunnalong on the Tyrone side.[7] The right to collect tribute from O'Doherty, however, had oscillated between O'Neill and O'Donnell, but apparently, in the early sixteenth century, O'Donnell had secured one strategic advantage: the establishment of a footing in the ecclesiastical enclave at Derry. The building of a small O'Donnell castle at Derry (erected, according to a later account, by O'Doherty on behalf of O'Donnell in lieu of certain duties, on a piece of ground acquired from one of the erenachs there)[8] may possibly have been also done to secure for O'Donnell control of the trade of Lough Foyle.[9] But here too recent change by the government had reduced O'Donnell power. In June 1588 John O'Doherty had been brought to engage in a surrender and regrant agreement whereby he would hold Inishowen directly from the crown,[10] though again Red Hugh O'Donnell won O'Doherty back, 'by the point and edge of the sword' in the words of his biographer Lughaidh O'Clery, in 1592.[11] However, with the landing of an army under Sir Henry Docwra at Lough Foyle in 1600, in what proved to be a decisive strategic move by the crown in the latter stages of the Nine Years' War, Derry became a base from which military operations against the confederates radiated.[12] Also, the military settlement at Derry itself evolved quickly into a small urban plantation which received a charter in July 1604.[13] The loss of this O'Donnell foothold – 'a house in Derry' as Rory later described it[14] – was to be permanent. Furthermore, just as Docwra's military force contributed to the defeat of the confederate rebellion, so also did his diplomacy, which unbared the tensions existing within the Gaelic world. Hence many of the minor adherents to the confederation were brought to surrender on promise of restoration to their lands. In the case of O'Doherty's country, the situation was complicated by the death of Shane (or Sir John) O'Doherty in 1601. Exercising his right of overlordship, Red Hugh O'Donnell nominated one candidate for the succession, while the supporters of another, Cahir, son of Sir John, procured Docwra's backing for him.[15] The subsequent pardon and patent to Sir Cahir of a slightly reduced Inishowen was designed to ensure the termination, once and for all, of O'Donnell influence over it.[16]

Much of the aim of the leading Ulster confederates in rebellion in the 1590s – themselves previously effectively ungoverned lords – had been to procure from the crown in some new form a legitimacy for claims to regional dominance which had been systematically under threat in the 1580s, while they were later to offer their allegiance to Spain, then the most powerful country in the world, promising to obey a Spanish king of Ireland.[17] Apart from the varied political influences over the dependent countries which these claims implied (cemented often by marriage alliances though often difficult to sustain), their implications for the smaller lordships in financial terms have been lost sight of because of the paucity of surviving evidence concerning them. Accounts surviving from the 1620s suggest that the costs of dependency, where it could be enforced, were high: in tribute, O'Doherty's Inishowen should supply O'Donnell with 120 cattle (beeves and milch cows) in the year; in military service, it must provide 60 horse and 120 foot and maintain O'Donnell's bonaghts (mercenary soldiers) 'be they ever so numerous for the space of nine nights'; and in the profits of justice, the *éiric* for killing a man was 168 cows.[18] Put simply, O'Donnell was greatly strengthened while he could enjoy this authority over satellite lords.[19] Now he was to be stripped of these claims.

More important, perhaps, was the nature of the settlement within Tyrconnell itself. The restoration of Rory O'Donnell (the first formally-completed surrender and regrant between the O'Donnells and the crown) needs, then, to be approached from two angles: to see what was granted to him and what was withheld. The two most important reservations in his patent concerned forts and monastic lands. Ever since direct rule in the 1530s, it had been recurrently suggested that the authority of the Dublin government on behalf of the crown over the outlying regions could best be made effective in those areas by a policy of fortification and related smallscale urban plantation within them. While the crown normally baulked at the cost of these proposals,[20] such progress as was made to this end in Ulster was bitterly resented by the Gaelic lords. However, the exigencies of the Nine Years' War made garrisons and fortifications imperative. Originally intended to be two parts of a single operation directed to both Derry and Ballyshannon, under two military commanders, Sir Henry Docwra and Sir Matthew Morgan (both with experience in the Netherlands), a military intervention in Donegal was brought about in two stages instead. Sir Henry Docwra's naval expedition, from Chester via Carrickfergus, with some 4,000 troops, which landed and fortified at Derry in May 1600 was all that could be achieved then,[21] but after Kinsale, in 1602, the castle at Ballyshannon was occupied by forces under Sir Henry Folliott, who, as a captain from Worcestershire, had been sent to Ireland in 1596 and had succeeded Morgan as colonel of a regiment in October 1601.[22]

Docwra's strategy, both militarily and diplomatically, played a major part in ending the Nine Years' War. Diplomatically, he secured the adhesion, of, amongst others, Niall Garbh O'Donnell, a dynastic competitor of Red Hugh's for power in Donegal; militarily, he occupied or built crucial strongholds in the area stretching between Derry and Lifford and took over other places of strength including the MacSweeney castle at Rathmullan, placing captains with forces within them.[23] Folliott, from his Ballyshannon base, pursued a similar military strategy which included the use of boats on the Erne to assault Maguire.[24]

Although financial constraints ensured that massive military reductions followed the peace in 1603, the importance of this initiative has to be stressed: the crown had now for the first time acquired footholds within the O'Donnell lordship and since these were mostly not new forts in new locations, it had deprived the O'Donnells and also some of their sub-lords of strongholds of immense practical and symbolic importance. When lord deputy Mountjoy returned to England in May 1603, he brought with him recommendations about army dispositions which he hoped to 'persuade' were essential, despite the ending of the rebellion and the failure of the associated Spanish invasion, for the future government of Ireland until a programme of social change, 'the reformation of religion and due obedience to the magistrate', were to be 'at least in some good measure settled' there.[25] In the north-west, along with Ballyshannon, Derry, Culmore, Rathmullan and Doe (which must all have been seen as essential against invasion), he felt that Lifford was a place 'most necessary to be held ... and guardable with 100 men to be maintained by land annexed to the town' while Coolmacatrean (near Newtowncunningham) was less essential. This question of government installations had to be decided on in London in the autumn of 1603 when the terms for the restoration of Rory O'Donnell, who, along with O'Connor Sligo ('two rebels of greatest power in those parts'), had submitted unconditionally to Mountjoy at Athlone on 14 December 1602,[26] were worked out. The outcome, conveyed in September to the Dublin government (which would have to deal with the implementation), was a compromise. The crown retained Ballyshannon castle and lands annexed to it 'adjoining the fishing there', assessed as 1,000 acres – Derry and Inishowen were, of course, excluded from the regrant – but reserved the right to build in the future any such forts as should be necessary for the 'service of the country'.[27]

The other significant change concerned monastic land. For Ireland, the Henrician policy for the dissolution of the monasteries had not proceeded at the pace of its English equivalent, leaving monasticism, in some form, to survive in the remoter localities. In the later sixteenth century it had furthermore become a recognised tenet of government policy that grants of monastic land, if they could be made effective, could provide one means of inserting controls into these localities. The termon *(tearmann)* lands, with origins in early Irish christianity, were seen to have the same capacity. However, to the O'Donnells and presumably also their sub-lords, notably the MacSweeneys, monasticism served a dual utility. The lands of the older orders and the termon lands were a source of taxation. Thus it was claimed that the termon of Derry had rendered Red Hugh O'Donnell a tribute of 18 beeves apparently three times a year and Kilmacrenan a 'supply of food' ('24 methers of butter and 40 methers of meal') in each quarter of the year.[28] The newer houses founded and endowed (however sparsely) by the chieftains, such as the Observant Franciscan friary dating from the 1470s at Donegal, as exercises in ecclesiastical patronage, served much wider cultural functions ranging from being places of burial for the O'Donnells to their members being found as part of the lordship's intelligensia engaged in its diplomacy.[29] On this matter, London's decision was an interim one: the earl-to-be should have a custodiam of them 'till we shall otherwise dispose of them'.[30] He should not receive, however, the presentation of 'spiritual livings'. Thereby such rights of patronage as the O'Donnells had enjoyed over the secular church would be severed, to remain at the disposal of the crown in accordance with the organisational principles of the English reformation.

These were the exceptions made on behalf of the crown. Finally, an exception was made on behalf of Niall Garbh O'Donnell, who should hold his own land around Castlefinn directly from the crown. Niall Garbh, a close relative of Rory's, was a competitor, in the Gaelic way, for the chieftainship. Linked with Docwra, the locally-placed agent of the crown, he had been granted a custodiam of Tír Chonaill in March 1601 on much the same terms as those now made with Rory[31] but had rebelled early in 1603[32] when it had become clear (to Docwra's subsequent regret) that the lord deputy in Dublin favoured his rival. Now, in satisfying one so relatively fully, the crown, however, had not solved the problem created by the aspirations of the other; it had, as it turned out, merely postponed it. Beyond that no precise guarantees were introduced at this stage governing the rights to land under the earl of the other occupiers, great or small, within Donegal.

It was left to Dublin to implement London's decisions. These it necessarily amplified, but also, at least in practice, slightly varied. The creation of the earldom followed quickly, Rory to have a seat in all parliaments and 'general' councils.[33] The patent of the land defined some important specifics which the outline decision of general principles in London had not attended to. The quit rent to be paid annually into the exchequer was set at 300 marks E (£200). The tenure was *in capite,* by the service of four knights' fees, and the military service required of him was 60 horse and 120 foot to serve in all general hostings.[34] Therein would lie the principal financial implications of tenure under the crown. However, before the patent was issued, commissioners (out of chancery) had to be appointed – on 24 October 1603 – to take inquisitions to record boundaries and to produce extents of the excluded lands.[35] In this way, while their work was far from complete, a record and valuation of some of the areas of monastic land was brought into existence and one which equated those of the termon lands (peculiar to the Gaelic parts of Ireland) as had been investigated with monastic property.[36] To these may be added the inquisitions taken at an earlier stage, in 1601 and 1602, recording other areas of such land in a piecemeal way (into one of which a piece of lay land – O'Doherty's rich island of Inch – got extra-legally slipped), the impulse behind which must have derived from the desire of a number of the captains in Docwra's Derry command, himself included, to obtain crown leases of the lands involved, and indeed also the recording of the property of the Cistercian abbey of St Bernard of Assaroe made as early as 1588.[37] In some of these inquisitions as well, the regalities (i.e. rights of royal authority) and the fisheries in both Lough Foyle and Lough Swilly were defined as crown property. When O'Donnell's patent was issued to him in February 1604, the crown specifically reserved the fishery both of the port of Ballyshannon and also of all rivers and lakes belonging to the castle 'or town' there.[38]

The process of granting out both the monastic land and some of the termon land which followed was a complex one but the ultimate beneficiaries were a small group of the local military commanders. The Dublin government did not have the initiative to dispose of major accretions of forfeited land unless authorised by commission from London. However, a practice grew up whereby grants of land in Ireland to various favoured individuals (often recompensing past service), which should amount to a specified valuation, were authorised by the king's signet. Their patents usually contained accumulated pieces of land ('books' of land) dispersed throughout Ireland, including at this time small areas formerly belonging to individuals attainted for their part in the recent rebellion. Commonly the beneficiary sold many of these pieces to somebody anxious to consolidate a holding in a particular area.

Ecclesiastical land in Donegal (which included at this time Termon Derry) was granted out in perpetuity in this way in patents to some six people between 1603 and 1609. They included two presidents of Munster, Sir George Carew and his successor Sir Henry Broncar. One Robert Leycester, whose father had held land in King's County, was favoured on the recommendation of Mountjoy and the Irish privy council. A grant authorised to the Old English countess of Delvin and her son, Richard, to compensate for the escheated lands of Gaelic owners in Longford and Cavan promised much earlier to her deceased husband, Christopher Nugent, baron Delvin but not realised, came, in 1609, after elaborate dealings, to include not monastic land but the valuable fisheries at Ballyshannon. Another beneficiary who received monastic land in Donegal in one of his many patents was a Scot, James Fullerton, who had come to Dublin as a schoolteacher in the later 1580s and had acted as an informant to James VI on Irish affairs prior to his succession and was now at court as one of James's numerous Scottish suitors. Finally, and exemplifying the advantage of holding office under the crown in London, a grant was made to Francis Goston, one of the auditors of the imprests (a financial official) of the abbey of Assaroe.[39]

Those who actually acquired the benefit of this land were, with one exception,[40] a small persistent group of the English military officers who managed to remain on (many, of course, got nothing and sought other outlets) as the war was brought to a close: principally Sir Henry Docwra (at Derry), Captain Ralph Bingley, Sir Henry Folliott, Captain Basil Brooke. Some of these had also acquired leases of the lands in question from the Dublin government.[41] Their entitling represented the tentative probes of Englishmen into one area of English expansion, Donegal (however limited its scope at this time), in the revival of a process, delayed by the Anglo-Spanish war, which now also included the early New England voyages and the establishment of the colony at Jamestown, Virginia. Bingley, whose connections included a relative, Sir John, an exchequer official, sought to act on this wider stage himself. However, his participation in an intended trans-Atlantic voyage with the *Triall* of London in 1606, financed by some London merchants, which degenerated into piratical activity in the Bay of Biscay, resulted in a trial before the high court of admiralty.[42] By contrast, Sir Henry Folliott was much more single-minded in approach. In June 1606, he was given a crown lease of Ballyshannon and the lands associated with it – that is to say, the area of secular land reserved from Rory O'Donnell's patent – and also of various fishing rights and tithes and a rectory which had belonged to the abbey of Assaroe, for the term of forty-one years. He was also given the valuable fishing rights of the ports and bays of Ballyshannon, Killybegs and Bundrowes and thereabouts, 'wherein fishes were accustomed to be taken'. In addition, to give him access to the centre of authority in Dublin, his lease included Tassagard (Saggart), county Dublin, the property of an owner recently attainted. In devolving away the 'castle or fortilage' of Ballyshannon with this lease, the only security provision made was that it should be held only for Sir Henry's lifetime.[43] The lease was renewed to him the following year, in July 1607.[44] By 1622, when he was granted a new patent, Folliott, who had become baron of Ballyshannon, had secured for himself, now in outright ownership, a substantial estate in this area (Tirhugh), which also included the lands of Assaroe abbey.[45] Two elements in his patent – the abbey of Assaroe and the bay of Ballyshannon 'from the sea to the salmon leap near the castle' and also an eel-weir 'called O'Donnell's weir' in the Erne – derived respectively from the earlier patents to Goston and to Lady Delvin and her son. It is not possible to establish what payment Folliott (or the others in like case) had made for these purchases.

What was being attempted more generally at this time was both simple and fundamental: the absorption of a major Gaelic Irish polity, the O'Donnell lordship, into a unitary administration of Ireland with forms and structures of power, central and local, deriving in part from those implanted in some areas of Ireland with the Anglo-Norman conquest and in part from refinements and modifications of these devised in the later sixteenth century. The changes that this process would require were extensive and would demand considerable adjustment on the part of a formerly quasi-autonomous lord. Thus appointments of customs officials to the ports took away rights formerly enjoyed by the lords and integrated the collection of this form of revenue into the crown's customs system. The first two appointments were made as early as November 1603: Richard Bingley (brother of Ralph) received a lease of the customs and subsidies on the imports and exports of the ports of Derry and Ballyshannon and their creeks and a certain Robert Kinsman was made searcher and gauger of these ports.[46] In a more limited way, further economic restrictions on local power, either of the O'Donnells or their vassal lords such as the MacSweeneys, are to be found in various grants of markets and fairs (more trivial, however, because of the crown rents laid down for them), made to some of these new figures, for example to Sir Henry Docwra at Lifford and to Sir Ralph Bingley at Rathmullan, at this time.[47] At another level entirely, the crown exercised the royal supremacy over the church, effectively here for the first time, in appointing the Protestant George Montgomery, a Scot who had moved to England in the 1580s and who had played some part in facilitating James VI's succession to the throne (rewarded with the office of one of the king's chaplains) and an administrator of marked ability, to be bishop of Raphoe, Derry and Clogher in February 1605.[48] This not only severed the relationship which had prevailed between the bishops of Raphoe and the lords, but had great potential importance for an area with leadership both lay and clerical which in recent times had been committed to a religiously-inspired ideology which had led them to seek in war a Spanish and Catholic rather than English and Protestant ruler for Ireland.[49]

Attempts at administrative change, to substitute the norms of county government in the place of lordly autonomy, also began to take some effect. The county Donegal had already been created in 1585 under lord deputy Perrot, an amalgamation of O'Donnell's and O'Doherty's countries with the recommendation that Donegal become the county town, but the government had been incapable of making it effective then.[50] Two of the first recorded sheriffs of the county, Oliver Scurlock, a palesman probably of Scurlockstown, county Meath, and very possibly a relation of Martin Scurlock, attorney in the council of Connacht, who appears before February 1605, and MacSweeney Banagh, one of the Donegal sub-lords, who appears in 1606 are, however, unlikely to have made much impact.[51] Nevertheless, there were probes by the assize judges into Donegal in 1603 and 1605, the first prior to the arrival in Ireland of solicitor-general Sir John Davies when, on his account, the chief baron, Sir Edward Pelham, was reverenced by 'the multitude ... as if he had been a good angel sent from heaven.'[52] Also in 1605 when, on Rory O'Donnell's account Captain Henry Vaughan, another of the military officers, was sheriff, beginnings were made towards erecting a sessions house, probably at Lifford, by levying £150 on the county.[53] However, it was probably effectively from 1607 when Sir Richard Hansard, who had been moved there late in 1606, was sheriff – a merging of civil and military functions in the hands of a man who commanded fifty horse – that Lifford came to be defined as the county town.[54] Behind Hansard's appointment, too, lay a more general point (not lost on the Earl of Tyrconnell who had written to principal secretary Salisbury in London from Donegal in May 1606 to petition that he be allowed the nomination of the office): the conviction of Sir Arthur Chichester, then lord deputy in Dublin, that a significant sprinkling of such New English figures – men of 'civility and understanding' was required in the remoter localities if the transition to county government was to be successfully achieved.[55] It had, however, been decided in England in 1605 that the earl himself should be awarded the important office of county lieutenant, whose functions were concerned primarily with the organisation of a militia, and should also be a justice of the peace.[56]

There, arguably, it was scarcely intended that matters should rest. In the later sixteenth century the Dublin government had decided on a policy for the remodelling of Irish landed society beyond the pale, degenerate Anglo-Norman and Gaelic Irish alike, along manorial lines. The lord would retain demesne, to use as he wished, and the heads of the other major landholding families – the 'ancient followers of the country' – would be redefined as freeholders, to owe to the lord no other major obligation than a fixed annual money rent. Although there were variations in this in practice, rents to the crown also from both lord and freeholder were normally part of it, thereby to satisfy the growing taxation requirements of an expanding administration. Revenue would arise as well, incrementally, from the tenures under which the land would be held. The purposes behind it in the composition of Connacht were lucidly summed up by one commentator:

> The plot of this composition was devised ... of purpose to take away the greatness of the Irish lords, with their names, macks and oes, that the inferior subject might be freed from their Irish customs, cuttings and unreasonable exactions, and (by knowing what was their own) be drawn to depend ever after upon the state (sic) and not on those Irish lords or gentlemen; which also might not only much avail her Majesty in time of any stirs or revolts, by drawing the common people from following the great chief lords, but also bring a more certainer yearly rent, or revenue, into her highness coffers than formerly was accustomed.[57]

In this way, then, the warlord of the late medieval *ancien regime* would be transformed into a landlord aristocrat, to exist within a framework embodying the controls and regulations of early modern government.[58] This was seen as the essential mechanism for the introduction of political stability through the demilitarisation of the localities. Since the process involved a detailed investigation of existing landownership, alongside it could go many other changes: monastic dissolutions, with the beneficiaries being normally New English; the defining and allocation of church lands, with the possibility that thereby the reformation might be advanced; the endowing of an occasional discoverer of 'concealed' land. In addition, counties could be created or resurrected, and seneschals or governors – themselves usually given small areas (so re-organisation could entail some loss of land) – could be appointed to stifle resistance. In the cases of Connacht and Munster, presidencies and councils had been instituted to regulate the new order. For their part, the freeholders would, amongst other things, provide the county electorate and be expected to fulfill, generally, the role of a gentry of large landholders in the affairs of their county. The response the scheme evoked amongst the lords varied: some indeed complied (seeing advantage in a fixed rental), many opposed. As far as Gaelic lords were concerned, it made chieftainship, with all its political claims, redundant, by introducing tenure under the crown. For them, too, given the tendency in the Gaelic lordships for the ruling family to branch into different segments, the outcome might be a division of the lordship amongst the heads of its various branches, each with freeholders under them. Also, the very bringing of definition of ownership, secular and ecclesiastical, in this way would be likely to cause considerable initial contention about who owned what.

While the government lacked the strength to introduce this universally in Ulster, some beginnings were also made there in the later 1580s and early 1590s, though these were confined to the lesser lordships. Thus, in the north-west, O'Doherty's patent of 1588 had divided Inishowen into six manors and laid down a crown rent of thirty beeves, though no freeholders were actually designated at that time.[59] Much more systematic had been the 'settlement' of Monaghan in 1591 where the land had been divided between six heads of the ruling MacMahon family and McKenna (the principal non-MacMahon landholder in the lordship) with freeholders assigned to each, to pay him a rent, grantee and freeholder to also pay an annual rent to Dublin. In addition, a seneschal was appointed and received the lands around Monaghan which had always appertained to the office of chieftain, on a twenty-one year lease. Finally, the erenach lands were granted to a number of people, both old English and new English, with the stipulation that each should build castles on them within five years.[60] It was the attempt to bring about similar changes in Fermanagh by the sending in there as sheriff of Captain Humphrey Willis (who had been in Donegal the previous year), in 1593, that had precipitated the Nine Years' War.[61]

The fundamental principle behind the restoration of O'Donnell and O'Neill as earls in the aftermath of the war was that they should not only sever their connections with Spain, but that, in turn, they would be capable of delivering an ordered and pacified society in Ulster and co-operate with what changes should be introduced. The beginnings of some of these changes in Donegal have already been detailed. The pressing urgency to end the war (Mountjoy's opportunist strategy) at a time of political and economic crisis in England, which had led to the restoration of O'Donnell and O'Neill, had meant that the detailed and systematic investigation of landholding through which only the manorialised structure of ownership with freeholders might have been brought into being, had not been carried out. Hence the brevity of O'Donnell's patent. That, arguably, it was not intended thereby to concede to him an untrammelled ownership of the entire territory seems, however, clear both from the use of the word 'manor' within it and also in the cautious phrase that he was granted it only 'in as large and ample manner' as his predecessors had enjoyed it.[62] By contrast, it was easy to insert the manorial divisions into Sir Cahir O'Doherty's patent of January 1605 which was essentially a re-issue of that of 1588, while O'Donnell's was the first ever to be granted.[63]

Where a thorough-going reorganisation had begun to be addressed, it was, again, in the smaller lordship of Fermanagh. A group of commissioners (including the judge Sir Edward Pelham) was, in June 1603, appointed by the lord deputy, Sir George Carey, Mountjoy's successor, to, amongst other things, investigate the landownership there and record the 'freeholders', and by January 1604 two leading members of the Maguire ruling family, Connor Roe and Cú Chonnacht, had been brought to agree in outline to a division of that 'country' between them.[64] It was not, however, until after Sir Arthur Chichester, whose background in Ireland had been a military one and who was energetically committed to the functions of the office, took over as lord deputy in 1605, that a more systematic 'reformation' of Ulster, including the greater lordships, was attempted over the years 1605 to 1607. In this he was backed by his law officer, Sir John Davies, who adopted the policies for social reconstruction of his sixteenth-century predecessors. Davies consistently argued the case that anyhow the real position of the lesser landholders in the Gaelic world approximated nearest to the English status of freeholder and so that they should not with propriety be treated by their lords as mere tenants-at-will.[65] To take away any ambiguity on which the lords – who had sought in the sixteenth century to negotiate on behalf of themselves and their 'followers' – might play, a proclamation was issued in Dublin in 1605 which hit at the whole separate basis of the Gaelic lordships as political entities. The lesser people were to be 'the free, natural and immediate subjects' of the king, not subjects of the lords: they were 'not to be reputed or called the natives or natural followers of any other lord or chieftain'.[66] In two major tours in the summers of 1605 and 1606, the former including Donegal, the latter Fermanagh, Chichester attempted to bring a reorganisation of Ulster into being involving efforts to establish freeholders: 'the honest liberty of that sort of man' he saw as being very much bound up with 'his Majesty's service and the commonwealth's'.[67]

Throughout these years Rory O'Donnell found himself confronted by numerous problems. Apart altogether from the presence of new men in his midst, with all the special tensions that engendered, his most immediate problem was that posed by Niall Garbh. Writing in April 1604, Sir John Davies contrasted the Earl of Tyrone's position with that of the Earl of Tyrconnell. While O'Neill appeared to be successfully re-asserting himself, O'Donnell was not. Thus '... in Tirconnell,' Davies reported, 'Neale Garve O'Donnell ... hath gotten many followers, hath possessed himself of the tenants and herds of cattle, and has grown so strong that the earl seems to hold it not safe to return thither, but lies here within the Pale very meanly attended.'[68] It was a classic situation of a challenger, Rory's rival as he had been his brother's (dissatisfied as well with his allocation under the crown) and himself no mean exponent of the rights of a Gaelic lord, competing for power.[69] Thus from the crown's point of view, it seemed that the two pillars of Mountjoy's restoration were proving to be of unequal stability. However, in August 1604, when he was still in Dublin, O'Donnell sent his secretary, Matthew Tully, to London to present a petition to the privy council[70] and by the end of that year he was in London himself, where he remained into the next year.[71] There he was seeking a clarification of his rights and the issuing of a new patent. The matters at issue, discussed between London and Dublin until July, reveal Rory's concerns: amongst them that the garrison be removed from Lifford, which had not been excepted from his patent, and that he should recover it; that his quit rent should be reduced; that he should receive the abbeys and their estates; that his complaints against Niall Garbh be upheld; that he should decide which land should be allocated to Ballyshannon; that he should receive payments for the fishing rights and that he should have the right to nominate the sheriffs.[72]

His attempts to assert his authority within Donegal also brought their tensions. His approach to the sub-lords appears to be borne out by his own evidence as well as that of government figures. 'The three McSwynes and O'Boyle,' he was to assert after the flight, 'who always held their lands from O'Donnell (sic) paying what rent he pleased to impose upon them and who consequently ought to hold from the earl (sic) on the same terms,' had been supported by the lord deputy against him, despite the fact that on foot of his patent and through recourse to English legal procedures they had been brought to 'make over all their estates and rights' to him and had 'taken their said lands again' from him 'by lease of years for certain rent'.[73] Thus he was seeking to become a landlord on his own terms. His attempts to raise a rental income emerge also from another tactic: between February 1604 and July 1607, he made mortgages and leases of considerable areas of land and fisheries to a group of Dublin merchants (newcomers of his own) – Nicholas Weston, John Arthur and Patrick Conley – which included MacSweeney's Doe castle and lands near Rathmullan, lands at Coolmacatrain and a substantial area in Portlough and Tirbrassil.[74] These commercialising decisions can scarcely have endeared the earl to the occupiers of these lands and they would seem to account for a number of incidents between him and some of the lesser figures which come to light in 1607. Thus it was reported in July 1607 that Caphar oge *(Cathbharr Óg)* O'Donnell had gone to the Scottish isle of Islay 'with thirty men in company', leading to fears that he would return with forces, 'for he is a malcontent and unsatisfied with the earl of Tyrconnell, who withholds most of his land from him, against right, as he affirms,' and that that had also been the cause of 'his and Neale McSwyne's last stirs', at the beginning of the year.[75] They may also go some way to account for the unexplained fracas at Rathmullan in September 1607, after the earls had boarded ship for the flight, between boatmen sent for water and firewood and MacSweeney Fanad's son and a party of supporters.[76]

It was into this context that Chichester, whose entourage included the assize judges, intervened in his northern journey of August 1605. Operating within the limits of the original decision, he sought, sitting at Lifford, to resolve the conflict between Rory and Niall Garbh, both of whom appeared with lawyers, by defining the latter's share (forty-three quarters in Glan Fyn and Munganagh) to him.[77] A central issue also was O'Donnell's relations with the MacSweeneys, O'Boyle and 'other ancient gents', because it raised the question of freeholders. The earl (whom Chichester found more compliant than he had been after his return from England) did not deny that he had 'procured' them 'to surrender their several estates in their lands' to him, but he was persuaded to name 'such of them as he deemed fit to be freeholders of part thereof, reserving their ancient rents in certainty'.[78] Sir Cahir O'Doherty was also asked to give the names of those to be created freeholders in Inishowen.[79]

On the issues raised by O'Donnell's petition, both London and Dublin had shown a willingness to make some little concessions, for example on the important appointment of the lieutenant. Some concessions proposed were also well-considered: he should only receive a regrant on condition that he relinquish all claim to the freeholders, and, he might suggest the names of six gentlemen from whom the sheriff would be chosen provided that they were 'freeholders of the country'.[80] On one point, however, the lord deputy, concerned as of first necessity he must be with security, would make no concession. Although O'Donnell's protest about Lifford had received a somewhat sympathetic response from the king, the lord deputy's judgement (which followed Mountjoy's that it was essential for security reasons) prevailed. The fact that he 'reserved' it (as a 'place of special importance to be kept and preserved in his Majesty's own hands' even preferable to Derry) and a small area of good lowland land nearby had the effect of depriving the earl of a strategic and economic resource in the north of the county.[81] The public purse, however, still heavily dependent on subvention from an England determined on financial retrenchment, was unable to stretch to his and the privy council's grander aspirations for Lifford that, in addition to the fort, it be 'walled about' and developed like Derry as an incorporated urban plantation, with houses and inns built and with merchants, tradesmen and artificers from England and Scotland commanded 'by authority' to come and work there, whereby (and this was a common belief about the value of urbanisation to bring about a change in life-style) 'obedience, peace, civility and plenty' would be established in the surrounding area, both on 'Tyrone and Tirconnell's side' of the river.[82] Eventually and in conjunction with the subsequent plantation, as will be seen, this goal was in fact to be devolved to private enterprise. Lifford and the adjacent land was subsequently leased[83] and later given in outright grant to Sir Richard Hansard, in a fall-back reliance on individual effort, on condition that he should bring about urban development there.[84] This was, however, to be in the future. Meanwhile, Chichester and the Dublin government furthermore recommended to London in 1605 that Culmore should also be retained and a small ward established there, to include a few cannoniers, as a means of challenging any invading vessels.[85] Finally, they claimed to have 'taken an exact note' of all the quarters of land in county Donegal with the intention of dividing them into six baronies. The precision of such a hasty survey must be doubted. If the intent behind it was indeed also to produce a record by which freeholds could be defined in a new patent, this did not happen. Chichester came to the view from the 'wastes and desolation' he had seen on his tour that the people were too poor to pay composition in the sense of the land tax to Dublin, and Rory's 1604 patent remained in operation.[86]

The northern tour of 1605 had, at any rate, set out the broad parameters within which the earl and Sir Cahir O'Doherty were expected to operate. The tour of 1606 into the small lordships, including Fermanagh, bade fair to bring about there – where after all beginnings had already been initiated – a land re-organisation with freeholders and left Cú Chonnacht Maguire particularly disaffected.[87] Also in 1606 a closeness was detected between him and Rory O'Donnell in what has all the appearance of a revival of the traditional relationship of *uir-ri* to overlord and at this time Dublin government suspicions were aroused by rumours that both intended to go to Spain or the Spanish Netherlands.[88] The departure of Maguire to Spanish Flanders the following year set in motion one of those chains of circumstances which culminated in the flight of the earls in September. The precise purpose of Maguire's secret journey is necessarily hard to determine: while on the one hand it may merely have been to seek employment in the newly-formed Irish regiment there, on the other, and perhaps more plausibly, it may well have been to test the waters, since the Archduke Albert (who with his wife, the Infanta Isabella, was now joint ruler there under Spain) had been the candidate proposed to be king of Ireland in 1596, for a possible renewed invasion of Ireland.[89]

The question is immediately raised as to whether the Ulster lords had indeed retained contact with Spain in the intervening years since 1603. In O'Donnell's case, at any rate, such a thread of contact can be found, mediated principally through Matthew Tully, a layman rather than an ecclesiastic – though the militant Franciscan intellectual Fr Florence Conry (formerly confessor to Hugh O'Donnell and subsequently absentee Catholic archbishop of Tuam) and various priests and friars can be found in the background – and a conspirator who had been in the pay of both the Spaniards and the O'Donnells.[90] Much of this contact had revolved around the quest for pensions for O'Neill and O'Donnell from a somewhat reluctant Spain, or even the suggestion that they might go to the Spanish court 'for protection and favour', with the skilful Matthew Tully arguing in February 1606, in a petition on behalf of both, that the former would be the preferable option, 'for if the earls come to Spain ... they would not be of such service if the opportunity arose'.[91] As early as December 1604, when O'Donnell, then in London, had himself approached the Spanish ambassador on this matter, he suggested that both he and O'Neill would be willing to renew the war in Ireland should the Spanish peace with England not hold, and the ambassador, conscious of Spain's recent grander aspirations with regard to England as well as Ireland, in reporting this to Spain, pointed to the fact that O'Donnell, through his marriage to Bridget, daughter of the deceased Earl of Kildare whose wife had been a daughter of the Earl of Nottingham, lord high admiral of England, had 'both in Ireland and in England ... relatives and rank'.[92] Eventually, in November 1606, a decision was made in Spain to grant a subvention to them, given the fact that 'should war break out again they could be of great use and so it is well to keep them well disposed,' and the resulting process for the payment of this through the Spanish Netherlands was underway in the spring of 1607, all dictated no doubt in part by wider issues in the current state of Anglo-Spanish relations, of which the formation of the English Virginia Company in April 1606 was one, as well as sympathy for their past actions and current decline.[93]

If, however, this new-found tentative Spanish interest, through which they might hope to achieve power as great potentates in Ireland, were to be converted to advantage, the earls must seek, as they had done in the later 1590s, to recreate a military alliance extending beyond the north which might attract Spanish armed intervention. It seems clear that O'Donnell at least was engaged in some explorations along these lines – towards the formation of a new Irish 'Catholic league' – at this time. In a powerfully-constructed essay in propaganda sent as a petition jointly by both earls to Philip III from Louvain in December 1607, after the flight, urging on him the ease with which he could take up their renewed request to be 'our lord and our king' and the advantages to Spain which would as a consequence accrue, they stated that 'one of us, the Earl O'Donnel, had secret dealings' with many of the 'nobles and the chief gentlemen' – except a few whom he did not trust – who had served Queen Elizabeth in the last war (that is, many of the Old English), and that they, out of fidelity to Catholicism, would now be willing, should Philip send 'some aid to them', to change allegiance 'and help us so that, by common consent, we should deliver the kingdom to your Majesty'.[94] In other words, they were seeking to argue that a crucial change had now taken place in Irish circumstances.

In fact O'Donnell's conspirings may not have gone as deeply or at any rate, perhaps, have evoked as positive a response as this memorial sought to suggest. His most well-known overture appears to have been made to Sir Richard Nugent, baron Delvin, a young Old English landowner living on the borders of the pale. At this time Delvin had good reason for disaffection. In May 1597 his father had received royal authorisation for a grant of attainted native Irish lands in Cavan or in the Anally, county Longford, to the value of £100.[95] However, no grant could be made until after the peace in 1603 and the Delvin claim to lands in Longford, which was engendering considerable ill-feeling just at this time, was ultimately not accepted, with the king ordering finally, in July 1607, that the O'Farrells in Longford be repossessed, Delvin and his widowed mother to receive escheated lands in Cavan and elsewhere.[96] Such was the context of O'Donnell's meetings with Nugent one of which had taken place, on the latter's confession of 6 November 1607, 'about Christmas twelve month' in the garden at Maynooth, Rory's wife's home. Nugent's confession also provides an outline of what was apparently being aired. Their discussions allegedly revolved around their discontents over land and also religion, with Rory accountedly complaining of his losses of Ballyshannon, Lifford and the fishings and expressing his determination to 'attempt something which might regain him his country in the same state his brother held it'. To this end Rory apparently proposed a coup to take Dublin castle when the lord deputy and council should be meeting there, and also some of the strongholds in the outlying localities including Ballyshannon and Lifford, arguing that O'Neill and Maguire and others, equally dis-contented, would join with him in doing so, and that in the resulting situation, 'the kingdom without other government than their own', he would have his 'lands and countries as [he] desire[d] it and make [his] friends peace with the king'. When pressed, at a later meeting, on the impracticality of the attempt, Rory, he said, stated that he had sent a messenger, a priest, to Fr Florence Conry in Spain to 'deal' with the king of Spain for 10,000 troops.[97] It was recognised therefore that success for such scheming would be contingent on Spanish intervention.

While it would be reasonable to assume that the earls had exaggerated the extent of Rory's conspirings in their December submission to Spain, Chichester's anxieties were aroused, when, conscious of the greatly reduced forces that were available to him, he received information, in the summer, from Sir Christopher St Lawrence, 22nd Baron of Howth, one of the lords of the pale and recently returned from Flanders, which suggested that a 'general revolt', with nobility (including some of the Mayo Burkes, Sir Randal McDonnell and the Earl of Tyrone as well as O'Donnell) and townsmen alike allegedly involved, had been planned and was intended, under promise of substantial Spanish military aid, to follow 'within twenty days after the peace should be broken', in order to 'shake off the yoke of the English government and adhere to the Spaniard' and that Fr Florence Conry had been employed by O'Donnell as his go-between with Spain and that the Spaniards had 'fed' O'Donnell with 'hope of great advancement and reward'. St Lawrence hoped to elicit more from O'Donnell, who was expected to come from the north for his countess early in September, and advised that he should be questioned on the matter. He expressed the view, however, that no pressing danger was presented since Spanish forces could not be ready to come for another year.[98]

On the strength of these allegations, made also in England, by St Lawrence, Chichester went down 'towards the borders of Ulster' in an effort to investigate and also perhaps, partly, to mollify O'Neill 'proceeding tenderly and slowly as with intemperate and desperate patients whom he could neither safely deal with nor yet abandon without imputation' and had decided to arrest and question O'Donnell when he should come into the pale.[99] At this point events overtook him. A ship with Maguire, Matthew Tully and Donagh O'Brien (a relative of the Earl of Thomond who had been in the Spanish service for some time) aboard arrived at Rathmullan. It was apparently promoted by the Archduke,[100] acting on the belief that O'Neill (who was just then about to go to England to defend a suit with his *uir-rí* O'Cahan, whose lands he had been granted in his patent) was also to be arrested and perhaps even executed since the plotting had been discovered, and it apparently offered the earls refuge in Flanders or Spain pending negotiations on their behalf with James I.[101] It became known, however, that only if the negotiations then in hand with the Dutch, to whom the Spaniards and the Archdukes' dependent government in Brussels were at this precise time, 1607-9, gradually capitulating, were to result in some English intervention on the Dutch side would the Spaniards, also coming to grips with the English landing in Virginia in April, break their peace with England.[102] As it happened, England and Spain remained at peace until 1625.

In the event, then, the earls sailed off, unaware perhaps of the declining power of Spain or, at any rate, its lack now of European imperial ambition, into a wider European politics in which they proved to be in some measure an embarrassment to their would-be deliverers. Their intended destination was Spain but they were blown ashore in France and went to the Spanish Netherlands which they left on 18 February 1608 and ended up in Rome two months later, where O'Donnell died on 18 July.[103] On their departure rumour was spread in Ireland that they would be returned. Thus Owen Groome Magrath, deputy to Fr Florence Conry as provincial of the Irish Franciscans, anxious to keep the conspiracy in Ireland alive, visited Nugent shortly after the flight to inform him (on the latter's account) that the earls would return by St Bridget's day bringing with them 'sufficient forces to make good their designs', and expressing confidence that although the king of Spain had refused to give assistance, the pope and the archduke would, 'at which the king of Spain will wink and perchance give some assistance under hand'.[104] However, the returning proved more difficult than the departure, although the earls bent their efforts to achieve it.

In their joint petition to Philip III, already referred to, they set out their case for Spanish reintervention. They stressed the benefits that had accrued to Spain through their involvement by its 'order and persuasions' in the last war, presented themselves as the 'principal leaders' in a 'kingdom consisting entirely of Catholics' then under great pressure from 'heretics' to conform in religion,[105] and, in calling for his renewed assistance, asserted that he was under a moral obligation to provide it because their 'present troubles' had arisen from the fact that they had refused 'the honourable conditions which the heretics offered us many times during the war' on account of royal letters from his father and himself. Spanish intervention now would not only conduce to a religious good, the advancement of catholicism against protestantism, but would lead as well to the expansion of the Spanish monarchy. They also pressed that it would serve much more transcendent Spanish ambitions, 'because once your Majesty is lord of Ireland, within a short time you will also be lord of England and of Scotland and you will have peace in the States of Flanders'. Nor would it be a disadvantage tactically that they were 'now away from our country': they could still control its responses from abroad. Militarily too, their proposal was feasible because the king of England had 'neither the experienced soldiers nor the financial resources' to oppose successfully. Also they argued that James was disliked by all his 'vassals' in England and Scotland, especially the Catholic ones, with those of Scotland being the earls' 'kinsfolk, friends and neighbours' to boot, and claimed that the Catholics of the 'three kingdoms' had placed all their hopes in the earls' intercession with him. Thus, then, if he would intervene he would become 'master of all the north, where you will establish the Catholic faith'.[106]

It was precisely this kind of strategy – however much it was, perhaps, now an anachronistic vision – that the English Protestant government must seek to pre-empt: that through Irish circumstances a new assault on their religion and independence was again gestating and might be launched.[107] Accordingly, English diplomacy was directed towards the forestalling of the earls' plans, with, amongst other things, the argument being advanced that, unlike Elizabeth, James I 'being possessed of Scotland' had in that country, itself 'near adjoining to the north part of Ireland', a people – 'of their own fashion, diet and disposition that can walk their bogs as well as themselves' – well qualified to repress any Spanish-incited Ulster rebellion.[108]

In these circumstances, with the Archdukes, anxious above all things that the peace negotiations with the United Provinces would not be impeded by the earls' presence, arguing that the earls had been received in Spanish Flanders as 'refugees' for religion and not as 'traitors',[109] and with them seeking to go by some route to a Spain which was reluctant to receive them, the question of what should be done with, let alone what should be done for, them became an issue between Spain and the papacy, reminiscent of the earlier contretemps between them in 1585-7 over the payment for an armada against England.[110] For their part, the earls sought not just Spanish, but also papal, military assistance. In a submission to Pope Paul V, which is couched in similar terms to that addressed to Philip III and in which they presented themselves again as leaders in the Catholic cause, they insisted that 'empty expressions of compassion' would be inadequate to their needs and asserted that they had 'special claims' upon him – a reference to the old papal claim to sovereignty over Ireland – since 'all their misfortunes' were due 'to the grant of Ireland to England by the Holy See'.[111] In coming to their aid militarily, the pope then would 'hand down to posterity a name that [could] never be forgotten').[112]

However, it was the immediate problem of where the earls should go, with its implications of who should take responsibility for them, which occupied some months after their arrival in Flanders, and the papal nuncio to Brussels, Cardinal Bentivoglio, found himself in the middle of the affair. His reports to the papal secretary of state, Cardinal Barberini, throw light on the predicament of the earls in Flanders prior to their departure to Rome. Acting on instructions of 17 November, Bentivoglio conveyed to Tyrone – who at that point had been forbidden to go to Spain pending further consideration, and who had indicated to him the earls' wish to go to Rome and from thence to Spain, in order to gain the pope's 'favour' and, through him, that of 'other Catholic princes' and especially Spain's, for their proposals – the 'great needs and difficulties of the Holy See', and made known to him that all hope must be placed in the king of Spain.[113] In a later interview with Conry, acting on behalf of the earls, Bentivoglio re-inforced the point. On Conry's admission that it was really the Spaniards who were seeking to direct the earls to Rome, Bentivoglio persuaded him of the 'artful cunning which lay behind this advice': were Tyrone to show a willingness to go to Rome, then the Spaniards would argue that 'since the earl wished to have recourse to the pope, it remained for the pope to help him' and thereby rid themselves of all future responsibility.[114] However by January-February 1608 the Spanish council of state had decided that they must go to Rome (where Spain would give them a monthly allowance), arguing that the pope should be persuaded to protect those who had lost their possessions 'for the Catholic faith'. Their presence in Rome could be used as a lever diplomatically to reduce pressure on Catholics in the English dominions to conform, while in the 'case of a break with England, the result will be the same as if they had come to Spain'.[115] Their eventual going to Rome, then, constituted a victory of the Spanish over the papal viewpoint. Not surprisingly, a mood of uncertainty and disillusion set in amongst the earls and their entourages as they awaited these decisions in Flanders, despite the sympathetic nature of their treatment there.[116]

In Rome the earls found themselves, despite persistent efforts, in a cul-de-sac from which there was neither exit nor return. Since the rebellion of old Irish and old English in Ireland, contingent anyhow in their view on Spanish support, did not materialise, it is difficult to judge the accuracy of the earls' assessment of its potential. In view of the expansionist tendencies of the O'Neills,[117] some doubt may perhaps be retained that the old English borderers of the pale would have been willing to risk themselves to a governance under Spain in which the old Irish lords of Ulster would expect to play such a prominent part.

The outcome for some of the principal figures drawn into O'Donnell's pre-flight conspirings throws light on how the affair was handled in Ireland. Delvin, initially destabilised, was arrested in November but escaped from Dublin castle and fled with a small following to Cloughowter in Cavan. He submitted, however, on 5 May 1608 and having been sent over to London was pardoned there in July.[118] When patronage was renewed to him, he (and his mother) did not refrain from accepting in a number of patents between 1 July 1609 and January 1613 substantial areas of land which, as has been seen, included property in Donegal.[119] For his part, St Lawrence was transferred to London but had been released by 1611.[120] The first of his family to become Protestant, he arranged a marriage between his son and heir, Nicholas, and the daughter of George Montgomery, now bishop of Meath. The Howth family estate of some 5,000 acres was retained up to 1641 and confirmed to them at the restoration.[121] The friar Owen Groome Magrath, sentenced to execution for high treason, was pardoned and released from Dublin castle in November 1609.[122] Pressure for religious conformity was also relaxed.

The rebellion which did break out was a purely local affair. O'Doherty's rising (18 April-5 July 1608), an attempt to expel both Captain Henry Harte from Culmore and the growing urban plantation from Derry, in which Bishop Montgomery was based and of which O'Doherty himself had been made one of the governing body, had arisen through ill-feeling with Docwra's successor there, Paulet, and because of delay in resolving his dispute over the possession of Inch island.[123] Although causing limited upheavals elsewhere in Ulster (for example Oghy oge *(Eochaidh Óg)* O'Hanlon's rebellion in Armagh, which did not peter out until September 1609)[124] and provoking Chichester to recriminations that his proposals for expenditure on fortifications had not received favour, O'Doherty's rising had been effectively suppressed with his death on 5 July.[125]

Seeking to seize on the opportunity thus presented, the earls, now in Rome, brought pressure on both Spain and the papacy to intervene and we are provided, as a result, with an interesting case of Spanish and papal interplay. In two submissions to Spain, on 30 June and 12 July, calling for armed assistance, they claimed that 4,000 of their 'vassals' had revolted in 'our province of Ulster' and that, crucially, the rising was spreading to the other provinces and causing reverberations in Scotland and England too.[126] The latter submission arose from a papal initiative: the pope had asked the Spanish ambassador to convey to Philip III the earls' proposal that Spain send forces to Ireland surreptitiously, 'doing so in the name of the pope'.[127] Spain's response to that was, however, dismissive: given the 'present lack of money and troops', there was too much in hand 'without undertaking anything new at the request of those who may be directly interested'.[128] However, for the next few months the issue was debated between Spain and the papacy. Thus, arising from a report from the Spanish ambassador in England which had spoken of financial difficulties and religious tensions there as well as events in Ireland, Philip III concluded that efforts now to 're-establish the holy faith in those parts' might succeed, and decided to urge the pope to take on the responsibility. The Spanish ambassador to Rome was accordingly instructed, on 19 July, to get both the English Jesuit Fr Robert Parsons (then employed in Rome) and the earls to test the pope's willingness to launch an assault to 'recover this patrimony of the church' (a reference it seems only to Ireland), given that 'Ireland belongs to the Apostolic See from ancient times' and given the precedent of Pope Gregory XIII's 'similar enterprise': the sending of a papal force to Ireland in 1580.[129] By September, however, the pope had made his decision: while in principle he would be 'glad to undertake this matter of Ireland', he could not in his present circumstances, being in conflict with Venice, levy the taxes for such a 'distant expedition' or offer any subvention to the Spaniards were they to take action.[130] At the same time the Spanish council of state and Philip III re-affirmed their earlier decision on the matter of Ireland.[131] Both instead sought to fall back on diplomacy – that because it was judged (with much exaggeration) that the English crown had been severely stretched by O'Doherty's rising, the restoration of O'Neill (O'Donnell had died in Rome on 18 July) could be negotiated and liberty of conscience achieved for at least Connacht and Ulster.[132] By now in fact, however, the process of planning a plantation for the lands in Ulster was already well underway. While it is impossible to know what the Spaniards might have done had the pope offered financial support, it is clear that they for their part had now fully accepted that their conflict with England, in which Ireland had, it can be seen, played a subordinate part, was over.[133] The death of O'Donnell (and Maguire) had also weakened the earls' effectiveness as a force for generating foreign involvement; however, the fear that O'Neill would be returned caused periodic anxieties in London and Dublin while he remained alive and indeed the ups and downs of Anglo-Spanish relations were to have reverberations in Ulster long after his death.

Plotting then, if manifestly not full-scale planning, on O'Donnell's part with a consequent fear of arrest and conviction for foreign conspiracy, had been a primary cause of the flight of the earls. That their fears of arrest or worse could have been very real ones can be seen in parallel with the treatment of the suspect north of England magnate, Henry Percy, ninth Earl of Northumberland, in the hardened atmosphere in the aftermath of the Gunpowder plot of 1605: he was imprisoned for life, only to be released in 1621.[134] To understand O'Donnell's actions, however, it is necessary to review briefly his position in the run-up to departure.

Although the broad outlines of his position in landholding were being laid down, as we have seen, they had not been confirmed in final detail. In the interim, as has also been shown, he had been actively seeking both a more favourable and a less regulated settlement. Thus in the summer of 1606 while Chichester was in Fermanagh, and at a time when the death of Mountjoy had taken away what the earl perceived as his 'patron' at court,[135] Rory approached him seeking arbitration of his land rights in south Donegal, a crucial area to him because much of the O'Donnell demesne land was located there. The matters at issue concerned the ownership of Bundrowes (and, effectively also, the defining of the county boundary there), boundary disputes arising from Folliott's lease, and in particular the future ownership of the large estate (15,768 acres) of the abbey of Assaroe. Rory, who up to this time still held much of the monastic property 'in commendam', was particularly anxious to procure a crown lease of this valuable estate. But Chichester, on visiting the area, was initially reluctant, as he informed Salisbury in London on 12 September, for security reasons, that this request be conceded: the abbey buildings stood in a valley close to Ballyshannon castle, with a hill rising between them 'by reason whereby the castle can discover nothing done in the abbey, which hath been a goodly house, and may yet shelter many people, who may in times of advantage lodge themselves within a caliver shot of the castle undiscovered ...'[136] By the end of November, he had, however, adopted a different attitude. If Rory, who remained 'very earnest' with him for this estate, could be got in return to disclaim his demand for Lifford and agree to demolish the abbey buildings (because of their proximity to Ballyshannon castle) and build elsewhere – a compromise which he hoped to bring him to – he would recommend London's approval for the grant.[137] Speed of decision-making now came into play. Although the matter was listed for discussion in London at the end of January 1607, London had not responded prior to the flight.[138] However, the decision, communicated to the lord deputy on 26 October 1607, to grant the estate to Goston was made after, rather than before, the flight of the earls.[139]

It is obvious, then, that Rory was actively seeking to recast O'Donnell power even in the altered circumstances of these years and it may be that his conspiratorial activities were engaged in as little more than a bargaining counter (or a threat as the astute Sir John Davies perceived them) to secure a more advantageous settlement. His problems were not, however, one-sided. The feud with Niall Garbh O'Donnell surfaced to full light also at this time, when the latter sought advantage through government contact. Hence in a statement made by him in Fermanagh in August 1606 to Chichester and chief justice Sir James Ley, on rumours then prevailing that Tyrconnell and Cuconnacht Maguire were about to depart the kingdom, he asserted that they and the earl of Tyrone and others had formed plans to seize the forts in Ulster, which they feared had now been discovered, and had links, through clerical agency, to Spain to boot.[140] However, whereas in the past such disputes between contestants for power would have been resolved by civil war with the stronger assuming control, the government now acted to pre-empt that by itself intervening in it. As a result, Rory and Niall Garbh, having 'submitted themselves to the order and arbitrament of the council table for all personal causes and variances ... between them' were obliged, early in December, to enter into recognisances in £3,000, each to the other, to abide by the order and decision of the lord deputy and privy council concerning 'all differences, controversies and challenges of goods' between them.[141] By this means (an example of government by recognisance),[142] Rory was debarred from the normal trial by strength which such circumstances threw up, and in agreeing to abide by Dublin's arbitration might possibly have had to accept a territorial adjustment in Niall Garbh's favour as well.[143] To Rory, whose personal financial circumstances were ones of considerable indebtedness, the forfeiture of that penalty would have presented an unsustainable burden: after the flight, Chichester expressed the view that 'that needy earl of Tyrconnell' had debts to the sum of £3,000.[144]

It is clear also, however, that O'Donnell's conspiratorial activities, which made the flight of the earls necessary (and in which his indebtedness may well have played some part), were ill-judged since the desired Spanish or papal army did not materialise and it looks likely that he had received a false impression about the prospects for Spanish intervention through the enthusiasm of his channels of communication with Spain, many of them priests, themselves with an interest in frustrating the extension of the reformation into Ulster now clearly signalled both by Montgomery's appointment as bishop and by the monastic dissolutions.[145] Conformity and compliance might have left O'Donnell in a position in landholding at least approaching to that which the astute Earl of Antrim (though by no means an entirely parallel figure) secured and sustained for himself in these years.[146] However, the loss of *uir-ri;* taxation through the quit rent; the loss of some castles; the insistence that the lesser lords must be freeholders paying only their 'ancient rents'; the loss of valuable fishing rights; the belief that some garrisons and some new owners must be an essential part of the new order as mechanisms of control all meant that in the Ireland whose 'settlement' was now being completed, the Earl of Tyrconnell's role, both politically and economically, would be a much restricted and transformed one. More a landlord now than a warlord, he would retain a personal estate (possibly enhanced by the 15,000 acres of Assaroe abbey lands) along with his principal castle at Donegal and (after a difficult transition) draw rents or services from much of the rest of the land as well. He could no longer, however, aspire to fill the role, embracing military virtues, personalised power and rights of patronage, of the 'independent' regional prince of the Gaelic world evoked so fulsomely in O'Clery's finely-honed obituary of his brother:

> ... He was the head of support and planning, of counsel and disputation of the greater number of the Gaels of Ireland whether in peace or in war. He was a mighty bountiful lord with the attributes of a prince and the maintenance of justice, a lion in strength and force, with threatening and admonishing so that it was not allowed to gainsay his word, for whatever he ordered had to be done on the spot, a dove in meekness and gentleness to privileged men of the church and the arts, and every one who did not oppose him. A man who impressed fear and terror of him on everyone far and near, and on whom no man at all put dread. A man who banished brigands, crushed evildoers, exalted the sons of life, and hanged the sons of death. A man who did not

allow himself to be injured or afflicted, cheated or insulted without repaying and avenging it immediately; a determined, fierce, and bold invader of districts; a warlike, aggressive plunderer of others' territories; a destroyer of any of the English and Irish that opposed him; a man who never failed to do all that befitted a prince so long as he lived; a sweet-sounding trumpet, with power of speech and eloquence, sense and counsel, with a look of affection on his face according to all who beheld him; a prophesied chosen one whom the prophets foretold long before his birth.[147]

There was, however, to be an aftermath to the earls' departure. Shortly after the outbreak of O'Doherty's rising, Niall Garbh, whose son Neachtan had gone to Trinity College, Dublin in what appears to have been a significant effort at adjustment, and who now professed his 'allegiance towards his king and country', sought the lord deputy's support with the king for a patent of 'the whole country and territory of Tyrconnell' ('the possessions of his ancestors'). In it he sought, on foot of a claimed previous promise of Chichester's, to have O'Doherty's Inishowen as well, and requested also a grant of the Lough Foyle fisheries. He avoided entirely the question of freehold status for the lesser owners, but was prepared to accept the exception of Lifford, Ballyshannon, Derry and, in effect, Culmore from his grant. He also sought patronage in various forms: the command, during the rebellion, of 300 foot and 50 horse which he would distribute to some of his supporters; the wardship of O'Boyle's son (which would give him power in south Donegal); and a pension for life.[148]

Chichester, in his replies, while temporising with him on the military command and offering some encouragement with regard to Inishowen, pointed out to Niall Garbh that since the earl was not yet attainted and the lands of the greater lordship not yet surveyed, whereby 'the king may know what he gives and that all subjects' rights may be preserved', he could not convey to him a sure estate of any more than had been formerly promised, and stressed also to him his need for loyalty and action in the context of the revolt.[149] He was reminded, too, that the king was now more powerful than Elizabeth had been 'by a populous and bordering kingdom' and urged not to so 'capitulate' with him 'as to cause his Majesty to believe him an ambitious and insatiable man, but one that would draw on his Majesty to do for him as a good and well-deserving subject'.[150] Also, in the ensuing correspondence with London, in May, Chichester expressed his concern about the deal Niall Garbh was attempting to negotiate. Referring to his 'spirit and vast desires', seeking by demanding the 'whole country' of Tyrconnell 'without any respect of other inferior rights and interests whatsoever' to become therein 'a Roytelett', he asked the privy council to direct him on 'how far to give him some reasonable satisfaction', and its view was that he should not make his 'fortune so great as may prove unfit should he show an evil mind hereafter'. Should he prove his loyalty by action against the rebels, they would, however, consent to his estate being enlarged (at Dublin's discretion) but he should not be made 'too powerful over his Majesty's other subjects'.[151] In fact, the effectiveness of the standing army in dealing with the revolt made Niall Garbh's proffered services redundant. In a campaign lasting from early May to late June, led by Sir Richard Wingfield, marshal of the army, lord treasurer Sir Thomas Ridgeway and Sir Oliver Lambert, a soldier of much experience, the revolt was brought under control through the recovery of the forts and the taking of O'Doherty's castles.[152] When they arrived (after a 'march so far and into such places of the North as no army has ever gone by land before'), they found Niall Garbh to be 'wavering and irresolute which side to take'.[153] By mid-June he had been arrested under suspicion and was conveyed to Dublin on the king's ship *Tramontane* to be eventually, after an abortive trial, transferred with his son to London where he died in the Tower.[154]

Thus ended O'Donnell power and with it a long crisis of integration between Gaelic lords and crown government. Direct-rule English government in sixteenth-century Ireland found itself confronted, beyond the pale, by a varying pattern of lordly power often expressed, as in the case of O'Donnell, through elaborate linkages which had created systems of regional dominance – which it sought to transform by creating a significantly disempowered nobility absorbed into a unitary administration with interlocking central and local elements. In secular terms, the model for change in Ulster lay in the arrangements for landownership devised in the 'settlement' of Monaghan in 1591, combined with its designation as a county in 1588.[155] A central assumption was that the ordinary people could only be ruled effectively if the barrier of lordly power was significantly reduced. Another aim was to achieve religious uniformity through the extension of the reformation to Ireland as well. At the time when social and political change was being attempted in Ulster in the 1580s and early 1590s, renewed and equally piecemeal efforts were made to extend the reformation into it also. In the course of the resulting Nine Years' War, religion and aristocratic power had come to be intertwined and eventually, and even more significantly, internationalised through the involvement of Spain.

Confronted by this gathering intensification of Tudor change, political and religious, the Ulster lords had been forced to think beyond the previous confines of regional power, and their own model for a unitary Ireland was put forward, without success, in 1599. The framework produced in a document ascribed to O'Neill, bears some of the character of the 'aristocratic constitutionalism' which surfaced from time to time elsewhere, as it had done, for example, in Sweden during a period of crisis in the monarchy in 1593-4.[156] The essence of the O'Neill proposal was simple: that, crucially, under a member of the English nobility representing the queen as lord deputy,[157] the nobility of Ireland should have access to all the offices of state and so form its government[158] and that the church of Ireland be 'wholly governed by the pope', in short, that the reformation should be reversed.[159] By now, therefore, the Ulster lords had come to a confirmed view that catholicism rather than protestantism was attuned 'best' to a right 'worldly policy' in which their kind of power should have its place.[160] However, as has been shown in the case of O'Donnell, lord deputy Chichester had, in the tense aftermath of the rebellion, renewed the programme for the 'settlement' of Ireland along opposing lines. Much of the 'lure of Spain' (by which one contemporary sought to explain the attempt at renewed conspiracy spearheaded by O'Donnell) must have resided in the expectation that under a Spanish dispensation the former kind of outcome might be achieved. Hence the strongly Catholic tone and aristocratic flavour of the appeals to Spain. However, a dispensation so favourable to aristocratic liberties was no longer easy to obtain in a period which tended everywhere in western Europe to be a 'time of collision between the authority of kings and local or national privileges, liberties and constitutions',[161] and least of all in Ireland which England still feared might become a base for Spanish aggression. The conjoining of aristocratic power with a requirement for religious diversity was an even more difficult demand to sustain. At first sight, it might appear that the Protestant Huguenot aristocracy in France had achieved it: the Edict of Nantes in 1598 conceded religious toleration. However, this privilege was gradually whittled away in Cardinal Richelieu's France, to be eventually revoked in 1685.[162] The outcome for the O'Donnells in Donegal may perhaps be understood more easily in this context. If Rory O'Donnell had hoped indeed to regain 'his country in the same state his brother held it' through a *coup d'etat* or by Spanish intervention he was to be disappointed, while Niall Garbh's attempts to achieve something slightly less through negotiation also proved abortive. Plantation followed.

References

1. *Cal. pat. rolls Ire., Jas I*, pp 10, 13. He was pardoned in October 1603 (Ibid., p. 35).
2. The peace with Spain was agreed in the Treaty of London in August 1604.

3. *Cal. S.P. Ire., 1606-8*, p. 365. For a careful examination of O'Donnell overlordship in Sligo see Mary O'Dowd, *Power, politics and land: early modern Sligo, 1568-1688* (Belfast, 1991), pp 20-44.

4. I intend to examine this point in more detail elsewhere.

5. H. Morgan, *Tyrone's rebellion: the outbreak of the Nine Years' War in Tudor Ireland* (Dublin, 1993), passim. I have benefited greatly from discussions with Dr Morgan.

6. On this see K. Simms, 'Niall Garbh II O'Donnell, king of Tír Conaill, 1422-39' in *Donegal Annual* 12 (1977-9), pp 7-21.

7. The castle at Dunnalong was built by Turlough Luineach O'Neill in 1568 (P.R.O., S.P. 63/23, no. 74, ix).

8. *Inq. cancell. Hib. repert.*, II, App. IV.

9. For a discussion of the O'Donnells and Derry in the early sixteenth century see B. Lacy, *Siege city: the story of Derry* and *Londonderry* (Belfast, 1990), pp 61-5.

10. *Fiants Ire., Eliz.*, nos 5190 and 5207.

11. P. Walsh (ed.), *The life of Aodh Ruadh Ó Domhnaill transcribed from the Book of Lughaidh Ó Cléirigh* (Dublin, 1948, 1957), 1, 55.

12. Sir Henry Docwra, 'A narration of the services done by the army employed to Lough Foyle' in John O'Donovan (ed.), *Miscellany of the celtic society*, passim.

13. *Cal. pat. rolls Ire., Jas I*, p. 52.

14. *Cal. S.P. Ire., 1606-8*, p. 365.

15. *A.F.M.*, 1601.

16. *Fiants Ire., Eliz.*, no. 6655; *Cal. pat. rolls Ire., Jas I*, p. 59.

17. For a full discussion of the issues at stake in the Nine Years' War see H. Morgan, *Tyrone's rebellion* (Dublin, 1993).

18. R.I.A., MS 14.B.7., pp 423-4. These accounts of the 'old customs' of O'Donnell, one by Teige McLinchy who had been steward to Red Hugh O'Donnell, suggest that the later O'Donnells had had difficulty in drawing revenue from North Connacht. There, only Tirawley is mentioned, where O'Donnell's 'rent' was 'ten pence in lieu of each cow'. Political influence might, of course, be exercised nonetheless. The document seems to imply, by mentioning it, that O'Donnell should receive the *eric*.

19. Interestingly, the conditions in Sir Cahir O'Doherty's patent under the crown in 1605 were less onerous than the ones demanded by O'Donnell had been: he should pay a rent of 30 beeves and provide a rising out of 6 horse and 20 foot; however, his tenure in capite would allow of the incidents of fiscal feudalism.

20. Lord deputy Perrott was informed by the privy council in August 1584 of 'how loth we are to be carried into charges and how we would rather spend a pound, forced by necessity, than a penny for prevention' (*Cal. S.P. Ire., 1574-85*, p. 525).

21. For his own account of this see Docwra, *Narration*.

22. *Cal. S.P. Ire., 1596-7*, pp 108, 146; *Cal. Carew MSS, 1603-24*, pp 284, 299, 397.

23. G. A. Hayes-McCoy (ed.), *Ulster and other Irish maps* (Dublin, 1964) pp 26-7.

24. *Cal. Carew MSS, 1601-3*, pp 284, 299, 397.

25. F. Moryson, *An history of Ireland from the year 1599 to 1603* (Dublin, 1735), ii, 347-51.

26. Ibid., p. 231.

27. Erck (ed.), *Pat. rolls Ire., Jas I*, pp 24-5.

28. R.I.A., MS 14.B.7, p. 424.

29. B. Lacy *et al.*, *Archaeological survey of county Donegal* (Lifford, 1983), pp 330-2. The friars of Donegal were witnesses of the agreement between O'Donnell and O'Connor Sligo in 1539 (M. Carney, 'Agreement between Ó Domhnaill and

Tadhg Ó Conchobhair concerning Sligo castle (23 June 1539)' in *I.H.S.*, 3 (1942-3), pp 282-96.

30. Erck (ed.), *Pat. rolls Ire., Jas I*, pp 24-5.

31. *Cal. pat. rolls Ire., Eliz.*, p. 587.

32. For accounts of these events see *A.F.M.*, 1603; F. Moryson, *An history of Ireland from the year 1599 to 1603*, ii, 154, 167, 256, 284, 335-6; Docwra, *Narration*, pp 263-81.

33. Erck, *Rep. pat. rolls Ire., Jas I*, p. 47; *Cal. pat. rolls Ire., Jas I*, p. 10. He received a pardon on 15 October (Ibid., p. 35).

34. *Cal. pat. rolls Ire., Jas I*, p. 13; Erck, *Rep. pat. rolls Ire., Jas I*, pp 59-60.

35. Erck, *Rep. pat. rolls Ire., Jas I*, pp 106-7; *Cal. pat. rolls Ire., Jas I*, pp 47-8. The commissioners were some of the local military commanders along with William Parsons, surveyor-general and Nicholas Kenney, escheator-general.

36. Ibid.; *Inq. cancell. Hib. repert.*, ii, Donegal (2), (3) Jas I.

37. N.A., R.C.9/1, pp 141-9.

38. *Cal. pat. rolls Ire. Jas I*, p. 13. A crown lease of some of the regalities was made to John Bingley, then of Dublin, in October 1603 (Ibid., p. 14).

39. *Cal. pat. rolls Ire., Jas I*, pp 12, 48, 57-8, 113, 129, 145; Erck, *Rep. pat. rolls Ire., Jas I*, pp 223, 40-1, 53, 54, 107-9, 112-14, 132-4.

40. The lands of St Patrick's Purgatory, Termon Magrath and Termonnemongan found by inquisition in November 1603 and granted to Robert Leicester in 1604, were granted to James Magrath in December 1610 (*Cal. pat. rolls Ire., Jas I*, p. 187). The influence of Archbishop Miler Magrath of Cashel is probably to be found here.

41. The commission to the lord deputy and other government officers empowering them to grant leases was dated 12 April 1603 (Erck, r*ep. pat. rolls Ire., Jas I*, pp 18-19).

42. R. J. Hunter, 'Sir Ralph Bingley, *c.*1570-1627: Ulster planter' in P. Roebuck (ed.), *Plantation to partition* (Belfast, 1981), pp 14-28, 253-6. For the *Triall* episode see D. B. Quinn, 'The voyage of *Triall* 1606-7: an abortive Virginia venture' in *The American Neptune*, XXXI, no. 2 (1971), 85-103.

43. *Cal. pat. rolls Ire., Jas I*, p. 95. Tassagard is modern Saggart, approximately 500 acres and 11 miles from Dublin.

44. Ibid., pp 101-2. On this occasion too, a fairly standard provision was inserted with regard to Ballyshannon castle, which again was granted only for Folliott's lifetime, that he should make no assignment of it to any person except of English birth or born in the Pale, without the deputy's consent.

45. Ibid., pp 541-2.

46. Ibid., p. 14 (bis).

47. Ibid., pp 10, 15.

48. *Cal. pat. rolls Ire., Jas I*, pp 84-5.

49. For the most recent exposition see H. Morgan, 'Hugh O'Neill and the Nine Years' War in Tudor Ireland' in *Historical Journal*, 36 (1993), 21-37. Niall O'Boyle who was Catholic bishop of Raphoe, 1591-1611, was therefore the last single bishop of the diocese.

50. *Inq. cancell. Hib. repert.*, ii, xvii.

51. H.M.C., *Egmont MSS*, i, 1, 29-30; *Fiants Ire., Eliz.*, no. 6501; *Cal. S.P. Ire., 1603-6*, pp 432, 567. There had been one appointment of sheriff prior to the Nine Years' War.

52. *Cal. S.P. Ire., 1603-6*, p. 111.

53. *Cal. S.P. Ire., 1606-8*, p. 369.

54. *Cal. S.P. Ire., 1606-8*, pp 2, 35.
55. H.M.C., *Salisbury (Cecil) MSS* 18, 140-41; *Cal. S.P. Ire. 1603-6*, p. 562.
56. *Cal. S.P. Ire., 1603-6*, pp 268, 296.
57. J. O'Donovan (ed.), *Miscellany of the Celtic Society* (Dublin, 1849), pp 190-1. The author, it may be noted, was Sir Henry Docwra.
58. I have adopted the term 'warlord' from Katharine Simms's important study *From kings to warlords: the changing political structure of Gaelic Ireland in the later middle ages* (Woodbridge, 1987), and suggest that the term 'landlord' conveys something useful about the changes that were intended. This paragraph is based on a reading of the sources for this policy in Connacht and Monaghan.
59. *Fiants Ire., Eliz.*, no. 5207.
60. *Inq. cancell. Hib. repert.*, 2, xxi-xxxi.
61. H. Morgan, *Tyrone's rebellion*, pp 130, 143-4.
62. *Cal. pat. rolls Ire., Jas I*, p. 13.
63. Ibid., p. 59.
64. *Inq. cancell. Hib. repert.*, 2, xxxi-xl; H.M.C., *Hastings MSS*, iv, 153.
65. G. A. Hayes-McCoy, 'Sir John Davies in Cavan in 1606 and 1610' in *Breifne*, i, no. 3 (1960), pp 177-91.
66. Printed in M. J. Bonn, *Die englische kolonisation in Ireland* i (Stuttgart & Berlin, 1906), 394-7; Aidan Clarke in *N.H.I.*, iii, 193.
67. *Cal. S.P. Ire., 1606-8*, p. 262.
68. *Cal. S.P. Ire., 1603-6*, p. 161.
69. K. Simms, *From kings to warlords*, p. 146; *Cal. S.P. Ire., 1600-1*, pp 289-90. Rory had, of course, been neither elected nor inaugurated, Gaelic-style, as lord. His brother Hugh had by will disponed the lordship to him (J. J. Silke, 'The last will of Red Hugh O'Donnell' in *Studia Hib.*, 24 (1984-8), 58.
70. *Cal. S.P. Ire., 1603-6*, p. 192.
71. Walsh, *Destruction by peace*, pp 152-3. His cause was finally heard by the privy council at Greenwich on 28 March 1605.
72. *Cal. S.P. Ire., 1603-6*, pp 296-8, 303-5. O'Donnell made no reference to religion in these articles. He was seeking the right to nominate the sheriff again in May 1606 (H.M.C., S*alisbury (Cecil) MSS* 18, 140-41).
73. *Cal. S.P. Ire., 1606-8*, p. 373.
74. *Cal. S.P. Ire., 1608-10*, pp 571-2.
75. *Cal S.P. Ire., 1606-8*, pp 85, 124, 225.
76. T. Ó Cianáin, *The flight of the earls*, ed. P. Walsh (Dublin, 1916), p. 9.
77. *Cal. S.P. Ire., 1603-6*, p. 319.
78. Ibid., p. 320. The most recent 'ancient rent' of MacSweeney Fanad appears to have been 18 beeves and 10 milch cows and 10 marks for the support of bonaghts, though he must send to the field 120 gallowglasses in time of warfare (R.I.A., MS 14.B.7., p. 423). The early sixteenth-century historian of the MacSweeneys claimed that an agreement had been reached a century earlier between MacSweeney Fanad and O'Donnell for the payment of a *martaigheacht* of six beeves no more than three times a year and an earlier MacSweeney, he asserted, had given no cows at all to O'Donnell, 'for he was strong and powerful and his own tribe was in submission to him' (P. Walsh (ed.), *Leabhar Chlainne Suibne* (Dublin, 1920), pp 51, 59). For analysis see K. Simms, *From kings to warlords*, pp 142-3. No wonder, then, that Rory should seek, in Englished circumstances, to reduce them to leaseholders for years.
79. *Cal. S.P. Ire., 1603-6*, p. 320.
80. Ibid., pp 297, 304.

81. Ibid., pp 319-20. For the loss of castles to the nobility in England see P. Williams, *The Tudor regime* (Oxford, 1979), p. 438. A segment at Carrigans was also retained though it is not mentioned at this time.

82. *Cal. S.P. Ire., 1603-6*, pp 319-20. Some sums of money were however spent in those years on improvements to the fortifications here and at Ballyshannon and Culmore (J. Buckley (ed.), 'Report of Sir Josias Bodley on some Ulster fortresses in 1608' in *U.J.A.*, 2nd ser. 16 (1910), 61-4).

83. *Cal. pat. rolls Ire., Jas I*, p. 182.

84. Ibid., pp 206-7.

85. *Cal. S.P. Ire., 1603-6*, p. 322. Capt. Henry Harte received a lease for twenty-one years of the castle and fort of Culmore and some 300 acres adjoining, reserved to the crown out of O'Doherty's patent, in February 1606 (*Cal. pat. rolls Ire., Jas I*, p. 83).

86. *Cal. S.P. Ire., 1603-6*, pp 320, 322. This exact note, which must have been very hastily done, does not appear to have survived. It could scarcely have been an adequate record on which to base land titles.

87. *Cal. S.P. Ire., 1603-6*, pp 558-68; N.P. Canny, 'The flight of the earls, 1607' in *I.H.S.* 17 (1970-71), 386-7.

88. *Cal. S.P. Ire., 1603-6*, pp 542, 560.

89. For the government of the Spanish Netherlands under the Archdukes and its relationship to Spain see H. de Schepper & G. Parker, 'The formation of government policy in the catholic Netherlands under the Archdukes, 1596-1621' in *E.H.R.*, 91 (1976), 241-54.

90. Walsh, *Destruction* by *peace*, passim.

91. Ibid., pp 164-7.

92. Ibid., pp 29-30, 152-3.

93. Ibid., pp 175-6, 179-80; D. B. Quinn, *Explorers and colonies: America, 1500-1625* (London and Ronceverte, 1990), pp 321-39.

94. Walsh, *Destruction by peace,* p. 192. In her introduction to this important collection of documents, the editor tends to refer to this and other joint statements of O'Neill and O'Donnell as documents of O'Neill only. For its part this chapter is concerned with O'Donnell; it is not its aim to give a full account of the flight of the earls.

95. *Cal. pat. rolls Ire., Eliz.*, pp 439-40.

96. *Cal. S.P. Ire., 1603-6*, pp 74, 312-14, 418-20, 52930, 536; *1606-8*, pp 45, 111, 116, 134, 220, 522-3. Richard Nugent's father is also an interesting case. During 'the doubtful time of the siege of Kinsale' he had come under suspicion of collusion with O'Neill and having been arrested had died in Dublin castle in 1602 before his trial had taken place (Moryson, *Ireland from 1599 to 1603*, ii, p. 154).

97. *Cal. S.P. Ire., 1606-8*, pp 320-1.

98. Ibid., pp 254-6.

99. Ibid., pp 259-62.

100. The only formal evidence of the Brussels government's involvement so far available lies in the issuing of a license to go to Ireland to O'Brien, then in the Irish regiment there, on 16 August (B. Jennings (ed.), *Wild geese in Spanish Flanders, 1582-1700* (Dublin, 1964), pp 91, 535). However, O'Brien appears to have been the Archdukes' emissary.

101. Walsh, *Destruction by peace*, pp 50-55; *Cal. S.P. Ire., 1606-8*, pp 297-300.

102. What would be sought on their behalf with James I was a pardon and an agreement 'to settle them in their countries in the same state that they were before the last rebellion, with liberty of conscience at least in their own

countries'. Evidence that this was the intention comes, indirectly, from views expressed by the Franciscan Owen Groome Magrath. Magrath also asserted that in the event of war, the pope had undertaken to provide financial support to the extent of 50,000 crowns and also some soldiers, 'if he could conveniently bring it to pass' (Ibid., p. 299).

103. Walsh, *Destruction by peace*, pp 73-4, 231.

104. *Cal. S.P. Ire., 1606-8*, p. 321 and also p. 299.

105. On the efforts to enforce the reformation in the years after 1603 see Aidan Clarke in *N.H.I.*, 3, 188-92.

106. Walsh, *Destruction by peace*, pp 189-95. The earls' view, as expressed here, would tend to suggest an earlier origin for the English civil war than is commonly now accepted. They may, however, have been referring to the anti-enclosure Midland Revolt of 1607. Undoubtedly, too, there were serious problems about taxation in England at this time, but on the other hand the burden of war taxation had been lifted given the peace with Spain.

107. Rumours of thinking about an assault on England surfaced in the alleged remark of Owen Groome Magrath to the baron of Delvin that it was the earls' strategy to return with foreign forces to Munster and, 'when they had well settled there', that 'they would soon after attempt England from thence' (*Cal. S.P. Ire.*, 1606-8, p. 321). Also Cuconnacht Maguire is said to have told the people around Rathmullan on his departure with the earls 'that they should shortly hear of their being in England with a powerful army, from whence they would return into Ireland' (Ibid., p. 275).

108. *Cal. S.P. Ire., 1606-8*, pp 311-13.

109. Jennings (ed.), *Wild geese*, pp 94, 97, 542.

110. C. Martin and G. Parker, *The Spanish armada* (London, 1988), pp 81-2, 96-8.

111. The reference was to Pope Adrian IV's bull *Laudabiliter*.

112. The document, which is undated, is published in *Archiv. Hib.*, 3, 302-10 where a much later date is suggested. However, it may be the 'letter from Tyrone' which Cardinal Bentivoglio sent to Rome on 24 November 1607 or perhaps have been produced in 1608, though before O'Doherty's rising since it makes no reference to it. It referred again to the grander issue of catholicism in the north of Europe. In May 1608 it was rumoured from Brussels that Tyrone sought from the pope 'the like allowance as he formerly gave for the maintenance of the war against the Turk' and that he should make a similar recommendation to Spain and that the earls sought only money and would themselves secure the soldiers (*Cal. S.P. Ire., 1606-8*, pp 660-1). It appears that Tyrone thought that no more than 12,000 men would be required 'to thrust all the English out of Ireland' (Ibid., pp 664-5) and it looks likely that he hoped to have the use of the Irish regiment in Spanish Flanders to advance his purposes.

113. Jennings (ed.), *Wild geese*, pp 538-9.

114. C. Giblin, 'Catalogue of material of Irish interest in the collection *Nunziatura di Fiandra*, Vatican archives' I, in *Collect. Hib.* 1 (1958), 556. Bentivoglio regretted the encouragement being offered to the earls by Archbishop Lombard in Rome.

115. Walsh, *Destruction by peace*, pp 197-200.

116. Jennings (ed.), *Wild geese*, p. 539; *Cal. S.P. Ire., 1606-8*, pp 641-3.

117. The petition of Cormac MacBaron O'Neill to Spain in 1596 to be granted the ownership of a substantial area of county Down, including Old English land in Lecale, may be worth taking into account in this context (H. Morgan, *Tyrone's rebellion*, pp 233-5). Given the O'Neill aspiration to control north of the Boyne, the palesmen of Louth might well have felt uneasy. Cormac MacBaron was

himself arrested after the flight of the earls and dispatched to the Tower of London.

118. *Cal. pat. rolls Ire., Jas I*, p. 134; *Cal. S.P. Ire., 1606-8*, p. 502.

119. *Cal. pat. rolls Ire., Jas I*, pp 197-8, 220-1, 238.

120. *Cal. S. P. Dom., 1611-18*, p. 65. He was also granted livery of his estate in succession to his father in December 1608 (*Cal. pat. rolls Ire., Jas I*, p. 139).

121. G. E. C., *Peerage*, VI, 607-8; V. J. McBrierty (ed.), *The Howth peninsula: its history, lore and legend* (Dublin, 1981), p. 26; L. J. Arnold, *The restoration land settlement in county Dublin, 1660-1688* (Dublin, 1993), pp 155, 158. The marriage took place in 1615 and St Lawrence died in 1619.

122. *Cal. pat. rolls Ire., Jas I*, p. 160.

123. O'Doherty may have expected the Spaniards to arrive at this time (*Cal. S.P. Ire., 1606-8*, p. 510).

124. *Cal. S.P. Ire., 1608-10*, pp 287, 305.

125. For an account of the rebellion, see B. Bonner, *That audacious traitor* (Dublin, 1975).

126. Walsh, *Destruction by peace*, pp 222-3, 226-8.

127. Ibid., p. 225. The very least that could, as a result, be achieved would be liberty of conscience.

128. Ibid., p. 226.

129. Ibid., pp 229-30.

130. Ibid., pp 234-6, where the Spanish ambassador summarises his discussion with the pope. For the conflict with Venice see W. J. Bouwsma, V*enice and the defense of republican liberty* (Berkeley and Los Angeles, 1968). An important study of the papal finances at this time is P. Partner, 'Papal financial policy in the renaissance and counterreformation' in *Past and Present* no. 88 (Aug. 1980), 17-62.

131. Walsh, *Destruction by peace*, p. 236.

132. Ibid., pp 237-40.

133. For Anglo-Spanish relations at this time see Quinn, *Explorers and colonies*, pp 321-39. Partner's study of the papal finances (p. 54) reveals that Pope Paul V spent 335,000 silver scudi on subsidies to Catholic powers and that he also allocated 1,000,000 silver scudi (4 per cent of income) to benefit members of his own family. See also W. Reinhard, 'Papal power and family strategy in the sixteenth and seventeenth centuries' in R. G. Asch and A. M. Birke (ed.), *Princes, patronage and the nobility* (Oxford, 1991), pp 329-56.

134. G. R. Batho, 'Henry Ninth Earl of Northumberland and Syon House, Middlesex, 1594-1632' in *Ancient Monument Society Transactions*, New ser., 4 (1956), 102, 108.

135. H.M.C., *Salisbury (Cecil) MSS* 18, 140-41.

136. *Cal. S.P. Ire., 1603-6*, pp 561, 564. For the acreage of the Assaroe abbey estate see Geraldine Carville, *Assaroe: 'Abbey of the morning star'* (Ballyshannon, n.d.), p. 15. The existence of the hill in question was confirmed by me on a field trip on 4 September 1993. On 18 September 1606 Donogh O'Connor Sligo was asserting that the castle of Bundrowes and twenty quarters of land associated with it should belong to him (H.M.C., *Salisbury (Cecil) MSS*, 18, 291-2).

137. *Cal. S.P. Ire., 1606-8*, p. 35.

138. Ibid., pp 95-6.

139. Ibid., p. 308.

140. *Cal. S.P. Ire., 1603-6*, pp 568-9. On this see p. 542.

141. B.L., Add MS 19,838, ff 35V-6.

142. For a discussion of the use of recognizances by the monarchy in England a century earlier see G. W. Bernard, *The Tudor nobility* (Manchester, 1992), pp 57-65.

143. For the earl's own account of this see *Cal. S.P. Ire., 1606-8*, p. 371. It is possible too that at this point a full freeholder 'settlement' might also have been attempted.

144. *Cal. S.P. Ire., 1606-8*, pp 296, 398. One element in his debts was incurred through efforts to purchase the monastic estate of Kilmacrenan, thereby to establish a territorial footing in the north of Donegal.

145. An informant in Brussels writing to London in January 1608 expressed the view that 'priests and friars are the doers of all' and said that those who had come with the earls had 'for the most part, a thousand times wished themselves safe back again' (Ibid., p. 643).

146. On Randal MacDonnell, earl of Antrim see Jane H. Ohlmeyer, *Civil war and restoration in the three Stuart kingdoms: the career of Randal MacDonnell marquis of Antrim, 1609-1683* (Cambridge, 1993), pp 18-36.

147. Ó Clerigh, *Aodh Ruadh Ó Domhnaill*, i, 345-7. The excellent paper by Michelle O'Riordan, 'The native Ulster *mentalite* as revealed in Gaelic sources, 1600-1650' in B. MacCuarta (ed.), *Ulster 1641: aspects of the rising* (Belfast, 1993), pp 61-91 was published just as this one, which is mainly concerned with government policy and the response it generated, was being written and should be read in conjunction with it.

148. *Cal. S.P. Ire., 1606-8*, pp 508-11, 530-4.

149. Niall Garbh had in fact asked for an interim custodiam of the lordship (Ibid., p. 510).

150. *Cal. S.P. Ire., 1606-8*, pp 511-14, 530-4.

151. Ibid., pp 499-502, 524-7, 528-9, 547-9.

152. Ibid., pp 580-1, 599-605.

153. Ibid., pp 542, 599.

154. Ibid., pp 573-4; Seán Ó Domhnaill, 'Sir Niall Garbh O'Donnell and the rebellion of Sir Cahir O'Doherty' in *I.H.S.*, 3 (1942-3), 34-8.

155. For the creation of the county see *Inq. cancell. Hib. repert.*, ii, 18-19.

156. Michael Roberts, 'On aristocratic constitutionalism in Swedish history' in his *Essays in Swedish history* (London, 1967), pp 14-55.

157. The title of Viceroy was used. Spain normally governed its dependencies through viceroys. Might the Earl of Essex (who himself had an Irish estate) have been in mind for this office?

158. Lordly power would be safe within such a constitutional framework.

159. *Cal. S.P. Ire., 1599-1600*, pp 279-80, 280-1 (a summary). This is the document which was endorsed by secretary of state Sir Robert Cecil with the word 'Ewtopia'. The alternative quest for a new Irish monarchy with O'Neill or a Spaniard as king, and how O'Donnell might be affected by it, cannot be dealt with here in any detail.

160. This derives from comments made by Bartholemew Owen, a confidante of Hugh O'Neill's, in January 1606 (P.R.O., S.P. 63/218, no. 18 (1)). In this context it may be worth noting that Hugh O'Neill had his marriage to Mabel Bagnal in 1591 conducted by the Protestant bishop of Meath (S. Ó Faoláin, *The great O'Neill: a biography of Hugh O'Neill Earl of Tyrone, 1550-1616* (London, 1942), pp 116-9).

161. The phrase is J.G.A. Pocock's, from his *The ancient constitution and the feudal law* (Cambridge, 2nd ed., 1987), p. 16. In Sweden, Erik Sparre and other exponents of aristocratic constitutionalist ideas were executed in 1600 (M. Roberts, *Swedish history*, p. 23).

162.   R. Bonney, *Political change in France under Richelieu and Mazarin, 1624-1661* (Oxford, 1978), pp 384-400. To reduce local independence in France Henri IV destroyed a number of castles and forts after 1593, while over 100 fortresses were razed by Richelieu in the 1630s after a series of Huguenot and aristocratic rebellions (G. Parker, *The military revolution* (Cambridge, 1988), pp 41-2).

All dates are given in the old style except that the year is taken to begin on 1 January and not 25 March.

Plate 8.1   Raphoe Castle.

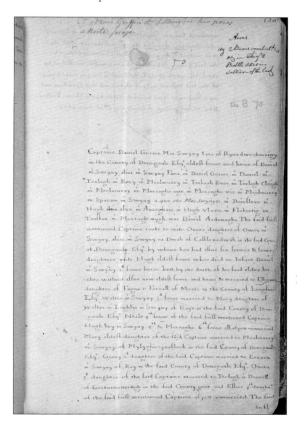

Plate 8.2   First page of copy
of funeral certificate
of Domhnall Gorm
Mac Suibhne, *obit*
17, February, 1636,
Genealogical Office,
Ms 70, p. 120,
dated June 1638
(Genealogical
Office).

Chapter 9

RAPHOE AND THE REFORMATION

JOHN J. SILKE

I

O'Donnell, paramount lord of Tír Chonaill, was, like O'Neill, powerful enough to leave to lesser kin-groups the spoils of ecclesiastical office. Thus in the period 1420-1561 the O'Gallagher sept, Sliocht an Easbuig, gave to the diocese three bishops (Lochloinn I, his grandson Lochloinn II, and the latter's grandson again Edmund), an abbot of Assaroe, Art son of Lochloinn II, and a dean, who was son to this Art; while Sliocht Áedha provided a bishop, Art son of Félim Fionn, whose cousin Eóghan (d. 1580) was dean of the diocese, although not a priest. The O'Gallaghers with their chief strongholds now along the Finn provided O'Donnell with his marshals and together with the gallowglass MacSweeneys formed the elite of the Tír Chonaill forces. A half-century after Bishop Art's death in 1561 it was said of him that he always went with a 'troupe of Horsemen under his collours'.[1]

In this dynastic clerical system of the native Irish, celibacy was naturally a casualty, and the increasing practice of papal provisions, with continuous and costly recourse to Rome for parishes as well as bishoprics, had furthered the decline of the secular clergy from the reform heights of the thirteenth and fourteenth centuries. From the time of Pope John XXII (1316-34) papal dispensations for the sons of priests as priests and even bishops were granted freely. Bishop Lochloinn II, unable as recidivist to persuade the primate to absolve him again from censures for breaches of celibacy, secured absolution in Rome in 1476, doubtless by sweetening officials there.

To give them their due, the O'Gallaghers were not the first Raphoe bishops who showed laxity in celibacy. In the fourteenth century two monks of Assaroe, of the family MacCormack O'Donnell of Corca Baiscinn, became bishops of Raphoe. Thomas (1319-37) mortgaged the lands of Tír mac Cáerthainn (apparently between Kerrykeel and Ramelton) to his concubine, Honora, daughter of 'McSwyne Ree' (of Fanad?). MacSweeney in turn mortgaged them to O'Donnell. Conor (1367-97) in his turn mortgaged Loughros to Margaret, daughter of Shiughey O'Boyle. Successive bishops sought in vain the return of these lands.[2]

In the parishes hereditary erenagh families managed the glebe lands and often supplied the clergy: the O'Devenneys in Kilteevogue and Raphoe parishes (as well as in Derry diocese); the O'Mulgeehs or Magees in Clondahorkey; the O'Friels in Termon and Kilmacrenan; the Conwells (Mic Congail) in Killybegs; and so on. As old families died out or lost out, new dynasties took their place.[3] The O'Clerys, established in the early fourteenth century in Kilbarron, became hereditary ollavs (chroniclers and poets) to the O'Donnells, and at times supplied Kilbarron parish with its priests.[4] Two of the Mac Congail family, Pádraig (d. 1366) and Domhnall (1562-89), became bishops. As did the MacCongail, so also the O'Gallaghers (in the persons of Bishops Edmund and Art) and the O'Devenneys (in that of Conor, OFM, bishop of Down and Connor, martyred in 1612) provided zealous counter-reformation bishops.

Although the medieval bishop received a third share of the produce of the parish glebe, he depended much more upon *refectiones,* whereby he and his retinue were quartered, once or oftener in a three-month period, on the freeholders. Thus all the copyhold, and not only the erenagh, lands contributed towards episcopal maintenance. It would appear that Bishop Conor O'Cahan, who had accepted the royal supremacy, abolished the system of refections, demanding instead of 'bread and beere' their monetary equivalent. That Conor ever enjoyed much recognition within the Tír Chonaill diocese is doubtful, and he may have wished to avoid 'lying upon'[5] the different erenaghs, vicars and parsons (or parish priests), as bishops coshering did. If the tenants found the monetary duty lighter, they in turn may have been tolerably satisfied with the change.

The revenues from church lands were sometimes appropriated by the O'Donnells, especially in a period of episcopal vacancy, to maintain their gallowglasses or to hire mercenaries from Scotland. Toirdhealbhach an Fhíona (1380-1422) detained lands and tithes belonging to the see of Derry. His son, Niall Garbh II, imposed a burdensome taxation to finance his struggle with the O'Neills for supremacy in Ulster. Niall's brother and successor, Nechtan, when an episcopal vacancy occurred in 1442, claimed spiritual and temporal custodianship of the diocese. Primate John Prene intervened strongly, declaring Nechtan a heretic and depriving dean and chapter of Raphoe of their benefices. He even removed the famous Cross of Raphoe to Armagh. Prene called upon the O'Neills as secular arm to execute the sentence of deposition upon Nechtan. This gave the O'Neills of west Tyrone the opportunity of seizing Cenél Móen, the territory (also known as Magh Íotha) lying between Lifford and Ballybofey, and Nechtan had to yield up his strategic Castle Finn.[6]

II

Raphoe had a number of male religious houses.[7] The Cistercian abbey of Samaria, or Assaroe, was founded between 1178 and 1184. A daughter-house, Kilfothuir (Churchminster, near Clonleigh), founded in 1194, was not successful and later became a grange, or outlying farm. At first noted for its fervour, Assaroe, like other Cistercian abbeys, suffered from laxity and laicisation. Giolla in Choimded (*fl. c.*1300), ancestor of the O'Gallagher septs, was it seems a Cistercian monk of Assaroe. In the last twenty years of the fourteenth century the monastery became an O'Donnell fortification against the O'Neills. In the following century the abbacy (whose fruits in 1426 were valued at 16 marks annually) was a prize to be contended for by ambitious clerics. Although Father Conway ranks Edmund O'Gallagher as only a commendatory abbot, he appointed the monk Patrick Obrayn to the grange of Kilfothuir in 1436.[8] A later struggle gained the abbacy for Canon Art O'Gallagher, son of Bishop Lochloinn II and rector of Killaghtee. He held it between 1489 and his death at Assaroe in 1502. His son, dean of Raphoe, died in 1538.[9]

There was, Conway believes, a great improvement in the quality of Irish Cistercianism in the years after 1498. But when we find Abbot Edmund Diver going to Donegal to take the Franciscan habit in which he died (1519), it appears as if now the *locus* for asceticism had shifted from Assaroe.

Of the four mendicant orders, the Dominicans had made foundations in Coleraine (1249) and Derry (1274), the latter foundation, in Tír Chonaill, being perhaps made by Donal O'Donnell. The Augustinians too were on the borders of Raphoe, at Devenish, Derry and Fahan. Inishowen, then, in Donegal but in Derry diocese, came under the influence of the Friars Preachers, the Augustinians and (at Balleghan in Raphoe) the Observant Franciscans. Equally, parts of Raphoe came under Dominican and Augustinian influences. Among both these last orders, the observant reform was adopted by houses which remained conventual but the Franciscan observants fashioned a new jurisdictional organisation. Given the piety of Mary MacSweeney, who founded or re-founded the Carmelites at Rathmullan in 1516,[10] and the strength of the observant reform in Tír Chonaill, it may be accepted that this St Mary's Priory shared in the reform ideals. It is notable how closely associated with this powerful observant movement of the fifteenth and sixteenth centuries were Tír Chonaill's leading families, particularly the O'Donnells and the three MacSweeneys, of Fanad, Doe and Banagh. These families vied with each other in setting up Third Order Regular (Order of Penitence) Franciscan friaries: Magherabeg (1430);

Ballymacswiney (1464), just south-west of Doe Castle; Killydonnell and Balleghan (both 1471); Ballysaggart, in St John's Point (after 1500); and Killybegs. At Kilmacrenan Magnus O'Donnell, probably the chief of that name (1537-63), founded a Third Order friary adjacent to the old Columban monastery.[11]

In founding the friaries the grandees no doubt saw various advantages: the recognition accorded a founder; spiritual benefits of masses and prayers; the opportunity for warrior chieftains to spend their last days in the penitential habit; and, by no means least, involvement in this exciting reform movement. O'Donnell, and to a lesser degree his sub-chieftains, were conscious of their obligation to maintain religious as well as civil order. At worst, this obligation was discharged by Aodh Dubh (1505-37), when he refused to tolerate the violation of churches by his troops on campaign; and at best when O'Donnell or his lady furthered the reform.

Something of the history of the friary of Donegal is known; of the house of 'the friars of Mary' at Rathmullan a little; of the rest of the Third Order Franciscan houses hardly anything. Donegal was founded as an observant friary by Aodh Rua and his wife Nuala O'Brien in 1474. One of their sons became a Franciscan; his father took the habit and was buried in the friary in 1505; and Nuala (who had become a Franciscan tertiary after her husband's death) was buried there in 1528. Donegal prospered, and in time sent friars to establish the reform in Carrickfergus (1497) and at Dromahair. The observant reform spread to the other Franciscan friaries in Ulster, including Cavan (1502) and, later, Armagh.[12]

The reform affected in the first place the brethren, but also secular clergy and laity. As well as leading lives of regular observance, the friars undertook both pastoral work and teaching of boys, this latter with obvious effect on the training of priests for the diocese. At Rathmullan, the Carmelite church was much frequented by the laity and clergy of the neighbouring district. Donal Ó Cradhain, a rich and charitable merchant, dropped dead at mass one morning in 1506 in Donegal (friary?).[13] The two things receiving incidental mention, mass attendance and the charity of a good man, are taken for granted. Much that was taken for granted is not mentioned, e.g. the prayer, work, preaching and teaching of the friars, their visitation of the sick and needy, the whole effect on the districts around of their presence.

Between old Assaroe and its granges (lying outside Raphoe), the eight Franciscan houses and Rathmullan Carmelite priory, there must have been quite a number of religious in Tír Chonaill for most of the fifteenth and all of the sixteenth centuries. In 1600 the Franciscans had rebuilt Donegal friary, which had been sacked and pillaged three times by the English, and again were forty in number. Must we think of years when regulars numbered a hundred at least and outnumbered the diocesan clergy by far? No record of nuns in Raphoe is found in Gwynn and Hadcock, but there appear to have been Augustinian and, later, Cistercian nuns at Derry.

There may be something in the claim that the parochial structure, even after three hundred years or more, had never really replaced in the hearts of the people the old monastic system. It can be no accident that the great literary work produced in Tír Chonaill before the shades were lowered on the Gaelic world was that masterwork accredited to Manus O'Donnell, *The Life of Colum Cille* (1532). But the *Life* betrays no bias against the secular clergy.[14] The authors know that the church has a hierarchy of bishops, priests, deacons and students preparing for the priesthood. They are very matter-of-fact in their acceptance of clerical failings and the failings of society generally. A famous lampoon, this time Manus's own composition, was directed not at one of the parish clergy but at some local Friar Tuck:

Bráthair boch brúite ó fhíon,
ná dúisgthear é, gion gur cóir . . .[15]

But sins, social and individual, are recognised for what they are, and a striking passage in the *Life* which relates the conquest of the Gael to crimes of injustice and the destruction of churches[16] sounds like an echo of the annals, when they attribute deaths to divine retribution, perhaps brought about by the prayers of the saints.[17] But when the *Life* goes on to speak of the sins of a cleric with someone's wife, it is in the tone of those who know that such misdemeanours must be.[18]

The *Life* and *Leabhar Chlainne Suibhne*, as Walsh names the manuscript (R.I.A., 24 P 25), written for Mary (d. 1523), wife of MacSweeney Fanad, by Ciothruadh Mac Fhionnghaill,[19] taken together reveal, unconsciously for the most part, a vigorous and strongly sacramental practice of religion in Tír Chonaill, with mass and confession, the latter with blessing by a priest and imposition of penance. Penance with good works is necessary for salvation, and penance is one motive for pilgrimage to Rome. One man went on pilgrimage himself and paid for fifty others who wanted to go but had not the means.[20] When the annals record the pilgrimage made by some great man, we are hardly to understand that he went unaccompanied. Hearing mass, St Colum Cille held his hands raised; was this a common practice? On Sundays the MacSweeney household (Turlough MacSweeney had a standing retinue of 150 men, besides wives and other womenfolk, musicians, poets, and inferior servants) went to mass to Clondavaddog parish church, where they used to lay eight score hilted swords, ornamented with gold and silver, on the altar. The party brought with them, at least on great feasts, twelve score satchels, made from dog-skins, filled with books and musical instruments.[21] Chance preserves this extraordinary account of one parish liturgy. A horn of the identical ram that Murchadh Mac Suibhne captured on the Fortunate Isle was used as wine vessel at Killydonnell Friary, having previously been in use at Gleann Éile, another parish church.[22] The matins bell, *cluic an medhóin*, was a sound familiar in Tír Chonaill, with its many friaries, and office in choir might have layfolk in attendance. The saints are honoured: Patrick, Brigid and a host of others paying tribute to Colum Cille, the (for Tír Chonaill) nonpareil; the masters of asceticism, led appropriately by Matthew the Evangelist (who presents Jesus as the Teacher), and including Ambrose, Augustine, Gregory, Bernard the Cistercian and Bonaventure the Franciscan; and above all Mary the mother of God. The companions of Mary's compassion will share with her in glory.[23]

As with the local church, so with the holy see. Renaissance moral decline or traffic in provisions do not enter into the *Life*'s view of the papacy, supreme spiritual and religious authority. Emphasising over and over the spiritual friendship which tradition held existed between Pope Gregory the Great – *Grighóir béil-óir* – and Columba, the *Life* puts stress on the holiness of the pope and on Colum Cille's approval by Rome. But the distinction between human and divine applies to the pope too, as the sixteenth-century authors are well aware: the mass is the same, whether offered by monk, priest (even unworthy), bishop, or even the pope – *ar altóir móir teampaill Petair sa Róim.*[24]

III

Sixtus IV sent an Italian reformer, Octavian, to Armagh, and in 1479 a Roman priest, Giovanni de Rogeriis, as bishop of Raphoe. In his brief reign of under three years he took stern action, including even interdiction of mass and the sacraments in the diocese, in an effort to recover the extensive church lands alienated (as noted above) by two of his predecessors.[25] His successor was Meanma MacCormack (1482-1514), an Oxford man, who had been dean under Giovanni. His adherence to the reform movement is evident in his collaboration with Primate Octavian: he took an oath of obedience to him on 16 July 1484 and attended four provincial synods summoned by Octavian. Incapacitated by old age and illness, it was said, he resigned on 6 February 1514 and died fifteen months later as a friar in the leading reform house of the north, Donegal.

But a major obstacle in the way of a thorough reformation 'in head and members' was the constricting embrace of the strong centralising new monarchs of western Europe. Henry VIII secured the appointment of the next bishop of Raphoe, Cornelius O'Cahan, clerk of Derry diocese, dispensed for illegitimacy.[26] Henry had a reason for so doing. Pope Julius II, fearful of the French threat to papal independence, had formed a Holy League, including Henry VIII, which in 1511 drove the French invaders of Italy back across the Alps.

France's defeat meant that James IV of Scotland was in great peril from Henry, now in aggressive mood against Scotland. Aodh Dubh O'Donnell was very keenly aware of this danger to Scotland – and to himself. His father Aodh Rua had broken the O'Neill supremacy in the north and had established O'Donnell as the great name in the whole northwest, in Tír Chonaill (including Inishowen), in Fermanagh, and in north Connacht. Vital to O'Donnell's strategy were the alliances with the Kildare FitzGeralds and with Edinburgh, which went back to the early 1490s. In 1510 Aodh Dubh visited London for sixteen weeks: went on to Rome; and returned again to the court of King Henry, who knighted him on 13 February 1511.[27] It would be much to have the record of the bold O'Donnell's conversations with Henry and with Julius II; but alas! no such record has come to light.

But it would seem that an English knighthood did not buy O'Donnell's allegiance. Hugh the Black took his politics neither from Rome nor from London. For him Henry's was a bear's embrace. It was England that threatened Tír Chonaill's independence. But he knew that Henry was in no position to do him injury if he remained resolute and maintained his alliances. Home he went to renew pressure upon Tír Eóghain and upon Connacht;[28] he failed however to take Sligo Castle. Meanwhile the warlike Henry VIII in the summer of 1513 invaded France. James invited O'Donnell to Edinburgh, and the Irish chief spent three months there, while James made preparations for war by land and sea. On 25 June James concluded a formal alliance with O'Donnell. The Scottish king was strong for an attack on England through Ireland, but O'Donnell knew that his failure to take Sligo made an assault from Tír Chonaill on the Pale too hazardous, and Garret More agreed with him. After much persuasion, Aodh Dubh managed to bring James around to this view. The death of the Great Earl of Kildare on 8 July was a terrible blow to the alliance. Nevertheless, James decided to go ahead with an attack upon England. But on 9 September his army was routed at Flodden, on which field James himself took his death-wound.

Sir Hugh O'Donnell wrote to King Henry from Donegal Castle, 12.1.1514, disavowing any sinister purpose in visiting James.[29] He was beyond the reach of Henry. But there was at hand a cleric whose people were O'Donnell's enemies and who was later to prove his loyalty to Henry in the latter's breach with Rome. How he came to the English monarch's notice we do not know for certain, but his appointment constituted a royal rap on O'Donnell's knuckles.

Over the next twenty years the main ecclesiastical interest in Raphoe and in Derry is the resurgence of the O'Gallaghers; this has been documented by the late Fr Gwynn, in his distinguished study of the Armagh registers.[30] In England Thomas Cromwell in 1533-4 pushed through the English parliament legislation that enacted schism between England and Rome. The house of Kildare fell in the years 1534-5, and in 1536 the 'reformation parliament' held in Dublin among other enactments recognised King Henry as 'supreme head on earth of the whole church of Ireland' (25 Hen VIII, c. 5) and forbade appeals to Rome (c. 6). In 1535 in England seven English Carthusians, a secular priest, and then Bishop John Fisher and Sir Thomas More were all executed for denying the supremacy.

These were dismaying events, 'directly repugnant' (said More) 'to the laws of God and his holy church'. Others thought so too, and in Ireland the revolt of Silken Thomas (who asserted that Henry, a heretic, had forfeited Ireland, granted by a pope to an English king) received support from some Anglo-Irish churchmen. This was, says Canon Jourdan, 'the first notable instance of ecclesiastics, for religious reasons', joining in rebellion against the English crown.[31] Rome now in a surprise move provided Edmund, son of Brian O'Gallagher, of Sliocht an Easbuig, dean of Derry, to the see of Raphoe, on 11 May 1534. The provision, asserting that the diocese was vacant since the death of Meanma MacCormack, ignored Conor O'Cahan.[32] Edmund was succeeded as dean of Derry by Art son of Féilim Fionn, of Sliocht Áedha.

In recording Edmund's death in 1543 the annals (Loch Cé, followed by the Four Masters) say that he had 'received great opposition'. This was indeed the case. Not only was he opposed by Conor, but also by his own first cousin, Edmund son of Art (d. 1538) and by Art son of Felim Fionn. For some years before he became chieftain in 1537 Manus O'Donnell had been in opposition to his father, with the support apparently of a section of Sliocht an Easbuig.[33] Bishop Edmund was Aodh Dubh's man, and he probably also had the support of Aodh Dubh's nephew, Bishop Rory O'Donnell of Derry (1520-50/51). Manus sought at Rome to have Edmund's appointment nullified, first proposing Edmund son of Art in his place and then, from at least July 1536, Art son of Féilim Fionn.

Clement VII's appointment of Edmund does not seem related to the Geraldine rebellion, for, contrary to what might have been expected,

Aodh Dubh had not only not supported Silken Thomas, but his threatened invasion of Tír Eóghain had forced O'Neill in November 1534 to withdraw from a planned attack on the Pale in support of FitzGerald.[34] The old O'Donnell-O'Neill conflict over local hegemony and over border lands was too strong for any shoot of nationalism to sprout in O'Donnell's garden. Fr Gwynn's guess that what brought about Bishop Edmund's appointment was his successful representation at Rome that Meanma's resignation had not been valid[35] would seem well founded.

But Manus was reported in June 1535, and perhaps with some truth, to be planning in concert with the king of Scotland and O'Neill to attack the Pale.[36] In supporting Manus's petition at Rome to be allowed to marry Eleanor, sister of Garret Óg and widow of Donal MacCarthy Reagh, James V argued that this would support the cause of religious opposition to Henry VIII's new doctrine and proposed that Art O'Gallagher be made bishop of Raphoe.[37] But in July Lord Deputy Skeffington won over O'Neill, and there was no invasion.[38] However, Edmund O'Gallagher consolidated his position sufficiently in Raphoe for Conor O'Cahan to remove to the Pale, where in 1536 he was granted English citizenship, afterwards being collated to Athlumney vicarage in Meath diocese. Doubts were now cast on the liceity of Edmund's provision, but efforts by James V, Bishop Rory O'Donnell and Manus (who succeeded as O'Donnell in 1537), to have Rome set aside Edmund's provision proved unavailing, in spite of a strong offer by Manus to lead, at Rome's bidding, a campaign by 'a great part of Ireland and all the bishops and religious houses' against the Antichrist Henry, who had assumed papal power.[39] However, Rome did appoint Manus's envoy, Canon Art O'Friel, to the archdiocese of Tuam.

IV

In April 1538 Manus O'Donnell married Eleanor FitzGerald, aunt of the boy Gerald, who was half-brother of Silken Thomas, in his castle of Donegal, with Conn O'Neill among those in attendance. In November or December Manus took Sligo Castle, a key position in any attack by O'Neill and O'Donnell on the Pale. And on 23 June 1539 a solemn treaty, witnessed by the poets, the entire community of friars at Donegal and Archbishop O'Friel, between Tadhg O'Conor Sligo and Manus made the latter's control of the castle secure. Among the signatories were Edmund, bishop of Raphoe, and Edmund, dean of Derry.[40] The Tudors had consolidated royal power in England and now, following upon the crushing of the Kildare rebellion, Henry VIII seemed bent on making monarchical control effective in Ireland. The forces of independence were, however, still strong in the country, and Gerald FitzGerald was made the figure-head of continuing resistance. Henry's programme included not only political and military supremacy but also religious, and this latter pretension, against 'the general council of Christendom',[41] had in Tír Chonaill proved a solvent of the difference between the two Edmunds and between one of them (the bishop) and Manus. Art O'Gallagher now recedes into the background, not to emerge again until four years after Edmund's death. As for Conor O'Cahan, it seems likely that he attended at least some sessions of the parliament of 1536-7. His grant of English liberty may have been, partly at least, to facilitate his attendance.

Thus, under the leadership of Manus O'Donnell and his cousin the bishop of Derry, the Geraldine League[42] forged very close bonds with the papacy. A number of Tír Conaill clerics – Bishop Rory and his dean, Edmund O'Gallagher; that dean's cousin, Bishop Edmund of Raphoe; and Archbishop O'Friel – were now emerging as among the first leaders of the counter-reformation clergy. O'Friel, because of local opposition, was ineffective in Tuam. But in Derry Rory O'Donnell was without rival; and in Raphoe Edmund O'Gallagher had ousted his Henrician rival. In Raphoe too the Franciscans of Donegal (and the other religious) were loyal to the holy see. Paul III hoped for some result from the alliance between the League and King James, and the pope's interest was known to, and indeed exaggerated by, the administration.[43]

Diplomatic activity between Donegal, Edinburgh and Rome now heightened; while Lord Leonard Grey, who in this summer had been successful in conciliating the southern chiefs, now made overtures to O'Donnell,[44] but without response. An envoy from O'Donnell to Rome, Roger O'Spellan, O.Cist., of Knockmoy, was captured and put to death. O'Donnell's letter to Paul III, dated 31.12.1538, which O'Spellan carried, disclosed that the four archbishops had now withdrawn their allegiance from Rome.[45] On June 17 Staples, bishop of Meath, recommended that bishops holding bulls from Rome be required to surrender them for cancellation,[46] and there can be little doubt that Conor O'Cahan, now in Staples' jurisdiction, was so required.

O'Donnell's plan was supported by an army of 6,000 Scots mercenaries, 'Redshanks' (to be provided by King James and MacDonnell of the Isles), to attack the Pale and destroy the English colony. This strategy, originating with Manus, who also sought aid from the emperor and the king of France, remained fundamental to the military thinking of the northern chieftains until the end of the sixteenth century.[47] Meanwhile, 'the friers and preestes of all the

Yrishtree, not oneley of Odownelles country', were preaching a religious war, in which death was viewed as martyrdom. In 1540 the vicar provincial of the Irish Franciscan Observants visited both emperor and pope, seeking aid to prevent Ireland being won for the reformation, as England had been.[48]

But the summer came without the large army of Redshanks sought. To keep the alliance alive it was necessary to risk a challenge to government. Soon after the pope had publicly announced his decision to suspend Primate Cromer (who had given spiritual allegiance to the crown) and appoint an administrator in his stead, the Irish armies, on their incursion into the Pale, were met and defeated at Lake Bellahoe, on the border of Meath and Monaghan. The insurrection of May 1540, after Grey's departure for England, seemed to nullify the lord deputy's victory, but the reality was different. Lady Eleanor's suspicions had been aroused that her nephew Gerald would be betrayed by her husband Manus, and in February she had the boy sent abroad. The coalition had lost its inspiration, and the way was open for a new lord deputy, St Leger, who landed in August 1540, to offer the chiefs a new and honourable relationship with the crown, in return for their submission.[49]

Thus it was that Manus, Conn Bacach and other lords submitted, accepting in effect the sovereign state and repudiating the pope's spiritual supremacy. Bishops Rory O'Donnell and Hugh O'Carolan of Clogher joined the ranks of bishops accepting royal supremacy.[50] There was no question of Edmund O'Gallagher seeking, or obtaining, recognition from the crown, so O'Cahan remained bishop of Raphoe. By late 1543 Henry could claim the allegiance of every bishop in Armagh province, except Edmund and the bishop of Dromore. Henry's bishops of course were expected to retain the familiar mass and sacraments. Prospects for the wide acceptance of the Anglican settlement in the north seemed very favourable, especially as there was now good prospect of political stability. But such a prospect was not to be realised, and this was fatal for the religious settlement.

Yet the counter-reformation had lost the first round in the independent north. The pope suspended Cromer in 1539 and appointed Robert Wauchop, a Scot, administrator of Armagh. Wauchop, unable to come to Ireland, turned to the Jesuits for help. But when two Jesuits, Salmeron and Broet, arrived in Derry from Edinburgh in March 1542, they were unable, although bearing credentials from the pope, to secure a meeting with O'Neill and O'Donnell. Manus, Nicodemus-like, offered to meet them secretly, but this was unacceptable to the papal envoys. They did meet one bishop, who can only have been Edmund O'Gallagher[51] and who must have made them aware that for the time being no support was to be hoped for from the chiefs.

Now, remarkably, the O'Gallagher dynasty produced its counter-reformation champions, Bishop Edmund; his successor Art; and Redmond, O.S.A. (?of what sept), bishop of Killala in 1545 and then of Derry from 1569 until his death at the hands of English soldiers in 1601. He was one of those bishops who made common cause of religion and politics and helped to launch the Nine Year's War.[52]

Rome delayed the appointment of a successor to Edmund O'Gallagher (d. 26.2.1543). The temporal lord, O'Donnell, and two bishops deep in his counsels had accepted royal supremacy. Besides (something that has gone unnoticed) Manus on Bishop Edmund's death imposed exactions on church lands and also raised the rents accruing to the bishop which, as declared custodian of the temporalities, he now appropriated. Up until the council of Trent, Rome did not provide to sees unless the temporalities were assured. Aware of Manus's game, the lord deputy and council in this year caused him to pledge himself, as they also did Conn O'Neill, to permit 'Bishops and other ecclesiastical persons ... to have their ecclesiastical patrimonies free from all exactions and bonaughts'.[53] But, true machiavellian, Manus ignored his own pledge. The demands of his war-chest and the splendid state maintained by him at his courts of Lifford and Donegal must be met.[54] In Armagh the seizure of primatial property by the O'Neill of the day (Bishop Montgomery incorrectly thought that Shane the Proud was the first to do so) was a recurring problem for the archbishops. In Tír Chonaill, Nechtan O'Donnell (1439-52) had anticipated his great-grandnephew Manus in such seizure. In the end, with his son Calvagh in revolt (as he himself had revolted against *his* father), Manus, who was depending upon Art's Sliocht Áedha for support, was, as it seems, at this juncture ready to remove a barrier to Art's provision by yielding up his unlawful custody of the temporalities of the diocese. Calvagh and his half-brother Hugh were now embarked upon a rivalry which their descendants would carry on until the end of the century.

Art was provided as bishop on 5.12.1547. It is unlikely that he received any real opposition from Conor O'Cahan. The Dublin administration treated O'Donnell with kid gloves. In 1543 they decided in his favour in his dispute with Con O'Neill over the lordship of Inishowen. As they wrote to the council of England (5.6.1543):

> ... for keeping galloglasses and for breaking all his promises to come to Parliament Odonell deserves to be scourged, yet considering bruit of war with Scotland and France, and the intended reformation of Laynster as soon as money comes, they dare not ruffle with him without express command.

They also secured the appointment by the king of Connacht O'Shiel, abbot of Assaroe and O'Donnell's chaplain, to the bishopric of Elphin in 1544.[55]

Bishop O'Cahan very likely assisted at the consecration of George Dowdall as king's archbishop of Armagh, late in 1543, and equally likely subscribed to the oath of supremacy.[56] Whether Rory O'Donnell did likewise, in both cases, may be in question. Conor was resident within the Pale, and so was more amenable to the administration's will. In 1544, styled bishop of Raphoe, he was one of the two presidents of a synod called by George Dowdall, primate by mandate of the king, to Drogheda in July.[57] But in 1550, when he was granted licence of absence from his vicarage for life, he was merely styled vicar of Athlumney.[58] Art O'Gallagher had so secured his position in Raphoe that Conor ceased even to lay claim to it. He probably did not long survive the grant of this licence.

Art O'Gallagher remained bishop through the reigns of Edward VI and Mary, dying in 1561 in Elizabeth's time. At his death the reformation had gained no footing in Raphoe, and churches and religious houses remained in place. It is unlikely that he did anything to reform the old hereditary ecclesiastical family system, of which he himself was a product, or to check the seeking of provisions from Rome. In fact, at his death Fr David Wolf, SJ, papal representative, noted that 'fourteen persons have left Ireland without letters from me', all seeking to be bishop. Wolf had to fall back on an associate, who happened to be a member of one of the old ecclesiastical families, Domhnall Mac Congail or Conwell, to send to Rome to be indoctrinated in the programme of the Council of Trent, then in session, and to be made bishop.[59] When as late as 1600 the two Hughs, O'Neill and O'Donnell, are found petitioning Rome that illegitimates, even sons of priests, may be ordained, it is obvious that little has changed.[60]

In fact, from 1596 these particular two allies had been seeking control over all ecclesiastical appointments in Ireland.[61] Thus, in Raphoe and in the north of Ireland generally, the confusion between politics and religion, which owed origin, natural perhaps in the circumstances, to the Geraldine League and was perpetuated by the two Hughs in their war, was compounded by the perdurance of the old hereditary system. Niall O'Boyle, bishop of Raphoe (1591-c.1611), was able, it seems, to make the distinction between faith and fatherland, but he was strongly opposed by his senior clergy.[62] Thus as, in the defeat of O'Neill and O'Donnell, the military shield collapsed, the question was, how would this traditional and divided church of Raphoe meet the challenge of the new century?

References

1. B.L., Add MS 4797, f. 48, A catalogue of the Bishops of Rapho to the year 1600 (hereafter *Cat.*) On the O'Gallaghers, see P. Walsh, 'Septs of Muintear Ghallchubhair' in *Irish Book Lover*, xxvii (1940) pp 194-200; repr. in P. Walsh, *Irish chiefs and leaders*, ed. C. Ó Lochlainn (Dublin, 1960), pp 206-15.

2. *Cat.; Inquisitionum in officio rotulorum cancellariae asservatarum repertorium*, 2 vols (Dublin, 1826-9), ii: *Ultonia*, app. v, 'Donegall' (hereafter *Inq.*). This is the place to correct a slip confusing the two McCormack bishops with Lochloinn II, in my 'Some aspects of the reformation in Armagh province' in *Clogher Rec.*, xi (1984), p. 346.

3. Details in *Annats, Ulster*. P. Ó Gallachair, 'Coarbs and erenaghs of county Donegal', in *Donegal Annual*, iv (1960), pp 272-81, lists the erenagh families as given in the 1609 inquisitions.

4. P. Walsh, *The Ó Cléirigh family of Tír Conaill* (Dublin, 1938).

5. *Inq.*

6. *A.F.M.*, 1442; W. Reeves (ed.), *Acts of Archbishop Colton* (Dublin, 1850), p. xv; W. Harris (ed.), *The whole works of Sir James Ware* (Dublin, 2nd ed., 1764), i, pp 273-4.

7. Details in A. Gwynn and R. N. Hadcock, *Medieval religious houses, Ireland* (London, 1970), *passim;* Colmcille Conway, 'Abbey Assaroe' in T. O'Donnell (ed.), *Father John Colgan, O.F.M., 1592-1658* (Dublin, 1959), pp 111-29; C. Mooney, 'The friars and friary of Donegal, 1474-1840' in T. O'Donnell (ed.), *Franciscan Donegal* (Ros Nuala, 1952), pp 3-49; P. O'Dwyer, 'The Carmelites in pre-reformation Ireland' in *I.E.R.*, cx (1968), pp 350-63.

8. *Annats Ulster*,pp 221-2.

9. A. Gwynn, *The medieval province of Armagh* (Dundalk, 1946), pp 199-200.

10. Gwynn and Hadcock, *Medieval religious houses*, p. 291, repeat Leask's error about the founder.

11. S. Ó Domhnaill, 'Some notes on Third Order Regular houses in Donegal' in O'Donnell (ed.), *Franciscan Donegal*, pp 97-104.

12. *A.F.M.*, 1507, 1508.

13. *A.F.M.*

14. A. O'Kelleher and G. Schoepperle (ed.), *Betha Colaim Chille: life of Columcille* (Urbana, 1918). Hereafter *B.C.C.*

15. T. F. O'Rahilly (ed.), *Dánfhocail* (Dublin, 1921), pp 77-8.

16. *B.C.C.*, par 127.

17. e.g. *A.U.*, 950.

18. *B.C.C.*, par 19.

19. Ciothruadh was from Tory. One suspects an old scribal tradition on the island.

20. *B.C.C.*, par 140.

21. *L.C.S.*, p. 36.

22. *L.C.S.*, p. 28.

23. *B.C.C.*, par 19.

24. *B.C.C.*, par 88.

25. The Catalogue's account of this bishop's activity was apparently overlooked by Gwynn, *Armagh*, p. 198.

26. Konrad Eubel, *Hierarchia catholica medii aevi* (3 vols, Münster, 1898-1910), iii (2n ed., 1923), p. 299.

27. *L.P.*, i, pt II, no 26 of App.; cf *A.U.*, 1511; E. Curtis, A *history of medieval Ireland, 1086-1513* (2nd ed., 1938), p. 360.

28. *A.F.M.*, 1512.

29. Curtis, *Medieval Ireland*, p. 362, citing H. Ellis, *Original letters illustrative of English history* (First and second series, London, 1827), i, pp 224-5.

30. Gwynn, *Armagh*, pp 201-9.

31. In W. A. Phillips (ed.), *History of the church of Ireland* (3 vols, Oxford, 1933-4), ii, pp 202-3.

32. Gwynn, *Armagh*, pp 201-2.

33. *A.L.C.*, 1531, 1536, 1537; *A.F.M.*, at same dates.

34. Cowley to Cromwell, 8.4.1539 (*S.P.*, 111.145).

35. Gwynn, *Armagh*, p. 202.

36. *L.P.*, viii, no 885.

37. James V to Pope Paul III, 1.7.1538 (*Anal. Hib.*, xii (1943), pp 179-81).

38. *Cal. pat. rolls Ire., Hen. VIII – Eliz.*, i, p. 23; Sir J. Ware, *Bishops* with annotations by Todd and Reeves. T.C.D., Ms 1120, p. 274; Gwynn, *Armagh*, p. 128.

39. James V to Paul III, 1.7.1538; Gwynn, *Armagh*, pp 207-8. The Irish gentleman mentioned, Cromwell to Cranmer, 14.1.1538 *L.P.*, xiii (i), nos 76, 77, is perceptively identified by Gwynn, *Armagh*, pp 224-6, as Manus. This has been missed by L. McCorristine, *Revolt of Silken Thomas* (Dublin, 1987), p. 165.

40. M. Carney (ed.), 'Agreement concerning Sligo Castle' in *I.H.S.*, iii (1944), p. 284.

41. More's careful phrase. R. S. Sylvester (ed.), *St Thomas More: action and contemplation* (New Haven, 1972), p. 45.

42. There is no good study of the League; but see B. Bradshaw, *The Irish constitutional revolution of the sixteenth century* (Cambridge, 1979), pp 174-83. The union of Manus and Eleanor brought in important allies (see *L.P.*, xiii (i), nos 1138, 1139, 1160, 1259, 1647).

43. Alen to Cromwell, 10.7.1539 (*S.P.*, iii. 136).

44. P. Wilson, *The beginnings of modern Ireland* (Dublin and London, 1912), p. 214. Deposition by Martin Pelles, 1540 (*L.P.*, xvi, no 304, p. 12; see ibid., xiii (ii), p. 830).

45. Gwynn, *Armagh*, pp 230-2.

46. *Cal. Carew MSS*, i, p. 141.

47. J. J. Silke, *Kinsale: the Spanish intervention in Ireland at the end of the Elizabethan wars* (Liverpool and New York, 1970), pp 6, 56, 76-87.

48. Thomas Lynch's deposition (shortly after midsummer) 1539 (*S.P.*, iii, p. 141, n.1 (*L.P.*, xiv (i), 1245.3).

49. Wilson, *Modern Ireland*, pp 223-9; Bradshaw, *Constitutional revolution*, p. 183.

50. Gwynn, *Armagh*, pp 253, 257-8.

51. Gwynn, *Armagh*, p. 252, inexplicably says that the bishop was 'almost certainly' Rory O'Donnell. He forgets about Edmund O'Gallagher. If the nuncios would not receive, even secretly, a compromised Manus, neither would they Rory.

52. J. J. Silke, 'Some aspects of the reformation in Armagh province' in *Clogher Rec.*, xi (1984), p. 353.

53. *Cal. Carew MSS*, i, p. 207.

54. Among loans to be repaid to the queen in an Account of Payments for 1563-4 we find, 'To Manus Odonnell, 23rd April, 1564, £200' (Fitzwilliam MSS, doc 11, cited *Anal. Hib.*, (1932) p. 296). B. Bradshaw, 'Manus "the Magnificent": O'Donnell as a renaissance prince' in D. McCartney *et al* (ed.), *Studies in Irish history presented to R. Dudley Edwards* (Dublin, 1979), pp 23-4, in advancing or, rather, reviving the thesis of Manus as renaissance prince, falls into the original error of making Manus the author of *B.C.C.* Again, in the 'evidence' he offers for making the Donegal friars exponents of Christian humanism (op. cit., p. 19; *The dissolution of the religious orders in Ireland under Henry VIII* (Cambridge, 1974),

pp 13-14), Bradshaw seems to confuse the shedding of blood with the just war. See Silke, 'Some aspects of the reformation', p. 348. Curiously, this scholar entirely misses Manus's strong-minded and clever manipulation of the episcopal revenues, which involved putting in some of his clients as erenaghs. There is of course a case to be made for Manus being affected by renaissance influences. His father had viewed at first hand the renaissance courts of Rome, London and Edinburgh, and he himself was familiar with Edinburgh at least. But he came of a formidable line of princes, well versed in statecraft and not entirely parochial in outlook.

55.   *L.P.*, xviii (i), no. 650.
56.   Gwynn, *Armagh*, p. 263.
57.   Public Library, Armagh. Dowdall Register (transcript), f 34v.
58.   Calendar of fiants, Edward VI (Public Record Office of Ireland, *Reports of Deputy-Keeper 7-22*), no. 38.
59.   M.V. Ronan, *The reformation in Ireland under Elizabeth, 1536-1558* (London, 1930), p. 91.
60.   *Archiv. Hib.*, ii (1913), p. 312.
61.   Ibid., pp 280-1.
62.   Ibid., pp 294-5.

Chapter 10

PLANTATION IN DONEGAL

R. J. HUNTER

This chapter seeks to present a short survey of the plantation in Donegal against a background of the general plan of plantation in Ulster and to examine in more detail its impact in one area of Donegal. It will also consider the circumstances and effects of its establishment prior to 1641.

The plantation plan

The decision to carry out a plantation in Ulster was based on two considerations: fear and opportunism. If the earls returned, argued Lord Deputy Chichester, expressing his anxieties for security, 'they will assuredly land in Ulster', while to Sir Geoffrey Fenton, an old government official with many years of Irish experience, a 'door [was] opened' to the king now 'to pull down for ever these two proud houses of O'Neill and O'Donnell'. Through plantation, Chichester went on to show, revenue would accrue to the government equal to that from Munster or Connacht and, with the Ulster problem solved, the recurring burden of military expenditure would be lifted.[1] By the end of September 1607, following on such advice, the decision for plantation had been made in London in outline form.[2] The process of designing what turned out to be a complex and systematic plantation plan for the escheated counties, as well as the carrying out of the necessary preliminaries to its implementation, took some two years and it was not until 1610 that the new ownership arrangements could be brought into being. Once implemented, though, it was expected that the many norms and ways of law, order and obedience to government could be made to apply in Ulster too.

The scheme eventually adopted embraced six counties – Donegal with Armagh, Tyrone, Cavan, Fermanagh and the subsequent county Londonderry – and in five of these (excluding the Londoners' plantation) a relatively uniform plan was followed. The ownership arrangements provided for two types of new proprietor, undertakers and servitors – the first, English and lowland Scottish (the latter arising from the linkage of Scotland with England incident on James I's succession to the English throne) in equal numbers, the second, as the name implies, mainly military officers – who received estates (called proportions) planned to range in size from 1,000 to 2,000 profitable acres. The other major group of owners comprised the Ulster Irish themselves. Although Dublin had not succeeded in redefining the larger lesser landholders as freeholders in the years before the flight (a policy so distasteful to the previous lords) and although now the patents of the departed were interpreted literally to allow a full-scale confiscation, Old Irish grantees, holding directly from the crown, formed an element in this plantation (as in most others), while pre-plantation grants to a small number of lesser Gaelic figures were also generally upheld where their patents had actually been taken out.

In addition to those three main groups, land was allocated for other purposes. Church-owned land – collectively the monastic estates; the termon and erenach lands, though their owners were by now much more secular than ecclesiastical; episcopal property and various small areas appertaining to parish clergy and other ecclesiastical dignitaries – had constituted a multi-form separate category in the old order, accounting for perhaps close on 20 per cent of the total acreage. While some of this had been secularised already with the monastic dissolutions in the years before the flight, decisions concerning substantial parts of these lands were made at the time of plantation. Thus along with the previous episcopal lands, the now established reformation episcopate received the extensive termon and erenach lands, distributed, as they were, throughout the parishes.[3] In addition, the parish clergy (the link with the erenach lands being now broken) were newly endowed with small areas of glebe taken out of the confis-cated secular property. To promote education, English-style, grammar schools, one to be established in each county, were provided with landed support and also the new university in Dublin received an Ulster estate.[4] In these ways, a financial basis for reform through religion and education was provided for. Finally, the scheme for plantation in Ulster contained urbanising proposals. In all twenty-five corporate towns were to be established – some to be based around the new forts (to the support of some of which land had already been allotted), many, to symbolise the changed order, to be centred on the focal points of the old regime – all of which were to receive an allocation of land to nurture them. Of the three main categories of grantee, the undertakers (with the Londoners) received over 40 per cent of the acreage, the servitors close on 15 per cent and the Irish about 20 per cent.[5]

Plantation, of course, implies settling or colonising; however, only the undertakers, hence the name, themselves forming the largest grantee category, were formally required to colonise. Precise obligations were laid down. Thus for estates of 1,000 acres and with proportionate increases for the larger ones – all estates to be manors – the undertaker should settle himself on a demesne of 300 acres, and plant on the rest of it, in accordance with a prescribed social structure, nine other families, to be made up of two fee-farmers (or freeholders) each with 120 acres, three leaseholders for three lives or twenty-one years on 100 acres each, and on the remaining 160 acres four families 'or more' of husbandmen, artificers or cottagers. These ten families should constitute between them twenty-four adult males. The undertakers were also tied to two specific building obligations. Their construction programme should involve buildings for themselves and buildings for their tenantry. The undertaker of a great proportion (a 2,000 acre estate) should erect 'a stone house with a strong court or bawne about it', that of a middle proportion (1,500 acres) might build either a stone or brick house also with a bawn, while the grantee of a small proportion (1,000 acres) must build 'a strong court or bawne at least'. This obligation reflects the defensive element which the plantation was supposed to serve. The second commitment concerned the tenantry. The undertakers should 'draw their tenants to build houses for themselves and their families ... near the principal house or bawne, as well for their mutual defence and strength, as for the making of villages and townships'. While this phrasing did not explicitly commit the undertakers to build the tenants' houses, elsewhere it was implied that they should 'erect habitations' for them.[6] Aside from that point, it is clear from this that the plantation planners were intent on ensuring that the settlement pattern on the undertakers' lands across the plantation should be one of village living protected by the landlords' bawns rather than one of dispersed settlement. The other categories of grantee (the servitors and native Irish), not being explicitly required to plant incoming tenantry, were tied only to build personal strongholds. The Irish grantees, for their part, however, must forgo the taking of 'Irish exactions' from those under them who must instead enjoy clearly defined tenancies with 'rents certaine'.[7] For all grantees, quit rents, a major source of government revenue, were set, which in the case of the undertakers were to be £5.6.8 per 1,000 acre estate. Faults in mensuration, however, subverted the government intention not to give out very large estates and had the effect, amongst others, that there were fewer grantees and less revenue gains than there might have been.

The original intention was that the estates should be allocated to their various grantees entirely by the haphazard mechanism of lottery. This, however, was not adhered to in the final plan. In 1609 a series of maps of the escheated counties, remarkable for their day, and given the speed of execution but not providing a means for the accurate calculation of acreages, on which the bounds of the estates were marked in, had been made. They were drawn by barony (the term normally used for the administrative sub-divisions of counties in Ireland), the Ulster counties having been divided into baronies in recent years. To satisfy the demands of the undertakers, many of whom had common local backgrounds in England or Scotland, that they might group together in Ulster for mutual support and to give them some re-assurance about their security, it was decided that estates should be allocated to 'consorts' of undertakers, English and Scottish, on a barony basis. This decision had implications for the other grantee categories as well: servitors and native Irish grantees grouped together were allocated other baronies. This pattern was duplicated across the five counties. This arrangement also had implications for the proposed treatment of all levels of the pre-existing Irish population. Those who were now to be restored to land would receive it only in the baronies allotted for servitors and Irish grantees. Also, and very significantly, since the undertakers must not 'alien', i.e. let, any land to Irish tenantry, the Irish occupiers on the estates in the baronies allocated to them (somewhat over 40 per cent of the acreage) must move entirely elsewhere and concentrate into the estates of any of the other grantee categories. Finally, and more generally, behind the plantation lay a broader ambition (though one perhaps both secondary and more long-term) concerning the native population as a whole: that in the Ulster re-organised in this way – before the source of internationalised rebellion and now to be set on a new course of development, social and economic – they would be protestantised through the concurrent advancement of the reformation, and integrated into an Ireland more unitary and more controlled.

Plantation in Donegal

The arrangements for the plantation in Donegal combined the elements of the general framework with some exceptional features. In accordance with the plan, estates were granted out on a barony or precinct basis in much of the county. Thus groups of Scottish undertakers were planted in two – Portlough and Boylagh joined with Banagh – English undertakers in just one – Lifford – while servitors and native Irish together got the barony of Kilmacrenan or Doe and Fanad. These were part of the general framework of the entire plantation, decided on in London with the assistance of the barony maps and the participation of officials from Ireland, and there is no conclusive evidence of what factors dictated the allocation. However, one factor which seems to have been influential in determining the allocation of Kilmacrenan to

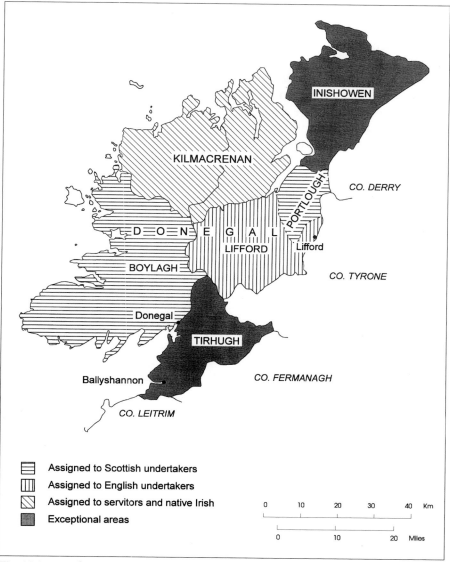

Fig. 10.1   Plantation Donegal.

servitors and Irish grantees was the notion that servitors already in place at strategic locations, for example, Rathmullan, should not be moved. Hence, in places, the plantation built on grants or leases already made, whether of monastic property, or of lands reserved for forts and defences or indeed of grants previously made to some individual Irish grantees. These may have been somewhat more numerous in Donegal than elsewhere.

The strategic consideration which had already entrenched Folliott as leaseholder at Ballyshannon with the lands reserved to it (the base from which he acquired the Assaroe monastic estate) in Tirhugh barony on the exposed south coast of county Donegal, may also account for the somewhat exceptional use to which yet more of that barony was put. Thus in November 1610, another military officer, Captain Basil Brooke, received a crown lease for twenty-one years of Donegal castle, O'Donnell's principal residence, its fishings, a small area of land nearby, which had supported it, and 'all customs and duties used and due to the said castle', at a rent of £1 Ir. per year.[8] Brooke, whose main estate was in Kilmacrenan, was later, in 1624, under a scheme for making economies in the forts, to be able to convert this title into one of outright ownership, on condition, however, that he should keep the castle under repair and permit the crown to place forces there in any 'time of rebellion or ... general disturbance'.[9] A third such figure, Captain Paul Gore, a member of a prominent London merchant family (and with Folliott a grantee in Fermanagh as well), acquired, by a purchase from the grantee Richard Nugent, baron Delvin, mediated through the lord deputy's secretary, Henry Perse, the property of the two Third Order Regular Franciscan friaries of Magherabeg (close to Donegal) and Flannacharta, the latter a small MacSweeney Banagh foundation on St. John's Point in the neighbouring barony.[10] Apart from this triumvirate, there was one major Irish grantee. Contrary to the decision that such lands should go to the local protestant episcopate, the lands of Termonmagrath with St Patrick's Purgatory and Termonomongan – a buffer zone inside and outside the county – were secured in December 1610 by James Magrath, son of archbishop Miler of Cashel and of the hereditary erenach family there. In the background to that lay a surrender and regrant ('for the purpose of reducing the lands to English tenure') involving Miler and his father in May 1596 and indeed the treatment of these termons fits in with the decisions concerning similar lands in Monaghan in 1591, including the obligation to build castles: James was required to build a 'capital house' within seven years.[11] The resulting structure – Castle Magrath – well underway in 1611, still stands.[12] In addition, a major beneficiary in Tirhugh, with about 25 per cent of the acreage, was the new university, Trinity College, Dublin. The college endowment (made up of lands in Armagh and Fermanagh too) came to include in Donegal, after complex post-war dealings in which Rory O'Donnell had been involved, the churchlands, originally Columban and latterly Franciscan, of Kilmacrenan as well.[13] Finally, the lands, assessed at 200 acres, allotted for the county grammar school (the 'royal school'), which it was proposed in 1609 to establish in the buildings of Donegal abbey, were located near Donegal in this barony.[14]

The treatment of the remaining barony, Inishowen, offers a striking contrast through its grant (church lands excluded)[15] to one man: Sir Arthur Chichester, the lord deputy. His entitling went through an evolution, reflected in instructions by 'king's letter' and one patent modified by another more careful in definition between June 1609 and July 1610 which amongst other things brought his grant to dovetail with that to the city of London of the future county of Londonderry, concerning which negotiations were finalised in January 1610. The principal difference related to Culmore and land adjacent. Initially intended to be granted to Chichester, who should receive the pay of a constable and gunner and the command of any warders maintained there, Culmore and this land was instead granted to the Londoners, they covenanting to maintain there 'at their own proper costs and charges' a ward of as many men and officers as should be necessary for its defence, without cost to the crown. This decision also had implications for the setting of the county boundary. Instead, however, and to increase coastal defences, Chichester was to receive the fees of a constable, gunner and ten warders to be kept at Greencastle castle. In his patents Inishowen was perceived as made up of four manors in each of which he might hold courts leet and courts baron before his seneschals, as well as markets and fairs. However, in his first – and this is missing from his second – he was given liberty (and by implication expected) to divide the territory into manors of 2,000 acres on each of which he should build a 'castle or capital messuage' within seven years, a reflection in the first instance of the estate-size norms of the plantation plan and in the second of the building prescriptions of earlier schemes. He was also given the quasi-medieval liberty to appoint four bailiffs 'to execute all writs and other processes ... no sheriff or bailiff of the crown to intermeddle'. He was not specifically required to colonise but he should institute 'free tenants' or freeholders, was allowed to hold in common soccage tenure and had his quit rent, set at £86.12.8 stg. in his patent of February 1610, reduced to £30 in his second in July.[16]

We now turn to the urbanising proposals for Donegal. In the English order, society was seen as divided between countryside and town or county and borough, distinctions which had had less meaning in the prior Gaelic world where lords may anyhow have sought to accumulate power to themselves. Towns should be both centres of trades and commerce and lanterns of local civility – hosts of schooling, law, church and administration – which when incorporated returned, like the counties, members to parliaments to participate in central consultation and law-making. To support these settlements, areas of land were to be assigned to their corporations and to 'people' them there was to be 'a levy or press of tradesmen and artificers' from England. For Donegal eight places – generally of some significance, political or ecclesiastical, in the old order and now to be re-orientated as symbols of the new – were chosen for incorporation and urbanisation and listed in the 'project' of the plantation produced in January 1609.[17] One of them, Derry, located in another traditional buffer zone between the lordships, like Termonmagrath, though more complex in make-up and at this stage placed in county Donegal, to which 1,000 acres of escheated land was to be allocated, need not concern us here because shortly it was to be placed instead in county Londonderry.[18] Of the remaining seven places, Lifford, Ballyshannon and Donegal were to receive 300 'acres' apiece while Killybegs, Raphoe, Rathmullan and, apparently, Carndonagh were each to be allotted 200 'acres'.[19] Some of the allocations failed, however, to materialise. Thus Chichester's patents of Inishowen passed without reservation of corporation land for a town there, and Raphoe, seated within episcopal land, received no extra endowment. Also the crown did not pursue the proposed plan for town planting by impressment or coercion; rather it devolved the responsibility for urbanisation to individual planters. Accordingly, a local grantee received the lands on condition that he should build and settle townsmen.[20]

The grant to Basil Brooke for Donegal embraced a rudimentary planning aesthetic. In March 1612 he agreed 'to set apart a convenient place for the site of the said town to be built' and 'for the market place ... church and church-yard'. The town should consist of twenty burgesses 'besides cottagers and other inferior inhabitants', to be accommodated with houses and lands within four years. In addition thirty acres should be set aside for common, to be called the burgess-field, and two acres for a school and exercise ground.[21] A year earlier, Sir Ralph Bingley had been tied to somewhat similar conditions for Rathmullan: he should plant within four years twenty Englishmen or Scots, 'chiefly artificers', to be burgesses and thereafter incorporated, each to receive two acres of ground, besides their houses and gardens, 'with the whole bog of Rathmullan for common of turf'.[22] Belatedly, in December 1615, Roger Jones, of Sligo (whose involvement highlights an old geographical link in a new, but reverse, form)[23] received the lands for Killybegs, again under similar conditions but with the variation that although he should build twenty houses, the burgesses should be twelve in number.[24] Even within this context of devolving responsibility to private men, the aspirations for Lifford, the county town, were grander. As early as October 1610 Sir Richard Hansard received a lease for twenty-one years at a rent of £2 Ir. of both the fort, 'commonly called Captain Brooke's fort', and of the lands (four quarters) which had already been reserved for Lifford by Chichester in 1605,[25] under specific urbanising conditions. Within five years he should allocate to sixty people sites for houses there, each with a 'curtilage or backside' and a garden plot 'adjoining', which they themselves should build, each to hold by rent from him for the remaining part of the twenty-one years. He should also assign and set out a specified area of land to be used by them as a common for meadow, pasture and turbary.[26] The final definitive plan for Lifford came in January 1612. At that point, Hansard received an outright grant of the four quarters of reserved land, with the exception of the fort, now to be called the king's fort, and the meadow of Stramore nearby (saving four acres of it granted to Hansard)[27] which the crown retained and which therefore now became a separate entity. Otherwise, he now became committed to a somewhat scaled-down colonising obligation. He was to settle within four years, thirty persons, English or Scots 'especially artificers or mechanics' to be burgesses and to be incorporated, fifteen of whom should receive two acres apiece and fifteen one acre apiece nearby, 'besides their several ... sufficient places ... for houses or messuages with backsides and gardens ... within the said town to be erected', to hold for ever as freeholders. They should likewise receive the 'moor or bog' of Roughan for a common turbary and 100 acres for a common pasture.[28]

The process of incorporation followed quickly for a number of these places, its context being the meeting of the 1613-15 parliament. However, only some of the places originally designated received charters. Those which did receive them were Lifford and Donegal in February 1613 followed by Ballyshannon one month later, while Killybegs was incorporated in December 1615. In each, the corporate body established was made up of a chief officer (called guardian in the Lifford charter) and twelve burgesses.[29]

It is necessary to revert now to some brief comments on the areas where the plantation was applied in its normal form, beginning with Kilmacrenan barony (some 300,000 acres) which was allocated to servitors and Irish grantees. Here there were seventeen servitor grantees as well as a section of the estate granted to Trinity College. The servitors included men such as Sir Ralph Bingley and the Vaughans (John and Henry) who had been part of Sir Henry Docwra's Lough Foyle expedition, Captain Henry Harte, who had been at Culmore, and Captain William Stewart, a Scot who had been sent to Ulster with 200 foot to suppress O'Doherty's rising.[30] The Irish grantees between them received about 60 per cent of the barony which represented (excluding

James Magrath's termon lands in Tirhugh) about 20 per cent of the county as a whole.

The Irish grantees, some fifty in all, divided into two groups. Thus six major figures received large estates within the framework of the plantation plan and there was also a second much more numerous category receiving smaller areas. The six included Donnell MacSweeney Fanad and Sir Mulmory MacSweeney a Doe, both from that area, and Donagh MacSweeney Banagh, the three heads of the MacSweeney sub-lord families, the latter transplanted from Banagh in south-west Donegal, and also a more minor figure, Walter McLoughlin MacSweeney. In addition, the young Turlough O'Boyle, the other major sub-lord under the O'Donnells, from Boylagh, received an estate, while Hugh McHugh Duff O'Donnell, head of a branch of the former ruling family, retained just a life interest in land based on Ramelton. For their part the lesser grantees may be taken to include many, though, of course, only a proportion of all, who would have been made freeholders had there been no plantation. One was Lughaidh O'Clery, 'chronicler', while another was a woman, Grainne ny Donnell. Two prominent widows received life interests – Ineen Dubh, Rory O'Donnell's Scottish mother and Honora Bourke (indicating a marriage alliance into old English Connacht), widow of the former O'Boyle.[31] In addition, the prior interests of the Dublin merchants with whom Rory O'Donnell had had dealings were compensated, and his own widow, Bridget, countess of Tyrconnell, was awarded a pension of £300 stg. per annum in 1616.[32]

The locations of the grants of the Irish suggest that a policy of interspersing them with the servitors was followed, though some of the latter were placed together from Letterkenny towards Ramelton (the 'lough shore' area). One factor, security-based, is also again clear. Only Hugh McHugh Duff retained his castle – for life – at Ramelton. Though tied to build in accordance with plantation regulations, neither Sir Mulmory nor Donnell MacSweeney regained their castles at Doe or Rathmullan – the latter being retained by Sir Ralph Bingley – and received their estates elsewhere, in Donnell's case further north and in Sir Mulmory's in the Dunfanaghy area. Nor did all these grantees, large or smaller, retain their lands up to 1641: varied pressures and problems of adjustment appear to have affected them. MacSweeney Banagh was one such casualty: he had lost much land by 1641. Another was Sir Mulmory MacSweeney a Doe, whose grandson was a captain in the rising of 1641. His entire estate had come into the hands of Sir Paul Davis, an exchequer and ward's official in Dublin since the mid-1620s and clerk of the privy council, by February 1640.[33] By contrast, MacSweeney Fanad had successfully retained his lands which were held in 1641, following an apparent practice of divided inheritance rather than primogeniture, by various members of his family.[34] Equally, the land granted to Walter McLoughlin MacSweeney, described in 1619 as 'a justice of the peace in the county and conformable to his Majesty's laws, serving the king and country upon all occasions', had by 1641 passed mainly to his son, Ervin, of Ray (then also a justice of the peace who wrote good English and an initial opponent of the rising in October of that year), though with provision for another son, Neale Mergagh and jointure for his widow Grainne Ni Gallogher.[35] Also a small number of MacSweeney proprietors in 1641, one of them the owner of a piece of land acquired from one of the servitor grantees, Henry Vaughan, had become converted to protestantism.[36] Overall, however, there had been a clear decline in the holdings of the Irish grantees by 1641. Also, although the servitors were not specifically tied to colonise, some pockets of settler settlement had come into being in this barony. Generally, too, the major Irish grantees had shown a reluctance, at least up to 1619, to grant leases to the tenantry under them.[37]

In Boylagh and Banagh the plantation brought about the foundation of eight estates, each granted to a Scottish undertaker. However, early on, all the original grantees in the barony disengaged (including Sir Robert McClelland who became tenant of the Haberdashers' and Clothworkers' estates in the Londonderry plantation) and the estates came to be engrossed into the hands of one man, originally Sir Robert Gordon of Lochinvar, Kirkcudbrightshire and then John Murray, a relative of one of the original grantees and one of James I's Scottish courtiers in London – a groom of the bedchamber and keeper of the privy purse – whom the king created Viscount Annan in 1622 and earl of Annandale in 1624.[38] There is a suggestion that Murray and Gordon were linked and that pressure was brought to bear on some of the original grantees, especially the family of George Murray of Broughton, Wigtownshire (who had died at Lifford in 1613), to sell their estates. On the other hand, the plantation had been making only limited initial success in what was a geographically remote barony, and when the king, in October 1618, authorised the legitimisation of Murray's acquisitions through the issuing of a new patent, promise appeared to be held out of a new energy in the colonisation of the region, even to the extent that the groom of the bedchamber would 'be at great charge' in building Murraystown, a new town within it. Murray was in fact a 'rising' figure on the wider stage of all three kingdoms, and was to be, like his son (born in 1617), the second earl (he himself died in 1640), a royalist peer in the context of the Scottish covenanting rebellion which began in 1637. His presence in Donegal must, however, at best have been no more than occasional, though an agent, Herbert Maxwell, was quickly in place. Moreover, when he took out a patent of the eight estates in December 1620 (now re-organised into two manors), he agreed to a doubled quit rent into the Irish exchequer of £106.13.4 stg., a figure just in excess of half of what Rory O'Donnell had been tied to for his entire earldom in 1604.[39] His ownership, at any rate, brought a measure of continuity and stability: he renewed his patents, in accordance with the regulations then applying in both 1629 and 1639, the latter (in which the eight proportions were re-organised now into three manors) tying him to an increased quit rent of £146.16.8 and opening him as well, through the introduction of tenure *in capite*, to the scrutiny of the court of wards. He received also the fisheries, 'of salmon, herring and whale', and his last patent conferred the mountains (which initially in the plantation at large had been treated as a separate entity) of the area as well.[40]

Various expedients for the letting of the lands, often in large blocs, and sometimes proving to be of only a short-term nature, were adopted by Murray. Thus by 1619 the proportion, or estate, of the Rosses had been let to Captain Thomas Dutton, an Englishman, while in 1626 the whole eight estates were leased to Sir George Hamilton of Greenlaw, brother to the earl of Abercorn and an energetic planter in the Strabane area and himself a Scottish Catholic who married a daughter of the earl of Ormond, for eleven years at £1,000 per annum. This may not have endured, however, because in May 1632 one Alexander Cunningham appears as agent of the earl of Annandale.[41]

While full and precise detail on the tenanting of these estates is missing, it appears that colonisation was mainly confined to the southern part of the barony and especially to the area from Killybegs, or beyond, to Donegal town: that was certainly the case up to the 1620s. Also while the new town of Murraystown, intended 'to be the principal town of the ... barony' failed precisely to materialise, the growth of the 'new borough town' of Killybegs, over the development of which Murray appears to have gained control, limited though it was by the early 1620s to 'seventeen British and Irish inhabitants', took its place. Estimates for the settler population (mainly Scottish but including an English minority) of the entire barony, for the period up to 1630, given in adult males, mostly suggest a figure of some 150, though one in 1626, which stands out from the rest, gave 340 and offered 739 as the number of Irish.[42] While some of these may have held big tenancies, it is clear that in much of the barony the Irish, rather than having been removed in accordance with the requirement for undertakers' areas, continued in occupation. Also while many of the settler tenants were said to hold for twenty-one years, they held often by 'minutes' rather than regular leases and no freeholders had been created by 1622.[43] This, however, may have changed later on. The conditions under which some of the Irish occupied land emerge from an enquiry in 1632, designed to investigate what had prevailed since Annandale had taken out his patent in 1629. Some held relatively large areas, either from those such as Dutton to whom Murray had demised whole estates or as undertenants to his lesser settler assignees, but their actual conditions of occupation were commonly only of a short-term nature, often from six months to six months. Thus Coochogery O'Clery held a half quarter of land (perhaps about 300 acres) in this way at £8 stg. per annum.[44] It also emerges from a report of a customs inspector in 1637 that, despite ownership change, a full ordered and disciplined society (a perennial obsession) had not been brought about. Referring to Killybegs, he saw a need for much more control.

> The place being wild and not inhabited with any men of power or quality and frequented especially in time of fishing by Redshanks and by divers of the Scotch Isles and other unruly and wild people that will do no right that is not enjoined on them by force.[45]

Thus both in terms of plantation and of social regulation, society in west Donegal remained transitional up to 1641.

By contrast the plantation in the barony of Raphoe (220,000 acres)[46] proceeded along much more orthodox lines. The forfeited land in this barony was divided into two precincts, Portlough and Lifford, the former, to the north-east of the barony, granted to Scottish undertakers, the latter (to its south-west) granted to English undertakers, with the churchlands of Raphoe forming one point of division between them. In Portlough, the land, considered to represent – in accordance with the estimations used by the plantation planners – 12,000 profitable acres, was allocated to nine Scottish grantees. The nine, which included Ludovic Stewart, duke of Lennox, a relative of the king's and both a privy councillor and lord high steward of the household in London and a one-time ambassador to France, as well as three others of that surname and also four Cunninghams from Ayrshire (a distinct sub-group) maintained, unlike their equivalents in Boylagh and Banagh, a reasonable level of continuity of ownership.[47] Many of the sites at which they built had previously been minor O'Donnell strongholds such as Dunboy or Coolmacitrain or Mongavlin, the latter Ineen Dubh's former place of residence.[48] This region came to be amongst the most effectively planted areas of the entire plantation in Ulster. By 1630 there were some 540 settler adult males in the area, about 180 of them on the estates of the absentee duke of Lennox and about 250 on the

Cunningham group of estates.[49] This figure represents close to double the minimum requirement of 288 adult males laid down in the conditions under which these undertakers had accepted their estates.

After this overview, we can turn now to focus in more depth on the plantation in one area – the precinct of Lifford, granted to English undertakers.

The English plantation in Lifford precinct

What was called the precinct of Lifford (the south-west part of Raphoe barony) is comprised of the basin of the rivers Finn and Deele and the southern half of the basin of the river Swilly. Where the Finn and Deele rivers merge with the Foyle is good fertile lowland. The Finn, Deele and Swilly rivers drain rolling countryside with potentially good farmland. Poor soils are scattered on the low hills throughout the area, but are largely confined to the mountainous fringe in the south-west and west of the precinct.

Those chosen to implement and benefit from the plantation in this area were a group of nine Englishmen selected in London in the spring of 1610 and assigned between them estates calculated to total in all 15,000 profitable acres.[50] Unlike most of the English undertakers elsewhere, they were not all people new to Ireland and simply with roots in English landed society. In fact they divided into two groups, of which the larger had already had Irish ex-military, or servitor, associations. Whether this latter arose from a need to grant patronage to those who had played a former military role, or because it was difficult to attract people to undertake in remoter west Ulster, or as a precaution against renewed sea-borne invasion, or through some combination of all, is difficult to determine.

One of this servitor group, Sir Henry Docwra, formerly governor of Lough Foyle and latterly one of the planners of the plantation, is already familiar. However, now building a career in Dublin, he immediately passed on his assignment to William Wilson, a lawyer and eldest son of deceased parents from Clare in Suffolk. Two others were captains: one the somewhat anonymous Ralph Mansfield, the other Edward Russell, then of London, who had served in Ireland (mainly at Newry) for two and a half years from 1595, and then returned to England claiming unpaid arrears of some £560, to be admitted to Gray's Inn in 1598, and who was probably a connection of a former lord deputy, Sir William Russell. Another former captain had achieved more prominence with both a knighthood (in 1603) and a pension (in 1606) and also enjoyed Lord Deputy Chichester's favour in 1610. He, Sir Thomas Coach, had been sent to Ireland late in 1598 in charge of men levied in Leicestershire, as part of wider re-inforcements sent at that time. He had fought at the battle of the Curlews in 1599, was at Lifford in 1601 and had married, prior to 1607, Dorcas Sidney, widow of Alexander Cosby of Stradbally, thereby forging a link with the earlier plantation in Leix and Offaly. Sir Robert Remington, a man of Yorkshire origin, was another grantee who fits broadly into this category, though he was to die, late in 1610, before he could play any effective part in the plantation. His most spectacular wartime involvement had taken place not in Ireland but directly against Spain: he took part in the Anglo-Dutch assault on Cadiz and the Spanish navy in 1596 (the 'counter armada') and was knighted by the earl of Essex, commander of the soldiers in that expedition, off Cadiz, at that time. Through that expedition, too, he had formed a link with Lord Thomas Howard who played a part in it and who now, as earl of Suffolk and lord chamberlain, had a role in the choosing of the grantees for this area of the plantation. He had, however, a further claim to favour: he had been employed briefly in Ireland after the Nine Years' War as vice-president of Connacht – securing permission to return to England late in 1607 because of legal and financial difficulties there – during which time he had unearthed suggestive indications that the earl of Tyrconnell was seeking to re-engage Spanish interest in Ireland. Sir Henry Clare, another grantee, was again a person of somewhat similar career and circumstances. A man of Norfolk landed origin and a 'cousin' of lord deputy Burgh, he took part with him, perilously, in an engagement with O'Neill at the Blackwater in Ulster in July 1597 and hoped to benefit through him from land in the Byrnes' Country in Wicklow. His subsequent career in Ireland saw him as lieutenant-colonel of the regiment of Donogh O'Brien, earl of Thomond, briefly in Ulster again in 1600, and later garrisoned in Galway, where complaints were made against him by the townsmen, until he was discharged with army reductions at the end of 1602. Absence in Ireland could also bring its problems and, knighted in 1603, he had returned to England about then to confront financial difficulties affecting his wife at that time, and, later, now out of employment, became an advocate of a project concerned with corn. An articulate and ambitious military officer, he kept up a correspondence while in Ireland with Sir Robert Cecil who as Earl of Salisbury was James I's principal secretary of state at the time that the plantation in Ulster was being inaugurated.

The remaining three, Sir Maurice Berkeley, Sir William Barne and Sir Thomas Cornewall, conform perhaps a little more nearly to the character of the more usual English undertakers elsewhere. Sir Thomas Cornewall was one of a family group which had applied for this entire precinct. Son and heir of Thomas Cornewall, baron of Burford

(d. 1615), a substantial Shropshire landowner, Sir Thomas (d. 1636), knighted on the king's accession in 1603 and known as the Great Baron, was a man active locally in county affairs and in favour centrally as a gentleman of the privy chamber of Prince Henry, James I's son. Of the others, Sir William Barnes (or Barne) although again a substantial property holder, was a man of entirely different origins. Of a London merchant background and son and grandson of two lord mayors, he had lived at Woolwich (eight miles from the capital) from at least the 1590s, was a justice of the peace of the county of Kent and had marriage connections with prominent Kentish men of affairs. Although his family had a well-established tradition of participation in numerous English long-distance mercantile enterprises, dating from the Muscovy company in the 1550s, Sir William (d. 1619) had however become drawn into the plantation through some connection with Sir Robert Remington. Finally, Sir Maurice Berkeley commands interest on many counts. A Somersetshire landowner, educated at Oxford and the Middle Temple, knighted at Cadiz in 1596, an active member of a number of parliaments and a leader in important negotiations about the royal finances just at this time, his family had already had Irish interests, both recent and medieval, and he was a relative of Sir Henry Folliott. He also played an active part in Virginia affairs, which appear to have taken precedence for him over the Ulster plantation. He died in 1617. Such were the people to whom the estates were assigned in 1610; not all of them retained a permanent association with them. While Berkeley and Barnes seem to be the only two with significant overseas connections, the military men as a whole will no doubt all have held anti-Spanish views and shared to some degree the religio-political sensibilities arising therefrom.[51]

Those assigned the estates were expected to meet the lord deputy and plantation commissioners from Dublin, who travelled through the escheated counties from August to mid-September, to receive possession. Only two in fact did so, Coach and Wilson, though Cornewall was to send over an agent, Edward Lyttleton, a likely relation of his wife's.[52] Indeed over the next few years there were to be a number of changes in ownership, with the effect that the plantation in the area got underway rather slowly.

By the end of the first year, when the first of a series of government inspections of it was carried out, by Sir George Carew, it was mainly some members of the servitor group, especially the two ex-captains, Mansfield and Russell, and also Sir Thomas Coach, all three of whom were already resident, along with the newcomer, Wilson, who were showing signs of activity, while the performance of the smaller civilian group of Berkeley, Barnes (who had already sold his estate), and even

Cornewall (who at least, in common with Clare, had sent over an agent) was much less promising.

Work on building and planting in accordance with regulation, which it was the main function of Carew's and subsequent government surveys to detail, was by this stage, on Carew's account, confined to just three estates. Wilson, through his agent Christopher Parmenter, a man from his home area in Suffolk, had begun the process of colonisation: there were 'some families of English resident who brought over good store of household stuff' and had as stock '21 cows and oxen, 9 mares, one service horse and some small cattle'. Russell's beginnings reveal another aspect of the plantation. He had imported a number of English labourers (but no tenants), presumably the builders of two timber-framed 'English houses' which had been erected, and his stock included six English cows. Finally, Sir Thomas Coach, who had four settler families on the land, none yet with leases, had made a start of another kind. He had chosen as site for his own residence the castle of Scarrifhollis, on the river Swilly, former residence of Caffar oge O'Donnell – who although destabilised (as has been seen) by Rory O'Donnell's behaviour towards him, had later gone into a 'kind of rebellion' capturing Doe castle and had been by 1608 lodged in Dublin Castle – and had already built a timber house adjoining it.[53]

The vacuum of absentee inactivity, evident now on most of the estates, was to be filled over the next few years, in some cases through people from neighbouring parts of the plantation acquiring some of them. One such was Sir Ralph Bingley – already holding land in Kilmacrenan – who by early 1613, when the next survey was carried out by Sir Thomas Bodley, had acquired control of the estates granted to both Remington and Berkeley, thereby bringing two estates into the hands of one man. Another new owner by this stage was Peter Benson, a London craftsman-entrepreneur and to be the contractor for the building of the walls of Derry, who acquired Clare's estate based on Stranorlar. Some of these changes evolved through partnership agreements, possibly surviving for many years, involving some of the local former military officers, or others, the evidence for which does not always survive in full detail. Thus initially Benson, for example, had as associate Arthur Terry, later a customs official in Derry. In the case of the Barnes estate, which stretched south and westward from near Lifford, more evidence is forthcoming, showing that it simply got split up. By 1613 also it had been sold, for £50 stg., to Russell and Thomas Wilson (brother of William who had acquired Docwra's proportion) from whom Sir Richard Hansard of Lifford had in turn acquired an interest in a part (for £100), with the obligation that he should carry out the building requirement and also plant one-third of the households.[54]

Another change in ownership, in September 1613, brought in a purchaser for the Cornewall estate from north Wales, Robert Davies of Gwysaney (near Mold and some ten miles from Chester) in Flintshire, whose home area and local links overlapped with those of Bingley and make it seem certain that it was through him that Davies was attracted to plantation Ulster. Of a self-anglicising Welsh family, Davies's career sprang from two roots: in Wales the family was consolidating an estate (some 1,750 acres) and engaging in coalmining, while through the act of union with Wales under Henry VIII a London connection was established – a grand-uncle had held military office at court. Robert (1581-1633), fresh from Oxford, had succeeded his father in 1603. His subsequent career suggests that, on the one hand, his presence in Donegal can have been no more than intermittent while, on the other, that he must have perceived his engagement there in some part in terms of advancing the Protestant cause. Certainly Davies and his brother Thomas (who was acting for Robert in Donegal towards the end of the decade), both of whom appear to have received military training in London, came soon to be involved at the cutting edge of religious warfare in Europe. They were in Prague in 1620 prior to the defeat – with catastrophic consequences for protestantism there – of the elector Frederick as king of Bohemia.[55]

Finally (as proof that so many of the original grantees lacked either the desire to stay or the financial resources to fulfil their plantation obligations), Russell's estate too passed to a new owner. By June 1614, Captain John Kingsmill (born 1579 and knighted in 1617), a younger son from Hampshire and one of a number of brothers who had had military careers in Ireland and himself (despite army reductions) recently placed in Glenfinn, Niall Garbh's former area of influence, in charge of some twenty-five horse, had acquired this estate.[56]

With these changes, a measure of stability in ownership of the estates had been achieved. Subsequent changes, down to 1641, including successions to heirs, were due mainly to family circumstances. In some cases, however, these brought new owners. In 1633 Robert Davies died, leaving an heir aged seventeen.[57] This ended the Gwysaney connection and the estate passed to Sir Paul Davis – not apparently a relation – a well-placed functionary in Dublin who held offices in the exchequer and the court of wards as well as being clerk of the privy council, and an absentee who, as has been seen, also acquired the lands of Sir Mulmory MacSweeney.[58] For his part, Sir Ralph Bingley, although an active enough planter, also maintained a London connection and was to seek a new military career in the context of a further English war with Spain and in France in the later 1620s. Living within an expansive mental world delineated by Anglo-Spanish conflict, he put forward at this time an elaborate plan, to be financed and manned from Ireland, for an intervention against Spain in the West Indies as a means of pre-empting a feared Spanish invasion of Ireland, which was before its time and came to nothing, but he was appointed instead a colonel in the English expedition to the Ile de Ré off La Rochelle (in support of a Huguenot rebellion) where he was killed in 1627.[59] Despite his death, the Bingley ownership of the estates continued for the time being, and following on the marriage of his widow to Robert Harrington, lessee of the Grocers' proportion in the Londonderry plantation, both took out a joint patent of them in May 1630, but they had passed by sale or possibly through a mortgage to Martin Basil of Essex and London by the end of the decade.[60] Of the original grantees, then, the families of William Wilson (replacing Docwra), whose son Sir John (d. 1636) became a baronet and married a daughter of the old English Sir Thomas Butler of Clogrenan, county Carlow,[61] Sir Thomas Coach (d. 1621) and Captain Ralph Mansfield (d. 1633) remained in continuous ownership down to 1641, while on many of the estates there had been ownership change in the initial years, with change again affecting a few of them in the 1630s. This provides the background for assessing the plantation which came about under them, both in building and tenanting, and its implications for the previous landholders.

Collectively, the estates as granted out were held to constitute 15,000 profitable acres. To conform to requirement, the undertakers must introduce between them, incrementally but within a few years, a settler colony of 150 families or 360 adult males. While that number was, broadly, to be reached, the process of achieving it proved slower than was expected. Given the initial wave of ownership change, it is not surprising that Sir Josias Bodley who carried out the second government survey of the plantation early in 1613 found that although building operations were beginning on a number of estates, the number of tenants in place was still relatively small. Of the more active, William Wilson, who was resident, had 'planted some few tenants' (none of them yet made either freeholders or leaseholders) and his brother was in England 'to draw over others'. Similarly, Mansfield had 'some tenants, albeit not his full number nor estated as they ought to be ... engaged on the land', and was himself engaged in litigation about the extent of his estate, while Coach had five English tenants with formal tenancy agreements concluded. These were amongst the owners who were to endure. On the estates of many of those who departed, little or simply no settling had taken place, while some of the newcomer owners had made a varying impact. Thus Benson and Terry, themselves resident, had some of their tenants present with 'the rest to come speedily thither'. On Sir Maurice Berkeley's estate, held at this stage in partnership by Sir Ralph Bingley and Captain John Vaughan, Bingley had built seven tenements with chimneys and had tenants in them already, while Vaughan for his part stated that when he took over 'at Allhallowtide last' (1 November 1612) Irish tenants were in place and entitled to hold until Michaelmas (29 September) and now had their corn sown – an indication of the early impact of plantation on the Irish landholders – but that he had recruited 'one Clinton and nine Englishmen more' to settle there the following summer and also build their own houses.[62]

By the spring of 1619 with the completion of Capt Nicholas Pynnar's survey of the plantation, a dramatically different picture is revealed. Across the nine estates he recorded 193 settler tenant families, ranging from 13 on one to 32 on another, with in some cases undertenants as well, and presented a total figure of 536 adult males in place. These tenantry were presented in gradations both in type, freeholders, leaseholders, and in some cases cottagers, and in sizes of tenancies, the latter all expressed with acreage figures. In many cases with regard to the latter, for example tenants with 120 acres, his figures can perhaps be seen as representing the conventional acreages of the land divisions of the time (in Donegal, quarters, with their sub-divisions into trians or sessiaghs, which form the basis of the more numerous townland divisions of the present day), but in the cases of many of the smaller tenancies they have a precision (for example as between tenancies of 60 acres and 62 and 66 and 67, or 10 and 11) which could scarcely be attained at the time.[63] Hence while his account may have been broadly accurate, it has a superficial precision which perhaps should not be taken to be totally reliable in every detail.

From the final government survey of the series, carried out in 1622, a more conservative picture emerges. The inspectors in 1622 found tenantry – the equivalents of Pynnar's tenant families – to the number of 135 on eight of the nine estates (including a few of Davies's who were then absent in Wales), having excluded Wilson's (where however they found 87 men present to Pynnar's 106, which had been made up, as Pynnar described them, of 20 tenant families with 50 more under them) on his admission that his conveyances did not follow due form. They also cast doubt on the status of some on a number of estates as 'reputed' freeholders or leaseholders for years or lives, which tends to suggest that some undertakers may not have given out such secure tenancies, particularly authentic freeholds, as the conditions of plantation laid down. Their total for 'British men present', in more striking contrast to Pynnar's, was no more than 263.[64] This discrepancy is a marked one. Apart from the likelihood of some errors, especially on Pynnar's part, in relatively quickly conducted surveys, it may possibly be accounted for in a number of ways. Some undertenants, who at any rate are not specifically mentioned, may have been omitted, while some building workers may now have moved away. However, it may also reflect an early plantation society, at Pynnar's time not fully settled down, in which some still moved elsewhere for better tenancies, or had decided (like some of the owners) not to stay, or were absentees, or held multiple tenancies. In the absence of estate papers, the surveys give the best impression available of the dimensions of the plantation they describe, though they may present an over-symmetrical picture of it.[65]

That also for some of the 1620s, when local tensions arising from renewed Anglo-Spanish conflict must have made Ulster at large less attractive to newcomers, there was no further major growth in settler numbers on these estates comes from the evidence of a muster in c.1630 at which 248 men presented themselves from eight of the nine estates. If allowance is made for those from the estate, Coach's, which somehow got left out, perhaps 20 or so, and for a small delinquency in attendance overall, that total might creep towards 300.[66] There is no systematic evidence for the 1630s when some expansion may well have occurred, though it must be remembered that opening opportunities in the English new world across the Atlantic in the 1620s and 1630s also provided migrants (though probably more so English than Scottish) with alternative outlets. However, with regard to the essential feature of the tenanting of the land by the undertakers, the plantation had mainly come into existence in the reign of James I.

For their part, a core element amongst the tenantry would seem to be made up of people recruited by the undertakers from their home areas in England and Wales. Thus many Welsh tenantry appear on the Davies and Bingley estates. However many others must have been freelance arrivers aware, through the spread of news, that land was available. A very significant group of these – revealed by the names on the muster roll of c.1630 – were Scots, arriving probably at Derry on Lough Foyle (though Lough Swilly may also have been used) and percolating through from the Scottish undertakers' area in Portlough or from the Strabane area which had also been granted to Scottish undertakers. Another element, since some of the undertakers here had had military backgrounds, was made up of former junior military officers and may even have included some former ordinary soldiers as well. Thus Lieutenants Edward Carter and John Dutton (d. 1629) are found as tenants on the Bingley estates. It is clear from a few names, Pitt and Babington for instance, that the plantation town of Londonderry, of which Peter Benson (d. 1642) became an alderman, was also a source of tenantry. Edward Torleton, who, as we will see, held a number of leases, himself lived in the new settler town of Lifford.[67] After all, Derry and Lifford were also the principal places giving access to sea-borne trade through which purchases were acquired and surpluses exported.

In the plantation, in Donegal as elsewhere, the settlement pattern laid down to the undertakers, whereby their tenantry should all live together in village communities, was not to be followed. Rather, a mix of dispersed and nucleated settlement emerged. A number of factors would appear to account for this. With the estates in fact very much larger than planned, the pursuit of a farming life would have been impeded (often to the point of impracticability) by time spent in travel, requiring in some Donegal estates the fording of rivers. Also the defensive considerations which partly underlay the proposal in the first place – otherwise it sprang from notions of the ordered society – were less imperative in the formative first decade of the plantation which was an interlude of international peace. Furthermore many of the undertakers appear to have lacked the resources to engage on any substantial scale, without government subsidy, in building tenant villages (seeking sometimes, as we have seen Capt John Vaughan do, to pass on the building obligation to the tenantry), which was an all the more decisive consideration given that there was so much ownership change in the early plantation years. In some cases, indeed, a little group of cottagers may have formed the initial core of a plantation settlement, but since the process of tenanting was not all effected neatly in a short space of time the ordained pattern of exclusively village living could not be easily imposed. Thus, as the settlement pattern stabilised, it came to be one of both small village and dispersed settlement.

Many who lived in the villages would appear to have held small acreages (with commons sometimes mentioned) with the adjacent land carved up to provide them, and must also have included workmen and artisans of various kinds amongst them. Sometimes, indeed, the houses varied in size and type, reflecting the differing sorts of people who lived in them. In some cases, the planter village beginnings of this period can be shown to form the basis of some present day towns, while the locations of others can only be tentatively identified. Thus Bingley on the estate acquired from Remington had erected by 1622 a village of twelve houses and cottages at Ballybofey 'inhabited for the most part with British' and had an estate residence under construction on the opposite side of the river Finn, 'near unto the ford' (still an identifiable location) and so in Drumboe Lower townland, a settlement seen at the time as well placed since the ford was on 'the chiefest passage' into the Barnesmore mountains and 'where a bridge is very needful to be built'. Likewise and closeby, Peter Benson on his Stranorlar estate, had constructed his residence 'near' the Finn, and 'near' to it a village of ten houses and cottages.[68] Some four miles further west on the Davies estate two little hamlets, recorded in 1622, which can plausibly be identified as Welchtown and Gorey or Welchtown Upper respectively, both at the easterly entrance to the estate, one 'near' the planter's house (which may possibly therefore have been at Glenafton) the other 'about half a mile distant from it', suggest that again a centre had been chosen at a crossing (now bridged at Glenmore bridge) of the river Finn.[69] Likewise, eastwards along the Finn, on his Killygordon estate, Mansfield had built 'near' the river, and also had by 1622 two little villages of cottages nearby, one of which was by then 'decayed' and in decline.[70] For his part, Kingsmill had occupied and rebuilt Niall Garbh O'Donnell's castle of Castle Finn, also on that river, and had nearby a village of another kind – one of twenty-five thatched cottages, 'where his troop lies in garrison'.[71] Equally, planters chose sites on the other major rivers for their settlements. Thus on the Deele, the Wilson site on a 'mount' in Killynure appears to be identifiable with the Killynure castle site in the townland of Killynure or Wilson's Fort and this would tend to suggest Convoy as the location of his little village.[72] On the divided Barnes estate the house and village settlement brought into existence by Sir Richard Hansard of Lifford can be identified with Ballindrait, also on the river Deele.[73] The remaining two estates were orientated towards Lough Swilly, in one case, that of Coach, involving a change from his original location. For his part, Sir Ralph Bingley established his own personal residence, on the estate acquired from Berkeley, at Farsetmore and had a little village nearly – 'within a mile' on Pynnar's account and 'in a place which is a continual passage' – the site of which may well be identifiable with one or other (probably Dromore Lower) of the little hamlets in the area.[74] Finally, the Coach estate was to undergo a change of centre and a consequent multiplication of minute concentrations of settler settlement. Sir Thomas abandoned Scarrifhollis, near which a little grouping of houses (perhaps Ardahee nowadays) had been erected, in favour of a new site and residence 'on Lough Swilly', which had four thatched houses near it – Pynnar found six – in 1622. The precise location of this 'mansion house' as it was called in the 1630s, when its location in Fycorranagh quarter was recorded, cannot easily be suggested because of the difficulty in establishing which group of modern townlands represents the quarter of that time; however a case can be made for a site in Coaghmill (erroneously gaelicised in spelling by the Ordnance Survey) townland, with the houses perhaps in Bunnagee, as may be suggested by the presence of some old lanes in the area which appear to interlink.[75]

Beyond the villages, the land on the estates was let out mainly in units comprised of the topographical entities of the time, either full quarters or their sub-denominations, to which Pynnar, for example, seeking to report in terms intelligible by reference to the plantation conditions, sought to ascribe acreage figures. Thus some tenancies were bigger than others. Those with the larger holdings constituted an emerging gentry class within the plantation society. However, with no collection of estate papers available for this area, it is not possible to establish, apart from the evidence of the government surveys, with certainty what the more common tenancies were, or even the amount of demesne land retained by the undertakers. Evidence, however, from a later period does reveal that commonly on each estate two or more freeholders had been created.[76]

Their building obligations constituted one of the principal demands for expenditure or investment which the undertakers had to meet. The residences that they built were not massive structures and were also completed slowly, mirroring the slow development of the plantation as a whole. Since none of these now survives substantially, it is necessary to rely on the contemporary descriptions of them, which are difficult to interpret and which can sometimes be inconsistent. The smallest and simplest, however, was on the Davies estate, described in 1622 as a stone house, thatched, and a bawn 40 feet square (rough cast with lime, according to Pynnar) with two thatched flankers. The other bawns were larger, ranging, according to 1622 descriptions, from 60 feet square (Coach's, which was similar, therefore, to the surviving Brackfield bawn in the Londonderry plantation) to 100 or 120 feet square and, in the case of Bingley's at Farsetmore (described as a bawn of brick), 150 feet square, though not all planter buildings had bawns.

The houses were generally of stone construction and slated. The one exception was Coach's where a 36-foot long thatched timber house had been added to a 24-foot stone and slated one of one and a half storeys, thereby spanning the width of his bawn. None was longer than 60 feet, as was Mansfield's at Killygordon. Many featured a main house to which had been added two 'returns', which may possibly suggest that a common 'architectural' hand – perhaps even Benson's or Hansard's (the latter a military engineer) – had been involved in their construction. The relationship of these structures to the bawns is conjectural as is also the location of their entrances, but it is perhaps possible that some of these 'returns' were in fact advancing or projecting wings, with an entrance porch between them, as appears to have been the case with Goldsmith's Hall at New Buildings. Most were two storeys or one and a half high, with some in varying ways uncompleted by the early 1620s. Thus Mansfield's, described by Pynnar as three storeys and in 1622 as two, had then some of the 'partitions and floors' not finished, while the upper rooms of Wilson's house were then 'unfloored'. Bingley's Ballybofey house, described by Pynnar as a 'strong castle with four large towers' and three storeys high, but unfinished because of controversy between him and Remington's heirs, was still not fully completed by the early 1620s when it is described as two and a half storeys high and with returns. Kingsmill's activity at Castlefinn was of a different order, because he had occupied and re-edified Niall Garbh's former castle or tower-house there and made 'good additions' to it. Described in 1622 as 40 feet square and 43 feet high, constituting three and a half storeys and slated and battlemented, it now had adjoining a strong flankered bawn, to which he intended to make 'an outwork of fortification'.[77] To the crown the grantees' building obligations constituted an exercise in the privatisation of defence. It is in that light that Kingsmill's promise to build his 'outwork', an echo of the fortifications of the contemporary 'military revolution', can be seen. That this was ever constructed (through private finance) may be doubted, but by 1629 a long stone house, 15 feet high (itself reflected, though on a grander scale, in the elegant extension to Donegal castle), had been added to the castle.[78]

These building costs, to which have to be added some mills and the undertakers' part in village construction, may well have had to be met in some degree by borrowing. Through the absence of their own papers, the incomes the undertakers were able to generate only became known (and that roughly) at the end of our period because the rental incomes 'in time of peace' (c.1640) of a few are given, 'to our best information', in the *Civil Survey*. Thus the Wilson estate yielded £430 per annum and the Benson one £109.[79] These may well represent increased rents negotiated in the mid-1630s when many early leases are likely to have expired. If we seek to go deeper, the economy of all lesser figures remains largely hidden.

The effects on the Irish population on these estates under the plantation is a question to which no precise and therefore entirely satisfactory answer can be given. Even though it meant the end of war and of the O'Donnell war taxation which had accompanied it and even though the plantation itself was a relatively thin one, plantation can scarcely have failed to be deeply traumatic for those who had held land in the previous society. In theory the native Irish population should move away entirely from the lands of the undertakers, in Donegal as elsewhere, to resettle on the lands of any of the other categories of grantee. That here, too, theory and practice diverged is well known, but how precisely is difficult to assess. That, in general terms no systematic and thorough government-conducted driving off of all of the native population from undertakers' lands was carried out to allow them free scope to plant on arrival, is clear. Equally, the government wished to see the regulation enforced (or at any rate to gain revenue through fines for its avoidance) and brought pressure to bear on the undertakers to do so, while they for their part, given the low intensity of the colonisation, actively sought modification of the rule.[80] Eventually in 1628 a compromise was reached, admitted in article 26 of the *Graces*. The grantees must take out new patents with a doubled quit rent and must covenant that three-quarters of each estate would be planted with settler tenants (with sound conveyances) or used as demesne. Apart from artificers holding small parcels of land who could remain on the three-quarters, Irish tenantry (who might also have leases) should be confined to the remaining quarter.[81] Since those refusing to comply with this compromise could be penalised, a large number of the undertakers were to take out new patents in the ensuing years. It is more difficult, however, to assess what actions may have been taken on the substantive point of Irish tenancies, though, in general, the one-quarter may have been approximating to reality as it then stood. A mechanism of enforcement was, however, found when in July 1630 the committee for Irish affairs of the English privy council recommended that the income from lands held by Irish tenants in excess of the Irish quarter since the dates of the new patents should be sequestered, and applied to satisfy the arrears of two army captains, one of whom, Sir Henry Tichborne, was stationed at Lifford, who should hold such lands during the king's pleasure. Following on enquiries in the counties, a patent of the lands in question, valued in all at some £400, was granted to the two beneficiaries in December 1631.[82] This was also the final government initiative on the matter prior to 1641.

For the Lifford precinct estates, there is no source which links each denomination of land precisely to a tenant on all the estates from the time the plantation was reaching its full pre-1641 extent in the early 1620s. The impression is left, however, that much of the land on most estates had been let by then to settler tenantry, but within a framework of low-intensity colonisation. For what it is worth, inquisitions designating the one-quarter for Irish tenantry survive for Davies's Corlackey estate, Harrington's Ballybofey estate, Benson's at Stranorlar and Kingsmill's based on Castlefinn.[83] Furthermore, land Irish-held in excess of one quarter was sequestered from the undertakers to the benefit of the two captains and granted to them on four estates – Davies's, Harrington's Ballybofey estate and also his Lough Swilly one and Wilson's, in the latter case involving only one tenancy.[84] What this evidence reveals is that the more westerly estates still offered greater opportunity to Irish tenantry and that also where two estates had come into single ownership – Bingley's, now held by his widow and Robert Harrington – plantation had been less effective. A further inquiry in 1632 revealed the same pattern.[85]

The evidence about Irish-held tenancies that emerges in these years (limited in extent though it be) shows that many of these tenancies were in fact sub-tenancies, indicating accordingly that many Irish land-holders had undergone a marked descent in status to sub-tenants. Thus, for example, on the Davies estate, Owen ballagh O'Galchor held the trian of Cashel (183 acres) from Peter Payne, Davies's tenant, at a rent of £1 stg. per annum, while the neighbouring trian of Altnapaste (nowadays 2,362 acres as triangulated by the Ordnance Survey) was held by Turlough ballagh McNulty and Donnagh McNulty at £2 stg. per annum. An Irish tenancy on the Ballybofey estate was held from the widow, Owny, – the name perhaps suggesting an intermarriage – of Edward Carter. Sometimes quite longstanding and complex relation-ships were revealed. Thus, again on the Ballybofey estate, in 1632 Hugh Mergagh O'Donnell and his Irish undertenants held a half quarter of ground for £3.10.0 stg. per annum, and had corn growing on it, originally by demise from Lieutenant John Dutton deceased, tenant to Sir Ralph Bingley, but now held from Edward Torleton, husband of Dutton's widow, under Robert Harrington who had married lady Anne Bingley. In a further complex instance on the same estate, also involving Dutton and Torleton as upper tenants, poignant evidence is revealed of what must have been a disturbance arising in the context of the Anglo-Spanish war: Hughe oge O'Mulwoath, a blacksmith, held a half quarter of land, having been tenant to Owen McFerganan O'Gallogher who had been executed for high treason at the last assizes for county Donegal.[86] The disposition of Torleton's own holdings in the plantation, which comes to light a few years later, may well give a rough indication of the position of Irish landholders generally. One of those with multiple tenancies, he held somewhat over a quarter (here a multiple of modern townlands) on the Ballybofey estate, which was all held by Irish sub-tenants. In addition, he held three quarters of episcopal land in the parish of Leck. One of these, Trimragh (325 acres), was held from him by five settler sub-tenants, while the other two were held by Irish sub-tenants – Toole McHugh oge O'Gallogher, Shane O'Mullarkye and Cahir McArt O'Gallogher.[87] Irish tenants and sub-tenants were, of course, the elite of their type in this area, as were any from it who were restored to land in Kilmacrenan barony. The remainder of the Irish population remains as hidden as most of their sixteenth-century predecessors, for whom there is little clear impression of either their numbers or their social structure, especially the proportion of labourers and artisans. A more general point made by the commissioners in 1622 is also worth noting: that on all the estates in Donegal the number of Irish far exceeded the number of settlers, and that many engaged still in the practice of 'creting' and were also subject to woodkerne 'who take meat and whatsoever else they think fit from them'.

Ecclesiastically, the estates in Lifford precinct were comprehended mainly in five parishes – three, Leck, Stranorlar and Raphoe, in the diocese of Raphoe and two, Lifford or Clonleigh and Donaghmore, in the diocese of Derry. In accordance with the widely-held confessional principles of contemporary European governments, the reformation was being advanced in tandem with the plantation and hence both the churches and the sources of clerical income came into the hands of clergy of the Church of Ireland at this time. The state of the medieval church buildings and what was being done to them emerges from the ecclesiastical visitation in 1622. The cathedral at Raphoe was described by the bishop, Andrew Knox, as 'ruinated and all decayed saving the walls' but for it a roof had been 'these two years past preparing ... which, God willing, will be set up this summer at the bishop's and parishioner's charges'. Here Sir John Wilson was buried in 1636. The other two churches in Raphoe diocese were described just as 'decayed', but 'in repairing at the parishoners charges'. Since the cure of these parishes was linked to the deanery, both had by this stage curates who were graduates – James Scott, M.A. 'a qualified man in doctrine and conversation' for Leck and Robert Connell, M.A. at Stranorlar – paid respectively by the dean, Archibald Adair and like him probably Scots, £20 and £13.6.8 a year. Adair, successor to Phelim O'Doherty who had been presented by the crown in 1609, and himself an M.A. and an 'eloquent scholar and good preacher of God's word', held the position for about twenty years, to be succeeded by a fellow Scot, Alexander Cunningham, M.A., who had been in the diocese since 1611 and was linked by marriage to George Murray of Broughton, one of the original grantees in the plantation in Boylagh and Banagh. At this time the two parishes in Derry diocese, Clonleigh and Donaghmore, shared a common incumbent, Thomas Turpin, M.A., probably an Oxford graduate and prominent in the church system as a prebend, who lived himself at Lifford and who was described by Bishop George Downame as 'an honest man and a good preacher and given to hospitality'. He maintained a curate, however, at Donaghmore, also a graduate, these two, on Downame's account 'preaching either of them in the said parishes *alterius vicibus* every week'. Their churches, however, were still a different matter. Donaghmore was described in 1622 as 'much decayed having neither roof nor good walls saving that the inhabitants have covered one end of it and made it fit for divine service'. In Lifford, though, change was underway. Although the church of Clonleigh was 'ruined', it was soon to be abandoned. Within the town itself, the foundations of an entirely new church of the plantation, provided for in the will of Sir Richard Hansard (d. 1619), had already been laid. From the mid 1620s, the two parishes too had each their own incumbent, Richard Walker of Clonleigh and William Warren of Donaghmore, both of them young graduates of Trinity College, Dublin and the latter, at any rate, himself a product of the plantation.[88] The Protestant clergy in an English-granted barony had thus come to be both Scots and English, with Bishop Knox of Raphoe willing to condone Presbyterian-style ordinations by the laying on of hands as well. Clergy were clearly important as an intelligentsia in the plantation, forming its culture and ethos and linking it to its intellectual roots in England and Scotland. Equally, it might be wrong to assume that such a number of clergy could have had a profound pastoral effect on all members of a rural plantation community. Such English-speaking clergy were also scarcely likely, if so inclined, to provide a mission to the native Irish of the area at least until some measure of bilingualism had begun to arise amongst them as part of the plantation impact. A more effective, if more expensive, church would have been created had each estate been made a parish, as had formed part of the original plantation plan.

Conclusion

In the baronies granted to undertakers colonisation was most intensive in Portlough, less so in Lifford and less again in Boylagh and Banagh. While the Irish were not universally removed from the estates in these baronies, they underwent a descent in status which was, ultimately, conditioned by the degree of new settlement which took place in any specific area of them. Yet over much of this area, the plantation, prior to 1641, can be seen as of relatively low intensity in type. However, some of the other new owners beyond the undertakers' areas, although not specifically required to do so, leased land to new settler tenants as well. Thus the over-riding part of the episcopal lands was leased by the bishops of Raphoe and Derry, generally by the quarter or in longer multiples of quarters, to new settler tenantry, both English and Scots. At Raphoe itself a more intensive pattern emerged. Here, and on a small area of adjacent land, a group of a dozen people, essentially Scots, can be found by the mid 1630s. These, the poor of the plantation, formed the nucleus of the settler town of Raphoe, and were very small holders of land, none with more than eight 'acres' as computed in the *Civil Survey* of the 1650s. Thus one of them, George Buchanan, had a house and garden plot containing two acres, and four acres of land, and the

grazing of four cows on the common of Raphoe. For this he paid
£3.5.0 per annum with 'duties' of 6 capons and 6 hens and three days
service of a man and a horse.[89] At Raphoe, too, Bishop John Leslie
(appointed 1633), his predecessor, Knox, having lived mainly at
Rathmullan and himself, like Knox, a Scot who was also formerly
bishop of the Isles, built his palace, a symbol of his status and one of
the architecturally-innovative glories of the plantation.[90] It is likely that
some of these smallholders were artisans – one held a 'kilroome' –
employed in the building of the bishop's castle or perhaps in the
restoration of the cathedral. This little concentration relates, however,
more to urbanisation than to the more normal settlement of the
countryside, which must now be reverted to. In this regard, some of
the servitors in Kilmacrenan also leased land to incomer tenantry,
though the number of them was quite small. For his part Chichester,
too, leased land in Inishowen to English and Scots but he also created
a body of native Irish freeholders there.[91]

The new urban beginnings in county Donegal of this period can
only be commented on briefly here more to note their scale than to
seek to examine in detail (anyhow without adequate sources) their
occupational structure. The borough and emerging county town of
Lifford, approachable by boats from Lough Foyle, had 'about' 54
houses in it by 1622, 'some of stone and slated, the rest of timber
thatched, inhabited for the most part with English'. It also remained a
garrison centre at this stage, the king's fort, its walls now 'in most part
decayed', having been reserved from the patent to Hansard. However,
the fort itself and its land was granted away (for a rent of £2 Ir. per
annum), as an economy measure, in 1627, though on condition that
the crown might garrison it 'in time of rebellion or war'.[92] Of the
original Lifford corporate body of thirteen, some had been soldiers.
One of the corporators, Thomas Perkins, was part of the pre-plantation
settlement at Derry which arose under Docwra's tutelage, became
lieutenant of Hansard's company and was an executor of his will, and
so occupied a prominent position in the town. His descendant, Richard
Perkins, came to hold the fort and its supply lands of Stramore. The
town had been planned by Hansard to include freeholders and
leaseholders or copyholders, fifty-four in all by the 1622 account. The
authors of the *Civil Survey* recorded (anyhow after 1641) a smaller
number, but confirmed that broad outline. They found twenty-five
freeholders and fourteen copyholders each with a house and garden
plot, two 'acres' of land nearby, and three cows grazing on Lifford
common.[93] The occupations of these people remain elusive: some were
probably artisans and there must have been a merchant or two
amongst them. In November 1613, William Kney of Chester, merchant

and his son (representing a place which was coming to have many links with Ulster) received a licence to keep a wine tavern in the town.[94] One who lived there was Edward Torleton, who, as has been seen, held a number of tenancies of land and may not have been an uncommon type of townsman: certainly a number of people who held land near Raphoe (in addition to the twelve smallholders) also had houses within it.[95] Lifford had many of the characteristics of a plantation town of the period, mainly English (though with some Welsh) in make-up. Also, on the Hansard lands in the immediate neighbourhood, including the little out-village of Ballindrait, there were quite a number of settler tenantry, constituting a small concentration of settlement and with the likely implication that not only was the O'Donnell entourage of c.1600 at Lifford dispersed, but that the immediately local occupiers of that time had been mainly dispersed too. Finally, Hansard's solicitude for the well-being of his new town and its future corporate identity was reflected in his will, providing for the building of the church and a school and for payments for the schoolmaster and his usher and members of the town's governing body.[96]

Although Lifford had a special status as county town and was distinctive given the freehold condition of many of its residents, a number of other of these settlements in Donegal were not dissimilar in size. Some were just the larger estate villages, their residents' occupations unknown, and not places designated for incorporation and urbanisation in the plantation plan. A number were in Portlough among the Scots, reflecting the degree of change there, and although there were none of this size in Lifford precinct, Letterkenny was just on its northern fringe. Thus the 'town' of St Johnstown (larger than Carrigans) 'erected' on the estate originally granted to the duke of Lennox 'which is intended to be made a borough town' and taking its name, we may safely assume, with deferential artifice, from that of Lord Deputy Sir Oliver St John, contained by 1622 some thirty thatched houses and cabins with a few more underway. Equally, by this time Newtowncunningham consisted of forty thatched houses and cabins 'with a stone cawsey in the middle thereof'. For its part, the 'market town' of Letterkenny consisted of fifty thatched houses and one watermill. Both Ramelton and Rathmullan in Kilmacrenan barony were similar in scale. At Ramelton under the aegis of Sir William Stewart there was a 'town' erected made up of forty thatched houses and cabins with a street 'well-paved from the castle to the foundations of a church'. Similarly, at Rathmullan held by Bishop Knox, who had married Bingley's daughter, there was a 'village' erected of fifteen stone houses and thirty timber houses and cabins. The three borough towns in south Donegal – Killybegs, Ballyshannon and Donegal – were somewhat smaller though they may have stood out more than those in Portlough precinct, being in a less colonised environment. Both Ballyshannon and Donegal (which contained the free school) each, by 1622, had some thirty households mainly English, though in the case of Ballyshannon where the English were mostly soldiers there were also some few Irish residents as well. In both cases, however, the townsmen (some of whom, especially at Ballyshannon, were probably involved with the fisheries) had no land given them in freehold and leasehold. The 'new borough town' of Killybegs was smaller, with seventeen British and Irish inhabitants, but here there was an area of common – thirty 'acres' – allotted to the town.[97] The size the towns attained related at least in some measure to the economic development of the resources that surrounded them.

Even with plantation, Donegal remained an agricultural economy (apart from the fisheries) based on arable and pasture, varying with its terrain, and with no decisive evidence available of how these components may have been altered prior to 1641. In the very sympathetic mid-seventeenth century description which accompanies the Down Survey map of the entire barony of Raphoe, the soil (which was 'finely watered' by the rivers 'gliding' through it and 'refreshing' it) was described as 'generally profitable consisting of arable and pasture chiefly ...'. While there was some 'woody land' and 'some bog', the first was 'advantageous ... for shelter, ornament and use' while the second was 'at some times of the year ... profitable and at all times fit for fuel'. The account in the *Civil Survey*, also of the 1650s, is, however, somewhat sharper and perhaps more informative: 'The soil is cold lying in patches intermixt with bog, heath, mountain and some parts towards Lough Foyle fens, most for oats, little for barley and less for wheat [and] reasonable pasturage for small cattle of all sorts'.[98] The effects which had been made, however, on the Donegal economy (subject anyhow to economic vagaries especially in the 1620s) in terms of its productivity, by the injection of new people – quantifiable numerically (about 1,500 adult males)[99] though not in terms of the range of skills amongst them – and of the capital they brought to invest – scarcely quantifiable at all – is not easy to assess through lack of sources. But it would be wrong to assume that there had been none. One area of innovation in the methods of production can, at any rate, be found – the erection of new mills. Many of these were manor mills, powered by water, and used for the grinding of corn. In the Lifford precinct area, for example, these are referred to in 1622 on the Benson estate at Stranorlar, on Hansard's lands at Ballindrait, and on Bingley's Farsetmore estate. However, there is evidence also for the erection of a second type of mill: tuck mills, used in the making of cloth. One such 'tucking mill' which comes to light from the general sources had been erected by 1622 near St Johnstown, where there was also a watermill, on the estate granted originally to the Duke of Lennox. Two mills, a corn mill and a 'tuke' mill, on the Trinity College estate near Mulroy Bay, are mentioned in the *Civil Survey*, while the 'two mills' at Raphoe, noted in the same source, may possibly also have included a tuck mill.[100] Their existence testifies to the emergence of an otherwise concealed settler cloth industry in Donegal. The two descriptions already cited of the barony of Raphoe pointed to more general infrastructural changes which had come about there. In the first, that area was seen as 'neither ... a place uncouth or unfrequented' because there were on it 'many improvements as castles, churches, mills, houses and craghts with other conveniences namely bridges [and] highways', though in the second many of these, especially the planters buildings and also Convoy bridge, were described as 'ruinous', which reflected the impact of war in the previous decade.

Administratively, the plantation period saw the effective beginnings of the integration of Donegal, as a county, into the structures and legal framework of a centralised Ireland. Hence the judges of the assizes were now able to make their regular circuits into the county. The establishment of county, or local, government there meant the appointment of commissions of justices of the peace, their members drawn from the local society but selected by the central government in Dublin, charged with legal and administrative functions. Both their names and their operation are obscure for this period, but, since power was a function of property, the upper levels of the plantation society will have predominated in county government. However, the fact that, as has been seen, Walter McLoughlin MacSweeney had been a justice of the peace, as was his son, shows that the justices were not chosen to be an exclusively settler body. The office of county sheriff (appointed annually) requiring of its holder a familiarity with legal procedures and bearing numerous administrative duties, was a crucial one in county administration. Where names survive for Donegal in a few intermittent years before 1641, the sheriff was always drawn from the settler society.[101] In these ways, common and statute law procedures could now be extended into Donegal and Gaelic procedures discontinued.

The creation of the county and the incorporation of many of the proposed borough towns meant also that constituencies now existed for the return of members to parliaments, three of which were summoned in this period: 1613-15, 1634 and 1640. In the first two, the two county members of the house of commons were Sir John Vaughan and Sir William Stewart, representing a balancing of Scots and English, and both of them military men in origin and grantees in the county. This changed for the 1640 parliament, however, when two English people occupied the seats, Sir Ralph Gore (d. 1642) who was successor to Paul Gore in south Donegal, and Sir Paul Davis, himself now a Donegal landowner but also, as has been seen, prominent in official circles in Dublin. In Ireland, as in England, the influence of government, or of some prominent figure, on the borough or its patron could lead to members being returned for the incorporated towns who had no direct local connection. This was true for some of the Donegal borough seats in all of these parliaments. Thus the election of Thomas Tallis, who was a rent collector for Trinity College, Dublin in the 1630s, as an M.P. for Killybegs (which had been incorporated too late to send members to the 1613-15 parliament), both in 1634 and 1640, may well have been secured as a means of upholding the interests of the college. However, a number had local interests, and a few of them may be mentioned to convey a brief impression of who they were. Of the two members for Ballyshannon in the first parliament, Paul Gore is already familiar while Edward Cherry must have had some local connection, since a Patrick Cherry appears as a tenant on Peter Benson's estate in 1630. Andrew Wilson, an M.P. for Donegal in 1640, derives from the Wilson undertaker family. Edward Torleton, already much mentioned, who lived at Lifford and who had been sheriff in the early 1630s and was also Lady Coach's estate manager, was an M.P. for Killybegs in 1640.[102] Obviously, then, the little plantation towns had not yet developed sufficient corporate identity and wealth to send members clearly their own to parliaments.

If thus 'one law' was beginning to be established, the achievement of 'one church' made little headway.[103] The effects of the extension of the reformation into Donegal at the same time as the plantation were much less profound. Some few, indeed, of the Irish population were drawn towards protestantism, for example those MacSweeney proprietors in Kilmacrenan who have been already noted. Another was the master of the free school (the 'royal school'), Brian Morrison, M.A., 'an Irish native who is conformable in religion and is a very good humanist', the school itself being then (1622) at Donegal rather than Raphoe.[104] It is clear, though, that no movement of any significance towards religious uniformity was underway prior to 1641. Although Bishop Knox on his appointment promised an active policy of evangelisation and sought from the secular arm a rigorous policy of suppression, including the banishing of Catholic priests, both prongs of this necessary partnership appear not to have been brought into action, a fact which may have ameliorated somewhat the difficult relationships of settler and native laities in the new circumstances of plantation.[105] No strenuous mission of conversion of the Irish laity backed by continuous coercive measures to ensure church attendance was systematically sustained.[106]

Furthermore, the reconstruction of the Catholic church in Donegal, to which, as well, commitment may have been heightened by the crisis of the Nine Years' War, began to get under way with the appointment by the papacy of Dr John O'Cullenan, first as vicar-apostolic in 1621, and then as bishop in 1625. Himself of south Donegal origin and with strong Cistercian links, he had studied in the Irish College at Salamanca in Spain, had a doctorate in theology from Rheims and was, by 1618, tutor in the Spanish Netherlands to the young Hugh O'Donnell, son of Rory the first earl of Tyrconnell, who lived there (d. 1642) and was from 1632 to occupy a high military command.[107]

His appointment as bishop coincided with the deteriorating relationship between England and Spain which led to a naval war between them, again, until 1630. During this period, the Franciscan archbishop Florence Conry and Owen Roe O'Neill, a major in the Irish regiment in the Spanish army in the Spanish Netherlands, and both natural leaders of their type, ecclesiastical and aristocratic, were actively seeking to get Spanish backing for the launching of an invasion of Ireland through Killybegs and 'the port of Londonderry', under the leadership of Colonel John O'Neill, son of Hugh and the commander of the Irish regiment, and Hugh O'Donnell – the exile second-generation earls. Their aim, which embraced some of the broader thinking which lay behind the Nine Years' War project in its later stages, was to initiate a military coup d'état from there, with the hope of raising sympathetic insurrections, to be brought about by their own nobilities, in the other parts of Ireland, designed to the creation of a new form of government for Ireland, separated from England, which would have linked it and its lords to the protection of the Spanish monarchy, and made it a part of the wider 'Catholic international' in the Europe of the time. That new form of government for Ireland, which necessarily would override the sensibilities of many of the Old English in Ireland, while conferring central power over Ireland as a whole, in some form, on the two northern 'earls' (each however concerned that the other would secure advantage), would presumably aim to do so in a way which would not disturb their pre-existing power-relationships in Ulster (prior to plantation) or their power over their 'followers' under them in their own lordships. It would, most likely then, reverse the innovations (which sought to curb the nobility) which had flowed from the drastic 'growth of governance' which had accompanied the Tudor and Stuart new departure in Ireland in the century since direct rule. Thus both plantation and the elevation of the freeholders, the two principal innovations with regard to landownership in the outreach parts of Ireland, would probably be ended, and possibly also such centralising tendencies as the extension of county government (so that there would be a plurality of law in Ireland), and also the Catholic Church, holding the church property, would become, in a very prominent way, the official church in Ireland. In the preparatory thinking which underlay all this was a desire to see only militant Catholic ecclesiastics, important as opinion-formers on the spot, appointed to Irish sees. This whole proposition created a short-term emergency because of English uncertainties as to whether Spain was powerful enough to support it, because in the altered balance of power between England and Spain which would flow from it (making Ireland a Spanish dependency garrisoned by Spanish soldiers), English ambitions, especially in the new world, which challenged Spain's claim to sole empire there, and also its influence in Europe, would be checked. As it happened, the whole scheme foundered on its inherent implausibility, and so the plantation in Donegal, which would have been particularly vulnerable to it, remained unchallenged.[108] When, however, even in peacetime with Spain, in the later 1630s, but just as another English crisis – rebellion in Scotland which led to the English civil war – was unfolding, the Countess Bridget sought to negotiate the restoration (within the existing *status quo*) of her son Hugh, Lord Deputy Wentworth's opinion was that it would be too dangerous: it 'might render him little less than a Prince in Ulster'.[109]

These more general points have been necessary because they provide the context of Dr O'Cullenan's appointment. Against this background, his political stance came under suspicion when Lord Deputy Falkland received an information in 1625 suggesting that he had been endeavouring to induce Philip IV's court at Madrid to attempt an invasion of Ireland.[110] Whatever the truth of that, and what in fact also he did preach, which remains unknowable except that his apparent distancing of himself from the exile earl O'Donnell is highly suggestive, he was arrested, and held prisoner for a time in Dublin, in January 1628.[111] His later career as bishop of Raphoe in peacetime (after 1630, the period of heightened tension in Ulster consequent on Anglo-Spanish uncertainties having probably been short-lived) was also not without its difficulties, because what, in effect, now existed in Donegal was an established Protestant Church and a disestablished Catholic one. The acute financial difficulties of a Catholic churchman within the plantation context are stressed in a letter he wrote to Rome in 1636 with the specific purpose of seeking to be transferred to the diocese of Derry instead.[112] In it he pointed out 'not without deep sadness of heart ... how thick [were] the weeds which the persistent heresy daily sows through the influx of the English and Scottish Protestants above all into [his] bishopric'. His poverty arose because as a result, he said, there were scarcely more than 700 Catholic men of 'some note' (that is, of some economic substance) there, and also he had no more than sixteen priests. Nor was this his only problem: he alluded also to his arrest in 1628. Through 'the storms of various calamities and disasters' stirred up by 'false brothers and ecclesiastics' – the former presumably Franciscan friars (which might reveal Cistercian and Franciscan antagonisms or even, perhaps, reinforce the view that he was not, after all, strongly committed to their political thinking which would have involved the renewal of warfare), the latter Bishop Knox and his clergy – he had been detained in Dublin for three months, when he had been twice brought before the lord deputy. His letter perhaps best reveals what had happened in the plantation period – he had been monitored but not expelled and he lacked the lands and revenues of his predecessors – and reveals too, more generally, that Donegal was emerging to be, in the main, in matters of religion a two-culture society.

A formidable exercise in government (though not without parallels in its time), the decision to have a plantation in Ulster was taken in an interlude in the European 'wars of religion' of the sixteenth and seventeenth centuries. Although itself still transitional in character up to 1641, for Donegal plantation had many consequences, not least the sweeping away of the O'Donnells as lords there and also of the landed base of medieval monasticism. Accompanying it, too, was the substitution of protestantism (itself not fully orthodox) for catholicism as the established church, though not to the exclusion of catholicism which survived even within the plantation context. It also laid the foundations of a new culture there, English and lowland Scottish, using the English language.[113] It survived through the 1620s, through the failure of Ulster Irish emigré schemes, just mentioned (themselves broader in conception), designed to achieve Spanish and papal backing for military intervention in Ireland. In the areas uncolonised, dues and revenues which had supported the old élite – henceforth taking mainly the form of rents, payable, in theory at any rate, in accordance with English property law conventions – now supported the beginnings of a new and more diffused replacement one of which some of the old owners formed a part. In the areas colonised the change, of course, meant much more than that. If the extent of economic expansion and re-orientation which resulted from plantation in its early decades is not fully apparent (in this context note must be taken of the 'improvements' and innovations and new urban beginnings mentioned above), and although the degree of concurrent religious change among the Donegal Irish was very slight, its political importance is clear: plantation saw the beginnings of the absorption of the former O'Donnell lordship into a centralised Ireland and therefore marked, in many ways, a decisive change from the past.

References

1. *Cal. S.P. Ire., 1606-8*, pp 268-9, 275-7.
2. Ibid., pp 289-90.
3. There were some exceptions to this arising from prior grants of some of this land.
4 Nothing came of a proposal to endow and establish a 'hospital' for 'diseased and maimed' soldiers.
5. For more detailed figures see P. Robinson, *The plantation of Ulster* (Dublin, 1984), p. 86.
6. *Conditions to be observed by the British undertakers of the escheated lands in Ulster* (London, 1610).
7. Conditions to be observed by the servitors and natives (7 April 1610) in *Anal. Hib.* viii, 220-22.
8. *Cal. pat. rolls Ire., Jas I*, p. 182.
9. Ibid., pp 195, 483, 561, 566, 572.
10. Ibid., pp 197-8 (patent to Nugent). For architectural descriptions see B. Lacy *et. al., Archaeological survey of county Donegal* (Lifford, 1983), pp 329-30, 340-41. Flannacharta was later acquired by Brooke and Gore built at Magherabeg.
11. *Cal. pat. rolls Ire., Jas I*, p. 187; *Cal. pat. rolls Ire., Eliz.*, pp 361-2; D. O'Connor, *St Patrick's purgatory, Lough Derg* (Dublin, 1931 ed.), pp 129-31; P. Ó Gallachair, The parish of Carn' in *Clogher Rec., 1975*, pp 301-80; Lacy, *Archaeological Survey*, pp 351-13. The conflicting claims of Bishop Montgomery and Archbishop Magrath came to a head in September 1609 (*Cal. S.P. Ire., 1608-10*, pp 288-9) and the decision to grant the land to Magrath was based on prior legal entitlement arising from the regrant of 1596. Magrath's patent (crown rent, £2 Ir.) also represented a defeat for Robert Leicester, whose general grant in 1604, procured by Lord Mountjoy, had included these territories. Uncertainty as to which county these lands were in – 'in the confines of the counties of Fermanagh, Tyrone and Donegal' in James Magrath's patent – permeates the official record.
12. Two existing castles are, however, referred to in 1596.
13. A. Gwynn and R. N. Hadcock, *Medieval religious houses: Ireland* (London, 1970), pp 39, 272.
14. *Anal. Hib.*, viii, 291. It was thought that the bishop of Raphoe might also live there.
15. There had been no recent late-wave monastic foundation in Inishowen by the O'Dohertys.
16. *Cal. pat. rolls Ire., Jas I*, pp 149, 153, 161, 169, 173. A decision that Chichester should enter into a recognizance to surrender within three years 1,000 acres of land for the better maintenance of the Londoners' new city was silently omitted from his second patent. This decision bears relation to a similar one, actually carried out, that Sir Randal MacDonnell should surrender lands near Coleraine to the Londoners to enhance their second town there.
17. *Anal. Hib.*, viii, 288, 291.
18. This is the origin of the proposal that Chichester should surrender 1,000 acres from his Inishowen grant.
19. Carndonagh was probably intended by 'Dowagh in Enishowen'. Another version of the 'project' does not include it (*Cal. Carew MSS, 1603-24*, p. 18).
20. I have set out the evolution of this policy in my 'Ulster plantation towns, 1609-41' in D. Harkness and M. O'Dowd (eds), *The town in Ireland: Historical Studies*, 13 (Belfast, 1981), pp 55-8.
21. *Cal. pat. rolls Ire., Jas I*, pp 219-20.

22. Ibid., pp 224-5.
23. On Jones see M. O'Dowd, *Power, politics and land: early modern Sligo, 1588-1688* (Belfast, 1991), passim.
24. *Cal. pat. rolls Ire., Jas I*, p. 300.
25. Strictly, then, additional corporation land was not made available in all places.
26. *Cal. pat. rolls Ire., Jas I*, p. 182. The area concerned was the Roughan, the Dorroghes and the remainder of the quarter of Liffer except the part called Stramore.
27. These 4 acres, to be measured at the rate of 21 foot to the perch, lay at the north-east of the meadow where the rivers of Deele and Finn joined.
28. *Cal. pat. rolls Ire., Jas I*, pp 206-7. Amongst other rights that Hansard received were ferries over the Finn and Deele.
29. The incorporation of St Johnstown came later.
30. G. Hill, *An historical account of the plantation in Ulster at the commencement of the seventeenth century, 1608-1620* (Belfast, 1877), pp 322-7; M. Percevel-Maxwell, *The Scottish migration to Ulster in the reign of James I* (London, 1973), pp 360-61.
31. The most convenient list is in Hill, *Plantation in Ulster*, pp 327-30. I have generally tried to retain the spellings of names as they appear at the time in an effort to minimise confusion in identifications.
32. *Cal. pat. rolls Ire., Jas I*, pp 248, 306, 309.
33. N.A.I., Lodge MSS, vi, 189.
34. *Cal. pat. rolls Ire., Jas I*, pp 210-11; *Civil Survey*, iii, 131-3.
35. *Cal. pat. rolls Ire., Jas I*, p. 184; *Civil Survey*, iii, 129-30; *Cal. S.P. Ire., 1633-47*, p. 344.
36. *Cal. pat. rolls Ire., Jas I*, p. 180; *Civil Survey*, iii, 106-7.
37. Hill, *Plantation in Ulster*, pp 526-7. MacSweeney Fanad's held 'from three years to three years' at that time.
38. M. Perceval-Maxwell, *Scottish migration*, passim; G. Donaldson, *Scotland: James V-James VII* (Edinburgh, 1971), p. 218; *Cal. pat.rolls Ire., Jas I*, pp 277, 483, 488.
39. B.L., Add. MS 36,775, ff 104ᵛ-5; *Cal. pat. rolls Ire., Jas I*, p. 488.
40. N.A.I., Lodge MSS, v, 135-9; vi, 247, 490-501. Rory O'Donnell had claimed in 1607 that the duties of the fishing of Killybegs had been worth £500 per annum (quoted in C. Conaghan, *History and antiquities of Killybegs* (Ballyshannon, 1974), p. 88.
41. Hill, *Plantation in Ulster*, p. 501; *Inq. cancell. Hib. repert.*, ii, Donegal (32) Chas I.
42. B.L., Sloane MS 3,827, f. 63.
43. This is based on Pynnar's survey of 1618-19 of the plantation in this area, printed in Hill, *Plantation in Ulster*, pp 500-4 and on the survey of 1622 [henceforth cited as Treadwell (ed.), '1622 survey'], printed in V. W. Treadwell (ed.), 'The plantation in Donegal: a survey' in *Donegal Annual* 2 (1951-4), 513-5.
44. *Inq. cancell. Hib. repert.*, ii, Donegal (17) Chas I.
45. B.L., Harleian MS 2138, ff 164-89.
46. This includes land drained and reclaimed prior to the mid-nineteenth century.
47. M. Percevel-Maxwell, *Scottish migration*, passim.
48. Coolmacitrain appears to be identifiable with Castle Forward.
49. M. Perceval-Maxwell, *Scottish migration*, p. 224.
50. *Anal. Hib.*, viii, 224-5.
51. Since this section is a preliminary part of a study of the English in the plantation as a whole, I have deferred the detailed footnoting of it to that time.
52. *Anal. Hib.*, viii, 209. In fact they met him outside Dublin late in September, and Lyttleton may not have come until 1611.

53. *Cal. Carew MSS, 1603-24*, pp 221-22. On Caphar oge see *Cal. S.P. Ire., 1606-8*, pp 124-5, 129-30, 513; *1608-10*, pp 29, 87, 104, 112,, 264.

54. *H. M. C., Hastings MSS*, iv, 171-2. T. W. Moody, *Londonderry plantation*, p. 351. Arthur Terry, who was from Southwark, sold his half of what had been a joint purchase from Clare, to Benson, his partner, in October 1615 (*Inq. Cancell. Hib. Repert.*, ii, Donegal (10) Chas I).

55. N.A.I., R.C. 9/1, p. 183; G. A. Usher, *Gwysaney and Owston: a history of the family of Davies-Cooke of Gwysaney, Flintshire and Owston, West Riding of Yorkshire* (Denbigh, 1964), pp 7-50. (The author was unaware of the Ulster plantation connection.)

56. *Inq. cancell. Hib. repert.* ii, Donegal (11) Chas I; *Cal. S.P. Ire., 1608-10*, p. 509; *Cal. Carew MSS, 1603-24*, pp 217-8, 385.

57. Usher, *Gwysaney and Owston*, p. 47.

58. N.A.I., Lodge MSS, vi, 304.

59. See my 'Sir Ralph Bingley, c.1570-1627: Ulster planter' in P. Roebuck (ed.), *Plantation to partition: Essays in Ulster history in honour of J.L. McCracken* (Belfast, 1981), pp 14-28, 253-6.

60. N.A.I., Lodge MSS, v, 219-20; vi, 190-92; T. W. Moody, *Londonderry plantation*, pp 301, 314, 323-5, 337, 446.

61. P.R.O.N.I., T 1021, pp 116-28. Some time after 1641 a Scot, Andrew Hamilton, succeeded to the Wilson estate through marriage.

62. *H. M. C., Hastings MSS*, iv, 171-2. Like Terry, Vaughan disengaged from Berkeley's estate, leaving it to be entirely owned by Bingley and with him probably went the arrangement with Clinton.

63. Pynnar's survey of this area is printed in Hill, *Plantation in Ulster*, pp 514-22.

64. For the text of the 1622 survey of this area see Treadwell (ed.), '1622 survey', pp 515-7.

65. With regard to Pynnar's survey, while there are instances throughout it of conscientious endeavour to probe really dubious information, he may have presented his evidence (for example the acreage figures) – and also have had it presented to him – too readily in a form that would be intelligible in terms of the plantation conditions the performance of which he was sent to investigate.

66. R. J. Hunter (ed.), 'The settler population of an Ulster plantation county' in *Donegal Annual*, 10 (1971-3), 124-54.

67. Ibid.; *Inq. cancell. Hib. repert.*, ii, Donegal (17) Chas I.

68. Treadwell (ed.), '1622 survey', p. 515.

69. Ibid.

70. Ibid. Pynnar found just one village 'standing on a passage very commodious for the king's service ...' (Hill, *Plantation in Ulster*, p. 517).

71. Given the size of Kingsmill's command, the 1622 commissioners' number of 25 cottages is to be preferred to Pynnar's 30.

72. Treadwell (ed.), '1622 survey', p. 516.

73. The Ordnance Survey memoir also gives a hint to its location (R.I.A., O.S. memoirs, Box 21/111, p. 20).

74. See my 'Sir Ralph Bingley' (fn 59 above). The Farsetmore site may have some archaeological potential and I would be delighted to be involved in an excavation there.

75. N.A.I., Lodge MSS, vi, 190. The site of the later manor house (now demolished) in Corravaddy has to be ruled out since Corravaddy was in a different quarter. I am indebted to Mr. J. Harris of Coachmills for his assistance with the local topography.

76. *Civil Survey*, iii, 24-37. More freeholds were created in the later seventeenth century.

77. This section is based on the surveys of Pynnar and the 1622 commissioners.
78. *Inq. cancell. Hib. repert.*, ii, Donegal (11) Chas I.
79. *Civil Survey*, iii, 24, 34.
80. T. W. Moody, 'The treatment of the native population under the scheme for the plantation in Ulster' in *I.H.S.*, i, no. 1 (Mar. 1938), pp 59-63.
81. *Cal. S.P. Ire., 1625-32*, pp 349-52.
82. N.A.I., Lodge MSS, v, 526-7.
83. *Inq. cancell. Hib. repert.*, ii, Donegal, (10), (11), (12) Chas I; N.A.I., R.C. 9/1. Only from the restoration do sources, especially the hearth money rolls, become available for Donegal that relate occupancy precisely to place names.
84. N.A.I., Lodge MSS, v, 526-7.
85. *Inq. cancell. Hib. Repert.*, ii, Donegal (17) Chas I.
86. Ibid., (14), (17) Chas I. Whether these were the original places of residence of these Irish tenants or whether they had moved from elsewhere is not clear.
87. N.A.I., R.C. 9/1. These British sub-tenants are not a hidden sub-tier of the plantation; most are on the muster roll of 1630.
88. T.C.D., MS 550, ff 193, 210; J. B. Leslie, *Derry clergy and parishes* (Enniskillen, 1937), pp 155-60, 195-200; Idem, *Raphoe clergy and parishes* (Enniskillen, 1940), pp 13-15, 102-3, 121-24. With regard to Lifford, the old Templebogan or Ballybogan church, of which parts still remain, some two miles from Lifford, may possibly have been used at first as an alternative to Clonleigh.
89. *Civil Survey*, iii, 46.
90. For the architectural genre see E. McParland, 'Rathfarnham castle, co. Dublin: a property of the Society of Jesus' in *Country Life*, 9 September 1982, 734-7.
91. *Inq. cancell. Hib. repert.*, ii Donegal (11) Jas I.
92. N.A.I., Lodge MSS, v, 52-3.
93. *Civil Survey*, iii, 38.
94. *Cal. pat. rolls Ire., Jas I*, p. 261.
95. *Civil Survey*, iii, 41-3.
96. The inscription on his monument in Lifford Church of Ireland church gives the details.
97. This section has been based mainly on Pynnar's survey and that made by the commissioners in 1622.
98. N.L.I., Down Survey maps, terrier to Raphoe barony map; *Civil Survey* iii, 23.
99. R. J. Hunter (ed.), 'The settler plantation of an Ulster plantation county' in *Donegal Annual*, 10 (1971-3), 124-54.
100. *Civil Survey*, iii, 45, 100.
101. For a partial list of sheriffs see P.R.O.N.I., D302, pp 55-6.
102. For lists of the MPs see T. W. Moody, 'The Irish parliament under Elizabeth and James I: a general survey' in *Proc. R.I.A.*, 45C (1939), 80; H. F. Kearney, *Strafford in Ireland, 1633-41* (Manchester, 1959), pp 255-6; *Commons' jn. Ire.*, i (Dublin, 1763), 217.
103. The reference is to the French crown's ideal: 'one law, one church, one king'.
104. T.C.D., MS 550, f. 220.
105. For Bishop Knox's efforts in this respect in his early years, and for the support he sought from the government, see Alan Ford, *The protestant reformation in Ireland, 1590-1641* (Frankfurt am Main, 1985), pp 166-8.
106. Even the churches themselves were in poor repair up to the early 1620s. There is little information available on the collection of recusants' fines in Ulster.
107. On Bishop O'Cullenan see Donal F. Cregan, 'The social and cultural background of a counter-reformation episcopate, 1618-60' in A. Cosgrove and D. McCartney

(eds), *Studies in Irish history presented to R. Dudley Edwards* (Dublin, 1979), pp 85-117. For Hugh O'Donnell see J. I. Casway, *Owen Roe O'Neill and the struggle for Catholic Ireland* (Philadelphia, 1984), pp 27, 29-33, 38.

108. I hope to return to this later. For a short analysis of Owen Roe O'Neill, see Raymond Gillespie, 'Owen Roe O'Neill, *c.*1582-1649: soldier and politician' in G. O'Brien and P. Roebuck (eds), *Nine Ulster lives* (Belfast, 1992), pp 149-68.

109. W. Knowler (ed.), *The earl of Strafforde's letters and despatches* (London, 1739), ii, 269.

110. *Cal. S.P. Ire., 1625-32*, p. 5.

111. Ibid., p. 304; Cregan, 'Counter-reformation episcopate', p. 94.

112. P. F. Moran (ed.), *Spicilegium Ossoriense: being a collection of original letters and papers illustrative of the history of the Irish church from the reformation to the year 1800* (Dublin, 1874), pp 212-3. I am indebted to Robert Martindale and Joy Rutherford of Cambridge and to Frank D'Arcy for translations.

113. A long-range reflection of that in the plantation society can be seen in the career (transcending Ireland) and writings (reflecting it) of William Allingham.

I am grateful to L. J. Arnold, Brian Lacy, Seán Connolly, Josephine Cowley, Laura Houghton, Henry Jefferies, Keith Lindley, John McCavitt, Michael McGuinness, Anne Moffett, Mary Monaghan, Winifred Montgomery and Hiram Morgan for their help in various ways, as well as to many people in Donegal who assisted with investigations on the ground and to the editors and publisher for their patience.

Chapter 11

BRITISH SETTLER SOCIETY IN DONEGAL, c. 1625-1685

KEVIN J. McKENNY

Traditionally the events of mid-seventeenth-century Ireland have been looked at from the perspective of a Catholic Ireland struggling against the colonising exploits of the Protestant English.[1] As a counter to this particular genre, this paper, while considering the fortunes of the Gaelic landholders, will focus primarily on the decades of warfare, confiscation and scramble for land (so characteristic of the Restoration period) through the experiences of the British settlers in Donegal.

As changes in land tenures are central to this study, it is essential to begin by enumerating the measured acres which comprised Donegal in the seventeenth century. The county was not comprehensively surveyed until the government commissioned such a project in the mid-1650s. The statistical results of these surveys are outlined in table 11.1.

Table 11.1[2]

Profitable and unprofitable acreage in county Donegal, by Barony, as admeasured by the Civil and Down Surveys

	Unprof.	%	Prof.	%	Total	%
Killmacrenan	17,273	29	41,745	71	59,018	100
Rapho	9,622	29	32,962	71	42,584	100
Boylagh-Banagh	6,852	26	19,495	74	26,347	100
Tirhugh	2,563	25	7,759	75	10,322	100
Inishowen	9,695	40	14,826	60	24,521	100
Donegal totals	**46,005**	**28**	**116,787**	**72**	**162,792**	**100**

These figures should not be taken as equivalent to the Ordnance Survey area of the respective baronies as it is obvious that much of the acreage values furnished by the Book of Survey and Distribution, especially those pertaining to Protestant holdings, were never measured in Petty's Down Survey. Instead, the figures provided by the less accurate Civil Survey were used.[3]

I

Until the end of Elizabeth I's reign in 1603, Ulster in general and Donegal in particular was an area still unfamiliar to the English.[4] The conclusion of the Nine Years' War in 1603, however, brought an end to the cultural insularity of the province.[5] The English government, aiming to achieve this policy, launched a deliberate scheme to diminish the lordly, particularly landed, powers of the Irish chieftains in the area.[6] That process has come to be termed the Plantation of Ulster, a particular event that has been dealt with extensively elsewhere.[7]

The departure in 1607 of many of Ulster's defeated Gaelic chieftains facilitated the escheat to the crown of their lands, including most of county Donegal.[8] In 1608 a special commission drew up plans for the planting of this confiscated land. The escheated lands were to be divided into great, middle and small proportions (2,000, 1,500 and 1,000 acres), each of which was to be passed, under dramatic new land tenures to one of three classes: undertakers, servitors or deserving natives.[9] The undertakers, who came from Scotland and England, were to convert the proportions granted them into exclusively British settlements by entering into an undertaking to bring tenants and artisans from either Scotland or England. The same restrictions were not, however, imposed on the other two classes of grantees.[10]

Between the plantation of Ulster and 1641 there was a significant decline in the numbers of original grantees[11] as a direct result of estate consolidation in the land market which evolved.[12] An elite planter society soon materialised from the fluid land market, and constituted, in effect, a new economic order.[13] The need to adapt to this market, money-orientated economy, which threatened the traditional values of many Gaelic septs, led to (as yet unmeasured) turnover of land in various parts of the island.[14] Tables 11.2 and 11.3, which relate to landholding and not ownership, represent the sum of individual land acquisitions or land losses in Donegal during this period.[15]

A striking feature of landholding patterns in 1641 Donegal is that a total of seventy Protestants from England (39 per cent) and an equal number from Scotland (also 39 per cent) held land in 1641. Similarly the acreage which each of these ethnic groups held (64,036 and 63,462 acres respectively) constituted 39 per cent of the total surveyed acres for Donegal.

It is also apparent from these tables that the barony of Rapho (by far the more densely populated), which originally was set aside for under-takers from England was, by 1641, densely populated by Protestant landholders from Scotland. Likewise the barony of Boylagh Banagh, which was originally parcelled out to undertakers from Scotland,

Table 11.2 [a]

The ethno-religious pattern of landholders in Donegal by Barony, 1641

	Kill.		Rapo.		Boy.		Tir.		Inis.		Donegal[b]	
EP	17	26%	45	48%	5	36%	4	33%	9	64%	70	39%[c]
SP	23	35%	43	46%	6	43%	2	17%	—	—	70	39%
RC	19	29%	—	—	—	—	1	8%	3	21%	23	13%
IP	3	5%	—	—	—	—	—	—	—	—	3	2%
DP	1	2%	—	—	—	—	—	—	—	—	1	1%
UP	—	—	4	4%	2	14%	—	—	—	—	6	3%
OT	2	3%	2	2%	1	7%	5	42%	2	14%	5	3%
Total	**65**	**100%**	**94**	**100%**	**14**	**100%**	**12**	**100%**	**14**	**100%**	**178**	**100%**

[a]   Tables 11.2 and 11.3 were constructed by categorising and aggregating landholders by their ethno-religious origins. This was facilitated by extracting values from three separate fields in my data-base. The Donegal totals are the actual number of landholders in the county (some held land in multiple baronies).

[b]   The codes used for the ethno-religious denominations in both tables include – EP: English Protestant; SP: Scottish Protestant; RC: Roman Catholic (Gaelic); IP: Irish Protestants; DP: Dutch Protestant; OP: Other Protestant (used where it is known that the subject is Protestant but whose ethnic origin cannot be ascertained); OT: Other (used for church, school and college lands). Donegal's baronies have been coded as follows; Kill: Killmacrenan; Rapo: Rapho; Boy: Boylagh Banagh; Tir: Tirhugh; Inis: Inishowen.

[c]   All percentages are to the nearest whole and are computed as portions of each of the respective baronies. For example, the 17 English Protestants in the Barony of Killmacrenan comprised 26 per cent of the 65 landholders in that barony in 1641. The Donegal percentages are portions of the total number of landholders in that county in 1641.

Table 11.3

The ethno-religious pattern of landholding in Donegal, by Barony, 1641 [a]

	Kill.		Rapo.		Boy.		Tir.		Inis.		Donegal	
EP	15,915	27%	20,262	48%	1,202	5%	3,345	32%	23,312	95%	64,036	39%
SP	19,318	33%	21,289	50%	21,717	82%	1,138	11%	—	—	63,462	39%[b]
RC	15,533	26%	—	—	—	—	500	5%	160	1%	16,193	10%
IP	360	1%	—	—	—	—	—	—	—	—	360	–1%
DP	1,166	2%	—	—	—	—	—	—	—	—	1,166	1%
UP	—	—	174	–1%	2,439	9%	—	—	—	—	2,613	2%
OT	6,726	11%	859	2%	989	4%	5,339	52%	1,049	4%	14,962	9%
Total	**59,018**	**100%**	**42,584**	**100%**	**26,347**	**100%**	**10,322**	**100%**	**24,521**	**100%**	**162,792**	**100%**

[a]   All acreage figures include profitable and unprofitable acres which the respective landholders had in their possession in 1641.

[b]   All percentages are to the nearest whole and are computed from the total acreage of the respective baronies. For example, the 15,915 acres held by English Protestants in the Barony of Killmacrenan comprised 27 per cent of the total surveyed acreage for that barony (59,018 acres) in 1641.

contained almost an equal number of Protestants from England by 1641.[15]

Protestants from Scotland predominate in the barony of Killmacrenan, originally parcelled out to servitors and deserving natives. Twenty-three people from this ethnic group held 19,318 acres, or 33 per cent of the area in 1641. A further seventeen Protestants from England held 15,915 (27 per cent); three Irish Protestants (of Gaelic Irish descent) and one Dutch Protestant (Wilbrant Olpherts) held land in this barony.[16] These shared Killmacrenan with nineteen Gaelic Irish Catholics who held 15,533 acres (26 per cent of the barony). The confinement of this ethnic group (comprised mainly of MacSweenys) to Killmacrenan in 1641 was determined largely by a conscious government policy which deliberately weakened the power structures of the major Gaelic families by reducing some to tenant level. This practice was pursued in order to diminish the power of the chieftain by undermining his economic and political power over his followers. To that end the state allotted a one or two ballyboe freehold (between 60 to 100 acres) to the natives in Killmacrenan, while the leaders of septs tended to received much larger grants which they, in turn, subdivided among lesser families.

The pattern of landholding in Donegal (both Gaelic and settler) on the eve of the rebellion in 1641 was mixed suggesting success by some and failure by others.[17] The process of land consolidation resulted in the estate system which evolved in settler society in Donegal. This pattern was produced by the initial plantation scheme, but was also the result of the land market, generated in the wake of the plantation.[18] Table 11.4, which shows the size distribution of settler estates in Donegal in 1641, illustrates this in statistical terms.

Thirty-nine planter estates in Donegal were 99 acres or less, estates small enough to be farmed by one family. In contrast, only 8 per cent of the land surveyed in the area (60,839 acres) was held by twelve individuals in estates of 3,000 acres or more.[20] While the initial

Table 11.4 [19]

Size distribution of settler estates in Donegal, 1641

Acres	Number of estates	% of estates	Number of acres	% of land surveyed
0-99	39	27%	1,349	1%
100-299	36	24%	6,307	5%
300-999	35	24%	21,676	17%
1,000-2,999	25	17%	41,106	31%
3,000 plus	12	8%	60,839	46%
Totals	**147**	**100%**	**131,277**	**100%**

plantation scheme doled out estates ranging in size from between 1,000 to 3,000 acres, estate consolidation led to the creation of much smaller estates. The largest proportion of holdings was held by seventy-five people (47 per cent) whose estates ranged in size from between 1 to 299 acres. In contrast, only seventeen per cent, or twenty-five individuals, held estates between 1,000 and 2,999 acres. Table 11.5 which shows the size distribution of Gaelic estates in the same period indicates a different pattern.

Table 11.5 [21]

Size distribution of Gaelic Irish estates in Donegal, 1641

Acres	Number of estates	% of estates	Number of acres	% of land surveyed
0-99	05	19%	319	1%
100-299	05	19%	934	6%
300-999	11	42%	5,953	36%
1,000-2,999	04	15%	5,030	30%
3,000 plus	01	04%	4,317	27%
Totals	**26**	**100%**	**16,553**	**100%**

Only one Catholic, Turlagh O'Boyle, held an estate larger than 3,000 acres in Donegal.[22] The four estates ranging between 1,000 and 2,999 acres were held by Turlagh O'Donnell and three MacSweenys, two of whom (Donell and Ervin, under Brehon Law, would be 'the MacSweeny Doe' and 'the MacSweeny Banagh' – chieftains of their respective septs) were originally granted great portions (2,000 acres) as deserving natives.[23] The third MacSweeny, Turlagh, appears to have obtained his large holding by combining some of the smaller original plantation grants.

While the branches of MacSweeny Doe and MacSweeny Banagh appear to have weathered the revolution in land tenures, brought about by the introduction of the new economic order into Ulster, the same cannot be said for Sir Mulmorry MacSweeny (head of the Fanad MacSweeny branch). While he was also originally granted a 'great portion' as a deserving native, his estate had diminished so much by sale and mortgage that his heirs only held 512 acres by 1641.

II

On 23 October 1641, claiming a commission from the king, the natives of Ulster rose and attacked the settlers in their immediate vicinity.[24] In west Ulster, Sir Phelim O'Neill initially managed to seize some places of note. The domicile of Lord Caulfield, Charlemont Castle, was one of his first objectives. He took this with no resistance as the unsuspecting Caulfield invited O'Neill and his retinue into the castle for pleasantries, learning too late the real objectives of the visit.[25] Charlemont was followed shortly afterwards by Dungannon, which the rebels got possession of on Saturday 23 October.[26]

While O'Neill was securing the Protestant strongholds in his local area, the dominant Donegal septs of MacSweenys and O'Donnells, after some hesitation, attempted to take the local strongholds but were everywhere repulsed by the levies hastily gathered by the settlers.[27]

By the middle of November almost all of Ulster outside of the north west, along with Antrim and north Down had been over-run with the exception of isolated garrisons, such as Enniskillen, which held out under Sir William Cole.[28]

While Dublin's magazine was well equipped, with a shortage of experienced soldiers to put the weapons there to good use, the same cannot be said for north-west Ulster, where there were no shortage of recruits but where no munitions were initially available to arm them.[29] That this was so was confirmed by the elders of Londonderry who, in January 1642, complained to the lords justices that there were only a few 'rotten culverins' and 'not 100 swords' in Londonderry. The blame for this crucial deficiency was assigned to Wentworth who 'caused our best and most useful ordinance to be carried away from us'.[30] In 1639 Strafford had seen to it that many settlers, especially those of Scottish origin, were disarmed and forbidden to hold or store any arms except those which they might receive from the magazine at Dublin.[31] While Strafford's earlier policies of disarming the settlers caused some handicaps, these were in some ways mitigated by advance warnings, along with indecisiveness on the part of the insurgents.[32] In addition to these warnings, refugees from mid-Ulster immediately began arriving in Coleraine and Londonderry, telling tales of rebel atrocities and apparent intentions.[33]

It appears that a combination of Sir William Cole's warnings, the arrival of refugees, hesitation on the part of the Donegal rebels, and the relative distance of the Lagan army's domiciles from the core of the rebellion ensured that they were, to a certain extent, ready to meet the challenge when it finally arrived. And it was perhaps this latter reason, combined with the verity that the rebels originally intended no harm to Scottish settlers, that allowed those from Donegal a slight reprieve which was all they required to prepare themselves for the assault when it came.

Sir William and Sir Robert Stewart are the two commanders credited with organising the Donegal settlers into what was to become one of the more efficient and impressive of all the military forces operating in Ireland at that time – the Lagan army, named after the Lagan valley, a fertile district in the barony of Rapho, county Donegal.[34]

Both Robert and William were at their residences – Newtownstewart – when the first of the warning horsemen carrying news of the rebel outburst reached them.[35] After dispatching warnings to the local strongholds, Sir William quickly gathered his family and relatives and hastened to Coleraine and later to Londonderry, where he dispatched all of them to Glasgow. His progeny secure, he immediately took steps to increase the size of his company which was then quartered at Rapho.[36] Simultaneously, Sir Robert, anticipating the king's commission, immediately recruited his regiment from among the British settlers in the area.[37]

The Lagan army's third regiment was raised by Sir Ralph Gore from a combination of refugees and settlers in the Ballyshannon area of Donegal. Once Ballyshannon was suitably fortified and garrisoned, Gore's regiment immediately marched northwards, successfully relieving the settlers in central Donegal then under siege by the MacSweenys and O'Donnells. This regiment acted as a protective cordon around a refugee camp which was hastily constructed. Their position grew ever more precarious as an increasing number of Gaelic septs converged on the area. Aid and succour arrived in the form of Sir Robert Stewart's regiment, however, which quickly marched over the Barnesmore Gap to Gore's relief and, together with the latter force, managed to convey the refugees Gore had been succouring back to Rapho.[38] Their route to safety took them back through the Barnesmore Gap which Stewart describes as 'being three miles long and not above a musket shot in breath'.[39] Here they were ambushed. The surviving women and children among the refugees were dispatched to Londonderry while the able-bodied were recruited into the Lagan army.[40] Sir Ralph Gore died shortly after his arrival in Rapho and his regiment came under the command of Audley Mervyn who, in his reports to the House of Commons, left the historian with an almost day-by-day account of the military manoeuvres of the Lagan army in north-west Ulster.[41] The fourth regiment was that of Sir William Cole who raised, under the king's commission, 500 men from Enniskillen and its surrounding districts. This effectively brought the strength of the Lagan corps to four regiments of foot and about fourteen other companies, from Londonderry, Coleraine and Limavady, who joined with the Laganeers at various times, depending on the campaign strategies.[42] Table 11.6 lists the foot raised in Donegal which became the nucleus of the Lagan army.

Table 11.6[43]

Soldiers raised in Donegal, 1641-2

Commander	Number	Place raised[a]		
Sir Robert Stewart	1,100	Donegal/Tyrone	KC	Y
Sir William Stewart	1,185	Donegal/Tyrone	KC	Y
Colonel Audley Mervyn	1,000	South Donegal	KC	Y[b]
Sir William Hamilton	100	North Donegal	PC	Y

a   These last two columns indicate the type of commission under which the regiment or company was raised, and whether or not they were taken into the pay of the parliament in 1643. KC: King's Commission; PC: Parliament's Commission; Y: taken into parliamentary pay.

b   Mervyn took over this regiment on the death of Sir Ralph Gore, who was the original recipient of the commission. Mervyn was also responsible for increasing the regiment to 1,000 from its originally commissioned strength of 500.

The Lagan force was initially formed to protect the settlers of Donegal, but as individuals, companies and regiments joined it from the surrounding counties, their area of protection and operation expanded to encompass Fermanagh, north and west Tyrone and those parts of Londonderry lying adjacent to county Donegal.[44]

The primary objectives of this force were to secure their quarters around Donegal and to rescue refugees from the outlying districts. The former objective was achieved when they decisively defeated the rebels in two battles towards the end of June 1642. Up until that time there had been no full-scale rebel assault on the north-west of the province. However, a combination of factors, not least of which was the presence of a large Scottish army in east Ulster,[45] forced the rebels out of that area in search of easier targets, which they assumed could be found in the north west.[46] Consequently, Irish rebels converged on Donegal only to find out too late that the settlers there were better prepared than had been anticipated. Commanded by Sir Phelim O'Neill, the rebel army, which was then comprised of members of many of the dominant Ulster septs, was drawn into a trap by the numerically inferior forces of Sir Robert Stewart.[47] The latter allowed the rebels to march unmolested into Donegal where they unsuspectingly struck camp at Glemaquin (near Rapho), on the evening of 15 June.[48] The next morning the rebels awoke to find a small party from Stewart's forces harassing them with musket fire. They charged the musketeers only to find too late that Stewart had brought in the main force of the Lagan army under cover of darkness and that they were standing in arms awaiting the rebel advance. O'Neill's forces were routed but not until after the Highlanders within the Irish ranks had nearly carried the day with a ferocious frontal assault on the Laganeers.[49]

This particular battle proved decisive in that it allowed the Lagan army to go on the offensive and not only retake many of the garrisons held by the rebels, but also to relieve those still holding out for the settlers. Strabane was retaken on 19 June, where the entire garrison, with the exception of their commander, Hugh Devine, was killed.[50] When word reached the Lagan men about Coleraine's predicament, they immediately convened a meeting whereby it was 'resolved, that notwithstanding our own wants we would endeavour by God's inheritance to relieve Coleraine'.[51]

Sir Robert Stewart and his men immediately crossed into county Londonderry with the intention of clearing the rebels who had been besieging Coleraine. Ballykelly and Limavady were quickly relieved. The rebels, commanded by Manus O'Cahan, attempted to check Stewart's progress in the vicinity of Magilligan but the Lagan force was again victorious, forcing the rebels to flee to the Sperrin Mountains. An engagement later took place at the foot of these mountains where the rebels, their backs literally against the wall, initially gained the upper hand but the military experience of Stewart eventually won the day and the rebels were forced to retreat towards Dungiven.[52] Dungiven Castle was then besieged and was soon yielded when the rebel garrison agreed to submit 'to the king's mercy'. While Stewart could have stormed the castle, it was a necessary expedient that he sought a peaceful surrender because many settler families were being held prisoner at Dungiven and an assault would have endangered their lives.[53] On surrendering, O'Cahan, the rebel leader was captured and sent prisoner to Derry.[54] Finally, the Lagan army relieved Coleraine which by then had been under siege for no less then six months. Eight hundred captured cows were delivered to the inhabitants and the Lagan men 'stayed with them until they furnished themselves with fire and what other necessaries the county could offer'.[55] Coleraine relieved, the Lagan forces withdrew, burning everything out of the immediate reach of the garrison which might prove of use to the remaining rebels in the vicinity. They returned to Donegal just in time to defeat another rebel force of 2,000 which had been intimidating Rapho, then garrisoned by Sir William Stewart.[56]

The number and frequency of these setbacks forced the rebels to retreat southward to Glasslough, county Monaghan, where their intention was apparently to disband and to fend for themselves. They had little choice as the Lagan army's successes had crushed or at least paralysed the rebellion in north and west Ulster.[57] They were on the verge of doing this when news arrived that Owen Roe O'Neill had landed at Doe Castle in Donegal.[58] The remnants of the rebel armies at Glasslough immediately raised about 1,500 foot and 9 troops of horse from the septs in the surrounding area.[59]

Once it became widely known that the Stewart brothers had taken the field and were recruiting, the north-west, especially Donegal, was regarded as the safest place in Ulster. This is proven by the number of non-combatants who made their way there, either on their own initiative or through being escorted there by local defence corps, eager to be rid of non-military personnel. The area became a funnel, into which refugees from south Donegal, Tyrone, Armagh and Fermanagh entered to be conveyed northwards by the Lagan army until eventually converging on the city of Londonderry – which was then perhaps the safest place in Ulster, if not in Ireland. Londonderry was a popular point of departure from which many of these refugees left Ireland for the relative safety of mainland Britain.[60] To ensure that these refugees would receive sympathetic help and be well looked after in Britain, the settler armies of Ulster caused to be published a pamphlet to 'excite the British nation to relieve our poor wives and children'.[61]

This export of refugees was probably the safety valve which ensured that the mortality rate within the walls of Londonderry remained slight, especially when compared with the other refugee centre of Coleraine. Once Coleraine's supplies ran out in early 1642 the death rate among the refugees was reputed to be between 100 to 150 persons each week.[62] Other refugee centres in the north-west were the strongholds of Ballycastle and Limavady. These were strategically placed between Londonderry and Coleraine and, consequently, used to shelter many refugees until such times as they could be conveyed to the larger centres of sanctuary.[63]

Once Donegal and the rest of north-west Ulster was secured the Lagan army, motivated by the need for supplies and for the rescue of other beleaguered settler garrisons, began to range afield. According to Hamilton:

> The immense area which relied on the Lagan force for protection called for an untiring energy on the part of the three regiments of which it was at that time formed.[64]

The greatest victory of the Lagan army in the initial stages of the civil war in Ireland, was that against Owen Roe O'Neill at Clones on Tuesday 13 June 1643. Since Donegal was secure, parties were often sent out for the purpose of bringing back any supplies, especially cattle, which they might happen to chance upon. On this occasion, however, their expedition was a deliberate offensive action. They had received intelligence that O'Neill's army was lying unserviceable and about to retreat into Connaught.[65] This provided a strategic moment for the Lagan army to solidify its position even further. To have destroyed

O'Neill's army would have given military supremacy to the settlers in the north and south-west, if not in the whole of the province of Ulster. If O'Neill were allowed to retreat into Connaught, however, he would then be in a position to threaten, or even attack, Donegal from its southern borders.[66] His retreat had to be prevented, and the strategy agreed upon was that the Lagan army would confront O'Neill in battle. Owen Roe, on receiving intelligence of this threat, attempted to move southward but was caught and decisively defeated by the Lagan men at Clones.[67]

Perhaps the most important consequence of the battle was that the Lagan army achieved military supremacy over north and south-west Ulster. In addition, the loss of many of O'Neill's continentally-trained officers was a blow not only to O'Neill's forces but to the Catholic cause in general. Shortly thereafter Dungannon was retaken and by September 1643, due mainly to the military experience and prowess of the Lagan army, Charlemont was the only place still in rebel hands in Ulster.

Throughout the initial stages of the rebellion the ideological divisions developing in England were evident only in the relative safety of Dublin where those who commiserated with the parliament continually opposed those with royalist sympathies. The further one got from Dublin (Donegal for example), the less important these political divisions were. Here the settlers were fighting for their lives, families and properties.[67] While the majority of non-combatants were dispatched to safety, those who remained and constituted the Lagan settler army had one goal and that was to preserve, as far as possible, the acres which had been given to them almost twenty-five to thirty years prior to the rebellion outbreak. These hardened frontiersmen were not ready to yield their estates, and exhibited a willingness to defend them to the end. Loyalty to property overshadowed all other political proclivities at this stage and remained their driving force until the signing of the cessation in September 1643 became a decisive factor in determining political ideology in Ireland.

The cessation was the first test of the political ideologies of the Protestants in Ireland.[68] Donegal settlers were able, for the first time since the outbreak of the rebellion, to assess the situation in England. While the initial responses of the settlers in Donegal to the threat posed by the rebellion can be explained in a religious context, where the polarisation of ideologies in England between the king and parliament was only of peripheral interest, the cessation, however, while satisfying the moderates on both sides, was also the 'most decisive factor in clarifying the attitude of the various parties in Ireland'.[69] The signing of the cessation ushered in a period in which the parliament and, to a lesser extent, the king, actively competed for the fealty of the Protestant colonist armies in Ireland.[70]

Once the independents gained the upperhand in the parliament in December 1648, and purged it of moderates, the situation in Ulster, which was technically under the leadership of parliamentary commanders, became quite complex.[71] Settlers, especially those originally from Scotland, did not know which way to turn. They could continue to support the parliament, but that body was more and more openly expressing opposition to Presbyterianism. Similarly, they could support the episcopalian royalists who, although not outwardly expressing it, also harboured a dislike for Presbyterianism. Faced by such a choice, many vacillated, as politics and parochial necessities dictated. The Lagan army, however, forged a path clear down the middle of this ideological dispute indicating that it would support neither side until the political situation had been sorted out. Events in England (especially the execution of the king in January 1649), however, were soon to force the Donegal settlers from this cautious middle course and begin a process in Ulster which divided the settlers to an unprecedented degree. By the middle of 1649, they were in open conflict.[72]

III

In December 1649 the defeat of the Ulster royalist settlers on the plains of Lisnagarvy made their position in Ulster untenable. Those who chose to continue the struggle against parliament crossed over to Scotland while those still in arms in Ireland awaited Cromwell's pleasure to know what was to become of them.[73] On 26 April 1650 Cromwell brought out 'general articles for the Protestant Party in Ireland' and indicated that certain commissioners would be constituted to determine under what terms the settlers, who had supported the royal cause, would retain possession of their estates.[74] In the meantime it was determined that Protestant royalists in Ulster should immediately proceed to Enniskillen where they were to take an oath not to do anything prejudicial to the parliamentary interests. After that they could, with their arms and horses, return to their homes in their respective areas of Ulster to await a parliamentary decision on their fate.[75]

In August 1652, two Acts of parliament which were to have monumental consequences for land tenures in Ireland were passed.[76] The entire substance of the so-called 'Cromwellian land settlement' was based on them. Traditionally the historiography of these acts has been examined only with reference to their effect on Catholic landholding patterns in Ireland. What is important to this present study, however, is that many Donegal settlers were encompassed within its various clauses. It is not commonly recognised that the 'Act of Settlement' categorised the people of Ireland (both Catholic and Protestant) according to their involvement in the rebellion and, perhaps more importantly, according to their loyalty to the king, or disloyalty to the parliament (a 'crime' which most of the British, especially Scottish, settlers of Donegal were charged with). The Act of Settlement did not single out Catholics for special treatment because it did not specifically distinguish between Catholic or Protestant. The only consequential difference was that between 'royalist' and 'parliamentarian'.

Five categories of people were exempt from pardon for life and estate. For these malefactors was reserved the punishment of loss of both life and land.[77] Clause three named no less than 103 people, among whom was the former leader of the Lagan army, Sir Robert Stewart, along with John Bramhall, late bishop of Londonderry.[78] Further clauses identified all who held commands in any armies which fought against the parliament and who were not comprehended in any of the former qualifications. These were to be banished from Ireland, while one-third of their estates was to be reserved for their wives and children who would be required to accept an exchange of equal value in some other area of Ireland. The next clause stipulated that those who had fought against the parliament were also to forfeit their estates in return for the same one-third compensation, wherever the parliament might determine. A further three clauses dealt with people who had not shown 'constant good affection' to the parliament. These were to receive two-thirds of their estates in a place yet to be determined by the parliament. The last category dealt with those who could not show 'good affection', and who were to retain only four-fifths of their original estate.

It appears that the main objective of this Act was an almost universal confiscation of all the lands of the Catholic Irish, along with the lands of those Protestant settlers who fought against the parliament at any time since the commencement of the rebellion in 1641. Table 11.7 lists the Protestant settlers of Donegal who were comprehended within its clauses and, therefore, liable to have their estates sequestered.

No less than twenty Donegal settlers (holding 18,642 acres) were to suffer the loss of their estates for their political proclivities throughout the preceding decade, especially their involvement with the pro-royalist Lagan army. With the exception of Sir William Stewart, who had died in 1648, they all were present at the 1649 siege of Londonderry.[80]

This malfeasance towards the commonwealth might have been ignored had they come over to the parliament forces after that siege was lifted in August 1649. Many of them, however, continued their struggle for the royalist cause by travelling south to join Ormonde's

Table 11.7 [79]

Forfeiting Protestants in Donegal[a]

	Name	Title	Rel	Acres	Barony
01	Arnet Edward		EP	0032	RO
02	Cunningham Alexander		SP	0221	RO/KN
03	Cunningham Anna		SP	1213	RO
04	Cunningham George		SP	0139	RO
05	Cunningham James	ESQ	SP	0850	RO
06	Cunningham William	LTC	SP	1549	RO
07	Galbraith Robert	GNT	SP	0210	RO
08	Hamilton Andrew	ESQ	SP	1953	RO
09	Hamilton James	ESQ	SP	1648	KN
10	Hamilton James	CPT	SP	1074	RO
11	Hamilton Robert		SP	0185	RO
12	Knox Andrew	MAJ	SP	0580	KN
13	Knox George		SP	1351	RO/TH
14	Knox James	GNT	SP	2349	KN
15	Nisbit John		SP	0686	RO
16	Parmenter Nicholas	GNT	EP	0128	RO
17	Pitt John GNT		EP	0158	RO
18	Stewart John SIR		SP	1005	RO
19	Stewart Thomas	ESQ	SP	2411	KN
20	Stewart William		SP	0900	RO
			Total	**18,642**	

a   EP: English Protestant; SP: Scottish Protestant; IP: Irish Protestant. The Barony abbreviations
   are RO: Rapho; TH: Tirhugh; KN: Killmacrenan. The title abbreviations are CPT: Captain,
   ESQ: Esquire; GNT: Gent; MAJ: Major; LTC: Lieutenant Colonel; SIR: Sir.

forces before Dublin and at Drogheda. Others, Captain James Hamilton
and George Cunningham, for example, crossed over to Scotland where
they fought alongside Charles II at his defeats at Dunbar (September
1650) and Worcester (September 1651).[81]

The specific clause of the Act of Settlement under which each of
these settlers was comprehended determined whether they would
suffer the same fate later handed down to Catholic landholders. In
other words, those who held a command in the Lagan (or any other)
army which opposed the parliament were to be banished from Ireland,
while their wives and children would receive one-third the size of their
original estate elsewhere in Ireland. Those (without commands) who
either fought against the parliament, or who couldn't prove 'constant
good affection' were to receive a portion of their estate in another area
of Ireland. Finally those who could only prove a 'good affection' to
parliament could remain on a portion of their original lands.

In early March 1653, Lord Deputy Fleetwood received intelligence
that certain septs in Scotland intended to rise with their fellow Scots in

Ulster. To counteract this threat, he dispatched seven people as commissioners for settling Ulster to deal with the problem.[82] The majority of the commissioners were Radicals and determined almost immediately to make more land available by removing the more popular Scots from Ulster.[83] Shortly thereafter, following 'serious consideration', the Council at Dublin issued a proclamation containing the names of those Scottish settlers who were to be transplanted out of Ulster.[84]

Within the space of a few months this policy was significantly amended by the intervention of Oliver Cromwell who realised that transplanting Protestants, despite their past political proclivities, would greatly weaken the English interest in Ireland at that time. He therefore thought it more expedient policy to transplant Catholics rather than Scottish Protestants. On 2 July 1654 Cromwell vetoed the transplantation of Ulster settlers and instructed Fleetwood to apply this policy to Irish Catholics only.[85]

To align the treatment of the settlers in Donegal with that meted out to their counterparts in England, Cromwell enacted an ordinance on 2 September 1654. This piece of legislation allowed them to compound for their estates at 'two years full value of such estate, as the same was worth to be let in the year one thousand six hundred and forty'. Payment of these fines freed their estates from 'all manner of sequestration, confiscation or forfeiture'.[86]

While the fines assessed on Protestant delinquent estates were not exceptionally high, they fell on an already straitened group.[87] The paucity of Donegal settler family papers prevents any useful quantification of their debt. Rents from land, the main source of landholders' income, had gone uncollected for over a decade.[88] Many estates were desolated by the effects of more than a decade of warfare and military impositions. In addition, a large number of tenants, particularly those who were not killed in the initial rebel onslaught or drafted into the Lagan army, were conveyed out of the country throughout the 1640s. All of this resulted in a large decrease in the settler population during the 1640s and 1650s.[89] In addition to the desolation and depopulation of planters' estates, many Lagan officers contracted enormous debts in their attempts to keep their regiments in the field for the king. Money to release their estates from escheatment was, therefore, in very short supply.[90]

The final outcome of this composition as regards Donegal remains obscure. What little evidence exists for elsewhere, indicates that a number of Ulster settlers had the sequestration of their estates lifted.[91] Other testimony indicates that settlers of Scottish origin were more quick than most to compound.[92] Suffice to say, whether they paid their fines or not, Donegal settlers, or their heirs (as many had been killed

Table 11.8

Forfeiting Catholics in Donegal, 1650s[96]

	Name	Title	Rel.	Acres	Barony
01	McDevitt Shane		RC	0060	EN
02	McDonnell Hugh		RC	0306	KN
03	McGrath James		RC	0500	TH[97]
04	McLaughlin Daniel		RC	0040	EN
05	MacSweeny Donagh		RC	0250	KN
06	MacSweeny Donnel		RC	2260	KN
07	MacSweeny Duffe		RC	0280	KN
08	MacSweeny Ervin		RC	1062	KN
09	MacSweeny Gomme		RC	0079	KN
10	MacSweeny(H) Mullmurry	SIR	RC	0512	KN
11	MacSweeny Neal		RC	0757	KN
12	MacSweeny Owen		RC	0889	KN
13	MacSweeny Oliver		RC	0383	KN
14	MacSweeny Turlagh	ESQ	RC	1016	KN
15	NyGallagher Gran		RC	0432	KN
16	NySweeny(R) Honora		RC	0836	KN
17	NySweeny(R) Mary		RC	0591	KN
18	NySweeny Seely		RC	0336	KN
19	O'Boyle Turlagh	ESQ	RC	4317	KN
20	O'Doherty Richard		RC	0060	EN
21	O'Donnell Turlagh		RC	0692	KN
22	O'Dungan Hugh		RC	0411	KN
23	O'Gallagher Turlagh		RC	0124	KN
			Total	**16,193**	

by parliament's forces in the latter days of the civil war), remained in possession of their estates throughout the interregnum period.

While Donegal's settlers were spared the sequestration of their estates, the same cannot be said for their former Catholic neighbours. Table 11.8 lists the forfeiting Catholic landholders from Donegal. These twenty-three landholders represent 100 per cent of the 1641 Catholic landholders as enumerated in the Donegal Book of Survey and Distribution. After some hesitation they had attacked Donegal settlers until they themselves were driven out of the county by the military prowess of the Lagan army.[93] Consequently they were liable to the forfeiture, not only of their estates, but also of their lives. While this latter sentence was almost always mitigated, none of these Catholics obtained any land set aside for transplanters in Connaught and Clare.[94] Their fate appears to have been either exile (as was the case for the more prominent MacSweenys) or reduction in status as tenants to the new landlords.[95]

The process whereby soldiers and adventurers were to settle down elsewhere in Ireland during the commonwealth period is quite complicated. The case of Donegal, however, does not have such complexities as it was omitted from the 'Cromwellian Settlement'. This came about as a result of the intricacies surrounding the group who had been granted the confiscated land in the county during the commonwealth period. Donegal was belatedly granted to the Protestant settler army from Munster.[98] They had, during certain stages of the campaign, given their allegiance to the king. Serving under Inchiquin since 1642, they revolted with him from the king's service to parliament in 1644. In 1648 they returned their allegiance to the king but shortly after Cromwell arrived in 1649 they revolted once again back to the parliament.[99] Their initial revolt from the parliament technically disqualified them from claiming the 'good affection' to parliament that was required of all Irish Protestants to prevent their transplantation or the sequestration of their estates. However, Cromwell rewarded them for the very timely return of their service to him in 1649 by granting, on 27 June 1654, an 'Indemnity to the English Protestants of the Province of Munster'.[100] The Munster army, however, due to the delay in stating their accounts, were never to set down.[101] Consequently, when the king was restored in 1660, all of the natives had been dispossessed while the escheated land was still available for distribution.

IV

In November 1660 the newly-restored king published a declaration for the settlement of Ireland. The substance of this document was that the Adventurers of the 1640s and the Cromwellian soldiers were to keep what they had got; the Protestants of Ireland (termed 1649 or '49 officers) who had actively supported the royalist cause (among whom the settlers of Donegal were well represented), and who had not yet received compensation for this service, were to receive their arrears of pay; Irish Catholics who had been deprived of their lands merely on the grounds of their religion were to be restored to what they had lost.[102] It is the clash of these interest groups that was the moulding forces behind what is known as the 'restoration land settlement'. It was based on two acts, the Act of Settlement, 1663, and the Act of Explanation, 1666. The former set out who was to receive lands and where. The latter explained and clarified the many conflicting clauses in the former.

There were two ways by which Donegal settlers sought and obtained satisfaction in the restoration period: either as individuals who, with powerful political patronage, obtained personal favours from the king, or by inclusion among a group (the 1649 Officers), whom Charles II identified as meriting special favour for their loyalty.[103] It is this latter group which had most impact on the confiscated land in Donegal. Many of the county's settlers claimed this status for their royalist service against the parliament. Additionally, because the '49 officers lay under much hardship during the commonwealth period, the king provided for them in his declaration by granting them all the undisposed lands in the counties of Donegal, Leitrim, Longford and Wicklow; the undisposed land within the mile-line;[104] all the undisposed properties within corporate and walled towns; the benefits of the redemption of mortgages and statute staples; and £100,000, which was to be paid by the adventurers and soldiers from the rents of the estates granted to them in the commonwealth period.[105]

Before the king had time to enjoy his newly-restored status, an enormous number of petitions began pouring in from various interest groups in Ireland.[106] Those from Donegal settlers were almost unanimous in requesting: commissions in the Irish restoration army; satisfaction for pay arrears and for debts incurred while supporting the royalist cause during the 1640s.[107] A particular weapon used by these settlers was the patronage of powerful royalists (such as Ormonde, Montgomery and Sir Robert Stewart) who were restored to former influential positions both at court and in Dublin.

One settler, Captain James Galbraith, for example, complaining of extreme poverty, petitioned the king for satisfaction of his arrears and a commission in the army.[108] To substantiate his claims, and to emphasise his loyalty and service in the Lagan army, a number of Ulster's more influential royalists also wrote to the king, attesting to Galbraith's service, not only against the Catholic insurgents, but also against the rebellious parliament.[109] Shortly thereafter Galbraith was given a commission as a lieutenant in the earl of Mountrath's horse regiment and later, he was also permitted to charge over £8,041 pay arrears on the '49 security.[110]

Belated rewards also came the way of the former leader of the Lagan army, Sir Robert Stewart. Before he was eventually satisfied, however, he spent the first eight months of the restoration imprisoned for debt. On 8 April 1661 the first of many petitions from Sir Robert was sent to the king. He indicated that a debt incurred for the royalist cause, particularly that of keeping the Lagan army in the field, was responsible for his incarceration. He requested that this debt be investigated and that he be immediately restored to his old commands on the military establishment and as governor of Culmore.[111] Shortly thereafter, Ormonde wrote to the king on his behalf and, after extensively eulogising Stewart, recommended that he be immediately released from his confinement.[112] The king ordered Stewart to be released and instructed the lords justices to put Sir Robert in possession of all the lands originally granted to Gregory Clement, the adventurer and regicide, who was attainted for high treason.[113]

Not all of Donegal's settlers petitioned for the settlement of their pay arrears, or for inclusion on the military establishment. Some, especially those originally from England, who had supported the parliament in the area found themselves in the position of having to obtain a general pardon for their parliamentary proclivities.[114]

As listed in table 11.8, a total of 16,193 acres was confiscated from twenty-three Catholics in Donegal during the commonwealth period. The 500 acres occupied by one of these, James McGrath, in fact belonged to the church, to which it reverted at the restoration.[115] A further three Catholics, Shane McDevitt, Daniel McLaughlin and Richard O'Doherty, who held 60, 40 and 60 acres respectively in the barony of Inishowen, appear, from the Book of Survey and Distribution, to have held on to this land in the restoration period. Finally, 60 acres belonging to the 1641 estate (250 acres) of Donagh Mac Sweeny remained undisposed of in the restoration period. The remaining 15,473 forfeited acres originally held by Catholics in the barony of Killmacrenan, were, with a further 166 acres which were held by Protestants in 1641, distributed between six people as indicated in table 11.9.

By virtue of the acts of settlement and explanation, these 15,639 confiscated acres were supposed to have gone to the '49 Security.[116] Only the 4,408 and 2,145 acres granted to Sir John Stephens and Sir Hans Hamilton, however, were disposed of in this way. These two parcels of land were held in trust for this group as portions of two separate lots.[117] Cary Dillon and William Cunningham received their portions (166 and 1,911 acres respectively) in satisfaction of their own outstanding pay arrears as '49 Officers.[120] The remaining 7,009 acres

Table 11.9 [118]

Grantees to confiscated land in Donegal in the 1660s

	Name	Rel.	Acres	Barony
1	Brasier Paul	P	4,338	Kill.
2	Cunningham William	P	1,911	Kill.
3	Dillon Cary	P	166	Kill.[119]
4	Hamilton Hans Sir	P	2,145	Kill.
5	Ponsonby John Sir	P	2,671	Kill.
6	Stephens John Sir	P	4,408	Kill.
		Total	**15,639**	

passed to two '49 Officers: Paul Brasier (a local merchant from Londonderry) and Sir John Ponsonby (a pre-1641 settler from Munster) in satisfaction of debentures which they had purchased during the commonwealth period.[121] It appears then that all of the forfeited acres in Donegal were granted to '49 Officers, although only 6,553 acres were distributed by lot through the actual '49 Security. The remaining 9,086 acres were passed as individual land grants. Therefore the forfeited land in Donegal was passed to the people it was intended for by virtue of the legislation implemented to facilitate the land settlement.

The same is not the case for other areas of north-west Ulster, where the land was eventually passed to people for whom it was not originally intended. The pattern that emerges in Londonderry and Tyrone, for example, was one whereby locally-established settlers, particularly merchants and company agents from Londonderry and Coleraine, dominated the fluid land market which resulted from the uncertainties of land tenure during the 1650s and 1660s. Ideally placed and quick to realise the market potential, they began buying debentures from the English soldiers eager to hurry home.[122] The failure of Cromwellian policy in Ireland, which aimed to colonise large numbers of people on numerous small estates, can be partly attributed to this sale of debentures because it ensured that fewer people settled on very large holdings. For instance, of the 41,290 acres disposed of in Donegal, Tyrone and Londonderry, it is certain that 38,664 acres (93 per cent) came into the possession of pre-1641, mainly local, settlers for whom they were not originally intended.[123] They did not confine their purchases exclusively to north-west Ulster land as many of them acquired vast holdings throughout Ireland. Paul Brasier, for example, purchased land in Westmeath, Limerick, Waterford, Clare, Kilkenny and Longford.[124] All of this ensured that the legislation implemented in the Cromwellian and Restoration period to facilitate a lasting settlement in Ireland became a blueprint for a house which was never built. Moreover, the fact that there were some willing to purchase and, more importantly, many eager to sell debentures and land, ushered in a period of predatory speculation, which alone was responsible for that scramble for land so characteristic of the years after the restoration.

References

1. This genre was established by J. P. Prendergast, *The Cromwellian settlement of Ireland* (3rd ed., Dublin, 1922); D. Murphy, *Cromwell in Ireland: a history of Cromwell's Irish campaigns* (Dublin, 1883), P. Beresford-Ellis, *Hell or Connaught: the Cromwellian colonisation of Ireland* (London, 1975).
2. Donegal Book of Survey and Distribution (N.A.); R. C. Simington (ed.), *The civil survey, A.D. 1654-56* (10 vols, Dublin, 1931), iii. I incorporated the acreage

figures from these sources into a data base, currently under construction, of the land tenurial upheavals in seventeenth-century Ireland. For more on my database see K. McKenny, 'The seventeenth-century land settlement in Ireland: towards a statistical interpretation' in J. Ohlmeyer (ed.), *From independence to occupation: Ireland, 1641-59* (Cambridge, 1995), pp 181-200; idem, *For King or Ulster: the landed interests, political ideologies and military campaigns of the British settler armies of north-west Ulster, 1620-85* (forthcoming).

3. The Civil Survey was taken by inquisitions from knowledgeable local inhabitants as opposed to exact measurement and mapping; two valuable attributes of the Down Survey. T. A. Larcom (ed.), *The Downe Survey by Doctor William Petty, 1655-56* (Dublin, 1851); J. H. Andrews, *Plantation acres: an historical study of the Irish land surveyor and his maps* (Omagh, 1985), pp 297-332; J. G. Simms, 'The Civil Survey, 1654-56' in *I.H.S.*, ix (1955), pp 253-63. Other problems with the acreage figures given in the Books of Survey and Distribution are identified in McKenny, 'Land settlement in Ireland', pp 183-85.

4. R. Loeber, *The geography and practice of English colonisation in Ireland from 1534 to 1609* (Athlone, 1991), pp 54-59; J. H. Andrews, 'Geography and government in Elizabethan Ireland' in N. Stephens and R. E. Glasscock (eds), *Irish geographical studies in honour of E. Estyn Evans* (Belfast, 1970), pp 178-91. To a certain extent, the insular Gaelic practices in Donegal were made known to the world through the woodcuts of John Derricke, *The image of Ireland, with a discovery of Woodkarne* (London, 1581). These are supposed to portray the Gaelic MacSweenys, although there is every reason to believe that Derricke never actually visited Donegal. D. B. Quinn, L. Miller, J. A. Gamble (eds), *The image of Ireland with a discovery of Woodkarne by John Derricke, 1581* (Belfast, 1985).

5. H. Morgan, *Tyrone's rebellion: the outbreak of the Nine Years' War in Tudor Ireland* (Dublin, 1993); idem, 'The end of Gaelic Ulster: a thematic interpretation of events between 1534-1610' in *I.H.S.*, xxvi (1988), pp 8-32; N. P. Canny, 'Hugh O'Neill and the changing face of Gaelic Ulster' in *Studia Hib.*, x (1970), pp 7-35.

6. N. P. Canny, 'The ideology of English colonisation from Ireland to America' in *William and Mary Quarterly*, xxx (1973), pp 585, 588, 592.

7. Some of these studies include: M. Perceval-Maxwell, *The Scottish migration to Ulster in the reign of James I* (London, 1973); P. Robinson, *The plantation of Ulster: British settlement in an Irish landscape, 1600-70* (Dublin, 1984); R. Gillespie, *Colonial Ulster: the settlement of East Ulster, 1600-41* (Cork, 1985). An older yet still indispensable work is G. Hill, *An historical account of the Plantation in Ulster at the commencement of the 17th century* (Belfast, 1877; reprint 1970).

8. C. Mooney, 'A noble shipload' in *Irish Sword*, ii (1962), pp 195-204; N. P. Canny, 'The flight of the earls, 1607' in *I.H.S.*, xvii (1971), pp 380-99; idem, 'The Treaty of Mellifont and the re-organisation of Ulster, 1603' in *Irish Sword*, ix (1969), pp 249-62.

9. R. Gillespie, 'Continuity and change: Ulster in the seventeenth century' in C. Brady, M. O'Dowd, B. Walker (eds), *Ulster: an illustrated history* (London, 1989), p. 108; J. G. Simms, 'Donegal in the Ulster plantation' in *Ir. Geog.*, vi (1972), pp 386-87.

10. Each undertaker was required to bring over 24 able-bodied men for every 1,000 acres received. Robinson, *Plantation of Ulster*, pp 129-49; Perceval-Maxwell, *Scottish migration to Ulster*, pp 114-37.

11. This fact has been adduced by comparing the 1641 landholding patterns

established from the data-base (see tables 11.2 and 11.3), with the appendices given in Robinson, *Plantation of Ulster*, pp 195-227 and from the 'Grants and Grantees' listed in Hill, *Plantation in Ulster*, pp 259-353. While Robinson only recorded grantees' names with the total acreage they received, Hill identified the townlands, quarters or ballyboes where each of the grantees received land. Tracing the movement patterns of each of these individual land units creates the aggregate of British (and other) land movement between the original plantation and 1641. See Appendix A in K. McKenny, The landed interests, political ideologies and military campaigns of the north-west Ulster settlers and their Lagan army in Ireland, 1641-1685' (Unpublished Ph.D. dissertation, State University of New York, Stony Brook, August, 1994), pp 403-5; idem, *For King or Ulster*.

12. A list of the Scottish estates which failed can be seen in J. M. Hill, 'The origins of the Scottish plantations in Ulster to 1625: a reinterpretation' in *Jn. Brit. Studies*, xxxii (1993), pp 24-43.

13. R. Gillespie, 'Lords and commons in seventeenth-century Mayo' in R. Gillespie and G. Moran (eds), *'A various country': essays in Mayo history, 1500-1900* (Castlebar, 1987), p. 45. Gaelic Irish literature of the period resonates with indignation at the destruction of their society by these market forces. T. J. Dunne, 'The Gaelic response to conquest and colonisation: the evidence of the poetry' in *Studia Hib.* xx (1980), pp 7-30; M. O'Riordan, *The Gaelic mind and the collapse of the Gaelic world* (Cork, 1990); B. Cunningham, 'Native Culture and political change in Ireland, 1580-1640' in C. Brady and R. Gillespie (eds), *Natives and newcomers: essays on the making of Irish colonial society, 1534-1641* (Dublin 1986), pp 148-70.

14. The extent of unofficial land acquisitions by settlers in Ulster has not yet been enumerated. Some inroads into this problem have already been made for areas outside of Ulster. W. J. Smyth, 'Property, patronage and population: reconstructing the human geography of mid-seventeenth century county Tipperary' in W. Nolan and T. G. McGrath (eds), *Tipperary: history and society: interdisciplinary essays on the history of an Irish county* (Dublin, 1985), pp 104-38; idem, 'Land values, landownership and population patterns in county Tipperary from 1641-1660 and 1841-50 – some comparisons' in L. M. Cullen and F. Furet (eds), *Ireland and France, 17th to 20th centuries: towards a comparative study of rural history* (Paris 1980), pp 60-84.

15. It is now evident that the survey column of the Books of Survey and Distribution contains the names of 1641 landowners together with lessees, freeholders and even, in some instances, tenants. It also omits many people who were freeholders, or who might have held the land in fee farm or fee simple, or, in certain cases, the actual owners. Consequently, it would be inaccurate to list them as landowners for the 1641 period. See McKenny, 'Land settlement in Ireland', pp 184-85; idem, *For King or Ulster*, chapter two; idem, 'The landed interests, political ideologies and military campaigns of the north-west Ulster settlers'.

16. It is not certain when the Olpherts settled in the area. They perhaps belonged to the group of Dutch engineers who, Chichester reported, had settled in Londonderry during the early stages of the plantation. The Olpherts soon ingratiated themselves with planter society, holding a number of houses in Derry and William became that city's mayor in 1633-34. He was later to distinguish himself, defending the city against the Jacobite threat in 1689 (British Library, Add. Ms 4756, fo. 117); 'Rent roll of Derry, 15 May 1628' in T. W. Moody and

J. G. Simms (eds), *The bishopric of Derry and the Irish society of London, 1602-1705*, 2 vols, (Dublin, 1968), i, 59; 'List of civil officials of Derry and Coleraine, 1613-41' in T. W. Moody, *The Londonderry plantation, 1609-41: the city of London and the plantation of Ulster* (Belfast, 1939), p. 449; Hill, *Plantation in Ulster*, pp 182-83. For a general introduction to the Dutch influence in Ireland see R. Loeber, 'English and Irish sources for the history of Dutch economic activity in Ireland, 1600-89' in *Journal of Irish economic and social history*, viii (1981), pp 70-85.

17. The problems of the English and Scottish planters are discussed in McKenny, 'Land settlement in Ireland', pp 188-92; idem, *For King or Ulster*; W. H. Crawford, 'The significance of landed estates in Ulster, 1600-1820' in *Journal of Irish economic and social history*, xvii (1990), p. 44; R. Hunter, 'The English undertakers in the plantation of Ulster, 1610-41' in *Breifne*, iv (1973), pp 471-99; Hill, 'Origins of Scottish plantations in Ulster', pp 24-43.

18. The emphasis here is on the rural land market. The urban market is explored in R. Gillespie, 'The origins and development of an Ulster urban network, 1600-41' in *I.H.S.*, xxiv (1984), pp 15-29; P. Robinson, 'Urbanization in north-west Ulster, 1609-70' in *Ir. Geog.*, xv (1982), pp 35-50.

19. This table includes the one Dutch Protestant and the six Protestants whose ethnic origin could not be ascertained and who were categorised as Unknown Protestants in tables 11.2 and 11.3.

20. Similar patterns are evident in other parts of Ireland. See, for example, D. Gahan, 'The estate system of county Wexford, 1641-1876' in K. Whelan and W. Nolan (eds), *Wexford history and society: interdisciplinary essays on the history of an Irish county* (Dublin, 1987), pp 201-21; Smyth, 'Land values, landownership and population patterns in county Tipperary', pp 59-84; P. J. Duffy, 'The evolution of estate properties in South Ulster, 1600-1900' in W. Smyth and K. Whelan (eds), *Common ground: essays on the historical geography of Ireland presented to T. Jones Hughes* (Cork, 1988), pp 84-109.

21. This table includes the three people categorised as Irish Protestants in table 11.2.

22. O'Boyle's holding of 4,317 acres in the barony of Killmacrenan was comprised of 1,085 unprofitable and 3,232 profitable acres.

23. P. Walsh (ed.), *Leabhar Chlainne Suibhne: an account of the MacSweeny families in Ireland, with pedigrees* (Dublin, 1920), pp xxx-xxxvi.

24. The complex origins of this rebellion can be seen in R. Gillespie, 'Destabilizing Ulster, 1641-2' in B. MacCuarta (ed.), *Ulster 1641: aspects of the rising* (Belfast, 1993) pp 107-21, pp 107-21, M. Perceval-Maxwell, *The outbreak of the Irish rebellion of 1641* (New York, 1994).

25. J. S. Reid, *History of the Presbyterian Church in Ireland comprising the civil history of the province of Ulster from the ascension of James I* (3 vols, London, 1853), i, 295; T. Carte, *Life of James, first duke of Ormonde* (6 vols, Oxford, 1851), i, 346-7.

26. A short summary of the rising in Tyrone can be seen in P. O'Gallachair, 'The 1641 war in Clogher' in *Clogher Record*, iv (1962), pp 135-47.

27. Carte is of the opinion that the organised settlers at this time had little trouble beating the poorly-armed rebels. His motive for asserting this is to suggest that if the lords justices followed the north-west Ulster settler's lead, the rebellion in the remainder of the country could have been ended at an early stage. *Life of Ormonde*, ii, 4.

28. Carte is incorrect in assuming that the rebels got control of all of Donegal and Londonderry because, as will become apparent below, these places were defended by the settlers under the leadership of the Stewart brothers. Carte, *Life of Ormonde*, i, 353.

29. The military situation in and around Dublin can be seen in H. Hazlett, History of the military forces operating in Ireland, 1641-9 (2 vols, unpublished Ph.D. dissertation, Queens University Belfast, 1938) i, 39.

30. 'The Mayor of Londonderry and others to the Lords Justices', 10 January 1642 (Bodl., Rawlinson MSS, B 507, fo. 4); J. Hogan (ed.), *Letters and papers relating to the Irish rebellion between 1642-46* (Dublin, IMC, 1935), pp 3-5.

31. Strafford's motives for disarming the Protestants (mainly Scots) in Ulster was due to their opposition to Bramhall's attempts to implement Laudian religious policy in Ireland, and because of the outbreak of the Bishop's War in Britain. M. Perceval-Maxwell, 'Strafford, the Ulster Scots and the covenanters' in *I.H.S.*, xviii (1973), pp 524-51; H. Kearney, *Strafford in Ireland, 1633-41: a study in absolutism* (Cambridge, 2nd ed., 1989), p. 187; C. V. Wedgwood, *Thomas Wentworth, first earl of Strafford, 1593-1641: a revaluation* (London, 1962 ed.), pp 177-80.

32. Sir William Cole not only apprised the Dublin government of the impending rebellion, but he was also instrumental in despatching messengers throughout the north-west. 'Sir William Cole to the Lords Justices of Ireland', Enniskillen, 11 October 1641 in Carte, *Life of Ormonde*, v, 254-55; i, 335: Reid, *History of Presbyterian Church*, i, 297.

33. 'Intelligence delivered to Irish House of Commons', 16 November 1641, *Commons Jn. Ire.*, i, 15. This report not only lists the areas holding out against the rebels, but also those garrisons favoured by the refugees as places of shelter.

34. Both these brothers (the *D.N.B.*, does not recognise this particular connection) served with distinction under King Gustavus Adolphus and later under King Sigismund III of Poland. *Cal. S.P. Dom.*, 1611-13, pp 51-52, 66, 98; *Reg. Privy Council Scot.*, 1638-43 (Edinburgh, 1906), p. 364.

35. An eyewitness account of the Stewart home that fateful day is printed in G. Hill (ed.), *The Montgomery manuscripts (1603-1706), compiled from the family papers by William Montgomery of Rosemont, esquire* (Belfast, 1869), pp 407-8.

36. 'Foot regiments raised by the king's commission', *H.M.C., Ormonde MSS*, i, 126; Hill, *Montgomery Manuscripts*, p. 407.

37. On 19 November commissions arrived from the king for Sir Robert and Sir William to each raise 1,000 foot, along with one troop of horse each. In addition, Sir Ralph Gore was commissioned to raise 1,000 foot and a troop of horse in Donegal and Sir William Cole was to do likewise in Fermanagh. 'A true and brief account of the services done by the seven British regiments and troops raised in the kingdom of Ireland by virtue of his majesties commission (in the beginning of this horrid rebellion) enabled by the ammunition sent by his majesty with arms, offensive and defensive, before they were entertained in the parliament's pay', by Sir Robert Stewart, *H.M.C. Coke MSS*, p. 298.

38. It took them seven days to reach the safety of Rapho as the Irish septs were attacking them constantly. *An exact relation of all such occurrences as have happened in the several counties of Donegal, Londonderry, Tyrone and Fermanagh, in the North of Ireland, since the beginning of this horrid, bloody and unparalleled rebellion there, beginning in October last. In all humility Presented to the honourable House of Commons in England by Lieutenant Colonel Audley Mervyn* (London, 4 June 1642), E149 (34). A copy of this is printed in J. T. Gilbert (ed.), *A contemporary history of affairs in Ireland from AD 1641 to 1652* (6 vols, Dublin, 1879), i, 464-75. All subsequent references to Mervyn's relation are from Gilbert.

39. 'True and perfect account by Robert Stewart', p. 299; 'Mervyn relation' in Gilbert, *Contemporary history*, i, 472-73

40. Stewart informs us that there were quite a few thousand of these refugees whom he called 'the unsuccessful people', which included men, women and children. 'True and perfect account by Robert Stewart', pp 298-99.

41. 'Mervyn relation' in Gilbert, *Contemporary history*, i, 464-75.

42. It is difficult to ascertain which of the 21 companies raised for defensive purposes in north-west Ulster came under the command of the Lagan army, but many of these companies, particularly those from Londonderry, took part in the offensive campaigns of the Lagan army.

43. H.M.C., Ormonde MSS, i, 125-26. 'Mayor and others of Coleraine to the Lords Justices', Coleraine, 14 January 1642 (Bodl., Rawlinson B 507, fo. 10), 'Muster Rolls of British Settlers in Ulster' (P.R.O., Commonwealth Exchequer Papers, S.P. 28/120).

44. McKenny, *For King or Ulster*, chapters two and three.

45. D. Stevenson, *Scottish covenanters and Irish confederates: Scottish-Irish relations in the mid-seventeenth century* (Belfast, 1981); E. M. Furgol, *A regimental history of the covenanting armies, 1639-51* (Edinburgh, 1990); H. Hazlett, 'The recruitment and organization of the Scottish Army in Ulster, 1642-49' in H. A. Crone, T. W. Moody, D. B. Quin (eds), *Essays in British and Irish history in honour of J. E. Todd* (London, 1949), pp 107-31. These tend to look at this army from the perspective of Scotland. More recently, however, Raymond Gillespie has looked at it from the perspective of the Ulster settlers. 'An Army sent from God: Scots at war in Ireland, 1642-49' in Norman MacDougall (ed.), *Scotland and war AD 79-1918* (Maryland, 1991), pp 13-32.

46. The situation in east Ulster can be gleaned from 'The state of the county of Antrim in 1641-42' in E. Berwick (ed.), *The Rawdon Papers, consisting of letters on various subjects, literary, political and ecclesiastical, to and from Dr John Bramhall, primate of Ireland* (London, 1819), pp 91-92; 'James MacDonnell to Archibald Stewart', Oldstowne, 10 January 1642 in Hogan, *Letters and papers of Irish rebellion*, pp 6-7; 'Sir John Vaughan to the Lords Justices', Londonderry, 10 January 1642 (Bodl., Rawlinson MSS, B 507, fo. 5); J. Turner, *Memoirs of his own life and times*, ed. T. Thomason (Bannatyne Club, vol. 28, Edinburgh, 1829).

47. Sir Robert indicates that this was the largest and best equipped rebel army yet to take the field. 'True and perfect account by Robert Stewart', pp 299-301; 'Mervyn relation' in Gilbert, *Contemporary history*, i, 473-74; Hogan, *War in Ireland*, p. 23.

48. *Special good news from Ireland being a true relation of a late and great victory obtained against the rebels in the North of Ireland by the pious, Prudent and courageous commander, Sir William Stewart, colonel. The truth whereof being confirmed by several letters directed to Mr Abraham Pont, solicitor to the said Sir William in London* (London, 27 January 1643), E86 (21).

49. The Highlanders were led by the celebrated Colla Ciotach who was himself wounded in the assault. 'Sir Robert Stewart to the Lords Justices', Culmore Castle, 21 June 1642 (Bodl., Rawlinson MSS, B 507, fos. 32-33); R. Black, 'Colla Ciotach' in *Transactions of the Gaelic society of Inverness*, xlviii (1972-74), pp 201-43.

50. Devine was sent as prisoner to Londonderry. In contrast to the other British forces in Ulster, Sir Robert Stewart realised the importance of keeping prisoner any rebel commanders he took. 'Mervyn relation' in Gilbert, *Contemporary history*, i, 474.

51. 'True and perfect account by Robert Stewart', p. 299; 'Mervyn relation' in Gilbert, *Contemporary history*, i, 474-5.

52. 'Sir William Stewart to the Lords Justices and Council', no date in Hogan, *Letters and papers of Irish rebellion*, pp 57-59. This particular letter also lists the rebel

army that opposed them and shows that it was comprised of a disorganised array of companies, each under a nominal sept leader; Hazlett, 'History of military forces', i, 86; Carte, *Life of Ormonde*, i, 380-81.

53. 'True and perfect account by Robert Stewart', p. 300.

54. 'Sir William Stewart to the Lords Justices and Council', no date in Hogan, *Letters and papers of Irish rebellion*, p. 58.

55. 'True and perfect account by Robert Stewart', p. 300.

56. *The last true and joyful news from Ireland declaring all the proceedings of the English and Scotch forces in Ireland, against the king of Spain's standard, which is now set up in defiance of the King of England, as it was reported to the House of Commons ... The battle fought in the Province of Ulster, where the standard was set up, by Sir William Stewart, Colonel Saunderson, Colonel Gore, Colonel Galbraith and Captain Thomas Newburgh, with 2,000 horse and foot, against 7,000 rebels, with the manner of their fight, and the victory over the rebels* (London, 22 September 1642), E118 (24).

57. Similarly east Ulster was by then virtually free from rebel encroachments. *A relation from the right honourable the Lord Viscount Conway, of the proceedings of the English army in Ulster from 17 June to this present 1642* (London, 30 July 1642) (Huntington Library California, Ms 230931).

58. Carte, *Life of Ormonde*, ii, 242-43, 318-22; J. Casway, *Owen Roe O'Neill and the struggle for Catholic Ireland* (Philadelphia, 1984), p. 63.

59. J. Casway, 'Owen Roe O'Neill's return to Ireland in 1642: the diplomatic background' in *Studia Hib.*, ix (1969), pp 48-64; idem, *Owen Roe O'Neill*, pp 62-64.

60. Many of them arrived in Scotland in terrible condition causing various presbyteries to solicit support for them. *Reg. Privy council Scot.*, 1638-43, pp 500-1; Stevenson, *Scottish covenanters and Irish confederates*, pp 53-55; The experiences of the refugees in Wales and England is explored in K. J. Lindley, 'The impact of the 1641 rebellion upon England and Wales, 1641-5' in *I.H.S.*, xviii (1972), pp 143-76.

61. *A brief declaration of the barbarous and inhumane dealings of the Northern Irish rebels, and many others in several counties uprising against the English, that dwelt both lovingly and securely among them. Written to excite the English nation to relieve our poor wives and children, that have escaped the rebel's savage cruelty, and that shall arrive safe among them in England; and in exchange to send aid of men, and means forthwith to quell their boundless insolencies, with certain encouragements to the work by G. S. Minister of God's Word in Ireland* (London, 1642), E181 (11).

62. 'The examination of William Skelton' in M. Hickson, *Ireland in the seventeenth century* (2 vols, London, 1884), i, 202-6; 'Deposition of John Redferne' in J. Temple, *The Irish rebellion: or, an history of the beginnings and first progress of the general rebellion raised in Ireland, 23 October 1641* (London, 27 April 1646), E508, p. 83; Reid, *History of Presbyterian Church*, i, 315.

63. Such was the strategic importance of Limavady and Ballycastle, that the lords justices petitioned that the two commanders who had raised companies without commissions (Dudley and Thomas Philips) should be entertained on the establishment. 'Lords Justices and Council to the Earl of Leicester, Lord Lieutenant', 4 April 1642 in *H.M.C., Ormonde MSS*, ns. II, 110-11; Hazlett, 'History of military forces', i, 167.

64. Hamilton, *Irish rebellion*, p. 265.

65. The intelligence was brought to the Lagan army by Rory O'Hara and Loughlin McRory. Hamilton, *Irish rebellion*, p. 287; Reid, *History of Presbyterian Church*, i,

411; Casway, *Owen Roe O'Neill*, p. 78.

66. Stewart was afraid that it was O'Neill's 'full intention to assault' west Ulster from Connaught. Robert Stewart to Ormonde, 19 July 1643 (Bodl., Carte MSS, vi, fo. 99). This letter also provides one of only two non-Gaelic, eye-witness account of the engagement. The other is in 'Robert Thornton, the Mayor of Londonderry to Ormonde', 17 October 1643 (Bodl., Carte MSS, vii, 104); Gilbert, *Contemporary history*, i, 793-94.

67. Contemporary accounts from the settler perspective can be seen in Hogan, *War in Ireland*, pp 29-31; Robert Stewart to Ormonde, 19 July 1643 (Bodl., Carte MSS, vi, fos. 99-101); Robert Stewart to Eglington, Culmore Castle, 23 June 1643 *Another extract of more letters sent out of Ireland, informing the condition of the kingdom as it now stands* (London, 1643), (British Library, Wing Collection, STC#406:13, pp 9-10). There is also a copy of this pamphlet in (N.L.I. Thorpe Collection, 3, no. 18). The Gaelic perspective can be seen in O'Mellan, 'A narrative of the wars of 1641' in R. M. Young (ed.), *Historical notices of old Belfast and its vicinity* (Belfast, 1896), pp 221-22; 'Aphorisimical discovery of treasonable faction' in Gilbert, *Contemporary history*, i, 49-50; 'An impartial relation of the most memorial transactions of General Owen Roe O'Neill and his party, from the year 1641, to the year 1650. Collected by Colonel Henry McTuoll O'Neill' in Gilbert, *Contemporary history*, iii, 199-200. See also Casway, *Owen Roe O'Neill*, pp 78-82; P. B. Ó Mordha, 'The Battle of Clones, 1643' in *Clogher Record*, iv (1962), pp 148-54.

68. 'Charles I to Lords Justices at Dublin', 31 July 1643 (Bodl., Carte MSS, vi, fo. 131); J. T. Gilbert (ed.), *History of the Irish confederation and the war in Ireland* (7 vols, Dublin, 1882-91), ii, 317-19; *A proclamation concerning the cessation of arms agreed and concluded on at Sigginstown in the county of Kildare* (Dublin, September 1643), E7 (29) and E69 (22). Carte is of the opinion that the king's motives for ordering the cessation was to alleviate the plight of his Protestant subjects in Ireland. *Life of Ormonde*, ii, 476.

69. Hazlett, 'History of military forces', i, 244. Carte holds that 'the news of the cessation was not agreeable to all of either party', *Life of Ormonde*, iii, 1.

70. For the complicated intricacy surrounding this topic see McKenny, 'The landed interests, political ideologies and military campaigns of the north-west Ulster settlers', pp 102-49, 178-232; idem, *For King or Ulster*, chapter three.

71. For the complex events surrounding this purge see D. Underdown, *Pride's purge: politics in the Puritan revolution* (Oxford, 1971). This purge and the preceding events in England, Scotland and Ireland, must be seen in the light of a second revolution. While the first revolution of 1642 was merely a reaction by conservative parliamentarians against the administrative, religious and fiscal policies of Charles I, this latter revolution was much more serious in that the new ideology of republicanism emerged to threaten the age-old institution of the monarchy.

72. For the complexities surrounding this topic, see McKenny, *For King or Ulster*, chapters two to five.

73. Others had long since left the field of battle, suing for individual articles from Sir Charles Coote in Ulster. These are printed in *A true relation of the transactions between Sir Charles Coote ... and Owen Roe O'Neill, as it was reported to the parliament from the council of state ...* (British Library, E571 (33), p. 10).

74. 'Until either the pleasure of the parliament be known concerning them respectively, or until there be commissioners or rules settled by authority from the parliament for the fines or compositions of persons in their quality of

delinquency'. 'Cromwell's articles for the Protestant Party in Ireland', 26 April 1650 (Bodl., Carte MSS, xxvii, fo. 244).

75. 'Cromwell's allowance of horses and arms for the Protestant Party' (Bodl., Carte MSS, xxvii, fo. 243); J. T. Gilbert (ed.), *Contemporary history*, ii, 396.

76. 'An act for the speedy and effectual satisfaction of the adventurers for lands in Ireland' (12 August); 'An act for determining the accounts of such officers and soldiers as are, or have been, employed in the service of this commonwealth in Ireland' (25 August). *Commons Jn.*, vii, 161, 169; C. H. Firth, R. S. Rait (eds), *Acts and ordinances of the interregnum, 1642-60* (3 vols, London, 1911), ii, 592-612; Gilbert, *Contemporary history*, iii, 341-46.

77. All who before the first general assembly at Kilkenny had abetted the rebellion, murders or massacres; all priests, particularly Jesuits, who had been involved in any way in the rebellion; one hundred and five named magnates; all who had been guilty of the murder of civilians; those who had refused to lay down their arms within twenty-eight days of the proclamation of the act in question. Firth and Rait, *Acts and ordinances*, ii, 598-601.

78. Firth and Rait, *Acts and ordinances*, ii, 599. It is quite probable that Sir William Stewart would also have been included had he not died in 1648. The other Lagan regiment commanders, Audley Mervyn and Sir William Cole, are not included because they went over to the parliament at a crucial time in 1649.

79. Donegal Book of Survey and Distribution (N.A.); Simington, *The Civil Survey*, iii; 'Forfeiting proprietors in Ireland under the Cromwellian settlement' in J. O'Hart (ed.), *Irish and Anglo-Irish landed gentry when Cromwell came to Ireland* (Dublin, 1887), pp 247-304.

80. For the ideological and political consequences of this particular siege see McKenny, *For King or Ulster*, idem, 'The landed interests, political ideologies and military campaigns of the north-west Ulster settlers', pp 178-233; idem, 'The first siege of Londonderry and civil war in Ireland' in G. O'Brien (ed.), *Derry history and society: interdisciplinary essays on the history of an Irish county* (forthcoming).

81. Others still saw action in England before the siege of Londonderry where they fought with Duke Hamilton's Engager Army in 1648. 'Henry Lawrence to the lord deputy and council', 15 April 1656, in R. Dunlop (ed.), *Ireland under the commonwealth being a selection of documents relating to the government of Ireland from 1651 to 1659* (2 vols, Manchester, 1913), ii, 592; 'Commissioners for settling Ulster to Council at Dublin', 24 April 1653 in R. M. Young (ed.), *Historical notices of Old Belfast*, p. 85; Furgol, *A regimental history of the covenanting armies*, pp 268-91.

82. Adjutant-General William Allen, Colonels Richard Lawrence, Robert Venables, Dr. Philip Carteret, Anthony Morgan, Henry Jones and Arthur Hill.

83. J. Ivimey, *A history of the English baptists* (4 vols, London, 1811), i, 241; Cheng Yuan, The politics of the English army in Ireland during the interregnum (unpublished Ph.D. dissertation, Brown University, 1981), p. 133.

84. The list for Antrim and Down can be seen in Young, *Historical notices of Old Belfast*, pp 80-83. While the list for north-west Ulster is not now extant, it certainly would have included the Scottish settlers listed in table 11.7. The preamble indicated that the commissioners thought the most expedient way for the peace and settlement of Ulster was, 'to transplant a certain number of such persons as we judge (by reason of their interest and disaffection) to be therein most dangerous, into the provinces of Leinster and Munster'. A transcription is in Reid, *History of the Presbyterian Church*, ii, 178-79.

85. 'Additional instructions to Charles Fleetwood, Lt. General of the Army in Ireland, Edmund Ludlow, Lt. General of the Horse, Miles Corbett and John Jones, Esquires', 2 July 1653, Dunlop, *Ireland under the commonwealth*, ii, 355-59.

86. An ordinance for admitting Protestants in Ireland to compound (London, 2 September 1654), E1064 (42); Firth and Rait, *Acts and ordinances*, ii, 1015-6.

87. T. C. Barnard, 'Planters and policies in Cromwellian Ireland' in *Past and Present*, cxi (1973), p. 37; R. Gillespie, 'Landed society and the interregnum in Ireland and Scotland' in R. Mitchinson, P. Roebuck (eds), *Economy and society in Scotland and Ireland 1500-1939* (Edinburgh, 1988), pp 38-47.

88. Raymond Gillespie concluded that the 1659 rental on some estates was around 37 per cent lower than it had been prior to 1641. R. Gillespie (ed.), *Settlement and survival on an Ulster estate: the Brownlow leasebook, 1667-1711* (Belfast, 1988); idem, 'Landed society and the interregnum in Ireland and Scotland', p. 39; T. C. Barnard, *Cromwellian Ireland. English government and reform in Ireland* (Oxford, 1975), pp 157-62.

89. W. Macafee, V. Morgan, 'Population in Ulster, 1660-1760' in P. Roebuck (ed.), *Plantation to partition: essays in Ulster history in honour of J. L. McCracken* (Belfast, 1981), pp 46-63.

90. Petition of Sir Robert Stewart to the King, 17 June 1661 (P.R.O., S.P. 63/307/100).

91. 'Commissioners to the Committee for Irish Affairs', 16 January 1652; 'Commissioners of Settlement to Lord Protector', 18 April, 1654 in Dunlop, *Ireland under the commonwealth*, i, 125-26, ii, 419-21; 'Order by the Commissioners appointed for relief upon Articles of War', 7 January 1653, (P.R.O., S.P. 63/282/66); 'George Rawdon to Colonel Edward Conway', 22 January 1651, S.P. 63/282/66).

92. 'The Council to the Lord Protector', 1 April 1656, in Dunlop, *Ireland under the commonwealth*, ii, 586-7.

93. McKenny, 'The landed interests, political ideologies and military campaign of the North-west Ulster settlers', pp 47-101.

94. This fact has been adduced from an analysis of R. C. Simington, *The transplantation to Connaught, 1654-58* (Shannon, 1970).

95. The MacSweenys and O'Boyles were still prominent in the area in 1659-60 period, S. Pender (ed.), *A census of Ireland circa 1659 with supplementary material from the poll money ordinances, 1660-61* (Dublin, 1939), pp 53-59. Many of the former sept, continuing their gallowglass tradition, left for the continent where they were to distinguish themselves in continental armies. J. C. O'Callaghan, *History of the Irish brigades in the service of France* (Glasgow, 1870).

96. Donegal Book of Survey and Distribution; *The Civil Survey*, iii; 'Forfeiting proprietors in Ireland under the Cromwellian settlement', in O'Hart, *Irish and Anglo-Irish landed gentry*, pp 247-304.

97. The Book of Survey does not indicate that McGrath leased these 500 acres from the church, to whom they reverted to at the Restoration. Simmington, *Civil Survey*, iii, p. 65. For an elaboration of this and other instances whereby errors in the Book of Survey artificially enhances the quantity of Catholic 1641 landholdings see McKenny, 'Land settlement in Ireland', p. 184.

98. 'Further instructions to our deputy of Ireland, and the Council there', August 1654 in T. Birch (ed.), *Collection of state papers of John Thurloe, esquire, secretary first to the council of state, and afterwards to the two protectors, Oliver and Richard Cromwell* (7 vols, London, 1742), ii, 509; 'Additional Instructions to the Lord Deputy and Council', 27 March 1656 in Dunlop, *Ireland under the*

commonwealth, ii, 578-85; 'An act for stating and determining the accounts of such officers and soldiers as are or have been employed in the service of this commonwealth in Ireland', 25 August 1652 in Firth and Rait, *Acts and ordinances*, ii, 603-11.

99. The circumstances surrounding their vacillating allegiances is explored in J. A. Murphy, 'The politics of the Munster Protestants, 1641-49' in *Cork Hist. Soc. Jn.*, cxxvi (1971), pp 1-20. Their reversion to Cromwell is discussed in Murphy, *A history of Cromwell's Irish campaign*, pp 192-217.

100. Firth and Rait, *Acts and ordinances*, ii, 933.

101. It was unfortunate for this group that the Restoration overtook their forthcoming disbandment because Charles II, remembering their support of Cromwell, refused to include them in the Restoration settlement. Prendergast, *Cromwellian settlement of Ireland*, pp 194-95.

102. For an analysis of this declaration see L. J. Arnold, *The restoration land settlement in county Dublin, 1660-1688: a history of the administration of the acts of settlement and explanation* (Dublin, 1993), pp 21-36.

103. The '49 Officers have been dealt with in K. McKenny, 'Charles II's Irish cavaliers: the 1649 officers and the restoration land settlement' in *I.H.S.*, xxviii (November, 1993), pp 409-25; idem, A seventeenth-century real estate company: the 1649 officers and the Irish land settlements, 1641-81 (Unpublished M.A. thesis, St Patrick's College, Maynooth, 1989).

104. The mile-line was the term used to identify land stretching from the coast one mile inland in the province of Connaught and one mile westward from the river Shannon.

105. Clause ix, *Irish statutes revised* (London, 1885), pp 94-95. A further clause stipulated that they were to receive 12s. 6d. in the pound of what was due to them, thus reducing their claim. McKenny, 'Charles II's Irish cavaliers', p. 410.

106. Many of these petitions can be seen in Bodl., Carte MSS, xli, xlii, xliii, passim; (P.R.O., S.P. 63/301-310).

107. 'Petition to the King of the Captains of the Old Establishment in Ireland', January 1661 (P.R.O., S.P. 63/306/9).

108. 'Petition to the King of Captain James Galbraith', July 1660 (P.R.O., S.P. 63/303/84).

109. 'Lord Montgomery, Sir Francis Hamilton, John, Bishop of Rapho and Sir Robert Stewart to the King', 31 July 1660 (P.R.O., S.P. 63/303/85).

110. All of the land and properties given to satisfy the pay arrears of the '49 officers became known as the '49 security. C. Dalton, *Irish army lists, 1661-1885* (London, 1907), pp 19, 25, 27, 53, 59; 'Memoranda of commissions', 28 July, 1662, *H. M .C., Ormonde MSS*, i, 241-2; ii, 187-192. Galbraith was also nominated a trustee for one of the '49 officer's lots.

111. 'Petition of Sir Robert Stewart to the King' (P.R.O., S.P. 63/307/9). Later he petitioned that his arrears be stated. 'Sir Robert Stewart to the King', April 1661 (P.R.O., S.P. 63/307/12). On 10 September 1660 the king had ordered that he be made governor of Londonderry. The King to the Lords Justices' (P.R.O., S.P. 63/304/10).

112. An investigation into the debt revealed that in September 1642 James Sanderson delivered 1,200 bolls of oatmeal to the Lagan army. No matter that parliament had indicated it would pay Sanderson for the oatmeal, the merchant forced Sir Robert and the other officers of the Lagan army to sign a contract that, if the parliament did not pay the £1,040 cost of the supplies, the Lagan officers would pay the sum of £3,000 to Sanderson. Sir Robert also provided the king with a

copy of this agreement, along with parliament's original order in 1642 to pay the debt. 'Petition of Sir Robert Stewart to the King', 17 June 1661 (P.R.O., S.P. 63/307/100; 63/307/103).

113. Notes of matters discussed at the Committee of the Privy Council for Irish affairs, 15 June 1661; 'King to the Lords Justices', April 1661 (P.R.O., S.P. 63/307/16: 63/307/98). Stewart experienced many problems in obtaining this land from its original Catholic owners whom the king had also ordered to be restored. 'Petition of Mary Coughlan, widow of Terence Coughlan to Ormonde', 28 August 1663 (Bodl., Carte MSS clix, fo. 2); Simington, *Transplantation to Connaught*, pp 124, 176; G. Tallon (ed.), *Act of Settlement, 1662, court of claims: claims appointed to be heard and determined by his majesty's commissioners appointed to execute the act for the settlement of Ireland, 1662-63* (forthcoming), pp 75-6. I am grateful to Dr Tallon for a page proof copy in advance of publication.

114. 'King to the Lords Justices', 21 January 1661 (P.R.O., S.P. 63/306/18); 'King to the Lords Justices for a general pardon', 25 April 1661, *Cal. S.P. Ire.*, 1660-1662, pp 316-19.

115. McGrath only leased this land from the church. See note 97.

116. All of the '49 security was eventually divided into 100 lots and parcelled out between 1,030 '49 officers, who themselves were divided into an equal number of lots. Each individual lot was then passed by patent to a trustee or trustees who were required to divide any profits from their lot among the specific '49 officers mentioned in the particular patents. McKenny, 'Charles II's Irish Cavaliers', pp 420-22.

117. 'Abstracts of grants of lands', *Rec. comm. Ire. Rep.*, 1821-25, pp 137-38, 173-74.

118. Donegal Book of Survey and Distribution, 'Abstracts of grants of lands and other hereditaments under the Acts of Settlement and Explanation, AD 1666-1684', *Rec. comm. Ire. Rep.*, 1821-25, pp 65, 100-101, 137-138, 173-4, 218.

119. Sixty-seven of these acres are listed as in the possession of Thomas Dutton, an English Protestant, in 1641. The remaining 99 were held by John Cunningham, a Scottish Protestant. A word of explanation is required to understand what appears to have been a Protestant forfeiture. John Cunningham held a mortgage on this 99 acres from Ervin MacSweeny, an Irish Papist. The land, therefore, belonging to a Catholic, reverted to MacSweeny and was consequently confiscated and given to Cary Dillon. Neither the Book of Survey, nor the Civil Survey, indicates why the remaining 67 acres (the half Quarter of Kill), which was held by a Protestant in 1641, was given over to Dillon (although the Book of Survey has Dillon only receiving 40 of these acres). Perhaps, as was the case in other similar instances, Dutton held a mortgage on this land from a Catholic. Thomas Dutton was a minor and was the son and heir of Ralph Dutton, deceased. Simmington, *Civil Survey*, iii, 101, 107.

120. 'Abstracts of grants of lands', *Rec. comm. Ire. Rep.*, 1821-25, p. 65.

121. 'Abstracts of grants of lands', *Rec. comm. Ire. Rep.*, 1821-25, pp 100-101, 218.

122. W. Petty, *The political anatomy of Ireland*, London, 1691), p. 26.

123. These figures are taken from my data-base of north-west Ulster. McKenny, 'Land settlement in Ireland', pp 198-200; idem, *For King or Ulster*.

124. 'Abstracts of grants of lands', *Rec. comm. Ire. Rep.*, 1821-25, pp 100-101, 153.

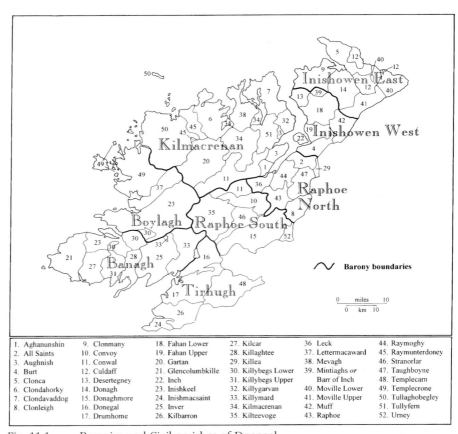

1. Aghanunshin	9. Clonmany	18. Fahan Lower	27. Kilcar	36. Leck	44. Raymoghy
2. All Saints	10. Convoy	19. Fahan Upper	28. Killaghtee	37. Lettermacaward	45. Raymunterdoney
3. Aughnish	11. Conwal	20. Gartan	29. Killea	38. Mevagh	46. Stranorlar
4. Burt	12. Culdaff	21. Glencolumbkille	30. Killybegs Lower	39. Mintiaghs or	47. Taughboyne
5. Clonca	13. Desertegney	22. Inch	31. Killybegs Upper	Barr of Inch	48. Templecarn
6. Clondahorky	14. Donagh	23. Inishkeel	32. Killygarvan	40. Moville Lower	49. Templecrone
7. Clondavaddog	15. Donaghmore	24. Inishmacsaint	33. Killymard	41. Moville Upper	50. Tullaghobegley
8. Clonleigh	16. Donegal	25. Inver	34. Kilmacrenan	42. Muff	51. Tullyfern
	17. Drumhome	26. Kilbarron	35. Kilteevoge	43. Raphoe	52. Urney

Fig. 11.1   Baronies and Civil parishes of Donegal.

Chapter 12

'NO MORE TO BE GOT OFF THE CAT BUT THE SKIN': MANAGEMENT, LANDHOLDING AND ECONOMIC CHANGE ON THE MURRAY OF BROUGHTON ESTATE, 1670-1755

GRAEME KIRKHAM

Late in 1699 Lady Ann Murray of Broughton made tentative enquiries of the Ulster landlord Thomas Knox of Dungannon about a match between her son John and Knox's eldest daughter. Before replying, Knox wrote to his cousin, also Thomas Knox, who was agent on the Murray estate in Donegal, asking for an account of the family and its concerns.[1] Knox replied enthusiastically: 'It is a very noble estate consisting of almost five large parishes and about a dozen of gentlemen that have their estates from him.'[2] Although currently set to Colonel Henry Conyngham at a yearly rent of £380, he knew the property 'to be worth £600 per annum clear rent over and above the King's rent ... the whole money he owes here is but about £1,000.' Knox had served the Murrays for almost ten years and was also agent on the adjoining Conyngham estate. He had recently obtained a freehold from the Murrays and had visited them in Scotland. He promptly sent Lady Murray copies of his correspondence with his cousin, with whom his loyalty to his patrons had made him less than candid.

The Murray estate in Donegal was certainly noble in size, totalling about 65,000 statute acres in parcels around Donegal town, Ardara and Killybegs, including large parts of the parishes of Killaghtee, Killymard, Killybegs, Kilcar and Inishkeel. In other respects, however, it was less impressive. Much of it was infertile upland and although there were areas of better land on the coast and assets in the herring and salmon fisheries, its potential was limited by its remoteness. Moreover, when Knox replied so positively to his cousin's enquiry a long running challenge to the Murrays' title to the estate had recently been revived, threatening a resumption of proceedings which had already proved ruinously expensive. In addition, the uncertainties and factional feeling arising from the dispute had created a schism between the Murray family and its major tenants. The 'dozen of gentlemen' Knox described as holding 'estates' from John Murray were freeholders occupying more than 12,000 acres of the property. Several of these freeholders also held leaseholds on the estate and they constituted a locally powerful and entrenched group with wide-ranging kinship ties between them, to the Conyngham family and, to a lesser extent, with the Murrays. Many of the families had been in the area for several generations. By 1700, however, these ties of kinship and obligation were breaking down and the support of this group – 'raised and bred up even from nothing' by their connection with the Murrays, as Knox put it – could no longer be relied upon.[3] In 1701 Knox reported: '[I] verily believe if £5 would save you and your family from ruin they would not advance it, on any other account than what they are obliged to; for most of the concerns there are now out of the old people's hands to their children'.[4] These themes – the problems of obtaining a return from a remote and poorly endowed property, of legal uncertainties and of troubled relations with tenants – were to persist in the affairs of the estate over a long period.

The Murray family seat was at Cally, near Gatehouse of Fleet in south-west Scotland. George Murray of Broughton had been one of a group of minor Scottish undertakers who obtained land in Boylagh and Banagh at the Plantation. By 1618 these proportions were forfeit and had been welded into one estate by John Murray of Cockpool, a distant relative of the Broughton family, subsequently created 1st Earl of Annandale.[5] In the early 1660s, however, following a complex legal dispute, possession was gained by Richard Murray of Broughton.[6] Murray and his wife resided in Killybegs for several years, returning to Scotland in 1672 during an acute downturn in the Irish economy. The Murray family was never again to reside on its Irish lands.

A survey of the tenures on the estate in 1673 listed two old leases for lives, a variety of leases for between 21 and 41 years and 19 freeholds.[7] Five off the latter predated Richard Murray's possession, but the remainder had been set by him during his recent residence and on at least two of these the previous determinable leases were still in being. Some of these perpetuity holdings had been set outright in return for cash payments, but in other instances it is probable that the 'freeholds' were unredeemed mortgages. Rents on many of them were subject to fixed annual rent charges throughout the eighteenth century, presumably representing interest on the original debts.[8] There were sporadic attempts over the next century to define these tenures and to regain possession, almost all unsuccessful.

The 1673 survey also attempted to assess the potential for increasing the rental from the estate, which then totalled £455 per annum. The entries for eight holdings included estimates of the possible rent for new leases when the current tenures expired, with a predicted rise of just under 40 per cent. Several holdings were reset in 1680 and several of these achieved significant increases; on one quarterland near Donegal town which included corn and tuck mills the rent doubled.[9] The difficult economic conditions of the late 1680s and the disruption caused by the Williamite War made it harder to keep the estate fully tenanted. In April 1688 Murray's agent commented on 'the extreme poverty of this country ... as to the settling of the lands it shall be my business that none go waste, though I cannot promise but that there will be some abatements of the rent, for I assure you unless some unexpected relief comes, this place and many more in the kingdom will go to perfect beggary'.[10] A month after the Treaty of Limerick, Thomas Knox, then agent for the neighbouring Conyngham estate, proposed that he should also act as agent for the Murrays and sought a power of attorney: 'There are now tenants of the Irish planting the lands and the law is so here that without a power in writing none can make any loyal defence.'[11] In 1694 Knox was commended for his 'care and pains in settling and setting' the estate.[12]

Richard Murray had sold a large area of the original Donegal property (including the Rosses and a significant estate around Mount Charles) to his cousin Sir Albert Conyngham in the 1660s. Richard died in 1690, leaving his heir, John, a minor. Sir Albert was killed in 1691, and was succeeded by his son, Colonel (later General) Henry Conyngham. The legal dispute over the title to the estate continued and the Murrays lost possession of at least part of it during this period. Henry Conyngham assumed responsibility for the continuing legal manouevres and for dealings with the tenants and possession was regained late in 1692. The dispute had been bitter: in November 1691 Knox reported that Lady Conyngham had arranged that a small military force was to be quartered near him for the winter, 'that I may not be run down by any of our enemies'; it is clear that he meant friends of the Scottish claimants to the estate.[13] It had also been expensive. It was proposed that the 1,200 guineas costs incurred in taking the dispute to the House of Lords be shared between the Murrays, Conyngham and the freeholders. In 1694 Henry Conyngham wrote to Lady Murray telling her of the

> difficulties I meet with from some of your tenants and my near relations who are so perverse in everything that relates to your interest or mine that I have found as much difficulty in managing them as I did in carrying our case, for they are so far from paying what was proposed to them on account of the suit that they

neither give thanks to me that saved them nor will pay a farthing
rent but what is extorted from them by the Collector for the
Crown Rent, for we durst not distrain them for fear of their
replevying and calling our title in question ... And though this
argument would cut their own throats, yet their ill nature would
prompt them to it ... I hope we might find a way to purchase out
some of your freeholders for I am heartily weary of them ...[14]

In 1696 it was agreed that Conyngham should 'farm' the estate for
two years for an annual rent of £243-10s.[15] When this agreement
expired Conyngham was granted a 21-year lease on a large part of the
property at £300 per annum, with an additional 99-year lease on the
remaining Loughros proportion – more than 21,000 statute acres – for
an additional yearly rent of £80.[16] In 1700 Conyngham obtained an
80-year extension to the remaining term of his lease for two smaller
proportions for an additional £18 per annum.[17] This arrangement
further emphasised the distance between the absentee Murrays and
their tenantry. In 1699, Knox pointed out to John Murray, now of age,
that 'were it not for the care and management of Col. Conyngham, as
matters now stand, there are but few tenants on your estate that would
acknowledge you in a sixpence, other than on their own terms'.[18]

Conyngham's tenure was potentially extremely advantageous but he
felt himself to be the loser almost from the outset. In February 1699 he
complained that

did not necessity for the good of both our concerns oblige me to
be farmer to your estate, I would not have the toil and trouble
together with the frequent losses that happens by insolvent
tenants and the expense of sending your money to Belfast for a
hundred guineas yearly. If Locrus [Loughros] were not a better
bargain than the rest I should have an ill time of it.[19]

The severe decline in the Irish economy from 1702 increased the
difficulties, and exchanges between the Murrays and Conyngham
became increasingly acrimonious, the former demanding severe
measures against tenants in arrears, the latter asserting the almost total
absence of cash in the north-west and the lack of markets by which to
generate it. John Murray died in March 1704 and was succeeded by his
younger brother, Alexander. In November 1704 Conyngham, en route
for military service in Portugal, informed Alexander that during the past
two years he had received only £50 from his own and the Murray
estate and from 'considerable farms' held from the bishop of Raphoe.

I took last year all the butter in the barony at 14s. per hundred
[cwt.] and after paying for the carriage of it to Dublin I shall not

get 7s. per hundred for my 14s. I took last year above 800 head of cattle and by those I could get sold I lost considerably, but the greatest part remaining still on my hands I believe I shall never get ⅓ of what they stood, the grazing considered. This is not all, but they owe me still about £1400 besides the half year's rent due the 1st of this instant and if all their lives depended on the raising one hundred pounds they could not do it ... for my part I can have no hand in sending hundreds of families a-begging, and abstracted from the charitable part I am sure it would not be common prudence ... all the cattle and other goods in our tenants' possession if now sold at the market rate would not near pay what the poor people now owe, and if all is taken there will be little comfort in a waste estate. It hath been the work of some time to get it planted.[20]

During Conyngham's absence his wife, Lady Mary Shelburne, maintained a spirited correspondence, urging Murray to grant an abatement of rent and an extension of the term of the 21-year lease, 'for no good improving, substantial tenants will take land for so short a time, which obliges us to set to the poorer sort, and makes the rent very ill paid; nay, sometimes they run away with all'.[21] Despite paying well above market rates for butter and cattle, and offering 2s. 6d per pound abatement for rents paid in cash, she was still unable to obtain significant remittances from Donegal.[22] Murray proposed that she should surrender the lease and pay him compensation for accepting it, to which latter proposal she replied that 'for as long as I have been a landlady (though I have had many leases thrown up) I never heard of it before; if that be the custom in Scotland I am sure it is nowhere else'.[23] The death of her husband in Spain early in 1706 meant that she was legally unable to relinquish what was now in effect part of her children's inheritance. Her brother-in-law, William Conolly, subsequently took on the management of her affairs and used his own resources to make full and regular payments to Murray, although it was probably some years before the Conyngham's tenure began to be profitable.[24] By 1718, however, with the 21-year lease on a large part of the estate about to expire, the property was evidently sufficiently attractive for Conolly to enquire 'whether you continue the resolution you once had of selling. If not, what you design about the lease my nephew holds which I think expires soon, and what you would do about reserving it to the family that hold it ...', suggesting obliquely that there could be unfortunate consequences were the estate to pass into 'other hands'.[25]

Alexander Murray resumed direct control of the property from 1719.

His annual income from it rose immediately, from £398 paid by the Conynghams to £710, reflecting the significantly higher rental the latter had received from their undertenants.[26] Rents were undoubtedly still low. In the following year Murray set new leases on almost 11,000 acres of the estate, in most cases renewing to existing tenants, and on those holdings for which a direct comparison can be made the new rents were almost 80 per cent higher than those being paid in 1719.[27] There was some recognition that tenants might find their new bargains difficult to hold at these rates: many of the leases included a clause allowing a surrender after four years. The new leases were also for the relatively short term of seven years, considerably less than the 21- and 31-year terms commonly granted in Ulster at this period, and considerably less advantageous than the tenures for lives often made as an enticement to substantial tenants. For Murray the short terms may have offered a period during which the prospects for the estate could be reassessed. Less than a month before the first of the new leases was signed, he was advised to make enquiries on the current value of the lands, to have the estate surveyed and that

> [I]n regard the value of land may still increase, the term given the tenant ought to be the shorter ... whereof a lease for seven years or less may be sufficient, if the true value be known. But where it is not, setting the land only from year to year appears most advisable until the full value can be certainly discovered, when it may with more advantage be demised for a longer time than probably it can now.[28]

These leases were due to expire in May 1727 and by early February that year the tenants of holdings totalling more than 13,500 acres had been canvassed for new proposals. The timing was unfortunate for the resetting became due during one of the most severe economic and subsistence crises of the century. Some gentry tenants offered substantial increases for grazing farms and holdings to be underset, but the non-gentry tenants holding partnership farms in the Mountcharles-Donegal town area refused to propose any rise.[29] As the crisis deepened, tenants who had agreed terms for new leases in 1727 refused to accept them; Murray held out against lower proposals because he apparently suspected that some tenants had 'combined' against increases. Some out-of-lease holdings were let from year to year on verbal agreements – arrears from some of these tenures were still unpaid in 1733 – but no new leases were made. This had unfortunate consequences, not least in keeping tenants on the lands. In February 1729 the agent, James Hamilton, pleaded with Murray to come to Donegal and negotiate with the tenants in person:

... it is not in my power, nor in the power of man, to settle it [the estate] to satisfaction until you come on the spot yourself, and it will always be the longer the worse. You will not believe the poor condition the country is in ... I had no small difficulty this season to persuade many of your tenants to plough their farms, always encouraging them and telling them that you would surely be here in February, and if they hear now that you won't come, I fear it will not be in my power to keep them any longer. But this I can assure you, if you are not here before May much of your estate will be turned waste. Land is like to fall to a great degree and bread is so exceedingly dear that a famine is feared among the poorer sort.[30]

By this time a number of holdings were already untenanted. Hamilton reported that on the Conyngham estate the tenants

tho' bound in firm leases for four years ending next May, are throwing them up daily. I have written pressingly to him [Conyngham] ... to come over this Spring and give his tenants abatement, otherwise he will have a waste estate ... There's a ship lying now at Killybegs belonging to New England that has indented with as many passengers as she can carry. Mr William Conyngham [one of Murray's freeholders] has a large ship which he intends to send off with more this Spring; I can't get any rent from him. I can assure you there is several in the Barony of Raphoe selling their freeholds and going to America.[31]

In July 1729 Hamilton wrote again, complaining that Murray gave no assistance in putting the estate on a 'better footing' and urging that he come to Donegal before November,

otherwise I doubt much if even the tenth man will plough their farms. There's two ships now in Killybegs ready to sail with passengers, wherein is some of your tenants and several other gentlemen's tenants gone off in arrear, and no help for it, for there's no more to be got off the cat but the skin. There's of these several that within this few years was accounted good tenants is now obliged to bind [indenture] themselves, their wives and children for three or four years to answer their passage, and I can assure you there's a great deal more rent due you in your estate that will never be paid you ... If you let your estate be once untenanted you will find more difficulty to plant it with as good tenants again than you imagine.[32]

Murray did not come but in February 1730 he sent Thomas Addi of Donaghadee, county Down, to investigate.[33] Addi confirmed much of what Hamilton had said: '[A]ll the tenants make a grievous complaint of the dearth of their holdings and most of them seems to be very poor.'[34] Without the protection of leases, tenants were refusing even to maintain their houses and some were refusing to grind their grain at the estate mills. Addi also urged Murray to come to Donegal:

> I assure you, your own concerns require you very much. I told all the tenants that you would infallibly be over about the beginning of April; many of them would not have ploughed their ground had I not assured them of this and I really think it a great disadvantage to you that your land is out of lease ... Whether they had a lesson learned them or not I cannot tell, but the generality of them say they will not hold your land any longer than May or All Saints if you do not set them leases.[35]

Addi came back to Donegal in July 1730 and sought new proposals for 19-year leases, informing the tenants that Murray 'would be soon with them to perfect leases to all of them that proposed in reason'.[36] However, having sought proposals, Murray then had a detailed schedule drawn up of the rents he expected.[37] In May 1731 Addi returned, accompanied by his brother-in-law, Henry McCulloch, and furnished with a power of attorney by which they and the agent, Hamilton, could set the lands on Murray's behalf. In early July they reported that a number of the new leases had been perfected at the rents Murray had specified, and that other tenants had signed 'articles' for new leases.[38] Addi recounted their efforts

> to have the tenants all in and to move them by fair or forcible means to do what is right. You may assure yourself Mr Hamilton is very careless in setting your land, and had not my brother McCulloch and I used more than ordinary diligence I believe we should have been in disgrace with you, and I assure you it grieved me very much to see your tenants in general stand out as if they had combined so to do. But thank God we have at last got some leases set ... All those that are perfected are according to your schedule and I assure you there has been broken heads about them, for we got some to take others farms over their heads which put them all a-steer [sic]; and had we not done so, we could not have set an inch of it ... as the ice is well broke I think there is no fear of those that are to be set, as to the rent etc., though with difficulty, and as so many leases are already taken it

will make the others set the better some time before May next, and I think you'll come the better to your purpose to defer setting the best farms 'til pretty near May next ... [39]

In their 'more than ordinary diligence' Addi and McCulloch also led some tenants to believe that a proportion of the rents they bound themselves to pay under the new leases would be 'reserved', that is, permanently abated. One was told that Murray would not charge him the full sum 'in regard he was one of the first of the tenants who took a lease at an advance rent'.[40] Another farm was set only after Addi had allowed the prospective lessees to discover that he intended bringing farmers from North Down – 'very able tenants and good honest Presbyterians' – to view it and other holdings on the estate.[41]

Table 12.1

	Rent per statute acre (new pence)	Total acreage set	No of leases	Average acreage per lease	Increase (%) in average rent/acre
Manor of Ballyboyle					
pre-1719	4.7	3366	—	—	—
1720	6.8	3366	11	306	45
1732-33	8.7	1596	7	228	28
1752	13.7	3366	21	160	57
Manor of Castlemurray					
pre-1719	1.7	15436	—	—	—
1720	3.5	7588	10	759	106
1732-33	3.6	4900	6	817	3
1752	6.2	10217	28	365	72

Sources: Acreages, see note 82; pre-1719 rents, see note 26; 1720 lettings, see P.R.O.N.I., D.2860/36, lease counterparts, 1720; 1732-33 lettings, see notes 38, 39, 40; 1752 lettings, see note 84.

Most of the remaining leases were signed during the spring of 1732, thus ending a five-year period of instability. On the better lands of the eastern, Ballyboyle, portion of the property the increase in rents since the previous resetting was a little over 25 per cent; on the much larger Castlemurray proportion, dominated by upland holdings, the rise was minimal (table 12.1). Again, the relatively short terms of the new leases may have depressed rents, but the underlying weakness of the local economy, particularly for graziers, was a more important limitation. Some effort was made to address this problem. Addi invited a number of major Belfast merchants to 'fix a company at Killybegs' to deal in local cattle, encouraging them with descriptions of the 'advantages of trade, the fine harbour, spacious cheap farms with all their good qualities and the fishings,' and conveying to them Murray's offer of £40 per annum 'for a clerk to attend the business'.[42] His contacts were concerned at the shortness of the lease and proposed that 'if the beef could be sent dead or alive to Belfast, they would buy it there ... I wish with all my heart it could be brought to a bearing, for I'm sure it would be much to the advantage of you and your tenants, as well as the company, and would make money circulate bravely in the country'.[43] This initiative failed, but Murray subsequently ordered that two out-of-lease townlands, from which the former tenants were to be ejected, should be secured as a grazing park. Cattle were bought from tenants, thereby buttressing the local market and returning cash to the local economy which would otherwise have been transmitted to Scotland.[44]

These moves emphasise the dependence of many households in the region on grazing, paralleling Charles O'Hara's observations on Sligo in the first half of the eighteenth century.[45] The rise of Munster as the centre for the fattening and dairying industries in Ireland narrowed the opportunities for peripheral regions such as the north-west, and the pastoral economy of the region was increasingly focused on external demand for store cattle. An embargo on beef shipments to France in 1741-42, affecting primarily the Munster ports, ruined markets in south Donegal and in November 1744, following a general embargo on beef exports, the grazier managing Murray's park reported that 'the markets are quite down; there's no such thing as selling any bullocks and very little demand for cows ... every grazier that bought cattle this year are considerably losers and have most of the cattle on their hands yet'.[46] On many parts of the estate cattle offered the sole source of income. Addi described one mountain farm in 1730 as 'coarse rocky ground, and but little grain ... they bring sea wrack from the [St John's] Point in boats to set their potatoes and draw it from the shore on cars to the farm ... a tolerable good farm for grazing'; another was noted as 'very coarse mountain ground and only fit for rearing young cattle. They have no grain but as they buy from others'.[47] There were areas of better soils along the coast, and holdings near Mountcharles and Donegal town were referred to in 1745 as 'grain farms'. Here too, however, the pastoral economy was important; proportions in this area were decribed as 'good for grain and grass' and 'good for grain, hay and pasture'.[48]

Alternative forms of economic activity were limited for much of the period. From the 1720s domestic production of linen yarn slowly introduced a new diversity to the regional economy, although it is difficult to trace the early progress of this change at a local level.[49] The Murray leases of 1720 included covenants binding the tenants to plant flax and hemp seed according to Act of Parliament (although there is no indication that the provision was enforced) and in 1726 James Hamilton sent some pieces of locally manufactured linen to Murray.[50] In the mid-1730s a tenant near Mountcharles complained to Murray of the difficulties he faced, asserting that were it not for the efforts of his son as a yarn dealer he would not have been able to continue to hold his lands.[51] When Arthur Young visited the Mountcharles area forty years later he found that 'all the women and children of ten years old and upwards spin', noting also '[T]he farmers here in general pay half a year's rent with fish, and half with yarn.'[52] Addi noted in 1730 that the tenants of several coastal farms 'have the benefit of herring fishing,' adding, in one case, 'by which they do some years make their whole rent'.[53] A decade later William Henry noted the 'infinite quantities of fish' to be had from the coast around Inver, observing that a 'vast number of carriers are employed in the season in supplying from hence the inland counties'.[54] The estate also included profitable salmon fisheries at Teelin and the mouth of the Owenea and the leases set in 1732 included new clauses specifically protecting these.[55] Another new covenant was added against tenants selling turf from their holdings, almost certainly a response to Addi's discovery that the tenants of two townlands were selling turf to the inhabitants of Killybegs, 'and by their turf as well as I can compute, the eleven tenants make the rent of their farm'.[56]

The early 1730s may have seen some improvement in the pastoral economy of the region and the rapid expansion of exports of linen yarn from Derry through the decade suggests the growing importance of domestic spinning as a source of household income.[57] These favourable indicators were fragile, however, and the following two decades saw a succession of further crises. With hindsight it is clear that the cumulative impact of these calamities put the affairs of the estate beyond effective management for almost 20 years. Harvests in 1734 and 1735 were severely deficient and early in 1736 Hamilton alerted Murray of his concern 'that there will be so much arrears, but I can assure [you] that it is not in my power to help it, for this was an unfortunate year in this country'.[58] Significantly, he repeated his previous requests for Murray to visit Donegal: 'I can assure you it will tend to your advantage and your affairs will be all put on a settled footing.' A fuller account of the 'unfortunate year' came from Alexander Crawford, one of the non-gentry tenants in the parish of Killymard, who wrote to his landlord in July 1736 to tell him of

the miserable condition that I have brought myself and my family to in staying in your Honour's land these years past, depending on your Honour's promise that you made to me when you were in this country last, and after that imposed rents and burdens that I am obliged to groan under the burden thereof, when I cannot provide for my children but am obliged to transport myself and my family to the deserts of America. And had it not been for depending upon your Honour's promise I and my family might be living in that land where we might be freed from those burdens that we are labouring under ... And there has been such famines for bread in these countries and great deaths of cattle and a kind of disease or murrain that the country is impoverished by it, which is the occasion, with rents and tithes, to cause the most part of the country to go to America. We are as bound hens to bishop[s and] minister[s], by their hurrying us into Bishop's Courts. If we do not meet their time and leisure they may do what they please for there is not one either to take part with us or to stand our cause or to plead our interest. We are obliged to your Honour's sparing us but at the same time the heavy burden continues the same and I's [sic] not able to stand it ... [59]

Alexander Crawford and his family had held the two balliboes [a *baile bó* or tate is about 480 arable Irish acres] of Drumark and Drumgun since before 1719 and signed a new lease for an annual rent of just under £24 in 1732.[60] Crawford's letter is one of the few direct testimonies from a prospective emigrant of this period of the 'burdens' which urged departure; the years 1735 and 1736 saw the largest short-term outflow of emigrants in the first half of the eighteenth century, prompted not only by economic distress but also by fears of an official ban on emigration. Crawford's appeal to Murray's 'promise' to him during a past visit – probably some ten years earlier – is revealing as evidence of the expectations of non-gentry tenants of a direct paternalistic relationship with their landlord, particularly during such periods of crisis. It was this expectation to which the repeated appeals of Hamilton and others for Murray's presence in Donegal to 'settle his affairs' made reference. Another of Murray's Ballyboyle tenants wrote to him in 1738: 'I think there is no landlords in this part of the world but comes and sees their tenants and gives them some encouragement that is under heavy rents ... the bearer will tell you what Colonel Henry Conyngham is doing for his tenants and how he is laying out schemes how to manage.'[61] Murray had not been entirely neglectful, however, for he had evidently supported a group of Presbyterian tenants in contesting a suit over tithe potatoes, probably the same case about which Alexander Crawford had complained two years earlier.[62]

Alexander Crawford did not emigrate but probably regretted the decision, for the economic difficulties of the region remained severe. From the mid-1730s arrears grew and a number of tenants offered Murray the surrender of their leases; others 'broke' and left their farms. The father and son who held Castletown, near Dunkineely, ran into arrears in the years 1735-37, 'then died for want of the necessaties of life'.[63] Once again, one of the immediate causes of distress was the lack of specie in the regional economy. In July 1738 another of Murray's tenants from the Ballyboyle area visited him in Scotland, carrying a letter from a neighbour: 'I and others has advised him to go to your Honour, him being a dealer in the country and brings in money ... ought to be encouraged.'[64] The letter cited the example of another absentee landlord who gave two local 'dealers' the 'return of [his] monies and it is kept in the country. They receive it from [his] agent and pays it by bill in Dublin and I do assure you they are of good circumstance by their dealing and I think there is none can live here by the benefit of farms'.

The subsistence crisis of 1740-41 was less catastrophic in the north-west than in many other parts of Ireland but was nonetheless severe. By the autumn of 1740 arrears on the estate totalled more than £670, almost two-thirds of the total annual rental.[65] Eighteen months later, after the immediate crisis had passed, Hamilton answered Murray's demands for greater rent remittances by informing him of the effect of the embargo on beef exports on local markets and observing, 'You do not consider the poverty of the tenants that I have to deal with,' adding that the occupiers of four large holdings were 'in more arrears than all they had in the world was worth'.[66] Henry McCulloch – then resident in Killybegs and probably acting as a receiver of rents – was critical of Hamilton's management and urged stronger measures: 'I beg it of you to give strict orders as to the arrears and I'll be bound I'll get you either money or cattle, for your little landlords are bad brutes on your estate, for the generality of middling tenants have paid 'til half year.'[67] His final observation is interesting. It is possible that the domestic economy of 'middling tenants' – now diversifying into spinning – was better able to generate a cash income than the hard-hit grazing trade of the 'little landlords', who would also have found it hard to prise cash from their undertenants. However, the comment may reflect profoundly different attitudes between the two groups towards debt and the importance of maintaining good relations with a landlord. A decade earlier Hamilton had reported that 'the bulk of arrears is owing by men of fortune' and Murray himself complained of the 'bad payments' by his freeholders.[68] In difficult times, given a choice between paying rent punctually and maintaining personal living standards, many middleman squires probably chose the latter.

In north-west Ulster the most serious crisis of the first half of the eighteenth century came in the mid-1740s. The unsettled political situation in Europe severely depressed trade from early in 1744 and in June, Hamilton was reporting that 'many of the tenants are much reduced'.[69] Rumours of a French invasion of the south of England added a new factor. On St Patrick's Day 1744 McCulloch informed Murray that

> [T]he man I set Derrylane and Teeling fishing to ... came here yesterday and told me positively he would waste it on Mayday next, for he would get better bargains soon ... I also wrote you of Gortnasillagh that I formerly set to Doctor Dunleavy. He told me the same day that he had provided himself otherwise and to make our best of it. I assure you our Irish are grown so superb on the account of this war that they don't know what end of them is uppermost ... We in these little villages are keeping what guard we can for we had an account privately they were to make a descent on us last night. They tell publicly Ireland is their property and will fight for it.[70]

This may provide a partial explanation for the disparity in rent payments between the two portions of the estate during this period: arrears in Ballyboyle were relatively small and declined in the year to May 1744; in Castlemurray, however, with a much higher Catholic population, arrears rose from £855 to almost £1100, near twice the annual rental for the manor.[71]

The harvest of 1744 failed catastrophically, 'so totally destroyed ... that not one acre in ten was worth reaping'.[72] An extremely hard winter followed and by the early spring of 1745 large numbers of cattle were dying of starvation. In April the usually optimistic Henry McCulloch was writing his seventh letter to Murray since the previous December, in a despairing attempt to impress him with the severity of the situation:

> [P]erhaps you may think I'm taking part with the tenants to wrong you, which if you do you'll find it to your great loss that it is not so. In the parish of Killcare [sic – Kilcar] ... there's not 30 barrels of any kind sown in the whole; the next parish which is Glen[columbkille] is the same for the people are starving since the carron [sic – carrion? = dead cattle] is over. There's not £40 worth of cattle in the quarterland of Largymore and Mucross men that formerly were able men tottering with perfect weakness ... I do assure you I see [sic] several tenants the other day, both of

Largymore and Mucross, that this time twelve months were good tenants, that were really begging from door to door ... there's not a landlord that had one inch of an estate in Ireland but sent their tenants relief, only you, and I assure you you're much exclaimed on for that. But it's your own loss and now past redemption, for your tenants are gone all to the South of Ireland where there's some victualling. Any that can pay their freight are going off to New England; those that can't bind themselves and families for 7 years. But I really believe you don't believe there's such terrible extremity here as is. If the Almighty does not order light out of darkness there will many suffer death for perfect want. They are already fallen on the ... cattle that survived ... For your waste land here you would not get stock for them in the county of Donegal – your parks are not half stocked by the death of both horses and black cattle.

Now to return to Killymard, they are broke horse and foot. Although they are grain farms the people gave the most of their grain to their cattle at the beginning to try to bring them through. Afterwards they all died and the people all starving ... [As] For your worthy Corporation [Killybegs] I'm persuaded you won't have 6 good tenants in it at May Day, for they are going off every day ... if ever you have an inclination to have those freeholds easy, if you advance them a little money now you may get them as you please, for I assure you they are as bad as any in the place for want of bread.[73]

In November 1745 Addi arrived in Donegal from county Down to assess the situation but was clearly unable to comprehend the severity of the crisis. He was critical of the handling of Murray's affairs and in March 1746 gloomily predicted that he feared Hamilton had 'let the arrear swell so large that I fear a great part of it will be lost'.[74] When the agent reported his receipts for the year to May 1746 he had been able to collect only £250, less than a quarter of the total rental. Of this his own rent for his lands in Ballyboyle contributed £80 and the Conyngham leases a further £98; the entire body of tenants had therefore paid only a little more than £70 during the preceding year, most of which derived from the freeholders.[75] The paucity of rent payments is hardly surprising. The harvest of 1745 was delayed by poor weather and was in any case much reduced by the small quantity of seed sown; by the end of the year the price of food grains was again rising and there were fears for the poor throughout the north-west.[76] In addition, the population of the region had been significantly reduced by increased mortality and migration, and many holdings had been abandoned.[77] In a few instances it had been possible to find new occupiers for these lands (at much reduced rents), but many of these also 'broke'. Other factors also continued to depress the economy. The outbreak of rebellion in Scotland in the summer of 1745 further dampened trade and the unstable political situation rendered many tenants unwilling to pay rent until there was a clearer indication of the outcome: in March 1746 Addi reported that the 'common people here are very uppish on all occasions and would be fond of a change in government ...'[78]

From the following year there were indications that conditions in the region were improving. Prices for cattle and yarn rose and food prices fell sharply.[79] Nonetheless, the accumulated burden of debt on the estate persisted for some time – in 1749 arrears still totalled £1100.[80] It is possible that some occupiers were loath to diminish their new prosperity by paying off old arrears – a number of those with significant debts were noted as 'certainly able to pay' and threatened with legal action – but even on the Abercorn estate, a much more tightly managed property with a significantly more developed local economy, arrears arising from the crisis were slow to clear.[81]

The leases set in the early 1730s were now approaching renewal. In 1749 a survey of much of the leasehold portion of the estate was commissioned, providing (for the first time) an assessment of the extent of the property and a basis for an informed estimate of its rental value.[82] When the new leases were set in 1752 average rents per acre soared: in Ballyboyle they rose by almost 60 per cent, in Castlemurray by more than 70 per cent (table 11.1). It is not clear whether tenants had been canvassed for proposals or whether a schedule of expected rents was compiled, as had taken place prior to the previous resetting, but there were in any case a number of factors which favoured an increase. The first of these was the extraordinary transformation in the economic outlook. By 1751, O'Hara observed, improved demand and rising prices had 'so enlivened our markets that people began to look cheerful again ... our people are grown rich and lands bear a higher price than ever was known before'.[83] Secondly, the lease terms were considerably longer than those which had been granted previously: four of the new lettings were for three lives or 31 years and the remainder for 31 years.[84] (One of the leases for lives was subsequently described as 'then known to be a very advantageous lease ... given to induce Mr. Foster to remove to Ballyboyle as a pattern to the rest of the tenants.'[85]) Finally, some large multi-townland proportions which had previously been set in one lease were divided between a number of lessees, many of them probably former undertenants to middlemen. This process of setting direct to occupiers was to go much further on the estate later in the century, but its limited adoption at this stage enabled the Murrays to profit to some extent from the real market value of land, rather than the considerably lower rents paid by those who held large areas and reset to others. In a number of instances holdings previously held in partnership were set in separate leases. This had some benefits for estate management, in simplifying the relationship between landlord and leaseholder and avoiding the problems likely to arise in collecting rents from a number of tenants on a holding. It may also reflect a developing individualism on the part of tenants, as they sought to focus within their own families the profits available from the more optimistic economic situation.[86] Between a third and half of the new leases were still held in partnership, however, and a note on a rent roll for the property after the resetting observed that it was 'not possible to place the number of acres to every person's possession because many of the farms are divided and part [of] a farm possessed by one tenant and another part of [the] same farm by another tenant'.[87]

Alexander Murray had died in c.1750 and his heir, James Murray, visited his Donegal property for the first time in 1754. By this time the prospects for the estate looked relatively auspicious; they were certainly so by comparison with almost any period since the Murray family resumed control of their property from the Conynghams in 1719. Nonetheless, the local economy was still relatively underdeveloped. James Murray was accompanied on his 'Irish expedition' by George Muir, who commented that he found the estate 'in many places very improvable ... it is greatly under-rated at present and if the improvements and manufactures which are so considerable in other parts of that country should reach there, it's difficult to say what that estate may be let for at the expiry of the present leases'.[88] However, Muir also noted that 'if at any time [the estate] should be under the management of a less able or honest man than your present agent, the rents might become more uncertain and precarious,' and other events at about this time also sounded a warning note. In November 1754 a tenant who had held over on his farm since the lands were reset was dispossessed. A number of houses on the farm 'were entirely burnt down and destroyed, and there was the greatest reason to believe, as [he] was so unwilling to quit the possession, that the same was done either by himself or by some employed and directed by him'.[89] The tenant claimed to hold a lease 'for a long number of years' set to him by Henry McCulloch, to whom he also claimed to have paid arrears of rent, and there was sufficient doubt about the details of past management for the story to be at least plausible. Murray eventually lost the arrears and had to compensate the incoming tenant for the delay in obtaining possession and the costs of rebuilding. When the estate was again reset thirty years later there were serious episodes of arson and cattle houghing attributed to ousted tenants. Murray also attempted to revive the issue of the validity of some of the reputed freeholds on the estate, not least because of their greater potential asset value as leaseholds if the estate were sold. This option had certainly been in James Murray's mind when he visited Donegal in 1754 and soon after he advertised the property for sale. The response was a public challenge to his title from one of the descendants of the heirs of the earl of Annandale, a suit believed settled for more than half a century.[90] This challenge appears not to have been pursued, but doubts about the validity of the title dogged repeated attempts to sell the estate until the 1840s.[91]

How typical was the Murray estate of others in Donegal or, for that matter, elsewhere in Ireland during this period? Absentee proprietorship was certainly not uncommon and the general chronology of economic change was shared very broadly. Other estates experienced equivalent histories of proprietorial indebtedness and the consequent setting of large areas as freeholds.[92] By comparison with more developed areas the return from the property was low – the gross average rent for the whole estate in the mid-1750s was less than three pence per acre – but not uniquely so. Neither can we be sure that the troubled history of management on the Murray estate was not more general. Certainly, comparisons with the Abercorn estate, another absentee property, draw a sharp contrast between apparent muddle and confusion on the one hand and an impression of well-defined policy and tight control on the other, but the lack of detailed case studies for this period makes it difficult to determine which was the more typical case. It is tempting to feel more than a little sympathy for both the Murrays and their agents in view of the problems they faced in dealing with a remote and generally unrewarding property, a frequently recalcitrant tenantry, a troubled legal history and a period of recurrent economic and subsistence crises.

Finally, what did the Murrays gain from their property? At the resetting in 1752 their annual notional income from it rose to £1,500, something more than three times the rental eighty years earlier.[93] It is clear, however, that their actual receipts rarely approached the totals which appeared on rent rolls. In addition to minor deductions such as crown rent, agent's fees, disbursements for minor improvements, rent charges on freeholds and losses on exchange between Ireland and Scotland, there were also frequent substantial arrears, often not recoverable, and major legal expenses. Neither were they able to rely on a regular income, for remittances of rents were unpredictable in frequency and were made piecemeal, in small sums. Commenting on James Murray's intention to sell the property in 1754, George Muir concluded

had you no other view than laying out so much as what that estate might produce upon sale, you could not have it better secured ... the common rates of land in Ireland does not exceed 25 years purchase; at that rate you have 4 per cent for your money ... as the world goes now I scarcely imagine you could make a purchase in Scotland would yield you more.[94]

His optimism was credible in the early 1750s but would have been untenable at almost any time over the nine decades since the Murrays took possession of the estate.

References

1. P.R.O.N.I., D.2860/4/6, Thomas Knox, Strabane, to Thomas Knox, 24 January 1699/1700 [copy]. Knox was cautious and the match did not eventually take place.
2. P.R.O.N.I., D.2860/4/5, Thomas Knox, Killigordon, to Thomas Knox [Dungannon], 2 February 1699/1700 [copy].
3. P.R.O.N.I., D.2860/4/1, Thomas Knox, Mount Charles, to Lady Broughton, 8 November 1691.
4. P.R.O.N.I., D.2860/4/9, Knox, Killigordon, to John Murray, 1 July 1701.
5. M. Perceval-Maxwell, *The Scottish migration to Ulster in the reign of James I* (London, 1973), pp 103, 170, 172; Denis Verschoyle, 'The background to a hidden age' in *Donegal Annual*, vi, 2 (1965), pp 110-128.
6. Verschoyle, 'Background to a hidden age,' p. 112. This source provides considerable detail on the earlier seventeenth century background.
7. P.R.O.N.I., D.2860/24/1, Rent roll of the lands of the proportions of Balliweell, Duncanally, Kilkarr and Monorgan in hands and possession of Richard Murray of Broughton Esq. as they now yield, or formerly been set for or may now be set at by lease of 21 years, 18 April 1673.
8. Verschoyle, 'Background to a hidden age', pp 113-4. Some of the notional freeholds are explicitly referred to as mortgages in an undated (probably late seventeenth century) rental of the property, accompanied by a calculation for six holdings headed 'gained by paying mortgages' (P.R.O.N.I., D.2860/25/11, [untitled]). One example of such an agreement survives: Richard Murray 'sold' the three balliboes of Castletown for £60 to a Derry merchant in 1672, with a proviso that he or his heirs could repossess the lands for a similar sum paid before 1 November 1679 (P.R.O.N.I., D.2860/36, Deed of mortgage, Richard Murray to James Fisher of Londonderry, effective 1 November 1672). The profit to the purchaser presumably lay in the rents from the land during the term of the agreement.
9. D.2860/36, Leases on quarterland of Drumrusk, 1680.
10. P.R.O.N.I., D.2860/3/1, George Nesbitt, Ballycroy, to Richard Murray, 18 April 1687/8.

11. P.R.O.N.I., D2860/4/1, Thomas Knox, Mount Charles, to Lady Broughton, 8 November 1691.

12. P.R.O.N.I., D.2860/5/1, Account between Col. Conyngham and Lady Broughton, 21 November 1694.

13. P.R.O.N.I., D2860/4/1, Thomas Knox, Mount Charles, to Lady Broughton, 8 November 1691.

14. N.L.I., PC 679 [unsorted collection], Henry Conyngham, Mount Charles, to [Lady Broughton], 21 November 1694.

15. N.L.I., PC 679, untitled agreement, Lady Broughton and Henry Conyngham, 17 October 1696. The minority of Richard Murray's heir, John, was probably a factor in this arrangement but it also served to secure the Murray's debts to Conyngham. An account of c. 1698 put the total debt at almost £1500, including £1200 which Conyngham had borrowed on behalf of the Murrays (D.2860/5/3, Account of Money expended in order to the composition with Lord James Murray [n.d.]).

16. D.2860/19/4, [memorandum respecting leases held by Conyngham family, n.d. (c.1791)].

17. Ibid.

18. P.R.O.N.I., D.2860/4/4, Thomas Knox, Killigordon, to John Murray, 9 June 1699.

19. P.R.O.N.I., D.2860/5/5, Henry Conyngham, Dublin, to Lady Murray, 13 February 1698/9.

20. P.R.O.N.I., D.2860/5/23, Henry Conyngham, Cork, to Alexander Murray, 11 November 1704.

21. P.R.O.N.I., D.2860/9/7, Lady Shelburne, Slane, to Alexander Murray, 22 November 1705.

22. P.R.O.N.I., D.2860/9/10, Lady Shelburne, n.p., to Alexander Murray, 5 January 1705/6.

23. P.R.O.N.I., D.2860/9/3, Lady Shelburne, Mount Charles, to Alexander Murray, 20 June 1705. Murray was at the same time encouraging proposals from a new prospective tenant for the estate (D.2860/6/3, Robert Spence, Donegal, to Alexander Murray, 25 October 1705; D.2860/6/4, same to same, 10 December 1705).

24. P.R.O.N.I., D.2860/7/2, William Conolly, Slane, to Alexander Murray, 7 December 1706; D2860/7/5-9, 11-16, [copies of rent receipts, Alexander Murray to William Conolly, 1711-19]. Conolly's willingness to undertake this role may have stemmed in part from the potential influence it gave him over the Killybegs seats in the Irish House of Commons: in 1711 most of the burgesses of Killybegs were said to be 'his relations and particular friends' (P.R.O.N.I., D.2860/4/21, Thomas Knox, Lougheaske, to Alexander Murray, 28 April 1711). In 1727, long after the Conyngham's main lease on the property had expired, Henry Conyngham's two sons stood for the two Killybegs seats. Conolly thanked Alexander Murray for writing to his agent in support of them but added significantly that Murray 'need not be at the trouble of writing to the Corporation' (Scottish Record Office [S.R.O.], G.D.10/1421/11/471, William Conolly, Dublin, to Alexander Murray, 10 August 1727).

25. S.R.O., G.D.10/1421/11/448, William Conolly, Dublin, to Alexander Murray, 27 August 1718. Three undated drafts of a deed of lease and release of the Donegal estate to Conolly suggest that negotiations may have proceeded further (N.L.I., P.C. 679 [unsorted collection]).

26. P.R.O.N.I., D.2860/4/25, Rent roll of Alexander Murray of Broughton Esquire's estate in the Barony of Boylagh and Banagh taken the 4th day of August 1719.

27. P.R.O.N.I., D.2860/4/25, Rent roll, 1719; P.R.O.N.I., D.2860/36, Leases, 1720. When Castlecummin, near Killybegs, was set in 1723 the rise was even greater, from £1-4s.-0d. per annum to £5 (S.R.O., G.D.10/1421/11/453, James Hamilton, Mountcharles, to Alexander Murray, 25 January 1723).

28. S.R.O., G.D.10/942, James Reid, Dublin, Memorandum for the Laird of Broughton in relation to setting his estate in Ireland, 22 April 1720. Leases for urban holdings in Killybegs were in fact set for one year in 1720, although at least one of these was reset in 1725 on a 21-year lease (S.R.O., G.D.10/944 [memorandum dated 17 June 1732 concerning surrender of lease held by Mr John Lawrence]).

29. P.R.O.N.I., D.2860/25/10, Rent roll of the estate ... as the several tenants now propose, 4 February 1726/7.

30. P.R.O.N.I., D.2860/12/21, James Hamilton, Mountcharles, to Alexander Murray, 4 February 1728/9.

31. Ibid. Only one emigrant, 'Michaell Offeeney [sic] who went to America ...', is identified in estate documents for this period (P.R.O.N.I., D.2860/12/28, Remarks on the arrears returned by Mr James Hamilton on the Manors of Castlemurray and Ballyboyle for one year ended the 1st day of May 1732 ... [dated] 16th Day of January 1732 [1733].)

32. P.R.O.N.I., D.2860/12/22, James Hamilton, Mountcharles, to Alexander Murray, 11 July 1729.

33. Addi was the brother-in-law of a Donaghadee merchant who frequently acted for Murray in transmitting money to Scotland. It is not clear what his qualifications for the commission may have been.

34. N.L.I., P.C. 679 [unsorted collection], Thomas Addi, Donaghadee, to Alexander Murray, 3 March 1729/30.

35. Ibid.

36. P.R.O.N.I., D.2860/25/3 [memorandum by Thomas Addi on Murray of Broughton estate, c. July-August 1730].

37. P.R.O.N.I., D.2860/25/2, Account of the rents and duties fixed on for leases in the estate of Alexander Murray Esq., n.d. [1730].

38. S.R.O., G.D.10/1421/11/478, James Hamilton, Thomas Addi and Henry McCulloch, Mountcharles, to Alexander Murray, 5 July 1731.

39. S.R.O., G.D.10/1421/11/480, Thomas Addi, Donaghadee, to Alexander Murray, 12 July 1731.

40. P.R.O.N.I., D.2860/12/54-6, Account of arrears returned by Capt. James Hamilton, 3 October 1751. These agreements caused considerable difficulties during the duration of the leases, in that the sums recorded as due in the rental did not correspond with the amounts the tenants themselves expected to pay. Considerable sums of disputed arrears therefore built up. (See also P.R.O.N.I., D.2860/24/11, Arrears of rent on Broughton's estate in the county of Donegal at first May 1749 [dated 29 December 1750]).

41. S.R.O., G.D.10/1421/11/485, Thomas Addi, Donaghadee, to Alexander Murray, 1 March 1732.

42. Ibid.

43. Ibid.

44. P.R.O.N.I., D.2860/15/7, Memorandum from Mr Murray of Broughton to Thomas Addi of Donaghadee, 20 March 1733. Murray ordered that the farms be meared by a 6 ft. high wall and a ditch 7 ft. wide and 4 ft. deep. See also S.R.O., G.D.10/1421/12/522, David Murray, Binroe Parks, to Alexander Murray, 3 November 1744; P.R.O.N.I., T.3250, Thomas Addi, Killybegs, to Alexander Murray, 18 March 1746.

45. P.R.O.N.I., T.2812/19/1, Charles O'Hara [manuscript survey of the economic development of county Sligo, c.1700-c.1755; n.d., but compiled c.1750-75].

46. S.R.O., G.D. 10/1421/12/500, James Hamilton, Mount Charles, to Alexander Murray, Scotland, 4 February 1742; G.D. 10/1421/12/522, David Murray, Binroe Parks, to Alexander Murray, 3 November 1744.

47. P.R.O.N.I., D.2860/25/3, Thomas Addi [responses to memoranda on the various holdings on the Murray of Broughton estate], July 1730.

48. S.R.O., G.D.10/1421/12/527, Henry McCulloch, Killybegs, to Alexander Murray, 27 April 1745; P.R.O.N.I., D.2860/25/3, Thomas Addi [responses to memoranda ... July 1730]. A contemporary description of the area is in William Henry, 'Hints towards a natural and topographical history of the counties Sligo, Donegal, Fermanagh and Lough Erne' (P.R.O.I., M.2533 [unpublished manuscript, 1739]).

49. G. E. Kirkham, '"To pay the rent and lay up riches": economic opportunity in eighteenth-century north-west Ulster' in R. Mitchison and P. Roebuck (ed.), Economy and society in Scotland and Ireland, 1500-1939 (Edinburgh, 1988), pp 95-100.

50. P.R.O.N.I., D.2860/36, Leases, 1720; S.R.O., G.D.10/1421/11/457, James Hamilton, Mountcharles, to Alexander Murray, 9 August 1726.

51. S.R.O., G.D.10/1421/12/489, Alexander Crawford, Drumgun, to Alexander Murray, 21 July 1736.

52. Arthur Young, A tour in Ireland, 1776-9, ed. A. W. Hutton (Dublin, 1892), i, pp 184-5.

53. P.R.O.N.I., D.2860/25/3, Addi [responses to memoranda ... July 1730].

54. Henry, 'Hints towards a history'.

55. P.R.O.N.I., D.2860/13/6-7, Robert Donaldson, Dublin, to Alexander Murray, 16 March 1731.

56. P.R.O.N.I., D.2860/25/3, Addi [responses to memoranda ... July 1730].

57. P.R.O.N.I., T.2812/19/1, O'Hara, county Sligo, Public Record Office [Kew], CUST 15, Ledgers of imports and exports of Ireland.

58. S.R.O., G.D.10/1421/12/487, James Hamilton, Mountcharles, to Alexander Murray, 8 March 1735/6.

59. S.R.O., G.D.10/1421/12/489, Alexander Crawford, Drumgun, to Alexander Murray, 21 July 1736.

60. P.R.O.N.I., D.2860/4/25, Rent roll, 1719; S.R.O., G.D.10/944, List of leases signed by the trustees of Alexander Murray of Broughton, Esq. since the 24th May 1731; P.R.O.N.I., D.2860/12/38, Abstract from the rent roll ended May 1744.

61. S.R.O., G.D.10/1421/12/494, Hugh Stephen, Drumighan [sic – Drumkighan], to Alexander Murray, 1 July 1738.

62. Ibid.

63. P.R.O.N.I., D.2860/12/54-6, Account of arrears ... 3 October 1751.

64. S.R.O., G.D.10/1421/12/494, Hugh Stephen, Drumighan [sic – Drumkighan], to Alexander Murray, 1 July 1738. For other comments on this problem, see Dublin Gazette, 19-23 October 1736; R. J. Dickson, Ulster emigration to colonial America, 1718-1775 (Belfast, 1988), p. 46.

65. P.R.O.N.I., D.2860/26/1, Memorandums from the Honourable Alexander Murray of Broughton to Henry McCulloch [includes list of arrears dated 23 September 1740].

66. S.R.O., G.D.10/1421/12/500, James Hamilton, Mountcharles, to Alexander Murray, 4 February 1741/2.

67. S.R.O., G.D.10/1421/12/501, Henry McCulloch, Killybegs, to Alexander Murray, 5 February 1741/2.

68. P.R.O.N.I., D.2860/12/27, James Hamilton, Mouncharles, to Alexander Murray, 16 January 1732/3; S.R.O., G.D.10/1421/12/493, James Hamilton, Mountcharles, to Alexander Murray, 30 June 1738.

69. S.R.O., G.D.10/1421/12/512, James Hamilton, Mountcharles, to Thomas Addi, Donaghadee, 19 June 1744. For additional comments on this period see P.R.O.N.I., T.2541/IA1/1B/6, John McClintock, Strabane, to Earl of Abercorn, 2 March 1743/4; T.2541/IA1/1B/7, Nathaniel Nisbitt, Lifford, to same, 5 March 1743/4; S.R.O., G.D.10/1421/Vol. 5/246, Thomas Addi, Donaghadee, to Alexander Murray, 2 July 1744.

70. S.R.O., G.D.10/1421/12/508, Henry McCulloch, Killybegs, to Alexander Murray, 17 March 1743/44.

71. P.R.O.N.I., D.2860/12/38, Abstract from the rent roll ended May 1744.

72. P.R.O.N.I., T.2812/19/1, O'Hara, county Sligo. For additional commentaries on this crisis see P.R.O.N.I., D.1449/12/51, John Lennox, Derry, to [William Lennox], 21 September 1744; T.2541/IA1/1B/23, John Colhoun, Strabane, to [Earl of Abercorn], 25 September 1744; T.2541/IA1/1B/40, John McClintock, Strabane, to Earl of Abercorn, 12 March 1744/5; T.2541/IA1/1B/41, John Colhoun, Strabane, to same, 18 March 1744/5; D.1449/12/51, John Lennox, Derry, to William Lennox, 5 March and 26 March 1745; T.2541/IA1/1B/47, John McClintock, Strabane, to same, 23 April 1745.

73. S.R.O., G.D.10/1421/12/527, Henry McCulloch, Killybegs, to Alexander Murray, 22 April 1745.

74. P.R.O.N.I., T.3250, Thomas Addi, Killybegs, to [Alexander Murray], 18 March 1745/6.

75. P.R.O.N.I., D.2860/12/40, Account of what James Hamilton received of the year's rent ended May 1746 [dated 30 August 1746].

76. P.R.O.N.I., T.2541/IA1/1B/73, John McClintock, [Strabane?], to Earl of Abercorn, 24 December 1745. By March 1746 oatmeal brought from Derry was being sold in the Killybegs area at 16d. per peck (P.R.O.N.I., T.3250, Thomas Addi, Killybegs, to [Alexander Murray], 18 March 1745/6).

77. D. Dickson, C. Ó Grada and S. Daultrey, 'Hearth tax, household size and Irish population change 1672-1821' in R.I.A. Proc., 82 C, 6, pp 168-9. Charles O'Hara estimated a fall of one-third in the number of households in county Sligo between 1744 and 1746 (P.R.O.N.I., T.2812/19/1, O'Hara, county Sligo).

78. P.R.O.N.I., T.3250, Thomas Addi, Killybegs, to [Alexander Murray], 18 March 1745/6. More explicit comments were made on political disaffection on the Abercorn estate; see P.R.O.N.I., T.2541/IA1/1B/58, John McClintock, [Strabane?], to Earl of Abercorn, 17 September 1745; T.2541/IA1/1B/60, Nathaniel Nisbitt, Lifford, to same, 6 October 1745; T.2541/IA1/1B/71, Jo. Colhoun, Strabane, to same, 12 November 1745.

79. P.R.O.N.I., T.2812/19/1, O'Hara, county Sligy; P.R.O.N.I., T.2541/IA1/1C/49, John McClintock, Strabane, to Earl of Abercorn, 30 June 1747.

80. P.R.O.N.I., D.2860/24/11, Arrears of rent on Broughton's estate in the county of Donegal at first May 1749.

81. P.R.O.N.I., D.2860/26/2, [memorandum re arrears from Lady Euphemia Murray (?) to James Hamilton, c.1749]. T.2541/IA1/1D/6, John McClintock, Strabane, to [Earl of Abercorn], 23 February 1748.

82. N.L.I., MS. 21.F.66, Survey and book of maps of the estate of Alexander Murray Esq. by John Bell of Cootehill, Co. Cavan, Land Surveyor, in the year 1749.

83. P.R.O.N.I., T.2812/19/1, O' Hara, county Sligo.

84. P.R.O.N.I., D.2860/16/2, Rent roll of the estate of Killybegs belonging to James

Murray Esq. of Broughton [n.d., c.1755]. A few minor leases in and around Killybegs were for shorter periods.

85. N.L.I., P.C. 679 [memorandum by Lady Katharine Murray on the value of holdings due to fall out of lease, n.d. (c.1785)].

86. See the discussion in Kirkham, '"To pay the rent and lay up riches"' in Mitchison and Roebuck (eds), *Economy and Society in Scotland and Ireland,* pp 95-104.

87. P.R.O.N.I., D.2860/16/2, Rent roll, c.1755.

88. P.R.O.N.I., D.2860/26/4, George Muir to James Murray, 7 October 1754.

89. S.R.O., GD.10/955 [memorandum by James Murray concerning James McClenaghan and Ravelin, n.d.].

90. N.L.I., P.C. 679 [unsorted collection], Memorial for James Murray of Broughton Esq. [n.d., c.1755].

91. Verschoyle, 'Background to a hidden age,' p. 113.

92. P. Roebuck, 'Rent movement, proprietorial incomes and agricultural development, 1730-1830' in P. Roebuck, (ed.), *Plantation to partition: essays in Ulster history in honour of J. L. McCracken* (Belfast, 1981) pp 95-6.

93. P.R.O.N.I., D.2860/16/2, Rent roll, c.1755.

94. P.R.O.N.I., D.2860/26/4, George Muir to James Murray, 7 October 1754.

Chapter 13

THE EVOLUTION OF THE URBAN NETWORK

W. H. CRAWFORD

Donegal is a world away from Dublin, maintaining its own culture where fashionable lifestyles are confronted by traditional values confirmed by extremes of climate and terrain. Yet life in Donegal has changed much over the centuries. Nowhere is this more apparent than in the development of the urban network and the spread of commerce. As Donegal is one of the most poorly endowed of Irish counties in terms of natural resources, the growth of towns has proved very difficult to sustain. They developed very slowly and only at first in the more fertile eastern districts, referred to as the Laggan or 'the low country' by the highlanders, and around the head of Donegal Bay. From the mid-eighteenth century much money was expended by the county grand jury in constructing a network of roads throughout the county and new settlements appeared like nodes at strategic points along them. From the mid-nineteenth century small steamboats were able to service ports such as Dunfanaghy, Milford and Letterkenny and later the narrow-gauge railways found their way from Londonderry and Strabane to Carndonagh in the heart of Inishowen, Burtonport on the west coast, Glenties further south, and Killybegs on the south coast. Communications were penetrating the valleys of Donegal and making it possible for small market centres to sustain urban community life with the help of money earned abroad by her emigrant children. These small towns did not grow spontaneously, however: they were promoted by members of the landlord class in order to improve the economic bases of their estates. The demise of the landlord class transferred this onus to other classes and groups.

I

This study will presume that the urban network of Donegal that we know today had its origin almost four centuries ago in the project for the plantation of Ulster devised by the London government. The project imposed on the landscape of Donegal a concept of civilisation that had evolved in countries with more advanced economies enjoying fertile lands, favourable climate, and abundant natural resources. In essence this concept presumed that the landlords of a realm should be allowed to develop estates as their personal property in return for serving the crown, while merchants and other entrepreneurs should be encouraged to speculate in markets and fairs. The plantation scheme, therefore, was designed to create landed estates in the form of manors to be governed by their owners (thus saving the crown considerable expense) and also to institute corporate towns where traders and craftsmen could thrive and merchants flourish while governing themselves. To launch so many estates and towns, however, would have required a vast input of both men and capital which the crown did not possess. Ambition had to be tempered with practicality. The first list of proposed corporate towns in 1609 for the escheated counties of Donegal, Coleraine, Tyrone, Armagh, Cavan and Fermanagh contained twenty-five names including Derry, Lifford, Donegal, Ballyshannon, Killybegs, Raphoe, Rathmullan, and Drong in north Inishowen. By 1611 this list had been reduced to Derry (transferred to become the county town of the new county of Londonderry), Lifford, Donegal, Ballyshannon, and Rathmullan: soon afterwards Rathmullan was dropped and in its place came Killybegs (incorporated in 1615) and St Johnstown (1618). The London government soon realised the enormity of the task and in some desperation agreed to a solution suggested by the lord deputy, Sir Arthur Chichester, that each of the corporate towns should be placed under the supervision of a neighbouring gentleman who would ensure that houses were built for tradesmen and then administer the town until it was ready for incorporation. To induce these gentlemen to take part they were issued with patents granting them the very lands destined to pay for the upkeep of the towns as well as the right to hold markets and fairs, and manor courts, and to receive profits from them. As a result, whenever these boroughs were ready to be incorporated, their incomes were found to be too small to maintain any real semblance of town government, and so they became 'thoroughly dependent on the local landlords'.[1]

Indeed, in the long run it became difficult to distinguish between these corporate towns and the settlements that grew up on the estates. Because these estates had been allocated as blocks of townlands they were compact and manageable and in the more fertile districts they should have been able to sustain towns to service them. At the first prospects of success, therefore, their owners were quick to take out patents for markets and fairs.

Table 13.1
Patents for Markets and Fairs predating 1641[2]
(corporate towns underlined)

BARONY OF INISHOWEN

DRONGE *als* CARROWLOUGH-IN-MALYNE ISLAND: Patent dated *22* Feb 1609 to Sir Arthur Chichester for a fair on 20/21 October.

BUNCRANA: Patent dated 22 Feb 1609 to Sir Arthur Chichester for a FRIDAY market and two two-day fairs commencing 30 April and 31 August. Patent confirmed 20 Nov 1621.

GREENCASTLE: Patent dated 22 Feb 1609 to Sir Arthur Chichester for a MONDAY market and two two-day fairs commencing 1 April and 30 Sept. Patent said to have been surrendered 5 July 1621.

REDCASTLE: Patent dated 20 Nov 1621 to Arthur Lord Chichester for a market (day not specified) and two two-day fairs commencing 1 Aug. and 1 Nov.

BARONY OF RAPHOE

CULMACATRYAN: Patent dated 10 March 1608 to Pat Conly for a TUESDAY market and a three-day fair commencing on the feast of St John the Baptist.

ALTHASON: Patent dated 7 July 1613 to William Stewart for a MONDAY market.

BALLYBOFEY: Patent dated 6 July 1619 to Sir Ralph Bingley for a SATURDAY market and two two-day fairs commencing 23 April [St George] and 18 Oct. [St Luke]. Patent renewed to Robert Harrington and his wife, Anne Bingley, dated 12 May 1630 for same markets and fairs.

LIFFORD: Patent dated 12 Sept 1603 to Sir Henry Docwra for a THURSDAY market. Patent dated 31 Jan 1612 to Sir Richard Hansard for two two-day fairs commencing on,Ascension Day and 21 Sept [St Matthew's Day].

ST JOHNSTOWN: Patent dated 6 Aug 1618 to Ludovic, Duke of Lennox, for a MONDAY market and two fairs on Easter Tuesday and the Tuesday after the feast of St Michael. Regranted to James, duke of Lennox, 24 January 1629.

CONVOY: Patent dated 24 Feb 1629 to Sir John Wilson for a MONDAY market and two two-day fairs commencing on 6 May and 15 Oct.

NEWTOWN CUNNINGHAM: Patent dated 13 May 1629 to Sir John Cunningham for a MONDAY market and a three-day fair commencing 18 Oct. [St Luke's Day].

MANORCUNNINGHAM (= MACHRIMORE near church of Raymoghy): Patent dated 29 May 1629 to James Cunningham for a THURSDAY market and two two-day fairs commencing 26 Jun and 24 Oct.

RAPHOE: Patent dated 25 Feb 1630 to Andrew, bishop of Raphoe, for a SATURDAY market and two fairs on 11 June [St Barnabas's Day] and 24 Oct.

CASTLEFINN: Patent dated 28 May 1631 to Sir John Kingsmill for a MONDAY market and two two-day fairs (Tues and Wed after Pentecost and commencing St Martin's Day = 11 Nov.).

BARONY OF KILMACRENAN

RATHMULLAN: Patent dated 8 Oct 1603 to Sir Ralph Bingley for a MONDAY market.

RATHMELTON: Patent dated 8 Dec 1610 to Sir Richard Hansard for a TUESDAY market and a three-day fair commencing St Luke's Day [18 Oct.].

LETTERKENNY: Patent dated 9 Dec 1616 to Sir George Marbury for a TUESDAY market and two fairs on 29 June [St Peter and St Paul] and 28 October [St Simon and St Jude]. Regranted to Sir William Semphill on 22 June 1639.

DUNFANAGHY: Patent dated 20 Aug 1630 to Sir Mulmurry McSuíbhne for a MONDAY market and two two-day fairs commencing on Whit Monday and 21 Sept. [St Matthew].

BARONY OF BANNAGH

DONEGAL: Patent dated 13 Mar 1611 to Sir Basil Brooke for a THURSDAY market and a two-day fair commencing 29 June [SS Peter and Paul]. Patent dated 12 Feb 1623 to same for a three-day fair commencing 18 Oct. [St Luke]. Patent dated 1 July 1639 to Henry Brooke for a one-day fair (no date).

KILLYBEGS: Patent dated 14 Dec 1611 to the Provost and Corporation of Killybegs for a TUESDAY market and a fair on Easter Monday and Tuesday.

DUNKINEELY: Patent dated 15 Dec 1620 to John Murray, Earl of Annandall for TUESDAY market and two three-day fairs commencing 21 June and 14 Sept [Holy Cross]. Regrant dated 8 July 1629 to same.

MACHREMORE (near ARDARA): Patent dated 13 Dec. 1620 to John Murray, earl of Annandall for FRIDAY market and a three-day fair commencing All Saints Day [1 Nov.].

BARONY OF TYRHUGH

ROSSKATT: Patent dated 10 March 1613 to A. Andrews for a TUESDAY market and a two-day fair commencing 10 May.

BALLYSHANNON: Patent dated 30 Aug 1639 to Lord ffolliott for a TUESDAY market and two fairs on 25 Mar [Annunciation] and 8 Sept. [Nativity of St Mary].

The table above, listing all the patents granted for markets and fairs in county Donegal before 1641, reveals a very noticeable surge in Raphoe barony between 1629-31: it would appear that in the rush four of the towns selected the same day, Monday, to be their market day. This lends weight to a suggestion by Raymond Gillespie that the landlord of such towns were most concerned that rivals might try to embarrass them by taking out patents for markets and fairs in their towns.[3] Many comments in the *Civil Survey* of 1654-6 suggest also that there had been an active land market in the Laggan in the mid-1630s.[4]

The plantation structure in Donegal seems to have been all but destroyed in the years following the 1641 rising. Consider this description of the Finn valley from the *Civil Survey* of 1654:

> ... upon which river is situated the ruins of a plantation belonging unto Sir Paul Davies called the Welsh Town next the castle of Drumbo belonging to Mr Bassill the attorney-general, near unto which castle is a famous passage over the mountains (towards Barnesmore leading to Donegal) called ford of Finn. Next unto it

is situated upon the river a ruinous house and bawn belonging to Mr Benson, another belonging to Mr Mansfield in which place the river is also passable. Next the house and bawn of Donaghmore, near which is situated a ruinous castle taking its name from the river, belonging to Mr Kingsmill where also is a passage and a stone house belonging to Mr William Warren and there the river beginneth to be navigable and continues in length yet three miles further where it empties itself in Lough Foyle at the town and fort of Lifford.[5]

Yet even if the settlements were destroyed these landlords retained ownership of the land and after the war they returned. Their resources were so slight, however, that towns throughout Donegal made a very slow recovery. The poll tax return of 1660 records that out of 12,001 who paid the tax, 8,589 or just over 71 per cent were Irish. The Irish formed a considerable percentage of town dwellers throughout the county. Indeed they outnumbered the British in the largest town, Ballyshannon, as well as in Donegal town and Killybegs. In Kilmacrenan barony Letterkenny, Ramelton and Doe Castle were the only significant settlements and in Inishowen barony only Cloncro near Redcastle where the Cary family had settled: in these four places the Irish made up one-third of the taxpayers. The only barony where the British outnumbered the Irish was Raphoe by about 7:5 and it was the only barony throughout which the British were dispersed, living on their farms. The dominance of the British, however, was not reflected in the size of the towns, if they warranted the term. Raphoe was the most considerable with 104 taxpayers, a quarter of them Irish, while Manor Cunningham had 46, St Johnstown 37, Culmaciltryan 26, Carrigans 35 and Lifford 68. Outside the towns, however, there were considerable numbers, especially in the Finn valley and along the Foyle from Lifford to Londonderry. It is clear that farming and the possession of land made up a more attractive proposition than living in the small towns. In Kilmacrenan barony this pattern of British settlement could be found only around Letterkenny in the parishes of Conwall and Aughnish, while it was absent from the baronies of Tyrhugh and Boylagh and Bannagh.[6]

Because land provided sustenance as well as status it is not surprising that so many men preferred to cultivate their own farms and raise their families in the countryside while evading the responsibilities for creating an urban community. Yet there were others who enjoyed the opportunities for personal contact that towns provided and were stimulated by the challenge of business. For them landlords were able to devise inducements that promised to combine the best of both worlds for the town dweller. Development leases granted for town properties were in effect perpetuities. Although many of them resembled the rural lease that terminated only on the expiry of three lives named in it, these urban leases contained an extra clause permitting the insertion of a new life on the fall of an old one on payment of a year's rent: the tenant's rent could not be increased and he could not be evicted, even for non-payment of rent. Businessmen and tradesmen in the town could indulge in farming only by taking fields in the 'town parks', parcelled out in the townlands adjoining the town, and operating from their own backyards.[7]

Town life could not flourish, however, or even survive, in a sterile environment. For its survival it depended throughout the seventeenth century on the character and commitment of individual landlords. With the exception of Ballyshannon, with its small colony of merchants, it is probable that the towns were no more than estate villages or service centres. Although in his absence a landlord might delegate authority to an agent, no-one else could take important decisions and the countryside watched for evidence of his ability and his commitment to the development of his town. The first major signal was his purchase from the crown of a patent for markets and fairs indicating that he was prepared to take responsibility for organising and administering markets and fairs. He might emphasise this engagement by building a market-house. Markets were held weekly for townspeople to purchase the necessities of life and so they had to attract buyers and sellers regularly throughout the year. Without regular supplies tradesmen and dealers would soon drift away from the town. Fairs were held once or twice in the year to sell off the surplus of the district and so they attracted merchants and jobbers from further afield. The landlord had to protect those who attended the fair and ensure that justice was speedily and effectively administered through his courts. If the success of the markets and fairs attracted potential tenants, the landlord's next task was to lay out tenements or plots of ground fronting on the main street on which the tenants could build substantial houses and out-offices.

In spite of considerable immigration into Donegal of settlers from Scotland in the late seventeenth century, there was no significant improvement in the towns. During these years no more than seven patents were taken out for the whole county of Donegal and even four of these are questionable. On 8 March 1677 a John Leslie took out patents for markets and fairs in four places: Magheralosky or Rosapenna in county Donegal, Lisbellaw in county Fermanagh, Moy in county Tyrone, and Callaghmore in county Sligo. On 28 February 1680 a certain Hugh Hamill took out similar patents for Ballindrait and

Dunfanaghy in county Donegal as well as Castlederg in county Tyrone. It is probable that one or both men were speculating in patents for places which landowners might wish to develop. More credible were the patents taken out for Mountcharles in 1676 and Dungloe in 1685, both by Sir Albert Conyngham who had recently purchased large districts in the Rosses, in the lower half (northern) of the barony of Boylagh, and half the parish of Inver. Mountcharles was to become his headquarters while Dungloe was to serve the Rosses.[8] In Inishowen the earl of Donegall in 1699 took out a patent for Muff near the city of Londonderry. There is also some evidence that the earlier patents for Buncrana had been confirmed in 1668.[9]

Of these seven patents it is surprising to find that only one, that for Mountcharles, contained a grant of four fairs in the year because such a grant was becoming commonplace in the rest of Ulster by the late seventeenth century. The dates for Mountcharles were 17 March (St Patrick's Day), 29 May, 11 September, and 11 November (St Martin's Day). A study of the fair dates granted in the period before 1641 rarely mentions dates in May and November and yet they were to become the commonest months for fairs because they suited the annual cycle of the cattle trade. In Ulster, cattle went out on the grass on the first of May and were brought home for the winter on the first of November: calendar customs confirm the importance of these dates in the farming year. It should not be forgotten, of course, that the dates of these fairs were altered by the parliamentary decision to adopt the Gregorian calendar by omitting eleven days in September 1751. As a result the dates were set back usually by eleven days but sometimes, as in the case of Mountcharles, the opportunity was taken to adjust the dates so that in 1785, for instance, the four fairs became 17 March, 9 June, 22 September and 18 November. The dates of moveable feasts such as Easter or Whitsun, however, would not have been altered.

II

For the late seventeenth and early eighteenth centuries there is very little evidence about Donegal towns and their markets. Almanacs annually listed the dates and locations of fairs throughout Ireland but since this information was obtained from patents, dead or dormant fairs had not been discarded. In April 1752 an Abercorn agent reported that he had attended the fair at St Johnstown on Easter Tuesday 'but found no people met, nor anything that looked like one; they say a parcel of idle people commonly meet in the evening to drink whiskey'.[10] Estate records do contain occasional references to fairs and markets while rentals may contain information about the payment of rents for them, but for a source that can be used to provide a comparative view of the progress of towns and villages it is necessary to search in the Registry of Deeds in Dublin where many thousands of legal transactions have been registered since its creation in 1708. Because leases for terms of more than twenty-one years were registered, it is possible to find out when individual landlords granted spates of building leases in order to develop their towns. Sales and mortgages were also enrolled and so often the value of properties can be ascertained. These memorials are indexed by county and both by placenames and family names so that searching can bring rapid results.[11]

Table 13.2
Patents for Markets and Fairs taken out in eighteenth century

STRANORLAR: Patent dated 27 February 1711 to Oliver McCausland for a THURSDAY market and fairs on 17 March, 24 June, 21 August and 29 December.

OLDTOWN: Patent dated 26 December 1725 to Nicholas, bishop of Raphoe for a WEDNESDAY market and fairs on 23 April, 28 May, 20 July, 20 October.

KILLYGORDON: Patent dated 9 July 1740 to Sir Ralph Mansfield for a FRIDAY market and fairs on 20 February, 20 May, 20 August, 20 November.

ARDARA: Patent dated 16 May 1760 to George Nesbitt for a TUESDAY market and fairs on 15 May, 1 August, 1 November, 22 December.

CARNDONAGH: Patent dated 23 May 1766 to William, bishop of Derry, for a MONDAY market and fairs on 21 February, 21 May, 21 August, 21 November.

BALLYNESS (FALCARRAGH): Patent dated 31 August 1769 to Wybrants Olphert for a TUESDAY market and fairs on 12 June, 24 August, 20 October, 30 November.

MALIN (CARROWMORE): Patent dated 19 December 1771 to Lord Donegall for a TUESDAY market and fairs on Easter Monday, 24 June, 12 August and 30 November.

FINTOWN: Patent dated 5 March 1772 to John Hamilton of Brownhall for a WEDNESDAY market and fairs on 16 May, 3 July, 3 September, 3 November.

CLOGHANBEG: Patent dated 23 February 1775 to Sir Charles and William Style for a market on the first MONDAY of each month and fairs on 1 February, 19 May, 25 August, 19 November.

BALLINDRAIT: Patent dated 22 February 1776 to Lord Erne for FRIDAY market.

CHURCHILL: Patent dated 11 July 1776 to Daniel Chambers for a market on the first THURSDAY of each month with fairs on 11 May, 15 August, 7 November.

AGHYGAULTS: Patent dated 8 July 1778 to Alexander Montgomery for a MONDAY market and fairs on 12 January, 20 March, 15 May, 20 July, 29 September, 1 November.

To test the effectiveness of this technique plenty of examples are needed. Throughout the first half of the eighteenth century, however, only three patents were taken out for the whole of Donegal county: Stranorlar in 1711, Oldtown near Letterkenny in 1725, and Killygordon in 1740. Nor does the Registry of Deeds contain the suggested spate of building leases for any of these places. The patent for markets and fairs in Stranorlar was taken out by Oliver McCausland of Rash in county Tyrone who had gone into partnership with the famous William Connolly of Castletown in county Kildare (himself born in Ballyshannon) to purchase the manor of Castlefinn in 1707/8.[12] This would suggest that McCausland was merely confirming his new title to Stranorlar. In contrast, it has to be admitted that although Buncrana recorded fewer references in the Registry of Deeds, its owner, Sir John Vaughan, in 1717 is known to have founded a new castle, built a bridge, and laid out a town with a market square. In the mid-1730s he established a 'college of weavers of Buncrana' and there is evidence that this settlement was in a healthy condition in 1744: by 1752, however, a visitor reported that this project had failed despite the landlord's efforts.[13] The second patent taken out in the eighteenth century was granted in 1725 to Nicholas Forster, the Church of Ireland bishop of Raphoe, for a Wednesday market and four fairs in Oldtown in the parish of Leck, which was really a suburb of Letterkenny. In 1739 Letterkenny was described as 'the largest market town in the whole county. Besides its communication with the sea by Lough Swilly, it has a very plentiful and thronged market for all kinds of country goods, especially for linen yarn and cloth, which manufacture has spread much about this place and is still increasing.'[14] In 1752 another traveller added that 'it was more beautiful in prospect than when one enters it, consisting of one street meanly built, with gardens behind the houses: and there are remains of an old square castle. The chief trade of the town consists of shops to furnish the country to the north, and a market for oats and barley, wheat, some yarn and flax.'[15] One of the Oldtown fairs – that in early June – survived as an important cattle fair, probably because there was a gap then in the list of Letterkenny fairs. The third patent was granted in 1740 for Killygordon to Sir Ralph Mansfield for a Friday market and four fairs following the registration of several property transactions in the Registry of Deeds. No substantial development followed until the 1780s and Killygordon was no more successful than Castlefinn in the same parish. A survey of Castlefinn about 1750 recorded:

> ... Tho' it is nothing at present but a heap of ruins, having scarcely either house or tenant in it worth taking notice of, is exceedingly

well situate for trade. It lies in the middle of a well planted country, by the side of a navigable river by which they may go every spring tide to and from Londonderry with boats or lighters of ten tuns ... The whole country about it is as remarkable for flax and yarn as any ... Would the proprietors get a bridge built over the river which would be done for less than £400, or lay out land in the adjacent farms to accommodate the town, which with the town tenements being set in freehold or long leases to traders of substance, it would turn to great advantage to both town and country.[16]

The reference here to 'the proprietors' and what they should do, confirms the importance in mid-eighteenth century Ulster of the landed proprietor as the mainspring of social change. The proprietors needed to induce tenants to come to live in Castlefinn by providing them with town fields 'in the adjacent farms', setting town tenements in freehold or by long leases, and getting a bridge built over the river for £400. (In fact the bridge was built by 1756.)[17]

III

After the misfortunes of the 1730s and 1740s the second half of the century ushered in a period of growing confidence and prosperity not only in Donegal but throughout Ulster. The most powerful engine of growth in each county was the grand jury because it was responsible for organising and administering a century of great activity in road-making and bridge-building throughout Ireland. Indeed, by the eve of the great famine Donegal had 2,482 miles of county roads, the fourth longest mileage in Ireland, exceeded only by Cork, Tipperary, and Down.[18] This is a very surprising record for the expenditure was raised within the county by the grand jury.

Before the Road Act of 1765 the initiative for maintaining and laying out new roads lay with individual parishes and to this end they held a vestry meeting in Easter week (a 1727 act switched this to the week after Michaelmas, 29 September), appointed overseers and organised the labour at their disposal. Every householder was required to provide labour for no wages for six days. The grand jury had responsibility for any work that required skilled tradesmen, such as masons, and it alone could raise money after the judge at the assize had given his approval to the 'presentment' or proposal.[19] An act of 1739 gave the grand jury authority to lay out new roads while insisting that they 'be carried in as direct a line as possible and of statutable breadth (30 feet broad in the clear) from any market town in the same county, or as far as the said county extends, to any other market-town in the next adjacent county', and providing that they should 'not be carried through any ground being built upon, or through any garden, orchard, yard, planted walk, or avenue to any house whatsoever'.[20] The problems generated by such changes required the mediation of landlords (see appendix). Individual landlords made themselves responsible for overseeing these new roads and one traveller paid tribute to Mr Wray of Ards for

> those fine roads which are made over Lough Salt mountain, and in other parts, laid out so as to be finished in about seven years, by allotting such a measure of road yearly to each house, according to the value of the land they hold: they are twenty-one feet broad, with a margin on each side of green turf about two feet wide; they are first raised with the earth that is thrown up to make a fosse on each side; then they lay a coat of broken quarry stones, on that some earth and gravel at the top. These roads considering the cheapness of carriage on little truckles drawn by one horse, almost answer the end of water carriage, for they will draw a hogshead of wine, or anything not exceeding 600 lbs in weight, and one man will attend three or four of them. They commonly feed their horses on the grass they find in the road so that they will carry a hundred and fifty miles for three shillings a load.[21]

The volumes of grand jury presentments for county Donegal, which have survived for the years 1753-1800, are full of references to the building of new roads and bridges.[22]

Because the six days labour requirement was abolished by a 1759 act, a 1765 act gave the grand jury responsibility for maintaining and constructing all the roads and bridges in the county and for levying and collecting the county cess. As James Hamilton of Strabane, an agent, explained to his master, the earl of Abercorn, in 1780:

> The mode of levying county taxes is, that the treasurer gets an order from the county to levy off the county at large, so much which is for building and repairing bridges, etc., and off each barony which is for roads, etc; the treasurer issues his warrants to the several barony constables who are to collect the taxes, in which is set forth the sum to be raised off the county at large, which with the barony charge is divided on the several parishes of the barony; for guiding him in this they have what they call an old key; in many cases that rule is very unequal, yet we find we can have no redress. The barony constable gives to each parish

applotters a copy of the warrant he receives, directing them to subdivide the tax which he is to levy from the parish; they also have a rule by which a proportion is fixed for the several districts or townlands in the parish ...[23]

Complaints about 'the old key' were due mainly to the great changes that had been made to the face of the countryside with the creation of so many new settlements, especially in the uplands: the outdated key took no account of them.[24] Further complaints might have come from Ulster after 1771 because an act of that year stipulated that 'whereas there are many public roads in the province of Ulster, which cannot without great expense and waste of ground be made of the breadth required by the said act, and which nevertheless, ought to be kept in proper repair,' parish vestries might levy one penny or twopence an acre and organise their repair.[25] This act was not repealed until 1796.

In spite of such complaints the most surprising consequence of the 1765 road act was its success in bringing in money, although it was remodelled in 1774. In the late 1760s and 1770s the annual figures for Donegal averaged about £4,300 but this increased to nearly £7,400 in the 1780s, £11,700 in the 1790s and almost £20,000 in the 1800s (in 1760 £1 was worth £1.64 in 1800).[26] There was no shortage of money for building roads and bridges and so landlords were quick to seize the opportunities to develop the wide expanses of waste lands on their estates. In this the landlord class was encouraged by parliament when it passed 'an act for the making of narrow roads through the mountainous unimproved parts of this Kingdom' in 1772: the intention of the act was set out in the preamble:

> Whereas there are in several parts of this Kingdom extensive tracts of land of a mountainous nature, and in a rude uncultivated state, and it would greatly contribute to the improvement thereof, if roads were made through the same; and yet from the nature of the country it would be in some cases impracticable, and from the poverty of the few inhabitants therein it would generally be inexpedient and unnecessary, to be at the expense of making such wide roads therein, as are proper in other places differently circumstanced: and whereas by the laws now in force no provision is made for the making and repairing of such narrow roads, as are suitable to the situation and circumstances of such mountainous tracts of land ...[27]

This act allowed the grand jury to build narrower and therefore cheaper roads across the mountains. It was followed in the statute book by 'an act to encourage the reclaiming of unprofitable bogs' by enabling landlords to lease bogland for terms of sixty-one years to improving tenants:[28] far too little attention has been paid to the exploitation of massive reserves of turf for fuel for both domestic and industrial consumers. Landlords knew also that if they took out patents for markets and fairs they could request the grand jury to link their new towns to the neighbouring market towns.

To visualise these requests the grand jury needed a map of the county. An act of 1774 had empowered grand juries to spend up to £100 on getting counties surveyed and in 1778 this was increased to £100 per 100,000 acres.[29] In 1785 James Hamilton, the agent for the Abercorn estates, reported:

> I send a letter I had from William McCrea, son to Samuel, with a list of subscribers for a survey and maps of the Counties of Tyrone and Donegal; the Tyrone map is said to be very well executed. It is hung up in the Grand Jury room during the assize, and often appealed to when new lines of road are proposed. I saw the Donegal map at last assize; it was then nearly finished, and I suppose by this time it is completed; he purposes going to London in March or April to have them engraved; they declare they are very much out of pocket, for many refuse paying their subscription till they get the maps, and I do believe it will be difficult for them to get them engraved. Their father died poor when these men were young, yet they have supported their mother and I believe three sisters decently ...[30]

The map of Donegal by McCrea was not engraved until 1801 although it was completed by 1793 but the Tyrone map had to wait until 1813.[31]

The McCrea map of county Donegal gives some concept of the great progress achieved in road construction by the close of the eighteenth century. The county had been bisected from east to west by two roads that left Letterkenny and Ballybofey respectively to meet at Fintown in the heart of the mountains and run on to Ardara by way of Glenties. A patent for markets and fairs in Ardara had been taken out in 1760 by George Nesbitt and during the 1760s a 'great road' was laid out from Killybegs to Ardara. The road from Ardara to Glenties was constructed about the same time.[32] Although no patent was ever taken out for markets and fairs in Glenties, it soon gained a reputation as 'one of the most considerable fairs ... for black cattle in the north of Ireland'.[33] A patent for a Wednesday market and four fairs at Fintown was taken out in 1772 by John Hamilton of Brownhall. In the following year the

London-Derry Journal and General Advertiser of 9 July 1773 announced a list of 'premiums to be given at the several fairs to be held at Fintown':

To the person who will buy the greatest number of black cattle, not less than one score	£0. 11. 4½d.
To the second, not less than half a score	6. 6d.
To the person who will buy the greatest quantity of linen yarn	11. 4½d.
To the second	5. 5d.
To the buyer of the greatest number of yarn stockings	11. 4½d.
To the person who will sell the greatest number of pairs of stockings of his/her own manufacture	11. 4½d.
To the person who will produce the finest and best knit pair of stockings of his/her own manufacture	2. 2d.

(The cash amounts are based on fractions of a guinea which was worth £1. 2. 9d in Ireland while the shilling was worth 1/1d in Ireland).

Two years later another patent was taken out for a new settlement on the road from Fintown to Letterkenny at Cloghanbeg (see table 13.2).

IV

The trade in linen yarn and black cattle impressed Arthur Young when he visited county Donegal in August 1776 but he devoted most of his account to the fisheries. Dean William Henry in 1739 had commented on the herring fishery at Inver and the 'vast number of carriers ... employed in the season in supplying from hence to the inland counties'.[34] Young pointed out that Inver had the only summer fishery for herrings: all the other places along the coast were winter herring fisheries employing more than two hundred and fifty boats in 1776.[35] So successful were the fisheries that a company was set up in 1783 with a grant from the Irish parliament to develop the fisheries on the marquess of Conyngham's estate around Dungloe. The company transformed the island of Inishmacadurn into Rutland Island with a well laid-out town, dockyard, storehouses and quays and encouraged the grand jury to link Rutland and Dungloe to Glenties. Unfortunately the fishery failed in 1793.[36] Enthusiasm for the fishery, however, was responsible for the development of other ports. An advertisement dated 13 June 1784 in the *Belfast News-Letter* offered:

> To be let for such term of lives or years as may be agreed on, in the town of Dunfanaghy in the Bay of Sheephaven and County of Donegal, several lots of ground for building houses and stores for the curing of cod, ling and herring in. There are stones, lime, and sand to be had upon the spot, slates within a mile, and water-carriage for timber into the centre of the town. The convenient situation of this place to the north-western fisheries is so well known to all persons that have been in that trade, as to render any further description of it unnecessary. The tenants will be accommodated with town parks and turbary ...

Herring fisheries, however, were notoriously unreliable and therefore speculative. The major generator of capital was the linen industry which exported great quantities of linen yarn to Lancashire through Londonderry. Exports of yarn through Londonderry rose steadily from the 1720s to 5,000 cwt. by 1735/6 and an average of over 16,000 cwt. by the 1770s, the peak decade. This figure fell in the 1780s to just under 14,000 cwt. but there was a corresponding increase in the export of linen cloth.[37] This suggests that it had been more profitable to export yarn to meet Lancashire's demands before the invention of Arkwright's water-frame made it possible for the Lancashire cotton-spinners to produce cotton warp yarns strong enough to withstand tension on the looms. The *Report of the state of the linen markets of the province of Ulster* by John Greer in 1783 recorded:

County Donegal

LETTERKENNY: Market on *Friday;* seven-eight wide linens, nine to twelve hundreds, and some yard wide fourteen to seventeen hundreds, all made of good stuff, but sleayed rather too light, and the linens exposed to sale in double pieces; the markets very uncertain, some being large similar to fairs, and the weekly average of the whole about £120.

RATHMELTON: Market on *Tuesday;* seven-eight wide, and yard wide linens, much like Letterkenny market in regard to quality, although there are some of a coarser fabric; the weekly average full £150 and the market held regularly: but a great misfortune attending these two (the only linen) markets in the county is, they are chiefly occupied by jobbers, who buy up the linens for Londonderry market, and it is extremely difficult to enforce the laws.

Observations

CONVOY, STRANORLAR, BALLYBOFEY, CASTLEFINN: No regular linen markets but that species of linens known by the name of Lagans is principally manufactured in the neighbourhood of these towns; they are twenty-six inches wide, of good stuff, wove in long pieces, and the weaver or manufacturer cutting the pieces in lengths of 10 yards each, whiten them without the use of mills, and thus expose them for sale; but through knavery this manufacture is declining, and the present yearly value about £2,000.[38]

The linen trade continued to develop, according to manuscript comments made in 1803 on this report. Both Letterkenny and Rathmelton had increased their weekly sales of seven-eight wide linens, Letterkenny to £350 and Rathmelton to £450 while at each of them about £50 worth of three-quarter linen was sold. A Saturday market had been established at Stranorlar for seven-eight linen. The location of these three markets indicates that much of the cloth woven in east Donegal was sold in Londonderry and Strabane. By 1803 no Lagans were offered for sale. The county was said to have seven bleachgreens capable of finishing 27,500 pieces yearly. One of them was probably the concern at Buncrana advertised for letting on 9 July 1773 in the *London-Derry Journal:*

> To be let, from All Saints last, a bleach-mill, buck-house, drying loft, with all convenience for carrying on the bleaching business, with any quantity of excellent land, not exceeding thirty acres, and plenty of water ... Said bleach-green, land and farm are situated close to the town of Buncrana in the county of Donegal, within ten miles of Londonderry, twelve of Letterkenny, sixteen of Strabane, and twenty of Omagh, all good market towns, and in the heart of a fine country for linen yarn and linen cloth, where provisions of all kinds are plenty and cheap, with abundance of firing, limestone, and sea-weed for manure, and on the shore of Lough Swilly, where there is plenty of fish and generally a good herring fishery. On the farm there is convenience for a bleach-green, and a constant supply of water. Those who are inclined to treat may apply to Mr John Bateman at Buncrana, Thomas Greg, or Waddell Cunningham of Belfast. There are monthly markets and fairs at Buncrana.

Of especial interest here are the names of the men empowered to treat for the new lease, Thomas Greg and Waddell Cunningham, for they were two of the chief merchants in Belfast and had made their fortunes in one of the largest shipping firms in New York during the wars with France in the 1760s. It is interesting that a business rival there, Redmond Conyngham of Philadelphia, had returned in the late 1760s to set up a branch of the house of Conyngham and Nesbitt in Letterkenny described as 'a newly established sea port near Londonderry': Conyngham and Nesbitt was reckoned to be 'perhaps the largest colonial firm involved in Irish commerce' with as many as fifteen vessels and especially strong links with Londonderry.[39]

The final sentence of the advertisement above draws attention to the existence of monthly markets and fairs in Buncrana. It was about this time that the 'monthly market' made its appearance in Ulster. Landlords, enthusiastic to develop their estate towns, would have preferred to establish a weekly market in order to obtain the status of 'market town'. Unless it was recognised as a market town the grand jury could not accept presentments for building roads linking it to other market towns. Landlords advertised in newspapers to attract buyers and sellers and once they were satisfied that a monthly market had been established, they were prepared to try to introduce a second market in the month. In 1758 Nathaniel Nisbitt, an agent for the absentee earl of Abercorn, reported on his attempts to establish a monthly market in St Johnstown:

> ... We had the 17th inst [April] at St Johnstown a very fine market for the first; there was about £100 worth of green linen bought, a large quantity of yarn; there were also several other sorts of goods, such as suit the markets of this country; our next is the 15th of May, for we were obliged to make it the *third Monday in the month* to steer clear of other markets; I would allow neither cock-fight, nor horse race, though the people of the town were for it, as all towns are indeed, but I satisfied them by saying that an inch gained by honest industry was worth a yard otherwise, and that we did not want to gather idle people at all.

Early in July Nisbitt added:

> St Johnstown market goes on, as yet, very well, though Castlefin fair interfered with the second market and Derry fair with the third, for we have had but three; I attended and notwithstanding the fairs, there was a good deal of cloth and yarn and all bought. Flax is very scarce in the country; I make no doubt but winter next will produce a very good market at St. Johnstown, for the fairs that hurt us a little, may not interfere in the same manner these fifty years.[40]

Unfortunately, there are no further letters in the Abercorn estate correspondence concerning this venture and no other evidence about the town's success. These two letters demonstrate, however, that some owners of market rights believed that they had the right to alter the dates of markets or fairs to suit the needs of the community as long as they avoided clashes with the dates of other markets whose owners might charge them with interference. If a quarrel arose it would be the province of the sheriff of the county to try the case by jury.

In all these circumstances it is not surprising that in county Donegal only two patents were taken out for markets and fairs in the decades that followed the burst of activity when six were taken out in the 1770s. The only two exceptions were for Buncrana in 1803 and Stranorlar in 1799 and in both cases the landlords used it for the traditional purpose of launching a new market. In contrast there was no patent for Glenties which the *Post-chaise companion* (1786) had described as 'one of the most considerable fairs ... for black-cattle in the North of Ireland'. Glenties was not mentioned in the almanacs but the *Belfast almanac* did note Pettigo and Rashedag while *Watson's* mentions Culdaff: for none of these three had patents been purchased. Half a century later the commissioners inquiring into the state of markets and fairs in Ireland noted a further twenty fairs in Donegal, all without patents. On this phenomenon they commented in general in their report:

> Markets are, at present, held in 349 towns and villages in Ireland. In 125 instances no patents can be discovered authorising the holding of markets; and in 103 towns, as to which patents exist, the markets are held on different days from those mentioned in the grants. Fairs are held at 1,297 different towns and places in Ireland. In 485 instances no patents can be traced, and in 324 the fairs are held on other days than those granted by the patent ...[41]

The great discrepancy between the dates granted in the original patents and those recorded in the almanacs was augmented by a *caveat* introducing the list of fairs in Ireland in *Thom's Directory* of 1845: 'Patents are extant for numerous fairs which have ceased to be held for some years.' Because almanacs merely advertised fairs their main value lies in drawing attention to newcomers. During the early nineteenth century, however, no more fairs were registered for county Donegal and so other sources have to be searched. The most comprehensive source (although not completely accurate) is an appendix to the report of the commissioners inquiring into the state of markets and fairs in Ireland, published in the 1852/3 session. To the list of places mentioned in the almanacs it adds in Kilmacrenan barony, Millford, Kilmacrenan, Glen, Creeslough, Gortahork and Derrybeg; in Inishowen barony, Moville, Carrowkeel and Burnfoot; in Boylagh barony, Glenties; in Banagh barony, Largy, Kilcar and Carrick; and in Tyrhugh barony, Laghy. Although most of these places were insubstantial villages noted mainly for seasonal or monthly cattle fairs, some of them were more significant, especially Moville and Millford. Moville had previously been known as Bunafobble and notorious for its great whiskey fairs but by the mid-nineteenth century it was challenging Buncrana as a seaside resort for Londonderry.[42] About the same time Millford was considered to be 'an improving place, sufficiently near the navigation of Mulroy Bay to command commerce by small trading vessels, and so situated in relation to the surrounding country as to be a fit market for a district of many square miles in extent'.[43]

Table 12.3 can be used to construct the urban hierarchy for Donegal in the mid-nineteenth century. The postal receipts have been introduced to indicate the relative commercial importance of each place.[44] It should not be forgotten that the most important commercial centre in north Donegal was Londonderry in the next county while the county town of Lifford had long been regarded as a suburb of Strabane in county Tyrone. Raphoe dominated its own barony but Kilmacrenan barony had two significant towns in Letterkenny and Rathmelton: Letterkenny was destined to eclipse Rathmelton, mainly because of its more central location. Ballyshannon enjoyed the best commercial reputation in the county although its prosperity was related to the Erne basin. Donegal town had begun to assume its modern character. Its importance helped to stimulate the twin towns of Stranorlar and Ballybofey which straddled the main route from Donegal and Ballyshannon to the north of the county. The importance of these towns as commercial centres was accentuated by the spread of a railway network and the provision of postal telegraphs.

V

By 1850 all the significant towns in the county had been established. While some of them were still little more than locations for cattle fairs, others had developed into communities that were able to service not only the local farmers but also their families by providing employment in textiles especially in the knitting of stockings, the embroidery of muslin and later linen, and the spinning and weaving of linen and wool.[45] The development of towns, however, was limited by the poverty of the countryside which had to support a population of

Table 13.3
Towns in the early nineteenth century

Post Office Established		1853 Weekly Market	1831 People	1831 Houses	1841 People	1841 Houses	1851 People	1851 Houses	Postal Receipts 1821	Postal Receipts 1823	Postal Receipts 1831
1820	ARDARA	M	456	—	603	102	651	102	£6	£19	£41
—	BALLINTRA	—	439	c.90	522	100	458	88	—	—	—
1784	BALLYSHANNON	M	3,775	620	3,513	597	3,697	661	£306	354	598
1793	BUNCRANA	M	1,059	190	961	176	794	144	£128	157	140
—	BUNDORAN	—	—	—	299	45	384	72	—	—	—
1796	CARNDONAGH	M	618	116	653	118	708	133	£54	42	70
—	CASTLEFIN	—	—	—	567	88	637	104	—	—	—
—	CONVOY	—	356	73	365	67	344	59	—	—	—
1785	DONEGAL	M	830	141	1,386	222	1,563	217	£62	39	367
1796	DUNFANAGHY	—	464	73	529	84	587	84	£53	83	189
—	DUNGLOE	—	—	—	449	78	484	75	—	—	—
—	DUNKINEELY	—	—	—	475	84	385	74	—	—	—
—	GLENTIES	—	—	—	317	45	506	63	—	—	—
1784	KILLYBEGS	—	724	126	798	136	819	146	—	—	£149
1784	LETTERKENNY	M	2,160	—	2,161	331	1,940	309	£113	156	378
—	LIFFORD	—	1,096	153	752	109	570	94	—	—	—
—	MILLFORD	—	—	—	406	66	437	70	—	—	—
1807	MOVILLE	M	—	—	595	91	776	118	£33	29	155
—	MOUNTCHARLES	—	508	83	539	88	444	78	—	—	—
1814	MUFF	—	—	—	248	43	138	30	£50	24	—
1787	NARIN	—	—	—	276	46	227	39	£18	12	26
—	PETTIGO	M	—	—	616	90	466	73	—	—	—
1801	RAMELTON	M	1,783	308	1,428	245	1,428	261	£226	208	340
1784	RAPHOE	M	1,408	266	1,362	240	1,492	265	£98	121	206
—	RATHMULLEN	—	—	—	639	123	639	100	—	—	—
1787	RUTLAND	—	—	—	125	22	108	17	—	£21	78
—	ST. JOHNSTOWN	—	—	—	344	61	330	62	—	—	—
1793	STRANORLAR/BALLYBOFEY	M	1,515	273	1,167	200	1,497	246	£80	134	195

almost 300,000 on the eve of the famine (compared with little more than 100,000 today). The system of landownership provided families with security of tenure on uneconomic holdings but the absence of local employment opportunities forced the young people to migrate, seasonally or permanently, in search of work. The cash they brought or sent back to Donegal maintained their families and hence the towns. This resource must have been responsible during the famine for the smaller proportion of population loss in Donegal than in the majority of Irish counties. Yet while the community may have been able to protect its dependants against economic catastrophe it could not partake in the growing prosperity of the British Isles without shedding population and consolidating farms. Although government policies, such as those instituted by the Congested Districts Board, served to ease the transition process by improving employment opportunities and the economic structure, they could not arrest change on such a vast scale.

Other social changes were making intrusions into Donegal towns. Some of the towns were singled out to provide locations for such services as law courts with the forces of constabulary and coastguards, union workhouses (at Ballyshannon, Carndonagh, Donegal, Dunfanaghy, Glenties, Letterkenny, Millford and Stranorlar), fever hospitals (at Letterkenny, Rathmelton, and Dunfanaghy) and the county infirmary at Lifford: even the smaller towns had dispensary districts. The Catholic Church too built its post-emancipation churches in the towns and established a powerful presence throughout the county. Its major ally was democracy in the new organs of local and national government while the authority of the old estate system was undermined by the Encumbered Estates Courts, then the Land Acts, and finally by the Land Purchase Acts.

Appendix

Two letters from the Abercorn correspondence concerning road-building in county Donegal in 1750 (T.2541/IA1/2/27 and 28)

21 Sept. 1750, Philip, Bishop of Raphoe, Raphoe, County Donegal to the Earl of Abercorn:

> Mr McClintock, I hope, has by this post acquainted your Lordship with the intention of the country gentlemen to alter the road from this town to Lifford, if they shall be so happy as to obtain your Lordship's consent to carry it through part of your lands to Ballindrait which will enable them to, shorten it between two and three miles. I need not inform your Lordship that 'tis necessary to cast the new road up the year before they are finished in order to settle them in such a manner that they shall be properly prepared for stoning and gravelling the year after. If your Lordship shall think proper to grant them this liberty, I could wish

you would signify your consent as soon as possible because the low ground cannot be properly cast up in the winter season which is absolutely necessary previous to finishing it next summer to which your Lordship's consent is only wanting.

22 Sept. 1750, John McClintock, Strabane, to the Earl of Abercorn:

Your Lordship may remember that when you were last at Baronscourt there was a new road talked of to be carried from Raphoe to Strabane through Ballindrait; at the last assizes of the County of Donegal the Bishop of Raphoe proposed it to the Grand Jury, but Mr Sinclair of Holly Hill would not suffer it to go through his estate, if he was not paid the value of his land taken up by the road, but as the value of the land was not ascertained or the other lands particularly mentioned through which the road should go there was no presentment made, and I had no farther account of it 'til Thursday last when John Houston of Drumnabratty and Samuel Marten of Culahymore came to acquaint me that there were men set to work to cut the road through their farms, on which I desired they should stop them from breaking the ground 'til they had your Lordship's consent, but before their return they had cut the road through a great part of John Houston's farm and broke down several of his ditches, and they came again yesterday morning to go on with the work but the tenants got them stopped (with difficulty) as I had desired. I went yesterday to see what was done and observed the new road cut out from the old road that leads from Raphoe to Derry 'til it came through part of John Houston's farm, and as far as I could observe, the new road will neither be straight or carried on the most level ground, which I always thought the two most principal things chosen in laying out new roads, and indeed I can't judge what is the motive to carry the road after the manner it is laid out, if it is not to save some of the parks at Raphoe or to avoid as much as possible the carrying it through Mr Sinclair's estate.

Acknowledgement

I wish to thank the Director of the Public Record Office of Northern Ireland and the following depositors for permission to quote from their material: the duke of Abercorn, the Hon. Desmond Guinness and the Viscount Massereene and Ferrard.

References

1. This paragraph is based mainly on R. J. Hunter, 'Towns in the Ulster plantation' in *Studia Hib.*, xi (1971), pp 40-79. The theme is developed in R. J. Hunter, 'Ulster plantation towns, 1609-41' in D. Harkness and M. O'Dowd (eds), *The town in Ireland* (Belfast, 1981), pp 55-79.

2. *Report of the commissioners appointed to inquire into the state of the fairs and markets in Ireland,* H.C. 1852-3 (1674), xli, appendix.

3. R. Gillespie, 'The origins and development of an Ulster urban network' in *I.H.S.*, xxiv, no. 93 (May 1984), p. 18.

4. R. C. Simington (ed.), *The civil survey AD. 1654-1656, iii, counties of Donegal, Londonderry and Tyrone* (Dublin, 1937), pp 24-7.

5. Ibid., p. 23.

6. S. Pender (ed.), *A census of Ireland circa 1659* (Dublin, 1939), pp 43-65.

7. R. Gillespie, *Settlement and survival on an Ulster estate: the Brownlow leasebook 1667-1711* (Belfast, 1988), pp xli-xliv; W. H. Crawford, 'Landlord-tenant relations in Ulster 1609-1820' in *Irish Economic and Social History*, ii (1975), pp 6-8.

8. D. Verschoyle, 'The background to a hidden age' in *Donegal Annual*, vi, no. 2 (1965), p. 113.

9. P.J. McGill, 'Some old fairs of county Donegal' in *Donegal Annual*, iv, no. 3 (1960), p. 228.

10. P.R.O.N.I. Abercorn papers, T.2541/IA1/2/121, Nathaniel Nisbitt, Lifford, to the earl of Abercorn, 10 April 1752.

11. P. Roebuck, 'The Irish Registry of Deeds' in *I.H.S.*, xviii, no. 69 (March 1972), pp 61-71.

12. P.R.O.N.I., Conolly papers, T.2825/C/39 includes conveyance by Kingsmill family to William Conolly and Oliver McCausland of Rash, county Tyrone who purchased it jointly *c*.1707-8.

13. S. Lewis, *Topographical dictionary of Ireland* (2 vols. London 1837), i, 230. *Dublin Evening Post*, 22-26 July 1735; D. Dickson, 'Buncrana and Derry in 1744' in *Donegal Annual* ix, no. 2 (1970), p. 234; G.T. Stokes (ed.), *Pococke's tour in Ireland in 1752* (Dublin, 1891), p. 46.

14. P.R.O.N.I. Mic.198 Natural and Topographical history of counties Sligo, Donegal and Fermanagh by Rev. William Henry *c*.1739.

15. Stokes, *Pococke's tour*, p. 52.

16. E. McCracken, 'Two eighteenth century surveys at Castlefin' in *Donegal Annual*, vii, no. 3 (1968), p. 318.

17. P.R.O.N.I. T.2541/IA1/3/66, Nathaniel Nisbitt, Lifford, to Earl of Abercorn, 4 March 1755.

18. *Report of the commissioners appointed to revise the grand jury laws of Ireland*, H.C. 1842, xxiv, appendix G, pp 191-4.

19. 9 Anne *c*.9 (1710), An act for the amending of the highways and roads in this Kingdom, and for the application of the six days labour; 1 George II *c*.13 (1727), An act for explaining and amending several laws made for amending the high-ways and roads in this Kingdom; and for the application of the six days labour.

20. 13 George II *c*.10 (1739), An act for better regulating the highways in this Kingdom, and for preventing the misappropriation of public money.

21. Stokes, *Pococke's tour*, p. 61.

22. R. Blair, 'An analysis of the Donegal grand jury presentment book for the years 1753 to 1762' in *Donegal Annual*, no. 36 (1984), pp 61-74; P. J. McGill, 'Ancient roadways of Donegal' in *Donegal Annual*, ii, no. 3 (1953-4), pp 478-84.

23. P.R O.N.I. Abercorn papers, T.2541/IA1/1343. James Hamilton, Strabane, to the earl of Abercorn, 6 August 1780.

24. E. Wakefield, *An account of Ireland, statistical and political* (2 vols, London, 1812), i, p. 661.

25. 11 George III *c*.9 (1771), An act to explain and amend an act passed in the fifth year of His Majesty King George the third, intitled, An act for amending the public roads.

26. *Devon commission*, evidence, pt iv, H.C. 1845 (672), xxii, appendix no. 70, pp 178-81.

27. 11 & 12 George III *c*.20, (1772), An act for the making of narrow roads through the mountainous unimproved parts of this Kingdom.

28. 11 & 12 George III *c*.21 (1772).

29. J. H. Andrews, *Plantation acres: an historical study of the Irish land surveyor and his maps* (Belfast, 1985), p. 349.

30. P.R.O.N.I. Abercorn papers, T.2541/IAI/15/27, James Hamilton, Strabane, to the Earl of Abercorn, 29 November 1785.
31. Andrews, *Plantation acres,* p. 352; the printed maps are dated.
32. P. J. McGill, *History of the parish of Ardara* (Donegal, 1970), p. 100.
33. *Post-chaise companion* (Dublin, 1786), p. 79.
34. See note 14.
35. A. Young, *A tour of Ireland,* ed. A.W. Hutton (2 vols, London, 1892), i, p. 178.
36. *Post-chaise companion,* p. 80; McGill, 'Ancient roadways', p. 482; A. Rowan, *The buildings of Ireland: north-west Ulster* (London, 1979), pp 480-1.
37. G. E. Kirkham, '"To pay the rent and lay up riches": economic opportunity in eighteenth-century North-West Ulster' in R. Mitchison and P. Roebuck, *Economy and society in Scotland and Ireland 1500-1939* (Edinburgh, 1988), pp 95, 99.
38. P.R.O.N.I. D.562/6225, John Greer, *Report of the state of the linen markets of the province of Ulster* (Dublin, 1784) annotated with market data for 1803.
39. T. Truxes, *Irish-American trade, 1660-1783* (Cambridge, 1988), pp 87, 114-5, 119, 240-1; see also D. Dickson, 'A Donegal revenue inspection of 1775' in *Donegal Annual,* x, no. 2 (1972), pp 172-82.
40. P.R.O.N.I. Abercorn papers T.2541/IA1/5/23, Nathaniel Nisbitt, Lifford to earl of Abercorn, 20 April 1758; and T.2541/IA1/5/37, Nathaniel Nisbitt, Lifford to earl of Abercorn, 2 July 1758.
41. *Report of the commissioners appointed to inquire into the state of the fairs and markets in Ireland,* part ii: minutes of evidence [1910] H.C. 1854-5, xix, 86.
42. *Slater's directory, 1846,* p. 501.
43. *Parliamentary gazetteer of Ireland* (3 vols, Dublin, 1844), ii, 769-70.
44. The weekly markets are listed in the report referred to in note 41; the population figures are taken from the census reports; the postal information is taken from two government reports: *19th report of the commissioners of inquiry into the collection and management of the revenus arising in Ireland and Great Britain: Post Office revenue, United Kingdom Part III – Ireland* (353) H.C. 1829, xii, 379, appendix 87; and *Report from the select committee on post communication with Ireland* (716) H.C. 1831/2, xvii, 349-52.
45. The most comprehensive account of these developments will be found in Judith Hoad, *This is Donegal tweed* (Inver, 1987).

Chapter 14

DERRY'S BACKYARD: THE BARONY OF INISHOWEN, 1650-1800

DAVID DICKSON

A cartographic image of Inishowen, the great peninsula in the far north, had not become firmly established in the official mind when the Dublin government was deciding in 1585 on the extent of a new north-western county. The fact that Sir John Perrot perversely chose to tack the peninsula on to the O'Donnell lordship to the west, thereby creating the new shire of 'Tyrconnel' or Donegal, reflected politics not administrative convenience. The decision to create such an odd-shaped county was a measure of the residual political influence in Dublin of the ailing Sir Hugh (Seán Óg) O'Donnell, who was as anxious as ever to assert his family's pre-eminence over the O'Dohertys and their 'country'. It was a precarious overlordship, for even in the government-brokered agreement forty years before when the lords of Inishowen had undertaken to pay a fixed tribute to the O'Donnells, the ancient counter-claims of the O'Neills had been recognized when they were also allowed to call on an albeit smaller tribute from the O'Dohertys. Inishowen's historic links were indeed multi-directional: the O'Dohertys had originally come from within Tír Chonaill, but the peninsula which they made their own in the fifteenth century – once the cradle of the O'Neills – had always been part of the diocese of Derry, and it was quite appropriate that the O'Dohertys in the sixteenth century should have held a castle beside the monastic settlement of Derry. The peninsula's autonomous status was reinforced by the marriage, trading and cultural links between the O'Doherty lordship and that of Argyll, traces of which continued even in the late sixteenth century.[1]

Inishowen's incorporation into the new county had no direct impact on the troubled history of the next three decades. Sir John O'Doherty went through the process of formally surrendering the lordship to the English crown in 1588, and accepting ownership of it under English patent, but this insulated neither the family nor the peninsula from the maelstrom of the 1590s.[2] However, the territory remained largely beyond direct English influence until the latter stages of the Nine Years' War; the decisive events which changed this were Sir Henry Docwra's

Foyle expedition in the summer of 1600 which led to the establishment of a fortified colonial settlement at Derry and, on the death the following year of Sir John, the Docwra-sponsored installation of a young friend of government, Cahir O'Doherty, as lord of Inishowen. Inishowen soldiery fought alongside Englishmen against the O'Cahans and the O'Neills in the final stages of the war. In English eyes, the peninsula had an unprecedented strategic importance, being seen as key to the security and provisioning of Derry and, after the 1603 peace, integral to the prosperity of the fledgling 'town of war and ... town of merchandize' on its southern border. Docwra allowed Sir Cahir to hold the key castles to the north of the city – at Elaghbeg and Burt (or 'Fort Lagin') – despite their defensive strength. Inch island however was resumed by the crown and in 1602 it was granted along with the entire fishing rights of Lough Swilly to Sir Ralph Bingley, a key military figure under Docwra.[3]

The reports of Docwra and others on the state of the peninsula provide some of the earliest documentary evidence on the local economy. The populated perimeter was contrasted with the interior, which was deemed 'good for feeding cows in summer only, but all waste, desolate and uninhabited ...'.[4] One coastal part of northern Inishowen, said to be 'the fertilest part', was in 1600 'so full of poor Irish houses, as it seems all in a manner but one town'.[5] Flax, oats and barley were the staples of the peninsula, 'wheat, rye, or peas it hath none, and, after the fashion of the country, lies all open, without any manner [of] inclosures'; as for 'wood it hath very little but turf exceeding much and passing good'.[6] Several estimates of Inishowen's wealth of cattle reached government during 1601: 'not so little as 20,000 cows' was one military guess.[7] And one of the reasons behind Docwra's decision in 1600 to erect six forts between Burt and Carrigans, across the south-west neck of the peninsula, was to seal this mobile larder, regarded as essential to the maintenance of the garrison and the conduct of the war.[8]

On the surface, the 'flight of the earls' did not affect the peace of Inishowen. But the fact that two of the McDevitt family, intimates and advisers of Sir Cahir, were part of the exodus in September 1607, seems to have made Sir Cahir's political judgement more erratic, as well as to have strengthened his opponents in Derry and further afield. His earlier agility in protecting the integrity of his lordship had created suspicion of his motives; thus when the lord deputy, Sir Arthur Chichester visited Derry for the first time in 1605, he warned of the precariousness of the colony 'being placed among neighbours who long for nothing more than the ruin thereof', and O'Doherty's Country was presumably the first object of suspicion.[9] Sir Francis Shaen, writing in the aftermath of the flight, was more explicit when he complained that 'the city of Derry, built by the English in hope that Inyshowen would be made an English colony, was not so much remembered [i.e. granted] ... with a poor common to grass their horses in'.[10]

Whatever the particular explanation for O'Doherty's shift from protégé of Docwra and burgess of the newly incorporated city of Derry to sudden exterminator of that colony in the rising of May 1608, there had been a palpable build-up of tension between the new citizens of Derry and their Gaelic hinterland, particularly after Docwra's departure in 1606. But the eleven-week revolt acted as a powerful catalyst, not just in Inishowen's but in Irish history. The way was 'now open', remarked Sir Geoffrey Fenton on the day of Sir Cahir's death, for 'a universal settlement of Ulster'.[11] If intended by Sir Cahir as a form of negotiation by deed, the rebellion had been entirely disastrous, for it played into the hands of those who had been calling for a vastly greater English intervention in Ulster. O'Doherty's death in rebellion laid the way open for the total forfeiture of Inishowen and its recreation as an English colony. Its future and that of Derry city were debated together, one writer in April 1609 arguing that the revival of Derry would only be possible if 'some great man, who shall be lord of O'Doghertie's country' were to make 'his principal residence there'.[12]

Following English law and the settlement of 1586, all but the churchland of Inishowen were deemed by due process to have been the personal property of Sir Cahir. Its recent prominence and the exaggerated estimations of its wealth made the territory an appropriate prize for the lord deputy, and Chichester – after intensive court intrigue – finally received his patent for the 170,000-acre estate in February 1610.[13] The grant envisaged the creation of precincts within Inishowen where internal arrangements could conform to 'the instructions of plantation in Ulster', but this was discretionary. Apart from specifying the location and time of fairs and markets (at Buncrana, Greencastle and Drung, near Malin), the grant allowed Chichester and his heirs to hold the 'palatinate' as a liberty in which the manorial officials could execute all writs and other legal processes, 'with no sheriff or bailiff of the Crown to intermeddle'.[14]

There was at first sight a paradox in the unconditional granting of a whole lordship to a single individual when two of the key elements in the wider plantation scheme precipitated by the Inishowen rising were tight upper limits on land grants, and rigorous colonial obligations attaching to them. Yet Chichester had not championed the kind of total forfeiture that was decided on in London during 1609; for several years he had argued for a less ambitious and cheaper method of securing and 'civilising' Ulster: he had argued that the implantation of a number of fortified British settlements and, more generally, the piecemeal infiltration of English gentlemen would allow English law and the institutions of local government to take root, without the necessity for a wholesale confiscation of Irish land or the elimination of Irish freeholders. In 1607 Chichester was the first to propose a role for lowland Scots in such a programme – they could be introduced as undertenants of English gentlemen. But in the wake of Sir Cahir's rising other views, notably those of the attorney-general Sir John Davies, prevailed, and London saw the solution to the Ulster problem in terms of a complete proprietorial revolution.[15] Chichester, with his Inishowen grant, was at liberty to pursue his alternative strategy to plantation if he so wished.

A large proportion, probably a majority, of the 1,400-odd persons pardoned in the wake of the rising were Inishowen men, among them 152 O'Dohertys, 100 McLaughlins, and 47 McDevitts,[16] and it can be assumed that despite the death and forced expatriation of some of the Gaelic elite of the peninsula, local structures of society remained intact as Chichester's lordship took shape. A pattern that was to endure for much of the seventeenth century was evident even in 1611: a handful of Englishmen – key veterans of the Derry garrison for the most part – had received leases with obligations to fortify and maintain specified castles, to invest specified amounts on house construction in the English or Scottish style, and to introduce settlers; Chichester's only direct involvement was in the reconstruction of Greencastle at Lough Foyle's entrance. It was asserted that 'divers other p[ar]cels of land are let to Englishmen w[i]th good bonds to build strong houses of stone or bricks for the chief tenants, and good English timber houses for their undertenants in townships after the manner of the English not scattering', although of this there was to be little evidence.[17] Chichester's role was in some respects analogous to that of the state itself: the active agents of plantation, the *de facto* undertakers of Inishowen, were to be Chichester's English chief tenants under whom, it was planned, English sub-lessees would settle. Chichester, soldier, statesman and courtier, was no entrepreneur in the Richard Boyle mould, and at no time were the great Chichester estates, in Donegal or elsewhere in Ulster, subject to the interventionist management that so transformed the Munster estates of the earl of Cork.[18] But this was entirely in keeping with Chichester's 'low intensity' approach to colonial policy.

The first survey and mapping of the estate was, it seems, carried out around 1609, even though it is only in a mid-seventeenth-century printed map that the evidence from 1609 survives (fig. 14.1): of the 150-odd townlands plotted, it is striking that two-thirds of them

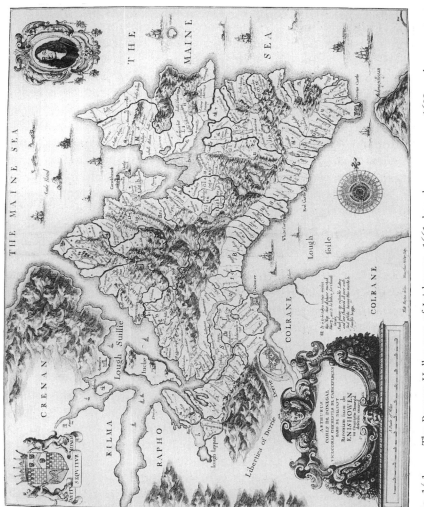

Fig. 14.1   The Parsons-Hollar map of Inishowen, 1661, based on a survey c.1609 no longer extant (Reproduced by permission of the Board of T.C.D.).

touched the coast, and that much of the interior was apparently *terra incognita* to the surveyor. The 'island' of Malin (as the northernmost appendage was called in Chichester's patent) was virtually cut off by the huge bogs to the south-east of the future Malin village. But the overriding impression given by the survey was of a peninsula more united by water and a coastline than by tracks and cattle paths. Of bridges and roads there is no evidence; and only in the shadow of Buncrana Castle is there a suggestion of embryonic urbanization (although that may be a later interpolation). Just before Chichester secured the grant of Inishowen, it was proposed that twenty-five new corporate towns should be created in Ulster, one of which would be located in Inishowen – on the Isle of Doagh; even by seventeenth-century standards, that was an optimistic aspiration.[19]

Two of the chief tenants in 1611 were Captains Henry Hart and Henry Vaughan, each the progenitor of an Inishowen landed family; George Cary, whose descendants proliferated in the region to a remarkable extent, took leases shortly afterwards. Hart, Henry Vaughan and his brother John were more than mere Chichester tenants; they received land in other parts of Donegal as servitors; they were among the twelve aldermen named in the new charter of Derry city; they were all to be mayors of Derry at least once; and John, beside much else, was military commander of the city until 1643 and an MP. George Cary, from Devon like Sir Arthur and a relative, was initially sent across to Derry by the Irish Society, and was Recorder there until his death in 1640. Two other large tenants of lands in Burt, Peter Benson and John Wray, were also mayors of the city before 1641. In other words, Chichester secured several of the most energetic, successful and resilient New Englishmen in the region as large tenants for his estate.[20]

By 1621 there were 17 English leaseholders in Chichester's Inishowen, all but two of whom were holding lands in the southern half of the peninsula. Their holdings varied in size from a single townland to the fourteen held by Henry Vaughan around his newly fortified castle at Buncrana. But the rental from English tenants, at about £600, was less than 45 per cent the valuation put on the estate at the end of that decade.[21] Thus, a very substantial part of the income from the Inishowen estate must have come from Irish head-tenants holding on short lease terms. A few were more favoured: three O'Dohertys and three McLaughlins, in deference to their previous social standing, held small perpetuity leases (i.e. freeholds) in 1621 for lands in the northern half of the peninsula. This was at least consistent with Chichester's original plantation philosophy.[22]

Very little is directly known about the early activities of the head-tenants beyond the fact that by 1630 there were substantial numbers of

English and Scottish undertenants on some parts of the estate. On the county muster-rolls for that year, 175 British males were listed for Inishowen, some 60 per cent of whom had English surnames; the fact that there were about 118 different names (and very few sharing the same patronymic) implies a heterogeneous and very recent colonial community.[23] At that stage English and Scottish settlement was heavily skewed towards the good land in the southern parishes of Burt, Inch, Fahan and Muff, and the number of Irish there had been drastically eroded – this was primarily a consequence of geographical location rather than the inherent soil quality, for the parishes were adjacent to two of the most dynamic elements in the Ulster Plantation, the London-financed and prospering port of Derry, and the heavily Scottish-settled precinct of Portlough in the barony of Raphoe.[24]

This southern *cordon sanitaire* helps explain the quiescence of Inishowen at the outbreak of the 1641 rising. There were settler fears then that the Irish in Inishowen would rise (which is itself telling), but there is no evidence in the loyalist depositions or elsewhere that conflict erupted.[25] The faction-ridden history of Derry city during the 1640s, culminating in Owen Roe's relief of the beseiged parliamentary adherents in 1649, allowed local war-lords their time in the sun, but judging by the evidence of the poll-money returns of 1660 and the hearth-tax lists of 1665, the social geography of Inishowen after the wars was not demonstably different from that *c.*1641.[26]

All but one of the half-dozen largest English families on the pre-war estate were still in evidence after the Restoration, and the 1660 returns list 15 English and 16 Irish tituladoes (i.e.gentlemen) on the peninsula. The north/south contrast was still obvious: eleven of the fifteen English tituladoes were in southern parishes, whereas ten of the sixteen Irish were in northern ones; even more starkly, of the 1,209 people listed in the 1660 returns for the northern parishes, a mere eight were returned as British, whereas of the 1,897 in the south 23.5 per cent were deemed British.[27] In the more exclusive hearth-tax lists of 1665, 27 per cent of all Inishowen householders eligible to pay the tax bore British names, but predictably these were nearly all in the southern parishes: in Fahan (which at that stage included Buncrana), 53 per cent of the 1665 taxpayers were British; in the Templemore group of parishes (Burt, Inch and Muff), 61 per cent. The relatively higher economic status of British households in these parishes is indicated by the significantly greater Irish share recorded there in the 1660 enumeration.[28]

In the 1654 Civil Survey, which is also extant for Inishowen, the contrast between settler and Irish zones was not so evident: in the albeit notional grading of land-use, 48.5 per cent of the profitable land in the northern parishes and 50.9 per cent in the southern were deemed arable. There is some suggestion however that population density in the south may have been somewhat higher than in the north: the average number of 'profitable' acres (plantation) in 1654 per person enumerated in 1660 was 3.27 in the north, 2.75 in the south. The overall judgement on the peninsula by the Civil Survey commissioners (who included George Cary of Redcastle) was decidedly more negative than some earlier appraisals: 'the greatest part of our soil is mountain and bog[;] that which is arable is hungry ground and the pasture worse[.] Our grain is most oats some barley little wheat and less rye.'[29]

Comparison of the 175 British surnames in the 1630 muster-roll with the total of about 244 in 1665 liable for hearth tax is also suggestive: 63 per cent of the pre-war names were not listed in the tax lists, and about 100 new names made their appearance. However, the survival rate of family names which had appeared more than once in 1630 was much higher: of the thirty-nine such cases, twenty-three of the surnames were still there three decades later. The Scottish proportion of surnames remained almost unchanged – at about two-fifths of the British total, but the most common names in 1665 – Porter and Browne – were held by Scots.[30]

Post-war continuity was also evident in Irish family-name distribution. The once dominant local septs still provided the chief Inishowen patronymics in the 1660 schedule of Irish names in the barony: 22 per cent were O'Doherty and 15 per cent McLaughlin. And in the 1665 hearth tax, 17 per cent of Irish-named tax-payers were O'Dohertys. But by that stage, O'Doherty Country had quite literally shrunk: in south Inishowen there was now only a handful bearing the O'Doherty name, whereas 56 per cent of all those bearing the name on the peninsula were by then concentrated in the three northern parishes of Clonmany, Clonca and Donagh.[31]

The housing of settlers and of Irish was uniformly modest in the 1660s – one-hearth houses being the standard. George Cary of Redcastle, son of the Derry Recorder, was unusual with ten hearths – it is not clear whether this refers to a fortified residence or not – and overlooking the Swilly at Fahan, a remarkably large structure with fifteen hearths was recorded in 1665. This was the bishop of Derry's house, built by Bishop Downham (1616-34) after he had failed to agree terms for a house in Derry with the Irish Society; it may have been fortified (although hardly in the spectacular manner of Bishop Leslie's contemporaneous Raphoe palace), but local tradition is that it was essentially an unfortified residence – Inishowen's first 'big house'.[32] Bramhall had chosen Fahan presumably because it was situated in the richest of the enclaves of the bishop's land that were reserved out of Chichester's 1610 grant. In all some 15 per cent of Inishowen was set aside, either as episcopal or glebe estate.[33] In the 1630s half-a-dozen chief tenants were in possession of church leases for terms similar to those held under the Chichesters, and at rents that were also comparable.[34]

The Church of Ireland, for all its territorial wealth in the peninsula, developed an active presence in the north very tentatively: Protestant clergy from outside the region had been appointed to the northern parishes in the 1620s and 1630s – 'the residence of a minister would be a great inducement to invite planters thither' – but there is evidence of only one new church – at Clonca – being built before 1641. Robert Young, appointed there in 1640, was unusual in being in continuous residence until his death c.1667; his son succeeded him and by the time of *his* death in 1706 the family, holding a large portfolio of Chichester and churchland leases, was well established among the leading tenant-gentry of the peninsula.[35] Clonmany parish boasted the remarkable distinction in the seventeenth century of having a local conformist, Daniel McLaughlin, as Church of Ireland rector (from 1672 to 1711), and his brother, Peter, as parish priest; they were grandsons of one of Chichester's few Irish freeholders.[36] But shifts in denominational allegiance and 'occasional conformity' may not have been particularly uncommon at that stage; at least fifteen of the forty-two persons named as parish clerks or church wardens of the northern parishes in the Church of Ireland visitation returns between 1661 and 1719 were McLaughlins, O'Dohertys or persons bearing other local Irish surnames.[37] Yet at a time of reviving Catholic fortunes as in the 1680s, north Inishowen could still seem a distinctly unpromising environment for the Protestant ministry; citing a complaint from the rector of Donagh about the swarms of friars locally active, the bishop of Derry informed the primate in 1682 that Inishowen, 'the most rude and uncivilized' part of his diocese, was a rendezvous for the Catholic priests and regulars, a situation which he claimed was facilitated by supine magistrates.[38]

Such fears of the residual potency of the old order in the peninsula were borne out in the Jacobite years. O'Dohertys – such as Daniel O'Doherty of Keenagh, descendant of another of Chichester's Irish freeholders, and Henry Doherty of Culdaff, Sarsfield's secretary – were again in lawful arms for the English crown, and the Protestant interest in the peninsula seems to have been close to collapse in 1688-89, in the lead-up to and during the siege on the southern horizon of Inishowen. During that siege and immediately after it was raised, settler housing and Protestant churches were extensively damaged, while many of Williamite sympathy took refuge on Inch island or shared in the defence of Derry itself.[39]

Before the war was over William King, the great polemicist for Protestant Ireland, was appointed to the bishopric of Derry; he was exceptional in his vigour in consolidating the established church in the region – at a time, in his view, not of triumph but of adversity. King's main concern was the new inflow of non-conformist Scottish migrants who seemed set to undermine the status and pre-eminence of the Church of Ireland. In Inishowen it was in southern parishes such as Moville and Fahan that the challenge of non-conformity was most clearly felt; in the former neighbourhood 'fanatical preachers' were reported in 1698 to be 'daily labouring to steal away our flock but thanks to God, [they] hath not as yet prevailed much, in adding to their former numbers'.[40] Bishop King maintained that Cary of Redcastle had been the first to bring in a dissenting minister into Inishowen, 'with a design to improve his lands, but I do not understand that it had that effect...'.[41] In 1718 the strongly Anglican George Vaughan of Buncrana appealed to King (long since departed to greater things in Dublin) to help prevent the construction of yet another meeting-house in Inishowen – and in so doing rather overestimated the power of magistrates to intervene. The earliest record of an established Presbyterian meeting in Inishowen is, not unexpectedly, for Burt, where a minister was ordained in 1673; Carndonagh's first minister was appointed in 1695, Moville in 1715, Malin in 1717, Fahan in 1719, and Knowhead (Muff) in 1749.[42]

The Chichester family in the later seventeenth century were at least benignly neutral towards the advancing tide of Presbyterianism, and tenant-gentry like the Carys played their part in encouraging Presbyterian colonisation out of economic interest; the major contribution of a branch of the Harvey family, providing three of the first Presbyterian ministers for Carndonagh, Moville and Malin – at a time when another branch of the family was emerging as leading Church of Ireland gentry in north Inishowen – implies a stronger religious motivation for some families.[43] But the overall pattern and timing of lowland Scottish/Presbyterian penetration into the peninsula would suggest that it was an unplanned process, with many migrating the short distance from the old Portlough precinct in the Laggan. It is not clear at what point in the eighteenth century Presbyterians outnumbered established church members on the peninsula; by the 1830s they formed three-fifths of the Protestant population, with two-thirds of the denomination being in the southern-most parishes of Burt, Inch, Muff and Fahan Upper.[44]

The delayed growth of a Protestant presence in the northern parishes is evident in eighteenth-century records: compared to the position in 1665 when less than 5 per cent of those with British surnames were to be found in the four northern parishes, one mid-eighteenth century return (in 1740) indicated that 25 per cent of Inishowen Protestant householders were located there, another (in 1766) that fully 32 per cent were in the north.[45] This erosion of the homogeneously Catholic character of the northern peninsula derived from three processes: a Presbyterian immigration dating from the last quarter of the seventeenth century, very little if any of which would have been primary colonisation from Scotland; a redistribution of Church of Ireland families within the peninsula; and, least important statistically but most exotic, an influx of West Highland episcopalians in the 1690s, fleeing from religious pogroms across the narrow channel. Bishop King was a willing patron of these Scots Gaelic-speaking conformists who settled in Moville, Culdaff and Clonmany parishes (as well as several coastal parishes in north Antrim and Derry). Twenty-two such families were said in 1695 to have recently settled in Culdaff parish, while those in Moville, on being supplied with a Gaelic prayer-book, 'answer the litany extreme well'.[46] Daniel McLaughlin of Clonmany was preaching and conducting prayers in Irish for his new parishoners in 1693, a practice continued by his son, curate in the parish until at least the 1720s; however, some of the Highlanders had gone home long before that.[47]

The Catholic church, after harsh initial persecution in the earliest days of the plantation, seems to have continued an effective if shadowy organisation for the rest of the seventeenth century, with north Inishowen as late as the 1680s being something of a refuge area for clergy harried in other parts of Derry diocese. Families of erenagh status such as the McColgans of Donagh and the O'Donnels of Fahan, continued to provide local clergy generation after generation, and it was of course one of the former family. John Colgan who became, in exile, the most famous seventeenth-century Inishowen man. Some measure of his anger and sense of cultural loss at events at home comes from the comments in his *Acta Sanctorum Hiberniae* (Louvain, 1645) on the old monastery at Fahan: 'the splendid relics of antiquity ... were preserved there until the arrival of the mad heretics who desecrated, demolished and plundered everything sacred. Thereafter that long-famous and noble monastery was laid waste and destroyed by the passage of time and the carelessness of those in charge. It was afterwards devastated and demolished and ended by being a parish church.'[48]

Active persecution peaked in the 1670s and again in the generation after the siege, with the main pressure for implementing anti-Catholic policy coming from outside. One of Colgan's relatives got the head-tenant of churchland in Carndonagh into trouble with Bishop King in 1701; the latter accused Tristram Cary, the tenant, of befriending and being 'infatuated by the 'lewd debauch'd priest', despite a clause in King's leases apparently prohibiting priestly sub-tenants.[49] King was much exercised at that time by the failure of Inishowen magistrates to enforce the penal code and to arrest either the numerous regular clergy in circulation or 'their harbourers'. One of those bullied by King to take action was George Vaughan, who was later involved in the notorious killing of Father James Hegarty during an attempted arrest c.1709; this elderly cleric, a native of the parish and dean of the diocese had been imprisoned in 1696, indicted in 1702 and officially registered in 1704.[50] But his murder was decidedly atypical; inscribed early eighteenth century grave-stones, erected in memory of long-serving priests in shared churchyards such as at Culdaff, hint at a more stable society.[51] The long-term problem of the Catholic church in a region like Inishowen was more the poverty of its leading lay families than the physical persecution of its clergy.[52]

*   *   *

The demands of public office, ill-health and financial difficulty had restricted Sir Arthur Chichester's direct involvement with Inishowen; his brother Edward, who inherited the property in 1625, apppears to have had a closer knowledge and interest,[53] but family charges and legal disputes forced him to continue a low-risk policy of 'benevolent' leasing, thereby consolidating the position of the original tenantry. The family appears to have drawn no revenue from any of their Ulster estates between 1641 and 1656, but under Edward's heir Arthur, raised to the earldom of Donegall in 1647, things improved and the much bruised title of the family to their huge estates was confirmed in 1668. Despite this, the first earl's regime continued the process of disengagement; for all the symbolism of the 'Donegall' earldom, the centre of gravity of the estate was in Antrim and, specifically, in the estate town of Belfast. The first earl's lack of a male heir was one incident in a long history of genetic misfortune for the family: in the six transfers of the Chichester estates between 1625 and 1757 only two were from father to son. The consequences were heightened encumbrances on the core properties, and intra-family litigation. In addition at least one link in the chain of inheritance, the fourth earl (1695-1757), was feeble-minded.[54]

By early eighteenth-century standards, rent levels on the Inishowen estate were exceptionally low. The most eloquent demonstration of this is the fact that in 1741 (at a period when entire reponsibility for the estate was in the hands of trustees), rental income at £2013 was only 50 per cent above the valuation made in the very diffferent world of 1630; the 1741 total implied that headrents averaged 3 pence per acre. There were seventy-six tenants on the rent-roll, all leaseholders on long terms of years or freeholders – but all the original Irish freeholds of Sir Arthur's day had passed into Protestant tenant-gentry hands, whether by marriage or by mortgage.[55] Most of the Chichester leases expired in the 1760s, and the consequent revaluation and resetting process held out the possibility of a transformation of the Inishowen head-tenantry.

A shift in the management of many Irish estates, favouring the breakup of large tenancies and the shortening of lease terms, was becoming evident in the later eighteenth century.[56] This occurred on the Inishowen estate, but on a much more modest scale than many expected. There was intense competition in the 1760s for new leases on what was regarded as a massively under-let property; but the spendthrift fifth earl of Donegall and his creditors saw little attraction in what would have a long-term programme of tenancy division and upward rent revision as against an immediate drive for large entry fines, discounted against future rent income, and for tenants wealthy enough to pay up-front.

Between 1767 and 1770, new leases for holdings (mainly in the range of 100 to 1,000 plantation acres) were tortuously negotiated with some 140 tenants to produce an annual rental of over £8,000, and a sum in excess of £20,000 was obtained in entry fines. The inability to raise loans to finance such fines excluded many would-be tenants. Around three-quarters of the successful bidders resided locally, but virtually all were – to use the new term coined by Arthur Young: – 'middlemen'. But, in the legal terminology of the day, the majority were also 'yeomen', particularly in the southern parishes, i.e. strong farmers who employed labour and sublet only a part of their tenancies. Further north was more clearly middleman country; the dominant lease-holders were the descendants of the first tenant-gentry – Carys, Harts, Sweetenhams and Youngs, now intermarried with the dynamic Harvey clan, who more than any gained in the reletting.[57] The patriarchal George Harvey, Inishowen agent for Donegall, reminded his heir in 1770, 'never let it slip of[f] y[ou]r mind that what we now have is of a short duration, that we must and ought to make a fortune out of our Donegal leases equal to what we now have'.[58]

The most striking feature of the new rent-roll was the fact that there were less than a dozen tenants with assumed Catholic names, including six O'Dohertys. Despite the continued existence of a shadow-gentry in the northern parishes – Catholics of old family who supplied sons to the priesthood – their inability to translate seventeenth-century informal power into eighteenth-century middleman fiefdoms seems to have gradually undone them.[59] One such family, the O'Dohertys of Kinea, Clonmany, revealed their resentment in 1765 to Morgan O'Connell, the

Liberator's uncle: George 'Dougherty', on his way to London and a career at sea, spoke of 'the enmity of those in whose power we are as agents [i.e. the Harveys], and the leases now out'; writing at the same time, his father John was more expansive: 'the original Irish are very happy in your part of the [?country]; the wicked brood of black-hearted heretics have got no foothold there as yet, although I believe they are creeping tow[ards] you; here are few else except hewers of wood & drawers of water; in short, we are in the most abject slavery in this barony of Inishowen especially, and not a foot of land to be renewed to any as prime tenant to our landlord the earl of Donegall, that is of the old stamp...'. There were particular circumstances inflaming O'Doherty at that point – a dispute over the ownership of a wreck as a result of which he was being threatened with an ejectment, and a vexatious prosecution of one of his sons for, as a Catholic, owning a hunting-piece (as it turned out, four O'Dohertys did manage to secure head leases in Clonmany parish several years later). In a somewhat archaic lament, he ended his letter: 'though people advanced in years are generally fond of making their exit in their native soil, yet I am tired of mine, and would rather traverse the globe than live under such tyranny...'.[60]

The marginalised status of the Catholic church, dependent still on the Mass rock and the itinerant friar, was one element in such alienation, yet the tyranny that O'Doherty complained of was not entirely different from that which was shortly to mobilise the Steelboys in Antrim: a sense of injustice at the way that resident families of modest substance were being denied the prospect of direct leases from Lord Donegall, and a resentment that tenant gentry and wealthy outsiders, better placed to raise the entry fines, were obtaining middleman tenancies over them.[61] The attraction of a direct lease was more than as a status symbol; it offered the prospect of abundant profit in the future, whether through farming or sub-letting. In the event, about a quarter of the new lessees of 1770 – and a higher proportion in the northern parishes – were non-resident, and for the most part these were men in Derry trade; many of the successful 'yeoman' lessees in the southern parishes were only able to afford the heavy renewal fines by securing loans from Derry merchants.[62]

The very long lease terms first granted in the 1610s (up to sixty-one years at fixed rent levels) had continued with little modification until the great re-letting. Slightly over half of the new leases after 1770 were for thirty-one years, and nearly all the rest were for three lives and forty-one years.[63] However, by contemporary standards these were loose agreements, not obliging tenants to make specific expenditures. Heavy entry fines and light annual rents continued to be the dominant tenancy arrangement for head tenants until well into the new century, by which time the Donegalls' debts were reaching another crisis, further diluting their control.[64] A collateral member of the family purchased Inch and much of Burt when the second marquess was in gaol for gambling debts around 1800, and the Harvey and Todd families bought out the head-rents for the rest of the western and southern parts of the estate between 1806 and 1812. Elsewhere, three-lives renewable leases were being offered between 1823 and 1838 to all who could afford to pay the heavy fines, and sixty-one years for those who could not. Previous to these loppings, the Chichester rent-roll had continued to grow, but nearly all the sub-division since 1770 took place on a few townlands in Burt and Muff.[65] The direct leaseholders as a whole, whether the big and usually Presbyterian farmers of the south or the gentry tenants elsewhere, were enjoying fixed-rent tenures during a long cycle of rising land values, and were acting 'as if they had become the actual proprietors'.[66] But despite this gradual empowering of the local elite, a surprisingly high proportion of the larger leaseholders, especially in the northern parishes, were non-resident; however most were living no further away than Derry or elsewhere in the Foyle valley region.[67] Neglect rather than oppression was the consequence.

The local administration of the Chichester estate had been in the hands of the indigenous tenant gentry for most of the eighteenth century, notably in those of George Harvey, the builder of Malin Hall. Little is known of his management style; his son, the Rev John, briefly the curate of Donagh before inheriting the family property, developed a high public profile, becoming the most enthusiastic sponsor of Volunteering in Inishowen; besides his own corps in Malin (1780-), he shared the captaincy of the Inishowen Rangers (1779-), was a correspondent of Charlemont, and later a partisan of Henry Flood; by 1784 he was reported to have included large numbers of Catholics in his Malin corp. There were also Volunteer corps based in Burt (1778-), Fahan [Buncrana] (1781-), and Inch (1781-), but none achieved the publicity of Harvey's corps.[68]

The Alexanders, one of the largest trading families in Derry, followed in the footsteps of the Malin Harveys, investing in extensive leasehold interests in Moville and Inch and holding (amid some controversy) the Inishowen agency. As well as overseeing rent collection these chief agents controlled the main machinery of local justice – the four manor courts – as well as being justices of the peace. There seems to have been something of a challenge to proprietorial legitimacy in the 1790s when for the first time in a century there was real difficulty in enforcing manorial authority and collecting head-rents.[69] Four yeomanry corps were raised in Inishowen between 1796 and June 1798, and both the Harveys, with a Malin cavalry corps, and the Alexanders, with a Moville cavalry corps, were centrally involved. The Youngs launched an infantry corps in Culdaff, but the only early one in south Inishowen was in Burt. The local yeomanries were in effect the first semi-permanent policing agency in Inishowen, to a very large extent controlled by their sponsoring officers, the gentry/magistracy, and in their first year there was a wave of supposedly United Irish inspired disturbances in the peninsula, leading to proclamation of the barony in January 1797. But there is little hard evidence of radical organization locally, and there was certainly no '98 in Inishowen.[70] However the expansion of local yeomanry tells its own story: additional corps were established at Buncrana (1798), Moville (1798), Donagh (c.1804), Muff (c.1804) and Malin (c.1804); the possibility of a French descent was very much in local minds from 1797 and, commencing in 1799, there was an unprecedented government fortification programme on Loughs Swilly and Foyle; this culminated in the string of coastal martello towers erected around 1812.[71]

Arthur Young, who travelled through south-west Inishowen in 1776, visiting Inch island and the herring-processing enterprise of the Alexanders, was informed that the gross rents received by the Inishowen chief tenants from their undertenants was £22,000, double their outgoings in head-rent. These suspiciously rounded estimates are nevertheless of the right order of magnitude; by the 1790s the ratio may

Plate 14.1   'View of Dunree Fort or Battery in 1800 (prior to the reform since made) seen as looking across Lough Swilly to Knockallan by Sir Wm. Smith 1800' (Reproduced by permission of the Board of T.C.D.).

have been nearer 5:2.[72] The level of head-tenant profit varied of course with the size of the under-tenancy; at one extreme, some held annual tenancies without written contract, paying their rent partly in kind; at the other, some under-tenants of the local gentry enjoyed relatively favourable tenancy terms – leases of thirty-one or even sixty-one years – and soft rents.[73] George Vaughan of Buncrana, one of the most active tenant-gentry of the first half of the eighteenth century, went so far as to include covenants of renewal in his leases to Protestant under-tenants and, as Catholics were debarred by statute from holding such priviliged terms, he considered that they should be offered premia for agricultural improvements in compensation.[74] And George Harvey, a nephew claimed many years later, had found his tenantry 'uncivilised, ignorant, barbarous', but had 'tamed them and introduced order, settling more difficulties by the whiskey-bottle and horse-whip than by a mittemus or the beadle'. His private correspondence does indeed hint at a rough paternalism.[75]

With the upswing in agricultural prices towards the end of the eighteenth century, expiring under-leases were either renewed for shorter periods or were replaced by tenancy at will – a phenomenon by no means peculiar to Inishowen.[76] By then a fairly active market in unexpired leases is evident from the advertisements in the recently founded *Londonderry Journal*. The majority of these emphasised the investment potential of such leases from under-letting rather than from direct farming. In some of them there were references to 'protection leases', which seem to have been contracts between head-landlord and under-tenant guaranteeing the latter's tenancy in the event of any change in the status or identity of the chief tenant.[77] The evolution of such legal peculiarities, together with the more general adoption locally of a kind of 'tenant right' – in the form of key-money payments by incoming tenants to those vacating a holding – imply a rural society where security of tenure and family continuity in a particular townland was the norm by 1800.[78] The auctioning by chief tenants of lands out of lease, publicly or privately, was becoming much rarer by then, and rent adjustments for tenancies at will were increasingly being made by means of valuation.[79]

Despite such broadening of the proprietorial base, change in the agricultural landscape was slow to reflect it. Apart from early enclosure on the best quality land in Burt, the peninsula remained by the criteria of agricultual reformers 'unimproved'. There is isolated eighteenth-century evidence that the tenant-gentry occasionally attempted to bind under-tenants to specific improvements in their leases, detailing a programme of ditching and field enclosure, but it was not until the late 1830s that this became at all widespread.[80] In 1773 the 'gentlemen of

Inishowen' had formed a farming society which adopted the fashionable strategy of offering premia to members' tenants for various improvements, but it was a short-lived initiative.[81]

Rent levels for occupying farmers taking new tenancies rose sharply during the inflationary Napoleonic years, a trend that was accentuated locally by the high prices for barley linked to the illicit distilling boom. The post-war decline in prices coupled with the later collapse of distilling had a more general effect on farm incomes. Population growth and the consequent demand for small holdings militated against a reduction in rents either on new or existing tenancies, and perforce 'agriculture improved to meet the rent'.[82] In response, in the 1820s and 1830s there was an unprecedented flurry of tenant-gentry projects involving reclamation, farm division, resettlement and enclosure in both southern and northern parishes, most spectacularly in the case of Inch island.[83] Enclosure of old mountain commons provoked a predictable reaction; there was a spate of fence destruction and ditch levelling in the north-west in the turbulent years of 1831-2, linked to anti-tithe agitation there.[84]

Most of Inishowen shares the drawbacks common to the north-west which hinder cereal farming – cool damp summers, and many a harvest lost in early autumn storms. But the rich soils of the southern parishes responded excellently to the plough, and much of the coastal land elsewhere gave good yields when regularly enriched with sea-sand or seaweed. The 1609 Inishowen survey would imply that it was the southern parishes and the Foyle-side coast that historically were the most intensively tilled and best populated. And on the Crow maps, produced at the time of the great reletting, the Foyle coast stands out as one of two areas of denser rural settlement, the other being a crescent stretching from the Clonmany coast in the north-west to Culdaff in the north-east. Settlement in Moville and the north was depicted by Crow in townland clusters, whereas in the south it was more obviously dispersed and dominated by large free-standing farm-houses.[85] The agricultural surplus was proportionately greater in the latter area, helped by proximity to Derry's wholesale markets. But across the peninsula small-scale tillage was universal: in the Culdaff tithe returns for 1773, 28 per cent more land was designated arable than pasture, and this cannot have been exceptional.[86] Barley was the commercial cereal in the eighteenth century, oats the subsistence crop, and the latter took up perhaps three times the acreage of barley.[87] Cattle rearing and stores production greatly expanded as a commercial activity in the course of the century, with stock from the Derry region being frequently summer-grazed on Inishowen farms, and stock from Burt farmers going north to the Mintiaghs and Donagh parish. However, the growth of independent cattle ownership by local farmers can be inferred from the establishment of successful tanneries at Carndonagh and Muff by the 1790s.[88]

The exceptional 'doorstep' demand for barley between the 1780s and 1820 transformed farming on the peninsula. Such was the scale of illicit distilling during the French wars that Inishowen was in effect a price centre in the north Ulster barley trade; mountain farms were 'unnaturally forced into cultivation', and there was a regular importation of barley and malt across the mouth of the Foyle.[89] The general Irish phenomenon of marginal land reclamation was pronounced in Inishowen; in Culdaff parish, land scheduled as arable rose from 1,465 acres (st.) in 1773 to 8,016 in 1834; in Moville parish 'every patch looking to the south is cultivated'.[90]

The sharp fall in the local demand for barley in the 1820s was one element in a post-war crisis that afflicted the small-farm economy of Inishowen, the other being the contraction of domestic industry.[91] One of the responses of farmers was to send to market, and probably to cultivate, far more oats. This new trade was directed via Derry and Moville to cross-channel markets; by the early 1830s there were grain stores and a grain market in Moville, and the market in Carndonagh was handling around 3,000 tons of oats p.a., as well as 1,000 tons of barley; it had the largest turnover of oats of any market in the county, and was in the top ten in Ulster.[92] This tillage-centred response to adversity was helped by the availability of cut-out bog for reclamation, of sea sand and, in Donagh, of lime (which was only used extensively as a fertiliser after 1800).[93] On the larger farms in the south, wheat became a cash crop in the 1830s, but as a winter-sown crop it was only an option when cultivated in longer crop rotations and in enclosed fields.[94] The heaviest tillage districts in the north remained by contrast quite unenclosed: in Clonmany 'the arable is too good to lose by enclosure, and as it is tilled in run and dale it does not require it'. Clonmany however was distinctive in the abundance of the seaweed harvest; this was used to fertilize short potato-led rotations on the family strips, and there was a trade in Clonmany potatoes reportedly worth £1,400 p.a. in 1814; a side-effect was that 'beggars flock [thither] from other districts'.[95]

The potato's importance in farming and diet was late in coming. For most of the eighteenth century, oats supplemented with fish had been more important than the potato in farming diets,[96] and even as late as 1814 it was being suggested that only 'in times of scarcity' were potatoes 'the chief aliment of the poor'.[97] Oatmeal in various forms remained the summer food, potatoes and fish the winter food, with eggs and milk products as regular elements, long after 1800. But as oats became the leading cash crop in the 1820s, the opportunity cost of holding back meal for family consumption was rising, and as a result the potato's dietary – and agricultural – importance was enhanced.[98]

There were two gentry-sponsored branches of the North-West Farming Society in Inishowen in the 1820s, with over 150 members; the gospel of improvement may have held little meaning for the predominantly small-scale and undercapitalised majority of farmers – it was to be half a century before the virtues of iron ploughs, potato drills and Scotch carts percolated downwards.[99] But the elimination of vegetation burning, the diffusion of clover, and improvements in the general quality of cattle were apparent by the 1840s. The rising demand for butter and milk in the Derry market was probably a stonger stimulus for change than the propaganda of the farming societies. And the shift on the mountain farms from the summer herding of the store cattle of others to building up their own flocks of sheep owed nothing to gentry enthusiasms.[100]

The rise of the oats trade in the 1820s had coincided with the introduction of fast and reliable steam-packet services from the Foyle to Glasgow and Liverpool. Oatmeal, flour, and fresh butter were among the perishable foodstuffs which benefited from the new accessibility of British markets. A trade in eggs was another dividend; up to a hundred tons of eggs per week were being shipped out from Derry in summertime in the 1830s, and vast numbers of Inishowen hens fed on Inishowen oats were obviously hard at work. Egg money, always in women's control, was some compensation for the contraction of domestic industrial earnings.[101]

'Domestic industry' covers two central elements of the peninsula's economic development between the 1720s and the 1820s: flax – or lint – spinning, and whiskey distilling. Linen yarn manufacture had the longer pedigree; Donegal already had an excellent reputation for its yarn in the 1720s, and in the following decade Dean Henry asserted that it was women's spinning that paid the rent. Young in the 1770s called Inishowen yarn 'the best ... in all the north',[102] and indeed the baronies of Raphoe and Inishowen seem to have been the main centres both of flax cultivation and spinning in the county, with most of the yarn being sent to Derry. The exporting merchants there were supplied by country yarn merchants who procured the unbleached thread from house to house and from local markets such as Buncrana and Carndonagh.[103] The bulk of the yarn was despatched to Liverpool for the Lancashire mixed-cloth manufacture.[104] At its peak in the 1760s, 500 tons of linen yarn p.a. were being shipped from Derry, the largest quantity from any Irish port; the substitution of pure cottons in the place of mixed cloths, and the growth of a stronger internal Ulster demand for Donegal yarn, explain the gradual decline of the export trade after 1770.[105]

The first 'infant industry', set up to capture added value from the yarn trade, was a vertically-integrated fine linen manufactory begun in the mid-1730s by George Vaughan, builder of Buncrana Castle and promoter of what was in effect a new estate village between the Cranagh and Mill rivers. His 'college of weavers' lasted less than twenty years; 'the people breaking [i.e. striking], his design came to nothing' was Bishop Pocock's verdict in 1752.[106] Yet commercial linen weaving did put down roots in the southern parishes, even before the great yarn export trade faltered in the 1770s.[107] In the wake of that, a mixed-cloth weaving and printing enterprise was begun by a Manchester-trained manufacturer in Buncrana, while, further north, George Harvey's son John started up a handloom hosiery business in his estate village of Malin in 1782, capitalising on 'the known excellence and low price of thread (both linen and woollen') in the neighbourhood'.[108] Enterprises such as these had a short life-span, but two indicators of the strength of linen in the Inishowen economy were the impressively large number of small farmers receiving a subsidy for flax cultivation in 1796 (1,527 farmers had sown a total of 681 acres (st.), with 73 per cent of the claimants and 78 per cent of the flax acreage being in the southern parishes);[109] and secondly, the presence of at least 5 bleach greens in 1800, four of them in southern parishes.[110]

By 1815 these small bleach-yards were gone, and the attempt by George Cary in 1811 to start a linen market in Carndonagh was an immediate failure; most of the peninsula's fine hand-spun yarn was still leaving the peninsula for sale in Derry and Coleraine, and what was woven up was despatched unbleached to the Derry market.[111] The new technology of water-powered machine-spinning had at first benign effects: until the development of wet-spinning in the mid-1820s, mechanisation was only successful in the production of coarse yarns, suitable for sacking and sail-cloth, and one such mill was located on the edge of Buncrana. Helped by wartime naval demand and government subsidy, a precociously large canvas and sailcloth venture commenced production in 1805; at its peak the mill, the adjacent loom-shops and out-work were said to have employed some 500 operatives, and was one of the largest such enterprises in the whole country. The original promoters from county Down went bankrupt in 1810, but a succession of Derry merchant partnerships kept it going until 1876. Buncrana's modest industrial success was built on the water-power resources of the Cranagh river, but the local availability of flax and semi-skilled labour was perhaps a distant legacy from George Vaughan.[112]

Whiskey distilling was domestic industry of a different hue. The remarkable ascendancy that the peninsula had achieved by 1800 in the production of unlicensed spirits was the result of three factors: firstly, cheap locally-distilled whiskey, licit and illicit, had long been the alcohol of popular choice across Ulster, and regions with an abundance of turf and a plentiful supply of barley had tended to generate surpluses for neighbouring districts and urban markets; Inishowen was one such region by the middle of the eighteenth century. Secondly, the trade in specifically illicit spirits tended to be linked with other excise frauds; Inishowen – lying along shipping routes, relatively inaccessible by land but adjacent to populous and wealthy markets – met the requirements of the eighteenth-century smuggler. Even in the 1730s Lough Swilly was notorious as a conduit for smuggling, mainly of tea, rum and brandy, and from the time of the American war northern Inishowen became an important illicit entry point for tobacco; one family apparently owned and operated a brig for running the product directly from the United States. In the 1780s legal processors of tobacco in Derry were shrinking in number, a result of unlicensed tobacco manufactories 'in different parts of Enishowen and the suburbs of Derry'.[113] A third and more direct catalyst of the rise of Inishowen distilling was geographical: the centre of legal distilling in Ulster up to the 1770s had been Coleraine, but within a relatively short period the industry there had almost disappeared. As elsewhere, its legal distillers were adversely affected by the changes in the distillery laws in 1779, and the new excise regulations seem to have had the effect of driving the Coleraine industry across the mouth of the Foyle and into Inishowen.[114]

At least a generation before the squeeze on the legal industry, a revenue report had claimed that Inishowen 'swarms with private stills', and in 1758 the illegal local market for grain was credited with boosting the Harveys' land values in Malin.[115] But it was only from around 1780 that the cat-and-mouse game between the forces of the Revenue and Inishowen's illicit distillers started to be played in earnest. A decade later every legal distiller in Derry had been put out of business, not by the old rivals of smuggled rum or brandy, but by a flood of illicit whiskey, coming mainly out of Inishowen.[116] By then few tillage farmers on the peninsula – and fewer millers – had not been drawn into the 'whiskey economy'. In the 1790s 'some respectable names' were rumoured to be linked with distilling and smuggling, and when in 1793 rewards were offered in connection with disturbances in the northern parishes – seemingly a smuggling vendetta – the chief 'delinquents' being sought were stated to have incomes in excess of £100 p.a. Indeed the price of illicit prosperity was evident by the 1790s – a general increase in violence in the form of armed clashes with revenue officers, which contrasted with the previous lack of rural disturbance in Inishowen.[117]

The roller-coaster fortunes of thousands of Inishowen families in the first two decades of the nineteenth century were to a surprising degree linked to whiskey, and the strong correlation between the distilling cycle, the smuggling cycle, and the linen yarn cycle conspired to produce extremes of prosperity and distress.[118] It was in this period that the peninsula established a national reputation as heartland of the illicit distillers and, equally, the source of the finest malt spirit in the country.[119] In the years up to 1814 many tried to guess the scale and profitability of the local black economy: one parliamentary witness in 1808 suggested that up to 1,300 stills existed in the barony; an estimate a decade later reckoned that before 1814 Inishowen had supplied 'all the neighbouring counties with spirits to the amount of several thousand gallons a day'.[120] Whatever the industry's true size, it was self-evident that until 1814 the forces deployed by the state – revenue officers backed up by local yeomanry or regular soldiers – were quite unable to smother the industry.

The proliferation of small stills and malt-houses spread the profits of distilling widely, but despite portrayals of the industry as an egalitarian collective enterprise, there were it seems 'godfathers': millers and strong farmers who – at least up to 1810 – played a central role. The larger stills (of around 100 gallons) were controlled, if not actually worked, by them, and they bought in much of their barley needs from their smaller neighbours; and larger farmers and millers were said to have been responsible for marketing the whiskey.[121] The most important such markets were at Moville and at Magilligan on the opposite shore, one or other being held 'almost every day' in the early years of the nineteenth century; barley from counties Derry and Antrim was sold or bartered against Inishowen whiskey. The survival of such markets, with established procedures for price-setting, were essential if smaller distillers and barley producers were to share in the bonanza.[122] Very substantial quantities of whiskey were also sold in Derry, albeit less publicly; it is not clear whether Moville/Magilligan or Derry was the main forwarding point for the product, but by whatever means it seems to have achieved 'brand' recognition across Ulster and even as far as Dublin by 1810.[123] A trade also existed across the North Channel: a seasonal traffic, specifically between Culdaff and Islay, was carried on in which barley, herrings and young horses were exchanged for Inishowen whiskey.[124]

The complicity of the tenant-gentry in the trade was often asserted by outsiders, but the evidence is ambiguous. Enhanced land values gave everyone a vested interest in the whiskey economy as long as it lasted, but most of those with a knowledge of the world outside seem to have been aware of the folly of relying on distilling, and saw in flax and linen a safer activity to promote.[125] But Henry Hart cannot have been unique in supplying a number of his Muff tenants with barley seed in 1798, to be paid off the following year partly in cash, partly in whiskey. Several of the gentry made highly publicised efforts, in conjunction with local yeomanry, to banish distilling from their property with very limited success; but the legal sanctions were inadequate for, as one Muff man said, his still-owning tenants 'had leases against me, and I could not get quit of them'.[126]

From 1810 there were more robust efforts by the Revenue board to put down the industry, but policy divisions in Dublin, problems of military and Revenue logistics, and extensive corruption on the ground allowed undiminished activity for several more years. 'The distillers', it was said in 1810, were 'well-armed, and would resist any force but the military, in which they would be joined by the whole population', and there was an escalation of violence, notably in the northern parishes.[127] Under pressure, the distillers began to organise more covertly behind the mask of Ribbonism, and several magistrates saw political, even sectarian designs in the reactive violence of the distillers – which culminated in 1816 in the assassination of one of the leaders of the north Inishowen gentry and a recent opponent of distilling, Norton Butler.[128] The most notorious breakdown of official authority occurred in the relatively inaccessible coastal plain of Urris in Clonmany: between 1811 and 1815 a mafia of local distillers sealed the neighbourhood off from Revenue, yeoman and army intervention; in the summer of 1814 there were said to have been 200 distillers at work, 'each man ... [having carried] thither a musket and ammunition with his still'.[129]

In the winter of 1813-4 a re-modelled system for the collective fining of all inhabitants in a townland where a still had been captured was introduced, but this was not fully enforced by the grand jury until the spring of 1815. From that point the penal size of the fines, the political will to enforce them, and the presence at last of a large, well-organised army presence tipped the balance of advantage for many. Dublin Castle, specifically Chief Secretary Peel, was determined to be rid of the embarrassment of Inishowen distilling, and thus a large army presence was maintained in the northern parishes for more than two years. The trade was driven out of the better-off districts into the 'barren mountains', and farmers of any substance dropped their involvement; the bigger stills disappeared, and the trade 'fell into the hands of the poorer sort'.[130] The bulk of townland fines between 1814 and 1818 were imposed on the four northern parishes, but there was an evident intensification of that pattern: in 1814-15, 43 per cent of the fines had been levied on the southern parishes, whereas from the Lent assizes in 1816 to the Lent assizes of 1818, they bore only 16 per cent of the total. Throughout the five-year fining offensive, the parishes of Culdaff and Clonmany between them received two-fifths of the total still fines levied on the barony.[131]

Fines owed by Inishowen townlands amounted to nearly £50,000 by 1817, a figure out of all proportion to the resources of the inhabitants. Some landlords made agreements with their tenants to pay outstanding fines in return for undertakings never to resume distilling.[132] But there were many 'guilty' townlands in arrears which were subjected to repeated cattle drives by revenue officials, and livestock numbers on the peninsula were said to have been greatly depleted as a result. By 1816 not just distilling but the whole agrarian economy was in crisis in the northern parishes; barley prices had collapsed, cattle had been impounded, and quite independent of the Revenue offensive there was the post-war slide in agricultural prices and a run of wretched harvests in 1815 and 1816. The typhus epidemic of 1817, particularly severe in Inishowen, was symptomatic of the thorough collapse in local fortunes.[133]

The end of townland fining in 1820, and the coming of low grain prices and occasional bumper harvests in the following twenty years, allowed some recovery of distilling in Moville, Culdaff and Donagh parishes. But although the reputation of Inishowen whiskey remained untarnished, the scale of illicit activity was always modest. The opening of a legal distillery in Burt (in 1813) and the re-birth of legal distilling in Derry did not offset the loss to the local black economy,[134] although the legal offspring of illicit 'Inishowen' that emerged in Derry was a remarkable product: the first commercially successful distillery there, Watt & Smyth's Bogside enterprise, was equipped with one of the first of the revolutionary 'patent' stills in Ireland, and patent spirit, suitably blended, became a cheap and acceptable alternative to illicit country malt; the Watts, who had made their first fortune in linen in Rathmelton and Derry, later became the undisputed whiskey princes of the north-west.[135]

*　*　*

The 1841 census enumerated 55,462 people in Inishowen, rather less than a fifth of the county Donegal total. The baronial population in 1660 had probably been less than 8,000, but the poll-money returns of that year suggest that its share of county population was over a quarter.[136] In other words, the demographic transformation on the peninsula, while being incontrovertibly the critical determinant of economic change, was not exceptional by Donegal or indeed national standards. From the parish returns for 1660, 1766 and the far more robust figures for 1821, it is possible to get some sense of the trajectory of growth and the shifting patterns of that growth within Inishowen over two centuries. Not adjusting for a myriad of possible statistical distortions, it would seem that the barony's population grew by around 1.0 per cent p.a. between 1660 and 1766, and by 1.3 per cent between 1766 and 1821; over the following two decades it grew by 0.7 per cent p.a. It is a fairly safe speculation that growth in the century after 1660 was punctuated by sharp reversals (war in the late 1680s, food shortages, epidemics and out-migration in the 1720s and mid-1740s), and short periods of rapid expansion (perhaps the 1660s, and probably the early 1680s, the 1690s, the 1710s, the late 1740s and early 1750s), episodes witnessing spurts of in-migration (prior to 1710) and trade-driven economic recovery.[137] The apparently higher rate of growth between the 1760s and 1821 is entirely consistent with the wider picture for late eighteenth-century Ulster, although the hearth-tax figures (available only at county level) imply that Inishowen growth was well below that of the county as a whole.[138] The hearth-tax trends suggest that Donegal's overall expansion was distinctly faster between mid-century and 1791 than in the subsequent thirty years; Inishowen's reported age structure in 1821 points to rates of growth that are themselves below the county average in the pre-1821 generation.[139]

As for shifts within Inishowen in the pace of growth, the figures hint at a not unexpected north/south contrast. Between 1660 and 1765 the southernmost group of parishes, the zone where linen weaving made most progress – Burt, Inch, Muff – had almost the highest growth rate in Inishowen, but over the longer run and taking the southern parishes as a whole (i.e. including Fahan, Desertegney and Moville), human expansion there was slightly lower than in the less well endowed northern parishes. The latter had 39.4 per cent of Inishowen's population in 1660, 42.3 in 1766, and 45.0 in 1821. (The northern share had edged back to 44.3 per cent in 1841, but this was mainly because of the strong expansion at the northern end of Moville parish, which included the new town of Moville.) Without closer parish analysis it is not possible to distinguish what may have been particular to Inishowen's population history, or to determine how far the demo-graphic behaviour of, for example, Presbyterian Inishowen differed from that of Catholic Inishowen. At first sight the atypically strong rate of growth in Clonmany, the most wholly Catholic parish on the peninsula, is suggestive, but its particularly rich supply of marine fertiliser may be more relevant in accounting for its 1.7 per cent growth rate between 1766 and 1821.[140] However, in accounting for later differentials in deceleration, contrasts in the denominational propensity to emigrate are of central relevance.[141] But whatever one's denominational label, relative proximity to Derry city – as employment magnet in its own right and stepping stone to the world beyond – was an important variable explaining out-migration by the early nineteenth century; it was after all primarily the inflow of Donegal migrants which inflated the city by more than 50 per cent between 1821 and 1841.[142]

It remains perhaps a little surprising that Inishowen's inland abundance of turf, its unreclaimed heart of blanket bog, was not more vigorously colonised in the early nineteenth century. Only 41 per cent of the total land area was cultivated (i.e. regularly cropped or intensively grazed) at the time of the first revision of the Ordnance Survey in 1847-8.[143] The huge rise in population had to a great extent been contained around the coast, and in that zone inherited agricultural practices – unenclosed fields, multi-household management of the arable ground in 'rundale', and short crop rotations – proved remarkably flexible in the face of an intensification of settlement and subdivision of farms.[144] However, without the growth of secondary employment – kelping, fishing, spinning, weaving, malting, distilling – the old agriculture would have been far less resilient.

Population density in several parishes was very high by Ulster standards in the 1840s: the northern parts of Fahan and Moville were close to 500 persons per squre mile of cultivated land, and Clonmany was over 600; Burt at 266 and Inch at 240 were a different agricultural world.[145] The long process of intaking or reclamation of marginal land continued, posssibly accelerated, in the pre-famine generation: between the first plotting of the Ordnance Survey, c.1833-4, and the first revision in 1847-8, there appears to have been 12.1 per cent added to the stock of cultivated land in the northern parishes and 9.6 per cent added in the barony overall; the range of reclamation recorded varied from 0.5 per cent added in Burt (between 1831 and 1847) to a remarkable 14.8 per cent in Donagh (between 1834 and 1848).[146]

There is little evidence of significant inter-parish migration in the era of rapid growth – although there was some overspill on to Magilligan in the early ninteenth century.[147] One indirect pointer to long-term settlement stability is the distribution of the O'Doherty patronymic: in the 1660s, as we have seen, 64 per cent of the Inishowen O'Dohertys paying hearth-tax were in the four northern parishes; 65 per cent of Inishowen O'Dohertys listed in the Griffith's Valuation c.1856 were similarly located; the only parish to show a relative influx of O'Dohertys was Fahan – and this reflected immigration into Buncrana town.[148]

An almost inevitable concomitant of rural population growth was increased inequality within farming society. In the three-quarters of the barony that became the Inishowen Poor Law Union, the top quartile of landholders in 1845 occupied 36 per cent of the agricultural land, the quartile with least land occupied collectively about 2 per cent. This is a somewhat more skewed distribution than that suggested in the one parish for which a comparison across time is possible – Culdaff: in a tithe survey of the parish carried out in 1773 the top quartile of landholders had held 48 per cent of the land, the bottom quartile about 11 per cent. In 1856, the top quartile there controlled 59 per cent of the tenanted land, the bottom a little over 3 per cent.[149] And while there are obvious dangers in comparing these returns, they do point to a self-evident central social process: the economic marginalisation of the poorest households, evident in the expansive eighteenth century, doubly so in the conditions of the early nineteenth century; in the 1831 census, just under a fifth of the adult males of Inishowen were returned as agricultural labourers; they formed a majority of the adult males in Muff and Burt, but a mere 2 per cent in Clonmany.[150] By contrast, every parish had its increasingly distinct knot of strong farmers or, to use the formula employed in the 1831 census, agricultural occupiers employing labourers; there were 856 such farmers enumerated in Inishowen that year (as against 6,780 who declared that they were not employing labour from outside their family); they ranged from the 54 solid farmers in Burt, to the 181 more modest employers in Lower Moville to the 13 in Clonmany (a mere 1 per cent of the parish's farmers).[151] Included among the latter were presumably some of the ex-godfathers of illicit distilling, including the remarkable Micky Shane (Micheál Mór) O'Doherty of Glen House, the wealthy miller, land agent, tithe proctor, and faction leader.[152] These *parvenu* gentlemen and strong farmers were able to weather the depressed state of farm prices because the labour-abundant environment favoured all who controlled access to land – and this included the larger tenant-farmers – allowing them to extract a greater share of the meagre surplus of under-tenants' and small-holders' output; in other words if they did not prosper as improving farmers, they did as rentiers.

For all the long history of population growth on the peninsula, there was no period in its post-conquest history as trend-breaking as the years between 1815 and 1850: by the time of the 1841 census, population growth had greatly slowed down, most emphatically in the southern parishes where there was actually a slight population decline recorded between 1831 and 1841 (the 1831 census is of course slightly suspect, but it was in the same district that the greatest population falls within the barony were to occur during the famine).[153] Low-level emigration to north America was nothing new – there was an out-agent for Derry emigration ships in Fahan parish in the 1760s and 1770s,[154] but it was only in the generation after 1820 that large-scale emigration out of the peninsula began.[155] Underlying the earlier stages of this haemorrhage was the multifaceted crisis in domestic and farm earnings which, for landholders, climaxed in the 1820s. This crisis was softened, not resolved, by the unprecedented intervention of the local gentry in tenant farming (squaring fields, breaking up rundale, consolidating some tenancies and displacing the already marginalised). It was also eased by the growth of male seasonal migration to Clydeside (from about 1820) and by female involvement in egg production, muslin sprigging and, later, shirt-making.[156] But it was the now highly visible migration to North America – several dozen were leaving each parish each year in the mid-thirties – that symbolised the changed state of the local economy.

Whatever about farming households, for those of agricultural labourers there is evidence only of immiseration in the 1830s and early 1840s. Their crisis climaxed in the famine years, but the relatively limited overall fall of population in Inishowen durng the 1840s suggests that the catastrophic rise in food prices hit the rural proletariat in the richer southern parishes even harder than the poorest families in the north; between them, the northern parishes had lost 9.4 per cent of their 1841 population by 1851, whereas there was a drop of slightly over 20 per cent in the combined parishes of Burt, Inch and Muff.[157] This heavier population loss in the south and west was presumably more a function of heavier migration – perhaps only to Derry – than of greater excess mortality.[158]

The pre-famine years were trend-breaking in other respects. The fall in the price of imported manufactured goods and the less obvious strengthening of stronger farmers' incomes led to a growth of shops and of other town-based services in the five towns of the peninsula. Proximity to Derry had previously held back urban development, but changing patterns of rural consumption were well in hand by 1845.[159] The factors at work stimulating urban growth varied somewhat from town to town: Buncrana was more factory village than market centre; Carndonagh was the principal fair and commercial centre north of Derry; Culdaff and even more clearly Malin were still little more than successful estate villages; and Moville, beyond being a secondary market centre for the east of the peninsula, was blossoming as the summer resort of the bourgeoisie of early Victorian Derry, thanks not a little to the regular steam-boat services.[160]

These towns were vanguards in less visible processes, the rise of popular literacy and the decline of Irish speaking: with 100 schools operating in Inishowen in the 1830s (half of which were autonomous or 'hedge' schools) it is not entirely surprising that 47 per cent of the over-fives in the barony claimed to be able to read (English) in 1841, and a third of these to write also. Reading and writing scores ranged from 32.0 per cent in Presbyterian Burt to 13.4 in Clonmany, but in the towns there was little north/south contrast: total literacy levels ranged from 49.1 in Buncrana to 40.1 per cent in Moville. The estate village of Malin in the north considerably excelled the less well-constructed Muff in the south in terms of literacy. The evidence on language use is much more problematic, but it would seem that an eighteenth-century language contrast between north and south was substantially removed by the 1840s, with probably only a small minority of townlands having at that stage a majority of Irish monoglots.[161]

And with the new literacy, the new politics. The peninsula, for all its religious heterogeneity, had not been convulsed by sectarian conflict in the 1790s or in the following generation; there was no Orange lodge on the peninsula, and the Chichesters' many freeholders were spared from being dragooned into electoral battles on behalf of their master. The only Inishowen figure to enter national politics in that period was George Vaughan Hart, a younger son who made a controversial fortune in the Indian army before becoming one of the county MPs in 1813; an ally of the Duke of Abercorn and a government supporter until his death in 1831, he was a less than strident opponent of Catholic Emancipation and did not stir up local animosities.[162]

There was however a distinct rise in the political temperature in the course of the 1820s, especially in the north where the Young family's evangelical enthusiasm had a political edge, and Brunswick Clubs

Plate 14.2   'Sketch of Dresden, the Minister's House, for the Parish of Clonmany as seen looking the way of the Mountain of Mamore by Sir Wm. Smith 1907' (Reproduced by kind permission of the Board of T.C.D.).

briefly sprouted up on the eve of Catholic Emancipation. Father Maginn, PP of Buncrana, informed the Poor Inquiry six years later that 'until ... 1829 all classes ... lived on the most amicable terms ... A Brunswick Club, however, was got up at that time by a few gentlemen who had more fear than prudence; and the Protestants ... were paraded before their Catholic friends and neighbours, as if it were in armed hostility towards them and their claims. Ever since a kind of mutual distrust and want of confidence in each other has prevailed: this has given something like a party complexion to society ...'.[163]

The Catholic clergy, with their own political divisions to contend with in the diocese, were not in general involved in forwarding national political isssues, but the tithe agitation of 1831-2 had strong local resonances.[164] Tithe reform was championed by the newly-appointed parish priest to Clonmany, Father William O'Donnell, whose personal and family biography encapsulates something of the transformation of Catholic fortunes underway. Known as the 'Waterloo priest', he was a military veteran, a fine horseman and a late vocation. His O'Donnell line had been erenaghs in Fahan; one of his paternal great-uncles had been the parish priest of Buncrana who had signed the Catholic qualification oath in 1782, another, Denis (Donncha) O'Donnell, the only Inishowen poet whose compositions in Irish survive;[165] his uncle Charles as curate in Clonca had overseen the building of the first post-Reformation Catholic church on the peninsula c.1784 and was later bishop of Derry; his two brothers, Charles and Denis, ordained before him, had both died in the 1817 epidemic.[166] Father O'Donnell became something of a folk-hero on being imprisoned in 1837 for non-payment of tithes, but even before this the tithe issue had brought to the surface less focussed discontents in several parishes.[167] A demonstration of a thousand people, calling for tithe and rent reductions, passed through Carndonagh in January 1832, and a correspondent to Dublin Castle told of an anti-tithe meeting held there in the hungry year of 1837 at which '16,000' had attended.[168] There were frightened claims from local JPs that an elaborate 'Rightboy' system was functioning, with a cellular committee system.[169]

Even if that was a wild exaggeration, northern and western Inishowen stands out as one of the most 'disturbed' regions of Ulster in the Poor Inquiry survey of 1835/6.[170] It was not directly sectarian, in the way that the campaign for Repeal in the early 'forties was. But it is hard to see how the popular politicisation of these years could fail to have had polarising effects; it was a time when local Catholicism was being re-empowered — whether in the appearance of chapel bells or in the spread of Catholic-managed 'national' schools — and self-confident priests like Fathers O'Donnell and Maginn with strong political instincts were leading towards a re-definition of the community.[171] By the 1840s O'Connell's message was being read in largely sectarian colours; it seems unlikely, for instance, that there were many Presbyterians or churchmen among the '7,000' who attended the monster meeting near Carndonagh in 1843. But perhaps the most potent sign that political power was beginning to slip from the hands of the old tenant gentry were the first elections for the Inishowen Board of Guardians. George Young recorded in his diary for November 1840 'our mortification' at being defeated for the chairmanship of the Board by 'Big Thomas Doherty, Muff', with the support of 'the Papists and two nominal Protestants'.[172] Doherty, like his namesake in Clonmany, had climbed from land agency to fragile gentility (having recently become proprietor of the old Cary estate at Redcastle); both enjoyed ambiguous social status and displayed uncertain denominational loyalty. It was men such as these who were the unlikely harbingers of democracy in O'Doherty's Country.[173]

References

1. *Cal. S.P. Ire.*, *1600-01*, p. 256; B. Lacy, *Siege city: The story of Derry and Londonderry* (Belfast, 1990), ch. 5; H. Morgan, *Tyrone's rebellion: the outbreak of the Nine Years' War in Tudor Ireland* (Dublin, 1993), pp 119-20. For early cartographic images see those of Mercator in Lacy, *Siege city*, p. 66, and of Francis Jobson on cover wraps of R. Bell, *The book of Ulster surnames* (Belfast, 1988).

2. B. Bonner, *That audacious traitor* (Dublin, 1975), chs. 3 and 4, passim.

3. Sir Henry Docwra to the Privy Council, 10 March 1600/01, *Cal. S.P. Ire.*, *1600-01*, p. 213; O. Davies & H. P. Swan, 'The castles of Inishowen' in *U.J.A.*, 3rd. ser., ii (1939), 185, 189; Bonner, *Traitor*, pp 135-42; R. J. Hunter, 'Sir Ralph Bingley, c.1570-1627: Ulster planter' in P. Roebuck (ed.), *Plantation to partition ...* (Belfast, 1981), pp 16-17; Lacy, *Siege city*, p. 77.

4. Docwra's 'Description of Lough Foyle ...', in *Cal. S.P. Ire.*, *1600-01*, p. 94.

5. It is not clear whether this refers to the 'island' of Malin or, more specifically, to the Isle of Doagh, which was one of the O'Doherty refuge areas.

6. Docwra's 'Description of Lough Foyle ...' in *Cal. S.P. Ire.*, *1600-01*, p. 94.

7. Capt. John Vaughan to [Sir Robert Cecil], 4 Sept. 1601, in *Cal. S.P. Ire.*, *1601-02*, pp 56-7.

8. Davies and Swan, 'Castles', p. 193.

9. Bonner, *Traitor*, pp 124-6; Lacy, *Siege city*, p. 77.

10. Sir Francis Shaen to the Earl of Salisbury, 30 Nov. 1607, in *Cal. S.P. Ire.*, *1606-08*, p. 340.

11. T. W. Moody, *The Londonderry plantation, 1609-40 ...* (Belfast, 1939), p. 161; John McCavitt, The lord deputyship of Sir Arthur Chichester in Ireland 1605-16 (unpublished PhD dissertation, Queen's University, Belfast, 1988), pp 307-9, 314.

12. Moody, *Londonderry plantation*, p. 60.

13. *Cal. pat. rolls. Irel., Jas. I*, p. 161.

14. Ibid.

15. M. Perceval-Maxwell, *The Scottish migration to Ulster in the reign of James I* (London, 1973), pp 54-5, 66-7, 76-7, 80-1; McCavitt, 'Chichester', pp 98, 306-19.

16. Bonner, *Traitor*, pp 267-71.

17. R. J. Hunter, 'Carew's survey of Ulster, 1611: The "voluntary works"' in *U.J.A.*, 3rd ser., xxxviii (1975), 82.

18. See P. Roebuck, 'The making of an Ulster great estate: The Chichesters ... 1599-1648', in *R.I.A. Proc.*, lxxix (1979), sect. C, 1-25.

19. J. H. Andrews, 'An early map of Inishowen' in *Long room*, vii (Spring 1973), 19-25; Hunter, 'Towns in the Ulster Plantation' in *Studia Hib.*, xi (1971), 25, 40-1, 45, 79. No roads are shown on the 1660 version of the survey, but a copy by Thomas Phillips [B.L. Maps K. Top. 52 (43)] in 1685 shows a road from Derry to Fahan, with a bridge at what later became Burnfoot.

20. A. Young, *Three hundred years in Inishowen* ... (Belfast, 1929), pp 35, 46, 51, 300 (and see also her working papers: P.R.O.N.I. D.3045); Moody, *Londonderry plantation*, pp 59, 131-2, 161, 173-4, 277, 280-3, 349. Sir Arthur's brother Thomas held leases for lands in Burt.

21. Hunter, 'Carew's survey'; Bonner, *Traitor*, pp 219-22; Roebuck, 'Great estate', p. 22.

22. Bonner, *Traitor*, pp 218-9. An O'Doherty and a MacLaughlin held lives leases as well. For the rights of an Irish tenant to damages if disturbed before the expiry of a lease, see Viscount Chichester to the Bishop of Derry, 22 June 1636 in T. W. Moody and J. G. Simms (ed.), *The bishops of Derry and the Irish Society*, i (Dublin, 1968), pp 209-10.

23. R. J. Hunter, 'The settler population of an Ulster plantation county' in *Donegal Annual*, x, 2 (1972), pp 147-9.

24. Perceval-Maxwell, *Scottish migration*, pp 293-302, 366. The scattering of the Irish population from the southern parishes may have been a consequence of Wingfield's scorched earth campaign carried out during Sir Cahir's rebellion; however, the thinning of the indigenous population may have occurred before 1603 and there may not have been a chance for it to recover before 1610.

25. Young, *Three hundred years*, p. 23; M. Perceval-Maxwell, *The outbreak of the Irish rebellion of 1641* (Dublin, 1994), p. 219.

26. J. P. Brown, *The MacLaughlins of Clan Owen: a study in Irish history* (Boston, 1879), pp 9, 62-3.

27. S. Pender, *A census of Ireland, circa 1659* (Dublin, 1939), pp 60-64.

28. For the 1665 returns, see P.R.O.N.I., T.6232. The Irish share in Templemore in 1665 was *c.* 64 per cent and in Fahan *c.*78 per cent. Bonner, *Traitor*, p. 226 understates the British presence in these returns. See also W. Macafee and V. Morgan, 'Population in Ulster, 1660-1760', in Roebuck, *Plantation to partition*, pp 47-53.

29. R. C. Simington (ed.), *The civil survey, A.D. 1654-1656*, iii: *Counties of Donegal, Londonderry and Tyrone* (Dublin, 1937), pp 1-19. Clonmany and Templemore have anomalous and oddly high ratios.

30. Hunter, 'Settler population', 147-9; P.R.O.N.I., T.6232.

31. Pender, *Census*, p. 64; [B. Mitchell], *O'Doherty information pack* (Derry, 1985), p. 20.

32. Moody and Simms, *Bishops of Derry*, pp 1, 184, 186.

33. For the grant of Inishowen churchland to the see of Derry, see ibid., pp 1, 54-71.

34. Rev. Edward Berwick (ed.), *The Rawdon papers* ... (London, 1819), pp 63-4, 75-6; Rev. J. B. Leslie, *Derry clergy and parishes* (Enniskillen, 1937), pp 8-9; Bonner, *Traitor*, pp 216-7; Alistair Rowan, *The buildings of Ireland: North-west Ulster* (London, 1979), pp 469-70.

35. Bishop of Derry to Visc. Chichester, 18 Aug, 1635, in Moody and Simms, *Bishops of Derry*, pp 202-3; Leslie, *Derry clergy*, p. 165; Rowan, *Buildings*, pp 224-5.

36. Leslie, *Derry clergy*, pp 161-2; Bonner, *Traitor*, p. 219. The MacLaughlins' mother was credited by Michael Harkin with the composition of a lament on her son's apostasy, and tales about the two brothers and their contrasting fortunes were still circulating 200 years later: 'Maghtochair' [Michael Harkin], *Inishowen: Its history, traditions and antiquities* (Carndonagh, 1935), pp 83-4; Young, *Three hundred years*, pp 83-4; C. McGlinchey, *The last of the name* (Belfast, 1986), pp 63-4.

37. Leslie, *Derry clergy*, pp 154, 162, 169, 190.

38. Ezechiel Hopkins, Bishop of Derry to the Duke of Ormonde, 1 Dec.1682, in *Report on the MSS of the Duke of Ormonde*, new ser., vi (H.M.C., 1911), pp 486-7.

39. Arthur Langford to Bishop King, 3 April 1691, King corr. (T.C.D. Lyons coll. MSS 1995-2008/117); copy, William King, Bishop of Derry to Arthur Upton, 23 June 1696, King out-letters (T.C.D. MS 750/1); 'Maghtochair', *Inishowen*, pp 98, 142, 168; *Jnl. of the Assoc. for the Preservation of the Memorials of the Dead in Irl.*, iv (1898-1900), 16; Young, *Three hundred years*, p. 46; Leslie, *Derry clergy*, pp 162, 190, 265; Simms, 'Donegal and the Jacobite War' in *Donegal Annual*, vii, 2 (1967), 215-220; B. Bonner, *Our Inis Eoghain heritage: the parishes of Culdaff and Cloncha* (Dublin, 1972), pp 268-9; McGlinchey, *Last of the name*, pp 60-1.

40. Patrick McLachlan to King, 20 Oct. 1698, King corr. (Lyons coll., 581). For a picture of the frightened state of mind of the Church of Ireland clergy in the face of the Presbyterian advance, see Rev John Humble, Donagh to King, 6 May 1698, King corr. (Lyons, /571).

41. Copy, King to Edward Cary, 12 April 1698, King out-letters.

42. George Vaughan, Buncrana to King, 22 Oct. 1717, King corr. (Lyons, /1829); Rev W .D. Killen, *History of the congregations of the Presbyterian church in Ireland ...* (Belfast, 1886), pp 73, 78, 143, 174, 192, 204.

43. Ibid., pp 78, 192, 204: Thomas Harvey – Carndonagh 1701-18; Thomas Harvey jr. – Moville 1715-18; John Harvey jr. – Malin 1717-33; Thomas, son of Thomas Harvey jr. – Moville *c*.1728-47. These ministers do not feature in A. Young's Harvey genealogy (*Three hundred years*, pp 128-33), but the father and grandfather of George Harvey, builder of Malin Hall, were evidently dissenters, and the genealogy omits many of the reputed 19 children of John Harvey of Derry (ibid., pp 122, 132-3). For oral tradition on the origins of the Inishowen Harveys' wealth, see 'Maghtochair', *Inishowen*, pp 142-3.

44. *First report of the commissioners of public instruction* (Parl. papers, 1835, xxxiii), pp 244a-267a. See also Alan Gailey, 'The Scots element in north Irish popular culture' in *Enthnologia Europea*, viii, 1 (1975), esp. maps on pp 6-7, 17.

45. Bonner, *Traitor*, p. 246. By 1834 the northern proportion had receded to 22 per cent: *Rep. Comm. Pub. Instr., 1836*. For a comparable case of delayed Protestant growth in west Donegal – at Inishkeel – see V. Treadwell, 'Background to a hidden age' in *Donegal Annual*, vi, 2 (1965), 119, and on the wider issue of delayed Presbyterian colonisation in west Ulster, see Macafee and Morgan, 'Population in Ulster', pp 58-60.

46. Patrick McLachlan to King, 22 Jan. 1694/5, King corr. (Lyons, /401; cf. /311, /366-7, /372).

47. Daniel McLachline to King, 9 Sept. 1701; Dean Bolton to King, n.d. [*c*.1704] King corr. (Lyons, /831, /1146b); Rev William Henry, 'Hints towards a natural and topographical history of the counties Sligo, Donegal, Fermanagh and Lough Erne' (N.A., M.2533), pp 68-9; Young, *Three hundred years*, p. 82. There were 80

Clonmany communicants who in 1703 did not understand English: McLachlan to King, 6 Nov. 1703 (Lyons, /1047).

48. Translation by Andrew Smith in *The Field Day anthology of Irish writing* (Derry, 1991), i, pp 261-2. For the Colgans' continuing associations with Carndonagh, see Bonner, 'The priests of Donagh' in *Donegal Annual*, xv (1990), 13-16.

49. Copy, King to Tristram Cary, 27 Dec. 1701, King out-letters 1701-02 (T.C.D. MS 750/2).

50. Copy, King to George Vaughan, 5 March 1701-02, King out-letters 1701-02; W. P. Burke, *Irish priests in penal times* (Waterford, 1914), p. 115; Bonner, *Derry: an outline history of the diocese* (Dublin, 1982), pp 212, 223-4.

51. *J.A.M.P.I.*, v, 168, 171; vi, 247.

52. Probably the most successful eighteenth-century men of Inishowen Catholic parentage were the London emigrés Charles Macklin the actor/dramatist (see Bonner, *Inis Eoghain heritage*, pp 257-68; W. W. Appleton, *Charles Macklin: an actor's life* (Cambridge, Mass., 1961)), and John Toland, the controversial philosopher and political lobbyist. There is a certain irony in the probability that Toland, the deracinated atheist, oversaw the first translation of Keating's *Foras feasa ar Éirinn* into English, doubly justifying the nickname he earned in local tradition, *Eoghan na leabhair* (see D. Berman and A. Harrison, 'John Toland and Keating's "History of Ireland (1723)"' in *Donegal Annual*, 36 (1984), 25-9); cf. 'Maghtochair', *Inishowen*, p. 100. For Inishowen resonances in Macklin's writing, see the extract from 'The True born Irishman' in Deane, *Field Day anthology*, i, pp 542-6.

53. Moody and Simms, *Bishops of Derry*, i, pp 209-10; Roebuck, 'Great estate', pp 14-19; Roebuck, 'Landlord indebtedness in Ulster in the seventeenth and eighteenth centuries' in J. M. Goldstrom and L. A. Clarkson (eds), *Irish population, economy, and society* ... (Oxford, 1981), pp 141-5.

54. Roebuck, 'Indebtednesss', pp 137-43.

55. Rental and valuation of Enishowen, 1741 (P.R.O.N.I., D. 835/3/1).

56. D. Dickson, 'Middlemen', in T. Bartlett and D. Hayton (eds), *Penal age and golden era* ... (Belfast, 1979), pp 162-85.

57. Rent roll of the Donegall estate, 1798 (P.R.O.N.I., D.835/3/2); D. Dickson, The barony of Inishowen in the century before the famine (unpublished B.A. dissertation, Dept. of Modern History, Trinity College Dublin, 1969), p. 71, fns. 7-9; W. A. Maguire, 'Lord Donegall and the hearts of steel' in *I.H.S.*, xxi, 84 (1979), 368-9.

58. George Harvey to Rev. John Harvey, 1 Dec. 1770, Harvey MSS (in possession of Mr Ian Harvey, Ballymena, county Antrim).

59. 1798 Donegall rent roll; 'Maghtochair', *Inishowen*, pp 98-9, 142-3; McGlinchey, *Last of the name*, p. 60. Cf. W. H. Crawford, 'The Ulster Irish in the eighteenth century' in *Ulster Folklife*, xxvii (1982), 25-6.

60. George Dougherty to Morgan O'Connell, 22 March 1765; John Dougherty to same, 22 March 1765 (N.L.I., Reports on MSS in private collections, ed. J. F. Ainsworth, no. 3, 61, O'Connell Fitzsimons papers); 1798 rent roll. Maghtochair suggests that this family had the unusual distinction of having served in the Williamite forces – unlike their Jacobite cousins in nearby Tullagh – and that they did indeed emigrate to America on selling their leasehold interests ('Maghtochair', *Inishowen*, p. 98).

61. George Harvey to Rev. John Harvey, 20 April 1771, Harvey MSS; Maguire, 'Donegall and the hearts of steel', 353-76.

62. 1798 Donegall rent roll; Reg. of Deeds, Dublin, 275/391/178091; 277/378/178512; 279/36/178373; 279/39/178375.

63. 1798 rent roll.

64. Ibid; rent roll of the Donegall estate, c.1825 (P.R.O.N.I. D.971/5/5A); Dickson, 'Barony of Inishowen', p. 72, fn. 18; p. 78, fns. 10-1l.

65. William Lyon to Chichester Skeffington, 22 March 1802, Foster MSS (P.R.O.N.I., D.562/2851); 1825 rent-roll; Dickson, Barony of Inishowe', p. 77, fns. 6-7.

66. Rev Edward Chichester, *The oppressions and cruelties of Irish revenue officers* (London, 1818), p. 31.

67. This was a frequent matter of comment in the Ordnance Survey memoirs, e.g. Statistical return of Donagh parish c.1825 (R.I.A., O.S. memoirs, Box 21, viii), pp 6-7.

68. Young, *Three hundred years*, p. 83; O. Snoddy, 'Notes on volunteers, yeomen and orangemen of county Donegal' in *Donegal Annual*, viii, 1 (1969), 49-73; D. Murphy, *Derry, Donegal and modern Ulster 1790-1921* (Culmore, 1981), pp 7-9.

69. See, for example, *The Londonderry Journal*, 30 Oct. 1792; 12, 26 Feb., 5, 12, March, 30 April 1793; 5 April 1796; 10 Jan. 1804. Cf. Murphy, *Derry, Donegal*, pp 6, 11-26.

70. *Ldy. Jnl.*, 31 Jan. 1797; *A list of the counties of Ireland and the respective yeomanry corps* ... (Dublin, 1798); W. S. Mason, *A statistical account, or parochial survey of Ireland* (Dublin, 1814-9), ii, pp 158, 170; Murphy, *Derry, Donegal*, pp 14, 19. The Youngs' Culdaff corps was still active in the 1830s: Journal of Mrs George Young, 12 Aug. 1835 (P.R.O.N.I., T.366/45).

71. Snoddy, 'Notes', 49-73; R. McKay, 'The fortifications of Lough Swilly and Lough Foyle ...' in *Donegal Annual*, xii, 1 (1977), 44-7.

72. A. Young, *A tour in Ireland* ..., ed. A. W. Hutton (London, 1892), i, p. 167; Dickson, Barony of Inishowen, p. 73, fn. 35.

73. Ardmalin rent roll, in Hart account-book 1757-1803, Hart MSS (N.L.I. MS 7,885); rent roll of Lord Wicklow in county Donegal, c. 1790 (N.L.I. MS 9,582); Edward Wakefield, *An account of Ireland, political and statistical* (London, 1812), i, p. 254; Dickson, Barony of Inishowen, p. 73, fn. 32. For a later illustration, see Robert Cary to Martha Rankin, 30 Sept. 1821, Cary MSS (P.R.O.N.I., Mic. 162).

74. Will of George Vaughan, 1753 (P.R.O.N.I., T. 187).

75. George Harvey to Rev. John Harvey, 20 April 1771, 14 July 1772, Harvey MSS; G. H. Harvey, *The Harvey families of Inishowen, Co. Donegal and Maen, Cornwall* (Folkestone, 1928), p. 94.

76. For example, see advertisements in *Ldy. Jnl.*, 3 Aug. 1790, 16 Jan. 1798, 17 Sept. 1799.

77. Dickson, 'Barony of Inishowen', p. 74, fns. 43-4, 46.

78. In the many references to leaseholds for sale in *The Londonderry Journal* in the 1780s and 1790s, no mention of tenant right has been encountered, whereas by the second decade of the nineteenth century it was regularly mentioned. For a detailed explanation of what was understood by the term, see an advertisement for land across the Swilly in Fanad: *Ldy. Jnl.*, 15 Nov. 1808.

79. There is no explicit reference to the growth in Inishowen of the practice of valuation, but its existence is implied in the many references to rents in the 1820s and 1830s, and was commented on by witnesses to the Devon Commission.

80. Dickson, Barony of Inishowen, p. 80, fns. 37, 49, 51.

81. *Ldy. Jnl.*, 23 Nov. 1773.

82. *Reports from the commissioners for inquiry into the condition of the poorer classes in Ireland* [hereafter *Poor inquiry*] (Parl. papers, 1836, xxxiii-iv), suppl. to append. F, pp 306-9; *Report from the commissioners of inquiry into the state of the law and practice in respect to the occupation of land in Ireland* [hereafter *Devon Commission*] (Parl. papers, 1845, xix et seq.), i, pp 710, 714.

83. *Devon Commission,* i, pp 689, 714-5, 722-4, 738-9, 741; Stat. ret. on Donagh, p. 7; Desmond MacCourt, 'The rundale system in Donegal...' in *Donegal Annual,* iii, 1 (1955), 52-3.

84. N.A., Registered papers 1832, 184, 194, 197, 199, 1082, 3047, 4104; Police reports 1838, 7/31, 7/56.

85. P.R.O.N.I., D.835/1/2.

86. A view of the tillage and pasture in the parish of Culdaff, 1773: Culdaff vestry book (P.R.O.N.I., D.803).

87. Young, *Tour,* i, p. 167. For Inishowen's vital role in provisioning Derry at a time of regional food shortage, see Dickson, 'Buncrana and Derry in 1744' in *Donegal Annual,* ix, 2(1970), 233-7.

88. G. T. Stokes (ed.), *Pococke's tour in Ireland,* 1752 (Dublin, 1891), p. 47; Dickson, Barony of Inishowen, pp 74-5, fns. 56, 58.

89. *Second report from the select committee on illicit distillation* (Parl. papers, 1816, ix), p. 89; A. Coffey, *Observations on the Rev. Edward Chichester's pamphlet ...* (London, 1818), pp 8-9; *Fifth report of the commissioners of inquiry into ... the revenue arising in Ireland* (Parl. papers, 1823, vii), p. 80.

90. View of Culdaff tillage, 1773; Statistical remarks on Moville Lower, 1833 (R.I.A., O.S. memoirs, Box 22, iii); *Returns relative to land reclaimed since the first publication of the Ordnance Survey maps* (Parl. papers, 1849, xlix), pp 424-5.

91. For an eloquent description of the impact of the price fall on the local economy, see Father Maginn's evidence in the *Poor inquiry,* supplement to append. E, p. 308. Cf. his evidence in *Devon Commission,* i, pp 768-72.

92. Field books, Moville Lower, 1833-4, N.A., General Valuation, O.L. 4.0344; *Third report from the select committee appointed to inquire into the state of agriculture* (Parl. papers, 1836, viii), pp 526-34. Note that the Carndonagh returns in the latter report are suspiciously rounded.

93. Statistical report on the Mintiaghs, 1834, p. 9; 'Lough Swilly no. 2', p. 4 (R.I.A., O.S. memoirs, Boxes 22, ii and vii); James McParlan, *Statistical survey of the county of Donegal* (Dublin, 1802), p. 61.

94. In the 1820s wheat was not even being grown in Burt or Inch, but by the late 1830s it was gaining ground in the southern parishes: Statistical report on Lough Swilly, no. 6, p. 3a (O.S. memoirs, Box 22, vii); S. Lewis, *Topographical dictionary of Ireland* (London, 1837), ii, p. 399; *Devon Commission,* i, p. 685.

95. Mason, *Parochial survey,* i, pp 183, 189.

96. *Pococke's tour,* p. 47; Dickson, 'Buncrana and Derry'.

97. Mason, *Parochial survey,* i, p. 183.

98. For some hint of this process, see Hart account book, passim; *Poor inquiry,* append. A, p. 463.

99. *North West of Ireland Society Magazine,* 2nd. ser., i, 79; ii, p. 384.

100. Dickson, Barony of Inishowen, pp 82, fns. 91, 96-8.

101. Mason, *Parochial survey,* ii, p. 156; Thomas Colby, *Ordnance Survey of the county of Londonderry: memoir of the city and north western liberties of Londonderry* (Dublin, 1837), p. 288.

102. *Precedents and abstracts ... of the Linen Board, 1711-37* (Dublin, 1784), p. 68; Young, *Tour,* i, p. 167; G. E. Kirkham, '"To pay the rent and lay up riches": Economic opportunity in eighteenth-century north-west Ulster' in R. Mitchison and P. Roebuck (eds), *Economy and society in Scotland and Ireland 1500-1939* (Edinburgh, 1988), p. 101.

103. R.D., 390/384/256865; *Ldy. Jnl.,* 28 May 1782; McParlan, *Donegal,* pp 50-3.

104. Robert Stephenson, *Reports and observations ... made to the Trustees of the linen*

manufacture, 1760-1 (Dublin, 1762), p. 9; Stephenson, *A review of part of the schemes proposed … towards extending and improving the linen manufacture of Ireland* (n.p., n.d.), p. 4; *Jnls. of the House of Commons Irl.*, xi (1783-85), append. p. dccliii.

105. M. M. Edwards, *The growth of the British cotton industry 1780-1815* (Manchester, 1967), p. 32; Kirkham, 'Economic opportunity', p. 99.

106. Henry's 'Hints', p. 47; *Pococke's tour*, p. 46; A. Spence, 'The antiquities of Fahan …' in *U.J.A.*, 2nd. ser., xvii (1911), 29; Kirkham, 'Economic opportunity', p. 97.

107. Stephenson, *Reports 1760-1*. The growth of linen weaving near Derry in the post-1780 period can be inferred from the sharp rise in linen sales at the market in Derry, the cloth 'mostly from County Donegal', from £1,000 per week in 1783 to around £2,000 per week in 1803: J. Greer, *Report of the state of the linen markets of … Ulster* (n.d, [c.1783] n.p.) [copy with MSS additions on 1803 in Foster MSS, P.R.O.N.I., D. 562/6225].

108. P.R.O.N.I., D. 562/5936; *Ldy. Jnl.*, 18 June 1782, 14 Jan. 1783, 22 May 1792; Kirkham, 'Economic opportunity', p. 97.

109. *County of Donegal: A list of persons to whom premiums for the sowing of flaxseed in the year 1796 have been adjudged by the Trustees of the linen manufacture* (n.d, n.p.); W. J. Smyth, 'Flax cultivation in Ireland…' in W. J. Smyth and K. Whelan (eds), *Common ground: essays on the historical geography of Ireland* (Cork, 1988), pp 237-40.

110. Dickson, Barony of Inishowen, p. 76, fn. 78.

111. Robert Cary to Rev William Rankin, 21 April, 5 Sept. 1811, Cary MSS; Statistical report on Moville Lower, 1825, sect. x; Mason, *Parochial survey*, i, p. 189; Dickson, Barony of Inishowen, p. 85, fn. 178.

112. Field books, Fahan Lower, 1833-4, N.A., Gen. Val., O.L. 4.0348; *Ldy. Jnl.*, 7 Aug., 4 Dec. 1810, 29 Nov. 1842; *Proceedings of the Linen Board …, 1808*, p. 4; James Corry, *Report of a tour of inspection …* (Dublin, 1817), pp 53-7; *Report on the select committee on the laws which regulate the linen trade of Ireland* (Parl. papers, 1822, vi), p. 660; Lewis, *Topographical dictionary*, i, p. 230; Akihiro Takei, 'The first Irish linen mills, 1800-24' in *Ir. Econ. Soc. Hist.*, xxi (1994), 34-7.

113. Henry, 'Hints', p. 69; abstacts of corr. of Collector of Derry, 22 Jan., 19 Oct. 1776, 18 June 1788 (Atton transcripts, Custom House Library, London, acc. 25,756); *Jnls. of the House of Commons, Irl.*, vi (1757-60), append., p. cxliii; *Ldy. Jnl.*, 21 Sept. 1784, 10, 24 Aug. 1790, 15 Feb. 1791; Dickson, Barony of Inishowen, p. 77, fns. 100, 102.

114. The evidence for this migration is indirect, but seems extremely probable given the prior trade in barley (and yarn) from Inishowen to the Coleraine market; see T. H. Mullin, *Coleraine in Georgian times* (Belfast, 1977), pp 87-8, 91.

115. *Jnls. of the House of Commons, Irl.*, vi (1757-60), append. p. cliii.

116. *Derry Rev.* corr., 7 July, 1783; *Ldy. Jnl.*, 15 Feb., 15 March 1791, 24 Jan. 1792.

117. *Ldy. Jnl.*, 11 May 1790, 26 Feb. 1793. Earlier in Feb. 1793 it had been reported that 'alarming depredations [have been] committed in various parts [of lower Inishowen] by several bodies of armed men, associated for the evil purposes of burning houses, destroying grain, extorting money, and writing threatening anonymous letters' (*Ldy. Jnl.*, 12 Feb. 1793), but the disturbances seemingly ceased after the capture of 'James Doo Butler, alias Capt. Fearnought, one of the Inishowen Break-of-Day men' (*Ldy. Jnl.*, 30 Apr. 1793). Another major incident occurred in 1800 when the High Constable of Inishowen was murdered: *Ldy. Jnl.*, 29 July 1800.

118. For early nineteenth-century tobacco smuggling, and its eclipse with the introduction of the coast guard in 1822, see *Derry Rev.* corr., 14 Apr. 1812; *Tenth report of the commissioners of inquiry ... into the revenue arising in Ireland* (Parl. papers, 1824, xi), pp 248-9, 312-4, 324.

119. *Belfast Magazine*, iii (1809), p. 91; *Report from the committee on distilleries in Ireland* (Parl. papers, 1812-3, vi), pp 12, 16; *Fifth rep. revenue in Irel.*, 1823, pp 23, 80.

120. *First report from the committee on ... the distillation of sugar and molasses* (Parl. papers, 1808, iv), p. 73; Coffey, *Observations*, p. 28.

121. Mason, *Parochial survey*, i, p. 156; Coffey, *Observations*, p. 31; *Fifth report of the committee of inquiry on fees, gratuities etc., Ireland* (Parl. papers, 1806-07, vi), pp 79, 230; *Report on distilleries*, 1812-3, p. 26.

122. Rev Edward Chichester to William Gregory, 3 Sept. 1813 (N.A., SOC papers, 1813 414/1537/42); Mason, *Parochial survey*, ii, p. 169; *Report on illicit distillation*, 1816, p. 89; *Fifth rep. revenue in Irel.*, 1823, p. 80.

123. *Report on distilleries*, 1812-3, pp 7-27.

124. Chichester to Gregory, 6 Aug. 1813 (N.A., SOC papers, 1813, 414/1537/42); *Fifth rep. fees and gratuities*, 1806-07, p. 76; Mason, *Parochial survey*, ii, p. 169.

125. *Report on illicit distillation*, 1816, pp 46-7; Coffey, *Observations*, pp 8-9.

126. *Report on illicit distillation*, 1816, p. 47.

127. *Report on distilleries*, 1812-3, p. 26; Chichester, *Oppressions*, passim; Robert Shipkey, 'Problems in alcoholic production and controls in early nineteenth-century Ireland' in *Hist. Jn.*, xvi, 2 (1973), 297-9; Murphy, *Derry, Donegal*, pp 60-1.

128. Chichester to Gregory, 6 Aug. 1813, 20 July 1816; Major T. D'Arcy to Robert Peel, 15 Oct. 1816 (N.A., SOC papers, 1813, 414/1537/42; 1816, 421/1766/18, /45); Murphy, *Derry, Donegal*, p. 61. For other attacks on gentry, see Chichester, *Oppressions*, pp 72ff.

129. Ibid., pp 69-70.

130. *Report on illicit distillation*, 1816, p. 46; Coffey, *Observations*, p. 29; *Fifth rep. revenue in Irel.*, 1823, p. 79; Shipkey, 'Alcoholic production', 298-300; Murphy, *Derry, Donegal*, pp 61-4.

131. *Papers relating to illicit distillation in Ireland, 1818* (Parl papers, 1818, xvi), 'Return of the number of fines for illicit distillation in the barony of Inishowen'.

132. *Papers relating to still fines* (Parl. papers, 1819, xvii), pp 15-6; Chichester, *Oppressions*, p. 33.

133. Samuel Lumsden to William Lumsden, 15 April 1816, 6 Aug. 1817, Lumsden MSS (P.R.O.N.I., D.649); copy, Robert Moore to Mrs [M.] Rankin, 30 July 1819, in William Thompson's Journal (P.R.O.N.I., Mic 162); *Report on illicit distillation*, 1816, p. 18; Chichester, *Oppressions*, pp 61, 107; *First report from the select committee on the state of disease and the condition of the labouring poor in Ireland* (Parl, papers, 1819, viii), p. 62; Murphy, *Derry, Donegal*, pp 62-3; Kirkham, 'Economic diversification in a marginal economy: A case study' in Roebuck, *Plantation to partition*, p. 79.

134. *Report on illicit distillation*, 1816, p. 139; *Fifth rep. revenue in Irel.*, 1823, p. 73; *Report from the select committee of inquiry into drunkenness* (Parl. papers, 1834, viii, pp 205, 401, 424); *Seventh report of the commissioners of inquiry into the excise establishment* (Parl. papers, 1834, xxv), p. 205; Lewis, *Topographical Dictionary*, ii, p. 301; *Return of the number of licensed distillers in Ireland, 1835 to 1850* (Parl. papers, i, p. 659).

135. A. Bielenberg, 'The Watt family and the distilling industry in Derry 1762-1921' in

Ulster Folklife, xl (1994), pp 2-3. Coffey had been a victim of the whiskey wars in Inishowen: *Fifth rep. revenue in Irel.*, 1823, p. 79.

136. Pender, *Census*, pp 60-5; *Report of the commissioners appointed to take the census of Ireland, 1841* (Parl. papers, 1843, xxiv), pp 306-7; W. J. Smyth, 'Society and settlement in seventeenth-century Ireland: the evidence of the 1659 census' in Smyth and Whelan (eds.), *Common ground*, pp 55-83.

137. Pender, *Census*, pp 60-5; for 1766 returns, Bonner, *Traitor*, p. 226; *Abstract of the ... returns under the Population Act, 1821* (Parl. papers, 1824, xxii), pp 268-71, 274. For a general discussion of medium-term trends, see S. Daultrey, D. Dickson and C. Ó Gráda, 'Hearth tax, household size and Irish population change 1672-1821' in *R.I.A. Proc.*, lxxxii, C (1982), 156-73.

138. Macafee and Morgan, 'Population in Ulster', pp 46-63; Macafee, 'Pre-famine population in Ulster: Evidence from the parish register of Killyman' in P. O'Flanagan, P. Ferguson and K. Whelan (eds), *Rural Ireland: modernisation and change 1600-1900* (Cork, 1987), pp 142-61; Daultrey, Dickson and Ó Gráda, 'Hearth tax', 171.

139. Daultrey, Dickson and Ó Grada, 'Hearth tax', 177-8. In 1821 the proportion of the under-fives in the Inishowen population was 4.14 per cent under the county Donegal cohort average, whereas the '50-60' year-old cohort was 8.48 per cent greater than the county average: *1821 census*, p. 274.

140. The growth of houses between 1767-70 (as plotted in the Crow survey of the Donegall estate) and 1841 (for Donegall-owned townlands, as reported in the 1851 census) confirms the particularly high rate of population growth in Clonmany; its rate of 1.1 per cent p.a. was bettered only by Burt/Muff/Inch where the rate (rather surprisingly) was 1.5 per cent: P.R.O.N.I., D.835/1/2; *Census of Ireland for the year 1851 ... Ulster* (Parl. papers, 1852-3, xcii); Dickson, 'Barony of Inishowen', append. B.

141. Whether arising exclusively from a differential in emigration, or from a combination of higher propensity to migrate and lower fertility, the Protestant share of the peninsula's population slipped from 23.7 per cent in 1834 to 20.56 in 1861, with the sharpest falls in Burt parish (64.4 per cent to 53.8), Inch (48.5 per cent to 40.7), and Donagh (18.3 to 13.3), with very small growth in Moville Lower (18.8 per cent to 19.1) and Culdaff (11.2 per cent to 12.3); the Protestant decline in the southern parishes was disproportionately Presbyterian: *First report of the commissioners of public instruction* (Parl. papers, 1835, xxxiii), pp 244a-267a; *Census of Ireland for the year 1861 ...: Ulster* (Parl. papers, 1863, lv).

142. Derry city population grew from 9,300 in 1821 to over 15,000 in 1841. Cf. Murphy, *Derry, Donegal*, pp 39-41, 47.

143. *Returns relative to land, 1849*, pp 430-1.

144. MacCourt, 'Rundale system', 52-3; Martina O'Donnell, 'Farm clusters in north-west Inishowen' in *Ir. Geog.*, xxvi, 2 (1993), 101-19.

145. 1841 census; *Returns relative to land, 1849*, pp 430-1. See also fig. 42 in T. W. Freeman, *Pre-famine Ireland* (Manchester, 1957), p. 297.

146. *Returns relative to land, 1849*, pp 430-1.

147. Kirkham, 'Economic diverification', p. 68.

148. [Mitchell], *O'Doherty*, pp 20-6.

149. View of Culdaff tillage, 1773; *General valuation ...: Union of Inishowen* (Dublin, 1857), pp 49-72.

150. *Return of the population... in Ireland* (Parl. papers, 1833, xxxix), pp 246-7. Cf. *Devon Commission*, i, pp 686, 690.

151. *1831 census*, pp 246-7.

152. N.A., Reg. papers, 1832, 184; Police reports 1838, 7/31, 7/36, 7/56; Thompson journal, p. 234; *Report on illicit distillation*, 1816, p. 57 et seq.; McGlinchey, *Last of the name*, pp 96-7.

153. *1831 census*, pp 246-7; *1841 census*, pp 306-7.

154. R. J. Dickson, *Ulster emigration to north America 1718-75* (London, 1966), pp 101, 139n.; S. Beattie, 'Emigration from north Donegal' in *Donegal Annual*, 44 (1992), 14-16. Cf. William Patterson to William Forward, 7 Oct. 1753, Forward corr. (N.L.I., MS 12,149/45(1)).

155. Beattie, 'Emigration', 17-9, 24-5.

156. Dickson, Barony of Inishowen, p. 65.

157. *1851 census*. See also Beattie, 'Workhouse and famine in Inishowen 1845-9' in *Donegal Annual*, xiii, 4 (1980), 508-28.

158. The uneven demographic impact of the Famine locally has yet to be properly investigated, but see Murphy, *Derry, Donegal*, pp 102-7; Beattie, 'Emigration', 19-20, 26-7.

159. The early nineteenth-century development of Rathmelton and Letterkenny offers an interesting comparison with Inishowen urbanisation.

160. Lewis, *Topographical dictionary*, ii, p. 398.

161. *1841 census*; C. K. Byrne, 'Hedge schools in Inishowen' in *Donegal Annual*, 33 (1981), 47-8. It is only in the denomination-specific literacy statistics of 1861 that sharp religious differentials are evident; at that stage 51.3 per cent of Catholics over 5 in Inishowen were illiterate, 21.7 of Church of Ireland members, and 16.4 per cent of Presbyterians, and while this must reflect income differentials to a considerable extent, there was a cultural residual present too. The 1861 religious returns also reveal that the Protestant component of Inishowen towns (22.7 per cent) was only slightly above the baronial average, but there was a large variation in the market towns – Carndonagh's population being 12.3 per cent Protestant, Moville 23.7 per cent, and Buncrana 30.2 per cent, and a huge variation in the villages for which data were published – Ballyliffin zero, nearby Clonmany 12.5 per cent, Malin 31.5 per cent and Culdaff 53.0 per cent: *1861 census*. For some preliminary discussion of the local history of language decline, see [Seán Beattie], 'The Irish language in Inishowen' in *Donegal Annual*, 45 (1993), 29-42.

162. R. G. Thorn (ed.), *History of parliament: The commons 1790-1820* (London,1986), ii, entry for G. V. Hart; Murphy, *Derry, Donegal*, pp 4-5, 33-38, 41, 78-9, 82-3; Cf. Rev Alexander Skipton to William Forward, 19 Dec. 1760, Forward corr. (N.L.I. 12149/47, p. 30). Despite the absence of Orange lodges in Inishowen, Protestant participants in fair-day riots, such as that at Carrowkeel in 1813, were described as 'Orangemen': *Ldy. Jnl.*, 1 June 1813. For reference to a Presbyterian teacher working in the Catholic church on Inch in the 1830s, and at the same time a Catholic teacher renting premises from the Presbyterian congregation in Carndonagh, see Byrne, 'Hedge schools', 50.

163. *Poor inquiry*, supplement to append. E, p. 308. Cf. Murphy, *Derry, Donegal*, p. 65; McGlinchey, *Last of the name*, p. 11.

164. Murphy, *Derry, Donegal*, pp 41-4, 49-50, 66.

165. McGlinchey, *Last of the name*, pp 54-6; [Beattie], 'Irish in Inishowen', p. 30. On the wider cultural role of Clonmany and its classical teachers, see J. Fitzgerald, 'The Waterloo priest' in *Donegal Annual*, xii, 1 (1977), 62-3; Byrne, 'Hedge schools', 51-3; McGlinchey, *Last of the name*, p. 110 [Beattie], 'Irish in Inishowen', 37-9.

166. 'Maghtochair', *Inishowen*, pp 88-91, 139; Fitzgerald, 'Waterloo priest', 62-3;

McGlinchey, *Last of the name*, pp 78-9; Bonner, *Diocese of Derry*, p. 356.

167. Murphy, *Derry, Donegal*, p. 66; Fitzgerald, 'Waterloo priest', p. 66.

168. N.A., Reg. papers, 1832, /184; Police reps. 1837, 7/41.

169. N.A., Reg. papers, 1832, /31; Murphy, *Derry, Donegal*, p. 66.

170. Only Inch, Fahan Upper and the two Movilles were reported as peaceable out of 9 parishes for which data were collected; however, 70 per cent of all Donegal parishes and 81 per cent of Ulster parishes were in this category: *Poor inquiry*, supplement to append. E, pp 306-9; C. Ó Gráda, *Ireland: A new economic history 1780-1939* (Oxford, 1994), p. 332.

171. N.A., Police reps. 1843, 7/15925; *Ldy. Jnl.*, 8 Aug. 1843; Murphy, *Derry, Donegal*, p. 67. Cf. K. Whelan, 'The regional impact of Irish Catholicism 1700-1850' in Smyth and Whelan, *Common ground*, pp 253-77.

172. Diary of George Young, 9 Nov, 1840, Young MSS (P.R.O.N.I., D.3045).

173. See fn. 152 above, and *Devon Commission*, i, 775-7.

Chapter 15

RUNDALE, RURAL ECONOMY AND AGRARIAN REVOLUTION: TIRHUGH 1715-1855

JAMES ANDERSON

Single farmsteads and compact farms with hawthorn hedges or dry-stone walls seem deeply rooted in the Tirhugh landscape. Between Donegal town and Ballyshannon, the farmer living among his own fields appears to perpetuate a rural economy hallowed by centuries of tradition. This dispersed settlement pattern is found throughout Ireland, and it was explained by Meitzen[1] and Demangeon[2] as stemming from ancient Celtic traditions of cattle-raising, in contrast to the large agricultural villages and tilled openfields traditional in lowland England and continental Europe.

Appearances are deceptive, the academic theory misleading. The present rural landscape of Tirhugh, as in much of northern and western Ireland, is largely the creation of an agrarian and social revolution of the nineteenth century. Before then, most of the rural population of Tirhugh had lived in clustered settlements, and had communally farmed an essentially openfield landscape bare of the present hedges and stone walls. Incongruous in the present pattern of dispersed farmsteads, it is the occasional house-clusters – often difficult to spot but seen very clearly on the coast at Kildoney for instance – which stem from older traditions.

This was first suggested by Evans[3] on the basis of research in the Gaeltacht of north-west Donegal. From survivals of openfield farming associated with house-clusters, he postulated that *rundale* and what he termed *clachans* had once been widespread in Ireland, and that enclosed farms with individual farmsteads were a late development in many parts of the country. He opened the way for detailed research into the Irish openfield or rundale system, most notably the pioneering work of McCourt.[4] McCourt's excellent series of original studies showed that rundale had indeed been widely distributed in Ireland, dominant over perhaps three-quarters of Ulster as late as 1750, and over most of Ireland's western seaboard into the nineteenth century. Emphasising the dynamic flexibility of the system, he showed how it had fitted into

Gaelic society, differing fundamentally from the feudal order of the English openfield village. Other researchers such as Buchanan,[5] Jones Hughes,[6] and Aalen[7] added significant details on rundale and its decline, and the various regional studies were well summarised by McCourt.

The present essay is based on one such regional study.[8] It shows how the inherent flexibility of the rundale system was strained to near breaking point in Tirhugh between 1715 and the 1820s; and how the system was subsequently eradicated in a landlord-imposed revolution which was virtually completed by 1855. But first the characteristic features of the system are outlined, and a different perspective is questioned. The 'red herring' that rundale decline matched Ulster Plantation settlement is also briefly dealt with by relating Tirhugh to county Donegal as a whole.

Rundale in outline

The system and its importance varied considerably in different parts of Ireland and in different historical periods, but some of its characteristics can be briefly outlined. It was based more on communal than on individual enterprise, originally in kinships groups, later in partnership farms. Co-operation and equity were among its guiding principles, though by the nineteenth century – which provides most of our evidence – the system was already in decline and more competitive and individualistic attitudes often prevailed.

The cultivated *infield* around the cluster of houses or clachan was divided into strips of varying soil quality, and individual holdings were intermingled and periodically (sometimes annually) redistributed, as a way of achieving 'fair shares' for the different individuals or households (Irish *roinn* can mean share or portion, while *dáil* can mean to distribute or portion out). The infield was continuously cultivated – typically with oats and barley from spring to September – and cultivation and harvesting seem to have been organised co-operatively. Livestock were grazed on the *outfield* at a safe distance from the unfenced crops in summer. In autumn they grazed the infield stubble, their manure helping to refertilise the infield for the next year's crops. The outfield could also be used for supplementary patches of unmanured and shifting cultivation; and there tended to be a proportionality between people's arable infield holdings and their rights to the use of the outfield whether for cultivation or grazing. Where outfield grazing was distant from the clachan, a type of transhumance, 'booleying' (Ir. *buailteachas*), was practised from May to November. In coastal areas rundale principles were extended to collecting seaweed for fertiliser and to fishing, with boats and nets shared by partnership teams. Many of these features were found in Tirhugh.

As can be seen from Tirhugh survivals, the *clachans*[9] were generally 'through-other' in layout. They generally lacked any formal plan for houses were simply added as population increased, shelter being the main consideration in choosing each new site. Up to the 1750s they averaged around four or five houses, but with the subsequent population explosion clachans of twenty or more houses were common by the 1820s. The townland, with one clachan and its communal farm, was probably the original unit of settlement. We shall see that some townlands were subdivided as the number of clachans increased in the eighteenth century, townland boundaries apparently being fairly fluid before they were finally fixed by the Ordnance Survey in the 1830s.

Rundale was inherently flexible and dynamic. The proportions of infield to outfield, and of cultivated to grazing land, could be varied. Land holdings were often subdivided equally among heirs, and when the size of the clachan increased, single farmsteads were hived off to create new infields, and eventually new clachans. This dynamic relationship between nucleated and dispersed settlement, coupled with the relatively small size of clachans and the greater importance of livestock (compared to the agricultural villages and tilled openfields of continental Europe), partly explains why Meitzen and Demangeon mistakenly thought that Irish agrarian settlement was traditionally dispersed.[10] In fact the fluid rundale system had counterparts throughout Atlantic Europe,[11] the Scottish *runrig* system being very similar.

Recently Whelan has argued that 'Rundale villages or clachans are not the degraded relics of an archaic, aboriginal settlement form ... They are instead a sophisticated solution to specific ecological, environmental and social problems ...'.[12] He emphasises their role as 'well-judged adaptations to marginal situations' in Ireland's western fringe areas, much of which were settled late in response to the population upsurge after 1750; this 'explains why they were so absent from good land, where such a system was unnecessary'. As we shall see, many individual clachans were indeed creations of the eighteenth century. The settlement form, however, and the associated farming system, are of course older; and in Tirhugh clachans were more numerous on the better land. Their pre-famine distribution was not as 'marginal' or spatially restricted as suggested, and they were also found further east in more fertile parts of Ireland according to McCourt. This debate has particular resonance for research in Donegal.[13] However, while the extent of rundale settlement in Ireland's western areas expanded because of population pressure in the eighteenth and early nineteenth centuries, the perspective of this essay is that population pressure also helped to undermine the system.

There were limits to the flexibility of what had traditionally been a mainly subsistence system of mixed farming in which livestock predominated. These limits became more marked in the eighteenth century with the growing commercialisation of agriculture, spiralling rents, rapid population increase, and a massive swing to tillage – even in areas (like Tirhugh) which were more naturally suited to grazing. There was severe land scarcity as Ireland's population doubled between 1780 and 1830. Less useable land was available for new clachan formation. Continuing subdivision among heirs, encouraged by rent-maximising landlords in the eighteenth century, led to swollen clachans; individual holdings became very small and fragmented. The shrinking outfields were overstocked; it became increasingly difficult to segregate livestock from the infield summer crops; and proportionally less stock meant less fertilising of the larger infields in winter. Increasingly, tenants had to rely on additional forms of income such as weaving and linen production, but in rural Ulster it declined in the 1820s.

The general results were extreme poverty, and sometimes famine, for the rundale farmers; low and unreliable rent returns for the landlords. This is what led the landlords finally to eradicate a system already severely under strain. They were also influenced by the fact that the continuous cultivation of the heavily populated infield led to soil impoverishment, while its use for grazing in winter precluded the introduction of the new crop rotations and winter root crops associated with the agrarian revolution in England. Furthermore, the communal and egalitarian element in rundale was completely antithetical to the liberal individualism of this 'age of agrarian improvements'.

Rundale decline in Donegal

McCourt,[14] following Mac Loinsigh,[15] showed that the agrarian revolution arrived in the Laggan of east Donegal in the late eighteenth century and spread westwards after 1800. Clachans, though mixed with dispersed farmsteads, were still the predominant settlement form in the county as a whole as late as the 1830s when the first Ordnance Survey maps were made. Although rundale declined first in the Laggan, where fertile soils and proximity to markets gave landlords more incentive to improve their estates, the changes there were more gradual or evolutionary and many clachans outlived the rundale system. In the west, by contrast, its later eradication was generally more rapid and revolutionary, both rundale and clachans being removed together. In most parts of Tirhugh they were removed very rapidly in the two decades before the famine.

Donegal parish was an exception, where McCourt suggests that 'Scottish Plantation settlements made for early social change'. This theme is taken up by Ó Cnáimhsí[16] with the implication that change progressed from the 'planted' east to the 'unplanted' west. But in fact there was no such simple progression. In Killymard parish, beside Donegal and also an area of Scottish settlement, rundale persisted until after the famine. It also lasted up to the mid-nineteenth century in parts of the heavily 'planted' Laggan – as late as in parts of the extreme west. In Gweedore, Fanad and northern Inishowen it survived into the second half of the century, but in Glencolumcille and in parts of the Rosses – Lettermacaward, Aranmore and around Dungloe and Crolly – it declined before the famine, as in Tirhugh, and it declined even earlier around Falcarragh. In short, the geographical pattern of decline was extremely uneven. What it reflected was not a difference between 'planted' and 'unplanted' areas, but rather the 'enormous variations in estate management' on the part of individual landlords or their sub-renting 'middlemen' and agents. It was not planted tenants but planter landlords who 'changed the face of the countryside'.[17]

Tirhugh 1715-1824

Most of settled Tirhugh lies on the twelve miles of coastal lowland between Donegal town and Ballyshannon (fig. 15.1). Drumlin-covered and less than five miles wide in the north, the lowland widens to over seven miles and has more limestone outcrops near Ballyshannon. It rises to turf-covered moorland in the east. The Ulster Plantation superimposed landlords and the two towns, and as in other parts of Ulster it may have led to improved methods of arable farming.[18] But it was probably not until the eighteenth century that the underlying rural economy experienced a more fundamental transformation, and not because of an influx of planted tenantry. Early eighteenth-century records of 'Speaker' Conolly's Ballyshannon estate[19] suggest that tenants with Scottish, English and Irish surnames all leased rundale farms in partnership on the same basis, and in some cases sub-rented land. The more detailed nineteenth-century reports of the area make no distinction between tenant-farmers of different ancestry, and it is possible that the predominantly Scottish incomers would have been familiar with runrig, the Scottish equivalent of rundale. In any case they were always a small minority of the Tirhugh population and they probably influenced their neighbours less than they were influenced by them, as is suggested for example by the strength of the Irish language in the area up to the early nineteenth century.[20]

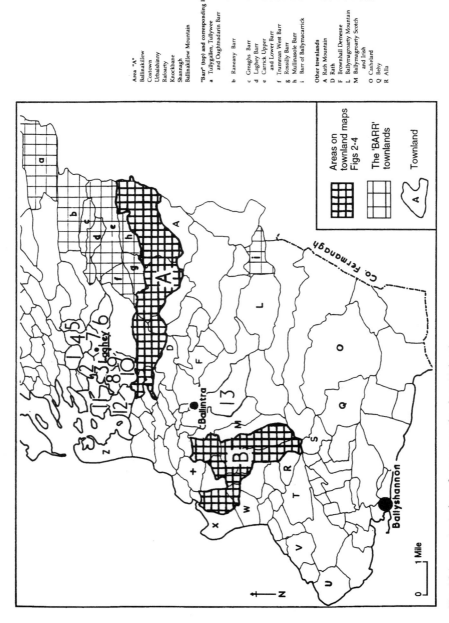

Area "A"
Ballinakillew
Coxtown
Urbalshinny
Rafoarty
Knockbane
Shannagh
Ballinakillew Mountain

Area "B"
Foyagh
Glasbolie
Lurgan
Dromore
Darnish
Rathfragan
Killinangill More

"Barr" (top) and corresponding lowland townlands
a Tullygallen, Tullywee
   and Oughtmadarin Barr
b Raneany Barr
c Greaghs Barr
d Laghey Barr
e Carrick Upper
   and Lower Barr
f Trumman West Barr
g Rossilly Barr
h Mullinasole Barr
i Barr of Ballymacarrick

lowland townlands
1 Tullygallen
2 Tullywee
3 Oughtmadarin
4 Raneany West
5 Raneany East
6 Greaghs
7 Laghey
8 Carrick West
9 Carrick East
10 Trumman West
11 Rossilly
12 Mullinasole
13 Ballymacarrick

Other townlands
A Rath Mountain
D Rath
F Brownhall Demesne
L Ballymagroarty Mountain
M Ballymagroarty Scotch
   and Irish
O Casheland
Q Behy
R Alla

S Cavangarden
T Cashel
U Kildoney Glebe
V Kilbarron
W Rossnowlagh Upper
X Rossnowlagh Lower
Z Lower Murvagh
+ Drumhome

Fig. 15.1   An index of some townlands in Tirhugh.

Under a special scheme of the Ulster Plantation, land in Tirhugh Barony was granted to Trinity College Dublin, to the established Church of Ireland, and to 'servitors' (ex-army officers).[21] Unlike other parts of Ulster, there was never any official requirement or any attempt to remove the existing Irish tenants. The area was very thinly planted, and a census in 1659 recorded only 244 Scottish and English adults; they accounted for less than 15 per cent of Tirhugh's total adult population which compared with a figure of over 50 per cent in the Laggan.[22]

The first detailed survey showing settlement and townlands in Tirhugh was made of Trinity College properties in 1715.[23] Trinity again surveyed its properties in 1824,[24] and a comparison of the respective maps (figs. 15.2, 15.3, and 15.4) indicates that the size and number of clachans increased significantly, and some townlands were subdivided. Settlement spread to previously 'unimproved' and 'unprofitable' moorland and coastal areas.

In 1715 townlands are referred to as 'farmes' – then the two were often synonymous. Along the border of some townlands (e.g. Dromore and Foyagh – fig. 15.2) there were strips of 'bog' which suggests they 5

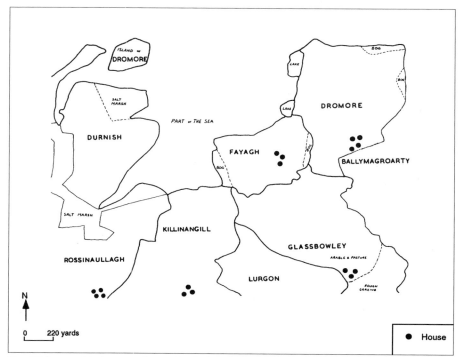

Fig. 15.2   Clachans and townlands in 1715 – Foyagh area ('B' on fig. 15.1).
Source: Trinity College Survey, 1715.

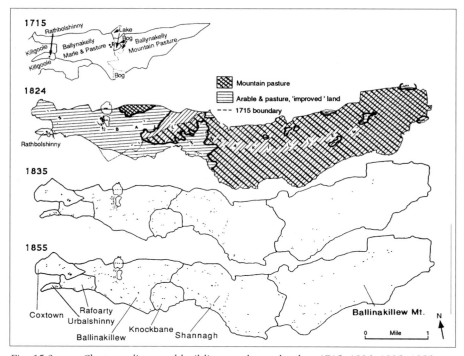

Fig. 15.3   Clusters, dispersed buildings and townlands – 1715, 1824, 1835, 1855
              Ballinakillew area ('A' in fig. 15.1).
              Source: Trinity College Surveys, 1715 and 1824; O.S. maps 1835 and 1855.

of the unimproved outfield, and that the cultivated infield was
expanded outwards from each clachan. The bogs are not shown on the
more accurate 1824 maps, indicating further reclamation and infield
expansion. Each townland generally had a clachan of three or four
houses. One exception was 'Rathbolshinny farme' which contained a
single house. However, by 1824 a sizeable clachan had developed – an
example perhaps of the 'dynamic relationship' between settlement
dispersal and nucleation in which single farmsteads were a stage in the
process of clachan formation (fig. 15.3).

Cunningham's detailed analysis of the Conolly estate records shows
that around 1720 whole townlands were sometimes the unit of renting.
The rundale tenants were simply listed as 'x and partners', so it is not
possible to tell the size or composition of the partnerships, but there
seems to have been a considerable turnover of the *named* tenants.[25]
Many of the larger townlands of 1715 had become two or more
separate townlands by 1824, some divided into 'East' and 'West', or
'Upper' and 'Lower' (and 'Irish' and 'Scotch' in the case of
Ballymagroarty). The 'Ballynakelly' of 1715 was six townlands by 1835

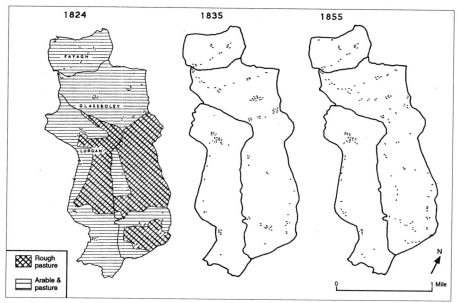

Fig. 15.4   Buildings and townlands in 1824, 1835 and 1855
Foyagh area ('B' in fig. 15.1).
Source: Trinity College Surveys, 1824 and O.S. maps 1835 and 1855.

(fig 15.3). Glassboley, shown with one three-house clachan in 1715, contained five clusters in 1824 (fig. 15.4). While the single clachan was typically located in the middle of the townland, the clachans in 1824 often straddled townland boundaries, indicating that the townland was losing its importance as a functional unit.

The 1824 survey notes that 'improvements' to 'mountain parts' since 1715 were 'very considerable'; and the area of arable land seems to have doubled between 1715 and 1824, while population and habitations increased even more, though some of the apparent increases may reflect inaccuracies in the earlier survey. In Ballinakillew a four-house clachan of 1715 had grown to over twenty houses by 1824, and there were several additional clachans as well as new dispersed houses (fig 15.3). Similarly, in 1715, upper Rossnowlagh had a cluster of four houses; by 1824 settlement had spread down to the coast and Lower Rossnowlagh now had a clachan on what had been 'pasturable rabbit warren' in 1715.

The 1715 survey indicates that oats, milk and fish were important for subsistence, but barley was grown for (illicit?) whiskey distilling and flax for linen manufacture which would have brought cash incomes. The swing to tillage, which helped undermine rundale, was already under way. According to a 1739 account, the drumlins between

Donegal town and Ballintra were fertilised with 'sea sand and limestone which some carry three or four miles' and they were 'thoroughly tilled to the top'; there were no large herds of cattle or sheep except around Ballyshannon.[26] The subsequent increase in arable farming, which required more labour, helped stimulate the extraordinary population growth in late eighteenth-century Tirhugh, as in Ireland generally, and there was increasing reliance on the potato for subsistence. Population growth and arable increase together helped destroy the fabric of rundale society: holdings became inefficiently small and fragmented while rents continued to rise, infield took over the outfield, and moorland reclamation the former 'booleying' pastures. This is clear from early nineteenth-century accounts in Tirhugh, even making allowance for the fact that most commentators were biased against rundale, seeing it as an obstacle to agrarian improvements and individual initiative.

Rural economy in crisis

To understand the perceived defects of rundale, and its subsequent break-up, we need to build up a picture of a local economy tottering on crisis. The 1824 survey notes that Trinity's lands were 'held in rundale, a system prejudicial to improvements, which prevents ... growing wheat, the lands not being fenced in'. But it was 'fertile country soon capable of paying a higher rental' and reclamation of 'mountain' would bring further rents. In 1802 hedges existed only on 'gentlemen's farms', and cattle had to be hobbled or herded 'to prevent them reaching the potato and corn sowings'.[27] In Drumhome parish 'the custom ... for the sheep of each townland to range at large as soon as the crop is taken off the ground [was] an absolute bar to the cultivation of green crops.'[28] Fences were 'insufficient ditches not of use to keep off any beast, which rendered a herd-boy necessary at all times'.[29] On the unenclosed infield, 'where a man had a piece here and a piece there' his neighbours' livestock would have trampled his wheat and winter green crops, and the landlords thought that 'few things could enable the tenantry better to pay their rents'.[30]

They wanted to introduce new crops and crop rotations, but the excessive subdivision of holdings meant that oats, flax and potatoes were grown 'in constant repetition to the ruin of the land', because to pay their rents the tenants 'couldn't afford any portion to rest'.[31] Population increase had accentuated the traditional 'gravelkind' division of property equally among heirs, and subdivision had been further encouraged by landlords, to increase rentals and also to secure votes when the 'forty shilling franchise' was extended to Catholics in 1793.[32] But in the early nineteenth century, they began to discourage subdivision and sub-letting by their tenants. The creation of larger as well as individual and enclosed holdings was a central objective of rundale break-up.

Believing in the virtues of individualism, the 'agrarian improvers' were opposed to the communal element in rundale. One observer in 1812 claimed (probably with exaggeration to bolster his case) that an annual reallocation of infield strips was typical throughout Donegal and 'as the fields pass from one hand to the other every year, no occupier takes the least pains to ameliorate the land'.[33] The paying of rents 'by townlands or in companies' was 'very injurious', the good tenants 'being subject to constant distress from the indolent or indigent'.[34] At the same time, rundale's co-operative character was weakened by commercialisation and the increasing social differentiation among tenants and subtenants; and disputes increased in the fragmented infields and over-crowded clachans. Tenants in Drumhome were described as living in 'miserable dwellings, congregated in villages', the clachans as 'consisting of a great number of poor houses crowded together'.[35] They were seen as insanitary, and removing them was another objective of rundale break-up.

Population increase and land scarcity also led to increasing numbers of landless labourers and 'cottiers' with only tiny subsistence plots. There was therefore more reliance on other sources of income, as an alternative or as a supplement to farming. Linen was a 'staple manufacture', some clachan-dwellers spinning and weaving their own flax while the landless bought the raw material.[36] But linen declined in the 1820s, a witness in Donegal town describing the 'failure of the linen trade' as 'the great misfortune of our country'.[37] Its decline contributed to the need for agrarian improvements because many tenants had depended on linen sales for rent money. Those near the coast got supplementary income from kelp manufacture, fishing and fish-salting; and seasonal migration for harvest work in Scotland and England was becoming common in the decades before the famine.[38] Local employment for smallholders and the landless was at best uncertain, and land reclamation schemes were widely seen as a solution.[39]

Tirhugh in 1802 was described as an area of small farms 'only adapted merely for the consumption of the tenants' who lived on potatoes, oaten-bread, milk, and 'the benefits of the sea-shore'. Barley 'in spite of every apprehension of want' was 'distilled privately' and 'cheerfully consumed in whiskey'.[40] Many had little to be cheerful about, however. According to the parish priest in Killbarron, the usual diet was 'potatoes, and buttermilk or herrings', but 'those not constantly employed can scarcely afford potatoes alone'.[41] In 1831 many Tirhugh tenants suffered famine conditions and the landlords got 'no rents to signify'. They had to import food which was either distributed free or in payment for reclamation work,[42] as would happen again in the famine of the 1840s.

Rundale breakup 1824-1855

Passing through Tirhugh on his Irish tour in the late 1770s, Arthur Young saw 'beautiful landscapes, swelling fields cultivated with the bay flowing up among them'. But 'partnership farms' were in a 'backward state', and in Ireland there was 'a severity towards the poor quite unknown in England'. Young helped to introduce Irish landlords to the 'improvements' of the agrarian revolution.[43] In 1800 the 'resident gentry of the barony' established the 'Tyrhugh Farmers Society' to encourage the introduction of new farming techniques, wheat and green crops, land reclamation, the subsidised sale of 'thorn quicks' for hedges and the enclosure of openfields.[44] In 1822 John Hamilton, one of the local landlords, described the 'improving society' as 'a considerable success', though adding that it was 'difficult to get through the conservatism of the people'.[45]

The landlords' main aim was to increase the size and reliability of their rental incomes, and they were stimulated to action both by the poor state of the local economy and by external factors. For example, the opening of the protected English grain market in 1806 brought a 50 per cent rise in Irish grain prices, which made an increase in the extent and the productivity of arable farming even more attractive. When Trinity College began to raise its rents in the 1820s, the sub-renting 'middlemen' (some of them small local landlords) were further pressured to put tenant farming on a more efficient basis. Improvement schemes were carried out jointly by landlord and tenants and some provided employment for tenant farmers and landless labourers.[46] Landlords assisted their tenants in buying seed grain, green crops and improved farm equipment.[47] But 'improvement' mainly meant the breakup of rundale, dispersal of the congested clachans, and the creation of enclosed compact farms of viable size.

The 'improving society's' ideas made earliest headway in Donegal parish, where by 1821 openfields had been 'enclosed with neat sod ditches in parks of about two acres'.[48] However, the really dramatic changes came later, in the fifteen years up to the famine, and especially on the estates of Colonel Conolly, Thomas Brooke, Rev. Edward Hamilton, John Hamilton, and Rev. William Foster. These estates were managed by the 'resident and careful agent', Alex Hamilton of Coxtown, and other estate owners were influenced by his methods.[49]

Hamilton outlined his methods to another Donegal estate owner in

1839.[50] He first ascertained the number and individual rents of the tenants in a townland, and then inserted new 'mearing lines' on a map, putting them 'as nearly at right angles with the public roads as possible'. In a large townland, where the new holdings would have been too long in proportion to their width, he 'ran a cross-line' and ensured that the new farms on each side of the line were as square in shape as the lie of the land allowed. Tenants drew lots for the individual holdings, and appointed two arbitrators who set the rent, land quality 'the only thing taken into consideration' (as in rundale). Sites for erecting new houses were chosen 'as central in the farm as can be, with regard to convenience to water, access etc.'. Where possible the size of tillage farms was increased by arranging sales between adjoining tenants, or by locating some tenants on improvable moorland with only nominal rent for the first three years. Each tenant had to enter his new holding when the mearings were fixed, and had responsibility for making half the fences dividing it from adjoining holdings. Old buildings had to be removed within two years.

'Excess of population' on lowland joint-farms was partly accommodated by 'allocating wasteland', 'unreclaimed mountain ... mere peat or turf'. Where 'village holding of a farm in common' prevailed, Alex Hamilton 'divided mountain districts into small lots, broke up the villages', and placed each tenant on a single holding of at least six acres. Tenants often gave the landlord the 'old materials of former dwellings in part payment', and in the first year of relocation they grew their subsistence potato crop on their former land, but left the cereal ground to the new occupant. Industrious tenants sometimes 'suffered when the new divisions were made', but 'tenant-right' was acknowledged by Tirhugh landlords, the 'rate of purchase of good-will' averaged £6 an acre, and dispossessed tenants were compensated 'from five to fifteen years' rent' (which sometimes paid the costs of emigration).[51]

Hamilton started to replan the Conolly properties in 1830 when many tenant leases expired on the death of George IV. In 1827 rundale had been 'almost universally prevalent [and] retarded improvement' on the estate, but by 1835 much of the 'squaring' of new farms had been completed and rundale had disappeared by 1839. Three types of new dwellings were erected 'according to the extent of the holding, or the circumstances of the occupant', the 'first-class' houses being slate-roofed, the 'third-class' being thatched cottages, and the landlord gave subsidies for each.[52] Altogether Conolly invested some £21,000 between 1830 and 1844, but he was reportedly 'well renumerated for his expenditure': his annual rental increased from £8,000 to £14,000, tenants paid their rents more promptly, while the 'labour and outlay of the tenant' gave him a personal interest in his own holding.[53]

On the various properties managed by Hamilton, the majority of them between Ballyshannon and Donegal, the scale of transformation in the period 1830-1844 is evident from the fact that 2,061 new houses were built and 2,639 new farms were 'squared'. Of these farms, 282 were 'exclusively on moor with tenants residing thereon', while nearly 1,000 consisted of 'small patches of arable' with 'a considerable extent of improvable moorland attached'.[54] On the Brownhall estate, the area of arable land was nearly doubled in the five years before the famine.[55] However, in favouring square-shaped fields and farms, Alex Hamilton spared Tirhugh some of the more doctrinaire manifestations of landlord improvement, such as the narrow 'ladder-farms' running to the top of the moorland in Glenfinn, or what McCourt refers to as George Hill's 'mathematical extravaganza' in Gweedore.[56]

Enclosed holdings had largely replaced 'run and dale' in Drumhome parish by 1834; by 1844 rundale had disappeared in Donegal parish; and it had been almost entirely replaced in the Ballyshannon area, except on church-owned 'glebe' lands and 'in the case of a few old leases still subsisting'.[57] But as already emphasised, landlords and agents had 'much influence' in determining the nature, speed, and extent of change, and 'small proprietors could not afford to assist and encourage'. On the mortgaged Reynold's estate near Rossnowlagh there was little change by 1844; and on glebe lands the frequent replacement of the 'incumbent' Church of Ireland clergyman 'prevented the tenants going on so well' and rundale persisted after the famine.[58] The clachans survived on such estates, and on some small freehold properties, but by 1855 it was only on glebes, such as Kildoney,[59] that they remained the dominant settlement form.

Comparing the 1824 survey with the O.S. maps of 1835 and 1855 shows the transformation of settlement and the eastward spread of dispersed houses on the moorland. The townland maps (figs 15.3 and 15.4) indicate that dispersed settlement already dominated in some areas by 1824; in others the pattern was more mixed, and some clachans continued to grow. But single farmsteads were increasingly an alternative to clachans, or products of clachan breakup, no longer a stage in the dynamic process of clachan formation. By 1855 many clachans were completely demolished. Others were partially broken up by removing the central houses (e.g., the main Ballinakillew cluster was split into three parts between 1835 and 1855), and today these 'hollowed-out' settlements are barely recognisable as clachan remnants.

The 1835 O.S. map (fig. 15.5) indicates that settlement dispersal had progressed significantly throughout Tirhugh, but clachans were still fairly widely distributed over the lowlands. They were noticeably absent on the northern moorland towards Donegal town (where

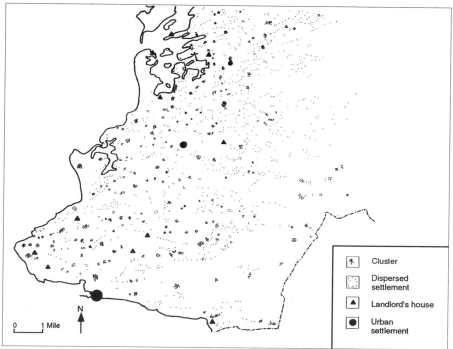

Fig. 15.5   Clustered and dispersed buildings, Tirhugh 1835.
Source: O.S. Six Inch maps, 1835.

'booleying' may have persisted longer on the 'Barr' townlands associated with townlands nearer the coast). However, there were some on the southern moorland which was settled earlier, possibly because the creation of some large grazing farms on the limestone near Ballyshannon had involved the 'clearance' of some lowlands tenants.[60] Clachans were also more numerous and tended to be larger on the southern lowland, perhaps because (in addition to variations between landlords) tillage had somewhat less predominance over pasture than on the lowlands to the north.

Quantitative analysis of the 'six-inch' O.S. maps for the area covered in figs 15.5 and 15.6 revealed that in 1835 there were nearly 200 clachans defined as clusters containing three or more houses. These clachans contained a total of over 1,130 houses, an average of six houses per clachan, though some contained over fifteen houses. There were slightly fewer dispersed houses – about 1,050 – giving an overall ratio of 0.9 dispersed houses for every clachan house, though the ratio was higher in the northern part of the area.

By 1855, when the Tirhugh 'improvements' had almost run their course, there were nearly four dispersed houses for every clachan

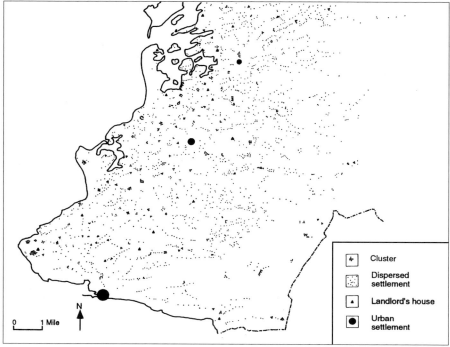

Fig. 15.6   Clustered and dispersed buildings, Tirhugh 1855.
                Source: O.S. Six Inch maps, 1835.

house, and the predominance of dispersed settlement continued to be most marked in the north. There were now over 1,600 dispersed farm-houses and approximately 430 in clachans. The number of clachans had fallen from nearly 200 in 1835 to just over 100, but many were 'hollowed-out' remnants, and the average clachan size had been reduced from six to four houses. However, some large clachans remained intact, particularly to the south near the coast, but also in the north, and one clachan in Kildoney actually increased in size between 1835 and 1855.

Rural crisis solved?

The overall settlement pattern was transformed, but were the incipient crisis conditions removed by eradicating rundale? In 1835, Tirhugh was under cultivation 'right to high-water mark' along the coast, and arable farming extended above the 400-foot contour. Farms were reportedly from six to twenty acres, and fields were 'generally well-sized, especially near (Donegal town), where quick-fences prevailed'. Farm equipment and fertilising techniques had been improved.[61] Thanks to the 'improving society', wheat was grown 'with the greatest success', and 'turnips, vetches, mangel-wurzel and other green crops [were] common'.[62] In 1844 it was reported that agriculture was more efficient, rentals were higher, rents were paid more punctually, and there were fewer evictions. The 'improvements' of Alex Hamilton 'gave a great quantity of work'. Potatoes, grain and oatmeal were exported from the ports of Ballyshannon and Donegal.[63] Previously flour had to be imported, but now the main imports were potash, iron, timber and slates, and 'the brisk demand for building materials ... gave great impetus to local enterprise'.[64] The growth of the two main towns, once mere military garrisons, now mirrored the growth of the commercial rural economy, as well as reflecting the urbanisation of some of the 'excess' rural population. Between 1821 and 1841 Ballyshannon's population grew from 2,482 to 3,231, Donegal town's from 696 to 1,031.

However, the rural population also continued to increase – by some 20 per cent to over 20,000 in the two decades before the famine[65] – and assessing the economic effects of the agrarian revolution is further complicated by the famine's almost immediate arrival. Subdivision of holdings continued even after enclosures; not all enclosed holdings were consolidated into compact farms; and just before the famine the land was 'still obliged to bear constant cropping' for rents had been raised and land scarcity persisted.[66] The 'improved' moorland farms were generally of poor quality and many would be abandoned after the famine. Although Alex Hamilton had set a six-acre minimum farm size, many holdings remained very small. In the central Ballintra area in 1851, 10 per cent of the holdings were under six acres (and half of those were only plots of one acre or less); 45 per cent of the farms were between five and fifteen acres and only 10 per cent were over thirty acres.[67] Despite the abolition of rundale, many Tirhugh tenants continued to live at near subsistence level, most of their cash income going in rents to the landlords. Meat consumption in the area did increase before the famine, but the 'ordinary diet' did not improve significantly with the 'improvements',[68] and in 1864 small farmers were reportedly little better off than constantly employed labourers.[69] The proportion of the Tirhugh population living in 'fourth class houses' dropped from 30 per cent to 10 per cent between 1841 and 1851,[70] but that probably had less to do with 'improvements' and more to do with the fact that the intervening famine had its worst effects on the poorest. The rural population, which had grown by nearly 20 per cent over the two previous decades, declined by over 20 per cent in the single decade of the famine.[71]

On the other hand, it is likely that the famine's effects would have been worse but for the previous 'improvements'. There are comparatively few traditions of famine in Tirhugh. There was starvation in lowland Cully and, despite fishing, in Mullinasole, while in some moorland townlands people had to take blood from cattle and drink it mixed with milk.[72] But improvement schemes organised by the landlords gave 'relief work'; at Ballyshannon they gave out 'thin porridge'; and proximity to food from the sea and sea-shore helped alleviate the worst effects of the potato blight.[73] John Hamilton reported that on his estate there were no deaths from famine, and not a single tenant had to go to the 'poor-house'.[74] While practically no rents were paid in Shannagh in 1846, some tenants in more fertile Foyagh were still able to pay.[75] The famine death rate in Tirhugh was below the Donegal average of 2.5 per cent, and markedly less than in adjacent county Leitrim where famine directly killed over 5 per cent of the population.[76] Conditions had improved again by 1850, and in 1853 Tirhugh was 'prospering better'.[77] The crisis incipient in the rural economy, however, had not been solved, and by 1911 the rural population had dropped to only 55 per cent of its pre-famine maximum.[78]

The viability of the rundale system in the eighteenth century had been undermined by rapid population growth and by the short-sighted policies of 'rack-renting' landlords. Then, influenced by the agrarian revolution in England, and a desire for higher and more reliable rentals, they made a relatively sudden attempt to eradicate inefficiencies for which they themselves were partly responsible. Implementing the innovations of the agrarian revolution meant enclosing the openfields and replacing the rundale system with individual consolidated farms. In removing rundale the landlord class created a largely 'replanned' landscape. But while individual local landlords were relatively humane during the Famine, landlord rentals continued to impose a heavy burden on the tenantry. The social revolution imposed 'from above' had left the landlords intact, but their removal is another story.

References

1. A. Meitzen, *Siedlung and agrarwesen* (Berlin, 1895).
2. A. Demangeon, *La geographie de l'habitat rural* (Paris, 1928).
3. E. E. Evans, 'Some survivals of the Irish openfield system, in *Geography*, xxiv (1939).
4. D. McCourt, 'Rundale and its social concomitants', unpublished M.A. thesis, Q.U.B. (1947); Ibid., 'The rundale system in Ireland; a study of its geographical distribution and social relations', unpublished Ph.D. thesis, Q.U.B. (1950); Ibid., 'Infield and outfield in Ireland' in *Econ. Hist. Rev.*, vii (1954-5); Ibid., 'Surviving openfield in county Londonderry' in *Ulster Folklife*, iv (1958); Ibid., 'The dynamic quality of Irish rural settlement' in R. Buchanan, E. Jones and D. McCourt (eds), *Man and his habitat* (London, 1971).
5. R. Buchanan, The barony of Lecale county Down – a study of regional

personality, unpublished Ph.D. thesis Q.U.B. (1958); Ibid., 'The achievement of Estyn Evans' in G. Dawe and J.W. Foster (eds), *The poet's place: Ulster literature and society. Essays in honour of John Hewitt, 1907-1987* (Belfast, 1991).

6. T. Jones Hughes, 'Landlordism in the Mullet of Mayo' in *Ir. Geog.*, iv (1959).

7. F. H. A. Aalen, 'Some historical aspects of landscape and rural life in Omeath, county Louth' in *Ir. Geog.*, iv (1962).

8. My B.A. dissertation, published as 'The decay and break-up of the rundale system in the barony of Tirhugh' in *Donegal Annual*, iv (1965). As an undergraduate in Derry I had the privilege of going on research trips with Desmond McCourt. This essay has benefited from suggestions made by Kevin Whelan, William Nolan and Desmond McCabe.

9. The term *clachan*, introduced by Estyn Evans into Irish settlement studies is not used locally in Donegal where terms such as 'cluster', 'town' or 'village' signify a collection of rural houses. The late P. J. McGill, Ardara, told me that house clusters were called *cloigeanns* in the Rosses and *cloghans* in Ardara. P. Mac Loinsigh in 'Rural villages and the rundale system' in *Donegal Annual*, ii (1948), wrote that people in the Glenfinn area called them *cladarns* and in Donaghmore *claigean tighte*. James Orr of Ballycarry, 'the weaver poet,' in his poem 'Donegore Hill' which laments the suppression of the 1798 rising in Antrim, wrote 'But wives and weans stript, cattle hought'/An' cots an' *claughin's* burnin' (emphasis added). Clearly words similiar to *clachan* were widely used in Ulster.

10. There were thousands of dispersed *rath* farmsteads in Ireland. Most had been abandoned by late medieval times. It is assumed that they may have been the settlements of a group with higher social status than *clachan* dwellers but in the absence of evidence such assumptions are mere speculation. There are about 50 surviving *raths* in Tirhugh. Known locally as 'Danish forts', *raths* here are generally located on the well-drained drumlin summits.

11. From western Iberia to the *aarkast* (annual change) system of Norway and including the *terres chaudes* of Brittany as well as rundale and runrig. For a wide-ranging discussion of the European contexts of Irish rural settlement see P. Flatres, *Geographie de quatre contrees Celtique* (Rennes, 1957).

12. K. Whelan, 'Settlement and society in eighteenth-century Ireland' in Dawe and Foster, *Essays in honour of John Hewitt*, pp 54-6.

13. The debate about *clachan* distribution is complicated by a number of factors. Agrarian improvements generally occurred earlier on the more fertile land in the east and south of the country before the advent of comprehensive cartographic surveys. Surviving house clusters there may be pre-Norman in origin but others are later (see J. Burtchaell, 'The south Kilkenny farm villages' in W. Smyth and K. Whelan (eds), *Common ground; essays on the historical geography of Ireland in honour of Tom Jones Hughes* (Cork, 1988) or may stem directly from the manorial system (see A. Simms, 'Newcastle-Lyons as a medieval settlement' in P. O'Sullivan (ed.), *Newcastle Lyons a parish of the Pale* (Dublin, 1986). Apparent continuities in settlement history often mask more complex interrelationships; see W. Nolan, 'Society and settlement in the valley of Glenasmole c.1750-1900' in F. H. A. Aalen and K. Whelan (eds), *Dublin city and county: from prehistory to present – studies in honour of J. H. Andrews* (Dublin, 1992). The debate is further complicated by contradictory political responses to Estyn Evans – for example his posthumous appropriation (in my view *mis*appropriation) by some Northern Unionists, or an over-emphasis on his insistence on a nine-county Ulster, on Ulster being the most Gaelic of Ireland's provinces and on the 'real Ireland' being 'the west' and particularly the far north-west in Donegal. Whelan (see note 12)

with some justification accuses Evans and his school of casting pre-famine Irish settlement into a monolithic peasant framework; of biasing settlement research towards areas such as the Rosses of west Donegal which are presented as timeless and classless repositories of Ireland's past; of over-identifying Gaelic Ireland with what were among its poorest communities; and of making unwarranted assumptions about settlement continuities from prehistoric times. However, the allegations about a homogeneous, classless 'clachan model' (Burtchaell, 'South Kilkenny farm villages'), hardly fit the detailed research on rundale and its decline by McCourt and others. Whelan argues that the real 'Hidden Ireland' of the eighteenth century was not to be found on the west coast or among the cos-mhuintir: 'the custodians of tradition were the comfortable, Catholic, strong farm class (a Norman-Gaelic hybrid) of south Leinster and east Munster'. However, the 'tradition' in this area of Norman colonization would have been rather different from uncolonized areas, such as the Rosses; and it is perhaps not very helpful to single out any one corner of the country as the 'real Ireland'.

14. McCourt, 'Infield and outfield'.
15. Mac Loinsigh, 'Rural villages'.
16. C. Ó Cnáimhsí, 'An historical geography of south Donegal 'in *Donegal Annual,* x (1971).
17. D. McCourt, 'The decline of rundale, 1750-1850' in P. Roebuck (ed.), *Plantation to partition* (Belfast, 1981); Mac Loinsigh, 'Rural villages'.
18. P. Robinson, *The plantation of Ulster* (Dublin, 1984), pp 178-82.
19. J. Cunningham, 'William Conolly's Ballyshannon estate, 1718-1726' in *Donegal Annual,* xxxiii (1981).
20. See G. Fitzgerald, 'Estimates for baronies of minimum levels of Irish-speaking amongst successive decennial cohorts, 1771-1881' in *R.I.A. Proc.* (1984). Fitzgerald's minimum estimates of Irish-speaking in Ireland's baronies show that in the 1790s at least 87 per cent of Tirhugh's total population (towns included) could speak Irish, second only to Boylagh (the Rosses area) which was 97 per cent Irish-speaking, while the figure for Raphoe North was only 6 per cent. But after 1810 Irish in Tirhugh declined rapidly, from around 80 per cent to less than 25 per cent in the three decades before the famine. This coincided with the main period of agrarian revolution and it is interesting to speculate on whether there was a casual connection.
21. For example, Sir Henry Folliott acquired the lands of the twelfth-century Cistercian Abbey of Assaroe, Ballyshannon, which extended northwards as far as the townland of Alla near Rossnowlagh (see fig. 15.1). In 1718 the Folliotts sold their estate to their legal advisor, locally-born Speaker, William Conolly. According to the 1655-8 *Civil survey,* Trinity College held 4,226 acres in Tirhugh, private landlords 3,256 acres, bishoprics 1,108 acres and local church glebes 288 acres. (Ó Cnáimhsí, 'An historical geography'). Before the Plantation, Bally-shannon and Donegal had been important as O'Donnell headquarters.
22. In 1659 Kilbarron parish to the south had 434 Irish and 126 Scots and English; Drumhome parish 698 Irish and 100 Scots and English (Ó Cnáimhsí, 'An historical geography'). The 'thinness' of Tirhugh's plantation can be seen by comparison with the Barony of Raphoe which includes the Laggan: it contained 1,825 Scots and English who comprised 58 per cent of the total population. See W. Macafee and V. Morgan, 'Population in Ulster, 1660-1760' in Roebuck, *Plantation to partition.*
23. *College lands in the counties Donegal and Fermanagh,* 1715, Muniments Room,

T.C.D. I was grateful to be told of this valuable and previously unused source by Robert Hunter and Fred Aalen.

24. *Valuation of Murvagh and Brownhall*, 1824, by Thomas Noble. Muniments Room, T.C.D.

25. Thus the named tenant in Alla (see note 21 above) in 1718 was William Gallagher, but by 1726 he was renting Beighey and Alla was now rented by 'McGrena and Partners'. There was substantial sub-renting by smaller local landlords (e.g. the Atkinsons of Cavangarden and the Hamiltons of Brownhall), acting as 'middlemen' as on the Trinity College estate. Cunningham ('William Conolly's Ballyshannon estate') notes that there was substantial sub-renting by Catholics (judged by the surnames O'Boyle, O'Coen, O'Gorman and Flanagan. In the 1820s, before rundale was removed, the tenants in Alla included 'James Thompson and Others,' the 'others' being George Thompson, William and Joseph Elliott, Thomas Anderson, John Vance, James Coyle, Andrew and Elizabeth Anderson and their brother John and his son John (my great-grandfather), suggesting familial subdivision and that partnerships were still at least partly kinship-based.

26. W. Henry, *Hints towards a natural and topographical history of the counties Sligo, Donegal, Fermanagh and Lough Erne*, 1739 (adapted by J. Simms in *Donegal Annual*, iv (1960).

27. J. McParlan, *Statistical survey of the county of Donegal* (Dublin, 1802).

28. O.S., MSS Box 22, Drumhome 1834, R.I.A. Dublin.

29. O.S., MSS Box 21, 1834.

30. *Devon Commission*, Part 2, 1844, p. 163; *Ballyshannon Herald*, August 1833.

31. O.S., Box 21, Drumhome 1834 and Donegal 1835.

32. A local nineteenth-century landlord John Hamilton, in *Sixty years' experience as an Irish landlord*, noted that this 'unhappy legislation ... had led my forefathers to encourage subdivision:' on a moorland part of his estate in 1821 he had 'not five or six substantial tenants' but nearly a hundred poor ones.

33. E. Wakefield, *Account of Ireland*, i, 1812, p. 372.

34. *Devon Commission*, part 2, 1844, p. 171.

35. Ibid., p. 179: and Trinity College survey. In 1802 McParlan, *Statistical survey*, p. 64 claimed county Donegal had 500 'villages' with 20 to 30 families in each. There were 38 houses in the partly fishing 'village' of Mullinasole in Drumhome in 1821, while Laghey had 30 houses (*Census abstracts*, 1821, P.R.O., Belfast).

36. McParlan, pp 90-93: O.S., MSS Box 21; Donegal 1821: *Census abstracts,* 1821.

37. *Devon Commission*, part 2, p. 163. The Ballyshannon linen mart, established by 'improving' landlords in the early 1800s, closed down in 1828 – H. Allingham, *Ballyshannon – its history and antiquities*, Ballyshannon, 1879, p. 102.

38. O.S., MSS Box 21, Drumhome 1834 and Donegal 1835. When fishing was good 'the whole population of the sea-coast ... (went) off to it'; and in Donegal parish 250 men had full-time employment fishing herring and white fish which were marketed in Derry, Omagh and Enniskillen – W. Mason, *Parochial survey of Ireland* 1816, p. 426; and O.S., MSS Box 21, Donegal, 1835.

39. O.S., MSS Box 21, Donegal 1821 and 1835, Drumhome 1834.

40. McParlan, *Statistical survey*, pp 30-31, 40, 59-60.

41. *Report from commissioners: poor laws (Ireland)*, 1836, p. 318.

42. Hamilton, *An Irish landlord*, p. 214: *Ballyshannon Herald*, June and July 1831: *Devon Commission*, part 2, p. 177.

43. A. Young, *Tour of Ireland*, 1776-9, ed. A. W. Hutton (Dublin, 1892), ii, pp 18 and 31.

44. McParlan, *Statistical survey*, pp 82-4. Six of the eight founder members were locally-resident landlords; there were two meetings a year, one in Ballyshannon and one in Donegal.

45. Hamilton, *An Irish landlord*, p. 47.

46. *Devon Commission*, part 2, p. 180.

47. Ibid., part 2, pp 172, 180; McParlan, *Statistical survey*, p. 28; Hamilton, *An Irish landlord*, p. 41. In 1802 wooden iron-shod ploughs were used only on lowlands; on many lowland and on moorland farms only spades were used. John Hamilton brought smiths and carpenters over from Scotland to improve the equipment of his tenants. He got orders for fifty carts. By 1844 every farmer 'had to have a cart' – previously panniers had sufficed – 'those near the sea to draw turf', while the 'mountainy men' needed carts to draw fertilising seaweed from the coast – *Devon Commission*, part 2, p. 171.

48. O.S., MSS Box 21, Donegal 1821.

49. *Devon Commission*, part 2, p. 166.

50. Ibid., part 2, pp 179-80.

51. Ibid., part 2, pp 169, 177, 179-80.

52. Ibid., part 2, pp 167, 177, 179. The subsidies – mainly for buying timber and slate- were £7.10s for a 'first class house' and £2.10s. for a cottage, both later increased.

53. Ibid., part 1, pp 76, 166, 167; and part 2, p. 178.

54. Ibid., part 2, p. 179.

55. Hamilton, *An Irish landlord*, p. 214.

56. McCourt, 'The decline of rundale' notes that in Gweedore some of the new holdings running from the coastal plain to the moorland 'were a mile long and so narrow – seven or eight feet on occasion – that new houses built on them had to be erected with gables to the road instead of fronting it in the usual way'. The motive, presumably, was to 'mirror' the rundale practice of ensuring equal shares of the different quality soils, but the results were much less efficient holdings and a new type of roadside 'clachan'.

57. O.S., MSS Box 21, Drumhome 1834; *Devon Commission*, part 2, pp 171, 180.

58. Ibid., part 2, pp 177-80; and part 1, p. 253.

59. Clachans still exist in Kildoney, on the coast near Ballyshannon and in 1964 there were vestiges of rundale: on jointly-owned lowland pasture five farmers had varying grazing rights, measured in 'a cow's grass,' which were proportional to their individual arable holdings.

60. On placename evidence (e.g. the *Barr* towlands, Cashel-Cashelard, Rath-Rath Mountain) many lowland townlands had their own part of the moorland, for 'booleying' summer pasture and turf cutting. The cows were milked in small enclosures on the moor in places called 'bolaise' (information from John H. Gallagher of Laghey Barr, and P. J. McGill of Ardara). Some turf cutting rights still continue. A widespread tradition in Tirhugh was that on 1 May, the start of summer, livestock were moved to upland pastures and old women swept the dew off the grass with a rope at sunrise – 'for taking the butter from the milk of other people's cows'. (*Irish folklore commission archives,* vol. 1033, p. 173; vol. 1030, pp 38, 117). There is an abandoned eight-house clachan high on the southern moorland in Cashelard Upper.

61. O.S., MSS Box 21, Donegal 1821 and 1835, Drumhome 1834. Poor farmers no longer burned the ground to 'set' potatoes in the ashes.

62. Lewis, *Topographical Dictionary*, 1837, p. 474.

63. *Devon Commission*, part 2, pp 162, 166-7, 171, 178-80.

64. Lewis, *Topographical Dictionary*, p. 474; Allingham, *Ballyshannon*, pp 89, 103; O.S., MSS Box 21, Donegal 1835.
65. The population of the parishes of Kilbarron, Drumhome and Donegal increased by 19 per cent -- from 19,095 to 22,691 – between 1821 and 1841.
66. O.S., MSS Box 21, Drumhome 1834; *Devon Commission*, part 2, pp 168-9, 173, 184.
67. 1851 *Census*. Ballintra Electoral Division. On these 'larger' farms 25 per cent of the arable land was 'meadow and clover;' 13 per cent was under potatoes; 33 per cent was under oats and the remaining 29 per cent was under barley, wheat, turnips and flax, in that order.
68. *Poor Law (Ireland)*, 1836, pp 318-9; *Devon Commission*, part 2, p. 173.
69. T. Foster, *Letters on the conditions of the people of Ireland* (London, 1864, pp 62, 264.
70. 1851 *Census*.
71. The population of the three parishes (see note 65 above) declined by over 21 per cent between 1841 and 1851 and most of that decline would have occurred in the second half of the decade.
72. *Folklore archives*, vol. 1035, p. 427; vol. 1032, p. 120; vol. 1028, p. 510.
73. In 1846-7, Brownhall tenants were employed building drains and roads, while other landlords organised the building of sea-walls and slobland reclamation – Hamilton, op. cit., p. 214. In moorland areas a member of each family periodically went to the sea-shore to gather 'a *Creanac* (dulse) ... dilisk, sloke, barnicles, winkles and crauther (carrigeen moss)'. *Folklore archives*, vol. 1029, p. 59; and vol. 1028, p. 510.
74. Hamilton, *An Irish landlord*, pp 216, 234.
75. Brownhall MSS Rental, 1846.
76. S. H. Cousens, 'The regional variation in mortality during the Great Famine' in *R.I.A. Proc.* lxiii (section C), Dublin.
77. Hamilton, *An Irish landlord*, pp 264-6.
78. In 1911 the population of the three parishes (see notes 65 and 71 above) was 12,282 compared to 22,691 in 1841.

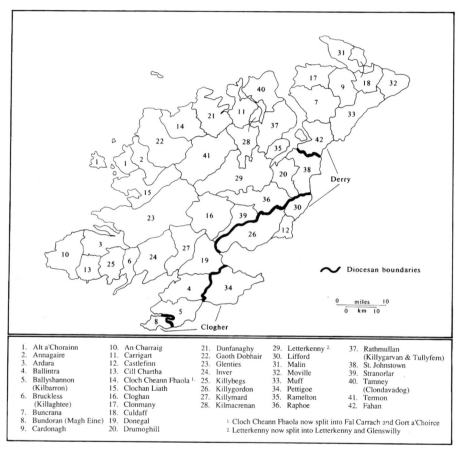

1.	Alt a'Chorainn	10.	An Charraig	21.	Dunfanaghy	29.	Letterkenny [2]
2.	Annagaire	11.	Carrigart	22.	Gaoth Dobhair	30.	Lifford
3.	Ardara	12.	Castlefinn	23.	Glenties	31.	Malin
4.	Ballintra	13.	Cill Chartha	24.	Inver	32.	Moville
5.	Ballyshannon	14.	Cloch Cheann Fhaola [1]	25.	Killybegs	33.	Muff
	(Kilbarron)	15.	Clochan Liath	26.	Killygordon	34.	Pettigoe
6.	Bruckless	16.	Cloghan	27.	Killymard	35.	Ramelton
	(Killaghtee)	17.	Clonmany	28.	Kilmacrenan	36.	Raphoe
7.	Buncrana	18.	Culdaff				
8.	Bundoran (Magh Eine)	19.	Donegal				
9.	Cardonagh	20.	Drumoghill				

37.	Rathmullan
	(Killygarvan & Tullyfern)
38.	St. Johnstown
39.	Stranorlar
40.	Tamney
	(Clondavadog)
41.	Termon
42.	Fahan

[1] Cloch Cheann Fhaola now split into Fal Carrach and Gort a'Choirce
[2] Letterkenny now split into Letterkenny and Glenswilly

Fig. 15.7   The Catholic Parishes of Donegal.

Chapter 16

CHANGING FARMING METHODS IN DONEGAL

JONATHAN BELL

For at least four hundred years, a distinction has been made between the fertile area of east Donegal, commonly known as 'the Lagan', and the much poorer west. The history of farming methods in the county to some extent reflects this divide.[1] The division can be taken as a microcosm of Ireland as a whole, where the east is often conceptualised as go-ahead, commercial and prosaic, and the west as poor, traditional and romantic.

It is important not to overemphasise differences.[2] Significant areas around Donegal town in the south of the county have fertile land, and this is also true of some small areas in the west. However, it is useful to bear the east-west division in mind when examining agricultural writings on Donegal. A clear difference of interest can be detected between eighteenth- and some early nineteenth-century agriculturalists, who were almost entirely concerned with developing the east of the county, and an increasing number of nineteenth century writers, who were more intrigued by the culturally distinctive, and impoverished, west.

The most famous eighteenth-century agriculturalist to write about Donegal was the English improver Arthur Young. He visited part of Inishowen, and went along the south coast to the Killybegs area, but his observations were made mostly on what he found in the eastern lowlands. Young was generally unimpressed with what he saw. At Clonleigh, near Raphoe, for example, he complained that 'tillage is exceeding bad, the land not half ploughed, and they like to have much grass among the corn for improving the fodder.'[3] Young fiercely denounced the home production of linen on small Ulster farms as disastrous for agriculture.[4] He found that 'the linen manufacture' was spreading slowly in to Donegal, the spinning of locally grown flax having become general.[5] As elsewhere in Ireland, Young did find a few 'gentlemen' farmers of whom he approved. The bishop of Raphoe, for example, and his dean, were commended for cultivating and hoeing turnips.[6] He also commented on some farming practices observed in less accessible parts of the county, particularly the use of seaweed and

sea-shells as fertilisers on Inishowen.[7] His description of how cultivation petered out in the hills, however, shows his lack of interest in
remote areas.

> It is curious to observe, how, as you advance towards the
> mountains, cultivation gradually declines; it is chequered with
> heath, till at last the heath is chequered with cultivation, spots of
> green on the mountainside, surrounded by the dreary wilderness.[8]

James McParlan, whose survey of Donegal was published in 1802,[9]
did attempt an overall description of the county. He also made a clear
distinction, however, between 'the mountain region' and 'the champain
region', which he described as including 'Lagan, blanket-nook, and
along the Fin-water'.[10] He described the western coast and hills as
being farmed on a very small scale, the main food crops being potatoes
and oats, while barley was cultivated for sale to distillers, both licit and
illicit. McParlan was unusual in that he recorded several distinctive
'common' implements. Two of these, steveens and loys, which he
found in the extreme south of the county are more usually associated
with county Leitrim (plate 16.1). Very unusually, McParlan praised the
efficiency of these local implements. He described loys as

> admirably well adapted to the weight and tenacity of the soil. A
> broad short spade, pushed into this ponderous gluey stuff, must
> remain there, as if in a locked vice, whereas this narrow one fits
> to its own breadth a portable weight, and the long handle
> answering as a lever and the back ... as a fulcrum in the operation
> of digging, very much facilitates the labour.[11]

By 1802, hay was produced in many parts of the county. In richer
areas, McParlan found scythes used for mowing the crop.[12] However,
he described pasture as generally poor, 'very bad indeed' in the
mountains, and even in the 'champain' parts, 'neither fit nor used for
fattening, except in a very few instances'.[13] Cattle were the only
livestock which McParlan discussed in detail. He found that in the
mountains very little attempt had been made to improve local breeds,
and that even in richer areas where the animals were of 'a somewhat
superior description', little systematic work at improvement had been
attempted.[14] Winter housing of cattle was very general, some richer
farmers feeding them turnips, potatoes, clover, and occasionally
carrots,[15] but in general, cattle fodder consisted of grass in summer, and
hay and straw in winter. In the 'mountain' regions many small farmers
housed their cattle even during summer, 'for the double purpose of
collecting the manure and avoiding the cruppan [a crippling disease]'.[16]

Plate 16.1   A digging match at Carrigallen, Co. Leitrim, Easter 1991. The one-sided
loys may be similar to those which were in use in south Donegal, in
1802 (Ulster Folk and Transport Museum Neg. No. L3280/2/11).

By 1802, two farming societies had been established in Donegal; the
Tyrhugh society, based in Ballyshannon and Donegal town, and the
Raphoe society. Both societies distributed premiums, and both proclaimed themselves anxious to encourage improvements by poorer
farmers as well as 'gentlemen'.[17] Premiums were awarded by the
Tyrhugh society for well-enclosed fields, drained ground, cultivating
wheat and clover, and the reclamation of marginal land. Prizes were
also given for the best farmers' servants, best and cleanest labourers'
cabins, best female servants and spinners, the best bull, best ram, best
draft stallion, best kitchen garden, best 'sallow' garden (osier bed), and
for raising forest trees and thorn quicks for sale.[18]

The work of these early societies was extended by the North West
of Ireland Society, which was founded in 1821, and became one of
the largest organisations of its kind in Ireland. The society held an
agricultural show in Derry each summer, with exhibits of horses,
cattle, sheep, swine, poultry, butter, farriery, green flax, and
agricultural implements.[19] An emphasis was also placed on organising
ploughing matches, seen as one of the most important contributions a
society could make to the improvement of local farming practice.[20]
Matches were organised at Raphoe in January 1823, and at Ramelton
in February of the same year.[21] In 1824, the society's general
ploughing match was held at Raphoe,[22] several weeks after the

Raphoe branch's own match, which took place on 4 February.

> The ploughing generally was very properly executed, and ... there was an evident improvement in that branch of husbandry, since the establishment of ploughing matches in this district, two years ago ... The horses were well harnessed, and the implements in good order. The attendance of spectators was very numerous, particularly of the higher classes, who evinced, from their conduct, a great deal of zeal for the promotion of such desirable work in the improvement of agriculture, and the crowded assembly behaved with very great decorum.[23]

The general history of ploughing in Donegal seems to have followed the broad pattern found in Ireland. By the 1820s Scottish swing ploughs, which could be pulled by two horses and operated by one ploughmans were replacing the large 'common' ploughs of the later eighteenth century which required four (or six) horses, and up to three men to operate. In Donegal, however, the debate on the relative merits of the Scottish and Irish ploughs seems to have gone on longer than in some other parts of Ireland, and 'common' Irish ploughs were still probably in use in the 1830s.[24] There are also isolated references from later in the nineteenth century which suggest that more unusual plough-types were used in the county. A reference from Carndonagh describes a plough which was 'a light wooden implement which a boy of eighteen could fix on one shoulder and carry from townland to townland,'[25] while John Hamilton wrote that on his estate at St Ernan, the plough used was 'a crooked stick with a second one grafted into it, to give two handles, and the point of the stick armed with a piece of iron'.[26] This is a fairly clear description of a plough type known in international agricultural literature as an 'ard'. Ard ploughs lack coulters and mouldboards. They were used in Ireland as early as the Bronze Age, and are still widely used in the modern Third World. There is evidence, however, that they were also used in parts of county Fermanagh until well into this century (fig. 16.1), and the nineteenth-century ploughs in neighbouring Donegal may have been of a similar kind.[27] Descriptions of wooden ploughs used around Hornhead in north Donegal, and Dunlewy, below Errigal, until early in the present century show a much more sophisticated development. These ploughs seem to have been similar to those used in parts of the Mourne mountains, county Down. They were fitted with wooden 'reests' which allowed them to be used for either turning ground or making potato drills, and like the 'Mourne' ploughs, may have been an ingenious local response to new methods of drill husbandry which became common in Ireland during the early nineteenth century plate 16.2).[28]

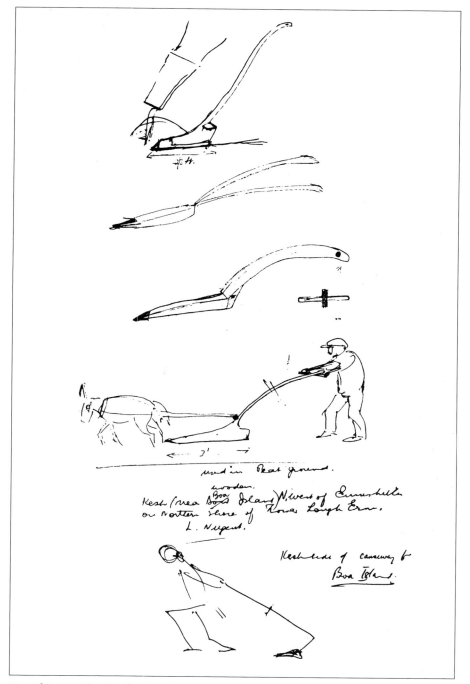

Fig. 16.1   Sketch of 'ard' ploughs used in county Fermanagh early this century. A similar plough may have been used at St Ernan in the mid-nineteenth century (Ulster Folk and Transport Museum archives).

Plate 16.2   A wooden plough from Dunlewy, which shows strong similarities to lea/drill ploughs used in the Mourne mountains, county Down (Photo: C. Ó Danachair (U.F.T.M. Neg. No. L3960/3)).

Agriculturalists became more interested in the large tracts of hilly moorland and bog in the west of Donegal, when the drive to reclaim such land for cultivation gathered momentum. Reclamation schemes became increasingly common throughout Ireland after the mid-eighteenth century, and involved the participation of some of the richest landlords, and their poorest tenants. The Devon Commission, published in 1847, recognised three main approaches taken to land reclamation by landlords:

> The landlord might organise the entire scheme, and only after it was complete, let it to tenants;
>
> the landlord might encourage tenants to settle on marginal land, offering them assistance such as monetary grants or loans, training in reclamation techniques, or the incentive of several years' reduced rent;
>
> the landlord could leave the whole operation to the unassisted labour of his tenants. Most contemporaries, and modern historians, accept that this last approach was the one most commonly taken, at least until the mid-nineteenth century.[29]

Land reclamation was labour intensive, requiring digging or ploughing, liming, and in some cases paring and burning. McParlan, discussing the possibilities for land reclamation in Donegal, found the principal obstacles to be 'a want of capital and knowledge in the poor, and of spirit and enterprize in the rich'.[30] The dependence of any scheme on the labour of the rural poor was recognised by McParlan when he commented, 'Emigration is a great obstacle to reclaiming bogs and mountains. In the course of last year, upwards of 4,000 persons left the single port of Derry.'[31] By the 1820s, however, the piecemeal reclamation of the west was well under way.

> A great deal of the Boylagh is reclaimed and cultivated, there being little other soil ... New cabins are rising in many places, and would still more rapidly if roads were open. Of these the most important seems to be the one from Rosses or Dungloe, by the river Gildore, to the road through Gortahork.[32]

The relationship between road-building, drainage and land reclamation was widely recognised. George Cecil Wray, a Donegal farmer who testified to the Devon Commission, was emphatic:

> There are immense tracts of improvable moorland totally neglected on two of the largest estates in this district. Many thousand acres, now only yielding a very small return from pasture, could, without any further cost to the proprietor than making roads through it, be made valuable land.[33]

One of the most publicised reclamation schemes in Donegal was carried out on the Cloghan estate in Glenfin, under the direction of the estate's agent, John Pitt Kennedy.[34] The estate was 16,000 acres in area, and in the 1820s about 14,000 of these were described as waste. Kennedy took possession of all the farms on the estate, which had been divided in rundale strips by the tenants. He laid out new compact holdings. About 160 new farms were situated on mountain land which was considered capable of improvement. It was claimed that Kennedy tried to give erstwhile tenants the same amount of arable land as they had previously held in rundale, and compensated those moved on to unreclaimed mountain. In cases where the arable land was considered insufficient to support a family, 'the claimant was placed on a waste-land farm, of improvable land, and dimensions suited to his capability – averaging twenty acres; and he besides received some compensation from those among whom his former small arable lots may have been divided.'[35]

Tenants of mountain farms were allowed to live rent free for between three and seven years, after which time the rent was gradually increased. Assistance was given with building new field walls and cottages and by 1841 twenty miles of road had been built through the estate.[36] Kennedy also set up a winter loan fund. Money from the fund was to be used for 'some reproductive object', such as liming land, or the purchase of new farm implements or a cow. To qualify for a loan, tenants had to carry out land drainage on their holdings, under the supervision of an 'agricultural teacher'.[37] The drainage project undertaken on the estate was described at length by the Devon Commission. One interesting aspect of the work was that it combined the use of thorough drains, an 'improved' technique, with the ancient technique of making cultivation ridges. The ridge and furrow pattern provided surface drainage in the early stages of reclamation.[38]

The teacher who inspected the drainage work on the Cloghan estate was employed on an agricultural school opened there in 1837. Tentative attempts at agricultural education had begun by 1802,[39] and the North West of Ireland Society had been actively investigating the possibility of establishing agricultural schools in the 1820s.[40] This eventually led to the founding of the well-known school at Templemoyle in county Derry.[41] The school on the Cloghan estate was smaller than Templemoyle, but attempted the same synthesis of practical and academic education. The surrounding moorland and bog was seen as an advantage of the site.

> The object in view of the establishment of [the school] ... was to qualify young men to fill the situations of capable land stewards, agriculturalists, and agents of estates; also teachers of agricultural schools. And the mode adopted was to select... [an estate] which

consisted almost entirely of waste land, when active operations were about to commence with a view to their reclamation and improvement in all requisite details.[42]

Girls were also taught at Cloghan, the object being 'to render them good servants'.[43] The well-known English travellers, Mr and Mrs S. C. Hall, who visited the estate, were impressed by the commitment of Captain Kennedy and his sister:

> It is surely enough to say of the boys' school, that while Miss Kennedy receives every day from the mistress a report of each pupil's progress, and inspects the school herself several times during the week, her brother ... watches over the boys with the deepest solicitude.[44]

An even better-known case of an estate energetically 'improved' by a landlord, was the project undertaken at Gweedore by Lord George Hill. Hill's account of his work[45] was widely discussed both by defenders of the landlord system in Ireland, and reformers who condemned it. Hill was influenced by the work at Cloghan,[46] and saw the abolition of the rundale system as his main achievement.[47] He was anxious to show the good effects of all aspects of his project, however, and he did this by contrasting the way of life of tenants on the Gweedore estate when he took it over, with the situation at the end of his proprietorship. He emphasised the destitution and backwardness of the people on the estate, but although this can be seen to lead to bias in his descriptions, his writings are some of the earliest to describe 'common' farming practices in detail.

Hill claimed that the way of life in Gweedore was essentially 'nomadic', tenants moving from the mountains to the coast and off-shore islands in search of grazing for cattle at different seasons of the year. This transhumance had been documented in Donegal since at least the early seventeenth century, although it may be that by the time Hill was writing the pattern of seasonal movement was less systematic and unchanging than he made it appear. Oral evidence and documentary records from Gweedore suggest that seasonal movements of people and livestock did occur, however, people often living in the hills for some period of the year, usually in a temporary dwelling known as a *bothóg* (plate 16.3).[48] Hill was certainly right to emphasise the importance of cattle for meat, milk, and dung. The collection of dung for manure in byre-dwellings was claimed to be common:

> Man and beast [are] housed together, i.e. the families at one end of the house, and the cattle in the other end of the kitchen. Some

houses having within their walls, from one cwt. to 30 cwts. of dung, others having from ten to fifteen tons of weight of dung; and are only cleaned out once a year![49]

Hill's descriptions of 'common' tillage practices were as dismissive as his account of livestock husbandry. He claimed, for example, that the most notorious Irish farming practice of all, harnessing implements to a horse's tail, had been observed on the estate.[50] He summarised the changes he had brought about in Gweedore by listing aspects of farming observed when he took over the estate in 1838, and comparing this to those established by 1866.

1838	**1866**
1. No carts used	1. 34 carts
2. No ploughs used	2. 10 ploughs
3. Land in common, or rundale	3. Almost every tenant has his own farm.
4. No progress in agriculture	4. 600 acres reclaimed since land was divided into farms. Flax, turnips, clover and grass seed sown in small quantities.
5. No market for produce	5. Corn store – more than 130 tons of oats purchased in 1865, also eggs, hides and butter.
6. No hay could be purchased within 12 miles	6. Model farm [beside Gweedore hotel] producing 50-60 tons of hay.
7. [No figures for livestock]	7. 1,700 cattle, 4,000 sheep and 300 horses.[51]

Hill's account provides an excellent case study of the different ways in which 'improving' activities were perceived by a landlord and his tenants.[52] Apart from conflicts over the abolition of rundale, Hill caused great resentment when he reserved 12,000 acres of mountain grazing, nearly half the area of the Gweedore estate, for his own use. In 1855 he let portions of the mountain to Scottish graziers who imported large numbers of sheep.[53] In 1858, ten priests sent a petition to parliament, protesting at this claiming, 'This fine old Gaelic race is about being crushed to make room for Scottish and English sheep.'[54]

Plate 16.3   A *bothóg*, in Gweedore in the late nineteenth century. Some very poor
people lived all year round in *bothógaí*, but in general they were used as
sleeping quarters for people tending livestock during the period of
summer mountain grazing (Glass Collection, Ulster Folk and Transport
Museum Neg. No. L440/2).

After the mid-nineteenth century, there was a long-term swing away
from arable farming all over Ireland, including Donegal. Within the
county, the rate of decline varied between crops. Potato cultivation
actually increased, and hay production rose in line with the shift to
livestock husbandry, but the major grain crops, and flax, all declined
sharply.

CROPS (acreage)	Wheat	Oats	Barley	Flax	Potatoes	Hay
1851	6,470	100,882	9,737	21,689	34,432	30,857
1901	301	81,084	607	6,823	39,343	65,652[55]

Several Donegal landlords who participated in this swing towards
pastoral farming took the same approach as Lord George Hill, and
developed sheep-farming instead of encouraging the reclamation of
mountain land for cultivation. Between 1851 and 1901 the number of
sheep in the country increased from 81,512 to 200,682.[56] The most
notorious example of this development took place on the Derryveagh
estate where the conflict between the landlord, John George Adair, and
his tenants over the introduction of Scottish sheep and Scottish

shepherds to the estate, eventually led to the eviction of 244 people, the landlord accusing these tenants of colluding in a crime of which they were in fact innocent.[57]

The introduction of new breeds of livestock by resident landlords during the later nineteenth century did have some effect on the types of animal kept by their tenants. On the small Hornhead estate outside Dunfanaghy, for example, the landlord imported Suffolk and Cheviot sheep. In return for working 'duty days', some of his tenants were given lambs bred from the sheep.[58] However, it seems that even these changes were often viewed in very different ways by tenants and landlords. Stephen Gwynn, writing about Lord Leitrim's career on his estate in Fanad, makes the point clearly:

> Nothing could be more characteristic of his tyranny even in bene-
> ficence, than the step he took to improve the breed of sheep and
> cattle. He imported bulls and rams of choice breeds from
> Scotland, but he simultaneously, to enforce the improvement,
> made away with all existing sires. Naturally, he compensated their
> owners, but no one likes to be done good by compulsion.[59]

Small scale projects undertaken by landlords did not effectively relieve the destitution experienced by many small west Donegal farmers, and during the later nineteenth century there was an increasing concern at the poverty of the area. For land reformers the fundamental problem was the landlord system itself, while other groups engaged in setting up self-help projects. Among the most effective of these bodies were the Congested Districts Board (CDB), established in 1891, and the Irish Agricultural Organisation Society (IAOS), founded in 1894. Leaders of both organisations wrote exten-sively about the problems of western Ireland, and these include detailed accounts of the way of life of the people of west Donegal. A picture emerges which has important parallels to the experience of farmers in many parts of the modern Third World; dependence on physical labour, lack of access to capital, a need for the income earned through migrant labour, and a crippling cycle of debt.[60] Leaders of the co-operative movement (IAOS) were especially hostile to the 'gombeen men' who were responsible for providing most farmers with credit for fertilisers and seed.[61] One notorious form of credit particularly associated with Donegal was the 'trust auction'. These seem to have started in the 1890s, when groups of neighbours combined to 'buy' and 'sell' one another's cattle. The auctioneer would pay the 'seller' on the spot, in return for bills from the ostensible buyer. These bills were granted for three or four months at an exorbitant rate of interest. The

Plate 16.4   Padaí Ó Dónaill of Gweedore, holding a racán which he made for
harrowing in seed (Ulster Folk and Transport Museum Neg. No.
L3360/4).

money obtained from the 'sale' was split among the participating
neighbours.[62]

We can use oral data to supplement the documentation available
around the turn of this century, to describe the farming methods
associated with the lifestyle of western farmers. Elements of the rundale
system survived until well within living memory. Small local communities, farming land associated with a cluster of houses, or *baile*,
made communal decisions on matters such as allocation of strips of
arable land, the control of livestock allowed to graze on lea land
(*talamh bán*), and dates when livestock were moved to hill grazing.[63]
In far western areas such as the Rosses and Gweedore, spades were
the most important tillage implements. The use of steep-sided
cultivation ridges (*iomairí*) was common for growing potatoes and
oats, the seed of the latter being harrowed in with an iron-toothed rake
(*racán*) (plate 16.4). Cereal crops were usually reaped using a sickle
(*corrán*). Gweedore men were especially famous for the speed at
which they could reap with sickles. The speed was partly achieved by

a technique which involved the reaper gathering grain against his leg as it was cut, until enough had been collected to make a sheaf. Elsewhere it seems to have been more common to lay each newly-cut handful individually in the ground.[64] The harvested grain was usually threshed using a flail (*súiste*), or seed was beaten from sheaves by lashing them against a stone or other hard surface.

On the small sandy coastal plains known as *machairí* the shallow soils were deepened by mixing in animal dung and *abar*, boggy soil taken from the mountains. Seaweed [*leathach* (broad-leaved seaweed) and *feamnach* (long thin seaweed)] was spread over the surface of the ground, and this acted both as a fertiliser, and as extra protection against wind erosion.[65] Planting potatoes in drills rather than in ridges became common in coastal areas early this century, and rye also grew well on the sandy soil.[66]

Along the coast, seaweed was often encouraged to grow by laying down stones on sandy soil. At Ardara and Carndonagh, for example, the stones were set below water level, and farmers had clearly demarcated boundaries within which they could cut weed.[67] Elsewhere, people depended on winter storms to wash seaweed ashore, or went out in boats to cut it in deeper water.[68]

The hoarding of animal dung as fertiliser was essential on small inland farms. On these farms the possession of a cow was necessary to provide the manure required to produce a subsistence potato crop. Cormac McFadden, whose family had a farm of three arable acres at Roshin in the north of the county, for example, said that he and his brother went to work in Scotland, to save the money with which to buy a cow. In the Roshin hills, if a farmer had no cow, he could 'dig potatoes all day and still carry everything he had dug home on his back'.[69]

Donkeys were common in the Rosses between Burtonport and Annagary, and other areas of moor and bog.[70] In the Rosses, in the late nineteenth century, a small local breed of pony was highly valued,[71] and horses were used where ploughing was common. The Congested Districts Board tried to encourage horse breeding in the Rosses by importing hackney horses. Bulls, rams, boars and improved poultry breeds were also introduced throughout the 'congested' districts,[72] but the extent to which these were accepted by local people varied. It has been claimed, for example, that apart from around Lochanure, people in the Rosses and Gweedore rarely kept pigs. One explanation given for this was that it was an established custom that a family killing a pig would share it with their neighbours, and people were reluctant to follow this practice.[73] After the mid-nineteenth century, however, there was a great increase of poultry in Donegal, numbers peaking around

1931, at 1,409,122.[74] On even the smallest farms in the Rosses early this century, farms commonly kept flocks of up to one hundred hens.[75] Poultry were managed by women and the money made from selling eggs gave them considerable purchasing power. It was estimated in 1899, for example, that the produce of forty hens equalled a cow in value, and many western small farms had only one cow.[76]

The co-operative movement (IAOS) had a considerable impact in Donegal. Several leaders of the movement had close ties with the county, including Cardinal O'Donnell, George (AE) Russell, and Sir Hugh Law of Marblehill. One of the movement's most charismatic figures, Paddy 'the Cope' Gallagher, attracted national attention by the success he made of the Templecrone Co-operative Society in Dungloe, in spite of the virulent opposition of local traders.[77] The Templecrone 'cope' was originally an agricultural supply society, but very soon extended its range of activities. The history of most Donegal co-operatives was much less dramatic than that of the Templecrone society,[78] but by 1910 Donegal had well-established co-operative creameries, which also organised trading in eggs, agricultural supply societies, co-operative credit societies, and others dealing with more specialised interests such as bee-keeping and flax-growing.[79]

In 1899 the Department of Agriculture and Technical Instruction for Ireland was established, and this body began work in Donegal which was to a large extent complementary to the work of the co-operative movement and the Congested Districts Board.[80] Like the CDB, the department was actively involved in agricultural education. Donegal was part of the catchment area for the North West Agricultural School at Strabane, county Tyrone. Here, short residential courses were organised in general agriculture, poultry keeping, and butter making.[81] Itinerant agricultural instructors were also employed, who organised winter classes in a wide range of subjects.[82]

Increasingly, the department became involved in schemes which led to the standardisation and centralised marketing of farm produce. This approach was consolidated soon after the establishment of Dáil Éireann, when a series of acts were passed which aimed at 'raising the quality, and ... expansion in exports of Irish farm produce'.[83] Throughout the present century there has been an increasing alignment between Donegal agricultural production and developments in national and international markets. This alignment has been accompanied by changes in farm technology. Many larger eastern farms had made use of nineteenth century technical developments, such as horse-powered reapers and threshing machines. Between 1860 and 1940 Kennedy's foundry in Coleraine, county Derry, for example, sold horse-operated threshing machines in Donegal.[84] On many western farms, smaller scale technology was more appropriate, however, and early this century the Congested Districts Board offered 'hand-and-foot' operated machines to farmers in these areas.[85]

Tractor technology has also spread throughout the county during the present century. Between 1851 and 1931 there were around 20,000 working horses in Donegal. After 1931, a decline began,[86] although it was not until 1965 that the number of tractors (3,322) exceeded the number of working horses (3,014).[87] By 1980, there were 7,592 tractors in the county, and only 324 working horses.[88] Between 1965 and 1980, other significant large-scale equipment used in the arable sector included corn drills, liquid manure spreaders, forage harvesters, fully mechanised potato harvesters, sugar-beet harvesters and milking installations of all kinds.[89] During the recent past, also, the number of combine harvesters in the county rose from 57 to 216.[90]

Paradoxically, the mechanisation of arable farming has not led to any long-term reversal in the swing away from tillage in Donegal. There were increases in crop acreages during both world wars, flax cultivation in particular rising sharply during the Emergency arising from the Second World War, but the revival did not last and by 1958, only 200 acres were grown.[91] The staple crops, oats and potatoes, have also declined dramatically.[92] Newer crops such as sugar beet and oil seed rape have not significantly altered the pattern of reduced tillage, the county sharing the low level found throughout much of the west and midlands of Ireland.[93]

Livestock husbandry has not shown the overall decline found in tillage. Working horses have almost all disappeared, and poultry numbers have declined sharply since their peak in 1931. Pig numbers, however, which declined sharply during both world wars, are now well over twice as high as they were in 1851, and the number of sheep and cattle in the county, despite temporary slumps, are now higher than they have ever been since the mid-nineteenth century.[94] Livestock breeds have become much more specialised. Sheep are mostly of the black-faced mountain and Cheviot breeds.[95] In 1900 the most common breeds of cattle all over Ireland were dual-purpose Shorthorns, with significant numbers of native breeds such as Kerrys and Irish 'moilies' (maolaithe).[96] By 1980, in Donegal, Friesian cattle were the most common breed but overall there has been a long-term swing away from dairy to beef cattle.[97]

Modern farmers in Donegal respond with alacrity to changes in the agricultural policies of the European Union. It is likely that the concentration on particular kinds of livestock and crops will be increasingly attuned to the provision of EU subsidies and other incentives. Co-existing with all of this international awareness and sensitivity to changing farming methods, however, it is still possible to find small Donegal farmers using techniques such as ridge making or lashing oats which would have been recognisable not only to their grandfathers, but to Irish farmers hundreds and possibly thousands of years ago.

References

1. Sporadic evidence for farming in Donegal goes back to the neolithic period. Ancient field systems, similar to those excavated at Belderg, county Mayo, have been found in coastal areas. B. Lacey *et al., Archaeological survey of county Donegal* (Lifford, 1983), pp 50-54; S. Caulfield, 'Neolithic fields: the Irish evidence' in H. Bowen and P. Fowler (eds), *British Archaeological Report*, 48 (Oxford, 1978).

   Literary evidence for farming in the county goes back to the early Christian period when ploughing, reaping, herding and milking cattle are all described. J. Marsden, *The illustrated Columcille* (London, 1991), pp 104, 113, 117. Archaeological evidence for farming in the medieval period has been uncovered, for example at Carrickfin, where evidence of cattle, pig, sheep and goat farming has been documented. F. McCormick, 'The animal bones from Carrickfin, county Donegal' (report for paleoecology centre, Queen's University Belfast, 1985). Documents relating to the plantations of the early seventeenth century also give some evidence of arable farming and transhumance. J. M. Graham, 'South-west Donegal in the seventeenth century' in *Ir. Geog.*, vi (1970).

2. The impossibility of making a rigid east-west division becomes clear when we try to define the boundaries of the fertile 'Lagan'. One early twentieth-century writer delimited the area fairly clearly. 'Immediately to the south of [Inishowen] ... is a fertile and comparatively flat country, lying between the river Foyle and the upper reaches of Lough Swilly, and extending in one direction from the City of Derry to Stranorlar, and in another from Lifford to Letterkenny.' The same writer points out, however, that the name Lagan is not widely used by the inhabitants of the area, but more by people from the mountainous western seaboard. A. G. Lecky *The Laggan, and its Presbyterianism* (Belfast, 1905), p. 1. People in west Donegal do still use the term, but define the area much more vaguely. Barney Gallagher, an Arranmore man, says that for many of his fellow islanders, 'the Lagan ... was any place east of Errigal mountain' – B. Gallagher, *Arranmore links* (Donegal, 1986), p. 5.

3. A. Young, *A tour in Ireland*, i (Dublin, 1780), p. 237.

4. Ibid., p. 162.

5. Ibid., p. 226.

6. Ibid., p. 239.

7. Ibid., p. 227.

8. Ibid., p. 240.

9. J. McParlan, *Statistical survey of the county of Donegal* (Dublin, 1802a).

10. Ibid., pp 31-32.

11. McParlan, *Statistical survey of the county of Leitrim* (Dublin, 1802), p. 30.

12. McParlan, *Survey of Donegal*, p. 56.

13. Ibid., pp 44-7.

14. Ibid., pp 43-8.

15. Ibid., p. 54.
16. Ibid.
17. Ibid., p. 85.
18. Ibid., p. 82.
19. Anon, 'The North West of Ireland Agricultural Society' in *Ireland industrial and agricultural* (Dublin, 1902), p. 214.
20. J. Bell and M. Watson, *Irish farming: implements and techniques 1750-1900* (Edinburgh, 1986), p. 9.
21. North West of Ireland Society, *Magazine*, i (Derry, 1823), pp 156, 132.
22. Ibid., ii, p. 113.
23. Ibid., pp 114-15.
24. Bell and Watson, *Irish farming*, pp 64-89. Ordnance Survey Memoirs – Donegal, Box 22/1/1 (1835), Box 22/2/1 (1834) North-west of Ireland Society, *Magazine*, p. 6.
25. M. Harkin and S. McCarroll, *Carndonagh* (Dublin, 1984), p. 20.
26. J. Hamilton, *Sixty years' experience as an Irish landlord* (London, 1894), p. 47.
27. J. Bell, 'Recent evidence for the use of *ard* ploughs in county Fermanagh' in *Sinsear* (Dublin, 1983), pp 30-34.
28. J. Bell, 'Wooden ploughs from Mourne' in Ulster Folklife Society, *Field excursions in Ulster 3. The Annalong district of the Mournes, county Down* (Belfast, 1985), p. 65.
29. Bell and Watson, *Irish farming*, p. 15.
30. McParlan, *Survey of Donegal* (1802a), p. 99.
31. Ibid.
32. North West of Ireland Society, *Magazine*, ii, p. 53.
33. [Devon Commission] *Digest of evidence taken before Her Majesty's Commissioners of Inquiry into the state of the law and practice in respect to the occupation of land in Ireland*, vol. 1 (Dublin, 1847), p. 603.
34. Ibid., pp 587-8.
35. Mr and Mrs S. C. Hall, *Ireland: its scenery and character*, iii (London, 1841), p. 262.
36. Ibid.
37. Ibid., p. 264.
38. Bell and Watson, *Irish farming*, p. 25.
39. McParlan, *Survey of Donegal*, p. 76.
40. North West of Ireland Society, *Magazine*, ii, pp 348-50.
41. Bell and Watson, *Irish farming*, pp 10-11.
42. *Devon Commission*, loc. cit., p. 42.
43. Hall, *Ireland*, p. 266.
44. Ibid.
45. Lord George Hill, *Facts from Gweedore* (5th ed.) (Belfast, 1971).
46. Ibid., p. xii.
47. Ibid., p. 3.
48. J. M. Graham, 'South-west Donegal', p. 141. F. Coll and J. Bell, 'An account of life at *Machaire Gathlán* (Magheragallan) county Donegal, early this century' in *Ulster Folklife*, xxxvi, p. 83; S. Ó Duilearga, 'Mountain shielings in Donegal', *Béaloideas*, ix (Dublin, 1939), pp 295-7.
49. Hill, *Facts*, p. 17.
50. Ibid., p. 21.
51. Ibid., pp 63-4.
52. An even more dramatic divergence of perceptions has, however, been recorded, on Lord Leitrim's estate in Fanad. Leitrim was eventually murdered. S. MacPhilib,

'Profile of a landlord in folk tradition and in contemporary accounts – the third Earl of Leitrim', *Ulster Folklife*, xxxiv (Holywood, 1988), pp 30-32.

53. Hill, *Facts*, p. xv.
54. Ibid.
55. Figures from Central Statistics Office, Dublin. I am grateful to Mr Frank Kelly of An Phríomh-Oifig Staidrimh for providing these and other statistics of agricultural output between 1851 and 1987.
56. Figures from Central Statistics Office, Dublin.
57. W. E. Vaughan, *Sin, sheep and Scotsmen* (Belfast, 1982).
58. J. Bell, Economic change in the Dunfanaghy area of north Donegal, 1900-1940, unpublished Ph.D. thesis – Queen's University Belfast, 1982, p. 88.
59. Quoted in MacPhilib, 'Profile of a landlord', p. 35.
60. W. L. Micks, *An account of the ... Congested Districts Board for Ireland from 1891 to 1923* (Dublin, 1925), pp 241-58.
61. P. Bolger, *The Irish co-operative movement* (Dublin, 1977), pp 158-60; see also P. Bolger, chapter in this volume.
62. Ibid., p. 164.
63. Coll and Bell, 'Life at *Machaire Gathlán*', pp 82-3.
64. Ibid., p. 85, and verbal information from Mr Anthony Glackin, Saltpans, county Donegal, 1987.
65. Coll and Bell, 'Life at *Machaire Gathlán*', p. 82.
66. Ibid., p. 81.
67. George H. Pethybridge 'Cultivation of seaweed in Ireland', *Journal of the Department of Agriculture and Technical Instruction for Ireland*, xv (Dublin, 1915), p. 547.
68. Verbal information from Mr Hugh Paddy Óg Ward, Keadew (Ulster Folk and Transport Museum tape no: R87.60).
69. Bell, *Economic change*, p. 58.
70. Hugh Paddy Óg Ward, Keadew.
71. Micks, *Congested Districts Board*, p. 244.
72. Ibid., p. 244.
73. Hugh Paddy Óg Ward, Keadew.
74. Figures from Central Statistics Office, Dublin (See note 94 for detailed figures).
75. Hugh Paddy Óg Ward, Keadew.
76. Bolger, *Co-operative movement*, p. 280.
77. P. Gallagher, *My story* (Dungloe, 1956).
78. J. Bell, 'An agricultural co-operative in county Donegal, Ireland' in *Peasant studies*, x (Salt Lake City, 1983), pp 191-211.
79. Bolger, *Co-operative movement*, p. 338.
80. Ibid., p. 293.
81. D. Hoctor, *The department's story* (Dublin, 1971), p. 61.
82. Ibid., p. 64.
83. Ibid., p. 164.
84. A. Gailey, 'Introduction and spread of the horsepowered threshing machine to Ulster's farms in the nineteenth century: some aspects' in *Ulster Folklife*, xxx, p. 4.
85. Congested Districts Board *Report* no. 12 (Dublin, 1903), p. 13.
86. Number of working horses in Donegal
    1851 – 22,689, 1901 – 22,032, 1918 – 21,558, 1931 – 18,288
    Figures from Central Statistics Office, Dublin.
87. Central Statistics Office, 'Agricultural statistics, 1965', *Irish Statistical Bulletin* (Dublin, March 1966), pp 23 and 27.

88. Central Statistics Office, 'Agricultural statistics, June 1980', *Irish Statistical Bulletin* (Dublin, March 1983), pp 33 and 34.

89. Ibid., pp 34-5.

90. Ibid., p. 34 and Central Statistics Office, *Irish Statistical Bulletin* (1966), p. 27.

91. Flax acreage: 1938 – 1,641 acres, 1944 – 9,409 acres
Figures from Central Statistics Office, Dublin.

92. *Acreage of oats and potatoes*

	Oats	Potatoes
1851	100,882	34,432
1980	4,468	6,053

93. A. A. Horner, J. A. Walsh and J. A. Williams, *Agriculture in Ireland: a census atlas* (Dublin, 1984), map 2.

94. *Numbers of livestock in Donegal, 1851-1987*

	Cattle	Sheep	Pigs	Poultry
1851	147,432	81,512	17,355	297,911
1901	187,457	200,682	26,443	863,217
1918	170,917	147,062	16,415	1,244,333
1926	154,351	164,453	17,997	1,325,080
1931	158,508	228,116	29,600	1,409,122
1938	145,777	176,006	14,651	1,008,902
1946	156,391	171,261	5,210	998,077
1953	155,779	215,539	11,577	1,100,142
1958	157,800	288,100	13,300	764,500
1965	172,888	290,744	21,848	529,400
1975	222,332	304,594	39,336	283,293
1980	200,082	318,008	44,747	190,498
1987	209,000	445,400	—	—

Figures from Central Statistics Office, Dublin.

95. Central Statistics Office, *Irish Statistical Bulletin* (1966), p. 17 (1977), p. 33 (1983), p. 31.

96. Anon. 'The Irish cattle industry' in *Ireland industrial and agricultural*, p. 359.

97. Central Statistics Office, *Irish Statistical Bulletin* (1983), pp 26-7.

Chapter 17

LOUGH DERG: THE MAKING OF THE MODERN PILGRIMAGE

JAMES S. DONNELLY, Jr

In the religious history of Ireland the holy island of Lough Derg, or St Patrick's Purgatory, has occupied a special place for centuries. Its Catholic chroniclers have never failed to stress its antiquity and continuity. Although a different interpretation will be presented in this essay, the view offered by devotional writers and other commentators is that of a highly distinctive religious experience whose core the passage of centuries has left virtually intact. Thus in a book which long remained the standard account of Lough Derg after its first publication in 1879, the young county Monaghan priest Father Daniel O'Connor described the famous pilgrimage to St Patrick's Purgatory as the 'oldest existing institution of the Irish church', with roots in the earliest Irish Christian era. 'It forms a connecting link', he declared, 'between the days of St Patrick and the present time. The penitential exercises of this pilgrimage constitute the most venerable and perhaps the only authorised surviving instance of the early Irish religious observances and penitential discipline – a discipline under which so many saints and scholars flourished.'[1]

Although hard evidence for direct Patrician links is lacking, there is abundant documentation for the national and indeed international celebrity of Lough Derg since at least the twelfth century. It was then that the story of the Knight Owein's pilgrimage to St Patrick's Purgatory, as written down by an English Cistercian monk, Brother H. of Saltery, first captured the literate imagination of medieval Europe with its vivid images of excruciating torments suffered there by sinful souls. By descending into a cave at Lough Derg, the Knight Owein supposedly was able to reach and explore the 'real' purgatory, the ecclesiastical doctrine of which was then in the process of more precise definition. As Laurence Flynn has succinctly pointed out, the enormous popularity of this story 'can be gauged from the fact that 150 manuscript copies of Brother H.'s text survive today in libraries throughout Europe, and as many manuscripts again give his story in translation'.[2]

For Protestant reformers, of course, the very notion of purgatory, tied up as it was with the scandalous sale of indulgences, was anathema, a classic instance of popish superstition which they sought to eradicate. Partly for this reason, Lough Derg and its pilgrimage became the focus of bitter controversy and conflict between Catholics and Protestants in Ireland during and after the Reformation. The pilgrimage epitomised their clashing world views. In the Protestant mind St Patrick's Purgatory was emblematic of the worst evils of popery, and the several attempts made by the government in the seventeenth century to suppress the pilgrimage and to desecrate the site were deemed to be highly praiseworthy, indeed part of God's work. In the Catholic mind, on the other hand, Lough Derg was emblematic of steadfastness in the faith in spite of the severest persecution. Catholic writers tended to regard the site of St Patrick's Purgatory as the holiest, or almost the holiest, place in all of Ireland, whereas with Protestant writers it occupied the foremost position in their demonology. As the Protestant rector, the Rev. John Richardson, observed of Lough Derg in 1727, 'it hath [the] most votaries and is the most remarkable in the kingdom, or perhaps in the whole world, for superstition and idolatry...'.[3] Even a century later, that inveterate traveller and Protestant evangelical Caesar Otway could scathingly write of Lough Derg as a place 'towards which the tide of human superstition had flowed for twelve centuries' and as 'the monstrous birth of a dreary and degraded superstition – the enemy of mental cultivation, and destined to keep the human understanding in the same dark, unproductive state as the moorland waste that lay outstretched around [it]'.[4]

It was this combination of factors (its antiquity, the severity of its penitential discipline, its early literary fame, and the bitter sectarian controversy long surrounding it), and not the number of pilgrims, that was responsible for Lough Derg's status as the premier Irish national centre of pilgrimage before 1845. Perhaps because of the rigours of its penitential rituals, St Patrick's Purgatory has never attracted vast crowds. At the beginning of the eighteenth century an entire pilgrimage season brought only about 5,000 visitors to Lough Derg,[5] and there is no reason to think that this figure had been exceeded in earlier periods. The pilgrimage traffic appears to have grown modestly by the 1780s, when one visitor reported a seasonal intake of 7,000 to 8,000 pilgrims.[6]

For the early nineteenth century there are numerous observations or estimates relating to the dimensions of the pilgrimage traffic at Lough Derg. But they display considerable variability and are not always reliable. The figures advanced by quite a few writers are much higher than those for the eighteenth or the late nineteenth centuries. Among the highest are those put forward by Father (later Canon) O'Connor in his history of St Patrick's Purgatory, the first edition of which, as previously noted, appeared in 1879. According to O'Connor, the 'average yearly number' from 1800 to 1824 was 'about 10,000'. In 1824 itself, he claims, the number exceeded 15,000; in 1834 it reached 19,000, and 'in the beginning of the famine years' (apparently, 1846 was meant) 'we are told that the total number of pilgrims could not have been much under 30,000'.[7]

How much contemporary support is there for the relatively high early nineteenth-century numbers advanced by O'Connor, and to what extent are these high figures reliable? O'Connor did not cite any specific sources either for his assertion that the number of pilgrims averaged 'about 10,000' a year from 1800 to 1824 or for his claim that in the first year of the famine the figure was close to 30,000. I know of no data that could possibly support the first statement, and the second also appears to lack any credible foundation. A special search of relevant newspapers failed to yield any evidence that Lough Derg was flooded with pilgrims in 1845 or 1846. But O'Connor's high numbers do find some corroboration. The experienced English traveller John Barrow, who toured Ireland in the autumn of 1835, 'was assured that during the last year the number of persons who had taken what is called "their rounds" at the purgatory was between nineteen and twenty thousand'.[8] In addition, the *Parliamentary Gazetteer for Ireland* for 1844-5 noted that the seasonal intake varied from 10,000 to 15,000 persons,[9] a figure repeated for the 1840s ('as many as fifteen thousand people') by a well-informed observer writing in *Household Words* in 1850.[10] On the other hand, the great antiquary John O'Donovan, who visited Lough Derg in 1835 while traversing county Donegal for the Ordnance Survey, took note of a report that 7,000 pilgrims arrived 'every year during the station season',[11] and even the writer in *Household Words* conceded that the attendance in 1851 was 'not likely to exceed six thousand'.[12] Although the available evidence is obviously conflicting, it is questionable whether the number of pilgrims ever approached 30,000 a year prior to 1850, and a *regular* seasonal intake of even 20,000 appears dubious. But annual attendances of 10,000 to 15,000, at least in some years, do seem probable. If this conclusion is correct, it would still mean that perhaps two or three times as many pilgrims came to Lough Derg in the 1830s and early 1840s as had visited in the eighteenth century.

In the second half of the nineteenth century, however, the pilgrimage traffic to Lough Derg went into steep decline. Systematic and reliable data on the number of pilgrims in each season survive for the years 1866-91. During most of that period fewer than 3,000 pilgrims visited St Patrick's Purgatory each year, and in no year of that period did the figure exceed 4,000. The highest number (3,683) came in 1872, the lowest (1,765) in 1879.[13] But even the heavier traffic which was evident in the decades immediately before the great famine was not all that impressive. The pilgrimages associated with many of the biggest regional patterns could boast traffic of similar magnitude, and these were occasions that lasted only a day or two (or three at most), in contrast to the season of two to three months at Lough Derg. Around 1840 the pattern at Ardmore, county Waterford, in honour of St Declan, which was a three-day affair in July, drew 12,000 to 15,000 persons, according to a careful calculation.[14] And the pilgrims who climbed Croagh Patrick, or 'the Reek' as it was popularly known, were said to number 'at least 30,000' in 1825.[15]

Change has manifested itself at Lough Derg in recent centuries not only in the fluctuating number of pilgrims but also and much more importantly in the character of the devotional exercises. This transformation has generally been overlooked or insufficiently appreciated by historians, and certain devotional writers have unwittingly turned the true story on its head. One of the myths repeatedly propagated about this ancient pilgrimage has been the alleged persistence of its traditional rituals. As Canon O'Connor insisted in his late nineteenth-century history of St Patrick's Purgatory, 'Elsewhere penitential austerities may have become modified in accordance with the circumstances of the age, but at Lough Derg the discipline of penance is as unchanged as when St Patrick and the holy cenobites, who imitated his extraordinary mortification, peopled those cells or beds round which a moving line of pilgrims may be seen reciting their devotions throughout the station season'.[16] In fact, the penitential severities for which Lough Derg had been famous in the medieval and early modern periods were greatly softened in the late eighteenth and early nineteenth centuries. In addition, or as a constituent part of this development, the traditional rituals were overhauled and reshaped by the ecclesiastical authorities so as to bring them much more closely into line with the demands of Tridentine Catholicism. It is not too much to say that at the hands of reforming bishops and priests a new religious regime was gradually put into place in the years 1750-1850. At the end of this process the Lough Derg experience as we know it today had essentially come into being.

What occurred at Lough Derg can be seen as a small but significant part of the much larger process by which the institutional church, in response to the fundamental challenge of the Protestant Reformation, set out to refashion the practice of religion by ordinary believers. In place of such traditional features as communal feasts celebrating local saints, held out of doors, and involving much lay control over ritual, the reformers inspired by the Council of Trent aimed to bring worship within the confines of the parish church, to focus it on the Mass and the sacraments, and to put the parish priest in complete charge of the storehouse of supernatural power. As John Bossy has pointed out in a seminal article, the realisation of these goals that made up the Tridentine agenda was a very protracted enterprise, which took 150 to 200 years of effort even in France and Italy.[17] Within the Irish historiographical context the name which has come to be applied to this transformation, following Emmet Larkin, is the Devotional Revolution. Although Larkin's view is that the Devotional Revolution in Ireland essentially took place in the period 1850-75, coinciding with and spurred on by the ecclesiastical primacy of Archbishop (later Cardinal) Paul Cullen,[18] other historians have seen it as a trend which began in the late eighteenth century and had already made deep inroads before the great famine.[19] The timing of devotional change at Lough Derg lends support to this latter revisionist view.

Before the character and dimensions of the major changes in ritual after 1750 can be grasped, it is necessary to provide an account of the strenuous ordeal which traditionally faced the conscientious Lough Derg pilgrim. All informed observers regarded the customary rites as a demanding test of repentance, and some commentators believed them to be unique in this respect. In his little Latin guide to Lough Derg, published at Louvain in 1735, Father Dominick Brullaughan declared that he had never 'read of any other place better for performing penance, nor of any severer purgatory in this world for a space of nine days'.[20] Bishop Thomas Burke, author of the famous *Hibernia Dominicana,* was led in 1748 to the same conclusion about Lough Derg by his review of the penances performed there, 'the like of which I do not believe take place at any other pilgrimage in the world'.[21]

St Patrick's Purgatory, then, was not a place for the fainthearted, the frivolous, or the laggard. Instead, it was far better suited to the religious athlete. Simply getting to this rugged and rather desolate corner of Donegal usually involved a long and arduous journey, generally on foot, at least for the poor. Immediately on coming in sight of the holy island, pilgrims were expected to remove their shoes and stockings and to bare their heads. After being ferried over to the island, they began a wearying and seemingly unceasing round of prayer, fasting, and other bodily mortifications that stretched over nine days. The fast was strict and must itself have been a severe test of endurance and commitment. Pilgrims were allowed only one meal a day, and this consisted merely of oaten bread or cakes and hot water, although the drinking of water (hot or cold) taken from the lake and the use of tobacco were apparently permitted at almost any time.[22] Such rigorous fasting no doubt contributed to the tendency of pilgrims to experience visions while on the island.[23]

Each day (except, usually, the last) the fasting pilgrim had to endure the pain and tribulation of doing the appointed stations barefoot and in all weathers. These stations, entailing an intricate pattern of prayer said in sacred spaces, were repeated three times a day around sunrise, noon, and sunset. It was estimated that in doing just one of the three required daily stations, a pilgrim walked as much as two miles. Over nine days the total distance amounted to well over fifty miles.[24] The most punishing and tedious part of the station was to traverse barefoot the seven so-called saints' beds while saying certain prayers.

Originally beehive-shaped oratories or cells dating back to perhaps the ninth century,[25] these sacred structures had suffered from the ravages of time and the destroying hands of Protestant 'heretics'. Now all that remained were low-walled circles of stone, about two feet high and from nine to eleven feet in diameter, with the exception of the so-called 'large bed', which was sixteen feet across.[26] On one side of each of the circular beds was a gap that allowed entry. The floors of the beds, inset with stones, were rough and uneven, besides being slippery when wet. Only the most hardened and nimble feet escaped without cuts and bruises. Indeed, the beds, declared a hostile Protestant clergyman in 1727, were 'so rugged and thick set with small, pointed stones that the greatest saint in the church of Rome could not bear it now and much less take any rest upon them', as the ancient saints were supposed to have done.[27] And besides the feet, knees also fared poorly, as the ritual required the pilgrim to kneel a dozen times in going over the penitential beds during each station, and thus 324 times in the course of nine days. At each of the saints' beds the pilgrim made three circuits of both the exterior and the interior of the stone circle, saying a prescribed number of prayers while making each circuit and the same number in a kneeling position upon entering and leaving each bed. Taking into account the three stations performed daily, the Dominican Bishop Burke calculated that each pilgrim said nearly three hundred paters and aves and about one hundred creeds, together with the whole of Our Lady's psalter (another 150 aves and 15 paters) three times.[28] In short, the praying was both mantra-like in its character and heroic in its proportions.

The circling of the penitential beds actually came in the middle of the station exercises. The arriving pilgrim first visited what was called St Patrick's altar, a pile of stones with the shank of a cross fixed in the middle of it, and the ruined chapel at the opposite side of the landing place; the pilgrim then made seven prayerful circuits of these two monuments. Following this ritual and that of the saints' beds, the pilgrim took his cut and bruised feet into the waters of Lough Derg itself, where the rites briefly focused on certain stones or rocks 'three or four paces' from the island shore. These included a group of sharp penitential stones known as the *Coaranach*. Pilgrims circled and knelt on these stones in order to 'redeem the punishment due to the sins of our five outward senses'.[29] But in contrast to the painful *Coaranach,* a smooth, flat stone called the *Leac na mbonn* reputedly had 'the singular virtue of curing the bruised and wounded feet of the pilgrims'.[30] The last act of the station, performed in the chapel, entailed the repetition of the exacting psalter or rosary of the Blessed Virgin, with its 150 aves and 15 paters.[31]

But the most famous, indeed notorious, ritual associated with the Lough Derg pilgrimage came on the ninth day (or some earlier day if crowding required it), when the pilgrim spent twenty-four hours without sleep or food in what was variously termed the cave, the pit, or purgatory. It was the descent into this purgatory that had fixed Lough Derg in the medieval literary imagination and that in the early centuries of the pilgrimage had attracted a steady stream of well-born penitents from foreign lands. According to the legend or foundation myth from which this ritual arose, St Patrick, wishing to convert the pagan Irish to Christianity, prayed to God that 'He might let them hear the lamentations of those who are in purgatory, in order that they might thereby be induced to believe', and the legend had it that 'from that hour onwards a perpetual lamentation and sighing has been heard out of this abyss'.[32]

Pilgrims to Lough Derg in the early eighteenth century encountered two caves, and it appears that neither of these was the original storied purgatory. If the topographical evidence of the Knight Owein story is accepted, then the original purgatory was located on Saints' Island, a larger nearby island that was also home to a monastic foundation of Augustinian canons, who long presided over the pilgrimage. The transfer of the purgatory to what became its permanent home on Station Island took place, it has been suggested, between the end of the twelfth century and about 1230. It was apparently this cave or purgatory that was closed in 1497 on the orders of Pope Alexander VI, reportedly on the grounds that it was an imposture and 'not the purgatory Patrick got from God, although they were, everyone, visiting it'.[33] Exactly what happened subsequently is unclear, but two caves were in use on Station Island in about 1630 at the time of a visit by a Protestant gentleman named Coppinger, one cave having been found to 'hinder the despatching of so many pilgrims', especially since custom prohibited mixing the sexes in this purgatory.[34] Although there was apparently a temporary reversion to a single cave by the late 1640s,[35] the same reasons that had first led to two caves prior to 1630 eventually brought about their return. In his Latin guide of 1735, Father

Brullaughan remarked that a new stone cave had been built because 'often there is so great a crowd of pilgrims that they cannot enter the old cave.' (And, said Brullaughan, 'if these two caves are not sufficient, they enter the chapel and watch, pray, and fast there for twenty-four hours.')[36]

Presumably, the so-called new cave was not unlike the old, of which numerous descriptions have survived. Writing in 1624, the Catholic bishop of Ossory, David Rothe, depicted it as 'a little stone house with such narrow sides and such a depressed arch that a man of big stature could not raise himself nor even sit unless with bended neck'. Into this confined space a relatively small number of pilgrims were crammed: 'They sit and lean next to each other in nines, pressing close, but a tenth could not join them except with the greatest trouble'.[37] A similar description came from the pen of an English Protestant gentleman who visited Lough Derg in 1765: 'This vault is only so long as to hold twelve penitents at once, who sit close to one another in a row, with their chins almost touching their knees...'.[38] If one assumes that two caves, each with a dozen penitents, were kept going daily for three months during the pilgrimage season, only slightly more than 2,000 persons could have had the experience of this purgatory, a figure that would represent from half to two-thirds of the 3,000 to 4,000 pilgrims said to be frequenting Lough Derg in the 1760s.[39]

Pilgrims intending to enter one of the caves were prepared psychologically and spiritually for their descent into purgatory by the dramatic religious ritual which directly preceded it. By immemorial custom the Mass of the Dead was said for all such pilgrims, 'just as if', observed the Catholic Bishop Hugh MacMahon of Clogher in 1714, 'they were dead to the world and ready for sepulture'.[40] The funeral drama was continued with a procession of pilgrims 'with cross and holy water to the door of the cave', where after the prior or his agent had bestowed a blessing, the pilgrims entered 'the sepulchre on bended knee', having been 'made like unto those who descend into the pit, as men without help, free among the dead, as wounded by the sorrow of penance but still keeping vigil in the sepulchre'.[41] These words have been taken from Father Brullaughan's guide to Lough Derg, English editions of which appeared from presses at Belfast and Dublin in 1752, and which remained 'much used at the pilgrimage' for almost a century.[42] Traditionally, the monks or friars in charge of the pilgrimage also ritually warned penitents against going into purgatory because of the trials, temptations, and terrors that awaited them there. Given this preparation, pilgrims were often emotionally stretched even before entering the cave. In his account of 1647 Henry Jones, the Protestant bishop of Clogher, pointed out, 'in what agony do they go, groaning and sighing,' or again 'with sighing, weeping, and tears'.[43]

Once pilgrims had been shut into purgatory, their physical and psychological distress intensified. Besides having to abstain from all food, pilgrims had fresh in their minds the friars' repeated cautions not to sleep, with the cautions underlined by the clerical declaration that 'the devil will certainly carry them away (as he hath done two cavefulls already) if he should catch them napping'.[44] This story of 1727 that the devil lay in wait to sweep off a third batch of dozing pilgrims, 'having a prophecy in his favour' to that effect, was repeated some forty years later by another Protestant visitor, who called the friars' cautionary tale 'more stimulating than even the pin' that was 'to be suddenly inserted into the elbow of his next neighbour at the first appearance of a nod'.[45] To remain awake throughout their twenty-four hours in the cave was, of all the penitential requirements, the hardest for pilgrims to satisfy, thus explaining why both psychological and physical coercion was needed to enforce adherence to it.

It is scarcely surprising that pilgrims deprived in this way of sleep and food, and crammed with others into a small, dark space after a funeral Mass and procession, should frequently have had fearful visions and dreams of the underworld and its torments. Writing in August 1517, shortly after his visit to Lough Derg, the papal nuncio Francesco Chiericati remarked that it was the practice of one of the Augustinian canons to station himself at a small opening into the cave and there to exhort the pilgrims periodically 'to be constant and not to be overcome by the temptations of the devil, for it is said that all manner of horrible visions appear to them, and many come out idiots or madmen because they have yielded to temptation'.[46] That at least some pilgrims appeared mad or psychologically disturbed on their release from purgatory is beyond doubt. Vividly recalling his visit, Chiericati also reported:

> Of those who entered the cave when I was present, two saw such fearful things that one went out of his mind, and when he was questioned, declared that he had been beaten violently, but he did not know by whom. Another had seen beautiful women, who had invited him to eat with them and offered him fruit and food of all sorts, and these [women] were almost vanquished. The others saw and felt nothing but great cold, hunger, and weakness and came out half-dead the next day.[47]

Emerging from purgatory at the end of the twenty-four-hour vigil, the exhausted pilgrims, as a last act of devotion, engaged in a bracing ritual of purification. Laying aside their clothes, they went completely naked into the lake and immersed themselves three times 'in the name of the

Holy Trinity in which we were first absolved by baptism'.[48] This purification ritual, with naked bathing to wash away sin, could also be found at other pilgrimage sites of the time. But at Lough Derg men and women performed the ritual separately and out of each other's sight. Only after the male pilgrims had immersed themselves and dressed did the prior or his agent call the women from the cave and invite them to do likewise.[49]

A pilgrim who had completed the severe penitential rituals of Lough Derg carried home emblems of his or her status and became an object of veneration and respect in the local community. The departing pilgrim took away a special staff previously used in making the stations but now with a cross peg fastened in a hole bored near the top of the staff. Besides bearing this emblem, pilgrims also carried away pebbles and water taken from the lake. The pebbles were treated as amulets with curative or protective powers and were presented by returned pilgrims to their relatives and friends. Similar significance was attached to the water of Lough Derg, which the pilgrims invariably called wine in obvious reference to the sacramental wine of the Mass, and which must have been popularly seen as more powerful than the curing waters of the innumerable local holy wells. Partly for these instrumental reasons and partly because of the status of Lough Derg in the popular religious psyche of Irish Catholics, the returned pilgrim was greatly revered as the embodiment of holiness. People would generally drop to their knees and beseech the pilgrim's blessing.[50]

If it was still accurate in 1750 to regard the Lough Derg pilgrimage as the most severe penitential test in western Christendom, by 1850 that reputation could no longer be sustained. This softening of penitential discipline was part of a fairly systematic restructuring of the traditional rites of the pilgrimage, which was itself a fascinating example of the great change in religious regimes that Ireland experienced in the late eighteenth and nineteenth centuries. Two of the most important modifications in ritual took place before 1800. In the first, the Franciscan managers of the pilgrimage greatly reduced its duration, certainly for some penitents and perhaps for most. The numerous early eighteenth-century sources – Archdeacon Hewson, Bishop MacMahon, the Rev. Richardson, Father Brullaughan – all indicate a pilgrimage lasting nine days, without ever mentioning shorter periods of penance at Lough Derg.[51] The first commentator to make reference to shorter periods was the anonymous English visitor of 1765 whose account appeared in the *Gentleman's Magazine* in February of the following year. According to this account, the pilgrim's stay lasted three, six, or nine days, depending on 'the quality of his sins, his leisure, or the judgement of his confessor'.[52] A later visitor, the Rev. William Bruce, noted in his journal for 1783 that nine days was 'a full term', thus implying that not all pilgrims went the entire distance.[53] The situation was further clarified in a report of 1804 by the Catholic Bishop James Murphy of Clogher, who observed that pilgrims made a '3, 6, or 9 days' station according to the nature of their vow or obligation, and in case of no vow or obligation, according to their devotion'.[54] Exactly how soon a majority of pilgrims availed themselves of the shortest duration – three days – is uncertain. But by 1850 the heroic nine-day stay was a distant memory except for the extremely devout. The anonymous author of a richly detailed account of Lough Derg published in *Household Words* in 1850 took three days to be the standard duration for the great majority, though he also remarked, 'There are some ... who accomplish six days' penance, and a few nine days'...'.[55] By this point, in fact, the general practice had almost settled into the invariable three-day length of today's pilgrimage.[56]

Just as important as the reduction in the length of the pilgrimage was the closure of the purgatorial cave or caves. Sometime in the 1780s – the exact date is uncertain – the caves were superseded by a modest new church dedicated to St Patrick but familiarly known as the 'prison chapel'. It was in the prison chapel, later repeatedly enlarged and improved, that pilgrims would keep the sleepless and foodless twenty-four-hour vigil for over a century.[57] The closing of the caves and the erection of the prison chapel in their place appear to have coincided with a fundamental change in the administration of the pilgrimage. Ever since the early seventeenth century, when they succeeded the Augustinian canons, Franciscans from the Donegal convent had supervised and staffed the pilgrimage, with one of the friars serving as the prior. But in 1780, or shortly thereafter, jurisdiction over the famous pilgrimage passed into the hands of the bishop of Clogher, the Rev. Dr Hugh O'Reilly, who appointed one of his diocesan priests, Father Patrick Murray, as prior. The new arrangement, which was attributed, perhaps too facilely, to the fact that the Franciscans' 'reduced numbers rendered them no longer equal to the work of the pilgrimage', proved permanent.[58] Father Murray, who also served as parish priest of Errigal-Truagh, was the first in an unbroken line of modern priors, most of them with remarkably long tenures, to be drawn from the secular clergy of Clogher diocese.[59] The Franciscan presence did not vanish immediately. The long-serving Franciscan prior, Father Anthony O'Doherty, who by 1783 had spent over thirty pilgrimage seasons at Lough Derg, continued to minister on the island after Murray took over, but the supervision of the pilgrimage was now firmly under diocesan control.[60]

Though lacking conclusive evidence, students of Lough Derg have tended to assume that it was Father Murray who built the prison chapel and shut the caves for good. This now appears certain. For when in July 1783 the Rev. William Bruce visited Lough Derg, he noted that pilgrims keeping the twenty-four-hour vigil were still 'sitting in purgatory or in the chapel', and on the back cover of his journal or diary he drew a sketch of the island site, with the mouth of the cave or purgatory clearly marked.[61] At some point before 1790 the cave or caves ceased forever to be used.[62] This strongly suggests that Bishop O'Reilly and perhaps his coadjutor, Bishop James Murphy, were decidedly hostile to the traditional ritual which above all others had defined Lough Derg in the eyes of ordinary Catholics as well as its many Protestant critics.

Other important consequences flowed from the takeover of the pilgrimage by the diocesan ordinary and his secular clergy. The pilgrimage was made to serve the goals of Tridentine Catholicism. Only a year after becoming bishop of Clogher, the Rev. Dr James Murphy issued in May 1802 what he called 'a few of the many regulations necessary for the orderly administration of the station at Lough Derg'. Among these was an injunction that the catechism be taught systematically to the pilgrims.[63] For 'many years' afterward two catechists were specially employed in this task, one for Irish-speakers and the other for English-speakers. In addition to 'instructing the rude and illiterate in their Christian doctrine', the two catechists also assisted the station priests in preparing pilgrims to receive the sacraments of Penance and the Eucharist.[64]

Confession and the Mass had long been essential parts of the Lough Derg experience, but beginning under Bishop Murphy there was a new emphasis on the preparation necessary for receiving Penance and the Eucharist worthily. Without sufficient knowledge of the catechism, pilgrims were not to be admitted to confession, nor even 'to the benefit of the station' at all. In addition, the clergy were said in 1814 to preach daily exhortations on the conditions necessary for a good confession and on 'the dreadful crime of approaching the tribunal' without satisfying these conditions. As confessors for the station, Bishop Murphy appointed only parish priests, 'the most learned and edifying I can procure', because some pilgrims had not 'for many years complied with any Christian duty' and presented 'difficult cases', that is, weighty sins. Pilgrims kept the confessors very busy. According to Bishop Murphy in 1814, six or seven priests sat in their confessionals for twelve hours or more every day for two months during the height of the pilgrimage season. And even this number was 'scarcely adequate' owing to 'the multiplicity of general confessions and the many penitents that come from every part of the kingdom for the purpose of getting strange confessors they will never see again'.[65]

In the new religious regime that began to take hold at Lough Derg in the 1780s, there was no longer any room for certain devotional practices that were now regarded as primitive, improper, or unseemly. At some point the Mass of the Dead that customarily preceded the descent into purgatory was abandoned, probably in conjunction with the shutting of the caves. Another casualty of the new regime was the purification rite that had traditionally followed the release from purgatory. This apparently fell foul of straight-laced Victorian sensibilities. Public immersion in the nude, even as part of sacred ceremonies and even if done separately by women and men, was hardly acceptable in that age. 'The practice of wading into the lake, which existed not long ago,' declared a careful observer in 1850, 'has been forbidden, as well as that of carrying stones away as memorials.'[66] 'Memorials' is not the right word here, nor is it likely that the prohibition arose from a reasonable fear that 'the island, being small and composed of stones, would by degrees be completely carried off by the pilgrims'.[67] Instead, what the church authorities wanted was to put an end to the superstitious use of Lough Derg pebbles as curative or protective amulets. Clearly, they had become hostile to such practices as that mentioned by William Carleton of laying two Lough Derg pebbles on the breast of every corpse as it was placed in the coffin.[68] Indeed, as Canon O'Connor noted in his history, the ban was not restricted to pebbles but also embraced 'water from the lake, branches of trees, ferns, heath, or such like' – all because of 'the danger that undue value might be attached to those things'. Even though, said O'Connor, 'this may seem a small matter, order and discipline even in small things should be observed'.[69]

The desire for order and discipline was manifested in yet another way. Religious ecstasy or enthusiasm had once been an accepted element of the Lough Derg pilgrimage. It was not only a matter of the visions, dreams, or nightmares experienced by penitents shut up in purgatory. Pilgrims also gave open expression to their feelings during the sermons preached several times daily. According to Bishop Hugh MacMahon in 1714, they frequently interrupted the preacher 'with copious tears, sobs, lamentations, and other marks of penance'.[70] How long clerical tolerance lasted for such exuberant lay behaviour is not exactly clear, but it had largely disappeared by the 1850s, if not earlier. A visitor in 1850, repairing to the chapel for evening prayers, heard the 'nightly warning' from the pulpit against impermissible practices on the holy island. Besides intoxicants and alms-giving, these included what were called exultations, that is, 'expressions of religious praise or joy, as unfit for a time of penance'.[71] If shouts of joy were prohibited, it hardly seems possible that loud laments were welcome any longer either. As with keening for the dead, this traditional style of religion was anathema to the modernising Catholic clergy.

In conclusion, during the half-century or so before the great famine, the Catholic bishops of Clogher and the secular priests they appointed as priors of Lough Derg took thorough control of this ancient pilgrimage and radically reshaped its rituals. In the case of Lough Derg, the imposition of a new or reformed religious regime was made easier by the general absence of those profane or secular elements that made the clerical struggle against other hybrid forms of traditional popular religion, above all the local patterns, so much more protracted, contentious, and difficult. In 1780, when the prelates of the ecclesiastical province of Armagh banned patterns and 'all the other stations of pilgrimage' in their dioceses, Lough Derg was exempted and, 'owing to its great utility, was by their unanimous suffrage judged worthy of being continued'.[72] The drinking, feasting, singing, dancing, and fighting that characterised the profane side of patterns never established themselves at Lough Derg. On the only apparent occasion when there was a serious danger that the pilgrimage would assume such detested features, in the year 1829, the ecclesiastical authorities simply suspended the station for that entire season. Justifying this drastic step in July of that year, Bishop Edward Kernan of Clogher observed that 'immorality and disorder shall never be permitted in that place, where penance and devotion should hold the first pre[e]minence'.[73] But as we have seen, the rites of penance and devotion now prevailing were of a new sort. The persistent notion of an unchanging set of rituals of mortification preserved through the ages at Lough Derg was and is yet another of Ireland's myths.

References

1. Rev D. O'Connor, *St Patrick's Purgatory, Lough Derg: its history, traditions, legends, antiquities, topography, and scenic surroundings* (rev. ed., Dublin, 1903), p. 11.

2. L. J. Flynn, *St Patrick's Purgatory, Lough Derg, County Donegal* (Irish Heritage Series, 54) (Dublin, n.d.), no pagination.

3. Rev. J. Richardson, *The great folly, superstition, and idolatry of pilgrimages in Ireland, especially of that to Patrick's Purgatory, together with an account of the loss that the public sustaineth thereby, truly and impartially represented* (Dublin, 1727), p. 85.

4. C. Otway, *Sketches in Ireland descriptive of interesting and hitherto unnoticed districts in the north and south* (Dublin, 1827), pp 149-50.

5. This figure of 5,000 is for the pilgrimage season of 1700 and comes from the Rev. Hewson, rector of St Andrew's parish, Dublin, who visited Lough Derg in 1701. See Rev. Hewson, *A description of Patrick's Purgatory in Lough Derg and an*

account of the pilgrims' business there [dated 1 Aug. 1701], printed at the end of the Rev. J. Richardson's work, *The great folly, superstition, and idolatry of pilgrimages in Ireland* (Dublin, 1727), p. 135. The length of the pilgrim season at Lough Derg has not always been the same. In the eighteenth century it usually lasted from the beginning of May until the middle of August, but during most of the nineteenth and twentieth centuries a shorter season of two and a half months (1 June-15 August) has generally prevailed (O'Connor, *St Patrick's Purgatory,* pp 208-9).

6.   Journal of a tour by the Rev. W. Bruce in the north of Ireland (June-Aug. 1783), 21 July 1783, p. 35 (N.L.I., Bruce papers, MS 20884). Earlier, an English Protestant visitor to Lough Derg in 1765 put the number of pilgrims in recent years at only 3,000 to 4,000 annually. See *Gentleman's Magazine,* xxxvi (Feb. 1766), p. 62.

7.   O'Connor, *St Patrick's Purgatory,* p. 195.

8.   J. Barrow, *A tour round Ireland through the seacoast counties in the autumn of 1835* (London, 1836), p. 142.

9.   *Parliamentary Gazetteer for Ireland* for 1844-5, ii, 10; *Household Words,* ii, no. 28 (5 Oct. 1850), p. 29.

10.   *Household Words,* ii, no. 28 (5 Oct. 1850), p. 29.

11.   Ordnance Survey letters, county Donegal, 1 Nov. 1835, p. 149 (MS pp 252-3). The author consulted the set of Ordnance Survey letters in typescript in the Pope John XXIII Library of St Patrick's College, Maynooth.

12.   *Household Words,* ii, no. 28 (5 Oct. 1850), p. 29.

13.   O'Connor, *St Patrick's Purgatory,* pp 195-7. Higher figures came to obtain during much of the twentieth century. Even in the first half of this century attendance was far above the depressed figures of the late nineteenth century (14,287 in 1919; 14,724 in 1942). The largest intake occurred in the early 1950s; a record of 34,645 pilgrims arrived during the 1953 season. Later decades witnessed a decline but certainly no collapse. In the 1970s the attendance was not far short of 20,000 (the average for the ten years ending in 1973 was 18,642), and the corresponding figure for the 1980s ranged from 22,000 to 25,000. See Rev. J. E. McKenna, *Lough Derg: Ireland's national pilgrimage* (Dublin, 1934), p. 20; A. Hopkin, *The living legend of St Patrick* (London, 1989), p. 104; Rev. Thomas Flood (Prior) to Bishop Patrick Mulligan, 16 Aug. 1978 (Lough Derg papers, Bishop's House, Monaghan).

14.   S. C. and A. M. Hall, *Ireland: its scenery, character, &c.* (3 vols, London, 1841-3), i, 284.

15.   Admittedly, this total comprised pilgrims who came to Croagh Patrick on one or more of the five main festival days or at other times during that year. See Rev. T. Walker, *A plea for spiritual religion, being the substance of a sermon delivered at Westport church ..., to which are added notes containing a detailed account of the pilgrimage to Croagh Patrick in the county of Mayo ...* (Castlebar, 1825), appendix, pp vi-vii.

16.   O'Connor, *St Patrick's Purgatory,* p. 238.

17.   J. Bossy, 'The Counter-Reformation and the people of Catholic Europe' in *Past & Present,* no. 47 (May 1970), pp 51-70.

18.   E. Larkin, 'The devotional revolution in Ireland, 1850-75' in *American Historical Review,* vol. 77, no. 3 (June 1972), pp 625-52.

19.   D. J. Keenan, *The Catholic church in nineteenth-century Ireland: a sociological study* (Dublin and Totowa, N.J., 1983), pp 243-4 and passim; K. Whelan, 'The regional impact of Irish Catholicism, 1700-1850' in W. J. Smyth and K. Whelan (ed.), *Common Ground* (Cork, 1988), pp 253-77.

20. Quoted in S. Leslie, *Saint Patrick's Purgatory: a record from history and literature* (London, 1932), p. 119.
21. Ibid., p. 121. Burke's book appeared in 1762, but what he wrote about Lough Derg was based on his visit in 1748.
22. Ibid., passim.
23. For the well-documented association between fasting and visions or hallucinations, see I. M. Lewis, *Ecstatic religion: a study of shamanism and spirit possession* (2nd ed., London and New York, 1989), pp 33-4.
24. Leslie, *Record*, pp 121-2.
25. O'Connor, *St Patrick's Purgatory*, p. 54.
26. Leslie, *Record*, p. 116.
27. Ibid.
28. O'Connor, *St Patrick's Purgatory*, p. 168.
29. P. D. Hardy, *The holy wells of Ireland, containing an authentic account of those various places of pilgrimage and penance which are still annually visited by thousands of the Roman Catholic peasantry, with a minute description of the patterns and stations periodically held in various districts of Ireland* (Dublin, 1840), p. 12.
30. Leslie, *Record*, p. 116.
31. Ibid., pp 115, 135.
32. R. A. S. Macalister, 'A German view of Ireland, 1720' in *R.S.A.I. Jn.*, 5th ser., xvi, pt 4 (1906), p. 397.
33. Leslie, *Record*, p. 63. See also Ludwig Bieler, 'St Patrick's Purgatory: contributions toward an historical topography' in *I.E.R.*, 5th ser., xciii, no. 3 (Mar. 1960), pp 143-4.
34. Leslie, *Record*, p. 96.
35. Ibid., pp 101-2.
36. Ibid., p. 118.
37. Ibid., p. 93. See also ibid., p. 125.
38. *Gentleman's Magazine*, xxxvi (Feb. 1766), p. 63.
39. Ibid., p. 62.
40. Leslie, *Record*, p. 113.
41. Ibid., p. 118.
42. Ibid., p. 211. See also O'Connor, *St Patrick's Purgatory*, pp 169-70.
43. Leslie, *Record*, p. 102.
44. Ibid., p. 115.
45. *Gentleman's Magazine*, xxxvi (Feb. 1766), p. 63.
46. Leslie, *Record*, p. 64.
47. Ibid., pp 64-5.
48. Ibid., p. 118.
49. Ibid.
50. Richardson, *Great folly*, p. 63; *Gentleman's Magazine*, xxxvi (Feb. 1766), p. 63; *The complete works of the late Rev. Philip Skelton ...*, ed. Rev. Robert Lynam (6 vols, London, 1824), v, 19; Journal of a tour by the Rev. William Bruce in the north of Ireland (June-Aug. 1783), 21 July 1783, pp 34-5 (N.L.I., Bruce papers, MS 20884, hereafter cited as Bruce journal).
51. Leslie, *Record*, pp 111-12, 115, 119.
52. *Gentleman's Magazine*, xxxvi (Feb. 1766), p. 62.
53. Bruce journal, 21 July 1783, p. 34 (N.L.I., Bruce papers, MS 20884).
54. Rev. S. Ó Dufaigh, 'James Murphy, bishop of Clogher, 1801-24' in *Clogher Rec.*, vi, no. 3 (1968), p. 458.

55. *Household Words*, ii, no. 28 (5 Oct. 1850), p. 32.
56. Canon O'Connor noted that some people in his day still chose to do pilgrimages lasting six or nine days (*St Patrick's Purgatory*, p. 209).
57. Ibid., p. 177; Flynn, *St Patrick's Purgatory*, n.p.
58. O'Connor, *St Patrick's Purgatory*, p. 182.
59. For the names of the priors of Lough Derg since Father Murray, and the periods of their tenures, see Rev. Dr P. Mulligan, 'The life and times of Bishop Edward Kernan' in *Clogher Rec.*, x, no. 3 (1981), pp 325, 327; O'Connor, *St Patrick's Purgatory*, pp 193-4; Flynn, *St Patrick's Purgatory*, n.p.
60. Bruce journal, 21 July 1783, pp 32-3 (N.L.I., Bruce papers, MS 20884); O'Connor, *St Patrick's Purgatory*, p. 173.
61. Bruce journal, 21 July 1783, p. 34 (N.L.I., Bruce papers, MS 20884).
62. Leslie, *Record,* p. 127.
63. O'Connor, *St Patrick's Purgatory*, pp 186-7.
64. Ibid., p. 188.
65. Ó Dufaigh, 'James Murphy', p. 462.
66. *Household Words*, ii, no. 28 (5 Oct. 1850), p. 31.
67. Ibid.
68. W. G. Wood-Martin, *Traces of the elder faiths of Ireland: a handbook of Irish pre-Christian traditions* (2 vols, London, 1902), i, p. 332. See also W. Carleton, *The works of William Carleton* (3 vols, New York, 1881), iii, p. 818.
69. O'Connor, *St Patrick's Purgatory*, p. 215.
70. Leslie, *Record*, p. 112.
71. *Household Words*, ii, no. 28 (5 Oct. 1850), p. 31.
72. Ó Dufaigh, 'James Murphy', p. 462.
73. Bishop Edward Kernan to Dean (and Prior) Patrick Bellew, 12 July 1829, quoted in Mulligan, 'Bishop Edward Kernan', p. 346.

Plate 17.1   St Patrick's Purgatory, Lough Derg *c.*1890 (Lawrence Print, N.L.I.).

Plate 17.2   Pilgrims at a station, Lough Derg, early twentieth century (N.L.I.).

Chapter 18

SETTLEMENT AND SOCIETY IN THE BARONY OF EAST INISHOWEN, *c.*1850

MARTINA O'DONNELL

This paper focuses on the landholding system that developed in the isolated barony of East Inishowen as a result of the prolonged absenteeism of the owner in fee. By 1850 the 'middlemen' system was well entrenched in the barony and the variety in character of the middle interest had clear settlement ramifications. The extent of rundale, openfield and cluster survival, as well as the degree of congestion, have been used as yardsticks to assess the effectiveness of management between estates. Some attention has been given to the working of this rundale/openfield/cluster system of land occupation, which was certainly prevalent over most of the barony up to the 1820s. The focus on the mid-nineteenth century also allows us to gain an insight into the economy of estates in the immediate post-famine period. For many proprietors in the study area, the depressed years of the 1840s proved to be a turning point, and some never managed to recover economic stability. For these the dismantling of the estate system that took place in the late-nineteenth or early-twentieth century was indeed welcomed. The earlier sections of the chapter are intended to place developments in the barony in the wider context of the county and country.

The physical endowment

A structural downfold of carboniferous rock, occupied by Lough Foyle, provides the starting point of the county boundary to the north-east. South of Muff in the Inishowen peninsula the boundary detours some 25 kilometres around the city of Derry and away from its more natural divide of the river Foyle. It rejoins this river in the vicinity of Carrigans and from hence meanders upstream to Lifford, and along the Finn to Clady, through the broad fertile valley encompassing the cultural region of the 'Laggan'. The Mourne Beg – tributary of the Foyle – carries the border west towards Lough Mourne. To the west and south the Barnesmore, Clogher Hill, Croaghnameal, Ardmore and Crockkinnagoe range provides a well defined boundary along with a bleak and

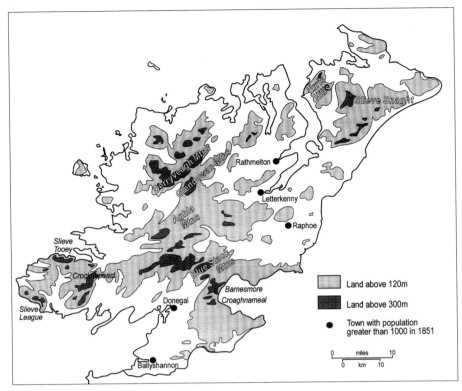

Fig. 18.1   Topography of county Donegal.

inhospitable terrain to envelop the penitential Station Island in Lough
Derg. From here it picks out minor streams and rivers as it runs east
then west, skirting Lower Lough Erne and dividing Pettigoe town with
neighbouring Fermanagh. Donegal also shares with this county some
of the lake-strewn lowlands north-west of the lough before the
boundary makes its way into Donegal Bay via the minor river Bradoge.
Within the county the physical geography is one of great diversity (see
fig. 18.1). Donegal's geology is primarily comprised of sedimentary
rocks, laid down over 600 million years ago and subsequently folded,
faulted and emplaced with massive granite plutons. Further basic
intrusions in the form of swarms of dykes add to the complexity and
provide lines of weakness to the forces of denudation. The north-
east/south-west structural trend of the Caledonian folding, however,
remains the salient feature of the physical geography – a feature that
has only been accentuated by the glaciation of more recent geological
times. In terms of elevation, the mountain/valley terrain of north and
west Donegal provides a sharp contrast to the more subdued and

510

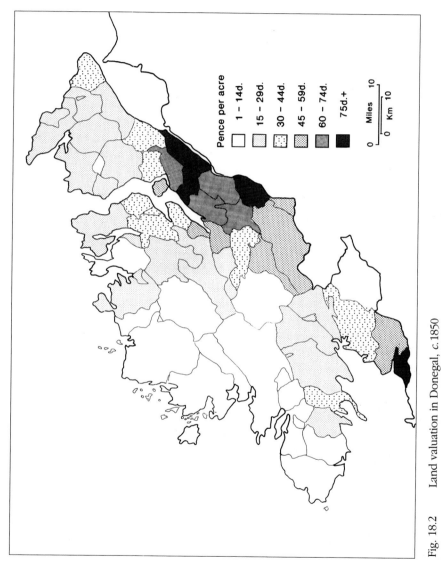

Fig. 18.2   Land valuation in Donegal, *c*.1850
Source: General Valuation, Co. Donegal, 1856-8.

rolling topography of the east and south, where the predominant schistose and limestone rocks have proved more susceptible to prolonged denudation. Fig. 18.2, which shows average land values at parish level, highlights that this broad east/west division of the county is also true in terms of soil fertility. Whereas most of the western coast has a valuation below 14 pence per acre, those in the east are generally above 45 pence.

In the south is a stretch of lowlands some 8-10 kilometres broad around Donegal Bay and comprising the northern-most extension of the limestone of the central plain. This is also an area of glacial deposition with swarms of drumlins producing a more subdued landscape than found elsewhere in the north or west. Grey-brown podzols dominate the area between Ballyshannon and Donegal town, forming some of the county's best agricultural land. This is enveloped in a wider band of gleys stretching west to Killybegs with the associated impeded drainage most evident in the lowlands north-west of Lower Lough Erne. Beyond the limb-shaped limestone peninsula of St John's Point is the broader peninsula of Slieve League, with the great quartzite cliffs of Slieve Tooey and Slieve League flanking its northern and southern coasts, respectively. Here we are back in the more familiar Dalradian landscape, and to the west of Killybegs the gleys give way to blanket bog interspersed with rock outcrops, with only the narrow valleys of Carrick, Malin Beg, Malin More and Glencolmbkille providing some semblance of cultivation in the otherwise barren countryside.

The complicated geology of the north-west mountain region results from the folding, thrusting, granite emplacement and severe tear-faulting that has mangled the different rock series. But this complexity has not succeeded in transcending the strong Caledonian trend characteristic of the area, and best seen in the parallel ridges of the quartzite Errigal/Muckish, and the granite of Derryveagh and Glendowan ranges. Indeed the displacement and rock shattering caused by the faulting has aided the development of the long deep glacial troughs as in the valley of Glenveagh. The granite mountains here cradled the local ice cap which escaped north and north-west leaving behind trains of erratics in the vicinity of Sheep Haven Bay. Glacio-fluvial deposits formed the extensive sand dunes of Ballyness Bay and the impressive tombolo of Horn Head, along with the well-drained and fertile pockets of land around Falcarragh and Dunfanaghy. North-west of the mountains the deep glacial breaching of Muckish Gap, the valley of Altan Lough and the impressive U-shaped valley of the Poisoned Glen, testify to the erosive power of the ice. However, it is in the islands and mainland that comprise the Rosses to the west that the work of the ice is best exemplified. Here is a low-lying plateau of *c.* 200 feet, strewn with erratics or thinly covered in drift with numerous lake-filled hollows. Lewis found nothing like this on his journey through the county: 'Even amidst the wilds of Boylagh and Banagh' there were 'cultivated and well peopled valleys, but the district of the Rosses presents mostly a desolate waste.'[1] East from the central uplands is the 'Laggan' region, stretching south from the Burnfoot depression in Inishowen to the valley of the Finn river. Glacial deposition rather than erosion predominated here, leaving behind a deep drift cover in many places. Several of the county's largest rivers – the Swilly, the Deele and the Finn – traverse this area in broad valleys, adding to its fertile quality.

It is the alternating bands of hard quartzite and granite, and less resistant schist that determine the overall physiography of Inishowen, as in the neighbouring peninsula of Fanad. Wedged in the intervening valleys of Slieve Snaght and the Urris Hills, or between hill and sea are the slices of arable land which in the nineteenth century were densely populated. East of Slieve Snaght a narrow belt of limestone running north from Buncrana to Culdaff forms a tract of low-lying ground picked out by the two main rivers – the Crana and Glentogher. This valley bisects the peninsula's mountain heartland, as eastwards the land again rises to about 1,000 feet in the range of hills including Scalp Mountain, Crockglass and Glencaw. The softer rocks of the east coast upland give way more gently to lowlands and settlement and cultivation here reaches almost to the summits. North of Burnfoot the chief soils of the lowlands are brown podzols and less fertile peaty podzols. However, in the vicinity of Culdaff these are interspersed with lowland blanket bog and limestone. In 1816 the Rev Chichester noted how this combination provided ideal conditions for reclamation. 'Nature', he wrote, 'seems to have diversified the soil in the manner most favourable to improvement; clay, peat moss and limestone being always near each other.'[2] Dotted along the coast from Tullagh to Trawbreaga Bay and north to Malin Head, the rising elevation of the land has provided, not only some of the most impressive raised beaches of the county, but also accumulations of alluvium forming potentially fertile soil.

Landholding in the nineteenth century: the national context
There has been some ambiguity associated with the term 'middlemen', even in the accounts of Arthur Young.[3] In general they filled the role – not unique to Ireland – of an intermediary between the occupiers of the soil and the landowners. In return for a potential profit rent that might accrue from holding long leases at relatively low rent, these

middle-tenants grappled with the risk and drudgery associated with dealing with a large number of under-tenants. In effect the system meant the alienation of the control of land from the owners in fee for a number of years, and the creation of a group of minor gentry with wide discretion in the shaping of the landscape. Two salient factors encouraged their emergence – the existence of underdeveloped regions and insolvent landowners – and the chronology of their appearance and demise varied regionally. On the Wandesforde estate in Fassadinin, Kilkenny, for example, yearly tenancies prevailed until 1746; thereafter leases were introduced in the hope of encouraging improvements on the estate.[4] Power's study of the Ormond estates in Tipperary[5] indicates an earlier introduction there. In the aftermath of the Williamite Wars large tracts of ground were left devastated, rents were stagnant or declining and creditors were demanding repayment of debts. Favourable conditions were necessary to attract solvent and industrious tenants to the estate, and some method to raise money quickly was needed. The solution was radical, involving the passing of several acts of parliament to enable Ormond to alienate part of his property by granting long leases or by outright sale.[6]

A similar situation prevailed on the estates of the Chichester family of Belfast. The first Chichester – Sir Arthur (d. 1625) – assembled his estate in a piecemeal fashion, firstly through his position as an undertaker in the Ulster Plantation and then as lord deputy of Ireland (1605-1615).[7] By 1797 the value of the family's Irish property, including some 90,000 acres in Antrim over 100,000 acres in Donegal and 11,000 in Wexford, was estimated at £48,000.[8] Although long leases and fee farm grants were available to principal tenants from the early seventeenth century,[9] alienation of land began in earnest from 1794, as a result of substantial debts. At that time George Agustus Chichester, the second marquis of Donegall, was indebted to several persons for the sum of £40,000 and therefore began selling the interest in land for terms of 1,000 years.[10] For both the Ormonds and the Chichesters a progressive process of upgrading tenure was evident, beginning with the granting of leases for terms of years or lives, to perpetual leases, fee farm grants and eventually the sale of land. Conversion from determinable to perpetually renewable leases was offered to tenants on the payment of a cash sum or 'fine' and these were usually given at a reduced rent. As more capital was required, leases were converted into fee farm grants whereby the tenant could purchase future renewal fines for a lump sum. By the 1840s most of the Chichester property including some 77,000 acres in Donegal and 70,000 in Antrim (apart from Belfast) had been alienated in perpetuity.[11]

It was the commercialisation of agriculture and the resultant rise in land values and rent, especially in the years from 1740-60 and 1790-1815, that eroded the advantages of the middlemen system, at least for solvent proprietors. Landowners now wanted to get their share of increasing profits from agriculture. In the more commercial areas of east Leinster and in the flourishing linen districts of Ulster, its demise took place earliest.[12] Reduction of the middleman's influence rather than complete removal was common in many instances. Whereas leases for three lives, or three lives renewable were given to middle-tenants on the O'Callaghan estate in county Tipperary in 1740, leases for thirty-one and twenty-one years were more common by the 1870s.[13] Offering smaller leasehold units was another means to ensure that no one tenant became too powerful.[14] For many landlords, however, the expiry date of leases was much later so the process of recovery could span over many decades. It was only in the early nineteenth century, and especially after the 1830s, that tenure on the Wandesforde estate was re-organised.[15] From 1819 to 1872 six of the London Companies recovered their properties in Londonderry in an attempt to rationalise their estates.[16] It is clear, therefore, that the Chichesters' policy of granting leases in perpetuity to middletenants was against the general trend apparent in nineteenth-century Ireland.

Curtis has stressed the need to assess landlords on their solvency and not on their apparent wealth,[17] and indebtedness certainly did plague Irish proprietors well before the mid-nineteenth century. It is also generally accepted that the provision for 'non-inheriting' family members in the form of marriage portions, education and jointures placed the greatest burdens on estates.[18] This was as true for the great estates such as Ormond and Donegall as it was for minor estates, because there was the tendency for gentry at all levels to emulate their wealthy peers in demonstrating social status. In eighteenth-century Tipperary, for example, Power found that portions for the daughters of the wealthier landowners generally ranged between £2,000 and £6,000 and those of the minor proprietors averaged £1,000.[19] In 1816, Henry Marquis Conyngham of Slane Castle was empowered to charge the estate with an 'additional' £60,000 for his four younger children. His successor, Francis Nathaniel, charged his estate with a total of £40,000 for five younger children.[20] Personal debts, estate administration, the building of great houses and ornamentation of demesnes were other areas of expenditure. Mortgaging of estates was the only means whereby many proprietors could fulfil obligations and keep their estates afloat. Sources of credit ranged from the local and personal, including relatives, neighbouring gentry, town merchants and solicitors, to the more formal banks and insurance companies. Lending opportunities and the rates of interest payable, depended on the standing and creditworthiness of individual borrowers and debts generally tended to be a greater burden to the smaller gentry. However, as long as interest repayments could be met the *status quo* remained.

The famine years effectively disrupted this income, expenditure and credit nexus. With stagnant or declining rents, expenditure eroded an increasing share of income, while credit became harder to acquire. The government's response to the growing indebtedness was the passing of the Encumbered Estates Act in 1849. By making the land of Ireland a more marketable commodity, it was hoped that a wealthier and more progressive investor would be attracted.[21] Indeed with rising land values in the economic prosperity of the 1850s to the mid-1870s it was not unreasonable to expect a lively interest in Irish land. Moreover, the social status residing in land ownership was a key if unquantifiable element in promoting demand. A new temporary body, the Encumbered Estates Commission, was given wide powers in dealing with encumbered estates (the Act defined encumbered as those estates with over half of their annual income absorbed in the repayment of interest on debts or other yearly charges) and in 1859 the scope of its successor, the Landed Estates Court, was further extended to include the sale of non-encumbered property. The scale of their work was impressive. From October 1849 to the final session of the commission in August 1858, there was a total of 4,413 petitions for partition, exchange and sale presented to the commission. The large number of encumbered estates by 1849 ensured that the earliest years were the most active, with 1,085 petitions presented in 1850 dwindling to 226 in 1857. Altogether 11,024 lots were sold for a total purchase price of £23,161,093.[22] A question of importance regarding the activities of the Encumbered Estates Commission and its successors is the extent to which 'new blood' was infused into the landownership class as a result of sales. Another issue is the degree of landholding continuity despite heavy encumbrances (which increased dramatically during the agrarian crisis of the late 1870s and 1880s) and the settlement ramifications of this indebtedness.

Landholding and settlement in Donegal, *c.* 1850

Three main factors are significant in the assessment of estate management in the county – the scale of estates, the level of absenteeism and the nature of the proprietor's interest – and this overall framework set the parameters for the development of the settlement pattern. The granting of perpetual leases by the Donegalls to middle-tenants was contrary to the prevailing pattern in nineteenth century Ireland, yet Inishowen was not an isolated case in the county. Perpetual leases were offered to holders of the scattered churchlands after the passing of the Church Temporalities Act of 1833. The 63,454 acres of the Trinity College property situated in the baronies of Tirhugh and Kilmacrenan was held by middle interests, all of whom were granted perpetual leases following the Trinity College Dublin, Leasing and Perpetuity Act of 1851. All except the earl of Leitrim received a perpetuity lease between 1854-56 (Leitrim was not granted one until 1870).[23] An overall lack of interest in the conditions on the estates, little pressure to increase income and the political clout of the principal tenants were the reasons given by McCarthy for the college board's acquiescence in granting perpetual leases.[24] Yet the extent to which the Trinity lessees were regarded as middlemen (even prior to 1851) is questionable. Most were substantial landowners in their own right. The earl of Leitrim, for example, held 28,235 acres from the college as well as a further 25,618 in fee in Donegal and 22,038 in Leitrim.[25] Conolly held the Rossnowlagh and Bundoran estates, comprising 15,660 acres from the college, in addition to 32,524 acres in Glencolumbkille, 4,738 acres in Killybegs, 20,220 acres in Lettermacaward and 8,082 in Iniskeel, all in perpetuity from the Church Temporalities Commissioners.[26] What was more significant was the quality of estate control. Altogether only 29 per cent of the value of land in the county was held by proprietors 'resident on or near their property' compared to 47.6 per cent for the country as a whole.[27] There is no doubt that this high level of absenteeism was detrimental for agricultural development. Non-residents included the earl of Leitrim and Conolly and most of the other principal proprietors in the county – the Marquis Conyngham of Slane Castle (estate valuation in the 1870s was £15,166), the duke of Abercorn, Newtownstewart (£10,382), H. G. Murray Stewart of Gullygate House, Scotland (£6,500), the earl of Erne, Newtownbutler (£4,324), the earl of Wicklow, Arklow (£4,818) and John Leslie of Glasslough, county Monaghan (£3,473) (see fig. 18.3). Alexander J. R. Stewart of Ards (£9,135), Sir E. S. Hayes of Drumboe Castle (£6,350) and Sir James Stewart of Rathmelton (£4,480) were the largest resident proprietors.[28] Extensive areas in the county were therefore left under the control of agents. Some like Alexander Hamilton of Coxtown, agent for Colonel Conolly, Rev Edward Hamilton, Rev William Forster and Thomas Brooke, managing altogether over 110,000 acres, were resident and progressive.[29] Others needed constant pressure from their employers to improve their efficiency and effectiveness. Correspondence between Lord Leitrim and his agent J. Murray Esq. (Millford) in the 1860s was full of landlord reprimands. In May 1865, for example, he complained about Murray's laxness in recording and reporting on money collected for seaweed and grazing, and money still in arrears. He wrote: 'I am sorry that you cannot continue to make as

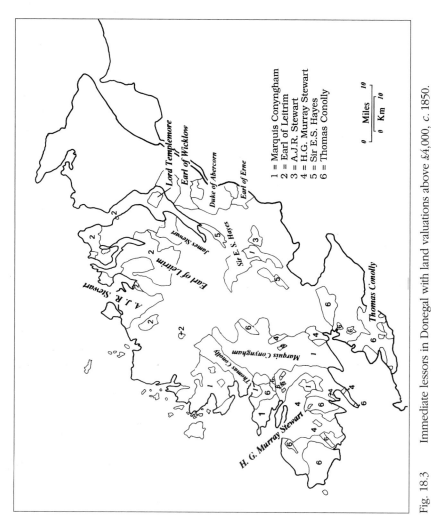

Fig. 18.3   Immediate lessors in Donegal with land valuations above £4,000, c. 1850.
Source: General Valuation, county Donegal, 1856; Townland Index, county Donegal, sheets 1-11, 1956.

clear a statement of the ordinary matters as my bailiffs do on other estates where there is no agent – and where the lettings are all made without the slightest difficulty or unnecessary correspondence'.[30] Some landlords were not so involved. In the parish of Killymard (Banagh), for example, 'the landlord (Murray Stewart) and agent were both absentees, to a great loss to the tenantry upon a large estate where it so happens.' Where they were resident there was a 'great deal of money laid out, and more labour given and many other things.'[31] Absenteeism was not so prevalent on the smaller estates, some of which were held by middle-tenants. These, unlike the Trinity College lessees, were viewed as such and had a reputation of less effective estate management, a common grievance on small estates.[32] In Letterkenny Union, for example, there were almost sixty estates, the majority of which were small. According to the witness, these 'very small estates (those belonging to persons who have risen from the farming class) are generally, I might say universally, the worst managed whether by the proprietors or their agents.'[33]

Where effective estate management was absent, population growth and sub-division was rampant and during the twenty years up to 1841 the population of the county rose almost 20 per cent, from 248,270 to 296,448.[34] Other indicators of neglect were the survival of partnership farming, rundale and openfield – all barriers to the development of agriculture. The system of holding land in partnership rather than in severalty had been general throughout the county at the turn of the nineteenth century.[35] These multiple tenancies originated with two or three tenants holding a single townland, and grew through the generations with subdivision.[36] In some places partnership farming had thwarted individual enterprise. Prior to the re-organisation of holdings effected by Alexander Hamilton in the 1830s, for example, 'rent was paid by the townland or in companies, the wealthy were subject to the constant distress for the indolent or indignant. On the expiration of the lease or term, new divisions were made, to the grievous injury to the industrious tenant.'[37] Elsewhere the responsibilities of the partnership farm had diminished by the nineteenth century and simply provided the most effective means of allocating non-arable resources.[38] Rundale had been prevalent prior to the 1830s. The principle of this system of fragmented holdings was to ensure access to shares in all land qualities. Rundale was found at its extreme where land quality was poor but variable and was vividly described by the landlord in Gweedore, Lord George Hill, in 1845:

> Every tenant considered himself entitled to a various portion of each quality of land in his townland: and the man who had some

good land at one extremity, was sure to have bad at the other, and a bit of middling in the centre, and bits of others in odd corners, each bounded by his neighbour's property and without any fence or ditch between them.[39]

Enclosure would have meant a great waste of precious arable land in such fragmented conditions, but even when holdings were consolidated many tenants were slow to properly enclose their lands. In Letterkenny, after rundale had been removed, there was still a dearth of fencing and in winter the sheep often ran 'in common over the lowlands, offering great obstacles to the introduction of green crops'.[40]

The clustering of dwellings was the rational response to this system of fragmented holdings. Not only did it minimise overall travel to the various patches of land but also preserved precious arable land for tillage, through the reduction of roads, paths and 'streets'. Where subdivision of holdings was rife, cluster size and internal kinship networks grew with each generation. Indeed some settlements comprised only one family group as the names Ballygorman, Ballycramsy, McCallionstown and Moorestown in Clonca parish in Inishowen testify. However, two or three family groups were more usual. The physical growth of the cluster was not totally devoid of planning as some geographers have suggested. According to Estyn Evans, for example, each dwelling in the 'loosely gathered' settlements he found in Gweedore had 'the air of ignoring the existence of its neighbour' because 'in the dense cluster of the nineteenth century new houses were evidently built where they could be squeezed in'.[41] Topography was central in determining cluster site and morphology. In Ballymagaraghy in East Inishowen, one large cluster was tucked in a shallow depression at the foothills with buildings aligned along the slope towards the coast.[42] In other exposed and wet Atlantic coastal areas, these considerations of shelter and drainage would certainly have been the most important factors. In low-lying tracts, the site and form of the cluster would have been determined by the nature of dry points. At a more intimate level, social factors including kinship and affinity between neighbours must have been significant in the siting and orientation of individual buildings.[43] For many landlords and agents, however, the apparent lack of organisation made the cluster settlements incomprehensible and threatening and they were often proclaimed as sources of corruption, idleness and disease.[44]

Openfield, partnership farms, rundale and clusters survived in Donegal only as long as they were beneficial to both landlord and tenant, or where neither the financial means nor will was available to remove them. As early as 1801, McParlan indicated that partnership farms were becoming less prevalent. Many tenant farmers had realised the benefits of holding in severalty and were 'themselves sub-dividing many of the old takes'.[45] The agricultural boom of the Napoleonic Wars (1793-1815) lifted many tenants above subsistence level. Even farmers in the most inaccessible areas found their marketing niche in the sale of illicitly distilled whiskey.[46] But in general the initiative lay with the proprietor to effect changes and only from the 1830s was there an accelerated drive towards rationalisation. The expiry of leases for royal lives on the death of King William IV in 1830[47] meant that some proprietors regained control of their estates and could only now begin to effect the prerequisites to agricultural innovation – consolidation, enclosure and drainage.[48] Concern for the condition of the tenants was certainly a motive of individual landlords and in the county, John Hamilton of Saint Ernans was particularly acclaimed for his work on the Fintown estate.[49]

But even here the landlord was not solely motivated by philan-thropic interest. In 1830, Hamilton began by 'squaring' the farms and building new houses for his tenants. In the following years every encouragement was given for the maintenance of dwellings and the reclamation of land. Altogether the estate comprised 8,168 acres, 3,400 of which was un-improved but reclaimable. Hamilton devised a forty-year plan to bring about this improvement, with 1,000 acres to be reclaimed by himself, the remainder by the tenantry. It was hoped that after ten years the rent would more than double from £462 to £995 and that 'ultimately there should not be above 160 farms on the estate; each would have on average at least twenty acres of arable – at a moderate rent and yet paying a handsome return to the landlord'.[50] Similar calculations emerged out of the valuation report carried out by James Frain in 1833 on the Pettigoe estate of Mr Leslie. In the townland of Crilley, where the farms were 'badly laid out' Frain noted that it 'would be advisable if profitable to arrange every man's division, together it would forward the improvement of the ground considerably' and the value of Ballinackavaney division would 'rise considerably at the next letting; the tenants are improving and breaking in considerable parts of the mountain which they will be able to do if they are accommodated with roads'.[51] Not all improvements generated an increase in rent. On the Conolly property in Glencolmbkille, Lettermacaward, Iniskeel and Killybegs there had been no rise in rent since 1818, despite rationalisation and in 1846 an abatement of 20 per cent was given to the tenants.[52]

From the 1830s improvements throughout the county were consider-able. All the properties managed by Alex Hamilton (with the exception of some leases) were 'surveyed, the farms squared and the owners of each placed on his own as centrally as could be, generally speaking, with reference to water, access, drainage, etc'. By 1844 some 2,639 farms had been reorganised and 9,061 houses built in the baronies of Boylagh, Banagh and Kilmacrenan.[53] The rentals of the Conolly estate confirm these improvements, depicting straightened holdings with dispersed dwellings and indicating only isolated cases of arable held in common (in the townlands of Derrynacarron, Derrynagrial, Derrynaspol, Stranasaggart and Cummine in the parish of Lettermacaward). In the 1840s the 200,000-acre Conyngham estate in Boylagh managed by Robert Russell was in the process of reorganisation. Partnerships of twenty to thirty farmers were not uncommon here, but now tenants were becoming more comfortable with the land better drained and cultivated.[54] But some small and isolated estates remained unaffected by this wave of innovation. The Conolly family had let 11,323 acres of the churchland in the parish of Glencolumbkille to the Humes from 1798.[55] Conditions of the tenantry were so bad in 1844 that the witness was ordered by the agent and bailiff to forgo giving evidence before the Devon Commission. The reason for the poverty was 'the extraordinary rent, without their having any earnings'. No aid was given for 'squaring the farms' or for improving the dwellings. This was in contrast with the adjoining Conolly estate which would 'give you 40s, and give you slates and timber for the house'.[56]

In his assessment of the role of the Encumbered Estates Court, Curtis refers to the relatively stable condition of landholding in Ulster in contrast to the other provinces.[57] He attributed this to more effective estate management and less extravagant provision for marriage settlements by the northern landlords. For Donegal relative stability is confirmed, at least for the early period of the court's work. By April 1853, the county had the third lowest value of sales in the court after Londonderry and Carlow.[58] However, the period of greatest activity was the decade after 1865 with over half (62 out of 113) of the total number of Donegal advertised sales occurring.[59] The increase in petitions for sale at this time may be a reflection of the changing nature of the new commission, which extended the provision of the Act to non-encumbered properties. The 'estates' listed, however, were a mixed lot. They included extensive properties held in fee simple like the 18,190 acre estate of Sir E. S. Hayes in Raphoe, offered for sale in 1857 and part again twenty years later.[60] In 1872, Thomas Conolly was selling his interest in the Ballyshannon estate, which to a large extent was merely the right to collect fixed fee farm rents from the middle-tenants.[61] Some of these middle-tenants, including Elizabeth Jones in 1867, were auctioning their interests – that is, fee farm grants.[62] Other rentals outlined particulars of town property. For example, a Mr John Laird was selling a 'dwelling house and premises in the town of Ballybofey' held under lease for lives renewal forever, in 1867.[63] Not all estates listed for sale in the court would have involved insolvent 'owners' nor would all have resulted in actual sale. But there is no doubt that many proprietors, including the principal ones, did face severe financial difficulties especially in the latter part of the century. The Conolly family troubles were evident from the eighteenth century when perpetual leases were granted to middle-tenants at old rents.[64] Attempts at the final alienation of the family's estates in Donegal began in 1867 when the Iniskeel, Lettermacaward, Glencolmbkille and Killybegs estates were put up for auction.[65] The interest in 1,744 acres of the Bundoran estate was sold in 1868 and that of the Ballyshannon some four years later.[66] In 1876 the earl of Wicklow sold 3,160 acres of his property in Raphoe North for a total purchase price of £40,343.[67] Debts on the duke of Abercorn's estates in Raphoe and Tyrone had reached c. £321,051 in 1886, a debt burden on a rental of £35,936.[68] His tenants were among the first in the county to benefit from the Land Purchase (Irl.) Acts. Some 162 holdings comprising 10,092 acres were sold in 1889 for a total purchase price of £125,278. In 1890 a further 7 holdings amounting to 453 acres were sold for £5,940.[69]

The Barony of East Inishowen (fig. 18.4)

Landholding

A survey of the Chichester Inishowen estate in the mid-eighteenth century indicated how grossly under-rented it was at the time with 160,000 acres valued at £10,600 but providing a nominal rental of only £1,766. The estate was divided into 76 holdings. Fourteen of these were either out of lease, held under fee farm grants, leases perpetually renewable or for an unknown number of years. Of the remainder, 47 were for terms over 40 years, 20 of which were made prior to 1700 for terms between 61 to 99 years.[70] An effort had been made during the eighteenth century to curb the influence of middle-tenants by reducing lease terms but due to the indebtedness of the Chichester family, this policy was abandoned by the end of the century when leases of up to 1,000 years were offered to principal tenants. Among the first principal tenants in the peninsula was George Cary of Devonshire, cousin of Sir Arthur Chichester,[71] who resided in Redcastle from 1622 and a fellow servitor Henry Hart.[72] The most successful and stable tenants in East Inishowen, however, arrived later – the Youngs of Culdaff and Harveys of Malin Hall. Robert Young first came to the area as rector of Clonca (1640) and later Culdaff (1661) and astute marriage arrangements aided the assemblage of townlands contiguous to the churchlands.[73] John Harvey (d. 1733), from a landed Bristol family, acquired capital through

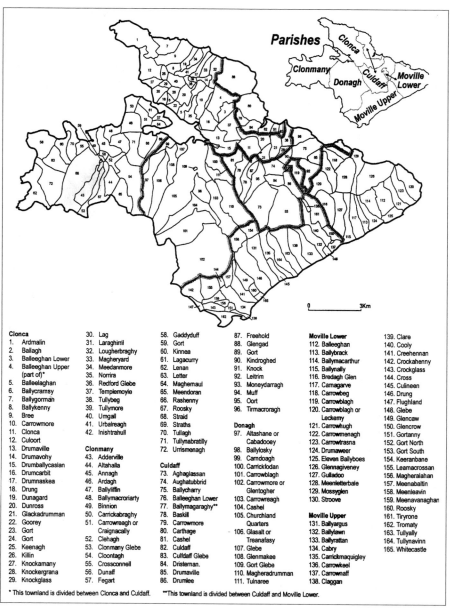

Parishes

Clonca
Clonmany
Donagh
Culdaff
Moville Lower
Moville Upper

0   3Km

Clonca
1. Ardmalin
2. Ballagh
3. Balleeghan Lower
4. Balleeghan Upper (part of)*
5. Balleelaghan
6. Ballycramsy
7. Ballygorman
8. Ballykenny
9. Bree
10. Carrowmore
11. Clonca
12. Culoort
13. Drumaville
14. Drumavohy
15. Drumballycasian
16. Drumcarbit
17. Drumnaskea
18. Drung
19. Dunagard
20. Dunross
21. Glackadrumman
22. Goorey
23. Gort
24. Gort
25. Keenagh
26. Killin
27. Knockamany
28. Knockergrana
29. Knockglass

30. Lag
31. Laraghirril
32. Lougherbraghy
33. Magheryard
34. Meedanmore
35. Norrira
36. Redford Glebe
37. Templemoyle
38. Tullybeg
39. Tullymore
40. Umgall
41. Urbalreagh
42. Inishtrahull

Clonmany
43. Adderville
44. Altahalla
45. Annagh
46. Ardagh
47. Ballyliffin
48. Ballymacroriarty
49. Binnion
50. Carrickabraghy
51. Carrowreagh or Craignacally
52. Clehagh
53. Clonmany Glebe
54. Cloontagh
55. Crossconnell
56. Dunaff
57. Fegart

58. Gaddyduff
59. Gort
60. Kinnea
61. Lagacurry
62. Lenan
63. Letter
64. Maghemaul
65. Meendoran
66. Rashenny
67. Roosky
68. Straid
69. Straths
70. Tullagh
71. Tullynabratilly
72. Urrismenagh

Culdaff
73. Aghaglassan
74. Aughatubbrid
75. Ballycharry
76. Balleeghan Lower
77. Ballymagaraghy**
78. Baskill
79. Carrowmore
80. Carthage
81. Cashel
82. Culdaff
83. Culdaff Glebe
84. Dristernan.
85. Drumaville
86. Drumlee

87. Freehold
88. Glengad
89. Gort
90. Kindroghed
91. Knock
92. Leitrim
93. Moneydarragh
94. Muff
95. Oort
96. Tirmacroragh

Donagh
97. Altashane or Cabadooey
98. Ballylosky
99. Carndoagh
100. Carrickfodan
101. Carrowblagh
102. Carrowmore or Glentogher
103. Carrowreagh
104. Cashel
105. Churchland Quarters
106. Glasalt or Treanafasy
107. Glebe
108. Glenmakee
109. Gort Glebe
110. Magheradrumman
111. Tulnaree

Moville Lower
112. Balleeghan
113. Ballybrack
114. Ballymacarthur
115. Ballynally
116. Bredagh Glen
117. Carnagarve
118. Carrowbeg
119. Carrowblagh
120. Carrowblagh or Leckemy
121. Carrowhugh
122. Carrowmenagh
123. Carrowtrasna
124. Drumaweer
125. Eleven Ballyboes
126. Glennagiveney
127. Gulladoo
128. Meenletterbale
129. Mossyglen
130. Stroove

Moville Upper
131. Ballyargus
132. Ballylawn
133. Ballyrattan
134. Cabry
135. Carrickmaquigley
136. Carrowkeel
137. Carrownaff
138. Claggan

139. Clare
140. Cooly
141. Creehennan
142. Crockahenny
143. Crockglass
144. Cross
145. Culineen
146. Drung
147. Flughland
148. Glebe
149. Glencaw
150. Glencrow
151. Gortanny
152. Gort North
153. Gort South
154. Keeranbane
155. Leamacrossan
156. Magheralahan
157. Meenabaltin
158. Meenleavin
159. Meenavanaghan
160. Roosky
161. Tiryrone
162. Tromaty
163. Tullyally
164. Tullynavinn
165. Whitecastle

* This townland is divided between Clonca and Culdaff.   **This townland is divided between Culdaff and Moville Lower.

Fig. 18.4   Townlands of East Inishowen.
Source: Townland Index, county Donegal, 1956.

work as a wine merchant in France and later as chamberlain of Derry. He took up residence in Malin some time after 1708 and at his death the family's holdings included the townlands of Keenagh, Ballagh, Killin and Evispagar (Tullymore, Lougherbraghy and Drumavohy). It was his son

George (1713-73) who was responsible for building up the estate and clearing his father's debts (John Harvey had four wives and nineteen children – a large drain on the estate)[74] through his strategic position as land agent for the Donegalls. With the rising economic prosperity of the late-eighteenth century the favourable conditions offered by Donegall on renewal of leases in 1769 were not expected to last and George warned his son to never 'let it slip from your mind that what we have now is of short duration, that we must and ought to make a fortune out of our Donegall leases equal to what we now have'.[75]

As a result of the Chichester family indebtedness, his fears were not to materialise and by the middle of the nineteenth century both the Harveys and the Youngs were managing their enlarged estates quite independently. Moreover, the gap between the head rent and rental income was significant. In 1856 George Young, for example, had in his possession 10,457 a. 4r. 22p., giving him a rental of £3,068 14s 9d. One townland, Clare, was held in fee simple. A further 6,076 acres were held from the marquis under a lease dated 1826 for lives renewable forever. The head rent was £210 compared to a rental income of £1,380. The remainder of his property was churchlands held under a lease in perpetuity from 1836 with a head rent of £252 and a rental income of £1,392.[76] A contemporary highlighted the distinctive position of men like Harvey and Young compared to other smaller gentry: 'I should hardly call the parties who have leases in perpetuity, under the Lord Donegall middlemen. I know many instances in which tenants holding under them are as comfortable as those holding under the proprietors: but where there are only small quantities of land held by the lessees of Lord Donegall the occupying tenants are not so well off'.[77] In his evidence before the Devon Commission, John Harvey expressed the same sentiments, indicating the enhanced status and security of holding land in perpetuity.[78]

Fig. 18.5 indicates the very fragmented nature of landholding in the barony outside the larger estates, by the mid-nineteenth century. Since the map is compiled from valuation material much of the complexity of landholding is hidden. A case study of one parish, for which landed estate rentals exist, will highlight the web of interests characteristic of less profitable land. Immediate lessors in Clonmany parish by the mid-1850s included J. W. Doherty who had purchased his father's property in the northeast of the parish in the Encumbered Estates Court, Lougherys of Binnion (lessors of the churchlands), Rev Young of Glebe and the sisters C. & G. Ball and McClintock (agent) in Cloontagh. The remainder of the parish was purchased by the Harvey family of Malin and the Meentiaghs (in the adjoining parish of Barr of Inch, West Inishowen) from the marquis of Donegall in 1810-11, for a term of

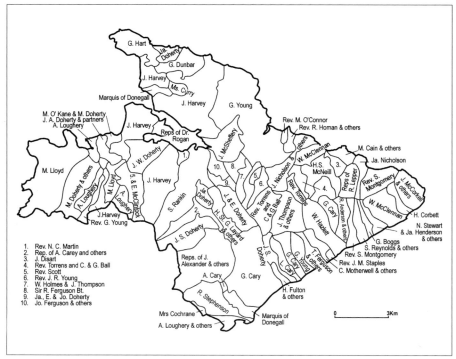

Fig. 18.5   Immediate lessors in East Inishowen, c.1850
Source: General Valuation Union of Inishowen, 1857.

1,000 years.[79] The townlands of Carrickabraghy, Ballymacroriarty, Carrowreagh, Fegart, Ardagh, Ballyliffin, Clehagh, Altahalla and Roosky were still in the ownership of Edward Harvey 'a lunatic' when the estate was advertised in the Landed Estates Court in 1879. In 1855 these lands were sub-let or just managed by John Harvey (Malin Hall), Minchin Lloyd (agent), J. Doherty, M. Doherty and M. O'Kane and the representatives of Dr Rogan. The estate to the west of the parish in Urris, purchased by Robert Harvey in 1811, was at this time managed by M. Lloyd, although in 1860 George Harvey was about to take it 'on his own hands'.[80]

Elsewhere in the barony information is patchy and it is difficult to determine the interest in property. Some smallholders were well established. In 1801, for example, Mr Henry Alexander was reclaiming 'into tillage and meadow' large areas around his new mansion sited in the 'blackest and wildest part' of Glentogher. According to McParlan, his efforts were at a scale not surpassed 'in the United Kingdom' and they were 'diffusing among the ignorant natives the spirit of industry and cultivation'.[81] J. S. Nicholson's (of Bangor, Down) father had purchased an unexpired lease from the marquis of Donegall earlier in the century.[82] Although he had a house in Leitrim townland, the estate was managed by Robert Lepper. The sisters C. & G. Ball, formerly of Leeson Street, Dublin, held scattered holdings throughout the peninsula which provided a stable income for the ageing spinsters augmented by interest on George Young's loans.[83] Robert Lepper of Foyle View, Redcastle, one of the principal land agents in the barony, by the 1870s managed *c.* 27,600 acres for about twenty proprietors, including Lord Donegall, J. S. Nicholson, G. Knox, D. Gilliland, B. McCorkell and S. Lawther.[84] Merchant capital from Londonderry was also invested in property in the peninsula. William Hazlett, merchant and 'mayor of Derry'[85] had been speculating in leases for some time. The lease of Cooly townland in Moville Upper was acquired after 1835 and in the early 1850s he considered purchasing Clare townland from Young. William McClennan, described as a 'herd' so presumably a land agent, had just purchased the interest of three townlands of the Greencastle estate previously held by the insolvent Sir Arthur Chichester.

Proprietors in the barony, who had a longer-term interest in their lands, proved to be better managers of their property but innovation, even on these estates, was late. Rundale, which greatly impeded agricultural improvements, prevailed throughout Inishowen in 1814. 'The want of enclosure' was another 'insuperable obstacle' with the arable becoming a common for cattle during the winter. The general rotation was 1. potatoes 2. barley 3. oats 4. oats 5. flax. 6. oats, 'after which the land is again prepared for potatoes, either with dung or seaweed, assisted sometimes with a little peat moss broke against it'. The pasture land was generally overstocked. 'Mere subsistence' was deemed sufficient for cattle in winter months and sheep were 'kept in great abundance, without sufficient pasturage'.[86] Some early initiatives were recorded. In 1801, for example, Rev Kennedy was using lime 'judiciously' in reclaiming bog south of Trawbreaga Bay and his exertions had 'induced numbers of the country people to follow his example, who were before strangers to the use of it'.[87] In the 1820s George Young began to experiment with drilling potatoes. He found them unsatisfactory, however, not being as dry as 'the old way in ridges'. They were 'larger and more productive but not near sufficient to pay the added expense of labour'. In 1828, Young was effecting consolidation of holdings on his estate, a process which took place in a piecemeal fashion. In Dunross townland he found that the farms had been 'badly laid out before, crossing and intersecting one another in several places, and in many cases one man's house being on his neighbour's cut, and in some places the land of one being a quarter of a mile distance from his own house and close to the door of another'.[88]

A joint effort among proprietors at innovation was also initiated in the 1820s. Many were members of the 'North West of Ireland Society' in Derry. A branch of this society was established for Culdaff, Clonca and Donagh parishes and ploughing matches were arranged in the region from 1825.[89] The society's magazine, reporting from the fourth annual ploughing match, found that 'an evident and progressive improvement in ploughing has taken place in this district, since the commencement of the society, and, we may also add, in the style and appearance of the cattle, etc.'[90] It seems that this and other local societies had only a limited impact on the mass of tenantry. A witness to the Devon Commission from Buncrana, in the barony of West Inishowen, highlighted how the recently established Union society was too exclusive to be effective.[91] These sentiments were repeated by Mr John McArthur, a chancery agent on the Greencastle estate. He noted that although societies had 'effected much good', for the majority of Irish farmers they proved 'quite ineffective'. The small farmers 'have got an opinion into their heads that there is no use trying'.[92] In the Buncrana district the embryonic agricultural school, initiated with the help of Captain Kennedy who had donated 3½ acres of land, showed more potential.[93] Still the progress by 1844 was limited. In a relatively commercial area south of Moville town, rundale was almost eliminated, some drainage effected and 'some green crops' introduced. But apart from the estate of Thomas Doherty Esq of Redcastle (2,800 acres with 36 tenants) no landlord in the district was aiding tenants to any great extent. This, Doherty suggested, was largely due to the increasing financial burdens such as the police and poor law taxes, imposed on the proprietors. Nor were the tenants free of blame. In 1823 Doherty had granted his tenants leases for years and lives at the 1780 rent, and encouragement was given through premiums for 1st, 2nd and 3rd class farmers. But as soon as the general agitation (concerning payment of tithes) commenced throughout Ireland they lost interest and in 1844 over 500 acres of easily reclaimable mountain remained barren.[94]

Without proper consolidation and enclosure any attempt at innovation was futile. On smaller estates and those characterised by several layers of property interest, rundale, openfield and partnerships still prevailed to the mid-nineteenth century. Holdings on the estate of J. S. Nicholson in Culdaff parish remained extremely fragmented and despite much potential, little reclamation had been effected. Nicholson was described as one of the best landlords in the district 'with the maxim of live and let live'[95] and seems to have adopted the policy of non-interference. This was also true for Oort, Moneydaragh and Leitrim townlands, all held by minor gentry. Poor land management was certainly a feature of Clonmany parish. In 1835, John O'Donovan described Clonmany as a 'very secluded and wild parish ... completely environed by mountains'.[96] More than half its area had several layers of proprietary interest. Of all the sub-lessors listed for the estate of Edward Harvey only John Harvey had any success in checking sub-division and reorganisation had been effected in several townlands under his management. Consolidation of holdings was planned, though not effected in Ardagh townland in the 1850s and instead was left to the Land Commission a century later.[97] Neither M. Doherty nor M. O'Kane were likely to have the means or will to carry out reform. Stray comments in the valuation books indicate high levels of stress in Urris, managed by M. Lloyd. In 1855 the tenants had received a '2/6 per £ of an abatement in the given rent in the last years all through Urris'. Little attention had been given to the management of the estate and the valuator understood that, 'Mr Harvey will change the boundaries of each farm in the seven townlands when it comes on his own hands which will be in the course of three years – at present the greater part is in rundale.'[98] The previous neglect of this remote region resulted in extreme congestion and fragmentation of holdings for which the easiest solution was the radical striping and dispersal of settlement, carried out in the early 1860s. Congestion was also evident on the Greencastle estate formerly held by Sir Arthur Chichester (see fig. 18.6). This property had been in receivership since the 1820s, over which time there had been several agents managing it. Chancery receivers had little or no authority of their own, acting merely as rent collectors, and it was only when Robert Lepper took over management of this estate in 1836 that rationalisation began. Despite consolidation, however, there was little evidence of adequate enclosure by 1848. Insecurity of tenure ensured that little improvement was carried out, with many of the tenants unable to pay their rents. In 1844 arrears amounted to £7,000 or over four times the rental of £1,600.[99] For the barony as a whole it was the estates of the principal proprietors, Young and Harvey, which were the most prosperous. With the exception of bog townlands like Lougherbraghy and Glengad, tenants held in severalty, fragmentation was no longer extreme and fields had been enclosed by the 1840s. A similar situation pertained in the more fertile land south of Moville town.

The mid-decades of the nineteenth century proved to be the turning point in the fortunes of many proprietors in the barony. Just when their discretionary power seemed to be strengthened as a result of perpetual leases, it was thwarted by their own financial difficulties. In the late eighteenth and early nineteenth centuries, the 'Golden Age' for the landed in the barony, profit rents of the larger proprietors like Youngs and Harvey allowed for lavish lifestyles. The diary of George Young,

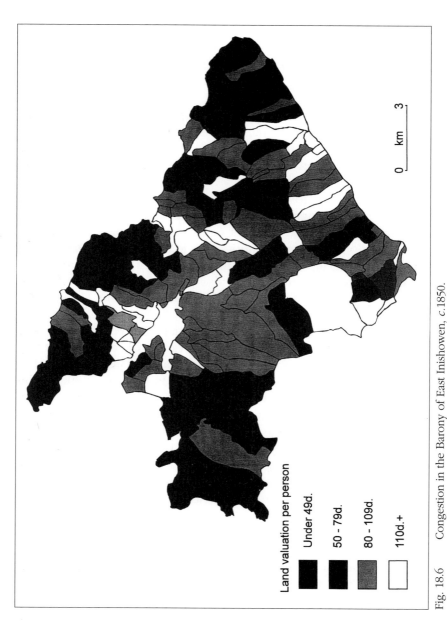

Land valuation per person

Under 49d.

50 - 79d.

80 - 109d.

110d. +

0   km   3

Fig. 18.6   Congestion in the Barony of East Inishowen, c.1850.
Source: General Valuation, Union of Inishowen, *Census of Population (Irl.),* 1851.

for example, outlines leisurely and prolonged family visits to England.[100] At home work as justice of the peace and regular entertaining of the neighbouring gentry absorbed income. Ornamentation of the 130-acre demesne in Culdaff absorbed much of Young's attention and income in the 1820s. In 1827 some 50,000 trees were planted. This taste for high living could not be sustained for long in the poorer economic climate of the post-Napoleonic era. Nor could the tradition of providing attractive settlements for younger children and wives on inheritance and marriage. By 1850 the Youngs were in severe financial straits and in 1856 Young presented a petition for the sale of his estate in the Encumbered Estates Court. A schedule of encumbrances and claims affecting the estate, lodged with the court in 1857, gives an insight into the sources of Young's indebtedness.[101] Altogether a principal sum of £30,807 was due as well as annuities amounting to £560. The earliest claims stemmed from the marriage settlement of Robert Young and Rebecca Hart in 1730 which provided for a portion of £600 for younger children of the union, and a jointure of £100 for Rebecca should she outlive her husband. Over the successive generations the amount of the portions and jointures increased to £2,000 and £200, respectively, on the marriage of the owner to Mary Anne Ffolliot in 1831. By 1857 nothing was owing from these charges. However, the legacies of the two generations placed a heavy burden on the estate. In her will of 1796 Rebecca Young (widow) left a total of £6,100 for her six 'non-inheriting' children, £1,153 of which was still unpaid.

Marcia Young was more extravagant, charging the estate in 1834 with £9,000 for three daughters and one younger son: all but £1,000 of this was still owing in 1857, and her will was promptly followed by a series of mortgages on the estate and judgements against George and his mother. Generally the amounts of credit were small and the sources primarily personal and localised. They included a judgement of £2,600 acquired by a close friend and relative, Rev Robert Harvey and his wife, from Malin in 1835, a judgement of £2,000 obtained by Rev James Knox of Carthage, Culdaff in 1839 and a further £4,900 judgement obtained by Sir Arthur Chichester MP in 1837. Financial sources further afield included a £10,000 mortgage on the churchlands from William Lecky Brown of Cumber House, Londonderry in 1846,[102] and a judgement of £1,846 acquired by the Rev William Cather, Joseph Cather and Henry Price of Londonderry two years later. Some tightening up of the credit pool in the 1850s is indicated by the borrowing of £100 at 5 per cent interest from a tenant, Alexander Douglas and £600 from his agent Robert Lepper.[103] Considering his growing indebtedness Young's estate improvements were somewhat badly timed. Loans totalling £5,000 received from the Board of Public Works in 1848 and 1850 burdened the estate with annual rent charges of £195 and £130 (to be paid over twenty-two years).[104]

Several efforts were made in the 1840s to reduce the debt burden. In 1842 Young attempted to sell his interest in Glenagivney townland to Hugh Lyle for £2,750. However, the offer was declined because of the 'wording of Donegall's leases reserving bog, etc'. Severe hardship among tenants exacerbated the problems and despite abatements, rents were not always collected. From 1845 to 1850 the tenants of Clare and Glenagivney had paid only two years' rents and Young was further pressed to tighten his purse strings in order to reduce his debts. In 1849 a Mr Campbell of Yorkshire replied to a Scottish newspaper's advertisement for the renting of 100 acres of Young's demesne. In 1851 he attempted to hire a new agent who would take some of the financial obligations on board. Mr Triall 'a very amusing, tho' plain, honest Scotchman' agreed to take on the agency if he could 'reside' and would 'advance £1,000 to pay off present bills, and also engage to pay head rents, interest, etc, as they became due'. However, it seems that Mr Triall could not reside, but did endeavour to find somebody who could. He also tried to raise a loan from a Scottish bank of which he was a director. Both attempts failed, the latter because the Edinburgh Insurance Company 'would not lend money on Irish estates at present'. In the same year he considered applying to the Sugar Company of Ireland, offering 200 acres for the production of sugar beet which was calculated to give a clear profit of £2,000 annually.[105] This adventurous scheme was not adopted but instead Young let his demesne for a five-year term. Pressure was further eased when he replaced George Mitchell with Mr Robert Lepper of Redcastle as his agent for Clare townland. This enabled him 'not only to settle the large bill with Mr Hazlett but also to meet some other very pressing demands'. Eventually only two townlands, Glenagivney and Clare, were sold. The proceeds may have been sufficient to meet the immediate demands and some of the family charges could be easily dealt with. In 1858, for example, he mortgaged the townland of Carthage to his spinster daughter Anne Angel in consideration of the debt he still owed her. At the same time the townland was charged with an annuity of £50 payable to his eldest son Robert to cover his debt of £990.[106] Young's financial problems were far from over. Interest on mortgages and family charges were still being paid in 1901 and from 1880 they absorbed all the income from the estate. In 1887 'when things were at their worst' some of the mortgagees again threatened to force the estate into the court, but it was calculated that the sale of the estate would not cover all the debts.[107]

The Harvey family faced similar trouble. John Harvey had mortgaged his property on several occasions around the mid-century. It was mortgaged in 1853 to Hugh Hawkshaw for £270.[108] In the same year William Wilson of Raphoe was attempting to recover a judgement debt of £209.[109] Other mortgages are listed for 1857 to a Robert Boyle Miller, commander in chief of HRM's navy, for £2,000,[110] and in 1858 to Jane Knox, Portrush, for £900.[111] By the end of the century, Harvey was more anxious than Young to take advantage of the Land Purchase Acts to sell off the interest in the property. In 1890, 4,968 acres comprising 193 holdings were purchased by the Irish Land Commission for £32,610.[112] Still his troubles continued and in 1903 a letter from Malin Hall to Letitia Young (daughter-in-law of George Young and Harvey's largest creditor) indicated that twenty-one of his thirty-five creditors had replied favourably to his terms of settlement.[113] Another heavily encumbered estate less successful in avoiding early sale was the Greencastle property of Sir Arthur Chichester; 1,202 acres of the 7,647 acre estate held in perpetuity and valued at £2,213 were sold in June 1851. On this part of the estate encumbrances amounted to £80,352.[114] The remainder of the estate was sold by 1856.[115]

The story of some of the more minor gentry of the barony was not unlike that of Harvey, Young and Chichester. They too built substantial houses surrounded by fine gardens, educated their sons and provided attractive financial settlements on their daughters' marriages. One family in difficulty by the mid-century was the Doherty family of the Glen House, Clonmany. The Dohertys were of local origin, only rising above tenant status in the early-nineteenth century through work as land agents to middlemen.[116] By mid-century they sub-leased land in parts of Annagh and Straid townlands which in turn was sub-let to under-tenants. However, the main part of the estate was in the north-east of the parish including Rasheny (765 acres) held in fee simple, Tullynabratilly (659) and Straths-Maghernaul (590) both held in perpetually renewable leases dating 1832.[117] The interest on this estate had been purchased in 1835[118] and since then had brought considerable profits. The chief rent of Straths, Maghernaul, for example, was £63. 6s. 8d. compared to £171. 3s. 1d. profit rent. But small estates were also vulnerable in the unsettled post-famine period and the canvass of the families' loans more restricted. The Dohertys' financial difficulties were evident from the early 1850s. In 1852 Michael Doherty still owed £300 of the £1,000 borrowed from his son J.W.[119] Family settlements remained to be paid, including over half of his daughter's marriage settlement of £800 to the local rector Rev Young.[120] However, the education and progression of his son in the legal profession[121] ensured that the estate was kept in the family for another decade. Through his position, J. W. was able to raise £5,000 of the total of £7,250 purchase price, from a Ms Jane Haig of Middlesex, though at a very steep interest rate of 7 per cent.[122] The estate was managed effectively by the new owner over the next decade, perhaps in an effort to ensure solvent tenants in the future. A rental of 1866 outlined the changes: 'Considerable improvements were effected on the lands by the late owner. The lands were surveyed and valued within the last 7 years, and the tenants who are now in very good circumstances, have lately built new dwelling houses on their own farms.' Despite the increased rental the Dohertys were unable to clear the estate of debts and it was re-sold in the Landed Estates Court on his death in 1866.[123]

In his study of the sale of Donegall's Belfast estate in the Encumbered Estates Court, Maguire highlighted the limited transfer of land that took place where long leases prevailed.[124] There was little attraction for outsiders to purchase what in effect were long-term fixed rents. For transfer of tenure below the status of freehold, the example of East Inishowen suggests only local interest. The principal estates listed for sale in the Encumbered and Landed Estates Courts, 1850 to 1885, were those of George Young (10,457 acres of which only 2,653 were sold in 1856), Sir Arthur Chichester of Greencastle (7,200 acres sold in the early 1850s), Edward Harvey in Clonmany, Donagh and in the adjoining parishes of Barr of Inch and Fahan (12,254 acres sold in 1879), Dohertys of Clonmany (2,013 acres which were lost from the family on the second sale in 1866) and L. Cary of Moville Upper (1,957 acres). The most substantial investors were Samuel Gilliland, Esq of Brookhall Londonderry and Ernest Cochrane (high sheriff of Donegal in 1879) who married the heiress of the Doherty estate of Redcastle. The notorious reputation for mismanagement, and the consequent decline in land values associated with estates under the management of the court of chancery receivers was confirmed in the barony. The Greencastle estate of Sir Arthur Chichester formed a substantial block of relatively fertile land bordering Moville town, and the greater part was held in perpetuity. However, it took almost five years and several attempts at auctioning before the townlands with determinable leases were purchased by local buyers.

Settlement

The predominant settlement form in the barony in the mid-nineteenth century was the cluster of farm dwellings and over 400 were mapped. (Five buildings were taken as the break-off point in the classification of cluster settlements.) Cluster morphology varied throughout the barony with the compact arrangement predominating. Lenan Keel in Clonmany, for example, was tucked in on slightly elevated ground at the foot of Croaghcarragh hill, safely removed from the risk of coastal floods. Dwellings here were aligned with their backs to the hill and their gables facing the westerly winds. Many other settlements formed a linear pattern, especially where they fringed arable and waste land. As the name suggests, Mullagh, in Annagh townland, Clonmany, developed at the extreme limits of cultivation on Binnion hill, strung out along a gently sloping tract. Behind the cluster the ground rose sharply but provided adequate grazing for the livestock. Below, tenant holdings formed elongated strips ensuring each tenant access to variable land qualities. A more formal layout of buildings, usually around a yard or green and with greater ornamentation by trees, was evident in the vicinity of the towns of Malin, Moville and Culdaff. In Knockglass, north of Malin town, for example, the engineer for the Ordnance Survey was struck by the appearance of the cluster 'being exceedingly neat and clean and more like an English colony' than any he had seen elsewhere in the neighbourhood.[125] The layout of other clusters was determined by the lines of communication including the large settlement of Carrowmenagh in Culdaff which developed at a crossroads.

Fig. 18.7 reveals variations in the scale of clusters, reflecting differences in soil quality and land management. Clusters were absent from areas of high relief running west from Leamacrossan Hill, Slieve Snaght, Bulbin Hill to the Urris Hills. The sand hills of Ballymacroriarty and Carrickabraghy in the Isle of Doagh, and in Lag in Clonca were of little agricultural value and settlement here was sparse. Considerable expanses of low-level blanket bog, such as in north-west Drumaville, Templemoyle, west Ballycharry, west Tirmacroragh, Knocknagrana, Leitrim, Leckemy and in the townlands north-west of Glengad repelled settlement. The greatest part of Dunagard, for example, was described in 1830 as 'uncultivated and used only for grazing'. Settlement developing on 'waste' lands like this was used for reclamation purposes as highlighted in the ordnance surveyor's description of the adjoining townland of Meedanmore: He noted that there was 'only one village in this townland and the ground in its neighbourhood is the entire part of the townland that is cultivated, not any road passes through it nor is there any object worth mentioning in it'.[126] Single clusters centrally located also developed in the small mountain townlands of Gortanny and Magheralan in Moville Upper where they acted as reclamation units. Under more favourable soil conditions, however, it was the quality of estate management that determined cluster scale. In the isolated and neglected estates in the west and north of Clonmany parish, around Ballymagaraghy, Ballycharry in Culdaff and in the former Chichester estate in Greencastle, large clusters flowered. They were also to be found in the extreme tip of the barony in the townland of Ardmalin and in Templemoyle and Drumaville in Clonca parish. The swelling of clusters was most evident in Culdaff. In Ballycharry

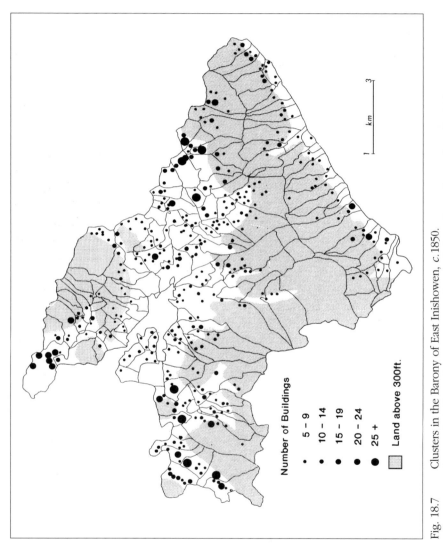

Fig. 18.7   Clusters in the Barony of East Inishowen, *c.*1850.

Source: O.S. Six inch maps, county Donegal, first edition (revised: 1846-1854)

townland (996 acres), for example, there was five clusters ranging in size from eight to thirty-three buildings and with an average size of sixteen buildings. The largest cluster of all was Ballymagaraghy in the adjoining townland, which consisted of forty-four buildings. Clusters also predominated in the central fertile plain of the barony, from the Isle of Doagh through the north of Donagh parish to Gleneely in Culdaff. Here, however, cluster size was smaller. In Moneydarragh townland, for example, there were fourteen clusters with an average size of six buildings. In the greater part of Moville Upper, south of Moville Lower and the area immediately north of Malin town in Clonca, both size and density of clusters were reduced.

There was nothing haphazard in the selection of cluster locations. All were strategically placed to take advantage of arable and waste land. An example of an isolated district, undisturbed by the re-organisation processes characteristic of the 1830s and 1840s, will serve to illustrate this. Rundale, openfield, partnership groups and clusters thrived in west Clonmany until the early 1860s. The region comprised a wedge of land between the Urris Hills and Lough Swilly with all the townlands forming oblong blocks to incorporate different land types. Each townland contained an average of four partnership farms which in turn were shaped to incorporate different resources, with clusters centrally located. The townland formed the basic resource unit and within each a progressively tighter system of resource organisation operated among the tenants. The first level was the mountain or coastal commonage which was shared between all resident occupiers, usually in proportion to their share of arable land. In this way the social cohesion of the townland was maintained. Within each partnership group there was also some form of commonage used primarily for grazing. The final tier of the system was the tenant's individual and permanent share in the arable land. The example of Lenan will demonstrate this townland hierarchy (see fig. 18.8). Lenan townland comprised 286 acres of low-lying alluvial soil, 560 acres of sandy and moory commonage and 837 acres of mountain. In 1848 definite field boundaries existed only where drainage or mountain reclamation had been effected, in the small gardens surrounding the clusters, separating arable from commonage and dividing the holdings of the different partnership groups. Five clusters had developed centrally within the partnership holdings and avoiding low-lying land liable to flooding. Lenan was the largest of these and about fifty metres away from it a break-away or secondary nucleation of five O'Donnell households which was still un-named by 1850, had developed. The two settlements formed part of the one partnership and the overspill was most likely an effort to prevent further overcrowding of an already congested settlement. Each of the resident

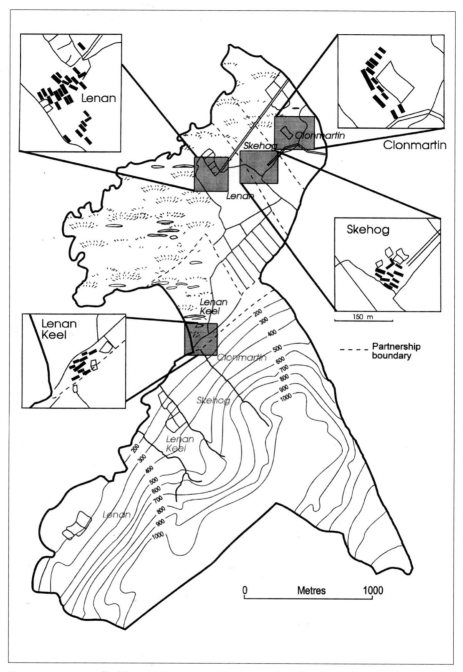

Fig. 18.8   Landholding and settlement in Lenan Townland, 1855.
          Source: O.S. Six inch map, county Donegal sheet 9 (revised, 1848);
          General Valuation, Union of Inishowen, 1857. Perambulation books,
          Clonmany, 1834.

occupiers of the townland held fragmented but fixed shares in the arable land, rights to grazing on the lowland commonage and access to the mountain in proportion to lowland valuation. Certain days during the year were allocated for tenants' use of the foreshore. The mountain share of each partnership was clearly demarcated on the ground either naturally by streams or by low earthen banks known locally as marches. No extra share of mountain or foreshore was given to tenants holding land outside their partnership farm.

Analysis of valuation material indicates that kinship and equality were features of these settlements. However, only Lenan Keel formed a true kin group cluster of five Kearneys, each having a building valuation of 15s and a total land valuation of £3 10s. The case study of Lenan cluster provides a more typical example (table 18.1). In 1855 the cluster consisted of one large partnership group of nineteen holdings. Being the largest settlement in the townland, it held almost half the mountain commonage ($^{342}/_{767}$th) and this was allotted to the partners in soums according to their shares in arable and rough grazing. The partnership was further divided into four sub-groups, each holding various proportions of 398th arable and lowland grazing. (The fractions were the valuators' means of dealing with the less quantifiable measures of soums.) Land and building valuations varied both between and within the sub-groups and perfect equality was found only among one family group – the Devlins. In the others one partner held a larger share than all others. For example, John Doherty held $^2/_6$ of the $^{70}/_{398}$th whereas his partners had only $^1/_6$. This level of inequality typified most settlements in the district and reflected a growing individualism among tenants.

Table 18.1

Partnership holdings in Lenan cluster, 1855

Names of sub-partners	Share in arable land	Average land valuation	Average building valuation
		£. s. d.	£. s. d.
Canny (1) Harkin (1) O'Donnell (5)	$^{171}/_{398}$	4 7 0	0 14 0
Kelly (3)	$^{87}/_{398}$	3 5 0	0 16 0
Doherty (3) Farrell (2)	$^{70}/_{398}$	2 1 0	0 13 0
Devlin (4)	$^{70}/_{398}$	3 5 0	0 15 0

Source: Valuation Manuscripts, Clonmany Parish, Ely Place.
Figures in brackets refer to number of partners.

It was not possible to reconstruct the fragmentation of holdings in Lenan because of the thorough eradication of rundale in the early 1860s. However, extreme fragmentation was common around clusters in the barony. In Doaghmore, in Lagacurry townland, Clonmany, for example, each tenant had an average of six parcels of land with a total area of eleven acres. The basic principle of rundale, access to all land types, was perhaps best illustrated in the Quig kin cluster in Bredagh Glen, Moville Lower. In 1855 the five Quigs held 137 acres (excluding mountain) valued at £51 15s, in partnership and in unequal shares. The complexity of fragmentation baffled the valuator who noted that 'tenement 35 is so minutely sub-divided it was impossible to show each occupier's portion.'[127] However, the valuator in 1827 was more successful. At that time, 101 acres were shared between four Quig households and the division of one parcel of 39 acres was as follows: fallow arable (6a. 1r. 0p.), meadow (2a. 0r. 1p.), bad arable (1a. 1r. 12p.), arable (12a. 3r. 32p.), bad arable (3a. 3r. 16p.), good arable (0a. 3r. 6p.), wet green pasture (4a. 3r. 32p.), bad arable and wet pasture (2a. 3r. 17p.).[128] This parcel alone was divided into at least thirty-two separate plots and the other sixty-two acres were equally as fragmented. Such excessive fragmentation of holdings could not be sustained in the latter part of the nineteenth century. In the 1870s, for example, John Loughery of Binnion, Clonmany, was 'pressed' to 'cut up' part of his estate. The two townlands were 'held in rundale, each of the tenants having from five to seven different parts of the townland. This made the place worthless – they were constantly trespassing on each other, and annoying each other, and quarrelling.'[129] Nor was extreme fragmentation always necessary. One or two open, elongated strips of land satisfied tenant access to different resources in other settlements including Ballyhillin, strung out along the highest ridge of the raised beach in Malin Head. Moreover, new clustered settlements developing at this time were less likely to adopt a farming system which was becoming increasingly frowned upon in the lowlands. Rundale was not so common among the later settlements of the marginal lands.[130]

The barony of East Inishowen provides an ideal example of the impact of prolonged absenteeism of the owner in fee, and the emergence of a system of middle-tenants with wide powers to shape the landscape. The barony had not been a hospitable place in the early-seventeenth century and even a century later little progress had been made in developing the agricultural economy.[131] Attractive leases were therefore necessary to encourage more progressive principal tenants to settle there, and the severe financial difficulties of the Chichester family in the late-eighteenth century consolidated the position of some of these families. Perpetual interest in land, granted mainly in the early decades of the nineteenth century, ensured that families like the Harveys and the Youngs were more interested in the long-term development of their property, and efforts at improvement were more evident from the 1820s. By 1850 these larger properties held in perpetuity were invariably the best managed. But middle-tenants comprised a mixed bag and ephemeral interest in land did remain significant over large parts of the barony to mid-century. Sub-leasing of land by the Harvey family to emerging local families, like the Dohertys, O'Kanes or the agent M. Lloyd, certainly eliminated the drudgery of dealing with numerous poor tenants, but it also removed the immediate opportunity, or indeed responsibility, to effectively manage the property. With only short-term interest in the land and limited finances, these lesser gentry were unlikely to expend on developing a more rational system of agriculture. Generally where this short-term interest prevailed up to mid-century, so too did rundale, openfield, partnership farms and clusters. The extreme undeveloped state of the Greencastle property managed by chancery receivers for over twenty years, perhaps best exemplifies the detrimental effect of short-term interest in land. The famine can be taken as a turning point for landholding in the barony in that it disrupted the very finely balanced system of gentry income and expenditure. Some estates were sold between 1850 and 1880 but due to the small-scale nature of property offered for sale and the complexity of interests involved, neither the Encumbered nor Landed Estates' Courts were generally successful in infusing progressive new blood into landholding. Other estates just managed to keep afloat for the remainder of the century, a situation not conducive to the development of agriculture.

One advantage of the management structure characteristic of the more isolated and poorly endowed areas is the opportunity it allows for examining a rapidly contracting system of land occupation. Where rundale, openfield and partnership farms survived to the mid-nineteenth century, they are well recorded by official sources. The example of Lenan townland showed how fine-tuned the system was to the physical endowment of the townland and how it ensured the maintenance of a social cohesion which survives within these units to this day. The example also revealed some heterogeneity in the nature of land occupation and settlement, a feature which is more evident when studying the wider area of the barony. It is important not to view clusters as homogeneous settlement forms combining all the associated features of rundale, openfield, partnership groupings and kinship ties.

The paper provides a detailed study of landholding and settlement in one of the more isolated baronies of the county. Similarities may be found for other Donegal districts characterised by relatively small and fragmented estates.

References

1. S. Lewis, *A topographical dictionary of Ireland*, i (Repr. Baltimore, 1984), p. 473.
2. W. S. Mason, *A statistical account or parochial survey of Ireland drawn up from the communication of the clergy*, ii (Dublin, 1816), p. 21.
3. See D. Dickson, 'Middlemen' in T. Barlett and D. W. Hayton (eds), *Penal era and golden age: essays in Irish history, 1690-1800* (Belfast, 1979), pp 162-85.
4. W. Nolan, *Fassadinin: land, settlement and society in south-east Ireland 1600-1850* (Dublin, 1979), p. 98.
5. T. P. Power, *Land, politics and society in eighteenth-century Tipperary* (Oxford, 1993), chapter 3.
6. For the significance of private acts as a 'last resort for hard pressed landowners' see D. Large, 'The wealth of the greater Irish landowners, 1750-1815' in *I.H.S.*, xv (Dublin, 1967), pp 21-45.
7. For an account of the building of the Chichester estate see P. Roebuck, 'The making of an Ulster great estate: the Chichesters, barons of Belfast and viscounts of Carrickfergus, 1599-1648' in *R.I.A. Proc.*, lxxix (Dublin, 1979), pp 1-25.
8. W. A. Maguire, 'Lord Donegall and the sale of Belfast: A case study from the Encumbered Estates Court' in *Econ. Hist. Rev.*, xxix (1976), p. 570.
9. Roebuck, 'Chichesters', pp 17-8.
10. *Rentals of estates for sale in the Encumbered and Landed Estates Courts, Ireland, 1850-85*, 135-29, P.R.O.I.
11. Maguire, 'Lord Donegall', p. 576.
12. See Dickson, 'Middlemen'.
13. W. J. Smyth, 'Estate records and the making of the Irish landscape: an example from county Tipperary,' in *Ir. Geography*, ix (1976), pp 29-49; Power, *Tipperary*, pp 138-42.
14. Nolan, *Fassadinin*, p. 125.
15. Ibid., chapter 5.
16. E. A. Currie, 'Settlement changes and their measurement: a case study from county Londonderry, 1833-1906' in C. Thomas (ed.), *Rural landscapes and communities: essays presented to Desmond McCourt* (Dublin, 1986), p. 117.
17. L. P. Curtis, Jr., 'Encumbered wealth: landed indebtedness in post-famine Ireland' in *American History Review*, lxxxv, no. ii (1980), p. 334.
18. See for example, Power, *Tipperary*, chapter 4; Large, 'Irish Landowners'; D. Cannidine, 'Aristocratic indebtedness in the nineteenth century: the case re-opened' in *Econ. Hist. Rev.*, second series, xxx (1977), pp 624-650.
19. Power, *Tipperary*, p. 93.
20. 'Final schedule of encumbrances, estate of Marquis Conyngham, county Donegal, 1912, N.L.I., PC. 351 (3).
21. *An act to further facilitate the sale and transfer of encumbered estates in Ireland, 12 and 13 Vict., C. 77*. For a discussion on the ineffectiveness of its predecessor – the Courts of Equity – and the widening remit of the Encumbered Estates Court – see: 'Encumbered Estate Court' in *Dublin University Magazine*, xxxvi (Dublin, September 1850), pp 311-28; W. L. Burn, 'Free trade in land: an aspect of the Irish question' in *R. Hist. Soc. Trans.*, xxxi (1949), pp 61-74; P. G. Lane, 'The management of estates by financial corporations in Ireland after the famine' in *Studia Hib.*, xiv (1974), pp 67-89.
22. 'Encumbered Estates Court (Ireland) ninth (and concluding) annual report' and article from '*Dublin Express*', 6/5/1858, in Larcom Papers, N.L.I., Ms. 7789.
23. *Trinity College Dublin estates commission; App. to report of the commissioners; minutes of evidence 2527, H.C.* (1905), xxvii, 157, pp 172-7 (The Fitzgibbon

Commission). Devon Commission, i, *evidence,* M. Collis, witness, p. 237.

24. R. McCarthy, *The Trinity college estates 1800-1923: corporate management in an age of reform* (Dundalk 1992), pp 112-3.

25. Ibid., p. 93.

26. *Rentals,* 87-64, 85-69.

27. *Return for 1870 of the number of landed proprietors in each county classed according to residence: H.C. P.P.,* 1872 (167), xlvii, 775.

28. *Landowners in Ireland; return of owners of land of one acre and upwards in the several counties, counties of cities, and counties of towns in Ireland* (Repr. Baltimore, 1988).

29. For an evaluation of the work of Alexander Hamilton of Coxtown, see *Ballyshannon Herald,* 2/11/1840, N.L.I.

30. 'Papers on the administration of Lord Leitrim's estate 1864-66', N.L.I., Ms. 1339 (1).

31. Devon commission, *evidence,* ii, John Crommer, witness, pp 159-60.

32. Ibid., ii, James Walker, witness, p. 157; James McCunningham, witness, p. 156; Alexander Hamilton, witness, p. 176.

33. Ibid., i, John V. Stewart, witness, p. 749.

34. *Census of population,* Ire., 1821, 1841 (Dublin).

35. J. M. D. McParlan, *Statistical survey of the county of Donegal with observations on the means of improvement drawn up in the year 1801, for the consideration, and under the direction of the Dublin Society* (Dublin, 1802), p. 59.

36. For a good account of how inequality developed among partnerships, see evidence from Mayo, in: Devon commission, *evidence,* ii, Rev Peter Geraghty and George Clending witnesses, pp 410-415.

37. Ibid., ii, Alexander Hamilton, witness, p. 179.

38. Ibid., i, Samuel Alexander, witness, p. 710.

39. Quoted in E. E. Evans, *Personality of Ireland: habitat, heritage and history* (Revised edition, Belfast, 1981), p. 96.

40. Devon commission, *evidence,* i, John V. Stewart, witness, pp 746-7.

41. E. Evans, 'Donegal survivals' in *Antiquity* xiii (1939), p. 209.

42. J. Tracey, 'Ulster vernacular housing – a study of the clachan of Ballymagaraghy, Co. Donegal,' Unpublished thesis for the Bartlett School of Architecture & Planning (1983), p. 8.

43. *Pers. Comm.,* Mark Dorrian, Institute of Irish Studies, Belfast.

44. Devon Commission, *evidence,* ii, Alexander Hamilton, witness, p. 179.

45. McParlan, *Statistical survey of Donegal,* p. 57.

46. Ibid., p. 67; S. Beattie, 'This destructive trade' in *Donegal Annual,* xxxxiii, pp 2-16.

47. See Devon Commission, *evidence,* ii, James Dunleavy, witness, p. 151; Robert Russell, witness, p. 165; T. J. Atkinson, witness, p. 171.

48. See evidence from John Pitt Kennedy on the lack of insight of proprietors who advocated new strains of crops and new breeds of animals without adequately enclosing and draining their land, Devon Commission, *App. to the evidence,* no. 16, p. 68.

49. For an account of the work in Fintown see *Ballyshannon Herald,* 6-11-1844.

50. Brownhall v/45 fol. 19r, T.C.D. I wish to thank John Hamilton of Brownhall, Ballintra and the Board of Trinity College Dublin for allowing access to this collection.

51. 'A valuation of the Pettigoe estate in the barony of Tierhugh', N.L.I., Ms. 5813.

52. *Rentals,* 85-69, 87-64.

53. Devon Commission *evidence*, ii, Alexander Hamilton, witness, p. 179.
54. Ibid., ii, Robert Russell, witness, p. 165.
55. *Rentals*, 44-40.
56. Devon Commission, *evidence*, ii, James McCunningham, witness, p. 156. See also ibid., i, John V. Stewart, witness, p. 748.
57. Curtis, 'Encumbered Wealth', pp 353-55.
58. *Return from the court for the sale of encumbered estates of Ireland up to the first day of April 1853, H.C. P.P.* (390) xciv, 599.
59. It is difficult to give an accurate figure for sales, owing to the fragmentation and incompleteness of the source material. Altogether there are four sets of rentals deposited in the Public Record Office (Ireland) and the National Library. In this calculation I have used the O'Brien Index to rentals (P.R.O.I.). Moreover, not all auctions resulted in sales and there are many instances of second and third attempts at sale.
60. *Rentals*, 46-13, 130-21.
61. Ibid., 108-24.
62. Ibid., 87-30.
63. Ibid., 87-3.
64. For the indebtedness of the Conolly family in the eighteenth century and the consequences for land management, see E. A. Currie, 'Fining down the rents: The management of the Conolly estates in Ireland 1734-1800' in *Derriana: the journal of the Derry diocesan historical society* (1979), pp 25-38.
65. *Rentals*, 87-64, 85-69.
66. McCarthy, *Trinity college estates*, p. 221; *Ballyshannon Herald*, 16/11/1872. Ebenzer Bustard Esq. of Belville Ho., Dunkineely purchased the interest on the 6,757-acre estate by private sale.
67. *Return of fee simple land exposed for sale or sold in the Landed Estates Court, Ireland, October 1874-6, H.C. P.P.*, 1877 (448), lxix, 569.
68. Curtis, 'Encumbered wealth', pp 355-7.
69. *Return of names of owners of properties under land purchase (Ire.) Act 1885, sanctioned by the Irish Land Commission 1889* (81), lxi 685: 1890 (115), lx 171.
70. P. Roebuck, 'Landlord indebtedness in Ulster in the seventeenth and eighteenth centuries' in J. M. Goldstrom and C. F. Clarkson (eds.), *Irish population, economy and society: essays in honour of the late K. H. Connell* (Oxford, 1981), p. 145.
71. A. I. Young, *Three hundred years in Inishowen* (Belfast, 1929), p. 60.
72. Ibid., pp 34-5.
73. Ibid., p. 29.
74. Ibid., p. 122.
75. Quoted in Dickson, 'Middlemen', p. 181 from Harvey manuscripts, George Harvey to John Harvey, 1 December, 1770.
76. *Rentals*, 43-120.
77. Devon Commission, *evidence*, i, Mr Gray, witness, p. 688.
78. Ibid., i, John Harvey, witness, pp 712-3.
79. *Rentals*, 135-29; Mason, *Parochial survey*, i (Dublin, 1814), p. 181.
80. Manuscript valuation books, *Clonmany*, Valuation Office, Dublin.
81. McParlan, *Statistical survey of Donegal*, p. 19.
82. *Report of her Majesty's Commission of Inquiry into the working of the Landlord and Tenant (Ireland) Act, 1870, and the Acts amending the same*: ii, Digest of evidence, minutes of evidence, part i, 1881, *c. 2779* – i, xviii (hereinafter *Bessborough Commission*), James McGlinchey, witness, ii p. 311.
83. Diary of George Young, Ms. D: 3045:6; 4: P.R.O.N.I.

84. *Bessborough commission*, ii, Robert Lepper, witness, p. 395.
85. Devon commission, *evidence*, i, William Hazlett, witness, p. 737.
86. Mason (1816), *parochial survey*, pp 163-5.
87. McParlan, *Statistical survey of Donegal*, p. 61.
88. D:3045:6; 4.
89. Ibid.
90. *North west society's magazine: a periodical publication intended to encourage and to improve agriculture, arts, manufacture and fishery*, second series, ii, no. 16 (1828), p. 384.
91. Devon commission, *evidence*, i, Samuel Alexander, witness, p. 710.
92. Ibid., *evidence*, i, John McArthur, witness, p. 723.
93. Ibid., *evidence*, i. Rev McGinn, witness, p. 706.
94. Ibid., Thomas Doherty, witness, pp 713-715.
95. *Bessborough commission*, ii, James McGlinchey, witness, p. 311.
96. J. O'Donovan, *Letters containing information relative to the antiquities of the county of Donegal with references to the Ordnance Survey* (1926), p. 10.
97. Pers. Comm., J. McElleney, Annagh.
98. Manuscript valuation books and cancelled valuation lists, Clonmany, Valuation Office, Dublin.
99. Devon Commission, *evidence,* i, Robert Lepper and Charles Hegarty, witnesses, pp 723-5.
100. D:3045: 6; 4.
101. D:3045:5; 11-20.
102. R.D., 1846-9-31.
103. R.D., 1855-4-231; D:3045:5; 11-20.
104. D:3045:5; 11-20.
105. D:3045:6; 4. This likely followed on from an advertisement in the *Londonderry Journal* of March 10, for tenders of 300-500 acres to follow on the success of the sugar factory at Mountmellick in Queen's county.
106. R.D., 1858-15-197 & 198.
107. D:3045:5; 31-40, no. 146, Young to O'Neill.
108. R.D., 1853-5-28.
109. Ibid., 1853-25-88.
110. Ibid., 1857-25-269.
111. Ibid., 1858-33-11.
112. *Return of names of landowners of properties under Land Purchase (Ire.) Act, 1885, sanctioned by the Irish Land Commission, H.C. P.P.,* 1890 (115), lx.171.
113. D:3045:5; 31-40, no. 171, Harvey to Young.
114. *Return of the proceedings of the commissioners for the sale of encumbered estates in Ireland, from their commencement up to the 1st day of January 1852, H.C. P.P.,* 1852 (167) xlvii 417.
115. *Rentals:* 3-22, 7-30, 10-18, 12-45, 34-27, 36-27
116. C. McGlinchey, *The last of the name, Charles McGlinchey; edited and with an introduction by Brian Friel* (Belfast, 1986), pp 96-100.
117. *Rentals:* 77-36.
118. R.D., 1836-2-44 & 45.
119. R.D., 1852-14-84.
120. R.D., 1852-23-175.
121. John Walker Doherty was apprentice solicitor for Isaac Colhoun in Londonderry. Colhoun was an important land agent in Donegal. See Devon Commission, *evidence*, i, J. W. Doherty, witness, p. 742.

122. R.D., 1855-29-212.
123. Rentals: 77-27; *Londonderry Journal*, 18-4-1866.
124. Maguire, 'Lord Donegall', p. 584.
125. *Ordnance Survey Name Books*, Donegal, no. 38.
126. Ibid., 42.
127. Manuscript valuation books, Moville Lower, Valuation Office, Dublin.
128. Composition of tithes, county Donegal, 1827, P.R.O.I.
129. *Bessborough Commission*, ii, John Loughery, witness, p. 407.
130. For a detailed discussion on clusters in Inishowen see M. O'Donnell, 'Farm clusters in north-west Inishowen, *c.*1850' in *Ir. Geography*, xxvi, no. 22 (1993), pp 101-19.
131. For a brief description of conditions in Inishowen in the early-eighteenth century, see the extract from the diary of Ludford Harvey (b. 1759), printed in Young, *Inishowen*, pp 124-5.

Chapter 19

AGRARIAN IMPROVEMENT AND SOCIAL UNREST: LORD GEORGE HILL AND THE GAOTH DOBHAIR SHEEP WAR

BREANDÁN Mac SUIBHNE

The Roman Catholic parish of West Tullaghobegley, commonly referred to as Gaoth Dobhair, was established in 1834. Bounded to the east and south by the Derryveagh mountains, it consists of an archipelago of islands, a *machaire* or coastal plain and large expanses of blanket bog. The parish is best known to students of nineteenth-century Ireland on account of *Facts from Gweedore* (London, 1845). In this self-congratulatory pamphlet, Lord George Hill (1801-79), describes the socio-economic condition of the district when he first invested there in 1838 and details his efforts to 'civilize Gweedore and raise its people to a higher social and moral level'.[1] The pamphlet includes a frequently-cited, though one-sided, assessment of rundale, the two-field system of land use which operated throughout Gaoth Dobhair until the 1840s. Under rundale, people lived in house-clusters on the edge of a townland's arable land or 'infield'.[2] They divided this land so that every household had a share of the various qualities of arable. Hence, a single holding might consist of several plots in a number of locations. There were no fences or ditches separating these plots which, according to Hill, the inhabitants periodically redistributed. In addition, households had turbary and grazing rights in the 'outfield', either a section of the townland or else a separate sparsely-populated townland. In Gaoth Dobhair transhumance was an important element of the system. In late spring some people, mainly young women, moved with the cattle of their townland to pastures on the hills and islands. Later, in autumn, the stock were driven back to the arable land where they grazed during the winter months.[3]

Hill and other 'improving' landlords who acquired property in the district in the decade before the famine believed rundale to be inherently inefficient and attempted to abolish it. They consolidated their tenants' plots and enclosed extensive tracts of commonage. Although the smallholders were initially reluctant to abandon customary practices, the landlords' initiatives provoked no violent opposition in the 1840s. Nevertheless, in the mid-1850s, when the landlords leased sections of the highlands to sheepfarmers, the smallholders vigorously reasserted their customary grazing rights. This culminated in a protracted campaign of anti-grazier activity known as the Gaoth Dobhair Sheep War.[4]

This chapter explores the tension between agrarian custom and 'improvement' in mid-nineteenth century Gaoth Dobhair. In particular, it examines the causes, forms and efficacy of popular opposition to landlord attempts to enclose sections of the highlands and develop commercial sheepfarming. Historians of rural Scotland have recently re-assessed the extent and efficacy of popular resistance to the great highland clearances which began in earnest about 1780 and continued until the mid-1850s. The background to the clearances is similar to that of the Sheep War, namely, the desire of market-oriented landowners to lease rough pastures to sheepfarmers. The most recent research rejects the widely held view that the highlanders were 'stoically passive and pathetically supine in their reaction to the landlord policy of clearance'. Nevertheless, it confirms that the highlanders' opposition resulted only in sporadic, unco-ordinated, petty violence which failed to prevent either the development of commercial sheepfarming or the clearances.[5] In contrast, the Gaoth Dobhair smallholders' opposition to enclosure and 'improvement' was relatively successful. Unlike the limited protests in the Scottish highlands, their resistance found expression in a well organised campaign of anti-grazier activity. This campaign entailed both agrarian outrages against specific targets and a political campaign aimed at discrediting the landlords and sheepfarmers and frustrating the state's response to the unrest. The willingness of the Roman Catholic clergy to sanction and encourage resistance and the involvement of some smallholders in a regional secret society are identified as critical factors in determining the character and course of the smallholders' opposition to 'improvement'.

Gaoth Dobhair before 1838

In 1833 the population of Gaoth Dobhair was 3,263. Despite emigration and a series of subsistence crises, it increased to 3,997 by 1841.[6] This small community, almost exclusively Roman Catholic and Gaelic-speaking, existed in the administrative and economic margins of Irish society. 'Disjoined from the world rather than connected to it', poor roads and the absence of bridges made it difficult to reach the area by land.[7] In 1838 the only institutions in the parish were a Roman Catholic chapel, an intermittently staffed police barracks and a national school. The nearest post office was ten miles away and the local corn mill was crude and inefficient. There was no village in Gaoth Dobhair and a small fair held at Doire Beaga brought few people into the parish. Although hucksters travelled to and from Letterkenny trading tea and sugar for eggs, the parish could not boast a shop or a dispensary and its only 'inns' were squalid *sibíní*. There was no pier or slipway and, with the exception of a salmon fishery established at An Bun Beag by Neidí Mór and Séamas Ó Gallchóir of Árainn Mhór in the early nineteenth century, no attempt had been made to commercialise fishing.[8]

Although Gaoth Dobhair was undoubtedly underdeveloped, there had already been significant commercial penetration of the local economy. There was a small trade in woollen goods, eggs and also *bodógaí* and *leathach,* seaweeds which were used to make iodine and kelp. Moreover, the inhabitants raised black cattle for sale and distilled the bulk of their corn crop into *poitín* or illicit whiskey. Illicit-distillation, a proto-industrial activity frequently practised in remote rural areas where transportation problems made it unprofitable to cart corn to market, was very important to Gaoth Dobhair's economy. James Dombrain, inspector general of the coastguard, who owned a small estate in the parish from 1829 to 1845, believed that the entire population was 'more or less concerned in it'. Other commentators corroborate this opinion.[9] Finally, by the 1830s seasonal migration to the tattiefields of the Laggan and Scotland had become an important means of supplementing income from agricultural production. Hill, for example, notes that 'many of them (the smallholders) go to Scotland in summer ... and also to the neighbourhood of Raphoe and Derry for work.'[10]

Although poteen-making, seasonal migration and the livestock and kelp trades were transforming the local economy, change was slow and frequently resisted by the smallholders. Two landowners who attempted to 'improve' their properties in the 1820s and early 1830s abandoned their plans – the routinisation of rent-collection and the replacement of incompetent agents – due to the inhabitants' opposition. Similarly, Dombrain's tenants initially opposed the surveying of his estate in the early 1830s.[11] Most landowners, however, took little interest in their small estates. Only Dombrain spent part of the year in Gaoth Dobhair and, according to his own account, despite surveying his property, he did not disturb the smallholders.[12] With the exception of Captain Stewart, who lived at Ards; Wybrant Olphert and James Copeland, who lived in the neighbouring parish of Cloich Cheann Fhaola, and James Watt who lived at Claragh near Milford, the owners rarely visited Gaoth Dobhair. They left estate management in the hands of local agents some of whom were only semi-literate. Rent collection was irregular and the agents rarely gave receipts. 'There were', according to Hill, 'arrears of eight, ten and even twenty years standing: some of the tenants not having paid rent for that period, and many lived on the estates quite unknown'.[13] He estimated that arrears on some 23,000 acres he purchased in 1838 totalled £1,000 even though the annual rent was only £429.[14]

In general, the landowners appear to have been reluctant to disturb customary practices as long as they received some return from their property. They accepted kelp, hides and *poitín* as payment for rent. Furthermore, those owners who lived near Gaoth Dobhair accepted 'duty days'. The tenants of Captain Stewart, for example, annually travelled to Horn Head where they spent a week labouring on his demesne, cutting turf or harvesting crops. On the Copeland Estate tenants were expected to pay rent and give the landlord 'eight days of a man and horse; thirty kishes of turf and six hens'. Besides these quasi-feudal customs, there were some totally irregular arrangements. In the 1840s, for example, the Copeland Estate was managed by an uncle of the owner, a minor. The young owner, however, gave the tenants rent-receipts if, rather than paying the rent in full to his uncle, they paid him two thirds of it.[15]

The owners' indifference to their poor estates facilitated the survival of rundale in Gaoth Dobhair. Rundale was a customary system of land use. E. P. Thompson has described agrarian custom in eighteenth-century England as a complex of 'practices, inherited expectations, rules which both determined limits to usages and disclosed possibilities, norms and sanctions both of law and neighbourhood pressure'.[16] Although not sanctioned by law, rundale might be described in similar terms. The system was predicated upon a concept of use-rights in land. The capitalist notion of private property which had been enshrined in eighteenth- and nineteenth-century land law was alien to rundale. Non-market notions of communal rights and responsibilities underpinned the designation of extensive areas as commonage and the division and redistribution of arable land. Similarly, the smallholders did not conceive the landlords to have the right to do as they pleased with the land. They regulated land use; bought and sold 'good will' or 'tenant-right' without any interference from the landowners or their agents and resisted the owners' attempts to survey their estates, appoint competent agents and routinise rent-collection.[17]

Nevertheless, the smallholders were not indifferent to the owners. Rather, an owner-occupier relationship based upon reciprocal obligations was at the centre of the smallholders' moral economy – 'their notions of economic justice and their working definition of exploitation'.[18] Notwithstanding the massive arrears in Gaoth Dobhair, many smallholders worked duty days for landowners or paid them in cash or kind. They also appear to have expected them to arbitrate in inter-tenant disputes and supply relief in times of dearth by either providing employment or distributing food. In 1858 Olphert recalled that before the Roman Catholic clergy established parish courts in the 1850s his tenants had regularly solicited his advice and asked him to settle disputes. Indeed, even during the disturbed 1850s, he claimed ten or twelve people would approach him during his daily ride and ask for advice, employment or credit. Similar relationships were evident on other estates.[19] In short, in return for labour and cash or kind payments, the smallholders expected the landowners to provide particular services, ranging from the provision of relief to arbitration in inter-tenant disputes.

By the 1830s this relationship was under strain. A potato diet and seasonal migration had allowed Gaoth Dobhair to sustain considerable population growth. Subdivision had reduced most arable holdings to about five acres made up of lilliputian plots. Hill claims that in one townland twenty-six families worked half an acre and that in another case a holding was in thirty-two plots.[20] These, like many of his more sensational and colourful claims, may be exaggerated or refer to atypical cases. It is clear, however, that population expansion had undermined the smallholders' capacity to tide themselves over during lean years without recourse to assistance from the landlords. They were becoming a burden on the owners. During a succession of subsistence crises in the 1830s, particularly in 1831, 1834, 1836 and 1837, some proprietors shirked their responsibilities. In a letter to the *Ballyshannon Herald* in 1835, Fr Hugh Friel, the parish priest, claimed that 'nine-tenths of the people' were starving and sharply criticized those landowners who chose to 'tie up their purses' in times of dearth.[21]

The failure of some landowners to fulfill their customary obligations prompted the smallholders to tap new sources of relief, specifically, the Roman Catholic Church and the state. Fr Friel, the lord lieutenant and Lieutenant Penfold, Royal Navy, repeatedly relieved the smallholders in the 1830s.[22] The emergence of the church and state as alternative sources of relief may have accelerated the erosion of the smallholders' sense of obligation to the owners. Nevertheless, Dombrain, Olphert and Watt perpetuated the ideal of the owner-occupier relationship as one of reciprocal obligations by assisting the smallholders in the 1830s.[23] Dombrain was particularly active on their behalf. In 1836 he invited Lord Mulgrave, the lord lieutenant, to tour Donegal and inspect those districts where 'distress has for some time past so generally prevailed'. In Mín a'Chladaigh, Patrick M'Kye, the national school teacher, presented a memorial to Mulgrave.[24] In this memorial M'Kye claimed that the inhabitants of the parish were 'in the most needy, hungry and naked condition of any people who ever came within the precincts of my knowledge'. Influenced by M'Kye's harrowing description of 'hardships and hunger' and the destitution which he had witnessed, Mulgrave secured food and clothing for the smallholders. The following extracts from the memorial and an inventory M'Kye made of the possessions of 'about 4,000 persons' give some indication of conditions in the parish on the eve of Hill's 'improvements':

> Their children crying and fainting with hunger and their parents weeping, being full of grief, hunger, debility and dejection, with glooming aspect, looking at their children likely to expire in the jaws of starvation. Also, in addition to all, their cattle and sheep are dying with hunger, and their owners forced by hunger to eat the flesh of such.
>
> One cart; no wheel car; no coach, or any other vehicle; one plough; sixteen harrows; eight saddles; two pillions; eleven bridles; twenty shovels; thirty-two rakes; seven table-forks; ninety-three chairs; two hundred and forty-three stools; ten iron grapes; no swine, hogs or pigs; twenty-seven geese; three turkeys; two feather-beds; eight chaff beds; two stables; six cow houses ...[25]

Gaoth Dobhair, 1838-47

Lord George Hill, the fifth and posthumous son of the second marquis of Downshire, was a member of one of the leading landed families in Ireland. Centred at Hillsborough in county Down, the Downshire Estates encompassed some of the best farmland in the country. Hill, however, was not an independently wealthy man. He received no part of the family estate in his father's will and it is unlikely that he accumulated any significant amount of capital during his early career as a major in the army and as representative of Carrickfergus in the House of Commons (1831-2). Money provided by his family, not personal savings, enabled him to purchase property in Gaoth Dobhair.[26] Following his first purchase in 1838, Hill quickly acquired three adjoining properties and so established an estate of some 23,000 acres. In 1862 he augmented the estate by buying Cnoc a'Stollaire and Mín Corrbhaic. He then owned 24,189 of the 44,000 acres in Gaoth Dobhair.[27]

Hill was not the only land speculator who invested in Gaoth Dobhair between 1838 and 1847. John Austen purchased his property in the early 1840s and James Russell, Rev A. B. Nixon and James Obins Woodhouse bought their estates in 1845. Indeed, the only townlands in Gaoth Dobhair which were not sold at this time were Mín na gCopóg and Cnoc Fola, the property of the Rev C. F. Stewart, and An Mhuine Mhór and Glaisdhobharchú which were owned by Lord Leitrim and Wybrant Olphert, respectively. Leitrim and Stewart both owned extensive estates in north Donegal while the Olphert family had owned their property, most of which was in Cloich Cheann Fhaola, since the seventeenth century. In contrast to the previous owners, the new proprietors regularly visited Gaoth Dobhair. Russell resided in the parish in Dunlewy House while Nixon lived in Cloich Cheann Fhaola where both he and Woodhouse had also bought property. Hill's main residence was at Ballyarr House in Rathmelton but he spent a considerable amount of time in Heath Cottage in An Bun Beag where he gained a proficiency in the Irish language and an intimate knowledge of his estate.[28]

Tenant-agitators later derided the new owners as rack-renting land speculators.[29] Profit undoubtedly motivated some of them. Nixon, for example, believed from the outset that the highlands would become valuable property if they were developed as sheep walks and later stated that he would not have purchased the Copeland Estate had it not included extensive 'wastes'. Woodhouse, a successful Dublin-based solicitor who bought land throughout Ireland in the 1840s and 1850s, also saw his Donegal properties as a good investment.[30] Nevertheless, it would be inaccurate to represent the new landlords as men driven solely by profit. A potent combination of both profit and philanthropy motivated Hill. In an introductory chapter to the third (1854) edition of *Facts from Gweedore* he stressed that his main objective was 'to ameliorate the condition of the people of the Gweedore district' and 'to endeavour to put them in a way of doing better for themselves', yet the chapter attempts to answer 'the oft-repeated and searching question – "DOES IT PAY?" '[31] Similarly, the Russells, whose estate was ideal for sheepfarming, were more concerned with establishing a Protestant community in Dún Lúiche than with exploiting the commercial potential of the highlands.[32]

The new owners took a keen interest in the management of their estates and made a determined effort to develop their properties. In this regard, Hill was the most dynamic. In 1839 he launched a comprehensive modernisation program by building a quay and corn store in An Bun Beag. By providing a new outlet for grain, Hill undermined the influence of the *poitín*-makers which he had identified as a major obstacle to change. The store was very successful:

> The first year (1839) that grain was purchased £479 9s 6½d was paid for oats at the store and for the year 1844 the amount brought in was upwards of £1,100.[33]

In 1840 it was extended to include a shop which sold goods previously unknown in Gaoth Dobhair and purchased hides, knitwear, poultry and dairy products from the smallholders. It too was a success:

> ... the first quarter's sales to the 19th of December, 1840, amounted to £40 12s . 10d. The sales for the quarter ending 19th December, 1842, amounted to £260 6s. 4d., whilst the corresponding quarter for 1848 was £550.

Cash-only dealings were conducted in both the shop and store and this further monetised the economy.[34]

Hill simultaneously introduced conventional management practices to Gaoth Dobhair. He appointed a new agent, Francis Forster, who abolished duty days and restructured rent-collection. Rent, be it the old rent, was now payable only in cash. Upon payment of two years' rent, Hill forgave arrears which he did not allow to accumulate again.[35] A notice from Forster, dated January 1842, reflects this new approach to management:

> I have received his Lordship's directions to give notice, that any more subdividing of the Farms will not be allowed, and that any Tenant selling, dividing or exchanging without leave, will be severely punished; and those that buy without leave will not be taken as Tenants ... and his Lordship desires me to direct their attention to the cleanliness and arrangement of the Furniture and Inside of their Houses ...[36]

Hill and Forster began the abolition of rundale. Between 1840 and 1841, Robert Montgomery, assisted by Charles Hazlitt Swiney, surveyed the estate.[37] The smallholders were served with notices to quit, ordered to demolish their houses and rebuild them, at their own expense, on squared holdings, or 'cuts', which Hill allocated to them. The smallholders objected to this scheme, pointing out that some holdings would have only good land while others would have only poor land. Fr Hugh MacFadden, the parish priest, established a tenant committee which proposed that the new holdings should be in two long narrow strips so that every tenant would have some of the best land in his townland. A compromise was reached. Most new holdings, on average 4.5 acres, were single strips.[38]

Hill's modernisation programme also threatened the other key elements of rundale: shoreline and highland commonages. As the estate was being surveyed, Hill designated over 12,000 acres of the highlands, over half of the estate, as his 'share'. In addition to appropriating this land for private use, Hill further violated the smallholders' customary grazing rights by allocating young landless couples 'new cuts' of six to nine acres on the rough pasture. The tenants had to reclaim this land and build houses on it at their own expense. Hill, however, did not charge any rent on these allotments until the tenants had been there for five or six years.[39] He also encouraged the permanent settlement of islands which, as part of the outfield, had been previously uninhabited or only sparsely occupied except during the summer months when cattle grazed there.[40]

From the smallholders' perspective, Hill's violation of their grazing rights was more apparent than real. Few fences were erected in the 1840s. Hill's bailiffs did not always impound animals trespassing in his share and, even when they did, the owners were not always fined.[41] Furthermore, after the initial period of displacement and resettlement, he allocated few new cuts. This tolerance of old practices and reluctance to fully assert his property rights may be credited to Hill's willingness to help the smallholders cope with the changes he had initiated on the estate. This, at least, was how he later explained his decision to allow his tenants to continue paying their original rent after he had increased the rents when the new holdings were allocated. On paper, however, Hill's agricultural rents rose from £429 to £875.[42]

Other 'rapid and progressive improvements' followed. Hill established a model farm in Mín a'Chuing and employed an agriculturist to demonstrate new farming methods and introduce new breeds and crops. He annually awarded premiums, donated by the Irish Peasantry Improvement Society of London and other such groups, for the 'best, neatest, and cleanest cottage', 'best pig-stye', 'best half dozen pairs of socks made on his Lordship's Estate', 'largest and best heap of compost', 'best colt from his Lordship's horse, the General' and so forth. A flax-mill; saw-mill; corn-mill; icehouse; bakery and a licensed tavern opened within six years of Hill's first purchase. Hill owned some of these businesses while others were owned by people from east Ulster and Scotland whom he brought to the parish. He also sought markets for local seafood, knitwear, poultry and dairy products and An Bun Beag gained a reputation as a good port to which steamers regularly called. He erected St Patrick's Church (Church of Ireland) in An Bun Beag, the building serving not only as a place of worship but also as a school, and in 1842 he opened the centre-piece of his highland arcadia, the Gweedore Hotel, at Mín a'Chuing.[43]

Hill's improvements effected tenants throughout Gaoth Dobhair. Moreover, other landlords, following his lead, attempted to abolish rundale and restructure rent collection. Some sponsored other developments. James and Jane Russell, for example, built an agricultural school in Dún Lúiche and erected a second Church of Ireland church.[44] State activity also increased. The Board of Works bridged the Gaoth Dobhair river and improved the parish's roads. By 1845 there was a post-office; coast guard accommodation; constabulary barracks and courthouse in the parish.[45] National schools had been established in Doire Beaga, An Luinneach, Mín a'Chladaigh, Dobhar and An Bun Beag.[46] In that year Hill marked (and marketed) his achievement by publishing *Facts from Gweedore,* which was followed in 1847 by a companion pamphlet, *Useful Hints to Donegal Tourists.*

Hill's 'curious social experiment' quickly became a *cause célèbre.*[47] In 1846 he attained the singular distinction of being praised by radical Irish nationalists and a conservative British prime minister. 'Heaven', the *Nation* enthused on 24 April, 'smiles upon his western Oasis of Gweedore ...' while Sir Robert Peel, speaking two days later in the House of Commons, lauded Hill as 'a public benefactor to his country'.[48] Hill made a profound impression on Thomas Carlyle when they met in March 1849 at the end of the novelist's Irish tour. Carlyle wrote in his diary that in all Ireland he had seen 'no such beautiful soul'.[49] Nevertheless, his comments also reveal the limitations of Hill's modernisation programme. He remarks on the 'crag and heather desolation' and refers to the inhabitants as the 'wretchedest "farmers" the sun now looks upon'. His impressionistic description of the area contrasts sharply with the *Nation's* rapturous prose:

> Black huts, bewildered rickety fences of crag; crag and heath; unsubduable by *this* population, damp peat, black heather, grey stones and ragged desolation of men and things.[50]

Hill's achievement, however, remains impressive. He had changed the settlement pattern of a sizeable area; improved agricultural production; stimulated a more monetised and market-oriented economy; increased the consumption of shop goods; created non-agricultural employment; developed the tourist industry and facilitated the expansion of state services in the area. Any one of these changes might easily have provoked either landlord-tenant or tenant-tenant conflict. Gaoth Dobhair, however, experienced no serious social unrest in the decade before the famine. Hill hints at some isolated outrages. He concedes that his tenants were initially opposed to the break-up of rundale but stresses that opposition, although 'vexatious and harrowing', was not violent. The only exception to this, according to Hill, was an attack on a 'fearless wanderer' who had been employed to fence the new holdings. Local people had refused to do this work. They threatened the labourer and attempted to level the fences. The culprits were caught and prosecuted.[51] In the 1842 notice quoted above, Forster also acknowledges the tenants' 'good behaviour'.[52]

The absence of agrarian outrages in Gaoth Dobhair can be explained by a combination of factors. First the recurring crises of the 1830s revealed that rundale had failed to maintain a balance between population and resources. This, coupled with a local tradition that *Oíche na Gaoithe Móire*/The Night of the Big Wind (6 January 1839) covered the arable land in some townlands with sand, causing the inhabitants to move inland and cultivate parts of the rough pasture, suggests that there may have been a willingness, born of necessity, to experiment with a new land system.[53] Second, many of Hill's early 'improvements', such as the store and shop, benefited the community. Moreover, during the famine, many of the landlords, particularly Hill and Olphert, helped their tenants. They drew heavily on their savings: Olphert claimed that in 1846 alone he and some neighbouring proprietors spent £4,000 on meal which they distributed to the smallholders.[54] They also secured 'substantial sympathy' from the Society of Friends, the Irish Peasantry Improvement Society of London and the Baptist Society. This enabled them to employ people making bridle roads and bridges and to distribute food to those incapable of working. In 1847 Hill's mill worked day and night to grind 688 tons of corn supplied by the government.[55] Such were their efforts that the population of Gaoth Dobhair in 1851 was 4,300, an increase of 303 since 1841. The smallholders were unlikely to bite the hand that was feeding them.[56]

Finally, and most importantly, the landlords' approach to estate management discouraged unrest. Although they regarded the land as a commodity which they as private owners could use as they pleased regardless of customary practices they also exhibited a readiness to compromise with their tenants which mitigated the impact of their 'improvements'. There were few evictions in Gaoth Dobhair. In 1858 Hill claimed that he had never evicted any tenants. He was being somewhat economical with the truth in that he had evicted five or six tenants but re-instated them shortly afterwards. Anti-landlord activists alleged that those evicted were entrepreneurs whom Hill wanted to prevent from competing with businesses he had established. Hill, however, denied these allegations.[57] Still, the general absence of evictions in Gaoth Dobhair, the amendment of plans for the allocation of new holdings after consultation with a tenant committee, and the postponement or partial implementation of the most controversial initiatives, such as rent increases and the restriction of grazing rights, reflect a non-confrontational approach to management. This, and the landlords' concern for the tenants' welfare during the famine, reinforced the smallholders' conception of the owner-occupier relationship as one of reciprocal obligations. In short, despite the rapid transformation of Gaoth Dobhair in the years before the famine, the moral economy still functioned.

Breakdown of landlord-tenant relations, 1848-56

National levels of agrarian crime fell in the decade after the famine.[58] In Gaoth Dobhair, however, there was a marked increase in agrarian crime between the famine and the outbreak of the sheep war in the winter of 1856-7. A constabulary return of outrages committed in the barony of Kilmacrenan in the 1850s lists sixteen outrages which occurred in the parish between February 1851 and December 1856. These outrages were sporadic and lacked any specific focus. Nevertheless, they had a vague anti-landlord character. In all but three cases the victims were associated with the landlords: two of Hill's bailiffs were assaulted when they attempted to distrain cattle for unpaid rent; timber, to be used for fencing work, was stolen from the Rev A. B. Nixon; a protective wall on a bridge on Hill's estate was destroyed; money was levied from the tenant on Hill's model farm; the tails were hacked from seven cattle belonging to Hill's agriculturist when he sent them to graze on land to which Nixon had denied his tenants free access; the business premises of John Masson, a baker and publican whom Hill had brought to Gaoth Dobhair, was broken into; Masson received threatening letters 'on account of him being a Scotchman'; rent-rolls and estate papers were stolen from Hill's office to frustrate his attempt to raise rents; a bailiff employed by both Hill and Nixon was assaulted; a threatening notice was posted to deter Hill's tenants from paying increased rents; a boat belonging to one of Hill's bailiffs was destroyed; Hill's gamekeeper was assaulted when he was accompanying a process server and a threatening letter was sent to Jane Russell to deter her from residing in Dún Lúiche.[59]

This increase in anti-landlord outrages was, in part, a consequence of a change in the proprietors' attitude to their tenants. By the early 1850s a more hard-headed approach to estate management had replaced the willingness to compromise which had previously complemented their reforming zeal. Gaoth Dobhair was not the only place in which such a change occurred. Throughout Ireland, landlords' benevolence, tolerance and, in many cases, savings had been exhausted by the famine. If not actually attempting to recoup losses incurred in the late 1840s, landlords were tightening their belts. The interpretation of *An Gorta Mór* as a consequence of over-population had already become an orthodoxy among Irish landlords. Viewed in this way, the calamity became a pretext for asserting property rights by clearing estates of

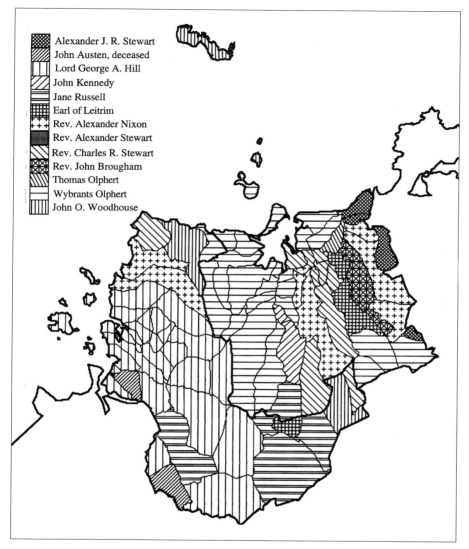

Fig. 19.1   Estates in Roman Catholic parishes of Gaoth Dobhair and Cloich Cheann
Fhaola, 1857.

'superfluous tenants', consolidating smallholdings and leasing mountain
pastures to graziers. W. E. Vaughan has calculated that 45,000 families
were evicted in the five-year period from 1849-53.[60]

The policies adopted by the Gaoth Dobhair landlords in the
aftermath of the famine must be seen in the context of this general
change. Here, as elsewhere, landlords were preoccupied with exercising stricter control over their estates. Nixon, for example, explained the
purpose of his new policies as 'merely to assert my

rights ... I wanted to show the people that the land was mine'.[61] Similarly, Hill's argument, in the introduction to the 1854 edition of *Facts from Gweedore,* that the national tragedy might ultimately prove advantageous, reflects the mood not only of his neighbours but also of his class:

> The Irish people have profited much by the famine, the lesson was severe; but so rooted were they in old prejudices and old ways, that no teacher could have induced them to make the changes which this visitation of Divine Providence has brought about, both in their habits of life and in the modes of agriculture.[62]

Regional forces, however, may also have precipitated the landlords' retreat from the philanthropy of the early 1840s. Rumours of gun-smuggling and secret society activity were common in north-west Donegal in the aftermath of the famine. In May 1850 the comptroller general of the coastguard reported to Dublin castle that Fr John Doherty, then a curate in Gaoth Dobhair, had informed him that the Inis Meáin islanders had subscribed money to import firearms from Scotland in order to resist coastguard raids for *poitín.* Doherty would not surrender the subscription paper, which he had been given 'as a clergyman', but he was afraid that he would be unable to control his parishioners. Similarly, in 1852, Wybrant Olphert whose family had lived near An Fál Carrach since the early seventeenth century reported that the tenants were smuggling guns from Liverpool and Glasgow. Later that year shots were fired near the Russell's residence and Nixon warned the authorities that the Ribbon Society, a masonic-type society of northern Roman Catholics, was organising in the district.[63]

There is no evidence of Ribbon activity in Gaoth Dobhair prior to these reports. Nixon's fears, however, were well-founded. Helped by the revival of *poitín*-making due to an increase in the duty on spirits, the Ribbon Society appears to have been extending into the poorer parts of Donegal.[64] Threatening notices denouncing landlords and fixing prices, posted in Gaoth Dobhair and Cloich Cheann Fhaola in the 1850s, were frequently signed 'Molly Maguire', a name commonly used in north Connaught and west Ulster since the early 1840s to refer to people labelled Ribbon Men by the authorities and press. The Molly Maguires/Ribbon Men remained active in the region in the 1860s and 1870s.[65]

Rent increases were one of the first consequences of this new approach to management. All the landlords, with the exception of John Austen and Rev Charles Stewart, raised their rents between 1852 and 1856.[66] In November 1854 Hill called for the rents which he had set when allocating the new holdings in 1840-3. Anti-landlord activists were able to cite cases where rents were quadrupled. Most increases, however, were in the region of 75 to 100 per cent.[67] On the Hill Estate, for example, Thomas McBride's rent for a house, valued at 10s., and four cow's grass, valued at £3, in Machaire Loiscthe increased from £2 12s. 6d. to £5 while Charles Gallagher's rent for a house, valued at 5s., and half a cow's grass, also valued at 5s., in Machaire Gathláin increased from 4s. to 8s.[68] The timing of these increases was unfortunate. The harvest was poor and the smallholders were facing a lean winter. A tenant-delegation asked Hill for an abatement. He refused it but agreed to accept two-thirds of the new rent on condition it be paid in full the following year.[69] No other landlord granted abatements. This unwillingness to compromise and the practice of annually serving 'notices-to-quit' generated considerable unease.[70]

The impact of these rent increases was exacerbated by the restriction of customary rights to turbary and pasture. Hill had technically excluded his tenants from some 12,000 acres of 'unoccupied land' when the estate was surveyed in 1840-3, yet his bailiffs had turned a blind eye to trespassing stock. In 1854, however, he introduced grazing fees in certain sections of the highlands. Stock straying in these areas were impounded and the owners were fined. In the same year, Hill, Woodhouse and Olphert leased extensive highland pastures to Scottish and English sheepfarmers. Hill leased 3,000 acres in Mín a'Chuing, Mín Doire Dhamh; Áit a'tSean Tí and An Tor to Joseph Huggup of Northumberland; Olphert leased land in An Caol Droim; Mín Doire (Tullaghobegley, Irish); Baile an Easa and Baile na mBó to William Hunter also of Northumberland and Woodhouse leased Altán to James Wright of Aberdeen. In 1854-5 much of this land was fenced and in 1855-6 Scottish black-faced sheep, known locally as *caoirigh bhrocacha*, were introduced.[71]

In addition to leasing sections of the old outfield to graziers, the landlords revived the new cuts schemes which they had initiated but abandoned in the 1840s. Young couples were again offered allotments on the rough pasture. Hill allocated these 'mountain farms' rent-free for five or six years. Other landlords were not so generous. Woodhouse, for example, charged rent immediately and also charged an 'entrance fee' of £1. These schemes strained the landlords' relationship with Fr John Doherty who had replaced Fr Hugh MacFadden as parish priest in 1852. He described the new cuts as 'a means of generating pauperism'.[72] The landlords also imposed fees on other customary rights. Nixon was particularly severe in this regard. He introduced charges for turf-cutting and prohibited the sale of turf. He demanded fees for the collection of seaweed, which the smallholders used both as a food and a fertilizer and also sold to kelp-making companies, and he compelled his tenants to use his lime-kilns, for which they had to pay, rather than their own kilns. Moreover, Nixon refused to allow the inhabitants of Bun a'Leaca and An Ghlaiseach to graze stock on 1,318 acres of highland pasture or 100 acres of grassland by the shore unless they paid a fee of 2s. 6d. Profit, rather than a desire to improve his estate, was the prime objective of these 'thrifty habits'. Although he had doubled his rents from 5d. to 10d. per acre, Nixon continued to demand 'duty fowl' and three duty days per annum – practices other proprietors were eager to abolish. He collected the Poor Rate from his tenants even though their holdings were of such a low valuation that he was legally bound to pay it.[73]

Rent increases, the loss of extensive areas of bog and rough pasture and the charges on customary rights had a devastating impact on the smallholders. Hill, for example, denied his seven tenants in An Tor (area: 3,115 acres) access to 2,858 acres of rough pasture which they had previously shared with the inhabitants of Machaire Clochair, yet increased their rents from £39 6s. to £72.[74] Throughout Gaoth Dobhair, smallholders claimed they had to sell cattle as they had either insufficient pasture or else needed to raise money to pay rent.[75]

Significantly, the violation of grazing-rights provoked serious disturbances before the introduction of the black-faced sheep. Fr Doherty played a conspicuous role in these disturbances. The first dispute occurred in 1851 in Mín a'Chladaigh when Woodhouse's bailiffs impounded cattle grazing on the old commonage. Doherty ordered a pound-keeper, Séamas Bán McBride, to release the animals. McBride, whose education had been paid for by Hill, was dismissed and fined. The priest, however, was believed to have paid his fine.[76] The second dispute, which occurred in 1854 in An Ghlaiseach and Bun a'Leaca, was more serious. According to Daniel Cruise, the resident magistrate, Doherty orchestrated a boycott of Nixon's pastures when the landlord introduced grazing fees. He allegedly 'fined' people 10s. for paying these fees and refused confession to the families of those who refused to pay his 'fines'. This boycott was also enforced by violence. In July, the tails were hacked from seven cattle grazing in An Ghlaiseach. Later, in September, the tenants changed tactics and attempted to graze the pasture by force. They clashed with bailiffs and armed constables on a number of occasions and violence was only averted by Doherty's intervention. Although the authorities believed that Doherty had fermented the disturbances, they decided against prosecuting him. Instead, Cruise, a Roman Catholic, complained to Patrick McGettigan, bishop of Raphoe, about his conduct. McGettigan reprimanded the priest.[77]

The disturbances on the Nixon Estate occurred at a tense time in Gaoth Dobhair. The landlords had raised rents; imposed fees on many practices which the smallholders regarded as rights and restricted access to extensive areas of common pasture, sections of which they had leased to 'outsiders'. In short, they had violated the moral economy. Moreover, they had refused rent abatements despite a poor harvest in 1854. Doherty assisted the smallholders through the winter of 1854-5 and in the spring he memorialised the lord lieutenant to allocate relief to the parish. His appeal was rejected as there had been no increase in the number of applications to the Dunfanaghy workhouse. Doherty then procured £1,500 worth of Indian Meal on credit from Henry Moffatt, a Dunfanaghy merchant, which he distributed to his parishioners. They repaid all but £30 by summer 1856. The harvest failed again that year.[78]

The Sheep War

The Gaoth Dobhair Sheep War began on the night of 10 December 1856 when an estimated forty young men entered the house of James Lillico, a Scottish shepherd in the isolated mountain townland of Altán. The raid was a classic Molly Maguire action. The raiders, one of whom was armed with a pistol, all wore white shirts. They claimed they were not from the area, a claim supported by the quality of their clothes, good English and disregard for disguises. They were well-disciplined and did not harm Lillico but searched his house and ordered him to leave the country within eight days.[79]

The campaign of anti-grazier activity initiated by this raid may be divided into two phases. In the first phase, from December 1856 to autumn 1857, agrarian outrage was the dominant mode of action. Encouraged by Doherty and occasionally assisted by people from outside the parish, the smallholders destroyed and stole black-faced sheep and raided shepherds' houses. In the autumn, legitimate political activity – petitions; lawful resistance to the state's response to the unrest and a propaganda campaign aimed at discrediting the landlords – replaced outrage as the dominant mode of action and the clergy and journalists replaced the smallholders as the main activists. Gaoth Dobhair and Cloich Cheann Fhaola became the subject of a major controversy when ten priests issued an appeal for aid, claiming that the policies adopted by the landlords in the early 1850s and the state's response to the outrages had left the tenants destitute. In July 1858 a select committee of the House of Commons dismissed these claims as unfounded. The agitation effectively ceased in mid-1858 and the authorities and community leaders in Gaoth Dobhair gradually adopted more conciliatory positions. The sheepfarmers, however, continued to report the theft of sheep. The affair only reached a definite conclusion at the summer assizes in August 1860 when Judge Monahan ruled that shepherds had fraudulently reported sheep missing.

Agrarian Outrage

The raid on Lillico's house was followed by a wave of anti-grazier activity. By 24 August a total of 974 black-faced sheep had been reported missing or destroyed in Gaoth Dobhair and Cloich Cheann Fhaola. The majority (618) were lost by mid-March.[80] Searches yielded few carcasses but sheep were found sheared, tied in pairs so that they could not move and starved or with cropped ears and broken horns and ribs. Pedigree rams also had strings tied around their testicles.[81] Four hundred and sixty three were from Huggup's flocks in Mín Doire Dhamh and An Tor and 212 from Wright's flocks in Altán. In addition, 299 sheep belonging to Hunter were maliciously destroyed in An Caol Droim and Barr Bhaile Chonaill in Cloich Cheann Fhaola. The campaign of theft and destruction was moderately successful. Wright, the first sheepfarmer to have lost stock, quit Gaoth Dobhair in April. Hunter, however, bought his sheep and replaced him as lessee of Altán.[82]

Daniel Cruise, the resident magistrate, co-ordinated the response of the state and landlords to this spate of anti-grazier activity. After the initial raid, three constables were posted in Lillico's house and the Gaoth Dobhair and Cloich Cheann Fhaola stations were augmented, each receiving two men.[83] When the unrest continued Cruise adopted two measures to restore order. First, to compensate the sheepfarmers, the grand jury levied an additional rate on the entire population of Gaoth Dobhair, with the exception of the Church of Ireland minister. This rate was referred to as the 'Sheep Tax'. Second, in February, at the request of the local magistrates, twenty-four constables from the constabulary reserve force were sent to the area under the Crime and Outrage (Ireland) Act (1847) and housed in temporary stations at An Bun Beag, An Tor, An Ghlaiseach in Gaoth Dobhair and An tArdach Beag in Cloich Cheann Fhaola. On 14 March, following a night-raid on one of Huggup's shepherds in An Tor and the destruction of a house and barracks which Hill was building there, an additional twenty constables were stationed in Gaoth Dobhair. These constables patrolled the district and made a number of searches of the mountains. The inhabitants of Gaoth Dobhair were levied for this force under the Peace Preservation (Ireland) Act (1856). This levy was known as the 'Police Tax'.[84]

Cruise's response to the unrest was hindered by the Roman Catholic clergy. In April, Doherty forwarded a petition to the House of

Commons which alleged that the loss of highland commonage and rent increases had impoverished the smallholders who would be left destitute if the sheep and police taxes were collected. The petition urged parliament to intervene in the affair and either relieve the people or assist them to emigrate. Doherty offered to emigrate with them. The petition, to which 2,027 signatures were attached, also claimed that no sheep had been killed or stolen. On 19 June parliament rejected the petition as only three of the 'signatures' were genuine. Doherty had read the petition at mass and asked the congregation if he should send it to the House of Commons. He had then signed his parishioners' names.[85]

Cruise was convinced that Doherty was not merely frustrating his efforts to stop the anti-grazier activity but actively fermenting unrest. 'Since those outrages commenced,' he reported to Thomas Larcom, the Under Secretary, 'the Rev. Mr Doherty as their clergyman took no part in punishing or checking them and further, from what has come to my knowledge and from what I am credibly informed, the part he has taken was calculated more to add to the excitement than to suppress it'.[86] Cruise met three members of the Roman Catholic hierarchy, Paul Cullen, archbishop of Dublin; Joseph Dixon, archbishop of Armagh and primate of All Ireland and Doherty's bishop, McGettigan, and complained about Doherty's behaviour. It is not known how Dixon responded but Cullen was sympathetic; McGettigan expressed his displeasure at the priest's behaviour[87] and promised Cruise to transfer Doherty.[88] He visited Gaoth Dobhair in mid-June and, in an address outside the chapel, publicly rebuked the priest and reprimanded his parishioners for stealing sheep:

> England has sent out an army to the Crimea, and she has conquered the Russians; she has now sent an army to China, and she has conquered the Chinese; and do you mean to tell me that you, a small corner of a parish in the County of Donegal, mean to stand up and say you will oppose the law of England.[89]

Several days after this speech, however, McGettigan expressed the opinion that the shepherds and sheepfarmers were killing and hiding sheep in order to collect compensation.[90]

The measures adopted by Cruise were slow to take effect. Removing a parish priest took time and 'the obnoxious priest Doherty', as Hill referred to him, remained in Gaoth Dobhair until September when McGettigan transferred him to Mevagh.[91] Levying the police tax was also difficult as Hugh McBride, the cess collector, refused to collect it. McBride, a brother of the dismissed poundkeeper, had to be replaced.

Nobody took his job, despite it being advertised as far away as Letterkenny that the collector would receive 10 per cent of all money collected (the usual rate was 2.5 per cent) and an additional £50 donated by the landlords. Parliament had to amend the law to allow the appointment of Head Constable William Young as cess collector and it was not until 25 August that he began to collect the £811 tax.[92]

Similarly, collecting the sheep tax proved problematic. Presentments for the sheep were not fiated by the grand jury until 8 July when the Donegal assizes were held at Lifford. Huggup, Wright and Hunter claimed £1,072 for the theft and destruction of sheep and Hill claimed £58 for the destruction of a house and barracks in An Tor. The Gaoth Dobhair smallholders disputed these claims. Doherty and Séamas Bán McBride engaged a solicitor to oppose the fiating of the presentments. Smallholders testified that large numbers of their own sheep had died during the severe winter of 1856-7 and others, who had been employed by the sheepfarmers to do fencing work, alleged that the shepherds had been negligent and allowed their flocks to stray. Under cross-examination, some shepherds confessed to having sold the fleeces of sheep which had drowned without telling the owners who were now seeking compensation. The grand jury, however, fiated presentments for £1,065 5s. This sum was collected in the winter of 1857-8.[93]

By early summer the augmented police force and the threat of sheep and police taxes had begun to take effect. Even a fortnight before the assizes, Cruise had reported to Dublin castle that there appeared to be a 'change for the better' in the district and that the people were beginning to accept that they would have to pay for their 'wanton and improper conduct'.[94] Only 274 black-faced sheep were reported stolen or destroyed in the latter half of the year and all but 96 of these had been grazing in townlands in Cloich Cheann Fhaola.[95] Determined that this trend would not be reversed, Cruise attempted to impress on the smallholders that 'the law is too strong for them'. In late-August and September, when Young was collecting the police tax, he marched between 170 and 300 constables from house to house to 'terrify the people'.[96] The replacement of Doherty by Fr Daniel McGee in September helped discourage further outrages. Although not immediately more amenable to the authorities, McGee was more moderate than Doherty – an ecclesiastical historian describes him as 'a shy, attractive insinuating democrat born to gain affection' – and he gradually adopted a more conciliatory position.[97]

Shortly after the replacement of Doherty and the *in terrorem* collection of the police tax, Cruise made a breakthrough in the sheep case. William McGarvey, a Gaoth Dobhair man serving a sentence in

Lifford Gaol for poaching, commented to a turnkey that James Boyle of An Seascann Beag knew a lot about the outrages and would divulge this information if arrested and brought to Lifford. This was promptly done on 28 September and Boyle, as predicted, swore several statements in which he admitted stealing sheep the previous Spring, killing them and hiding the mutton in tubs which he then buried. Boyle named a number of accomplices. The constabulary arrested these people in a series of night raids and intensive searches. Several of those arrested made short statements admitting their involvement, corroborating Boyle's statements or implicating others. They were refused bail and remanded in custody to stand trial at the March assizes. Including Boyle and his wife, Maggy, the police detained thirty men and two women.[98]

This breakthrough was very significant. Those arrested included several of the most prominent people in Gaoth Dobhair. A number of them had close connections to Doherty. John Coll, of Doire Beaga, for example, was Doherty's brother-in-law. He had allegedly told Boyle that 'the priest, Mr Doherty, gave them leave to do it (steal sheep).' Coll's son, Thomas, was also implicated in anti-grazier activity although he escaped arrest until late Spring 1858. Séamas Bán McBride, the dismissed pound keeper, was a prosperous cattle dealer and an acknowledged community leader. He had been treasurer of the money collected by the smallholders to defray legal expenses at the summer assizes. Doherty had allegedly paid him £14 for helping to prepare the case. Cruise was convinced that McBride, 'the principal adviser of the people of Gweedore and the great friend of the Rev Mr Doherty', was 'at the head of all the parties who committed these outrages'.[99]

Some of those arrested can be identified from the General Valuation of Tenements, which was completed in Gaoth Dobhair in 1857, as among the most prosperous tenants in the parish. McBride, for example, was renting 21a. 2r. 5p., a house and offices in Baile an Droichid (Cnoc a'Stollaire). The valuation of this holding was £2. This was the highest valuation of any holding in the townland and one of the largest holdings in Gaoth Dobhair (average holding: 4.5a.). Similarly, John Coll, Doire Beaga; John McGee, An Charraig and Connell and Biddy Coyle, Áit a'tSean Tí were all relatively well off. Coll's holding (exact area unspecified but almost 10a.) was valued at £2 14s. while the valuation of the Coyles' holding (unspecified area) was £2 5s. McGee, on the other hand, was renting a house and 8a. 0r. 30p. valued at £1 10s. and he also held two houses and 15a. 2r. 10p. with Michael McGee, his portion of which was valued at £2 5s.[100]

It would be a mistake, however, to see the alleged sheepstealers as representing only the more commercially-oriented tenants who feared financial loss if the graziers remained in the parish. Although several of those arrested were quite prosperous, others were more typical tenants. Neal Gallagher, An Charraig, for example, held only 4a. valued at 15s. and a house valued at 5s. while John Coll; Hugh Coll; Denis Coll, sen. and Denis Coll, jr., of Mín Doire Dhamh, were renting very small holdings – between 1a. 2r. and 2a. 1r. – valued only at 10s. and houses valued only at 5s. Similarly, in An Seascann Beag, James Boyle's holding – a house, offices and 3a. 1r. 30p. – was valued at 15s., although, with a neighbour, he also held 10a. 2r. of mountain, valued at 4s.[101] The involvement of people of different socio-economic status in anti-grazier activity suggests that the sheep war was a community protest.

The effect of the arrests surprised even Cruise. The day after the first arrests a group of smallholders approached him and asked that the additional police be withdrawn. He refused but noted in a report to Dublin Castle that 'they seem the most altered and subdued people I ever saw and seem fully to feel the folly of their former conduct.'[102] Doherty was equally surprised. He returned to Gaoth Dobhair, ostensibly to say a valedictory mass, on Sunday 4 October. His sermon, delivered in Irish, was transcribed in English by constables in the chapel. In it he reminded the congregation that although the bishop had promised that they would not have to pay taxes if he was transferred, it was now certain that they would have to pay all the taxes even though he was leaving them. Doherty advised the people to keep their own 'secrets' or else the landlords and police might drive them from their homes. He urged them not to criticize the sheepstealers or blame them for their troubles as they had done nothing for personal gain but rather for the good of the country. He denied that those arrested had anything to do with the theft of sheep.[103]

Gaoth Dobhair remained calm through the winter of 1857-8. Other than the loss of thirty-two sheep in An Tor in late November, no sheep were reported missing until February. The smallholders paid their rents and the sheep tax without incident. Nevertheless, despite the fall-off in the numbers of sheep reported missing or destroyed, Huggup decided to leave Gaoth Dobhair. In November he sold his flocks and leases to Hunter who was then the only sheepfarmer in the district.[104]

'In Search of Public Commiseration'

Although outrages abated, anti-grazier activity continued. The sensational claims and counterclaims at the Assizes had aroused considerable press interest in the affair. Predictably, both the conservative *Ballyshannon Herald* and *Londonderry Sentinel* supported the landlords. The smallholders' champions represented a broader spectrum of political opinion. Their most trenchant supporters were Dr James McKnight, editor of the *Londonderry Standard;* Denis Holland, editor of the *Ulsterman* and A. M. Sullivan, editor of the *Nation*. The *Londonderry Standard,* the paper with the largest circulation in the north-west, was a staunchly Presbyterian, radical tenant-right organ which held Church of Ireland landlords and Roman Catholic priests in equal disdain.[105] The *Ulsterman* was a Belfast newspaper with a small circulation. Its editor, a Corkman, articulated a sectarian nationalism which made him anathema to McKnight who frequently criticized him in the *Londonderry Standard.*[106] In addition, Holland had an acrimonious relationship with Sullivan. Their rivalry, and Holland's disregard for the libel laws, resulted in a court case in which Sullivan was awarded token compensation.[107]

Suppplied with information by Doherty, these newspapers formulated a comprehensive critique of landlord management and the state's response to the unrest. They highlighted the deprivation suffered by the smallholders due to the restriction of their grazing rights and rent increases and attacked the injustice of punishing an entire community for the crimes of a minority. They argued that by making the smallholders pay for all the sheep reported missing the state was charging them not only for those stolen and destroyed but also for those which died of natural causes or neglect. Emphasising that the compensation had been fixed above the market value of the sheep the newspapers fuelled speculation that the sheepfarmers and shepherds were inflating the numbers reported missing.[108]

Controversy increased in the winter. Holland toured north-west Donegal with Doherty and published a series of articles on landlord-tenant relations in the region. These articles were serialised in many newspapers in Ireland and abroad and republished as a pamphlet, *The Landlord in Donegal: pictures from the wilds,* two editions of which appeared in 1858. Holland castigated the Gaoth Dobhair landlords, reserving particular spleen for Hill, 'a pretentious philanthrope' and 'proselytiser', whose pamphlet he dismissed as 'the cheapest engine by which any man ever won a good name'. He argued that the raising of rents, allocation of 'new cuts' and restriction of grazing rights had impoverished the smallholders and that the subsequent levying of police and sheep taxes had left them destitute.[109]

An editorial on the affair in the Christmas edition of the *Nation* heightened the controversy. It included a graphic, though highly exaggerated, description of 'poor persecuted Celts' being 'driven to death by the mechanism of British laws':

Along the shores of the coast crawl crowds of gaunt spectres, prowling for shellfish and scraping the rocks for seaweed, with which to prolong life's span another day. Houseless, homeless, shelterless, naked, cold and starving are the once happy, virtuous and warmhearted people of Donegal. Day by day they droop and die; and the sheep will soon thrive gloriously on the rank verdure on the mounds where they moulder.

The editorial concluded by suggesting that a relief fund be established for Gaoth Dobhair to which nationalists could contribute instead of the 'pro-British' Indian Relief Fund.[110]

The suggestion did not fall on deaf ears. On 14 January 1858 ten priests met at Dunfanaghy, established a relief committee and issued a public appeal for assistance. The appeal, which was published in sympathetic newspapers, repeated the claim that the smallholders were facing starvation having sold stock, crops and furniture to pay increased rents, police and sheep taxes. It attributed the loss of sheep to the shepherds' negligence. The appeal detailed extreme poverty allegedly prevalent in Gaoth Dobhair and Cloich Cheann Fhaola:

> There are at the moment 800 families subsisting on seaweed, crabs, cockles or any other edible matter they can pick up along the seashore, or scrape off the rocks ... Thousands of the male population have only one *cotton* shirt, and wear none whilst it is being washed, *while thousands have not even one.* The females are still in a worse condition. There are about 400 families, in which there may be half-a-dozen full grown females, who have only one dress among them, in which they can appear in public; mothers and daughters alternatively using this common wardrobe when they go out of doors. There are about 600 families who have *now* neither cow, sheep, nor goat; and who from the beginning of the year to its close, hardly ever know the taste of milk or butter. There are thousands of youths, of both sex, verging on the age of puberty, who are so partially clothed that modesty forbids one to look at them ...

'This fine old Celtic race', it concluded, 'is about to be crushed aside to make room for Scotch and English sheep'.[111]

The publication of the appeal brought the controversy to fever-pitch. Conservatives were outraged. The *Londonderry Sentinel* dubbed the relief fund a defence fund for sheepstealers; the *Ballyshannon Herald* believed it to be a 'device of popery to replenish its failing coffers' while a contributor to the *Dublin University Magazine* warned that 'in this obscure corner of Ireland a flame is being kindled which will, if unextinguished, spread far and wide, and shake the rights of property, if not defy the power of British law.'[112] Liberals, nationalists and the tenant-right lobby supported the appeal. Sympathisers established relief committees in large towns throughout the country, organised public meetings and made collections. Newspaper reports reveal considerable Presbyterian support from Donegal, Derry and Tyrone. The appeal, however, struck its most responsive chord among Roman Catholics. Dublin students donated money, as did the students and staff of seminaries in Ireland, France and Spain. Irish emigrants in Britain, North America and Australia made large contributions through their priests or the press and countless individuals sent money or clothing direct to the committee. Members of the Roman Catholic hierarchy donated money. In Ireland, Archbishops McHale, Cullen and McGettigan made donations. Abroad, Bishop Mullock of St John's Newfoundland and Abbé Peraud, later bishop of Autun, both took a keen interest in the affair.[113] Gaoth Dobhair's local row had become an international controversy.

It is not known how much money, food and clothing the appeal raised. An estimate of £2,000, made by a judge at the summer assizes, may be quite moderate. In Australia the Donegal Relief Fund of Victoria and New South Wales collected £3,800 in the latter half of the year when considerable doubt had been cast on the claims in the appeal. This particular committee raised a total of £5,725 between 1 June 1858 and 30 June 1860. This money was used to assist young people, many, if not most, of whom were from Gaoth Dobhair and Cloich Cheann Fhaola, to emigrate. Between 1859 and 1860 some 1,500 Donegal people travelled to Australia on ships chartered by the Donegal Relief Fund of Victoria and New South Wales.[114]

The landlords responded to the appeal through the Board of Guardians of the Dunfanaghy Poor Law Union. On 16 February, at the board's instigation, Richard Hamilton, a senior civil servant in the Poor Law Commission, was directed to investigate the claims made in the appeal. Anticipating that Hamilton would draw attention to the absence of anybody from Gaoth Dobhair in the Dunfanaghy Workhouse, the relief committee memorialised the lord lieutenant to repeal the 'Gregory Clause'. This clause in the Poor Law Extension (Ireland) Act (1847) stipulated that occupiers of quarter of an acre could not be considered destitute and were ineligible for outdoor relief or admission to a workhouse. The publication of the Hamilton Report in early March served only to intensify public debate. Hamilton found that there were five or six head of cattle per household, that everyone had potatoes and that the only hungry children were those of a well-fed father and stepmother. He alluded to attempts to hide cattle, clothes and furniture during his investigation and concluded that the people of Gaoth Dobhair and Cloich Cheann Fhaola were not destitute but rather 'far better at present than at any time since the famine'. The relief committee rejected the report, claiming that the majority of those who had given evidence to Hamilton were either connected with the landlords or had never visited the parish. The appeal continued to appear in the press supported by applications for relief which McGee received from parishioners claiming to be starving. A. M. Sullivan, Sharman Crawford and other tenant-right activists visited Gaoth Dobhair to demonstrate support for the smallholders.[115]

In addition to the increasing controversy, there was a resurgence of sheep-stealing in Gaoth Dobhair. Between 4 February and 22 April, 217 of Hunter's sheep were reported missing from Altán, Áit a'tSean Tí, An Tor and Mín Doire Dhamh. The majority of these sheep (122) disappeared within ten days of the destruction of Doire Beaga chapel in a mysterious fire on 12 February. Following the fire, Doherty and McGee delivered sectarian, scare-mongering speeches blaming the blaze on the landlords and local Protestants. Doherty claimed that the landlords had a 'spiteful feeling' against Roman Catholics and that their object was 'to reduce them to poverty and drive them from the country at large'. Alluding to Jane Russell's agricultural school in Dún Lúiche, he warned his congregation that the landlords planned to build a school for Protestant orphans who would replace them as tenants.[116]

The authorities, meanwhile, continued to pursue hard-line policies. At the spring assizes a presentment for £53 was fiated; the Gaoth Dobhair prisoners were refused bail and two men from Gartán, a neighbouring parish, were convicted of stealing five black-faced sheep. The Gartán men, a father and son, were sentenced to eighteen months and six years penal servitude, respectively. Cruise felt that such stiff sentences for 'a minor offence' would have 'a most salutary effect' in Gaoth Dobhair. The pro-tenant press, however, emphasised that the conviction created a legal dilemma as the inhabitants of Gaoth Dobhair had been levied for these sheep.[117]

In mid-April John Bagwell, a liberal MP, moved that a House of Commons select committee be established to investigate the claims in the appeal. The conservative government supported the motion. The Select Committee on Destitution (Gweedore and Cloughaneely) met at Westminster from 8 June to 2 July. It heard evidence from 31 witnesses. The committee found that the people of Gaoth Dobhair and Cloich Cheann Fhaola were not destitute. Its report, published on 12 July, concluded that 'there are among them many who are very needy, who, on the failure of their crops, are subject to more or less distress and poverty in consequence at one portion of the year but ... destitution such as complained of in the appeal of 18th January, 1858 ... did not and does not exist.' Despite this emphatic rejection of the appeal, two members of the committee, Bagwell and J. F. Maguire, an Independent MP, published separate reports which, although not alleging that the people were destitute, attributed their poverty to the changes made by landlords in the 1850s. The report had exonerated the landlords, however, and later that year they took the unusual step of publishing in pamphlet-form the evidence refuting the appeal.[118]

Two days before the report was published, Thomas Coll had been sentenced to 10 years penal servitude at the Donegal assizes. Séamas Bán McBride, his co-accused, was acquitted. The other suspects were not tried but were bound over to appear at the assizes until discharged in due course of law. The grand jury fiated presentments totalling £335 for the destruction of 207 black-faced sheep.[119]

By late summer the smallholders were prepared to accept defeat. In mid-September representatives from most of the townlands on the Hill, Russell and Leitrim estates signed a petition to the lord lieutenant prepared by Hill and his agent. They expressed their 'most unfeigned regret and entire disapprobation of the late barbarous outrages' and 'our firm determination to suppress (as far as we are able) such disgraceful proceedings for the future'. Pointing out that they had already paid over £2,500 police and sheep tax, they said they feared that the payment of any additional taxes might result in 'the very state of distress, hitherto untruely alleged'. To save them from 'utter ruin' they asked that the police be withdrawn and that the outstanding police tax be remitted. The local magistrates believed the sentiments expressed in the petition to be sincere. Nevertheless, an assassination attempt on Nixon in Cloich Cheann Fhaola on 24 October made the petition a dead letter. Ironically, although the conservative press was convinced that Nixon's evidence to the select committee led to the murder attempt, the authorities never suspected anyone from Gaoth Dobhair of involvement in the attack for which nobody was ever convicted.[120]

The sheep war, however, was now effectively over. Only six sheep were lost in Gaoth Dobhair between 1 July and 31 December 1858. The culprits, apparently driven by hunger to steal the sheep, were arrested almost immediately afterwards on 17 December. A further 704 black-faced sheep were reported missing or destroyed by January 1861. At the summer assizes in 1860, however, Chief Justice Monahan refused to fiat presentments for sheep allegedly stolen in December 1859 after hearing evidence about the shepherds' negligence and the suspiciously large quantities of wool and mutton which they often had in their possession. The decision cast doubt on earlier presentments. In all 1,933 sheep were reported destroyed or stolen in Gaoth Dobhair between December 1856 and January 1861. Presentments were not fiated for 15 per cent of these sheep.[121]

Cruise, who had become embroiled in a dispute about non-payment of rent with his own landlord, the marquis of Conyngham, was transferred in early 1859.[122] His replacement, Thomas Dillon, had a less truculent approach to law enforcement. In February he reported to Dublin castle that he believed the most recent thefts had been committed by people from neighbouring districts and that the smallholders were 'showing a disposition to assist in putting down the outrages'. His reports in spring 1859 reveal a growing frustration at having to deploy large numbers of constables in atrocious weather to collect the taxes from increasingly impoverished people. In June, when the smallholders' resources were at a low ebb, he postponed collection of the police tax. When the police eventually collected it in October, Dillon reported that they did so with 'good temper and forbearance and apparently feeling much for the poverty of these people'. 'I really do not know', he continued, 'how they can support themselves during the coming winter as their potatoes and corn were partly blighted and their cattle, also, are very poor and wretched looking.'[123]

Conditions deteriorated in the winter of 1859-60. McGee, who had appointed two men in every townland as 'special constables' to protect Hunter's sheep and search for those reported missing, pressed Dillon for a public inquiry. Dillon staved off this demand but in February he, Constable Young, and County Inspector MacMahon informed Dublin Castle that they felt the collection of the sheep and police taxes would be inhumane given the extreme poverty in Gaoth Dobhair. Government accepted their advice and ordered the collection of the taxes 'provided the sum be not oppressive to the parties from whom it is to be levied'.[124] The authorities were now aware that some of the presentments fiated at the 1859 assizes were suspect. In May Dillon again postponed the collection of £541 police tax when Young warned that 'if any of them (the smallholders) were driven for this tax a good number of them would be lost'. Monahan's refusal to fiat presentments at the summer assizes in 1860 brought the affair to an end.[125] The additional police were withdrawn shortly after this. They had been stationed in the parish for three years, longer than any additional force was in a disturbed community between 1848 and 1861, yet the authorities only ever collected one year's police tax (£1,605).[126]

Conclusion

The sheep war was a subject of intense debate in the late 1850s. There were a number of contemporary explanations of the unrest. Defenders of the shallholders attributed the anti-grazier activity to the deprivation suffered due to the restriction of grazing rights; the raising of rents and poor harvests.[127] The landlords and magistrates, on the other hand, viewed the affair as a consequence of 'the part the Roman Catholic clergymen of the district are taking in the affairs of the landlords', while the conservative press raised the spectre of Ribbonism and argued that the unrest had been fermented by a secret society with the intention of driving the settlers from the parish.[128] Occasionally both pro- and anti-landlord commentators presented the sheep war as a consequence of modernisation. The emphases were, of course, different. One side focused on the 'instinctive obstinacy' and irrational opposition of the tenantry to progress while the other depicted the landlords driving the people off the land 'like the American Red Men'.[129] Impartial observers attributed the unrest to modernisation. 'The truth', according to a Scottish writer, 'is that in that part of Ireland, as well as in many other parts of that country, a transition is being made from an old to a new state of things, and that neither party is entitled to unqualified blame or praise.'[130]

None of these explanations – deprivation; clerical interference; secret society activity or modernisation – accounts fully for the outbreak of the sheep war in December 1856. The contention that the smallholders had no legitimate grievances but were rather duped by priests and Ribbonmen into opposing the graziers is least persuasive. Although it is clear that the smallholders suffered due to rent increases and the loss of grazing rights, the deprivation explanation is unconvincing. Deprivation brought the agitation to an end, it did not begin it. Taken in tandem the deprivation and modernisation explanations can account for the widespread discontent in Gaoth Dobhair in the 1850s, but they do not explain how this discontent was translated into a major campaign of agrarian unrest.

The analysis of the Sheep War offered here is a synthesis of these explanations. It has argued that when the new landlords invested in the parish the smallholders did not perceive land to be the private property of any individual. Rather, the central concepts in their moral economy were use rights and reciprocal obligations. The 'curious social experiment' of the 1840s threatened this moral economy. Nevertheless, by consulting with the smallholders and their community leaders, particularly the parish priest, about the most contentious proposals and by responding sympathetically to the smallholders' plight during the famine, the new landlords obscured the contradiction between their concept of land as private property, a commodity which they could buy, sell, let as they pleased, and that of the smallholders. The famine, however, prompted the landlords to assert more vigorously their property rights by allocating new cuts, restricting access to highland pastures, introducing turbary fees, refusing rent abatements during poor harvests and raising rents. These measures constituted serious infractions of the smallholders' moral economy and generated considerable discontent in the period between the famine and the sheep war.

The discontent of 1847-56 fizzled out in sporadic and unco-ordinated outrages. Although anti-landlord, these outrages lacked a specific focus. Hence, this initial unrest is quite similar to the sporadic petty violence in the Scottish highlands during the clearances.[131] The Sheep War, however, was a highly organised campaign against specific targets which entailed both outrages and political activity. Although blind to the smallholders' grievances, conservative commentators were correct to emphasise the importance of Doherty and the Molly Maguires in the development of the agitation. The Mollies, by raiding Lillico's house, started the Sheep War. They appear to have had a well-organised network in Gaoth Dobhair and links with Mollies elsewhere in the county. This facilitated the safe disposal of stolen sheep and successful attacks, such as the raids on shepherds' houses and the burning of the barracks in An Tor. Doherty, on the other hand, was the most prominent community leader in Gaoth Dobhair. His support for the sheepstealers was critical. More importantly, he was the smallholders' most trenchant defender. Through petitions and appeals he developed a paper campaign which complemented and ultimately replaced the theft of sheep as the dominant form of anti-grazier activity.

The Sheep War exacted a heavy price on the smallholders. Even if the claims in the 1858 appeal were exaggerated, as no doubt they were, it is clear that sheep and police taxes produced considerable poverty in Gaoth Dobhair, particularly in 1859-60. Nevertheless, the anti-grazier activity was relatively successful. Two of the three sheepfarmers quit Gaoth Dobhair in the first year of the Sheep War. Significantly, both Wright and Huggup left before the political campaign replaced agrarian outrage as the main mode of action. Although the third sheepfarmer, Hunter, subsequently leased the lands held by Wright and Huggup, his heir left Gaoth Dobhair shortly after Monahan's refusal to fiat presentments and the smallholders regained access to almost all the highland pastures, with the exception of an area reserved by Hill for private use. The landlords, however, apparently incorporated grazing fees into increased rents.[132]

Outside Gaoth Dobhair, the Sheep War was quickly forgotten. In 1868, Hill wrote in a preface to the fourth edition of *Facts from Gweedore* that 'peaceable and orderly behaviour' had prevailed in the district since he began his improvements.Nationalists and land-agitators had nothing to gain by pointing out that this was untrue. In 1861 they had found a starker example of rapacious landlordism in Donegal when Hill's neighbour, John George Adair, cleared forty-seven families from Derryveagh in Gartán. Recalling the protracted campaign of anti-grazier activity and rumours of secret society activity on the nearby estate of a celebrated improving landlord would only have clouded the popular image of Adair as a profit-hungry land speculator, eager to replace tenants with sheep.[133]

References

1. The quotation is from a commemorative plaque in St Patrick's Church, An Bun Beag.

2. The term 'clachan' is used in the geographical literature to describe house-clusters. J. Coll, 'Continuity and change in the parish of Gaoth Dobhair, 1850-1980' in W. J. Smyth and K. Whelan (ed.), *Common ground: essays on the historical geography of Ireland* (Cork, 1988), p. 279, claims house-clusters were referred to as *bailte (s. baile)* in Gaoth Dobhair.

3. On rundale see Lord George Hill, *Facts from Gweedore; compiled from the notes of Lord George Hill: a facsimile reprint of the fifth edition (1887) with an introduction by E. Estyn Evans* (Belfast, 1971), pp 21-7; *Digest of evidence taken before her majesty's commissioners of inquiry into the state of law and practice in respect to the occupation of land in Ireland*, part iii (1847), [657] xxi, [hereafter cited as *Devon Commission*], pp 797-800; D. McCourt, 'The rundale system in Donegal: its distribution and decline' in *Donegal Annual*, iii (1955), pp 47-60; E. Estyn Evans, *The personality of Ireland: habitat, heritage and history* (Cambridge, 1973), pp 85-105; F. Coll and J. Bell, 'An account of life in Machaire Gathláin (Magheragallan), north-west Donegal, early this century' in *Ulster Folklife*, xxxvi (1990), pp 80-85.

4. For accounts of the Sheep War by local historians see P. Ó Gallchobhair, *The history of landlordism in Donegal* (Ballyshannon, 1962); B. Mac Cnáimhsí, 'Northwest Donegal after the great famine' in *Donegal Annual* (1983), pp 60-82; N. Ó Gallchóir, 'Gan saoirse gan só' in *Scathlán 3* (1986), pp 1-24; D. Ó Baoill, 'Seanchas agus dinnsheanchas i nGaoth Dobhair' in Idem, pp 48-64.

5. E. Richards, *A history of highland clearances, emigration, protest, reasons* (London, 1985), ii, pp 287-369. Also E. Richards, 'Patterns of highland discontent, 1790-1860' in R. Quinault and J. Stevenson (ed.), *Popular protest and public order: six studies in British history, 1790-1920* (London, 1974), pp 75-114 and T. M. Devine, 'Social responses to agrarian "improvement": the highland and lowland clearances in Scotland,' in R. A. Houston and I. D. Whyte (ed.), *Scottish society 1500-1800* (Cambridge, 1989), pp 148-69.

6. *Abstract of population returns*, H. C. 1833 (634), xxxix, pp 248-9 includes data for Ryetullaghobegley West, presumably Gaoth Dobhair which was often called Tullaghobegley West. The population of Gaoth Dobhair in 1841 was computed from townland data in *The Census of Ireland for the year 1851*, H.C. 1852 (36), xcii (hereafter cited as *1851 Census*), pp 131-2.

7. Hill, *Facts*, pp 27-9; *Ballyshannon Herald* (hereafter *B.H.*) 9 July 1858; [Anonymous], 'Gweedore,' *Dublin University Magazine*, xli (1853), p. 10.

8. For Gaoth Dobhair prior to 1838 see *B.H.*, 24 June 1835; *Devon Commission*, pp 797-99; Hill, *Facts*, pp 15-35, 63-4; [Anonymous], 'Gweedore,' pp 9-22.

For different views of the success of the fishery see *B.H.*, 9 July 1858 and S. 'Ac Fhionnlaoich, *Scéal Gaoth Dobhair* (Baile Átha Cliath, 1983), p. 53.

9. *B.H.*, 9 July 1858; Hill, *Facts*, pp 29-30.

10. Hill, *Facts*, p. 35; *Report from the select committee on destitution (Gweedore and Cloughaneely); together with the proceedings of the committee, minutes of evidence, appendix and index*, H.C. 1857-8 (412), xiii, 89 (hereafter cited as *Destitution*), pp 9, 79.

11. Hill, *Facts*, pp 18-21, 29; *B.H.*, 9 July 1858.

12. *B.H.*, 9 July 1858.

13. Hill, *Facts*, p. 18.

14. Ibid., p. 64; *Destitution*, p. 45.

15. Mac Fhionnlaoich, *Scéal*, p. 54; *Destitution*, pp 308-9.

16. E. P. Thompson, 'Custom, law and common right' in *Customs in common* (London, 1991), p. 102.

17. Hill, *Facts*, p. 23.

18. J. C. Scott, *The moral economy of the peasant: rebellion and subsistence in south-east Asia* (London, 1976), p. 3.

19. *Destitution*, pp 191, 234, 302.

20. Hill, *Facts*, pp 22, 25-6.

21. *B.H.*, 24 June 1835.

22. Hill, *Facts*, pp 15-8, 34; *B.H.*, 24 June 1835.

23. *B.H.*, 24 June 1835.

24. *B.H.*, 19 Aug., 2 Sept. 1836.

25. Hill, *Facts*, pp 16-7. Evans, *Personality of Ireland*, p. 93, claims that M'Kye underestimated the population of Gaoth Dobhair. It is clear from references in the memorial to the absence of resident gentlemen and the inhabitants of the district being all Roman Catholics that M'Kye's estimate is for the Roman Catholic parish of Gaoth Dobhair or West Tullaghobegley and not the civil parish of Tullaghobegley. The population of Gaoth Dobhair in 1841, computed from the townland data in the census, was 3,997. Hence, M'Kye's estimate was quite accurate.

26. Evans, *Personality of Ireland*, pp 87-8. For the administration of the Downshire estates see W. A. Maguire, *The Downshire estates in Ireland, 1801-1845: the management of Irish landed estates in the early nineteenth century* (Oxford, 1972), passim.

27. It is unclear when Hill first visited Gaoth Dobhair. In a letter to the *Times*, dated 27 June 1858, Dombrain recounts his first visit to Gaoth Dobhair in 1821 and his visit with Hill, which he says was in 1829. The letter was reprinted in *B.H.*, 9 July 1858. In his evidence to the select committee in 1858, however, Hill cites 1834 as the date of his tour of Ireland with Dombrain and his first visit to Gaoth Dobhair, *Destitution*, p. 277.

28. Hill, *Facts*, p. 36. Hill had 'some knowledge of the Irish language' when he came to Gaoth Dobhair.

29. D. Holland, *The landlord in Donegal: pictures from the wilds* (Belfast, n.d.), passim.

30. *Destitution*, pp 286-7, 310; *Devon Commission*, pp 801-2.

31. Hill, *Facts*, p. 40.

32. E. Maguire, *A history of the diocese of Raphoe*, part 1, ii (Dublin, 1920), pp 265-6.

33. Hill, *Facts*, p. 40.

34. Ibid., p. 38.

35. Ibid., p. 6; *Devon Commission*, p. 799.

36. Hill, *Facts*, p. 54. See also Hill's 'Notice to tenants' in Ibid., p. 55.
37. *Destitution*, pp 345-8.
38. Ibid., pp 44, 346; Hill, *Facts*, pp 40-3.
39. *Destitution*, pp 44-5, 52, 280-1, 289-90, 304.
40. Coll and Bell, 'An account of life in Machaire Gathláin', p. 85.
41. *Destitution*, pp 29, 111, 289-91, 303-4.
42. Ibid., pp 44, 52-5, 306.
43. Hill, *Facts*, pp 43-7, 51-3.
44. *Destitution*, pp 265-6.
45. Ibid., pp 284-6; *Devon Commission*, pp 799-800.
46. Maguire, *Diocese of Raphoe*, p. 309.
47. For favourable impressions of Hill see James Hack Tuke, *Irish distress and its remedies – a visit to Donegal and Connaught in the spring of 1880* (London, 1880); A. Pichot, *L'Irlande et le Pays de Galle*, Deux Tomes (Paris, 1850); J. O'Hagan, 'Ulster in the summer of 1845' in *Irish Monthly*, May-September (1913); T. Carlyle, *Reminiscences of my Irish journey in 1849* (London, 1882); [Anonymous], 'Gweedore,' pp 9-22; [Anonymous], 'The state of Donegal – Gweedore and Cloughaneely' in *Dublin University Magazine*, li (1858), Mrs Craik, 'An unknown country' in *The English Illustrated Magazine* (1887), pp 477-558. The last author's father, Thomas Mulock, championed the evicted during the highland clearances. See J. Prebble, *The highland clearances* (London, 1963), pp 239-69.
48. Quoted on back cover of Hill, *Facts*.
49. Carlyle, *My Irish journey*, p. 262.
50. Ibid., pp 239-40.
51. Hill, *Facts*, pp 40-2; see NAI, OR, 1840, 7/16219, E. J. Baron to Inspector General.
52. Ibid., p. 55.
53. For confirmation of this tradition see *Destitution*, p. 313.
54. *Destitution*, pp 191, 260.
55. Ibid., pp 31-3, 281, 288; Hill, *Facts*, p. 5.
56. Computed from *1851 Census*, pp 131-2.
57. *Destitution*, pp 106, 245, 286-8; Holland, *Landlord in Donegal*, pp 68-70.
58. *Return of outrages reported to the Royal Irish Constabulary Office from 1st January 1844 to 31st December 1880*, H. C. 1881 (C2756), lxxvii, pp 887-914.
59. *A return of the outrages specially reported by the constabularly as committed within the barony of Kilmacrenan, county Donegal, during the last ten years*, H. C. 1861 (404), lii, 585 (hereafter cited as *Outrages Kilmacrenan*), pp 2-7. These outrages occurred on 20 Feb. 1851; 8 Nov. 1852; 14 Mar., 30 Mar., 2 July, 31 Aug., 25 Sept. 1854; 4 Jan., 19 Feb., 9 Dec. 1855; 5 Jan. and 23 Feb. 1856.
60. W. E. Vaughan, *Sin sheep and Scotchmen: John George Adair and the Derryveagh evictions*, 1861 (Belfast, 1983), p. 27.
61. *Destitution*, pp 191-2, 280-2, 311-4, 323-4.
62. Hill, *Facts*, p. 9.
63. NAI, OR, 1850, 7/162, 4 May 1850, Comptroller General of coastguard to Under-Secretary 7/347, 9 Dec. 1850, Sir J. Stewart to J. N. Redington; OR, 1852, 7/406, 10 Nov. 1852, P. J. Newman to Under-Secretary; 7/407, 13 Nov. 1852, W. Olphert to Under Secretary; 7/424, 22 Nov. 1852, V. Hanlon to W. Olphert.
64. For the revival of the *poitín* trade see Hill, *Facts*, pp 6-7; *Destitution*, pp 79-80, 236. At the Donegal assizes in 1857, Master McGlynn, a national school teacher in Beagh, Ardara, gave an insight into the structure, membership and aims of the Molly Maguires/Ribbon Society when he testified against fellow Mollies. See

Londonderry Standard, 12 Mar. 1857. See also CSORP, 1858/18151.

65. *L.S.*, 16 July 1857; Holland, *Landlord in Donegal*, pp 94-9; CSORP, 1862/19409 'Information of Edward Diver'. Andy O'Donnell of Dungloe, named by Diver as 'head man' of the Molly's men in 1862, was identified as a leading Ribbonman in a confidential report twenty years later. See NAI, Crime Department B Files Carton 1, B134.

66. *Destitution*, pp 53, 332.

67. Ibid., pp 298-9, 306.

68. Ibid., p. 109; *General valuation of the rateable property in Ireland – Union of Dunfanaghy – valuation of the several tenements comprised in the above named union situate in the county of Donegal* (Dublin, 1857), [hereafter cited as *Griffith's Valuation Dunfanaghy*], pp 73, 81.

69. *Destitution*, pp 44, 306-7.

70. Ibid., pp 55-6, 128.

71. Ibid., pp 239, 250-6, 289-90, 310.

72. Ibid., pp 52, 304.

73. Ibid., pp 311-2; Holland, *Landlord in Donegal*, pp 26-31, 54-57.

74. *Destitution*, p. 57.

75. Ibid., pp 100-18.

76. Ibid., pp 246-50.

77. Ibid., pp 349-52; CSORP, 1860/15527, Cruise to Larcom 2 July 1854; 12 July 1854; 9 Oct. 1854 and 4 Nov. 1854.

78. *Destitution*, p. 467.

79. Ibid., p. 352.

80. *Outrages Kilmacrenan*, pp 7-8.

81. Ibid., p. 7; *Destitution*, pp 253, 349-54, 373-4, 380-1.

82. CSORP, 1860/15527 Cruise to Larcom, 3 April 1857.

83. Ibid., Resolutions of the Dunfanaghy Magistrates, 17 Dec. 1856.

84. Ibid., Cruise also sent two disposable men (detectives, disguised as peddlers) to Gaoth Dobhair. This tactic was abandoned with unseemly haste on 1 April when he discovered that the 'peddlers' were staying in the Gweedore Hotel. Cruise to Larcom, 3 April 1857.

85. Ibid., Cruise to Larcom, 3 April 1857. The genuine signatures were those of Doherty; Fr MacFadden of Cloughaneely and Fr O'Donnell of Dungloe; *Destitution*, p. 389.

86. CSORP, 1860/15527 Cruise to Larcom, 3 April 1857.

87. CSORP, 1857/5335 Cruise to Larcom, 20 June 1857; Ibid., 1860/15527 Cruise to Larcom, 3 April 1857.

88. It was later alleged that this was a *quid pro quo*, Cruise having promised that the sheep and police taxes would not be levied if McGettigan transferred Doherty. See Holland, *Landlord in Donegal*, p. 14; *Destitution*, pp 355, 371; CSORP, 1860/15527 Young to Cruise, 7 Oct. 1857.

89. *Destitution*, p. 355.

90. *Londonderry Standard*, 25 June 1857.

91. N.L.I., MS 7632, 9 Larcom Papers, Hill to Larcom, 9 Oct. 1857.

92. *Destitution*, p. 375; N.L.I., Ms 7632 Larcom Papers, Precis of reports and proceedings, with respect to the destruction of sheep belonging to settlers on mountain farms in the county of Donegal; CSORP, 1860/15527 Cruise to Larcom, 27 Feb. 1857; Hill to the Lord Lieutenant, 24 Mar. 1857. The police tax charged for the forty-four additional constables stationed in Gaoth Dobhair was £386 per quarter.

93. *L.S.*, 16 July 1857; CSORP, 1860/15527 Young to Cruise, 7 Oct. 1857; Queen v

Daniel Gallagher and others – information of James McBride, 29 Dec. 1857.
94. CSORP, 1857/5335 Cruise to Larcom, 20 June 1857.
95. *Outrages Kilmacrenan*, p. 8.
96. *Destitution*, p. 356.
97. CSORP, 1860/15527 Cruise to Larcom, 22 Feb. 1858; Maguire, *Diocese of Raphoe*, i, p. 487.
98. CSORP, 1860/15527 Queen v Daniel Gallagher and others – further information of James Boyle, 2 Oct. 1857.
99. Ibid., Cruise to Larcom, 6 Oct. 1857; Young to Cruise, 7 Oct. 1857.
100. *Griffith's Valuation Dunfanaghy*, pp 75-76, 83-4, 88-9.
101. Ibid., pp 77, 82, 89.
102. CSORP, 1860/15527 Cruise to Larcom, 6 Oct 1857.
103. Ibid., Young to Cruise, 7 Oct. 1857.
104. *Outrages Kilmacrenan*, p. 8; *Destitution*, pp 250-6.
105. Brian M. Walker, *Ulster politics: the formative years, 1868-86* (Belfast, 1989), p. 37.
106. *L.S.*, 23 July 1857; 31 Dec. 1857.
107. T.D. Sullivan, *A. M. Sullivan: a memoir* (Dublin, 1885), pp 64-6. For biographical notes on Holland see *Irish Book Lover*, vi (1914), p. 46, and Idem, viii (1916-7), p. 67.
108. *L.S.*, 27 Aug. 1857.
109. Holland, *Landlord in Donegal*, pp 58-72.
110. *Nation*, 26 Dec. 1857.
111. *Destitution*, pp 391-3. The signatories of the appeal were John Doherty, P.P., Carrigart, Rosgill; Hugh MacFadden, P.P., Falcarragh, Cloughaneely; Daniel McGee, P.P., Bunbeg, Gweedore; John O'Donnell, P.P., Dungloe, Rosses; John Flanagan, P.P., Rathmelton; Hugh McFadden, C.C., All Saints; James McFadden, C.C., Falcarragh, Cloughaneely; Bernard McMonagle, C.C., Dunfanaghy, Doe; John McGroarty, C.C., Cashelmore, Doe; Hugh Cullen, C.C., Rosgill.
112. *B.H.*, 23 July 1858; [Anonymous], 'State of Donegal', p. 731.
113. *Nation*, 20 Feb. 1858; 6 Mar. 1858; 13 Mar. 1858; 20 Mar. 1858; *B.H.*, 23 Apr. 1858; 14 May 1858; *Catholic Directory* (1860), see entry for 9 April 1859.
114. One hundred and forty three 'young men and women' who had been evicted by John George Adair were among the passengers on the *Lady Eglington*, the last of the five ships which embarked for Melbourne on 18 January 1862. For a discussion of the Donegal relief fund in Australia, focusing on the assisted emigration of the Derryveagh tenants, see B. Barrett, 'The mystery of a long-lost Irish village' in C. Kiernan (ed.), *Australia and Ireland, 1788-1988, bicentenary essays* (Dublin, 1986), pp 207-14.
115. *Nation*, 28 Feb. 1858; 27 Mar. 1858; *Destitution*, pp 73, 140, 391-408; CSORP, 1860/15527 Hamilton's report.
116. CSORP, 1860/15527 Young to Cruise, 12 Feb. 1858; Slyne to Cruise, 14 Feb. 1858; Young to Cruise 14 Feb. 1858; Cruise to Larcom, 22 Feb. 1858; *Destitution*, pp 362-4; Maguire, *Diocese of Raphoe*, ii, p. 266.
117. CSORP, 1860/15527 Cruise to Larcom, 8 Mar. 1858; Ibid., 1858/14827 Cruise to Larcom, 11 June 1858; *L.S.*, 11 Mar. 1858.
118. *Destitution*, p. iii; p. vii; pp ix-xi; The landlord committee, *Evidence given by the Donegal landlords before the committee of the House of Commons in reply to charges made against them by the Gweedore priests in the public papers and in their celebrated 'Appeal'* (n.d., 1858?).
119. *L.S.*, 15 July 1858; CSORP, 1858/15603 Cruise to Larcom, 10 July 1858.
120. *B.H.*, 5 Nov. 1858. For the investigation into the attempt on Nixon's life see

N.L.I., Ms 7633 Larcom Papers; CSORP, 1860/15527 Dillon to Larcom, 1 Mar. 1859; Considine to Larcom, 12 Nov., 14 Nov., 16 Nov. 1859.

121. *Londonderry Journal*, 16 Nov. 1858; A. M. Sullivan, *New Ireland* (London, n.d.), pp 221-3.

122. CSORP, 1858/18151.

123. CSORP, 1860/15527 Dillon to Larcom, 6 Mar. 1859; Dillon to Larcom, 1 Apr. 1859; Dillon to Larcom, 19 Oct. 1859.

124. Ibid., MacMahon to Larcom, 20 Feb. 1860; Dillon to Larcom, 21 Feb. 1860; McGee to Dillon, 21 Feb. 1860; N.L.I., MS 7633 Larcom Papers.

125. CSORP, 1860/15527 Dillon to Larcom, 21 Feb. 1860; Young to Larcom, 15 May 1860.

126. Ibid., Return of the special stations formed under the crime and outrage and peace preservation acts.

127. Holland, *Landlord in Donegal*, passim.

128. [Anonymous], 'State of Donegal,' passim; *B.H.*, 23 July 1858; for suggestions of Ribbon involvement see newspaper articles reprinted in *The landlord committee, evidence of the Donegal landlords*.

129. *Daily Express*, 19 Nov. 1860; Holland, *Landlord in Donegal*, p. 66.

130. *Morning Advertiser* quoted in *B.H.*, 7 May 1858.

131. Richards, *History of the highland clearances*, ii, p. 317.

132. J. MacFadden, *The present and past of the agrarian struggle in Gweedore with letters on railway extension in Donegal* (Londonderry, 1889), p. 15; Hill, *Facts*, pp 58-9.

133. Hill, *Facts*, p. 13; Sullivan, *New Ireland*, pp 221-3 briefly discusses the Sheep War in a chapter on the Derryveagh clearances but does not refer to Gaoth Dobhair by name.

Chapter 20

THE POLITICS OF NATION-BUILDING IN POST-FAMINE DONEGAL

JIM MacLAUGHLIN

Introduction

Deeply rooted in an empirical tradition of regional analysis and historical detail, historical geography and local history in Ireland still carry many of the birthmarks of their Victorian origins and have not been noted for their theoretical strengths. With few exceptions, they have been better at describing than explaining social and historical change.[1] Thus they have scarcely confronted the wider theoretical issues raised by historical sociology, structuration theory, cultural Marxism and postmodernism. To the extent that they even consider theory useful in historical explanation, Irish historians and historical geographers alike have either discussed regional and social change in terms of modernisation theory or have taken strong nation-centred, or revisionist perspectives on Irish historical and geographical problems. Local histories in particular have been deeply rooted in narrow parochial traditions. They have also exhibited a high degree of national exceptionalism.[2] Thus they describe their communities as exceptionally nationalist, or exceptionally unionist, or, less frequently, treat their communities as exceptions to the national rule. In so doing they deny even the possibility of cross-cultural or trans-national comparisons with the many nationalist, and nationalist separatist movements in other nineteenth-century European contexts.

This chapter uses the theoretical logic of Gramsci's cultural Marxism to analyse the role of the Catholic intelligentsia in the nationalisation of society and landscape in post-famine Donegal and to account for the political and economic success of the nationalist bourgeoisie in late nineteenth- and early twentieth-century Donegal. Section one briefly outlines a Gramscian framework for explaining social and political change in post-famine Donegal. Section two discusses the role of nineteenth-century local historians, and histories, in the rationalisation of nationalism and the nationalisation of people and places in Donegal in this time period. Section three focuses on the forgotten 'local heroes' of Irish nationalism in Donegal, namely the nationalist intelligentsia, especially Catholic priests and teachers. It also examines the relationship between 'priestly politics' and nationalist hegemony in Donegal in the late nineteenth and early twentieth century.

Hegemony and state-formation: a theoretical framework for understanding political and economic change in post-famine Donegal

The Italian Marxist Antonio Gramsci was the first to outline a historical geographical as opposed to an economic reductionist approach to state-formation and regional development within a materialist frame-work.[3] The category of hegemony occupied a central position in his analysis and referred to the cultural and economic modes of incorporation adopted by dominant sectors of class-structured societies to establish control over subordinate sectors and thereby legitimise their monopoly of state apparatuses of local government and education.[4] As used by Gramsci the concept 'hegemony' is not simply synonymous with ideological domination – it constitutes the substance and limit of common sense for most people and corresponds to the reality of social experience very much more clearly than any notion derived from the formula 'base' and 'superstructure'.[5]

Gramsci's mode of theorising also recognised the centrality of human agency in historical change. Thus he stressed that the dialectic was more than the blind clash of 'physical forces' that it was in orthodox Marxist-Leninist accounts of state-formation.[6] It was instead a historical movement to which real people contributed by making their own history, not least by constructing their own 'homelands'. Gramsci also managed to evade the voluntarism of idealist accounts of social and historical change, and the determinism of structuralist explanations, by building a model of social behaviour which recognised social groups as both determined and determining agents of regional and historical development. For Gramsci, writing in an Italian context, a hegemony had distinctive geographical correlates, and was not just a question of how a state related to society in any abstract terms. The way in which the largely peasant Italian South had been integrated into the Italian nation-state in the late nineteenth century particularly attracted Gramsci's attention. Northern industrialists, he argued, in alliance with southern landowners established hegemonic control over all of Italy, with the southern intelligentsia, a predominantly professional class, serving as intermediaries between peasants and landowners while also managing the links between both groups and the state.[7]

Gramsci's approach is particularly suited to an analysis of Irish nationalism in post-famine Donegal for a number of reasons. Firstly, unlike Marx, Gramsci recognised the rural poor as important actors in the political arena and showed that, through their links with the petty bourgeoisie, better-off peasants and small farmers had a debilitating effect on working class movements for revolutionary change.[8] Secondly, Gramsci explained the anomaly of subordinate social classes being led by a petty middle class intelligentsia in terms of the latter's social class origins, especially their close links with the rural poor and the urban working-class. He demonstrated that the national intelligentsia, particularly the clergy, were social mediators between dominant and subordinate social classes in class-structured nation-states. Peasants and small farmers in turn, he argued, often regarded priests, teachers and others set above them in a deeply ambivalent manner. On the one hand they looked up to them as their political 'betters' and 'natural' leaders, not least because so many of them were their own flesh and blood.[9] This was especially the case not only in the impoverished south of Italy but also in late nineteenth-century Donegal, where priests, teachers, and other members of the intelligentsia had disproportionate social and political influence, and acted as social intermediaries between the rural poor on the one hand and the local petty bourgeoisie and nation-building classes on the other. Having a son or daughter in the clergy, or in the teaching or any other white-collar profession, here, as in rural Italy, also often gave local families status and influence in the community.

However, the rural poor could also envy, or even despise, their clergy and political 'betters' for their easy way of life, and for the fact that they often identified with dominant social classes rather than siding with those from whom they literally sprung. The intelligentsia, including priests, were central to the consolidation of bourgeois nationalist hegemony. They cultivated deferential attitudes among the poor, contributed to the process of ethnogenesis, and helped prevent outbreaks of class conflict in late nineteenth- and early twentieth-century national societies. Finally, Gramsci insisted that the rural poor were as much subjects as objects of history, and showed that history was not only shaped by intellectual elites operating outside of time and space but was also made by the lesser intelligentsia who were conscious of being organically linked to national-popular masses.[10]

This chapter suggests that nationalist hegemony in post-famine Donegal was not so much the product of ethnic geography or ideological manipulation but was rooted in the political landscape and in the local political and economic structures of Donegal. It argues that Catholic nationalism saturated every aspect of community life and culture in Donegal at the beginning of the twentieth century. It also suggests that nationalist hegemony here described a process of structural and cultural negotiation which allowed certain social groups, notably well-off farmers and the shopocracy, to exert moral leadership, through the clergy, over the rest of Donegal society in such a way that their ideological outlook came to be regarded as 'common sense'. This suggests that nationalism in Donegal is best viewed not so much as an autonomous social force, or as a political ideology imposed from above by a national intelligentsia, but as a political ideology and social movement that literally developed out of the county's socio-economic and ethnic geography.[11] As such it was widely regarded as a cultural and political force which released Donegal's rural poor from the 'idiocy of rural life' and gave those at the bottom of a colonial society a new nationalist sense of value, and a national sense of place in nationalist Ireland.[12] The section that follows examines the role of history in the nationalisation of people and places, and in the consolidation of bourgeois nationalist hegemony in Donegal in the latter half of the nineteenth and the opening decades of the twentieth century.

Nationalist history and bourgeois nationalist hegemony in late nineteenth-century Donegal

Gellner has argued that nationalism is an attribute of people rather than places.[13] Nationalism in nineteenth-century Donegal was transformed into an attribute of places and reflected the socio-regional contexts within which it evolved. As such it constituted a 'Balkanising' force which set Donegal apart from unionist Ulster while simultaneously uniting it with nation-building Ireland. However, contrary to the claims of either Irish nationalists or Ulster unionists, places were neither naturally unionist or naturally nationalist. Yet this was precisely what one unionist politician suggested when, claiming Derry for unionist Ulster, he insisted that:

> No candidate or truthful person can deny that the city of Derry is unionist. It is unionist in its representative citizens, in its industry and in its social life, aye, its very bricks and mortar are unionist.[14]

However, it is possible to propose an alternative perspective on nationalism and unionism to that held by Irish nationalists and Ulster unionists, and to treat states in late nineteenth-century Ireland as propagators and enforcers of regionally-based hegemonies.[15] This at least allows for a critical geography of nationalism and unionism in Ulster, including Donegal, and does not take national or unionist geographies as socio-spatial or historical 'givens'. Irish nationalism and unionism certainly had clearly identifiable heartlands and 'shatter-belts' in late nineteenth- and early twentieth-century Ulster. Just as there were areas over which nationalists and unionists fought for hegemonic control, there were others where Irish nationalism and Ulster unionism literally had to be constructed from the ground up. Indeed within Ulster it is possible to identify three distinct zones where nationalism and unionism evolved and were either hegemonically successful, or failed to develop. Firstly, there was the predominantly Presbyterian and prosperous heartland of eastern Ulster, the heartland of unionist Ulster where unionist hegemony was practically unchallenged. Secondly, there was the mixed Catholic and Protestant 'shatter-belt' of mid-Ulster. This was a 'contested terrain' over which Irish nationalists and Ulster unionists struggled to assert political and cultural hegemony. Finally there was the 'other Ulster', the overwhelmingly Catholic and under-developed west of the province, a region that was of peripheral interest to Ulster unionists but of considerable strategic and symbolic signi-ficance to Irish nationalists ever anxious to acquire 'lebensraum', or 'living space', for an Irish Catholic nation.[15]

In Ireland as elsewhere in mid-nineteenth century Europe, there was a fundamental difference between the movement to found the nation-state and 'nationalism', in the sense that one was an ideological programme for constructing a political artefact claiming to be based on the other. Moreover, given its nature and political programme, nationalism in late nineteenth-century Ireland implied significant political changes, just as unionism sought to defend the territorial integrity of the United Kingdom, and this is what made both movements essentially 'nationalist'. In ethnically-divided Ulster nationalists, including historians and antiquarians, played a crucial role in the nationalisation of people and places, not least in Donegal and the 'Other Ulster'. Thus Catholic priests and cultural nationalists in Donegal sought to contain unionist influence and to resist the encroachment of unionist power beyond the heartlands of east and mid-Ulster into the county's agricultural heartland centred on Letterkenny. Protestant influence was concentrated in this area, especially in the Lagan Valley where Catholics were between 50 and 65 per cent of the population on the eve of the Great War.[16] That this part of the county was considered by some to be a contested terrain over which nationalists and unionists would have to contend for power is clear from the following statement. In his *In the days of the Laggan presbytery*, published in 1908, the Reverend G. A. Lecky suggested:

> It should be remembered that there are two Donegals – an outer and an inner. The former, which is almost wholly Roman Catholic, and from which the county to a large extent takes its character and complexion in the eye of the public, consists of extensive mountainous districts that lie along the western seaboard, and at some points run far inland. The latter consists of the more flat and

fertile country that lies between the mountains and the river Foyle – the eastern boundary of the county. It is largely Protestant and from a very early period in history has been known as the Laggan, i.e. the low and level country.[17]

Historians and antiquarians in late nineteenth-century Donegal as elsewhere in Ireland and nation-building Europe were also so conditioned by the 'history-saturated cultures' within which they operated that they required little justification for writing history, and interpreting the past, from a nationalist perspective.[18] Donegal was in no way exceptional in this regard. Thus Sheehy has argued:

> People in nineteenth-century Ireland looked more and more to the past: they looked at the church and plate jewellery which had survived from the Early Christian period, they examined the not inconsiderable architectural remains scattered around the country, and most of all they studied ancient manuscripts for information about Irish history and civilisation. They realised that vestiges of this ancient culture remained in the music, storytelling and customs of the Irish-speaking population, and began to study those too. Such interests were already apparent in the late eighteenth century, and they gained momentum in the nineteenth. They began among scholars – historians and antiquarians – who were essentially the middle class, but then gradually filtered through the whole country, so that a people who had been told for years that they were savages, with a barbarous language and no evidence of civilisation, were persuaded that this was not so.[19]

Neither was Ireland in any way exceptional in constructing a national identity from a mixture of ethnic folk customs and complementary images of a prehistoric Golden Age. Historians, artists, and indeed social scientists throughout nation-building Europe mobilised history in order to construct national identities, to create national styles, and to establish the ethnic credentials and legitimacy of their nations. In underpinning the political legitimacy of nation-building, they also 'nationalised' folk culture and insisted that the growth of strong nations was a moral evolution as spontaneous and uncontrollable as the evolution of the human organism. This idea was based on two premises – that advanced nation-states were 'natural' developments', and that powerful nation-states were the most desirable forms of political organisation in a world composed of self-governing strong nations and colonial dominions.[20] Separatist and ethnonationalist movements which claimed autonomy on the basis of distinctive religious or cultural traits were branded retrogressive because they threatened the territorial integrity of powerful nations and sapped the geopolitical vigour of national societies.[21]

The power of place and race in Irish nationalism: some Donegal examples

Myth and myth-making were mixed in equal proportions both in regional and nationalist history, and in the state-centred ideology which it spawned. Thus, far from disproving myths and dispensing with tradition, nationalist historians and the intelligentsia nourished the political imagination of modern nations with myths and folk history and introduced a strong element of tradition into the political consciousness of nineteenth-century national societies.[22] Such was the position in post-famine Donegal, where nationalist myths and folk beliefs often supplemented, but less frequently substituted for, religious modes of explanation for social and historical developments. Here also they gave the rural poor a new national sense of place and elevated the 'native', including the native landscape and native iconography, to a new position in modern Irish society (See figs 20.1 and 20.2). Daniel Corkery well described the symbolic and cultural significance of 'the sterile tracts' and 'back places' of the Atlantic fringe to the whole process of ethnogenesis in late nineteenth- and early twentieth-century Ireland. Thus he argued:

> The hard mountain lands of West Cork and Kerry, the wild seaboard of the West, the back places of Connemara and Donegal – in such places only was the Gael at liberty to live his own way. In them he was not put upon. Big houses were few or none. Travellers were rare; officials short at the very aspect of the landscape; coaches found no fare. To reach them one must, leaving the cities and town behind, venture among the bogs and hills, far into the mountains even, where the native Irish, as the pamphleteers and politicians loved to call them, still lurked.[23]

In Donegal, cultural nationalists and nationalist historians regarded the west of the county as the very 'core of Gaeldom'. Here, they argued, were the perfect specimens of an Irish race, the remnants of a folk society and 'the mental heirs of the historic past'. In quasi-racial accounts of the history of Celtic civilisation, 'back places' like Donegal, Galway, Cork and Kerry were valued because they were a world apart from urban Ireland, and were inhabited by a people set apart from Ireland's 'West Britons' by their linguistic heritage and social psychological characteristics. Thus, in *Education and the Nation*, a

Fig. 20.1   Inishowen, Gaelic fortifications and the 'Gaelicised' landscape.

Catholic Truth Society pamphlet which was published in 1915 and which circulated widely among Donegal priests, the Reverend J. Fahy argued that 'in spite of severe privations', the inhabitants of 'core areas of Gaeldom' like west Donegal were:

> among the finest specimens of the race; mentally, in spite of want

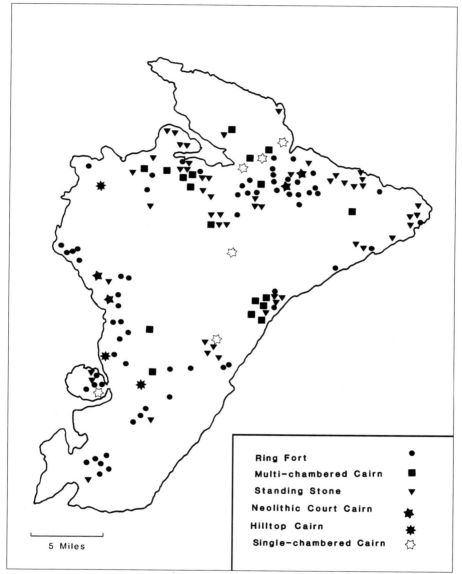

Ring Fort	●
Multi-chambered Cairn	■
Standing Stone	▼
Neolithic Court Cairn	★
Hilltop Cairn	✳
Single-chambered Cairn	☆

5 Miles

Fig. 20.2   Pre-historic Inishowen – relics on the landscape.

of education – perhaps because of that want – they are the equals or the superiors of their English-speaking neighbours. Classed as 'illiterates', because unable to speak or write English, they are equipped with a store of folk-lore, proverbs, and legends, and endowed with an acuteness which their neighbours entirely lack. Masters of vocabulary ten times greater than that of the English peasant, they speak their language with a fluency and accuracy he knows nothing of and many of the best English-speakers never attain. In respect of courtesy, reverence, or morality, there is no comparison between them.[24]

Similarly, in stressing the centrality of the Irish language both as a basis of national identity and as a defense against cultural imperialism, the bishop of Raphoe urged his parishioners to take their example from the Gaelic-speaking 'people of the mountain':

> The language is still in the air there. It is in the blast that blows from the mountains, and it is our duty to see that it is the breeze that fans the plains.[25]

Gallagher called these 'the people of the rock' and they possessed all the characteristics of the peasants in Carlo Levi's *Christ stopped at Eboli*, a classic account of peasant life in southern Italy in the 1930s.[26] Indeed Levi's portrayal of relations between the rural poor and the state in this part of Italy could equally be applied to the rural poor of Donegal in the late nineteenth century. In Levi's classic such poor communities 'existed outside the framework of time' and were 'confined to that which is changeless and timeless'. Thus, he argued:

> Governments, theocracies and armies are stronger than peasants. So the peasants have to resign themselves to being dominated, but they cannot feel as their own the glories and undertakings of a civilisation that is radically their enemy. The only wars that touch their hearts are those in which they have fought to defend themselves against that civilisation, against history and government. These wars they fought under their own pennants, without military leadership or training. The peasant world has neither government nor training; its wars are only sporadic outbursts of revolt, doomed to repression. Still it survives, yielding up the fruits of the earth to the conquerors, but imposing upon them its measurement, its earthly divinities and its language.[27]

Donegal historians and cultural nationalists were in no way unique in mythologising the past and idolising the rural poor in order to rationalise nationalism and defend a national route to capitalism and modernisation. Myths, mythical history and folklore were widely used to legitimise state-centred objectives throughout nation-building Europe.[28] Thus in nineteenth-century Russia 'Saintly Princes' and 'Princely Saints' featured prominently in the political landscape, and

Plate 20.1   Mud cabin in South Inishowen, early twentieth century.

Plate 20.2   Glentogher National School, North Inishowen, April 1925.
Source: Harkin and McCarroll, 1984.

were also 'beatified' in the history books.[29] This was also the case with the Reverend William James Doherty's *Inis-Owen and Tirconnell: an account of antiquities and writers* published in 1895.[30] Born in Buncrana in 1864, Doherty served as a Catholic curate in Omagh (1890-94), Coleraine (1894-1900), Dungiven (1900-05) and Moville (1905-20). He was appointed parish priest of Ardstraw West in 1920.[31] His account is not so much a history as a celebration of Donegal's Celtic and pre-historic past and a homage to its saints and scholars. Doherty argued that, prior to the Young Irelanders,

> The history of Ireland had to be written to satisfy the English conscience, generally by showing that everything noble and exalted had been done by English statesmen, and their army of *heroes* and *divines* sent for the reclaiming, extirpation, extinction, and good example to the Irish savage.[32]

Eulogizing the Carndonagh-born Franciscan monk John Colgan for his patriotism in recording so much Irish ecclesiastical history, Doherty argued that:

> Ireland, though the possessor of ancient historical manuscripts, unsurpassed by those of any other nation in their present spoken language, had been unable from the vicissitudes of ever-recurring conquests, to do much more than preserve her historic treasures from extinction. Her ancient manuscripts, like her people, breathed an heroic and lively imagination. Full of sentiment, with Christian feeling even to exultation. This tended to impress on the Irish mind that strong veneration which at all times has ever been rendered to the patron saints of Ireland. These manuscripts were interwoven with a crowd of traditions, the very framework of the history of every ancient nation, so difficult of comprehension to the uninitiated critic, and which has found a place in the lives of several of her saints.[33]

Doherty's original objective was to provide 'a popular and homely rendering of John Colgan's place as a writer of the seventeenth century'. In Inishowen and Tirconnell this was extended to include 'other prominent writers of Donegal, who, in ancient and modern times, by their genius and learning, at home and abroad, have upheld the name, and extended the fame of the Irish race'.[34] This in turn brought the author on a literary tour which included not only Donegal's most famous saints and scholars, but also those who were only remotely connected with the county by accident of birth.

In late nineteenth-century Donegal, as in other parts of rural Ireland, the writing of history went hand in hand with the Catholicisation of people and places. Here the writing of history was frequently the work of amateurs, Catholic curates and antiquarians who literally 'Christened' places in Donegal and claimed them for nationalist rule. Thus, writing on 'the place occupied by Donegal in early Christian civilisation', Father Doherty stated:

> ... we find her present from the first, sending forth apostles of religion, recording in the pages of history its progress, successes and vicissitudes, founding schools and universities abroad to impart knowledge, and extending literature. The children of Donegal rescued many treasured relics of antiquity, thereby contributing towards the distinction we claim as a nation, as pioneers in the cause of progress, Christianity, and civilisation throughout Western Europe.[35]

That Catholic cultural nationalism still informed local history in Donegal until recently is evident in the following passage from Brian Bonner's *Our Inis Eoghain heritage* which was published in 1972.[36] The author's objective was 'to make the people of Inishowen aware of the achievements, the sufferings and the heroism of their ancestors'. He went on to add:

> The example of the past generations will, it is hoped, help them to retain their true sense of values and so stimulate a better informed line of action in community life. The earnest hope is that the present inhabitants of Inis Eoghain will become more fully aware of their rich inheritance and appreciate adequately its great and unique character. They will then, no doubt, take steps to restore what has been lost and retain, from deep conviction, what is best in their traditional mode of life. A renewed and dynamic community will be the result. Inis Eoghain will thus be able to make a major contribution to the whole Irish nation in the coming years, as it did so effectively once before, in the period following the introduction of Christianity.[37]

For Bonner, as for many Catholic nationalist historians in late nineteenth- and early twentieth-century Ireland, the writing of history was a strategy for dispelling 'a superficial sense of values', a way of protecting 'an old and precious order of things' from 'a new and materialistic culture devoid of spiritual values'. Bonner believed that only a proper recording and reading of history will set Inis Eoghain apart from 'that pagan, de-Christianised society which is such a disturbing feature of the present day'.[38]

Catholic nationalist historians such as Reverend William James Doherty nationalised the Donegal landscape and peopled it with nationalist heroes and Catholic saints. Discussing Cahir O'Doherty's rebellion against English rule under Sir Arthur Chichester he claimed that the 'crumbling ruins' of the castle of O'Doherty were more worthy of respect than the 'alabaster monument' erected to the memory of Chichester.[39] Local historians and antiquarians like Doherty also literally made places in Donegal pregnant with history by making them reverberate with calls from a heroic and largely mythical past. Using data from Bonner's accounts, and from the more recent archaeological survey of Donegal, figures 20.1 and 20.2 have reconstructed the pre-plantation and Gaelic landscapes of Inishowen that would be recognisable to late nineteenth- and early twentieth-century nationalist historians in Inishowen.[40] They also emphasise the density and depth of the Celtic and pre-historic geography of this part of the county. In imprinting this local historical geography on the consciousness of the local community, nationalists helped to instil a strong sense of place in rural Inishowen and taught the rural poor to revere the past.

Michael Harkin, also of Inishowen, was equally aware of the role of local history and ethnic geography in the cultivation of a nationalist sense of place. Writing on the history, traditions and antiquities of Inishowen in 1867, he described his philosophy of history as follows:

> I wished to draw the attention of the people of Inishowen to the prominent and proud position which this territory holds in the ancient history of our country; to the illustrious line of princes of the Kinel-Owen, born and reared within the wall of Aileach, who wielded monarchical sceptre, who proved themselves the fathers of their people and the defenders of the rights of their country; to notice the old druidical temples, and other remains of pagan times, as illustrating the colonisation of the district and the form of worship of that remote period; *to show the childlike docility with which its people received the light of the gospel*, and to point to the churches and monasteries which they founded; to call to remembrance the struggles which our fathers sustained with the Dane and Saxon, successfully against the first, and though to the other they were forced to yield, it was not until after a most obstinate defense, when all Ireland besides had been subdued, and more than four centuries after Henry II received the submission of the southern princes (Emphasis added).[41]

Stephen Gwynn, whose *Highways and byways of Donegal and Antrim* was published in 1899, argued that although Donegal had long been 'a worthless appendage of the Empire' under English rule, it would one day be of considerable strategic and economic significance to nation-building Ireland. Thus Gwynn argued that Donegal could never be:

> ... a thriving county, but it may cease to be clouded by the shadow of famine. While human beings in these islands increase and multiply as they are doing, every year will give an added value to these lonely places which become the breathing spaces and playgrounds of our laborious race.[42]

Like other Victorian visitors to Donegal, Gwynn was 'enchanted' by its 'remote, lonely, and storm-beaten character', and by the fact that 'many districts here are so wild and barren that no industry of man has yet reclaimed them'.[43]

Nationalist myths, geographies and historiographies like these performed a number of other functions in rural Ireland. Firstly, in recalling the past in heroic terms, they mobilised popular support for the nationalist cause and bolstered the political confidence of nationalists. Secondly, they gave the struggling nationalist movement in Donegal an ancient and respectable lineage by 'ethnicising' the historical record and reducing all past struggles to clear-cut conflicts between native and foreigner. Finally, they portrayed the local bourgeoisie as the 'natural' leaders of the Irish nation, and praised them for thwarting foreign rule, and for leading 'their people' out of the 'idiocy of rural life' on to national pathways of political righteousness.

Nationalism in late nineteenth- and early twentieth-century Donegal and Ulster was not just a cultural phenomenon but a regional expression of a European-wide tradition of racial and ethnic theorising whereby nationalists ranked nations hierarchically and placed their nation at the apex of an evolving world order. In ethnically-divided nations, nationalists and national separatists also emphasised the dangers of cultural miscegenation and stressed the centrality of nation-building to the preservation and accumulation of individual aptitudes. This was particularly the case in early twentieth-century Ulster where nationalism, as in Irish nationalism, and national separatism, as in Ulster unionism, reflected the political and economic concerns of regionally-based social blocs and contending ethnic collectivities.[44] These ideologies were also inherently geographical in that they had clear geographical domains and clear territorial imperatives by the beginning of the twentieth century. Ideological expressions of Irish nationalism, including nationalist literature, were most clearly associated with the agricultural heartlands of southern Ireland and the Atlantic fringe of Ulster.[45] Unionist ideology on the other hand, particularly in the opening decades of the twentieth century when Ulster unionism had emerged as a powerful regional expression of political separatism, was most strongly articulated in the heartland of east and mid-Ulster, where it also had considerable support from defenders of Empire and visiting MPs from Britain. Nationalist historiography had its intellectual roots in the political pamphleteering of the Young Irelanders in the 1840s.[46] It not only attacked the ideological kernel at the heart of Anglo-Irish historiography which suggested that the Irish were unfit to govern themselves – it also condemned cattle ranching and *laissez faire* capitalism as contrary to the best interests of the Irish people. Indeed, while English political pamphlets 'simianised' the 'Paddy' and caricatured Irish politics as irrational at best and conspiratorial at worst, nationalists characterised English rule in Ireland as a crime against Irish civilisation.[47]

Legitimising nationalism: 'native custom' versus 'alien rule'

Local historians and nationalists provided nationalists with political legitimacy and insisted on the superiority of indigenous Irish customs and practices over foreign customs. Opposing what they categorised as the 'alien rule' of landlords and the principles of free market rural capitalism, they conveniently ignored the role of the native middling Catholic tenantry in the consolidation of a native capitalist system from the mid-nineteenth century onwards.

Micheal Harkin, the Inishowen historian, was clear in his attribution of culpability for post-famine agricultural conditions in Donegal:

> The cause of all this misery is palpably plain, though many pretend not to see it. Ireland is an agricultural country. The few who own the soil till it not, and the millions who till the soil own it not; and while tillage and occupation impart increased value to the land, landlord-made law steps in and says to the tenant – I disown your improvements or I leave the landlord to appropriate them to himself, to rent you for them, and tax you for your own industry; you are his serf, his engine, his machine; the trust which the legislature confers on you is partially his; you are wholly and completely in his power, and he may evict and exterminate you without let or hindrance.[48]

Harkin, of 'middling tenantry' background and ideologically closer to Donegal's rural petty bourgeoisie than to the landless poor, proffered solutions to the social and economic problems of Donegal which stopped short of any radical restructuring of social class and property relations in the county. Steering a clear course between the extremes of *laissez faire* rural capitalism and the doctrinaire socialism of continental Europe, he argued that:

> In treating of the relations which should exist between landlord and tenant in Ireland, I wish at the very outset not to be understood as advocating socialism; for God forbid I should be found on the side of socialism, or to advocate the doctrines of Rousseau, nor those of Diderot or D'Alembert, as circulated through the medium of the infidel Encyclopaedia, and which led to the horrors of the revolution.[49]

Harkin made repeated historicist claims that the rightful rulers of Donegal were not 'alien landlords and their agents' but 'the descendants of its old Celtic tribes'. Like the late nineteenth-century Basque separatist Sabino de Arana, Harkin also made attachment to place, and rootedness in rural society, the legitimate basis for nationalist rule in Donegal.[50] Central to both of these nationalisms was the concept of race as the fulcrum of the nation. In Donegal, as in the Basque country, nationalism was depicted as an historic obligation and Donegal historians and cultural nationalists transformed elements from folk history and pre-industrial society into symbols of national legitimacy. These symbols in turn were harnessed in the struggle for hegemony over cultural, economic and political resources in the county. Thus Harkin pointed out that 'the title deed of many of our landed properties do not extend beyond the revolution of 1688', and argued that most large landholders in Donegal 'derived their grants from the confiscation of Ulster'.[51] In so doing he not only regularly exaggerated the historical lineage of nationalism in Donegal, which, he suggested, was suspended through the Plantation of Ulster in the seventeenth century – he also claimed that:

> the title deed of occupancy is as good as any title which the Crown can confer, and should shield the inhabitants of the country from the irresponsible exterminator; should warrant the law to secure them the full value of the improvements which their labour or capital, or both, have conferred upon the soil.[52]

Ignoring the role of middling tenantry in consolidating rural capitalism in Donegal, local historians and political leaders went on to systematically refute each assimilationist premise underlying the

Plate 20.3   The re-inauguration of the Inishowen Society, Carndonagh, 1897. The
              society, patronised by the Earl of Shaftesbury, had a mixed membership
              of Catholics, Church of Ireland Protestants and Presbyterians and was
              typical of other nineteenth century 'self-improvement' societies through-
              out Donegal. It was open to 'improving' landholders, small merchants
              and the substantial tenantry alike. The photograph shows, front row,
              left to right: Unknown; Charles McColgan; Robert Doherty, Culdaff;
              Mr. Quigley, Isle of Doagh; Unknown Culdaff resident; J. Reid; J. McIvor;
              Captain Scott, Burt; and Robert Moore. Back row, left to right: second
              from left, Ned Smith; fifth, B. Moore; sixth, George Doherty; seventh,
              William Crampsey.
              Source: Harkin and McCarroll, 1984.

Anglicisation and modernisation of Donegal society in the nineteenth
century. Inchoate though it was, this historicist reaction to 'English
misrule' revolutionised the treatment of many questions concerning
social life and work in Donegal, including the political future and
development of the county. In so doing it constructed a new political
agenda and re-opened questions that were supposed to have been
settled with the introduction of progressive farming from the early
nineteenth-century onwards. Discussing the role of historicist claims
and Celtic agrarian legislation on nationalist politics, Clive Dewey has
argued that historicists in late nineteenth-century Ireland and Scotland
shifted the cause of agrarian conflict from population pressure to a
conflict of laws – a conflict between Celtic custom and English
commercialism.[53] Dewey demonstrated that confident rationalist con-
clusions were embodied across the whole spectrum of social issues,
and has argued that nationalist historians attacked as erroneous the
assumption that rancherism was necessarily more productive than
'petite culture' in rural Ireland and Scotland.[54]

Plate 20.4   By the 1920s 'genteel' sports like lawn tennis were played by middle class and lower middle class elements in Donegal society. This picture, taken in the mid-1920s, shows members of the Carrick Tennis Club, Carndonagh. Judging by members' names, it also shows that the game was not confined to the Protestant minority, and that Catholics and Protestants mixed freely on sporting and social occasions. Back row, left to right: Miss Binns, Mrs Gillespie, Nurse Mitchell, Mrs Meehan. Centre row, left to right: Eileen Cowey, Nancy Moore, Susie White, Lila Smith, Nan Porter, Harry Workman. Front row: Tom Moore, Garda O'Hagan, Reverend Boyd, Garda McGurk, Michael White, George Scott.
Source: Harkin and McCarroll, 1984.

This was particularly the case in Donegal, where local historians and antiquarians came of political and intellectual age at a time when the hegemonic status of the county's beleaguered aristocracy was under attack from an emergent Catholic bourgeoisie. As the century progressed the latter gradually dominated local government and claimed Donegal for nationalist Ireland. Meanwhile, local priests, teachers and historians established the petty bourgeoisie and improving farmers as the 'natural leaders' of Donegal and gave the rural poor a new political destiny, a national sense of place in a new Ireland. The failure of the county's landed ascendancy to ameliorate the massive problems of rural underdevelopment facilitated the new pathfinders. Thus, after considering the options available for the alleviation of poverty in late nineteenth-century Donegal, one state official argued:

What seems to be needed for the relief of these districts is the establishment on a permanent basis of an emigration department, which, with a competent staff, and the co-operation of a voluntary committee, combined with systematic and careful oversight at ports of departure and arrival, shall from year to year, and not spasmodically, deal with all applications for assisted emigration, and advise or make grants in each case as may seem for the best.[55]

The wife of a prominent landlord in south Donegal suggested that the only remedy for the endemic poverty of Donegal in the late nineteenth century was for the people:

to rely on their own industry and efforts, instead of becoming public beggars, or beseeching the government to help them – in other words requesting the government to hand over to them the result of other people's labours. If a healthier tone could be infused, and the people roused from their old indolent ways, Donegal's great curses – misrepresentations, beggings, and laziness – would vanish, and we should hear no more pitiable appeals. Doling out meal, abusing landlords, and blaming Government can never be the cure for the evils from which these congested districts suffer. At present there is neither industry nor the desire for improvement. When seasons do not fail the people can exist, and are happy, and do not care for settled work. They have their warm cabins, and all the winter the men lounge about doing nothing. To get the people away from the crowded districts and into more profitable fields of labour, if possible at home, if not, abroad, is the only cure for Donegal. Thousands of girls could find employment in the factories of Belfast and vicinity, but as long as meal can be had for the asking, the people will not exert themselves.[56]

This statement is all the more remarkable because it referred to subjects of the crown in an Ulster county in terms redolent of the paternalism, racism and ethnocentrism normally reserved for subordinate communities in colonial Africa and India. Many of the poor 'vanished' from Donegal not only to Belfast but also to England, Scotland, and North America with hardly enough English to write their names.[57] Thus nationalists made political capital out of the fact that from the late nineteenth century onwards Donegal became an 'emigrant nursery' which exported surplus labourers to the core areas of world capitalism in order to make room for 'graziers and their bullocks' in rural Catholic Ireland.[58]

Creating a national imagination of late-nineteenth- and early twentieth-century Donegal

Cultural nationalists and the nationalist intelligentsia in late nineteenth-century Donegal also coupled a concern for tenant right and legislative reform with a concern for denominational education. They extolled the virtues of Catholic teaching as the best means for transforming the county's rural poor into citizens of an Irish Catholic nation. As Eugene Weber's study of the transformation of French peasants to French citizens has shown, Irish nationalists were not exceptional in regarding national schools as social modes for incorporating the rural poor into a bourgeois nationalist world in the late nineteenth century.[59] Local historians and the nationalist intelligentsia defended nationalist education not just because it was their own creation, but because it provided employment opportunities for the petty bourgeoisie while simultaneously disciplining the children of the poor and disseminating 'good taste' and the 'Three Rs' to those occupying the lowest ranks of late nineteenth-century Irish society. By the opening decades of the twentieth century, a Catholic education was widely regarded as a buffer against 'Music Hall culture', secularism, socialism and radical ideas emanating from Scotland and England. Catholic schools were defended because these imparted a moral code and educational values which eclipsed any training in 'the mechanical arts'. From the cultural nationalist perspective, the purpose of state education under English rule in Ireland was 'to steal the love of their faith and the love for their motherland from the young hearts of little ones'. *Catholicity and progress in Ireland*, a veritable handbook of Irish Catholic nationalism published in 1905, and certainly one familiar to priests and nationalists in Donegal, claimed that:

> Irish Catholic children, while their hearts were plastic, were brought under un-Catholic influences, and were trained to think of Ireland as a western province of England with no more national individuality than an English shire. ... The effect of the thing called National Education on the Irish mind and character has been to lessen or to destroy that genuine idea of patriotism which is a positive principle of thought and action.[60]

Donegal nationalists adapted these arguments to local conditions and had little difficulty in making them the guiding principles of national education. Thus Michael Harkin was a strong advocate of Catholic education who preferred to have the children of Inishowen steeped in Catholic values, and in Celtic beliefs and mythology, rather than having them 'raised in a knowledge of the mechanical arts'. He argued:

Plate 20.5   Inaugural meeting of the North-West Gaelic League in Gortahork. The photograph was taken *c.*1914. Seated from left to right are: J. L. Murrin, Anthony Doherty, Reverend James McGettigan, Unknown, Douglas Hyde, P. O'Daly, Reverend John O'Doherty, P. J. Flanagan (former editor of *Derry Journal*). Standing from left to right are: Harry Coll, James McGill, Mrs Nellie Flanagan, Nora Glass, Sheila McGuinness, Thomas McCarter (*Derry Journal* employee), Ned McDermott, Cissy Casey, Reverend Doherty, H. Duffy.

> Education does not consist in reading, writing, music and the like. These are mere mechanical arts. They form part of the grand educational system, but it is only a subordinate one. Religion should be the beginning, the middle and the end of all educational systems.[61]

Later in the century Catholic priests echoed Harkin's views, declaring that 'imparting knowledge without religion' meant that schools were 'only making so many clever devils'. They also stressed the role of schools in the formation of national character, insisting that:

> A nation is what its schools have made it. Schoolmasters are the teachers of the race – as they mould the child's mind, so is the nation moulded. The school is the nation's home, where its children are trained; as home-life leaves its impress on the family, so is the imprint of the school left on the civic and national life. The schoolboys of today are the men who will rule our destinies tomorrow.[62]

Plate 20.6   Members of Inishowen District Council, June 1920. This photograph was taken on the occasion of the Council's decision to recognise Dáil Éireann as the legitimate government of the country. Seated in front row from left to right are: Councillor Bradley, Desertegney; Councillor Kavanagh, Sledrin; Robert Doherty, Malin; Patrick Quigley, Ballyliffen; Edward Doherty, Ballyloskey; Dan McMullin, Mossy Glen. Middle row, left to right: Frank O'Connor, Illies; E. Smith, Culdaff; W. McKinney, Bootagh, Culdaff; P. H. O'Doherty, Carndonagh; J. Ruddy, Clonmany; Patrick Canny, Gortinney; Edward O'Donnell. Back row, left to right: Patrick McCallion, Malin; Brian Douglas, Magheramore; Councillor McGonagle, Clonmany; James McSheffrey, Redcastle; Dan O'Kane, Clar, Moville; M. Quigley, Workhouse Master; Robert Moore, Clerk of Workhouse. *Source:* Harkin and McCarroll, 1984.

In 1905 the Catholic bishop of Derry, whose diocese extended into north Donegal and supplied the county with many of its priests, exhorted local priests and teachers in the following terms:

> In their anxiety about secular education men appear to forget that there is a knowledge of greater importance than that which facts of history or scientific knowledge can impart. They seem to lose sight of the truth that man is not a mere animal, but he possesses an immortal soul, the salvation of which is the supreme good.[63]

In statements such as these the clergy elevated the rural poor of Donegal to a status above that of the 'accomplished linguist', the 'eloquent orator' and 'successful businessman'. *The literature crusade in Ireland*, a Catholic Truth Society pamphlet which circulated widely in Donegal, Derry and Tyrone on the eve of partition, claimed that:

Since the barrier of the Irish language was broken down, and since Ireland has become practically an English-speaking country, there is no natural breakwater to prevent the flood of English literature flowing through the land. Day and night it is constantly coming, and in ever-increasing quantities. Some of the new Crusade have been struck by the number of cross-channel publications which find their way to the small towns and villages of Ireland. The larger towns have been almost deluged with them.[64]

This author also warned against the dangers of secularism, stressed the relationship between 'literature and infidelity', and insisted that the connection between the two was 'only too often lost sight of by the petty philosophers of our own day'. He went on to argue that:

There is indeed a striking contrast between the profound respect with which the great minds of all time have approached the deep questions of pure existence, and our relations with our Creator, and the flippancy with which many of your modern quill drivers treat of them. Yet the disrespect of up-to-date novelists and review writers will have its effect on the unthinking, and even the best literature crusade imaginable will not save them from moral ruin. If the 'little philosophy' which is only too often apparent in the flippancy and shallowness of current literature does not openly preach atheism, it very often attacks us Catholics, and everything that is dear to us. This is especially the case since so much of the Press has got into Masonic hands.[65]

However, that it was not so much colonial literature and colonial ideology, but the 'baser elements' of that ideology which worried Catholic nationalists and priests is clear from the following statement from the Reverend J. Fahy:

We have no quarrel with the best forms of English life, manners and literature. They are no doubt excellent and they suit English people. But it is exactly the worst forms which Ireland absorbs and assimilates, and which eat into her marrow, transmuting our people beyond the power of pulpit or platform to resist.[66]

In rural Catholic Donegal, as in Catholic enclaves elsewhere in Ulster, Catholic literature, including Catholic newspapers, were not only a means for protecting 'the unthinking' from 'pernicious influences' of 'foreign literature' – they also created a unified field of communication which linked the isolated Catholic population of Ulster to the rest of Catholic Ireland. Catholic newspapers and political pamphlets in particular provided cultural nationalists here with an alternative to the hegemonic culture of Ulster unionism, and provided priests and nationalists alike with the means to tighten their hegemonic control over 'their own people'. This concern to resist anglicisation and contain class conflict was particularly evident in urban areas, especially in and around Derry and its hinterland in Donegal. Here, it was suggested,

> the Gael has been crying for help to beat back the anglicisation he saw dragging its slimy length along – the immoral literature, the smutty postcards, the lewd plays and suggestive songs were bad, yet they were mere puffs from the foul breath of a paganised society.[67]

Worse than the 'full sewerage' of immoral literature was 'the black devil of socialism, hoop and horns', which, priests and cultural nationalists claimed, was 'invading' Donegal and other Ulster counties. The Reverend Phelan, whose speeches featured regularly in newspapers circulating throughout east Donegal, argued that:

> Our workmen are Catholic, but borrow their thoughts, phrases and standards from the infidel socialism. They denounce the power which denies their country the right to manage their own affairs, and then hitch themselves on to English trade unions and ask foreigners to dictate to Irish trade.[68]

In a statement aimed as much against the principles of trade unionism as against English-based trade unions in Ireland, Phelan declared:

> The day may come when the interest of the 'foreign union' may require you to thrust a knife into the commercial heart of your country. You answer 'Never', but I reply 'Is not the watchword of socialists "Patriotism is a Crime"?' The foreign tradesman's interest above Ireland's interest. This is treason. When Irish workers hand themselves over to foreign control they place Ireland's heart in the grip of the foreigner; and he will squeeze it every time it dares to beat against his own self-interests.[69]

Local priests together with factory-owners in Donegal and Derry defended low wages on the grounds that small factories in country districts would be 'crushed by kind friends of Ireland under the guise of coming to the relief of the low wage-earner'. An employer of outdoor labour in Inishowen's shirt industry insisted:

> employers are not philanthropists, and do not send work to the country to lose money by. Yet if wages were too high the Inishowen cottage industry would be completely destroyed.[70]

In this context thus, Catholic employers and clergy reminded workers of their duty to give employers a 'fair' day's work for what they deemed a 'fair wage', treated trade unionism and labour unrest as a threat to nationalist unity in Donegal, and extended patriotism from the political realm to the workplace.

Natural leaders and the rural bourgeoisie in nationalist Donegal

In portraying the rural bourgeoisie as the natural defenders of Donegal's moral economy, writers like Harkin, Doherty and Gwynn depicted the Hungry Forties as the final indictment of landlord rule in Ireland. In so doing they completely ignored the parsimonious response of Catholic tenant farmers, and shopkeepers, to rural poverty during and after the famine. Both these social groups held strategically important positions in mid-nineteenth century Donegal society, not least as poor law guardians responsible for indoor and outdoor relief. Like their social class peers in England and Scotland, they took great care to ensure that the local poor would not become a burden on the local rates, and that relief would be distributed only on condition that its recipients abandon all claims to land and other property. In mid-nineteenth century Donegal this led to a glut of small holdings on the market and these were frequently bought up, or rented, by 'improving' tenants and independent small farmers. Thus did the disintegration of peasant society augment the socio-economic status, heighten the political status of improving tenant farmers and consolidate bourgeois nationalist hegemony.[71] The 'emptying' of the county through emigration also extended the range of commercial farming and consolidated the power of the 'thirty acre men' and the petty bourgeoisie. The proletarianisation of Donegal's rural poor into overseas labour markets allowed those who stayed behind to add field to field, and to enter the ranks of the small but substantial propertied classes. As early as mid-century, members of this class in west Donegal were already proclaiming Ireland's right to self-determination. Thus in 1845 the guardians of Glenties poor law union claimed:

> The Irish Nation in extent of territory, in fertility of soil, in the number and industry of its inhabitants furnishes abundant means

for the maintenance of an independent legislature and requires such legislature for the due attention to the local interests and general prosperity of Ireland.[72]

Glenties poor law petitioners defended the right of the Irish race to self-determination, and argued that nationhood did not derive from 'any ordnance or statute of English Parliament' but sprang instead 'spontaneously and of necessity from the principles of self-government inherent in the position of free-born subjects of the English Crown'. Written on the eve of the great famine, this petition ironically added that:

The Union has produced the most disastrous results to Ireland. It has inhibited the Irish manufactures that existed and substituted but few indeed in their place, it has merely extinguished all legitimate commerce, it has made the exports of Ireland consist of provisions and cattle, and her imported goods manufactured in foreign countries. It has covered the land with poverty, distress and destitution. It produced the astounding spectacle of more than 2,300,000 paupers, being more than one quarter of the inhabitants of one of the most fruitful countries on the face of the globe, and these evils instead of diminishing are manifestly augmenting and spreading into a wide circle.[73]

By the late nineteenth century this petty bourgeoisie owed its hegemonic status to its economic strength, and to the fact that it had by then practically monopolised political and cultural life in Donegal. It controlled the market for agricultural produce. It practically dominated local government and was on the verge of securing property rights from the beleaguered landed ascendancy. It had long sought to ensure that poor law rates would not pose an obstacle to development in the county, including the development of modern farming practices with their revulsion against farm fragmentation.

By the turn of the century the Catholic petty bourgeoisie in Donegal had clearly come of age, and were dominant in the professions as well as in economic life. This is borne out by an analysis of the social class structure of Donegal in table 20.1 which shows that Catholic representation in selected professional and commercial occupations increased quite significantly between 1881 and 1911. These figures also show that Donegal had become a more commercialised society at the end of this period, and that the Catholic middle class, although still quite small by 1911, had benefited significantly from the breakdown of peasant society and the emergence of native capitalism. There were a

Table 20.1

Roman Catholic Representation in Business and Selected Middle Class Occupations

Occupation	1881		1911	
	Total Employed	% R.C.	Total Employed	% R.C.
Catholic Priest	88	100	121	100%
Schoolmaster/Assistant	241	73	301	80
Teacher/Professor	74	51	26	66
Civil Service Official	54	39	101	48
County and Local Official	53	23	73	36
Parish/Union/District Officer	39	33	53	76
General Shopkeeper	262	77	336	85
Merchant	145	61	160	67
Broker	15	47	33	58
Commercial Traveller	12	58	39	64
Commercial Clerk	69	55	87	49
Banker	3	00	1	00
Bank Service	44	16	52	25
Auctioneer	18	72	20	15
Barrister/Solicitor	25	20	42	36
Law Clerk	47	49	39	49
Physician	62	29	64	45
Civil Engineer	14	14	17	41
Insurance Agent	1	00	28	75
Total	1,266	60%	1,593	68%

Source: *Census of Population, County of Donegal,* 1881, 1911. Her Majesty's Stationery Office, Dublin.

number of occupations where Catholic strength was on the increase, notably civil service officers and clerks, and parish, county and poor law union officials. Catholics were also dominant in the teaching profession, and were increasingly dominant in the merchant class. However, as table 20.1 shows, Donegal's middle class was still very small in the late-nineteenth and early-twentieth centuries and Catholic priests constituted a very significant social force in the county. The total number of Catholics in these occupations was only 1,266 in 1881, and Catholic representation in this broad socio-economic grouping increased by 25 per cent in 1911.[74] Priests as a percentage of listed occupations in 1881 and 1911 was 10.6 per cent and 11.2 per cent respectively. Priests, schoolmasters and teachers formed a cohesive intelligentsia and accounted for just over 35 per cent of all Catholics in the occupations listed in table 19.1 in 1881 and 1911. However, combined they were over 25 per cent of all Catholics in a middle class socio-economic grouping comprising civil service officers and clerks, county and local officials, parish and union officials, barristers, physicians, teachers, civil engineers, merchants, brokers, auctioneers and bankers. The fact that they had state interests and were engaged in national and county politics, meant that the rural bourgeoisie were a class apart from their social subordinates in Donegal who struggled against the vicissitudes of rural capitalism.

The Catholic shopocracy and petty bourgeoisie, contrary to the assumptions of nationalist historians, were never the natural successors to the landed ascendancy in Donegal. They achieved hegemonic status by occupying socially-strategic positions, by controlling the rural economy of the county, by mixing with their social peers in the Protestant middle class, and by co-operating with such of the landed ascendancy as had survived the regular depressions affecting rural Donegal from the 1830s onwards. The section that follows focuses more centrally on the relationship between Catholic priests and the petty middle class, and discusses their contribution to the consolidation of bourgeois nationalist hegemony in Donegal in the late-nineteenth and early- twentieth centuries.

Priestly politics and nationalist hegemony in Donegal

The population of Donegal in 1881 was 206,035, of whom 76 per cent were Roman Catholics, 12 per cent belonged to the Church of Ireland, and 10 per cent were Presbyterians.[75] By 1911 the population of the county had dropped by almost 20 per cent, but Roman Catholics constituted 79 per cent of the total population of 168,537, while the Church of Ireland congregation was only 10.7 per cent and Presbyterians 8.9 per cent of the total (tables 20.2, 20.3).[76] The ratio of clergy to population increased for all denominations in this period, particularly in respect of the overall Catholic population, as the numbers of priests and nuns in the county increased by 38 per cent and 124 per cent respectively. This meant that the ratio of priests and nuns to the overall Catholic population had risen sharply from 1:1,260 in 1881 to 1:652 in 1911.

As leaders of 'their people', priests were responsible for instilling a sense of patriotism in the Donegal poor while simultaneously reminding them of their Christian and political duties as Irishmen and Irishwomen to support Catholic nationalists. Far from being mere instruments in the hands of the petty bourgeoisie, Catholic priests occupied socially strategic positions within the petty bourgeois world and were at once structured by, and had a powerful structuring influence within, that world. Their numerical strength and political

Table 20.2

The Population of Donegal by Religious Affiliation, 1881

Religion	Population	Percentage Total
Roman Catholic	157,608	76.5
Protestant Episcopalian	24,759	12.0
Presbyterian	20,784	10.1
Methodist	2,014	1.0
Other Persuasions	870	0.4
Total	206,035	100

Source: Census of Population, county of Donegal, 1881, Her Majesty's Stationery Office, Dublin.

pragmatism cast Donegal priests in the role of 'organisational men' in the late-nineteenth century and early-twentieth century. One priest-historian described fellow priests in Clogher diocese in the early twentieth century as follows:

> ... they were men of zeal and activity and solid piety. It is administrative and apostolic activity that they favour rather than literary and intellectual activity. In this the differ from their confrères in mainland Europe. They prefer to build and develop church, school and parochial house, as generally their pre-decessors did when they restored the faith to Western Europe in the eighth and ninth centuries. They are men of deep and remark-able prayer and piety, of upright and sensible Christian lives. They are very much men of the church, faithful to their bishop, regular and methodical in their spirituality and their duties. There is a subtle interplay of action and reaction between these men and their parishioners, those faithful, modest, critical and humorous people with whom they deal ... Above all they are people's priests, sprung from the people and though coming back to them after years of higher education in seminary or university in Ireland or abroad, they are at one with the people ... They were never revolutionaries though sometimes innovators. They adhered to what was tried and found to be good.[77]

A better description of priests as a Gramscian 'organic intelligentsia' could scarcely be found. However, this depiction of priests as men who were 'at one with their people' requires considerable qualification in the case of rural Donegal. Far from simply being 'sprung from the people', priests in Donegal tended to derive from small farming and middle-class families as these alone could afford the expense of training a son for the priesthood. As the organisers of their communities, Catholic priests were able to dictate social and political morality in Donegal. They used their considerable social influence to police the political consciousness of their communities and, like their political confrères in the richer heartlands of the south of Ireland, supported the political objectives of the rural middle class against the landed ascendancy during the Land War in the 1880s. They condemned all expressions of rural radicalism when this threatened the interests of the middling tenantry, and preached the politics of moderation and national consensus. To have acted otherwise would have been to attack the social and political edifice upon which they depended.

Table 20.3

The Population of Donegal by Religious Affiliation, 1911

Religion	Population	Percentage Total
Roman Catholic	133,021	78.9
Protestant Episcopalian	18,020	10.7
Presbyterian	15,016	10.1
Methodist	1,698	8.9
Other Persuasions	782	1.4
Total	168,537	100

Source: Census of Population, County of Donegal, 1911, Her Majesty's Stationery Office, Dublin.

Recent studies of the social outlook and political role of priests throughout late nineteenth- and early twentieth-century Ireland have stressed the fact that priests often acted as social and political mediators between dominant and subordinate sectors of rural and urban society.[78] This was particularly the case in Donegal where priests were the chief, and often the only, mediators between the rural poor and the emergent bourgeoisie. In his political portrait of priests in mid-nineteenth century Tipperary, O'Shea has argued that the priesthood here by the 1860s had:

> largely come to grips with spiritual and ecclesiastical problems. Aided by synodical guidelines these priests imposed a large measure of Catholic discipline on society, as well as making frequent examinations of their consciences. Following the dramatical upheaval of the famine ... they found themselves in a

Plate 20.7   The official opening of Carndonagh Alcohol Factory, 1936. One of five
               alcohol factories opened in underdeveloped rural areas by the
               government, the turf-fired Carndonagh factory was one of the few
               industrial projects sponsored by the government in Donegal. It used
               potatoes and molasses to produce industrial alcohol. The two-tier social
               division in this photograph illustrates the strong class distinctions
               separating workers from the Catholic petty bourgeoisie in Donegal in the
               1930s. It also emphasises the central 'organisational' role of Catholic
               priests in regional industrial development in Donegal.
               Source: Harkin and McCarroll, 1984.

> society dominated by their own kith and kin, the tenant farmers
> who were the bastions of this church spiritually and financially.
> Not only could the clergy identify with this class on a social and
> spiritual level, but their respective politics were ... comfortingly
> compatible.[79]

O'Shea has shown that a mixture of Catholic theology, social class
influence, and public opinion directed the socio-political actions of
priests in Tipperary. He also argued that it was precisely through their
affinity with the middling tenantry that priests were 'sucked into the
vortex of politics'. However, while O'Shea has painted an excellent
portrait of 'priestly politics' in one of the richer heartlands of post-
famine Ireland, he fails to allow for regional differences in the social
class origins and political functions of priests in peripheral counties like
Donegal, Mayo, Clare and Kerry. His categorisation of Tipperary priests
as a 'peasant priesthood' is particularly inappropriate, given, as he
himself has shown, that most priests here derived from the substantial
tenantry and from the middle-class shopocracy. Smyth's survey of the

Plate 20.8   *The forgotten 'local heroes' of Catholic Donegal.*
This group photograph, taken in October 1945, shows workers responsible for building the imposing Church of the Sacred Heart, Carndonagh. Front row: John McLaughlin, John Doherty, John Canny, Laurence McFarland, Paddy McDermott, Barney McLaughlin, Denis Harkin. Second row: Hugh Doherty, Sam Irwin, Denis McLaughlin, Paddy O'Neill, Father Bonner, Denis Doherty, Dick Doherty, Mickey Gibbons, Hughie McGonagle. Third row: Pat McClure, Jack McDermott, Michael Thomas McLaughlin, Unknown, Patsy Doherty, Barney Lafferty, Benny Doherty, Eddie Grant, Tommy Hirrell, Mickey Canny, Leslie Finton. Back row: Barney Long, Hugh Toye, John McGuinness, John McLaughlin, Jimmy Long, Jack McDaid, Willie Gordon, E. McEleny.
Source: Harkin and McCarroll, 1984.

class origins of Catholic priests originating in one Tipperary parish, Clogheen-Burncourt, in the period 1900-1950, confirms this and suggests that the most fertile breeding grounds for priests were rich agricultural lowlands and county towns.[80] O'Shea, Smyth and Whelan point to the fact that the big farmer was the progenitor of the vast majority of Tipperary priests, especially the diocesan clergy, and that small farms were barren ground for vocations.[81]

Preliminary analysis of the social origins of priests in late nineteenth- and early twentieth-century Donegal suggest that here, as in other rural Ulster counties, Catholic priests were of humbler origins than their confrères in the richer heartlands of southern Ireland. Thus they were as likely to derive from medium, as opposed to large, farms throughout Donegal, Derry and Tyrone, and a significant proportion originated from the emergent middle class comprising shopkeepers, publicans, grocers, Gardaí Siochána, hoteliers, butchers, and clerical workers.[82]

Their humbler social class origins not only reduced the social distance between priests and poorer parishioners in Donegal – it also made it all the easier for them to act as an organic intelligentsia who not only represented but actively articulated what they considered the best interests of 'their' people. Those Donegal priests raised in the mixed nationalist and unionist shatter-belt of mid-Ulster were often brought up with an awareness of the second-class status of Catholic nationalists in unionist Ulster and brought to their pastoral duties in Donegal a missionary zeal to simultaneously elevate and nationalise those under their care.

However, in Donegal, as elsewhere in rural Ireland, the Catholic clergy was not a monolithic group, and the politics of its members could range from political indifference, through Romantic nationalism to constitutional nationalism. Thus, while the overtly political clergy could present themselves as 'at one with their people', they shared the social class outlook of the substantial tenantry and petty middle class from whom they derived and the politics of both groups were almost completely compatible. Moreover, even the politically indifferent among the clergy could be classified as nationalists in the wider sense of being nation-builders who instilled nationalist sentiments in those under their charge and defended nation-building as a political project that was above party politics. As O'Shea's study has also shown, priests in post-famine Ireland had specific class interests and rarely behaved in a socially altruistic manner. His description of the political role of priests in post-famine Tipperary could equally be applied to the clergy in late nineteenth-century Donegal:

> The slowness and limited extent of clerical involvement in labour reform underline an unwillingness by many priests to ruffle the harmony between themselves and their kinsfolk. The clergy, for all their concern with famine, emigration, starvation and clearances, did not highlight the plight of the labourers on any notable scale because it was not part of the Tenant League, a body composed mainly of the wealthier type farmers.[83]

Social class background and territorial context were not the only factors influencing the political outlook of priests in Donegal. As spiritual leaders in areas practically devoid of a secular intelligentsia priests were perceived as the 'natural leaders' of their communities which in turn meant that Catholic social teaching and religious morality met very little opposition. Priests in Donegal, for example, acted as social catalysts and served as convenors of, and orators at, social and political gatherings throughout the county. They frequently acted as political and moral censors, whose approval was crucial to the success, or failure, of local political or other initiatives.

By the turn of the century Catholic priests invariably made patriotism and loyalty to Catholic Ireland a moral obligation binding on all Catholics in Donegal:

> Patriotism is a Christian virtue, just as really as truthfulness, obedience, gratitude are virtues. It is a virtue that binds us in conscience, in the first place, to honour and reverence the country of our birth, and in the second place, to make sacrifices proportionate to the need of our country when she requires them. Patriotism is not a matter that we are free to practise or disregard according to our pleasure. The man who acts unpatriotically is guilty in the sight of God, just as the man who lies or is intemperate is guilty in the sight of God; and if the unpatriotic act be of a grave nature, it is a crime which, unatoned for, will carry with it the penalty of eternal damnation. Patriotism is really a subdivision of the virtue of piety that obliges us to honour and reverence our parents as the authors of our being.[84]

In a Lenten pastoral letter read at all masses in one Donegal diocese on the first Sunday of Lent, 1901, Bishop O'Doherty of Derry prayed that 'God in his mercy would send a man who will not seek his own exaltation but to raise Ireland and her people to her proper place among the nations of the world'. He also urged his priests to play an active role in nation-building and insisted that:

> ... with us the cause of faith and fatherland have ever been inseparably intertwined; that priests and people have worked together as one body; and we have reason to fear those who would try to separate them now, and to teach the people that politics and religion are no longer one, but two distinct issues.[85]

In March 1913 the bishop of Raphoe was similarly stressing the links between priests and their people, and prayed that:

> under God's grace and mercy, the bonds between priests and people, so indispensable to national concord, would never be broken, while the Irish priest found, as he did, his place by preference among the poor and the toilers, giving them the priceless sympathy of his warm heart.[86]

In another sermon Bishop O'Doherty of Derry defended political caution, gradualism and a constitutional route to national self-determination as preferable to any radical break with the past, including, not least, any radical fracture between priests and 'their people', arguing:

> It is with nations as it is with individuals, nature knows no harsh transition. A crushed bone does not recover in a day. We could only abandon ourselves to despair if, without remembering our respective historical conditions, we were to compare our historical conditions with that of any of the European nations whose homes are hives of industry and whose traditions of industry are the growth of centuries. Their government was sunshine and love, when ours was a boulder from an iceberg when it was not a gibbet.[87]

From sermons like these a paternalism or hegemony was constructed which was accepted by both the dominated and the dominant, and afforded a fragile bridge across the social contradictions separating priests and the rural poor. For men like O'Doherty, as indeed for the priests and nuns under his charge, Catholic nationalism was not only a strategy for underpinning solidarity among the poor by linking them to their social and political 'betters' – it was furthermore a cultural defence against 'pernicious' influences from England and Scotland.

Bishops and priests in Donegal frequently defended Catholicism against unionist charges that Irish Catholics were innately inferior to Ulster Protestants and that 'Catholicity' was an obstacle to social and economic development. The fact that they were responsible for building schools, churches, and parochial halls throughout the county made it easier for Donegal's poor to see priests as socially progressive and worthy of respect. To many indeed it appeared that they were literally constructing a Roman Catholic Ireland among the hills and fields of Donegal. The parish priest of Buncrana described the relationship between Roman Catholicism and nation-building in Ireland:

> We are the children of long ages of struggling and servile existence. Throughout a struggle which would have crushed the heart of any other people we clung to the jewel of religion though we lost the casket, nationality; and if our national character has not been preserved so well as our national faith, we have surely good reason as a people to thank God that so many splendid virtues have survived the wreck. It is from the records of our past enforced degradation that we acquire confidence in our future destiny. The degradation of a country is the work of centuries, and though its freedom can be achieved with the swiftness of a storm, yet the recovery of a nation's liberty is often a gradual, uphill work.[88]

Sermons like these were regularly preached at Sunday mass throughout Donegal in the late-nineteenth and early-twentieth centuries. They not only suggested that patriotism was a Christian duty and nationalism was the epitome of political virtue – they made the poor of Donegal defer to 'their betters' in matters political, and made it difficult for those attending mass on Sunday to know where religion left off and where middle-class social morality and nationalist politics began.

Conclusion

This chapter began with a discussion on the relevance of Gramscian theory to the study of nationalism. It then proceeded to stress that people and places throughout late nineteenth- and early twentieth-century Donegal were never naturally or primordially nationalist or unionist. Instead, it has been shown, they became such through a process of capitalist modernisation and state-centralisation. However, it has also shown that, contrary to Gellner, nationalism, as in Irish nationalism, and national separatism, as in Ulster unionism, were attributes to places as well as people.[89] For that reason, as this chapter has argued, places matter both to nationalists and to students of nationalism, not least because they are the lifeworlds wherein the process of ethnogenesis occur, and because they have regularly been invested with a high degree of symbolic, geopolitical and economic significance by nationalists and national separatists. Thus, for example, late nineteenth-century Donegal was regularly paraded as a heartland of Gaeldom and rural conservatism and was widely regarded as an important building block of a Catholic nationalist Ireland. The fact that unionists here were in no position to assert hegemonic control over a county that was literally a world apart from the heartlands of unionist Ulster made it all the easier for Catholic nationalists, including nationalist historians, antiquarians and the indigenous petty bourgeoisie, to hold Donegal for 'Mother Ireland'.

The dialectical approach to political regionalism adopted in this chapter has a number of advantages over autonomist, reductionist and structuralist models of nationalism favoured by Smith, Gellner, Nairn and Wallerstein.[90] Firstly, it accommodates a political geography of nationalism which avoids the pitfalls in Hechter's internal colonialist and in Smith's cultural explanation of nationalist resurgence. It also avoids the excesses of 'two nations' theory and economic reductionism in Nairn's account of nationalism and national separatism. Secondly, while recognising the centrality of the *intelligentsia* to the processes of state centralisation and ethnogenesis, unlike Smith I have treated them less as an autonomous social force and more as representatives of bourgeois interests, including bourgeois cultural and political interests.

Finally, it transcends the nationalist parameters within which so much local history and so much discussion about nationalism have been entrapped. Where the nationalist historiographical tradition has not 'naturalised' nationalism, it has traced its roots to exogenous causes, notably to 'English misrule' in Ireland. In so doing nationalists have ignored the indigenous roots of bourgeois nationalist hegemony in rural Donegal and the very rootedness of nationalism to the cultural and economic landscape of the county from at least the late nineteenth-century.

This chapter has also focused on nation-building and nationalism in Donegal in order to redress an imbalance in existing literature which has tended to adopt either a national focus, and therefore devalued place in the study of nationalism, or concentrated on historic heartlands of Irish nationalism outside Ulster. It has been as much a study of failed unionism as a study of successful nationalism in the forgotten 'other Ulster' beyond the heartlands of unionist power. This 'other Ulster' was far less urbanised and indeed less commercialised than the industrialised east of the province. It was also far more homogeneous than the mixed Catholic and Protestant shatter belt of mid-Ulster, the great 'contested terrain' over which unionists and nationalists struggled to assert hegemonic control. By the late nineteenth century it was politically and economically integrated into nation-building Ireland and was nationalised from within by Catholic priests and teachers and other 'local heroes' of the nationalist cause.

Winning the plebian sectors of Donegal society to an acceptance of the statist goals of the nationalist bourgeoisie proved a more difficult task than the latter had anticipated. However, it was made all the more easier after the famine, which not only depleted the ranks of the plebian poor but hastened the 'kulakisation' of Donegal society and facilitated, not least through emigration and a reduction in farm fragmentation, the emergence of substantial peasant and petty bourgeois sectors. In this way nation-building forces operating at the national level intersected with those operating at the local level to form a social bloc of petty bourgeois interest groups capable of exerting hegemonic control over all aspects of the political and economic life of the county. This was achieved not so much by the conversion of the rural poor of Donegal to the political creed of the petty bourgeoisie as by a 'long revolution' led by Donegal amateur historians, priests, teachers, merchants and substantial farmers. Cultural nationalists here also forged local with national identities by literally highlighting relics on the Celtic landscape and stressing the authenticity of local over 'foreign' customs. Thus priests and their lay subordinates used chapel and school to 'nationalise' the rural poor and to 'Gaelicise' the landscape of Donegal by peopling it with pre-colonial saints and scholars and littering it with 'mass rocks', holy wells and the relics of a pre-colonial culture.

Far from being political mediators who carried the gospel of nationalism from dominant to subordinate sectors in Donegal society, Catholic priests were organisational men in their own right. The cultural and ideological markers which they used to define Irishmen and Irishwomen accorded well with the political and economic interests of the petty bourgeoisie from whom they derived. Their socially-strategic, and often unchallenged positions in Donegal society meant that they were able to lay the bare architectural framework of a cultural Irish nationalism such that alternatives to their worldview were often literally unthinkable. Thus they facilitated the ethnicisation and the controlled modernisation of Donegal society and made ethnic identity superior to class identity by treating class conflict as 'foreign' to Gaelic Catholic Ireland. In so doing they channelled class identities into ethnic moulds, portrayed the subservient sectors of rural society as paragons of Gaelic virtue, and 'sanctified' people and places throughout Donegal for the cause of Catholic nationalism.

Acknowledgements

The author would like to thank Maura Harkin and Eileen McCarroll for permission to use photographs from their pictorial study, *Carndonagh*; Seán Beattie, Croragh, Culdaff, for his help in identifying individuals in several of the group photographs in this chapter, and Dr Willie Nolan, Department of Geography, University College Dublin, for reading and commenting upon an earlier draft of this chapter. The usual *caveat* applies regarding the author's responsibility.

References
1. S. Clark, 'Agrarian class structure and collective action in nineteenth-century Ireland' in *British Journal of Sociology*, 29 (1978), pp 23-39; S. Clark and J. S. Donnelly (eds), *Irish peasants: violence and political unrest 1780-1914* (Manchester, 1983); D. Fitzpatrick, *Politics and Irish life* (Dublin, 1976); P. Gibbon, *The origins of Ulster unionism* (Manchester, 1979); W. Nolan, *Fassadinin: land, settlement and society in south-east Ireland* (Dublin, 1979).
2. P. Ó Gallachobhair, *The history of landlordism in Donegal* (Ballyshannon, 1975); B. Bonner, *Our Inis Eoghain heritage* (Dublin, 1972).
3. J. MacLaughlin and J. Agnew, 'Hegemony and the regional question: the political geography of regional industrial policy in Northern Ireland, 1945-1972' in *Annals of the Association of American Geographers*, 76 (1986), pp 247-61.
4. A. Gramsci, *Selections from political writings* (London, 1977), p. 56.
5. R. Williams, *Problems in materialism and culture* (London, 1980), p. 37.
6. MacLaughlin and Agnew, 'Regional industrial policy', p. 249.
7. A. Gramsci, 'The southern question' in *The modern prince and other writings* (New York, 1957), pp 25-96.
8. Gramsci, 'Southern question', p. 57.

9.   Gramsci, 'Political writings', pp 2-23; 44-51.
10. J. Joll, *Antonio Gramsci* (London, 1978), p. 124.
11. MacLaughlin and Agnew, 'Regional industrial policy', p. 249.
12. K. Marx, 'The class struggles in France 1848-1850' in K. Marx and F. Engels, *Selected works* (London, 1950), p. 231.
13. E. Gellner, *Thought and change* (Chicago, 1969); Idem, *Nations and nationalism* (London, 1983).
14. *Londonderry Standard*, 25 March, 1912.
15. J. MacLaughlin, 'Towards a critical geography of Irish partition' in *Espace, Populations, Societes* (1992-3), pp 292-4; J. MacLaughlin, The political geography of unionism and nationalism in nineteenth- and early twentieth-century Ulster, unpublished Ph.D. thesis (1987), Department of Geography, Syracuse University, New York.
16. *Census of Ireland*, 1911.
17. G. A. Lecky, *In the days of the Laggan presbytery* (Dublin, 1908), p. 12.
18. W. J. Hudson, 'The historian's social function', in J. Moses (ed.), *Historical disciplines and culture in Australia* (St Lucia, 1979), pp 56-79.
19. J. Sheehy, *The rediscovery of Ireland's past: the celtic revival, 1833-1930* (London, 1980), p. 7.
20. J. MacLaughlin, 'The political geography of nation-building and nationalism in social sciences' in *Political Geography Quarterly*, 5 (1986), p. 300.
21. E. Hobsbawm, 'Some reflections on the break-up of Britain' in *New Left Review* 105 (1977), pp 3-23.
22. B. Anderson, *Imagined communities: reflections on the origins and spread of nationalism* (London, 1983); See also J. MacLaughlin, 'Reflections on nations as imagined communities' in *Journal of Multicultural and Multilingual Development*, 9 (1988), pp 449-57.
23. D. Corkery, *The hidden Ireland* (Dublin, 1924), pp 19-24.
24. J. Fahy, *Education and the nation* (Dublin, 1901), p. 7.
25. *Irish Catholic Directory*, 1915, p. 519.
26. P. Gallagher, *My story* (Dungloe, 1936), p. 45.
27. C. Levi, *Christ stopped at Eboli* (London, 1983), pp 35-7.
28. M. Cherniavsky, *Tsar and people: studies in Russian myths* (New Haven, 1961); L. Poliakov, *The aryan myth* (London, 1982); G. A. Williams, Madoc: *the making of a myth* (London, 1979); W. A. Wilson, *Folklore and nationalism in modern Finland* (Bloomington, 1976).
29. Cherniavsky, *Tsar and people*, pp 91-4.
30. W. J. Doherty, *Inis-Owen and Tir Connell* (Dublin, 1895).
31. Private correspondence from Bishop E. Daly, Derry.
32. Doherty, *Inis-Owen*, p. 488.
33. Ibid., p. 85.
34. Ibid., p. 10.
35. Ibid., p. 7.
36. Bonner, *Inish Eoghain Heritage* (Dublin, 1972).
37. Ibid., pp 1-2.
38. Ibid., p. 1.
39. Doherty, *Inis-Owen*, p. 7.
40. Bonner, *Inish Eoghain Heritage;* B. Lacy, *Archaeological survey of county Donegal* (Lifford, Co. Donegal, 1983).
41. M. Harkin, *Inishowen: history, traditions and antiquities* (Londonderry, 1867), p. 199.

42. S. Gwynn, *Highways and byways of Donegal and Antrim* (London, 1899), p. 4.
43. Ibid., p. 15.
44. E. Balibar, *Race and nationalism* (New York, 1991), p. 43.
45. James Anderson, 'Ideological variations in Ulster during Ireland's first home rule crisis' in E. Kofman and C. Williams (eds), *Community, conflict, partition and nationalism* (London, 1955).
46. J. Mac Laughlin, 'Regional social history, nationalists and the famine', in *Journal of North West Archaeological and Historical Society*, 1 (1984), pp 26-37.
47. E. Curtis, *Apes and angels* (London, 1972), p. 124.
48. Harkin, *Inishowen*, p. 46.
49. Ibid., p. 47.
50. M. Heiberg and M. Escudero, 'Sabino de Arana, la logico del nacionalismo' in *Materiales*, 5 (Barcelona, 1977), pp 32-47.
51. Harkin, *Inishowen*, p. 45.
52. Ibid., p. 47.
53. C. Dewey, 'Celtic agrarian legislation and the celtic revival' in *Past and Present*, 64 (1974), pp 30-71.
54. Ibid., pp 32-5.
55. J. H. Tukes, *Donegal: suggestions for improvement of congested districts and extension of railways, fisheries etc.* (London, 1889), p. 44.
56. J. Maurice (ed.), *Letters from Donegal* (London, 1886), p. 56.
57. J. MacLaughlin, 'Ireland: an "emigrant nursery" in the world economy' in *International Migration*, xxxi, 1 (1993), pp 149-70.
58. G. R. C. Keep, 'Official opinion on Irish emigration in the later nineteenth century' in *I.E.R.*, lxxxi (1954), p. 413; J. MacLaughlin, *Ireland: The Emigrant Nursery of the World* (Cork, 1994).
59. E. Weber, *Peasants into Frenchmen; the modernisation of rural France* (Stanford, 1977).
60. M. O'Riordan, *Catholicity and progress in Ireland* (London, 1905), pp 446-7.
61. Harkin, *Inishowen*, p. 167.
62. *Christian Brothers handbook* (Dublin, 1952), p. 11.
63. Lenten pastoral, St Columb's College, Derry (1905).
64. T. A. Murphy, *The literature crusade in Ireland* (Limerick, 1912), p. 21.
65. Ibid., pp 18-20.
66. Fahy, *Education and the nation*, p. 7.
67. M. J. Phelan, 'A gaelicised or socialised Ireland – which?' in *The Catholic Bulletin* (1913), p. 773.
68. Ibid., p. 772.
69. Ibid., p. 773.
70. *The Derry Journal*, October 25, 1915.
71. Mac Laughlin, 'Regional social history', pp 26-8.
72. Minutes, Glenties Poor Law Union, September 26, 1846.
73. Ibid., September 26, 1846.
74. *Census of Ireland*, 1881; 1911.
75. *Census of Ireland*, 1881.
76. *Census of Ireland*, 1911.
77. P. Donnelly, *A history of the parish of Ardstraw West and Castlederg* (Strabane, 1978), pp 113-17.
78. J. O'Shea, *Priests and people in post-famine Tipperary* (Dublin, 1983); K. Whelan, 'The Catholic Church in Co. Tipperary, 1700-1900' in W. Nolan (ed.), *Tipperary: history and society* (Dublin, 1985), pp 215-55.

79. O'Shea, *Priests and people,* pp 232-3.
80. W. J. Smyth, 'The social geography of an Irish rural parish: a case study from South Tipperary', unpublished Ph.D. thesis (1969), Department of Geography, University College, Dublin, 1969.
81. Whelan, 'The Catholic Church in Co. Tipperary', p. 244.
82. Donnelly, *A history of the parish of Ardstraw West;* E. Daly, 'Priests of Derry, 1820-1905' in *Derriana: Journal of the Derry Diocesan Historical Society* (1980), pp 26-34.
83. O'Shea, *Priests and people,* pp 241-6.
84. C. Burbage, 'The obligation of patriotism' in *The Catholic Bulletin,* iii, 11 (1913), 593-607.
85. Lenten Pastoral, St Columb's College, Derry, 1901.
86. *The Irish Catholic Directory* (1915), p. 519.
87. Ibid.
88. *The Derry Journal,* June 5, 1905.
89. Gellner, *Thought and change,* p. 210.
90. A. D. Smith, *Theories of nationalism* (London, 1971); E. Gellner, *Nations and nationalism* (London, 1983); T. Nairn, *The break-up of Britain* (London, 1977); I. Wallerstein, *The modern world system* (New York, 1974).

Chapter 21

SEASONAL MIGRATION TO THE LAGAN AND SCOTLAND

ANNE O'DOWD

*Níl fear ar bith is fearr a dtig leis scéal innse fá'n ampla ná an fear a
tháinig fríd a' tsúisteáil féin.*[1]

Hiúdaí Sheáinín first went away from his home to work when he was
fourteen years old. He had not started school until he was ten but, by
his own admission, he was never a great scholar and he was not too
upset when his father sent him to work with a farmer in the Lagan.
Hiúdaí told his story to Eoghan Ó Domhnaill and it was published in
1940. He is not alone in having his story recorded but, thanks to him,
several other Donegal writers and the diligence of folklore collectors,
the facts and figures relating to seasonal and temporary wanderings of
Donegal men, women and children can be fairly accurately told.

Hiúdaí's story is similar in many respects to so many from county
Donegal who have left us details of their lives. The other Donegal
writers who have published autobiographies, including Micí
MacGabhann, Patrick Gallagher and Máire (Séamus Ó Grianna), also
Patrick MacGill, whose work is semi-autobiographical, and Peadar
O'Donnell who wrote about the people he knew, give remarkably
similar details in their work in respect to the boys and girls hired at the
hiring fairs and working in the Lagan, and the older men working with
farmers at various farm jobs in the Lothians of Scotland.[2] The repetitive
mentioning of specific issues, which on the one hand might be seen as
plagiarism, can also be viewed as emphasising the importance of
impressions and perceptions of the outside world created in the home
communities of the migratory labourers.

Aodh Ó Domhnaill, the Hiúdaí of *Scéal Hiúdaí Sheáinín,* was born
in Rann na Feirste, county Donegal, in 1853. His story telling us about
his time as a migratory worker is the most straight-forward, the least
romanticised and the earliest of the writings about these workers.
Hiúdaí was first hired at the hiring fair in Letterkenny in 1867 at which
time the hiring fair was still held in the old town; it was later to move
to the main street. Typical of so many first timers he was delighted

when his father told him to get himself ready to go to the Lagan; he had never been away from home before and, in his innocence, did not anticipate the loneliness which was to hit him within a fortnight of arriving there.

His mother had made a pair of footless stockings and had prepared his bundle in the couple of days before he left home. This was not an onerous task as the bundle consisted only of an old shirt and a pair of working trousers. As he set out with his friend, Seán Ó Baoighill, who was already crying with loneliness just a few miles from home, Hiúdaí began to feel the pangs of regret but quickly steeled himself with the reminder that the reason for his journey was the dire poverty of his family's circumstances. They walked to Letterkenny – a tough journey of some thirty miles – and frequently got lost along the way. It was not until they met two others on the same errand, two experienced workers, that they found courage. They arrived in Letterkenny on the evening of their departure from home and got lodgings there for the night. The following morning they arose early and wandered through the town wondering at all they saw – the size of the buildings and even the size of the windows in them. Hiúdaí was hired by a farmer in Drum Caoin at a rate of £1 for the six-month term.

When he arrived at the farmer's house he felt immediately lonely in a strange place where no one spoke Irish – his mother tongue. His supper was a bowl of buttermilk and a few potatoes; his bed a load of straw thrown on the ground and an old blanket and a couple of empty bags. The work he had to do was to herd cattle all day, a lonely enough job but, in Hiúdaí's circumstances, made all the more lonely when we consider that he could not converse with anybody he met. His employer was obviously a sensitive man and he soon introduced Hiúdaí to a local woman who could speak Irish. Hiúdaí put in the season until the November fair when he walked into Letterkenny again for the journey home. He got a pair of shoes made for himself from his earnings.

Hiúdaí spent the subsequent five or six seasons working on the Lagan and when he was around twenty years of age, he made the adventurous journey to Scotland as his people before him had done for at least two generations. The Lagan had toughened him in preparation for his future life as a migratory worker. The workers traditionally set out on St John's day and walked to Letterkenny where they stayed for the night, continuing on the tramp to Derry the following day.

They arrived at the quayside already 'briste, brúighte, brónach, cumhadheamhail' (broken, beaten, sad, lonely) only to face a sickening passage to Glasgow. A bed in a lodging house in the city gave them rest for the night, but also advice from one of the lodgers that they might find work on the railway at Wishaw. They journeyed out on the chance that some work would be available for them at their destination. They did not get a start as navvies, but the helpful gaffer on the job suggested that they might get work thinning turnips near Carluke. For the majority of workers the vagaries of the weather meant unpredictability in the timing of the ripening of the crops; when the farmers did not have work for them they tramped about the country-side and suffered subsequent hardship and hunger until the situation improved.

In Hiúdaí's case, he did get work thinning turnips near Carluke. He had no previous experience of this task, but was taught the necessary skills by one of his companions. From Carluke, he journeyed on to Kelso as soon as news filtered through that the early harvest was ready for reaping. He had a hard time keeping up the pace set by the older and more experienced harvesters, but did remain on the farm until the end of the season. When he returned home he was no longer a boy or a youth; in the eyes of the community, from his experiences of his first season working with the farmers in Scotland, he had passed through a rite of passage and become a man.[3]

Mící Mac Gabhann's story was published in 1958 and in it he tells us about his working life from the age of nine years in 1874, when he had his first taste of service and left his home in Doire Chonaire, Cloghaneely, for the hiring fair in Letterkenny. Mící spent six, six-month terms hired in the Lagan. In Glenveigh he worked as a herd boy and in Drom Eochaille (some five miles on the Lifford side of Letterkenny) he worked milking cows. His mother had gone with him to the hiring fair in Letterkenny to make the bargain with the farmer and to ensure, as much as she could in the brief encounter with the farmer at the fair, that her son was in safe hands. Mící's memory of his time as a servant boy in the Lagan he described tersely and alliterately with the words: 'Sclábhaíocht, slathaíocht, streachailt agus síorobair gan sos gan scíth'. (slavery, slimness, struggling and working all the time without a rest.) He continued to Scotland in 1880, when he was just fifteen years old, and spent five seasons coming and going, working at various jobs from mining in Coatbridge, to thinning turnips in Berwickshire and thinning turnips and harvesting in Dunbar. At the mature age of twenty, Mící Mac Gabhann grew tired of life as a migratory worker and set sail for America.[4]

Máire, like Hiúdaí Sheáinín, was also from Rann na Feirste, and he went to the Lagan for the first time in 1903. However, unlike Hiúdaí, he was hired at the hiring fair in Strabane having walked from his home to Croithlí via Tom na hAithnighe, Bean na Lochlannach and Carracamáin. In Croithlí he journeyed by train to Manorcunningham where he again took to his feet and walked the remaining eight miles to Strabane. Like Hiúdaí, he observed much and was filled with wonder and amazement at all that he saw in Strabane. He, too, was struck with loneliness when he went out to the farm at Guirtín, where he worked herding and milking cattle, so much so that he ran away and returned home complaining that he had been sent to the worst farm on the Lagan!

When he was sixteen, Máire set off for Scotland with his father and neighbour, but he did not experience anything like the same hardship that Aodh Ó Domhnaill had suffered some years previously. They went straight to Dolphintown where they worked thinning turnips – his father and their neighbour being readily at hand to show the young Máire how to do the work. He was still young, however, and not strong enough for the first few years to work at the harvest. He did find work gathering the soft fruit crop and in his years working in Scotland he thinned turnips, gathered soft fruit, picked potatoes and harvested corn.[5]

These three stories give us some idea of the lifestyle of the migratory worker from Donegal: their apprenticeship on the Lagan; the excitement they experienced in going to the hiring fair; the different language and culture which they met while they were away from home; the loneliness which struck so many of the youngsters; the workers' experiences in Scotland in places throughout the Lothians and in Berwickshire, Ayrshire, Stirling, Perth and Fife as general farmworkers, potato pickers, navvies and mineworkers.

In fact, throughout the time that Donegal workers were travelling as migratory labourers to Scotland they were graded in terms of what they themselves saw as a hierarchy of workers. On the one hand there was the *imirce shóisearach* – the migration of young people to the Lagan – and on the other there was the *imirce shinsearach,* which consisted of the various groups of older men who worked in Scotland as general farm labourers, navvies and miners, the groups of men, women and children who worked as potato diggers and pickers from Ayrshire to Perth and the men and women who were employed as herring gutters and packers.

At the bottom of the scale were the young and inexperienced boys and girls who went to the Lagan, and the older men who were not fit for any onerous tasks, who worked during the summer months harvesting the soft fruit crop in Scotland; those who did not have a great deal of general farm experience went potato picking in squads consisting of men, women and children; any man able to reap with a sickle worked with the farmers throughout the summer as soon as the harvest was ready to reap; men and women travelled around the Irish, Scottish and English coasts as herring gutters and packers, and men interspersed periods of general farm work which they found here and there with working in the mines and as navvies.[6] However, before we look at the migratory movement from one county we will see how the Donegal workers fit into an overall picture of Irish migratory labourers.

Working in Ireland – the early years

As with all population movements the history of the temporary worker moving away from home in order that he could afford to continue living there, has a history of its own. Aodh Ó Domhnaill, Micí Mac Gabhann and Séamus Ó Grianna, we remember, told us of their experiences hired in the Lagan. Working in the Lagan formed one part of an internal movement of workers which, in an Irish context, was predominantly from western areas of Ireland to counties in the east. The external and internal movements were of comparable size around the 1830s, by which time it is quite probable that the internal movement had already passed its peak. We first read about the internal wanderings of workers at the relatively late date of the seventeenth century, and the evidence for these early years survives mainly in the poetry and lives of the poets. These early references refer to fairly restricted parts of the country; workers from Armagh travelled to Meath, for example, Roscommon *spailpíní* worked in Leinster and Kerry *spailpíní* worked in east Munster. The tradition of the hiring fair, which had its origin in medieval statutes, was also introduced to Ireland at this time primarily to facilitate the new landholders in Ulster, after the plantation, to find a convenient and available labour supply at specific times of the year.

The extent and scale of the internal movement had increased significantly by the opening decades of the nineteenth century when, by 1815, the economy collapsed at the end of the Napoleonic wars. The subsequent decrease in demand for agricultural produce and the ensuing poverty, two very wet years in 1816 and 1817 and attendant fevers, combined to produce destitution in many areas. As a result, thousands upon thousands of people began to move out of their home areas to beg and seek work elsewhere. As many as 3,000 people from Roscommon and Mayo had travelled to Kilcock, county Kildare; hundreds of destitute poor from Sligo, Leitrim, Cavan and Monaghan found their way to Dunboyne and Swords while workers from Westmeath, Longford, Laois and Offaly found harvest work in Kildare. Many thousands of others made the journey across the Irish sea, a journey which they saw as their only means of survival.[7]

Working in England – the early years

Ireland has long had contact with her sister island but it was in the middle ages that the first door was opened for what was in a matter of centuries to become a flood of seasonal and migratory workers travelling to Great Britain. An ordinance issued in 1349 was supposedly concerned with the survival of master-workman arrangements; in effect the ordinance marked the beginning of the infringement of the English labourer's freedom of movement in that he was instructed to work specifically for those who most required his services and to accept the fixed rate of pay for the area.

These restrictions led to a shortage of labourers in many areas and we know that already by 1388 a statute compelled the non-agricultural labourer population – the craftsmen and others whose work was not deemed to be urgent – to help at the harvest whenever the added assistance was required. Undoubtedly, news of available harvest work in England percolated through to some areas of Ireland and a trickle of workers began to cross over at this time. We do not know how many might have made the journey or where they went to work. What undoubtedly started as a trickle, however, soon gained a level of significance, as already by 1413 a statute of Henry V ordered all Irish from the realm of England.

Irish workers continued to travel to England for temporary employ-ment throughout the sixteenth and seventeenth centuries, but any acceleration in the numbers travelling to Great Britain did not commence in earnest until population pressures caused their own problems in Ireland at the end of the eighteenth century. Improved communications throughout the century in road and canal building provided much needed employment, but also provided channels for the easier spread of news and, in the present context, information about the availability of work elsewhere. The Irish presence was noted throughout Great Britain in the 1700s, implying an already considerable movement of temporary agricultural workers. At the beginning of the nineteenth century the establishment of the first regular passenger steamship service in 1815 made travel between the two countries so much easier and, within a few years, competition between the different steamship companies brought fares to a level affordable by all.

Already by the late 1820s the British authorities were becoming overtly concerned about the increasing numbers of Irish migratory workers and the expressions of this concern were a sure sign that the migration had attained a momentum of its own. One estimate of the number of migratory workers in the 1830s puts the figure between 35-40,000. It was to rise to 100,000 within thirty years.[8] Up to the 1830s the main movement of migratory workers, however, had been an internal one. In Donegal this centred around the institution of the hiring fair.

Hiring fairs

There seems to be no doubt that the hiring fairs were introduced to Ulster during the early plantation years to facilitate the new landowners to find a convenient labour supply. It was a method of finding temporary labourers which the planters had been familiar with for some hundreds of years, at least since 1350 in England in the reign of Edward III when it was ordered that hiring arrangements were only to be entered into at designated centres on specific dates.[8] Hiring fairs were held in the market towns of all the Ulster counties and the important fairs still operating at the beginning of the twentieth century were held in Antrim, Armagh, Aughnacloy, Ballymena, Ballymoney, Bailieboro', Banbridge, Ballynahinch, Cavan, Cookstown, Coleraine, Cootehill, Comber, Dungannon, Derrygonnelly, Enniskillen, Irvinestown, Killyleagh, Lisbellaw, Letterkenny, Monaghan, Magherafelt, Newry, Newtownards, Newtownhamilton and Strabane.[10]

Essentially the Donegal workers were first sent to the hiring fairs to find employment and gain experience with Ulster farmers as young teenagers – sometimes even children from the ages of nine or ten were hired – before embarking on a career as migratory workers to Scotland.[11]

They served their apprenticeships in the Lagan to toughen them for their future lives – apprenticeships which entailed 5-6 years of working with severe taskmasters herding, milking and working as farm servants. Older men went to work in the Lagan as general farm workers pulling flax, cutting corn, threshing, draining land and making and repairing stone walls.

There was very little variation in the dates of the hiring fairs or the nature of the hiring agreement. They were nearly always held twice a year with the more important hiring fairs coinciding with the large annual May and November fairs and the business of the day included both the selling of livestock and the hiring of farm servants. The largest and most important of the hiring fairs was that which was held in Newry on the eastern side of the province, but important hiring fairs were also available in the west for the benefit of the huge supply of Donegal workers.

A hiring fair was, for example, held on the Diamond in Donegal town on the second Friday in May; in Milford the dates of the hiring fairs were 23 May and 23 November and they were known respectively as the May fair and the Halliday fair. In Ballybofey, Carndonagh, Raphoe and Letterkenny the hiring fairs were known as the Rabbles – the etymology of which is unclear, but perhaps refers to the hordes of workers converging on the town on the hiring day. Other Donegal hiring fairs for which we have some reference were held in

Ballyshannon, Pettigo and in an unspecified location in Cloghaneely.

Many of the Donegal hiring fairs were local fairs in that the young boys and girls did not have to travel outside the county boundary to find a farmer to employ them for a six-month term. Undoubtedly, the largest of the Donegal hiring fairs was the Letterkenny fair, or Rabbles, which was held on the Fridays after 12 May and 12 November and the workers attending travelled from a wide area including Cloghaneely, Gweedore, The Rosses, Falcarragh, Creeslough, Fanad, Beltany, Killybegs, the Inishowen Peninsula and the Donegal islands. Those not hired in Letterkenny might walk to Milford and be at the fair there for example for 23 May. But we must look outside the county boundary to find the other hiring fairs which were important for the Donegal workers looking for a 'place'. In neighbouring Tyrone, the Rabble in Strabane in May and November (and in an earlier time on 1 February) attracted workers from The Rosses, Gweedore and Glenties either as a first choice or as an alternative to the fair in Letterkenny. A few from The Rosses and the Inishowen Peninsula also went to the hiring fairs in Omagh and Derry. Here the Donegal workers were especially sought by the Lagan farmers as they could be hired at a cheaper rate than the workers from other counties who also attended the fairs.

The workers who were hired at the fairs in Letterkenny, Strabane, Omagh and Derry went to work on farms in counties Derry, Tyrone and east Donegal in an area which became known as the Lagan, the boundaries of which have been variously described by the workers themselves. For example, it is an area around the towns of Newtowncunningham, Manorcunningham, Plumbridge, Gortin and Omagh; it is '200 square miles of the best agricultural land in Europe', between the rivers Foyle and Swilly; it is an area east of Muckish mountain as far as county Antrim and it is a triangle joining Derry, Lifford and Letterkenny. To others it was the land along the banks of the river Finn and the land just east and west of a line drawn from Letterkenny to Omagh. The core of the Lagan area lies between Letterkenny and Derry and its boundaries can really only be defined by the distance travelled by the farmers to the hiring fairs where the workers made themselves available.[12]

While all the hiring fairs were held in May and November, the dates varied with priority toward the beginning of the month being given to the larger fairs. This staggering of dates, of course, facilitated workers who did not find an employer at the first fair and afforded them an opportunity to try their luck a second time. Other fairs at which Donegal workers might have found an employer included Claudy, Dungiven and Limavady in county Derry and Irvinestown, county Fermanagh.

The boys and girls attending the fairs might not have been hired for very tenuous reasons such as being too scruffily dressed, or too well dressed, or because they were not known, in which case they would continue to another, and possibly, bigger fair. This happened around about 1890 to Sorcha Bean Nic Grianna from Rann na Feirste, who told her story to Aodh Ó Domhnaill in 1938 when she was about sixty-two years old. She left home without her parents' permission and walked with her companion to Letterkenny where they got lodgings for the night and rose early the following morning to attend the fair:

Agus ar maidin d'éirigh muid agus tháinig anuas agus rinne réidh ár mbricfeasta, agus chóirigh suas muid fhéin. Nigh achan duine a aghaidh, agus a lámha, a chuir air a bhróga, agus chuir rud beag blaicín ionnta, agus chuaidh amach na sráide.

Bhí an t-ám olc. Ní raibh fastaidheacha ar bith a' gabhail a b'fhiú nó b'fheáirrde. 'N seanduine a bhí 'cúteáilte' agus a rabh aithne aige ar chor fhórmar, labhairfeadh siad leobtha, agus b'fhéidir go bhfuigheadh siad áit de n-a gcuid páistí fhéin, agus ní raibh aon duine le labhairt air ár son-inne.

Bhí muidne ansin go dtí gur bhánuigh an t-aonach.

'Mary,' arsa mise, 'ní bhfuigh muid fastódh indiu.'

'Diabhal a feárr liom fághail,' arsa sise.

'Cá tuige,' arsa mise, 'nach mbeidh muid náirighthe pilleadh. Is cuma duitse, acht mise d'imthigh i gan fhios, beidh mé náirighthe.'

'Mar bhfágh tú náire acht sin,' arsa sise, 'Déanfaidh tu gnaithe. Tá rabble i nDoire,' arsa sise, 'Dia Céadaoine.'

'O Dhia! sé,' arsa mise, 'acht ní fhuil ár sáith airgid againn le sinn féin 'a chongbhail a' gabhail.'

'O! mhálaid,' arsa sise. 'Chár cailleadh mise ariamh anns an gheimhreadh,' arsa sise, 'agus chá mhuirbhfeadh 'n diabhal anns a' tSamhradh mé. Rachaidh muid síos i dtoigh Sam Wallace go Burnfoot. Chaith mise dhá bhliadhain ann agus óch! óch! is muid a gheobhas a' loistín fo Ceadaoine seo-chugann ann.'[13]

(And in the morning we got up and came down and prepared our breakfast and got ourselves ready. Everyone washed face and hands, put on shoes and rubbed them with some boot blacking and went out onto the street.

The time was bad. There was no hiring going, good or bad. The old person who was cute and who knew some of them, would speak to them, and perhaps they would get a space for their own children, and we had no one to speak for us.

We were there until the fair dispersed.

'Mary,' I said, 'we won't hire today.'

633

'Indeed, I'd prefer to leave,' she said.

'Why?' I asked, 'won't we be ashamed to return. It's alright for you, but I left without telling anyone. I'll be ashamed.'

'If that's all that will make you ashamed,' she said, 'you'll be alright. There's a Rabble in Derry,' she said, 'on Wednesday.'

'Oh! God! Yes,' I said, 'but we haven't enough money to keep going.'

'Oh! you silly woman,' she said. 'I was never lost in the winter,' she said, 'and the devil wouldn't kill me in the summer. We'll go down to Sam Wallace's house in Burnfoot. I spent two years there and Oh! Oh! we'll get lodgings there until next Wednesday.')

Because the workers were generally so young, they were accompanied, unlike Sorcha and her companion, by one or other of their parents who made the bargain with the farmer as regards pay and work to be done and who ensured that a specific, and frequently mentioned, condition be observed – that the young person be allowed to attend mass at least every second Sunday.[14] The rates of pay varied from one fair to the other – higher rates were demanded at the larger fairs and were related to the ability of the worker. Experienced men, for example, who could work with horses and hire as ploughmen bargained for £12 for the six-month term at the end of the nineteenth century. This, of course, included their board. Men who had only what were rated as lower skills, reaping and sowing, for example, would hire for between £6-£8. Small boys, who were hired as herds and to look after pigs, were hired for rates of around £2.10s-£3. Girls were hired for work in the farm house and for milking. Their rate of pay for the six-month term also depended on their size and ability and was in the range £2-£5.10s.[15]

At some fairs we know that the workers would wear or carry some emblem such as a straw or a stick. The stick was sometimes described as a white rod such as a peeled sally or willow rod. The straw might have been held in the hand or sewn on to a coat or jacket. In all probability the recent references to the carrying or wearing of the emblem by available workers are vestiges of a much older custom instituted at a time when the worker's demeanour alone did not betray the fact that he was looking for work. One wonders, however, just how important in fact the wearing of the emblem might have been. Certainly as regards the Donegal workers at hiring fairs it would have been obvious to any farmer that the young, apprehensive and fearful looking boys and girls, with their bundles containing their working clothes, were for hire.

That the farmers played on the young people's insecurities there seems to be no doubt and one observer summed up his impression of the scene at the fair with the words: 'D'aithneodh na feirmeoirí na páistí bochta seo le féachaint ortha gur as an Ghaeltacht iad – bhíodh siad faiteach, critheaglach, cúthalta agus ar bheagán Béarla – agus bhéadh fhios ag na feirmeoirí seo.'[16] (The farmers would recognise by looking at them that these poor children were from the Gaeltacht – they were fearful, terrified, shy and with very little English – and the farmer would know this.)

Descriptions of the bargaining process show us that it was essentially no different to the haggling and banter which went on at most fairs. Those who could, made their own bargains with the farmers, while the parents of the younger workers looked after their children's interests. There was no shortage of advice and assistance from the onlookers. The reputations of good and bad farmers accompanied them wherever they went and stories spread quickly among the crowd gathered at the fair. Farmers who did not treat their workers well in a previous six-month term found it difficult, or even impossible, to find a worker to make a bargain with him. Young and inexperienced boys and girls had the protection of parents or older and wiser workers to help them assess the character of a farmer. In some cases, as a consequence of their bad reputations, farmers were immortalised forever in songs or legends. Two tellings of one legend concerning a notoriously miserable farmer have been told in recent years in Donegal. The farmer in question is not named, but the curiously named Hungersmother townland is mentioned as the place where he lived.

> Workers were generally treated well by employers though there were always miserly farmers who stinted food to their employees but this sort of treatment usually rebounded on the miser, giving him difficulty in procuring workers. There is a townland in the Raphoe area often referred to as Hunger's Mother. How it came to be so called is that a farm hand was so scantily fed there that he declined further engagement. Instead he presented himself at the next Raphoe 'Rabble' seeking work. His late boss went there too, looking for another hand, closely watched by his late employee. When finally the farmer had met and made a bargain with a likely worker, and final details were being settled, the worker asked: 'Where do you live?' Quick as lightning the answer came from the ex-employee: 'Hunger's Mother,' and Hunger's Mother it has remained ever since.[17]

Hungersmother is a townland in Raymoghy parish, about fifteen miles from Raphoe. This aetiological legend explaining the townland name is a lasting testimony to the conditions endured by so many thousands of young workers from Donegal. There is no doubt that many of them did suffer great hardship going to an alien place to people who did not even speak the same language as themselves, for the most part. As one worker observed, they went to 'Daoine Gallda. Gallda ina gcroidhe agus Gallda ina gcreidimh'.[18] (Foreign people. Foreign in their hearts and foreign in their belief.) Andrew McLaughlin from Middle Illies in Ballymagan townland on the Inishowen peninsula first hired as a youngster of fourteen years at Letterkenny on 15 May, 1936 and his memories of the hiring fair and his experiences as a hired servant give us some idea of the life of the workers:

I was so glad to get away from school. I was not fourteen until June. A few of my pals were also for the road. It was the discussion among us for quite a while. And what we were mostly afraid of was getting hired with Protestants. I had a bundle with some old things tied up in a brown paper. Old clothing. I got to the Diamond and it was packed with farmers and farmers' boys.

I listened to the bargaining for a while. I could hear each farmer asking anyone he was bargaining with could he do all work. This meant milking, ploughing ... everything. A man came to me and asked me was I for hiring. I said I was. He said to me 'Can you plough?'

I told him I could plough but I was not hiring as a ploughman. I could plough alright because I ploughed plenty at home. I used to take the plough off my father when I would come home from school. This was a method the farmers used. He had chance of cutting you down in money if he could find something that you couldn't or didn't want to do. He might then ask what kind of work you could do. He asked me what I wanted for the term until November. I said I wanted £8. He said he would get a ploughman for that. He left me but I could see that he was still keeping his eye on me. It was a short (while) after that I could find something pulling at my arm. I turned round and it was another man with a moustache. He says to me, 'Hie, young fellow. Are you for hiring?' I said I was so he held on to my coat sleeve and took me away down the street away from the crowd. He says, 'Tell me. Are you a Catholic?' I said I was. He says, 'So am I.' But he knew well that I was a Catholic because I was wearing a Sacred Heart pin on my coat. Anyway he started to hire me. I would have very little to do with him as he only wanted someone to clean out a byre, do a bit of herding and work at turf. He asked me did I ever work at turf. I told him I did. He told me I would have to be in for the rosary at 10 o'clock and that I would get to mass every second Sunday. He says to me, 'How much do you want?' I said £8. He laughed. He says, 'The Rabble is full of boys today that won't get hired.' He told me ploughmen were hiring for that. I thought it would be terrible if I had to go home without getting hired and I also thought this was a great chance getting into a Catholic house. So, I was hired for £7.15s. I was put on a bus going out county Derry way, but I don't remember getting off the bus nor I don't mind how I got to the house. The house was a long way from any bus route. But the rosary was said that night and I was up early next morning, cleaned the byres and away to the hill. And I holed turf for six long weeks as hard as that man could cut them. I was strong and a good holer of turf. I was well used to doing this at home for my father but he would cut at a slow pace and cut the turf small in case he do me any harm. It was different when I went to the stranger.

I worked in those banks to 9 o'clock at night. I couldn't but be in for the rosary. Next morning the boss would be up and waken me. Nobody else in the house got up. He would make the tea for me and him. He would be on the stocking feet and all the time while he was making the tea he would be saying, 'Our father who art in heaven,' and 'Holy Mary Mother of God,' out loud. He was a proper rogue. It was only on a Sunday I got the job of herding. One Sunday near the end of June I was herding and I climbed up a tree and out on a branch which broke and I fell to the ground. Two of his boys saw me as they were out with me. They were about school age. I hurted my back but next morning he had me out on the banks again. I tried to hole but I wasn't fit as the back was very sore. So he told me I was no good to him if I couldn't work. So I left him and headed for home. His name was Arthur ————, Slaghtmans, Co. Derry (a bad man).

I hired the following November in Altaghoney, Claudy for £7 until May 15. But it was a better place. At least there was plenty to eat. (This was not the case in Slaghtmans as I could not get enough bread to eat while I was there.)

These people in Altaghoney were the name of Kane. They were good enough but I was not finished work until 11 o'clock at night milking, fothering, and looking after sheep, hens, pigs, cattle, horses. They bought me a pair of nailed boots 14s and they were good ones. They said no rosaries but went to the chapel every Sunday and me too.[19]

It was important for the workers at the Ulster hiring fairs especially to include in the bargain that they be allowed to attend mass at least every second Sunday. Most of the farmers, the potential employers, were Protestants and there is some indication that the workers would seek out the Catholic farmers in preference to the Protestants in the belief that they would automatically get time on a Sunday morning to go to mass. This did not, of course, always work out as expected, and servants and hired workers were often prevented by farmers of both religious persuasions from attending to their spiritual duties on a Sunday, while others were only allowed occasional visits.[20]

At most of the hiring fairs once the bargain was agreed it was sealed with a money token – a form of luck money known either as earls or earnest. The amount of this token varied from about a shilling to half a crown and as much as five or even ten shillings over the years. It was 'money given as a token of good faith' and both parties were expected to respect it as a sign that the bargain could not be broken. Owing, however, to the very young age of so many of the Donegal workers, the giving of a money token to seal the bargain was not as commonly practised as in the other Ulster counties. In many cases the farmer might have taken the young person's bundle to prevent them hiring with another farmer at the fair.[21]

Conditions were, in many cases, appalling for the workers and they made complaints about the loneliness, the long hours worked, their accommodation and especially their food; the porridge of Indian meal given to some workers in the Lagan was described as 'brachán buí ... chomh lom go rachadh sé de rása ón tine go dtí an doras'[22] (porridge so thin that it would run from the fire to the door). 'No one hired with farmers ever saw butter or meat,' summed up one man's opinion of the quality of the food given to those from Donegal who hired in the Lagan[23] and it is no wonder, in the circumstances, that workers ran away from their hired place before the agreed term had expired. Séamus Ó Gríanna has told us that he ran away from the farm at Guirtín on his first and only venture to the Lagan, and he was not the only worker to break the unwritten agreement.[24]

Not surprisingly, the theme of running away from an employer is one which was especially taken up by the schoolchildren in the 1930s when they wrote down the folklore of their area for the Irish Folklore Commission's Schools' Scheme. The stories relate the fantastic experiences which occurred when the young workers were trying to find their way home.[25]

The young people were not alone in feeling lonely – parents also anguished over sending children away at such a tender age and looked forward to seeing them at the end of the term. Niall Ó Dubhthaigh from Beltany, county Donegal, described the parents' loneliness to Seán Ó hEochaidh in 1941 when the hiring fair in Letterkenny was still held.

Bhí aonach fastóidh ariamh anseo in Leitir Ceanann; gcuimhne m'athara-móire, agus tá go dtí an lá indiú. Bhíodh páisdí beaga ó ocht mbliadhna go dtí dhá bhliadhain déag agus ó sin go dtí ocht mbliadhain déag, cailíní agus buachaillí. B'fhéidir go mbéadh athair ag 'ul amach agus beirt nó triúr leis astoigh ins na feadhnógaí ar dhruim na mbeathadhach go dtí go mbéadh sé amuigh i Leitir Ceanainn. Ní raibh siad ábalta siubhal bhí siad comh h-óg sin agus an turas comh fada. Tiocfadh maighistir gallta aníos fhad leóbhtha annsan agus labhairfeadh sé i mBéarla, agus dheanfadh sé a bhfastódh b'fhéidir ar chúig scilling déag. Tá fhios agam bean annseo a bhí ar fastódh ar feadh sé mí ar deich scillinge, chualadh mé í a rádh go raibh sí 'na bean comh láidir ins an am sin agus a bhí sí nuair a pósadh í.

Bhí tuarasdal beag agus am cruaidh ag na creatúir seo, agus droch bhiadh agus droch ghléas luigheacháin, agus beagán meas ortha siocair gur Caitlicigh a bhí ionntú agus gan focal Béarla acú. Bheireadh na maighistrí íde na madadh ar na créatúir seo ins an am sin, agus eadar achan seórt bhí droch bheó ortha.

Tá aonach an fhastóidh seo ag 'ul i Leitir Ceanainn go fóill. Théid corr dhuine amach anois agus arais go Leitir Ceanainn agus gnidh siad fastódh, ach tá tuarasdal mór ag 'ul thar mar bhí fad ó shoin, agus tá gléas níos fearr ortha ar achan ndóigh. Tá an biadh níos fearr acú agus tá urraim agus meas ortha, an rud nach raibh ortha ins na laethibh sin ...

D'fhúigeadh imtheacht na bpáisdi seo am brónach ins na toighthe. Bhéadh an mháthair brónach agus a caoineadh, agus a fiafruigh gach lá fá dtaobh díobhtha, agus an t-athair mura gcéadna. B'fhéidir anonn i dtrathaibh na Lughnasa, nuair a bhéadh siad trí mhí amuigh, dá mba rud go mbéadh a muinntir ag 'ul amach go turas Thobar a' Dúin – turas mór atá amuigh annseo ar an taobh seo de Leitir Ceanainn, agus théid na céadtaí annsin gach bliadhain a' dhéanamh turais – nuair a bhéadh siad a' fad sin is minic a rachadh siad go Leitir Ceanainn, agus thiocfadh a gcuid páisdí an fad sin a d'amharc ortha. B'fhéidir go bhfanochadh siad oidhche annsin agus phillfeadh siad 'na bhaile annsin arais, a' fuireóchadh agus a' fanacht leis an lá a dtiocfadh a gcuid páisdí 'na bhaile thart fá 'n dóghadh lá déag do mhí na Samhna.[26]

(There was always a hiring fair in Letterkenny in my grandfather's memory, and there is still today. Young children from eight to twelve years and from that to eighteen years, boys and girls. Perhaps the father would be going out and two or three with him in the panniers on the back of the beast until they reached Letterkenny. They weren't able to walk, they were that young and the journey so long. A strange master would come up to them then and he would speak in English, and he would make the bargain for perhaps fifteen shillings. I know a woman here who was hired for six months for ten shillings. I heard her saying she was as strong a woman then as when she married.

These poor creatures had small wages and a hard time, and bad food and bedding and little respect as they were Catholics without a word of English. The masters gave these creatures dog's abuse at this time and between everything they had a bad living. This hiring fair is going in Letterkenny still. An odd person goes out now and again to Letterkenny and they arrange a hiring, but there are good wages, beyond what they were years ago, and in every way things are better for them. The food is better for them and they have esteem and respect, a thing they hadn't got in those days ...

The children's going would be a sad time in the houses. The mother would be sad and crying, and asking every day about them, and the father the same way. Perhaps around Lughnasa when they would be three months away, if it was a thing that their parents were going out to the pilgrimage at Doon well – a big pilgrimage out here on this side of Letterkenny, and hundreds go every year to do the pilgrimage – when they would be that far often they would go to Letterkenny, and their children would come that distance to see them. Perhaps they would stay a night there and they would return back home, expecting and waiting for the day that their children would come home around about the 12th of November.)

Disputes sometimes between farmers and their hired labourers became the subject of legal proceedings and it is likely that the majority of these cases were brought by the workers, rather than the farmers, despite the fact that there was a belief among many hired farm workers that the farmer could take them to court if they left before the expiry of the agreed term.[27] In reality, however, it was generally not in the farmer's interest to instigate court proceedings against a runaway temporary worker. The farmer was only bound to pay the labourer when the work was done and the agreed term had expired.

The poor inquiry commissioners in the 1830s attempted to ascertain the nature and extent of disputes between farmers and labourers. They asked magistrates who presided over petty sessions hearings throughout the country for the years 1831-33 to submit details on the cases which came before them concerning the recovery of wages.

The Petty Sessions Order Books record the nature of the dispute and the names of those involved. At Bunbeg court on 5 July 1909, for example, Ellen McFadden on behalf of Sarah McFadden (her daughter) was the complainant in a hearing in which she sought the payment of £2 for the said Sarah, for wages due until the following 12 November, from the defendant Ellen Coyle of Knockfulla (Bloody Foreland). The court ordered that the defendant pay a sum of nine shillings and fourpence with two shillings costs. Is this a case of the servant girl leaving her place before the term had expired and only receiving payment for the period worked, i.e. from May, the hiring time, until some date in June? At the Falcarragh court on 5 July 1898 Anna Doherty, a hired servant, sought the payment of one pound sterling from Neal Boyle. Mr Boyle was ordered to pay fifteen shillings, less two shillings already paid to Anna Doherty, and he was also liable for costs of one shilling and sixpence. The two shillings already paid probably represents the earls or earnest – the money token traditionally given to the hired person when the bargain was made. At Bunbeg court on 18 October 1915, James Ferry, on behalf of his daughter Mary Ferry, from Brinlack, Kilmacrenan, faced the defendant Daniel Gallagher in seeking the payment of two pounds for work done by his daughter from 7 April to 6 August 1915. In this instance the case did not proceed as neither the defendant nor the complainant appeared and we might assume that the matter was settled out of court.[28]

The years' experience of dealing with the vagaries of the Lagan farmers hardened them for what was, for most of the men, to become a regular way of life – crossing over and back to Scotland as migratory workers.

Working in Scotland

There was a significant movement of seasonal workers from some Donegal parishes to Scotland already in the 1830s. As it was absorbed into the kingdom of Great Britain in the early eighteenth century so began several decades of great agricultural change in Scotland – a change which had attained significant momentum by 1800. In the climate of the time – the success of the Industrial Revolution in the various industries of linen, wool, cotton, iron and steel – a demand was created for increased agricultural production. Agricultural improvements were tried out and met with varying levels of success from Aberdeenshire to Berwickshire and Galloway. Agricultural expansion occurred especially in Berwick, Roxburgh and the Lothians and farms ranging up to thousands of acres developed. Annual requirements of hands to harvest the crops were necessary. Many of the Scottish workers were finding employment in the new factories and the search for seasonal agricultural workers extended to Ireland – especially Ulster.

The expansion of agriculture and the availability of at least part-time employment for the destitute Irish coincided with the establishment of a regular passenger steamship service between Ireland and Great Britain. By the beginning of the 1830s, there were nine to ten vessels crossing between Glasgow to Belfast, Derry and Dublin a few times a week in the busy season. Fares on the Derry route were reduced in the steerage class to an affordable one shilling to entice the Irish agricultural workers.[29]

By the mid 1830s the competition among the steamship companies was paying off and a growing movement of Donegal workers to Scotland from several parishes including Leck, Desertegny, Clonmany, Moville, Conwal and Mevagh was recorded. Furthermore, the knowledge of the availability of work in Scotland spread to several other parishes throughout Donegal. The work undertaken by the workers, as mentioned in the reports of the time, includes harvesting and working in spinning and carding factories. We do not know in detail to which areas in Scotland the migrants travelled.[30] However, for the reasons cited above, we can be sure that they visited the Lothians, and also Berwick and Roxburgh, where the harvest was, as a rule, the earliest. They would also have found some work on farms if they travelled in a north-west direction as the harvest ripened to Stirlingshire, along the Valley of the Forth, round the southern borders of Fifeshire and even as far North as the Carse of Gowrie. We do know from newspaper reports, the published autobiographies and the recorded stories of several other seasonal workers that places especially familiar to them included Paisley, Armadale, Dalkeith, Haddington, Linton, Lauder, Biggar, Peebles, Carluke, Coatbridge and also Kelso, Dunbar, Greenlaw and Jedburgh. It was not until after the extension of the railway in the 1840s that the workers were able to reach what in later years, and up until more recent times, was to become lucrative employment – the tattie hoking. This has been written about especially by Patrick MacGill and the tattie hokers' struggles throughout the decades up to the early 1970s have been described elsewhere.[31] Counties visited by the tattie hokers included Ayrshire and Wigtownshire, for the early potato harvest, continuing north for the main potato crop harvest in Bute, Renfrewshire and Dunbartonshire and north-east to Perthshire and Fifeshire.

In many parts of Ireland improvements in labourers' wages were recorded from the 1860s. These increases, in a matter of a few years, led to a significant reduction in the number of migratory workers travelling to Great Britain. For the most part throughout the country, the 1870s were good years with continuous, if gradual, improvements in living conditions. However, it was during these years that the numbers of seasonal migrants continued to increase in a large area from Donegal in the north to Galway in the south. The temporary migrations from this area, and especially from west Mayo and west Donegal, was a predominantly post-famine phenomenon.[32]

In the 1830s, witnesses from only a few parishes in Donegal had recorded a significant number of seasonal workers. By 1841, 16 per 1,000 of the county's population migrated to Great Britain and this figure represented 27 per cent of the Ulster total.[33] The relative importance of the county as a home for seasonal workers increased dramatically throughout the century and in the decades after the famine the migration was to become regionalised in the west of the county. Already by 1858 all the able-bodied men from Gweedore and Cloghaneely left home every spring to work in Scotland;[34] they were going in large numbers from west Donegal in the 1870s[35] and in 1895 the men who left the Rosses, Gweedore and Cloghaneely as soon as they had planted their own crops in the springtime, did not return again until Christmas.[36] In 1880 seasonal migrants from Donegal accounted for 47 per cent of the Ulster total. In 1910 they were 80 per cent of that total and the direction of the movement was predominantly to Scotland.[37]

Congestion and continued migration

At that end of the nineteenth century the Congested Districts Board attempted to find out about the extent of poverty in the so-called congested districts, and from the information which the Board's inspectors gathered at this time we see just how dependent on the annual seasonal migration so many areas in Donegal had become. The CDB delineated eighty-four congested districts, twenty of which were in Donegal. Fourteen of these listed migratory labour as an occupation of the inhabitants in addition to the management of small holdings. However, in eleven Donegal congested districts – Clonmany, Desertegny, Dunfanaghy, Fanad, Gartan, Cloghaneely, Rosguill, Brockagh, Gweedore, The Rosses and Arranmore – there was no doubt that migratory earnings from both the hirings in the Lagan and working with farmers in Scotland, in addition to the savings to be made when the workers were not eating from the family's budget (reckoned at 2s 6d a week in 1890s), were vitally important to the household income. For example, in Dunfanaghy the earnings accounted for 27 per cent of the annual income; in The Rosses and Gweedore comparable figures were 37 per cent and in Fanad the earnings contributed 39 per cent of the household income.[38]

In terms of numbers of workers, the Dunfanaghy Poor Law Union was home for most of them at this time. Fifty-one per 1,000 of the population of the Union left for migratory work in Scotland in 1880. This figure reached a high of more than 57.4 per 1,000 in 1896 and was as high as 31.9 in 1915, the last year for which such figures were recorded.[39] The most numerous group consisted of those who worked as traditional farm workers – c.3,000 were making the annual journey from Donegal to Scotland in 1905 and spent the season turnip thinning, haymaking, potato lifting and working at the harvest in the Lothians and south-east of Scotland. Some workers also found their way north to Stirling, Perth and Fife, south into Northumberland and south-west into Galloway. Despite the decrease in the number of these workers since the closing decades of the nineteenth century, the earnings from the work were still vital to several thousands at the beginning of this century. The wages they received and the work they did is described in some detail in the agricultural statistics reports.

In addition to the general farm workers there was another important group of migratory labourers leaving Donegal at this time. The tattie hoking squads came from The Rosses, Arranmore and the islands and they worked alongside Mayo men, women and children especially in Ayrshire, Renfrewshire and Dumbartonshire. In 1905 it was estimated that there were about 1,500 tattie hokers in Scotland.[40] They remained an important group of migratory workers up to the 1940s and the most poignant reminder of them is the sad event, now popularly known as the Arranmore disaster, which occurred in 1935 in which nine workers lost their lives in a boating accident on their return to Arranmore after their season's work.[41]

A much smaller number of Donegal men and women travelled to the English, Irish and Scottish fishing ports as herring gutters and packers at the beginning of the century and up to the late 1930s. The 'gutters', as they were known, visited such ports as Lerwick, Peterhead, Wick, Stornaway, Peel, Lowestoft, Holyhead, Schull, Howth and Ardglass. They were engaged for the duration of the herring fishing season and were paid piecework rates.[42]

There is no doubt that the earnings from the migratory work were depended on in large areas of west Donegal as late as the 1930s and 1940s and the irony of their way of life could not have been lost on the workers themselves. They were going away from their home place for anything up to nine months of the year in order that they and their families could afford to continue living at home. This irony was certainly not lost on Seán Ó Duibheanaigh, a farmer from Rann na Feirste, who talked to Aodh Ó Duibheanaigh in 1938 and described the way of life of the workers as he saw it in the second half of the nineteenth century. Seán started his account talking about the generation of workers who migrated in the 1870s – the generation to which Aodh Ó Domhnaill (Hiúdaí Sheáinín) belonged – who traditionally went to the early harvest in Kelso, reaping it with hooks which they bought in Scotland.

Bhail ansin de réir a chéile thoisigh corr dhuine ag imeacht anonn ag foghmhar an fhéir, ansin thoisigh siad a' trácht Féil' Eoin, go dtí sa deireadh gurabh é mar bhí: dá luathas a mbeadh an obair críochnaithe 'sa bhaile aca i dtrátha na Féil' Eoin nó bfhéidir roimhe sin – go raibh an t-iomlán ar shiubhal go h-Albain agus ní thiocfadh siad 'na bhaile go dtí ... 28adh de Shamhain agus cuid mhaith de na buachaillí óga nach dtiocfadh 'na bhaile ar chor ar bith – a chaithfeadh an geimhreadh ar shiubhal.

Nuair a thiocfadh na fir sin 'na bhaile annsan agus a saothrughadh leo; an áit nach raibh ach fear amháin agus é a' streachailt leis an tsaoghal ag iarraidh a bheith a' togáil mná agus teaglaigh. Bhéadh buanadhas a shaothruigh uilig le díol síos aige sin le lucht na siopaí ar shon an méid a thóg siad ar cairde an t-earrach roimhe sin. Ní raibh am ar bith ins an bliadhain a ba mheasa agus a ba cruaidhe a chuirfeadh ar créatúir bochta nó an t-earrach. Bhéadh cibé saothrughadh a dhéanfadh an fear in Alban, caithte an uair sin; agus bhéadh an bárr le cur agus móin le baint agus fiche cineál eile mar sin le déanamh agus na créatúir ar phócaí folamha. Tá sean fhocal ráidthe agus chluinfeá ag chuid mhór daoiní ins an earrach an t-am sin é: 'Ní thig cruadhta go dtarraidh Earrach nó go raibh dhá uibh ag an fheannóig.'

Bhail ansin a' teach a mbéadh sgaifte mór fear ann, nuair a thiocfadh siad 'na bhaile agus a saothrughadh leo, ní bheadh a dhath a' cur buadhartha ortha ach cá h-áit a bhfuigheadh siad giota talaimh le ceannacht. Bhí rachtabhairt mhór ar thalamh an uair sin rud nach bhfuil anois ... Do réir mar bhí na daoine ag mirighe ins an tsaoghail bhí siad ag éirighe bródamhail agus ní raibh a dhath ar a n-áird ach cé is breaghtha a mbéadh teach aige. D'fhág siad na botógaí a' chéad uair agus rinne siad toighthe cloiche agus an t-eallach agus na cearca i gcionn an toighe. Ansin rinne siad boithigh amuigh agus cuir siad an t-eallach agus na cearca ionnta agus rinne siad seomra síos de áit an eallaigh.[43]

(Well then an odd person started going over for the haymaking and they started travelling on St John's Day, until at the end that's how it was: as soon as they had their work finished at home around about St John's Day or perhaps before that – until all of them were off to Scotland and they wouldn't come home until ... November 28th and a lot of the young boys that wouldn't come home at all – that would spend the winter wandering.

When those men came home then and their wages with them; the place where there would only be one man and he struggling with life trying to keep a wife and family. He would have to pay out the majority of his wages to the shops for the amount they took on credit the spring before. There was no worse or harder time for the creatures than the springtime. Whatever wages the man had earned in Scotland was spent by then; and the crop had to be sown and the turf cut and twenty things like that to do and the creatures with empty pockets. There is a saying and you would hear it from quite a few people in the spring at that time: 'Hardship doesn't come until the spring or until the grey crow have two eggs.'

Well then in a house where there would be a group of men, when they would come home and their wages with them nothing would be worrying them but where they might buy a piece of land. There was great selling of land at that time something that is not there now... As people's living standards were rising they were becoming proud and their sole interest was who had the nicest house. They left the huts first and made stone houses and the cattle and hens at one end of the house. And they made outhouses and they put the cattle and hens in them and they made a bedroom of the cattle's place.)

Overall, there were advantages in going away. As Seán Ó Duibheanaigh has described, the earnings went a long way toward improving living conditions. Initially cash was available to pay off debts at home and gradually newer and more comfortable houses were built until grants and Irish colleges arrived in the 1930s to further boost the developing cash economy. It is really only the individuals who went who could assess the merits of the advantages over the disadvantages of continued seasonal migration back and forward to Scotland. Some workers mention the skills they learned while working away from home. Others were enterprising and invested some of their earnings in livestock such as sheep and lambs while many spent part of their savings on clothes, pieces of household furnishings and agricultural hand tools. It remains for us to wonder how the seasonal work wanderings survived for so long and to continue to ask the question, 'Was it all worthwhile?'[44]

Acknowledgement
I am grateful to the Head of the Department of Irish Folklore, University College, Dublin, Professor Bo Almqvist, for permission to quote from the manuscripts.

References
1. Eoghan Ó Domhnaill (ed.), *Scéal Hiúdaí Sheáinín* (Dublin, 1940), p. 74.
2. Mici Mac Gabhann, *Rotha mór an tsaoil* (Dublin, 1959); Patrick Gallagher (Paddy the Cope), *My story* (Dungloe, n.d.); Séamus Ó Grianna (Máire), *Nuair a bhí me óg* (Dublin, 1942); Patrick MacGill, *Children of the dead end* (Dingle, 1982); idem. *The rat pit* (Dingle, 1983); Peadar O'Donnell, *Islanders* (London, 1928); idem, *Adrigoole* (London, 1929).
3. Ó Domhnaill (ed.), *Scéal Hiúdaí*, pp 20-101.
4. Mac Gabhann, *Rotha mór*, pp 33-85.
5. Máire, *Nuair a bhí*, pp 197-238.
6. Máire, *Nuair a bhí*, p. 230; Niall Ó Domhnaill, *Na Glúnta Rosannacha* (Dublin, 1952), pp 64-5.
7. Anne O'Dowd, *Spalpeens and tattie hokers. History and folklore of the Irish migratory agricultural worker in Ireland and Britain* (Dublin, 1991), pp 9-17.
8. ibid., pp 1-8. Cormac Ó Gráda discusses the changing numbers of seasonal migrants in 'Seasonal migration and post-famine adjustment in the west of Ireland', *Studia Hibernica, 13* (1973, pp 48-76).
9. *The statutes of the realm printed by command of His Majesty King George the Third ... from original records and authentic manuscripts, volume the first up to 1377* (1810), p. 311.
10. *Second report by Mr. Wilson Fox on the wages and earnings of agricultural labourers in the UK*, P.P. 1905, xcvii, cd. 2376, p. 117.
11. The following discussion on hiring fairs is based on information in the Irish Folklore Collections' Main Manuscripts (hereinafter I.F.C. MS), the Schools' Manuscripts (I.F.C. S MS), the questionnaire *Seasonal workers,* I.F.C. Q 80 and also the Ulster Folk and Transport Museum Archive. See O'Dowd, *Spalpeens,* pp 103-26.
12. I.F.C. Q 80/Donegal 6, Inishkeel, Boylagh; I.F.C. Q 80/Donegal 10, Portnoo; I.F.C. Q 80/Donegal 12, St Johnstown; Mac Gabhann, *Rotha mór*, p. 37.
13. I.F.C. MS 478:227-276 (1938).
14. See *Royal Commission on labour, the agricultural labourer*, vol. iv, Ireland, 1893-4. Part 1, Report by Mr R. McCrea, pp 58-9, P.P. 1893-4, xxxvii.
15. Congested Districts' Board, *Baseline reports* (Dublin 1892-8).
16. I.F.C. Q 80/Donegal 1, Meenmore, Inishkeel, Boylagh.
17. I.F.C. Q 80/Donegal 4, Killybegs, Banagh. A second telling of the legend is contained in I.F.C. Q 80/Donegal 12, St. Johnstown.
18. I.F.C. MS 799:412, Beltany, Tullaghobegley, 1941.
19. I.F.C. Q 80/Donegal 13, Ballymagan, Fahan.
20. See I.F.C. Ms 644:355-6, 1939; I.F.C. Q 80/Donegal 2, I.F.C. Q 80/Donegal 13, Mac Gabhann, *Rotha mór*, p. 55; Ó Domhnaill, *Scéal Hiúdaí*, p. 31 ; I.F.C. MS 1744: 12, 1966; I.F.C. MS 478: 50 , 1937; I.F.C. MS 1004: 147, 1937.
21. O'Dowd, *Spalpeens*, p. 123.
22. Ibid., p. 144.
23. Ibid.
24. Ó Grianna, *Nuair a bhí*, pp 206-9; Mac Gill, *Children,* pp 64-5; I.F.C. MS 644: 355-8.

25. See, for example, I.F.C. S MS 1075: 37; 54-5; 66-7; 85; 284-5.

26. I.F.C. MS 799: 407-9.

27. See O'Dowd, *Spalpeens*, p. 224.

28. The Petty Sessions Order Books for the last years of the nineteenth century and the first years of the twentieth century are stored by the National Archives. The cases cited are entries in the Petty Sessions Order Books.

29. James Handley, in two important publications, discusses at length both the permanent and temporary migration to Scotland. His sources are primarily contemporary newspaper accounts. See *The Irish in Scotland, 1799-1845* and *The Irish in modern Scotland* (Cork, 1945 and 1947).

30. See, for example, the Ordnance Survey Memoirs for the parishes of Leck (21, ix, 2, p. 25, 1835); Desertegny (21, vii, 1, p. 11, 1835); Clonmany (21, iv, 1, p. 22, 1835) and information pertaining to the parishes of Iniskeel, Inver, Killymard, Kilgarvan, Mevagh, Conwal and Moville in *First Report from H.M. commissioners of inquiry into the condition of the poorer classes in Ireland, 1835* (Poor Inquiry). Appendix A and supplement. P.P. 1835, xxxiv.

31. MacGill, *Children* and *The rat pit*. See also O'Dowd, *Spalpeens*, pp 176-202.

32. See O'Dowd, *Spalpeens*, pp 23-6.

33. S. H. Cousens, 'The regional variations in emigration from Ireland between 1821 and 1841,' *Transactions of the Institute of British Geographers*, no. 37, 1965, pp 15-30.

34. *Report from the select committee on destitution (Gweedore and Cloghaneely)*, 1858, P.P. 1857-8, xiii, p. 79.

35. *Reports from Poor Law Inspectors in Ireland as to the existing relations between landlord and tenant in respect of improvements on farms, etc... 1870*, P.P. 1870, xvi.

36. *Minutes of evidence taken before the Royal Commission on the financial relations between Great Britain and Ireland, 1894.* P.P. 1895, xxxvi, p. 130.

37. *Agricultural statistics, Ireland. Reports and tables relating to migratory agricultural labourers, 1880.* P.P. 1181, xciii and P.P. 1909-1910, cviii.

38. Congested Districts' Board, *Baseline*.

39. See O'Dowd, *Spalpeens*, p. 74.

40. *Agricultural statistics, Ireland. Reports and tables relating to migratory agricultural labourers, 1905*, P.P. 1906, cxxxiii, pp 6-13 and *1908*, P.P. 1909, cii, pp 7-8.

41. An evocative and detailed account of the boating tragedy was written down by Barney Gallagher and published in *Arranmore links* (Aidan Gallagher, 1986), pp 128-37.

42. To date very little has been written about the Donegal herring 'gutters'. Two questionnaire replies contain some information; I.F.C. Q 80/Donegal 3, Ballyshannon and I.F.C. Q 80/Donegal 4, Killybegs.

43. I.F.C. MS 477: 394-6.

44. See O'Dowd, *Spalpeens*, pp 291-4.

Chapter 22

THE CONGESTED DISTRICTS BOARD AND THE CO-OPS IN DONEGAL

PAT BOLGER

We have in Ireland a poor country, practically without manufactures – except for the linen and ship building of the north and the brewing and distilling of Dublin – dependent upon agriculture with its soil imperfectly tilled, its area under cultivation decreasing, and a diminishing population without industrial habits or technical skill.

(Report of the Recess Committee) [1]

This picture of Ireland in the 1890s was generally applicable to the county of Donegal – the images of rural poverty as starkly outlined as the profile of its barren mountains, the hills of Donegal. This is not to discount the thrift and industry of farmers in the Laggan area where the land was better, the holdings larger and the tenants enjoyed that fixity of tenure which had come to be known as the 'Ulster custom'. [2]

Even there the appearance and dress of the farmers and their farm labourers (in tied cottages) were hardly indicative of any great degree of affluence. Shirt-making in the Derry hinterland had moved out of the cottages into factory centres, [3] but further west, tweedweaving, embroidery and knitting were still home based. These home industries did engender industrial habits and technical skill: industrial habits which came from the grim necessity of spending long hours of toil to supplement meagre family incomes. The drudgery of craftwork, often pursued to the point of injury to eye-sight and general health, was alleviated (indeed motivated) by a remarkable pride in skills of manual dexterity and design that verged on artistry. In the spriggers or embroiderers and the hand-weavers we had the epitome of Donegal cheerfulness and patience in adversity. These cottage industries involved considerable numbers of people but for many of the workers they provided bare economic survival rather than the build-up of modest prosperity.

West of a line through Stranorlar and Letterkenny the agricultural resource base is very limited. In 1910, the poet AE (George William Russell) marvelled at the survival of a community in 'the Rosses of

Donegal where the bare bones protrude through the starved skin of earth'.[4] This apparently inhospitable place was home to a large number of 'farmers' though the holding might be no more than a few acres of 'green' land with limited rights to turbary and mountain or moorland commonage for grazing.

The most striking social feature of West Donegal was the close interaction with Scotland mediated through the large-scale annual migration in search of work. Although farming in Britain had become more mechanised in the latter half of the nineteenth century there was still a good deal of employment for farm labourers in Scotland,where Lothian farmers in particular specialised in labour-intensive crops like potatoes and turnips (neeps). Whole families often moved to Scotland for the 'tatie-hoking', leaving only the very youngest children in the care of grandparents. Work on farms in the 'Laggan' and in counties Tyrone and Londonderry was often a prelude to migration further afield. Teenage boys and girls (and sometimes children as young as ten years) were hired to work for six-month periods at the 'rabbles' (hiring fairs) in Letterkenny and Strabane. The official statistics (based on 'male landless labourers' migrating to Scotland) are notoriously inaccurate, but the trend was towards an increased migration during the 1890s, peaking at a notional 2,500 in 1899. The poor-law union of Dunfanaghy had a migration rate of 45.6 per 1,000 with the Glenties union at 35.8.[5]

Although Donegal lost over 37 per cent of its pre-famine population[6] in the 50 years up to 1891 the problem of overcrowding was hardly relieved at all. Indeed in some coastal districts the population increased again after 1861. Added to the hardship of small farms, poor soils and high rainfall were the fragmentation of holdings, poor infrastructure, lack of transport and inadequate markets for the produce of land or sea.

The seas along Donegal's 400 miles of coastline contributed to local subsistence. Sea fish, shellfish and river salmon alleviated the worst effects of famine in some areas. The burning of kelp gave a little cash income to some island and coastal dwellers; but these maritime resources were not generally exploited, due to lack of boats and proper equipment. Conditions in the West of Ireland had always proved an intractable problem for government. Landlord/tenant relationships were far from satisfactory and agrarian unrest flared at fairly regular intervals, usually coinciding with bad harvests. The various Land Acts enacted from 1870 onward had little effect on the western situation because distressed tenants were in no condition to participate in any scheme of land purchase. Attempts to relieve congestion by schemes of 'assisted emigration' were hardly more popular than the compulsory emigration through eviction practised by the more determined landlords. There were no co-ordinated plans to tackle the complex socio-economic tangle, and for the most part little was done except by piecemeal crisis measures such as food kitchens and relief works where local distress and unrest became particularly acute.

The Congested Districts Board

Plans to tackle specific aspects of the western problem were put forward from time to time, but gradually the idea of a comprehensive integrated approach developed. In the House of Commons, Mayo MP John O'Connor Power championed the idea of a government commission with statutory powers particularly with regard to the problem of farm size.[7] 'The chronic distress prevailing in certain congested parts of Ireland', he stated, 'can be most safely and efficaciously relieved by a judicious and economic system of migration and optional emigration with a consolidation of the holdings from which tenants are removed.'

Chief secretary Arthur Balfour decided in his new Land Act (1891) to tackle the problem at an appropriate level. In this, Balfour, a perceptive politician of considerable vision, was perhaps influenced more by 'philanthropic' canvassing rather than political motives. He was greatly impressed by the work of men like Fr Charles Davis and Rev W.S. Green, businessmen Thomas P. Cairnes (Drogheda), Charles Kennedy (Dublin) and the indefatigable Quaker, James Hack Tuke, a Yorkshire man with a legendary reputation for his famine relief work in Ireland. Balfour was particularly attracted to the self-help philosophy of Horace Plunkett MP founder of the Co-operative Movement which was giving Irish farmers big, and small, an identity of interest. Consequently the Purchase of Land (Ireland) Act 1891, Part II, enacted that 'for twenty years after the passing of the Act and thereafter until Parliament should otherwise determine there should be a Board called the Congested Districts Board for Ireland'.

The act became law on 5 August 1891 and the Congested Districts Board held its first meeting on 2 November in that year. The funding of the Board came from a sum of £1.5 million, part of the surplus of the Disestablished Church, with interest at 2¾ per cent which gave an annual income of £41,250. The Board also received the greater part of two Fishery Loan Funds amounting to approximately £84,000. It could spend part of the principal (£1.5m) subject to Treasury approval but this was never forthcoming so the capital sum remained intact.[8]

The Board was to concern itself with improving living conditions in the designated Congested Districts by becoming involved in (i) agricultural development, (ii) forestry, (iii) breeding of livestock and poultry, (iv) sale of seed potatoes and seed oats, (v) amalgamation of small holdings, (vi) migration, (vii) emigration, (viii) fishing and matters subservient to fishing, (ix) weaving and spinning, (x) any other suitable industry. The powers to enable the purchase by tenants of interest in their holdings and to arrange emigration or migration or amalgamation of holdings were never used.[9] The power to purchase estates was conferred in 1910 but this was used but little in county Donegal. The major functions of the Board were in aiding and developing agriculture, forestry, livestock, weaving, spinning and fishing.

The CDB was limited geographically to areas where the total rateable valuation when divided by the total population, gave a sum of less than one pound ten shillings (£1.50) for each individual. Under this criterion, the Board's jurisdiction extended over a great part of all the counties of Connacht together with Donegal, Kerry and West Cork; small parts of Clare, Limerick and Tipperary benefited from some of the Board's schemes. Districts in CDB remit in county Donegal were North Inishowen, Clonmany, Desertegney, Fanad, Rossguill, Gartan, Brockagh, Dunfanaghy, Cloghaneely, Tory Island, Gweedore, The Rosses, Arranmore, Glenties, Glencolumbkille, Teelin, Killybegs, Inver, Lough Eske and Ballyshannon.

The Board was composed exclusively of honorary and ex-officio members who received no remuneration for their services. As laid down in the Act it was to consist of the chief secretary, a member of the Land Commission[10] plus five other members appointed by the queen. Her majesty was also authorised to appoint up to three temporary members for business relating to fisheries, agriculture and other special matters.

The first Board comprised the chairman Rt Hon Arthur J Balfour, chief secretary for Ireland; Rt Hon Frederick Wrench (Land Commission); Rev Charles Davis, PP Baltimore; Rt Hon Horace Plunkett; Mr Thomas Plunkett Cairnes; Mr Charles Kennedy; Mr James Hack Tuke. Rev William Spotswood Green, chief fishery inspector was added to the Board a few weeks after its constitution because of his special expertise and knowledge of the Irish fishing industry. A few years previously, he had with other experts completed a valuable survey of Irish fishing grounds which was funded by the Royal Dublin Society. Mr William L Micks was appointed secretary and was the only employee of the Board for the first month. Mr Micks was a local government board inspector on secondment to the CDB. Six inspectors were appointed and the Congested Districts Board commenced operations. Concurrent with their development work, one of the first tasks was to carry out basic assessments along with simple surveys and to submit a report on each 'Congested District'. Eighty-four districts had been identified[11] and reports on these were completed between 1892 and 1898. These 'baseline' reports give a fascinating insight to conditions in the 1890s. One of the first was W. L. Micks' baseline report on the district of the Rosses which was completed by 27 May 1892.[12] The baseline reports confirmed previous findings and alerted public conscience to the fact that there was a state of chronic destitution in the west of Ireland.

The Donegal baseline surveys bore out the contention that the maritime Donegal congest was at once 'a labourer, a farmer and a fisherman'. Fishing was merely a supplement to subsistence agriculture. No resource was efficiently developed; marketing was largely chaotic. Though there were many common problems, each district had its own particular deficiencies and peculiarities. The sight of people carrying bags of meal on their backs was common in Donegal. There were few horses or donkeys – 'only 70 badly fed, badly housed, badly treated horses in the 37,018 acres around Glencolmkille'. There was no single area in North Inishowen with sufficient cows to support a creamery. In 1891 Ardara weavers rarely made more than £4 from tweed in the year. The Dungloe home knitters were paid at the rate of ten pence (10d) per dozen pairs of socks in 1835 and this continued to be the accepted rate up to the turn of the century.

The baseline reports have perceptive observations on the character and attitudes of the people. Horace Plunkett neatly summarised community characteristics:

> Clever in their resourcefulness and shrewd in bargaining, they lack the qualities which secure the fruits of industry, perseverance and self-confidence, due to lack of education and favourable economic circumstances ... Through a long and sad history, almost every influence that has operated upon the minds of these people has militated against the application of the only principles which have been found to be effective in elevating rural communities similarly depressed in other countries.[13]

With commendable speed the Board began action on several fronts – farming, industry and fishing. A large number of demonstration plots together with a number of 'example' holdings were established to demonstrate improved agricultural practices. Small iron ploughs which could be drawn by a team of donkeys were supplied – a nice touch of appropriate technology!

In the year 1892-3, twenty-seven bulls and fifty-six improved large white boars were located in Donegal. Later ten stallions were brought in[14] as well as a number of sturdy Spanish jackasses. A large number of good rams were sent in autumn to be overwintered at Ards and

Plate 22.1   Downings' Pier 1890s(?).

Plate 22.2   Stacks at Mulroy. Donegal climate favours growth of fine oats.
Workers on estate of Lord Leitrim.

Glencolumbkille. Sheep dipping was encouraged and the Board supplied portable dipping troughs for use at Doon (county Galway), Clifden and Glenties. A £50 grant was offered for the training of machinists at a shirt factory in the old army barracks in Ballyshannon which was run by the Tillie & Henderson company of Derry.

A weaving school and tweed depot was established at Ardara. Webs at the monthly fair were inspected. A bonus of a penny'halfpenny was paid on all webs which were of sufficiently high standard to be given a quality mark. A grant of £350 was given for setting up the school and there was an annual allocation for running costs and for the administration of the 'quality' scheme. These developments were directed by W. T. D. Walker, a county Down textile manufacturer, who also established centres at Carrick and Milford. The training and quality schemes were so successful that by 1896 it was decided that no further premia on quality were needed – the rewards were coming from the market.

In 1891 the condition of the fishing industry was such that the Board decided to help the existing industry in the southern counties but north of a line from Galway to Dublin it was necessary to create the industry anew. Fifteen curing stations were recommended – five each in counties Galway, Mayo and Donegal. By 1893 all these were operational except the one for Tory island. Two years later eight curing stations were working in county Donegal and the CDB voted an additional £1,000 for fish curing – filleting, salting and smoking.

In 1894 Alexander Duthie, an astute and experienced Aberdeen fish trader, was appointed CDB fishery inspector for Donegal. Duthie was greatly impressed by the superb quality of the Sheephaven herrings landed at Downings. Crews from Teelin had been provided with 'Zulu' type fishing boats, 40 ft long. Duthie recommended the same for Downings but arranged to put a Scottish instructor on each boat as skipper in charge of six young local men. Scots personnel were also brought over to supervise the curing of fish. In reciprocation a great number of Donegal girls, mainly from the Rosses, were sent for training to Scottish curing stations. The pay at 3d per hour was satisfactory and (with free lodging and travel) money was remitted home. Duthie set up a cooperage yard making barrels at Teelin and later at Downings. Coopering was also carried on in Burtonport and boat-building in Killybegs. Instruction was given in net-mending. The Board of National Education bore half the cost of this training. Fishermen were introduced to the art of long lining.

There was great pressure for the improvement of harbours, piers and slipways. During 1892 nearly all the areas of fishing activity (however small) were visited by Horace Plunkett and the Rev W. S. Green, chief fisheries inspector. By 1894 forty-nine items of marine works (seven in

Donegal) were either completed or in progress. By 1896 the overall figure had increased to sixty-three (twelve in Donegal). A new pier was approved for Killybegs at a cost of £10,000 – a third of the cost to be borne by the CDB and the balance by way of a direct grant from the Treasury. For the first three years the Board had a chartered vessel, the *Fingal,* constantly employed carrying fish to markets and returning with salt and other requisites. Then their own ship *Granuaile* was built at a cost of £10,252. Road access to fishing ports was very important. By 1896, thirty-one road projects in Donegal (eighty-eight in all CDB areas) had been completed. A major engineering feat was the construction of a viaduct over the Gweebarra estuary (Balfour's bridge) and the most troublesome was the 'so-called road' to Kincasslagh pier because of its very steep gradient.

There was a general feeling that the Congested Districts Board had gained the confidence of the people. Much of this success could be attributed to the dedication of the Board members and their understanding of the psyche and condition of the people. Notable newcomers to the Board were two remarkable clerics who were to give lengthy and valuable service. These were Most Rev Patrick O'Donnell, the tall handsome bishop of Raphoe, later to be cardinal archbishop of Armagh, who joined the Board in October 1892 and remained during its existence. Rev Denis O'Hara, the amiable but energetic parish priest of Kiltimagh, came on in 1893 and remained until his death in 1922. These two men greatly enhanced the reputation of the Board particularly through their 'meet the people' visitations in the promotion of the Parish Improvement Schemes, wherein prizes and grants locally administered were given for a great variety of improvement works.

Matching the enthusiasm and persistence of the Board members was the expertise and pragmatism of the inspectors and other employees which reduced bureaucratic delays to a minimum. Rigorous and exacting training was the prerequisite of every CDB business venture. No boat ventured on the sea except in command of an experienced skipper. No fish was processed except under the eyes of trained supervisors. Similarly no work in factory, workshop, boatyard or farm school but had its own training and supervision. Great pride was taken all round in imparting or acquiring new skills.

Stories of many of the CDB officials are enshrined in the folklore of the West. Individually unexceptional these tales focus on skills and teaching ability, insistence on high standards and, not infrequently, courage in resisting pressure from highly-placed influentials to appoint or qualify unfitted candidates. So great was the local admiration for Alexander Duthie, the doughty Scot fish merchant and seaman, that the Duthie Memorial Hall was erected in Downings to commemorate him.

Co-operative societies

The Lagan Co-operative Creamery established in 1896 was the first in county Donegal. Two more co-operative creameries followed shortly afterwards, Ramelton (1897) and Finn Valley (1898). These business enterprises started up in a landscape quite different from the typical congested district. They were in the better land areas of east Donegal where the holdings were larger and farming better. Were it not for its heavy rainfall the Laggan area could be considered very good farmland.

The formation of co-operatives was encouraged by the gentry and substantial landowners who had followed with interest the happenings in Munster from the founding of the first co-operative at Drumcollogher in 1889. Plunkett and many of the early founder members of the movement belonged to the aristocracy and landlord classes. Notable proponents of the movement were the Hamilton family in south Donegal, Hugh Law MP of Marblehill and Sir James Musgrave who was landlord of an extensive though not overly productive acreage in the Slieve League peninsula. Sam Marshall in the Laggan, Andrew Hunter, Ramelton and Captain John Riky in the Finn valley worked hard to set up co-op creameries in their own localities.

The foundation in 1894 of the IAOS (Irish Agricultural Organisation Society) gave the movement a much wider base. The first national committee of the IAOS was carefully contrived to include well-balanced representation between all shades of class, creed, political opinion and occupational pursuit. An outstanding member of that first IAOS committee in 1894 was Dr Patrick O'Donnell who, six years previously on his appointment to the diocese of Raphoe, was hailed as the youngest bishop in christendom. Other members included Lord Monteagle, Count Arthur Moore, Christopher Digges la Touche, managing director of Guinness, Father Tom Finlay, Sir James Musgrave of the Belfast engineering company and C. T. Redington, commissioner of national education. Dr W. J. Weir, an enthusiastic co-operator from Ballindrait, Lifford, joined the board in 1908.

Plunkett's co-operative movement had the enthusiastic backing of prominent and progressive industrialists and businessmen. Opposition came from small town merchants and money lenders (gombeen-men) who saw Plunkett's move to have the farmers and country people set up their own businesses as posing a threat to the 'legitimate traders'. Plunkett endeavoured to establish co-operation on the British and European models – starting as a 'consumer' system of co-operative retail shops as initiated by such as the Rochdale pioneers. The consumer arm would be paralleled by a credit/savings bank system to enable people to be free of the clutches of money lenders. The growth of co-operative retail shops would in time make it necessary to have co-operative wholesaling. From there it was hoped to proceed to manufacture and 'producer' co-operation.

In Ireland every attempt at consumer co-operation was frustrated by the vested interests of merchants who exerted enormous influence particularly in the congested districts. Plunkett and his supporters were thus compelled to begin at the 'producer' end in the dairy industry, which was admirably suited to the practice of co-operation. The production of high quality butter in quantities sufficient to gain market advantage was something beyond the competence of even the largest individual farmer.

Table 22.1

Co-operative Creameries established in Donegal

Creameries	Year established
The Laggan	1896
Ramelton	1987
Finn Valley	1898
Pettigo	1899
Drumholm	1900
Sessiaghoneill	1901
Termon	1901
Carndonagh	1902
Donegal	1902
Glenfin	1902
Gleneely	1903
Inishkeel	1903
Inver	1903
Kilbarron	1903
Taughboyne	1903
Kilteevogue	1903
Bruckless	1905

Between 1896 and 1905 some seventeen co-operative creameries were set up in county Donegal. Of these only ten survived until 1920 – Bruckless, Drumholm, Finn Valley, Inver, Kilbarron, Laggan, Pettigo, Ramelton, Termon and Taughboyne. Donegal was never a great dairying county. Tyrone to the east had thirty-eight co-operative creameries in 1920.

As the creameries organised by the IAOS gained a footing, they ventured into trading in farm supplies such as seeds, manures, feed-stuffs and hardware. The organising society did not lend its support to any co-operative proposal that resembled a grocers shop or 'consumer co-operation'. This policy of appeasement did little to diminish the virulent merchant opposition to co-operatives of any kind.

In non-dairying areas, co-operative agricultural societies on the pattern of the *syndicats agricoles* of rural France and the *consorzio agrario* of Italy were supported by the IAOS but viewed with great suspicion by traders. These co-operative agricultural societies, or store societies as they came to be known, were to become the dominant feature of the co-operative movement in Donegal. Before the establishment of the Department of Agriculture and Technical Instruction (DATI) the IAOS played a considerable role in agricultural instruction. Co-operative store societies were to varying degrees centres of agricultural innovation. Their main purpose was to provide the farmer members with the raw materials and requisites for their industry – seeds, fertilisers, animal feed, tools, building materials, machinery and equipment. They also aspired to purchase and market farm produce and generally concerned themselves with agricultural improvement and the provision of useful services. Many of the early stores, as well as marketing the farmers' grain, potatoes, wool and eggs kept sire animals to promote better breeds of livestock, bulls, boars, rams and even stallions. These societies introduced the spraying of potatoes as a standard farm practice. The efficacy of spraying potatoes against the dreaded blight had been demonstrated both by the RDS and the Congested Districts Board but success was only achieved when the farmers had the spraying equipment available in their own co-op. By the turn of the century it was reported that 'nearly every one of the 106 Co-operative Agricultural Societies in Ireland was the proud owner of an efficient horse-drawn sprayer'.

The pioneering work of the CDB in blight control and trial-growing of different varieties of potato was continued by the Department of Agriculture and Technical Instruction (DATI) and the co-operatives from the turn of the century.[15] In this way the foundation of successful Donegal potato growing was laid. It was also the co-operative movement that established and made effective the analysis of fertilisers and feeding stuffs for quality and the testing of seeds for purity and germination. Existing regulations were not enforced until the co-operative wholesale society (IAWS Ltd) was established in 1897. It set standards and merchants were compelled to follow.

The first co-operative agricultural society in Donegal was a small store set up at Copany close to Donegal town in 1901. This was followed by Templecrone, founded five years later. Templecrone Co-operative is very much the story of Patrick Gallagher (Paddy the Cope) who became the great folk hero of the co-operative movement and won national and international fame. Gallagher, a country boy from Cleendra in the Rosses, worked as a miner in Scotland where he and his wife Sally made their purchases and saved their money with the

Pumperstown Co-operative Society, a small retail co-operative on the Rochdale model. On his return he was dismayed to find that the same facilities were not only unavailable in his homeland, but the formation of co-operatives was actively opposed. The story of the beginnings of Templecrone Co-op is told with appealing simplicity in Gallagher's autobiography.[16]

Paddy inveigled the IAOS into supporting the establishment of an agricultural store in Dungloe whilst his real intention was to set up a full retail consumer co-operative shop of the type he had known in Scotland.[17] Opposition to farmer trading (even in farm requisites) was intense. The merchants and gombeen men were powerful as many country people were in debt to them. Many community leaders – clergy, doctors, professional men and local politicians had ties of kinship or friendship with the merchants. Nationalist politicians, obsessed with political rather than economic solutions to Ireland's problems, looked on the co-operative efforts for economic improvement as 'a red herring dragged across the path of Home Rule'. Some unionists, on the other hand, believed that too much had already been conceded to the tenantry and believed that Plunkett's co-operative organisation would only raise their expectations.

Co-operative credit societies

Before any real progress could be made in co-operative trading it was necessary to do something about the community indebtedness to gombeen shopkeepers. Some families were always 'in the shopkeeper's book'. This was particularly so in the case of migrant labourers. Goods were taken on credit throughout the summer with the expectation that the shop bill would be cleared when the migrant workers returned before Christmas with their season's earnings. The book though was rarely fully cleared. Excessive prices and outrageous interest charges as high as 100 per cent per annum or more ensured that the family was constantly in debt.

George Russell (Æ) gives some graphic descriptions of the exactions of gombeen shopkeepers and their local dominance:

> In the maps of ancient Ireland we see pictures of famous chiefs standing over their territories – MacSwineys of the Battle Axes and their peers. In the maps of modern congested Ireland pictured in the same way we should find swollen gombeen men straddling right across whole parishes, sucking up like a sponge all the wealth in the district, ruling everything, presiding over county councils, rural councils boards of guardians, and placing their relatives in every position which their public functions allow them

to interfere with. In congested Ireland every job which can be filled by the kith and kin of gombeen kings and queens is filled accordingly, and you get every kind of inefficiency and jobbery. They are all publicans, and their friends are all strong drinkers. They beget people of their own character and appoint them lieutenants and non-commissioned officers in their service. All the local appointments are in their gift, and hence you get drunken doctors, drunken rate-collectors, drunken J.P.s, drunken inspectors – in fact round the gombeen system reels the whole drunken congested world, and underneath this revelry and jobbery the unfortunate peasant labours and gets no return for his labour. Another enters in and takes his cattle, his eggs, his oats, his potatoes, his pigs, and gives what he will for them, and the peasant toils on from year to year, being doled out Indian meal, flour, tea and sugar enough to keep him alive. He is a slave almost as much as if he were an indentured native or had been sold in the slave market.[18]

Fr Tom Finlay SJ was one of the prime movers in the establishment of the agricultural credit societies. The first of these was opened in Doneraile county Cork in February 1895. The agricultural banks or village banks as they came to be called, operated on the same Raiffeisen principles as our modern-day credit unions.

In 1897 the poet AE (George William Russell) then working as a clerk in Pim's drapery store in Dublin was befriended by W.B. Yeats and Horace Plunkett and given the job of co-op organiser for Connacht and Donegal with a special remit with regard to co-operative credit societies. AE performed brilliantly and a whole network of village banks was in place throughout the west of Ireland before AE returned to Dublin in 1905 to become editor of the co-operative weekly newspaper *The Irish Homestead*. Four village banks were in place in Donegal by 1898 – Glenswilly, Inver, Killybegs and Kilmacrenan. By 1905, twenty-four banks were active. AE as organiser had powerful support from Bishop O'Donnell and from Hugh Law MP, benevolent landlord of Marblehill.

In areas where the people were too poor to have sufficient savings to get the lending process started the CDB and later the Department of Agriculture provided seed capital, usually £50 to £100 by way of loan to the bank. These were small but not inconsiderable sums in the days when a good milch cow could be bought for £15 and small pigs from five to ten shillings. Law and O'Donnell subscribed personally to help a bank get started and the bishop often persuaded the clergy to back the system with their approval and some funds. Four more village banks were founded in 1899 – Burtonport, Clondahorkey, Cloughaneely and Termon, ten more in 1901 and a further five in 1903.

Table 22.2

Co-operative Banks in Donegal

Bank	Year established	Bank	Year established
Glenswilly	1898	Malin	1901
Inver	1898	Townawily	1901
Killybegs	1989	Tullynaught	1901
Kilmacrennan	1898	Gleneely	1901
Burtonport	1899	Lough Eske	1901
Clondahorkey	1899	Ardmalin	1903
Cloughaneely	1899	Creeslough	1903
Termon	1899	Dunaff	1903
Ballydevitt	1901	Dungloe	1903
Clogher	1901	Straid	1903
Killygarvan	1901	Kilbarron	1904
Knockalla	1901	Bruckless	1905
Lough Eske	1901	Porteous	1913

Village banks such as these were tremendously popular. Fashion suggested that they had a special charm – their money was 'lucky money'. Some put it down to the essential goodness of the neighbourly helping hand or the fact that the bishop had given it his blessing. In material terms success could be attributed to the practical way in which the business of the bank was done. The rate of interest charged – 5 or 6 per cent compared to the 60 to 100 per cent per annum commonly charged by merchants. One of the most famous of the village banks was that at Malin established in 1901. By 1908 the Malin Bank had over 300 members, deposits (savings) of nearly £1,500 and over £1,000 disbursed annually in loans. The village banks declined after 1912 when support from the CDB and DATI was discontinued making it difficult to establish or expand in the more peripheral areas. Donegal held on to its twenty banks, losing only Glenswilly and Kilmacrennan in 1910. The spurious prosperity of the war years (1914-18) also had its effect due primarily to the laxness of creameries and other co-operatives in giving credit casually to members and bypassing the formalities of a loan through the village bank. Relations between the village banks and the local co-operatives were generally good. Sometimes the banks operated from offices in the local creamery or store co-operative. During the euphoric years of good farm prices during World War I the village bank enjoyed little of the cash flow experienced by the trading co-operatives. By 1922 the number of village banks in Donegal was reduced to thirteen; in the next decade they almost disappeared with only Inver, Tullynaught and Gleneely remaining, mainly due to financial support from the Department of Agriculture to offset the ravages of a serious outbreak of liver fluke in sheep and cattle in the winter of 1924-5. Inver bank closed in 1944 but the others survived until at least 1950 and it is not known how long thereafter. The modern credit union system, based on the same Raiffeisenist principles, began in Ireland in the late 1950s. This new movement especially in its early years was an urban rather than a rural phenomenon. The village bank helped the farmer to buy a cow; the credit union helps the housewife to buy a cooker and a washing machine!

Co-operative credit societies provided a most valuable and necessary service and in the words of Horace Plunkett performed 'the apparent miracle of giving solvency to a community composed almost entirely of insolvent individuals'. By the turn of the century the co-operative movement had gained strength and there was a nationwide trend towards diversification. Co-operative societies were set up for a wide variety of purposes – farm and garden societies (horticulture); home industry societies (homecrafts); poultry societies for the marketing of eggs and fowl; bee-keeping societies. Attempts were also made to establish fishing co-ops and livestock insurance societies but without much success. It became apparent that small single-purpose societies were often quite unable to stand on their own and it was recommended that they merge with the stronger creamery or store societies to ensure better facilities and better management.

Poultry societies

Six co-operative poultry societies were established in Donegal in 1899 – Clonmany, Milford, Glenvar, Tamney, Kincasslagh and Lettermacaward. Very little is known of their activities. Tamney was still operating separately in 1909. The North-West Poultry Society was planned in 1900 with headquarters at Strabane, a poultry fattening station at Lifford and several egg collecting depots at various centres along the Donegal and Great Northern railway systems, but it failed to materialise. But these small independent poultry societies performed a very useful function in basing their main business on packing fresh eggs for export. Emphasis was placed on freshness and it became a common practice that children on their way to school brought the day's supply of eggs to the packing station. The poultry co-op could pay a handsome premium for good quality fresh eggs delivered promptly to selected market outlets.

The reputation heretofore of Irish eggs was very poor, mainly due to the practice of withholding eggs from the market until a large number was accumulated, particularly coming into winter in anticipation of scarcity and rising prices. The marketing of eggs was generally chaotic. 'The Irish egg', noted Horace Plunkett, 'has acted as a depreciated currency. In its too long life it became as dirty as a one pound note, and the process of securing for it its proper place in the English wholesale trade aroused the wrath of those who profited by its humble place in the Irish retail trade.' Eggs were exchanged in the local shop for everything from porter to postage stamps.There was a role too for the travelling dealer:

> It is the same as regards eggs. The jobber will come to the cross-roads to collect them. He will take them whether they are small or big, whether they are clean or dirty, new laid or old. He will say he is giving the highest price for them, and thus he has the good eggs for the price of the stale, dirty ones.[19]

In the late 1890s the CDB sought to develop a deep litter poultry enterprise in Carrigart but with very limited success. The most successful poultry society in Donegal was the Sessiagh O'Neill society (Ballybofey) founded in 1903 which did a flourishing egg trade for many years. When it experienced management difficulties in 1915, the IAWS supplied a manager and the society eventually became a co-operative wholesale, part of IAWS Ltd in 1924 and continued as such into the 1970s.

Co-operative beekeeping
The CDB assiduously promoted beekeeping in Donegal. In 1897 the Board reported a good honey season in Fanad where 1,627 sections of honey were produced from fifty-three stocks of bees. The formation of three co-operative beekeeping societies – Inishowen, Glenties and Milford – in 1902 could have passed unnoticed by the general public, as no elaborate structures were involved, but merely the coming together of a number by local beekeepers to market their honey and buy their beekeeping requisites. Another society was planned for Dunkineely following a visit there of the outstanding beekeeper and co-operator, Rev J. G. Digges, who founded Ireland's first beekeeping co-operative in south Leitrim.[20] Unfortunately, bad weather in three successive years following 1902 virtually destroyed all efforts at co-operative bee-keeping.

Home industries societies
From its earliest days the Congested Districts Board promoted industry and crafts with particular emphasis on indigenous crafts and traditional skills. The Board established training centres and classes for lace-

making, crochet and knitwear throughout the county. With its encouragement, Ayrshire carpet manufacturer, Messrs Morton & Co, established factories at Killybegs (1901), Crolly (1903) and later at Kilcar and Annagry.

An attempt to set up a boyswear clothing factory in Glenties (Albion Manufacturing Co) was abandoned because railway freight charges were deemed excessive. Not all the locally-based training efforts resulted in establishing conventional factories, but the cottage crafts contributed significantly to family incomes. By 1900, lace and crochet were taught by CDB instructors in a number of local centres. A common arrangement was that learners at these centres were fed and paid 3d per day. Established workers earned five shilling and six pence a week. A very high degree of proficiency was achieved in some areas: Bruckless lace or crochet gained not only an identity but a national reputation. In 1908 there were eleven lace centres throughout the county from Culdaff to Ardara.

A number of Donegal groups sent exhibits to the International Exposition (World Fair) in St Louis in June 1904. Amongst these were co-operative home industries societies from Ballyshannon, Bundoran (both registered in 1900) and Ramelton (1902). The Ballyshannon society with eighty-five members sold £600 worth of goods in 1902. Bundoran, after a weak start, flourished for a brief period. The Ramelton Society (fifty-nine members) concentrated most of its effort on teaching the crafts and had very little sales. All three co-operatives had ceased to function by 1909.

Even the foundation of the women's section of the co-operative movement, the United Irishwomen in 1910 (later to evolve into the ICA), failed to arrest the decline of the home-industries co-operatives nationwide. Very few of these small single-purpose societies were financially or organisationally strong enough to put their industry on a sound business-like footing.

The exception was Templecrone. With a membership of 200 women the second guild of the United Irishwomen to be established in Ireland was started in Dungloe, December 1910. Paddy the Cope persuaded his co-operative committee (Templecrone Agricultural Co-operative Society Ltd) to equip the co-operative village hall as a knitwear factory.[21] At the annual general meeting of IAOS in 1916, Fr Tom Finlay, then vice-president, reported on progress and stressed the co-operative moral:

> ... they have set up a factory built and equipped by themselves, where 96 girls are employed finishing the work and hundreds more in the homes round about. Instead of the 5/= or 6/= a week

Plate 22.3   Photo taken in Alex Jacob's field ?1927 shows 10½ lbs. Arran Banner potatoes, planted on 6 May 1927, lifted 5 Oct; they were grown on a reclaimed bog at Ballymore, between Creeslough and Dunfanaghy. The crop gave an extraordinary yield of 17 cwts. 3 grs. 21 lbs. From l. to r.: Jim Thompson, Dick Moffett [?], Alex Jacob, James Algeo, J. J. Silke. Photo is believed to have been taken by Capt. W. G. Hamilton.

Plate 22.4   'Burning off' of A. Pilot Crop, 1940 in Jim Algeo's field. L. to r.: Allan Baird, Ballymore, Jim Algeo.

which they had formerly earned under trying circumstances, these 96 girls now receive as I saw by the pay sheet £101 per week. And they have succeeded because they do honest work. One of the men representing these workers went over to London lately and brought over an order for 5,000 dozen pairs of gloves. These workers in Dungloe are now invading the British market and are able to supply goods which formerly came from Germany. These people in the North have succeeded because they are imbued with the co-operative spirit.[22]

A number of co-operative flax societies were set up in 1905 – Castlefin, Letterkenny, River Finn and Stranorlar. The Pluck Society and the Swilly Valley Society followed in 1907. They were to concern themselves with improving the condition of the flax growing industry – better quality and varieties of seed, better husbandry and primary processing and marketing of this raw material for the linen industry. For the most part these co-ops scutched their members' flax in rented premises, many of them dating back to the days when the acreage of flax grown in the county was so much greater. In the 1840s some 40,000 acres of flax were grown in Donegal and it remained an important cash crop on east Donegal farms for many years despite market aberrations.

The great advocate of co-operation in flax production was Harold Barbour (1874-1938) of the great linen firm of William Barbour of Lisburn. He was for many years chairman of the co-operative wholesale IAWS Ltd. A regular visitor to Donegal, he had a profound influence on the development of co-operatives of all kinds in the county. The Castlefin Flax Society was the most successful. It owned its own premises and was in fact a combination flax and corn mill.[23]

The milling of grain ensured that the premises were in use and some staff employed all year round. All the flax societies did good business during the years of World War I. Two new co-operatives were founded in 1918 – Raymochey and Convoy. The post-war slump and decline in flax growing led to the winding up of most of these societies but the Raymochey and Convoy mills survived to do some business when flax growing boomed briefly again in the 1940s.

Around the time that Birrell's Land Act came into force in 1910 the Congested Districts Board became a corporate body legally entitled to purchase, hold and sell land and to acquire land compulsorily. Although there was a large transfer of land in counties Mayo and Galway, only thirty-three estates changed hands in Donegal. The largest was that of the marquess of Conyngham – 62,976 acres of west Donegal – nearly all the parish of Templecrone. Most of the acquisitions were completed before the war as between 1914-18 only five estates were vested. After 1915 the CDB was not as active on any front as it had been. In 1920 its income was still £231,000, the same as in 1910, although it then needed £2.50 to have the purchasing power of the pre-war pound. The total figure for land transfer in Donegal (up to 1919) was thirty-four estates at a cost of £271,045, approximately 170,000 acres of tenanted and 24,000 acres of untenanted land (appendix 22.2). This compares to total CDB purchases of 733 estates, 1.77 million acres for £6.73 million. The Donegal lands were for the most part allocated to sitting tenants. No co-operative farming societies, as was attempted in other counties, were formed in Donegal to lease or farm land collectively.[24]

Co-operative societies in the county did not get greatly involved in the 'Grow More Food' campaign during World War I. Whilst co-operatives in the south of Ireland were operating machinery and implement hire as well as bacon curing and corn milling, the Donegal societies, with the exception of multi-purpose Templecrone, took remarkably little part and seemed content to leave these activities to private enterprise. The Laggan creamery undertook corn milling in a small way and in Ardara a co-operative milling society was registered distinct from the store co-operative founded there in 1911.

During World War I farmers got good prices for their produce and money was relatively plentiful. Euphoria grew as good times continued even when hostilities had ceased. Co-operatives gave credit freely and in turn took almost unlimited credit from wholesalers, notably IAWS. The co-operative idea was taking hold as farmers were coming to realise the advantages of owning their own business. As early as 1913, Fr Tom Finlay SJ, a man never given to undue optimism, was already talking of the ideal of a 'co-operative commonwealth' when the whole economic system of the nation would be a co-operative one.

In Donegal by 1917 as well as fourteen co-operative creameries, twenty village banks and various other societies there were eleven agricultural store societies all serving the farmers' needs and becoming increasingly involved in the supply of grocery and household goods. They earned respect by their even-handed distribution of food and goods that were in short supply, and acted as a countervailing force against the profiteering of some unscrupulous shopkeepers. Six new store societies were founded in 1919 and ten more in 1920.[25]

Suddenly towards the end of 1920 the bad times came. Widespread unemployment had reduced the purchasing power of British workers and matters were aggravated by the flood of cheap food products coming into Britain from America and the colonies. Farm prices slumped and co-operatives with supplies of scarce and expensive shop goods found them seriously devalued almost overnight. This hit co-operatives all over Ireland and seriously affected the wholesale IAWS Ltd. It undertook a drastic programme of retrenchment in 1922. Exceptionally hard hit were the recently formed co-operative stores in Donegal, the seventeen formed since 1917 (see table 22.1). Many of these were, one might say, crippled from birth. Nevertheless, a third of Donegal's twenty-seven store co-operatives (in 1922) struggled on and survived until the 1950s. These were Buncrana, Corkey, Doe, Downstrandes, Gartan, Glassagh, Inniskeel, Moville and Templecrone.

Nearly all the Donegal societies owed money to the IAWS centre in Derry. In certain cases where co-operatives had serious problems the IAWS operated a kind of informal consultancy in conjunction with the IAOS. A young Mr Mellett from IAWS headquarters who had rescued the Maryborough Society (Laois) was assigned to Letterkenny where the Conwal store society (established 1919) was in serious trouble. Here, however, the rescue operation proved more difficult and eventually involved a takeover. Conwal Society thus became the successful Letterkenny branch of IAWS with Michael Mellett as manager. He was in due course succeeded by his son, Michael; so the Melletts, father and son, managed IAWS Letterkenny for over half a century.

Fishing co-operatives

Despite repeated efforts to establish co-operative fishing, the first such society was not founded until 1915. This was in the Aran Islands and enjoyed fairly spectacular success during the war years. In Donegal there were ups and downs. In the summer herring fishing in Downings in 1904 one local boat landed £200 worth of herring in one night. A year later, November 1905, the report was of massive mounds of herring piled high in a field outside Falcarragh, the huge catch having outstripped the onshore capacity to cope. However, thanks to the superb efforts of the CDB in seeking to integrate catching, processing and marketing, the foundations of a sound fishing industry were laid. It was a matter of annoyance and envy that the cream of the fishing earnings was going to the crews of Scottish steam drifters, coming more and more to the Donegal coast. Fishing off the Donegal coast was banned during World War I because of the presence of German submarines threatening the security of the Royal Navy in its Lough Swilly base but a good deal of inshore fishing continued.

Apart from the basic co-operation of the 'share' system in the individual boats there was very little done towards involving the industry in formal co-operation. On CDB boats the proceeds of each catch were divided on the basis of nine shares: one share for each of the five crew members and the remaining four between the skipper/ instructor and the sinking fund for boat costs and gear. To some extent the infrastructure provided by the CDB and the assistance which it gave on marketing and in every aspect of the industry gave little incentive to Donegal fishermen to set up co-operatives to handle all the complex sides of the business on their own.

It was not until 1920 that two co-operative fishing societies were established in Donegal – the Tory Sound Fishing Society and the West Donegal Fishing Society. The driving force behind the latter society, based in Kincasslagh, was Patrick Gallagher *alias* Paddy Pat Bawn *alias* Paddy the Cope. Both societies were short-lived. The disastrous decline in the German and American markets and enormous increases in freight charges rendered fishing with large boats, as used by these societies, unprofitable. Paddy the Cope and his Templecrone Society continued with a limited level of activity, both in fishing and shipping of goods. The Tory men never really got started. Their large boat, the *Ferry Bank,* which they had purchased to bring their island catches to the mainland, was consumed by fire when at anchorage in circumstances described non-committally in the official IAOS report as 'lost through burning in the war conditions then prevailing'. No first-hand evidence was produced but it was widely held that crown forces were responsible for the burning.

During the nineteen twenties and thirties co-operative societies began a period of retrenchment and isolation. The Congested Districts Board was dissolved in 1923. Civil war, worldwide recession and in Ireland the 'economic war' left the country beset by poverty, disease and emigration. There was a general air of apathy; meetings were poorly attended. They bore little resemblance to the 'large, enthusiastic and turbulent assemblies of co-operative democracy'[26] of former years. Much of the members' sense of belonging was lost, and with it any understanding of what co-operation was, or should be, about. Educational programmes were hardly ever undertaken. Few general meetings were held other than the statutory a.g.m. and the notice given of such meetings was frequently no more than the bare minimum. Management boards and paid managers became secretive about co-operative affairs. They feared that if a small trading surplus was achieved and highlighted the ordinary members would demand a dividend. When dividends ceased to be paid the last tangible feature of member involvement disappeared and the co-operative became little more than another trading post. Expansion during the years of World War II (1939-45) was unthinkable because of shortage of supplies of all kinds. It was not until the 1950s that any worthwhile development could be considered.

When this post-war upsurge came it favoured the creameries and co-operatives with a strong agricultural base, including a number of new store societies serving east Donegal and Inishowen. Other work was now undertaken through the spread of co-operative marts, credit unions and stronger fishing societies in the main ports. There was also a fair amount of diversification primarily through community co-operatives. Templecrone staggered but survived; but unfortunately most of its contemporary pre-war store societies which had followed Paddy the Cope along the lines of consumer co-operation and based their main business on the supply of grocery and household goods, went into decline. They provided honourable service in their small communities during the years of wartime and immediate post-war scarcity, but supermarkets and modern developments in retailing were on the way. In Donegal the possibility of cross-border shopping and price differentials made life very difficult for small shops of all kinds. Small co-operative shops on the Rochdale model had flourished in Northern Ireland, particularly in the Belfast hinterland, but for them as for their Donegal counterparts the tinkle of electronic cash registers sounded a death knell as they faced liquidation or amalgamation with stronger societies.

References

1. *Report of the Recess Committee, on the establishment of a Department of Agriculture and Industries for Ireland* (Dublin, 1896).
2. By custom, but not by law, tenants in Ulster were not subjected to eviction except for non-payment of rent. They could also sell the goodwill (tenant right) of their holding to anyone whom the landlord accepted as a suitable tenant.
3. Following the invention of the sewing machine c.1853.
4. Pamphlet detailing achievements of Templecrone Co-op – IAOS, 1910.
5. D. Murphy, Derry, *Donegal and modern Ulster 1790-1921* (Derry, 1981), pp 222-3.
6. From 296,448 in 1841 to 185,635 in 1891. Of the population loss of 110,813, 41,290 was recorded between 1841 and 1851 with 38,260 over the subsequent decade.
7. Hansard, 10 April 1883. See also J. H. Tuke, *Irish distress and its remedies: the land question; a visit to Donegal and Connaught in spring 1880* (London, 1880).
8. The Board could also benefit from any gifts or loans, directly or indirectly.
9. Under the main part of the same 1891 Act, £33 million was made available for tenants' loans.
10. Nominated by the lord lieutenant.
11. Eighty-four Congested Districts comprising 3,608,567 acres with a population of 549,516 persons and a total P.L.V. of £556,141 i.e. £1.0.2 valuation per head of population. The figure for county Donegal was eighteen shillings. By 1901 the average for all districts was £1. 2. 9. (Donegal: nineteen shillings and five pence).
12. Following the dissolution of the Board, the eighty-four original reports were presented to Trinity College Dublin in May 1927.
13. Horace Plunkett evidence to the *Royal commission on congestion in Ireland.*
14. A quality Arab stallion called Tirassin was donated by the queen and located in the Glenties area.

15. In 1896 the CDB experimented with twelve different potato varieties in Carrigart and Glenties.

16. P. Gallagher, *My story – Paddy the Cope* (London, 1927). A revised paperback edition published by Templecrone Co-op Society Ltd is currently in print.

17. P. Bolger, *The Irish co-operative movement* (Dublin, 1977), p. 241.

18. G. W. Russell, *Co-operation and nationality* (Dublin, 1912). pp 13-14.

19. IAOS, *Annual report* (Dublin, 1904), p. 18.

20. Rev Digges is commemorated by a beautiful stained-glass window in his church in Farnaught, county Leitrim, depicting a Welsh saint with his hive of bees.

21. This hall was built with the help of a prize of £200 from an IAOS prize scheme sponsored by the Pembroke Irish Charities Trustees in 1908, for the co-operatives which had done most to improve the social as well as the material well-being of the people.

22. IAOS, *Annual report* (Dublin, 1917).

23. A similar combination of flax/corn mill at Newmills, Letterkenny has recently been restored to working order by the Office of Public Works.

24. Bolger, *Co-operative movement*, pp 386-7.

25. Ibid., pp 325-32 and passim.

26. *Agricultural co-operation in Ireland: a survey by the Plunkett foundation* (London, 1931), p. 400.

Appendix 22.1

Donegal Districts included in CDB remit

North Inishowen	Gweedore
Clonmany	The Rosses
Desertegney	Aranmore Island
Fanad	Glenties
Rossguill	Glencolumbkille
Gartan	Teelin
Brockagh	Killybegs
Dunfanaghy	Inver
Cloghaneely	Lough Eske
Tory Island	Ballyshannon

Appendix 22.2

Estates purchased by CDB in Donegal for migration of Tenants and enlargement of Holdings

Name of Owner of Estate	Total Purchase Price including Estate Tenants' interests etc.	Area of Estate in statute acres
Carrowcannon Estate	678	93
W. R. Tredennick	6,281	459
Charley Estate (Arranmore)	7,987	4,412
C. J. Tredennick	6,628	420
Fawcett Estate	1,331	170
B. St. J. B. Joule (Tory Island)	1,206	4,222
N. McLoone	2,171	889
General Tredennick	15,932	4,736
G. Williams	1,357	124
H. Hamilton and another	1,089	84
W. H. M. Sinclair	13,445	5,776
Sir E. E. Hayes Bart	27,214	12,863
Viscount Lifford	14,900	11,199
William Wilson	5,543	349
Canon B. Kelly	3,610	1,330
H. and E. Musgrave	43,478	48,592
Rev. G. N. Tredennick	2,509	1,220
G. H. Johnstone	4,331	4,313
James McNulty	349	228
Murray Stewart Estate	1,820	2,508
T. J. Gorringe	4,269	2,965
The Earl of Shaftesbury	3,496	2,484
Rose O'Donnell	1,893	2,873
The Marquess Conyngham (Glenties and Downstrands)	64,008	62,973
Lackenagh Farm (Conyngham, Rosses)	600	63
Sir John Olphert	20,620	15,611
H. & W. Elliott	338	65
H. & C. F. Becher	20,620	13,611
Hon. W. C. Pepys	2,705	704
Marquis of Donegal	1,496	591
George Bustard	16,400	2,965
Ulster Bank, Limited	1,237	1,325
W. F. Marwood and others	2,461	1,470
James Johnston	1,780	1,106
Hart Minors	4,094	1,359
E. C. Mansfield	5,811	453
Miss A. Mahaffy	616	191
Rev. J. S. Stevenson	476	336
Henry Musgrave	10,082	1,834
John Craig	651	479

Source: W. L. Micks, *An account of the constitution, administration and dissolution of the Congested District Board.*

Plate 22.5
Patrick Gallagher
(Paddy the Cope).

Plate 22.6   Hugh Law of
                          Marblehill.

Chapter 23

THE MARQUIS, THE REVEREND, THE GRANDMASTER AND THE MAJOR: PROTESTANT POLITICS IN DONEGAL, 1868-1933

JOHN TUNNEY

It is, perhaps, technically correct to see the 'Protestant Ascendancy' as an eighteenth-century reality, a power, privilege and wealth monopoly vested in one religious denomination under the constitutional and legal framework and underpinning all social relations. Such a view, however, leaves one with the problem of defining the dominant position that Protestants continued to enjoy for most of the nineteenth century as a hangover from the earlier era. Certainly in a county such as Donegal, while the ascendancy *per se* may have gone, it continued to exist insofar as the minority controlled almost every aspect of life in the community. Gradually this position changed and its political fortunes may prove to be a useful index of wider economic and social contexts. This paper will trace the course of Protestant political involvement in county Donegal from the 1860s to the early years of the Free State.

In the general election of 1868, the year after the Fenian Rising, two Tories, the marquis of Donegall and Thomas Connolly were elected to represent county Donegal. Both men, like the other MPs elected to Westminster from the province of Ulster that year, were members of the Church of Ireland. All belonged to the landed gentry, being either major landowners themselves or kinsfolk of such landowners. In terms of the influence they had on public life, however, these bare facts tell only part of the story. As B. M. Walker has put it:

> Besides owning nearly all the land, these men occupied an important social position in the countryside. They acted as magistrates, were members of grand juries, as well as boards of guardians and often presided over local societies and organisations.[1]

This short comment perfectly describes the situation that pertained in Donegal and later we will explore the complex web of religious, social and blood ties that, in combination with land ownership, was at the heart, not just of this class influence but of its very cohesion.

In the decade 1870 to 1880 the Liberal Party endeavoured to overthrow the long monopoly of comfortable control that the Tories had enjoyed. In this situation the marquis of Donegall, being the son of the duke of Abercorn, was much less vulnerable than his colleague Connolly who, in 1875, had a mere forty votes to spare over the Liberal candidate, Tristram Kennedy. Connolly's untimely death in 1876 caused a by-election, but this time the local Tory, William Wilson of Raphoe, had almost one hundred votes to spare over the Liberal candidate, Thomas Lea, a British manufacturer from Kidderminster. For a short time it seemed that the Tories had found the measure of their opponents and perhaps had even checked the tide of change. This was, however, an illusion and soon yet another Donegal by-election provided evidence that not just change but a cataclysm was to dramatically alter the Ulster political landscape.

It was December 1879 and Lea again stood for the Liberals. Although there had been scarcely any change in the electorate since the previous by-election three years earlier, he swept to victory transforming a deficit of ninety-nine votes into a winning margin of 683. The evidence was irrefutable; the result had turned on a direct transfer of support from the conservative to the liberal cause. But why? It appears that several factors were at work, not least of which was unrest generated by a serious agricultural depression. In addition, as Bew and Wright have correctly pointed out: 'Far from leaving the Protestant farmers of the North cold the land war had important consequences in Ulster.'[2]

Many Presbyterians believed that the land question was of primary economic importance and they were not prepared to allow long-held suspicions of Catholics retard progress on this issue. Why, for example, should the Presbyterian farmers of east Donegal vote for landed Tories when the Liberal Party represented their own quite separate interests. Just four months after their first breakthrough in the county, the Liberals got the opportunity to build on this success when Gladstone called a general election in April 1880.

The redoubtable Marquis Hamilton was again in the contest for the Tory Party. Thomas Lea represented the Liberal interest but this time he had as running-mate, Rev John Kinnear, pastor to Letterkenny's Presbyterian congregation. Kinnear is one of those colourful personalities who, though deserving of the historian's attention, have been unfortunately neglected. He had spent much of his early life in America, which may well explain his open, democratic views, which almost appear radical when compared to those of many of his contemporaries. Kinnear had campaigned for tenant rights in the 1850s and had taken a pragmatic approach to co-operation with Catholics and nationalists in such campaigns. He was a fine orator though sometimes regarded by his enemies as a demagogue. Kinnear was surprised by the ignorance in Britain regarding Ireland's problems and was convinced of the 'persistent misgovernment of Ireland by the constituted authorities of the empire'.[3] Many of his ideas were revolutionary: he wanted the grand juries scrapped and replaced by county boards elected by all ratepayers. As early as 1881 he was developing the idea of compulsory purchase as a solution to the land problem and in 1885 he advocated Home Rule for Ireland.[4] Recognising the strength of the Liberal ticket, the Tories tried to negotiate an arrangement to share the constituency's two seats. The Liberals, 'scorning a compromise', went for a clean sweep[5] and the results fractured the old political mould. Although the margin of victory was small, both seats went to the Liberal Party. With the defeat of the marquis of Donegall, no titled aristocrat and no major land-holder was ever again to contest a parliamentary election in the county.

In the general election of 1880 similar Liberal successes occurred throughout Ulster, fashioned by the alliance which the land reform campaign had forged. The prospect of such reform allowed a variety of interest groups 'with divergent strategies and ultimate objectives' to work together, at least temporarily.[6] Thus Presbyterians, Catholics and Orangemen became involved in the Land League despite their very different backgrounds and the very different ways they perceived themselves within the polity. On the other hand, Presbyterian support for the Liberals in Donegal has been estimated at around 23 per cent of the electorate.[7] It is therefore ironic that the election of a British industrialist and a Presbyterian minister to the Westminster parliament was dependent largely on the county's Catholic voters. But in the years between 1880 and 1885 a combination of factors ensured that this support would not continue.

Donegal had begun to show signs of a growing popular nationalism since the mid-1870s. This explains, for example, the large and enthusiastic St Patrick's Day demonstration that occurred in 1877 and which continued in the years that followed.[8] The militant turn that the Land War took in 1884, particularly in west Donegal, led Catholics to insist that their demands be presented with greater vehemence and by public representatives who actually shared them. The jailing of Fr McFadden of Gweedore and the subsequent unwise use of coercion by the authorities politicised many priests. These priests were to prove vital in getting voters registered for the general election that came in the following year and ensured that the Irish Parliamentary Party would benefit most from the electoral reforms that had gone through parliament during the life of the previous government.

If the 1880 election had cracked the political mould it was shattered forever in 1885. The most critical factor influencing the result in 1885 was the enormous change in the electorate. In 1880 the county had two seats and 4,612 electors. Five years later there were four one-seat constituencies, with a total electorate of over 30,000.[9] Many of the new electors were small farmers and agricultural labourers who had no sympathy whatsoever for the substantial farmers, who were the backbone of the Liberal support. Indeed in east Donegal there was a tradition of enmity between the Protestant farmers and their largely Catholic labourers – an enmity that continued well into the present century.[10]

The electoral changes, the talk of Home Rule and the very determined effort that the National Party was making to win seats in Ulster, led Tories and Liberals to co-operate in some constituencies to avoid splitting the unionist vote. A pact of this type was made in Donegal. The Rev Kinnear was ruled out of the contest through illness, so the Tories agreed to leave the field open to the other sitting MP, Thomas Lea.[11] In two of the county's other constituencies unambiguous conservative-unionist candidates opposed the nationalists. In the north, Sir Henry Hayes Stewart entered the contest at the last possible moment, while in south Donegal the task of carrying the unionist banner fell to the county grand master of the Orange Order, A. H. Foster. No attempt was made to fight west Donegal and as things transpired, the Irish Parliamentary Party won the other three seats with a crushing display of political muscle-flexing by Donegal's Catholic majority.

The result of the 1885 election must have been a terrible blow to the morale of Donegal's Protestant community. Never again would one of its members represent its interests in the Westminster parliament. Thereafter, until the advent of Sinn Féin, there was no chance that Irish Parliament Party candidates standing for election in Donegal would be defeated. However, this was by no means the last occasion on which unionists were to fight parliamentary elections in the county. Of all the elections up until 1918, only the general election of 1906 and the second general election of 1910 were uncontested in the four Donegal constituencies. T. B. Stoney, E. T. Herdman, D. B. McCorkell, Henry Stubbs and J. Cooke QC were just some of the prominent citizens that represented the unionist interest. Still, it was impossible to escape the harsh reality that Protestant participation in parliamentary elections only served to confirm their own impotence in this aspect of public life. Further discussion of the matter would hold little interest were it not for the fascinating role which a uniquely Protestant institution began to play in the community's political life; enter the Orange Order.

The Orange Order had traditionally been of limited significance in Donegal.[12] Concentrated chiefly in the south of the county, it was largely ignored by Presbyterians and avoided by the more prosperous, both of whom saw it as tainted with the whiff of society's 'riff-raff'.[13] In the northern half of the county this state of affairs continued until the 1900s. South of the Barnesmore Gap, however, in the second half of the nineteenth century the Order gradually came to enjoy the patronage of local wealthy landowners and consequently it grew in importance. At this time the Orange Society's role was that of guardian of Protestant values and Protestant freedoms. Its badges and emblems, marches and demonstrations had a strong cultural dimension, expressing the community's closed identity and celebrating a history which set them apart from their Catholic neighbours. It could not be said to have played an overtly political role, nor did it see itself as having one. All this was to change and again it was the 1885 general election that was the catalyst.

Electoral reforms in 1885 replaced Donegal's one constituency by four. Each of the new constituencies had more electors than the entire county had five years earlier. These changes highlighted organisational weakness in Tory-Unionist election machinery and this, in the south Donegal constituency, the Order moved, at first hesitantly, to fill. True to its original *raison d'etre*, the county Grand Orange Lodge (GOL) was primarily concerned with candidate suitability. In November of that year the following resolution was passed:

> That we, the district lodge, assembled recommend the brethren to look out for an Orange candidate and that the county lodge draw up a code of questions relating to the principles of Christian religion and that in the event of us not finding a suitable candidate we abstain from voting unless otherwise determined at a subsequent meeting of the brethren.[14]

This amazing threat to withold Orange support from any unionist candidate whose Protestant principles did not measure up to those of the GOL was not yet put to the test since an unimpeachable candidate was found in the person of A. H. Foster, county grand master of the Orange Order. He was soundly beaten by the nationalist Bernard Kelly, but the defeat was not considered a complete waste by the GOL which felt that Foster should be congratulated on 'illiciting the support of so large a number of electors and of infusing a hopeful spirit into the loyalists generally'. Thanks were also considered due to:

> ... the self sacrificing exertions of the polling agents, chiefly though not exclusively of our institution, who worked as if the result depended on their single exertions.[15]

Thus the brethren were at the coal face of local unionist election efforts and were to remain there for some time.

The general election of 1886 gave the Orange Order an opportunity to build on its initial entry into Donegal politics. Grand Master Foster initially refused the invitation from the GOL to enter the race. No doubt the hopelessness of trying to overhaul a nationalist majority of over 3,500 (there was not even that number of unionist electors in the constituency) was a central consideration. But the GOL was determined that the seat be contested and it is testimony to the increase in the political temperature raised by the threat of Home Rule that the Lodge's attitude had changed significantly since the previous year. Gone was the careful concern over correct Protestant principles; the general membership was now urged to support 'any loyal' candidate who would stand for the cause. There was evidence too of a hardening of attitudes and a motion passed in January 1886 stated that: '... the brethren shall use their utmost legal efforts to prevent any Protestant countenancing or in any way compromising himself with the nationalist candidates or their party'.[16]

Unequivocally, religious and political principles are identified as being, as it were, coterminous. However, this concern with preventing any member from contaminating the purity of the tribe or the integrity of its cause is even more remarkable for the ethnocentric, exclusivist, almost apartheid assumptions that underlie it. Foster relented late in the day agreeing to let his name go forward for the election and although he improved slightly on his previous performance, he was again trounced by Kelly.

A pattern had now been established in south Donegal whereby the members of the Orange institution had become the political machinery of the unionist cause. When Henry Stubbs of Ballyshannon, a non-Orange candidate, stood for election in 1892 he unquestioningly was given the backing of the Order and the GOL urged: 'the private lodges under the Grand Lodge to make every exertion to canvass the division and to bring every unionist vote to the poll at the pending election'.[17]

As ever, defeat was certain and the concern was simply to demonstrate to those outside that there was a unionist presence in the constituency and to boost local morale in the face of Catholic triumphalism. In fact Stubbs did better than Foster had in his two attempts, but not dramatically so.

In 1893 Gladstone made his final attempt to enact Home Rule; it was not to become a pressing issue in British politics for almost twenty years. The Donegal GOL passed the following resolution full of rhetoric and overflowing with pride in the British connection:

That this County Donegal Lodge protests at the attempts at present being made to weaken if not sever the connection that binds this country to the greatest empire the world has even seen and believe that the bill at present before the parliament will, if it passes into law, be ruinous to the best interests of the country and we pledge ourselves to oppose the same by every means in our power.[18]

Copies of the resolution were sent to the Grand Orange Lodge of Ireland, the marquis of Salisbury, Col. Saunderson and other prominent British politicians, including A. J. Balfour and Joseph Chamberlain. Perhaps one has here in the phrase 'every means in our power' the seeds of an attitude that made possible at a later date support for the UVF, illegal gun-running and even the threat of civil war.

Thus far we have described how Protestant domination of Donegal politics had finally been broken. This did not mean that their political influence within the county had ended, for there was still the important matter of local politics and local government. For most of the nineteenth century local government throughout rural Ireland was administered by two institutions, the grand juries and the boards of guardians. The former operated at a county level while the latter presided over the poor law unions. Poor law union boundaries were dictated by geographical and administrative convenience rather than tradition and they often crossed the older boundaries of barony and county. All of the seven unions of Donegal, Dunfanaghy, Glenties, Inishowen, Letterkenny, Milford and Stranorlar, and, parts of the three unions of Ballyshannon, Londonderry No. 2 and Strabane No. 2 were in Donegal.

The Donegal grand jury had responsibility for a wide range of functions including maintenance of roads and bridges, a lunatic asylum in Letterkenny, the county infirmary in Lifford, the cost of extra police when needed, the conveyance of prisoners, the upkeep of court houses and the remuneration of county officials. Furthermore it had to provide compensation in malicious injury cases. The grand jury met only twice a year so, despite its considerable ability to dispense patronage through awarding contracts for such things as road maintenance and the undoubted prestige attached to membership of such an exclusive club, it was not responsible for the day-to-day running of local government in the county. This role belonged to the poor law guardians, who met weekly. They administered the poor law, oversaw the workhouses, controlled the dispensary medical system, acted through paid officials and were empowered to raise finances to cover the costs of these activities.[19]

To understand how these bodies operated it is vital to outline the means and mechanisms by which they were constituted. The grand jury was selected by the county sheriff, who in turn was appointed by the lord lieutenant of the county. Traditionally, and for almost all the period under scrutiny here, the position of lord lieutenant for Donegal belonged to the duke of Abercorn. After 1885 the incumbent was James, second duke of Abercorn, ex-Tory MP for Donegal. In 1878 the Abercorn estates in Donegal amounted to 16,000 acres, although this was by no means the full extent of the Hamilton family holdings in the county.

High sheriffs appointed by the Abercorns – men like Major James Henry Todd Thornton, Robert McClintock and Sir Samuel Hayes – were all unmistakably members of the landed gentry. Indeed in 1901, shortly after the county council had been instituted sixteen of the county's twenty deputy lieutenants had served in the past as high sheriffs. All were members of the Church of Ireland and owned large estates; many were to become directly involved in the great unionist, anti-Home Rule campaign of 1910-14.

There were virtually no limits under law as to whom the high sheriff might select as grand jurors. So long as he appointed one person from each barony holding freehold land to the value of £50, or leasehold to the value of £100 above the rent, he could choose whomsoever he liked. It is not surprising, therefore, that the grand jury was a bulwark of Protestant, or more specifically, Church of Ireland, privilege, comprised of the petty aristocracy, the gentry and retired military. It was not surprising either that it excluded not only Catholics but Presbyterians as well. Those outside the select club had hoped in vain that some change would follow the local government reforms of 1898. Fourteen years later, however, Presbyterians and Catholics on the county council were combining to call for the suspension of the high sheriff's salary until such time as he explained why both these denominations were being ignored as possible candidates for the grand jury. In the council debate that followed it emerged that only one Presbyterian was then sitting as a grand juror and that only one Catholic had ever done so.[20]

Although the selection of the poor law guardians did involve an elective element it was not in any real sense democratic. Half of each board was made up of justices of the peace resident in the union in question. Where these proved to be too few in number, the deficit was made up by drawing in non-resident JPs. The other half of the board was elected by rate-payers and property owners. In these elections there was, in theory, a maximum of 6 votes per person but it was possible for an individual to have up to 36 votes in one electoral division.[21] Predictably, such an arrangement left control in the hands of the largely Protestant propertied class.

Not surprisingly, the majority considered this system of local government totally unsatisfactory. Nevertheless, throughout the nineteenth century all attempts to have it reformed failed. In the long term the old arrangements were doomed and as the decades passed, the forces of popular democracy grew in strength. When reform did come in the Local Government of Ireland Act 1898, the result was a transformation that virtually stripped the traditional order of its powers overnight.

The purpose of the 1898 Act was to make local government more democratic. This involved not only the alteration of the way that existing local bodies were constituted but the creation of new institutions, which were to take over the functions of the old. Most of the powers of the grand jury were transferred to the newly established county council; the older body being left with very limited legal functions. County Donegal was restructured into ten new rural district councils, which assumed many of the functions of the boards of guardians. The new rural district councillors automatically became poor law guardians, so although the old institution remained in existence, its powers were reduced and its membership changed. Additional changes to the electoral system added to the transformation. Plural voting was abolished and the electorate enlarged.

Roche implies that Catholic farmers were the sole beneficiaries of these changes, but his assessment is too simplistic to accurately describe the situation in Donegal.[22] For the Protestant farmers in the east of the county, for example, and for Presbyterians in particular, the new legislation meant that for the first time they had a real voice in local administration. Up until 1922 Protestants had working majorities in the rural district councils of Strabane No. 2 and Londonderry No. 2. The RDCs however, were subject to the county council which remained dominated by a Catholic/nationalist majority (fig. 23.1).

The grand jury was in no doubt about the hidden agenda behind the reforms. It was to them an attack on the role of Protestants, particularly the landed gentry in public life. At the 1898 spring assizes it passed a detailed motion which essentially sought to have the new Local Government Act overturned.[23] Copies of the motion, like many an Orange Order motion before and after, were sent to such people as the prominent Ulster unionist Col. Saunderson and the Tory MP, A. J. Balfour. It was to no avail; the authorities simply ignored the grand jury's concerns and representations. Within twenty years the total control that Protestants had enjoyed over the county's local and parliamentary politics had disappeared. These developments have to be viewed in the wider context of the equally sobering socio-economic changes that were taking place simultaneously.

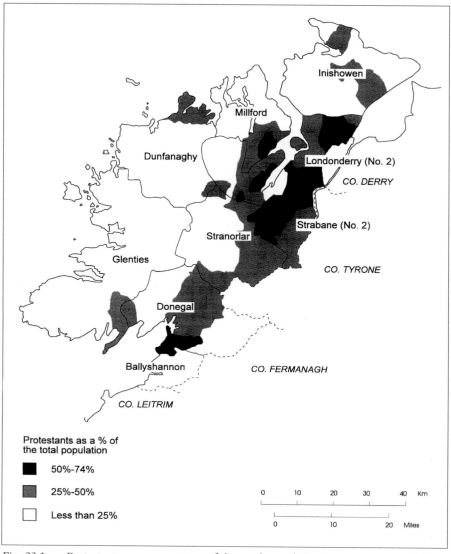

Fig. 23.1   Protestants as a percentage of the total population in county Donegal by
rural district, 1911.

In the period between the great famine and the First World War, a
remarkable transformation was reshaping almost every aspect of
Donegal life. Slowly but relentlessly Catholics began to replace
Protestants as the influential and dominant faction in society. While the
total population of the county fell, with the numbers of every
denomination suffering a very significant decline, Catholics were
increasing as a proportion of that total. Literacy rates and general

Table 23.1

Major religious denominations as a % of the total population of Donegal 1861-1926

	1861	1881	1901	1926
Total population	237,395	206,035	173,722	152,508
Catholics	75.1%	76.5%	77.7%	81.9%
Church of Ireland	12.2.%	12.0%	11.5%	9%
Presbyterians	11.4%	10.1%	9.3%	8%
Others	1.3%	1.4%	1.5%	1.1%

Decline in the numbers of the two major Protestant denominations in Donegal 1861-1926

Church of Ireland	29,943	24,759	19,908	13,774
Presbyterians	26,215	20,784	16,212	12,162

educational standards among Catholics improved dramatically and were reflected in ever more positions within local government going to the majority community. This change was mirrored by a rise in the percentage of locally-based national government officials who were Roman Catholics. In almost every area of the professions, commerce and business the once dominant position enjoyed by the Protestant minority was being encroached upon – banking and financial services being the sole exception. At the same time the land purchase acts were eating away at the monopoly that Protestants had once enjoyed over the primary economic resource.[24]

Some sociological models of minority-majority conflicts see them in terms of the competition between the two communities for the limited prestige, power and economic resources available within society.[25] Viewed in these terms, the collapse of control in the political arena becomes just one more sector in which Protestants were losing out to the majority. Fear, tension and feelings of being under siege were the result. Clearly, from a Protestant perspective, the Home Rule scare of 1910-14 takes on an even greater significance. For them it came to represent a dreaded confirmation that they had lost any hope of arresting their declining fortunes and that they would be abandoned to the tender mercies of those over whom they had lorded for so long. It must have seemed a frightening prospect, something to be opposed with the ballot box in one hand and the cavalry carbine in the other.

In the decade-and-a-half leading up to 1910, apart from fighting hopeless election battles and trying to mitigate the effects of the new local government reforms, Protestant political activity was at a minimum. As the immediate threat of Home Rule disappeared after 1893, so did the enthusiasm for active participation in the Irish Unionist Alliance or the Ulster Defence Union. As a result it proved impossible to sustain a local political network. Individuals such as T. B. Stoney, W. H. Boyd or T. J. Atkinson attended meetings in Belfast, or occasionally took part in delegations to prominent British politicians, but that was the extent of their involvement. An indication of local stagnation is the fact that the county committee of the IUA changed scarcely at all between 1906 and 1912.[26] Despite this committee's inactivity we shall use its composition to investigate the nature of the Protestant community's traditional leadership.

The committee had thirteen members, drawn evenly from all parts of the county. The honorary president was a Boer War veteran and Donegal's third largest land-owner, the fifth earl of Leitrim, who was not to play any active role in unionist affairs until 1912. There was a Church of Ireland clergyman (a member of the Orange Order), and the remainder were prominent members of the local gentry. Yet here's the crux: What do we mean by this term 'gentry'? What qualifications allowed one to be classed as a member of this exclusive club?

Wealth was not the key, as many prosperous farmers and even more prosperous merchants could testify. Membership was a function of a more complex, more subtle set of variables, the most important of which was family pedigree. Thus, the fact that one's family had owned, and lived on, an estate for hundreds of years was of primary significance. Next, and for historical reasons usually linked to the first, came religion, which was almost always Church of Ireland. Growing up, the children were sent to the same schools and colleges and so had a shared educational experience. Later they would enter the same clubs, sit on the diocesan committees, be nominated as grand jurors, maybe even get a turn as high sheriff, judge the produce competitions at the local agricultural show and so on. The network of relationships was reinforced partly by marriage and partly by a system of visits and 'calls' between families who could claim such pedigree. Until such time as one succeeded to one's estate it was common to go into the military or some other branch of the imperial services for a time. This had the added advantage of conferring an attractive military title, which was no impediment when one returned to civilian life. Further integration into wider gentry networks came through invitations to attend state functions, such as the balls staged by the viceroy in Dublin Castle.

The traditional leaders of the Protestant community were then, 'chosen' through a combination of family pedigree, religion, education, social arrangements and in the last analysis, tradition itself. It was not absolutely necessary to have all the qualifications that have just been listed, but some combination of them was imperative. To illustrate the previous discussion we will look briefly at a typical case, a father and son, members of the Hamilton family of Brownhall, near Ballintra.

The Hamiltons held estates in Donegal since the 1660s. By the second half of the nineteenth century the Brownhall branch of the family owned 8,500 acres. Major James S. Hamilton sat on the Donegal IUA committee during the years of the Home Rule crises. Both he and his son, Captain John, had earned their military titles serving with the Donegal Militia, and in this respect they had only occasionally been 'embodied'. This, for example, had seen the son serve in England for four years during the Boer War.

Both men had been educated mainly in Britain. In John Hamilton's case he had been to Skyrne preparatory school. Then, after a short spell at St Columba's, county Dublin, he went to Uppingham Public School. From there it was on to Cambridge, where he studied electrical engineering. During this time his schoolmates had included members of the Knoxes and Olpherts of Lifford-Strabane and the Moores, Pomeroys and Herdmans. The major's wife was related to the Stewarts of Hornhead, while his sister was married to the prominent unionist and one-time county grand master of the Orange Order, A. H. Foster. When at home, the Hamiltons were regular visitors to, and were in turn visited by, the Moores of Molenan and Cliff, the Watts of Thornhill, the Stoneys of Raphoe and the McClintocks of Hansted. All of these were prominent landed people in north-west Ulster.

Both father and son served as grand jurors and were deputy lieutenants of the county. John was the sitting high sheriff when the county council was instituted and was one of the three nominees that the grand jury was entitled to make to the first council. Predictably, these wheels within wheels allowed them to rub shoulders with many prominent personages. John Hamilton was a very close friend of Sir Emerson Herdman. At university he had been an acquaintance of a future lord chancellor of England, F. H. Maugham. He had met and struck up a close friendship with Cecilia Wray, when the latter was on holiday in south Donegal. In the future course of her life she was to marry the politically powerful, if ill-fated, Sir Henry Wilson.[27] In this way, through a veritable tapestry of contacts and relationships the family not only had its finger on the pulse of prestige and power in its own corner of Ulster, but was integrated into the more sublime reaches of the British establishment. Its class led the Protestant community into the great anti-Home Rule battle which was their swan song. Even during the campaign their position was being challenged by a combination of business men, solicitors, shopkeepers and big farmers. This new breed seemed more comfortable with the fire-brand rhetoric of extreme unionism and had more stomach for bending the law in ways that had become unacceptable to many of the gentry.

The result of the 1910 general election catapulted the Irish Home Rule question to centre stage. John Redmond's Irish Parliamentary Party held the balance of power and their price for supporting the new Liberal government was a parliament in Dublin. The tide was stemmed by the House of Lords but reforms saw to it that when Asquith introduced his new Home Rule bill in April 1912, the Lords could do no more than offer a stay of execution. Protestant Ulster sprang to the defence of the Union and Donegal did all that was asked of it.

Having whipped up an initial flurry of enthusiasm the next step was to demonstrate to the outside world the full extent of the unionist opposition. The signing of a Solemn League and Covenant was decided upon for 28 September; a day declared a public holiday by the Ulster Unionist Council. Throughout Donegal, from Hornhead to Dunkineely, unionists of every creed and hue gathered in schools, private houses, churches, Orange and Masonic halls to sign the covenant. The number who signed (8,300 men and 8,730 women) represented a major organisational effort by the entire community.[28]

. To sustain the interest and channel the available energy, a network of Ulster Unionist Clubs was put in place. When it became apparent that the government planned to stick to its guns, the unionist leaders decided to up the ante and establish their own army, the Ulster Volunteer Force (UVF). The entry on to the scene of Charles Clements, earl of Leitrim, ensured that even in this respect Donegal would keep pace with the rest of the province. A full discussion of the organisation, structure, and activities of the UVF is inappropriate here.[29] It belongs more properly to the realms of paramilitary history than to any account of the role of democratic politics. Suffice it to say that when Carson visited Raphoe for a major rally in October 1913, amongst the ten thousand who were in attendance were 1,500 uniformed and armed UVF members, many carrying cavalry carbine rifles, smuggled into the country, disguised as Congested Districts Board supplies on the orders of the earl of Leitrim himself. By the summer of 1914, Donegal's unionists were as ready for the imminent civil war as anyone could reasonably have expected. The Kaiser, however, intervened and for the time being Irish men, particularly the Protestant communities, had someone else to fight.

During the years of World War 1, as Europe tore itself asunder and pierced the hearts of almost every family on the continent the Protestant community in Donegal suffered traumas that rocked it to its foundations. Its young men in the Ulster Division suffered horrendous casualties with over one-third killed and almost as many seriously

Plate 23.1   Edward Carson arriving at Strabane station on his way to UVF demonstration at Raphoe, 1913 (Cooper Collection, P.R.O.N.I.).

Plate 23.2   View of crowd and platform party, UVF demonstration at Raphoe, 1913 (Cooper Collection, P.R.O.N.I.).

Plate 23.3   Section of the crowd, UVF demonstration at Raphoe, 1913 (Cooper Collection, P.R.O.N.I.).

wounded. Political developments were almost equally shattering. During the course of the Buckingham Palace negotiations in 1916, it became clear that the Ulster unionist leadership were ready to drop their brethren in Cavan, Donegal and Monaghan without so much as a by-your-leave. The collapse of this initiative held out hopes for a more favourable settlement when peace finally came, but such hopes were in vain.

Preliminary post-war negotiations started from the assumption that the proposed northern state would be comprised of only six counties. The members of the Donegal Unionist Association were appalled. They protested to the UUC secretary, to Carson, to their contacts in the establishment and to the government itself. They worked under Lord Farnham's leadership with the unionists in Cavan and Monaghan to try to persuade the UUC to change its stance. It was all to no avail. Even some of those on the council, whose homes and property were within the new statelet, were shocked at the particular turn of events. Sir James Stronge felt that 'the three counties have been thrown to the wolves with very little compunction'.[30] In any event, the deed was done. Many witnesses who testified to the boundary commission a few years later recalled the events with bitterness. To this day many older Protestants still discuss the 1920 settlement in terms of being 'sold down the river'.

Plate 23.4   Edward Carson addressing the crowd at UVF demonstration at Raphoe, 1913 (Cooper Collection, P.R.O.N.I.).

The feelings of betrayal, of a solemn covenant having been broken, were very strong. But more was to follow over the next three years, as their worst nightmares became reality.

In the War of Independence, the Civil War and even more especially through the intervening peace, Protestants throughout the county suffered terribly. They had the big houses where troops could be billeted; they had the cars that could be requisitioned; they owned many of the big shops and stores that were raided for provisions, but the widespread attacks amounted to much more than that. Arson, theft, kidnapping, intimidation and every kind of abuse was hurled at them. Some of this was in retaliation for what was seen as anti-Catholic pogroms in Belfast. Much of it, however, can be put down to a complete breakdown of law and order which allowed every yahoo, every embittered tenant, labourer or competitor with an axe to grind, to settle old scores with very little chance of ever being caught.[31] In retrospect, the manner in which the Free State troops had conducted themselves provided the only glimmer of hope from a Protestant point of view. In fact, the respect engendered by the Cosgrave government was to have important long-term political implications which were evident even during the general elections of the 1920s.

A unionist candidate, Major Moore of Cliff, contested the 1918 election, standing in the east Donegal constituency. With two nationalist candidates in the field to split the Catholic vote, he could in theory have been elected. But the local voters bucked the national trend, didn't vote Sinn Féin and instead handsomely elected the Irish Parliamentary Party candidate.[32] No unionist contested the 1922 election but the 1923 general election was a very different affair from 1918, since the entire county was now a single multi-seat constituency which clearly had a Protestant quota if only it could be mobilised. The problem, of course, was finding a suitable candidate. From where would the political leadership come under the new and very different circumstances? The answer, when it came, seemed obvious in retrospect. It would have to be from among the returned war veterans. As matters transpired, the actual choice of candidate could scarcely have been more suitable. Major J. S. Myles proved to be a winner in every respect.

Myles came from a long established Protestant family that had extensive trading interests throughout south Donegal, but were by no means members of the landed gentry. In the period before the First World War he had been a local commander of the UVF in the Ballyshannon area. At the outbreak of hostilities he had received a commission as a captain in the Ulster Division and went on to fight on the Somme and elsewhere. He returned home a major, having been decorated by the king. During the troubles he had significant amounts of property destroyed and more significantly, in February 1922, he was one of the prominent border unionists kidnapped by republicans. While not a member of the Orange Order, he thought it prudent not to antagonise Orange interests.[33] He was known as a moderate and effective county councillor, who was popular even with Catholics. In summation then, Myles had played a full part in the pre-war anti-Home Rule campaign, had served the empire with distinction, suffered more than most during the troubles and his views were such as not to alienate any strand of Protestant opinion. Finally, while it may not have been a great help though unlikely to have been a hindrance, he was a Freemason.

His campaign manager, Captain Scott of Birdstown – one time secretary of the county's Unionist Association – was a close personal friend. They had been at school together and had served in the same battalion during the war. Other prominent unionists rallied behind Myles. His candidacy was proposed by James Clarke of Porthall and seconded by Colonel Wagentreiber, soon to be elected to the county council. Because of the security situation there was none of the traditional canvassing by Myles. In a policy statement in a local newspaper he clearly aligned himself with the forces of 'law and order' indicating that he stood with the pro-Treaty forces. He pledged to work to have 'property restored' and to achieve 'the most economical administration combined with efficiency'.[34]

The election result – Myles topped the poll and was elected on the first count – was a great triumph for unionism. Civil war politics split the nationalist vote between Free Staters and Republicans but his first preference vote of 6,954 was all the more impressive given that the other Protestant candidate in the field, Lowery, representing the Farmer's Party, polled over 1,100 votes. Unionists, virtually unrepresented in parliament for some forty years, now had one of their own in Dáil Éireann. In the general election of June 1927, Myles received 7,557 first preference votes and in September of the same year he increased this to 8,000. His performance in the election of 1933 was even more spectacular when, despite a reduction through emigration of the previous electorate by some 3,000, Myles polled 10,789 votes. Clearly 'the Major' as he was known in Donegal was attracting support across the religious divide.

The distribution of Myles's second preference votes may inform us more about the nature of Protestant politics in Donegal in this period. Table 23.2 shows the percentage distribution of his surplus votes in the elections between 1923 and 1933.[35]

Table 23.2

	1923	1927	1927	1932	1933
Govt. (C na nG)	6.8%	41%	45%	93.6%	93.4%
Repn. (FF)	1.8%	2.5%	2.4%	1.8%	1.2%
Labour	1.8%	8.1%	4.3%	4.6%	—
Farmers	86.6%	42%	48%	—	—
Centre*	—	—	—	—	5.4%

(*There was a selection of smaller parties and a number of independents in the elections prior to 1933).

Predictably in 1923 most of the transfers went to Lowery, the only other Protestant candidate. The pain of the immediate past was still too fresh for Protestants to be able to cast aside the weight of history and transfer their second preferences to Cumann na nGaedhael. By 1927, however, it is clear that a significant change had taken place. The Farmer's Party was still the natural home for the bulk of Myles's transfers but the swing to the party of government was most impressive. By 1933 almost 95 per cent of Myles's transferable surplus was going to Cumann na nGaedheal and Donegal Protestant loyalty to Fine Gael, its successor, continued this distinctive voting pattern.

In January 1987, Deputy Dick Spring led the Labour Party out of coalition with Dr Garret FitzGerald's Fine Gael and a general election was called. At the time Donegal north-east was considered one of the most predictable constituencies in the country. Then a charity worker from Belfast, Michael Boomer-Brookes, described by southern political journalists as a 'Bible-wielding Ulster Protestant candidate' entered the field as an independent unionist.[36] Although he canvassed scarcely at all, Boomer-Brookes finished ahead of the Labour Party candidate with 696 votes. Down the years Protestants had continued to elect their own county councillors and so, locally, no one was particularly shocked. Nationally, however, political commentators were surprised at his performance, surprised perhaps that, sixty-five years after the treaty, Donegal's Protestant political tradition still lived. It was confirmation, if such were needed, that political traditions have much in common with old soldiers; they don't so much die as fade into the background until someone gives them an opportunity to re-assert themselves. It's an old lesson and one which in the wider Irish context should not be forgotten.

References

1. B. M. Walker, 'The land question in Ulster 1868-85' in J. Donnelly Jr. and S. Clarke (eds), *Irish peasants and land agitation in modern Ireland* (Wisconsin, 1983), p. 234.
2. P. Bew and F. Wright, 'The agrarian opposition in Ulster politics, 1848-87' in Donnelly and Clarke, *Peasants and land agitation*, p. 149.
3. P.R.O.N.I., D1374/4. From a speech made in the House of Commons, May 1881 and collected in bound MS form as 'The speeches of John Kinnear'.
4. Ibid., Nov. 1885.
5. *Derry Sentinel*, 27 March 1880.
6. Bew and Wright, 'Ulster politics,' p. 203.
7. Walker, 'Land Question in Ulster,' p. 246.
8. T. D. Murphy, *Derry, Donegal and modern Ulster 1790-1921* (Derry, 1981), pp 137-58.
9. B. M. Walker, *Parliamentary elections in Ireland 1800-1922.*

10.   J. Tunney, From ascendency to alienation: Donegal's Protestant community 1880-1932, unpublished M.A. thesis, Department of History, University College Galway (1985), pp 129-36.

11.   The speeches of John Kinnear, Nov. 1885.

12.   P. Ó Snodaigh, 'Volunteers, militia and yeoman in Donegal' in *Donegal Annual* (1969), and Tunney, Donegal's Protestant Community, pp 53-60.

13.   Ibid.

14.   Minutes of the Donegal Grand Orange Lodge, 10 Nov. 1885, MS in private hands in county Donegal.

15.   Ibid., 18 Jan. 1886.

16.   Ibid., 19 June 1886.

17.   Ibid., 1 July 1892.

18.   Ibid., 16 March 1893.

19.   J. D. Williams, *Seventy-five years of local government in Donegal* (Donegal, 1974), p. 2.

20.   *Derry Sentinel*, 28 August 1912.

21.   Williams, *Local government*, p. 5.

22.   D. Roche, *Local government in Ireland* (Dublin,1982), pp 45-7.

23.   Murphy, *Modern Ulster*, p. 147.

24.   A detailed analysis of this entire process is given in Tunney, 'Donegal's Protestant community', pp 1-50.

25.   Rosemary Harris, *Prejudice and tolerance in Ulster* (Manchester,1972).

26.   P.R.O.N.I., D 989/C/56, Irish Unionist Alliance, bound reports for 1901-11.

27.   This account of the Hamiltons draws extensively on J. S. Hamilton, *My times and other times* (Ballyshannon, 1950).

28.   P.R.O.N.I., D 1098/1 boxes 33-39, covenant signatories.

29.   See Tunney, Donegal's Protestant community, pp 87-103.

30.   P.R.O.N.I., D 627/435, letter from J. Stronge to Hugh de Fellenberg-Montgomery.

31.   Tunney, Donegal's Protestant community, pp 137-54.

32.   General Joseph Sweeney claimed that Sinn Féin did not contest the constituency so as not to split the nationalist vote. Walker, however, lists a Sinn Féin candidate and records his vote in *Parliamentary elections*.

33.   Myles did not attend the Orange Order's commemorations in 1924 but was careful to send an apology, *Londonderry Standard*, 14 July 1924.

34.   *Donegal Democrat*, 17 Aug. 1923.

35.   The table is based on the election results published in the *Donegal Democrat*, 4 Sept. 1923, 18 June 1927, 24 Sept. 1927, 27 Feb. 1932 and 4 Feb. 1933.

36.   Shane Kenny and Fergal Keane, *Irish politics now* (Dublin, 1987), pp 119-21.

Plate 23.5   Cardinal Patrick O'Donnell.

Chapter 24

STAIR LITRÍOCHT GHAEILGE DHÚN NA nGALL LE CÉAD BLIAIN ANUAS

NOLLAIG MAC CONGÁIL

Tá Dún na nGall ar cheann den bheagán contaetha sa tír ina bhfuil an Ghaeilge á labhairt go fairsing i gcónaí. Tá an Ghaeilge le cluinstin timpeall an tuaiscirt, san iardheisceart agus í lár an chontae,[1] gí go bhfuil na ceantracha Gaeltachta ansin á ngannú agus á dtanú go millteanach le fada an lá. É sin ar neamhchead do na plandálacha, don chóras ghallda oideachais, don ghorta, don imirce, do mhaorlathas ghallda an Rialtais, na heaglaise, na turasóireachta agus na tionsclaíochta, do naimhdeas an phobail i gcoitinne agus uile, a chuidigh lena meath le cian d'aimsir.[2] Maireann an Ghaeilge léi, áfach, agus mairfidh, isteach san aois seo chugainn ar scor ar bith. Teist mhór í sin ar dhúchas láidir Ghaelach bhunadh an chontae san am atá caite.

De réir dhaonáireamh 1851, an chéad daonáireamh inar fiosraíodh cás na Gaeilge, bhí amach is isteach ar sheachtó míle duine i nDún na nGall a raibh an Ghaeilge acu, sin trian de phobal uile an chontae. Dáiríre, ba líonmhaire an pobal Gaeilge i nDún na nGall ag an am ná in ocht gcontae eile Chúige Uladh ar fad.[3] Rud eile atá ar shlí a ráite fán líon Gaeilgeoirí sin ná nach raibh Béarla ar bith ag a leath. Agus é sin uilig a ghlacadh le chéile, ní hiontas ar bith é ainm an chontae a bheith in airde ó thaobh na Gaeilge de, fiú amháin san aois seo. Tá tábhacht mhór ag baint le dúchas Gaelach seo an chontae nuair a chuimhnítear go bhfuil amach is isteach ar thrí scór scríbhneoir Gaeilge[4] maíte ar an chontae agus nach bhfuil ach dornán iontach beag díobh sin ar fad nach raibh ina gcainteoirí dúchais. Rud eile de, is iomaí glúin scríbhneoirí Gaeilge eile nár Chonallaigh iad a tháinig faoi anáil throm na Gaeltachta i nDún na nGall, bunadh na Sé Chontae ach go háirithe.[5]

Córas gallda oideachais an chontae

Má chruthaigh an contae go maith i dtaca le holc maidir le líon agus fairsinge a chuid ceantracha Gaeltachta, go háirid i gcomórtas le contaetha eile, bhí sé fágtha ó thaobh léann foirmeálta na Gaeilge de. Bunús na gcainteoirí Gaeilge sin, anuas go dtí bunú an Stáit sa bhliain 1922 ar scor ar bith, cha raibh siad ábalta an Ghaeilge a léamh ná a scríobh. Chan iontas ar bith sin óir bhí toirmeasc iomlán ar an Ghaeilge mar ábhar teagaisc agus mar mheán teagaisc faoi chóras na bunscolaíochta náisiúnta san aois seo caite ó thús na 1830í go dtí deireadh na 1870í.[6] Sa bhliain 1879 tugadh cead an Ghaeilge a theagasc sa bhunscoil mar ábhar deonach breise i ndiaidh uaireanta scoile ach is beag leas a baineadh as seo óir, faoin am a bunaíodh Conradh na Gaeilge, ní raibh ach tuairim is caoga bunscoil sa tír ar fad a ghlac an deis seo.

Mar léiriú ar ghéarchéim theagasc na Gaeilge sa chontae sa tréimhse seo, breathnaítear bomaite ar an eolas seo a leanas. I dtuarascáil Chumann Buan-Chosanta na Gaedhilge (Society for the Preservation of the Irish Language) don bhliain 1892, tugadh liosta iomlán de na múinteoirí in Éirinn a raibh teastas sa Ghaeilge acu agus de na scoileanna a raibh siad ag teagasc iontu. I gcás Dhún na nGall, tá ceathrar luaite, mar atá: J. A. Doherty, Cruit Island; D. Heraghty, Churchill, Letterkenny; John C. O'Boyçe, Fanad, Tamney; J. C. Ward, Killybegs. Cuirtear an líon beag múinteoirí sin i gcomórtas leis an líon múinteoirí sna contaetha eile ab fhairsinge ceantracha Gaeltachta sa tír: contae Chorcaí, naonúr déag, contae na Gaillimhe, naonúr déag, contae Chiarraí, ochtar is fiche, contae Mhaigh Eo, ochtar déag agus contae Phort Láirge, naonúr.[7] Is léir ón phíosa eolais sin amháin cé chomh fágtha is a bhí an contae sa chomhthéacs seo.

Bhisigh an scéal go mór ina dhiaidh sin nuair a throid Conradh na Gaeilge go láidir ar son na Gaeilge sa chóras bunscolaíochta. Sa bhliain 1900 tugadh cead an Ghaeilge a theagasc taobh istigh d'uaireanta scoile agus, cúpla bliain ní ba mhoille, ceadaíodh an Clár Dátheangach sna scoileanna Gaeltachta, rud a d'fhág go bhféadfaí úsáid a bhaint as an Ghaeilge chomh maith leis an Bhéarla mar mheán teagaisc. Próiseas fadálach a bhí anseo nár fhág a lorg go dtí blianta fada ina dhiaidh sin, go háirid ar ábhair scríbhneoirí.

Má b'fhearr scéal na Gaeilge sa mheánscoil. Sa bhliain 1899, cuir i gcás, ní raibh ach tuairim is deich meánscoil do bhuachaillí sa tír ar fad ar sheas níos mó ná duisín dalta dá gcuid scrúdú Gaeilge an Stáit. I dtaca le meánscoileanna do chailíní de sa bhliain chéanna, níor bhain ach corradh beag le dhá scór cailín pas amach i scrúdú Stáit na Gaeilge agus bhain siad sin uilig, chóir a bheith, leis an aon scoil amháin, mar atá, Clochar Lughaidh, contae Mhuineacháin, áit, dála an scéil, a raibh Bríd Ní Dhochartaigh, bean den bheagán banscríbhneoirí Conallacha atá againn, ar an fhoireann teagaisc lá ab fhaide anonn. Mar a tharla i gcás na bunscolaíochta, áfach, bhisigh an scéal sna meánscoileanna le himeacht ama, go háirid nuair a rinneadh ábhar éigeantach den Ghaeilge le haghaidh Scrúdú an Mháithreánaigh sa bhliain 1913. Ach arís, próiseas fadálach a bhí ann a ghlac na blianta fada sular aithníodh a thoradh.

Ó tharla scéal na Gaeilge a bheith mar a bhí sa chóras oideachais sa cheathrú dheireanach den aois seo caite agus i mblianta tosaigh na haoise seo, chan ansin a d'fhaibhir síolta tosaigh litríocht Ghaeilge Dhún na nGall. Ach, ní miste cuimhneamh san am chéanna gur chuir an córas gallda oideachais sin ar chumas daoine áirithe léann Gaeilge a lorg agus a shealbhú lá ab fhaide anonn agus is as an phróiseas sin ar fad a tháinig luathscríbhneoirí Gaeilge Dhún na nGall chun boinn. Sop in áit na scuaibe a bhí sa chóras ghallda oideachais sin ach b'fhearr é ná a bheith ar an bhlár fholamh ar fad mar a bhí na daoine le fada an lá roimhe sin.

Tá cúpla focal eile ar shlí a ráite fá cheist na litearthachta i gcoitinne i nDún na nGall san aois seo caite agus isteach go maith san aois seo fosta. Chuir saol eacnamaíoch an chontae cúl mór ar scaipeadh an léinn i measc na gConallach. Má bhreathnaítear ar an chineál saoil a chaith an mhuintir óga ansin san am atá caite, aithneofar nár fhreastail siad i dtólamh ar na háiseanna léinn a bhí ar fáil san am. Cuir i gcás, is minic a chaill siad leath na scoilbhliana agus iad ar fostú ar an Lagán. Is minic a coinníodh sa bhaile iad fosta le lámh chuidithe a thabhairt amuigh agus istigh ag dioscaireacht agus ag timireacht. Is iomaí lá scoile a cailleadh chomh maith de bharr easláinte. Sin an teachtaireacht atá le baint as caint seo Mháire agus é ag cur síos ar an drochthinreamh ina scoil féin nuair a bhí sé ag iarraidh foireann dráma a bhailiú:

Bhí Cassius ar an Lagán agus bhí Brutus ar fostó i mBun an Bhaic. Bhí Portia ag bogadh an chliabháin dá mháthair sa bhaile, agus bhí Caesar ina luí sa bhruitínigh.[8]

Traidisiúin litríochta an chontae roimh thús an chéid – sean-léann na Gaeilge

Bhí traidisiún liteartha Gaeilge sa chontae i bhfad siar sa stair, rud is fíor fán chuid eile den tír fosta. Bhí fáil ar an tsaibhreas sin i lámhscríbhinní agus i leabhair scolártha amháin, rud a d'fhág a éifeacht ceilte ar na scríbhneoirí Conallacha Gaeilge de bharr a ndíobháil léinn i gcúrsaí Gaeilge. Ní raibh ach duine nó beirt ar fad as a measc a bhainfeadh ceart de Mhaoilíosa Ó Brolcháin nó d'Annála Ríochta Éireann nó de bhairdne chlann Mhic an Bhaird. Chuir beagán acu spéis i saothar Mhánais Uí Dhónaill óir ba chóngaraí é dá n-am agus dá gcanúint agus dá dtallann féin ach ba é an beagán é. Ba bheag an tairbhe dóibh, mar sin, an réimse áirithe sin dá dtraidisiún dúchasach léinn. Bhí mearchuimhne acu ar an litríocht sin mar a bhí acu ar a gcéimíocht shinseartha.

An léann béil

Easpa léinn ina dteanga dhúchais féin a d'fhág an *corpus* litríochta sin ceilte orthu ach bhí an traidisiún béil acu mar a bhí ag a ndaoine maithe muinteartha riamh anall. Bhí an Rúraíocht agus an Fhiannaíocht acu, scéalta gaile agus gaisce, seanchas fán uile rud a bhaineas leis an tsaol seo agus leis an tsaol úd eile. Bhí amhráin bhinne acu fosta chomh maith leis na scéalta filiúnta agus rud mór sílte acu díobh: achan dream agus achan cheantar ag maíomh as dream s'acu féin – filí Rann na Feirste, filí Ghleann Fhinne agus Ghleann tSúilí, filí Theilinn agus a thuilleadh eile nach iad – mhair cumraíocht na bhfilí gan iomrá sin i mbéal agus i gcuimhne na ndaoine go dtí tús na haoise seo agus ina dhiaidh. Is maith mar a chuireas Niall Ó Dónaill síos ar an traidisiún chéanna:

> Na glúnta daoine gan áireamh nach raibh léann leabhar acu, chothaigh siad a n-intinn ar scéalaíocht agus ar cheol. Tharraing lucht gach linne orthu na heachtraí a dtáinig a n-iomrá chucu ó chianaimsir agus chóirigh go húr iad in aice lena dtoil féin ar phearsana agus ar áiteacha a bhí ar aithne acu.[9]

Mar theist éigin ar shaibhreas an traidisiúin bhéil sa chontae, d'fhéadfaí tagairt a dhéanamh don chnuasach mhór béaloidis a chruinnigh leithéidí Sheáin Uí Eochaidh, Liam Mhic Mheanman agus Aodha Uí Dhónaill do Choimisiún Béaloidis Éireann in imeacht na mblianta agus don ábhar fhairsing béaloidis ó achan chearn den chontae a foilsíodh i bhfoirm leabhair mar na cinn seo a leanas: *Cruach Chonaill* le Seosamh Laoide, *Zehn Irische Volkserzöhlungen Aus Süd-Donegal* le Ludwig Mülhausen, *Na Cruacha, scéalta agus seanchas* le hÁine Ní Dhíoraí, *Uair an chloig cois teallaigh* le Séamas Ó Catháin, *Scian a caitheadh le toinn* le Cosslett Ó Cuinn, *Maighdean an tsoluis agus sgéalta eile, Oidhche áirneáil i dTír Chonaill, Daoine beaga agus daoine móra* – iad sin a dtriúr le Feargus Mac Róigh – *Maith thú, a Mhicí* agus *Lá de na laethaibh* le Micí Sheáin Néill Ó Baoill, *Scéalta Johnny Sheimisín* srl. Sin beagán den stóras ar fad a rinneadh a chur i míotar agus a fhoilsiú.

Timirí agus múinteoirí taistil

Is luath a tuigeadh do lucht na hAthbheochana má bhíothas leis an Ghaeilge a choinneáil beo agus a chur chun cinn ar fud na tíre go gcaithfí an Ghaeilge a chothú agus a neartú i measc bhunadh na Gaeltachta, chan i measc lucht an léinn agus mhuintir na mbailte móra amháin mar a bhí ag tarlú cuid mhaith go dtí sin. Ceapadh timirí agus múinteoirí taistil go fada leitheadach ar fud na tíre le craobhacha den

Chonradh a bhunú agus le soláthar do na craobhacha céanna ar an uile bhealach a bhí riachtanach. B'fhearr ar an ócáid lucht Gaeltachta a chur ina bhun seo in áit Gaeilgeoirí, rud a rinneadh. Seo a leanas cuid de na dualgais a bhí ar na timirí céanna:

> To establish Irish classes and branches of the Gaelic League, to teach persons to read Irish, who would in turn be capable of teaching and influencing others, to distribute Irish literature, to interview the principals of the districts visited, and to inform and arouse local opinion on the Irish language question.[10]

I dtaca leis na múinteoirí taistil de, seo a leanas an cineál duine a bhí a dhíth:

> The type of teacher wanted is a man who can teach Irish independently of books, more especially in the initial stages. He must be expert at *modh díreach* and *clár dubh* work, and must have a competent knowledge both of Irish and English. While sound teaching methods are essential, personality is more so. The *múinteoir taistil* should know his Ireland past and present; should have a thorough grasp of what Irish Ireland means; should be able to appeal to the sentiments of the people as well as to their intellectual side; should be a patriot and an enthusiast; good-humoured and an optimist ... A knowledge of Irish songs, music, dances and games will help ... *Múinteoirí* should feel that they are soldiers of Ireland and should talk to young and grown of Ireland's heroes and Ireland's glories, thus infusing the right spirit of nationality into all with whom they come in contact.[11]

I ndáiríre, bhí siad ina múinteoirí, ina lucht bolscaireachta, ina n-eagraithe siamsaíochta agus fostaíochta, ina mbailitheoirí béaloidis 7rl. – na cúraimí líonmhara sin ar fad a mbíonn freagracht astu ar chuid mhór eagraíochtaí Stáit agus deonacha faoi láthair. É sin uilig gan trácht ar an tsíorthaisteal ar rothar, olc maith an aimsir, ar bheagán tuarastail.

Ní minic a chuimhnítear go raibh na timirí agus na múinteoirí taistil seo gnóthach i nDún na nGall fosta. Is iad a bhí agus ní bheadh an cháil chéanna ar an chontae ó thaobh na Gaeilge de agus ó thaobh na scríbhneoireachta de ach ab é go raibh. Ní miste a rá anseo go raibh líon mór de na scríbhneoirí Gaeilge as Dún na nGall sáite sa chineál sin oibre. Cuir i gcás, bhí Séamas Ó Searcaigh ina mhúinteoir taistil agus gan é ach sé bliana déag d'aois agus bhí Antoine Ó Dochartaigh, arbh as oileán na Cruite dó fosta, i mbun na gairme céanna. Ar na Conallaigh eile a bhí ag gabháil don chineál sin oibre bhí Séamas Mac an Bhaird, Aodh Ó Dubhthaigh, Aindrias Ó Baoill, Seán Bán Mac

Meanman agus Séamas Ó Grianna. Ní hamháin go raibh siad sin ag obair i gcontae Dhún na nGall ach chuaigh siad isteach sna contaetha a bhí ag críochantacht leis fosta, rud a chuidigh go mór le haontú na Gluaiseachta sa chúige ar fad.

Má fuair na daoine seo cuid mhór masla agus anró agus iad i mbun na hoibre seo, is cinnte os a choinne sin go ndeachaigh sí chun tairbhe dóibh féin ar go leor bealaí gan trácht ar an leas a rinne sí do Ghluaiseacht na Gaeilge sa chontae i gcoitinne. Thug sé isteach i nGluaiseacht Oifigiúil na Gaeilge iad, den chéad uair ina lán cásanna; thug sé eolas dóibh ar aidhmeanna uile an Chonartha: ar na modhanna oibre, ar a gcuid comórtas liteartha, ceoil srl., ar thábhacht stair na hÉireann, ar eagraíochtaí Gaeilge, ar lucht na Gaeilge ó áiteanna eile, ar Ghaeltachtaí eile, go háirid ina gcontae féin. I mbeagán focal, chuir sé i mbealach shaol na Gaeilge iad i dtéarmaí fostaíochta, fealsúnachta agus gairme. Scar sé iad ó shaol thraidisiúnta na feirmeoireachta agus na hiascaireachta, ón spád is ón tsleán. Chuir sé cuid mhór acu ar dhréimire léann na Gaeilge agus na scríbhneoireachta. Ó tharla sin amhlaidh, tá tábhacht mhór ag baint leis na timirí agus na múinteoirí taistil seo i stair scríbhneoireacht Ghaeilge Dhún na nGall. Gan amhras, baineann an scéal seo leis an chéad scór bliain den aois seo amháin óir tháinig deireadh cuid mhaith leis an chleachtadh seo le bunú an tSaorstáit nuair a thit cúram Athbheochan na Gaeilge ar an Rialtas.

Coláistí Gaeilge

Aithníodh i ndiaidh bhunú Chonradh na Gaeilge nach bhféadfaí aidhmeanna na hAthbheochana a chur i gcrích go sásúil mura bhféadfadh lucht na Gaeilge an Ghaeilge a scríobh agus a léamh. Gí go raibh feabhas ag teacht ar stádas oifigiúil na Gaeilge sa chóras oideachais le himeacht aimsire, cha raibh go leor daoine oilte i léann na Gaeilge leis an obair seo a chur chun cinn go gasta agus go héifeachtach. Chuige sin, cuireadh Coláistí Gaeilge ar bun, mar a deir Donncha Ó Súilleabháin, 'chun múinteoirí Gaeilge a chur ar fáil do na craobhacha agus chun oiliúint a thabhairt do na múinteoirí taistil a bhí ann agus chun daoine le Gaeilge a oiliúint i modhanna múinte teanga'.[12]

Rinneadh an chéad cheann de na Coláistí Gaeilge seo, mar atá, Coláiste Múinteoireachta na Mumhan, a oscailt i mí Iúil, 1904. Cuireadh triúr eile ar bun sa bhliain 1905: Coláiste Chonnacht i dTuar Mhic Éadaigh, Iolscoil na Mumhan sa Rinn agus Coláiste Chomhghaill a bhí ina Choláiste Geimhridh i mBéal Feirste. Cuireadh Ardscoil Cholmcille ar bun sa bhliain 1906 i gCloch Cheann Fhaolaidh. Tá tábhacht mhór ag baint leis na coláistí luatha Gaeilge seo maidir le scéal agus cinniúint na Gaeilge agus na Gaeltachta, le spreagadh scríbhneoireachta agus le hoiliúint scríbhneoirí.

Má ghlacaimid le cás Ardscoil Cholmcille de arbh é an chéad choláiste Gaeilge é a bunaíodh i nDún na nGall agus arbh é a rinne an t-eolas do líon mhór coláistí eile ar fud an chontae ó shin i leith, aithnímid a thábhacht ach breathnú ar liosta na n-údar Conallach Gaeilge sin a rinne freastal ar a chuid cúrsaí nó a bhí ag teagasc ann: Seaghán Mac a' Bhaird, Fionn Mac Cumhaill, Seán Bán Mac Meanman, Síle Ní Dhúgáin, Aindrias Ó Baoill, Antoine Ó Dochartaigh, Domhnall Ó Grianna, Séamas Ó Grianna, Séamas Ó Searcaigh agus Tadhg Ó Rabhartaigh. Is fiú a lua anseo gur fhreastail Aindrias Ó Baoill agus Séamas Ó Searcaigh ar Choláiste Gaeilge Thuar Mhic Éadaigh fosta agus gur fhreastail Séamas Ó Searcaigh ar Choláiste na Mumhan agus ar Choláiste Chomhghaill. Sin tromlach na luathscríbhneoirí Gaeilge Conallacha.

Ní luaitear ansin na daoine eile a rinne freastal ní ba mhoille ar Ardscoil Cholmcille — Máiréad Nic Mhaicín agus Bríd Ní Dhochartaigh ina measc, mar shampla — ná ar choláistí Gaeilge eile sa chontae agus sa chúige a bunaíodh ar thoradh moille: Coláiste na gCeithre Maighistrí, Leitir Ceanainn sa bhliain 1907 (Seaghán Mac a' Bhaird agus Séamus Craig ar na hoidí ann); idir 1911 agus 1912 bunaíodh Scoil an Chaisleáin Ghlais, Tír Eoghain, Coláiste Bhríde, Ó Méith, Ardscoil Ultach, Béal Feirste, Coláiste Mhaolmhaodhóg, Oileán Reachrann (1913), Ardscoil Bhreifne, Gleann Ghaibhleann, contae an Chabháin (1920), Coláiste Theilinn (1920). Sa bhliain 1926 aistríodh Coláiste Bhríde ó Ó Méith go Rann na Feirste. Bunaíodh lear mór coláistí Gaeilge i nDún na nGall ó shin, mar shampla, Coláiste Cholmcille i nGaoth Dobhair sa bhliain 1936. D'imir na coláistí céanna seo tionchar mór ar scríbhneoireacht Ghaeilge an chontae agus ar lucht a scríofa. Is léir mar sin go bhfuil áit lárnach ag na coláistí sin sa scéal atá faoi chaibidil anseo.

Tá sé ar shlí a ráite anseo gur bheag ab fhiú cinniúint na Gaeilge i nDún na nGall ach ab é muintir na Sé Chontae riamh anall. Tá an méid seo a leanas le rá ar an tséala ag Seán Mac Meanman faoi luathstair Choláiste Uladh nó Ardscoil Cholmcille:

As cathair Dhoire a thigeadh an mhór-chuid de na macaibh léighinn a casadh orm féin i gCloich Cheann Fhaolaidh ins an am seo … Chluinfeá daoine ag rádh, agus bhí sé inchreidte i gceart, go gcaithfidhe an Coláiste a dhruid na chéad bhliadhanta acht go bé na buachaillí agus na cailíní agus an t-airgead a tháinig as Doire. Acht leoga ní raibh bunadh Bhéal Feirste, nó Árd Mhacha, nó contae Thír-Eoghain i bhfad na ndiaidh. Go dearbhtha daoibh ba hiad muinntear na Sé gConndae a choinnigh an druithleog gan a ghabháil as go dtí go dtáinig bunadh Thír Chonaill chucu féin agus go bhfuaradar ar a mbonnaibh.[13]

Nuair a chuimhnítear ar choláiste Gaeilge sa lá atá inniu ann, cuimhnítear ar na mílte de pháistí bunscoile agus meánscoile ag tarraingt chun na Gaeltachta i rith mhíonna an tsamhraidh. Caitear an t-am ansin le teagasc na Gaeilge, le ceol agus le damhsaí Gaelacha – le sealbhú dhúchas na Gaeilge agus na Gaeltachta, más fíor. Is mó go mór an spéis a chuireas na daoine óga seo sa tsiamsaíocht, sa chuideachta agus sa chaidreamh. Níorbh ionann na Coláistí Gaeilge sa tsean-am, áfach. Cúrsaí do dhaoine fásta amháin a bhí i gceist ansin ach, gan amhras, ní raibh toirmeasc ar an tsiamsaíocht. Caithfear deoch gharg na foghlama a shnáthadh i dtólamh leis an chuideachta má táthar le daoine a mhealladh.

Ba mhó ba chosúla na chéad choláistí Gaeilge le coláistí le haghaidh an oideachais aosaigh ná rud ar bith eile. Bhí clár trom léinn agus oibre i bhfeidhm iontu: modhanna múinte, foghraíocht, stair na litríochta ó ré na sean-Ghaeilge i leith. Bhí béim ar léachtaí ócáide ar an uile chineál ábhair agus, gan amhras, ar stair agus ar thraidisiún béil na Gaeltachta. Is é Conradh na Gaeilge a chuir ar an tsaol an chéad lá riamh iad le haidhmeanna éagsúla an Chonartha a chur i bhfeidhm agus chun cinn, rud a rinne siad.

Is anseo go minic is túisce agus is iomláine a tháinig scríbhneoirí luatha Gaeilge Dhún na nGall faoi anáil léann oifigiúil na Gaeilge, Chonradh na Gaeilge agus Ghluaiseacht uile na hAthbheochana agus a gcuid feidhmeannach agus lucht tacaíochta. Fuair siad an léann a bhí ag gabháil ansin agus dhírigh a smaointe sa treo chéanna go minic. Ní hiontas ar bith go mbeadh lorg obair uile na gcoláistí Gaeilge seo ar chuid mhór de luathfhoilseacháin na n-údar Conallach. Ach, chomh maith le gach rud eile, spreag na coláistí Gaeilge seo iad, thug siad ardú meanman dóibh, thug siad le fios dóibh gurb éadáil luachmhar í an traidisiún béil agus an Ghaeilge, agus go raibh ráchairt ar an Ghaeilge taobh amuigh den Ghaeltacht. Bhí baint ag daoine céimiúla leo, m.sh. Íde Nic Néill, An tEaspag Ó Dónaill, Roger Casement, Lord Ashbourne, Pádraig Mac Piarais, Éamonn Ó Tuathail agus Úna Ní Fhairchilligh. Spreagadh agus broslaíodh iad lena gcion féin a dhéanamh ar son na Gaeilge. Chuir siad deiseanna fostaíochta ar fáil dóibh fosta a chuir ar a gcumas scríbhneoireacht a dhéanamh lá ab fhaide anonn in áit a bheith ag úspaireacht sa bhaile mar a rinne a gcuid sinsear rompu.

Luathstair na scríbhneoireachta

Ag cuimhneamh dúinn ar an chúlra sin ar fad, caithfear a fháil amach anois cérbh iad na chéad scríbhneoirí Gaeilge Conallacha ag deireadh na haoise seo caite agus ag tús na haoise seo, cad é an sórt scríbhneoireachta a rinne siad, cad é a spreag i mbun pinn iad agus cé air a raibh a gcuid scríbhneoireachta dírithe.

Is eol dúinn sular bunaíodh Conradh na Gaeilge sa bhliain 1893 nach raibh ach fíorbheagán leabhar Gaeilge i gcló sa tír ar fad, amach is isteach ar scór acu.[14] I gcás chéadscríbhneoireacht Ghaeilge Dhún na nGall de, chan le leabhair a cuireadh tús léi. Tosaíodh le cineál áirithe scríbhneoireachta, cuid mhaith de réamhdhéanta nó meicniúil, a foilsíodh in irisleabhair luatha na Gaeilge, m.sh. amhráin nó scéalta béaloidis nó pointí teanga/canúna nó filíocht a cuireadh i gcló in *An Gaodhal* thall i Meiriceá ag leithéidí Phádraig Uí Bheirn nó Antoine Uí Dhochartaigh nó Sheagháin Mhic a' Bhaird, nó abhus in Éirinn in *Irisleabhar na Gaedhilge* agus i bhfoilseacháin eile de chuid Chonradh na Gaeilge ar thoradh moille. Le hiarrachtaí laga nó trialacha ach tábhachtacha san am chéanna a cuireadh tús le scríbhneoireacht Ghaeilge Dhún na nGall agus is ón dúshraith sin a shíolraigh *corpus* iomlán litríochta lá ab fhaide anonn.

I dtaca le scéal na leabhar de, níor foilsíodh ach dhá leabhar as Gaeilge nó ag plé leis an Ghaeilge le húdair Chonallacha ó thús na hAthbheochana go dtí tús an chéid seo, mar atá, *Modern Irish* le J. P. Craig sa bhliain 1896 agus *An Teagasg Criostaighe fá choinne Díoghóise Rátha-Bhoth* sa bhliain 1891 le Seaghán Mac a' Bhaird, glactar leis gí nach bhfuil a ainm leis. Léiriú iad an dá leabhar sin agus na leabhair Chonallacha eile a foilsíodh go ceann tamaill ina dhiaidh sin ar chás na foilsitheoireachta Gaeilge sa chontae – agus sa tír ar fad – san am. An chéad chuspóir a bhí taobh thiar den scríbhneoireacht chéanna sin, cuspóir oideachasúil. Mura raibh ach beagán daoine sa chontae ar fad a bhí ábalta an Ghaeilge a léamh nó a scríobh, chaithfí an scéal sin a leigheas láithreach trí ábhar fóirsteanach teagaisc/foghlama a sholáthar ar mhaithe le lucht foghlamtha agus teagaisc na Gaeilge faoi *aegis* Ghluaiseacht na Gaeilge ach go háirid. Sin *raison d'être* thromlach na leabhar a scríobh J. P. Craig: *Modern Irish* (1896), *Modern Irish grammar* (1900), *Modern Irish composition* (1901), *Studies in composition* (1901) srl. Rinne Conallaigh eile an cineál céanna leabhar a sholáthar thart ar an am chéanna ar na cúiseanna céanna, mar shampla P. T. Mac Ginley le *Handbook of Irish teaching* (1902) nó Mícheal Ó Dochartaigh le *Ceachta agus comhradh ar neithibh* (1906).

Ach dá riachtanaí iad na saothair nó na téacsleabhair chéanna sin chomh maith leis na leabhair staire agus chreidimh, níor leor iad amháin le daoine a mhealladh ar bhealach léann agus litearthacht na Gaeilge. Rinneadh ábhar éadrom scríbhneoireachta a sholáthar fosta le cuidiú le próiseas na foghlama. Cuir i gcás scríobh J. P. Craig leaganacha athchóirithe de scéalta traidisiúnta, mar shampla *Clann Lir* (1901), *Clann Tuireann* (1902), *Clann Uisnigh* (1902) chomh maith le leabhair cheoil, mar shampla *An ceoltóir* (1903) agus nuacheapadóireacht éadrom ar nós *Iasgaireacht Shéamuis Bhig* (1904).

Chomh maith le leabhair a scríobh ar chúrsaí staire agus teagaisc agus athchóiriú a dhéanamh ar ábhar thraidisiúnta, chuir Peadar Mhag Fhionnlaoich spéis ar leith sa drámaíocht mar bhealach éifeachtach le teanga agus Gluaiseacht na Gaeilge a chur chun cinn, rud a rinne an tAth. Peadar Ua Laoghaire agus an tAth. Pádraig Ó Duinnín ag an am chéanna sa taobh eile den tír. Scríobh sé na bundrámaí *Miondrámanna* (1902) chomh maith le *Tá na Francaighe ar an muir* (1905) a raibh leagan Béarla ag gabháil leis. D'aistrigh sé an dráma *An pléidhseam* (1903) a scríobh Seamus Mac Manus, scríbhneoir cáiliúil Béarla de chuid an chontae a raibh a ainm in airde ó thaobh na scríbhneoireachta de agus a thug tacaíocht d'Athbheochan na Gaeilge ar go leor bealaí.

Is léir, mar sin, gur scríobhadh cuid mhór den luathscríbhneoireacht Ghaeilge Chonallach seo faoi anáil Ghluaiseacht na hAthbheochana idir ábhar, chuspóir, *genre* agus fhriotal, agus, i gcásanna áirithe, faoi anáil na cléire i bpearsa an Easpaig Uí Dhónaill go dtí gur éirigh idir é féin agus lucht an Chonartha. Cuireadh síol san ithir nár saothraíodh le fada roimhe sin.

Le himeacht ama, tháinig bachlóga ar na síolta céanna. Ní hamhlaidh gur tháinig deireadh leis an ábhar a scríobhadh d'aon toisc ar mhaithe le lucht foghlama na Gaeilge nó le scríbhneoireacht ar mó an leas a baineadh aisti mar ábhar foghlama seach aon rud eile. Níor imigh scríbhneoireacht Ghaeilge na linne seo i dtréimhse ar bith i gcearn ar bith den tír ar an chinniúint mhínádúrtha sin. B'éigean do na scríbhneoirí Conallacha Gaeilge freastal ar an mhargadh sin i gcónaí, a chomhartha sin na leabhair staire iomadúla a scríobh siad, na leabhair aistí, na leabhair nach raibh iontu ach ceachtanna teanga i ndáiríre gona ngluaiseanna, gona bhfoclóirí, gona gceisteanna ag deireadh na leabhar. Isteach leis sin caithfear cuimhneamh gurbh oidí múinte de chineál éigin a bhí i mbunús na scríbhneoirí Conallacha Gaeilge, rud a d'fhág luí acu go nádúrtha leis an chineál sin scríbhneoireachta.

Ach thosaigh clann na Gaeltachta a theacht chun béil nó chun pinn. Seo dream a raibh an Ghaeilge as a leanbaíocht acu, a bhí ar maos i dtraidisiún béil a gcuid sinsear, a raibh teanga ar a dtoil acu a bhí ligthe i ndearmad, a chaith saol a raibh an bás daite dó agus a chronaigh siad go mór. Tosaíodh ar an saol sin a nochtadh de réir a chéile i gcanúint a d'fhóir dó. Scríobh Séamas Mac a' Bhaird *Troid Bhaile an Droichid* a foilsíodh sa bhliain 1907 inar léiríodh seansaol Gaelach na gConallach. Cuireadh cuid d'amhráin na gConallach i láthair an tsaoil ag Seaghán Mac an Bhaird agus ag Donnchadh Ó Searcaigh. Chuir Niall Mac Giolla Bhríde cnuasach dá chuid filíochta amach in *Blátha fraoich / Heather blossoms* sa bhliain 1905. Ba mhaith ann iad uilig mar chlocha míle i stair scríbhneoireacht Ghaeilge Dhún na nGall.

Duine a bhfuil tábhacht mhór leis sa tréimhse seo ar an uile dhóigh is ea Séamas Ó Searcaigh. I measc na saothar luath a scríobh sé tá *Cloich Cheann Fhaolaidh* a foilsíodh sa bhliain 1908. Tráchtar ann ar sheanchas agus ar ghnéithe de bhéaloideas iarthar Dhún na nGall. Ina dhiaidh sin tháinig *Faire Phaidí Mhóir* leis sa bhliain 1914 agus an cnuasach tábhachtach béaloidis *Cú na gcleas agus scéalta eile* sa bhliain chéanna a chuir sé amach i gcomhar le híde Nic Néill. Seo saol na Gaeltachta i nDún na nGall, seanchas na Gaeltachta agus canúint na Gaeltachta. Mura raibh féith láidir na scríbhneoireachta le sonrú ina chuid scríbhneoireachta féin, ba mhór a thionchar ar scríbhneoirí Gaeilge eile agus ar ábhair scríbhneoirí a thiocfadh ina dhiaidh.

Cuimhnítear gurbh é Séamas Ó Searcaigh an duine ba thábhachtaí i saol iomlán na Gaeilge sa chontae sa tréimhse sin agus go ceann na mblianta ina dhiaidh sin. Ba chainteoir dúchais as oileán na Cruite é, ba dhuine tábhachtach i nGluaiseacht na Gaeilge é, ba dhuine é a raibh léann trom air, bhí dlúthbhaint aige ar feadh na mblianta le hArdscoil Cholmcille, áit a raibh deis aige cainteoirí dúchais eile a spreagadh agus a bhroslú i dtreo léann na Gaeilge agus na scríbhneoireachta mar a rinne sé i gcás Shéamais Uí Ghrianna, cuir i gcás. Ba mhó den mhúinteoir agus den fhear léinn é ná den scríbhneoir chruthaitheach agus tá a shliocht ar a shaothar scríbhneoireachta. Chuidigh a bhuanna iomadúla agus a shaothar ilghnéitheach, áfach, le Conallaigh eile ó na ceantracha Gaeltachta ach go háirithe a chur ar bhealach na scríbhneoireachta.

I ndéaga an chéid seo tháinig fear Gaeltachta chun cinn ar dhual dó saol fada a chaitheamh i gceann na scríbhneoireachta, mar atá, Seaghán Mac Meanman, crann taca na gConallach i rith a shaoil. Tháinig Seaghán Bán, mar a thugtaí air, ar an tsaol ag tús na nóchaidí san aois seo caite ar an Cheann Gharbh i gceartlár an chontae. Bhí d'ádh air gur cheantar láidir seanchais agus béaloidis a bhí ina cheantar dúchais agus é ag éirí aníos. Teach mór airneáil fosta a bhí i dteach a mhuintire agus bhíodh scoth na seanchaithe ag cuartaíocht nó ag aíochtaigh ann in aimsir a óige. D'fhág sin lorg mór ar a intinn agus ar an chineál scríbhneoireachta a rinne sé lá ab fhaide anonn.

Is éard a chuir sé roimhe féin léargas a thabhairt ina shaothar ar sheansaol na Gaeltachta i nDún na nGall, ar an tsaol dhúchasach Ghaelach sin a bhlais sé féin agus é ina bhrian óg agus a bhí á bhánú ag saol ghallda nua-aimseartha na hÉireann san aois seo. Thosaigh sé i dtús báire mar a rinne a chomhghleacaithe Gaeltachta sa taobh ó dheas den tír tamall de bhlianta roimhe sin, mar atá, an tAthair Peadar Ua Laoghaire, le leaganacha athchóirithe de scéalta béaloidis ina chéad leabhar *Scéalta goiride geimhridh* sa bhliain 1915. Seo a leanas ina chuid focal féin a chuspóir leis na scéalta seo aige:

Tá súil agam go dtaitneoidh na scéalta nuadhéanta seo leis an léitheoir. Baineann an t-iomlán acu le saol na hÉireann agus na nÉireannach, is ó thús go deireadh tá iarraidh tugtha na modha smaointe, na béasa agus na cora cainte a bhíodh ag ár seanaithreacha is ár ngaraithreacha a tharraingt isteach san insin. Na seanóirí Gaelacha seo a d'imigh go formhothaithe mar shneachta earraigh le fiche bliain, bhí mórán mór nós agus abairteach acu nach bhfuil ag a sóisir leathGhallda. Bhí Gaeilge bhríomhar bheacht acu fosta, ach tá sí ag meath, is ag crupadh, is ag gannú i mbéal na ndaoine a tháinig ina ndiaidh. Agus in áit an chreidimh láidir a bhí acusan i neacha spioradálta agus i ngníomhachas dofheicseana, síogaithe, taibhsí, taiseacha, áibheirseoirí, Liamanna Sopóg, samhailteacha, ádh, dán is cinniúint, níl ag cuid againne ach creidiúnas marbhánta nach síneann leathorlach taobh thall d'amharc ár súl.

I gcead don údar, ní scéalta nuadhéanta a bhí iontu seo ach leaganacha dá chuid féin de scéalta béaloidis a chóirigh sé ar mhaithe le pobal léitheoireachta. Scríobh sé ar an téad chéanna sin i rith a shaoil agus ba é a dhálta céanna é ag cuid mhór de scríbhneoirí na Gaeltachta i nDún na nGall ina dhiaidh sin. Tuigimid dó agus dá liacht eile. Ní scríbhneoir coinsiasach cruthaitheach a bhí ann den chineál a bhfuil eolas againn ar a gcuid saothar i litríochtaí forbartha eile na cruinne. Níor fhoghlaim sé ceird na scríbhneoireachta, níor chaith sé saol an scríbhneora, ní raibh dearcadh ná léargas an scríbhneora nua-aimseartha aige. Oidhre ar an traidisiún béil a bhí ann a bhí ag iarraidh an traidisiún béil agus ar bhain leis a thabhairt isteach i saol an léinn scríofa. Bhí neart scríbhneoirí Conallacha eile ar an dóigh chéanna ó shin i leith ach go ndearnadh maolú ar thréithe láidre an bhéaloidis ina gcuid saothar de réir a chéile. Thug dúchas agus oiliúint chaomhnóirí seo an dúchais, a bhfealsúnacht liteartha agus a gcuspóir scríbhneoireachta orthu cineál áirithe scríbhneoireachta a scríobh arís agus arís eile a bhí ag cur le mian na léitheoirí a bhí ag léamh a gcuid saothar. Scríobh siad saothair a bhí préamhaithe go domhain in ithir na Gaeltachta, a léirigh seansaol na ndaoine mar a bhí, a chuir síos ar a gcreideamh, a nósanna, a stair, a saol sóisialta, a gcuid scéalta agus amhrán. Rinne siad seansaol Gaelach na Gaeltachta beo beathach arís agus níor fhéach siad mórán le drannadh le saol achrannach cheisteach aimhréiteach na linne seo. Ní tógtha orthu é. Cha raibh ciall acu dá athrach.

Scríbhneoir Conallach amháin a gcuirtear ina leith i gcónaí gurbh é ba mháistir ar an chineál sin scríbhneoireachta agus gurbh é ba mhó a chuaigh i bhfeidhm ar na glúnta scríbhneoirí Gaeilge Conallacha ina dhiaidh Séamas Ó Grianna nó Máire mar ab fhearr aithne air. B'ionann dúchas láidir Gaelach dó féin agus do Sheaghán Mac Meanman agus tháinig sé faoi anáil fhealsúnacht Shéamais Uí Shearcaigh agus é ag freastal ar Ardscoil Uladh. Ach nuair a d'fhéach Máire le tabhairt faoin scríbhneoireacht chruthaitheach i ndáiríre den chéad uair, is mó a bhí sé ag cuimhneamh ar thábhacht litríocht an Bhéarla agus ar cháil liteartha a chomhChonallaigh Patrick MacGill san am ná ar a dhúchas Ghaelach. Tá a shliocht ar an chéad úrscéal leis a foilsíodh riamh, mar atá, *Castar na daoine ar a chéile is ní chastar na cnuic nó na sléibhte* a foilsíodh in aghaidh na seachtaine in *The Irish Weekly and Ulster Examiner* sa bhliain 1915. Cuirtear síos do Mháire na smaointe seo a leanas faoi chuspóir an tsaothair seo sa nóta bolscaireachta a cuireadh leis an tsraithscéal seo:

In looking through the different Irish books recently published, it occurred to me that little attempt was being made to describe modern life in Irish – that the language was solely devoted to describing Finn Mac Cool and other myths, who had very little interest for the ordinary Irish reader, and that if Irish is to become a popular language it must become a vehicle of modern thought.

Ba mhaith an smaoineamh é seo aige agus ba dhúshlánach fosta san áit agus san am sin ach cha raibh an saothar ag cur lena chuspóir. Tá plota an úrscéil dochreidte agus ní hiontas sin agus é suite i saol nach bhfuil aon chur amach ag Máire air. Tá ceist na carachtrachta go dona fosta agus, idir sin agus lochtanna iomadúla eile, níor foilsíodh an saothar i bhfoirm leabhair ná níor thug sé go leor uchtaigh do Mháire leanstan ar aghaidh ar an téad scríbhneoireachta sin lá ab fhaide anonn.[15]

Is léir nár scar sé go hiomlán le céadchuspóir a chuid scríbhneoireachta nuair a scríobh sé *Mo dhá Róisín* áfach, ach le foilsiú *Caisleáin óir* sa bhliain 1924, bhí a chúrsa scríbhneoireachta faoina shúil aige a gcloífeadh sé leis a bheag nó a mhór an chuid eile dá shaol. D'aithin sé an bua a bhí aige mar scríbhneoir. D'aimsigh sé an saol a thuig sé, a raibh cur amach aige air, na daoine a raibh aithne aige orthu agus dáimh aige leo, an friotal a nocht intinn na ndaoine céanna. Lean sé air ag scríobh ar an téad seo bliain i ndiaidh bliana agus *genres* uile na scríbhneoireachta á gcleachtadh aige: gearrscéalta, úrscéalta, dírbheathaisnéis, leabhar seanchais 7rl.

Is é Máire is mó a d'fheidhmigh mar cheannaire neamhoifigiúil ar scoil scríbhneoireachta Gaeilge an chontae le samplaí líonmhara a chuid leabhar agus, níos tábhachtaí arís, leis na haistí iomadúla leis a foilsíodh sna fichidí ach go háirithe. An manadh liteartha ar chloígh sé leis tromlach a shaoil, ábhar éadrom scríbhneoireachta a sholáthar i nGaeilge dhúchasach na Gaeltachta, ábhar a bheadh scríofa ar dhóigh nach dtabharfaí snamh dó i measc ghnáthmhuintir na Gaeltachta. Le sin a chur i gcrích chaithfí modhanna teibí nua-aimseartha scríbhneoireachta a sheachaint, chaithfí ábhair gharbha choimhthíocha a sheachaint, chaithfí reacaireacht dhothuigthe a sheachaint. Bhí agus tá i gcónaí blas ar leabhair Mháire i measc mhuintir na Gaeltachta i nDún na nGall agus i measc an lucht foghlama a tharraing ar thobar sin na Gaeilge agus an dúchais Ghaelaigh.

Ó tharla gur éirigh chomh maith sin le saothar Mháire, ba líonmhar iad a lucht leanúna mar scríbhneoirí Conallacha, go háirid ina chontae dúchais féin. Ba dhaoine iad nach bhféadfaí litríocht ardchruthaitheach a shamhailt leo, daoine a bhí teoranta ó thaobh na scríbhneoireachta de. Na cáilíochtaí liteartha is mó a bhí acu an dúchas láidir Gaelach a bhlais siad óna leanbaíocht ina gcuid ceantar féin agus ar chuir comhlacht foilsitheoireachta an Stáit, mar atá, an Gúm, fáilte roimhe mar ábhar téacsleabhar agus mar lón fóirsteanach intinne do dhaltaí scoile na tíre. Sin é a d'fhág scríbhneoirí Conallacha againn ar nós Fhinn Mhic Cumhaill, Thaidhg Uí Rabhartaigh, Mhuirghein, Aindriais Uí Bhaoill, Sheáin 'ic Fhionnlaoich 7rl. chomh maith le lucht scríofa na ndírbheathaisnéisí. Is slua líonmhar scríbhneoirí iad agus baineann a mbunús, a bheagán nó a mhórán, leis an tsruth chéanna scríbhneoireachta atá préamhaithe in ithir na Gaeltachta ar an uile dhóigh.

Ní féidir aon bhail amháin a thabhairt orthu uilig, áfach, óir bhí agus tá corrdhuine ina measc a raibh tuigbheáil acu do chúrsaí litríochta. Is fada anois ó d'aithin Seosamh Mac Grianna cé na deacrachtaí a bhí i mbealach an scríbhneora i nGaeltacht Thír Chonaill:

> Ach ní dhearna a gcuid aithreacha rompu dada lena n-inchinn ach ag smaoineamh cad é mar ab fhearr a leasódh siad cuibhreann de thalamh fhuar, nó cad é mar ab fhearr a chothódh siad bullán faoi choinne an mhargaidh. Ní dhearna siad mórán smaoinimh riamh ar cheisteanna domhaine; níor shiúil siad mórán riamh, agus ní fhaca siad mórán den saol; agus ní raibh de litríocht acu ach seanscéalta agus amhráin nach raibh iontu ach páirt de litríocht nach dtáinig i gcrann riamh. Nach doiligh don té a shíolraigh ó na daoine seo, a bhfuil a n-intinn maol ag smaoineamh cad é an dóigh lena mbéal a líonadh, dála mar atá a gcuid lámh garbh ag obair leis an spáid – nach doiligh do mhac an dóirnealaigh bheith chomh héasca san intleacht agus go mbeirfidh sé ar an rud a dtug file an Bhéarla *'The light that never was on sea or land'* air?[16]

Ba dheacair agus b'amaideach a bheith ag dúil le litríocht shofaisticiúil nua-aimseartha chomh gasta sin ó dhaoine nach raibh an léann agus an t-oideachas sa dúchas acu. Seo daoine ar ceileadh léann agus oideachas foirmeálta orthu sa dá theanga leis na cianta, daoine nach dtáinig deiseanna léinn chucu ach go fadálach san aois seo.

Duine den bheagán scríbhneoirí Conallacha Gaeilge a stróic a bhealach isteach i saol na haoise seo agus a thug leis friotal agus saol na Gaeltachta lena chois i gcuibhreann na scríbhneoireachta, Seosamh Mac Grianna. Seo an scríbhneoir is éifeachtaí a thóg an contae, duine a shíolraigh ó shaol na Gaeltachta agus a bhí ar maos in iomlán a cuid traidisiún ach duine, san am chéanna, a chuir a bhinid i litríocht an Bhéarla ó bhí sé ina leanbh. Chuaigh an dá thraidisiún i bhfostó ann ón tús ach nuair a thosaigh sé ar a shaol mar scríbhneoir Gaeilge, ba threise tionchar a dhúchais Ghaelaigh air ná aon tionchar eachtrach mar is léir ó *Dochartach Dhuibhlionna* agus *Filidh gan iomrádh* agus *An grá is an ghruaim*. Ach ba léir fiú amháin ó na hiarrachtaí luatha sin go raibh mianach litríochta ann nach bhfacthas i scríbhneoirí Gaeilge eile an chontae roimhe sin ná mórán ó shin. Is féidir a theacht i méadaíocht a aithint ó leabhar go leabhar agus é ag tarraingt go tréan ar phríomhshruth na litríochta comhaimseartha a bhfeictear a chruthúnas go soiléir ina shaothar dheireanach nár críochnaíodh *Dá mbíodh ruball ar an éan*. Seo, den chéad uair i scríbhneoireacht Ghaeilge Dhún na nGall, scríbhneoir lánaibí lánoilte lánliteartha ag scríobh go gairmiúil cruthaitheach agus nach gá aon leithscéal a ghabháil faoi i dtéarmaí litríochta.

Tháinig beirt eile ar an fhód ó shin ar mó a luí le scoil scríbhneoireachta Sheosaimh ná le scoil na muintire eile. Is iad an bheirt atá i gceist, Niall Ó Dónaill agus Cathal Ó Searcaigh. Ba chara le Seosamh é an Dálach agus ba mhinic iad ag caibidil cúrsaí litríochta agus iad ina bhfir óga i mBaile Átha Cliath. Is léir cumas scríbhneoireachta an Dálaigh in *Na glúnta Rosannacha* agus ina chuid gearrscéalta. Ní fios nach dtiocfadh sé in aibíocht mar scríbhneoir mar a tharla i gcás Sheosaimh ach ab é gur chaith sé iomlán a dhúthrachta le saol an léinn i rith a shaoil.

Is duine de ghlúin úr na scríbhneoirí Gaeilge é Cathal Ó Searcaigh, file ó Ghaeltacht Ghort an Choirce. Is duine é a bhaineas le saol an oideachais, na n-ilteangacha, na n-ilchultúr, na n-ilfhealsúnachtaí agus na n-ilmheán cumarsáide. Tá a shliocht ar a shaothar fhoilsithe go dtí seo a bhfuil eolas fada fairsing air ní hamháin i measc lucht na Gaeilge ach i measc lucht an Bhéarla abhus in Éirinn agus thar lear. Má tá aon chinniúint i ndán do litríocht Ghaeilge Dhún na nGall san am atá le teacht, is é an Searcach ach go háirithe as measc scríbhneoirí Gaeilge comhaimseartha Chlann Chonaill a dhéanfas an t-eolas do lucht a saothraithe isteach san aois atá romhainn.

Nótaí

1. Is deacair a rá go cruinn neamhchlaonta cá bhfuil na ceantracha Gaeltachta sa lá atá inniu ann ná a rá fiú amháin cad é an rud Gaeltacht. Níl sé i gceist an cheist sin a chíoradh go mion anseo ach, le leid éigin a thabhairt faoin scéal, d'fhéadfaí na Gaeltachtaí sin i nDún na nGall a lua a dtug Wagner cuairt orthu sna caogaidí agus an *Linguistic atlas and survey of Irish dialects* á ullmhú aige. Ina measc bhí: Baile Fhuaruisce, Gleann Bhairr, Ros Goill, an Craoslach, Cill Darach, Gort an Choirce, Oileán Thoraí, Dún Lúiche, Loch an Iúir, Rinn na Feirste, Árainn Mhór, Leitir Mhic an Bhaird, An Ceann Garbh, Na Cruacha Gorma, Ard an Rátha, Teileann agus Mín an Chearrbhaigh. Caithfear a rá, gan amhras, gur mhaígh Wagner fiú amháin ag an am sin go raibh an Ghaeilge ar an dé deiridh i gcuid de na ceantracha sin agus is i ndonacht go mór a chuaigh an scéal ó shin. Más mionanailís chomhaimseartha ar staid na Gaeltachta i nDún na nGall atá a dhíobháil, d'fhéadfaí breathnú ar a bhfuil le rá ag Reg Hindley in *The death of the Irish language* (London, 1990), leathanaigh 65-79, 287-9 nó ag Mícheál Ó Gliasáin in *Language shift among schoolchildren in Gaeltacht areas 1974-1984: an analysis of the distribution of £10 grant qualifiers* (Baile Áth Cliath, 1990).

2. Tá mionstaidéar déanta ag John Coll ar stair Ghaoth Dobhair le céad go leith bliain anuas: 'Continuity and change in the parish of Gaoth Dobhair 1850-1980,' in W. J. Smyth and K. Whelan (eds), *Common ground: essays on the historical geography of Ireland* (Cork, 1988), pp 278-95. Baineann an staidéar sin go dlúth le stair na nGaeltachtaí i nDún na nGall. Féach fosta ar a bhfuil le rá ag Maitiú Ó Murchú in 'An Ghaeilge i dTír Chonaill le céad bliain anuas' in N. Mac Congáil (eag.), *Scríbhneoireacht na gConallach* (Áth Cliath, 1990), leathanaigh 26-44.

3. B. Ó Cuív, *Irish dialects and Irish-speaking districts* (Dublin, 1967), leathanach 25.

4. An chiall atá le scríbhneoir anseo, duine a bhfuil leabha(i)r de chineál ar bith scríofa aige. Gan amhras, cuid mhaith acu sin, níor scríbhneoirí cruthaitheacha ar chor ar bith iad ach aistritheoirí, lucht léinn, seanchaithe srl. Os a choinne sin arís, áfach, bhí scríbhneoirí ann a rinne scríbhneoireacht chruthaitheach ach nach bhfuil aon leabhar maíte orthu. Is cuid bhunúsach thábhachtach iad seo uilig de ghréasán aimhréiteach scríbhneoireacht Ghaeilge Dhún na nGall.

5. Orthu sin tá Séamas Ó Néill, Seán Mac Maoláin, Proinsias Mac an Bheatha, Ciarán Ó Nualláin srl. Tá suas le céad údar Gaeilge den uile chineál maíte ar na Sé Chontae agus d'fhoghlaim a mbunús sin a gcuid Gaeilge i nGaeltachtaí Dhún na nGall.

6. T. Ó Fiaich, 'The great controversy' in S. Ó Tuama, *The Gaelic League idea* (Cork, 1972), leathanach 64.

7. Eolas bainte as *An Gaodhal* iml. 9 uimh. 11 (Aibr. 1893), leathanaigh 272-3.

8. *Saol corrach* (Corcaigh, 1981), leathanach 130.

9. *Na glúnta Rosannacha* (Baile Átha Cliath, 1974), leathanach 71.

10. D. Ó Súilleabháin, *Na timirí i ré tosaigh an chonartha 1893-1927* (Baile Áth Cliath, 1990), leathanach 3.

11. *An tUltach* (M. Fómh. 1981), leathanach 18.

12. Ibid.

13. *Coláiste Uladh* 1906-1931 (Cló na dTrí gCoinneal, g.d.), leathanaigh 32-3.

14. 'Foillseacháin an chonartha', *Connradh na Gaedhilge 1893-1943 Leabhar Cuimhne* (1943), leathanach 57.

15. Tá cuntas iomlán scríofa agam ar an leabhar atá faoi thrácht againn anseo in 'Úrscéal dearmadta le Máire' in N. Mac Congáil, *Scríbhneoirí Thír Chonaill* (Foilseacháin Náisiúnta Teoranta, 1983), leathanaigh 121-30.

16. *Ailt* (Comhaltas Uladh, 1977), leathanach 15.

Chapter 25

THE DONEGAL FIDDLE TRADITION: AN ETHNOGRAPHIC PERSPECTIVE

DAMHNAIT NIC SUIBHNE

One of the central conditions for the development of Irish traditional music has undoubtedly been the geographical isolation of the country itself. The physical separation of Ireland from the European mainland has contributed to the distinctiveness of an Irish culture which has endured into the present time. Within the country this 'island' concept also obtains, where isolated pockets of individual musical tradition have developed and flourished by virtue of geographical boundaries. It is the plurality of these individual regional traditions that forms the varied layers of Irish traditional music.

In recent years both the decline of the rural lifestyle and the emergence of an urban-based musical revival have helped to obscure the various regional identities. Media influences have precipitated the fashion towards eclectic playing styles which led to the neglect of the rich body of localised styles and repertoires still accessible in many parts of the island. Nevertheless Donegal, by virtue of its location, has been fortunate in avoiding much of the acquisitive and potentially destructive interest shown by the media and other organisations. The rich body of fiddle music associated with the county has survived intact and this tradition contrasts sharply with the styles of the South of Ireland.

In analysing the individuality of Donegal music I have found it important to examine the cultural and economic conditions that have shaped and formed the Donegal style. I believe that the factor of geographical isolation is, perhaps, the most significant contributor to the insular development of the cultural lifestyle which nurtured this music. The rugged terrain and the inadequate road systems which hindered communication between townlands meant that the majority of people lived on small land holdings for generations at, or close to, subsistence level. Their source of income was dependent on small-scale farming, agricultural and fishing, and these limited means necessitated a pattern of seasonal migration in search of work as a means of survival. The sheer effort of existence in this difficult terrain bound people together into self-sufficient structured communities.

Their identity was based on a sense of kinship, religion, the Irish language, a shared oral history and a strong musical tradition. Music, song, dance and storytelling were the mainstays of their communal social activities, and it was in this environment that fiddle music flourished and functioned as an integral part of everyday life. In my opinion, therefore, a reflection of the harsh cultural and economic conditions that shaped this lifestyle can be seen in the ruggedness and individuality of the Donegal style. This concept is not a new one. Éamonn Ó Gallchobhair suggested that music is conditioned by its environment in the same way that speech, customs and manners are. In his view the Donegal musical form is:

> ... geometrical and aesthetic with something of the rugged grandeur of our cliffs and mountains ... It has a hard core which serves to check the swelling surge of passion. ..... (and in it) one senses the logic of the hard-headed Northerner who recognises that winter cold and bleak must inevitably follow in the path of the loveliest summer ...

In contrast, he finds that Kerry music is more multi-coloured.

> it has more charm with, perhaps, a suggestion of effeminacy; its passionate intensity is nearer the surface, more easily discernible; in pattern it is more luxuriant ...[1]

It is, perhaps, because of its rugged and almost foreign character that Donegal music has until recently been ignored by most scholars and collectors. Now, at a time when traditional music is tiring of standardisation and conformity, the Donegal fiddle tradition is emerging as something of a phenomenon. The singularity of its idiom and the provincialism of its accent makes it a worthwhile topic for study.

The introduction of the fiddle to Donegal

It is not possible to pinpoint with any degree of accuracy the introduction of the fiddle to Donegal. Documentary evidence is negligible and, as yet, little research has been carried out in this area. Breathnach suggests[2] that the pipes preceded the fiddle in Ireland as the instrument most commonly used for providing dance music, and the many references to pipes and pipers in accounts from the eighteenth century seem to confirm this view. The pipes in question are the mouth-blown pipes (modern day uilleann pipes only developed in the late eighteenth century). Subsequently during the eighteenth century the fiddle had been established as the instrument most commonly used to accompany dancing. Several printed sources verify this; the Englishman Richard Head, writing about Ireland in 1674 describes the Sunday amusement:

> in every field a fiddle and the lasses footing it till they are all of a foam.[3]

The fiddle in its modern form arrived in Ireland in the late seventeenth century. Its use in traditional music quickly became widespread, due principally to its adoption by the travelling dancing masters.[4]

One of the earliest references to fiddle playing in Donegal is of the late eighteenth century when Hugh Doherty b.1790, a native of Dungloe, played the fiddle, uilleann pipes and highland bagpipes. He was the great grandfather of John Doherty, well-known Donegal fiddle player and travelling musician.[5] From the late eighteenth century and early nineteenth century oral tradition carries information on renowned fiddle characters of the region such as 'fiddler Doyle', Anthony Helferty and Paddy Mc Sweeney.

Fiddle types in Donegal

It seems likely that bowed instruments were known in Ireland prior to the introduction of the violin. Breathnach notes several sources where such instruments are mentioned.[6] The late Mickey Byrne of Kilcar remembered hearing of the existence of a bowed instrument that preceded the violin in Donegal:

> When the fiddle first came to Donegal it wasn't the flat ones that's in it now you know. In that time, there were fiddles that had a stoop to the neck you see; the neck was sort of bent. They used to call them the crooked-necked fiddles. They called it in Irish *an fhidéal cham;* there was a turn in the neck. They kept at those till these [violins] come across the water from Scotland. These were a different make then. If you didn't learn to play these crooked-neck fiddles first (before the standard violin) you'd never get on to them.[7]

Judging from this description of the *fidéal cham*, its construction and melodic range seems to be akin to the medieval rebec. A similar instrument called the *gue* was known in the Shetland Islands.[8] This suggests the presence of a common type of instrument among the inhabitants of the northern regions of Ireland, Scotland and Scandinavia. A carving in St Finian's church in Waterville *c.*1200 shows a bowed instrument played under the chin that corresponds in form to the medieval rebec.[9]

The harsh economic conditions of the isolated farming communities did not enable many of the inhabitants the luxury of affording a finely crafted or perhaps even an imported violin. Besides, there was a certain reluctance to buy a new fiddle:

> People wouldn't believe in buying a new fiddle. They would wait and wait until somebody got really hard up for money and then sell their fiddle, which was in some cases the last thing that would leave the house. The kitchen chairs would go before the fiddle would go. But they had a thing about the new fiddle, that it took a long time to break it in – the older the fiddle, the sweeter the tune, they always reckoned.[10]

Some people did attempt to make their own fiddles but the lack of materials and rudimentary skills in the art of violin-making did not produce instruments of comparable tone with the imported variety. In Donegal, however, such straightened economic and geographical circumstances inspired an unusual and perhaps unique innovation in terms of fiddle-making. These were the brass and tin fiddles made by the travelling tinsmith musicians. Bachmann suggests that the craft of fiddle making in rural societies in medieval times tended to be based on oral tradition and was generally the province of the players themselves.[11] Apparently one of the main skills expected of a medieval minstrel was the ability not only to master the techniques of various instruments, but also to make and repair them. This may indicate a connection between the travelling tinsmith musicians, in nineteenth- and twentieth-century Donegal, and medieval minstrel musicians.

The instruments made by these travellers seemed to be of a remarkably high standard and to the ears of the musicians compared very favourably with the local wooden fiddles and were much sought-after and prized articles. The tinsmith musicians made instruments available to aspiring fiddlers who would otherwise have been unable to locate or indeed afford a standard violin. The O'Doherty family were among the most famous of these travelling musicians. Mickey Byrne recalled:

> They made the fiddle popular – they made fiddles of their own: square fiddles. They used to call it the box fiddle. They were putting the right neck on it. If you were outside you would not know the difference between them and the violins; it was a terrible good strong sound.[12]

Simon Doherty in conversation with Feldman explained in detail how these tin fiddles were constructed:

My grand-uncles Mickey and Alec Mc Connell were the first to make tin fiddles. They were at a big dance and the fiddle got broke. They had nothing left but the bow and the peg head and the strings. Well, fiddles were scarce at them times so they didn't know what to do. Well my grand-uncle was sitting looking at the broken fiddle – 'Oh!' he says, 'I'm thinking of some remedy,' and he just reached for a sheet of tin and he split the sheet of tin in two. He marked it round and round and cut out the identical same shape as the ordinary fiddle; he raised her [the tin], put the head on her and played time about in the morning. That was the Mc Connells from Connaught. They delighted in smith work and it was them that was the first to draw a plan of it ... To make a tin fiddle she has to be cut just the same as that wooden fiddle there, but the belly and the back have to be raised together. And you put two flanges around the rim to connect the belly and back together. You would use no solder only for the neck. There is a drop of solder that goes on the two sides of the neck to hold it firm, but for the body the less solder you use the better. You might use a wee bit on the inside of the rim before you put on the belly, to keep it in its place till you get it properly seamed and when it's well seamed it would be a lovely job. The 'S' hole you put in is called a chiselled 'S' hole with a hole here and a hole there (he points to either side of the bridge) ... with the sides bent down and a bar in the middle. Then you would put a bass rod in under the third string to give her a lovely soft tone but the back and front have to be plumb level together, and would have to hammer it out the back the same as the belly – the verse on her has to be one depth all round ... and then you would carve your own fingerboard – ash for the head and a bit of sycamore for the fingerboard – that's for the tone of a tin violin – and a nice piece of glass to smooth it out and leave it level. A bit of sycamore for the bridge is just as good as ebony and ash is the best timber for the pegs. It's not a splitful kind of timber; it's long in the grain ...[13]

An example of this type of tin fiddle which was made by Mickey Doherty (father of Simon, John and Mickey) is in the possession of John Gallagher (fiddler) of Ardara. There is also a very interesting example of a brass fiddle owned by Charlie McDevitt from Kilcar which was made in the 1920s by Frank and John Cassidy. The body of the instrument is made from heavy brass obtained from a brass drum washed ashore at the bottom of the cliffs at Bun Glás near Sliabh Líag.[14]

Plate 25.1   Tin fiddle made by Mickey Doherty.

Plate 25.2   Myles Tinney (Inver), playing a handcrafted box fiddle.

The fiddle in Donegal society

There is little doubt that the fiddle is intimately associated with the music of Donegal just as the concertina has come to be associated with the music of Clare. Certainly fiddle players were plentiful throughout the county, though they tended to be concentrated in certain areas. It is generally acknowledged that south-west and west Donegal was rich in fiddle playing. The boundaries of this musical region extend westwards from the glens of Glenties to the south Rosses and southwards towards Teelin, Kilcar and Glencolmkille. Research has shown that this area undoubtedly had the greatest proliferation of fiddle players (fig. 25.1). Certain other parts of the county such as the Inishowen peninsula and pockets in the centre of the county around Killygordon and Drumkeen were also significant areas for music-making, although perhaps not quite as prolific in fiddle players. Packie Manus Byrne recalls:

> Fiddles were as plentiful as stones in our area. There were fiddles all over the place – in nearly every house. That was part of the furniture! You went into a house and the first thing that struck

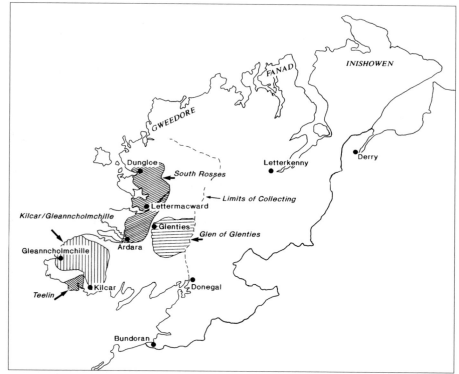

Fig. 25.1   Donegal fiddling styles.
Source: Damhnait Nic Suibhne.

your eyes was a fiddle and the fiddle was always hung in one particular place, above the fireplace, on what they used to call the brace of the house.[15]

In this extract Packie Manus is talking about his homeplace – a townland called Conkermore situated between the towns of Ardara and Dunkineely in south-west Donegal. Similarly, several other printed sources refer to the richness of the musical tradition in this part of the county. When there were large numbers of fiddlers in every parish. Con Cassidy of Teelin (Teileann) talks of as many as thirty. The higher incidence of fiddle playing in south-west Donegal is largely due to the influence of the travelling tinsmith musicians.

Peter Cooke in his study of the Shetland Island fiddle tradition points out that virtually all men on the islands earlier this century attempted to acquire some skill on the instrument. He found that the well-known fiddlers represented only the apex of a pyramid consisting of countless men and a few women who could play the fiddle to some standard or other.[16] I found a similar situation in south-west Donegal. A considerable variation in standards of ability existed among the musicians. The ability of each individual was monitored by his fellow musicians who categorised him accordingly. Con Cassidy said that few players were regarded as good solo players, possibly as few as two or three in a region of thirty. He talked of fiddlers who were considered to be good 'dance players', yet you couldn't sit down and listen to them. James Byrne said:

> Well you had fiddle players who specialised in playing jigs and other players that favoured reels you know, and then you had the great hornpipe players ... You had people then like Johnny Doherty and them who could play anything very well, Johnny Doherty, Frank Cassidy, and Francie Byrne ... anything![17]

The existence of a hierarchy of musical accomplishment among these players is important because it illustrates not only the function of music within society but also the medium through which the tradition regenerated itself. This hierarchy can be viewed as a three-tiered structure.

- *The house fiddler* who could manage to play a tune or two for dancing in his own home but who didn't regard himself as a real fiddler and who would not be asked to play at functions of any kind.

- *The local fiddler* who was considerably skilled and would be expected to take his fiddle around with him to social evenings, or whose home was used as a centre for the big nights or for house dances during the winter evenings.

- *The fiddle expert:* the travelling musicians and the professional players undoubtedly responsible for promoting and developing the highly distinctive Donegal fiddle style.

The influence of the travelling tinsmith musicians on the music of the community has already been discussed with regard to their popularising of the fiddle as an instrument in the area. One cannot, however, ignore the enormous effect their music had on the local musicians who came in contact with them. Who then were these itinerant musicians? And how could such a small minority group have such an effect on a large community?

The origins of this travelling group in Donegal can be traced from the early nineteenth century and their influence extended well into this century. In south-west Donegal there were four families of itinerant musicians, all related: Dohertys, Mac Sweeneys, McConnells and Gallaghers. Together they formed a highly skilled musical sub-culture in the south-west region. Through their travels they continually cross-fertilised the various local musical traditions of isolated farming communities. They travelled from parish to parish where they were treated as honoured guests. They moved from house to house supplying music for big nights, house dances and country fairs. Within the region, they frequented the areas where music and musicians were plentiful and where they felt their music was more keenly understood and appreciated. The local musicians who were exposed to the music of the travellers were anxious and quick to pick up new tunes. As well as influencing their repertoire, the travellers had an effect on the playing style and standards of the farmer fiddlers. The average fiddler was usually a part-time player who restricted his playing to the idle winter months, his musical activity being tied to agrarian work cycles. The travelling musicians, in contrast, were professional players involved in relatively light work such as tinsmithing and their economy was not tied to seasonal work cycles. Therefore they had time and opportunity to develop their music to a high degree of proficiency. They were also in continuous contact with other players, whether sedentary players or other travelling musicians like themselves. As a result of these factors the travelling players often had a wider range of music than the isolated farmer fiddler. That is not to say that the local fiddlers were lacking in musical talent. On the contrary, many virtuoso and expert fiddlers such as John Mosey McGinly, Jimmy Lyons, John Frank Cassidy and Nealy Boyle were from localised farming

Plate 25.3   Nealy Boyle, Dungloe.

Plate 25.4   Jimmy Lyons, Teelin.

communities; but it is significant that all of these maintained close relationships with the travelling musicians.[18]

Seamus Grant from north Inishowen talked of travelling musicians named McGinley, Gallagher and McDonald who frequented his area, and a travelling piper called Gillespie who came around away back before the turn of the century. He himself remembers a fiddler named McDonald who frequented Inishowen until around the 1930s. McDonald was a well-known character who used to spend a lot of his time travelling over and back on the Derry boat entertaining the groups of migratory workers going to Scotland for the harvest. One of his favourite platforms was a herring barrel on the quay in Derry where it was said that even after drinking half a bottle of whiskey, he could still balance remarkably well and play his fiddle.[19]

The last and perhaps the most famous of these travelling musicians in Donegal was John Doherty (1895-1980) who was, in Paddy Tunney's words: 'the last living link with the great wandering minstrels and harpers of the eighteenth century'.[20]

A member of the Doherty family, he could trace his descent through four generations of travelling musicians.[21] Although they are best known in this century for their fiddling, the mouth-blown pipe was originally their main instrument. Their unique repertoire derives in a large part from that experience as pipe players. A considerable amount of John Doherty's music consisted of tunes derived from the piping tradition of his own clan and that of his cousins, the Gallagher brothers. Some of these piping pieces date back to the sixteenth century, the most archaic being the funeral laments that he claimed were played to accompany the dead on their last journey.[22] What is most interesting, I believe, is the way in which these piping tunes were transferred to the fiddle and how the highland piping techniques such as the staccato sound of the chanter and general rhythmic precision were imitated and assimilated by John Doherty and his relations and subsequently by local fiddlers into a distinctive regional style.

Music in society

It must be remembered that the core of musicians within the Donegal fiddle tradition belongs to the early decades of the twentieth century, the era of the country house dance, when the people of the neighbour-hood gathered into a household for a night's céiligh-ing. Dances were important social events in the life of the community and bearing in mind the comparative isolation of country folk in remote mountainous regions, they were for many the only opportunity for social intercourse. Con Cassidy from Teelin recalls a typical house dance scene in south-west Donegal:

Plate 25.5   Travelling itinerant musicians.
Mickey Mór Doherty & Sons – John and Simon.

Plate 25.6   Expert fiddler, John Doherty.

> We used to play three or four together. I was maybe sixteen or seventeen; before that we weren't allowed to dance. They were all in country houses; every kitchen was big and they were always overcrowded. There'd be half as many outside the door dancing. I often seen them dancing on the pier. Oh! that was great go in the summertime. I remember Francie Byrne ... he would come across the water by boat and everytime he came he had a new tune with him, a new highland or jig every time. They would always start the time of October on the hay stacks. There might be four or five haystacks to make on one day; well they couldn't have four or five dances. There would be one or two girls in those houses who could invite the other girls to the area. The highland, quicksteps, quadrilles, barndances and lancers were all the go. You would pull the girl out whether she danced or not; she soon came on the step. The old stepdance was called the breakdown. The dancer would change the steps any time he wanted. They had every sort of trick. Sometimes the door would be taken off the hinges and placed on the floor; that way the dancer could make plenty of noise. There would be two facing the other. Then they would change; the man who was up would go down ...[23]

The musician's role was to provide lively music for the dancers; the maintenance of a strict tempo with plenty of lift was of prime importance. It is understandable, then, that much of the musical material presented by these musicians has a close affinity to the dance as this aspect of their repertoire was moulded to suit the needs of the dancers and it reflects the kind of dances in vogue at the time.

Occasions for music-making

The occasions for these house dances varied somewhat in different parts of the county. South-west Donegal was noted for the frequency of these big nights; any excuse for music-making was welcomed, whereas in the Rosses and west Donegal the big occasions were less frequent.[24]

Small unorganised gatherings of an informal nature were common in all areas. These took place mostly on Sunday nights. Sunday was a day of rest when farm work was done; it was customarily a day for visiting, and for *rambling and raking*. On these occasions just a few neighbours and locals gathered together for a dancing session.[25] There would always be a fiddle player in the company who willingly provided the music.

The organised gatherings or the *big nights* however were un-doubtedly important social events.

We all looked forward to the big nights. There was the dancing and the singing, and the music, and of course the females ... The musicians would be appointed three or four days in advance. The girls would be invited for miles and miles around. There was no need to ask the men, because they would come anyway. But all the girls would be invited and if they weren't invited they didn't go ...[26]

In south-west Donegal the 'harvest gatherings' were important occasions for big nights. On the 'night of the stacks' there would be a gathering in almost every house after the final haystacks were taken in. Other occasions for big nights in the south-west were when visitors came to the area. There would be two or three big nights organised in their honour to give them a chance to meet the locals and to experience the customs of the region.

On all of these 'house' occasions refreshments were provided for the dancers. There was tea, sometimes even a few bottles of whiskey and poteen and some Guinness porter or stout. The musicians were the honoured guests, and they had to be treated well:

There were usually two chairs put up on the kitchen table and they sat away out up there. For two reasons; one was they were right above the dancers and they could see the figures of the dance ... and along with that they were out of the way because some of the dances were a bit hectic and they were all very proud of their fiddles and if there was a hectic dance going on and four or five people collapsed on a fiddle that was the end of it. So the fiddle player was away safe, away in a corner or up on a table somewhere so, let the dancers kill each other, who cared, the fiddles were safe anyway.[27]

While the custom of celebrating the night of the stacks was less common in the Rosses, they had their own particular occasions for the big nights, one of which was a variation on the harvest gathering theme of the south-west. The Rosses event was called a 'fiddler'. This was initiated in situations whereby neighbours would gather together in households who were without young male members to help them carry out seasonal farm work, such as the sowing and harvesting of crops. When all the work was completed the householder repaid his/her neighbours for their much appreciated help by holding a dance. A fiddler was engaged for the evening; food and drink were given to the workers in the kitchen and then the floor was cleared for a dance.[28] This feature of a 'party' accompanying joint work is found in most societies where a system of mutual aid exists.[29]

Emigration provided further cause for 'big occasions'. Farewell parties were held for locals who were emigrating to America. These were known in the Rosses as 'convoys', although in other parts of the county they were sometimes called 'American wakes'. The 'convoy' took place the night before the departure. The locals wanted to ensure that the emigrant's last night would be a lively and entertaining one. Music and dancing commenced in the early evening and continued throughout the night until morning. The emigrants were then escorted to the local Lough Swilly railway station – 'Kincaslagh Road' – where they departed for the boat at Derry.[30]

In more recent times the school house or the parochial hall were also popular venues for the big nights. These were usually held on specific days throughout the calendar year – Christmas night, New Year's eve, St Patrick's night and Easter Sunday. The aim of these events was to raise funds for the upkeep of the school or church property.

> The people, of course, were young and old. They would all come out and support those things ... it didn't cost very much ... the standard admission would be a shilling for the man and sixpence for the girls ... Just one fiddler played the whole night and there was no such thing as stopping at three o'clock that time ... it went on till clear daylight in the morning, in fact there was an old fiddler told me he remembers playing down in Cruit school (beyond Kincaslagh chapel) .... it was a lively place for those dances ... and when daylight started to come on they'd pull down the blinds on the window to keep out the daylight so they could dance some more ...[31]

Weddings and wakes

Weddings were ideal occasions for partying and merrymaking. After the ceremony the wedding party returned to the bride's home and they entertained themselves for two, three or maybe four days.

> I was at a wedding myself, and it started about four o'clock in the afternoon of the day of the wedding, and it finished up sometime in the small hours of the third day after. People would stay up and dance, oh! crikey yes, dance and drink. It was a known fact that some of them would go home and sleep for about two hours and get up and come back again. And drink more. Whilst there was whiskey or poteen or Guinness going, they wouldn't leave – when all was eaten up and all was drank they'd leave.[32]

As in the normal house dance situation, the role of the fiddler was simply to provide music for the dancers. However, there were usually several musicians invited, so that they could take turns in keeping the entertainment going continuously throughout the day and night. The invited musicians were never paid but were assured of plenty to eat and drink.

Wakes, on the other hand, were occasions where no instrumental music or dancing took place. The dead and relatives of the dead were highly respected. Should there be a death in a family, no member of that family danced, played music or attended a dance for the duration of twelve months afterwards. At least one representative from each family for miles around went to the funeral. Everyone in the townland stopped work for the two days of the wake while the remains was in the house. Even in summer, when the hay had to be saved, no-one worked if a neighbour had just died.[33]

The only musical form that took place at these wakes was the *caoineadh,* the singing of a lament over the dead. Sometimes, as in Inishowen, this was done by the relatives and as each of these arrived he/she stood over the corpse and chanted praise of the dead and sorrow at the death. In other areas, notably Tory Island, the *caoine* was sung not necessarily by the relatives but by the women of the area who were skilled in the art. There the singing took place at the graveside.[34]

The dance repertoire

Dancing was the main entertainment of the big nights. The dances performed were those which involved the whole gathering. Solo dances were not particularly common as no formal teaching of step dancing ever took place in Donegal. The dance repertoire in its entirety was very extensive and included the following: sets, lancers, quadrilles, highland schottisches, mazurkas, barndances, polkas, germans, waltzes, *Maggie Pickins,* and the *Versa Vienna.* Each region had its particular selection of popular dances. Some of the less common dances were, *The Marine, Kit O'Connor, Larry Agow, Erin Ó, The Coté Longue, The Tokyo* and *The Allemande.* These, according to Vincent Campbell, were among the popular dances in his locality of Eadan Infagh, in the upper part of the Glen of Glenties. *The Corn Riggs* was particularly common in the Rosses area while in Inis Eoghain, the *Pin Polka,* the *Heel and Toe Polka,* and the *Cripple Dance* were popular and seemed to be unknown elsewhere in the county. Generally speaking, however, the most popular dances throughout the county were the group dances such as the sets, lancers and quadrilles and the couple dances – the highlands, germans, barndances, mazurkas, waltzes and *Versa Vienna.*

The highland was undoubtedly the most popular of these dances and was often performed several times a night. This tune-type seems to be a variation on the strathspey which is widely recognised as a classic Scottish fiddle metre. In Donegal, the Scottish strathspey tunes were regularly played as highlands whereas in Scotland they were used purely as exhibition pieces and were played in a highly stylised and rigid manner. The highland dance called for a faster tempo than the regular strathspey, therefore the musicians tended to speed up and simplify the rhythmic complexities of the Scottish model.

Furthermore, many highland tunes have been composed in Donegal for the dance using a hybrid strathspey derived form. There is also a rather unique practice whereby reels are broken down or adapted to highlands for the purpose of the dance.

This practice of composing new tunes and reworking old ones is mostly confined to the highland repertoire. It is probably due to the popularity of the dance which demanded a constant supply of new melodies. The musicians, therefore, were forced to devise a means of expanding and varying their highland repertoire.

Fig. 25.2   The reworking process. Reel – Highland.
Source: Field recording. Damhnait Nic Suibhne (1988).

The most common method of adapting reels for the highland dance was to slow down the reel tempo and simplify the melodic line, and also to eliminate any intricate ornamentation. Fig. 25.2 provides an ideal example of the 'reworking process'. It is taken from the playing of Francie Mooney.

The highland retains the same overall structure as its source tune – *The High Road to Linton*. An interesting feature is the playing of the 'peak notes' in the melody which invariably occur in different positions to those of the model (the reel). The most important differences between the two tunes are the slower tempo in the highland and the use of the 'scotch snap'[35] particularly in the 'tune' (first part) where it usually occurs in the first beat of each bar, thereby helping to emphasise the characteristic highland rhythm.

There were at least two categories of highland danced, (a) the highland schottische and (b) the Irish highland. The schottische dance-form is widely documented in Scottish printed sources. Dating from around 1800, it was said to be a dance in four-four time with a pleasant easy-going tempo and a prominent dotted rhythm. It was popular all over Europe and was known as the écossaise or schottische.

The music associated with the dance was similar to the strathspey in its tempo and use of 'scotch snap'. The dance itself was a kind of polka of continental, not Scottish, origin. According to G. Vuillier's *A history of dance* (1898), it was invented by Markowski, who brought the mazurka to Western Europe. The highland schottische, however, contained a more elaborate step resembling, and perhaps derived from, the 'highland fling' style of dancing and this is regarded as a Scottish schottische.[36]

The following illustration shows examples of both the Scottish and Donegal versions of the highland schottische dance:

The highland – Donegal version[37]

Steps	Bars
Partners stand as for 'Shoe the Donkey.'	
Two slipping steps in line of direction.	1
Two slipping steps back to place.	1
Four slipping steps in line of direction.	2
Repeat going the other way first.	4
Turn partner as in Military Two Step.	4
Partners swing.	4

Highland Schottische step[38]

There were a number of versions of this step in use before 1914, but within living memory the following was the most common.

A. 1 Hop on LF and point R toe in 2nd position
    2 Hop on LF and bring RF to rear leg position
    3 Hop on LF and point R toe in 2nd position
    4 Hop on LF and bring RF to front leg position.

B. 1 Step to the right on RF
    2 Close LF to rear 5th position
    3 Step to the right on RF
    4 Hop on RF and bring LF to rear leg position.

It is difficult to make an accurate comparison of both forms since the Scottish example refers only to what is commonly known as the highland schottische step. This particular step, it seems, occurred in both *The Highland Schottische* and *The Common Schottische*. Both steps (A & B above) were used in country dances in strathspey tempo and *The Highland Schottische Step* was also used in reels. In each of the dances this pattern was used whenever the period of setting occupied two bars; it was then performed once with the right foot and once with the left. This accounted for four bars of the tune.[39] If we compare this to the Donegal version there appears to be no semblance of the Scottish step present at any point in the dance. In contrast, the steps used seem to be simple and uncomplicated. Since the method of learning the dances in Donegal was of an oral nature it was, perhaps, inevitable that intricate movements and steps would be simplified to suit the dancers' capabilities. Nevertheless, both Packie Manus Byrne and Danny O'Donnell pointed out that it was only in later years people began to simplify the dance in this way.

> In later years the people started doing the dances sort of in slow motion – in time with the music, but with no beat action, only just doing the bare steps and not the in-between things ...[40]
> ... As the jazz music came in they lost the old steps. It was originally a very graceful dance, but as the generations passed by, the old steps were gone by the board. Kilcar and Glencolumbcille are the only places in Donegal where they dance the old form of the highland in good style.[41]

Unfortunately, there appears to be no printed source for this more elaborate account of the highland. The above illustration is taken from a collection of dances collected in Donegal by Grace Orpen and published in 1931.

The *Irish* highland is possibly a variant of the previous dance, but as I could find no evidence of a four-hand highland in the Scottish dance books, it is possible that it may be an indigenous form,

> ... four danced that ... and they formed a circle you know. Two men and two girls and they joined hands first and went around in a semi-circle and back again, and with the other foot then swung back with the music ....[42]

The tune-type associated with these dances is notable for its lively swing. It is in four-four time with an obvious characteristic rhythmic pattern – this is, a very definite accent on the first beat of the bar and a precise manner of playing with the slight 'scotch snap'. The average tempo for the highland is ♩ = 184. It is taken at a slower tempo than a reel ♩ = 224.[43]

The fiddler's repertoire

One of the defining features of a region's music personality is its indigenous repertoire which is very much dictated by certain social factors in that society. Within the house dance situation, the fiddler's role was to provide lively music for the dancers. It is understandable then that much of the musical material presented by these musicians has a close affinity to the dance. This aspect of their repertoire has been moulded to suit the needs of the dancers and consequently reflects the kind of dances in vogue at the time. All of the fiddlers I interviewed had played mostly for dancing when they were younger and as a consequence, their repertoire included imported waltzes, foxtrots and music hall airs which co-existed with the traditional dances.

This corpus of repertoire material breaks down into two sections according to the functional nature of the music. These are the dance tunes and listening tunes. The dance tune category deals with the dance music, the tunes that musicians associated with a particular dance. The listening tune section contains the tunes which were not part of the dancing repertoire and were played as 'solo pieces', usually to a listening audience. This group contains a variety of unusual tune-types, many of a rather complex nature which the fiddlers learned as a challenge to their technical mastery of the instrument.

The tune-types were distributed between the groups as follows:

Dance tunes	Listening tunes
Highland Schottische	Reels
Mazurkas	Jigs
Barndances	Single jigs

Polkas

Germans

Set dance tunes (for example:

The Corn Riggs, Maggie Pickins)

Waltzes

Lancers

Quadrilles

(This section also includes those
tune-types already quoted earlier)

Slip jigs

Pipe and brass band marches

Hornpipes

Strathspeys

Airs – Laments

Programmatic pieces (tunes or
a series of tunes expressing a
certain theme, for example:
The Foxchase)

These divisions should not imply that dancers do not listen to music played for them, or that dance tunes are not played as listening pieces whenever fiddlers meet or entertain their friends or families. I must also point out that my study is based on only a portion of the *corpus* of dance music as played in the county today. It includes only those tunes which the musicians considered to be locally indigenous, whereas the repertoire of most Donegal fiddlers today, especially the younger generation, contains much else besides.

I have chosen these categories because it appears to me that the musicians divide their repertoire in this way. In my interviews they presented their material either as dance-related tunes or as solo tunes. For them, the division was a tangible one. The boundaries of each category were clearly defined. The most obvious distinction between these two groups is the way in which they differ in tune-type content. But what is not readily perceivable, at least by ourselves, is the extent to which they diverge in terms of their range of technical capacity. It appears, therefore, that the fiddler's repertoire functioned on two levels. This dichotomy can be viewed more readily like this:

Dance tunes

1-2 or more players
(less complex)

Listening tunes

Solo
(complex)

The dance tunes were played specifically for dancing to and were always played by one, two or more musicians, depending on the number of fiddlers in the locality. The function of these musicians was to provide a solid rhythmic base for the dancers and this, combined with the group factor, allowed no opportunity for individual inter-pretation in performance. This group then was viewed as being less complex in nature. The tunes were, generally speaking, thought to be simple in construction and the manner of playing straight-forward. James Byrne put it like this:

... The mazurkas, highlands, barndances, ah! they would be just for dancing away back ... they wouldn't be playing them for listening at all you know; any player that would play those sort of tunes for listening ... nobody would listen to them anyway. They'd figure they were too simple for listening to. Though indeed, some of the highlands are very complicated ...[44]

The listening tunes were associated with the solo performer, and as such were considered to be the more complex group. The individual musician in this case was free to explore tune-types unrelated to the dance, and to interpret the tune in whatever manner his creativity allowed him. In these, he was no longer tied to the rigid rhythmic boundaries of the dance. Vincent Campbell refers to it in this way:

... highlands, mazurkas, barndances, germans and polkas, they were all dancing tunes. They're wasn't much put on those, only to play them for dancing.[45]

Such deviations in complexity between the categories points to the question of standards in technical ability among the musicians. It would appear that a higher standard of musicianship was required in the performance of material from the listening tune section. The evolvement of this listening tune section, I would suggest, was dependent on the more technically proficient musicians, the fiddle experts and the skilled local fiddlers. As all the fiddlers had an extensive range of dance tunes in their repertoire, the dance tune section was said to be the larger of the two groups. The material in the listening tune category was the province of the better players. Only those musicians who were considered to be of solo standard would have developed this side of their repertoire. This minority group then was the sole contributor to the listening tune section and it was regarded as the smaller of the two, since the tunes within this section were too complicated for dancing, and the house dance was the main outlet for musical activity. Where, then, were these listening tunes performed?

The platform for the listening repertoire varied throughout the region. Vincent Campbell told me that in some areas there were music nights where no dancing took place. A group of fiddle players gathered together in a household and entertained their audience by holding competitions. The musicians performed to the best of their ability, devising complex variations and composing new parts for their tunes. At the end of the night, the audience selected the best fiddler of the evening.[46]

In other areas the listening tunes would be played at the end of a night's dancing. James Byrne describes it like this:

Plate 25.7   Vincent Campbell, Glenties.

> They would dance at the beginning of the night, and when the
> music would get complicated towards the end of the night, they
> would get tired and they would sit down and listen, you know ...
> that's when you'd hear the good music, you see, the hard jigs and
> the hard reels and hornpipes and all, because most of those hard
> tunes weren't really good for dancing at all. There were more
> straight-forward ones played for dancing, you know.[47]

The combination of both groups provides the complete repertoire
picture as it existed, or still exists today (however altered) in the
Donegal fiddler's repertoire. The extensive nature of its contents, both
in terms of diversity and volume of tune-type is, I would suggest, rather
unusual among traditional music repertoires in other regions. The
dancing dictated the type of dance tunes played, and their repertoire
reflected the categories of dances in vogue in a particular region at that
time. As a result, in particular areas, certain tunes and dance types were
more common than in other areas. Take for example, the high proportion of polkas and slides in musicians' repertoires in the Sliabh
Luachra area compared to that of musicians in Donegal and
elsewhere.[48]

One of the most significant differentiating factors of the Donegal
fiddler's repertoire is tune-type variety. The number of individual tune

types and the variety of rhythms contained within both groups differ substantially from many other regional traditions. The dance tune section already discussed provides a wide variety of rhythms and types. The listening tune section contains, besides mainstream traditional music genres, tunes such as pipe marches, brass band marches, strathspeys, programmatic pieces and ancient laments. I am not suggesting that these pieces were not played at some stage in other parts of Ireland, but that in most areas they do not seem to have survived the passage of time so well as in Donegal; and that, at the present time, few regions seem to possess, as a *corpus*, such a wide, ranging variety of musical material in their repertoire, material which has remained intact over a considerable length of time. It is interesting to examine the repertoire picture of an equally important musical region in southern Ireland. Compare the above with Alan Ward's study of the repertoire material in the Sliabh Luachra area (the Cork/Kerry borderlands).

> ... Most of it is dance music. The dance music of the region has developed to suit the type of social dancing which had been popular since the mid-nineteenth century – the sets. The set had six figures, the first four danced to polkas, the fifth called the *slide* danced to a fast single jig (these tunes are hence always called slides) and the sixth to a hornpipe or reel ... The present-day incidence of the various types of dance tunes in the district is directly related to their use in the polka set and hence polkas predominate with jigs and slides a long way behind in second and third place, hornpipes fourth, and reels, the dominant rhythm elsewhere in Ireland, a poor fifth. Most musicians know only a few reels and these are usually very common like the *Mountain Road, Miss Mc Leod's* or *My love she's in America* ...
>
> ... A small proportion of the current repertoire has never been associated with dancing and most musicians know one or two song airs at least ... the fashion for playing airs is a relatively recent one among dance musicians, having developed according to existing evidence only in this century, and in Sliabh Luachra there is reason to believe that Pádraig O'Keeffe was partly responsible for any popularity the playing of airs might have ... other forms of listening music are also encountered such as Pádraig's *Johnny Cope* and Tom Billy's *The drunken piper* which Maurice O'Keeffe plays, but such pieces are rare on the whole.[49]

There are notable similarities in both traditions. Of particular significance is the similar grouping of the repertoire material. In both regions the music is classified either as dance music or as listening music. The dance music has developed to suit the type of social dancing which had been popular in each area, the preference being for sets in Sliabh Luachra and couple dances in Donegal. Consequently the presence of the various types of dance tunes in their repertoire is directly related to their use in these dances.

It is in the area of listening tunes, however, that both traditions differ considerably. The Sliabh Luachra musicians did not concentrate on this side of their repertoire to any substantial extent, whereas in Donegal the listening repertoire is an extensive one. This recalls my previous suggestion that the evolution of a listening tune repertoire was dependent on the more technically proficient musicians, the solo performers, or those musicians who were not satisfied to play for dancing only. Note that Alan Ward attributes much of the small listening tune repertoire in Sliabh Luachra to the influence of Pádraig O'Keeffe (a noted fiddle player from this area). Furthermore, can this mean that the ratio of good fiddlers in a region possibly dictated the extent of the listening tune repertoire?

Influences on the repertoire

The creative and challenging nature of the listening tune repertoire made it somewhat vulnerable to the pressure of external influences. For example, the presence of brass band marches and certain hornpipes reveals the influence of the Victorian classical style, with their unusual scales and tricky fingerwork and testify to the growing influence of external culture in the county. Simultaneously, the presence of highlands, strathspeys and pipe marches implies a strong Scottish influence on the music. Indeed this obvious Scottish element in the Donegal fiddle tradition has been a source of contention for decades. It seems that much of the repertoire and fiddling styles of Donegal, and indeed of Ulster in general, challenge certain assumptions concerning the nature of Irish fiddling as characterised by the more familiar Connacht and Munster traditions. This divergence in styles is accounted for by a number of factors: geography and history have long promoted trade, cultural exchange and military contacts between Donegal and Scotland, interaction was facilitated historically through a common language and in more recent times by the large-scale movement of migratory labourers. Musicians identified more easily with the Scottish tradition than with the mainstream Irish music culture.[50]

The presence of these Scottish elements, I would suggest, was not the result of direct borrowing from Scotland but part of a native tradition which shared common elements with the music tradition of the Scottish Highlands. Perhaps it was part of a common Gaelic culture that was prevalent in the Celtic regions of Northern Europe. This common Gaelic culture formed the foundation of the 'Northern style' and would, in part, account for the presence of these so-called Scottish elements in the music. Central to this relationship between Donegal and Scotland was the longstanding shared highland piping tradition dating from the 1700s, which continued in Donegal up to the turn of this century. Its principal exponents were the travelling itinerant musicians. The presence of a large number of piping tunes in the fiddler's repertoire is directly related to the influence of these versatile musicians. What is even more significant is the way in which the highland piping techniques have been transferred to the fiddle and have been assimilated into the fiddler's playing technique. Particularly evident are the use of drones to produce a harmonic effect at selected points and the familiar bowed triplets which are reminiscent of the piper's cran. Indeed, more general stylistic features such as the bowing styles and the fairly stark unadorned fingerwork are also marks of the piping tradition. Fig. 25.3 provides an example of this 'transformation process'. It is taken from the playing of Francie and Mickey Byrne (Dearg) of Kilcar.

Fig. 25.3   The transformation process – piping tradition to fiddle tradition.
Source: Feldman and O'Doherty, *The northern fiddler*, p. 177.

The presence of strathspeys and programmatic pieces in the repertoire points to a later period in our historical relationship with Scotland. Earlier this century, with the ongoing practice of migratory labour and the profusion of shipping links between Ulster and Scotland, Donegal folk travelled frequently between these two countries. The people going there were caught up in the surge of a musical revival lead by James Scott Skinner (1843-1927). He was a virtuoso player and composer with a mixed background in traditional and classical violin playing. Skinner played and composed in a style that attempted to graft on to Scottish fiddle music the playing technique and romantic flourishes of European classical violin playing. The Donegal fiddlers looked to Skinner's music for repertoire and playing technique. There was a keen interest in improving one's technique. A popular tutor was published at this time called *The young violinist and duet book* by William C. Honeyman, which became the bible of most fiddlers both Irish and Scottish. Seamus Grant, a fiddler from Inishowen, had a copy of this tutor and considered it to be most useful. It contained technical elements such as changing positions and many tunes in simplified notation. Danny O'Donnell from the Rosses also mentioned this tutor and how popular it was in his area; he considered it to be: 'marvellous – you could almost teach yourself from it ...'[51]

The widespread circulation of Skinner's recordings played a crucial part in establishing his popularity throughout Scotland and Ulster. Most Donegal fiddlers today would have in their repertoire tunes composed by Scott Skinner. It is generally recognised in Scotland that Skinner's followers have lost contact with the element of traditional dance music in his work and have tended to play his tunes in even a more classical style than Skinner originally played. In contrast, the Donegal players that I have heard play Skinner's music concentrate on the traditional element in his compositions and have assimilated them into the native oral tradition.

It is these accumulated influences that give to the 'Donegal style' an ambience that contrasts sharply with the more homogenous musical styles of the south of Ireland. The influences are readily recognisable, but their absorption into the Donegal tradition has given them a wholly local flavour and has produced, through time, a distinct and personal musical culture. It is precisely this distinctive quality that has recently generated such interest and attention in the Donegal fiddle tradition. The last decade has brought due acclaim to the long forgotten 'expert fiddlers' of the county and has brought them directly into line with the Colemans and Killorans of the past.

The tradition is alive and vibrant and wholly indigenous, significantly at a time when media influences have contributed to a large degree to the erosion of many distinctive local and regional styles. In Donegal, the *corpus* of musical material has, to a large extent, survived intact. However, the notion of the fiddler's divided repertoire no longer pertains. With the social changes of the last few decades and the disappearance of the country house big nights, many of the older dances have by now become obsolete. Although the steps and figures of these dances may be forgotten, the tunes remain in the repertoire of the musicians who now play them as listening tunes. The dance tune section is slowly evolving as a separate musical genre totally divorced from its roots, and the listening tune section, which in the past was regarded as the smaller of the two sections, is being extended to incorporate it. Nowadays, although the older musicians remember clearly the original division in repertoire material, they are no longer concerned with it. They have no hesitation in playing a highland or any of the dance tunes as listening pieces. The younger musicians, on the other hand, have have no perception of the original division in repertoire and their own repertoire can be seen instead, to be a merging of the two categories.

References

1.　A. MacLoone, 'Music in Donegal' in *Donegal Annual*, ii, pt. 1 (1951), p. 301.
2.　B. Breathnach, *Folk music and dances of Ireland* (Dublin and Cork, 1971), p. 79.
3.　Ibid., p. 55.
4.　Ibid., Chapter 5.
5.　A. Feldman and E. O'Doherty, *The northern fiddler – music and musicians of Donegal and Tyrone* (Belfast, 1979), p. 36.
6.　Breathnach, *Folk music*, p. 69.
7.　Feldman and O'Doherty, *Northern fiddler*, p. 142.
8.　P. Cooke, 'The fiddle tradition of the Shetland Islands, unpublished Ph.D. thesis, School of Scottish Studies, University of Edinburgh (1986).
9.　W. Bachmann, *The origins of bowing* (London, 1969), pl. no. 93.
10.　S. Jones (ed.), Packie Manus Byrne, *Recollections of a Donegal man* (Lampeter, 1988), p. 81.
11.　Bachmann, *Bowing*, p. 71.
12.　Feldman and O'Doherty, *Northern fiddler*, p. 142; for a detailed account of the Doherty family and its music see Comhairle Bhéaloideas Éireann, *The gravel walks: Mickey Doherty*.
13.　Ibid., p. 44.
14.　D. McLaughlin, Sleeve notes on the recording 'The brass fiddle' (Dublin, 1986).
15.　Jones, *Packie Manus Byrne*, p. 80.
16.　Cooke, 'The fiddle traditions'.
17.　Field recording (1990) of James Byrne by Damhnait Nic Suibhne, Traditional Music Archives, University College Cork.
18.　Feldman and O'Doherty, *Northern fiddler*, pp 34-5.
19.　Field recording (1988) of Seamus Grant by Damhnait Nic Suibhne, Traditional Music Archives, University College Cork.

20. P. Tunney, *The stone fiddle – my way to traditional song* (Dublin, 1979), p. 142.
21. Feldman and O'Doherty, *Northern fiddler*, p. 36.
22. Ibid., p. 47.
23. Ibid., p. 131.
24. Field recording of Danny O'Donnell (1991) by Damhnait Nic Suibhne, Traditional Music Archives, University College Cork.
25. Jones, *Packie Manus Byrne*, p. 71.
26. Ibid., p. 72.
27. Ibid., p. 73.
28. O'Donnell field recording (1991).
29. C. Foley, Irish traditional stepdancing in north Kerry – a contextual and structural analysis, unpublished Ph.D. thesis, Goldsmith College, University of London (1988).
30. O'Donnell field recording (1991).
31. Ibid.
32. Jones, *Packie Manus Byrne*, p. 56.
33. See K. Danaher, *In Ireland long ago* (Dublin and Cork, 1962), pp 153, 169 for a detailed account of both events.
34. D. Nic Suibhne, Song airs in the repertoire of Dinny Doogan, Tory Island unpublished undergraduate dissertation, Department of Music, University College Cork.
35. Scotch snap – name for a rhythmic figure consisting of a short note on the beat followed by a longer one held until the next beat. See A. Jacobs, *A new dictionary of music* (London, 1958).
36. H. A. Thurston, *Scotland's dances* (London, 1954), p. 51.
37. G. Orpen, *Dances of Donegal* (London, 1931), p. 28.
38. J. F. and T. M. Flett, *Traditional dancing in Scotland* (London, 1964), p. 103.
39. Ibid., p. 102.
40. Jones, *Packie Manus Byrne*, p. 75.
41. Feldman and O'Doherty, *Northern fiddler*, reference to Danny O'Donnell, p. 149.
42. Field recording (1988) of Francie Mooney by Domhnait Nic Suibhne, Traditional Music Archives, University College Cork.
43. B. Breathnach, *Ceol rince na hÉireann*, i (Baile Átha Cliath, 1963).
44. Field recording of James Byrne (1989) by Damhnait Nic Suibhne, Traditional Music Archives, University College Cork.
45. Field recording of Vincent Campbell by Damhnait Nic Suibhne in ibid.
46. Ibid.
47. Byrne field recording.
48. A. Ward, 'Music from Sliabh Luachra' in *Traditional Music Magazine*, v (London, 1970).
49. Ibid., p. 19.
50. D. Nic Suibhne, Scottish influences in the Donegal fiddle tradition, unpublished undergraduate dissertation, Department of Music, University College Cork (1988).
51. Feldman and O'Doherty, *Northern fiddler*, p. 147.

Chapter 26

AN CEOL DÚCHAIS I dTÍR CHONAILL

LILLIS Ó LAOIRE

Bhí urraim agus ómós riamh daite don cheol i dTír Chonaill agus tá an scéal i gcónaí amhlaidh. Tá sé i gceist agam gearrchuntas a thabhairt anseo ar dhúchas na n-amhrán sa cheantar. Beidh mé ag díriú go háirithe ar amhránaíocht na Gaeilge ós uirthi is mó atá eolas agam ach beidh corrthagairt agam fosta do thraidisiún na n-amhrán Béarla. Baineann dúchas an cheoil Ghaelige, mar a thugtar air, le traidisiún cultúir i bhfad níos leithne a shíneas ó thuaisceart na hAlban go deisceart na hÉireann agus is cuid de shean-dúchas Eorpach é atá, nach mór, caillte sa chuid is mó d'Iarthar na hEorpa seachas againn féin agus ag cúpla shainghrúpa eile. Is féidir ceangail a fheiceáil idir cuid ceoltóirí na nEipicí Slavacha, ar bhuail Albert Lord[1] leo sna tríochaidí, agus dúchas na tíre seo. Síleann daoine go bhfuil cultúr na Gaeltachta cúng siocair go bhfuil an Ghaeltacht cúng ó thaobh talaimh ach ní fíor sin. Tá claonadh ann fosta sa tír seo amharc ar an Ghaeltacht mar iarsmalann mhór a bhfuil an oidhreacht náisiúnta idir theanga agus bhéaloideas ar buantaispeáint inti. Ar ndóigh thiocfadh a rá gurb iad na daoine a bhfuil an cultúr seo ina seilbh na príomh-iarsmaí. Is iomaí uair a chuirtear an cheist ar amhránaithe: 'Do bharúil an iarsma é an cultúr seo den tsean-am a chuaigh thart?' Tá aithne agam ar dhuine amháin a thug an freagra borb, 'Ní iarsma mise ar scor ar bith.'

Tá claonadh ann dearmad a dhéanamh go bhfuil an cultúr seo sean agus comhaimseartha ag an am chéanna. Baineann sé leis an am i láthair chomh maith leis an tsean-am. Ar ndóighe sin ceann de na gnéithe is speisialta fá dtaobh de. Sin an rud a bheir leanúnachas dó agus a ní traidisiúnta é. Le blianta beaga anuas, deacair go leor a bhíonn sé amanna teacht ar an chultúr traidisiúnta agus tá an amhránaíocht ar an ghné is seachantaí ar fad b'fhéidir, ó tharla gur ealaín an-phearsanta í nach réitíonn rómhaith le tithe tábhairne agus an gleo agus an callán a bhíos ag gabháil ar aghaidh iontu. Ina dhiaidh sin maireann na hamhráin i gcuimhne an phobail. Ar na saolta deireanacha seo tá claonadh ann a mheas go bhfuil siad ag gabháil i léig ach níl ann ach go bhfuil siad ag fáil a n-anála arís. Tá spéis mhór á cur sna hamhráin Ghaeilge arís le tamall anuas agus glúin ceoltóirí óga ag teacht chun tosaigh a fhágfas a lorg ar an dúchas go fóill nuair a thiocfas siad in inmhe. Tá an dúchas atá acusan difriúil go maith ón rud atá ag an ghlúin is sine. Tá an amhránaíocht níos teirce anois ná mar a bhíodh tráth agus fiú amháin nuair a bhíonn seisiún amhrán ann, go minic chan iad na seanamhráin a bhíos in uachtar. Mar a dúirt an scoláire béaloidis as Meiriceá, Julie Henigan,

> Now that traditional singing is less common, however, it becomes increasingly necessary for young singers to seek out and imitate 'a proper thing'. They must more consciously master the stylistic features that characterise sean-nós singing.[2]

Ní thuigeann an óige sa lá atá inniu an t-ionad tábhachtach a bhí ag an amhránaíocht i saol na ndaoine fiú glúin ó shin. Ba dhlúthchuid iad na hamhráin de ghnáthshaol na ndaoine. Líonann an ceol go leor de na spásanna inár saol anois, nuair a bhímid ag siopadóireacht, nuair a bhímid ag obair sa teach, nó fiú nuair a bhímid ag ar an ghuthán ag iarraidh teangmháil a dhéanamh le duine. Cuirtear an ceol sa chúlra sa saol nua-aimseartha ach fada ó shin ba é a mhalairt glan a bhí fíor. Seo fianaise ó Áine Ní Ghallchóir, a fuair bás in 1994, grásta ó Dhia uirthi, as Dobhar, ceoltóir a thabhaigh cliú dá ceantar dúchais sna caogaidí agus sna seascaidí ag an Oireachtas:

> Bhínn ag ceol achan áit – trasna na bpáirceanna agus ag léimnigh thar na claíocha – bhínn ag ceol achan áit, domh féin.[3]

Le gairid dúirt Hannah Mhic Ruairí agus Treasa Mhic Laifeartaigh as Toraigh liom faoina n-uncal Jimí Shéamais Bháin Ó Mianáin agus faoi bhean mhuinteartha dó, Ciot Tom Ní Mhianáin, gurb é an caitheamh aimseartha a bhíodh acu, ag fiafraí dá chéile – 'Cén tús a bhí ar a leithéid seo de cheathrú?' – agus ansin á cheol le déanamh cinnte go raibh sé i gceart acu. Léiríonn an fhianaise sin chomh leitheadach agus a bhí na hamhráin fiú le dhá ghlúin anuas, ach tá an oiread athruithe ar an tsaol ón am sin gur geall le brionglóid anois é.[4]

Le dhá chéad bliain anuas nó mar sin is iad na hamhráin ghrá bun agus barr an dúchais amhránaíochta sa Ghaeilge go speisialta. Bhí cineál eile filíochta a chantaí go fairsing ar fud na hÉireann agus na hAlban sa tsean-am fada ó shin ach a d'imigh as cuimhne na ndaoine sa dá ghlúin dheireanacha. Sin iad na laoithe Fiannaíochta. Dánta iad seo a cumadh sna meadarachtaí siollacha a bhí in úsáid ag na filí gairmiúla tráth a mhair siad. Tugann Hugh Shields cuntas ar na laoithe agus deir sé,

> The ... lays were culturally remote from mainstream Western thought and art, and what was of universal human interest in them was not articulated in easily accessible form. No less than in

their earlier history, they were known and appreciated in the nineteenth century by the native Gaelic communities alone – in both Scotland and Ireland – which were now growing smaller while the popularity of imported ballads in English and native imitations increased.[5]

Nuair a bhí an traidisiún seo ina neart ba ghnáth na laoithe seo a cheol ach ní foinn mar atá le hamhráin an lae inniu atá i gceist. Mar a dúirt Peadar Mac Fhionnlaoich (Cú Uladh) ar an *Chlaidheamh Solais* faoi Phroinias Mac Loinsigh, 'Chan fonn amhráin do bhí leis ar chor ar bith acht ceol mar bheadh ag sagart ag canadh Aifrinn'.[6]

Tá samplaí ar taifead de chuid de na laoithe á gcanadh agus tá cosúlacht idir an stíl agus ceol eaglasta ceart go leor. Bailíodh píosa de *Laoi an Amadáin Mhóir* ó Sheán Bán Mac Grianna agus fuarthas píosaí de *Laoi na bhFiann* agus de *Laoi na Mná Móire* ó bheirt de mhuintir Ighne as paróiste Glinne in Iardheisceart na contae. Tá fear acu le cluinstin ag ceol *Laoi na Mná Móire* ar chaiséad a cuireadh amach dornán blianta ó shin.[7] Deir Hugh Shields gur dócha gur i nDún na nGall a b'fhaide a mhair na laoithe a gcanstan le guth:

> Another fact suggests that Donegal, more reliant on oral trans-mission, preserved the singing of lays the longest: from that county comes the strongest evidence, in the form of description and sound recording, of narrative lays being sung in the twentieth century.[8]

Gné eile de dhúchas na hamhránaíochta atá ar shiúl i léig go mór, an chaointeoireacht. Mhair an chaointeoireacht go láidir sa Ghaeltacht i dTír Chonaill go háirid san Iarthuaisceart. Ar ndóighe is le Carraig Airt a bhaineas *Caoineadh Dhoimnic Uí Dhomhnaill* nó *Pill, Pill a Rún Ó,* mar is fearr aithne air. Amhrán é seo a chuirtear i mbéal mháthair Uí Dhomhnaill nuair a thiontaigh sé ina mhinistir mar gheall ar bhean ar thit sé i ngrá léi.[9] Léirigh Breandán Ó Madagáin go bhfuil an-chosúlacht idir an fonn seo agus foinn chaointeoireachta as ceantair eile in Éirinn.[10] Is cosúil go mbíodh an ceol céanna á úsáid arís agus arís eile do chaointe éagsúla. Tá cuimhne ag go leor daoine go fóill ar na mná caointe a fheiceáil ag caoineadh coirp agus tá corrdhuine beo i gcónaí a rinne an caoineadh iad féin. Chonaic mé féin iarsma de ar thórramh a raibh mé air tá ceithre bliana ó shin. Seo cuntas air a tógadh ó Niall Ó Dubhthaigh as an Bhealtaine i dtús na ndaicheadaí:

> Go dtí ar na moillibh fhéin chuirfead sé crith ort a bheith ag éisteacht le cuid de na daoine seo, nó bhí sé 'na ghrás acú na

muirbh a chaoineadh. Dá mbeadh duine annsin nach mbéadh curtha ach mí nó cupla mí nó b'fhéidir seachtmhain, rachadh a mhuinntir fhad le na n-uaigh agus chluinfeá iad míle ar shiúl a caoineadh sa roilig sin. Stad sin ar fad le seal 'e bhliadhanta agus bhí na sagairt 'na gcuideadh mhaith le deireadh a chur leis.[11]

Deasghnáth agus dualgas poiblí a bhí sa chaoineadh ina ndéantaí an té a bhí ar lár a mholadh. Ní mheastaí fada ó shin go raibh an corp curtha i gceart mura gcaoinfí é. Tá cuntas eile againn ar an chaoineadh a dhéanamh os cionn an choirp i dteach na faire ó Chonall Ó Domhnaill as Rinn na Feirste. Ba é Eoghan Ó Dubhthaigh a bhí marbh agus ba í Máire John Nic Gairbheith a bhean chéile a chaoin é. Bhí cáil ar an bhean seo mar bhean a níodh cleamhnais, baisteadh urláir agus mar cheoltóir fosta. Ní raibh i gConall ach tachrán ag an am agus cuireadh ina luí é ach d'éirigh sé agus bhí sé ag culéisteacht leis an rud a bhí ag gabháil ar aghaidh.

Théadh Máire John anonn chun na cónra ó am go ham agus ligfeadh sí amach a racht le dreas caointe. Faoi cheann tamaill bhí a raibh istigh i dteach na faire ag smeacharnaigh ina cuideachta. De réir mar bhí a mbrón ag méadú thosaigh siad ag longadán anonn agus anall agus iad snadhmtha ina chéile. Dúirt Conall gurbh éigean Máire a tharraingt ar shiúl ón chorp nuair a bhíothas ag cur an chláir ar an chónair. Féach fig. 26.1.[12]

Ceol iontach simplí atá ann, líne amháin dáiríre, athráite arís agus arís eile de réir mar a d'fhóir sin dá racht. Ar ndóigh ní hiad seo na focla ceanann céanna a dúirt Máire ach cuimhne Chonaill orthu. Tá cosúlacht idir an ceol agus *Pill Pill a Rún Ó,* fosta cé go bhfuil níos mó ná líne amháin sa cheol sin. Tá gné eile den traidisiún a mheath go mór, is é sin na hamhráin diaga. Tá ceangal idir cuid acu seo agus an caoineadh sa méid is go gcuirtear cuid acu i mbéal Mhuire nuair a bhí Íosa á chéasadh. Ba iad na mná a ba mhó a chaomhnaigh na caointe agus dánta diaga eile, leithéidí Mháire Ní Dhonnagáin as Teileann agus Nóra Ní Ghallchóir as an tSruthán i nGort a' Choirce.[13] Táimid faoi chomaoin mhór ag Enrí Ó Muirgheasa a rinne cnuasach mór de na dánta seo.[14] Faraoir go bhfuil an leabhar as cló anois. Tá corrcheann de na dánta seo le fáil ar bhéala daoine i dTír Chonaill i dtólamh, an *Dán a' Bháis* mar shampla, a fuair Caitlín Ní Dhomhnaill as Rinn na Feirste óna máthair, Gráinne.[15]

An gcluin sibh mise anois a pheacachaí
Ná déanaigí faillí in bhur gcás
Ní raibh sibh tarrthaithe ins na hAifrinn
Is sibh go tapaidh ag triall 'un báis

Fig. 26.1   Píosa ceol caointe ó Chonall Ó Domhnaill, Rinn na Feirste.

Beidh na haingle ar uachtar uisce
'S iad go cliste anonn is anall
Níl a'n anam dá bhfuil saor ó pheacadh
Nach rachaidh ar eiteogaí go Cuan na nGeall

Bhí dán eile ag Joe Dhónaill Sheáin Mac Eachmharcaigh as Doire Chonaire[16] a raibh an teideal *Dán na Marbh* air ach chan ionann é agus ceann Chaitlín. Théid na téamaí sna dánta seo siar chomh fada leis na meánaoiseanna agus díríonn an spioradáltacht a bhaineann leo ar thruacántacht na Páise ar leibhéal pearsanta. Bíonn teagasc i gcuid eile acu ar na rudaí a ba chóir do dhuine a dhéanamh lena anam a shábháil. Chantaí iad go minic i rith an Chargais agus is cosúil go mbítí á rá sna tithe pobail le linn Aifreann an Domhnaigh agus na mná ina mbun. Deir Niall Ó Dubhthaigh:

Ins na laethibh sin bhí dánta diadha ag 'ul i dtoigh a' phobail gach Domhnach fríd a' bhliadhain. Bhíodh piocadh na gceoltóirí a b'fhearr ins a' pharaiste annsin cruinn fá theach a' phobail agus iad ag gabháil na ndánta diadha seo ar feadh an Domhnaigh. Stad sin tá corradh agus dhá fhichead bliadhain ó shoin. Thug siad oideas mór de'n mhuinntir a bhí ag 'ul san am sin.[17]

Agus cuntas eile ón fhear chéanna:

Bhéadh an ceol ag 'ul annsin go díreach mar atá sé indiú ach amháin ins an am sin in m'óige féin go mbíodh achan nduine i dtoigh an phobail ag 'ul cheoil mar sin Lá Nodlag. Bhí sean-dántaí ag na sean-mhrá agus bhíodh siad a crónán leobhtha ag 'ul daobhtha cé acu a bhí ceol acu nó nach rabh. Chualaidh mé seandaoine a rádh go minic gurb é an chéad cheol uirnéise a chualaidh siad ariamh i dtoigh pobail Ghort a' Choirce cupla fideóg – sin tuairim ar chéad bliadhain ó shoin nuair a bhí mo mháthair, na giorrsuigh. Bhíod sise ag innse dúinne ins na laethibh sin go rabh ceoltóirí an-mhaith ar fad ann. Tháinic athrach mór ar sin fhéin agus chan fhoscluigheann a'n duine astoigh toigh a' phobail a mbéal ach amháin na cupla duine a bíos ar an lafta ag bocsa an cheoil.[18]

Ní dheir Niall cad chuige ar stadadh de chanstan na n-amhrán diaga i dteach pobail Ghort a' Choirce, ach is féidir a bheith measartha cinnte go raibh baint ag cúrsaí eaglasta na linne leis. Deir an diagaire Seán Ó Ríordáin linn:

The nineteenth century apostles of the Church achieved their aims in Ireland, not necessarily because of their personal worth or the message they had to offer, but because of the vast reserves of faith in the hearts of the people. At the same time, these nineteenth-century churchmen virtually ignored, and sometimes openly opposed, what were in fact the very sources of the faith, namely fourteen centuries of unbroken and life-giving Christian tradition passed on in the erstwhile vernacular – Irish and the tradition which it embodied.[19]

Bhain an t-athrú le teacht Phaul Cullen mar Ardeaspag Ard Mhacha agus mar chairdinéal in 1849. Bhí tríocha bliain caite ag an fhear seo sa Róimh agus bhí fonn air béasa na Róimhe a chur i bhfeidhm ar an chreideamh Chaitliceach sa tír seo. Is dócha gurb é sin an rud a ba chúis le go leor den mheath a tháinig ar na dánta diaga sna Gaeltachtaí le céad bliain agus corradh anuas. Tá an t-ádh orainn mar sin féin go bhfuil go leor fágtha againn agus is rudaí iad a d'fhóirfeadh go maith do chuid de shearmanais eaglasta an lae inniu.

Is mithid dúinn aird a dhíriú ar an traidisiún comhaimseartha agus ar na coda de a bhfuil mothú i dtólamh iontu. Tharraing na hamhráin ghrá sa Ghaeilge go leor airde ó bhailitheoirí éagsúla, siocair iad a bheith chomh leitheadach i measc na ndaoine agus siocair friotal glinn, gonta bheith iontu. Gan amhras is gné an-phríobháideach den tsaol é an grá atá doiligh fiú inniu a phlé go foscailte. Ba mhó arís an bang a bhí ar an ghrá a phlé go foscailte fada ó shin. Bhí dóigheanna thart air sin agus is fríd na hamhráin a thigeadh an scéal amach go minic – an rud nach raibh cead a rá sa ghnáthchaint dúradh i modh filíochta é. Dálta an chaointe, bhaintí úsáid as an fhilíocht le racht a ligean a bhí ina luí go trom ar chroí duine. Mar a dúirt Aodh Ó Duibhneannaigh:

> ... poetry wasn't composed merely for the sake of composing a song; it came straight from the heart – and therefore it meant every word of what was said... you were *driven* to poetry... It was like crying your eyes out over something: you put it into words and you got *relief* after composing something that you were satisfied with.[20]

Ag caint ar dhaoine a raibh cumas filíochta iontu a bhí Aodh ansin. Bhí an cumas sin níba leitheadaí ag na daoine fada ó shin ná mar atá sé anois. Mar sin féin ní raibh bac ar bith ar an té nach raibh ábalta filíocht a chumadh amhrán a chum duine éigin eile a tharraingt air féin le faoiseamh a fháil nuair a bheadh na mothúcháin faoi bhrú. Tá na hamhráin ghrá lom lán de phaisean agus de chrá croí agus caint ghlan ghéar iontu. Nuair a chuirtear guth, is é sin ceol, leo tá earra fíorghreanta snoite againn. Chuir Éamonn Mac Ruairí as Toraigh amhrán maith i gcompáráid le pictiúr de chuid a chomhoileánaigh Ruairí L Mac Ruairí – é glan, soiléir gan a dhath de bharraíocht curtha leis.

Ba mhaith leis na daoine na hamhráin bheith soiléir agus ba mhaith leo na focail a chluinstin. Go minic ní bhíonn scéal sna hamhráin Ghaeilge mar a bhíos sna bailéid Bhéarla. Ba ghnách i gcónaí údar nó brí an amhráin a insint roimh ré. Is minic mar sin féin nach raibh brí nó údar ar eolas ag daoine agus fágann sin deacair in amanna scéal an amhráin a fháil. Dúirt amhránaí amháin liom gurbh fhusa na scéalta a leanúint sna hamhráin Bhéarla agus is fíor sin. Deir Hugh Shields: 'Ambiguity after all invites intelligent listeners to interpret what they can of a text',[21] agus pléann sé ceist an údair sna hamhráin ar bhealach íogair tuisceanach. Sna hamhráin ghrá cuirtear go leor in iúl i mbeagán focal – a leithéid seo mar shampla a fuarthas ó Róise Nic Grianna, Róise na nAmhrán as Árainn Mhór:

Ansacht na n-ansacht a dtug mé m'ansacht go léir duit
An é nach cumhan leat mo mhealladh is rinne tú an fheall orm 'na
  dhiaidh sin
Anois ó tá mé folamh is go bhfuil m'intinn lánbhuartha
'S mé ag amharc ar mo leannán ag fear eile á bréagadh.[22]

Tá draíocht ar leith ag baint le bheith ag éisteacht le Róise a cheol. Tá
neart den chineál seo le fáil againn. Seo sampla eile a fuair mé ó bheirt
dheirfiúracha as Toraigh, Treasa Mhic Laifeartaigh agus Sorcha Uí Bhaoill:

Ag an phobal Dé Domhnaigh thug mé mórchion don chailín
Is í ba deise is ba bhreácha dar tógadh riamh i mbaile
Bhí a béilín mar bheadh an rós ann is a caoinchom mar an
  sneachta
Ó is a Rí nach bhfuil mo lóistín san áit a gcóiríonn sí a leabaidh.[23]

Nó ceathrú as amhrán a fuarthas ó Neilí Ní Dhomhnaill fá fhear a
fágadh gan a chéile Cití Ní Eaghra:

Is fada mé ag triall fá mhullaigh na nArdán Donn
Mar i ndúil is go bhfeicfinn mo leanbh nó scáil a cinn
A cúilín deas triopallach fite a bhí fáinneach fionn
Is nach seo mé ag triall chugaibh is gan mo Chití Ní Eaghra liom.[24]

Bhí a sciar féin den fhilíocht ag na mná fosta, rud a léiríos an cheathrú
seo:

B'fhurast domh aithne ort nach tú a bhí i ndán dom
Chuir tú amach mé oíche na báistí
Bhain truisle díom ag giall na bearnadh
Is char dhúirt tú Dia leat is char chroith tú lámh liom.[25]

Nó cás an chailín óig sa rann seo:

Nach trua mé inniu is nach trua mé amárach
Mo theach mór folamh is gan agam preáta
Níl aon deoir bhainne agam is gile ná'n t-uisce
Tá babaí óg agam is tá m'fhortún briste.[26]

Nó an bheirt a bhí pósta ar dhaoine eile agus iad i ngrá le chéile i rith
an ama:

Mhuire is a Rí an Domhnaigh
Ná nach bhfuil cabhair ar bith i ndán domh

Ná nach mbím go brách sé mo chónaí
In aon lóistín amháin leis?

Sé mo chreach agus mo ghéarbhrón
Nach ár bpósadh anocht atá muid
M'fhearsa bheith faoin fhód
Is tusa ar thórramh do mhnása.[27]

Sin, dar liom féin ceann de na ráitis is géire agus is breácha dá bhfuil
againn sa stór amhrán ar fad. Léiríonn sé go beacht an fhírinne fá na
hamhráin seo – go minic bíonn cead rudaí a rá i véarsaíocht nach
gceadófaí go brách i ngnáthchomhrá. Tá tuigse iontach don
choincheap sin ar a dtugtar an dúchas i véarsaí na n-amhrán seo. 'Guth
na treibhe' a bheir Máire Mhac a' tSaoi air. Tá cinnteacht agus muinín
sna ráitis a insíonn dúinn – 'seo sinne agus sinn féin sinn féin.' Ní léir
aon cheistiú ar na luachanna atá ar a gcúl. Is filíocht í seo a thig ó
phobal a bhí an-chinnte díobh féin agus dá gcultúr. Dream ar bith
daoine a chothaigh agus a chaomhnaigh ceolta den chineál seo,
chaithfí a rá go raibh tuigbheáil iontach don teanga agus don cheol acu
agus go dearfa don áilleacht. Tá níos mó ná an áilleacht le fáil sna
hamhráin. Tá amhráin ann a bhaineas le rudaí nach maith linn díriú
orthu –

Idir Caiseal agus Úrchoill a casadh domh an cúilín
Is í ag teacht go ciúin céillí fá mo choinne ins a' ród
Rug mé greim cúil uirthi agus leag mé ar an drúcht í
Agus d'fhág mé an croí dúnta aici is í ag sileadh na ndeor.[28]

Tá fonn álainn leis an amhrán seo agus bíonn iontas ar dhaoine go
minic go bhfuil an téama ann chomh gránna. Bhí bean i rang agam
bliain nó dhó ó shin a dúirt nach dtiocfadh léi é a cheol ar an ábhar go
dtug sé tacaíocht don bhanéigean. Seo sampla eile den chineál
chéanna:

Casadh fear mire uirthi ar mhullaigh Shliabh Báine
Nó i dtom ghlas na coilleadh san áit a gcroitear na húllaí
Chuir sé cor coise uirthi agus leag sé ar an drúcht í
Ba ródheas an obair is ba doiligh a diúltú.[29]

Go fiú go bhfaighimid a leithéid seo in *Maidin Fhómhair* atá ar cheann
de na hamhráin is mó a bhfuil tóir air:

Leag mé mo lámh ar a brollach ródheas
Is d'iarr mé póg uirthi stór mo chroí.[30]

Ar cheart dúinn stad de bheith ag rá na n-amhrán seo? Tá a fhios agam gur ghnách le cuid de na ceoltóirí na focail a athrú nuair nár thaitin siad leo. Tá na leaganacha seo le fáil mar mhalairt ar an líne thuas:

> Thug mé spéis don chailín ródheas
> Leag mé mo lámh ar a mínchrobh ródheas

Níl amhras orm ná gurb é an *brollach* an rud is sine a bhí ann agus gur ina dhiaidh a tháinig na malairteacha. Caithfidh mé rá nach mothaím mé féin bheith ag tacú le foiréigean in éadan na mban nuair a cheolaim na línte seo. Baineann siad le ré eile agus ní féidir dearcadh agus ceart polaitiúil na linne seo a chur i bhfeidhm orthu. Caithfear é a fhágáil ag an cheoltóir féin i ndeireadh na dála. Meabhraítear scéal domh a d'insíodh Áine Ní Ghallchóir (Annie Eoghain Éamoinn) fá amhrán a thug Síle Mhicí di. Seo mar a fuair sí an chéad cheathrú ó Shíle:

> D'éirigh mé go luath luath agus ghluais mé fán choill
> A bhaint beairtín den luachair a b'fhearr a gheobhainn ann
> Caidé tharla domh ar an uaigneas ach an gruagach deas donn
> Is é dúirt sé a chailín óg deas caidé a ghluais tú fán choill?

Fuair Áine leagan eile ina dhiaidh sin ó Mháire Mhicí, deirfiúr do Shíle, agus ba í an líne dheireanach a bhí aicise sa cheathrú:

> Ruaig sé aníos agus anuas orm agus d'fhág sé mé trom.

Nuair a bhí sin ráite aici thiontaigh sí chuig Áine agus ar sise, 'Tá a fhios agat caidé sin, a thaiscidh?'

Mar sin de bhí daoine riamh ann nach raibh sásta rudaí a rá agus daoine eile a déarfadh amach iad. Ceist í, cad chuige ar athraigh Síle na focail. Chaith sí seal i nGlaschú agus b'fhéidir gurbh é sin a ba chúis leis, sin nó go mbíodh malairt leagain ag daoine i gcónaí agus go n-athraíodh siad na focail de réir na hócáide a bhí ann. Mar shampla, tá an véarsa seo san amhrán choitianta *Fuígfidh mise an baile seo* —

> Mhuire nach mé an truaigh is mé pósta ar an sclábhaí
> Nach ligfeadh amach 'un Aifrinn mé lá saoire ná Dé Domhnaigh
> Nach dtabharfadh toigh a' leanna mé is nach gcaithfeadh giní óir
> liom
> 'S nach dteannfadh lena chroí mé mar dhéanfadh an buachaill óg
> liom.

Sin an leagan a cuireadh i gcló in *Cnuasacht de Cheoltaí Uladh.*[31] Ach tá leagan eile ag imeacht sa bhéaloideas i dtólamh agus is mar seo atá sé –

Mhuire nach mé an truaigh agus mé pósta ar an sclábhaí
Nach ligfeadh amach 'un Aifrinn mé lá saoire ná Dé Domhnaigh
Nach gcaithfeadh siar sa leabaidh mé is nach dtabharfadh cúpla
   póg domh
'S nach dteannfadh lena chroí mé mar dhéanfadh an buachaill óg
   liom.

Tá mé cinnte de go mbíonn ócáidí príobháideacha ann ar a mbíonn an
dara ceann fóirsteanach ach go gcoinnítear an ceann eile d'ócáidí
poiblí. Is cinnte go raibh an piúratánachas fairsing i ré Victoria agus go
ndeachaigh sé i bhfeidhm ar chuid mhaith de na Gaeil chomh maith. Is
minic a d'athraigh bailitheoirí leaganacha a bhí sna hamhráin a mheas
siad bheith lán de 'shuarachas agus de ghairsiúlacht'.[32] Is iomaí cineál
eile amhráin beo sa traidisiún sa lá atá inniu ann. Tá na caointe móra
againn, *Amhrán Phádraig Shéamais* mar shampla agus rudaí eile dálta
Scairteach Áranna –

Tá scairteach mhór á dhéanamh in Árainn
Ag iarraidh orainne na cladaí a fhágáil
Ach imígí sibhse ós sibh atá sáraithe
'S cha choraíonn muidinne go raibh lucht den leathach linn.

Chuir bean chupaí in iúl do Mháire
Go mbeadh siad chuici ar thús na mbádaí
Ach chrom sí a cionn agus rinne sí paidir
Is ar dheireadh na scéaltaí bhí an báthadh déanta

Cuirimse scrios agus léan ar Árainn
Is é bhain domhsa mo thriúr fear breácha
Ba deise méin agus a b'fhearr nádúr
Agus a bhí ar aghaidh ins na leabharthaí Gaeilge.[33]

Is annamh a chluintear an t-amhrán sin cé gur amhrán an-
chumhachtach é. Mar is dual do dhaoine atá i muinín na farraige le slí
bheatha a bhaint amach, tá go leor eile de na hamhráin seo ann. Tá
siad a gcumadh anuas go dtí ár linn féin cé gur i mBéarla is mó a
chumtar anois iad.

Réimse eile amhrán atá torthúil ar fad é an t-amhrán áite/dúlra. Tá
cur síos déanta agam in áit eile[34] ar an choimhlint a bhí idir Eoghan
Mac Niallais agus Séamas Ó Doraidheáin in Iardheisceart na contae san
ochtú aois déag. Tá samplaí eile againn fosta atá inchurtha lena gcuid
amhrán siúd – *An Fial-Athair Dónall* mar shampla.[35] Amhráin iad sin a
bhfuil blas láidir na meánaoiseanna orthu, lena n-áibhéil neartmhar fá

thorthúlacht agus fá fhlúirse. Coimhthíoch go leor, is iad na hamhráin a cumadh níos maille ná sin is mó a bhéarfadh traidisiún filíochta na manach in aimsir na Sean-Ghaeilge chun cuimhne. Tá mé ag smaointiú go háirithe anseo ar amhrán beag a chum bean as ceantar lár Thír Chonaill. *Ceol Loch Aoidh* a bheirtear ar an amhrán de ghnáth ach tá barúil agam gur *Loch Fhia* an t-ainm ceart atá air. Seo mar a chuireas Énrí Ó Muirgheasa síos ar údar an amhráin:

> Bean tuaithe a bhí 'na comhnuidhe le taoibh Loch Aoidh a rinne an t-amhrán seo. Sinéid Nic Mhaongail a bhí uirthi, agus pósadh í ar Phádraig Ó Tiománaidhe i Mín na Sróna comhgarach do'n droichead úr – Droichead Ríothlúin. Cé nach rabh an dá áit ach sé nó seacht de mhílte óna chéile bhí cumhaidh uirthi i nGleann Fhinne, agus as a' chumhaidh rinne sí an t-amhrán. D'éag sí tuairim 1915 is tá sí adhlaicthe i gCill Taobhóig. Tá a fear Pádraig Ó Tiománaidhe beo go fóill (1929). Is cosúil gur cumadh an t-amhrán thart fá 1904.[36]

Tá soineantacht agus neamhurchóid iontach sa liric bheag seo a cheanglaíos í go díreach leis an chéad fhilíocht dhúlra a cumadh sa Ghaeilge corradh agus míle bliain ó shin:

> Is iomaí maidin shamhraidh ann a d'éirigh mé in m'óige
> A dh'éisteacht leis na héanacha ag déanamh a gcuid ceoil bhinn
> Iad ag gabháil ó thom go tom ag eiteallaigh go ceolmhar,
> Is a nguth lánbhinn ag teacht faoi dhuilliúr ghlas na gcrannaibh
> óga.

> Is iomaí lá breá fada ansin a chaith mé ar bheagán buartha
> Is is iomaí lá breá fada ansin a chaith mé ag déanamh uabhair
> Ag seoladh na mbó breac amach fríd ghleanntáin deas na luachra
> I ndiaidh bheith ins an loch ó theas na gréine ag iarraidh
> fuaraithe.

Is féidir *Gaoth Beara na dTonn* a chum Dónall Mac Diarmada a áireamh ar na hamhráin atá sa ghrúpa seo agus tá siad a gcumadh i gcónaí. Más uaigneas a spreag bean amháin i mbun cumadóireachta tá an nóta ceiliúrtha in uachtar san amhrán a rinne bean eile fána cónaí úr:

> In uaigneas an tsléibhe tráthnóna deas samhraidh
> Is mé ag éisteacht le ceol binn na n-éan ar gach tom
> Ag coimhéad na gréine ag dul síos cúl an tsléibhe
> Is í ag dealramh mar ór ar an loch ins an ghleann.[37]

Ceanglaítear téama na háite le téama na himirce i gceann eile de na hamhráin nua-chumtha:

Tá togha agus rogha gach ní sna bailte móra
Ach tá an chontúirt ann ó thús go deireadh an lae
Nárbh aoibhinn tús mo shaoil is mé i mo pháiste
Is mé ag imirt síos fán reannaigh i bhfad i gcéin.[38]

Ní mhaireann na hamhráin gan na daoine a chothaíos agus a chaomhnaíos iad, na ceoltóirí. Céad bliain ó shin bhí drochbharúil ag Énrí Ó Muigheasa go mairfeadh an traidisiún, le linn dó bheith ag gabháil thart ag cruinniú amhrán:

... the young generation of Irish speakers are little more than semi-Irish in mind and spirit and they have ceased to memorise and sing or rehearse Irish poetry as their forebears did, so that when the last of the *seanachies* and singers die out they will be succeeded by a race no longer steeped in poetry and song.[39]

Ar ndóigh bhí cuid den cheart aige agus is fíor go dtáinig crapadh mór ar an Ghaeltacht, ach d'éirigh glúnta eile aníos ó shin a bhí inchurtha lena n-oidhreacht. Ní raibh sna daoine a dtugaimidinne máistrí agus máistreásaí an tsean-nóis Chonallaigh orthu anois ach naonáin nuair a scríobhadh an méid sin. Cuimhnímid go háirithe orthu sin atá ar shlua na marbh – Aodh Ó Duibheannaigh agus Neilí Ní Dhomhnaill – go ndéana Dia trócaire orthu. Tá cuid acu inár measc i gcónaí, Conall Ó Domhnaill agus Máire Rua Bean Uí Mhaí a bhfuil saibhreas mór amhrán agus seanchais acu – gura fada buan iad. Tá neart ceoltóirí ar oileán uasal Thoraí go fóill agus ceolta acu nach bhfuil ar taifead fuaime in áit ar bith. Chomh maith leis sin tá stíl amhránaíochta acu atá an-dúchasach agus ag éirí an-annamh le blianta beaga anuas. Mura ndéanaimid ach éisteacht leo agus comparáid a dhéanamh eatarthu agus Róise na nAmhrán nó Síle Mhicí Uí Ghallchóir cluinfimid na cosúlachtaí láithreach bonn. Aithneoimid fosta go dtáinig athruithe móra ar an tsean-nós le leathchéad bliain anuas. Ní locht ar bith sin ar an dúchas. Ach gurb é an t-athrú, bheadh an traidisiún chomh marbh le scadán agus bhí cead riamh ag an duine aonair a stampa féin a leagan air ar scor ar bith. Mar a deir údar amháin:

Tá traidisiún na hamhránaíochta breá láidir ach tá sé ag athrú. In áit amhráin a bheith á bhfoghlaim agus á n-aithris sa teaghlach dúchasach, bíonn siad á bhfoghlaim go minic anois le haghaidh an ardáin agus le haghaidh comórtas; bíonn siad á ngiortú, agus tá

claonadh ann glacadh le hinsint amháin mar théacs caighdeánach
... cé go bhfuil meas i gcónaí ar an traidisiún béil...is le
téipthafeadán a bhítear ag foghlaim amhrán sa lá atá inniu ann.[40]

Sílim nach miste tagairt a dhéanamh don pháirt eile sin dár ndúchas –
na hamhráin Bhéarla. Tá claonadh ann a mheas gur oidhreacht den
dara grád iad. Séanann sé seo an bhunfhírinne gur chuir glúnta de
mhuintir na hÉireann spéis iontu agus go ndearna siad a gcuid féin
díobh, idir amhráin a tháinig isteach agus ceolta a cumadh in Éirinn. Tá
an dá dhúchas measctha le chéile an oiread sin gur brainsí iad den aon
chrann amháin agus má táthar le staidéar iomlán cuimsitheach a
dhéanamh ar an ghné seo dár gcultúr caithfear an dúchas a ghlacadh
mar tá sé agus ní mar ba mhaith linn é a bheith. Ráiteas conspóideach
é sin agus tá a fhios agam go bhfuil daoine ann a mbeidh fearg orthu
liom dá thairbhe. Sílfidh na daoine sin go bhfuil contúirt ann go
mbainfidh an Béarla an bláth d'amhránaíocht na Gaeilge. Tá sé sin ag
tarlú le céad go leith bliain ar a laghad agus tá sé chomh maith an
fhírinne a inse fá dtaobh de. Agus tá rud eile ann fosta. Is minic gurb
iad na hamhránaithe nach bhfuil acu ach Béarla is fearr a thuigeas an
easbhaidh atá orthu agus gur mó an meas atá acu ar cheol Gaeilge ná
mar tá ag bunús na ndaoine a bhfuil Gaeilge acu. Dúirt bean as Tír
Eoghain le gairid agus í ag cur síos ar bheith ag éisteacht le hamhrán
Gaeilge – 'It's like sitting in a beautiful room, with the light off.' Is é a
bhí sí a mhaíomh gur thuig sí áilleacht na n-amhrán Gaeilge ach nach
raibh sí ábalta na focail a thuigbheáil. Bhí sí mar bheadh sí dall. Shíl mé
ag an am gurbh iontach an chiall don ealaín agus don dúchas a léirigh
an abairt bheag shimplí amháin sin agus gur abairt í a bhí iontach
cóngarach do thraidisiún na Gaeilge. Baineann na daoine seo linn agus
tuigeann siad muid. Is saibhrede muidinne aithne agus eolas a bheith
againn ar a ndúchas siúd. Gan amhras bhí daoine riamh ann agus tá go
fóill a shíl gurbh fhearr an rud i mBéarla siocair gur i mBéarla a bhí sé,
agus cé go bhfuil an dearcadh sin ag athrú sa Ghaeltacht, is go mall
righin é. Táimid uilig ar an taobh chéanna i ndeireadh báire.

Tá an traidisiún ag athrú agus tá feidhm le bealaí úra ionas go
gcoinneofar an traidisiún bríomhar os comhair an phobail. Sampla
iontach maith den rud a thig a dhéanamh é Ciorcal Ceoltóirí Inis
Eoghain (Inis Eoghain Traditional Singers' Circle) a bhunaigh Jimí Mac
Giolla Bhríde tá dornán blianta ó shin. Tugann an club seo deis do
lucht leanúna na n-amhrán ar fud na leithinse, sean agus óg, a theacht
le chéile agus bheith ag ceol. Tá obair éachtach déanta ag Jimí agus
cuid mhór ábhair chartlainne bailithe aige. Le cúig bliana anuas ritear
seiminéar deireadh seachtaine ar bhonn bliantúil. Tarraingíonn sé seo
amhránaithe ó áiteacha chomh fada ar shiúl le deisceart na Sasana agus

bíonn tinreamh maith ón Ghaeltacht ann fosta. B'fhiú do phobail eile ar fud na contae aithris a dhéanamh ar an dea-shampla sin. I dtaca le cúrsaí stíle de, mar sin, an té ar mhaith leis bheith ina amhránaí san am i láthair caithfidh sé saothar a chur air féin an stíl cheart a fháil. Cé go bhfuil an traidisiún i mbaol i gcónaí tá comharthaí dóchais ann go mairfidh sé slán, gan bhriseadh, isteach san aois seo chugainn.

Nótaí

1.   A. B. Lord, *The singer of tales* (New York, 1960).
2.   J. Henigan, 'Sean-nós in Donegal: in search of a definition'in *Ulster Folklife*, 37 (1991), p. 98.
3.   Ibid., p. 104 (Gaeilge curtha agam féin air).
4.   Gheofar cúntas bríomhar ar ócáid den chinéal in H. Wagner, *Gaeilge Theilinn* (Baile Átha Cliath, 1959), lch. 254.
5.   H. Shields, *Narrative singing in Ireland* (Dublin, 1993), pp 14-15.
6.   Ibid., p. 22.
7.   Ibid.
8.   Ibid., p. 25.
9.   E. Ó Muirgheasa, *Céad de cheoltaibh Uladh* (Baile Átha Cliath, 1915), lgh 15, 186, 333.
10. B. Ó Madagáin, 'Irish vocal music of lament and syllabic verse' in R. O'Driscoll (ed.), *The Celtic consciousness* (Toronto, 1981), pp 311-32.
11. Cnuasach Bhéaloideas Éireann (CBE), Roinn Bhéaloideas Éireann, Coláiste na hOllscoile, Baile Átha Cliath. CBE 933:83. Is le caoinchead Cheann na Roinne a fhoilsítear na sliochtáin, CBE 933:83 agus CBE 818:86-87 agus CBE 932 446-447.
12. Cartlann Raidió na Gaeltachta, Doirí Beaga, Gaoth Dobhair. Taifeadadh an t-ábhar le linn cheardlann amhránaíochta agus scéalaíochta an Oireachtais 4 Samhain 1977. Tá mé buíoch do Phat Ó Rabhartaigh, nach maireann, a chuir an t-eolas ar fáil dom agus do Breandán Ó Madagáin a scríobh amach an ceol dom.
13. A. Partridge, *Caoineadh na dtrí muire,Téama na Páise i bhFilíocht na Gaeilge*, lgh 38 & *passim*, 218.
14. E. Ó Muirgheasa, *Dánta diadha Uladh* (Baile Átha Cliath, 1936; athchló 1963).
15. C. Ní Dhomhnaill, Seal mo chuarta, cáiséad amhrán (Indreabhán), CIC 070.
16. Le cluinstin ar an téip Ceolta agus seanchas as Tír Chonaill, H. Shields agus C.Goan (eag.), (Baile Atha Cliath, 1984).
17. CBE 818, 86-87.
18. CBE 932, 446-447.
19. J. J. Ó Riordáin, *Irish Catholics – tradition and transition* (Baile Átha Cliath, 1984), p. 64. M. Mac Craith, 'An intinn Ghaelach agus an diagacht' in *Comhar* (Bealtaine, 1992), lgh 116-28.
20. Henigan, 'Sean-nós in Donegal', lch 101.
21. Shields, *Narrative singing*, p. 71.
22. C. Goan (eag.), Róise na namhrán, songs of a Donegal woman, dlúthcheirnín/ caiséad agus leabhrán (Baile Átha Cliath, 1994). Tá cuntas spéisiúil ar shaol na mná seo le fáil sa leabhar *Róise Rua* le Pádraig Ua Cnáimhsí (Baile Átha Cliath, 1988).
23. L. Ó Laoire, Bláth gach géag dá dtig, cáiséad amhrán (Indreabhán, 1992), CIC 075.

24. C. Goan, 'Dhá amhrán ó Neilí Ní Dhomhnaill' in *Ceol*, vi (Aibreán, 1983).

25. E. agus P. Mac Ruairí, Toraigh ó thuaidh, caiséad amhrán (Indreabhán), CIC 023, Dónall Og.

26. Ibid., san amhrán 'Thiar i gConnachta'.

27. E. Ó Mhuirgheasa, *Dhá chéad de cheoltaibh Uladh (DDCU amach anseo)* (Baile Átha Cliath, 1934), lch. 145. Fuair mé leagan eile den amhrán seo ó Shéamus Ó Dubhgáin an t-amhránaí as Toraigh. Níl na véarsaí seo ina leagan siúd.

28. P. Kennedy, *Folksongs of Britain and Ireland* (London, 1975), p. 86. Ó Chonall Ó Domhnaill a fuarthas an leagan seo.

29. Leagan Thoraí den amhrán *Peigí Ní Shléibhín*. Tá leagan eile in *DDCU*, lch. 49 ach gan trácht ar bith ann ar an véarsa seo.

30. Leagan atá fairsing i dTír Chonaill.

31. S. Ó Baoill, R. Ó Frighil agus A. Ó Duibheannaigh, *Cnuasacht de cheoltaí Uladh* (Comhaltas Uladh, 1944), lgh 32-3.

32. P. MacSeáin, *Ceolta Theilinn* (Béal Feirste, 1973), lch. 11.

33. N. Hamilton, *The Irish of Tory Island* (Belfast, 1974), p. 47. Tá fonn an-mhaith leis an amhrán seo a chuirfeadh fonn caointe i do cheann. Ceolann Séamus Ó Dubhgáin é agus is uaidh a fuair Brian Ó Domhnaill é.

34. L. Ó Laoire, 'Traidisiún na namhrán in Iardheisceart Thír Chonaill' in S. Watson (eag.), *Oidhreacht Ghleann Cholm Cille* (Baile Átha Cliath, 1989), lgh 123-42.

35. C. Goan, 'An Fial-Athair Dónall' in *Ceol*, vii (1984), lgh 46-9. Leagan ar taifead agam féin. Féach n. 19 thuas.

36. Ó Muirgheasa, *Dhá chéad de cheoltaibh Uladh*, lch. 187. Fuair mé leagan eile ó Chonall Ó Domhnaill, Rinn na Feirste.

37. Gearóidín Neidí Frainc Nic Grianna a chum fána baile úr, An Aird Mhín, Croithlí. Tá mé buíoch do Shéan Mac Corraigh as Béal Feirste a chuir na focail ar fáil dom.

38. C. Ní Dhomhnaill, Bean an fhir ruaidh, caiséad amhrán (Indreabhán), CIC 009.

39. Ó Muirgheasa, *Céad de cheoltaibh Uladh*, lch. x.

40. Partridge, *Caoineadh na dtrí muire*, lch. 141.

Chapter 27

GAELIC FAMILIES OF COUNTY DONEGAL

Fergus Gillespie: Fearghus Mac Giolla Easpaig

Introduction

In Séamus Ó Grianna's *Caisleáin Óir* the four-year-old hero Séimí returns from his first day at school, having been beaten over the head by the schoolmaster for not responding when his name was called out at roll-call.[1] The bewildered child explains to his mother:

> ... ní m'ainm féin a thug sé orm,' arsa an gasúr, 'ach ainm eile. James ... Níl cuimhne agam ar an chuid eile de.'
>
> 'Gallagher, a leanbh,' arsa an mháthair ...
>
> 'Agus, a mháthair,' arsa an gasúr, 'nár shíl mise riamh gur Séimí Phádraig Duibh a bhí orm. Nach é sin an t-ainm a tugadh i gcónaí orm?'
>
> 'Is é, a thaisce,' arsa an mháthair, 'ach seo d'ainm i mBéarla. Agus Béarla a bhíos i gcónaí i dteach na scoile.'[2]

What is very evident here is that at the end of the last century the use of patronymics to distinguish one person or family from another was the norm in little Séimí's community in north-west Donegal and that surnames – in the English language – were for more formal use such as in the school-roll. It goes without saying that in all dealings with church and state only English forms of surnames were permitted when Séimí was growing up.[3] The extent to which surnames in Irish, rather than patronymics or English language forms of surnames, were used in Irish speaking areas is difficult to assess, and for north-west Donegal the evidence from local writers such as Seosamh Mac Grianna is not conclusive.[4]

The account in Myles na Gopaleen's satire *An Béal Bocht* of the hero, Bónapáirt Ó Cúnasa's first day at school in the boundless Gaeltacht of Corca Dorcha presents us with another – and very cynical – view of the use of surnames. Here, the schoolmaster, who goes by the name of Aimeirgean Ó Lúnasa, enquires of the child, 'Phwat is yer nam?' and receives the reply: 'Bónapáirt Mícheálangaló Pheadair Eoghain Shorcha Thomáis Mháire' (and so on). This infuriates the master who gives the seemingly obligatory blow on the head to young

Bónapáirt and tells him: 'Yer nam is Jams O'Donnell.' All the other children on giving their names and patronymics are treated in the same fashion and all are given the same name, Jams O'Donnell.[5]

The implication here is, of course, that surnames were more often than not supplied by the authorities, in this case the schoolmaster, who showed a singular lack of originality in his choice of nomenclature. That the surname chosen for his pupils should be that of the most famous of Donegal families, Ó Domhnaill, echoes a doubt that I have often heard expressed regarding surnames: are all Gallaghers, Boyles and Dohertys of Donegal, for example, genuine descendants in the male line of the once powerful families of Ó Gallchobhair, Ó Baoighill and Ó Dochartaigh, who ruled large tracts of the county in the later Middle Ages and beyond? Even taking into account the wholescale confiscations of Irish land at the time of the plantation of Donegal at the beginning of the seventeenth century and the subsequent change in social status of so much of the local population, the problem of Gaelic surnames remains a vexed one and one that deserves careful approach and treatment.[6]

Surnames made their appearance in Ireland for the first time in the tenth and eleventh centuries. Cathbarr Ó Domnaill, for example, who died in 1106,[7] belonged to the first generation of his immediate kin to have a surname. That surname was derived from the name of his great-grandfather, Domnall, son of Éicnechán.[8] Cathbarr was king of Cenél Luigdech, an obscure branch of Cenél Conaill. The territory of Cenél Luigdech lay around Kilmacrenan[9] and they came to power as kings of Tír Conaill in 1201 only after the collapse of the dynasties of Ó Maíl Doraid and Ó Canannáin, two bitter rivals who between them had ruled Tír Conaill for well on three centuries before that time.[10] The fame of these Ó Domhnaill kings has obscured the fact that they ruled Tír Conaill for a mere four centuries, since they and their Cenél Luigdech ancestors had been excluded from the kingship for over six centuries, finally attaining power only at the beginning of the thirteenth century.[11]

A further factor to be taken into account in this connection is that the name of Saint Colum Cille has been linked in the popular mind almost exclusively with the Ó Domhnaill dynasty. Certainly, they and Colum Cille share a common ancestor, Conall, son of Niall Nóigiallach, but that circumstance does not entitle them to claim the saint as its own.[12]

The great Gaelic families of late medieval Donegal were of the Northern Uí Néill, descendants of Niall Noígiallach, king of Tara, through his sons, Conall and Eógan, who with their brother, Éndae, had conquered the territory in the fifth century.[13] From Conall and Eógan are descended Cenél Conaill, 'the race of Conall' and Cenél Eógain, 'the race of Eógan', respectively, and from these two also come the names of the territories in Donegal over which they ruled, Tír Conaill[14] and Inis Eógain (Inishowen).[15]

Little is known, on the other hand, of the Cenél Éndai, the descendants of the third brother, whose territory lay in the parishes of Raymoghey and Taughboyne.[16] They are ignored by the genealogists and the few mentions of their kings in the annals are no earlier than the eleventh century. In 1177, at his death, Niall Ó Gailmredaig of Cenél Eógain was king of Cenél Éndai[17] and by the end of the century their territory was ruled by the Ó Dochartaigh family, a branch of the Cenél Conaill.[18]

The latest formation of a surname in Donegal that I know of is that of Mac Daibhid, *anglice* MacDevitt, the name of a family who derive their name from Daibid Dub Ó Dochartaig, who died in 1208.[19]

This article treats of thirty county Donegal families listed in alphabetical order in their standard Irish forms, with commonly occurring English language variants:[20]

Mac Ailín: 'MacAllen', MacCallion, Campbell
Mac an Bhaird: 'Macaward', Ward
Mac Carmaic, Mac Cormaic: MacCormick
Mac Colgan: MacColgan, Colgan
Mac Conghail: MacGonigle, Magonigle
Mac Daibhid: MacDevitt, MacDaid
Mac Duinnshléibhe, Mac an Ultaigh, Ultach: Donleavy, MacNulty, 'Ultagh'
Mac Giolla Bhrighde: 'McKilbridey', MacBride
Mac Giolla Easpaig: Gillespie
Mac Lochlainn: MacLaughlin, MacLoughlin
Mac Niallghuis: MacNelis, 'McEnelis'
Mac Robhartaigh: Magroarty
Mac Suibhne: MacSweeney
Ó Baoighill: O Boyle
O Breisléin: O Breslin, Bryce
Ó Brolcháin: 'O Brillaghan', Bradley
Ó Canannáin: O Cannon, Canning
Ó Cléirigh: O Clery, Clarke
Ó Dochartaigh: O Doherty
Ó Dubhthaigh: O Duffy
Ó Duibh Dhíorma: 'O Dooyeearma', MacDermot
Ó hEarcáin: O Harkin
Ó Firghil, Ó Frighil: O Friel
Ó Gairmleadhaigh: O Gormley
Ó Gallchobhair: O Gallagher
Ó Maoil Doraidh: O Mulderry

Ó Maoil Fhábhaill: O Mulfail, Faul, MacFall
Ó Maoil Mhoichéirghe: 'O Mulmogheery', Early
Ó Muirgheasáin: O Morrison, Bryson
Ó Robhartaigh: O Roarty

The Families
Mac Ailín: 'Mac Allen', Mac Callion, Campbell

The Mac Ailín family of Inishowen are most likely to be a branch of the Mac Ailín family of Galloway in Scotland. In Scots Gaelic, the name is MacCailein, which is also the style of the Campbell dukes of Argyll.[21]

In 1555 An Calbhach Ó Domhnaill went to Scotland and returned with mercenaries from Giolla Easpuig Donn Mac Cailín which he used to ravage Inishowen, and Tír Conaill, demolishing the castle of Greencastle and imprisoning his father, Mághnas, the reigning lord.[22] In 1557, Seán an Díomuis Ó Néill invaded Tír Conaill and pitched his camp at Balleeghan. One of the two spies that An Calbhach sent to spy in Ó Neill's camp was Muiris Mac Ailín, who is described as a trusty friend of his. When Muiris returned with news of Ó Néill's forces, An Calbhach attacked the unprepared camp and Ó Néill was defeated.[23]

The following year two young constables of gallóglaigh in Tír Conaill, Domhnall and Giolla Easpuig Mac Ailín, set out with their Scots to seek fame in Connacht. Risteárd an Iarainn de Búrca of Tirawley agreed to help the Scots against his own enemies, but the combined forces were attacked and defeated by Ricard Sasanach, earl of Clanricard, and Domhnall and Giolla Easpuig were killed. The annals tell us that the victory would have been greater if the two had been captured alive, for the ransom for them would have been great.[24]

The family would appear to have become powerful in Inishowen. In 1601 when Seán Óg Ó Dochartaigh died his son, Cathaoir, was styled Ó Dochartaigh with the help of the Clann Daibhid and the Clann Ailín, despite Ó Domhnaill's having chosen Feilim Óg, Cathaoir's uncle.[25] At an inquisition taken at Derry in 1602 'Dowill oge McAllin' of Gleneely is named as one of the jurors.[26] In the same year twelve of the Clann Ailín were pardoned for rebellion.[27]

In Bishop Montgomery's survey of the diocese of Raphoe at the beginning of the seventeenth century (ca. 1605), 'Nellanus M'Callen' is mentioned as one of the distinguished clergymen 'beyond the mountains' who had been a good student at Glasgow and who spoke Irish, Latin and Scots.[28]

The census of 1659 lists Domhnall Mac Ailín, gentleman, as a titulado in the parish of Culdaff.[29] In the same census there are fifteen families under the form McCallin and twelve under O Callane and O Cullane listed for Inishowen.[30] In the Hearth Money Rolls most householders with this surname are found in east Donegal, in the parishes of Culdaff, Fahan, Clonmany and Conwal.[31]

At Clonca Old Church there is a slab which is decorated with a cross, foliage, a camán and ball, and a sword, bearing the inscription 'Fergus mak Allan do rini in clach sa'.[32]

The strong evidence that exists for the Scottish origins of the family does not stop Lughaidh Ó Cléirigh, however, from stating that the Clann Ailín were a branch of the Ó Dochartaigh family and that the eponymous ancestor, Ailín, was a brother of Daibhid, ancestor of Clann Daibhid of Inishowen.[33] The genealogists had their own reasons for sometimes falsifying the record as I have shown elsewhere.[34]

Mac an Bhaird: 'Macaward', Ward

The Mac an Bhaird family of Tír Conaill, who gave their name to the parish of Leitir Mac an Bhaird, *anglice* Lettermacaward, in the barony of Boylagh, were professional *filedha* or poets to the Ó Domhnaill rulers of Tír Conaill from the fifteenth to the seventeenth century.

The origins of the family are obscure. The surname itself means 'son of the bard'. A bard in the hierarchy of Irish learned men occupied an inferior position: the *fili*, on the other hand, was not only a poet, but also a historian, a man of learning whose position in society was close to that of his king or lord.[35] By the time the Mic an Bhaird appear in the records for Tír Conaill, however, their rank is very definitely that of *fili*.

The earliest mention of the name in the annals is in 1173 when Máel Ísa Mac in Baird, bishop of Clonfert (county Galway), died.[36] In 1408 we read of the death of Mac an Bhaird of Cooloorta in county Galway.[37] Another entry, in 1488, shows that a family of the name was established in Oriel, for in that year Mac an Bhaird Oirghiall died. (He was, no doubt, a poet – the entry also contains the death of Maol Mhuire Ó hUiginn, 'oide Éreann le dán'.)[38] We cannot be certain of the relationship of these two to Mac an Bhaird of Tír Conaill, as the Ó Cléirigh genealogies totally ignore our family.

The first of the name in Tír Conaill to be mentioned in the annals is Gofraidh, head of his family, who died of plague in 1478.[39] However, the earliest mention that I know of the family's connections with the Ó Domhnaill family is to be found in a poem by Eoghan Mac an Bhaird on the death of Domhnall Ó Domhnaill, a brother of two early fifteenth century kings of Tír Conaill, Niall Garbh and Neachtain.[40] In 1510 Mac an Bhaird 'Tíre Conaill' (Eoghan Ruadh) died in Inishmacadurn in the Rosses[41] and in 1522 Aodh (mac Aodha) Mac an Bhaird, son of another head of the family, was slain when Ó Néill took Ballyshannon, seat of Ó Domhnaill.[42]

In 1541 Conchobhar Ruadh (mac Fearghail) Mac an Bhaird is

described at his death as chief poet to Ó Domhnaill, head of a school and as being expert in poetry and the arts.[43] In 1572 Eoghan Ruadh (mac Fearghail) Mac an Bhaird, who 'was learned in history and poetry', was hanged along with Muiris Ballach Ó Cléirigh, another poet and historian, by Conchobhar Ó Briain, earl of Thomond.[44] Uilliam Óg Mac an Bhaird, from whom we have a poem in honour of Cú Chonnacht Maguidhir lord of Fermanagh[45] died in 1576 at Druim Mór, which may be in the parish of Drumhome. He is described at his death as ollamh to Ó Domhnaill in poetry, a head of schools and a patron of the learned classes.[46]

The unfortunate Eoghan Ruadh's brother, Fearghal Óg, is better known to us. Among his poems is one written to Aodh Ruadh Ó Domhnaill, lord of Tír Conaill, *Ionmhas ollaimh onóir ríogh* (Ollamh's wealth is prince's glory).[47] Fearghal Óg spent some time in Scotland where he wrote the beautiful poem, *Beannacht siar uaim go hÉirinn* (A blessing westward from me to Ireland), which is addressed to one of the Mac Aonghusa lords of Iveagh.[48] In another poem where he bids farewell to Munster he uses the clever device of praising it, then bidding farewell to its people and dwellings, while at the same time naming the places to which he is going in the North – Aileach, Derry, Tír Conaill, which brings a certain excitement and anticipation to his verse.[49] Like many poets of his generation he saw the downfall of the Gaelic order, and his lament for the house of Ó Domhnaill, *Truagh liom Máire agus Mairgrég,* is full of the despair and desolation of the times.[50] He also wrote poems in honour of Cormac Ó hEadhra lord of Luighne in county Sligo.[51] In 1618 he went to Louvain[52] from where he wrote a poem to Flaithrí Ó Maoilchonaire, archbishop of Tuam, asking for help in his exile.[53] He died in Louvain in 1618, in poverty.[54]

Maol Mhuire Mac an Bhaird, son of Cú Uladh, has left us a poem on the destruction of Donegal Castle by Aodh Ruadh Ó Domhnall, *A dhúin thíos atá it éanar.*[55] Maol Mhuire was active on Aodh Ruadh's side and he was killed fighting the English in 1597.[56]

From Gofraidh Mac an Bhaird, son of Brian, we have a poem satirising the sloppy work of a fellow poet.[57] Gofraidh's son, Gofraidh Óg, was also a poet and long after the destruction of Ó Domhnaill rule he wrote a poem *Treoin an cheannais Clann Dálaigh* (the Clann Dálaigh are the powerful ones of lordship), addressed to An Calbhach Ruadh Ó Domhnaill, grandson of Conn Óg, a brother of Niall Garbh.[58] An Calbhach was probably the first of his family to settle in county Mayo.[59] Gofraidh Óg, who died sometime after 1655,[60] may well be the 'Gory McAward', gentleman and *titulado* of Corr, 'Ye capitall of Letter McAward', and of other townlands in that parish.[61]

Another poet of the name was the well-known Eoghan Ruadh, son of Uilliam. In 1603 Ruaidhrí Ó Domhnaill, brother of Aodh Ruadh was in Dublin, having made peace with the English in 1602,[62] and Eoghan Ruadh showed his disapproval of this in a poem entitled *Dána an turas tríalltar sonn*.[63] Another poem complains of Ruaidhrí's acceptance of the earldom of Tirconnell the same year.[64] In September of 1607 Ruaidhrí and Aodh Ó Néill, earl of Tyrone sailed into exile from Rathmullan,[65] and Eoghan Ruadh, who was one of the ship's company composed a poem lamenting their departure, *Anocht is uaigneach Éire* (Ireland is lonely tonight).[66] Perhaps his most famous poem is *A bhean fuair faill ar an bhfeart*, addressed to Nuala Ní Dhomhnaill, which sees her as lamenting alone at the tomb of her brother, Ruaidhrí, who died in Rome in 1608.[67] We know nothing of where, or when, the poet died.[68]

Aodh Buidhe Mac an Bhaird, who is also called Hugh Ward, or Hugo Wardeus in contemporary sources, was born in Tirhugh about 1593 according to his oath taken when enrolling in Salamanca University in 1612.[69] He took orders as a Franciscan on the persuasion of Fr Luke Wadding, O.F.M., and was sent as lector to the Irish College in Louvain, where he later became guardian. In Louvain he collected material for a work on the lives of Irish saints.[70] The lives were edited and published in Louvain after his death by his fellow Franciscan, John Colgan.[71] In the *praefatio* to his great work, Colgan acknowledges Aodh Buidhe's labours and mentions that he also wrote a life of Saint Rumold, archbishop of Dublin, which was published in Louvain in 1662.[72] Aodh Buidhe died in Louvain in November 1635.[73]

Pádraig Óg Mac an Bhaird, son of Cormac Óg, who may have lived to see the end of the seventeenth century, was probably the last of his family to compose poetry, at least in *dán díreach,* or strict versification. Among his poems is one written for Ruaidhrí Ó hEadhra of the noble family of that name in county Sligo. Ruaidhrí was alive about 1700.[74]

None of the family received grants in the plantation of Ulster, but we have seen that 'Gory McAward' is listed in the census on 1659 as a *titulado* in Lettermacaward in the barony of Boylagh and Banagh. In the same census eleven families in all are numbered for the barony.[75] In the Hearth Money Roll for county Donegal (1665) householders are listed for the parishes of Killybegs, Inishkeel, Killymard, Killaghtee, Leck and Lettermacaward.[76]

Mac Carmaic, Mac Cormaic: MacCormick

The Mac Carmaic family were of the Cenél Eógain, being descended from Ailill, son of Eógan.[77] Their territory was in An Bhrédach, or Bredagh, the eastern part of Inishowen.[78]

The name does not occur often in the annals for Donegal and the family is mostly known to us in the late medieval period from papal registers. In 1430 we read there of the death of 'Gilbert' Mac Carmaic, sacristan,[79] and in 1469 'Meanalaus' Mac Cormaic is mentioned in connection with the deanery of Raphoe.[80] Two of the name were bishops of Raphoe: Eoin who died in 1419[81] and Meanma. Meanma was educated in Oxford and appears to have been a Franciscan. He died in 1515 and was buried in Donegal friary.[82] He may well have been the Meanalaus mentioned above.

Among those who received pardons from the English authorities in 1601 were 'Mannema' and 'Donill M'Carmack', in a list headed by Niall Garbh Ó Domhnaill, 'chief of his name'.[83] Later, in 1608, Domhnall Ó Dochartaigh in a confession claimed that 'Brene Crossach M'Cormac' had promised to join Cathaoir Ó Dochartaigh in his revolt against the English.[84]

In 1630 'Hugh Mc.cormack' is listed as a tenant in Agharin in the precinct of Lifford.[85] In the census of 1659 there are seven families of the name numbered for the barony of Raphoe.[86] In the Hearth Money Rolls the name is also found in the parishes of Clonca in Inishowen and in Drumhome in the south of the county.[87]

Mac Colgan: Mac Colgan

Mac Colgan is an Inishowen name, the form of their eponymous ancestor being Colgu, a first name often found in the early Middle Ages.[88] According to John O'Donovan almost all of the 'aboriginal' inhabitants of the parish of Donagh were Mac Colgans in 1835 and the name was extremely common in the surrounding parishes.[89] The earliest reference to a surname containing Colgu is in a Midland context when Gilla Críst Ó Colgan was slain in battle between members of the Ó Maíl Sechlainn family of Meath in 1212.[90] The surname Ó Colgan was also borne by the lords of Uí Mhac Carthainn in Airghialla in late medieval times but whether they and the Midland families of the name were related to the Inishowen family is impossible to say with any certainty.[91]

The family in Inishowen were *airchinnigh*[92] in the parish of Donagh, the name of the holder in 1609 being Domhnall Mac Colgan.[93] Many of them were in holy orders. In 1421 the death of 'Nemeas' Mac Colgan, vicar of Donagh, is noted in the papal registers.[94] In the same year Domhnall Mac Colgan was appointee to the rectory of the same parish.[95] In 1430 'Henry' Mac Colgan was in unlawful possession of the vicarage of Moville[96] and in 1436 'John' Mac Colgan was assigned the rectory of Donagh parish.[97] 'John' was the son of a priest. In 1630 Ruaidhrí and Éamann Mac Colgan attended a secret meeting of clergy in the Derry diocese.[98]

The most famous of the family was John Colgan, the Franciscan, who was born in Donagh about 1592. He became professor of theology in the Irish College of Louvain, and died there.[99] His published works include *Acta Sanctorum*, lives of Irish saints whose feast days were in January, February and March.[100] The preparatory work for this volume had been done by his colleague at Louvain, Father Aodh Buidhe Mac an Bhaird.[101] He also published *Triadis Thaumaturgae Acta* which contains the lives of Patrick, Brigid and Colum Cille.[102] These works were in Latin. He died in 1658.

There are thirty families of the name listed in the census of 1659, all in Inishowen.[103] In the Hearth Money Rolls for Donegal (1665) all taxpayers of the name are listed for Inishowen, the parish with most householders being Donagh.[104]

Mac Conghail: MacGonigle, Magonigle

The surname Mac Conghail is particularly associated with the Church in early records. In 1429 Cornelius Mac Conghail is mentioned in connection with the rectory of Kilaghtee,[105] and in 1439 he was nominated as vicar of Killybegs.[106] 'Bernard' Mac Conghail, although the son of a priest and an unmarried woman, was assigned to the vicarage of Tullyfern in 1432.[107] Besides being parish priests, members of the family held higher office in the diocese of Raphoe. In 1513 we read of the death of one of the name who had been diocesan official of Raphoe,[108] and in 1586 we read of the death of another official, 'An t-Oficel Mag Conghail .i. Eoghan Ballach', who died on Saint Brigid's day.[109] In the same year Cormac, son of a Domhnall Mac Conghail, died on Saint Patrick's day.[110]

The Domhnall mentioned above may have been Domhnall, bishop of Raphoe, who died in 1589.[111] Bishop Mac Conghail attended the Council of Trent, and it is interesting to note that he died in Killybegs,[112] in which parish, according to the Lifford Inquisition of 1609, the 'Clanmagonegill' were *airchinnigh*.[113]

In February 1603 Tadhg Óg Mac Conghail, who is described as a natural follower of Ruaidhrí Ó Domhnaill, received a pardon from the English authorities.[114]

In the Hearth Money Rolls (1665) the name is found mostly in Inishowen, but also in the parish of Inver.[115]

Mac Daibhid: MacDevitt, MacDaid

The eponymous ancestor of the family of Mac Daibhid of Inishowen was Daibhid Ó Dochartaigh, a man already possessed of a surname.[116] All we know about this Daibhid from the annals is that he was killed in battle in 1208 along with other lords of Cenél Conaill, while pursuing a party of Cenél Eógain who had plundered Inishowen.[117]

The annals tell us nothing of his descendants in the centuries that followed and it is not until the year 1595 that any mention is made there of the name. In the autumn of that year Aodh Ruadh Ó Domhnaill, lord of Tír Conaill, was in lower Connacht with an army of Scottish mercenaries in his war with Sir Richard Bingham, governor of Connaught. Bingham had occupied the monastery of Sligo in an attempt to take Ó Domnaill's castle of Sligo and Aodh Ruadh devised a plan whereby Feilim Riabhach Mac Daibhid and others would act as a decoy to lure the English out over the bridge of Sligo and into an ambush. The plan went wrong, however, because Feilim's horse was slow, but Feilim succeeded in killing Bingham's nephew, Captain Martin, after which the English retreated back over the bridge into Sligo.[118]

Feilim's brother, the famous Aodh Buidhe Mac Daibhid, was described by Sir Henry Docwra, governor of Derry, as being 'subtle, wise and civil',[119] and by Captain Humphrey Covert as being 'tall, comely, young, active, bold of countenance and practiced in stratagems'.[120] In October 1598 Aodh Buidhe went to Spain on a mission for Ó Néill (Aodh) to seek men, money and ammunition for the war against the English.[121] Elsewhere he was described as a 'creature of O'Donnell'[122] and much trusted by him.[123]

In May of 1600 Sir Henry Docwra had arrived in Lough Foyle and proceeded to build forts at Culmore in Inishowen, at Derry and at Dunalong in Ó Cathain's country.[124] While Sir Seán Óg Ó Dochartaigh, lord of Inishowen, was parleying with Docwra, Aodh Buidhe, his close ally, was regarded with deep suspicion by the Englishman because of his loyalty to Ó Domhnaill (Aodh Ruadh).[125] In December of 1600 Docwra feared for the truce he had made with Ó Dochartaigh since, as he says, Ó Dochartaigh had taken to drink and the country (i.e. Inishowen) was being led to ruin by Aodh Buidhe and his brothers.[126] Docwra's suspicions of Aodh Buidhe were confirmed when a plot was discovered whereby Culmore fort would be betrayed to Ó Dochartaigh by a certain Captain Alford, the officer in command, and then handed over to Aodh Ruadh. In this Aodh Buidhe and his brother Feilim Riabhach played a large part,[127] to which Aodh Buidhe later confessed.[128]

Ó Dochartaigh, who had fled Inishowen to Ó Domhnaill, died in January of 1601 and Ó Domhnaill proclaimed his brother, Feilim Óg Ó Dochartaigh, lord of Inishowen.[129] This caused great offence to Aodh Buidhe and Feilim Riabhach who were fosterers of Sir Seán Óg's young son, Cathaoir, who was then in Ó Domhnaill's hands as a guarantee of his father's loyalty.[130] Aodh Buidhe approached Docwra asking him to support Cathaoir; Docwra, after hesitating between Feilim Óg and Cathaoir, opted for Cathaoir, and in February 1601 articles of agreement were drawn up between Docwra and Aodh Buidhe, on his own behalf and on behalf of his brothers, Éadhmann Gruama and Feilim Riabhach, and on behalf of the young Cathaoir Ó Dochartaigh. According to the agreement the brothers would fully submit themselves to Queen Elizabeth and renounce all allegiance to O Néill, Ó Domhnaill and other Irish lords. Docwra, for his part, would proclaim Cathaoir, lord of Inishowen, and procure for Aodh Buidhe and his brothers, and for their heirs, all lands formerly held by them from Sir Seán Óg Ó Dochartaigh under Ó Domhnaill.[131] Docwra did not fully trust Aodh Buidhe, however, and took his children as pledges.[132]

Cathaoir Ó Dochartaigh was still being held by Aodh Ruadh Ó Domhnaill which meant that Aodh Buidhe was the effective ruler of Inishowen; but in May of 1601 Cathaoir was back in Inishowen, 'having been allowed by O'Donnell or escaped from him'.[133] In the same month Ó Domhnaill attacked Inishowen in order to drive off cattle, but was repulsed by Feilim Riabhach. Despite this act of 'loyalty', Docwra took Burt Castle from Aodh Buidhe in June and took one of his brothers as a hostage.[134]

In August Docwra was writing from Derry to the privy council expressing his anxiety about Aodh Buidhe's pretended loyalty and a few weeks later Docwra received a letter from Niall Garbh Ó Domhnaill alleging that Aodh Buidhe had asked Aodh Ruadh to invade Inishowen.[135] However, Docwra kept Aodh Buidhe close to him and stressed to the privy council that he (Docwra) now held Burt Castle, that had previously been in Aodh Buidhe's possession.[136] The Clann Daibhid kept faith with the English, and in the winter of 1601 Éamann Gruama accompanied Docwra on an invasion of Ó Catháin's territory of Ciannachta (county Derry).[137]

Aodh Buidhe was killed after a visit to Docwra in August 1602 'by a party of loose fellows that fell upon him by chance' and in his *Narration*, Docwra expresses his high regard for him and for his brothers, Feilim Riabhach, Éadhmann Gruama and Seán Crón, who 'were all men of good parts'.[138] Aodh Buidhe had been head of the Clann Daibhid and he was succeeded by Feilim Riabhach who guided the young Cathaoir Ó Dochartaigh until 1605, when he was able to rule the Peninsula himself.[139] In 1607 Feilim's brothers, Éadhmann Gruama and Seán Crón, were among those who accompanied Ruaidhrí Ó Domhnaill, earl of Tyrconnell, on his journey into exile from Rathmullan in September of 1607.[140]

In April 1608, Feilim Riabhach took part in Cathaoir Ó Dochartaigh's revolt against the English, and may have been the main instigator of it.[141] Together they took the fort of Culmore and marched on Derry where Feilim killed the governor.[142] Ó Dochartaigh's revolt lasted for eleven weeks and at the end of the summer Feilim Riabhach was discovered by the English in a wood, and although he defended himself he was captured and brought to Lifford.[143] The following August he was executed there along with nineteen others.[144] With Cathaoir Ó Dochartaigh's death in Kilmacrenan and with Clann Daibhid reduced to impotence, Inishowen lay at the mercy of the English. The peninsula was confiscated and in 1609 it was granted to Sir Arthur Chichester.[145] The Clann Daibhid, for their part in the sack of Derry, were, known at least until the nineteenth century by the nickname 'Burnderry!'[146]

In 1601 Aodh Buidhe was living at Greencastle and a brother of his was living at Moymill (Moville) three miles to landwards.[147] According to an inquisition taken at Derry in 1602, Éadhmann Gruama was living at Carrick McCowlin and 'Connor McDavy' had a residence in Malin.[148]

There is only one proprietor of the name listed in the Civil Survey (1640), 'Shane Crone McDevitt, Irish papist' who held forty acres in the parish of Fahan.[149] In the census of 1659 'Owen McDevet, gentleman, is listed as a *titulado* in the parish of Culdaff.[150] In all there are twenty-seven Mac Daibhid families listed in the census for Inishowen.[151] In the Hearth Money Rolls (1665) there are families of the name listed for the parishes of Moville, Fahan and Culdaff. There are also householders listed for parishes outside Inishowen, such as Conwal, Leck and Lettermacaward.[152]

Mac Duinnshléibhe, Mac an Ultaigh, Ultach: Donleavy, MacNulty, Ultagh

The family of Mac Duinnshléibhe of Donegal are descended from the Dál Fiatach kings of Ulaid, the ancient province of Ulster which by the eighth century had so dwindled that it comprised only the modern counties of Antrim, Down and part of Louth.[153] Although under constant threat from Uí Néill ambitions from the ninth century onwards, and later from the Normans, who conquered their territory in the late twelfth century,[154] Ruaidrí Mac Duinn Sléibe, who was killed fighting the Normans in 1201, is still described by the *Annals of Ulster* as 'king of Ulaid'.[155] The same annals do not style the Ó Néill family kings of Ulster until 1364, at the death of Áed Ó Néill,[156] which is significant, and helps to explain why the family of Mac Duinnshléibhe in later centuries were also known as Mac an Ultaigh 'Son of the Ulsterman' and Ultach 'Ulsterman',[157] thus distinguishing them from the later Uí Néill of which the leading families of Tír Conaill were branches.

The first of the name to be mentioned in connection with Donegal is Muirchertach Mac an Ultaig who was slain in 1281 alongside Domnall

Óc Ó Domnaill, king of Tír Conaill, and nobles of Cenél Conaill.[158] The first of the family that we know was a physician was Muiris mac Póil Ultaigh who died in 1395, and who is described as *ollamh leighis Chenél cConaill* 'chief physician of Cenél Conaill'.[159] Another physician, Cormac Mac Duinn Shléibhe, who is described as a bachelor of physic, has left us an example of the type of medicine practised in Ireland in late medieval times. It is a translation done by him into Irish of the *Gaulterus de dosibus*, a medical tract on mainly herbal cures for various ailments. The translation was done for Diarmaid Ó Laighin, a member of another medical family, at Cloyne in county Cork in 1459.[160] In 1497 another physician of the name was on a campaign in the Curlews with Con Ó Domhnaill, king of Tír Conaill, when he was taken prisoner. He is merely referred to as the son of Eoghan Ultach, 'mac Eoccain Ultaigh'.[161] In 1527, Donnchadh, 'an doctuir ua duinnsleibhe', died. He is described as a doctor of medicine, learned in other sciences, a man of great influence and wealth and one who kept a house of hospitality. His father was Eoghan, perhaps the Eoghan mentioned in 1497.[162] (Unfortunately, we know little of the descent of the family of Mac Duinnshléibhe of Donegal since they are completely ignored by Cú Choigríche Ó Cléirigh in his *Book of Genealogies*). In 1586 Eoghan Ultach, son of Donnchadh, died. The annals tell us that he excelled all the physicians of Ireland during his time,[163] and he is probably the 'Eugene' Ultach who attended the lord lieutenant, the earl of Sussex, in the winter of 1563 and certified a description of his illness.[164] He is the last physician of the family to be mentioned in the annals.

In a general pardon by Queen Elizabeth in the spring of 1603 the following names occur: 'Francis Ultagh, Donogh Ultagh' and 'Owen Ultagh', but we have no other information regarding them.[165]

Muiris Ultach, a Franciscan, was confessor to Aodh Ruadh Ó Domhnaill, last lord of Tír Conaill, and was with him at his death.[165a] Muiris was in Spain in 1607. He returned to Donegal in the autumn with letters for Ruaidhrí Ó Domhnaill, earl of Tyrconnell, who was soon to go into exile from Rathmullen in 1607. Ruaidhrí, on receipt of the letters, gave him a horse and £10.00, after which Muiris went on to Dungannon, the centre of Ó Néill power before Kinsale.[166] In 1610 Muiris, 'a doctor of some kind of divinity' is named by the Protestant bishop of Limerick as an envoy of the pope and is stated to be living in Multyfarnham.[167] We have a letter of Muiris' which he wrote from Multyfarnham, as minister provincial of his order, to the Irish Franciscan community in Saint Anthony's College in Louvain.[168] In 1626 he was on a final list of candidates for the See of Armagh, but was not selected.[169] In 1636 he was in Donegal and was one of the four Franciscans who signed the certificate of approbation on completion of the *Annals of the Four Masters* in Donegal abbey.[170] Among the other signatories was another Muiris Ultach, who is mentioned elsewhere as having sent money from Ireland for the support of the Irish College in Louvain.[171]

None of the family received grants in the Plantation of Ulster, but in 1632 we hear of 'Dermot Ultagh' who is described as 'meere Irish' being evicted from his tenancy in Aghalacky in the barony of Boylagh and Banagh.[172] 'Gabriell Ultagh', gentleman, is listed in the census of 1659 as a *titulado* in the parish of Mevagh in the barony of Kilmacrenan.[173] In all six families of the name are listed for the Barony.[174] The sobriquet *Ultach* persisted long after the seventeenth century, and John O'Donovan tells us that it was still commonly used for Mac Duinnshléibhe in the first half of the nineteenth century.[175]

Mac Giolla Bhrighde: 'McKilbridey', MacBride

The family of Mac Giolla Bhrighde were *airchinnigh* in the parish of Raymunterdoney in the modern barony of Kilmacrenan.[176] They were a famous ecclesiastical family and most of our information about them comes to us from papal sources, and that mostly in the fifteenth and early sixteenth centuries.

'Cornelius' Mac Giolla Bhrighde was bishop of Raphoe from 1440.[177] His life as far as we know, was blameless, but the same cannot be said for other clerics of the name. Domhnall Mac Giolla Bhríde, we are told, held the rectory of Taughboyne without ever having been ordained a priest.[178] 'Maurice' Mac Giolla Bhrighde, abbot of the Augustinian monastery of Derry, was accused by a fellow cleric of keeping a married woman as his concubine and of using monastery goods for his own use.[179]

'John' Mac Giolla Bhrighde, clerk of the diocese of Derry, although he was the son of a priest and an unmarried woman, was assigned the parish church of Moville in 1478[180] and in 1499 we read of another 'Johannes Margyllubryde' in connection with the canonry of Raphoe.[181] In 1504 he was still a canon of the church there.[182]

In the census of 1659 thirteen families under the anglicised form McIlbreedy are listed for the barony of Kilmacrenan.[183] In 1665 Tadhg Mac Giolla Bhrighde was living in the parish of Leck[184] and Mághnas Mac Giolla Bhrighde in the parish of Templecarn.[185]

The Ó Cléirigh genealogies state that the family of Mac Giolla Bhrighde are an offshoot of the Ó Dochartaigh family.[186] Since in the same entry they claim the same for the family of Mac Ailín, who were Scottish, the link has to be treated with some caution.

Mac Giolla Easpaig: Gillespie

The name Mac Giolla Easpaig in the earliest sources is found in the ancient kingdom of Ulaid in east Ulster. In 1165 Echmarcach, son of Mac Gilla Espuic, was killed by an invading force of the Northern Uí Néill and the Airgialla.[187] They are more firmly placed in what is now county Down by the death in 1172 of Mac Gilla Espuic, lord of Clann Ailebra and legislator of Cath Monaig who was treacherously slain by Donn Sléibe Ó hEochada, king of Ulaid.[188] It is possible that members of the family may have later migrated to Donegal with the defeated Mac Duinn Sléibe kings of Ulaid sometime in, or after, the twelfth century.[189]

The family were *archinnigh* in the parishes of Killybegs and Kilcar.[190] In 1471 a papal mandate was issued granting permission to Diarmaid Ó Doirnín and Diarmaid Mac Giolla Easpuic, brothers of the Third Order of Saint Francis, to build a monastery of the order at Cill Ó dTomhrair (*anglice* Killydonnell) on the banks of Lough Swilly.[191]

In the census of 1659 there are eight of the family numbered for the barony of Boylagh and Banagh.[192] In the Hearth Money Roll for Donegal, families are listed for the parishes of Killybegs, Glencolumbkille, Kilcar, Inishkeele and Kilbarron.[193]

Mac Lochlainn: MacLaughlin, MacLoughlin

The Mac Lochlainn family of Inisowen (i.e. Inis Eoghain) provided eleven kings of Cenél Eógain and two high-kings between the years 1061 and 1241.[194] It is surprising, then, that the immediate forebears of their eponymous ancestor, Lochlann, who lived about the middle of the eleventh century should have been a matter of dispute among the genealogists. According to some sources Lochlann was a descendant of Niall Glúndubh, the eponymous ancestor of Ó Néill of Tír Eoghain;[195] others have him descend from Niall's brother Domnall, who had preceded Niall in the kingship of Aileach, and who died in 915.[196] It is highly likely that Lochlann himself was the king of Inis Eoghain mentioned in the annals in 1023 as having been killed by his own people.[197]

From the seventh century the Cenél Eógain had begun to expand eastward from Aileach into the territory of the Airgialla, and by 1012 Telach Óc, modern Tullyhogue, near Dungannon, the ancient inauguration site of at least one branch of the Airgialla, is described as being firmly in the territory of Cenél Eógain.[198] It most likely that the Ó Néill dynasty had made their headquarters at Telach Óc at the beginning of the eleventh century[199] and a clear distinction is made from that time onwards between the two main branches of Cenél Eógain: the family of Mac Lochlainn, known as Cenél Eógain na hInnse (of the Island, i.e. Inishowen), and that of Ó Néill, Cenél Eógain Telcha Óc.[200]

Lochlann's son Ardgar is first mentioned in the annals in 1051 when he was expelled from the kingship of Telach Óc which he had previously wrested from his kindred, the Ó Néill family, who were now restored to it.[201] In 1061 Ardgar became overking of Cenél Eógain at Aileach[202] and the following year he invaded Connacht, carrying off 6,000 cows and a thousand prisoners.[203] He invaded Connacht again in 1063 and in Tirawley received the submission of the kings of Connacht, including Áed Ó Conchobhair, the overking.[204] Ardgar died in Ó Néill territory, in Telach Óc, in 1064, and was buried in Armagh in *mausolio regum*.[205] The following year Áed Ó Ualgairg took the kingship of Cenél Eógain,[206] which was lost to the Mac Lochlainn family until 1083 when Ardgar's son, Domnall, became king.[207]

One of Domnall's first acts as king was his invasion, in 1084, of east Ulster, the much reduced territory of the Ulaid, the pre-Uí Néill Ulstermen, whose king Donn Sléibe Mac Eochada had asserted his ancient rights of kingship over the ancient *cúige* in defiance of Cenél Eógain.[208] In 1088 Domnall invaded Connacht and was given hostages by Ruaidrí Ó Conchobhair, king of Connacht, and together they burned Limerick and destroyed Kincora, the ancient Ó Briain stronghold.[209] In 1090 Muirchertach Ó Briain, king of Munster, Ruaidrí Ó Conchobhair and Domnall Ó Maíl Sechlainn, king of Meath, delivered hostages to him which made him effective high-king.[210] In 1091 he turned his attentions to the Ulaid and killed Donn Sléibe.[211] By 1093 Muirchertach Ó Briain was high-king 'with opposition' to Domnall,[212] and although a peace was concluded between them in 1099,[213] Muirchertach brought a Viking fleet to Derry in 1100 but was defeated.[214] The following year Muirchertach invaded Tír Eoghain and razed Aileach in revenge for Kincora.[215] In 1103 at Magh Coba, Domnall defeated Muirchertach, who had allied himself with the Ulaid.[216] In 1104 the Ulaid submitted[217] and a peace was made between Domnall and Muirchertach in 1105.[218] In 1113 Domnall banished Donnchadh mac Duinn Sléibe from the kingship of Ulaid and divided his territory.[219] Muirchertach resigned his kingship in 1114 because of illness, and in that year Domnall made peace with Munster.[220] Domnall died in 1121 at the age of 73 and was buried in Derry.[221] He was succeeded in the kingship of Aileach by his son, Conchobhar, who at his death in 1136 is described as king of Cenél Eógain, Cenél Conaill, Ulaid and Airgialla.[222]

The next king of Aileach was Conchobhar's nephew, Muirchertach, son of Niall, one time king of Tír Conaill, who reigned from 1136.[223] Little is known of Muirchertach until 1148 when he invaded the territory of the Ulaid, defeating them at Dundrum. He divided their territory, as his grandfather, Domnall, had done before him, which not only turned the Ulaid against Muirchertach, but also alienated his vassal Donnchad Ó Cerbaill, king of Airgialla. Later in the year Donnchad made peace with Muirchertach,[224] and in 1149 Cú Ulad, king of the Ulaid, submitted to him.[225]

In 1149, too, he received the submission of Tigernán Ó Ruairc of Breifne and of Diarmait Mac Murchada, king of Leinster, at which time he assumed the high kingship in opposition to Toirdelbhach Ó Conchobair of Connacht.[226] To further demonstrate his power he expelled Murchad Ó Maíl Sechnaill, king of Meath, and divided his kingdom between Toirdelbach Ó Conchobair of Connacht, Ó Ruairc and Ó Cerbaill.[227] In 1153 he helped restore Toirdelbach Ó Briain to half of his kingdom in Thomond after the southern king had been expelled by Toirdelbach Ó Conchobair.[228] Ó Conchobair retaliated the following year by sending a fleet against Muirchertach. Muirchertach hired fleets of mercenaries from the Hebrides and Man to help him, but these foreign fleets were defeated off Inishowen.[229] By 1156 Muirchertach's power was at its height and in that year he 'gave' Leinster to its reigning king, Diarmait Mac Murchada, a feudal act and not one in accordance with Irish law.[230] He repeated this policy in 1161 when he 'gave' Connacht to its reigning king, Ruaidrí Ó Conchobhair.[231]

Muirchertach was a patron of the Church and in 1157 was present at the consecration of the Cistercian monastery of Mellifont,[232] and in 1162 he and Flaithbertach Ó Brolcháin, abbot of Derry, reconstructed Derry after demolishing eighty houses there.[233] In 1164 they together began the building of the 'Great Church of Derry', Tempall Mór Doire, from which the present parish of Templemore gets its name.[234]

In 1165 after the Ulaid had revolted he expelled their king Eochaid Mac Duinn Sléibe, who was restored only on the intercession of Donnchad Ó Cerbaill, king of Airgialla.[235] When Muirchertach treacherously blinded Eochaid the following year in violation of the pledges of the bishop of Armagh, Donnchad turned against him and switched his allegiance to Ruaidrí Ó Conchobair, king of Connacht. Donnchad then invaded Tír Eógain having been invited there by Muirchertach's own people who had deserted him because of his sacrilege in killing Mac Duinn Sléibe. When his remaining followers deserted him he died. He was buried in Armagh.[236]

In 1167 Ruaidrí Ó Conchobhair, now high-king of Ireland, invaded Cenél Eógain and divided Tír Eógain (which included Inishowen) giving the north to Muirchertach's son, Niall, and the south to Áed Ó Néill, 'in Macáem Tóinlesc'[237] and the following year the sub-kings of Cenél Eógain submitted to Ruaidrí as high-king at Athlone.[238] Niall was not among those kings who submitted to Henry II of England in 1171. He was slain in 1176 by the Muintir Branáin, whose territory lay around Lough Neagh in Antrim. That same year his brother and successor in the kingship, Máel Séchlainn, destroyed Richard Fleming's castle at

Slane, killing over a hundred of the inhabitants.[239] In 1177 Máel Sechlainn had Áed Ó Néill killed and so became king of all Tír Eógain.[240] He was killed in Meath in 1185 by William le Petit.[241]

Máel Sechlainn was succeeded in the kingship of Tír Eógain by his third cousin, Domnall, who continued the war with the Normans. In 1188 he was killed by a raiding party of the Normans of Iveagh.[242]

The last Mac Lochlainn king of Tír Eógain was Domnall, son of Muirchertach, who had also been king.[243] Domnall was driven from his kingship twice, once by Domnall Ó Néill, whom he killed in 1234,[244] and again in 1238 by the lord justice Maurice Fitzgerald and Hugo de Lacy, earl of Ulster, who gave the kingship to Brian Ó Néill.[245] The following year after a victory at Carnteel (in county Tyrone) Domnall assumed the kingship again.[246] In 1241 the ousted Brian Ó Néill sought the help of Máel Sechlainn Ó Domnaill, king of Tír Conaill, and together they invaded Tír Eógain where they defeated Domnall's army at Cam Éirghe. Domnall was killed in the battle and with him ended the Mac Lochlainn kingship of Cenél Eógain.[247] From then on until the beginning of the seventeenth century the kings of Cenél Eógain came exclusively from the Ó Néill family.[248] After Cam Éirghe the family of Mac Lochlainn sank into obscurity and there is little about them in the annals after that date, or in any other sources, until the end of Gaelic rule in Inishowen at the beginning of the seventeenth century.[249]

Among the strongholds of Inishowen mentioned in the state papers in 1601 are two castles, one at Caire MacEwlyn (Redcastle) where 'Hugh Carrogh McLaughlin, chief of his sept' lived and another at Garnagall (Whitecastle), the home of 'Brian Oge McLaughlin'.[250] Among the Irish gentlemen present at an inquisition held at Derry in November of 1602 was 'Hugh Carragh Mclaghlin de Bullibrack'.[251] In the *Civil Survey,* 'Daniel McGloghlin', Irish Papist, is listed as a proprietor in 1640 in the parish of Moville.[252] 'Edmund Moder McLaughlin and Hugh his sonn, gentlemen' as well as 'Donnell Ballagh McGlaghlin, gent:' are mentioned as *tituladoes* in the parish of Clonca in the census of 1659.[253] Sixty-three families of the name in all are listed for Inishowen in the census.[254] In the Hearth Money Roll for Donegal most families of the name are found in the parishes of Moville, Clonca and Culdaff.[255]

In August, 1835, the antiquarian John O'Donovan visited Ishkaheen, in Inishowen, and the grave of Eógan, fifth century ancestor of the Cenél Eógain, and of the Mac Lochlainn family. There he met 'MacLoughlin', chief of his name, and owner of the graveyard where Eógan was buried.[256] Unfortunately, he does not give MacLoughlin's first name, and so the descendants of this 'princely figure' are unknown to us.

Mac Niallghuis: MacNelis, 'McEnellis'

The Mac Niallghuis family were *airchinnigh*[257] in the parish of Glencolumbkille. In an inquisition in 1609 at Lifford it is stated that 'William oge, McEneilis is corbe and herenagh of th' one moitie' of the termon land there and that 'Neale McEneilis is corbe of th' other moitie; ... in former times there was only one corbe of the whole landes but that uppon discontent conceived by one of the sept, for that he was not named corbe of the moitie, he adhered to O'Donnell, and by his power was made corbe to the moitie thereof, and soe continued in possession of his moitie untill O'Donnell's late defeccion'. Half of the royalty of the fishing of 'Tullin', no doubt Teelin, belonged to 'Neale McEneillus' and half to Mac Suibhne Boghaineach.[258]

In the early years of the seventeenth century 'Bernardus M'Nellus' was curate of Glencolumbkille. According to Bishop Montgomery of Derry, Bernardus 'speaks Irish, Latin and Scots' and 'paints cleverly'.[259]

In the census of 1659 there are nine families numbered for the barony of Boylagh and Banagh.[260] In the Hearth Money Rolls there is only one householder of the name listed, 'Michael', of Glencolumbkille.[261]

Mac Robhartaigh: Magroarty

The name of Mac Robhartaigh is commemorated in two townlands, Ballymagrorty in the parish of Drumhome in the south of county Donegal and a place of the same name in Templemore, which includes part of the present city of Derry.[262]

The head of the family was the traditional keeper of the *Cathach*, a sixth century manuscript copy of Saint Jerome's translation of the Psalter, which has been ascribed to Saint Colum Cille. *Cathach* can be translated 'battler', and according to Mághnas Ó Domhnaill, lord of Tír Conaill, in his life of the saint, the shrine of the manuscript was carried around the host of Cenél Conaill before going into battle in order to ensure victory.[263] And so, in 1497, we read of how, in a battle between Con Ó Domhnaill, king of Tír Conaill, and Mac Diarmada of Moylurg the *Cathach* was taken and Mac Robhartaigh, its keeper, was slain. In 1567 another head of the family was slain at Farsetmore, near Letterkenny, in an engagement between a contingent of Aodh Ó Domhnaill's men and the army of Seán an Díomais Ó Néill. Here Mac Robhartaigh is again said to be the keeper of the *Cathach*.[264]

The shrine, which is now in the National Museum of Ireland, bears the following inscription: [*Or]oit do [Ch]lathbarr Ua Domnaill las indernad in cumtachs'a agus do Sittriuc mac Meic Aeda do rigne acus do Domnall mac Robartaig do comarba Canasa* [i.e. abbot of Kells]. Domnall's death is noted in the annals at 1098; in *A.F.M.*, where he is called *ua* Robartaig, he is said to have been abbot for a time.[264a] In the early seventeenth century the shrine was kept at Ballymagrorty, in Drumhome, which was a Columban foundation. Although the family is found in the sources in Inishowen, their close associations with Colum Cille and the family of Ó Domhnaill would suggest that they were of the Cenél Conaill.[264b]

The Irish name of the famous anchorite, biblical scholar and scribe, Marianus Scotus, was Muiredach mac Robartaig, who very likely was born in Ballymagrorty in Donegal. In 1067 he set out on pilgrimage to Rome with six companions but when they reached Ratisbon in Germany they decided to stay there as anchorites. Muiredach died in Ratisbon in 1088.[265]

Members of the family are found in the papal registers. In 1405, for instance, a mandate was given to appoint 'Philip' Mac Robhartaigh vicar of Taughboyne.[266]

According to an inquisition at Lifford in September, 1609, the Mac Robhartaigh family held the grange of Burt in Inishowen, which had previously belonged to the monastery of Moycoskin in the present county of Derry.[267] In the same month in an inquisition held at Derry one of the sworn jurors was 'Manus McRoarty'.[268]

The name does not appear once for Donegal in the census of 1659. In the Hearth Money Rolls (1665) three householders of the name are listed for the parish of Conwal.[269]

The eponymous ancestor of Mac Robhartaigh (i.e. Robartach) may well be the same as that of Ó Robhartaigh, long associated with Tory island. For the latter family the reader is directed to the section under Ó Robhartaigh.

Mac Suibhne: MacSweeney

The Mac Suibhne family are of Scottish origin and did not settle permanently in Tír Conaill until the beginning of the fourteenth century, when they became *gallóglaigh,* or hired mercenaries, to the Ó Domhnaill kings.[270] They did, however, claim a remote Irish ancestry, tracing their descent from Ánrothán, son of Áed, son of Flaithbertach Ó Néill, king of Cenél Eógain, who died in 1036.[271]

According to *Leabhar Chlainne Suibhne,* after Áed's death his son Ánrothán was chosen as king despite his brother, Domnall, who was the rightful heir. Domnall then cursed Ánrothán who gave up the kingship and departed for Scotland with his followers. There he married the daughter of the king of Scotland. His great-grandson was Suibne from whom the Clann tSuibhne descend.[272] The story of the descent of Clann tSuibhne from the Ó Néill kings of Cenél Eógain may have been a convenient fabrication in order to give the family a

Milesian pedigree and thus an accepted place in medieval Tír Conaill.[273] W. D. H. Sellar, however, has argued most convincingly that the story is not unlikely and that Clann tSuibhne and other Scottish families such as Lamont may well be descended from the Ó Néill family.[274]

As *gallóglaigh* the Mac Suibhne family were certainly unusual, for they soon became lords of vast territories in Tír Conaill and developed a special relationship with its Ó Domhnaill kings. In this they differed greatly from other *gallóglaigh* families in medieval Ireland, such as those of Mac Cába and Mac Somhairle, who were totally dependent on whoever wished to hire their services.[275]

The earliest reference to Mac Suibhne in Ireland is in 1267 when Murchad Mac Suibne was taken prisoner by Domnall Ó Conchobair and delivered to the earl of Ulster, in whose prison he died.[276] This Murchadh was a son of Máel Muire an Sparáin, a Scottish lord whose seat was the modern Castle Sween in Kintyre, and whose father was Suibne, the eponymous ancestor of the *Clann*. Suibne's floruit was 1200 and we know that Máel Muire was still alive in 1262.[277] (Murchad's mother, Ben Mide, daughter of Toirdelbach Ó Conchobair, king of Connacht, died in 1269.)[278]

(a) *Mac Suibhne Fánad*

The first Mac Suibhne to settle in Tír Conaill was Eoin, grandson of Máel Muire. Having expelled the ruling Ó Breisléin family from Fanad sometime after 1263, he became lord of that territory and his daughter Caterína married Domnall Óc Ó Domnaill, king of Tír Conaill. His son, Suibne, succeeded him, but died without issue within the year, and with the death of Suibne's brother, Toirdelbach, the Mac Suibhne lordship of Fanad ceased for the time being.[279]

After the battle of Bannockburn in 1314 Murchad Mear, great-grandson of Máel Muire an Sparáin and grandson of the Murchad who died while a captive of the earl of Ulster, arrived at Lough Swilly with his followers. According to *Leabhar Chlainne Suibhne* he and his son, Murchad Óc, conquered part of Inishowen, Fanad, Ros Guill, Ó Maíl Gaíthe's Tuath and the two tuatha of Tír Boghaine, and on these territories, with the exception of Inishowen, he settled his people.[280] It is unlikely, however, that Murchad penetrated as far south as Tír Boghaine.

Murchad Mear was succeeded by his son, Murchad Óc, as lord of the conquered lands east of Bearnas Mór. Of Murchad Óc's sons, Máel Muire became lord of Fanad and Donnchad Mór became lord of the Trí Tuatha in north-west Donegal, previously the territory of Ó Báegill.[281]

Máel Muire defeated Niall Ó Domhnaill in battle at Achadh Móna but later was present as an ally of Niall when the latter killed his brother,

Conchobhar Ó Domhnaill, king of Tír Chonaill, at Murvagh, near Donegal town, in 1342. For his trouble Máel Muire was granted Moross in the north of Fanad. He also extended his territory by taking Ray and Glenalla, in the present day barony of Kilmacrenan, from Ó Tairchirt.[282]

The next lord of Fanad was Máel Muire's son, Toirdhealbhach Caoch, who was granted certain privileges by Ó Domhnaill, such as the right to sit on Ó Domhnaill's right hand side and the right to spend three nights in each house in Tír Conaill. This, and the agreement that Toirdhealbhach Caoch and his successors would supply two *gallóglaigh* for every quarter of land in his territory when Ó Domhnaill went to war,[283] is indicative of the growing interdependence of Ó Domhnaill and Mac Suibhne Fanad.

Toirdhealbhach Caoch's son, Toirdhealbhach Ruadh, assumed the lordship in 1399,[284] but not without a struggle with his two uncles, Eoin and Murchadh. In this he was helped by Toirdhealbhach an Fhíona Ó Domhnaill, king of Tír Conaill, who himself inaugurated Toirdhealbhach Ruadh at Kilmacrenan, the traditional site of inauguration of Ó Domhnaill. According to *Leabhar Chlainne Suibhne* Mac Suibhne of Scotland had been inaugurated by the successor of Colum Cille at Iona, but after the family's removal to Ireland the ceremony had been sometimes performed by Ó Firghil (O Friel) at Kilmacrenan, 'baile Choluimchille', rather than by the abbots of Iona.[285] Toirdhealbhach Ruadh was present in Meath in 1423 with Ó Domhnaill (Niall) and Ó Néill (Domhnall) when they defeated the army of the English lord deputy, although it is Mac Suibhne Connacht who is mentioned in A.F.M.[286] In 1434 Niall Ó Domhnaill was captured by the English during a skirmish and his army was rescued with difficulty by Toirdhealbhach Ruadh after their defeat.[287] He and Neachtain Ó Domhnaill, Ó Domhnaill's brother, were defeated in the Rosses in 1435 by Ó Néill (Eoghan), but *Leabhar Chlainne Suibhne* loyally claimed that Toirdhealbhach and Neachtain were the victors![288]

Toirdhealbhach Ruadh died, probably in 1438, having ruled for thirty-nine years. He was succeeded by his son, Ruaidhrí, but not until a dispute over the succession with his uncle, Donnchadh Garbh, had been resolved by Ruaidhrí's defeating his uncle in a wrestling match. During Ruaidhrí's lordship a beef tax was levied on Fanad by Neachtain Ó Domhnaill. Ruaidhrí died after ruling for thirteen years, and was succeeded by his brother, Domhnall.[289]

In 1456 Énrí Ó Néill, king of Tír Eoghain, along with the sons of Neachtain Ó Domhnaill, who were in exile with Ó Néill, invaded Inishowen. They were opposed by Neachtain's nephew, Domhnall, the ruling Ó Domhnaill, who was aided by Maol Mhuire Mac Suibhne, son of Toirdhealbhach Ruadh and brother of Domhnall. Ó Domhnaill was killed in the subsequent battle near Cúl Mic an Treoin (Castleforward), and Maol Mhuire and Ó Domhnaill's brother, Aodh Ruadh, were taken prisoner. Neachtain's son, Toirdhealbhach Cairbreach Ó Domhnaill, then assumed the kingship of Tír Conaill,[290] and after Domhnall Mac Suibhne's death at the hands of his nephews, the sons of his brother, Ruaidhrí, Toirdhealbhach Cairbreach proclaimed Domhnall's cousin, Toirdhealbhach Bacach, lord of Fanad.[291]

Aodh Ruadh Ó Domhnaill and Maol Mhuire were released in 1460[292] and the following year they defeated Toirdelbach Cairbreach at Kinnaweer on Mulroy Bay. After Aodh Ruadh's victory he was inaugurated as Ó Domhnaill at Kilmacrenan and immediately set up Maol Mhuire as lord of Fanad.[293] Maol Mhuire ruled for eleven years. He was killed on Easter Tuesday, 1472, at the river Finn, fighting beside Aodh Ruadh against Ó Néill (Énrí). After the battle, his body was taken to Derry for burial covered with the flag of another captain of *gallóglaigh,* Mac Domhnaill of Antrim, which he had captured in the battle.[294]

Maol Mhuire was succeeded by his son Ruaidhrí, who built Rathmullan castle. His wife was Máire, daughter of Ó Máille (Eoghan), and a woman of great piety. Together they built the Carmelite priory at Rathmullan, which was completed in 1516, the first prior of which was Suibhne Mac Suibhne of the Connacht branch. *Leabhar Chlainne Suibhne* tells us that the priory was built to honour Ruaidhrí's son, Ruaidhrí Óg, a man who had travelled abroad and who could speak many languages.

Ruaidhrí's successful campaigns with Ó Domhnaill, both Aodh Ruadh and his successor Conn, are given great prominence in *Leabhar Chlainne Suibhne.*[295] But other campaigns, where he suffered defeat, get no mention, such as in 1497 when Ó Domhnaill (Conn) was defeated in battle by Mac Diarmada (Tadhg) of Moylurg and Ruaidhrí taken prisoner, and later in the same year when Conn was defeated and killed at Béal-Átha-Daire in Fanad and Ruaidhrí's son taken prisoner by Ó Néill (Énrí Óg)![296]

Ruaidhrí was famed for his patronage of poets and learning. He died in 1518 and was buried in Rathmullan 'in the habit of the friars of Mary.' His wife, Máire, survived Ruaidhrí by four years. She is remembered as being generous, a good mother, pious, and a great builder of churches, both in Ulster and in Connacht, and, of course, the person who caused the 'leabhar díadhacht', which forms the first part of the manuscript of which *Leabhar Chlainne Suibhne* is the second part, to be written.[297]

After Ruaidhrí's death there was a fierce struggle for the lordship of Fanad until Domhnall Óg, son of Domhnall Mór and cousin of

Ruaidhrí, the previous lord, was proclaimed Mac Suibhne by the chiefs of Cenél Conaill at Kilmacrenan. Ruaidhrí's son, Toirdhealbhach, however, would not submit to Domhnall Óg and continued to defy him, and when Domhnall Óg died in 1529, Toirdhealbhach gathered his followers and had Ó Firghil inaugurate him at Kilmacrenan, which greatly angered Ó Domhnaill (Aodh Dubh), for Ó Domhnaill claimed that he alone had the right to inaugurate his sub-chief. Toirdhealbhach was killed in 1544 by the sons of Domhnall Óg Mac Suibhne, the previous lord, as revenge for the death of their brother, Maol Mhuire. It was during his lifetime that *Leabhar Chlainne Suibhne* was compiled.[298]

Ruaidhrí Carrach, son of Domhnall Óg, ruled for ten years until he was slain in 1552 with two of his kin 'in a monastery'.[299] The next Mac Suibhne to be mentioned in the annals is Domhnall Gorm, leader of 'Sliocht Domhnaill', when he was with Calbhach Ó Domhnaill in a victory over Seán an Díomais Ó Néill in 1557.[300] He was slain in 1568 by some of his own kin, Muintir Sruithéin[301] and was succeeded by Toirdhealbhach Óg, son of Toirdhealbhach (who had died in 1544). Toirdhealbhach Óg and Mac Suibhne na dTuath were slain at Dún na Long on the Foyle near Strabane in 1570 in battle against Ó Néill (Toirdhealbhach Luineach). Toirdhealbhach Óg was succeeded by his brother, Domhnall,[302] who was the last inaugurated lord of Fanad, for he lived well into the seventeenth century and witnessed the destruction of the Gaelic order in Tír Conaill.

When Aodh Ruadh Ó Domhnaill was captured aboard an English ship at Rathmullan in 1587, Domhnall's son, Domhnall Gorm, was, most likely, one of the captives who was taken to Dublin with him. (Domhnall Gorm escaped from Dublin Castle in February 1588).[303] In 1592 Domhnall was present at Aodh Ruadh's inauguration.[304] He gets little mention in the annals, except for the year 1599, when he accompanied Aodh Ruadh on a raid into Thomond.[305]

In October of 1600 the English authorities were informed that Domhnall was with Aodh Ruadh.[306] In March of the following year there was an English garrison installed in Rathmullan[307] and in May Domhnall submitted.[308] In September he rose out again,[309] but finally submmitted in January, 1602.[310] When Ó Néill and Ruaidhrí Ó Domhnaill sailed from Rathmullan in September 1607, some of the ship's company, who had gone ashore for water, were attacked by Mac Suibhne's son, but succeeded in routing him and his party.[311]

In 1608 Domhnall was on a list of jurors which indicted the earls of Tyrconnell and Tyrone for treason.[312] For his loyalty he received a grant of land in the Plantation of Ulster,[313] and in 1619 he is reported to have '2000 acres, called Roindoberg and Caroocomony. 'He hath built a good bawne, and a house, all of lime and stone, in which with his family, he dwelleth.'[314]

His son, Domhnall Gorm, was married to 'Honora' daughter of Mac Suibhne na dTuath (Eoghan Óg) and had ten children. He died on 12 February, 1637, and is buried in Clondavaddog, in Fanad.[315]

Among the Mac Suibhne Fanad proprietors listed in the *Civil Survey* whose lands were held forfeit after the 1641 rising were Domhnall Óg and Aodh Buidhe, sons of Domhnall Gorm, both of whom held lands in the parish of Clondavaddog in the north of Fanad.[316] A leading insurgent in the rising was Éiremhón Mac Suibhne, son of Uaitéar, whose lands in the parishes of Aughnish and Tully were forfeited.[317]

In the census of 1659 the only Mac Suibhne *titulado* mentioned for Donegal is 'Donell McSwyne' in Clondavaddog.[318] Some thirty-nine McSwyne families are counted for the barony of Kilmacrenan.[319] In the Hearth Money Rolls, most taxpayers of the name listed for the barony are found in the parishes of Clondavaddog, Clondahorky, and Tullaghobegley.[320]

(b) *Mac Suibhne na dTuath*

Compared with the sources we have for the history of Mac Suibhne Fanad, those for Mac Suibhne na dTuath are quite meagre.

The district called Na Trí Tuatha, or Tuatha Toraighe, an area west of Fanad and including the modern parish of Gweedore and Tory Island, was ruled by the family of Ó Báegill until shortly after 1360, when it was conquered by Clann tSuibhne.[321] The first Mac Suibhne na dTuath was Donnchadh Mór, grandson of Murchad Mear, who, as we have seen, made large conquests in Tír Conaill about the year 1314 with the help of his son Murchad Óc, the father of Donnchadh Mór. Eoghan Connachtach, son of Donnachadh, was taken prisoner by Cathal Óg Ó Conchobhair, son of Ó Conchobhair Shligigh in 1359 when the latter defeated an army led by Ó Domhnaill (Seán).[322] Later Eoghan helped Seán's family to defeat Toirdhealbhach an Fhíona Ó Domhnaill at Sliabh Malair. They also plundered Glencolumkille, where Eoghan perished as a result of his violating the monastery there.[323] At the beginning of the fifteenth century his son, Toirdhealbhach Óg, was lord of Na Tuatha according, to his pedigree in the *Book of Ballymote*.[324] Another son, Donnchadh, was drowned at sea in 1413.[325] There is little else to be heard of Mac Suibhne na dTuath after that date until the middle of the sixteenth century.

In 1543 Mac Suibhne na dTuath – most likely Eoghan, who died in 1545, in Umhall Uí Mháille[326] – and his son, Brian, were taken prisoner at Inis Mhic an Doirn (Rutland Island in the parish of Templecrone) by a fleet from Iar-Chonnacht,[327] and in 1544 we read that Murchadh, his son, and Donnchadh, his brother died.[328] Eoghan's son, Eoghan Óg, lord of Na Tuatha, was slain fighting his own kin in 1554 at Ceann Salach in Cloghaneely,[329] and was succeeded by his son Murchadh Mall, who in 1567 helped Ó Domhnaill (Sir Aodh) defeat Seán an Díomuis Ó Néill at Scarriffhollis, near Letterkenny.[330] He and Mac Suibhne Fánad (Toirdhealbhach Óg) were slain at Dún na Long near Strabane in 1570 by the Clann Domhnaill Gallóglaigh.[331] Murchadh Mall was succeeded by his brother, Eoghan Óg.[332]

In 1588 the English were expressing concern that Eoghan Óg was aiding Spaniards from the Armada who had landed in his territory[333] and that he had allowed one of their ships to be prepared for their onward journey.[334] In 1590 he gave shelter to Ó Ruairc (Brian) of Breifne who had fled north after a disastrous defeat by the English. Ó Ruairc remained with Mac Suibhne for a year after which, in 1591, he went to Scotland, and to his death in London.[335] In 1592 Eoghan Óg attended the inauguration at Kilmacrenan of Aodh Ruadh Ó Domhnaill as lord of Tír Conaill.[336] He died in 1596 and was succeeded by his nephew, Maol Mhuire, son of Murchadh Mall.[337] Maol Mhuire was the last lord of Na Tuatha.

At the beginning of 1598 Sir Conyers Clifford, the English president of Connaught, writing to the privy council was confident that Maol Mhuire would join him in the war against Aodh Ruadh Ó Domhnaill.[338] By the spring Maol Mhuire had joined the English and revolted against Ó Domhnaill, but suffered defeat and had been banished from his territory.[339] In August of 1599 he was with Clifford when the latter was defeated and killed in battle against Ó Domhnaill (Aodh Ruadh).[340] He was knighted for his services in May of 1600,[341] but in August of the same year he was in contact with Aodh Ruadh. Having been captured by the English he was imprisoned on a ship on the Foyle near Derry. However, with the aid of a prostitute, who had been brought aboard to keep him company, he escaped and swam across the river to Ó Catháin's country,[342] after which he rejoined Ó Domhnaill.[343] In the late spring of 1601 he gave pledges of submission to the English[344] but by the summer he was again at war against them.[345] In April 1603 Doagh Castle fell to Sir Henry Docwra, governor of the Derry garrison, and so finally Docwra was 'possessed of the country of Tyrconnell for the king'.[346] Maol Mhuire was pardoned in 1604,[347] but in 1608 he was arraigned for treason and was in danger of imprisonment.[348] He obviously succeeded in escaping punishment, however, and was granted 2000 acres in the plantation of Ulster.[349] There is some evidence that there were some changes in Maol Mhuire's affairs in 1621 for the crown was in possession of his lands. His lands, however, were regranted to him, his heirs and assigns in 1630.[350]

Maol Mhuire's grandson, Colonel Maol Mhuire Mac Suibhne, is named as a leading rebel in 1641.[351] His lands in Dunlewy in the parish of Gweedore were held forfeit after the rising.[352]

In 1835 John O'Donovan saw a tall and stately man, three women, and some children on the strand at Dunfanaghy, accompanied by a donkey, greyhounds and a goat. On enquiring who the group was, he was told by a local fisherman that it was Mac Suibhne na dTuath and his family. He later met 'Mac Suibhne', who was a travelling man and was given the latter's genealogy back through Colonel Maol Mhuire to Sir Maol Mhuire. This 'Mac Suibhne' was respected and acknowledged by 'all the old Milesians from Fanaid to Ballyshannon' who 'acknowledge him to be the senior and agree in the number of generations up to Sir Malmurry'.[353] O'Donovan was very impressed by the Mac Suibhnes who 'are a glorious race, warm-hearted, humane, obliging, manly and honourable and easily distinguished from the other tribes by the peculiar cast of their physiognomy'.[354]

(c) *Mac Suibhne Boghaineach*

The third branch of Clann tSuibhne in Tír Conaill was that of Mac Suibhne Boghaineach, who according to *Leabhar Chlainne Suibhne*, were descended from Dubhghall Mac Suibhne, who was granted the territory of Tír Boghaine by his grandfather, Murchadh Mear, who, as we have seen, died about the year 1320.[355] The district of Boghaine comprised the modern barony of Banagh in south-west Donegal, as well as a part of Boylagh.[356]

The story of this branch of the *Clann*, because of a lack of early sources, is less clear than those of the branches in Na Tuatha and Fanad. Dubhghall, the founder of the branch according to *Leabhar Chlainne Suibhne*, was slain in 1356,[357] although in the *Book of Ballymote* (ca. 1400) six of his grandsons are said to belong to Mac Suibhne of Connacht.[358] The eldest of these, Toirdhealbhach, who is described in *A.F.M.* as Ard Chonsapal Connacht, or High Constable of Connacht, was slain in battle with two of his brothers, Donnchadh and Donn Sléibhe in 1397.[359] It is interesting, however, that he is included in the seventeenth-century Ó Cléirigh genealogies as being of Boghaine.[360] From him descend the later lords of Banagh.[361]

The first clear mention of a Mac Suibhne of Banagh in the annals is as late as 1496, when Maol Mhuire, 'Mac Suibhne Thíre Boghaine', died.[362] The following year another lord of Banagh is mentioned as follows: 'Mac Suibhne Connachtach .i. Mac Suibhne Baghnineach (i.e. of Banagh), Eoghan décc'. This and other evidence led Father Paul Walsh to argue, and to show very clearly, that the Banagh branch were, in fact, a late offshoot of the Connacht branch whose territory was Cúil

Chnámh in the civil parish of Dromard, county Sligo.[363]

At the end of the sixteenth century the seat of Mac Suibhne Boghaineach was at Rahan in the parish of Killaghtee near Dunkineely, overlooking MacSwyne's Bay,[364] and it was there that Mac Suibhne Thíre Boghaine (Niall Mór mac Eoghain) died in 1524, 'a constable of hardest hand'.[365] It was at this castle, too, that his son Maol Mhuire Mór, lord of Banagh, was killed in 1535 by another son, Niall Óg.[366]

Also within their territory was Killybegs, *Na Cealla Beaga* or 'the small churches', in which stood the church of Saint Catherine.[367] In 1513 Killybegs was plundered by Eoghan Ó Máille and the crews of three ships, who were, however, unable to return home to Connacht with their prisoners because of stormy weather. The leaders of Banagh were away in Ó Domhnaill's army at the time, but a youth called Brian Mac Suibhne, along with some shepherds and farmers, rescued the prisoners and slew Eoghan Ó Máille.[368] We hear of another raid by sea in 1542 when the crew of a ship under the son of Ó Flaithbheartaigh of Iar-Chonnacht landed at Rathlin O'Beirne. This time they were taken by Toirdhealbhach Mac Suibhne, son of the then Mac Suibhne Boghaineach, Niall Óg, and slaughtered, with the exception of Ó Flaithbheartaigh's son, who was pardoned by Mac Suibhne and sent home.[369]

Niall Óg, himself, was killed in 1547 at Badhbhdhún Nua by the sons of his brother, Maol Mhuire, because of Maol Mhuire's death at the hands of Niall Óg, in 1535.[370] He was succeeded in the lordship by Toirdhealbhach Meirgeach Mac Suibhne, who had a short rule, being slain at Baile Mhic Suibhne by the Clann Coilín and the Clann Coinneigéin in January of 1550.

After Toirdhealbhach's death, Ruaidhrí Ballach Mac Suibhne requested Maghnus Ó Domhnaill to create him lord of Banagh and when Ó Domhnaill refused Ruaidhrí plundered Killybegs. He was, however, killed by Maol Mhuire, son of Aodh Mac Suibhne,[371] who then became lord.[372]

During Maol Mhuire's rule, in August of 1569, the MacCleans of Scotland, who were in the service of Ó Néill (Toirdhealbhach Luineach), arrived in Banagh and killed 'Hue Boy Row and eighteen galloglas more'.[373] In 1581 Maol Mhuire himself was slain fighting under Ó Domhnaill (Aodh) against Ó Néill (Toirdhealbhach Luineach), when the latter defeated the Cinél Conaill at Kiltole, near Raphoe. Also slain in this battle were Maol Mhuire's sons, Murchadh and Toirdhealbhach Meirgeach and many others of his kin.[374]

The rule of the next lord, Maol Mhuire Óg, son of Maol Mhuire, lasted only a year – he was slain in 1582 by a party of Scots while attending a meeting between Ó Néill and Ó Domhnaill on the shores of Lough Foyle.[375] He was succeeded by Brian Óg, son of Maolmhuire Mór (lord of Banagh, who died in 1535).[376] He, in his turn, was slain in 1586 by Niall Meirgeach son of Maol Mhuire (lord of Banagh who died in 1581), who was next to rule, but Niall, like his predecessors, did not rule for long and was killed on St Brigid's day in 1588 by Donnchadh son of Maol Mhuire Meirgeach (lord who died in 1564), at Derryness,[377] an island off the coast of the parish of Inishkeele in the barony of Boylagh.

In 1590 while Aodh Ruadh Ó Domhnaill was still imprisoned in Dublin Castle his half brother, Domhnall, made an attempt to wrest the lordship of Tír Conaill from his ageing father, Aodh. Aodh Ruadh's mother, An Inghean Dubh Nic Dhomhnaill, mustered Ó Dochartaigh, a large army of Scots and the Mac Suibhne branches of Na Tuatha and Fanad to oppose him, as she wanted the lordship for her own son, Aodh Ruadh. Donnchadh, however, who was now lord of Banagh, took Domhnall's side, as did Ó Baoighill, and on the fourteenth day of September the opposing forces met near Glencolumbkille, where Domhnall's forces were defeated and Domhnall, himself, killed at Derrylahan near Teelin harbour.[378] In 1592 Aodh Ruadh was at liberty and Donnchadh, who was back in favour, attended his inauguration the same year at Kilmacrenan.[379]

In September 1596 it was reported that ten Spanish ships had arrived in Banagh and that Aodh Ó Néill, lord of Tír Eoghain, had gone to meet them.[380] In June 1600 we hear that Spanish and French ships came daily there 'with all manner of relief, to the comfort of the rebels'.[381] However, in April of 1601, Donnchadh was sending signals that he wanted to join the English and help expel Aodh Ruadh from Tír Conaill.[382] In the autumn of that year Mac Suibhne's Castle had fallen to the English, but was later recaptured by Ó Domhnaill.[383] In November, with Aodh Ruadh out of Tír Conaill, Donnchadh submitted to Niall Garbh Ó Domhnaill, who was acting on behalf of the English.[384] We hear little else of him until the beginning of 1608 when he was one of the jurors who indicted Ó Néill and Ruaidhrí Ó Domhnaill, earl of Tirconnell, after their flight from Rathmullan in 1607.[385] Later in the year the English authorities had reports that he was plotting to help restore the earls to their lands[386] and that he had attacked the ward of Donegal.[387] In November he was in prison for having joined Sir Cathair Ó Dochartaigh's uprising[388] and in 1609 he was arraigned for having entered 'Calebegg with sixty or eighty men' the day that Cathair Ó Dochartaigh burned Derry. The jury would not find him guilty, however, and he was acquitted. At this time the English could report that the only people of account left in Tír Conaill were the 'McSwynes'.[389]

In the subsequent plantation of Donegal, Donnchadh received 2,000 acres in the barony of Kilmacrenan.[390] A son of his, 'Hugh Mc. Donnogh bane Mc. Swyne' and others were renting the half-quarter of Mullagh in the Rosses in 1633, 'meere Irishmen, whoe are not of English or British descent.'[391] Donnchadh, himself, died about this time.[392] Donnchadh's eldest son, Niall Meirgeach, is probably the 'best MacSwyne' who was killed in a skirmish near Killybegs by a settler force under Andrew Knox in 1641.[393]

Niall Meirgeach is not listed in the Books of Survey and Distribution, but the lands held by his son, Donnchadh Óg, in Dore, now in the parish of Gweedore, were held forfeit after the Rising.[394]

Ó Baoighill: O Boyle

The Ó Baoighill family, a branch of the Cenél Conaill, were originally lords of Cloghineely in north-west Donegal,[395] of Tír Ainmhireach, which comprises the modern barony of Boylagh,[396] and of Tír Boghaine, later the barony of Banagh in the south-west of the county:[397]

> Cloch Cinn Fhaoladh na ngeileach,
> Is Tír áloinn Ainmireach,
> do-chím go colgdha an cuire,
> Is Tír mborbdha mBághuine.
> Ag sin cuid na clógh sotla,
> tír Ó mBaoighill mbélchorcra.[398]

The earliest references to the name in the annals are from the twelfth century – in 1131 Garbánach Ó Báegill was slain in the Curlew mountains when Conchobhar Mac Lochlainn was defeated by the Connachtaigh, and in 1137 we read of the death of a Bishop Ó Báegill.[399]

In 1202 a number of the Uí Báegill slew Ó Dochartaig, lord of Ard Miodhair, because of his plundering of churches[400] and in 1212 Gilla Fiaclach Ó Báegill drove off cattle belonging to people of Cenél Eógain who were under the protection of Ó Tairchirt, lord of Clann Sneidgile, who himself was killed in the fray.[401] Who this Gilla Fiachlach was it is impossible to tell, for the annals are full of names which give little information about those who bear them. For instance in 1222 a Tadg Ó Báegill, who is described as the 'splendour of the north of Ireland, died',[402] in 1251 Cellach Balb Ó Báegill killed Gilla Críst Ó Breisléin, lord of Fanad,[403] and in 1259 we read that an unfortunate Sidraid Ó Báegill was killed by his own *derbfine* or 'true kin'.[404]

Máel Ruanaid Ó Báegill, lord of the Trí Tuatha, was slain in battle against Áed Buide Ó Néill at Desertcreaght in county Tyrone, in which

Ó Domnaill (Domnall Óc), king of Tír Conaill, was defeated and killed in 1281.[405] The first inkling in the annals that there were different branches of Ó Baoighill at this time is when we read that Cellach Ó Báegill, another lord, was slain in the same battle.[406] Later on, in 1284, Dubgall Ó Báegill lord of Cloghaneely (in the Trí Tuatha) was slain by the people of Ó Maíl Gaíthe,[407] and in 1343, a year in which Domnall Dub Ó Báegill helped to depose Niall Ó Domnaill, king of Tír Conaill, the lord of Tír Ainmhirech, Aindíles Ó Báegill was slain at Aghawoney in a battle between rival factions of the Ó Domnaill family.[408] It may have been this Aindíles' son, Lochlann, who was slain in battle in Breifne between different Ó Ruairc factions in 1349.[409]

In 1360 Maol Ruanaidh Ó Baoighill, son of An Cammhuinéalach, lord of the Trí Tuatha, 'a man illustrious for his hospitality, nobleness, wisdom, conquests and protection, died'.[410] With him the lordship of Ó Baoighill in the Trí Tuatha came to an end, with the conquest of that territory by the Clann tSuibhne.[411] After that the annals refer only to the Ó Baoighill *clann* in Boylagh and Banagh, and no territory is appended to the name of any lord of the name. We can assume from this that subsequent to 1360 there was only one Ó Baoighill lord in Tír Conaill.

In the fifteenth century Ó Baoighill had a castle at Baile Uí Bhaoighill (Ballyboyle) on the north side of Donegal Bay which is described much later in 1601 as the chief residence of 'O'Boyle'.[412] The castle was taken by Domhnall, son of Ó Domhnall (Neachtain), in 1440 when it was left unguarded, and money, clothing and armour were stolen. However, Ó Domhnaill himself retook the castle and returned it to Ó Baoighill.[413]

The succession in the lordship of Ó Baoighill becomes less uncertain towards the end of the fifteenth century. In 1485 Toirdhealbhach Óg, son of Toirdhealbhach Mór Ó Baoighill, resigned and his son, Niall, took his place.[414] Toirdhealbhach Óg himself died in 1489.[415] Niall's brother, Toirdhealbhach, was killed when thrown from a horse while riding on the ridge of Murvagh in south Donegal in 1490, and in 1495 his son, Tadhg, was killed at Sligo fighting beside Ó Domhnaill against the Uí Ruairc and the Uí Chonchobhair of Connacht.[416]

In 1502 Niall Buidhe, brother of Toirdhealbhach Óg, was lord of Banagh and we are told that he and his sons were slain in battle by the brothers of the previous chief, Niall, son of Toirdhealbhach Óg.[417] In 1509 Éamann Buidhe, the ruling Ó Baoighill, was slain in the dark of night at Loughros by the cast of a javelin thrown by Conchobhar Óg Ó Baoill.[418] Another Ó Baoighill lord was killed in most unusual circumstances in 1536. This time Niall Ó Baoighill was with Ó Domhnaill (Aodh Dubh), who had pitched his camp between the rivers Drowse and Duff to watch out for the invading army of

Ó Conchobhair. Both Ó Baoighill and Ó Domhnaill's son went out to reconnoitre and each mistaking the other for the enemy they came to blows in the dark, resulting in Ó Baoighill's death.[419]

One of the most tragic stories concerning the family at this time was that of the savage deaths of two brothers, Niall Ruadh and Conchobhar, both sons of the ruling Ó Baoighill, who were at odds with one another. Niall went to Loughros to seek out his brother who lived there and, on arriving, hid at night in the nearby church of Saint Seanchán. In the morning Conchobhar climbed a hill near the church, whereupon Niall rushed to attack him. Conchobhar, who had no one with him who could bear arms, fled along Loughros strand. When Niall overtook him Conchobhar gave him a blow from a weapon which left him prostrate, and continued his flight across the sands, although he was wounded. Niall then told his companions to pursue his brother and when they caught up with him at a neighbouring lake they knocked him down with stones and then killed him with their weapons. When they returned to Niall he was already dead. According to the annals, this dreadful event was the cause of great sorrow in Tír Conaill. The tragedy may have been related to the inauguration of Domhnall son of Niall Ó Baoighill the same year.[420] Another poignant entry, in 1576, tells us that Siubhán Óg, the daughter of Toirdhealbhach Ó Baoighill, was drowned in 1576 while learning to swim in the Srath Buidhe river in the parish of Inishkeel.[421]

In 1591, Toirdhealbhach, the ruling Ó Baoighill, died and was buried in Donegal.[422] About the time of Aodh Ruadh Ó Domhnaill's escape from Dublin Castle in December 1591 English forces were billeted in Ó Baoighill's castle at Ballyboyle, which was situated 2,000 paces west of Donegal, as well as in Donegal Abbey, from where they terrorised the neighbouring countryside. When confronted with Aodh Ruadh's growing power, however, they gladly gave up their positions and returned to Connacht in February of 1592.[423] In May of the same year Ó Baoighill was one of the lords who was present at Aodh Ruadh's inauguration as Ó Domhnaill at Kilmacrenan.[424] This was apparently Tadhg Óg (son of Tadhg) who died in 1607.[425]

In 1601 the English governor at Lough Foyle, near Derry, Henry Docwra, was writing to the privy council that 'O'Boyle' wished to surrender and 'come in',[426] but there is no evidence that he did at this time. Some years later it was stated that in 1606 Ruaidhrí Ó Domhnaill, Earl of Tirconnell and Ó Baoighill had gone aboard the ship of one Gawen More, and asked if it were fit to sail for France or Spain.[427]

By the time of the plantation of Ulster Tadhg Óg was dead and his son Toirdhealbhach Ruadh, 'Tirlagh O'Boyle', son of 'Honora Bourk', widow of Ó Baoighill, was granted lands in the barony of Kilmacrenan, far from his father's patrimony.[428] In Nicholas Pynnar's survey of the planted lands in 1619 'Tirlagh', who at the time of the original grant was only a child, was still in possession of his lands in the parishes of Clondahorky and Tullaghobegley.[429]

In 1611 a servitor, Captain Paul Gore, is reported to have 'erected a fair stone house out of the ruins of O'Boyle's castle upon the sea' at Ballyboyle.[430]

By the year 1622 Toirdhealbhach Ruadh was back in Ó Baoighill territory, in Kiltoorish, in the parish of Iniskeel where he had English and Irish tenants. His house in Kiltoorish came to the notice of the authorities as a refuge for outlaws and for meetings with Spaniards, and he was imprisoned in Lifford in 1628. He was active in the uprising of 1641, along with his son, Toirdhealbhach Óg, and his brother Tadhg Óg.[431]

The ancient enmity between Cenél Eoghain and Cenél Conaill caused jealousy among the insurgents in Donegal and most ignored or deserted the Ulster commander, Eoghan Ruadh Ó Néill, especially in 1647 and 1648. Toirdhealbhach Ruadh and his son Toirdhealbhach Óg, however, remained loyal to Eoghan Ruadh. Toirdhealbhach Óg was slain at the battle of Scariffhollis in 1650.[432] It is uncertain what became of Toirdhealbhach Ruadh after the Rising but his lands were held forfeit because of his part in it.[433]

In the census of 1651 'Teage O Boyle' is listed as *titulado* in seven townlands including Mulvagh and Samagh[434] and 'Torlagh O Boyle' in Loughros and adjacent townlands, all holdings in traditional Ó Baoighill territory.[435] Forty-one families of the name are counted for the barony of Boylagh and Banagh[436] and fifteen for the barony of Kilmacrenan in the Census.[437] In the Hearth Money Roll for Donegal (1665) most taxpayers of the name listed are in the parishes of Inishkeele, Templecarn, Clondahorky, Killybegs, Glencolumbkille and Kilcar.[438]

O Breisléin: O Breslin, Bryce

The Ó Breisléin family, a branch of the Cenél Conaill[439] are first mentioned in the annals in 1168 when we read that Conn Ó Breisléin, lord of Fanad, was killed by the son of Mac Lochlainn, and that Inishowen was spoiled in vengeance.[440] In 1213 Donn Ó Breisléin, lord of Fanad, was slain by his own people,[441] and in 1261 another Donn, also lord of Fanad, avenged the murder of sixteen distinguished clergy by killing Conchobhar Ó Néill, the perpetrator of the crime.[442] It may have been this Donn, no longer described as lord of Fanad, who was slain in 1263 by Domhnall Ó Domhnaill in the bishop's house at Raphoe.[443] About this time the lordship of Ó Breisléin in Fanad came to an end when the family were ousted by the Clann tSuibhne of Scotland.

791

According to the early sixteenth century *Leabhar Chlainne Suibhne*, Eoin Mac Suibhne, the youthful grandson of Máel Muire an Spáráin, of what is now Castle Sween in Scotland, while on a visit to Ireland with his foster-father, put in at Ceann Maghair Átha in Fanad and while there was asked by Ó Breisléin to eat at his house at Dún an Chairbrigh. Ó Breisléin's intent was to murder Eoin because he feared that his lordship was in danger from the Scots, but in the subsequent fray at Dún an Chairbrigh Ó Breisléin and his household were slain. After this (post-1263), the lordship of Fanad passed to the Mac Suibhne family.[444]

The Ó Breisléin family, like other families who had lost political power, later adopted a learned profession,[445] and we next hear of them in 1322 with the death of Petrus Ó Breisléin, chief judge of Fermanagh.[446] Among other entries in the annals relating to the family are the deaths of Eoghan, son of Petrus, in 1447, Tadhg in 1478 and Eoghan Óg in 1524, all of them chief judges to the Mág Uidhir kings of Fermanagh.[447] In the text *Mc Guidhir Fhearmanach* there is an actual account of a judgement given by Ó Breisléin, sometime in the thirteenth century, in a case involving the tribute owed by Ó Flannagáin of Tuath Rátha to Mághnas Mag Uidhir, king of Fermanagh. After the judgement Ó Breisléin was accused of partiality because the Ó Flannagáin family, it seemed, had their origins in Fanad![448]

As well as being chief judge to the king of Fermanagh, Ó Breisléin is also mentioned as being airchinneach of Derryvullen in the barony of Tirkennedy in that county.[449]

Sir John Davies, attorney general of Ireland, who took an active part in the plantation of Ulster, in a letter to Lord Salisbury, mentions meeting 'O Brislan' in Fermanagh, whom he describes as 'a chronicler and principal brehon of that country'. Davies wanted to find out about the rents that had been due to Mág Uidhir out of his mensal lands. Ó Breisléin, who was 'aged and decrepid', finally, with much reluctance, took a scroll 'out of his bosom where he did continually bear it about him'. The scroll was then translated for Davies and returned to Ó Breisléin.[450]

In September of 1610 Davies officiated at an inquisition held at Lifford where another O Breslin, this time of Donegal, is mentioned as one of the three *airchinnigh* of Inishkeele.[451] John O'Donovan, in 1835, describes how in his own time the senior member of 'the O'Breslin house' attended the *turas* on Inishkeele island near the mouth of Gweebarra. Here O Breslin sat at a place called Saint Conall's bed and praying in Latin, held up the Bearnán Chonaill, the Saint's bell, of which he was the hereditary keeper, for the pilgrims to kiss. When the pilgrimage was stopped by the parish priest, O Breslin moved to Glengesh outside Ardara and his son Conall sold the bell to a Major

Nesbitt sometime before 1835. It is interesting what O Donovan has to say about the sale: 'Some say that Connell, the son of Michael O'Breslin had no right to dispose of this bell as others contend with him for the seniority of the chieftainship.'[452] This, if correct, is an interesting survival of early Irish law in the nineteenth century!

None of the family received grants in the plantation of Ulster. In 1659 there are eight families of the name numbered for the barony of Boylagh and Banagh and nowhere else in Donegal.[453] Five are listed in Fermanagh.[454] In the Hearth Money Roll (1665) three tax-payers of the name are listed for the parish of Inishkeele.[455]

Ó Brolcháin: O Brillaghan, Bradley

The Ó Brolcháin family were of the Cenél Eógain and claimed descent from Suibne Menn, the Northern Uí Néill high-king who died in 628.[456] The earliest reference in the annals to the surname is in 1086, when Máel Ísu Ó Brolcháin died, a 'learned senior of Ireland, a paragon of wisdom and piety, as well as in poetry and both languages'.[457] Máel Ísu has left us some beautiful Middle Irish verse including the well-known bilingual *Deus meus, adiuva me*,[458] a poem to Saint Michael the Archangel,[459] and a poem on an old and treasured psalm-book that he had lost and found again.[460]

He was born in Inishowen, and educated in the monastery of Both Chonais which is likely to have been in the vicinity of Gleneely or Culdaff.[461] He was later a member of the monastic community of Armagh, and was probably the author of *Homilarium*, a collection of sermons in Latin.[462] In 1095 Máel Ísu's son Áed, a monastic chief lector, died of plague in 1095.[463] Máel Coluim Ó Brolcháin, bishop of Armagh, died in Derry[464] and in 1139 his kinsman, Máel Brigde, also bishop of Armagh died.[465] In 1150 Flaithbertach Ó Brolcháin, abbot of Derry, made a visitation of Cenél Eógain – which included Inishowen – and received tribute from its people in horses and cattle, as well as a ring and battle-dress from Muirchertach Mac Lochlainn, king of Aileach.[466] He was made a bishop (or a mitred abbot) and arch-abbot of all Columban foundations in Ireland in 1158.[467] Flaithbertach is remembered as a great builder. In 1162 he and Muirchertach Mac Lochlainn, king of Aileach, demolished about eighty houses in Derry so that the area of church sanctuary could be better defined.[468] In 1163 he constructed a large lime kiln in Derry in twenty days,[469] and in 1164 the building of the Tempul Mór or 'Great Church' of Derry was completed by him and by Muirchertach Mac Lochlainn. In the same year he was offered the abbacy of Iona by the community there but was prevented from accepting it by Mac Lochlainn and the archbishop of Armagh.[470] He died in Derry in 1175.[471]

In 1213 Finn Ó Brolcháin, steward of Domnall Mór Ó Domnaill, king of Tír Conaill, was killed with an axe by Muiredach Ó Dálaig, a poet, while collecting the king's tribute in lower Connacht. Ó Domnaill pursued Muiredach through Clanrickarde, Thomond, and Dublin, until the poet finally was compelled to flee to Scotland.[472]

There are few other references to the name in early sources after that. Flann Ó Brolcháin was chosen as abbot of Kells in 1220 by the Cenél Eógain against the wishes of the monastic community there, but was ousted the same year.[473] Two centuries later 'Solomon' Ó Brolcháin was professed as an Augustinian canon in Derry,[474] and in 1425 'Sitrig' Ó Brolcháin is mentioned as having been vicar of Culdaff.[475]

Twenty-three families of the name are numbered for Inishowen and eight for the barony of Kilmacrenan under the anglicised form of O'Brillaghan in the census of 1659.[476] The later form, Bradley, which is an English name, is unfortunate.[477]

In 1665 Eoghan Ó Brolcháin was a resident in the parish of Culdaff, with others of the surname living in Moville, Clonmany, and as far distant as Glencolumkille.[478]

Ó Canannáin: O Cannon, Canning

The history of the Ó Canannáin family has been largely forgotten, despite the fact that they produced more than twenty kings of Tír Conaill between the first half of the tenth century and the death of the last king of the name, Ruaidrí, in 1247. It is even more surprising that their genealogy is not included in the early seventeenth century Ó Cléirigh *Book of Genealogies*, although that of their kinsmen and their rivals for the kingship, the Uí Maíl Doraidh, is.[479]

The family take their name from Canannán, a ninth or tenth century local king who was fifth in descent from Flaithbertach, Cenél Conaill king of Tara.[480] Canannán himself is described as a 'brave and generous chieftain' and one whom the famous Munster poet, Flann mac Lonáin, was urged to visit.[481] Their original territory would seem to have been in the most northerly tuath of Tír Áeda (Tirhugh), that is, Mag Seired.[482]

Ruaidrí ua Canannáin, probably a grandson of Canannán,[483] is the first of the name to be mentioned as king of Cenél Conaill and is first so described in 937.[484] In the year that Muirchertach mac Néill Glúndub, Cenél Eógain king of Ailech, was killed in battle against the Vikings, Ruaidrí seized his chance and invaded Cenél Eógain. In the ensuing battle of Tracht Muga the dominant Cenél Eógain were defeated and their *rígdamna* (or heir-apparant to the kingship), Máel Ruanaid mac Flainn, killed.[485] Having established his supremacy in the North, Ruaidrí marched into Meath, where he defeated Congalach mac Maíl Mithig of

Síl nÁedo Sláine, king of Tara, and billeted part of his army on him.[486] In 945 at Slane he again defeated Congalach and his Viking allies from Dublin.[487] In 948 after defeating Congalach in Meath and later in Brega he was proclaimed king of Ireland.[488] His reign was short-lived: he remained at Muine Brocáin in Meath for six months, but was killed there in battle against the Vikings at the end of that time.[489] Congalach died in 956 and according to the *Annals of Inisfallen* he and Ruaidrí were kings of Tara for twelve years *inter se*.[490]

Most of the subsequent entries in the annals for the next three centuries deal with the family's warfare with the family of Ó Maíl Doraid,[491] their kinsmen and their rivals for the kingship of Tír Conaill, and with the Cenél Eógain of Inishowen and Tír Eógain, the dominant power in the North.[492] In 965 at Formael, Máel Ísu ua Canannáin was slain in battle with Cenél Eógain. In 1093 Áed Ó Canannáin was blinded by Domnall ua Lochlainn, king of Aileach, and in 1103 the reigning Ó Canannáin was driven from the kingship by the same Domnall.[493] Ruaidrí Ó Canannáin, king of Tír Conaill, was slain by Máel Ruanaid Ó Cairealláin of Mag Itha in 1135, after which the Cenél Conaill inflicted great slaughter on the Cenél Eógain.[494]

Three Ó Canannáin kings of Tír Conaill are mentioned as having been slain by their own people: Muirchertach in 962, Flaithbertach in 999 and Domnall in 1083.[495] Int Athchléireach Ó Canannáin was killed by Ó Báegill and the Cenél Conaill in 1160 when his house was burned around him. This was in revenge for the killing of two of the Ó Máil Doraid family who were under the protection of the clergy of Cenél Conaill.[496] (The reader is directed to the section under Ó Maíl Doraidh below for more on the strife between these two families who for three centuries disputed the kingship of Tír Conaill.)

We read of the death of Ruaidrí Ó Canannáin in 1188, sometime king of Tír Conaill and 'Rioghdamhna Ereann', on the bridge of Sligo, at the hands of Flaithbertach Ó Maíl Doraid.[497] According to Professor Cannon it was this Ruaidrí who, as king of Tír Conaill, refused to submit to Henry II of England as lord of Ireland in 1171; however by 1181 it is Flaithbertach Ó Maíl Doraid who is called king of Tír Conaill in the annals.[498] Some authorities claim that it was Ruaidrí who founded the Cistercian abbey of Assaroe in 1178, but this is disputed by the *Annals of the Four Masters*, which clearly states that his rival, Flaithbertach Ó Maíl Doraid, was the founder in 1184.[499]

After Ruaidrí's death no Ó Canannáin regained the kingship of Tír Conaill until 1247. In that year the reigning Ó Domnaill king, Máel Sechlainn, was killed in battle against the one time justiciar of Ireland, Maurice fitzGerald, who had led an army to Assaroe on the Erne. After Máel Sechlainn's death another Ruaidrí Ó Canannáin took the kingship according to the *Annals of Ulster*, but the *Annals of the Four Masters* says that he was given it by Maurice.[500] The following year Maurice banished Ruaidrí and gave the kingship to Gofraid Ó Domnaill; Ruaidrí with the help of the Cenél Eógain marched against Gofraid but was slain in the attempt.[501] However, the following year, in 1249, Niall Ó Canannáin wrested the kingship from Ó Domnaill for a time.[502] In 1250 he was taken prisoner by Maurice fitzGerald, who was now Gofraid's ally, and was later killed trying to escape.[503] After that date the family of Ó Canannáin does not merit one single mention in any of the annals.

It is not until the seventeenth century that we meet the *clann* again in contemporary sources, when five of the name were pardoned by Queen Elizabeth for 'rebellion'.[504] In 1603 'Donal' and 'Conor O Cannon' were likewise pardoned and described as 'natural followers' of Ruaidhrí Ó Domhnaill,[505] brother of Aodh Ruadh, who had died in Spain in 1602. None of the family received grants in the plantation of Ulster. In the rising of 1641 'Dermot O Cannon' is mentioned as one of the leading insurgents from the barony of Kilmacrenan.[506] In the census of 1659 eight families of the name are counted for the barony of Boylagh and Banagh[507] and nine for the barony of Kilmacrenan.[508] In the Hearth Money Roll (1665) Uí Chanannáin are listed for the parishes of Clondavaddog, Tullaghobegley, Kilmacrenan and Tullyfern in the barony of Kilmacrenan, and Inver in the barony of Banagh, among others.[509]

Ó Cléirigh: O Clery, Clarke

Most of what we know concerning the history of Donegal families in the later Middle Ages, and often beyond, comes to us from the writings of the Ó Cléirigh family, a learned professional family, whose patrons were the Ó Domhnaill kings of Tír Conaill. The family themselves were not of Donegal origin, but could rightly claim to be as royal as their patrons. They were, according to their own genealogies, descended from the kings of the Uí Fiachrach Aidni in south County Galway, and traced their ancestry back through the famous Guaire, king of that territory, who died in 663, and who was remembered ever after by the learned classes for his patronage of poets and learned men.[510]

The first mention of their eponymous ancestor Cléirech is in the year 887 when Máel Fábail, son of Cléirech and king of Uí Fiachrach Aidni died.[511] Cléirech's great-grandson, Comaltán, king of Uí Fiachrach Aidni (obit 976), was the first person we know of to use Ó Cléirigh as a fixed surname,[512] thus making it one of the oldest recorded surnames in Europe. Besides being kings of Aidne, the family also produced churchmen, for instance Eógan Ó Cléirig, archbishop of Tuam, who died in 967.[513]

Shortly after the Norman invasion of Ireland the Uí Chléirigh were dispossessed by the de Burgos, and some of them moved north to their kinsmen the Uí Fiachrach Muaide, in Tirawley in north-east Mayo. Little is heard of them after that time until the fourteenth century, when the young Cormac Ó Cléirigh went from Tirawley to Tír Conaill, where he first stayed with the monks of Assaroe who 'loved him for his education and good morals, for his wisdom and intellect'. Niall Garbh Ó Domnaill, who died in 1348, was king of Tír Conaill at the time and his ollamh, or chief man in learning, was Matha Ó Sginginn. Ó Sginghin had no son, but only a daughter, whom Cormac married. They had a son, Giolla Brighde, who in turn had a son, Giolla Riabhach, who at his death in 1421 was described as 'a learned historian'. Giolla Riabhach's son was Diarmaid na tTrí Sgol, 'of the Three Schools', to whom Niall Ó Domhnaill, king of Tír Conaill, granted the lands of Creevagh in the parish of Kilbarron.[514] Two of Diarmaid's poems have come down to us which deal with the capture of Niall Garbh by the English in 1434 and his subsequent death in 1439 in the Isle of Man.[515]

Tadhg Cam was Diarmaid's son and at his death in 1492 he is described as ollamh to Ó Domhnaill in literature, poetry and history.[516] Tadhg Cam, himself, had three sons, Tuathal, Giolla Riabhach, and Diarmaid, who all built stone houses in Kilbarron. Besides having other estates the family were freeholders of part of the lands of Assaroe Abbey.[517] Giolla Riabhach died in 1527 and is described as head of the family, i.e. Ó Cléirigh, and as being adept in history, poetry and literature.[518] Little is known of his progeny,[519] and it is the descendants of his brothers Tuathal and Diarmaid who made the Ó Cléirigh family of Tír Conaill one of the most famous and most revered of the learned dynasties of Ireland.

Tuathal Ó Cléirigh died in 1512.[520] Among his great-grandsons were three of the best known of the name – Conaire, Maol Mhuire, or Father Bernardín, a Franciscan, and Brother Micheál, who, before he entered the Franciscan order, was called Tadhg an tSléibhe. These three were brothers and two of them, Conaire and Micheál, worked on the monumental compilation, *Annála Ríoghachta Éireann*, more commonly known as the *Annals of the Four Masters*.[521] Of the three brothers, Brother Micheál was the giant, and his output was truly astounding, considering the difficulties under which he worked.

Micheál was born probably in the last decade of the sixteenth century. He became a Franciscan brother and in 1626 was sent from Louvain to Ireland by the guardian of the Irish monastery there, Father Aodh Mac an Bhaird, to collect material on Irish saints. While in Ireland he remained for most of the time at the Monastery of Donegal which was then not actually on the site of the ruined monastery in the town of Donegal, but at Bundrowes on the Donegal-Leitrim border.[522] Among his manuscript compilations were the *Réim Ríoghraidhe*,[523] which contains a list of Irish kings and the genealogies of Irish saints, the *Leabhar Gabhála*, a pseudo-history which tells the history of the different peoples who invaded Ireland before, and including, the Gaelic peoples,[524] and of course, the *Annals of the Four Masters*. His kinsman, Cú Choigcríche, son of Diarmaid Ó Cléirigh, also worked with him on the *Annals*. The great work was begun in January of 1632 and completed in 1636 in the Monastery of Donegal.[525] Brother Micheál left Ireland again in 1637, and died in Louvain in 1643.

Much of the period 1586-1602 in the *Annals of the Four Masters* is taken from the life of Aodh Ruadh Ó Domhnaill which was written by Lughaidh, son of Mac Con Ó Cléirigh of Sliocht Diarmada.[526] Lughaidh was also a poet and took part in that curious poetic debate between northern and southern parts called *Iomarbhágh na bhFileadh* or 'Contention of the Poets', to which he contributed four poems.[527] He was, no doubt, the same 'Lewys O Clery' who was appointed as one of the jurors in an inquisition held at Lifford in 1609 just before the Plantation of Ulster to determine which lands in Donegal belonged to the Church and which to the Crown.[528] He is also most probably the 'Loy O'Cleary' who with 'Shane O'Cleary' and nine others were later granted 960 acres in the precinct of Doadh and Fanad in the Plantation.[529]

Lughaidh's son, Cú Choigcríche, 'a mere Irishman, and not of English or British descent or sirname' held land from William Farrell in the barony of Boylagh and Banagh in 1631 and 1632, but was forced to relinquish his tenancy in the latter year.[530] He moved with other Tír Conaill families to Ballycroy in the barony of Erris in county Mayo, taking his manuscripts with him.[531]

Among the manuscript compilations attributed to Cú Choigcríche now in the Royal Irish Academy are the *Topographical Poems* of Seaán Mór Ó Dubhagáin and Giolla na Naomh Ó hUidhrín,[532] the former's work being often cited in this article, and the famous *Book of Genealogies*.[533] The latter work begins with the genealogy of Philip V of Spain and goes back in time honoured fashion to Adam.[534] The inclusion of Philip's genealogy is, no doubt, a tribute to the aid afforded by Spain to the Irish lords, including Aodh Ruadh Ó Domhnaill, during the Nine Years War, and afterwards.[535] It must also be remembered that the Gaelic Irish traced their descent from Míl of Spain.[536] As Séamus Pender points out in his introduction to the work, precedence is given to Cenél Conaill, and within Cenél Conaill, to the family of Ó Domhnaill, patrons of the Uí Chléirigh.[537]

Cú Choigcríche's will, much of which is indecipherable, is to be found pasted to a page of the R.I.A. manuscript containing the *Genealogies*. The will is dated 8 February, 1664, and the extract here quoted makes for poignant reading: *Fágbhaim an mhaoin dob annsa liom dar chuires am sheilbh isin saoghal (mar atá mo leabhair) ag mo dhias mac, Diarmaid, agus Seaan. Benaid a ttarbha eistibh gan milleadh [agus do] reir a riachtanais, agus tabhraid a radharc agus a ngnathughadh do chloinn Cairbre* [i.e. his brother] *mar iad féin ...* 'I bequeath the property most dear to me that ever I possessed in the world, namely my books, to my sons, Dermot and John. Let them copy from them without injuring them, whatever may be necessary for their purpose, and let them be equally seen and used by the children of my brother Carbry as by themselves ...'.[538]

According to John O'Donovan, Cú Choigríche's son, Diarmaid, had a son, Cairbre, who moved to the parish of Drung in county Cavan. Cairbre had a son, Cosnamhach, who was born in 1693 and died in 1759. Cosnamhach had one son, Pádraig, who married Anne, daughter of Bernard O Gowan of Lara, in county Cavan. Their second son, John, went to live in Dublin in 1817, taking with him the *Leabhar Gabhála, Beatha Aodha Ruaidh Uí Dhomhnaill,* and the *Book of Genealogies* and *Topographical Poems* mentioned above. All of the manuscripts containing these works are attributed to Cú Choigcríche, John's ancestor.[539] They are now in the Royal Irish Academy.[540] Another important Ó Cléirigh manuscript once in John O'Clery's possession is National Library Ms. G. 50, which contains early poetry such as the *Amra Coluim Cille.* By far the most important works in the manuscript, however, are poems attributed to Blathmac, son of Cú Brettan, which can be dated to the eighth century according to the late James Carney, and which are not known to us from any other source.[541]

In a letter to John O'Donovan in 1842, John's son, John, told how his father came to lose his treasured manuscripts. He lent five of them to Edward O'Reilly, and when the latter died John senior discovered, too late, that four of them were listed in a sales catalogue – the fifth had already been sold – and although he signed an affidavit that he had only *lent* his books to O'Reilly, the manuscripts were bought by the Royal Irish Academy. John, junior, continues in his letter: 'Little did Cucogry think that these very books, on which he set so high a value, as seen by his own will, would ever, by any means, pass out of the hands of his descendants.'

John O'Clery, the elder, died on 28 December 1846, at 10 Hamilton Row in Dublin. He himself was a 'good scholar and scribe' according to O'Donovan,[542] but the only employment he would appear to have had was a humble position in Ringsend Road gas works.[543] Of the descendants of his son, John, we know nothing at present.[544]

There is no mention of any Ó Cléirigh landholders either in the *Books of Survey and Distribution* or in the census of 1659. In the census, nine families of the name are counted for the barony of Tirhugh, the ancient homeland of the family.[545] In 1665 there are four Ó Cléirigh householders listed for the parish of Kilbarron.[546]

Ó Dochartaigh: O Dogherty

The Ó Dochartaigh family were a branch of Cenél Conaill and traced their descent from Dochartach, who was ninth in descent from Conall Gulban.[547] They were also known as Clann Fiamhain from Dochartach's grandfather, Fiamhan.[548] We know nothing of either Dochartach or Fiamhan.

The earliest mention of the surname in the annals is at 1180 when Aindíles Ó Dochartaig died in Derry and his son was slain by Mágnas Ó Cellecháin.[549] Who this father and son were remains a mystery, but clearly they were of some importance – compared to other leading families such as Ó Gallchobhair early references to the name in the annals are scarce. On the death of Flaithbertach Ó Maíl Doraid, Echmarcach Ó Dochartaig broke the bloody hold which the Uí Chanannáin and the Uí Maíl Doraid had on the kingship of Tír Conaill by taking it in 1197. Echmarcach's reign was short-lived, however, and he was killed a fortnight later opposing the Norman, John de Courcy, who had plundered Inishowen.[550] In 1199 Domnall Ó Dochartaig, lord of Cenél Énna and Ard Midair, in the barony of Raphoe, died,[551] which is the first indication we have of where the homeland of the *clann* was before their removal to Inishowen. Cenél Énna lay between Lough Foyle and Lough Swilly, in the Lagan, between Lifford and Letterkenny.[552] Ard Midair lay west of that towards Lough Finn.[553] In 1203 Domnall Carrach Ó Dochartaig lord of Ard Midair was slain by the Uí Báegill after he had plundered churches.[554] It is interesting that the entry here in the *Annals of Ulster* refers to him as king of Tír Conaill at his death, while the *Annals of the Fours Masters*, which is reluctant to call any local potentate king in the post-Norman period, calls him *riogh-thaoiseach Árda Miodhair*, 'royal chief of Ardmire'.[555]

Conchobar Ó Dochartaig, lord of Ard Midair, died in 1252.[556] Two important developments took place after his death which led to Ó Dochartaigh rule in Inishowen. The first was the ending of the Mac Lochlainn kingship of Cenél Eógain, which included Inishowen, in 1241,[557] and the second was the occupation of the peninsula by the Normans and the building of the great castle of Greencastle in 1305 by Richard de Burgh 'the Red Earl'.[558] By the time Domnall Ó Dochartaig, lord of Ard Miodhair and Tír Énna died in 1342,[559] Norman power had come to an end in Inishowen.[560] The entry regarding Domnall's death in the *Annals of Ulster* is significant for it says that he was *almost lord of Inishowen*: *'uair is bec nach raibhi tighernus Innsi-hEoghain [aige]*. The same annals are unusually full in their praise of him and claim that few lords in Ireland had more subjects or a greater cavalry than he had.[561] His son Seán, who is described as lord of Ard Midair, helped to depose Ó Domhnaill, Niall mac Aodha, in 1343, and to set up Áenghus Ó Domhnaill in his place.[562] In 1380 the ruling Ó Dochartaigh was killed in battle while involved in another power struggle within the Ó Domhnaill camp.[563]

Conchobhar an Einigh Ó Dochartaigh at his death in 1413 is the first of the name to be called lord of Inishowen as well as of Ard Midair, 'a man full of generosity and general hospitality to the wretched and the poor ...'[564] although three of his sons are described as lords of Ard Midair, but not of Inishowen. These were Domhnall[565] from whom, through his son, Brian Dubh, descended the main branch of the family, that of Elagh,[566] and from whom through his son, Eachmharcach, the Greencastle branch;[567] and Seán Balbh, from whom descended the Inch and Buncrana branches.[568] The Doagh branch is very early, descending from Toimilín, most likely to have been the brother of the lord of Ard Midair, Domnall, who died in 1342.[569]

On Domhnall mac Conchobhair's death in 1440 two of the family were nominated as Ó Dochartaigh, Brian Dubh, Domhnall's son and his nephew, Aodh, son of Seán Balbh.[570] This would indicate that there were now two lordships, one of Ard Midair, and one of Inishowen, and that the Ó Dochartaigh lordship was firmly established in Inishowen. This is borne out much later by an entry in the *Annals of Ulster* which says that Aodh Carrach son of the western Ó Dochartaigh was slain by Gofraidh Ó Catháin, 'western' here meaning Ard Midair.[571] In the same year that the two lords were nominated, Neachtain Ó Domhnaill, who no doubt resented Ó Dochartaigh ambitions, attacked the castle of Culmactraine in the south of Inishowen.[572]

After the death of Brian Dubh, son of Domhnall in 1496 it is clear that Ó Dochartaigh was now a subject lord of Ó Domhnaill, for the annals tell us: *Ó Dochartaigh (Brian mac Domhnaill) d'écc agus Ó Domhnaill (Aodh Ruadh) do ghairm tighearna ina ionad do Sheán ua nDochartaigh.*[573] (Neither Brian nor Seán are called lords of Inishowen in the annals, but their brother Eachmharcach is so styled when he died in 1526.)[574]

In the year of Seán's death in 1511 and the accession of his nephew, Conchobhar Carrach, son of Brian Dubh, Art Ó Néill, lord of Tír Eógain, invaded Tír Conaill and took hostages from Conchobhar.[575] It must be remembered that Inishowen was part of Cenél Eógain territory, that most of the leading families there, like that of Mac

Lochlainn were themselves of the Cenél Eógain and that the Ó Néill rulers of Tír Eógain naturally laid claim to it.[576] However, that claim was dropped in 1512 when Ó Domhnaill, Aodh mac Aoidh Ruaidh, plundered Tír Eógain and forced Art Ó Néill to give up all claims he had on Inishowen,[577] thus clearly demonstrating that Ó Dochartaigh was his subject lord. This agreement with Ó Néill was confirmed by charters in 1514 after hostilities had broken out again with Ó Domhnaill being the victor.[578] In 1522 in another war with Ó Néill, Ó Dochartaigh is called Ó Domhnaill's loyal follower, along with Ó Baoighill, Ó Gallchobhair and Clann tSuibhne.[579]

Conchobhar Carrach was succeeded by his uncle, Eachmharcach, who died in 1526, after which a contention arose about the succession. An outsider, Gearalt, of the Doagh branch, none of whose members had ever held the lordship of Inishowen, was finally chosen,[580] but not to everybody's satisfaction, for in 1537 Gearalt's son, Niall, was killed by Ruaidhrí, son of Feilim Ó Dochartaigh, of the main branch of Elagh.[581] On Gearalt's death the lordship returned to the Elagh branch where it remained until 1608.[582] Even after Gearalt's death in 1540 the enmity between the two branches continued, and in 1543 Ruadhraighe and Seán, two sons of Feilim, who had succeeded Gearalt, murdered the latter's son, Cathaoir. This deed was speedily dealt with by Mághnas Ó Domhnaill[583] who wished to display his own authority over Feilim and Inishowen. Feilim died in 1556[584] and was succeeded by his son, Seán Mór.

In October 1566 a garrison of English soldiers was established at Derry and at Culmore some miles along the Foyle to the north. Seán Mór provided the garrisons with provisions, including cattle, and helped to defeat Seán an Díomuis Ó Néill of Tír Eógain when he attacked the English there the same month.[585] In the ongoing hostilities between Ó Néill and Ó Domhnaill Seán suffered at the hands of Toirdhealbhach Luineach Ó Néill's Scottish mercenaries in 1579, when they carried off 3,000 cattle from Inishowen.[586] Seán Mór died in 1582, and his son Seán Óg was elected in preference to Cathaoir, brother of the dead lord, which resulted in the different factions going to war.[587] Seán Óg, had married a daughter of Seán an Díomuis Ó Néill, and one of his sons by this marriage was the famous Cathaoir, last lord of Inishowen.[588] In 1585 along with other lords of the North, he attended a parliament in Dublin[589] and in 1588 he is listed as one of those lords who had surrendered their lands to Queen Elizabeth I and been regranted them.[590] In 1588 when he received reports that ships of the Spanish Armada had arrived in Inishowen he sent word to Richard and Henry Hovenden, who were in charge of a garrison at Burt Castle, that 700 Spaniards had arrived at Kinnago, where 200 or 300 had perished.

Seán Óg played a tight game, wanting to save the Spaniards but fearful of offending the English. He actually blamed Mac Suibhne [na dTuath?] for having directed the Spaniards to Inishowen. In any case the Spaniards were attacked by the English near Elagh, Ó Dochartaigh's main residence, stripped naked and many were slaughtered. Those that managed to get away were helped by Ó Dochartaigh, but his involvement in the whole affair is unclear. Later in the year he was imprisoned by Lord Deputy Fitzwilliam, who had demanded Spanish treasure but got none. He was not released until 1590.[591]

Seán Óg did not attend the inauguration of Aodh Ruadh Ó Domhnaill at Kilmacrenan in 1592, and for this disloyalty was taken prisoner and forced to submit to the new lord of Tír Conaill.[592] He remained loyal, perhaps reluctantly, to Aodh Ruadh until his death in January, 1601.[593]

Aodh Ruadh Ó Domhnaill then had Feilim Óg, who was Seán Óg's brother, inaugurated[594] which infuriated the fosterers of Seán Óg's son, Cathaoir. Cathaoir's fosterers' were Aodh Buidhe Mac Daibhid and his brother Feilim Riabhach and they approached Sir Henry Docwra, the English governor of Derry, on their foster son's behalf. Docwra, who mistrusted the Mac Daibhid *clann,* reluctantly agreed to support the young Cathaoir, realising that Feilim Ó Dochartaigh had declared for Ó Domhnaill against Elizabeth, and that Cathaoir, who was a prisoner of Ó Domhnaill, had promised to submit, along with his fosterers. The following summer Cathaoir was released by Ó Domhnaill through the guile of Aodh Buidhe mac Daibhid and on his return to Inishowen was well received. He was then styled Ó Dochartaigh by Docwra.[595] Cathaoir remained loyal to the English, was knighted, and in 1603 he visited King James I in London. The same year he was granted all lands that had been granted to his father Sir Seán Óg with the remainder to his brother, Sir Seán, and his brother Ruaidhrí.[596]

In 1606 Sir Henry Docwra surrendered the governorship of Derry to George Pawlett. A man who proved unpopular with everyone including his own soldiers, Pawlett wrote to the lord deputy, Chichester, that Cathaoir was preparing for revolt, a charge which Cathaoir denied.[597] In 1608 Cathaoir was foreman of a jury that indicted the earls, Ruaidhrí Ó Domhnaill and Aodh Ó Néill, after their flight from Rathmullan.[598] In April of the same year as a result of a grave insult to his person by the governor, he surprised Derry, burned it and Pawlett was slain. Soon afterwards a proclamation was issued against Cathaoir and his fosterer, Feilim Riabhach, and by June, Cathaoir had fled Inishowen. When help from Ó Gallchobhair was not forthcoming, Cathaoir left Glenveagh, where he was in hiding, and on 5 July he was overcome and slain at Kilmacrenan.[599] His lands were held forfeit,[600] and his wife, Mary Preston, daughter of Viscount Gormanstown, was held under arrest in Dublin.[601] She was later given a pension of £40 per annum.[602] In May of 1609 Cathaoir Ó Dochartaigh's lands were granted to Sir Arthur Chichester.[603]

In an inquisition taken at Derry in November, 1602, the following Ó Dochartaigh gentlemen are listed: 'Hugh Boy McCahir' and 'Averkagh McShan', both of Greencastle, 'Dwaltagh McHugh' in Buncrana, 'Shane' in Glannoganell, 'Shan McDwalty' in Gleneely, 'Brian McTirlogh Chy' in Malin, among others.[604] In another inquisition, in November, 1603, the following Ó Dochartaigh gentlemen are mentioned: 'William' of Dungrennon and 'Ferdoragh McCahir' of Termon Neile.[605]

Only one proprietor of the name is mentioned in the *Civil Survey,* as having been in possession in Inishowen in 1640 – 'Richard Oge O Dogherty' of Kenogh in the parish of Clonca.[606] In the census of 1659 among those listed as *tituladoes* in Inishowen were: 'Rory' and 'Phelomy' in the parish of Desertegney;[607] 'Cahair, Thomas' and 'Rory' in the parish of Clonca;[608] 'Gerauld' and 'Cahair' in the parish of Donagh;[609] Conn in Clonmany.[610] In all there are over two hundred families of the name noted for the peninsula, by far the most numerous of any *clann*.[611] On the other hand there are only sixteen numbered for the barony of Raphoe, the original homeland of the family, and none for the barony of Kilmacrenan.[612] The Hearth Money Rolls list more than one hundred and thirty-taxpayers of the name![613]

In 1989 Dr Ramón Ó Dochartaigh of Cádiz in Spain was recognised as head of the family by the Chief Herald. He is a direct descendant of Cathaoir Ó Dochartaigh's brother, Seán.[614] In 1790 Dr Ó Dochartaigh's ancestor, John, a minor, with his two brothers were sent to Spain, where John became a naval officer. The three brothers were granted arms by the chief herald's predecessor in 1790 about the time of their departure from Ireland.[615]

Ó Dubhthaigh: O Duffy

The earliest references in the annals to the name Ó Dubhthaigh are found in Connacht, almost all in an ecclesiastical context. For instance, in 1172 a synod of the clergy of Ireland was convened at Tuam by Ruaidrí Ó Conchobair, the high-king, and Cadla Ó Dubthaig, archbishop of Tuam.[616] In 1223 another high churchman, Dubthach Ó Dubthaig, abbot of Cong, died.[617] The earliest mentions of the Ó Dubhthaigh family in Donegal are late, and we cannot be certain that the family there are related to the Connacht family of the name. However, it is interesting to find that in Donegal the Uí Dhubhthaigh are again mostly found in an ecclesiastical context. They were *airchinnigh* in the parish of Culdaff, according to an inquisition at Lifford in 1609. A branch of the family were also *airchinnigh* in the parish of Templecrone.[618]

Many of the family were in holy orders. In 1463 Domhnall Ó Dubhthaigh is mentioned as the late rector of Clonca. In the same year 'Patrick' Ó Dubhthaigh, the actual rector, is described as an open fornicator, a perjurer and guilty of simony with regard to the collation of the vicarage of Moville.[619] He was later deprived of his living.[620]

In 1602 'O'Douthie' of Inishowen, head of his *clann*, was 'pardoned' by the English authorities.[621] In the census of 1659 six of the name are numbered for the barony of Kilmacrenan[622] and six for Inishowen.[623] In the Hearth Money Rolls (1665) the name is found in the anglicised form of O'Dowey in the parishes of Tullyfern and Lettermacaward, among others in the diocese of Raphoe, as well as in the parish of Culdaff.[624] However 'Brian *O'Duffy*' is also listed in the same source for the parish of Clonca.[625]

Ó Duibh Dhíorma: O Dooyeearma, MacDermot

The Ó Duibh Dhíorma family were a branch of the Cenél Eógain[626] and were lords of the An Bhréadach, in English Bredagh, which lay in east Inishowen. The placename is still preserved in the Bredagh river which flows into the sea at Moville, and in Bredagh Glen through which it flows.[627] The surname, unfortunately, is now rendered MacDermot – the name of a family with which it has no connection – and this was already happening when John O Donovan visited the district in 1835.[628]

The earliest mention of the name in the annals is in 1043 when Gilla Mo Chonna ua Duib Dírma, about whom we know nothing else, died *in pace*.[629] Later, in 1122, Áed Ó Duib Dírma, lord of Brédach and 'head of the hospitality of the North of Ireland', died the same year as his brother Domnall.[630] There is no mention of the family holding the lordship of the territory until this date. In 1167 Muirchertach Ó Duib Dírma, king of Fardrum, a man who is highly praised by the annalists, was killed in the middle of Moville by Donnchad Ó Duib Dírma and the people of An Bhréadach.[631] The reason for his death is unknown, but it is interesting to note that his kingdom was Fardrum and not An Bhréadach. Fardrum, or Tardrum, which originally stretched from Greencastle to Shrove at Inishowen Head is now confined to the townland of Eleven Ballyboes outside Greencastle.[632] A small kingdom indeed! In 1196 after the death of Muirchertach Mac Lochlainn, king of Cenél Eógain, the kingship was taken by Áed Méith Ó Néill of Telach Óc.[633] Áed invaded Mag Itha in 1198 where Ó Duib Dírma was killed fighting on behalf of the rival Cenél Conaill,[634] no doubt because of his enmity towards the usurping Ó Néill.

In 1452 when Inishowen was firmly under Ó Domhnaill control, Neachtain Ó Domhnaill, lord of Tír Conaill, was murdered by his nephews, Domhnall and Aodh Ruadh, after which war broke out about the succession between Domhnall and Neachtain's son, Rudhraighe.[635] Domhnall was inaugurated in 1454 but was seized by Ó Dochartaigh and imprisoned at Inch, an island on the Swilly, which was guarded by, among others, Cathal Ó Duibh Dhíorma. Rudhraighe, having mustered an army, burned the door and stairs of the castle, whereupon Domhnall implored Cathal Ó Duibh Dhíorma to release him from his fetters. This he did, and Domhnall went to the top of the tower of the castle and taking a stone hurled it down on Rudhraighe, killing him, and so he retook the kingship of Tír Conaill.[636] No doubt Cathal was duly rewarded by Ó Domhnaill, as he saw fit!

After that date the Uí Dhuibh Dhíorma sank into obscurity because of the rising power of the Ó Dochartaigh family in Inishowen, especially in the Fardrum region, where a branch of Uí Dhochartaigh had settled in Greencastle.[637] There is little mention of Ó Duibh Dhíorma in English sources. 'Owin O Dughierma' was granted a pardon during the reign of Elizabeth I but we know nothing of his status.[638] In the census of 1659 there are thirty-five families of the name listed for Inishowen under the form of 'O Dermond'.[639] In the Hearth Money Roll (1665) the name is found mainly in the original homeland, about the parish of Moville.[640]

Ó hEarcáin: O Harkin

The Ó hEarcáin family were descended from Dallán, son of Eógan, son of Niall Nóigiallach, and their original homeland was in Bredagh in Inishowen.[641] They were one of several *airchinnigh* in the parish of Clonca.[642] In Bishop Montgomery's survey of Derry diocese about 1606, the airchinneach is named as 'John O'Harkan'.[643] In the papal registers is a mandate in 1419 to confer the rectory of Clonca on 'Solomon' Ó hEarcáin, if found fit,[644] and in 1455 in the same source we learn of the death of 'Roger' Ó hEarcáin.[645]

Domhnall Ó hEarcáin of Inishowen received a pardon from the English authorities in 1602, no doubt for 'rebellion'.[646] In October 1608 Brian Ó hEarcáin made a deposition regarding the rebellion of Cathaoir Ó Dochartaigh.[647]

In the census of 1659 there are twenty-one families of the name numbered for Inishowen.[648] In the Hearth Money Rolls most house-holders of the name are found in Clonca including 'Shan O'Harken' and 'Patrick O'Harken'. One, 'Owen', is found as far away as the parish of Iniskeele.[649]

Ó Firghil: O Friel

The earliest reference to Ó Firghil in the annals is in 1261, when

Conchobar Ó Firghil, along with fifteen others of the most distinguished clergy of Cenél Conaill were slain in Derry by Conchobar Ó Néill of Cenél Eógain, a deed that was later avenged by Donn Ó Bresléin, lord of Fanad.[650] In 1299, another Ó Firghil cleric, Fergal, bishop of Raphoe, 'the most celebrated man of his time for charity, humanity, piety and benevolent actions' died and in 1328 we read of the death of Gilla Adamnáin, coarb or successor of Saint Adamnán at Raphoe.[651] But it is with the Columban foundation of Kilmacrenan[652] that Ó Firghil is especially associated. There they were *airchinnigh* and responsible for the inauguration of the Ó Domhnaill kings of Tír Conaill and of Mac Suibhne Fánad.

The Mac Suibhne family before their removal from Scotland to Ireland in the late thirteenth and early fourteenth centuries had the elected Mac Suibhne inaugurated at Iona by Colum Cille's successor there. When they settled in Tír Conaill they gave the task of inauguration to Ó Firghil 'when they were not at enmity with one another, and they had power', instead of having the ceremony performed at Iona. According to *Leabhar Chlainne Suibhne* a Mac Suibhne could only be truly inaugurated in Colum Cille's precinct, in other words, at Kilmacrenan.[653] Ó Firghil, at the time of the writing of the *Leabhar* (ca. 1540) got five marks for every Mac Suibhne proclaimed there.

In 1581 Kilmacrenan was plundered by a raiding party of Cenél Conaill after which they were cursed by Bishop (sic) Ó Firghil.[654] In consequence of this Aodh Ó Domhnaill, lord of Tír Conaill, suffered defeat in battle at the hands of his nephew, Con Ó Domhnaill and Ó Néill (Toirdhealbhach Luineach).[655]

In the summer of 1592 at a gathering in Kilmacrenan when some, but not all, of the heads of the ruling families of Tír Conaill attended Sir Aodh Ó Domhnaill, their lord, it was decided that the ailing Ó Domhnaill should relinquish his rule to his son, Aodh Ruadh. The *Annals of the Four Masters* tells us what occurred on this occasion:

> This resolution was universally applauded by all, and accordingly adopted, for Ó Firghil the erenagh was sent for; and he inaugurated Hugh Roe chief of the country, by order and with the blessing of his father; and the ceremony of conferring the name was legally performed and he styled him O'Donnell on the third day of May.[656]

The last Ó Domhnaill to be inaugurated by Ó Firghil at Kilmacrenan was Niall Garbh, son of Con, who had allied himself with the English against Aodh Ruadh Ó Domhnaill. This was in 1603, and Niall was proclaimed there in defiance of the English.[657] How seriously this inauguration was taken by the people of Tír Conaill is shown by a subsequent entry in the *Annals of the Four Masters* where he is just referred to as Niall Garbh Ó Domhnaill.[658] In the same year 'Clement' and 'Hugh Oge' Ó Firghil were pardoned by Queen Elizabeth.[659]

None of the name received a grant in the plantation of Ulster. In the census of 1659 there are seven families of the name numbered for O Friell and nine for O Ferill in the barony of Kilmacrenan, which is interesting, in that it shows that metathesis in the first syllable had already begun in the early seventeenth century.[660] In the Hearth Money Rolls (1665) the name is listed for the parishes of Kilmacrenan, Clondavaddog, Clondahorky, Mevagh and Leck.[661]

One of the registers at the Genealogical Office contains the pedigree of Jacobus O Friell, gentleman. The date of the entry in the folio is 1744 which was certified by William Hawkins, Ulster king of arms, and later certified by George Newport, archbishop of Armagh. It further certifies that Nicholaus O Friell is brother to Jacobus, or James. The genealogy is traced back through six generations to Gildusius, or Giolla Dé, Ó Firghil of Kilmacrenan, gentleman, who would have been alive in 1600. Among the names of the wives mentioned are Catherina O Hegarty, Cecilia O Boyle and Gildusius' wife, Susana O Donell.[662] The Ó Cléirigh genealogies completely ignore this important *airchinneach* family, so we know nothing about Giolla Dé. If he was alive in 1600 then it is most likely that he was present at the inauguration of his lord, Aodh Ruadh Ó Domhnaill, and, who knows, it may have been he who proclaimed the last legitimate lord of Tír Conaill.

The entry in the register is without doubt a copy of the certificate issued by the Office of Arms for the naturalisation and recognition of nobility of an O'Friel by the French Court in 1750 which is listed in the *Grand Armorial de France*.[663] The arms of Jacobus in the Genealogical Office register and in the Grand Armorial contain a sheaf of wheat and a hand holding a cross, the latter being a reference to their function in the proclamation of Ó Domhnaill.[664] Of the progeny of Jacobus, nothing is known.

Ó Gairmleadhaigh: O Gormley

The Ó Gairmleadhaigh family were of the Cenél Eógain and until the twelfth century were lords of Cenél Moein whose territory lay in Mag Itha in the present barony of Raphoe. Their remote eponymous ancestor was Moan, son of Muiredach, son of Eógan, son of Niall Nóigiallach.[665]

The early mention of the family in the annals is in 1084 when Domnall Ó Gailmredaig was slain by Domnall ua Lochlainn, king of

Aileach.[666] In 1119 Conchobhar Ó Gailmredaig, king of Cenél Moéin, was slain by the Uí Dubdai and the Uí Flaithbertaig.[667]

In 1128 Domnall Ó Gailmredaig and the men of Mag Itha entered the house of Fáelán Ó Duib Dara king of Fir Manach and killed him and many of his nobles.[668] Domnall later, in 1143, seized the kingship of Cenél Eógain after the expulsion of Muirchertach Mac Lochlainn, king of Aileach.[669] However, Domnall was ousted two years later and Muirchertach was reinstated as king with the help of the Cenél Conaill,[670] and in 1148 he banished Domnall to Connacht.[671] In 1160 Domnall was killed by Domnall Ó Maíl Ruanaid, king of Fir Manach, at the instigation of Muirchertach.[672] In 1175 the people of Cenél Énna were defeated, and many slaughtered, by Echmarach Ó Catháin and Niall Ó Gailmredaig.[673] In 1177 Niall was slain while escaping from a burning house by Donnchad Ó Cairelláin of Clann Diarmata. At his death he is described as king of Cenél Énna as well as of Mag Itha.[674]

The following year Conchobhar Ó Luinig usurped the kingship of Cenél Moein and Domnall Ó Gailmredaig was forced to flee to Donnchad Ó Duib Dírma in Inishowen. However, after a revolt against Conchobhar's rule, Domnall was restored. He was deposed soon afterwards by his own people, who gave his kingship to Ruaidrí Ó Flaithbertaig. Ó Flaithbertaig's three sons afterwards murdered Domnall, and eight nobles of Cenél Moein.[675] However, in 1179 Amlaim Ó Gailmredaig was king of Cenél Moein, when he was treacherously murdered by Donnchad Ó Cairealláin of Clann Diarmata after the two kings had made peace at the church of Ardstraw.[676]

After 1177 no Ó Gailmredaig was called king of Mag Itha and it is reasonable to assume that it was soon afterwards that they abandoned their territory there and settled east of the Foyle in Ardstraw in present day county Tyrone.[677]

I know of no other early source where the name is found again in a county Donegal context except for the mention in 1419 of the death of 'Dionisius Ogormali', late vicar of Moville.[678]

Ó Gallchobhair: O Gallagher

The Ó Gallchobhair family were a branch of the Cenél Conaill and claimed descent from Gallchobar, who was sixth in descent from the mid-seventh century high king of Uí Néill, Cellach son of Máel Cobo.[679]

One of the earliest references to the name in the annals is in 1022 when Máel Cobo ua Gallchobair, comharba or abbot of Scrín Adamnáin, died.[680] However, most of the references to the family in the annals are late and date to the late fifteenth and sixteenth centuries.

The families were remarkable for the great number of ecclesiastics they produced, many of whom, despite their calling, were fathers of children. For instance Gilla Coimded Ó Gallchobair, 'the Monk', had at least two children, Fearghal, whose son Domhnall, died in 1377[681] and Niocol. Niocol was grandfather of Lochlann Ó Gallchobhair bishop of Raphoe, who died in 1438.[682] Lochlann had sons, one of whom was Domhnall, grandfather of Réamann, vicar of Drumhome in south Donegal, who was himself the father of a son, Cathal Dubh Ó Gallchobhair.[683] In 1469 another Lochlann Ó Gallchobhair, also bishop of Raphoe, was proceeded against for incontinence before John Bole, archbishop of Armagh. He was absolved after penance by direction of Bishop Bole so as 'not to bring a scandal on religion and the episcopal dignity we conceal [his crimes]'.[684] Lochlann died in 1477.[685]

The succession of the Ó Gallchobhair lordship in the fifteenth century is extremely difficult to determine. In 1494 the annals tell us that Uilliam, son of Ó Gallchobhair (Émann) was killed when Aodh Ruadh Ó Domhnaill, king of Tír Conaill, laid siege to Sligo Castle.[686] In 1497 after the defeat of Conn Ó Domhnaill, king of Tír Conaill, at the Curlew mountains, two sons of Tuathal Ó Gallchobhair, Eoin and Toirdhealbhach, were taken prisoner by Mac Diarmada.[687] They were released however the following year, no doubt after a large ransom had been paid.[688] Eoin was father of Éamann, head of his *clann*, who died in 1534.[689]

The next Ó Gallchobhair was Tuathal Balbh, who by all accounts was deeply influenced by the teachings of the church. At his death in 1541 we are told that he imprisoned captives taken in battle rather than having them killed, having heard a sermon in his youth preached by one of the friars of Donegal against the evils of wounding and killing![690]

The sixteenth century had its own share of Ó Gallchobhair churchmen. In 1502, for instance we are told that Art Ó Gallchobhair and Eoin Ó Lóiste, who had contended for the abbacy of the Cistercian monastery of Assaroe, died on the same day.[691] In 1543 we read of the death of Éamann Ó Gallchobhair, bishop of Raphoe, when his bishopric was opposed, why we do not know.[692] But the most famous of these aristocratic divines in the sixteenth century was Réamann Ó Gallchobhair, bishop of Derry from 1569 to 1601.[693] In the autumn of 1588 the English authorities were aware that the Bishop was helping survivors from the Spanish Armada who had landed in Mac Suibhne na dTuath's country[694] and in 1590 in a report to the English authorities in Dublin the archbishop of Cashel, Myler MacGrath, has this to say of him: 'In Ulster there is one Redmond O'Gallagher, bishop of Derry, pope's legate and custos of Armagh, one of three bishops who were in the Council of Trent. He rides from place to place with pomp and ceremony as was the custom in Queen Mary's days.' The archbishop goes on: 'The clergy there have even changed the time according to the pope's new invention. He has been several times before the governors of the land upon protection, and yet he is suffered to enjoy his bishopric these twenty years past or more.'[695] Réamonn is elsewhere described as Ó Domhnaill's 'most traitorous bishop ... who this year [1595] took the profits of the bishopric of Killala.'[696] The English had reason to be wary of the bishop: in 1597, among copies of letters found on 'Fr Bernard O Donnell' was one from Réamonn to the pope asking for help for the Irish nobility in their struggle against England.[697] Réamonn was murdered by English forces in Ó Catháin's territory in 1601.[698]

In 1546 the head of the family was Eoghan mac Éamainn, whose wife was Onóra, daughter of Tuathal Balbh. Together they treacherously killed Domhnall Ó Domhnaill – son of Aodh Dubh, king of Tír Conaill who had died in 1537 – after inviting him to Inis Saimhéir on Lough Erne.[699] This may have been related to the seizure in 1543 of Lifford Castle, the property of Mághnas Ó Domhnaill, king of Tír Conaill by a party of the Uí Ghallchobhair. When Mághnas' son, An Calbhach, recaptured the Castle in 1544 the Ó Gallchobhair faction 'then left the country'.[700]

That there was enmity between some members of the *clann* and Ó Domhnaill (Aodh) is evident in 1567 when, after the defeat of Seán an Díomais by Aodh on the Swilly, a party of Uí Ghallchobhair helped Seán to escape home to Tír Eoghain.[701]

It is difficult to know who succeeded Eoghan but it is probably safe to assume that Eoin, son of Tuathal Balbh, was already chief in 1573 when he was writing to the Dublin authorities in relation to his lord, Aodh Ó Domhnaill.[702] In 1574 he is described as Ó Domhnaill's 'trusty counsellor'[703] and in 1581 there is mention of payment to 'Sir Owen O Gallougher, Knt., ... one of the chief pillars for the stay of the North'.[704] In 1585 Eoin attended a parliament in Dublin with other lords of the North, including Ó Domhnaill (Aodh).[705]

Aodh Ó Domhnaill, however, had an inveterate enemy in another Ó Gallchobhair, Aodh, son of the dean of Raphoe, but reputed to be the illegitimate son of An Calbhach Ó Domhnaill,[706] brother of Aodh. Aodh 'mac an Déccanaigh' had allied himself with An Calbhach's sons in opposition to their uncle's lordship of Tír Conaill and in this way they were helped by Toirdhealbhach Luineach Ó Néill, lord of Tír Eoghain. In 1586 Aodh 'mac an Déccanaigh' slew Alasdrann Mac Dhòmhnaill, son of the Lord of the Isles and brother of An Inghean Dubh, Ó Domhnaill's wife.[707] Two years later An Inghean Dubh had her revenge when she had her brother's killer slain at Mongavlin in the parish of Taughboyne.[708]

Four years after that, in 1592, at the inauguration of Aodh Ruadh, 'Red Hugh', Ó Domhnaill at Kilmacrenan, certain Uí Ghallchobhair did not attend because of the malice they bore the young Ó Domhnaill and his mother.[709] Sir Eoin Ó Gallchobhair himself was not present either, but for a different reason. In the winter of 1588 after the survivors of the Armada had been helped by certain Ulster lords, including Aodh Ó Néill, earl of Tyrone,[710] and Mac Suibhne na dTuath,[711] Fitzwilliam, the lord deputy, journeyed to Tír Conaill in search of survivors and during his time there he had Ó Gallchobhair and Ó Dochartaigh arrested and detained in Dublin, ostensibly as a pledge for the rents of Tír Conaill owed by the two lords.[712] Sir Eoin was not released for over six years, when he died, old and infirm, in 1595.[713] In 1588 his son, 'Owen' had also been a prisoner in Dublin but he managed to escape in January of 1589, without being recaptured.[714]

In the winter of 1601 when Aodh Ruadh Ó Domhnaill had gone with Aodh Ó Néill to meet the Spaniards at Kinsale, the ruling Ó Gallchobhair, Eoghan, son of Seán, kept the castle of Ballymote for Ó Domhnaill. When Ó Domhnaill did not return Ó Gallchobhair dutifully surrendered the castle to his brother, Ruaidhrí, the future earl of Tirconnell.[715]

During the short-lived uprising of Cathaoir Ó Dochartaigh in April of 1608 he was helped in his capture of Culmore Fort, near Derry, by some of the Uí Ghallchobhair,[716] and in June when Cathaoir had retreated to the wilderness of Glenveagh he wrote a letter (in Irish) – one of the last we have written by a Gaelic lord – to Ó Gallchobhair asking for his help. But unknown to Cathaoir, Ó Gallchobhair had already surrendered Lough Eske, which had been Aodh Ruadh Ó Domhnaill's storehouse, to Sir Henry Folliott.[717]

According to the Irish state papers the territory of the Uí Ghallchobhair lay in 'the midland of Tyrconnell', and in Ballakill some eleven miles from Lifford stood a fort where 'Donnell O'Gallocor, one of O'Donnells chief counsellors' lived,[718] and it may have been to this 'Donnell' that Cathaoir Ó Dochartaigh sent his desperate plea.

In 1607 five Uí Ghallchobhair left with the earls from Rathmullan and remained in the Spanish Netherlands.[719] Those that remained at home fared badly in the subsequent plantation of Ulster. The only grants to any of the name was a meagre one in the barony of Kilmacrenan to 'Donnell Ballagh O'Galchor' and a grant of sixty-four acres in Rosgill to 'Farroll McHugh O'Galchor'.[720] 'Torlagh og McOwen O'Gallogher' was proprietor of seventy-seven acres in Beltany in the parish of Tullaghobegley, land which was held forfeit after the rising of 1641.[721] Two leading insurgents of the name in the rising are mentioned as being from Magheroarty, Dubhaltach and Tuathal.[722]

In the census of 1659 fifty-two families of the name are listed for the barony of Kilmacrenan,[723] nineteen for the barony of Raphoe,[724] fifty-one for the barony of Boylagh and Banagh,[725] and twenty-six for the barony of Tirhugh.[726] In the Tax-Money Roll for Donegal (1665) the most numerous Ó Gallchobhair tax-payers listed are in the parishes of Inishkeel, Drumhome, Conwal, Tullaghobegley, Mevagh and Kilbarron.[727]

Ó Maoil Doraidh: O Mulderry

Uí Mhaoil Doraidh dá mardais
ní thiocfaid 's do thiocfadais
gan mhoille agus gan mhalldál
'nar ccoinne is Uí Chanannán.

So wrote Seán Mór Ó Dubhagáin in his topographical poems.[728] Seán Mór died in 1372[729] and for him and the annalists of the late Middle Ages the name and fame of the Ó Maoil Doraidh family were but a memory. Their genealogy, although it is included in the Ó Cléirigh *Book of Genealogies* cuts off early at Máel Ruanaid[730] who died in 1027,[731] and it is clearly defective, although ten kings of the name are mentioned by the Four Masters.

The family were descended from Máel Doraid, the eponymous ancestor, who was fourth in descent from Flaithbertach, Cenél Conaill high-king, who died in 765.[732] Their chief stronghold was at Leac Uí Mhaoil Doraidh (Ó Maol Doraidh's Flagstone) at Narrow Water on the Donegal-Fermanagh border at Beleek.[733] According to O Hart they were keepers of the *Cathach* before it passed into the hands of the Ó Domhnaill kings of Tír Conaill, who succeeded them.[734]

The entries for the first two kings of the name reflect the violence of the times: in 960 Óengus ua Maíl Doraid, king of Tír Conaill, was slain by his own people,[735] and in 980 the same fate befell his kinsman Tigernán, also king of Tír Conaill.[736] Until the end of the twelfth century the Uí Maíl Doraid and their rivals, the Uí Chanannáin, fought bitterly for the kingship of Tír Conaill.[737] In 1004 two of the Uí Chanannáin were killed by Ó Maíl Doraid,[738] and in 1037 three of the Uí Mhaíl Doraid were killed by the Ó Canannáin.[739]

In 1026 Máel Ruanaid Ó Maíl Doraid, king of Tír Conaill, went overseas on pilgrimage[740] and died there,[741] a peaceful death compared to that of his son, Domnall, who like so many other kings of the name, was slain in 1032, in this case by the Clann Fiangusa.[742] The feuding between the two rival families continued throughout the eleventh century: for instance in 1061 Domnall Ó Maíl Doraid was slain in battle by Ruaidrí Ó Cannanáin,[743] who was in turn, when king of Tír Conaill, slain by Óengus Ó Maíl Doraid, head of his *clann*.[744]

The last of the family to rule Tír Conaill was Flaithbertach. In 1172, he defeated the Cenél Eógain in vengeance for their having plundered the churches of Colum Cille and Patrick.[745] Four years later, his wife, the daughter of the king of Connacht, Ruaidrí Ó Conchobhair, was slain by the sons of Ó Cairelláin of Clann Diarmata, a branch of the Cenél Eógain,[746] and the following year Flaithbertach was defeated in battle by Conchobar Ó Cairelláin.[747] In 1181 Flaithbertach is described as king of Cenél Conaill. In that year he defeated the sons of the kings of Connacht after which he laid Connacht under tribute.[748] In 1184 he granted the monastery of Assaroe to the Cistercians, although the actual foundation may have been begun by Ruaidrí Ó Canannáin, whom Flaithbertach had supplanted.[749] In 1197 he pursued a party of Normans from the Bann under Rotsel Fitton, after they had despoiled the churches of Derry, and defeated them at Faughanvale, county Derry. He died shortly afterwards, in the same year, aged fifty-nine years and was buried at Drumhome.[750]

After his death Echmarcach Ó Dochartaig took the kingship and although it was shortlived – a fortnight – it broke the hold that the Uí Chanannáin and the Uí Mháil Doraid had on the kingship of Tír Conaill. The family were never again to produce a king of Tír Conaill and quickly sank into obscurity. With the death of Flaithbertach all entries in the annals concerning them cease; they are not mentioned in English sources of the sixteenth and seventeenth centuries, and in the early nineteenth century there is only one householder of the name listed, in the parish of Inver.[751]

Ó Maoil Fhábhaill: O Mulfail, Faul, MacFaul

The family of Ó Maoil Fábhaill were of Cenél Fergusa, a branch of Cenél Eógain.[751a] The earliest mention of the name in the annals is in 1082 when Gilla Críst ua Maíl Fábaill, king of Carraic Brachaide in Inishowen, was slain.[752] Twenty years later, in 1102, another king of Carraic Brachaide, Sitriuc Ó Maíl Fábaill, was with an invading party of Cenél Eógain in Uí Eachach when he was killed at night by a party of the Ulaid.[753] In 1166 Áed Ó Maíl Fábaill, king of Carraic Brachaide, was treacherously slain by Muirchertach Mac Lochlainn, king of Aileach and high-king.[754] The last of the name to be definitely mentioned as king of Carraic Brachaide was Cathalán, who was slain by Ó Déráin in 1199.[755] In 1216 Trad Ó Maíl Fábaill was killed by Muiredech, son of the Great Steward (Mór Máer) of Leamhain in Scotland. Trad is described as king of Cenél Fergusa in north-west Inishowen.[756] After that date the family are no longer mentioned in the annals.

In 1665 Murrogh O'Mulfail was a resident in the parish of Conwal.[757] The name, also in an anglicised from, O'Mullfoyle, is found in the barony of Tirkeeran in county Derry in the Census of 1659.[758] It is likely that many of the *clann* migrated there about 1200.[759]

In the 1820s and 1850s the name is found in Inishowen, anglicised as McFall, McFawl, McFalls, etc.[760]

Ó Maoil Mhoichéirghe: 'O Mulmogheery', Early

The family of Ó Maoil Mhoichéirghe were originally from Inishowen and, like the Uí Maoil Fhábhaill, were of the Cenél Fergusa, a branch of the Cenél Eógain.[761]

The earliest mention of the name in the annals is in 1149 when Muirchertach Ó Maíl Moichéirge, abbot of Uí Briuin Breifne, in counties Cavan and Leitrim, died.[762] The family were *comharbaí* of Druim Lethan, *anglice* Drumlane, in the former county, one of whom, Aodh, was drowned in 1512.[763]

References to the family in Donegal come to us mostly from papal letters. In 1419 there is a mandate to assign the vicarage of Moville to 'David' Ó Maoil Mhoichéirghe.[764] However, in 1430, we learn that he claims to have been unjustly deprived of his living there.[765] In 1455 he, or another 'David', was accused of fornication, simony and perjury.[766] In 1459 there is mention of a 'David' Ó Maoil Mhoichéirghe being a canon of Derry.[767]

In the census of 1659, six families of the name are listed for the barony of Boylagh and Banagh, none for Inishowen.[768] However, in the Hearth Money Roll (1665) there are two householders listed for the parish of Moville, with others in Inishkeele, Desertegny, and Drumhome.[769]

Ó Muirgheasáin: O Morrison, Bryson

In 1609 Donnchadh Ó Muirgheasáin, *anglice* Donnogh O'Morreeson, was described in an English source as 'the abbot's corbe and the busshop [of] Derrie's herenagh' in three quarters, or divisions, of church land in the parish of Clonmany. One of these was rent free to Donnchadh and another three had been given to his ancestors 'whoe in those daies were servaunts of Collumkill'. Ó Muirgheasáin, as *airchinneach*, also collected the dues of the bishop of Derry throughout the Inishowen peninsula.[770]

Considering their importance in Church affairs, it is surprising that most of our information regarding the family comes to us from non-Gaelic sources. Many of the *clann* were in holy orders and in fact all pre-seventeenth century references to them are in this regard. In 1438, for instance, 'Solomon' Ó Muirgheasáin, the rector of Clonca, had died and 'John' Ó Muirgheasáin was in unlawful possession of it, and was to be removed by papal mandate.[771] In 1447 'Henry' Ó Muirgheasáin, rector of the parish church of Clonca was accused of keeping a woman,[772] and in 1470 Comedinus Ó Muirgheasáin, clerk of the diocese of Derry was assigned the rectory of Clonca, notwithstanding his being the son of a priest and an unmarried woman.[773]

In the census of 1659 there are seven 'Omrisane' families listed for Inishowen,[774] a pronunciation, which with the dropping of the prefix, O, explains the anglicised form Bryson.[775] In the Hearth Money Roll (1664) 'Donnell O Morison' of the parish of Clonmany is the only one of the name listed.[776]

Ó Robhartaigh: O Roarty

The Ó Robhartaigh family were particularly associated with the island of Tory in the parish of Tullaghobegley where they were *airchinnigh* and *comharbaí*. At the beginning of the seventeenth century we are told that as part of the rent paid by Ó Robhartaigh to the bishop of Raphoe were 'fortie tercian madders of maulte and thirtie yards of brackan cloath of their owne making soe thin as beinge laid uppon the grounde the grasse might appear through the same ...'. Ó Robhartaigh also held the tenure of Kilultagh and Glosagh in the parish of Tullaghobegley, 'being Collumkillie's land'.[777] Just opposite Tory on the mainland, in the modern parish of Gortahork, is another place associated with the name, Machaire Uí Robhartaigh (*anglice* Magheroarty), 'Ó Robhartaigh's Plain'.[778]

The church in Tory was a foundation of Saint Colum Cille,[779] but the Domnall ua Robartaig mentioned in the *Annals of the Four Masters* as being *comharba* of Colum Cille at his death in 1098 bore the surname Mac Robartaig and was abbot of Kells.[780] It must be borne in mind that *ua* here merely means 'grandson' and is not part of a surname.

According to tradition, a small square castle noted by John O'Donovan in 1835 was built by 'O'Roarty, who was it seems, some time ago powerful on the island'.[781]

In 1542 Brian Dorcha Mac Con Midhe died through the miracles of God and Colum Cille and the curse of Ó Robhartaigh for having dishonoured the 'Crois Mhór' by striking it.[782] The Great Cross was an altar cross kept in Tory. It would appear to have been cased in metal with glass bosses and was reputedly a gift sent by Pope Gregory to Colum Cille.[783]

In 1486 'Edmond' Ó Robhartaigh is named as a possible abbot of Raphoe.[784]

In February of 1603 'Donnell grana O Rowarty', who is described as a natural follower of Ruaidhrí Ó Domhnaill, received a pardon for rebellion.[785]

Of thirty-two families of the name listed in the first half of the last century, twenty-six still lived in the original homeland of Tullaghobegley.[786]

References

1. I should like to thank the former Chief Herald, Mr Dónal Begley, for his encouragement and advice. My thanks also to Ms Margaret Doolan for her typing, and for her vigilance, which saved me from many an orthographic inaccuracy.
2. S. Ó Grianna, *Caisleáin óir* (Baile Átha Cliath, 1976), pp 1-2.
3. An examination of records of the last century, such as the registers of births and baptisms, will verify this.
4. Cf. Ó Grianna, *Caisleáin óir*, p. 55, where in a conversation two men are given their patronymics and one his surname.
5. Myles na Gopaleen (pseud., i.e. Brian Ó Nualláin), *An béal bocht* (Dublin, 1975), p. 25.
6. Very few Donegal families received grants of land in the plantation of Ulster; see Rev. G. Hill, *An historical account of the plantation of Ulster at the commencement of the seventeenth century, 1608-1620* (1877), pp 327-30.
7. *A.U.*, sub anno.
8. S. Pender (ed.), 'The O'Clery book of genealogies' in *Anal. Hib.*, 18 (1951), par. 191.
9. Hogan, *Onomasticon*, pp 221-2.
10. See sections under Ó Maoil Doraidh and Ó Canannáin.
11. None of the Cenél Luigdech are mentioned in the early sources as being kings of Cenél Conaill. Dálach, grandfather of the eponymous ancestor of the Ó Domhnaill family, is described at his death as *dux generis Conaill* (*A.U.²* 870), but this merely means that he was a chief of Cenél Conaill, not 'king of', cf. *A.U.²*, 754 where Loingsech mac Flaithbertaig is described as *rex* ['king'] *generis Conaill* at his death. From Dálach the Uí Dhomhnaill got their tribal name, Clann Dálaigh. For the genealogy of Ó Domhnaill see *Anal. Hib.*, 18, pars. 54-196.
12. For the relationship of Colum Cille to Cenél Luigdech see Byrne, *Irish kings*, p. 258.
13. For the pedigrees of Cenél Conaill see *Anal. Hib.*, 18, pars. 8-300; for those of Cenél Eógain, ibid., pars. 407-92, 523-727. For the conquest of Donegal by the sons of Niall Noígiallach see Byrne, *Irish kings*, pp 83-84: 'We have no trustworthy account of the actual conquest of the north-west Ulster by Conall, Eógan and Éndae ...'
14. Also called Cenél Conaill, see Hogan, *Onomasticon*, pp 217-8, 636.
15. Ibid., p. 464, also called *Tír Eógain na hInnse*, 'T. of the Island', i.e. Inishowen (ibid., p. 637).
16. Ibid., pp 219, 636.
17. *A.U.*, sub anno; for other kings of Cenél Éndai (later Énna), see *A.U.²*, 1011, 1057, 1078.
18. See *A.F.M.*, 1199, and section on Ó Dochartaigh below.
19. *A.F.M.*, sub anno; for Clann Daibhid see *Anal. Hib.*, 18, par. 300.
20. There are, or course, other anglicisations of these surnames; for further variations see the current Irish telephone directory and *An Index of surnames of householders in Griffith's primary valuation and tithe applotment books: county Donegal* (1967). The original Ó has, for the most part, been dropped.
21. For Mac Cailein see W. J. Watson (ed.), *Bardachd Ghaidhlig: specimens of Gaelic poetry 1550-1900* (1959), p. 275. It is notable that *A.F.M.* notes the death in 1573 of the head of the *clann* in Scotland: *Mac Ailin .i. Giolla Epscoip mac Giolla Epscoip ... décc.*
22. Ibid., sub anno.

23. Ibid., sub anno. Balleeghan is in the parish of Raymoghy, barony of Raphoe (*A.F.M.*, p. 1553, note u).

24. Ibid., 1558.

25. Ibid., sub anno; see section under Mac Daibhid.

26. T. W. Moody and J. G. Simms (eds), *The bishopric of Derry and the Irish Society of London, 1602-1705*, i: 1602-70 (1968), p. 27.

27. *Fiants Ire., Eliz. I*, 6655.

28. A. F. O'D. Alexander (ed.), 'The O'Kane papers' in *Anal. Hib.*, 12 (1943), p. 104. 'Beyond the mountains' means west of Barnesmore. As early as 1500 'John Macallen' is mentioned as canon of Raphoe (*Cal. papal letters* 1495-1503, p. 157).

29. *Census Ire.*, p. 61.

30. Ibid., p. 64.

31. N.L.I., Ms. 9583 contains a transcription of the Hearth Money Roll for county Donegal; see The Mac Carthy Mór, 'Index to the 1665 Co. Donegal Hearthmoney Roll' [typescript], pp 15, 16, under McAllen, McCallen, etc.

32. Brian Lacy (ed.), *Archaeological survey of county Donegal* (Lifford, 1983), par. 1539: the translation is 'Fergus MacAllan made this stone.' In R. A. S. Macalister, *Corpus inscriptionum Insularum Celticarum*, ii, p. 117, it is emphasised that *clach* is the Scots-Gaelic form of Irish *cloch*.

33. *Anal. Hib.*, 18, par. 300; see section under Mac Daibhid.

34. The Scottish Clann tSuibhne of Donegal, too, were provided with an early Irish ancestor by the genealogists; see F. Gillespie, 'Genealogy and pseudo-genealogy in early Ireland' in *Aspects of Irish genealogy: proceedings of the 1st Irish genealogical congress* (1992), pp 123-37, for this and other learned fabrications.

35. R.I.A. (*Contributions to a dictionary of the Irish language* (1913-67) = ((*C*)*DIL*), A-C, column 36; F-H, cols. 132-3; E. Knott, *Irish classical poetry* (Dublin, 1960), p. 7.

36. *A.F.M.*, sub anno: Cluain Ferta Brénainn was in the barony of Longford, county Galway (Hogan, *Onomasticon*, p. 263).

37. *A.F.M.*, sub anno. For Cooloorta see ibid., p. 797, note a.

38. *A.F.M.*, sub anno. In 1507 another Mac an Bhaird of Oriel, Giolla Phádraig, was slain (Ibid., sub anno). For the Uí Uiginn see E. Knott (ed.), *The bardic poems of Tadhg Dall Ó hUiginn, 1550-1591*, i (Dublin, 1922), pp xiv-xxxii.

39. *A.F.M.*, sub anno. The reader is referred to P. Walsh, *Irish men of learning: studies* (Dublin, 1947): 'The learned family of Mac an Bhaird', pp 151-9, for more on the family.

40. The poem, 'Leasg an aghuidhsi ar Eas Ruaidh' was edited by Lambert McKenna in *Studies*, 39 (1950), pp 187-92; for Domhnall's death see *A.F.M.*, 1420, and *N.H.I.*, ix, p. 145 for Ó Domhnaill genealogical chart.

41. *A.F.M.*, sub anno. Inishmacadurn, or Rutland Island, lies off the coast of the Rosses (Ibid., p. 1304, note t).

42. Ibid., sub anno. For Ballyshannon castle see Lacy, *Archaeological survey*, par. 1952.

43. *A.F.M.*, sub anno.

44. Ibid., sub anno.

45. In D. Greene (ed.), *Duanaire Mhéig Uidhir* (Baile Átha Cliath, 1972), pp 158-69: 'Trí coin chosnus clú Gaoidheil'.

46. *A.F.M.*, sub anno. Druim Mór is probably the townland of Drumore in the parish of Drumhome (*A.F.M.*, p. 1684, note f).

47. Edited by L. McKenna in *Studies*, 41 (1952), pp 99-104. Aodh Ruadh died in Spain in 1602 (*A.F.M.*, sub anno).

48. Edited by O. Bergin in *Studies*, 9 (1920), pp 565-70.

49. 'Slán agaibh, a fhiora Mumhan', edited by O. Bergin in *An Reult*, i, no. 4 (1925), pp 24-25.

50. Edited by O. Bergin in *Irish Review*, 3 (1913-14), pp 136-9. Máire and Mairgréag, Aodh Ruadh's sisters, were his only surviving siblings (ibid., p. 139).

51. L. McKenna (ed.), *The book of O'Hara: Leabhar Í Eadhra* (Dublin, 1951), pp 112-53, 250-7. Cormac Ó hEádhra was lord of Leyny from about 1581 to 1612 (ibid., pp xxiv-xxv).

52. C. Mhág Craith (ed.), *Dán na mBráthar Mionúr*, ii (Baile Átha Cliath, 1980), p. 153.

53. 'Fúarus iongnadh a fhir chumainn', edited by O. Bergin in *Studies*, 8 (1919), pp 72-76.

54. Mhág Craith, *Dán na mBráthar Mionúr*, p. 153.

55. Edited by T. F. Ó Rathille in *Measgra dánta* (Baile Átha Cliath, 1927), pp 150-5. Donegal Castle was destroyed in 1595 (*A.F.M.*, sub anno).

56. *A.F.M.*, sub anno.

57. 'A fhir shealbhas duit an dán', edited by L. MacKenna in *Studies*, 40 (1951), pp 217-22.

58. Edited by O. McKernan in *Éigse*, 5, part 1 (Samhradh, 1945), pp 8-24. For the descent of Niall Garbh and Conn Óg see *N.H.I.*, ix, p. 145.

59. *A.F.M.*, pp 2401-2.

60. See *Éigse*, 5, part 1, p. 8.

61. *Census Ire.*, p. 48; Lettermacaward parish was in the barony of Boylagh and Banagh.

62. *A.F.M.*, sub annis.

63. Edited by O. Bergin in *Studies*, 8 (1919), pp 255-9: 'Bold is the journey attempted here; long has it been debated; the expedition is equal to a tragic fate; hard is the end of nobility.'

64. *Diomdhach mé an mhacdhacht ríogh*: 'I am dissatisfied with the son of a king' in P. Walsh (ed.), *The life of Aodh Ruadh Ó Domhnaill transcribed from the Book of Lughaidh Ó Cléirigh* (Dublin, 1948), pp 104-17.

65. *A.F.M.*, sub anno.

66. In Walsh, *Life of Aodh Ruadh*, pp 137-48; see P. de Barra and T. Ó Fiaich (eds), *Imeacht na nIarlaí* (Baile Átha Cliath, 1972), p. 26.

67. *O woman that has found the tomb unguarded*, edited by E. Knott in *Celtica*, 5 (1960), pp 161-71; translated by James Clarence Mangan as *O woman of the piercing wail*, in E. Hull, *The poem-book of the Gael* (Dublin, 1913), pp 176-81.

68. The study of Eoghan Ruadh's life is fraught with difficulties: he may or may not have been a Franciscan; there may have been two men of the same name who were contemporaries, see C. McGrath, 'Eoghan Ruadh Mac Uilliam Óig Mhic an Bhaird' in S. O'Brien (ed.), *Measgra i gcuimhne Mhicíl Uí Chléirigh* ... (Dublin, 1944), pp 108-16; Walsh, *Irish men of learning*, chapter xiii: 'The book of O'Donnell's daughter', passim.

69. D. O'Doherty, 'Students of the Irish College in Salamanca' in *Archiv. Hib.*, 2 (1913), p. 29.

70. L. Wadding, *Scriptores Ordinis Minorum* ... (Rome, 1650), p. 179; in his work on the lives of the saint he was helped by Father Patrick Fleming, O.F.M., who on a journey to Rome called on libraries in Clairvaux, Lyons and Bobbio, all the time writing to Aodh; see 'Irish Franciscan historians of Saint Anthony's College, Louvain' by Fr. Felim O'Brien in *I.E.R.*, 32 (July, 1928), pp 115-24.

71. Iohannes Colganus, *Acta santorum veteris et maioris Scotiae seu Hiberniae sanctorum insula* ... (Louvain, 1645).

72. Hugo Wardeus, *Sancti Rumoldi martyris* ... (Louvain, 1662).
73. Colgan, *Acta sanctorum*, preface.
74. *Clú gach fheadhma ar fhuil Chéin* in *Poems on the O'Haras*, edited by L. McKenna (Dublin, 1980), pp 276-85; for Ruaidhrí and his family see ibid., pp xi-xxvii.
75. *Census Ire.*, p. 48.
76. Mac Carthy Mór, 'Index', pp 15, 27.
77. *Anal. Hib.*, 18, par. 717.
78. Hogan, *Onomasticon*, p. 123.
79. *Cal. papal letters*, 1427-47, p. 208.
80. Ibid., 1458-71, p. 299.
81. *A.F.M.*, sub anno; see Sir James Ware, *The works of Sir James Ware concerning Ireland ... containing the history of the bishops of that kingdom ...* i (1739), p. 273.
82. *A.F.M.*, sub anno; Ware, *History of the bishops*, p. 274.
83. *Fiants Ire., Eliz. I*, 6483.
84. *Cal. S.P. Ire.*, 1606-8, p. 583.
85. *Inq. Ult.*, Donagall, 11 – Charles I.
86. *Census Ire.*, p. 53.
87. Mac Carthy Mór, 'Index', pp 16, 18.
88. *A.U.*, index, p. 82.
89. *O.S. letters, Donegal*, 19 Aug., 1835.
90. *A.F.M.*, sub anno.
91. See J. Carney (ed.), *Topographical poems by Seán Mór Ó Dubhagáin and Giolla-na-Naomh Ó hUidhrín* (Dublin, 1943), p. 14, ll. 361-4. For the midland families of Ó Colgan see Fr P. Woulfe, *Sloinnte Gaedheal is Gall* (Dublin, 1923), p. 335.
92. An *airchinneach, anglice* (h)erenagh, in the late medieval period and beyond was a layman who held church lands from a bishop in return for rent, refection and part maintenance of the parish church; see F. Kelly, *A guide to early Irish law* (Dublin, 1988), p. 42, note 26; J. Barry, 'The distinction between coarb and erenagh', in *I.E.R.*, 94 (1960), pp 90-95.
93. Mackolligan, as it is written in the Lifford inquisition of that year; see *Inq. Ult.*, appendix v.
94. *Cal. papal letters*, 1417-31, p. 186.
95. Idem.
96. *Cal. papal letters*, 1427-47, p. 179.
97. Ibid., 1427-47, p. 596.
98. *Cal. S.P. Ire.*, 1625-32, p. 512; cf. B. Bonner, 'MacColgan: airchinneach of Domhnach Mór Mhaighe Tochair' in *Donegal Annual*, 39 (1987), p. 26.
99. The Irish language form of his first name is not found in any contemporary source. However, he may be the S. Mhá Colgan who wrote a poem about 1607 for Toirdhealbhach Ó Néill, grandson of Toirdhealbhach Luineach: 'Rob soraidh an séad-sa soir', edited by C. Mhág Craith in T. O'Donnell (ed.), *Father John Colgan, O.F.M., 1592-1658: essays in commemoration of the third centenary of his death* (1959), pp 60-62; for his life and works see Fr C. Mooney, 'Father John Colgan, O.F.M., his work and times and literary milieu', ibid., pp 7-40; B. Jennings (ed.), *Louvain papers 1606-1827* (1968), passim.
100. See note 71 above.
101. See section on Mac an Bhaird above.
102. Iohannes Colganus, *Triadis thaumaturgae seu divorum Patricii, Columbae, et Brigidae, trium veteris et maioris Scotiae, seu Hiberniae, Sanctorum Insulae, communium patronorum acta, a variis, iisque pervetustis, ac sanctis authoribus scripta ...* (Louvain, 1647).

103. *Census, Ire.*, p. 64.
104. Mac Carthy Mór, 'Index', p. 17.
105. *Cal. papal letters*, 1427-47, p. 99. The parish of Killaghtee is in the barony of Banagh.
106. Ibid., 1427-47, p. 154.
107. Ibid., 1427-47, p. 429.
108. *A.F.M.*, sub anno.
109. Ibid., sub anno.
110. Ibid., 1586.
111. Ibid., sub anno.
112. Ware, *History of the bishops*, p. 275.
113. *Inq. Ult.*, appendix v; see note 92 above.
114. *Fiants Ire., Eliz. I*, 6761.
115. Mac Carthy Mór, 'Index', pp 18, 21, under McCongill, McGongill.
116. *Anal. Hib.*, 18, par. 300.
117. *A.F.M.*, sub anno and note d.
118. Ibid., sub anno.
119. *Cal. S.P. Ire.*, 1600-1, p. 263.
120. Ibid., 1600-1, p. 235.
121. Ibid., 1598-9, p. 423; 1599-1600, pp 33-34.
122. Ibid., 1600, p. 195.
123. Ibid., 1600-1, p. 235.
124. *A.F.M.*, 1600; see also extract from Sir Henry Docwra, 'Narration of his services at Lough Foyle' in *A.F.M.*, pp 2189-91, note y.
125. *Cal. S.P. Ire.*, 1600-1, p. 10.
126. Ibid., 1600-1, p. 95.
127. Docwra's 'Narration' in *A.F.M.*, pp 2236-7; cf. *Cal. S.P. Ire.*, 1600-1, p. 158.
128. Ibid., 1600-1, p. 90.
129. *A.F.M.*, sub anno and Docwra's 'Narration' in *A.F.M.*, pp 2237-8.
130. Idem.
131. *Cal. S.P. Ire.*, 1600-1, pp 191-3.
132. Ibid., 1600-1, p. 218.
133. Ibid., 1600-1, p. 339, but see ibid., p. 363 where Aodh Buidhe is reported to have tricked Ó Domhnaill into releasing Cathaoir.
134. Ibid., 1600-1, p. 375; see ibid., 1600-1, p. 364.
135. Ibid., 1601-3, p. 47.
136. Ibid., 1601-3, p. 171.
137. B. Bonner, *That audacious traitor* (1975), pp 136-7.
138. Docwra's 'Narration' in *A.F.M.*, p. 2321.
139. Bonner, *Audacious traitor*, p. 144.
140. De Barra and Ó Fiach, *Imeacht na nIarlaí*, p. 24, see *A.F.M.* sub anno.
141. *Cal. S.P. Ire.*, 1606-8, pp 485-6.
142. Ibid., 1606-8, pp 505-6.
143. Ibid., 1608-10, p. 8.
144. Ibid., 1608-10, p. 26.
145. Ibid., 1608-10, p. 580.
146. *O.S. letters, Donegal*, 18 Sept., 1835 (par. 110).
147. *Cal S.P. Ire.*, 1600-1, p. 276.
148. Moody and Simms, *Bishopric of Derry*, p. 27; Carrick McCowlin is the present-day Redcastle on the coast south of Moville (Bonner, *Audacious traitor*, p. 86).
149. *Civil Survey*, iii, p. 8.

150. *Census Ire.*, p. 61.
151. Ibid., p. 64.
152. Mac Carthy Mór, 'Index', p. 19.
153. For the pedigree of Mac Duinn Sléibe, kings of Ulaid, see *Anal. Hib.* 18, par. 1789; for convenient chart of the same see *N.H.I.*, ix, p. 132.
154. Byrne, *Irish kings*, pp 124-9.
155. *A.U.*, sub anno.
156. Ibid., sub anno.
157. See below. It is tempting to think that there may have been another family of Mac Duinnshléibhe in Donegal: in *Leabhar Chlainne Suibhne*, Eoin, the first Mac Suibhne to settle in Fanad, had a great-grandson, Eoin, who was also known as Mac Duinn Sléibe; see P. Walsh (ed.), *Leabhar Chlainne Suibhne: an account of the MacSweeney families in Ireland, with pedigrees* (1920) (=*LCS*), par. 17.
158. *A.F.M.*, sub anno.
159. Ibid., sub anno and note f.
160. M. Dunleavy, 'The medical families of medieval Ireland' in W. Doolin and O. Fitzgerald (eds), *What's past is prologue: a retrospect of Irish medicine* (1952), p. 19.
161. *A.F.M.*, sub anno.
162. Ibid., sub anno.
163. Ibid., sub anno.
164. *Cal. S.P. Ire.*, 1509-73, p. 228.
165. *Fiants Ire. Eliz. I*, 6761.
165a. *A.F.M.*, 1602 (p. 2297).
166. *Cal. S.P. Ire.*, 1606-8, pp 257-8.
167. Ibid., 1608-10, p. 463.
168. Jennings, *Louvain papers*, pp 30-31.
169. Jennings, *Wadding papers, 1614-38* (1953), pp 177-8.
170. *A.F.M.*, p. lxvii; see section under Ó Cléirigh for this monumental work.
171. Jennings, *Louvain papers*, p. 88.
172. *Inq. Ult.*, Donagall, 17-Charles I.
173. *Census Ire.*, p. 54.
174. Under the form Wltagh, *Census Ire.*, p. 59.
175. *A.F.M.* 1395, note f.
176. *Inq. Ult.*, appendix v. For the term *airchinneach* see note 92 above.
177. Rev. M. A. Costello (ed.), *De annatis Hiberniae: a calendar of the first fruits' fees levied on papal appointments ... in Ireland, A.D. 1400 to 1535...* i: Ulster (1909) [=De Ann. Hib.], p. 288.
178. *Cal. papal letters*, 1427-47, p. 139.
179. Ibid., 1458-71, pp 536-7.
180. Ibid., 1471-84, p. 604.
181. *De Ann. Hib.*, p. 270.
182. *Cal. papal letters*, 1503-13, p. 273.
183. *Census Ire.*, p. 59.
184. Mac Carthy Mór, 'Index', p. 20.
185. Idem.
186. *Anal Hib.*, 18, par. 300. See section on Mac Ailín above.
187. *A.U.*, sub anno.
188. *A.F.M.*, sub anno. For Clann Ailebra see Hogan, *Onomasticon*, p. 236.
189. See section above on Mac Duinnshléibhe. Both families were settled in the south of the present county.

190. *Inq. Ult.*, appendix v.

191. *Cal. papal letters*, 1458-71, p. 643. For the monastery of Cill Ó dTomhrair see Lacy, *Archaeological survey*, par. 1888.

192. *Census Ire.*, p. 48.

193. Mac Carthy Mór, 'Index', p. 20.

194. See *N.H.I.*, ix, pp 129, 140.

195. For Lochlann's genealogy see the *Book of Leinster*, fol. 338a. Niall died in 919 (*A.U.²*, sub anno).

196. *N.H.I.*, ix, pp 128, 194. Domnall's death is recorded *A.U.²*, 915. For Lochlann's descent from Domnall se the *Book of Lecan*, 56b.

197. *A.U.²*, sub anno, where he is described as son of Máel Sechnaill, the name of Domnall's great-grandson, who died in 997 and who is described in *A.U.* as heir designate of Aileach (*A.U.²*, sub anno). *A.I.*, sub anno 1023, calls Lochlann king of Inishowen at his death. For genealogical chart see *N.H.I.*, ix, p. 128. For discussion see J. Hogan, 'The Ua Briain kingship in Telach Óc' in E. Ua Riain, *Féil-sgríbhinn Eoin Mhic Néill* (Baile Átha Cliath, 1940), pp 425-6.

198. *A.U.²*, sub anno, when Máel Sechnaill mac Domnaill, king of the Southern Uí Néill and high-king led an army into 'Tír Eógain' and burned Telach Óc. For the expansion of the Cenél Eógain into Airgialla territory see Byrne, *Irish kings*, chap. 7 and map on pp 120-1.

199. Hogan, 'Ua Briain kingship', p. 427.

200. 'Of the Island', i.e. Inishowen, see Hogan, 'Ua Briain kingship', pp 422-3.

201. *A.U.²*, sub anno, see Hogan, 'Ua Briain kingship', p. 427.

202. Niall, son of Máel Sechnaill, king of Aileach, died in 1061 (*A.U.²*, sub anno), see *N.H.I.*, ix, for genealogical chart.

203. *A.U.²*, 1062.

204. Ibid., sub anno. For genealogical chart of the Ó Conchobair kings of Connacht see *N.H.I.*, ix, pp 138, 158.

205. Ibid., sub anno: 'in the cemetry of the kings'.

206. Ibid., 1065; Áed was of the Uí Duibinnrecht, a people I know nothing about.

207. Ibid., sub anno. For kings before 1083 see *N.H.I.*, ix, p. 195.

208. Ibid., sub anno. For the Ulaid see Byrne, *Irish kings*, chap. 7 and map on pp 120-1.

209. Ibid., sub anno. For Cenn Corad (Kincora) see Hogan, *Onomasticon*, p. 224.

210. *A.F.M.*, sub anno, cf. *A.U.²*, sub anno.

211. Ibid., sub anno.

212. See *N.H.I.*, ix, p. 192.

213. *A.U.²*, sub anno.

214. *A.F.M.*, sub anno, see *A.U.²*, sub anno.

215. *A.F.M.*, 1101, cf. *A.U.²*, sub anno.

216. *A.U.²*, sub anno: Muirchertach, himself, was not present at the battle; cf. *A.I.*, sub anno.

217. Ibid., sub anno.

218. Ibid., sub anno, cf. *A.F.M.*, sub anno.

219. Ibid., sub anno.

220. Ibid., sub anno.

221. Ibid., sub anno.

222. *A.F.M.*, sub anno: Conchobar met his death through treachery at the hands of the men of Mag Itha (part of the barony of Raphoe – Hogan, *Onomasticon*, p. 522).

223. See *N.H.I.*, ix, p. 129 for Muirchertach, and Niall, who reigned as king of Tír Conaill from 1101 to 1119.

224. *A.F.M.*, sub anno.

225. Ibid., sub anno.
226. Ibid., sub anno, cf. *N.H.I.*, ix, p. 192.
227. *A.F.M.*, 1150.
228. Ibid., sub anno.
229. Ibid., 1154.
230. *A.U.*, sub anno, cf. *A.F.M.*, sub anno.
231. *A.U.*, sub anno.
232. *N.H.I.*, viii, cf. *A.U.*, sub anno.
233. Ibid., sub anno, see section under Ó Brolcháin below.
234. *A.U.*, sub anno; for Templemore see Hogan, *Onomasticon*, p. 631.
235. *A.U.*, sub anno.
236. Ibid., 1166.
237. *A.F.M.*, sub anno, cf. *A.U.*, sub anno; for Ruaidrí's accession to the high-kingship see *N.H.I.*, ix, p. 192. for the genealogy of Áed Ó Néill see F. Gillespie, 'Gaelic Chart 1', in the Genealogical Office, Dublin.
238. *A.F.M.*, 1168.
239. *A.U.*, sub anno. For Muintir Bránáin see Hogan, *Onomasticon*, p. 546. For Máel Sechlainn see *N.H.I.*, ix, pp 129, 195.
240. *A.U.*, sub anno.
241. *N.H.I.*, viii, sub anno; *A.U.*, sub anno. William le Petit was later created lord justice of Ireland (*N.H.I.*, ix, p. 470).
242. *A.U.*, sub anno.
243. For the regnal succession see *N.H.I.*, ix, p. 129.
244. Domnall Mac Lochlainn was king of Tír Eógain in 1232 (*A.F.M.*, sub anno); Domnall Ó Néill was king of Tír Eógain at his death in 1234, after which Mac Lochlainn assumed the kingship (ibid., sub anno).
245. Ibid., sub anno and note g.
246. *A.U.*, 1239.
247. Ibid., sub anno.
248. For the genealogical chart of the Ó Néill kings of Tír Eógain see *N.H.I.*, ix, pp 140-2.
249. Aodh Mac Lochlainn was drowned in 1421 according to *A.F.M.* and in 1431 'Donaldus Maglathlaind' is mentioned as being parish priest of Moville (*De Ann. Hib.*, p. 193).
250. *Cal. S.P. Ire.*, 1600-1, p. 276; see Bonner, *Audacious traitor*, p. 86.
251. Moody and Simms, *Bishopric of Derry*, i, p. 27.
252. *Civil Survey*, iii, p. 7.
253. *Census Ire.*, pp 62, 63.
254. Ibid., p. 64.
255. Mac Carthy Mór, 'Index', pp 24, 25.
256. *O.S. letters, Donegal*, 27 Aug., 1835.
257. For the office of *airchinneach* see note 92 above.
258. *Inq. Ult.*, appendix v.
259. *Anal. Hib.*, 12, p. 104.
260. *Census Ire.*, p. 48.
261. Mac Carthy Mór, 'Index', p. 26.
262. *General index to the townlands and towns, parishes and baronies of Ireland, based on the census of Ireland for the year, 1851* (Baltimore, 1992), p. 99.
263. For the *Cathach* of Colum Cille see F. Henry, *Irish art in the early Christian period* (Dublin, 1965), pp 58-67; R. Ó Floinn, *Irish shrines and reliquaries of the middle ages* (1994), p. 12; A. O'Kelleher and G. Schoepperle (eds), *Betha Colaim*

Cille: life of Columcille, compiled by Manus O'Donnell in 1532 (1918), pp 182-3. For a discussion of the manuscript and its ascription to Colum Cille, see the article on reliquaries by Raghnall Ó Floinn in this volume.

264. *A.F.M.*, sub annis.

264a. *A.U.²*, sub anno, see *N.H.I.*, ix, p. 258.

264b. See Colgan, *Triadis thaumaturgae*, p. 145 for the location of the shrine. For monasteries founded by Colum Cille see J. O'Donovan (ed.), *The martyrology of Donegal: a calender of Irish saints* (Dublin, 1864), p. 151.

265. *New Catholic Encyclopedia* (New York, 1967), ix, pp 216-7, where his name is given wrongly in Irish as Muirchertach, see J. J. Silke, 'Blessed Murray Mac Groarty' in *Donegal Annual*, 40 (1988), pp 75-77.

266. *Cal. papal letters*, 1404-15, p. 36.

267. *Inq. Ult.*, appendix v.

268. Ibid., appendix iv.

269. Mac Carthy Mór, 'Index', p. 21.

270. For the early history of Clann tSuibhne see Walsh, *Leabhar Chlainne Suibhne* [=*L.C.S.*], pars. 1-13. The text deals mainly with the branch of the *Clann* that settled in Fanad.

271. *A.F.M.*, sub anno.

272. *L.C.S.*, pars. 1-2; for the early genealogy of the family see *Anal. Hib.*, 18, par. 336.

273. Cf. E. F. Skene, *Celtic Scotland* (1886-90), iii, p. 339. For the forging of genealogies see F. Gillespie in *Proceedings of the 1st Irish genealogical congress*, pp 133-6.

274. W. D. J. Sellar, 'Family origins in Cowal and Knapdale', in *Scottish Studies*, 15 (1971), pp 21-35.

275. For these 'foreign warriors' see G. A. Hayes-McCoy, *Scots mercenary forces in Ireland, 1565-1603* (Dublin, 1937).

276. *A.F.M.*, sub anno. For Murchad's descent see *Anal. Hib.*, 18, par. 493; for Mac Suibhne genealogies in Ireland see also pars. 336-86, 493-522.

277. Máel Muire is mentioned in a charter in that year (*L.C.S.*, p. xvii).

278. *A.F.M.*, sub anno.

279. *L.C.S.*, pars. 13-17. Domnall Óc died in 1281 (*A.F.M.*, sub anno).

280. *L.C.S.*, pars. 18-23. For Bannockburn (Sruibhshliabh) see *L.C.S.*, pp xxi-xxii. For Ó Maíl Gaíthe's Tuath see *L.C.S.*, p. 141. Tír Boghaine comprised the modern barony of Banagh; see Hogan, *Onomasticon*, p. 635.

281. *L.C.S.*, par. 20-24; for the Trí Tuatha see section under Ó Baoighill.

282. *L.C.S.*, par. 25, and see pars. 26-27 for anecdotes concerning him. For Conchobhar's death see *A.F.M.*, sub anno. Ó Tairchirt was lord of Clann Sneidgile *anglice* Clannelly, west of Letterkenny (Ibid., ii, p. 995, note i).

283. *L.C.S.*, pars. 30-31.

284. *A.F.M.*, sub anno.

285. *L.C.S.*, par. 37; for Kilmacrenan as the Ó Domhnaill inauguration site see section under Ó Firghil below.

286. *L.C.S.*, par. 38; *A.F.M.*, sub anno.

287. Ibid., sub anno, *L.C.S.*, par. 39.

288. Ibid., par. 39; for Ó Domhnaill's defeat see *A.F.M.*, sub anno.

289. *L.C.S.*, pars. 43-45.

290. *A.F.M.*, sub anno; for Castleforward see *A.F.M.*, 1440, note y.

291. *L.C.S.*, par. 46.

292. *A.F.M.*, sub anno, cf. *L.C.S.*, loc. cit.

293. *A.F.M.*, 1461, cf. *L.C.S.*, loc. cit.

294. Ibid., par. 47, cf. *A.F.M.*, sub anno.

295. For Ruaidhrí, Máire Ní Mháille and their family see *L.C.S.*, pars. 49-52.
296. *A.F.M.*, sub anno.
297. See *L.C.S.*, pp xliv-lviii. The manuscript containing the text is now in *R.I.A.*, numbered 24 P 25.
298. For Toirdhealbhach's rule see *L.C.S.*, par. 54. For Domhnall Óg's death see *A.F.M.*, sub anno. For Toirdhealbhach's death see ibid., sub anno. For dating of the writing of the text see *L.C.S.*, p. lviii.
299. *A.F.M.*, sub anno.
300. Ibid., sub anno.
301. Ibid., sub anno.
302. Ibid., sub anno.
303. He is on a list of pledges in Dublin in Aug., 1588 (*Cal. S.P. Ire.*, 1588-92, p. 11). See *A.F.M.*, 1587 for Aodh Ruadh's capture.
304. Ibid., sub anno.
305. Ibid., sub anno.
306. *Cal. S.P. Ire.*, 1600, p. 478.
307. Ibid., 1600-1, p. 223.
308. Ibid., 1600-1, p. 325.
309. Ibid., 1601-3, p. 93.
310. Ibid., 1601-3, p. 262.
311. De Barra and Ó Fiaich, *Imeacht na nIarlaí*, p. 60.
312. *Cal. S.P. Ire.*, 1606-8, p. 556.
313. Hill, *Plantation*, pp 228, 327.
314. Ibid., pp 526-7.
315. Genealogical Office Ms. 70, p. 114, contemporary funeral entry.
316. *Civil Survey*, iii, p. 131.
317. Ibid., iii, pp 129, 130; see Rev. P. Ó Gallachair, 'Tirconaill in 1641', in O'Donnell, *Father John Colgan*, p. 79.
318. *Census Ire.*, p. 58.
319. Ibid., p. 59. Not all of these would be of Mac Suibhne Fánad. Includes families of Mac Suibhne na dTuath.
320. Mac Carthy Mór, 'Index', p. 27.
321. See section under Ó Baoighill. Na Trí Tuatha comprised the parishes of Tullaghobegley, Raymunterdoney, Clondahorky and Mevagh (Hogan, *Onomasticon*, p. 649).
322. *A.F.M.*, sub anno, see *L.C.S.*, xxxiv and par. 61.
323. Ibid., par. 28. Toirdhealbhach an Fhíona died in 1423 (*A.F.M.*, sub anno).
324. *L.C.S.*, par. 61 and p. xxxiv.
325. *A.F.M.*, sub anno.
326. Ibid., sub anno.
327. Ibid., sub anno.
328. Ibid., sub anno.
329. Ibid., sub anno.
330. Ibid., sub anno.
331. Ibid., sub anno; for the Clann Domhnaill (the MacDonnells of Antrim and Scotland) see *L.C.S.*, p. xviii, *Anal Hib.*, 18, pars. 301, 1696-1715; Hayes-McCoy, *Scots mercenaries*, passim.
332. For the most likely succession of Mac Subihne na dTuath in the sixteenth century, see *L.C.S.*, p. xxxiv.
333. *Cal. S.P. Ire.*, 1588-92, pp 43-44.
334. Ibid., 1588-92, p. 63.

335. *A.F.M.*, sub annis.
336. Ibid., sub anno.
337. Ibid., sub anno. He is popularly known as Maol Mhuire an Bhata Bhuí.
338. *Cal. S.P. Ire.*, 1598-99, p. 25.
339. Ibid., 1598-99, p. 130.
340. *A.F.M.*, sub anno.
341. *Cal. S.P. Ire.*, 1600, p. 234.
342. Ibid., 1600, pp 383-4.
343. Ibid., 1600, p. 433.
344. Ibid., 1600-1, p. 335.
345. Ibid., 1600-1, p. 426.
346. Ibid., 1603-6, pp 23-24.
347. Ibid., 1603-6, p. 196.
348. Ibid., pp 1606-8, p. 486.
349. Hill, *Plantation*, pp 327, 526.
350. Ibid., p. 526, note 217.
351. Ó Gallachair, 'Tirconaill in 1641', p. 79.
352. *Civil Survey*, iii, p. 137.
353. *O.S. letters, Donegal*, 5 Sept., 1835.
354. Ibid., *Donegal*, 13 Sept., 1835.
355. *L.C.S.*, par. 20.
356. Hogan, *Onomasticon*, p. 217.
357. *A.F.M.*, sub anno.
358. Book of Ballymote, fol. 77, cf. *L.C.S.*, par. 62.
359. *A.F.M.*, sub anno, cf. *L.C.S.*, p. xxxvii.
360. *Anal. Hib.*, 18, par. 513.
361. *L.C.S.*, par. 20; for the genealogies see *Anal. Hib.*, 18, pars. 376-83, 497-9; for the lords of Boghaine, ibid., pars. 500-14.
362. *A.F.M.*, sub anno.
363. Eoghan died in 1497 (*A.F.M.*, sub anno); see *L.C.S.*, xxxvii-xxxviii.
364. For a description of the Castle see Lacy, *Archaeological survey*, par. 1926; see *Cal. S.P. Ire.*, 1600-1, p. 278.
365. *A.F.M.*, sub anno.
366. Ibid., sub anno.
367. A. Gwynn, and R. N. Hadcock, *Medieval religious houses* (Dublin, 1970), p. 272; Lacy, *Archaelogical survey*, par. 1885.
368. *A.F.M.*, sub anno.
369. Ibid., sub anno.
370. Ibid., sub annis. Badhbhdhún Nua was probably in Bawan in the parish of Kilcar, see *O.S. Letters, Donegal*, 24 October, 1835.
371. *A.F.M.*, sub anno. In *Anal. Hib.*, 18, par. 505, we find *Toirrdelbach meirgech .ix. ráithi.* I have found it impossible to determine his relationship to Niall Óg.
372. Ibid., 18, par. 504.
373. *Cal. S.P. Ire.*, 1509-73, p. 417.
374. *A.F.M.*, sub anno.
375. Ibid., sub anno.
376. Ibid., sub annis.
377. Ibid., sub annis; for Derryness see ibid., sub anno 1588, note b. For a chart showing the familial relationship of the Mac Suibhne lords of Banagh from Niall Mór (obit 1524) onwards, see *L.C.S.*, p. xxxix.
378. *A.F.M.*, sub anno.

379. Ibid., sub anno.
380. *Cal. S.P. Ire.*, 1596-7, p. 141.
381. Ibid., 1600, p. 259.
382. Ibid., 1600-1, p. 289.
383. Ibid., 1601-3, p. 54.
384. Ibid., 1601-3, p. 165.
385. Ibid., 1606-8, pp 555-6 and note 1, p. 555.
386. Ibid., 1606-8, pp 439-40.
387. Ibid., 1606-8, p. 482.
388. Ibid., 1608-10, p. 95.
389. Ibid., 1608-10, pp 194-5.
390. Hill, *Plantation*, pp 328, 527.
391. *Inq. Ult.*, Donagall, 16 – Charles I.
392. *L.C.S.,* p. xl. I have found no reference to his date of death in earlier sources.
393. Ó Gallachair, *Tirconaill in 1641*, p. 81.
394. *Civil Survey*, iii, p. 137.
395. Cloghineely comprised the parishes of Tullaghobegley and Raymunterdoney (Hogan, *Onomasticon*, p. 250).
396. Ibid., p. 635.
397. Ibid., p. 217, under Cenél mBogaine.
398. Carney, *Topographical poems*, p. 17; for Ó Baoighill genealogies see *Anal. Hib.*, 18, pars. 197-8, 387-396.
399. *A.F.M.*, sub annis.
400. Ibid., sub anno.
401. Ibid., sub anno; Clann Sneidgile, *anglice* Clanelly was in Glenswilly, west of Letterkenny (Hogan, *Onomasticon*, p. 245).
402. *A.F.M.*, sub anno.
403. Ibid., sub anno.
404. Ibid., sub anno. for the *derbfine* see Kelly, *A guide to early Irish law*, pp 12, 104; Byrne, *Irish kings*, pp 122-3. The Tuatha were in north-west Donegal; see note 321 above.
405. *A.F.M.*, sub anno; Desertcreaght is in the barony of Dungannon (note x, sub anno 1281).
406. Ibid., sub anno.
407. Ibid., sub anno.
408. Ibid., sub anno.
409. Ibid., sub anno.
410. Ibid., sub anno.
411. See section under Mac Suibhne na dTuath above, and *L.C.S.,* par. 24.
412. *Cal. S.P. Ire.*, 1600-1, p. 278; for a description of the present site of the castle see Lacy, *Archaeological survey*, par. 1928.
413. *A.F.M.*, sub anno; Neachtain was king 1439-52 (*N.H.I.*, ix., p. 145).
414. *A.F.M.*, sub anno.
415. Ibid., sub anno.
416. Ibid., sub annis.
417. Ibid., sub anno.
418. Ibid., sub anno.
419. Ibid., sub anno.
420. Ibid., 1540. Domhnall died in 1549 (*A.F.M.*, sub anno).
421. Ibid., sub anno. Srath Buidhe *anglice* Straboy is also a townland (Hogan, *Onomasticon*, p. 616).

422. *A.F.M.*, sub anno.
423. Ibid., 1592, see *Life of Aodh Ruadh*, ii, pp 32-37.
424. *A.F.M.*, 1592.
425. Ibid., sub anno.
426. *Cal. S.P. Ire.*, 1600-1, p. 289.
427. Ibid., 1603-6, p. 542.
428. Hill, *Plantation*, p. 328.
429. Ibid., p. 526 and note 219.
430. *Cal. S.P. Ire.*, 1611-14, p. 123.
431. Ó Gallchair, 'Tirconaill in 1641', pp 83-84.
432. Ibid., pp 102-4.
433. *Civil Survey*, iii, pp 135-7.
434. *Census Ire.*, p. 47.
435. Ibid., pp 47-48.
436. Ibid., p. 48.
437. Ibid., p. 59.
438. Mac Carthy Mór, 'Index', p. 30.
439. See Carney, *Topographical poems*, p. 18.
440. *A.F.M.*, sub anno.
441. Ibid., sub anno.
442. Ibid., sub anno.
443. Ibid., sub anno.
444. *L.C.S.*, pars. 10-13; see section under Mac Suibhne.
445. Other learned families in Donegal who once held political power were those of Ó Cléirigh and Mac Duinnshléibhe, which see under sections on those families.
446. *A.F.M.*, sub anno.
447. Ibid., sub annis.
448. An tAth. P. Ua Duinnín (ed.), *McGuidhir Fhearmanach: the Maguires of Fermanagh .i. Maghnas agus Giolla Íosa ...* (Dublin, 1917), pp 32-32, 78-79.
449. *A.F.M.*, 1447; *A.U.*, 1495.
450. The portion relating to Ó Breisléin is quoted in Ua Duinnín, *McGuidhir Fhearmanach*, pp 105-6.
451. *Inq. Ult.*, appendix v.
452. *O.S. letters, Donegal*, 18 Oct., 1835; for a description of the bell and a further description of the *turas* see ibid., 19 Oct., 1835; for the antiquities of Iniskeele see Lacy, *Archaeological survey*, par. 1573.
453. *Census Ire.*, p. 48.
454. Ibid., p. 119.
455. Mac Carthy Mór, 'Index', p. 30.
456. For their genealogy see M. Ní Bhrolcháin, *Maol Íosa Ó Brolcháin* (1986), p. 9, from Ms. Laud 610; *Anal. Hib.*, 18, par. 607; for the descent of the kings of the Northern Uí Néill see *N.H.I.*, ix, p. 127.
457. *A.F.M.*, sub anno; 'sruith senóir Ereann, saoi i neaccna, i ccrabadh 7 hi filidhecht an bherla cechtardha'.
458. Ní Bhrolcháin, *Maol Íosa*, p. 9.
459. Ibid., p. 42.
460. Ibid., p. 80; the ascription is uncertain.
461. Colgan, *Acta Sanctorum*, p. 108. Muireann Ní Bhrolcháin has gathered all the available material on Máel Ísu in her book and has set it in its historical context.
462. F. Mac Donncha, 'Medieval Irish homilies' in M. McNamara (ed.), *Biblical studies: the Irish contribution* (Dublin, 1976), pp 67-68.

463. *A.F.M.*, sub anno. For 'lector', *fer léiginn*, see *(C)DIL*, F-fochraic, col. 82, l. 12. Another son, Máel Brigde, bishop of Kildare, also died of plague in 1095 (*A.I.*, sub anno).

464. *A.F.M.*, sub anno; see Ware, *History of the bishops*, p. 53 – Máel Coluim was suffragan bishop under Archbishop Cellach.

465. Ibid., sub anno; not archbishop; see *N.H.I.*, ix, p. 240.

466. Ibid., sub anno. For Muirchertach see section under Mac Lochlainn.

467. *A.U.*, sub anno, cf. *A.F.M.*, sub anno.

468. *A.U.*, sub anno and note sub anno, cf. *A.F.M.*, sub anno.

469. *A.F.M.*, sub anno.

470. *A.U.*, sub anno.

471. *A.F.M.*, sub anno.

472. Ibid., sub anno.

473. *A.U.*, sub anno.

474. *Cal. papal letters*, 1417-31, p. 547.

475. Ibid., 1417-31, p. 396.

476. *Census Ire.*, p. 64.

477. For anglicisations of some Irish surnames see P. Hanks and F. Hodges, *Dictionary of surnames* (Oxford, 1990).

478. Mac Carthy Mór, 'Index', pp 30, 31.

479. For a history of the family see T. G. Cannon, 'A history of the O'Cannons of Tír Chonaill' in *Donegal Annual*, 12, no. 2 (1978), pp 276-315. For a genealogical chart see J. O'Donovan (ed.), *The banquet of Dún na n-Gedh and the battle of Magh Rath, an ancient historical tale* (Dublin, 1842), p. 335.

480. Idem. Flaithbertach died in 765 (*A.U.*, sub anno).

481. Cannon, 'History of the O'Cannons', p. 284.

482. Cannon, 'A forgotten medieval placename' in *Donegal Annual*, 18 (1986), especially pp 37-38.

483. *A.I.*, p. li, note 2.

484. *Ann. Clon.*, sub anno: 'prince of Tireconnell'.

485. The dates in the annals are confusing here. Muirchertach's death according to *A.U.²* and *A.I.* took place in 943; in *A.F.M.* in 941. The invasion of Cenél Eógain took place in 941 according to *A.U.²* and *A.F.M.*. For the dating in *A.F.M.* a year should be added.

486. *A.F.M.*, sub anno.

487. Ibid., sub anno.

488. Ibid., sub anno.

489. Ibid., 948; *A.U.²* and *A.I.* have 950.

490. In the *Irish World Chronicle*, Ruaidrí is described as *leth-rí* or joint king of Ireland with Congalach; see *A.I.*, p. 44. His death is recorded in *A.U.²*, sub anno.

491. See Section under Ó Maoil Doraidh, also O'Donovan, *Dún na n-Gedh*, p. 335.

492. See Byrne, *Irish kings*, pp 114-29, for the Cenél Eógain.

493. *A.F.M.*, sub annis.

494. Ibid., sub anno.

495. Ibid., sub annis.

496. *A.U.*, sub anno; cf. *A.F.M.*, sub anno.

497. *A.F.M.*, sub anno.

498. Ibid., sub anno.

499. Ibid., sub anno; for discussion see Fr. Colmcille, 'Abbey Assaroe' in O'Donnell, *Father John Colgan ... essays in commemoration*, pp 111-29; see Cannon, 'O'Cannons of Tir Chonaill', p. 294.

500. *A.U.*, sub anno, *A.F.M.*, sub anno.

501. Ibid., 1248.

502. *A.U.*, sub anno.

503. *A.F.M.*, sub anno.

504. In the year 1602 (*Fiants Ire., Eliz. I*, 6713).

505. Ibid., 6565.

506. Ó Gallachair, 'Tirconaill in 1641', p. 80.

507. *Census Ire.*, p. 48.

508. Ibid., p. 59.

509. Mac Carthy Mór, 'Index', p. 31.

510. *Anal. Hib.*, 18, par. 1546-1588. For Guaire see *A.U.²*, sub anno 663, *A.F.M.*, 662 and note f. For the Uí Fiachrach Aidni see Hogan, *Onomasticon*, p. 67.

511. *Anal. Hib.*, 18, par. 1547.

512. Ibid., 18, par. 1551.

513. Ibid., 18, par. 1556.

514. Ibid., 18, pars. 1560-1565. For Niall Garbh's death see *A.F.M.*, 1348. For Giolla Riabhach's death see *A.F.M.*, 1421. For the Uí Fiachrach see Hogan, *Onomasticon*, pp 670-1.

515. *A.F.M.*, sub annis for Niall. The first poem is addressed to Colum Cille asking him to help Ó Domhnaill, the second is on his death. Both are published in *Irish Texts* II, pp 87-91, 91-96, see P. Walsh, *The Ó Cléirigh family of Tír Conaill ...* (1938), pp 3-4, for Diarmaid.

516. *A.F.M.*, sub anno, where he is also named as head of his *clann*, i.e. Ua Cléiricch.

517. *Anal. Hib.*, 18, par. 1566.

518. *A.F.M.*, sub anno.

519. His son Muiris 'a man learned in history and literature' died in 1573 (ibid., sub anno); see Walsh, *Ó Cléirigh family*, p. 11.

520. *A.F.M.*, sub anno. For a convenient chart showing Ó Cléirigh pedigrees see Walsh, ibid., fold-out at end of book.

521. Edited and translated by John O'Donovan, Dublin, 1856 (=*A.F.M.*).

522. See Brendan Jennings, 'Brother Michael O'Clery' in *Assisi*, 5 (Oct., 1933), pp 458-61 for an account of Brother Micheál. For the monastery of Bundrowes see Walsh, *Ó Cléirigh family*, p. 10.

523. P. Walsh (ed.), *Genealogiae regum et sanctorum Hiberniae by the Four Masters, edited from the manuscript of Micheál Ó Cléirigh* (1918).

524. See R. A. S. Macalister (ed.), *Lebor gabála Érenn: the book of the taking of Ireland*, part I (1938), pp vi, xxv. For other works see Fr S. O'Brien (ed.), *Measgra i gcuimhne Mhichíl Uí Chléirigh ...* (1944), p. xviii.

525. *A.F.M.*, pp lxiii-lxvii.

526. P. Walsh (ed.), *The life of Aodh Ruadh Ó Domhnaill, transcribed from the book of Lughaidh Ó Cléirigh*, vols. I-II (1948); see also Walsh, *Ó Cléirigh family*, pp 15-16.

527. L. Mac Kenna (ed.), *Iomarbhágh na bhfileadh: the contention of the bards*, part I (1918), pp 18-27, 54-95, 102-7.

528. *Inq. Ult.*, appendix v.

529. Hill, *Plantation*, p. 330.

530. *Inq. Ult.*, 17 – Charles I.

531. *A.F.M.*, p. xxvii.

532. Ed. by James Carney, see note 91 above.

533. *Anal. Hib.*, 18, see note 8 above.

534. Ibid., 18, Par. 3.

535. As at Kinsale in the winter of 1601, *A.F.M.*, sub anno.
536. See Macalister, *Lebor gabála*, parts 1-5 (1938-56), for the story of the sons of Míl.
537. *Anal. Hib.*, 18, p. xix.
538. Ibid., 18, p. xvii; translation by John O Donovan in *A.F.M.*, pp xxvii-viii. The original will was much damaged when Pender edited the *Genealogies* in 1951.
539. *A.F.M.*, p. xxviii. O'Donovan is mistaken here when he calls Cú Choigcríche 'the annalist'. Walsh clearly shows that he was not (*O Cléirigh family*, pp 19-20).
540. Ibid., pp 18-19.
541. J. Carney (ed.), *The poems of Blathmac son of Cú Brettan together with the Irish gospel of Thomas and a poem on the Virgin Mary* (Dublin, 1964). For the contents and history of the manuscript see pp ix-xiii.
542. *Anal. Hib.*, 18, pp xii-xiv.
543. Carney, *Poems of Blathmac*, p. 10.
544. For the other descendants of Tadhg Cam (d. 1492, *A.F.M.*), see Walsh, *Ó Cléirigh family*, pp 4-22, and fold-out genealogical chart in the same work.
545. *Census Ire.*, p. 45.
546. Mac Carthy Mór, 'Index', pp 31-32.
547. *Anal. Hib.*, 18, par. 199.
548. D. H. Kelly (ed.), *the Book of Fenagh in Irish and English originally compiled by Saint Caillin* ... (1875), p. 347.
549. *A.F.M.*, sub anno.
550. Ibid., sub anno; de Courcy had invaded Ulster in 1177, built a castle at Downpatrick from which he made forays into the territory of Ulaid, Tír Eógain and the north in general; see *N.H.I.*, viii, sub anno 1177 et seq.
551. *A.F.M.*, sub anno.
552. Ibid., 1177, note d.
553. Ibid., 1199, note s.
554. *A.U.*, sub anno.
555. *A.F.M.*, 1202.
556. Ibid., sub anno.
557. Ibid., sub anno; see section under Mac Lochlainn.
558. Ibid., sub anno.
559. Ibid., sub anno.
560. O. Davis and H. P. Swan, 'The castles of Inishowen' in *U.J.A.*, series 3, ii, p. 180: Norman power in Inishowen ended about 1333.
561. *A.U.*, 1342.
562. *A.F.M.*, sub anno.
563. Ibid., sub anno.
564. Ibid., sub anno.
565. Obit 1440 (Ibid., sub anno).
566. Obit 1496 (Ibid., sub anno): Brian's territory is not mentioned. He is simply called Ó Dochartaigh. For his descendants see *Anal. Hib.* 18, pars. 199, 237; F. Gillespie, Gaelic Chart 3, for an idea of the general descent of the family.
567. Obit 1526 (*A.F.M.*, sub anno). He was lord of Inishowen. See *Anal. Hib.*, 18, pars. 224-8.
568. Obit 1439 (*A.F.M.*, sub anno). For the Inch branch see *Anal. Hib.*, 18, pars. 267-74; for the Buncrana branch see pars. 263-66.
569. Ibid., 18, pars. 275-287; *A.F.M.*, sub anno.
570. Ibid., sub anno.
571. *A.U.*, 1524.
572. *A.F.M.*, 1440. For the history and location of this castle see Davis and Swan,

Castles of Inishowen, pp 200-1 and Lacy, *Archaelogical survey*, par. 1937.

573. *A.F.M.*, sub anno.
574. Ibid., sub anno.
575. Ibid., sub anno.
576. See *Anal. Hib.*, 18, pars. 523-724, passim and section under Mac Lochlainn in this article.
577. *A.F.M.*, sub anno.
578. Ibid., sub anno.
579. Ibid., sub anno.
580. Ibid., sub anno; see F. Gillespie, Gaelic Chart 3.
581. *A.F.M.*, sub anno.
582. Ibid., sub anno.
583. Ibid., sub anno.
584. Ibid., sub anno.
585. Bonner, *Audacious traitor*, pp 44-45. See footnote 137. This is the most complete work on the Ó Dochartaigh family published to date, and treats very fully of the rule of Seán Óg and his son, Cathaoir Ruadh.
586. Ibid., p. 49.
587. *A.F.M.*, sub anno; see Bonner, *Audacious traitor*, p. 53.
588. Idem.
589. *A.F.M.*, sub anno.
590. Bonner, *Audacious traitor*, pp 55-56.
591. Ibid., pp 57-68: this gives a good account of the Spanish in Inishowen. Later it was claimed Ó Dochartaigh had actually killed many Saniards (*Cal. S.P. Ire.*, 1588-92, p. 453).
592. Walsh, *Life of Aodh Ruadh*, ii, p. 57, cf. *Cal. S.P. Ire.*, 1592-6, p. 215.
593. Bonner, *Audacious traitor*, pp 75-76, *Life of Aodh Ruadh*, pp 117, 189, etc.; also *Cal. S.P. Ire.*, 1600, pp 9-10, for Ó Dochartaigh's many offers to submit to Queen Elizabeth.
594. *A.F.M.*, sub anno.
595. Bonner, *Audacious traitor*, pp 112-6: Docwra's 'Narration' in *A.F.M.*, pp 2236-8 and *A.F.M.*, 1601.
596. *Cal. S.P. Ire.*, 1603-6, pp 78-79.
597. Ibid., 1606-8, pp 316-8.
598. Ibid., 1606-8, p. 406.
599. For a detailed account of Cathaoir's rising see Bonner, *Auadacious traitor*, pp 153-197: see also *A.F.M.*, 1608.
600. *Cal. S.P. Ire.*, 1606-8, p. 613.
601. Ibid., 1608-10, p. 227; Bonner, *Audacious traitor*, p. 251.
602. *Cal. S.P. Ire.*, 1608-10, p. 216.
603. Bonner, *Audacious traitor*, p. 215.
604. Moody and Simms, *Bishopric of Derry*, i, p. 27.
605. Ibid., p. 28.
606. *Civil Survey*, iii, p. 4.
607. *Census Ire.*, p. 61.
608. Ibid., p. 62.
609. Ibid., p. 63.
610. Idem.
611. Ibid., p. 64.
612. Ibid., p. 53.
613. Mac Carthy Mór, 'Index', pp 33-36.

614. In Genealogical Office register of Chiefs of the Name, Ms. 527.
615. G.O. Ms. 165: 'Irish pedigrees', pp 407-10.
616. *A.F.M.*, sub anno.
617. Ibid., sub anno.
618. *Inq. Ult.*, appendix v.
619. *Cal. papal letters*, 1455-64, p. 485: Patrick's being 'a fornicator' may here mean no more than that he was in an irregular union, a common enough occurrence at the time.
620. *Cal. papal letters*, 1458-71, p. 748.
621. *Fiants Ire., Eliz. I*, 6655.
622. *Census Ire.*, p. 59 under the form 'O Dowy'.
623. Ibid., p. 64 under the form 'O Doy'.
624. Mac Carthy Mór, 'Index', p. 36.
625. Idem.
626. *Anal. Hib.*, 18, par. 720.
627. Hogan, *Onomasticon*, p. 123; *O.S. letters, Donegal*, 17 Aug., 1835.
628. Idem.
629. *A.F.M.*, sub anno.
630. Ibid., sub anno.
631. Ibid., sub anno.
632. B. Bonner, *Where Aileach guards: a millenium of Gaelic civilisation* (1974), p. 53. My thanks to Dónal Mac Giolla Easpaig for information on this point.
633. See section under Mac Lochlainn above.
634. *A.F.M.*, sub anno. His name was Niall according to *A.U.* (sub anno). Mag Itha is the present day Lagan according to *A.F.M.*, sub anno 1199, note a.
635. Ibid., sub anno.
636. Ibid., sub anno.
637. See section under Ó Dochartaigh above.
638. *Fiants Ire., Eliz. I*, 6655.
639. *Census Ire.*, p. 64; for the pronunciation of the name in the last century see *A.F.M.*, sub anno 1454, note q.
640. Mac Carthy Mór, 'Index', p. 33 under forms O'Dierma, O'Diermond, etc.
641. *Anal. Hib.*, 18, par. 716, where the form Ó hEircinn is found. However, it is more likely that the name of the eponymous ancestor was Ercán, a diminutive of Erc. For An Bhrédach see note 627 above.
642. *Inq. Ult.*, appendix v.
643. *Anal. Hib.*, 12, p. 78.
644. *De Ann. Hib.*, p. 215.
645. *Cal. papal letters*, 1455-64, p. 285.
646. *Fiants Ire., Eliz. I*, 6655.
647. *Cal. S.P. Ire.*, 1608-10, p. 45; see section under Ó Dochartaigh.
648. *Census Ire.*, p. 64.
649. Mac Carthy Mór, 'Index', pp 39-40.
650. *A.F.M.*, sub anno.
651. Ibid., sub annis.
652. Hogan, *Onomasticon*, p. 201; Henthorn and Reeves, *The martyrology of Donegal*, pp 150-1.
653. *L.C.S.*, par. 37.
654. There is no mention of a Bishop Ó Firghil in Ware's *Bishops* for this time: he was, no doubt, the abbot of the Franciscan house founded by Mághnas Ó Domhnaill; see Lacy, *Archaeological survey*, par. 1889.

655. *A.F.M.*, 1581.

656. Ibid., sub anno, O'Donovan's translation.

657. Ibid., sub anno. For Niall Garbh's career see ibid., pp 2385-90.

658. In 1608, the year he was taken prisoner by the English. He died in the Tower of London in 1626 (*A.F.M.*, 1608, note m. and p. 2389).

659. *Fiants Ire., Eliz. I,* 6761.

660. *Census Ire.*, p. 59.

661. Mac Carthy Mór, 'Index', p. 37.

662. Genealogical Office, Ms. 162, pp 24-25.

663. *Grand armorial de France,* v (Paris, 1948), p. 178.

664. The arms of Ruaidhrí Ó Domhnaill, earl of Tirconnell, are to be found in a certificate in the Genealogical Office issued in 1709 by James Terry, Athlone Pursuivant at Saint Germain, to Daniel O'Donnell of Ramelton. The blason of the shield is as follows: Or out of the dexter an arm vested azure cuffed argent the hand holding a cross crosslet fitchy gules.

665. *Anal. Hib.*, 18, pars. 560, 572 for the genealogy. See Carney, *Topographical poems*, p. 8, ll. 193-6. The territory of Cenél Moein in Donegal lay in the barony of Raphoe (Hogan, *Onomasticon*, p. 222). The form of the name was originally Ó Gailmredaig with metathesis occurring later, giving Ó Gairmledaig.

666. *A.U.²*, sub anno. For Domnall's reign see *N.H.I.*, ix, p. 129.

667. *A.F.M.*, sub anno. Ó Dubdai, *anglice* O Duddy; Ó Flaithbertaig, *anglice* O'Laverty, a name found in Donegal, Tyrone and Derry (*A.F.M.*, sub anno 1119, notes y, z, respectively).

668. Ibid., sub anno: Fir Manach, the people who gave their name to Fermanagh.

669. Ibid., sub anno; see section on Mac Lochlainn.

670. *A.F.M.*, 1145.

671. Ibid., sub anno.

672. Ibid., sub anno.

673. Ibid., sub anno. Cenél Énna were descendants of Éndae, son of Niall Noígiallach; see introduction: they originally inhabited Tír Énna which extended from Glas nEnncha, probably the Errity river near Manorcunningham, to the parish of Killymard in the barony of Banagh (*Bk. Fen.*, p. 314, note 4); Tír Énna comprised the modern barony of Raphoe (Hogan, *Onomasticon*, p. 636).

674. Ibid., sub anno. The territory of Clann Diarmata (*anglice* Clondermot) lay east of the river Foyle in the barony of Tirkeeran, county Derry (Hogan, *Onomasticon*, p. 240).

675. Ibid., 1178.

676. Ibid., sub anno. Ardstraw is near Newtownstewart in county Tyrone (Hogan, *Onomasticon*, p. 48).

677. For their migration to present-day county Tyrone see S. Ó Ceallaigh, *Gleanings from Ulster history* (1951), pp 24-25 and N. J. A. Williams (ed.), *The poems of Giolla Brighde Mac Con Midhe* (1980), p. 3. Giolla Brighde was poet to the Uí Gailmredaig. He died about 1272 (ibid., p. 4).

678. *De Ann. Hib.*, p. 216.

679. For convenient chart showing the descent of the family of Ó Gallchobhair see O'Donovan, *The banquet of Dún na n-Gedh and the battle of Magh Rath*, pp 335-6; see also *Anal. Hib.*, 18, par. 201-223. For pedigree of the high-kings of the Northern Uí Néill see *N.H.I.*, ix, pp 127-9.

680. *A.F.M.*, sub anno. Scrín Adamnáin, *anglice* Skreen, is in county Sligo.

681. Ibid., sub anno.

682. Ibid., sub anno.

683. For the descent of Cathal Dubh from Gilla Coimded see *Anal. Hib.*, 18, par. 206. I have assumed that the pedigree includes the first Bishop Lochlann rather than the second, who died in 1477, because of the time span between Gilla Coimded and the earlier Lochlann.
684. Ware, *History of the bishops*, p. 274.
685. Idem.
686. *A.F.M.*, sub anno.
687. Ibid., sub anno.
688. Ibid., 1498.
689. Ibid., sub anno: Émann mac Eóin mic Tuathail, cf. *Anal. Hib.*, 18, par. 203.
690. *A.F.M.*, sub anno.
691. Ibid., sub anno.
692. Ibid., sub anno. In the decades following 1515 the dates and the succession for Raphoe bishops are uncertain according to Ware, *History of the bishops*, p. 274, but see Genealogical Office Ms. 619, p. 284A for Catholic bishops during the century following the reformation.
693. Genealogical Office Ms. 619, p. 298A.
694. *Cal. S.P. Ire.*, 1588-92, pp 44, 63.
695. Ibid., 1588-92, p. 375. For Bishop MacGrath see Ware, *History of the bishops*, pp 483-5.
696. *Cal. S.P. Ire.*, 1592-6, p. 434. Réamann had been bishop of Killala before his translation to Derry (Genealogical Office Ms. 619, p. 298A).
697. *Cal. S.P. Ire.*, 1596-7, p. 354.
698. *A.F.M.*, sub anno.
699. Ibid., sub anno; for Aodh Dubh's death see ibid., 1537.
700. Ibid., sub anno.
701. Ibid., sub anno.
702. *Cal. S.P. Ire.*, 1509-73, p. 530.
703. Ibid., 1574-85, p. 29.
704. Ibid., 1574-85, p. 321.
705. *A.F.M.*, sub anno.
706. An Calbhach, who succeeded his father, Mághnas, in 1555, held the lordship until 1566, see *N.H.I.*, ix, p. 145.
707. *A.F.M.*, sub anno.
708. Ibid., 1588.
709. Ibid., sub anno and pp 1928-9.
710. Hill, *Plantation*, pp 32-33 and note 28.
711. See section under Mac Suibhne na dTuath above.
712. *Cal. S.P. Ire.*, 1588-92, p. 93.
713. Hill, *Plantation*, p. 45 and note 55; cf. *A.F.M.*, 1595.
714. *Cal. S.P. Ire.*, 1588-92, p. 195.
715. *A.F.M.*, sub anno and 1602.
716. *Cal. S.P. Ire.*, 1606-8, p. 505.
717. Ibid., 1606-8, p. 598; for Ó Domhnaill's storehouse see ibid., 1600-1, p. 278.
718. Idem.
719. De Barra and Ó Fiaich, *Imeacht na nIarlaí*, p. 25.
720. Hill, *Plantation*, pp 329-30.
721. *Civil Survey*, iii, p. 137.
722. Ó Gallchair, 'Tirconaill in 1641', p. 80.
723. *Census Ire.*, p. 59.
724. Ibid., p. 53.

725. Ibid., p. 48.
726. Ibid., p. 45.
727. Mac Carthy Mór, 'Index', pp 37-38.
728. Carney, *Topographical poems*, p. 17, ll. 443-6: 'The Uí Mhaoil Doraidh will not come – if they lived they would come to meet us immediately and without delay, and the Uí Chanannáin too.'
729. Ibid., p. viii.
730. *Anal. Hib.*, 18, par. 229; for a genealogical chart showing the Ó Maíl Doraid descent see O'Donovan, *The banquet of Dún na n-Gedh*, p. 335.
731. *A.F.M.*, sub anno.
732. *A.U.²*, sub anno, see *New hist. Ire.*, ix, p. 127 for Flaithbertach.
733. *A.F.M.*, 1200, note k. See Cannon, *Donegal Annual*, 38 (1986), pp 36-38.
734. John O'Hart, *Irish pedigrees*, ii (1915), p. 573; see section under Mac Robhartaigh.
735. *A.U.²*, 962.
736. Ibid., sub anno, *A.F.M.*, 978.
737. See section under Ó Canannáin above.
738. *A.U.²*, sub anno; cf. *A.F.M.*, 1003.
739. Ibid., sub anno.
740. *A.U.²*, sub anno.
741. *A.F.M.*, 1027.
742. Ibid., sub anno. The Clann Fiangusa are unidentified.
743. *A.U.²*, sub anno.
744. Ibid., 1072.
745. *A.F.M.*, sub anno.
746. Ibid., 1176. For the Clann Diarmata see note 674 above.
747. Ibid., 1177.
748. Ibid., 1181; *A.U.* describes him as 'king': *A.F.M.* uses *tigherna*, 'lord'.
749. *A.F.M.*, sub anno, see note 499 above for the monastery of Assaroe.
750. *A.F.M.*, sub anno.
751. *An index of surnames of householders in Griffith's valuation and tithe applotment book: county Donegal* (1967), p. 142. For Echmarcach see section on Ó Dochartaigh.
751a. See *Anal. Hib.*, 18, par. 700 for pedigree.
752. *A.U.²*, sub anno. Carraic Brachaide, according to O'Donovan, was in the north-west of Inishowen (*A.F.M.*, 834, note e); see Ó Ceallaigh, *Gleanings from Ulster history*, map I.
753. *A.U.²*, 1102. The territory of Uí Eachach, *anglice* Iveagh, was in the modern county of Down (Hogan, *Onomasticon*, p. 669).
754. *A.U.²*, sub anno. For Muirchertach see section on Mac Lochlainn above.
755. Ibid., sub anno.
756. Ibid., sub anno. Leamhain, *anglice* Lennox, was in the territory of Dumbartonshire in Scotland (Hogan, *Onomasticon*, p. 482). The territory of Cenél Fergusa was in north-west Inishowen (*A.F.M.*, 1215, note s).
757. Mac Carthy Mór, 'Index', p. 42.
758. *Census Ire.*, p. 128.
759. See Ó Ceallaigh, *Gleanings from Ulster history*, pp 6-8: the eastward expansion of Cenél Eógain and the rise of Ó Dochartaigh power were reasons for the demise of Ó Maíl Fábaill power in Inishowen.
760. *Index of surnames, Donegal*, pp 61, 63, 65, 96 for examples.
761. *Anal. Hib.*, 18, par. 705.
762. *A.F.M.*, sub anno.

763. Ibid., sub anno; for the term comharba see note 92 above.
764. *Cal. papal letters*, 1417-31, p. 104.
765. Ibid., 1427-47, p. 179.
766. Ibid., 1455-64, p. 251.
767. Ibid., 1457-71, p. 35.
768. *Census Ire.*, p. 48.
769. Mac Carthy Mór, 'Index', p. 43 under the form O'Mulloghery.
770. *Inq. Ult.*, appendix v.
771. *Cal. papal letters*, 1431-47, p. 17.
772. Ibid., 1447-55, p. 287.
773. Ibid., 1458-71, p. 748.
774. *Census Ire.*, p. 64.
775. The dropping of the prefix 'O' leaves the impossible combination in English, initial 'mr-': the nearest labial, the voiced plosive 'b' was later substituted for 'm', bringing the pronunciation into line with normal English phonology.
776. Mac Carthy Mór, 'Index', p. 42.
777. *Inq. Ult.*, appendix v.
778. In an English survey dated 1608 the form of this townland is 'Maghery Irourty' (*Anal. Hib.*, 3, p. 172). I am grateful to Dónal Mac Giolla Easpaig for information on this point.
779. O'Donovan, *Martyrology of Donegal*, p. 151.
780. *A.U.*, sub anno; *N.H.I.*, ix, p. 258. See section under Mac Robhartaigh.
781. *O.S. letters, Donegal*, 15 Sept., 1835.
782. *A.F.M.*, sub anno.
783. Canon E. Maguire, *A history of the diocese of Raphoe*, ii (1920), pp 293-4. I am grateful to Raghnall Ó Floinn for information on this point.
784. *Cal. papal letters*, 1484-92 (vol. xiv), p. 134.
785. *Fiants Ire., Eliz. I*, 6761.
786. *Index of surnames, Donegal*, p. 50.

Chapter 28

DONEGAL HISTORY AND SOCIETY: A SELECT BIBLIOGRAPHY

Liam Ronayne

This is a select bibliography of monographs on the history and topography of Donegal, arranged under a number of broad headings, together with a representative listing of poetry, fiction and other writings, in Irish and English, by Donegal authors. Brenda O'Hanrahan's *Donegal authors: a bibliography* remains the leading work in this area, but as the title indicates, does not cover titles about the county written by people not from Donegal. Journal articles are not included here, although they are of the utmost importance. The main journal for Donegal local studies is the *Donegal Annual*, published by the County Donegal Historical Society. Other journals which regularly include articles of Donegal interest are the *Clogher Record, Ulster Folklife, Ulster Local Studies, An tUltach* and *The Donegal Association Yearbook*. The *Donegal Annual* has in recent years included a listing of monographs, journal articles and other materials on Donegal local studies in each issue.

The bibliography is arranged under the following headings:
Official reports; Religion/Ecclesiastical history; Economy and Society; Education; Transport and Communications; Folklife/Folklore; Gaeilge/An Gaeltacht; Natural History/Environment; Architecture/Arts/Crafts; Music; Sport and Outdoor Life; Biography; Archaeology; General Histories; County Guides and Miscellanea; Local History and Topography: Gaeltacht/West Donegal; Local History and Topography: East and Central Donegal; Local History and Topography: South Donegal; Local History and Topography: Inishowen; Litríocht agus Léirmheastóireacht; Filíocht; Dramaíocht; Scéalaíocht; Prós; Litríocht Páisti; Literature Language and Literary Criticism; Poetry; Drama; Fiction; Children's Stories.

Official reports
Donegal is a Border county, and, chiefly because of this, it has been the subject of a considerable number of studies commisioned by regional bodies, the Irish and British Governments, and the European Communities. These provide valuable background information on the social and economic condition of the county.

Anson, Brian. *North West Donegal Gaeltacht: a social and environmental study*. Doirí Beaga: Údarás na Gaeltachta, 1982.

Cross-border communications study for the Londonderry and Donegal area. Dublin: Stokes Kennedy Crowley, 1977.

*Donegal-Leitrim-Sligo regional strategy/*prepared by Brady Shipman Martin for Donegal RDO, Sligo/Leitrim RDO, and the Commission of the EC (in 4 volumes) Dublin: Brady Shipman, Martin, 1987.

European Communities. Economic and Social Committee. Irish border areas: information report. Brussels: ESC, 1983.

European Communities. Economic and Social Committee. Information report on the cross-border communications study for the Londonderry and Donegal area. Brussels: ESC, 1978.

Foras Talúntais. *West Donegal Resource Survey* (in 4 parts). Dublin: An Foras Talúntais, 1969.

North West Study: final study report. Dublin: Coopers & Lybrand (Ireland), 1990.

North-West sub-region: submission for CSF (1994-97) and Cohesion Fund Support (S.l.) North-West Sub-Region Review Committee, 1992.

Priorities for public investment in the Strabane, Londonderry and Donegal areas in the cross-border context: joint report by Foyle Development Organisation, Donegal Regional Development Organisation and Strabane District Council. Lifford etc: RDO etc., 1980.

Proposed whaling stations in county Donegal: Report of inquiries held at Burtonport, Co. Donegal on 17th and 18th February 1908 and at Londonderry on 19th and 20th February 1908. Dublin: HMSO, 1908.

Religion/Ecclesiastical history

Bonner, Brian. *Derry: an outline history of the Diocese*. B.Á.C.: Foilseacháin Náisiúnta, 1982.

Bourke, J. *Rev. James O'Gallagher's sermons: Irish & English*. Dublin: Gill, 1877.

Catechism of Christan doctrine approved for the Diocese of Raphoe. 5th ed. Letterkenny: County Donegal Printing, 1926.

Cave, Stephen A. *Our church in history*. Donegal: Published by author, 1954.

Colm Cille. *Prophecies of St Colmcille*. Ballyshannon: Donegal Vindicator (19-).

Crooks, D.W.T. *In the footsteps of Saint Báithín: a history of the parishes of Taughboyne with Craigadooish, All Saints, Newtowncunningham, Christ Church, Burt and Killie, Carrigans* (Ballyshannon: Donegal Democrat) 1993.

David, Fr. *A history of Ards*. Creeslough: Capuchin Friary, 1991.

Dill, Richard. *Prelatica-Presbyterianism or curious chapters.* London: McGlashan and Gill, 1856.

Doherty, W. J. *The abbey of Fahan in Inishowen, Co. Donegal.* Dublin: P. Traynor, 1881.

Evans, Robert Rees. *Pantheisticon: the career of John Toland.* New York: Lang, 1991.

Fitzgerald, John. *Holy wells of Inishowen.* Carndonagh: Foyle Press [198-].

Fitzgerald, John. *Mass rocks of Inishowen.* Carndonagh: Foyle Press [198-].

Gebbie, J. H. and others. *In his hand 1870-1970.* (s.l.): Universal, 1970 (history of C of I parishes, Derry & Raphoe Diocese).

Gibbons, Margaret. *The ownership of Station Island, Lough Derg.* Dublin: James Duffy 1937.

Giblin, Cathaldus, (ed). *The Diocese of Raphoe 1773-1805: documents illustrating the history of the Diocese from the Congress volumes in the archives of the Congregation of Propaganda Fide, Rome.* Dublin: [Franciscan Order], 1980.

Jackson, Bernard. *Places of pilgrimage.* London: Geoffrey Chapman, 1989.

Lecky, Alexander G. *The Laggan and its Presbyterianism.* Belfast: Davidson & McCormack, 1905.

Lecky, Alexander G. *In the days of the Laggan Presbytery.* Belfast: Davidson & McCormack, 1908.

Leslie, James B. *Clogher clergy and parishes.* Enniskillen: [s.n.], 1929.

Leslie, James B. *Derry clergy and parishes.* Enniskillen: [s.n.], 1937.

Leslie, James B. *Raphoe clergy and parishes.* Enniskillen: [s.n.], 1940.

Mac a' Bháird, Seaghán. *An Teagasg Criostaighe fá choinne Díoghóise Rátha-Bhoth.* Leitir Ceannain: [s.n.], 1891.

Mac a' Bháird, Seaghán. *Turus na Croiche agus an Choróin Mhuire* [s.l.]: [s.n.], 1902.

McAteer, John. *The apparitions of Kerrytown: an account compiled from the stories of the eye-witnesses* [s.l.]: [s.n.], 1946.

McAuley, Joan P. *Take five: 31 reflections and prayers with an everyday housewife as broadcast on Highland Radio.* Belfast: Ambassador, 1993.

McElderry, Nevill. *Methodism in the Pettigo area* [s.l.]: [s.n.], 1991.

Maguire, Edward. *A history of the Diocese of Raphoe.* Dublin, 1920 in 2 vols.

Meehan, Denis. *Adamnan's De locis sanctis.* Dublin: Dublin Institute for Advanced Studies, 1958.

Mullen, E. J. *Mount Silver looks down (a supplement to Maguire's History of Raphoe)*. Glenties: Quinn, 1952.

O'Boyle, Philip. *My Holy Year pilgrimage, March 19-26 1950*. Letterkenny: printed by Letterkenny Printing, 1950.

O'Byrne, Sinion. *The Franciscans of Rossnowlagh*. Rossnowlagh: Franciscan Friary, n.d.

O'Donnell, Terence. *Franciscan Donegal*. Ros Nuala: Franciscan Friary, 1952.

Ó Gallachair, P. *Where Erne and Drowes meet the sea: fragments from a Patrician parish* [Ballyshannon: printed by Donegal Democrat], 1961.

Swan, Harry Percival. *Presbyterianism in Ulster: Story of Buncrana Church. Ulster Presbyterian history. Moral and spiritual anthology* [s.l.: s.n.] 1961.

Economy and Society

Dolan, Liam. *Land war and eviction in Derryveagh 1840-65*. Dundalk: Annaverma Press, 1980.

Fox, Robin. *The Tory islanders: a people of the Celtic fringe*. Cambridge: Cambridge UP., 1978.

Hill, George. *Facts from Gweedore,* London: Hatchards, 1887.

Inishowen Community Development Group. *Resources and development in Inishowen*. Carndonagh: ICDG, 1985.

Holland, D. *The landlord in Donegal: pictures from the wilds*. Belfast: 'Ulsterman', 1863.

McFadden, James. *The present and the past of the agrarian struggle in Gweedore with letters on railway extension in Donegal*. Londonderry: printed at the Derry Journal, 1889.

McGinley, Joan. *Ireland's fishery policy*. Teelin: Croaghlin Press, 1991.

McParlan, James. *Statistical survey of the county of Donegal with observations on the means of improvement: drawn up in the year 1801 for the consideration, and under the direction of the Dublin Society*. Dublin: Dublin Society, 1802.

Micks, William L. *An account of the Congested Districts Board for Ireland*. Dublin: Eason & Son, 1925.

Ó Cinnéide, Mícheál and Ronan Mac Gearailt. *Developing the indigenous resources of Cloughaneely*. Galway: Department of Geography, UCG, 1988.

Ó Gallachobhair, Prionnsias. *History of landlordism in Donegal*. Ballyshannon: printed by Donegal Democrat, 1962.

Sacks, Paul Martin. *The Donegal Mafia: an Irish political machine*. New Haven: Yale U.P., 1976.

Vaughan, W. E. *Sin, sheep and Scotsmen: John George Adair and the Derryveagh evictions, 1861.* Belfast: Appletree Press, 1983.

Education

McClintock, May. *The heart of the Laggan: the history of Raymoghy and Ray National School* [Letterkenny: printed by Donegal Printing Co.], 1991.

MacGiolla Ruaidh, Pádraig. *Ollscoil shaor Ghaelach: tús leighis ar easpa bhasmar.* Gaoth Dobhair: Coiste Comórtha an tAthair Mícheál O hIcí, 1991.

Transport and Communications

Bourke, Edward J. *Shipwrecks of the Irish coast.* Dublin: [the author], 1993.

Boyd, J. I. C. *The Londonderry and Lough Swilly Railway.* Truro: Bradford Barton, [198-].

Mac Polin, Dónal. *The Drontheim: forgotten sailing boat of the North Irish coast.* Dublin: [printed by PlayPrint], 1993.

Patterson, Edward M. *The county Donegal railways.* Newton Abbott: David & Charles, 1962.

Patterson, Edward M. *The Londonderry & Lough Swilly railway.* Newton Abbot: David & Charles, 1988.

The South Donegal railway: an introduction to the project to re-open a section of the old county Donegal railway. Donegal Town: South Donegal Railway Restoration Society, 1992.

Folklife/Folklore

Bernan, Robert. *The hills: more tales from the Blue Stacks.* London: Hamilton, 1983.

Bernen, Robert. *Tales from the blue stacks.* London: Hamilton, 1978.

Campbell, Patrick. *From silent glen to noisy street.* Cork: Mercier, 1983.

Campbell, Patrick. *Rambles round Donegal.* Cork: Mercier, 1981.

Cassidy, Patrick Sarsfield. *The borrowed bride: a fairy love legend of Donegal.* New York: Holt, 1892.

Doherty, Jenni and Liz Doherty. *That land beyond.* Derry: Guildhall Press, 1993.

Gallagher, Michael. *Traditional weather signs* [s.l.: s.n.], 1991.

Mac Grianna, Seaghán Bán. *Céoltaí agus seanchas* [s.l.: s.n.], 1976.

Mac Manus, Seamus. *Donegal fairy stories.* New York: Doubleday & Doran, 1900.

Mac Manus, Seamus. *In chimney corners: Irish folk tales*. London: Harper, 1899.

Mac Manus, Seamus. *The Donegal wonder book*. New York: Stokes, 1926.

Mac an Luain, Pádraig. *Uair an chloig cois teallaigh = An hour by the hearth: scéalta dá n-inse ag Pádraig Eoghain Phádraig Mac an Luain*/Seamas Ó Catháin a bhailigh, a d'aistrigh agus a chuir notaí leo. B.Á.C.: Comhairle Bhéaloideas Éireann, 1985 (leabhar is téip).

McGlinchey, Charles. *The last of the name*. Belfast: Blackstaff, 1986.

Mac Roigh, Feargus. *Daoine beaga, daoine móra: Donegal folk tales*. Dún Dealgan: Preas Dhún Dealgan, [192-].

Mac Roigh, Feargus. *Oidhche áirnéail i dTír Chonaill*. Dún Dealgan: Preas Dhún Dealgan, 1924.

Nic Aodhain, Medhbh Fionnuala, eag. *Baitheadh iadsan agus tháinig mise (tiomsú de bhéaloideas na Gaeltachta Láir)*. B.Á.C.: Coiscéim, 1993.

Ní Dhioraí, Áine (eag). *Na Cruacha: scéalta agus seanchas*. B.Á.C.: Clóchomar, 1985.

Ní Dhochartaigh, Brighid. *Cómhradh cois teineadh* [s.l.: s.n., 192-].

Ní Dhochartaigh, Brighid. *Seamróg na gceithre nduilleóg* [s.l.: s.n., 192-].

Ó Baoill, Dónal. *Amach as ucht an sliabh. Iml. 1*. Doirí Beaga: Cumann Stáire agus Seanchas Ghaoth Dobhair, 1992.

Ó Baoill, Micí Shéaín Néill. *Lá de na laethaibh: scéalta, dánta agus paidreacha/arna gcur in eagar ag Lorcán Ó Searcaigh*. Muineachán: Cló Oirghialla, 1983.

Ó Cuinn, Cosslett. *Scian a caitheamh le toinn: scéalta agus amhráin as Inis Eoghainn agus cuimhne ar Ghaeltacht Iorrais*. B.Á.C.: Coisceim, 1990.

Ó Domhnaill, Conal. *Oiche airnéail i dTír Chonail*. Bun Beag: Cló an Eargail, 1986.

Ó Domhnaill, Eoghan. *Na laetha a bhí* [s.l.: s.n.],1953.

Ó Domhnaill, Niall. *Na glúanta rossanacha*. B.Á.C.: Oifig an tSolathair, 1952.

Ó Donaill, Niall. *Seanchas na Féinne I, II, III*. 1942, 1943, 1943.

O'Donnell, Michael. *By the Kilcar hearth* [Ballyshannon: printed by Donegal Democrat], 1987.

Ó hEochaidh, Seán. *Síscéalta ó Thír Chonaill = Fairy legends from Donegal*/Máire Ní Néill a d'aistrigh go Béarla. B.Á.C.: Comhairle Bhéaloideas Éireann, 1977.

Ó Searcaigh, Seamus, *Cloich cheann Fhaolaidh*. B.Á.C.: Gill, 1911.

Ó Searcaigh, Seamus. *Sgéalta as an tsean-litrídheacht* [s.l.: s.n.], 1945.

Shanklin, Eugenia. *Donegal's changing traditions: an ethnographic study.* New York: Gordon and Breach, 1985.

Therman, Dorothy Harrison. *Stories from Tory Island.* Dublin: Country House, 1989.

Ua Cnaimhsí, Pádraig/Mhic Ghrianna, Róise. *Róise Rua.* B.Á.C.: Sairséal/Ó Marcaigh, 1988.

Gaeilge/An Gaeltacht

Coláiste Uladh, Cloch Cheann Fhaolaidh: an Fheile Airgeadta 1906-1931. B.Á.C.: Trí Coinneal, 1931.

Coláiste Uladh: leabhar cuimhne iubhaile leith-chéad blian 1906-1956. Séamus Ó Néill agus Bernard Ó Dubhtaigh a chuir in eagar. An Fál Carrach: Colaiste Uladh, 1956.

Éigse Uladh 1991: Bás no beatha, na teangacha Ceilteacha san Eoraip. Gaoth Dobhair: Coiste Éigse Uladh, 1991.

Hamilton, J. N. *The Irish of Tory Island.* Belfast: Institute of Irish Studies, Queens University, 1974.

Lucas, Leslie W. *Cnuasach focal as Ros Goill.* B.Á.C.: Acadamh Ríoga na hÉireann, 1986.

Lucas, Leslie W. *Grammar of Ros Goill, Irish, Co. Donegal.* Belfast: Institute of Irish Studies, Queens University, 1979.

Mac Maoláin, Seán. *Cora cainnte as Tír Chonaill.* B.Á.C.: An Gum, 1993.

Ní Dhochartaigh, Brighid. *Cainnt choitcheannta ó'n Ghaedhealtacht = Everyday phrases from the Gaeltacht.* Dun Dealgan: Preas Dhun Dealgan, [192-].

Ó Baoill, Colm. *Contributions to a comparative study of Ulster Irish and Scottish Gaelic.* Belfast: Institute of Irish Studies, Queens University, 1978.

Ó Ciosáin, Eamon, *An t-Éireannach 1934-1937: páipéir sóisíalach Gaeltachta.* B.Á.C.: An Clóchomhar, 1993.

Ó Corráin, Ailbhe. *A concordance of idiomatic expressions in the writings of Seamus Ó Grianna.* Belfast: Institute of Irish Studies, QUB, 1989.

Ó Creag, Séamus. *Modern Irish.* Dublin: Browne & Nolan, 1896.

Ó Creag, Séamus. *Modern Irish Grammar.* Dublin: Sealy, Bryers & Walker, 1900.

Ó Creag, Séamus. *Modern Irish Composition.* Dublin: Sealy, Bryers & Walker, 1901.

Ó Creag, Séamus. *Studies in Composition.* Dublin: Sealy, Bryers & Walker, 1901.

Ó Creag, Séamus. *Progressive Studies in Irish.* Derry: Craig, 1906.

Ó Dochartaigh, Mícheál. *Ceachta agus comhradh ar neithibh* [s.l.: s.n.], 1906.

Ó Domhnaill, Niall, *Forbairt na Gaeilge*. B.Á.C.: Sáirséal agus Dill, 1951.

Ó hEochaidh, Seán. *Sean-chainnt Theilinn.* B.Á.C.: Institiúid Árd-Léighinn Bhaile Átha Cliath, 1955.

Ó hEochaidh, Seán. *Sean-chainnt na gCruach, Co. Dhun na nGall = Alte Redensarten aus den Cruacha County Donegal*/phonetisch transkribiert und ins Deutsche übersetzt von Heinrich Wagner. Tübingen: Niemeyer Verlag, 1963.

Ó Muirí, Damien. *Comhréir Ghaeilge Ghaoth Dobhair.* B.Á.C.: Coisceim, 1982.

Ó Muirí, Damien. *Comhréir Ghaeilge Ghaoth Dobhair: patrúin na nabairtí.* B.Á.C.: Coiscéim. 1982.

Ó Searcaigh, Seamus. *Foghraidheacht Ghaedhilge an Tuaiscirt* [s.l.: s.n.], 1925.

Ó Searcaigh, Seamus. *Coimhréir Ghaedhilg an Tuaiscirt* [s.l.: s.n.], 1939.

Quiggin, E. C. *A dialect of Donegal: being the speech of Meenawanna in the parish of Glenties; phonology and texts.* Cambridge: Cambridge UP, 1906.

Sommersfelt, Alf. *The dialect of Torr, Co. Donegal. 1: Phonology.* Christiania: Dybwad, 1922.

Uí Bheirn, Úna. *Cnuasach focal as Teileann.* B.Á.C.: Acadamh Ríoga na hEireann, 1989.

Uí Bheirn, Una, *Teileann inné 's inniu: Coláiste Aoidh Mhic Bhricne, Teileann 1955-1980.* Teileann: Coiste an Choláiste, 1980.

Wagner, Heinrich. *Gaeilge Theilinn.* B.Á.C.: Institiúid Árd-Léinn Átha Cliath, 1959.

Natural History/Environment
Boyle, Elizabeth. *The Irish flowers.* Cultra: Ulster Folk & Transport Museum, 1971.

Carleton, R. *Wild mammals of Donegal* [s.l.: s.n.], 1978.

Cole, Grenville A. J. *On a hillside in Donegal: a glimpse into the great earth-caldrons* [London: s.n., 1906].

O'Connor, P. J., C. Reimann, and H. Kurgh. *A geochemical survey of Inishowen, Co. Donegal.* Dublin: Geological Survey of Ireland, 1988.

Hart, Henry C. *The flora of Donegal.* Dublin: Sealy, Bryers and Walker, 1898.

Perry, Kenneth W. *The birds of the Inishowen peninsula: their distribution and habitats.* Belfast: Litho Printers, 1975.

Pitcher, Wallace Spencer, and Anthony Robert Berger. *The geology of Donegal: a study of granite emplacement and unroofing.* New York: Wiley-Interscience, 1972.

Sheppard, Liz. *Donegal for all seasons*. Ballyshannon: Donegal Democrat, 1992.

Taylor, P. J. et al. *The environmental impact of a projected uranium development in Co. Donegal, Ireland*. Oxford: Political Ecology Research Group, [198-].

Architecture/Arts/Crafts

Folan, Andrew. *Works 4*. Dublin: Gandon, 1991.

Gallagher, Patrick M. *Donemars from the Hills of Donegal*. New York: Donemar, 1922.

Gowrie, Grey, Earl of Gowrie. *Derek Hill, an appreciation*. London: Quartet, 1987.

Hoad, Judith. *This is Donegal tweed*. Inver: Shoestring Publications, 1987.

Irish rural life and industry, with suggestions for the future. Dublin: Hely, 1907.

Manners, John. *Irish crafts and craftsmen*. Belfast: Appletree Press, 1982.

Mitchell, Lillias. *Irish spinning, dying and weaving*. Dundalk: Dundalgan Press, 1978.

Rowan, Alistair. *North West Ulster*. Harmonsworth: Penguin, 1979 [The buildings of Ireland].

Shaw Smith, David. *Ireland's traditional crafts*. London: Thames & Hudson, 1984.

Sutton, E. F. *Weaving: the Irish inheritance*. Dublin: Dalton, 1980.

Music

Bantock, Granville. *The Grianan of Aileach; for chorus of mixed voices*/music by Granville Bantock, text from the *Dinnseanchas*. London: Curwen, 1924.

Feldman, Allen and Eamonn O'Doherty. *The northern fiddler: music and musicians of Donegal and Tyrone*. Belfast: Blackstaff Press, 1979.

Ferry, Paddy. *The story of Keadue Band* [Ballyshannon: printed by Donegal Democrat], 1988.

Galwey, Honoria. *Old Irish croonauns and other tunes*. London: Boosey, 1910.

McBride, Jimmy. *The flowers of Dunaff hill and more traditional songs sung in Inishowen*. Buncrana: Crana, 1988.

McBride, Jimmy and Jim Mc Farland. *My parents reared me tenderly and other traditional songs sung in Inishowen* [Buncrana: printed by Doherty], 1985.

Mac Giolla Bhrighde, Niall. *Blátha fraoich = Heather blossoms*. Dublin: Whaley, 1905.

Mac Seáin, Pádraig, *Ceolta Theilinn*. Belfast: Institute of Irish Studies, QUB, 1973.

Ó Creag, Séamus. *An craoibhín ceoil.* Dublin: [s.n.], 1908.

O'Grady, Paddy. *Donegal in song and story.* Dublin: the author, 1992.

Orpen, Grace. *Dances of Donegal.* Norwich: London and Norwich Press, 1931.

Tunney, Paddy. *The stone fiddle.* Dublin: Dalton, 1978.

Tunney, Paddy. *Where songs do thunder.* Belfast: Appletree Press, 1992.

Vallely, Eithne, *Learn to play the tin whistle.* Belfast: Regency Press, 1972.

Vallely, Eithne, *Sing a song and play it.* Belfast: Regency Press, 1975.

Vallely, Eithne, *Learn to play the fiddle.* Belfast: Regency Press, 1977.

Sport and Outdoor life

Begley, Anthony. *History of Bundoran Golf Club 1894-1994* [Ballyshannon: printed by Donegal Democrat], 1994.

Irish Mountaineering Club. *Donegal rock climbs.* Dublin: IMC, 1962.

Kerr, Michael, *Portsalon Golf Club: centenary 1891-1991.* Portsalon: Portsalon GC, 1992.

McLaughlin, Michael. *The Donegal connection: Italia 90* [s.l.: s.n.] 1990.

Ó Gallchóir, Seán. *The Donegal Democrat book of Donegal GAA facts* [Ballyshannon: printed by Donegal Democrat], 1985.

The Packie Bonner Story. Dublin: Irish Permanent, 1991.

Simms, Patrick, and Gerard Foley. *Irish walk guides: North West.* Dublin: Gill & Macmillan, 1979.

Stelfox, Dawson (ed). *Rock climbs in Donegal.* Dublin: Federation of Mountaineering Clubs in Ireland, 1985.

Biography

Adhamhnán *[Beatha Cholmcille]. Life of Saint Columba, founder of Hy.* Edmonston: Historians of Scotland, 1874.

Adhnamhnán *[Beatha Cholmcille]. Adomnan's life of Columba.* Edited by Alan Orr Anderson and Marjorie Ogilvie Anderson. London: Nelson, 1961.

Allen, Samuel, *Memoir of the Rev. George Vance, D.D. of the Irish Methodist Conference.* Dublin: Hodges Figgis, 1901.

Appleton, William W. *Charles Macklin: an actor's life.* Cambridge, Mass: Harvard UP, 1961.

Barkeley, John M. *Blackmouth & dissenter.* Belfast: White Row Press, 1991.

Betha Adamnán: The Irish life of Adamnán. Edited by Máire Herbert and Pádraig Ó Riain. London: Irish Text Society, 1988.

Biographical sketch of the Rev. John Boyce, D.D. (1810-1864) [Dublin: printed by Javerne Press], 1941.

Bishop, Alan. *Gentleman rider: a life of Joyce Cary.* London: Joseph, 1988.

Boyle, Darinagh. *Half-hanged McNaghten.* Derry: Guildhall Press, 1993.

Burdy, S. *The life of Philip Skelton.* Oxford: Clarendon Press, 1914.

Byrne, Packie Manus. *Recollections of a Donegal man.* Lampeter: Millington, 1988.

Byrne, Conall. *John Colgan 1592-1992.* Carndonagh: Foyle Press, 1991.

Canning, Bernard J., *Bishop Neil Farren 1893-1980, Bishop of Derry 1939-1973* [Limavady: printed by Limavady Printing Co., 1993].

Carlin, Kathleen. *George Farquhar: restoration dramatist.* Derry: Guildhall Press, 1987.

Clann Dálaigh: a concise history of the O'Donnell Clan from 1600 to the present: on the occasion of the Clan gathering, at Doon Rock 1989 [Letterkenny: printed by Donegal Printing], 1989.

Congreve, F. *Authentic memoirs of Mr. Charles Macklin, comedian.* London: Barker, 1798.

Cooke, Edward Alexander. *Saint Columba, his life and work.* Edinburgh: St. Giles, 1893.

Cuimhne Coluimcille or the Gartan Festival, being a record of the celebration held at Gartan on the 9th June 1897, the thirteenth centennial of St. Columba. Dublin: Gill, 1898.

de Vere White, Terence. *The road of excess.* Dublin: Brown and Nolan, 1945. (biography of Butt).

Devlin, Ernest. *Life is a broad road* [s.l: s.n.] 1974.

Dill, James Reid. *Autobiography of a country parson.* Belfast: Witness, 1888.

Dolan, Liam. *The third Earl of Leitrim* [Letterkenny: printed by McKinney & O'Callaghan], 1978.

Edwards, John. *Recollections of the Edwards family of Castlehill, Burt, County Donegal.* Londonderry: [printed at the Sentinel Office]. 1916.

Falkiner, C. Litton, *Memoir of the late John Kells Ingram.* Dublin: Sealy, Bryers & Walker, 1907.

Finlay, Ian. *Columba.* London: Gollancz, 1979.

Fisher, Barbara. *Joyce Cary remembered in letters and interviews by his family and others.* Gerrands Cross: Smythe, 1988.

Foster, M., *Joyce Cary: a biography.* Boston: Houghton Mifflin, 1968.

Fowweather, Arthur. *One small head* [Downpatrick: printed by Down Recorder] 1980.

Gallagher, Patrick [Paddy the Cope]. *My story.* Dungloe: Templecrone Co-op, [19-].

Hamilton, John Stewart. *My times and other times.* Ballyshannon: Donegal Democrat. 1950.

Hamilton, John. *Sixty years' experience as an Irish landlord*/edited by H.C. White. London: Digby, Long, [n.d.].

Hart, Henry Travers, *The family history of Hart of Donegal.* London: Mitchell, Hughes & Clarke, 1907.

Hayward, Pat (ed). *Surgeon Henry's trifles.* London: Chatto & Windus, 1970.

Herdman, Rex. *They all made me.* Omagh: Montgomery, 1970.

Higgins, Michael D. (ed). *Monkeys in the superstructure: reminiscences of Peadar O'Donnell.* Galway: Salmon, 1986.

How, Frederick Douglas. *A hero of Donegal, Dr. William Smyth.* London: Ibister, 1902.

Jackson, Robert Wyse, *Archbishop Magrath, the scoundrel of Cashel.* Cork: Mercier Press, 1974.

Jackson, Robert Wyse, *Charles Inglis of Glencolmcille.* Dublin: APCK, 1962.

James Haggerty of Tir Conaill: Irish patriot – American hero. New York: Donegal Association of New York, 1992.

Jennings, Brenda. *Michael Ó Cléirigh, Chief of the Four Masters and his associates.* Dublin: Talbot Press 1976.

King, Cecil. *Memorabilia: musings on sixty odd years of life as a newspaperman.* Ballyshannon: Donegal Democrat, 1988.

Kingsley Porter, Lucy. *AE's letters to Mín an Labáin.* New York: Macmillan, 1937.

Kirkman, J. T., *Memoirs of the life of Charles Macklin.* London: Lackington, Allen, 1799.

Mac a' Bháird, Seaghán. *Beatha Naoimh Adhamhnain* [s.l.: s.n.], 1911.

MacDevitt, John. *The most Reverend James MacDevitt, bishop of Raphoe: a memoir.* Dublin: Gill, 1880.

Mac Donagh, J. C. *Isaac Butt 1813-1879* [Dublin: printed by Mahon], 1945.

McDyer, James. *The island of the setting sun*. Dublin: Veritas, 1986.

McDyer, James. *Fr McDyer of Glencolumbkille: an autobiography*. Dingle: Brandon, 1982.

Mac Fhionnghaile, Niall. *Donegal: their native soil (biographies of 10 men and women from North Donegal)*. Letterkenny: An Crann, 1989.

Mac Gabhann, Mící. *Rotha mór an tsaoil*. B.Á.C.: Foilseacháin Náisiúnta, 1959.

Mac Gabhann, Mící. *The hard road to Klondike*. Translated by Valentin Iremonger. London: Routledge and Kegan Paul, 1962.

MacGill, Patrick. *The great push*. London: Jenkins, 1916.

MacGill, Patrick. *The red horizon*. London: Jenkins, 1916.

Mac Giolla Bhrighde, Niall. *Dírbheathaisnéis Néill Mhic Ghiolla Bhrighde*. B.Á.C.: Oifig an tSoláthair, 1938.

Mac Giolla Chomhaill, Anraí. *Beatha Cholm Cille*. B.Á.C.: Foilseacháin Naisiúnta, 1981.

MacGinley, Niall. *Dr McGinley and his times*. Leitir Ceanainn: An Crann, 1985.

Mac Manus, Seamus. *The rocky road to Dublin*. Dublin: Talbot Press, 1947.

Mac Manus, Shaun B. *Yesterdays; part one: schooldays*. [Ballyshannon: printed by Donegal Democrat], 1964.

McCarron, Edward. *Life in Donegal 1850-1900 (Reminiscences of a lighthouse keeper)*. Dublin: Mercier, 1981.

McCullagh, Thomas. *Sir William McArthur K.C.M.G.: a biography, religious, parliamentary, municipal, commercial*. London: Hodder and Stoughton, 1891.

McGarrigle, Joe. *Donegal profiles*. Ballyshannon: Donegal Democrat [198-].

McGarvie, Michael. *Fanad on foot. Genealogical explorations in Donegal* [Glastonbury: printed by Direct Offset], 1989.

McGee, Thomas D'Arcy. *A life of the Rt Rev. Edward Maginn, coadjutor bishop of Derry, with selections from his correspondence*. New York: O'Shea, 1857.

McInerney, Michael. *Peadar O'Donnell, Irish social rebel*. Dublin: O'Brien Press, 1974.

McLaughlin, Raymond. *Inside an English jail*. Dublin: Borderline Press, 1987.

McStay, Margaret. *Colin*. Dublin: Poolbeg, 1986.

Maguire, Edward. *Life of Saint Adamnán, patron of Raphoe*. Dublin: Gill, 1917.

Maguire, Edward. *St Barron*. Dublin: Browne and Nolan, 1923.

Maguire, W. A. *Living like a lord: the second marquis of Donegall 1769-1824.* Belfast: Appletree Press, 1984.

Marsden, John. *The illustrated Columcille.* London: Macmillan, 1991.

Meehan, C. P. *The fate and fortunes of Hugh O'Neill, earl of Tyrone and Rory O'Donnell, earl of Tyrconnel; their flight from Ireland and death in exile.* Dublin: Derry, 1870.

Montgomery, Brian. *A field marshall in the family.* London: Constable, 1973.

Montgomery, Brian. *Monty's grandfather: Sir Robert Montgomery, GCSI, KCB, LCD 1809-1887; a life's service for the Raj.* Poole: Bladford Press, 1984.

Moody, George. *Rev. George Moody, M.A. of Buncrana, Co. Donegal, Ireland: a brief autobiographical sketch of his life and work, with an appreciation by the Very Rev. Henry Montgomery* [Belfast: printed by Graham and Heslip], 1935.

Nic Giolla Easpaig, Áine, agus Nic Giolla Easpaig, Eibhlín. *Girseacha i ngéibheann.* B.Á.C.: Foilseacháin Náisiúnta, 1986.

Nic Giolla Easpaig, Áine, and Nic Giolla Easpaig, Eibhlín. *Sisters in cells.* Westport: Foilseacháin Náisiúnta, 1987.

O'Brien, Sylvester. *Measgra i gcúimhne Mhíchíl uí Chléirigh: miscellany of historical and linguistic studies in honour of Brother Michael Ó Cléirigh, OFM, Chief of the Four Masters 1643-1943.* Dublin: Assisi Press, 1944.

Ó Cléirigh, Lughaidh. *Beatha Aodha Ruaidh ui Dhomhnaill = The life of Hugh Roe O'Donnell, prince of Tirconnell (1586-1602).* Edited by Denis Murphy. Dublin: Fallon, 1895.

Ó Domhnaill, Aodh agus Eoghan Ó Domhnaill. *Scéal Hiúdaí Sheáinín.* B.Á.C.: [s.n.], 1940.

Ó Domhnaill, Maghnus. *Betha Colaim Chille = Life of Colmcille.* Compiled by Manus O'Donnell in 1532; edited and translated ... by A. O'Kelleher and G. Schoepperle. Urbana: University of Illinois Press, 1918.

O'Donnell, Brigid. *The jew that Shakespeare drew (Charles Macklin).* Culdaff: Charles Macklin Autumn School, 1990.

O'Donnell, Daniel with Eddie Rowley. *Follow your dream.* Dublin: O'Brien Press, 1992.

O'Donnell, Peadar. *The gates flew open.* London: Cape, 1932.

O'Donnell, Peadar. *Salud! An Irishman in Spain.* London: Methuen, 1937.

O'Donnell, Peadar. *There will be another day.* Dublin: Dolmen Press, 1963.

O'Donnell, Terence, (ed). *Father John Colgan OFM 1592-1658.* Dublin. Assisi Press. 1959.

O'Grady, Standish. *Red Hugh's captivity.* London: Ward & Downey, 1889.

Ó Searcaigh, Séamus, *Beatha Cholm Cille* [s.l.: s.n.], 1967.

Parry, E. A. *Charles Macklin.* London: Kegan Paul, 1891.

Peacocke, J. Irvine. *Peacocke of Derry and Raphoe: an autobiographical sketch* [Dublin: printed by Church of Ireland Printing], 1946.

Rafter, Kevin. *Neil Blaney: a soldier of destiny.* Dublin: Blackwater Press, 1993.

Read, Maureen Hay. *Earthen vessel: James Hay, ordinary man.* Elverson, PA: Olde Springfield Shoppe, 1993.

Rentoul, James A. *Stray thoughts and memories.* London: Parsons, 1921.

Sheppard, Victor. *Michael O Clery, knight errant of Irish history.* Dublin: Assisi Press, 1943.

Sheridan, John. *Dawn to dusk.* Dublin: Fahy, 1991.

Simpson, W. Douglas. *The historical Saint Columba.* Aberdeen: Milne & Hutchinson, 1927.

Smith, John. *The life of St Columba, the apostle and patron saint of the ancient Scots and Picts, and joint patron of the Irish; commonly called Colum-Kille, the apostle of the Highlands.* Edinburgh: Mundell, 1798.

Sweeney, George. *'What about the workers': the story of John Doherty, trade unionist and factory reformer.* Derry: Guildhall Press, 1988.

Thornley, David. *Isaac Butt and home rule.* London: Macgibbon & Kee, 1964.

Trench, Charlotte Violet. *The Wrays of Donegal, Londonderry and Antrim.* Oxford: Oxford UP, 1945.

Tunney, John. *Saint Colmcille and the Columban heritage* [Gartan: Columba Heritage Trust], 1987.

Walsh, Paul. *The O'Cléirigh family of Tír Chonaill.* Dublin: Three Candles, [19-].

Walsh, Paul. *Irish chiefs and leaders.* Edited by Colm Ó Lochlainn. Dublin: Three Candles. 1960.

Walsh, Paul. *The Four Masters and their work.* Dublin: Three Candles. 1944.

Walsh Paul. *Leabhar Chloinne Suibhne.* Dublin: Three Candles, [19-].

Whiteside, Lesley. *George Otto Simms: a biography.* Gerrards Cross: Smythe, 1990.

Archaeology

Archaeological Survey of County Donegal: a description of the field antiquities of the county from the Mesolithic Period to the 17th century A.D. Brian Lacey et al. Lifford: Donegal County Council, 1983.

Commissioners of Public Works in Ireland. *Grianán of Aileach; Grey Abbey, Co. Down.* Dublin: HMSO, 1919.

Davies, O. and H. P. Swan. *The castles of Inishowen* [Belfast: printed by Gratan and Heslip, 194-].

Ireland. Office of Public Works. *Sites and monuments record, County Donegal.* Dublin: OPW, 1987.

Ó Donnabháin, Pádraig. *The archaeology of Inishowen = Seandálaíocht Inis Eoghain.* Carndonagh: Inishowen Tourism, 1988 (folded sheet).

General Histories

Campbell, Patrick. *A Molly Maguire story.* Jersey City, N.J: Templecrone Press, 1992.

The Civil Survey A.D. 1654-1656. Counties of Donegal, Londonderry and Tyrone vol. III. Prepared by Robert C. Simington. Dublin: Stationery Office, 1937.

Doherty, William James. *Inis-Owen and Tirconnell: being some account of antiquities and writers of the county of Donegal.* Dublin: Traynor, 1895.

McGinley, Niall. *Donegal, Ireland and the First World War.* Letterkenny: An Crann, 1987.

Moody, T. W. and J. G. Simms (eds). *The bishopric of Derry and the Irish Society of London, 1602-1705. vol. I: 1602-70.* Dublin: Stationery Office for Coimisiún Láimhscribhinni na hÉireann, 1968.

Moody, T.W. and J. G. Simms (eds). *The bishopric of Derry and the Irish Society of London, 1602-1705. vol. II: 1670-1705.* Dublin: Stationery Office for Coimisiún Láimhscríbhinni na nÉireann, 1983.

Murphy, Desmond. *Derry, Donegal and Modern Ulster, 1790-1921* Derry: Aileach Press, 1981.

Ó Cianán, Tadhg. *The flight of the Earls.* Edited by Paul Walsh. Dublin: McGill, 1916.

Ó Cléirigh, Micheál *[Annála Rioghachta Eireann]. The annals of Ireland, translated from the original Irish of the Four Masters.* By Owen Connellan. Dublin: Geraghty, 1846.

Ó Cléirigh, Michéal *[Annála Rioghachta Eireann]. Annals of the Kingdom of Ireland, by the Four Masters, from the earliest period to the year 1616.* Edited ... by John O'Donovan. 7 vols. Dublin: Hodges, Smith, 1856.

O'Donovan, John. *Letters containing information relative to the antiquities of the county of Donegal collected during the progress of the Ordnance Survey in 1835.* Lifford: [s.n.], 1946.

Quinn, J. *The story of the Drumboe martyrs.* Letterkenny: [printed by McKinney & O'Callaghan], 1976.

Quinn, John. *Wartime crashes and forced landings in Co. Donegal.* Belfast: WWII Irish Wreckology Group, 1990.

Tuke, James, H. *A visit to Donegal and Connaught.* London: Ridgway, 1880.

County Guides and Miscellanea

Bayne, S.G. *On an Irish jaunting-car: through Donegal and Connemara.* New York: Harper & Brothers, 1902.

Campbell, Joseph. *Mearing stones: leaves from my notebook on tramps in Donegal.* Dublin: Mansell, 1911.

Derwent, Eugene. *In the shadow of an Irish mountain.* Dublin: Clontarf Press, [19-].

Donegal Democrat Yearbook 1989. Ballyshannon: Donegal Democrat, 1989.

Donegal Democrat Yearbook 1990-91. Ballyshannon: Donegal Democrat, 1990.

McDevitt, James, *The Donegal Highlands.* Dublin: Murray, 1865.

Feehan, John M. *The secret places of Donegal.* Cork: Royal Carberry, 1988.

Fox, Arthur W. *Haunts of the eagle: man and wild nature in Donegal.* London: Methuen, 1924.

Gwynn, Stephen. *Highways and byeways in Donegal and Antrim.* London: Macmillan, 1903.

Hill, George. *Useful hints to Donegal tourists, with a brief notice of Rathlin Island, being the third part of Lord George Hill's 'Facts from Gweedore'.* Dublin: Philip Dixon, Handy, 1947.

Hill George. *Facts from Gweedore with useful hints to Donegal tourists.* Dublin: Philip Dixon, Handy, 1845.

Mason, William Shaw. *A statistical account, or parochial survey, drawn up from the communications of the clergy.* 3 vols. Dublin: Graisberry and Campbell, 1814 [covers six Donegal parishes].

Official guide to county Donegal. Castleblayney: Condor, 1989.

Shrubsole, Edgar S. *The land of lakes; being the Midland Railway company's illustrated guide to the sporting and touring grounds of County Donegal.* London: Cate, 1906.

Shrubsole, Edgar S. *Picturesque Donegal: its mountains, rivers and lakes; being the Great Northern Railway (Ireland) Copey's illustrated guide.* London: Cate, 1908.

Tohill. J. J. *Donegal: an exploration* [Ballyshannon: printed by Donegal Democrat], 1976.

Waddington's practical and pictorial guide to Londonderry and the Donegal highlands. York: Waddington, [19-].

Local History and Topography
Gaeltacht/West Donegal

Aalen, F. H. and H. Brody. *Gola: the life and last days of an island community.* Cork: Mercier Press, 1969.

'Ac Fhionnlaoich, Seán. *Scéal Ghaoth Dobhair.* B.Á.C.: Foilseacháin Náisiúnta, 1983.

Briody, Liam. *Glenties and Inniskeel* [Ballyshannon: printed by Donegal Democrat], 1986.

Campbell, Patrick. *Memories of Dungloe.* Jersey City, N.J.: [the author], 1993.

Cannon, Karl. *A tour of Lettermacaward* [s.l.: s.n.], 1985.

Devenney, Donnchadh. *Footprints through the Rosses* [s.l.: s.n.], 1993.

Gallagher, Barney. *Arranmore links* [s.l.: s.n.], 1986.

Giese, Rachel. *The Donegal pictures.* London: Faber & Faber, 1987.

Harkin, William. *Scenery & antiquities of north-west Donegal.* Londonderry: Irvine, 1893.

Herity, Michael. *Gleanncholmcille: a guide to 5,000 years of history in stone.* Dublin: John Augustine Press, 1971.

Manning, Aidan. *Glencolumbkille 3000 BC-1985 AD* [Ballyshannon: printed by Donegal Democrat], 1985.

Mac an Bháird, Seamas. *Troid Bhaile an Droichid: scéal faoi bhrúion chaorthainn a troideach i dTír Chonaill.* Beal Feirste: (s.n.), 1980.

Mac Aoidh, Seamus. *Oidhreacht Fhionáin.* An Fál Carrach: Glór na nGael, 1988.

McClintock, May. *After the battering ram: the trail of the dispossessed from Derryveagh, 1861.* Letterkenny: An Taisce, 1991.

Mac Menamin, Liam. *Glenfinn* [s.l.: s.n., n.d.],.

Ó Colm, Eoghan. *Toraigh na dtonn.* B.Á.C.: Foilseacháin Náisiúnta, 1971.

O'Donnell, Jimmy. *The Arranmore disaster: Saturday 9th November 1935* [Ballyshannon: printed by Donegal Democrat], 1993.

Swan, Henry Percival. *Highlights of the Donegal highlands.* Belfast: Carter, 1955.

Toraigh/Cloich Cheann Fhaola/Cnoc Fola: turas oidhreachta thart ar iarthuaisceart Thír Chonaill. An Fál Carrach: Cumann Stáire is Seanchais Chloich Cheann Fhaola, 1992.

Toraigh = Tory Island. Toraigh: An Comhar Cumann, 1992.

Treoir leabhar ar Ghaoth Dobhair-Cloich Cheannfhaola = Ein Miniführer durch Gweedore-Cloughaneely = Un guide abrégé de Gweedore-Cloughaneely = A mini guide to Gweedore-Cloughaneely [Ballyshannon: printed by Donegal Democrat], 1993.

Treoir leabhar ar na Rosa = Ein Miniführer durch die Rosses = une guide abrégé des Rosses = A mini guide to the Rosses [Ballyshannon: printed by Donegal Democrat], 1992.

Tullach Beaglaoich inné agus inniu. Taighde agus téacs (le) Cathal Ó Searcaigh. An Fálcarrach: Glór na nGael, 1993.

Watson, Seosamh, (eag.) *Oidhreacht Ghleann Cholm Cille.* B.Á.C.: An Clóchomhar, 1989. (leagan Gaeilge ar saothar Herity thuas).

Local History and Topography
East and Central Donegal

A sign-posted walking tour of Letterkenny. Sligo: D/L/S Tourism, 1988.

Bailey, Frances. *The Glebe House and Gallery.* Dublin: OPW, 1990.

Carton, Margaret. *Kilmacrennan: guided trails.* Kilmacrennan: Kilmacrennan Development Association, 1985.

Creeslough-Dunfanaghy: a guide [Creeslough]: Doe Historical Committee, [198-].

Cuimhne Adhamhnáin or a guide to St Eunan's Cathedral. Letterkenny: [s.n.], 1901.

Fitzgerald, John and John McCreadie. *Glenvar & Oughterlin.* Carndonagh: Foyle Press, [198-].

Fleming, Sam. *Letterkenny, past and present* [Ballyshannon: printed by Donegal Democrat], [197-].

Gartan and Churchill: a travellers guide [s.l.: s.n.], 1993.

Haggan, Mary. *Ramelton: an illustrated guide to the town.* Ramelton: RHDA, 1990.

Harrison, Graham. *St Eunan's Cathedral, Letterkenny.* Dublin: Eason, 1989.

Historical notes of Raphoe, Finn Valley, Lifford and Twin towns. Stranorlar: Knights of Columbanus, 1991.

Kelly, David. *Rambles round the Finn* (Ballyshannon: printed by Donegal Democrat), 1992.

Lucas, Leslie. *Mevagh down the years*. Belfast: Appletree Press. 1983.

Lucas, Leslie. *More about Mevagh*. Belfast: Appletree Press, 1982.

Maguire, Edward. *Letterkenny past and present*. Letterkenny: McKinney & O'Callaghan [192-].

Milford: photographs and memories. Milford: Tidy Towns Committee, 1989.

Mullin, T.H. *The Kirk and lands of Convoy since the Scottish settlement*. Belfast: Newsletter, 1960.

O'Carroll, Declan. *Rockhill House, Letterkenny, Co. Donegal: a history* [Ballyshannon: printed by Donegal Democrat], 1984.

Souvenir of the First Civic Week in Co. Donegal, Ballybofey and Stranorlar 28th April to 5th May, 1946 [s.l.: s.n.], 1946.

Wall, Maureen. *Glenswilly: a talk on her native glen* [s.l.: s.n., 197-].

Ward, Kevin. *Doe Castle, Creeslough, Co. Donegal: a visitors guide* [s.l.: s.n., 198-].

Local History and Topography
South Donegal

Allingham, Hugh. *Ballyshannon: its history and antiquities* [Ballyshannon: printed by Donegal Democrat], 1937.

Ballyshannon town study 1985. Commissioned by the Ballyshannon Chamber of Commerce, and carried out by the Department of Architecture, Bolton St College, DIT. Dublin: DIT, 1985.

Barron, Edward. *Ballyshannon: the rare old times* (Ballyshannon: printed by Donegal Democrat), 1989.

Carville, Geraldine. *Assaroe: abbey of the morning star*. Ballyshannon: Abbey Mill Wheel Trust, 1988.

Conaghan, Charles. *History and antiquities of Killybegs*. Ballyshannon: [printed by Donegal Democrat, 1975].

Conaghan, Pat. *Bygones: new horizons on the history of Killybegs* [s.l: s.n.], 1989.

Cunningham, John B. *Lough Derg: legendary pilgrimage* [Monaghan: printed by R & S Printers], 1984.

Curtayne, Alice. *Lough Derg, St Patrick's Purgatory* [Monaghan: printed by R & S Printers], 1962.

Duffy, Patrick J. *Landscapes of South Ulster: a parish atlas of the Diocese of Clogher*. Belfast: Institute of Irish Studies, QUB, 1993 (2 South Donegal parishes are in Clogher).

Egan, Bernard. *Drumhome* [Ballyshannon: printed by Donegal Democrat], 1986.

Flynn, Lawrence J. *St Patrick's Purgatory, Lough Derg, County Donegal.* Dublin: Eason, [198-].

Gibbons, Margaret. *Station Island, Lough Derg, with a brief historic sketch of the pilgrimage.* Dublin: Duffy, 1950.

'Kinnfaela'. *The cliff scenery of South-western Donegal, embracing detailed notices of St John's Point, Killybegs. Sliabh Liag, and Glen-Head.* Londonderry: Journal, 1867.

Leslie, Shane. *Saint Patrick's Purgatory: a record from history and literature.* London: Burn Oats and Washbourne, 1932.

Lough Erne, Bundoran and Donegal Highlands. From photographs by William Lawrence. Dublin: Lawrence, 1899.

Maguire, Edward. *Ballyshannon, past and present.* Bundoran Stepless, [193-].

McGee, William, *Upper Lough Erne in 1739.* Dublin: William McGee, 1892.

McGill, Lochlann. *In Conall's footsteps.* Dingle: Brandon Press, 1992.

Ó Gallachair, Pádraig. *The parish of Carn* [s.l.: s.n., 19-].

O'Connor, D. *St Patrick's Purgatory, Lough Derg: its history, traditions, legends, antiquities, topography and scenic surroundings.* Dublin: Duffy, 1885.

Patterson, W. J. *Rossnowlagh remembered* [Ballyshannon: printed by Donegal Democrat], 1991.

Purcell, Deirdre and Liam Blake. *On Lough Derg.* Dublin: Veritas, 1988.

Seymour, St John D. *Saint Patrick's Purgatory: a medieval pilgrimage in Ireland.* Dundalk: Dundalgen Press: 1918.

St Patrick's Purgatory, Lough Derg, county Donegal [s.l.: s.n., 193-].

Stephens, James, *Illustrated handbook of the scenery and antiquities of south-western Donegal.* Dublin: McGlashan & McGill, 1872.

Tractatus de Purgatorio sancti Patricii. St Patrick's Purgatory; a twilight century tale of a journey to the other world. Translated by Jean-Michel Picard. Dublin: Four Courts Press, 1985.

Wright, Thomas. *St Patrick's Purgatory; an essay on the legends of purgatory, hell, and paradise current during the middle ages.* London: Smith, 1844.

Local History and Topography
Inishowen
Beattie, Seán. *The book of Inistrahull.* Carndonagh: Lighthouse, 1992.

Beattie, Seán. Ancient monuments of Inishowen, North Donegal [Carndonagh]: Lighthouse, 1994.

Bonner, Brian. Our Inis Eoghain heritage. B.Á.C.: Foilseacháin Náisiúnta, 1974.

Bonner, Brian. That audacious traitor. B.Á.C.: Foilseacháin Náisiúnta, 1975.

Bonner, Brian. The homeland of the Ó Dochartaigh: an historical conspectus of Inis Eoghain. Pallaskenry: Salesian Press, 1985.

Bonner, Brian. Where Aileach guards. B.Á.C.: Foilseacháin Náisiúnta, 1974.

Doherty, William J. The Abbey of Fahan in Inis-Owen, county of Donegal. Dublin: Traynor, 1881.

Dougherty, Murray. The O'Doherty historic trail in counties Derry and Donegal. Derry: Guildhall Press, 1989.

Fitzgerald, John. Inishowen's fairyland [Ballyshannon: printed by Donegal Democrat, 197-].

Gailey's guide to Derry and its suburbs and county of Donegal. Londonderry: William Gailey, 1892.

A Guide to Inishowen, Co. Donegal. Carndonagh: Inishowen Tourism, 1993.

Harkin, Michael (ie. 'Maghtochair). Inishowen: its history, traditions and antiquities. Derry: [printed by the Journal], 1867.

Harkin, Maura and McCarroll, Sheila. Carndonagh [s.l.: s.n.], 1984.

McFadden, Vera. Dunree – guardian of Lough Swilly. Omagh: Montgomery, 1986.

McGrory, Neil. Inishowen: a journey through its past; an illustrated guide to the historical sites of Inishowen. Culdaff: [s.n.], 1988.

Montgomery, Henry. A history of Moville and its neighbourhood. Moville: [s.n.], 1991.

Swan, Harry Percival. 'Twixt Foyle and Swilly. Dublin: Hodges Figgis, [19-].

Swan, Harry Percival. Romantic Inishowen: Ireland's wonderful peninsula. Dublin: Hodges Figgis, 1947.

Swan, Harry Percival. The book of Inishowen. Buncrana: Doherty 1938.

Young, Amy Isabel, Three hundred years in Inishowen. Belfast: McCan, Stevenson & Orr, 1929.

Litríocht agus Léirmheastóireacht

MacCongáil, Nollaig, Léargas ar 'Cith is dealán' Mháire. B.Á.C.: Náisiúnta Teoranta, 1982.

Mac Congáil, Nollaig, *Scríbhneoirí Thír Chonaill.* B.Á.C.: Foilseacháin Náisiúnta Teoranta, 1983.

Mac Congáil, Nollaig, *Máire – Clár Saothair.* B.Á.C.: Coiscéim, 1990.

Mac Congáil, Nollaig, *Seosamh MacGrianna/Iolann fionn (Clár Saothair).* B.Á.C.: Coiscéim, 1990.

Mac Congáil, Nollaig, (eag). *Scríbhneoireacht na gConallach.* B.Á.C.: Coiscéim, 1990.

Mag Fhionnlaoigh, Peadar [i. Cú Uladh]. *Scríobhnóirí móra Chúige Uladh.* B.Á.C.: [an t-údar], 1925.

Ó Corráin, Ailbhe, *A concordance of idiomatic expressions in the writings of Seámus Ó Grianna.* Belfast, Queens University, 1989.

Ó Gallchóir, Seán [i Peigí Rose], *Peigí ar 'Mháire'.* B.Á.C.: Coiscéim, 1992.

Ó Searcaigh, Seamus, *Nua Sgríbhneoirí na Gaedhilge.* B.Á.C.: Brún agus Ó Nualláin, 1933.

Póirtéir, Cathal. *Micí Sheáin Néill: scéalaí agus scéalta.* B.Á.C.: Coiscéim, 1993.

Filíocht

Mac a' Bháird, Seaghán. *Leabhar filidheachta fá choinne na scoil.* Dublin: Gill, 1909.

Mac Grianna, Seosamh. *Filí gan Iomrádh.* Béal Feirste: Cló-oifig Shéin Uí Mháta, 1926.

Ní Bhrolcháin, Muireann, (eag). *= Maol Íosa Ó Brolcháin.* Maigh Nuad: An Sagart, 1986.

Ó Gallchóir, Cathal [*Japanese text = Beautiful Irish Language. Dublin City & Errigal Mountain*]. Tokyo: [s.n.], 1990.

Ó Searcaigh, Cathal. *Miontraigéide Chatrach* [s.l.: s.n.], 1975.

Ó Searcaigh, Cathal. *Tuirlingt.* B.Á.C.: Earlsfort Press, 1978.

Ó Searcaigh, Cathal. *Suíle Shuibhne.* B.Á.C.: Coiscéim, 1983.

Ó Searcaigh, Cathal. *Suibhne.* B.Á.C.: Coiscéim, 1987.

Ó Searcaigh, Cathal. *An bealach 'na bhaile,* Indreabhan: Cló Iar-Chonnachta Teo, 1991.

Ó Searcaigh, Cathal, *Homecoming = An bealach 'na bhaile: selected poems = rogha dánta.* Indreabhán: Cló Iar Chonnachta, 1993.

Dramaíocht

Mag Fhionnlaoigh, Peadar [i. Cú Uladh]. *Miondrámanna.* B.Á.C.: Conradh na Gaedhilge, 1902.

Mag Fhionnlaoigh, Peadar [i. Cú Uladh]. *Tá na Francaighe ar an Muir.* Dublin: Gill, 1905.

Mag Fhionnlaoigh, Peadar, i. Cú Uladh. *Eachtra Aodh Ruaidh Uí Dhomhnaill.* B.Á.C.: [s.n.], 1911.

Mac Meanman, Seaghán, *Trí mhion-dráma.* B.Á.C.: Oifig Díolta Foillseacháin Rialtais, 1936.

Scéalaíocht

'Ac Fhionnlaoich, Seán. *Ó rabharta go mallmhuir.* B.Á.C.: Foilseacháin Náisiúnta, 1975.

'Ac Fhionnlaoich, Seán. *Is glas na cnoic.* B.Á.C.: Foilseacháin Náisiúnta, 1977.

Mag Fhionnlaoigh, Peadar [i. Cú Uladh]. *Ciall na sean ráidhte.* Belfast: Irish News, 1914.

Mag Fhionnlaoigh, Peadar [i. Cú Uladh]. *An cogadh dearg agus scéalta eile.* B.Á.C.: [an t-údar], 1918.

Mag Fhionnlaoigh, Peadar [i. Cú Uladh]. *Bliain na haiséirí.* B.Á.C.: Coiscéim, 1992.

Mac Grianna, Seosamh. *Dochartach Dhuibhlionna agus sgéaltai eile* B.Á.C.: Cú Uladh, 1925.

Mac Grianna, Seosamh. *An Grádh is an ghruaim* B.Á.C.: Oifig an tSoláthair, 1929.

Mac Grianna, Seosamh. *Eoghan Ruadh Ó Neill.* B.Á.C.: Oifig Díolta Foillseacháin Rialtais, 1931.

Mac Grianna, Seosamh. *Pádraic Ó Conaire agus aistí eile.* B.Á.C.: Oifig an tSoláthair, 1936.

Mac Grianna, Seosamh. *An Bhreatain Bheag.* B.Á.C.: Oifig an tSoláthair, 1937.

Mac Grianna, Seosamh. *Na Lochlannaigh.* B.Á.C.: Oifig an tSoláthair, 1938.

Mac Grianna, Seosamh. *Mo bhealach féin agus dá mbiodh ruball ar an éan.* B.Á.C.: Oifig an tSoláthair, 1940.

Mac Grianna, Seosamh. *An Druma Mór.* B.Á.C.: Oifig an tSoláthair, 1969.

Mac Grianna, Seosamh. *Ailt.* Cabhán: [s.n.], 1977.

Mac Grianna, Seosamh. *Filí agus felons.* Cathair na Mart: FNT, 1987.

Mac Meanman, Seaghán Bán. *Sgéalta goiride geimhridh.* B.Á.C.: Connradh na Gaedhilge, 1915.

Mac Meanman, Seaghán Bán. *Fear siubhail a's a chuid comharsannagh agus daoine eile.* B.Á.C.: Oifig Díolta Foillseacháin Rialtais, 1924.

Mac Meanman, Seaghán Bán. *Indé agus indiu*. B.Á.C.: Oifig an tSoláthair, 1929.

Mac Meanman, Seaghán Bán. *Mám as mo mhála*. B.Á.C.: Oifig an tSoláthair, 1940.

Mac Meanman, Seaghán Bán. *Ó chamhaoir go clap-sholas*. B.Á.C.: Oifig an tSoláthair, 1940.

Mac Meanman, Seaghán Bán. *Eachtraí chois teineadh*. B.Á.C.: Oifig an tSoláthair, 1945.

Mac Meanman, Seaghán Bán. *An margadh dubh*. B.Á.C.: Oifig an tSoláthair, 1952.

Mac Meanman, Seaghán Bán. *Mám eile as an mhála chéadna*. B.Á.C.: Oifig an tSoláthair, 1954.

Mac Meanman, Seaghán Bán. *Crathadh an phocáin*. B.Á.C.: Oifig an tSoláthair, 1955.

Mac Meanman, Seaghán Bán. *Rácáil agus scuabadh*. B.Á.C.: Oifig an tSoláthair, 1955.

Mac Meanman, Seaghán Bán. *Cnuasach chéad conlach*. B.Á.C.: Coiscéim, 1988.

Mac Meanman, Seaghán Bán. *An chéad mhám*. B.Á.C.: Coiscéim, 1990.

Mac Meanman, Seaghán Bán. *An dara mám*. B.Á.C.: Coiscéim, 1991.

Mac Meanman, Seaghán Bán. *An tríú mám*. B.Á.C.: Coiscéim, 1992.

Mac Suibhne, Pádraig. *Táibhsí an chreagáin* [s.l.: s.n.], 1976.

Mac Suibhne, Pádraig. *Spaisteoireacht* [s.l.: s.n.], 1980.

Mac Suibhne, Pádraig. *Solas uaigneach* [s.l.: s.n.], 1992.

Máire (Séamus Ó Grianna). *Mo dhá Róisín*. B.Á.C.: Trí gCoinneal, 1920.

Máire (Séamus Ó Grianna). *Caisleáin óir*. Dún Dealgan: Preas Dhún Dealgan, 1924.

Máire (Séamus Ó Grianna). *Micheál Ruadh*. Dún Dealgan: Preas Dhún Dealgan, 1925.

Máire (Seéamus Ó Grianna). *Cioth is dealán*. Dún Dealgan: Preas Dhún Dealgan, 1926.

Máire (Séamus Ó Grianna). *Feara fáil*. Dún Dealgan: Cló-lucht an Scrúduightheoir, 1933.

Máire (Séamus Ó Grianna). *Thiar i dTir Chonaill*. B.Á.C.: Trí gCoinneal, 1940.

Máire (Séamus Ó Grianna). *Nuair a bhí mé óg*. B.Á.C.: Cló an Talbóidigh, 1942.

Máire (Séamus Ó Grianna). *Rann na Feirste*. B.Á.C. An Press Náisiúnta, 1942.

Máire (Séamus Ó Grianna). *An aibidil a rinne Cadmus*. B.Á.C.: An Press Náisiúnta, 1944.

Máire (Séamus Ó Grianna). *Saoghal corrach*. B.Á.C.: An Press Náisiúnta, 1945.

Máire (Séamus Ó Grianna). *Scéal úr agus sean scéal*. B.Á.C.: Oifig an tSoláthair, 1945.

Máire (Séamus Ó Grianna). *An teach nár tógadh*. B.Á.C.: Oifig an tSoláthair, 1948.

Máire (Séamus Ó Grianna). *Ó neamh go h-Árainn*. B.Á.C.: Oifig an tSoláthair, 1953.

Máire (Séamus Ó Grianna). *An clár is an fhoireann*. B.Á.C.: Oifig an tSoláthair, 1955.

Máire (Séamus Ó Grianna). *Fód a' bháis*. B.Á.C.: Oifig an tSoláthair, 1955.

Máire (Séamus Ó Grianna). *Tráigh is tuile*. B.Á.C.: Oifig an tSoláthair, 1955.

Máire (Séamus Ó Grianna). *Fallaing shíoda*. B.Á.C.: Oifig an tSoláthair, 1956.

Máire (Séamus Ó Grianna). *Tarngaireacht mhiseóige*. B.Á.C.: Oifig an tSoláthair, 1958.

Máire (Séamus Ó Grianna). *An draoidín*. B.Á.C.: Oifig an tSoláthair, 1959.

Máire (Séamus Ó Grianna). *An bhratach*. B.Á.C.: Oifig an tSoláthair, 1959.

Máire (Séamus Ó Grianna). *Ó mhuir go sliabh*. B.Á.C.: Oifig an tSoláthair, 1961.

Máire (Séamus Ó Grianna). *Cúl le muir*. B.Á.C.: Oifig an tSoláthair, 1961.

Máire (Séamus Ó Grianna). *Suipín an iolar*. B.Á.C.: Oifig an tSoláthair, 1962.

Máire (Séamus Ó Grianna). *Úna Bhán*. B.Á.C.: Oifig an tSoláthair, 1962.

Máire (Séamus Ó Grianna). *Bean Ruadh de Dhálach*. Oifig an tSoláthair, 1966.

Máire (Séamus Ó Grianna). *Le clap-sholus*. B.Á.C.: Oifig an tSoláthair, 1967.

Máire (Séamus Ó Grianna). *Oidhche shamhraidh agus scéalta eile*. B.Á.C.: Oifig an tSoláthair, 1968.

Máire (Séamus Ó Grianna). *An sean-teach*. B.Á.C.: Oifig an tSoláthair, 1968.

Máire (Séamus Ó Grianna). *Cora cinniúna 1*. B.Á.C.: An Gúm, 1993.

Máire (Séamus Ó Grianna). *Cora cinniúna 2*. B.Á.C.: An Gúm, 1994.

Ó Baoighill, Aindrias. *Fir mhóra na hÉireann*: Dún Dealgan: Phreas Dhún Dealgan, 1925.

Ó Baoighill, Aindrias. *Sgéilíní na Finne*. B.Á.C.: Oifig an tSoláthair, 1928.

Ó Baoighill, Aindrias. *An dílidhe*. B.Á.C.: Oifig an tSoláthair, 1930.

Ó Baoighill, Aindrias. *Cnuasach na Finne*. B.Á.C.: Coiscéim, 1993.

Ó Baoighill, Pádraig. *An coileach troda agus scéalta eile*. B.Á.C.: Coiscéim, 1993.

Ó Dochartaigh, Mícheál. *Scéaltaí beaga.* Letterkenny: McKinney, 1910.

Ó Domhnaill, Maghnus [i. Fionn Mac Cumhaill]. *Sraith 'sgian go mbuaidh'.* B.Á.C.: Brún agus Ó Nóláin, 1922.

Ó Domhnaill, Maghnus [i. Fionn Mac Cumhaill]. *Maicín.* Dún Dealgan: Tempest, 192?.

Ó Domhnaill, Maghnus [i. Fionn Mac Cumhaill]. *Tusa a mhaicín.* Derry: McCool and Green, 1922.

Ó Domhnaill, Maghnus [i. Fionn Mac Cumhaill]. *An dochartach.* Dundalk: Dundalgan Press, [192?].

Ó Domhnaill, Maghnus [i. Fionn Mac Cumhaill]. *'Sé Dia an fear is fearr.* B.Á.C.: Oifig an tSoláthair, 1928.

Ó Domhnaill, Maghnus [i. Fionn Mac Cumhaill]. *Na Rosa go brathach.* B.Á.C.: Oifig an tSoláthair, 1939.

Ó Domhnaill, Maghnus [i. Fionn Mac Cumhaill]. *Gleann na coilleadh uaignighe* [s.l.: s.n., 19-].

Ó Domhnaill, Maghnus [i. Fionn Mac Cumhaill]. *Iascaire na gciabhfholt-fionn* [s.l.: s.n.], 1955.

Ó Domhnaill, Maghnus [i. Fionn Mac Cumhaill]. *Gura slán le m'óige* [s.l.: s.n.], 1967.

Ó Domhnaill, Maghnus [i. Fionn Mac Cumhaill]. *An sean-fhód* [s.l.: s.n.], 1969.

Ó Rabhartaigh, Tadhg. *Mian na marbh* [s.l.: s.n.], 1937.

Ó Rabhartaigh, Tadhg. *Thiar in nGleann Ceo.* B.Á.C.: Oifig an tSoláthair, 1953.

Ó Rabhartaigh, Tadhg. *Gasúr de chuid bhaile na nGrág* [s.l.: s.n.], 1955.

Ó Searcaigh, Séamus. *Faire Pháidí Mhóir.* B.Á.C.: Connradh na Gaedhilge, 1909.

Ó Searcaigh, Séamus. *Cú na gcleas agus sgéalta eile* [s.l.: s.n.], 1914.

Ó Searcaigh, Séamus. *Ceol na n-éan.* Dundalk: Tempest, 1919.

Ó Searcaigh, Séamus. *Buaidh na tuigse* [s.l.: s.n.], 1940.

Prós

Ó Baoill, Aindrias. *Fiach fánach: Díolann aistí as an tUltach 1951-1971.* B.Á.C.: Coiscéim, 1992.

Rose, Peigí, *An chéad chnuasach,* B.Á.C., Coiscéim, 1991.

Mag Fhionnlaoigh, Peadar [i Cú Uladh]. *An léightheoir Gaedhealach.* B.Á.C.: [an tÚdar], 1907.

Litríocht Paistí

Ó Creag, Séamus. *Clann Lir.* Dublin: Sealy, Bryers & Walker, 1901.

Ó Creag, Séamus. *Clann Tuireann.* Dublin: Sealy, Bryers & Walker, 1902.

Ó Creag, Séamus. *Clann Uisnigh.* Dublin: Sealy, Bryers & Walker, 1902.

Ó Searcaigh, Séamus. *Laochas.* B.Á.C.: Augustine, 1945.

Literature, Language and Literary Criticism

Christian, Edwin Ernest. *Joyce Cary's creative imigination.* New York: Lang, 1988.

Cook, Cornelia. *Joyce Cary, liberal principles.* London: Vision Press, 1981.

Dantanus, Ulf. *Brian Friel, a study.* London: Faber & Faber, 1988.

Freyer, Grattan. *Peadar O'Donnell.* Lewisburg, Ky: Bucknell U. P., 1973.

Hall, Denis. *Joyce Cary, a reappraisal.* London: Macmillan Press, 1983.

Hart, H. C. *Notes on Ulster dialect, chiefly Donegal.* Hertford: Austin, 1899.

Mahood, M. M. *Joyce Cary's Africa.* London: Methuen, 1964.

Maxwell, D. E. S. *Brian Friel.* Lewisburg, Ky: Bucknell U.P., 1973.

O'Brien, George. *Brian Friel.* Dublin: Gill & Macmillan , 1989.

O'Connor, Ulick. *Brian Friel: crisis & commitment: the writer & Northern Ireland.* Dublin: Elo Publications, 1989.

Peacock, Alan J. (ed). *The achievement of Brian Friel.* Gerrard's Cross: Colin Smythe, 1993.

Pine, Richard. *Brian Friel and Ireland's drama.* London: Routledge, 1990.

Traynor, Michael. *The English dialect of Donegal: a glossary.* Dublin: RIA, 1953.

Warner, Alan. *William Allingham.* Lewisburg, Ky: Bucknell U.P., 1975.

Wright, Andrew. *Joyce Cary: a preface to his novels.* London: Chatto & Windus, 1958.

See also Biography.

Poetry

Alexander, Cecil Frances. *Poems.* London: Macmillan, 1896.

Alexander, William. *Selected poems.* Dublin: Talbot Press, 1932.

Allingham, William. *The music master, A love story and two series of day and night songs*. London: Routledge, 1855.

Allingham, William. *The ballad book*. London: Macmillan, 1864.

Allingham, William. *Fifty modern poems*. London: Bell and Daldy, 1865.

Allingham, William. *Songs, ballads and stories*. London: Bell, 1877.

Allingham, William. *Day and night songs*. London: Philip, 1884.

Allingham, William. *Laurence Bloomfield or Rich and poor in Ireland*. London: Reeves & Turner, 1888.

Allingham, William. *Life and phantasy*. London: Reeves and Turner, 1889.

Allingham, William. *Irish songs and poems*. London: Longmans Green, 1901.

Allingham, William. *Sixteen poems by William Allingham*. Selected by William Butler Yeats. Dublin: Dún Emer Press, 1905.

Allingham, William. *By the way*. London: Longmans, Green, 1912.

Allingham, William. *Poems*. London: Macmillan, 1912.

Allingham, William. *The poems of William Allingham*. Edited by John Hewitt. Dublin: Dolmen Press, 1967.

Brooke, Richard Sinclair A. B. *Poems (grace-creation-suffering)*. Dublin: McGlashan, 1852.

Brooke, Stopford A. *Studies in poetry*. London: Duckworth, 1907.

Burke, Ulick. *Donegal rhymes*. London: Claude Stacey [192?].

Campbell, Una. *The tapestry of life*. Killarney: Mac, 1989.

Cannon, Moya. *Oar*. Galway: Salmon, 1990.

Carbery, Ethna, Seamus MacManus, and Alice Milligan. *We sang for Ireland*. Dublin: Gill, & Son, 1950.

Doherty, Alexander. *Through the lens* [Sligo: printed by the Champion], 1981.

Gallagher, Patrick. *Land I love*. Ilfracombe: Stockwell, 1969.

Gallagher, Patrick. *Selected Poetry*. New York: Exposition Press, 1979.

Gallagher, William J. *From sod to star*. London: Smith. 1920.

Gallagher, H.G. *The lays of a 'lad'*. Letterkenny: [Printed by Donegal Printing Co.], 1917.

Galligan, Frank, *A cold forbidding Irish green*. Coleraine: University of Ulster, 1990.

'Gallion Slieve' & 'Cruck-A-Leaghan', *Lays and legends of the North of Ireland*. Dublin: Gill & Son, 1884.

Gage, Gervais (J. Laurence Rentoul). *From far lands*. London: Macmillan, 1914.

Gillespie, Brigid. *Milestones along the way*. Letterkenny: (printed by Donegal Printing Co), [19-].

Gorevan, T. G. *Flight of the earls*. Devon: Stockwell, 1982.

Graham, John. *Poems, chiefly historical*. Belfast: [printed by Stuart and Gregg], 1929.

Harvey, Francis. *In the light of the stones*. Dublin: Gallery Press, 1978.

Harvey, Francis. *The rainmakers*. Dublin: Gallery Press, 1988.

Henderson, James. *The wanderer's dream and other poems*. Belfast: Baird, 1912.

Holmes, Theodore. *Poems from Donegal*. London: The Mitre Press, [19-].

Ingram, John K. *Sonnets and other poems*. London: Black, 1900.

Johnston, James Nicoll. *Donegal memories and other poems*. New York: Mathews-Northrup Works, 1910.

MacGill, Patrick. *Songs of the dead end*. London: Year Book Press, 1913.

MacGill, Patrick. *Soldier songs*. London: Jenkins, 1917.

MacGill, Patrick. *Songs of Donegal*. London: Jenkins, 1921.

MacGill, Patrick. *The navy poet: the collected poetry of Patrick MacGill*. Dingle: Brandon, 1984.

McGinniss, John J. *Flights of the fairies and other verses*. New York: Celtic Publishing, 1917.

McKelvie, James. *A wheen o' Finnside verses* [s.l.: s.n.], 1991.

M'Loughlin, J. Bawn. *Gems from the heather and songs of Donegal*. Letterkenny: [printed by McConnell & O'Callaghan], 1903.

MacManus, Seamus. *Shuilers from heathy hills*. Donegal: G. Kirke, 1893.

MacManus, Anna (Ethna Carbery). *The four winds of Éirinn*. Dublin: Gill, 1902.

MacManus, Seamus. *Ballads of a country boy*. Dublin: Gill, 1905.

Melvin, O.P. *Selected poems*. Killybegs: Banba Press, 1978.

Ó Domhnaill, Mícheál. *From the cradle to the grave* [Ballyshannon: printed by Donegal Democrat], 1990.

O'Boyce, John Clinton. *Rustic rhymes or idle hours*. Dundalk: Dundalgan Press, [19-].

O'Boyle, Charles J. *Oldtime poetry from Donegal* [s.l.]: Owenteskna, 1993.

O'Byrne, Cathal and Cahir Healy. *The lane of the thrushes*. Dublin: Sealy, Bryers & Walker, 1905.

O'Donnell, F. Hugh. *The message of the masters*. London: Long, 1901.

O'Donnell, Michael. *By the Kilcar hearth* [Ballyshannon: printed by Donegal Democrat], 1989.

O'Kelly, Dominic. *Sky sea sod*. Ballyshannon: Donegal Democrat, 1960.

O'Neill, John. *The rock of Arranmore*. Dublin: Gill, 1904.

O'Sullivan, Seumas. *The Rosses and other poems*. Dublin: Maunsel, 1918.

O'Sullivan, D. J. *Lightkeepers lyrics*. Dundalk: Dundalgan Press, 1947.

O'Sullivan, D. J. *From Fastnet to Inishtrahull*. Belfast: Lapwing Press, 1993.

Scott, Rebecca. *Echoes from Tyrconnel: a collection of legendary and other poems*. Londonderry: Colhoun, 1880.

Shane, Elizabeth. *Tales of the Donegal coast and islands*. London: Selwyn & Blount, 1921.

Shane, Elizabeth. *By bog and sea in Donegal*. London: Selwyn & Blount, 1923.

Shane, Elizabeth. *The collected poems of Elizabeth Shane*. Dundalk: Dundalgan Press, 1945.

Shane, Elizabeth. *Piper's tunes*. London: Selwyn & Blount, [19-].

Sheridan, John D. *Joe's no saint and other poems*. Dublin: Gill, 1951.

Sweeney, Mathew. *Without shores*. Leicester: Omens, 1978.

Sweeney, Mathew. *Empty trains*. London: Oasis, 1978.

Sweeney, Mathew. *A dream of maps*. Dublin: Raven Arts, 1981.

Sweeney, Mathew. *A round house*. Dublin: Raven Arts, 1983.

Sweeney, Mathew. *The lame waltzer*. Dublin: Raven Arts, 1985.

Sweeney, Mathew. *Blue shoes*. London: Secker & Warburg, 1989.

Sweeney, Mathew. *Cacti*. London: Secker & Warburg, 1992.

Sweeney, Mathew. *The flying spring onion*. London: Faber & Faber, 1992.

Tunney, Paddy. *Dáchas and other poems*. Letterkenny: Eagráin Dhun na nGall, 1990.

Ward, Thomas E. *Blossoms from the song time*. Derry: [printed by the Derry Journal], 1914.

Wilson, R. A. *The reliques of 'Barney Maglone'*. Dublin: Griffin O'Donoghue, 1894.

Drama

Carr, Hugh. *Encounter in the wilderness*. Baltimore: Proscenium Press, 1980.

Friel, Brian. *Philadelphia, here I come!*. London: Faber & Faber, 1965.

Friel, Brian. *The loves of Cass Maguire*. London: French, 1966.

Friel, Brian. *Lovers*. London: Faber & Faber, 1969.

Friel, Brian. *Crystal and fox*. London: Faber & Faber, 1970.

Friel, Brian. *The mundy scheme*. London: French, 1970.

Friel, Brian. *The gentle island*. London: Davis Poynter, 1973.

Friel, Brian. *The freedom of the city*. London: Faber & Faber, 1974.

Friel, Brian. *The enemy within*. Newark, Del.: Proscenium Press, 1979.

Friel, Brian. *Living quarters*. London: Faber & Faber, 1978.

Friel, Brian. *Volunteers*. London: Faber & Faber, 1979.

Friel Brian. *Faith healer*. London: Faber & Faber, 1980.

Friel, Brian. *Aristocrats*. Dublin: Gallery Press, 1980.

Friel, Brian. *Translations*. London: Faber & Faber, 1981.

Friel, Brian. *Communication cord*. London: Faber & Faber, 1983.

Friel, Brian. *Dancing at Lúghnasa*. London: Faber & Faber, 1990.

Friel, Brian. *Wonderful Tennessee*. Oldcastle: Gallery Press, 1993.

Friel, Brian. *[The freedom of the city] Les citoyens d'honneur*. Lille: Presses universitaires, (1986).

Friel, Brian. *[Philadelphia, here I come! The loves of Cass McGuire. Lovers] Théâtre: Philadelphie, mon amour. Les amours de Cass McGuire. Les saisons d'amour*. Lille: Presses universitaires, 1982.

Friel, Brian. *Selected plays*. London: Faber & Faber, 1990.

Friel, Brian. *The London vertigo,* based on a play *'The honest Irishman'* by Charles Macklin. Oldcastle: Gallery Press, 1990.

Friel, Brian. *The three sisters,* by Anton Chekov, adapted by Brian Friel. Dublin: Gallery Press, 1981.

Mac Manus, Seamus. *The hard-hearted man,* with Thomas O'Concannon. Dublin: Gill, 1905.

Mac Manus, Seamus. *Women of seven sorrows*. Dublin: Gill, 1905.

Mac Manus, Seamus. *The lad from Largymore*. Donegal: O'Molloy [1909?].

Mac Manus, Seamus. *Mrs Connolly's cashmere*. Donegal: O'Molloy [1909?].

Mac Manus, Seamus. *Rory wins*. Donegal: O'Molloy [1909?].

Mac Manus, Seamus. *The resurrection of Dinny O'Dowd*. Donegal: O'Molloy [1909?].

Mac Manus, Seamus. *The rale true doctor*. Donegal: O'Molloy, 1934.

McGuinness, Frank. *The factory girls*. Dublin: Monarch Line, 1982.

McGuinness, Frank. *Observe the sons of Ulster marching towards the Somme*. London: Faber & Faber, 1986.

McGuinness, Frank. *Mary & Lizzie*. London: Faber & Faber, 1989.

McGuinness, Frank. *Innocence*. London: Faber & Faber, 1987.

McGuinness, Frank. *The Carthaginians*. London: Faber & Faber, 1988.

McGuinness, Frank. *Baglady*. London: Faber & Faber, 1988.

McGuinness, Frank, *Someone who'll watch over me*. London: Faber & Faber, 1993.

McGuinness, Frank, *Three sisters,* by Anton Chekhov, adapted by Frank McGuinness. London: Faber & Faber, 1990.

McGuinness, Frank. *Peer Gynt,* by Henrik Ibsen, adapted by Frank McGuinness London: Faber & Faber, 1990.

Macklin, Charles. *Four Comedies a) Love a la mode b) The true-born Irishman c) The school of husbands d) The man of the world*. London: Sidgwick & Jackson, 1968.

O'Donnell, Frank J. Hugh. *The dawn-mist: a play of the rebellion*. Dublin: Gail Cooperative, 1922.

O'Donnell, Peadar. *Wrack*. London: Cape, 1933.

Fiction

Barlow, Jane. *Irish ways*. London: Allen, 1911.

Barrington, Margaret. *David's daughter Tamar*. Dublin: Wolfhound Press, 1982.

Bodkin, M. *Halt, invader*. Dublin: Browne & Nolan, 1940.

Brooke, Richard Sinclair. *The story of parson Annaly*. Dublin: Drought, 1870.

Butt, Isaac. *The Gap of Barnesmore: A tale of the Irish highlands and the revolution of 1688*, Vol. I. London: Smith, 1848.

Butt, Isaac. *The Gap of Barnesmore: A tale of the Irish highlands and the revolution of 1688*, Vol. II. London: Smith, 1848.

Carbery, Ethne. *The passionate hearts*. Dublin: Gill, 1903.

Carbery, Eithne. *In the Irish past*. Cork: Mercier, 1978.

Carbery, Eithne. *In the Celtic past*. Dublin: Gill, 1907.

Cary, Joyce. *An American visitor*. London: Joseph, 1933.

Cary, Joyce. *Castle corner*. London: Joseph Ltd, 1938.

Cary, Joyce. *Power in men*. London: Nicholson & Watson, 1939.

Cary, Joyce. *Herself surprised*. London: Joseph, 1941.

Cary, Joyce. *A house of children*. London: Joseph, 1941.

Cary Joyce. *The moonlight*. London: Joseph, 1946.

Cary, Joyce. *Mister Johnson*. London: Joseph, 1947.

Cary, Joyce. *A fearful joy*. London: Joseph, 1949.

Cary, Joyce. *Except the Lord*. London: Joseph, 1953.

Cary, Joyce. *Prisoner of grace*. London: Joseph, 1954.

Cary, Joyce. *Not honour more*. London: Joseph, 1955.

Cary, Joyce. *Charley is my darling*. New York: Harper & Brothers, [1956].

Cary, Joyce. *The captive and the free*. London: Joseph, 1959.

Cary, Joyce. *Memoir of the Bobotes*. London: Joseph, 1965.

Cary, Joyce. *Triptych*. London: Penguin, 1985.

Cassidy, P.S. *Glenveigh or the victims of vengeance*. Boston: Donahoe, 1870.

Coyle, Edmund. *Bird in the window*. Letterkenny: [printed by the Ballyraine Training Centre], 1986.

Coyle, Edmund. *Derrymen*. Letterkenny: [printed by Donegal Printing Co.], 1988.

Davidson, F. *Loan-ends stories in Ulster*. Belfast: Quota Press, 1933.

Derwent, Eugene. *The welcome in the glen*. Dublin: Gill, 1951.

Doherty, Angela. *Constant friends*. London: Orion, 1993.

Dorman, Seán. *Valley of Graneen*. London: Davies, 1944.

Edwards, R. W. K. *The mermaid of Inish-uig*. London: Arnold, 1898.

Esler, E. R. *A maid of the manse*. London: Sampson Low, Marston, 1895.

Esler, E. R. *Mid green pastures*. London: Sampson Low, Marston, 1895.

Esler, E. R. *Youth at the prow*. London: Long, 1898.

Fleming, W. H. *Life-line lad*. New York: Comet Press, 1957.

Floredice, W. H. *Derryreel: a collection of stones from North West Donegal*. London: Hamilton,1889.

Floredice, W. H. *'Mere Irish' stories*. London: Kegan Paul, Trench, 1886.

Friel, Brian. *The saucer of larks*. London: Gollancz, 1962.

Friel, Brian. *The gold in the sea*. London: Gollancz, 1966.

Friel, Brian. *Selected stories*. Dublin: Gallery Press, 1979.

Gaffney, Gertrude. *Towards the dawn*. Dublin: Talbot Press, 1930.

Galligan, Frank. *Out of the blue*. Coleraine: Clegnagh House, 1992.

Gee, D.P. *Hotel at the edge of the world*. Dingle: Brandon, 1989.

Healy, Cahir. *A sower of the wind*. Dublin: Sealy,Bryers & Walker, 1903.

Mac Carron, Daniel. *The waters of Donegal*. Dublin: D.M.C. Universal, 1982.

Mac Carron, Daniel. *Mac Carron's Dubliners*. Dublin: D.M.C. Universal, 1983.

Mac Carron, Daniel. *The mountains of Donegal*. Dublin: D.M.C. Universal, 1984.

Mac Manus, Seamus. *'Twas in Dhroll Donegal*. Dublin: Duffy, 1897.

Mac Manus, Seamus. *The humours of Donegal*. London: Unwin, 1898.

Mac Manus, Seamus. *Through the turf smoke*. London. Unwin, 1901.

Mac Manus, Seamus. *A lad of the O'Friel's*. London: Isbister, 1903.

Mac Manus, Seamus. *The red poocher*. New York: Funk & Wagnall, 1903.

Mac Manus, Seamus. *Doctor Kilgannon*. Dublin: Gill, 1907.

Mac Manus, Seamus. *The leadin' road to Donegal*. London: Digby, Long, 1909.

Mac Manus, Seamus. *Yourself and the neighbours*. New York: Devin-Adair, 1914.

Mac Manus, Seamus. *Tales that were told*. Dublin: Talbot Press, 1920.

Mac Manus, Seamus. *O do you remember*. Dublin: Duffy, 1926.

Mac Manus, Seamus. *Bold blades of Donegal*. London: Sampson Low, 1935.

Mac Manus, Seamus. *Dark Patrick*. New York: Macmillan, 1939.

Mac Manus, Seamus. *The well o' the worlds' end*. New York: Devin-Adair, 1949.

Mac Manus, Seamus. *Heavy hangs the golden grain*. Dublin: Talbot Press, 1950.

Mac Manus, Seamus. *The bold heroes of hungry hill and other tales*. London. Dent, 1951.

Mac Manus, Seamus. *The little mistress of the Eskar Mór*. Dublin: Gill, 1960.

Mac Manus, Seamus. *Hibernian nights*. New York: Macmillan, 1963.

Mac Manus, J. *The bend of the road*. London: Downey, 1898.

MacGill, Patrick. *Children of the dead end*. London: Jenkins, 1914.

MacGill, Patrick. *The amateur army*. London: Jenkins, 1915.

Mac Gill, Patrick. *The rat pit,* London: Jenkins, 1915.

MacGill, Patrick. *The brown brethren*. London: Jenkins, 1917.

MacGill, Patrick. *The diggers*. London: Jenkins, 1919.

MacGill, Patrick. *The dough-boys*. London: Jenkins, 1919.

MacGill, Patrick. *Glenmornan,* London: Jenkins, 1919.

MacGill, Patrick. *Maureen*. London: Jenkins, 1920.

MacGill, Patrick. *Fear!* London: Jenkins, 1921.

MacGill, Patrick. *Lanty Hanlon*. London: Jenkins, 1922.

MacGill, Patrick. *Moleskin Joe*. London: Jenkins, 1923.

MacGill, Patrick. *The carpenter of Orra*. London: Jenkins, 1924.

MacGill, Patrick. *Sid Puddiefoot*. London: Jenkins, 1926.

MacGill, Patrick. *Black Bonar*. London: Jenkins, 1928.

MacGill, Patrick. *The Glen of Carra*. London: Jenkins, 1934.

MacGill, Patrick. *Tulliver's mill*. London: Jenkins, 1934.

MacGill, Patrick. *The house at the world's end*. London: Jenkins, 1935.

MacGill, Patrick. *Helen Spenser*. London: Jenkins, 1937.

Martin, David. *The road to Ballyshannon*. London: Secker & Warburg, 1981.

Maturin, William and Henry Hogan. *Pioneers and partners*. Dublin: Jenkins, & Simms, 1885.

McGeown, Patrick. *Heat the furnace seven times more*. London: Hutchinson, 1967.

McGinley, Patrick. *Bogmail*. London: Transworld, 1978.

McGinley, Patrick. *Goosefoot*. London: Weidenfeld and Nicolson, 1983.

McGinley, Patrick. *Foxprints*. London: Weidenfeld and Nicolson, 1983.

McGinley Patrick. *Foggage*. London: Cape, 1984.

McGinley, Patrick. *The trick of the Ga Bolga*. London: Cape, 1985.

McGinley, Patrick. *The red men*. London: Cape, 1987.

McGinley, Patrick. *The fantasist*. London: Flamingo, 1987.

McGinley, Patrick. *The devil's diary*. London: Cape, 1988.

McGinley, Patrick. *The lost soldier's song*. London: Sinclair-Stephenson, 1994.

McGowan, Hugh. *The board of management and other stories* [Ballyshannon: printed by Donegal Democrat], 1979.

McLaughlin, Enda. *Memoir for the WASP*. Dublin: Glendale Press, 1989.

Moody, Laurence. *The lantern men*. Belfast: Carter, 1951.

O'Donnell, Peadar. *Storm*. Dublin: Talbot Press, 1925.

O'Donnell, Peadar. *Islanders*. London: Cape, 1928.

O'Donnell, Peadar. *The way it was with them*. New York: Knickerbocker Press, 1928.

O'Donnell, Peadar. *Adrigoole*. London: Putnam, 1929.

O'Donnell, Peadar. *The knife*. London: Jonathan Cape, 1930.

O'Donnell, Peadar. *On the edge of the stream*. London: Cape, 1934.

O'Donnell, Peadar. *The bothy fire and all that*. Dublin: Irish People Pub., 1937.

O'Donnell, Peadar. *The big windows*. Dublin: O'Brien Press, 1975.

O'Donnell, Peadar. *Proud island*. Dublin: O'Brien Press, 1975.

O'Grady, Standish. *The flight of the eagle*. London: Lawrence and Bullen, 1897.

Pender, M. T. *Last of the Irish chiefs*. Dublin: Lester, 1923.

Pender, M. T. *The spearmen of the North*. Dublin: Talbot Press, 1931.

Peppergrass, Paul, [i.e John Boyce]. *Shandy Maguire or tricks upon travellers*. Boston: Merlier, Callanan, 1863.

Peppergrass, Paul [i.e. John Boyce]. *Mary Lee, or the Yankee in Ireland*. Boston: Kelly & Piet, 1864.

Robertson, E. A. *The signpost*. Dublin: Macmillan, 1944.

Rogers, Nan. C. *A romance of 'troubled' Ireland*. London: Caldwell Press, 1935.

Sadlier, J. *The daughter of Tyrconnell*. Dublin: Duffy, 1863.

Children's Stories

Bodkin, M. *Halt, invader!* Dublin: Browne & Nolan, 1940.

Browne, Frances. *Granny's wonderful chair and its tales of fairy times*. London: Partridge, 1856.

Cavanagh, Kit. *A Dunleary legend and other tales*. Belfast: The Quota Press, [19-].

Gamble, John. *Sarsfield or wanderings of youth*. An Irish Tale, vol. 1. London: Cradock & Joy, 1814.

Gorman, Danny. *The crow-killer's revenge*. Tralee: Kerryman Ltd., 1983.

Jones, Shelagh. *Save the unicorns*. Dublin: Children's Press, 1989.

McClintock, Letitia. *Sir Spangle and the dingy hen*. London: King, 1877.

McClintock, Letitia. *A little candle*. London: Nelson, 1887.

McGrory, Yvonne. *The secret of the ruby ring*. Dublin: Children's Press, 1991.

McGrory, Yvonne. *Martha and the ruby ring*. Dublin: Children's Press, 1994.

McLoone, Tess. *Pognolia*. Ashbourne: Skylark Books, 1994.

McMahon, Seán. *The light on Illancrone*. Dublin: Poolbeg, 1990.

McManus, L. *Nuala, the story of a perilious quest*. Dublin: Browne and Nolan, [19-].

The maid of Erin or the lily of Tyrconnel. London: 'The Star', 1885.

Mullen, Michael. *The four masters*. Dublin: Poolbeg, 1992.

Murray, Paul. *A tale of Ireland, Culann and the leprechauns*. Cork: Mercier, 1987.

Ní Dhuibhne, Eilís. *Hugo and the sunshine girl*. Dublin: Poolbeg, 1991.

Parkinson, Siobhán. *Off we go. The Dublin adventure*. Dublin: O'Brien Press, 1992.

Reilly, Robert T. *Red Hugh, prince of Donegal*. Milwaukee: Bruce, 1957.

Scoltock, Jack. *Seek the enchanted antlers*. Dublin: Wolfhound, 1992.

Sweeney, Mathew. *The Chinese dressing gown*. London: Faber & Faber, 1987.

Sweeney, Mathew. *The snow vulture*. London: Faber & Faber, 1992.

Sarr, Kenneth. *The white bolle-trie*. Dublin: Talbot Press,1927.

Tanguay, Mary. *The accident*. Dublin: Coram, 1983.

Tunney, Paddy. *Ulster folk stories for children*. Cork: Mercier, 1990.

General Index

Place Index

Bredagh Glen, 805
Bredagh mountain, 540
Bredagh river, 805
Breifne, 187, 192, 213,
    784, 789, 815
Brinlack, 641,
Bristol, 206, 207, 210, 523
Britain, 2, 5, 76, 85, 96,
    160, 334, 571, 598,
    650, 668, 677, 687
British Isles, 401
Brittany, 206, 209-10, 223
Brockagh, 643, 652
Brookhall, 534
Broughton, 293, 310, 357,
    358
Brownhall, 393, 687
Bruckless, 658
Brussels, 247, 249
Buckingham Palace, 690
Buda, 224
Bulbin Hill, 535
Bullibrack, 776
Bun a' Leaca, 562
Bun an Bhaic, 699
Bun Beag, An, 549
Bun Droabhaoise, 206
Bun Glas, 717
Bunafobble, 399
Bunbeg, 91, 95, 98
Buncrana, 85, 383, 387,
    389, 396-400, 407,
    410-411, 414, 419-
    421, 424-5, 431, 433-
    5, 513, 528, 594, 618,
    669, 801, 804
Buncrana Castle, 410, 425
Bundoran, 9, 86, 89, 400,
    517, 523, 665, 720
Bundrowes, 185, 252,
    798
Bunnagee, 305
Burgundy, 219, 223
Burnderry, 770
Burnfoot, 333, 513, 634
Burt, 406, 410-11, 414,
    419-21, 429-34, 778
Burt Castle, 769, 802
Burtonport, 381, 484, 655,
    662
Bute, 642

Cadiz, 297, 298
Caher Island, 37, 46
Cahercommaun, 95
Cairbre, 184
Cairbre Droma Cliabh,
    183
Cairbre Ua (g)Ciardha,
    176
Caire McEwlyn, 776
Caiseal, 751
Caithness, 47
Calebegg, 787
Call Cháin, 157
Callaghmore, 386
Cally, 358
Cam Éirghe, 776
Cambridge, 77, 687
Camlin, 106
Camus Comhghaill, 129
Camus Macosquin, 129
Camuston, 66
Caol, An, 166
Caoránach, 497
Carbury Drumcliff, 183
Carlow, 301, 522
Carluke, 627, 642
Carn Domhnach, 170
Carnaclug, 112
Carndonagh, 19, 43-5, 54-
    9, 60, 62, 66-7, 81,
    112, 132, 162, 170,
    290, 381, 388, 400,
    401, 414, 415, 423,
    424-5, 433, 435-6,
    484, 594, 600-1, 605,
    614-15
Carnteel, 776
Carocomony, 782
Carracamin, 627
Carraic Brachaidhe, 102,
    103, 814
Carraig Allen, 473
Carrick, 512, 601, 655
Carrick McCowlin, 770
Carrickabraghy, 103, 526,
    535
Carrickfergus, 77, 270, 552
Carrickfergus Castle, 189
Carrickfin, 16
Carrigans, 230, 313, 406,
    509

Carrigart, 664
Carrontlieve, 15
Carrowen, 101
Carrowlough-in-Malin,
    383
Carrowmenagh, 535
Carrowmore, 66, 100,
    101, 388
Carrowntemple, 46
Carrowreagh, 526
Carse of Gowrie, 642
Carthage, 531, 532
Cashel, 176, 288, 810
Cashel, Trian of, 309
Cashelnavean, 19
Castle Doe, 75, 76, 154
Castle Magrath, 288
Castle Sween, 779, 792
Castlederg, 387
Castlefinn, 3, 13, 159,
    186, 194, 206, 234,
    268, 305, 307-8, 383,
    389, 390, 396, 400,
    667
Castlemurray, 365, 370,
    372
Castleport, 91
Castletown, 369, 389
Cath Monaig, 773
Cavan, 52, 96, 192, 212,
    235, 245, 250, 283,
    382, 629, 631, 690,
    799, 815
Cealla Beaga, Na, 786
Ceann Maghair, 152
Ceann Maghair Átha, 792
Ceann Sáile, 173
Ceann Salach, 784
Ceannaclug, 112
Cell Erca, 130
Celtic Regions, 739
Cenél Móen, 268
Cenn Maghair, 101, 102,
    103
Cenn Ríg, 101, 103
Charlemont, 335
Charlemont Castle, 330
Chester, 300, 312
Cheviot, 486
China, 565
Church Island, 168